Economics

THIRD EDITION

Economics

THIRD EDITION

Joseph E. Stiglitz
Columbia University

Carl E. Walsh
University of California, Santa Cruz

W • W • NORTON & COMPANY
NEW YORK • LONDON

The text of this book is composed in Bulmer
with the display set in Cholla Slab Bold
Composition by TSI Graphics
Manufacturing by R. R. Donnelley
Editor: Ed Parsons
Associate Managing Editor—College: Jane Carter
Manuscript Editor: Mary Babcock
Project Editor: Mary Kelly
Editorial Assistants: Sarah Chamberlin, Chris Swart
Book designer: Rubina Yeh

Library of Congress Cataloging-in-Publication Data

Stiglitz, Joseph E.
    Economics/Joseph E. Stiglitz, Carl E. Walsh.—3rd ed.
        p.   cm.
    Includes index.
    ISBN 0-393-97518-5
    1. Economics.   I. Walsh, Carl E.

  HB171.5   .S884   2002
  330—dc21   2001044943

W. W. Norton & Company, Inc., 500 Fifth Avenue, New York, N.Y. 10110
  www.wwnorton.com

W. W. Norton & Company Ltd., Castle House, 75/76 Wells Street, London W1T 3QT

1 2 3 4 5 6 7 8 9 0

About the Authors

Joseph E. Stiglitz is professor of economics, business, and international and public affairs at Columbia University. Before joining the Columbia faculty, he held appointments at Yale, Oxford, Princeton, and Stanford. Internationally recognized as one of the leading economists of his generation, Professor Stiglitz has made important contributions to virtually all of the major subfields of economics. He was a corecipient of the Nobel Prize in Economic Science in 2001 and earlier in his career received the American Economic Association's John Bates Clark Medal, which is given every two years to the most outstanding economist under the age of forty. Professor Stiglitz is the author and editor of hundreds of scholarly articles and books, including the best-selling undergraduate textbook *Economics of the Public Sector* (Norton) and, with Anthony Atkinson, the classic graduate textbook *Lectures in Public Economics*. He was the founding editor of the *Journal of Economic Perspectives*. Professor Stiglitz has also played a prominent role at the highest levels of economic policy making. He was a member and then chairman of President Clinton's Council of Economic Advisers and later served as chief economist of the World Bank.

Carl E. Walsh is professor of economics at the University of California, Santa Cruz, where he teaches principles of economics. He previously held faculty appointments at Princeton and at the University of Auckland, New Zealand, and has been a visiting professor at Stanford. He is widely known for his research in monetary economics and is the author of a leading graduate text, *Monetary Theory and Policy* (MIT Press). Before joining the Santa Cruz faculty, Professor Walsh was senior economist at the Federal Reserve Bank of San Francisco, where he continues to serve as a visiting scholar. He has also been a visiting scholar at the Federal Reserve Banks of Kansas City and Philadelphia, and at the Board of Governors, and has taught courses in monetary economics at the Bank of England, the Bank of Spain, the Bank of Portugal, and the International Monetary Fund. He is a past member of the board of editors of the *American Economic Review* and is currently an associate editor of the *Journal of Money, Credit, and Banking* and the *Journal of Economics and Business*. He is also on the editorial board of the *Journal of Macroeconomics*.

contents in brief

PART 5   Introduction to Macroeconomics

PART 6   Full-Employment Macroeconomics

PART 7   Macroeconomic Fluctuations

PART 8   Topics in Macroeconomics

contents

ix

PART 3   Imperfect Markets

Chapter 11   Introduction to Imperfect Markets • 226

PART 4   Topics in Microeconomics

CHAPTER 17   A Student's Guide to Investing • 344

CHAPTER 18   Trade Policy • 364

preface

The Third Edition of this textbook has a number of significant changes. To begin with, it is now a collaborative effort. By working together, we have been able to broaden dramatically the range of experience and expertise that informs our book. The result is a new edition that improves substantially over its predecessors while still retaining their guiding principles.

As we worked on the revision we kept our sites on four main objectives. The first was to ensure that the book continues to provide students with a clear presentation of the basic competitive model, while also ensuring that students can quickly move on to explore the richness of modern economic analysis in areas such as the economics of information, imperfect competition, and the economics of technology and innovation. These areas, prominent in the previous editions, have taken on an even greater relevance as information technologies change the marketplace. Our second objective was to present macroeconomics in a manner that builds on the way economic researchers and economists in policymaking positions frame their analysis, while doing so in a manner that prepares students for understanding the public debates on monetary and fiscal policy. Our third objective was to present modern economics in a way that is conducive to good teaching and student learning. Here, we stress core concepts and have reorganized the book so that instructors will find it flexible enough for a variety of classroom and lecture settings. Whether it is used for a one-semester course covering the principles of microeconomics and macroeconomics or for a one-quarter course devoted solely to either micro or macro, the new edition allows instructors to combine core chapters with a selection of additional chapters that contain extensions, more in depth coverage of various topics, or that focus on issues of current policy debate.

Much has changed in the modern economy and in modern economics since the Second Edition of this textbook. The productivity slowdown that gripped the economy in the twenty years after 1973 was replaced in the last half of the 1990s by an apparent productivity acceleration. The fiscal deficits of the 1990s were replaced, as the century ended, with fiscal surplus, although the economic slowdown and the War on Terrorism have quickly eroded these surpluses. The long economic expansion of the 1990s came to an end when the book was in the last stages of preparation. New technologies, particularly those associated with information-based systems, are transforming the economy to such a degree that many observers have come to describe the contemporary economic environment as a *new economy*. Our fourth objective was to write a textbook that reflects the contemporary scene. Thus, the Third Edition integrates the recent developments associated with innovation and the digital economy by using examples from the new economy.

Principles of Microeconomics

As we began work on this edition, we were repeatedly reminded of the importance of writing a textbook that reflects *modern* microeconomics—one that recognizes the importance of incentives, limited information, innovation, and technology. The new economy has provided many new examples and case studies to illustrate the core principles of economics. And the new economy provides further evidence of the importance of information and technology, topics whose treatment has always been one of the strengths of the previous editions. The new economy, despite its current slump, has forcefully driven home the critical role new technologies play in the modern economy. For students to make sense of competition policy in the twenty-first century, they need to understand what network externalities are and how information and ideas are different from traditional goods and services.

In the presentation of microeconomics, previous editions of this book have been distinguished by their emphasis on information, imperfect markets, innovation, and technology. This distinction continues to mark the Third Edition.

Key changes for the Third Edition:

A number of key changes have been made to the structure of the microeconomic sections. These include:

- The opening chapter (Chapter 1) uses the story of the Internet to introduce basic concepts in economics. Five core concepts (incentives, trade-offs, exchange, information, and distribution) are explained in this opening chapter and then woven throughout the book in Thinking Like an Economist boxes that serve to illustrate how these key concepts help students understand issues from overloaded AOL modem servers (Chapter 1) to why developing economies have supported trade liberalization for information technologies but not for financial services (Chapter 18).

- The organization has been streamlined to allow the core material for the basic competitive model to be covered in the first ten chapters. This is followed in Part 3 by six chapters covering imperfect markets, information, and the role of the government.

- A new introductory chapter to Part 3 (Chapter 11) provides an overview of imperfect competition in the goods market, imperfect information, and imperfections in the labor market. This is followed by individual chapters that deal with each topic in greater depth. This allows instructors to introduce students to all these important topics even in shorter courses or when both microeconomics and macroeconomics need to be covered within a single course.

- Optional chapters have been collected together in Part 4. Teachers who wish to go beyond the basic course comprised in Chapters 1 through 16 may add in chapters from Part 4 as they see fit. For instance, after covering the labor and capital markets in Chapter 9, some teachers may wish to cover investment decisions, discussed in Chapter 17, "A Student's Guide to Investing." Similarly, the other chapters of Part 4 can be used to satisfy particular course objectives according to the teacher's needs. The flow chart below shows the chapter dependencies for the book.

- Strategic behavior permeates modern economic analysis, so we have added a new chapter (Chapter 19) that

uses simple examples to introduce students to the concepts of Nash equilibrium, dominant strategies, backward induction, and sequential and repeated games.

Principles of Macroeconomics

The year 2001 saw an unprecedented period of sustained economic growth coming to an end, reinforcing the need to provide students with a macroeconomic framework that encompasses both growth *and* fluctuations. The model of fluctuations in the Third Edition is ideal for helping students understand the Fed's interest rate cuts during 2001, as well as the impact of fiscal policies designed to cut taxes and increase expenditures.

The basic organization of macroeconomics remains from the second edition, with the full-employment model with flexible wages and prices developed first, followed by a treatment of economic fluctuations. Each part has seen major restructuring, however.

Key changes for the Third Edition:

- The macroeconomic presentation kicks off with a new introductory chapter that deals with the major issues in macroeconomics.

- The material on the full-employment model now places greater stress on the role of the capital market and the real rate of interest in ensuring aggregate demand and supply balance at full-employment output.

- The pickup in economic growth at the end of the 1990s and the debate over the role of new technologies have meant that issues of growth and productivity have re-emerged as ones of critical importance. Because the full-employment model of Part 6 provides the basis for understanding the economics of growth and productivity, we now devote a complete chapter to these issues at an early stage in the macro presentation.

- Because major central banks around the world no longer implement monetary policy through explicit control of the money supply, the traditional discussion of money demand and supply has been de-emphasized. Instead, monetary policy is discussed in terms of nominal interest-rate control. The book focuses on the federal funds market so that students can gain an understanding of what the Federal Reserve actually does when it intervenes to raise or lower the rate.

- Over the last decade, both academic researchers and economists in central bank research departments world-

wide have increasingly made use of a basic foundation for macroeconomic policy analysis that relies on three components. First, underlying wage and price rigidities lead inflation to adjust in response to movements of output around its full-employment level and to expectations of inflation. Second, aggregate demand depends on the real interest rate and expectations of future income. And third, monetary policy is represented by either a rule for setting the nominal rate of interest or by the specification of the central bank's objectives, such as is typified by an inflation-targeting policy regime. The model of economic fluctuations we use reflects this framework.

- The model of fluctuations is developed in terms of *inflation* and *output,* and it integrates monetary policy based on the federal funds rate. Thus, rather than develop an aggregate demand and supply model based on the price level and then append a model of price level adjustment to explain inflation, the entire discussion is carried out in terms of inflation and output. This provides a more integrated framework and is ideal for getting students to understand monetary policy actions. It is also ideal for analyzing both the inflation-targeting policies adopted by major central banks such as the Bank of England and the Bank of Canada and the actions of other central banks such as the Federal Reserve and the European Central Bank.

In revising the macroeconomics presentation, we have continued to honor one of the central objectives that motivated the earlier editions: to write a modern textbook that reflects, as much as possible, the way economists approach their subject. The treatment of macroeconomics in the new edition does this while also presenting a model that students can apply directly to the policy debates they read about in newspapers or hear reported on the television.

Pedagogical Elements   This book provides a complete pedagogical package designed to help students master basic principles and then apply them to a wide range of situations. The following special elements, which have various applications and real-world connections, appear throughout the book:

e-Insight boxes, appearing in most chapters of the book, apply economic principles to new developments in information technology and the Internet.

e-Case boxes, which conclude each part of the book, explore "new economy" themes in greater depth.

International Perspective boxes present applications on international issues.

Thinking Like an Economist features, which appear in each chapter of the book, reinforce the core ideas presented in the book's opening chapter.

CASE IN POINT vignettes, which highlight real-world applications in each chapter, are integrated into the body of the text.

Internet Connection boxes provide useful links to Web resources and home pages.

In addition to these elements, students will find guidance through other important pedagogical features. Each chapter opens with a set of key questions to help the reader get oriented to the main issues in the chapter. Within the chapter, Wrap-Up boxes track key concepts as they are developed in the text. And a chapter summary, list of key terms, set of review questions, and a problem set appear at the end of each chapter.

Ancillary Package   A variety of valuable supplements are available to students and teachers who use the textbook.

Student Web Site   Stephen Erfle (Dickinson College), David Gillette (Truman State University), and Rosemary Rossiter (Ohio University) have contributed to the textbook's exciting companion Web site, which may be accessed at www.wwnorton.com/StiglitzWalsh . This innovative tool will help students improve their command of economic principles. Features include:

- *Conceptual quizzes* that pair challenging questions with thought-provoking feedback. This highly effective combination encourages critical thinking and drives home the central themes and ideas of each chapter.
- *Interactive tutorials* that guide students through a sequence of analytical applications of the most important principles in the textbook. By working through these tutorials, students strengthen not only their understanding

of economic principles but also their ability to solve economic problems.

- *Mini lectures* that review the main ideas covered in each chapter of the textbook in a multimedia format featuring animated graphs and audio narration.
- *FAQs* that alert students to common misunderstandings and clarify essential material in each chapter.
- *Practice quizzes* that test students' mastery of the information presented in each chapter.

Norton's Economics News Service　By subscribing to a listserv created specifically for users of the textbook, students and instructors will receive e-mail messages directing them to current business-related articles from sources like NYTimes.com and CBSnews.com. Each article is prefaced by a brief annotation that explains its pertinence to material in the text.

Study Guide　This innovative Study Guide, prepared by Lawrence Martin of Michigan State University, uses reviews, practice exams, and problem sets to reinforce the major ideas of each chapter. Unique problem-solving sections called "Doing Economics" give students the opportunity to apply what they have learned. Each section contains a series of "Tool-kits," which walk students through a specific problem-solving technique, several worked problems, and practice problems that apply the relevant technique.

Instructor's Resource Site and Manual　The Instructor's Manual, prepared by Gerald McIntrye of Occidental College, includes annotated chapter outlines, lecture objectives, lecture modules, PowerPoint slides to accompany each lecture module, solutions to review questions in the textbook, solutions to problems in the textbook, alternative problem sets, and solutions to alternative problems sets. For more details, visit www.wwnorton.com/StiglitzWalsh .

PowerPoint Lectures and Color Transparencies　A rich source of lecture supplements, this CD-ROM features one set of PowerPoint slides that corresponds to the lecture modules in the Instructor's Manual and a second set of slides that contains all of the figures from the text. Color transparencies for all figures in the text are available to qualified instructors upon adoption.

Test-Item File and Computerized Test-Item File　The Test-Item File has been revised by David Gillette of Truman State University. It contains 3,500 multiple-choice questions and is available in book or electronic form to qualified instructors.

Acknowledgments　Although this Third Edition has been the collaborative effort of its two authors, it has also been a collective effort involving many, many other contributors, to all of whom we offer our profound thanks.

No project like this can succeed without the constant encouragement, advice, and gentle prodding of an editor. Ed Parsons fulfilled all these roles superbly, serving as a critical sounding board for our ideas, sharing our desire to present the ideas of modern economics to today's students. He has been invaluable, and it has been a pleasure working with him. Over the course of preparing this edition, editorial assistants Ann Marcy, Sarah Chamberlin, and Christopher Swart were always there to deal with problems ranging from locating photos to ensuring research assistants were paid. Mary Babcock (manuscript editor), Mary Kelly (project editor), and Jane Carter (managing editor), have all contributed their considerable skills to translating our manuscript into its final form. Rubina Yeh created the book's wonderful design, and Roy Tedoff served as production manager, coordinating the book's manufacturing. Finally, Jamie Marshall has helped promote our ideas of modern economics in his service as the book's marketer.

The book's first two editions were improved immeasurably by the input of numerous reviewers. In particular, we thank Robert T. Averitt, Smith College; Mohsen Bahmani-Oskooee, University of Wisconsin, Milwaukee; H. Scott Bierman, Carleton College; John Payne Bigelow, University of Missouri; Bruce R. Bolnick, Northeastern University; Adhip Chaudhuri, Georgetown University; Michael D. Curley, Kennesaw State College; John Devereux, University of Miami; K. K. Fung, Memphis State; Christopher Georges, Hamilton College; Ronald D. Gilbert, Texas Tech University; Robert E. Graf, Jr., United States Military Academy; Glenn W. Harrison, University of South Carolina; Marc Hayford, Loyola University; Yutaka Horiba, Tulane University; Charles Howe, University of Colorado; Sheng Cheng Hu, Purdue University; Glenn Hubbard, Columbia University; Allen C. Kelley, Duke University; Michael M. Knetter, Dartmouth College; Stefan Lutz, Purdue University; Mark J. Machina, University of California, San Diego; Burton G. Malkiel, Princeton University; Lawrence Martin, Michigan State University; Thomas Mayer, University of California, Davis; Craig J. McCann, University of South Carolina; Henry N. McCarl, University of Alabama, Birmingham;

John McDermott, University of South Carolina; Marshall H. Medoff, University of California, Irvine; Peter Mieszkowski, Rice University; W. Douglas Morgan, University of California, Santa Barbara; John S. Murphy, Canisius College; William Nielson, Texas A&M University; Neil B. Niman, University of New Hampshire; David H. Papell, University of Houston; James E. Price, Syracuse University; Daniel M. G. Raff, Harvard Business School; Christina D. Romer, University of California, Berkeley; Richard Rosenberg, Pennsylvania State University; Christopher J. Ruhm, Boston University; Suzanne A. Scotchmer, University of California, Berkeley; Richard Selden, University of Virginia; Andrei Shleifer, Harvard University; John L. Solow, University of Iowa; George Spiva, University of Tennessee; Mark Sproul, University of California at Los Angeles; Frank P. Stafford, University of Michigan; Raghu Sundaram, University of Rochester; Hal R. Varian, University of Michigan; Franklin V. Walker, State University of New York at Albany; James M. Walker, Indiana University; Andrew Weiss, Boston University; Gilbert R. Yochum, Old Dominion University.

Many additional reviewers guided us in our preparations of the Third Edition. Our thanks to Richard Barret, University of Montana; Howard Bodenhorn, Lafayette College; Stephen Erfle, Dickinson College; Rudy Fichtenbaum, Wright State University; Kevin Forbes, Catholic University; Nancy Jianakoplos, Colorado State University; Lori Kletzer, University of California, Santa Cruz; Kevin Lang, Boston University; William Lastrapes, University of Georgia; John Leahy, Boston University; Eric Leeper, Indiana University; Colin Linsley, St. John Fisher College; Lawrence Martin, Michigan State University; Myra Moore, University of Georgia; Michael Nelson, University of Akron; Douglas Pearce, North Carolina State University; Jerrold Peterson, University of Minnesota, Duluth; Rosemary Rossiter, Ohio University; David F. Ruccio, University of Notre Dame; Nirvikar Singh, University of California, Santa Cruz; and Mark Wohar, University of Nebraska, Omaha.

We also thank our research assistants—Alessandra Cassar, Wei Chen, Peter Kriz, Garrett Milam, and Roger White—who devoted their substantial time and efforts to the project and often went well beyond the call of duty in their determination to improve the book.

Finally, we would like to thank our families—not only for their love and encouragement as we worked on the book but also, in so many different instances, for their insightful suggestions and eager assistance as we tackled various facets of the project.

A special note of thanks is owed to Judy Walsh for her contributions to the Third Edition. Judy has been an invaluable sounding board. Not only has she been an astute editor, providing ideas for examples and illustrations and offering numerous suggestions for expressing ideas more clearly, but she has always been there to offer needed encouragement and support.

Alternative Course Outlines In the Third Edition, we have improved the flexibility of the book for easy adaptability to courses with very different time constraints and objectives. One aspect of the book's flexibility is the two optional parts: **Part 4, Topics in Microeconomics,** and **Part 8: Topics in Macroeconomics.** The chapters in these parts may be used selectively at different points in the preceding core discussion of microeconomics and macroeconomics, or they may be discussed at the end of the course, if time permits. The following course outlines, which represent only a small subset of those that might be devised, reflect this structure.

Outline for a one-semester course in microeconomics

Chapter	Title
1	Economics and the New Economy
2	Thinking Like an Economist
3	Trade
4	Demand, Supply, and Price
5	Using Supply and Demand
6	The Consumption Decision
7	The Firm's Costs
8	The Competitive Firm
9	Labor and Capital Markets
10	The Efficiency of Competitive Markets
11	Introduction to Imperfect Markets
12	Monopoly, Monopolistic Competition, and Oligopoly
13	Government Policies Toward Competition
14	Imperfect Information in the Product Market
15	Imperfections in the Labor Market
16	The Public Sector

Plus any of the optional chapters comprising Part 4

Outline for a short course in microeconomics

Outline for a one-semester course in macroeconomics

Core macroeconomics presentation

Plus any of the optional chapters comprising Part 8

Outline for a short course in macroeconomics

Economics

THIRD EDITION

Part 1

Introduction

Chapter 1

Economics and the New Economy

Key Questions

1. What *is* economics? What are the key concepts that define core ideas in economics?

2. In economies such as the U.S. economy, what are the respective roles of government and the private, or "market" sector?

3. What are markets, and what are the principal markets that make up the economy?

4. Why is economics called a science?

5. Why, if economics is a science, do economists disagree so often?

Newspapers, magazines, and television are filled today with stories of the "new economy." New technologies are transforming everything, from how airlines sell tickets to how automobiles are produced, from the way we buy books to the way we communicate with one another. The Internet is playing a rapidly growing role in the modern economy. It is estimated that the number of Web sites in use grew from 26,000 in 1993 to 5 million in 1999, while the number of Americans connected to the Internet rose from 3 million to 80 million over this same period.

Like the industrial revolution of the eighteenth and nineteenth centuries that transformed first Britain and then other countries from agricultural to manufacturing-based economies, the information revolution promises to transform virtually all aspects of our daily lives. In 1999 in recognition of the growing importance of new high-tech firms, Microsoft—the producer of the Windows computer operating system—and Intel—the major producer of the microprocessors at the heart of personal computers—were added to the Dow Jones industrial average, the most widely followed index of prices on U.S. stock markets.

But the old economy is still alive and kicking. It is estimated that the new "digital" economy accounts for less than 10 percent of the U.S. economy. Four of the five largest U.S. corporations in *Fortune* magazine's top five-hundred list for 2000 were traditional industrial firms—General Motors, Ford, Exxon, and General Electric (GE). IBM, at number 8 was the only "tech" firm in the top twenty. Microsoft only managed to make it to number 79.

So the old economy and the new economy coexist side by side. But it is not just the emergence of new software and Internet companies that represents the effects of new technologies. The way all firms do business is being changed, and their customers are being affected too. Assembly lines now rely on computer-aided and -controlled robots, making them far different from the old assembly line. Car repair shops with grease-stained floors have been replaced by clean, quiet garages where computers diagnose each car's problems. The way we buy things is changing. Whether we purchase a car, book, or compact disc, book a hotel or plane reservation, or even apply to college through the Internet, our relationships with each other and with firms are evolving. New technologies are changing the way courses are taught too—textbooks like this one have Web sites that provide students with help, with interactive exercises, and with links to news, policy debates, and the latest economic information. The address for the home page for this textbook is www.wwnorton.com/StiglitzWalsh .

With such wide-reaching changes, what insights and understandings does the study of economics have to offer? After all, economics is a field of study that usually looks to Adam Smith, a Scottish professor of the late 1700s, as its founder. Smith published his famous book, *The Wealth of Nations,* in 1776, a time when economies were still overwhelmingly agricultural. Surely, you might think, ideas developed to understand the nature of, say, wheat prices have little relevance in today's modern economy.

In fact, the basic insights gained from studying economics continue to provide a critical understanding of today's global economy. As Carl Shapiro and Hal Varian of the University of California, Berkeley, put it, "Technology changes. Economic laws do not."[1] The way we produce things, what we produce, and how goods are exchanged have varied tremendously since Smith wrote. But the same fundamental laws of economics that explained agricultural prices in the eighteenth century can help us to understand how economies function at the dawn of the twenty-first century. And during the past two hundred years, economists have refined and expanded our understanding of economic behavior in many ways. The foundation laid by Smith and built upon by generations of economists has yielded insights that will continue to offer guidance to anyone wishing to make sense of the modern economy.

But what are these insights? What do economists study? And what can we learn from looking at things from the perspective of economics? How can economics help us understand why we need to worry about the extinction of salmon but not of sheep, about why auto manufacturers advertise but wheat farmers don't, about why countries that rely on market systems have done better than countries that rely on government planners, and about why letting a single firm dominate an industry is bad?

Looking at the story of one of the newest phenomena, the Internet, and the computer revolution that created it, can help to illustrate the perspective of economics and can teach us a great deal about the economic way of thinking.

The Story of Computers and the Internet

Walk into any office today and there is sure to be evidence of the revolution that has occurred in computing and information technology. The most prominent piece of evidence will be the personal computer at each desk. And increasingly, both at home and at the office, people are using computers to access information, to shop, and to conduct business through the Internet.

Not just offices—the modern cash register is a far cry from its 1970s ancestor. Today, the cash register does more than just add up sales and calculate change. It also keeps track of what items are being sold, allowing firms to have up-to-date information on what's hot and what's not. A grocery store can use this information to know whether it needs to order more boxes of raisin bran or more cornflakes. A bookstore can know how many copies of the latest best-seller it still has on its shelves and use that information to decide whether it should order more from the publisher.

To trace the rise of one aspect of this information and technological revolution, the Internet, we need to start with the rise of the computer.

The Rise of IBM

In the 1950s, computers meant huge mainframe machines. Their million-dollar price tag limited them to large corporations or government agencies. In fact, the first customer for the first computer designed for business use, the UNIVAC, was the U.S. Census Bureau, which took delivery in 1951.[2] The general public got its introduction to the UNIVAC when one was used as part of CBS's coverage of the presidential election in 1952. At 8:30 P.M. on election night, UNIVAC predicted an Eisenhower landslide over Stevenson. Even the computer operators couldn't believe

---

[1]Carl Shapiro and Hal R. Varian, *Information Rules* (Cambridge: Harvard Business School Press, 1999), p. 2.

[2]The software for the first UNIVAC was programmed by Grace Murray Hooper, one of the few women among computer experts of the time.

this, as most polls were projecting a close election. Rather than risk what they feared would be an embarrassing error, they adjusted the program to produce a closer election forecast. They needn't have feared—the final results were a landslide for Eisenhower, who received 442 electoral college votes to Stevenson's 89, not far off UNIVAC's original prediction of 438 to 93.

While UNIVAC, produced by Remington Rand, was probably the first computer most Americans had heard of, IBM soon became the major force in this industry. In the late 1950s and early 1960s, IBM stock became the standard example of exceptional growth, much as the stocks of Microsoft, Intel, and other high-tech firms were in the 1990s. But IBM only established true dominance in this industry with the introduction of its model 1401 in 1959, and it did so for reasons not directly related to the computing power of this machine. Instead, the success of the 1401 was largely due to the new printing technology that IBM developed to accompany it. The 1401 had the capacity to print 600 lines per minute, four times that of IBM's most popular pre-computer accounting machine. Even though the cost of the 1401 was about twice that of the standard accounting machine it replaced, the fourfold increase in printing capacity more than justified the expense.

By the early 1960s, the computer industry consisted of IBM and the Seven Dwarfs—seven smaller firms that had managed to survive by supplying computers to a small segment of the market.[3] But the lack of compatibility among different types of computers was a major problem for the industry. IBM alone produced seven different computer models, each with its own sales force, separate production line, and unique components.

Software compatibility was also a major problem. A firm that wanted to buy a bigger computer needed to completely rewrite its software applications for the new machine. This was time-consuming and expensive. Because IBM controlled a large share of the market, it could afford to develop software program suites for business applications and then give them away free to purchasers of IBM machines. Smaller firms tended to specialize, developing software applications for only one or two industries.

Even so, it was clear that standardization would help reduce production and software development costs. So in March 1964, IBM announced System/360, a complete line of compatible computers. Dubbed "the computer that IBM made that made IBM," System/360 fueled the growth of IBM. To meet the huge number of orders it received, IBM had to build new assembly plants and expand its workforce. In the three years after System/360 was introduced, the number of IBM employees jumped by 50 percent.

IBM continued to dominate the computer industry through the 1970s, entering the decade controlling about 75 percent of the mainframe market. During an economic downturn in the early 1970s, when production and employment fell in many industrialized economies, RCA and GE dropped their computer lines, reducing the industry to IBM and the BUNCH (Burroughs, UNIVAC, NCR, Control Data, and Honeywell). These smaller firms often survived by finding niches in the market that IBM did not serve—for example, Control Data become the leading producer of supercomputers. The basic design of mainframe computers, however, and the software they run have changed little in the past thirty years. "The world's mainframes and the software that runs on them have become like the aging sewers beneath British city streets, laid in the Victorian era. Not very exciting infrastructure, and largely unseen—but they work, and life would be totally different without them."[4]

The Fall of IBM and the Rise of Microsoft

During the 1970s, while IBM continued to dominate the market for mainframe computers, its share of the total computer market declined as new technological discoveries allowed computers to become more powerful and smaller, leading to the introduction of minicomputers. Firms such as Digital Equipment Corporation (DEC), Data General, and Xerox Data Systems were able to compete successfully for the minicomputer market. IBM failed to capture this expanding segment of the market, and with few new design innovations in mainframes, the special service and support offered by IBM to its customers no longer seemed as necessary.

Instead, time-sharing systems that allowed many users to simultaneously use a single mainframe were growing in importance, particularly in universities. Time sharing made sense because it was cheaper to have several users sharing

---

[3]The Seven Dwarfs were Sperry Rand, Burroughs, NCR, RCA, Honeywell, GE, and Control Data Corp.

[4]Martin Campbell-Kelly and William Aspray, *Computer: A History of the Information Machine* (New York: BasicBooks, 1996), p. 150.

the same computer than buying a computer for each user. Many began to think of parallels with the electrical utility industry—a "computer utility" would provide computing services to individuals and firms by linking them to a central computer. This vision of computing was temporarily killed by technological and economic factors. First, developing the software to manage a computer utility system proved too difficult. Second, falling prices for computer hardware—caused in part by the introduction of the integrated circuit—reduced the economic incentive for time sharing. It became cheaper to buy small minicomputers, each capable of handling a few users. The number of minicomputers in use worldwide leaped from 3,600 in 1966 to 19,000 in 1969 to 150,000 by 1974.

The next stage in this story of computers was set by Intel's development, around 1970, of the microprocessor. Advertised as a "computer on a chip," the programmable microprocessor served to lower the price of a computer to within the reach of almost everyone. The first "personal computer"—the Altair 8800—was introduced in 1975. It came as a kit for the user to build. Programs were entered by flipping the switches on the front, but it lacked the power or memory to do very much.

However, with the Altair 8800 came opportunities for small firms to offer accessories, like extra memory and storage devices. It also offered an opportunity for someone to provide software programs. Two old high school friends from Seattle, Bill Gates and Paul Allen, saw this opportunity. They contracted with Altair to produce a programmable system for the Altair 8800. The two formed a partnership, initially called Micro-Soft. In a strategic move, Gates and Allen decided not to sell the software system to Altair; instead, they licensed it, receiving a royalty for each copy sold.

Between the introduction of the Altair in 1975 and the introduction of the IBM PC in 1981, many firms entered the personal computer market. New computers could be produced or software developed with relatively low start-up costs—the huge production costs of mainframes that created barriers to the entry of new firms were absent in the personal computer arena. That changed with the introduction of IBM's personal computer. The IBM PC quickly became the industry standard, forcing other firms either to produce clones of the IBM PC or to face bankruptcy. Only Apple Computer managed to survive as the producer of a distinct line of computers.

To compete, Apple needed to differentiate its product. It had to clearly distinguish itself from the IBM clones and give people a reason to buy its product. The launch of the Macintosh in 1984, with its user-friendly graphical interface, dramatically differentiated Apple from other personal computers running Microsoft's operating system, MS-DOS. Unfortunately, the Macintosh was not powerful enough to challenge the IBM name in business applications, and sales were disappointing.

Because the IBM PC had been constructed from parts such as Intel's 8088 microprocessor that other firms could also purchase, many firms were able to market IBM clones. Many of these clones were made in Asia where lower labor costs gave these firms a competitive advantage. High-cost producers of personal computer hardware such as IBM were eventually supplanted, and as personal computers grew in popularity, software, not hardware, became the key factor. Between 1981 and 1984, sales of personal computer software grew from $140 million to $1.6 billion.

With software the key factor, Microsoft owned the key—MS-DOS, which was running on virtually every IBM-compatible personal computer. Competition drove down the prices of hardware, but Microsoft retained almost sole control over the operating system, first through DOS and then through its Windows programs. The revenue generated by its dominance of the operating systems market allowed Microsoft to enter the market for software applications. Its word processor (Word) and spreadsheet (Excel) software eventually became the market leaders. As computers became more complicated, so did the software. When software programs were relatively simple, two or three people could write a program and start a company to market it. As programs became more complex, hundreds of programmers needed to be involved in their development.[5] This created a barrier that limited the ability of new firms to enter the market.

No firm better symbolizes the rise of the computer industry to most people today than Microsoft. Bill Gates, its cofounder, is the wealthiest person in the world, and just as the huge rise in the value of IBM stock was a widely cited phenomenon in the 1950s and 1960s, the same was true of Microsoft in the 1990s. But just as the dominance of IBM was threatened first by the introduction of minicomputers and then by the personal computer, Microsoft's dominance was threatened in the 1990s by the rise of the World Wide Web.

---

[5]The original spreadsheet program for personal computers, VisiCalc, contained about 10,000 lines of code. Lotus 1-2-3, which replaced it, contained around 400,000 lines of code.

The World Wide Web and the Internet

Time sharing represented one way of making more efficient use of mainframe computers, allowing many users to work simultaneously on a single computer. But time-sharing systems were not the only avenue for using computing resources more efficiently. The U.S. Defense Department's Advanced Research Projects Agency (ARPA) wanted to find a more efficient way to utilize all computers around the country that it had funded. At 9 A.M. on the East Coast, a researcher at MIT might find the local computer busy and be unable to run programs, while a computer at Stanford or the University of California at Berkeley sat idle since it was only 6 A.M. and no one was at work yet. How could the MIT researcher access the Stanford computer?

The answer was to link different computers through a network. This network, called the ARPANET, was launched in late 1969, linking four different computers at UCLA, the University of California at Santa Barbara, the University of Utah, and The Stanford Research Institute, a nonprofit research organization.[6] Out of this beginning can be traced today's Internet. Funded by the Defense Department, the ARPANET expanded to link fifteen computers by 1971. While the ARPANET continued to expand in the 1970s, the decline in the cost of computers reduced the demand for shared computer services. Computer resources were no longer scarce. "Had the ARPANET's only value been as a tool for resource sharing, the network might be remembered today as a minor failure rather than a spectacular success."[7] Instead, users of the ARPANET found a different way to use the network—electronic mail.

By the early 1970s, ARPA had set up several networks. The next step was to link these networks, developing a network of networks—an Internet. The Internet was first demonstrated successfully in 1977. But the Internet primarily linked universities and Defense Department locations. The Defense Department's need for secure communications between its facilities had played an important role in many aspects of the technical design of the network. Not until 1982 were the military sites on the network separated from the ARPANET. But the Internet was still a far cry from what we know today.

What transformed the Internet was the development of a new application, the World Wide Web. The Web was created in 1990, at the CERN research center in Switzerland. By developing a system of "hypertext" to allow users to move from one piece of information to another, the Web produced an environment that opened up new opportunities for using the Internet. But what was still needed was a means of navigating through all the information on the Web, a need that was filled by the development of Web browsers like Netscape's Navigator and Microsoft's Internet Explorer.

The phenomenal growth of the Internet in the 1990s posed a direct threat to Microsoft's dominance of the market for personal computer operating systems, just as the rise of the minicomputer and the PC had robbed IBM of its dominant position in the computer industry twenty years earlier. The operating system was critical for the personal computer, but the Internet opened up new possibilities for developing applications that could operate on any operating system. No longer would the operating system be the interface between the computer and the user—instead, it would be a browser such as Navigator. Naturally, Microsoft did not sit idly by while this threat developed. It launched its own browser. And to maintain control over the interface between users and computers, Microsoft bundled its browser with the Windows operating system, a practice that led to a major court battle between Microsoft and the U.S. government. This court case highlights one of the important ways the government plays a role in the economy.

The Government and the Computer Industry

When we think of the computer industry, we think of major firms such as IBM, Microsoft, and Intel. But the government also has played a critical role in the development of new information technologies. After all, it was the government's needs during World War II that spurred research into the technologies that later made the personal computer and the Internet possible.

Government funding of basic research has long played a critical role in supporting activities that lead to new ideas and expand our knowledge. These ideas form the basis from which new technologies, new ways of producing goods, and new products arise. The government also has been an important consumer of new technologies, from the Census Bureau's purchase of the first UNIVAC to the Defense Department's purchase of satellite communications

---

[6]For a history of the Internet, see Janet Abbate, *Inventing the Internet* (Cambridge: MIT Press, 1999).

[7]*Ibid.*, p. 106.

equipment. But government plays a further role—it regulates the activities of firms in a market to ensure healthy competition, and in markets where a single firm is dominant, it makes sure that firm does not take advantage of its dominant position.

This last role of the government—as the watchdog that ensures fair competition—has figured prominently in the news in recent years, with the U.S. Justice Department and nineteen states accusing Microsoft of abusing its power as the dominant producer of personal computer operating systems. The same arguments that led the U.S. government to break up John D. Rockefeller's Standard Oil Company in the early twentieth century were used by government lawyers in their case against Bill Gates's Microsoft Corporation at the end of the twentieth century. In 1999, a federal judge ruled that Microsoft did have dominant power in the market for operating systems and that it had used that power to stifle innovation.

Microsoft, in its defense, argued that its dominant position was constantly threatened by new technologies—much as IBM's position in the 1970s had been undercut by the rise of personal computers. In the case of Microsoft, the threat was from the Internet. As we await the final outcome of this case, debate centers on how the government can ensure fair competition in the fast-changing high-tech industries while allowing innovation to flourish.

Internet Connection

Tracking the Digital Economy

Since 1998, the U.S. Department of Commerce has issued an annual report on the digital economy. You can find the latest report at http://www.ecommerce.gov.

What Is Economics?

The story of computers and the Internet illustrates many of the important issues with which economics deals, but now a definition of our subject is in order. *Economics* studies how individuals, firms, government, and other organizations within our society make *choices*, and how these choices determine society's use of its resources. Why did consumers choose to buy small, energy-efficient cars in the 1970s and large sports utility vehicles in the 1990s? What determines how many individuals work in health care industries and how many work in the computer industry? Why did the income gap between rich and poor rise in the 1980s? To understand how choices are made and how these choices affect the use of society's resources, we must examine five concepts that play an important role: trade-offs, incentives, exchange, information, and distribution.

Choices involve **trade-offs**—deciding to spend more on one thing leaves less to spend on something else. Your weekly entertainment budget might allow you to see two movies and have a pizza *or* buy two new compact discs (CDs), but it does not allow you to see two movies, have a pizza, *and* buy two CDs. You can spend the next few years after graduating from college getting an MBA *or* a law degree, but not both. In making choices, individuals respond to **incentives.** If the price of a CD falls, so that now you can buy three CDs for the price of two movies and a pizza, there is a greater incentive to spend your money on CDs. If the salaries of lawyers rise relative to the salaries for people with an MBA, there is an increased incentive to choose law school over business school. When we **exchange** with others, the range of choices we each face becomes larger. Making intelligent choices requires that we have, and utilize, **information.** And the choices we make—about how much education to have, what occupation to enter, what goods and services to buy—determine the **distribution** of wealth and income in our society. These five concepts—trade-offs, incentives, exchange, information, and distribution—define the core ideas that are critical to understanding economics. They also guide the way economists think about issues and problems. Learning to "think like an economist" means learning how to discover the trade-offs and incentives being faced, the implications of exchange, the role of information, and the consequences for distribution. These key concepts are emphasized through the text in "Thinking Like an Economist" boxes.

Trade-offs

Each of us is constantly making choices—students decide to study at the library rather than in the dorm, to have pizza rather than sushi, to go to college rather than work full-time.

Societies, too, make choices—to preserve open spaces rather than provide more housing, to produce computers and import televisions rather than produce televisions and import computers, to cut taxes rather than increase government expenditures. In some cases, individuals or governments explicitly make these choices. You decided to study economics rather than some other subject. The government decides each year whether to cut taxes or increase spending. In other cases, however, the choices were the result of the uncoordinated actions of millions of individuals. Neither the government nor any one individual decided that the United States would import cars from Japan and export wheat to India. But in each case, choice involves trade-offs—to get more of one thing involves having less of something else. We are forced to make trade-offs because of **scarcity.**

Scarcity figures prominently in economics; choices matter because resources are scarce. For most of us, our limited income forces us to make choices. We cannot afford everything we might want. Spending more on rent means there is less available for clothes and entertainment. Getting a sunroof on a new car may mean giving up leather seats for upholstered seats to stay within budget. Limited income is not the only reason why we are forced to make trade-offs. Imagine an enormously wealthy individual who can have everything he or she wants. We might think that scarcity is of no concern to such an individual—until we consider that time is also a resource, and even the wealthiest individual must decide what expensive toy to play with each day. Taking time into account, we realize scarcity is a fact of life for everyone.

One of the most important points on which economists agree concerns the critical role of scarcity. We can summarize this point in the following way: *There is no free lunch. Having more of one thing requires giving up something else. Scarcity means that* trade-offs *are a basic fact of life.*

Incentives

It is one thing to say we all face trade-offs in the choices we make. It is quite another to understand how individuals and firms make choices and how those choices might change as economic circumstances change. If new technologies are developed, will firms decide to increase or decrease the amount of labor they employ? If the price of gasoline rises, will individuals decide to buy different types of automobiles?

When faced with a choice, people evaluate the pros and cons of the different options. In deciding what to eat for dinner, you and your roommates might weigh the advantages and disadvantages of having a frozen pizza again tonight over going out for sushi. Similarly, a firm evaluates the pros and cons of its alternatives in terms of the effects different choices will have on its profits. For example, a retail chain deciding on the location for a new store must weigh the relative advantages of different locations. One location might have more foot traffic but come with a higher rent. Another location might be less desirable but have lower rent.

When decision makers systematically weigh the pros and cons of the alternatives they face, we can predict how they will respond to changing economic conditions. Higher gas prices raise the cost of driving, but the cost of driving a fuel-efficient car rises less than the cost of driving a sports utility vehicle. Therefore, households weighing a car purchase face a greater incentive to choose the fuel-efficient car. If a firm starts selling more of its goods through the Internet, it will rely less on foot traffic into its retail store. This reduces its incentive to pay a high rent for a good location.

Economists analyze choices by focusing on incentives. In an economic context, incentives are benefits (including reduced costs) that motivate a decision maker in favor of a particular choice. Many things can affect incentives, but among the most important are *prices*. If the price of gasoline rises, people have a greater incentive to drive less. If the price of MP3 players falls, people have a greater incentive to buy one. When the price of a good rises, firms are induced to produce more of that good, to increase their profits. If a resource used in production, such as labor or equipment, becomes more expensive, firms have an incentive to find new methods of production that economize on that resource. Incentives also are affected by the return people expect to earn from different activities. If the income of college graduates rises relative to that of people with only a high school diploma, people have a greater incentive to attend college.

When economists study the behavior of people or firms, they look at the incentives being faced. Sometimes these incentives are straightforward. Increasing the number of courses required to major in biology reduces the incentive to pick that major. In other circumstances, they may not be so obvious. For example, safer cars may create incentives to drive faster. Identifying the incentives, and disincentives, to take different actions is one of the first things economists do when they want to understand the choices individuals or firms make.

Decision makers respond to incentives; for understanding choices, incentives matter.

Thinking Like an Economist

Incentives and the Price of AOL

Today, most on-line services such as AOL charge their customers a fixed monthly fee for Internet access. In the earlier days of the Internet, it was common to charge a fee based on how many minutes the member was connected to the Internet. In 1997, AOL announced that it would change its pricing policy and move to a flat monthly fee with unlimited minutes of connect time. AOL's servers were quickly overwhelmed and members found it virtually impossible to log on. Why? With charges no longer based on the number of minutes a member was logged on, many customers never logged off. Once connected, they simply left AOL running, tying up its modem capacity. When members had to pay on a per-minute basis, they had an incentive to log off when the service was not being used. When this incentive was removed, there was no longer any incentive to economize on connect time. Thinking about incentives would have shown AOL that it needed to greatly increase its modem capacity *before* announcing the new pricing plan.

Exchange

Even a Robinson Crusoe, living alone on a desert island, faces choices and responds to incentives in making those choices. But for most of us, our economic lives are interwoven with the lives of millions of other individuals. The food we eat may be grown in Mexico, our shoes may be produced in Taiwan, and our car in Detroit. To produce a single product like an automobile or a computer, thousands of decisions and choices have to be made. Since the economy is made up of millions of different products, not just automobiles and computers, it is a marvel that the modern industrial economy functions at all, let alone as well as it does most of the time. This marvel is particularly clear if we consider instances when things have not worked so well: during the Great Depression of the 1930s; in Russia, where the painful transition to a market economy has left some workers going months without being paid; and in the less developed economies of many countries in Africa, Asia, and Latin America, where standards of living have remained stubbornly low or have even declined.

Somehow, decisions that are made—by individuals, households, firms, and government—together determine how the economy's limited resources, including its land, labor, machines, oil, and other natural resources, are used. Why is it that land used at one time for growing crops may be used at another time for a silicon chip plant? How was it that over the space of a couple of decades early in the last century, resources were transferred from making horse carriages to making automobile bodies? That blacksmiths were replaced by auto mechanics? How do the decisions of millions of consumers, workers, investors, managers, and government officials interact to determine how the scarce resources available to society are used? How is it that modern economies are able to produce millions of different goods in a seemingly uncoordinated fashion? And since resources are scarce, is there any mechanism that ensures the best possible use of them? The key to these questions lies in the role of *voluntary* exchange in *markets*.

Long before the rise of modern industrial societies, the benefits of exchange were well understood. Coastal societies with access to fishing resources, for example, would trade some of their fish to inland societies in return for meat and furs. The coastal group exchanged fish for meat and furs that were worth more to them than the fish they gave up; the inland group exchanged meat and furs for fish that were worth more to them than the things they gave up. Both groups benefited from voluntary exchange.

In modern societies, millions of exchanges take place. Few individuals produce any of the goods and services they themselves want to consume. Instead, teachers, police officers, lawyers, or construction workers sell their labor services to a school district, a city, a client, or a home-builder and then exchange the income they earn for all the various goods and services they wish to consume and that have been produced by others. An important insight in economics is the recognition that *both* parties in a voluntary exchange gain. Whether it is voluntary exchange between two individuals, between an individual and a firm, or between residents of two different countries, exchange can improve the well-being of both parties.

Economists describe any situation in which exchange takes place as a market. For thousands of years, societies have established physical locations such as village markets or periodic trading fairs where people have brought their products, haggled over the prices at which one item would trade for another, and reaped the benefits of trade. The economic concept of markets is used to include any situation in which exchange takes place, though this exchange may not necessarily resemble a traditional village market or a modern stock exchange market. In department stores and shopping malls, customers rarely haggle over the price. When manufacturers purchase the materials they need for production, they exchange money, not other goods, for them. Most goods, from cameras to clothes, are not sold directly from producers to consumers. Instead they are sold from producers to distributors, from distributors to retailers, and from retailers to consumers. All of these transactions are embraced by the concept of markets and a **market economy.**

Today's consumers shop at both traditional markets as well as online markets such as eBay.com.

In a market economy like the United States, most exchanges take place through markets, and these exchanges are guided by the prices of the goods and services involved. The goods and services that are scarcer, or require more resources for their production, come at a higher price. Automobiles are more expensive than paper cups; lawyers charge more than janitors. As a result, markets enable consumers and firms to make choices that reflect scarcity, and therefore lead to efficient uses of resources.

Market economies thus rely primarily on market exchanges to resolve the most basic economic questions: What and how much is produced? How is it produced? For whom is it produced? And who makes the economic decisions? Individuals and firms make the decisions. Individuals make decisions that reflect their own desires as they respond to the incentives they face. Firms make decisions that maximize their profits, and to do so they strive to produce the goods that consumers want at the lowest possible cost. This process determines what is produced, how it is produced, and for whom. As firms compete in the quest for profits, consumers benefit, both from the kinds of goods produced and from the prices at which they are supplied. On the whole, markets ensure that society's resources are used efficiently.

In some areas, however, markets lead to outcomes that society may find inadequate. There may be too much pollution, too much inequality, and too little concern about education, health, and safety. When the market is not perceived to be working well, people often turn to government. An economy such as in the United States is often called a *mixed economy*—one that relies primarily but not exclusively on the free interaction of producers and consumers to determine what is produced, how, and for whom. In some areas, the government makes the decisions, in others it imposes

Internet Connection

Auction Sites

An auction is one form of market that used to require potential buyers to be physically present in a single location. Now auctions are held over the Internet and can involve participants from around the world. Some sites such as eBay (http://www.ebay.com/) offer just about everything for sale. Other sites specialize. For instance, Heritage Coins (http://www.heritagecoin.com/) provides an auction site for rare coins. Even the U.S. government has gotten into the act. The U.S. Treasury does not actually auction items on-line, but it uses the Web to publicize the locations at which confiscated property will be auctioned (http://www.treas.gov/auctions/customs/) .

The Basic Economic Questions

1. What is produced, and in what quantities?
2. How are these goods produced?
3. For whom are these goods produced?
4. Who makes economic decisions, and by what process?

regulations that affect the incentives firms and households face, and in many areas, both the private and the public sector are involved (education is a good example).

Government plays a critical role in all market economies. In the United States, the government sets the legal structure under which private firms and individuals operate. It regulates businesses to ensure that they do not discriminate by race or sex, do not mislead consumers, are careful about the safety of their employees, and do not pollute the air and water. In some industries, the government operates like a private business: the government-owned Tennessee Valley Authority (TVA) is one of the nation's largest producers of electricity; most children attend government-owned public schools; most mail is still delivered by the government-owned postal service. In other cases, the government supplies goods and services that the private sector does not, such as the national defense, roads, and currency. Government programs provide for the elderly through Social Security (which pays income to retired individuals) and Medicare (which funds medical needs of the aged). The government helps those who have suffered economic dislocation, through unemployment insurance for those temporarily unemployed and disability insurance for those who are no longer able to work. The government also provides a safety net of support for the poor, particularly children, through various welfare programs.

One can easily imagine the government controlling the economy more directly. In countries where decision making is centralized and concentrated in the government, government bureaucrats might decide what and how much a factory should produce and set the wages that should be paid. At least until recently, governments in countries like the former Soviet Union and China attempted to control practically all major decisions regarding resource allocation. Even in Europe, not long ago many governments ran oil companies, coal mines, and the telephone system. Increasingly, however, governments have sold these enterprises to the private sector, a process called *privatization*.

Market economies in which individuals and firms make the decisions about what to produce and how much to pay have proven adept at developing new technologies and products. It is hard to imagine government bureaucrats developing MP3 players or iMacs in neon colors. Markets also generally ensure that resources are used efficiently.

Exchange in markets is a key to understanding how resources are allocated, what is produced, and who earns what.

Information

Making informed choices requires information. After all, it is hard to weigh the costs and benefits of alternative choices if you do not know what they are! A firm that is contemplating the purchase of a new software system needs to know not only the costs of the various alternatives but also the capabilities and limitations of each alternative. Information is, in many ways, like other goods and services. Firms and individuals are willing to purchase information, and specialized institutions develop to sell information. In many areas, separate organizations are designed solely to provide information to consumers. *Consumer Reports* is a prime example. The Internet also now serves as a major source of independent information for buyers. But there are some fundamental ways in which information differs from other goods. A car seller will let you test-drive a vehicle before you buy, but a seller of information cannot let you see the information before you buy. Once you have seen the information, you have no incentive to pay for it. Another way information differs from other goods is that unlike a can of soft drink or a bagel, information can be freely shared. When I tell you something, it does not subtract from what I know (though it may subtract from the profits I might earn from the information).

In some key areas of the economy, the role of information is so critical that it affects the nature of the market. In the used-car market, buyers and sellers negotiating over the price of a used car may have quite different information about its quality. The seller may have better information about the quality of the car but also has an incentive to misrepresent the condition of the car since better-quality cars command higher prices. As a result, the buyer will be reluctant to trust claims that the car is in perfect shape. When consumers lack adequate information to make informed choices, government frequently intervenes to require that firms provide information. The Securities and Exchange Commission (SEC) that oversees American stock markets requires that firms meet certain reporting requirements before their stock can be listed on exchanges such as the New York Stock Exchange. This helps to ensure that private investors have reliable information on which to base their investment decisions. The SEC also enforces laws against "insider trading" to ensure a company's managers do not profit by trading on information not yet available to the public. Even in the absence of regulations, firms have incentives to signal to buyers that their products are of high quality. One way they do this is to offer guarantees that a producer of low-quality goods could not afford to offer.

Imperfect information also can interfere with incentives. Employers want to create incentives for employees to work hard. One way to do this is to base pay on a measure of how productive each worker is. Often, however, it is difficult to measure a worker's productivity. If performance can be measured only imperfectly, it is difficult to link pay to performance. For example, a major debate in the United States concerns tying teacher salaries to performance. Because it is hard to measure teaching performance, the pay of most teachers is based primarily on how long they have been teaching.

Information, or its absence, plays a key role in determining the shape of markets and the ability of private markets to ensure the economy's scarce resources are used efficiently.

Distribution

The market economy not only determines what goods are produced and how they are produced but also determines for whom they are produced. Many people find unacceptable the way the market distributes goods among households. "While recognizing the efficacy of capitalism to produce wealth, there remains considerable unease among some segments about the way markets distribute that wealth and about the effects of raw competition on society."[8] Like bidders at an auction, what market participants are willing and able to pay depends on their income. Incomes differ markedly across occupations, as Figure 1.1 shows. Some

[8]Alan Greenspan, speech at the Federal Reserve Bank of Kansas City Jackson Hole Conference, August 25, 2000.

groups of individuals—including those without skills that are valued by the market—may receive such a low income that they cannot feed and educate their children without outside assistance. Government provides the assistance by taking steps to increase income equality.

Steps that soften the distributional impact of markets may blunt economic incentives. While welfare payments provide an important safety net for the poor, the taxation required to finance them may discourage people from working and saving. If the government takes one out of every two or three dollars that an individual earns, that individual may not be inclined to work as much. And if the government takes one out of every two or three dollars a person earns from interest on savings, the person may decide to spend more and save less. Thus, efforts by the government to redistribute income may came at the cost of reduced economic efficiency.

The primary reliance on private decision making in the United States reflects economists' beliefs that this reliance is appropriate and necessary for economic efficiency. However, economists also believe that certain interventions by government are desirable. Like the appropriate balance between public and private sectors, the appropriate balance between concerns about equality (often referred to as *equity concerns*) and efficiency is a central issue of modern economies. As elsewhere, trade-offs must be made.

WRAP-UP

Five Core Ideas

1. *Trade-offs*: resources are scarce, so trade-offs are a basic fact of life.
2. *Incentives*: in making choices, decision makers respond to incentives.
3. *Exchange*: people benefit from voluntary exchange, and in market economies, market exchanges lead to the efficient use of resources.
4. *Information*: the structure that markets take and how well they can function depend critically on the information available to decision makers.
5. *Distribution*: markets determine how the goods and services produced by the economy are allocated to members of society.

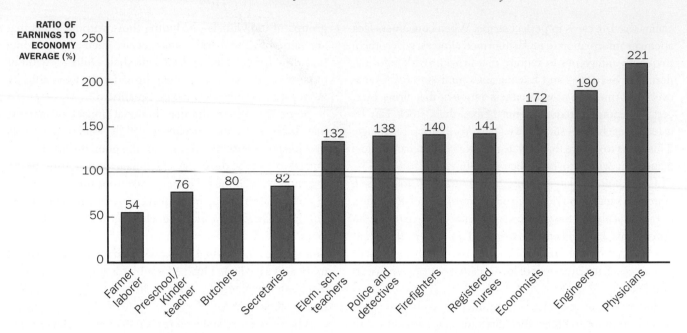

FIGURE 1.1 *Who Takes Home America's Output?*

This chart measures the median earnings of a variety of professions relative to the wages of an average worker. Farm workers earn only 54 percent of the average worker's income, elementary school teachers make 32 percent more than an average worker, while physicians make over twice as much.

SOURCE: Bureau of Labor Statistics, *Current Population Survey of Employment and Earnings* (January 1999).

The Three Major Markets

The market economy revolves around exchange between individuals (or households) who buy goods and services from firms, and firms, which take *inputs,* the various materials of production, and produce *outputs,* the goods and services that they sell. In thinking about a market economy, economists focus their attention on three broad categories of markets in which individuals and firms interact. The markets in which firms sell their outputs to households are referred to collectively as the **product market.** Many firms also sell goods to other firms; the output of the first firm becomes the input of the second. These transactions too are said to occur in the product market.

On the input side, firms need (besides the materials they buy in the product market) some combination of labor and machinery to produce their output. They purchase the services of workers in the **labor market.** They raise funds to buy inputs in the **capital market.** Traditionally, economists also have highlighted the importance of a third input, land, but in modern industrial economies, land is of secondary importance. For most purposes, it suffices to focus attention on the three major markets—product, labor, and capital—and this text will follow this pattern.

As Figure 1.2 shows, individuals participate in all three markets. When individuals buy goods and services, they act as *consumers* in the product market. When people act as *workers,* economists say they "sell their labor services" in the labor market. When people buy shares of stock in a firm, deposit money in a savings account, or lend money to a business, they are participating in the capital market as *investors.*

Keeping Track of Tricky Terms

Terms in economics often are similar to terms in ordinary usage, but they can have special meanings. The terms *markets* and *capital* illustrate this problem.

Though the term *market* is used to conjure up an image of a busy *marketplace,* there is no formal marketplace for most goods and services. There are buyers and

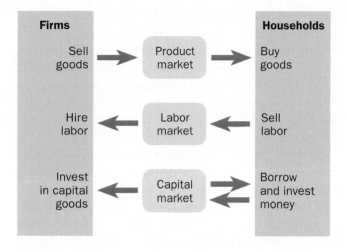

FIGURE 1.2   *The Three Markets*

To economists, people wear different hats. They are usually consumers in the product market, workers in the labor market, and borrowers or lenders in the capital market.

sellers, and economists analyze the outcomes *as if* there were a single marketplace in which all transactions occur. For example, economists analyze the "market for books," even though the buyers and sellers in the market for books interact in thousands of individual bookstores and on-line selling locations.

Moreover, economists often talk about the "market for labor" as if all workers were identical. But workers differ in countless ways. In some cases, these differences are important. We might then talk about the "market for skilled workers" or the "market for computer engineers." In other cases—such as when we are talking about the overall state of the economy and focusing on the overall unemployment

WRAP-UP

The Three Major Markets

1. *The product market*: the markets in which firms sell the goods they produce.
2. *The labor market*: the market in which households sell labor services and firms buy labor services.
3. *The capital market*: the market in which funds are borrowed and lent.

rate (the proportion of workers who are looking for jobs but cannot find them)—these differences can be ignored.

When newspapers refer to the *capital market,* they mean the bond traders and stockbrokers and the companies they work for on Wall Street and other financial districts. When economists use the term *capital market,* they have in mind a broader concept that includes all the institutions concerned with raising funds (and, as we will see later, sharing and insuring risk), including banks and insurance companies.

The term *capital* is used in still another way—to refer to the machines and buildings used in production. To distinguish this particular usage, in this book we refer to machines and buildings as **capital goods.** The term *capital markets* thus refers to the markets in which funds are raised, borrowed, and lent. *Capital goods markets* refers to the markets in which capital goods are bought and sold.

Microeconomics and Macroeconomics: The Two Branches of Economics

Economists have developed two different ways to look at the economy. The detailed study of the decisions of firms and households, and of prices and production in specific industries, is called **microeconomics.** Microeconomics (*micro* is derived from the Greek word meaning "small") focuses on the behavior of the units—the firms, households, and individuals—that make up the economy. It is concerned with how the individual units make decisions and what affects those decisions.

By contrast, **macroeconomics** (*macro* is derived from the Greek word meaning "large") looks at the behavior of the economy as a whole, in particular the behavior of such aggregate measures as the overall rates of unemployment, inflation, and economic growth and the balance of trade. The aggregate numbers do not tell us what any one firm or household is doing. They tell us what is happening in total, or on average. In a dynamic economy, there are always some industries expanding and others contracting. For instance, the economic expansion of the late 1990s saw rapid growth in Internet-related industries, while oil firms in Texas contracted. But why does the overall growth in an economy sometimes slow and at times, the level of economic activity actually decline, not just in an isolated industry but seemingly across all or almost all industries?

In macroeconomics, we also look at the behavior of the general level of prices, interest rates, and exchange rates. Why do prices of almost all goods and services seem to rise at rapid rates during some periods, while at other times they remain stable? Why do interest rates fluctuate? And what determines the value of the dollar relative to other currencies?

In approaching these questions, it is important to remember that the behavior of the economy as a whole is dependent on the decisions made by the millions of households and firms in the economy, as well as the decisions made by the government. Micro and macro perspectives are simply two ways of looking at the same thing. Microeconomics is the bottom-up view of the economy; macroeconomics is the top-down view.

WRAP-UP

The Branches of Economics

Microeconomics: focuses on the decisions of households and firms and the detailed study of prices and production in specific industries.

Macroeconomics: focuses on the behavior of the economy as a whole and the behavior of aggregate variables such as overall employment, output, economic growth, the price level, and inflation.

The Science of Economics

Economics is a *social science*. It studies the social problem of choice from a scientific viewpoint, which means that it is built on a systematic exploration of the problem of choice. This systematic exploration involves both the formulation of theories and the examination of data.

A **theory** consists of a set of assumptions (or hypotheses) and conclusions derived from those assumptions. Theories are logical exercises: *if* the assumptions are correct, *then* the results follow. If all college graduates have a

better chance of getting jobs and Ellen is a college graduate, then Ellen has a better chance of getting a job than a nongraduate. Economists make predictions with their theories. They might use their theory to predict what would happen if a tax is increased or if imports of foreign cars are limited. The predictions of a theory are of the form, "If a tax is increased and if the market is competitive, then output will decrease and prices will increase."

In developing their theories, economists use *models*. To understand how models are used in economics, consider a modern car manufacturer trying to design a new automobile. It is extremely expensive to construct a new car. Rather than creating a separate, fully developed car for every conception of what engineers or designers would like the new car to be, the company uses models. The designers might use a plastic model to study the general shape of the vehicle and to assess reactions to the car's aesthetics. The engineers might use a computer model to study air resistance, from which they can calculate fuel consumption.

Just as engineers construct different models to study particular features of a car, economists construct different models of the economy—in words or equations—to depict particular features of the economy. An economic model might describe a general relationship ("When incomes rise, the number of cars purchased increases"), describe a quantitative relationship ("When incomes rise by 10 percent, the number of cars purchased rises, on average, by 12 percent"), or make a general prediction ("An increase in the tax on gasoline will decrease the demand for cars").

Discovering and Interpreting Relationships

A *variable* is any item that can be measured and that changes. Prices, wages, interest rates, and quantities bought and sold are variables. What interests economists is the connection between variables. When economists see what appears to be a systematic relationship among variables, they ask, could it have arisen by change or is there indeed a relationship? This is the question of **correlation.**

Economists use statistical tests to measure and test correlations. Consider the problem of deciding whether a coin is biased. If you flip the coin 10 times and get 6 heads and 4 tails, is the coin a fair one? Or is it weighted toward heads? Statistical tests will show that the result of 6 heads and 4 tails easily could have happened by chance, so the evidence does not prove that the coin is weighted. It also does not prove that it is *not* weighted. The evidence is not strong enough for either conclusion. But if you flip the coin 100 times and get 80 heads, statistical tests will tell you that the possibility of this happening by blind chance with a fair coin is extremely small. The evidence supports the assertion that the coin is weighted.

A similar logic can be used on correlations among economic variables. People with more education tend to earn higher wages. Is the connection merely chance? Statistical tests show whether the evidence is too weak for a conclusion, or whether it supports the existence of a systematic relationship between education and wages.

Causation and Correlation

Economists would like to accomplish more than just assertions that different variables are indeed correlated. They would like to conclude that changes in one variable *cause* the changes in another variable. This distinction between correlations and **causation** is important. If one variable "causes" the other, then changing one variable necessarily will change the other. If the relationship is just a correlation, this may not be true.

During the 1970s, imports of Japanese cars into the United States increased while sales of U.S. cars decreased. The two variables were negatively correlated. But did that prove that increased Japanese car sales caused the decrease in American sales? If the decline in U.S. car production during this period was because American companies were producing large gas guzzlers that people no longer wanted, reducing Japanese car sales might not increase the sales of U.S.-made cars. In short, if there was a common cause to both changes—increased oil prices after 1973 leading to increased sales of fuel-efficient Japanese cars and decreased sales of U.S. cars—then these trends would be reversed only when American companies started producing fuel-efficient cars or gas prices decreased.

In some cases, the *direction* of causation is not clear: did high Japanese sales cause low U.S. sales, or vice versa? For instance, it might have turned out, upon closer investigation, that the true explanation of decreased sales of U.S. cars was strikes that caused production shortages. When U.S. cars were not available, consumers turned to Japanese cars. To tell which explanation is valid—whether high Japanese car sales caused low U.S. car sales, whether low U.S. production caused high Japanese sales, or whether both were caused by a third factor—requires closer examination of, for example,

the circumstances in which the two variables moved in directions different from those normally observed.

Why Economists Disagree

Economists are frequently called on to make judgments on matters of public policy. Should the government cut taxes? Should Internet commerce be taxed? Should the government impose environmental regulations, and if so, how should they be designed? In these public policy discussions, economists often disagree. They differ in their views of how the world works, in their *descriptions* of the economy, or in their predictions of the consequences of certain actions. Or they differ in their values, in how they evaluate these consequences.

When they describe the economy and construct models that predict either how the economy will change or the effects of different policies, economists are engaged in what is called **positive economics.** When they evaluate alternative policies, weighing the various benefits and costs, they are engaged in what is called **normative economics.** Positive economics is concerned with what "is," with describing how the economy functions. Normative economics deals with what "should be," with making judgments about the desirability of various courses of action. Normative economics makes use of positive economics. We cannot make judgments about whether a policy is desirable unless we have a clear picture of its consequences. Good normative economics also tries to be explicit about precisely what values or objectives it is incorporating. It tries to couch its statement in the form, "If these are your objectives, then this is the best possible policy."

Consider the normative and positive aspects of a proposal to restrict imports of Japanese cars. Positive economics would describe the consequences: the increased prices consumers have to pay, the increased sales of American cars, the increased employment and profits, and the increased pollution and oil imports because American cars on average are less fuel efficient than Japanese cars. Economists might disagree over the consequences of restricting imports because they differ over the appropriate model of the economy or because they differ over quantitative magnitudes, perhaps agreeing that prices to consumers would rise but disagreeing over how much prices would rise.

In the end, though, the policy question is, *should there be restraints on imports of Japanese cars?* This is a normative question. Normative economics would weigh these various effects—the losses to consumers, the gains to workers, the increased profits and pollution—to reach an overall judgment. Normative economics develops frameworks within which these complicated judgments can be conducted in a systematic way.

Economists, like members of any other profession, often have different values. Two economists might agree that a particular tax change would increase saving but would benefit the wealthy more than the poor. However, they might reach different conclusions about the desirability of the tax change. One might oppose the tax change because it increases income inequality; the other might support it because it promotes saving. They differ in the values they place on the effects of the policy change, so they reach different conclusions even when they agree on the positive analysis of the proposed policy.

While economists may often seem to differ greatly among themselves, in fact they agree more than they disagree. When they do disagree, economists try to be clear about the source of their disagreement: (1) to what extent does it arise out of differences in models, (2) to what extent does it arise out of differences in estimates of quantitative relationships, and (3) to what extent does it arise out of differences in values? Clarifying the source of and reasons for disagreement can be a very productive way of learning more.

Review and Practice

Summary

1. Economics is the study of how individuals, firms, and governments within our society make choices. Choices are unavoidable because desired goods, services, and resources are inevitably scarce.

2. Economists study how individuals, firms, and governments within our society make choices by focusing on incentives. People respond to changes in incentives by altering the decisions they make.

3. Exchange occurs in markets. With voluntary exchange, both parties to the exchange can benefit.

4. Making choices requires information. Limited or imperfect information can interfere with incentives and affect the ability of the private market to ensure an efficient use of society's scarce resources.

5. The incomes people receive are determined by the market economy. Concerns over the equitable distribution of wealth and income in the economy lead to government programs that increase income equality.

6. The United States has a mixed economy, one in which there is a mix between public and private decision making. The economy relies primarily on the private interaction of individuals and firms to determine how resources are allocated, but government plays a large role as well. A central question for any mixed economy is the balance between the private and public sectors.

7. The term *market* is used to describe any situation where exchange takes place. In the U.S. market economy, individuals, firms, and government interact in product markets, labor markets, and capital markets.

8. The two major branches of economics are microeconomics and macroeconomics. Microeconomics focuses on the behavior of the firms, households, and individuals that make up the economy. Macroeconomics focuses on the behavior of the economy as a whole.

9. Economists use models to study how the economy works and to make predictions about what will happen if something is changed. A model can be expressed in words or equations and is designed to mirror the essential characteristics of the particular phenomena under study.

10. A correlation exists when two variables tend to change together in a predictable way. However, the simple existence of a correlation does not prove that one factor causes the other to change. Additional outside factors may be influencing both.

11. Positive economics is the study of how the economy works. Disagreements in positive economics center on the appropriate model of the economy or market and the quantitative magnitudes characterizing the models.

12. Normative economics deals with the desirability of various actions. Disagreements in normative economics center on differences in the values placed on the various costs and benefits of different actions.

Key Terms

trade-offs
incentives
exchange
information
distribution
scarcity
market economy
product market
labor market
capital market
capital goods
microeconomics
macroeconomics
theory
correlation
causation
positive economics
normative economics

Review Questions

1. Why are trade-offs unavoidable? Why are incentives important in understanding choices?

2. After a voluntary exchange, why are both parties better off?

3. How does information differ from standard goods? How do information imperfections affect markets?

4. Why might there be a trade-off between equity and efficiency?

5. What is a mixed economy? Describe some of the roles government might play, or not play, in a mixed economy.

6. Name the three main economic markets, and describe how an individual might participate in each one as a buyer or a seller.

7. Give two examples of economic issues that are primarily microeconomic and two examples that are primarily macroeconomic. What is the general difference between microeconomics and macroeconomics?

8. What is a model? Why do economists use models?

9. Give two examples of variables that you would expect to be positively correlated. For each example, explain whether causation exists between the two variables.

10. "All disagreements between economists are purely subjective." Comment.

Problems

1. How does each of the following affect the incentive to go to college?

    (a) An increase in tuition costs

    (b) A fall in the interest rate on student loans

    (c) A rise in wages for unskilled jobs

    (d) An increase in incomes of college graduates

2. Characterize the following events as microeconomic, macroeconomic, or both.

    (a) Unemployment increases this month.

    (b) A drug company invents and begins to market a new medicine.

    (c) A bank loans money to a large company but turns down a small business.

    (d) Interest rates decline for all borrowers.

    (e) A union negotiates for higher pay and better health insurance.

    (f) The price of oil increases.

3. Characterize the following events as part of the labor market, the capital market, or the product market.

    (a) An investor tries to decide which company to invest in.

    (b) With practice, the workers on an assembly line become more efficient.

    (c) The opening up of economies in Eastern Europe offers new markets for American products.

    (d) A big company that is losing money decides to offer its workers special incentives to retire early, hoping to reduce its costs.

    (e) A consumer roams around a shopping mall looking for birthday gifts.

(f) The federal government uses a surplus to pay off some of its debt.

4. The back of a bag of cat litter claims, "Cats that use cat litter live three years longer than cats that don't." Do you think that cat litter actually causes an increased life expectancy for cats, or can you think of some other factors to explain this correlation? What evidence might you collect to test your explanation?

5. Life expectancy in Sweden is seventy-nine years; life expectancy in India is sixty-two years. Does this prove that if an Indian moved to Sweden, he would live longer? That is, does this prove that living in Sweden causes an increase in life expectancy, or can you think of some other factors to explain these facts? What evidence might you collect to test your explanation?

6. During 2000, some economists argued that the Federal Reserve should undertake policies to slow the economic expansion in the United States to ensure low inflation. Other economists opposed such policies, arguing that the dangers of inflation were exaggerated and attempts by the Federal Reserve to slow the economy would lead to higher unemployment. Is this a disagreement about positive or normative economics? Explain.

Chapter 2

Thinking Like an Economist

Key Questions

1. What is the basic competitive model of the economy?

2. What are incentives, property rights, prices, and profit motive, and what role do these essential ingredients of a market economy play?

3. What alternatives for allocating resources are there to the market system, and why do economists tend not to favor these alternatives?

4. What are some of the basic techniques economists use in their study of how people make choices? What are the various concepts of costs that economists use?

*E*veryone thinks about economics, at least some of the time. We think about money (we wish we had more of it) and about work (we wish we had less of it). But there is a distinctive way that economists approach economic issues, and one of the purposes of this course is to introduce you to that way of thinking. This chapter begins with a basic model of the economy. We follow this with a closer look at how the basic units that comprise the economy—individuals, firms, and government—make choices in situations where they are faced with scarcity. Choice involves trade-offs—spending money on one item means less is available for others. Understanding how economists study these trade-offs and how they analyze decisions by individuals, firms, and government is key to learning to think like an economist. In Chapters 3 through 5, we study ways in which individuals and firms interact with one another in markets to carry out exchanges, and how these interactions "add up" to determine how society's resources are allocated.

The Basic Competitive Model

Every day, millions of people take part in thousands of exchanges in hundreds of different markets. Somehow, out of all these exchanges, computers get produced and end up in student dorm rooms, food is grown and ends up on the dinner tables of households, and electricity is delivered to millions of homes and offices at the flick of a switch. In an economy like that of the United States, markets play a critical role in ensuring that workers find jobs, things get produced, and firms sell their goods. Exchange and the role of markets are important, but what makes them work? How can you be sure your local grocery store will have bread in the morning? And how can you be sure that the grocery store won't try to charge you $20 for that loaf of bread?

25

The answer can be given in one word—**competition.** Firms compete with one another for customers, and in doing so offer them the products they want at the lowest possible price. Consumers also compete with one another. Only a limited number of goods are available, and they come at a price. Consumers who meet the price can enjoy the goods, but others are left empty-handed. This competitive picture of markets, which economists call the **basic competitive model,** provides the point of departure for studying the economy. It consists of three parts: assumptions about how consumers behave, assumptions about how firms behave, and assumptions about how markets in which these consumers and firms interact and in which exchange takes place behave. Consumers are assumed to be *rational,* firms are assumed to be *profit maximizing,* and the markets in which they interact are assumed to be highly *competitive.* The model ignores government, because we need to see how an economy without a government might function before we can understand the role of government.

Rational Consumers and Profit-Maximizing Firms

Scarcity, which we encountered in Chapter 1, implies that individuals and firms face trade-offs and must make choices. Underlying much of economic analysis is the basic assumption of **rational choice,** that people weigh the costs and benefits of each possibility whenever they must make a choice. This assumption is based on the expectation that individuals and firms will act in a consistent manner, with a reasonably well-defined notion of what they like and what their objectives are, and with a reasonable understanding of how to attain those objectives.

In the case of individuals, the rationality assumption is taken to mean that they make choices and decisions in pursuit of their own *self-interest.* Of course, different people will have different goals and desires. Sarah may want to drive a Porsche, own a yacht, and have a large house; to attain those objectives, she knows she needs to work long hours and sacrifice time with her familiy. Andrew is willing to accept a lower income to get longer vacations and more leisure time throughout the year.

Economists make no judgment about whether Sarah's preferences are "better" or "worse" than Andrew's. They do not even spend much time asking why different individuals have different views on these matters, or why tastes change over time. These are important issues, but they are more the province of psychology and sociology. Economists are concerned with the consequences of these different preferences. What decisions can they expect Sarah and Andrew to make when each is rationally pursuing their respective interests?

In the case of firms, the rationality assumption is taken to mean that firms operate to maximize their profits.

Competitive Markets

To complete the model, economists make assumptions about the places where self-interested consumers and profit-maximizing firms meet: markets. Economists begin by focusing on the case where there are many buyers and sellers, all buying and selling the same thing. You might picture a crowded farmers' market to get a sense of the number of buyers and sellers—except that you have to picture everyone buying and selling just one good. Let's say we are in Florida, and the booths are full of oranges.

Each of the farmers would like to raise his prices. That way, if he can still sell his oranges, his profits go up. Yet with a large number of sellers, each is forced to charge close to the same price, since if any farmer charged much more, he would lose business to the farmer next door. Profit-maximizing firms are in the same position. In an extreme case, if a firm charged any more than the going price, it would lose *all* its sales. Economists label this case **perfect competition.** In perfect competition, each firm is a **price taker,** which simply means that because it cannot influence the market price, it must accept that price. The firm takes the market price as given because it cannot raise its price without losing all sales, and at the market price it can sell as much as it wishes. Even if it sold ten times as much, this would have a negligible effect on the total quantity marketed or the price prevailing in the market. Markets for agricultural goods would be, in the absence of government intervention, perfectly competitive. There are so many wheat farmers, for instance, that each farmer believes he can grow and sell as much wheat as he wishes and have no effect on the price of wheat. (Later in the book, we will encounter markets with limited or no competition, like monopolies, where firms can raise prices without losing all their sales.)

On the other side of our farmers' market are rational individuals, each of whom would like to pay as little as possible for oranges. Why can't any consumer pay less than the going price? Because the seller sees another buyer in the crowd who will pay the going price. Thus, the consumers also have to compete against each other for the limited

e-Insight

Markets, Exchange, and E-Commerce

In traditional societies, markets are places where people get together to exchange goods. They are active, bustling places, full of life. In the modern economy, goods and services are being exchanged *as if* there was a well-defined marketplace. The Internet has created this new kind of marketplace where people all over the world can exchange goods and services without ever getting together.

In traditional economies, prices for similar goods in different marketplaces could differ markedly. Traders would buy goods in a marketplace where it was cheap, and transport the goods to where the price was higher, making a handsome profit in doing so. These merchants helped make markets work better. Much of their high income could be thought of as a return on their information—on knowing where to buy cheap and sell dear. And by moving goods from places where they were valued less to places where they were valued more, they performed an important social function.

The Internet has enabled all of this to be done far more efficiently, at lower cost, with more complete information. Markets all over the world can be joined instantaneously, creating a global marketplace. Now any buyer (not just a merchant) can find the place where the good is selling at the lowest price, and any seller can find the place where the good is selling at the highest price.

Some have worried that this will eliminate the role of the middleman, of merchants. But there is more to trade than just information about price. Many goods differ in a variety of dimensions, such as quality and durability. E-markets work best for well-defined goods, for which these issues are not relevant, goods like wheat or steel or products like this textbook.

---

number of oranges in the market, and as a result each takes the market price as given.

While a farmers' market provides one illustration of what economists mean by a market, most markets do not take this form. The modern-day market is more likely to involve buyers and sellers interacting over the Internet. But the same basic principles apply. When there are lots of buyers and sellers, each will take the price as given in deciding how much to buy or sell.

Efficiency and Distribution in the Basic Competitive Model

The basic competitive model, assuming it accurately represents actual markets, has one very strong implication: the economy will be efficient. Scarce resources will not be wasted. It will not be possible to produce more of one good without producing less of another, and it will not be possible to make any person better off without making someone else worse off. These results are obtained in the absence of any government activity.

Competitive markets also determine the distribution of goods—who gets to consume how much of the goods that are available. High levels of competition for the services of an individual with a rare and valuable skill will result in a very high income for that individual. On the other hand, competition among suppliers of unskilled labor may result in these workers facing very low wages, so low that even long work hours fail to achieve a decent standard of living. This raises the question of the fairness of competitive distribution. Though efficiency is a desirable property of any economic system, the question of fairness is a seperate issue. Later in this book we will discuss how economists and policymakers think about the inequalities that inevitably emerge from the workings of the competitive market.

The Basic Competitive Model as a Benchmark

Virtually all economists recognize that the competitive model is not a *perfect* representation of actual economies, but most economists still use it as a convenient benchmark—

as we will throughout this book. After all, as you learned in Chapter 1, a *model* is never a complete and accurate description—it is not meant to be—but instead is designed to highlight critical aspects of the economy that provide insight and help us understand particular features of the economy. We will point out important differences between the predictions of the basic competitive model and observed outcomes, and in Part Three, we will show how this model can be extended to offer new insights for understanding markets and situations that cannot be understood fully just using the basic competitive model. Differences between the predictions of the basic competitive model and observed outcomes can help guide us to other models that provide a better understanding of particular markets and situations. While the basic competitive model may not provide a *perfect* description of some markets, economists recognize that it may provide a good description—with its predictions matching actual outcomes well, though not perfectly. In fact, most economists believe that the basic competitive model gives us tremendous insights into a wide range of economic issues, and for that reason, it is the foundation on which economists build.

WRAP-UP

Ingredients in the Basic Competitive Model

1. Rational, self-interested consumers
2. Rational, profit-maximizing firms
3. Competitive markets with price-taking behavior

Incentives and Information: Prices, Property Rights, and Profits

For market economies to work efficiently, firms and individuals must be informed and have incentives to act on available information. Indeed, incentives can be viewed as at the heart of economics. Without incentives, why would individuals go to work in the morning? Who would under-

take the risks of bringing out new products? Who would put aside savings for a rainy day? There is an old expression about the importance of having someone "mind the store." But without incentives, why would anyone bother?

Market economies provide information and incentives through *prices, profits,* and *property rights.* Prices provide information about the relative scarcity of different goods. The **price system** ensures that goods go to those individuals and firms who are most willing and able to pay for them. Prices convey information to consumers about scarcity, and consumers respond by adjusting their consumption. Similarly, prices convey information to firms about how individuals value different goods.

The desire for profits motivates firms to respond to the information provided by prices. By producing what consumers want in the most efficient way, in ways that least use scarce resources, they increase their profits. Similarly, rational individuals' pursuit of self-interest induces them to respond to prices: They buy goods which are more expensive—in a sense relatively more scarce—only if they provide commensurately greater benefits. If a good such as oil becomes scarcer, its price rises. In order to make rational decisions about how much heating oil to use, consumers do not need to know why the price of oil has risen. Perhaps a particularly cold winter has increased demand. Or perhaps troubles in the Middle East have decreased supply. In either case, the higher price signals to consumers to reduce their purchases of oil products. If the price of home-heating oil rises, that signals to oil refineries to produce more heating oil. Prices provide the information individuals and firms need to make rational decisions.

For the profit motive to be effective, firms need to be able to keep at least some of their profits. Households, in turn, need to be able to keep at least some of what they earn or receive as a return on their investments. (The return on their investments is simply what they receive back in excess of what they invested. If they receive back less than they invested, the return is negative.) There must, in short, be **private property,** with its attendant **property rights.** Property rights include both the right of the owner to use the property as she sees fit and the right to sell it.

These two attributes of property rights give individuals the incentive to use property under their control efficiently. The owner of a piece of land tries to figure out the most profitable use of the land; for example, whether to build a store or a restaurant. If he makes a mistake and opens a restaurant when he should have opened a store, he bears the consequences: the loss in income. The profits he earns if he makes the right decisions—and the lossess he bears if he makes the wrong ones—give him an incentive to think carefully about the decision and do the requisite research. The owner of a store tries to make sure that her customers get the kind of merchandise and the quality of service they want. She has an incentive to establish a good reputation, because if she does so, she will do more business and earn more profits.

The store owner will also want to maintain her property—which is not just the land anymore, but includes the store as well—because she will get more for it when the time comes to sell her business to someone else. Similarly, the owner of a house has an incentive to maintain *his* property, so that he can sell it for more when he wishes to move. Again, the profit motive combines with private property to provide incentives.

WRAP-UP

How the Profit Motive Drives the Market System

In market economies, incentives are supplied to individuals and firms by prices, profits, and property rights.

Incentives Versus Equality

While incentives are at the heart of market economies, they come with a cost: inequality. Any system of incentives must tie compensation with performance. Whether through differences in luck or ability, performance of different individuals will differ. In many cases, it will not be possible to identify why performance is high. The salesperson may claim that the reason his sales are high is superior skill and effort, while his colleague may argue that it is luck.

If pay is tied to performance, there will inevitably be some inequality. And the more closely compensation is tied to performance, the greater the inequality. The fact that the greater the incentives, the greater the resulting inequality is called the *incentive-equality trade-off*. If society provides greater incentives, total output is likely to be higher, but there will also probably be greater inequality.

One of the basic questions facing society in the choice of tax rates and welfare systems is how much would incentives be diminished by an increase in tax rates to finance a better welfare system and thus reduce inequality? What would be the results of those reduced incentives?

When Property Rights Fail

Prices, profits, and property rights are the three essential ingredients of market economies. We can learn a lot about why they are so important by examining a few cases where property rights and prices are interfered with. Each example highlights a general point. Any time society fails to define the owner of its resources and does not allow the highest bidder to use them, inefficiencies result. Resources will be wasted or not used in the most productive way.

Ill-Defined Property Rights: The Grand Banks   Fish are a valuable resource. Not long ago, the area between Newfoundland and Maine, called the Grand Banks, was teeming with fish. Not surprisingly, it was also teeming with fishermen, who saw an easy livelihood scooping out the fish from the sea. Since there were no property rights, everyone tried to catch as many fish as they could. A self-interested fisherman would rationally reason that if he did not catch the fish, someone else would. The result was a tragedy: The Grand Banks was overfished, to the point where not only was it not teeming with fish, but commercial fishing became unprofitable. Today Canada and the United States have a treaty limiting the amount of fish that fishermen from each country can take from the Grand Banks, and gradually, over the years, the fish population has been restored.

Restricted Property Rights   In California the government allocates water rights among various groups. Water is scarce. Hence these rights to water are extremely valuable. But they come with a restriction. They are not transferable; they cannot be sold. Cattle ranchers currently have the right to about 10 percent of the state's water, slightly less than the fraction consumed by residences. Government charges ranchers as little as $50 per acre-foot for their water, in contrast to $256 per acre-foot charged to residences in San Francisco and much more in some towns. The value of water to thirsty urban consumers—what they would be willing to pay for the additional water—exceeds the profits from raising cattle. If the water rights could be sold, those in the cattle industry would have a strong incentive to sell their rights to the towns. If cattle owners could get out of the cattle business and sell their water rights to urban residents instead, everyone would be better off.[1] In this case, restrictions on property rights have led to inefficiencies.

Entitlements as Property Rights   Property rights do not always mean that you have full ownership or control. A *legal entitlement,* such as the right to occupy an apartment for life at a rent that is controlled, common in some large cities, is viewed by economists as a property right. Individuals do not own the apartment and thus cannot sell it, but they cannot be thrown out either.

These partial and restricted property rights result in many inefficiencies. Because the individual in a rent-controlled apartment cannot (legally) sell the right to live in her apartment, as she gets older she may have limited incentives to maintain its condition, let alone improve it.

Incentives, prices, profits, and property rights are central features of any economy, and highlight an important area of consensus among economists: *Providing appropriate incentives is a fundamental economic problem. In modern market economies, profits provide incentives for firms to produce the goods individuals want, and wages provide incentives for individuals to work. Property rights also provide people with important incentives, not only to invest and to save but also to put their assets to the best possible use.*

Rationing

The price system is only one way of allocating resources, and a comparison with other systems will help to clarify the advantages of markets. When individuals get less of a good than they would like at the terms being offered, the good is said to be *rationed.* Different **rationing systems** are different ways of deciding who gets society's scarce resources.

Rationing by Queues   Rather than supplying goods to those willing and able to pay the most for them, a society could give them instead to those most willing to wait in line. This system is called *rationing by queues,* after the British term for lines. Tickets are often allocated by queues, whether they are for movies, sporting events, or rock concerts. A price is set, and it will not change no matter how many people line up to buy at that price. (The high price that scalpers can get for "hot" tickets is a good indication of how much more than the ticket price people would be willing to pay.)

Rationing by queues is thought by many to be a more desirable way of supplying medical services than the price system. Why, it is argued, should the rich—who are most able to pay for medical services—be the ones to get better or more medical care? Using this reasoning, Britain provides free medical care to everyone on its soil. To see a doctor there, all you have to do is wait in line. Rationing medicine by queues turns the allocation problem around: since the value of time for low-wage workers is lower, they are more willing to wait, and therefore they get a disproportionate share of (government-supplied) medical services.

In general, rationing by queues is an inefficient way of distributing resources because the time spent in line is a wasted resource. There are usually ways of achieving the same goal within a price system that can make everyone better off. Returning to the medical example, if some individuals were allowed to pay for doctors' services instead of waiting in line, more doctors could be hired with the proceeds, and the lines for those unable or unwilling to pay could actually be reduced.

Rationing by Lotteries   *Lotteries* allocate goods by a random process, like picking a name from a hat. University dormitory rooms are usually assigned by lottery. So are seats in popular courses; when more students want to enroll in a section of a principles of economics course than the size of the section allows, there may be a lottery to determine who gets to enroll. The United States used to allocate certain mining rights and licenses to radio airwaves by lottery. Like queue systems, lotteries are thought to be fair because everyone has an equal chance. However, they are also inefficient, because the scarce resources do not go to the individual or firm who is willing and able to pay (and therefore values them) the most.

Rationing by Coupons   Most governments in wartime use *coupon rationing.* People are allowed so many gallons of gasoline, so many pounds of sugar, and so much flour

---

[1]The calculation of benefits and losses does not take into account the feelings of the cattle.

each month. To get the good, you have to pay the market price *and* produce a coupon. The reason for coupon rationing is that without coupons, prices might soar, inflicting a hardship on poorer members of society.

Coupon systems take two forms, depending on whether coupons are tradable or not. Coupons that are not tradable give rise to the same inefficiency that occurs with most of the other nonprice systems—goods do not in general go to the individuals who are willing and able to pay the most. There is generally room for a trade that will make all parties better off. For instance, I might be willing to trade some of my flour ration for some of your sugar ration. But in a nontradable coupon system, the law prohibits such transactions. When coupons cannot be legally traded, there are strong incentives for the establishment of a *black market*, an illegal market in which the goods or the coupons for goods are traded.

Opportunity Sets and Trade-offs

We have covered a lot of ground so far this chapter. We have described the economist's basic model, which relies on competitive markets. We have seen how prices, the profit motive, and private property supply the incentives that drive a market economy. And we have gotten our first glimpse at why economists believe that market systems, which supply goods to those who are willing and able to pay the most, provide the most efficient means of allocating what the economy produces. Market systems are more efficient than the nonprice rationing schemes that have been employed. It is time now to return to the question of choice. Market systems leave to individuals and firms the question of what to consume and what to produce. How are these decisions made?

For a rational individual or firm, the first step in the economic analysis of any choice is to identify what is possible—what economists call the **opportunity set,** which is simply the group of available options. If you want a sandwich and have only tuna fish and cheese in the refridgerator, then your opportunity set consists of a tuna fish sandwich, a cheese sandwich, a tuna and cheese sandwich, or no sandwich. A ham sandwich is out of the question. Defining the limitations facing an individual or firm is a critical step in any analysis of choice. One can spend time yearning after

TABLE 2.1

Michelle's Opportunity Set	
CDs	**DVDs**
0	6
2	5
4	4
6	3
8	2
10	1
12	0

the ham sandwich, or anything else outside the opportunity set, but when it comes to making choices and facing decisions, only what is within the opportunity set is relevant.

So the first step in analyzing choice is to identify what is within the opportunity set.

Budget and Time Constraints

Constraints limit choice and define the opportunity set. In most economic situations, the constraints that limit a person's choices—that is, those constraints that actually are relevant—are time and money. Opportunity sets whose constraints are imposed by money are referred to as **budget constraints**; opportunity sets whose constraints are prescribed by time are called **time constraints**. A billionaire may feel his choices are not limited by money but by time, while for an unemployed worker, lack of money rather than time limits his choices.

The budget constraint defines a typical opportunity set. Consider the budget constraint of Michelle, who has decided to spend $120 on either CDs or DVDs. A CD costs $10, a DVD $20. So Michelle can buy 12 CDs *or* 6 DVDs; or 8 CDs and 2 DVDs; or 4 CDs and 4 DVDs. The various possibilities are set forth in Table 2.1. And they are depicted graphically in Figure 2.1.[2] Along the vertical axis, we measure the number of CDs purchased, and along the horizontal axis, we measure the number of DVDs. The line marked B_1B_2 is Michelle's budget constraint. The extreme cases, where Michelle buys only DVDs or only CDs, are represented by the points B_1 and B_2, respectively. The dots between these

---

[2]See the chapter appendix for help in reading graphs. Economists have found graphs to be extremely useful and they will be employed throughout this book. It is important that you learn to read and understand graphs.

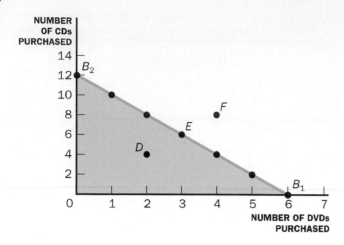

FIGURE 2.1   *Michelle's Budget Constraint*

The budget constraint identifies the limits of an individual's opportunity set between CDs and DVDs. Points B_1 and B_2 are extreme options, where she chooses all of one or the other. Her actual choice corresponds to point E. Choices from the shaded area are possible but less attractive than choices actually on the budget constraint.

two points, along the budget constraint, represent the other possible combinations. The cost of each combination of CDs and DVDs must add up to $120. If Michelle decides to buy more DVDs, she will have to settle for fewer CDs. The point actually chosen by Michelle is labeled *E,* where she purchases 6 CDs (for $60) and 3 DVDs (for $60).

Michelle's budget constraint is the line that defines the outer limits of her opportunity set. But the whole opportunity set is larger. It also includes all points below the budget constraint. This is the shaded area in the figure. The budget constraint shows the maximum number of DVDs Michelle can buy for each number of CDs purchased, and vice versa. Michelle is always happiest when she chooses a point on her budget constraint rather than below it. To see why, compare the points *E* and *D.* At point *E,* she has more of both goods than at point *D.* She would be even happier at point *F,* where she has still more DVDs and CDs, but that point, by definition, is unattainable.

Figure 2.2 depicts a time constraint. The most common time constraint simply says that the sum of what an individual spends her time on each day—including sleep—must add up to 24 hours. The figure plots the hours spent watching television on the horizontal axis and the hours spent on all other activities on the vertical axis. People—no matter how rich or poor—have only 24 hours a day to

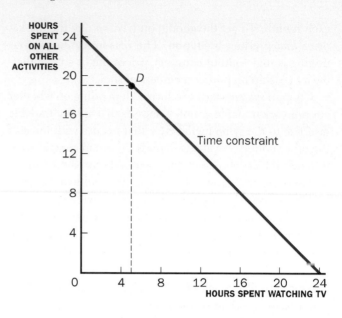

FIGURE 2.2   *An Opportunity Set for Watching TV and Other Activities*

This opportunity set is limited by a time constraint, which shows the trade-off a person faces between spending time watching television and spending it on other activities. At 5 hours of TV time per day, point *D* represents a typical choice for an American.

spend on different activities. The time constraint is quite like the budget constraint. A person cannot spend more than 24 hours or fewer than zero hours a day watching TV. The more time she spends watching television the less time she has available for all other activities. If she wants to watch more TV, she faces a trade-off—the only way to have more time to watch TV is to reduce time spent in some other activity. Point *D* (for dazed) has been added to the diagram at 5 hours a day—this is the amount of time the typical American chooses to spend watching TV.

The Production Possiblities Curve

Business firms and whole societies face constraints. They too must make choices limited to opportunity sets. The amount of goods a firm or society could produce, given a fixed amount of land, labor, and other inputs, are referred to as its **production possibilities.**

As one commonly discussed example, consider a simple description of a society in which all economic production is divided into two categories, military spending and civilian spending. Of course, each of these two kinds of spending has many different elements, but for the moment, let's discuss the choice between the two broad categories. For simplicity, Figure 2.3 refers to military spending as "guns" and civilian spending as "butter." The production of guns is given along the vertical axis, the production of butter along the horizontal. The possible combinations of military and civilian spending—of guns and butter—is the opportunity set. Table 2.2 sets out some of the posible combinations: 90 million guns and 40 million tons of butter, or 40 million guns and 90 million tons of butter. These possibilities are depicted in the figure. In the case of a choice involving production decisions, the boundary of the opportunity set—giving the maximum amount of guns that can be produced for

TABLE 2.2

Production Possibilities for the Economy	
Guns (millions)	**Butter (millions of tons)**
100	0
90	40
70	70
40	90
0	100

each amount of butter and vice versa—is called the **production possibilities curve.**

When we compare the individual's opportunity set and that of society, we notice one major difference. The individual's budget constraint is a straight line, while the production possibilities curve bows outward. There is a good reason for this. An individual typically faces fixed *trade-offs:* if Michelle spends $20 more on DVDs (that is, she buys one more DVD), she has $20 less to spend on CDs (she can buy two fewer CDs).

On the other hand, the trade-offs faced by society are not fixed. If a society produces only a few guns, it will use those resources—the men and machines—that are best equipped for gun making. But as society tries to produce more and more guns, doing so becomes more difficult; it will increasingly depend on those resources that are less good at producing guns. It will be drawing these resources out of the production of other goods, in this case, butter. Thus, when the economy increases its production of guns from 40 million a year (point *A*) to 70 million (*B*), butter production falls by 20 million tons, from 90 million tons to 70 million tons. But if production of guns is increased further, to 90 million (*C*), an increase of only 20 million, butter production has to decrease by 30 million tons, to only 40 million tons. For each increase in the number of guns, the reduction in the number of tons of butter produced gets larger. That is why the production possibilities curve is curved.

In another example, assume that a firm owns land that can be used for growing wheat but not corn, and land that can grow corn but not wheat. In this case, the only way to increase wheat production is to move workers from the cornfields to the wheat fields. As more and more workers are put into the wheat fields, production of wheat goes up, but each successive worker increases production less. The

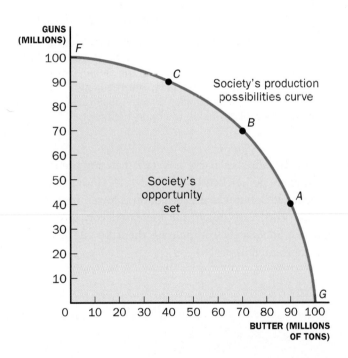

FIGURE 2.3   *The Guns and Butter Trade-off*

A production possibilities curve can show society's opportunity set. This one describes the trade-off between military spending ("guns") and civilian spending ("butter"). Points *F* and *G* show the extreme choices, where the economy produces all guns or all butter. Notice that unlike the budget and time constraint lines, the production possibilities line curves, reflecting diminishing returns.

first workers might pick the largest and most destructive weeds. Additional workers lead to better weeding, and better weeding leads to higher output. But the additional weeds rooted up are smaller and less destructive, so output is increased by a correspondingly smaller amount. This is an example of the general principle of **diminishing returns.** Adding successive units of any input such as fertilizer, labor, or machines to a fixed amount of other inputs—seeds or land—increases the output, or amount produced, but by less and less.

Table 2.3 shows the output of the corn and wheat fields as labor is increased in each field. Assume the firm has 6,000 workers to divide between wheat production and corn production. Thus, the second and fourth columns together give the firm's production possibilities, which are depicted in Figure 2.4.

Inefficiencies: Being off the Production Possibilities Curve

There is no reason to assume that a firm or an economy will always be on its production possibilities curve. Any inefficiency in the economy will result in a point such as *A* in Figure 2.4, below the production possibilities curve. One of the major quests of economists is to look for instances in which the economy is inefficient in this way.

Whenever the economy is operating below the production possibilities curve, it is possible for us to have more of every good—more wheat and more corn, more guns and more butter. No matter what goods we like, we can have more of them. That is why we can unambiguously say that points below the production possibilities curve are undesirable. But this does not mean that every point on the pro-

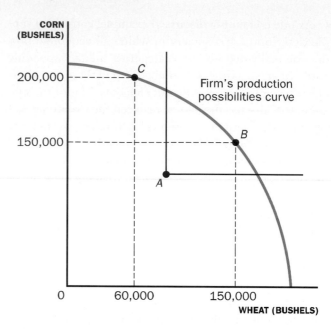

FIGURE 2.4   *The Wheat and Corn Trade-off*

This production possibilities curve shows that as wheat production increases, it becomes necessary to give up larger and larger amounts of corn. Or to put the same point a different way, as corn production falls, the resulting increase in wheat production gets smaller. Point *A* illustrates an inefficient outcome, falling inside the opportunity set.

duction possibilities curve is better than any point below it. Compare points *A* and *C* in Figure 2.4. Corn production is higher at *C*, but wheat production is lower. If people do not like corn very much, the increased corn production may not adequately compensate them for the decreased wheat production.

TABLE 2.3

Diminishing Returns			
	Corn		**Wheat**
Labor in cornfield	**output**	**Labor in wheat field**	**output**
(no. of workers)	**(bushels)**	**(no. of workers)**	**(bushels)**
1,000	60,000	5,000	200,000
2,000	110,000	4,000	180,000
3,000	150,000	3,000	150,000
4,000	180,000	2,000	110,000
5,000	200,000	1,000	60,000

There are many reasons why the economy may be below the production possibilities curve. If land better suited for the production of corn is mistakenly devoted to the production of wheat, the economy will operate below its production possibilities curve. If some of society's resources—its land, labor, and capital goods—are simply left idle, as happens when there is a recession, the economy operates below the production possibilities curve. The kinds of inefficiencies discussed earlier in the chapter with inadequately or improperly defined property rights also result in operating below the production possibilities curve.

Costs

Making trade-offs always involves weighing costs and benefits. What you gain is the benefit; what you give up is the cost.

Thinking Like an Economist

Trade-offs

Whenever you see an opportunity set, a budget or time constraint, or a production possibilities curve, think *trade-off.* The variables on the two axes identify the objects of the trade-offs, whether it is CDs and DVDs, guns and butter, or something else. The line or curve drawn from one axis to the other provides quantities for the trade-off. The opportunity set shows the choices that are available. The budget constraint illustrates the trade-offs that must be made because of limited money to spend, while the time constraint reflects the limited time we all have. The production possibilities curve gives the trade-offs faced in deciding what to produce when the amount of land, labor, and other inputs is limited. All three focus attention on the necessity of making trade-offs.

Many people think economists only study situations that involve money and budget constraints, but time constraints are also very important for defining trade-offs in many situations. Political elections provide a good example of the importance of time constraints. As the 2000 presidential election campaign entered its final stages, each candidate faced tough choices because of the time constraint. The election date was fixed, so there was only so much time available for campaigning before the election. A week before the election on November 7, 2000, Vice President Gore's lead in California was shrinking, but to come to California to campaign would mean he could not spend time in some other state like Tennessee or Michigan where the outcome was also in doubt. Similarly, if Governor Bush spent more time in Florida, he would have less time to visit other states. Each candidate had to decide how best to allocate the time remaining before the election.

Economists find it useful to distinguish between budget constraints and time constraints, but often we study trade-offs that involve both time *and* money. Choosing how to spend your Saturday evening ususally involves both. You might decide to go to a movie that lasts for 2 hours and costs $8 or go to a concert that lasts 4 hours and costs $35. Both your budget and time constraints are important for defining your opportunity set.

With only a week to go before the presidential election, Vice President Gore had to decide in which states to spend his remaining campaigning time.

Often, the benefits depend on an individual's personal preferences—some people would gladly skip a tennis game to go play golf, and others would just as gladly make the opposite choice. Economists generally do not try to explain why people have different preferences; instead, when it comes to understanding the choices individuals make, economists focus on costs. An opportunity set like the budget constraint, the time constraint, or the production possibilities curve specifies the cost of one option in terms of another. If the individual, the firm, or society is operating on the constraint or curve, then it is possible to get more of one thing only by sacrificing some of another. The "cost" of one more unit of one good is how much you have to give up of the other.

Economists think about costs in terms of trade-offs within opportunity sets. Let's go back to Michelle choosing between CDs and DVDs in Figure 2.1. The trade-off is given by the **relative price,** the ratio of the prices of CDs and DVDs. In our example, a CD costs $10, and DVD $20. The relative price is $20/$10 = 2. For every DVD Michelle gives up, she can buy 2 CDs. Likewise, societies and firms face trade-offs along the production possibilities curve, like the one shown in Figure 2.3. There, point *A* is the choice where 40 million guns and 90 million tons of butter are produced. The trade-off can be calculated by comparing points *A* and *B*. Society can have 30 million more guns by giving up 20 million tons of butter.

Trade-offs are necessary because resources are scarce. If you want something, you have to pay for it—you have to give up something. If you want to go to the library tomorrow night, you have to give up going to the movies. If a sawmill wants to make more two-by-four beams from its stock of wood, it will not be able to make as many one-by-four boards.

Opportunity Costs

If someone were to ask you right now what it costs to go to a movie, you would probably answer, "Eight dollars," or whatever you paid the last time you went to the movies. But with the concept of trade-offs, you can see that a *full* answer is not that simple. To begin with, the cost is not the $8 but what that $8 could otherwise buy. Furthermore, your time is a scarce resource that must be figured into the calculation. Both the money and the time represent opportunities forgone in favor of going to the movie, or what economists refer to as the **opportunity cost** of the movie. To apply a resource to one use means that it cannot be put to any other use. Thus, we should consider the next-best, alternative use of any resource when we think about putting it to any particular use. This next-best use is the formal measurement of opportunity cost.

Some examples will help to clarify the idea of opportunity cost. Consider a college student, Sarah, who works during the summer. She has a chance to go surfing in Costa Rica with friends, but to do so she has to quit her summer job two weeks early. The friends have found a cheap airfare and place to stay, and they tell Sarah the trip will only cost $1,000. To the economist, $1,000 is not the total cost of the trip for Sarah. Since she would have continued working in her summer job for an extra two weeks if she did not go to Costa Rica, the income she would have earned is part of the opportunity cost of her time. This forgone income must be added to the airfare and hotel costs in calculating the total economic cost of the surfing trip.

Now consider a business firm that has bought a building for its headquarters that is bigger than necessary. If the firm could receive $3 per month in rent for each square foot of space that is not needed, then this is the opportunity cost of leaving the space idle.

The analysis can be applied to the government as well. The federal government owns a vast amount of wilderness. In deciding whether it is worthwhile to convert some of the land into a national park, the government needs to take into account the opportunity cost of the land. The land might be used for growing timber or for grazing sheep. Whatever the value of the land in its next best use, this is the economic cost of the national park. The fact that the government does not have to buy the land does not mean that the land should be treated as a free good.

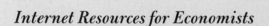

Internet Connection

Internet Resources for Economists

A guide to Internet resources for economists can be found at http://www.rfe.wustl.edu/ . The American Economic Association sponsors this guide. It lists over 1,200 resources in sixty-nine sections and subsections that are of interest to professional economists as well as those simply interested in economics.

Thus, in the economist's view, when rational firms and individuals make decisions—whether to undertake one investment project rather than another, whether to buy one product rather than another—they take into account *all* of the costs, the full opportunity costs, not just the direct expenditures.

CASE IN POINT

The Opportunity Cost of Attending College

Opportunity cost is a key concept in economics. It is the correct measure of the cost of everything we do. As a college student, what is your opportunity cost of attending college? If you (or your parents) are asking how much your college costs, you probably think of the tuition, room and board, and books as major costs. But a consideration of the opportunity cost suggests that such a list includes both too much and too little.

Since you would need a place to live, and you would certainly need to eat, even if you were not in school, these costs do not represent part of the opportunity cost of attending college. Only if your college charges higher rent than you would otherwise pay would your dorm costs be part of your opportunity cost.

To correctly evaluate opportunity cost, you need to think about what you would be doing if you had decided not to continue in school. The economist's mind immediately turns to the job you might have had if you had not enrolled in college and the income you could have earned. While it will vary from student to student, according to the U.S. Department of Education, non-college-bound high school graduates work just under 10 months on average and earn just over $10,000 per year.[3] This *forgone income* must be added to the direct costs such as tuition to obtain the opportunity cost of attending school. For most students, this forgone income is a major component of the opportunity cost of college.

Test your understanding: Use the concept of opportunity cost to explain why great college basketball players often fail to complete four years of college.

[3]U.S. Department of Education, National Center for Education Statistics, http://www.nces.ed.gov/pubs/ce/c9730a01.html , October 2000.

Sunk Costs

Economic cost includes costs, as we have just seen, that noneconomists often exclude, but it also ignores costs that noneconomists include. If an expenditure has already been made and cannot be recovered no matter what choice is made, a rational person would ignore it. Such expenditures are called **sunk costs.**

To understand sunk costs, let's go back to the movies, assuming now that you have spent $8 to buy a movie ticket. You were skeptical about whether the movie was worth $8. Half an hour into the movie, your worst suspicions are realized: the movie is a disaster. Should you leave the movie theater? In making that decision, the $8 should be ignored. It is a sunk cost; your money is gone whether you stay or leave. The only relevant choice now is how to spend the next 60 minutes of your time: watch a terrible movie or go do something else.

Or assume you have just purchased a fancy laptop computer for $2,000. But the next week, the manufacturer announces a new computer with twice the power for $1,000; you can trade in your old computer for the new one by paying an additional $400. You are angry. You feel you have just paid $2,000 for a computer that is now almost worthless, and you have gotten hardly any use out of it.

Internet Connection

The Dismal Scientist

One way to start thinking like an economist is to read what economists have to say about current events. Economy.com's "The dismal scientist" Web site at http://www.dismal.com/ provides a portal to many resources for economists, to articles about current economic issues, and to sources of information about the economy. Economics has been known as the "dismal science" ever since the nineteenth-century economist Thomas Malthus predicted that any rise in living standards would be quickly erased because improved living standards lead to population growth that would outstrip the capacity of the economy to support it.

You decide not to buy the new computer for another year, until you have gotten at least some return for your investment. Again, an economist would say that you are not approaching the question rationally. The past decision is a sunk cost. The only question you should ask yourself is whether the extra power of the fancier computer is worth the additional $400. If it is, buy it. If not, don't.

Marginal Costs

The third aspect of cost that economists emphasize is the extra costs of doing something, what economists call the **marginal costs.** These are weighed against the (additional) **marginal benefits** of doing it. The most difficult decisions we make are not whether to do something or not. They are whether to do a little more or a little less of something. Few of us waste much time deciding whether or not to work. We have to work; the decision is whether to work a few more or a few less hours. A country does not consider whether or not to have an army; it decides whether to have a larger or smaller army.

Jim has just obtained a job for which he needs a car. He must decide how much to spend on the car. By spending more, he can get a bigger and more luxurious car. But he has to decide whether it is worth a few hundred (or thousand) marginal dollars for a larger car or for extra items like fancy hubcaps, power windows, and so on.

Polly is considering flying to Colorado for a ski weekend. She has three days off from work. The airfare is $200, the hotel room costs $100 a night, and the ski ticket costs $35 a day. Food costs the same as at home. She is trying to decide whether to go for two or three days. The *marginal* cost of the third day is $135, the hotel cost plus the cost of the ski ticket. There are no additional transportation costs involved in staying the third day. She needs to compare the marginal cost with the additional enjoyment she will have from the third day.

People, consciously or not, think about the trade-offs at the margin in most of their decisions. Economists, however, bring them into the foreground. Like opportunity costs and sunk costs, marginal analysis is one of the critical concepts that enable economists to think systematically about the costs of alternative choices.

This kind of marginal analysis has come to play an increasingly important role in policy discussions. For instance, the key issue in various environmental regulations and safety standards is not whether there should be such

regulations, but how tight they should be. Higher standards have both marginal benefits and marginal costs. From an economic standpoint, justification of higher standards hinges on whether the benefits outweigh the costs. Consider, for instance, auto safety. For the past two decades, the government has taken an active role in ensuring auto safety. It sets standards that all automobiles must meet. For instance, an automobile must be able to withstand a side collision of a particular velocity. One of the most difficult problems the government faces is deciding what those standards should be. It recently considered tightening standards for withstanding side collisions on trucks. The government calculated that the higher standards would result on average in 79 fewer deaths per year. It calculated that to meet the higher standards would increase the cost of an automobile by $81. (In addition, the heavier trucks would use more fuel.) In deciding whether to impose the higher standard, it used marginal analysis. It looked at the *additional* lives saved and at the *additional* costs.

WRAP-UP

Basic Steps of Rational Choice

Identify the opportunity sets.

Define the trade-offs.

Calculate the costs correctly, taking into account opportunity costs, sunk costs, and marginal costs.

CASE IN POINT

Investment Tax Credits

Investment tax credits have been a popular tool of policymakers. With a 10 percent investment tax credit, a firm that invests $100 million—say, in the construction of a new factory—gets a credit against its taxes of $10 million. The government is in effect paying 10 percent of the investment. In 1993, the Clinton administration proposed a new form of tax credit, one that would have

The government has offered firms tax credits for investment in new capital expenditures, such as the construction of a new factory.

rewarded businesses for increasing the amount they spend on new investment over what they spent the previous year. This proposal differs from the usual investment tax credit, which rewards all new investment equally (including the vast amount that would have been invested anyway). The Clinton proposal, which Congress failed to pass, made good economic sense. Because it focused on the additional (marginal) dollar, which is the focus of a business's investment decision, it offered more for the tax buck.

Here is the logic. As we have seen, an investment tax credit that allows firms to reduce their tax bill by 10 percent of their investment expenditures effectively reduces the cost of investment by 10 percent. This is a strong incentive to invest. But it comes at a high cost, because most of the investment would have been undertaken anyway. If, for example, the economy would have undertaken $750 billion of investment, and the tax credit increases this to $810 billion, the cost of the $60 billion in increased investment is $81 billion in lost federal revenue.

The intent of a net investment tax credit, as noted, is to reward investment that would not have happened without the credit. How do we know what that is? We don't. But an acceptable if imperfect substitute is to provide the credit on investment increases over the previous year. In terms of the previous example, suppose that last year's investment was in fact $700 billion—an imperfect estimate of the $750 billion that would have occurred without the tax credit. Since it is only the marginal cost that is relevant to investment decision makers, a 10 percent net investment tax credit will increase investment to $810 billion, as before. But because the credit is only paid on $110 billion ($810 billion minus $700 billion), the Treasury loses only $11 billion ($110 billion × 10 percent)—$70 billion less than the revenues lost from the regular investment tax credit. ●

Review and Practice

Summary

1. The basic competitive model consists of rational, self-interested individuals and profit-maximizing firms, interacting in competitive markets.

2. The profit motive and private property provide incentives for rational individuals and firms to work hard and efficiently. Ill-defined or restricted property rights can lead to inefficient behavior.

3. Society often faces choices between efficiency, which requires incentives that enable people or firms to receive different benefits depending on their performance, and equality, which entail people receiving more or less equal benefits.

4. The price system in a market economy is one way of allocating goods and services. Other methods include rationing by queue, by lottery, and by coupon.

5. An opportunity set illustrates what choices are possible. Budget constraints and time constraints define individuals' opportunity sets. Both show the trade-offs of how much of one thing a person must give up to get more of another.

6. A production possibilities curve defines a firm or society's opportunity set, representing the possible combinations of goods that the firm or society can produce. If a firm or society is producing below its production possibilities curve, it is said to be inefficient, since it could produce more of either good without producing less of the other.

7. The opportunity cost is the cost of using any resource. It is measured by looking at the next-best use to which that resource could be put.

8. A sunk cost is a past expenditure that cannot be recovered, no matter what choice is made in the present. Thus, rational decision-makers ignore them.

9. Most economic decisions concentrate on choices at the margin, where the marginal (or extra) cost of a course of action is compared with its extra benefits.

Key Terms

competition
basic competitive model
rational choice
perfect competition
price taker
price system
private property
property rights
rationing systems
opportunity set
budget constraints
time constraints
production possibilities
production possibilities curve
diminishing returns
relative price
opportunity cost
sunk costs
marginal costs
marginal benefits

Review Questions

1. What are the essential elements of the basic competitive model?

2. Consider a lake in a state park where everyone is allowed to fish as much as they want. What outcome do you predict? Might this problem be averted if the lake were privately owned and fishing licenses were sold?

3. Why might government policy to make the distribution of income more equitable lead to less efficiency?

4. List advantages and disadvantages of rationing by queue, by lottery, and by coupon. If the government permitted a black market to develop, might some of the disadvantages of these systems be reduced?

5. What are some of the opportunity costs of going to college? What are some of the opportunity costs a state should consider when deciding whether to widen a highway?

6. Give two examples of a sunk cost, and explain why they should be irrelevant to current decisions.

7. How is marginal analysis relevant in the decision about which car to purchase? After deciding the kind of car to purchase, how is marginal analysis relevant?

Problems

1. Imagine that many businesses are located beside a river, into which they discharge industrial waste. There is a city downstream, which uses the river as a water supply and for recreation. If property rights to the river are ill-defined, what problems may occur?

2. Suppose an underground reservoir of oil may reside under properties owned by several different individuals. As each well is drilled, it reduces the amount of oil that others can take out. Compare how quickly the oil is likely to be extracted in this situation with how quickly it would be extracted if one person owned the property rights to drill for the entire pool of oil.

3. In some states, hunting licenses are allocated by lottery; if you want a license, you send in your name to enter the lottery. If the purpose of the system is to ensure that those who want to hunt the most get a chance to do so, what are the flaws of this system? How would the situation improve if people who won licenses were allowed to sell them to others?

4. Imagine that during time of war, the government imposes coupon rationing. What are the advantages of al-

lowing people to buy and sell their coupons? What are the disadvantages?

5. Kathy, a college student, has $20 a week to spend; she spends it either on junk food at $2.50 a snack, or on gasoline at $1 per gallon. Draw Kathy's opportunity set. What is the trade-off between junk food and gasoline? Now draw each new budget constraint she would face if

   (a) a kind relative started sending her an additional $10 per week;

   (b) the price of a junk food snack fell to $2;

   (c) the price of gasoline rose to $1.20 per gallon.

   In each case, how does the trade-off between junk food and gasoline change?

6. Why is the opportunity cost of going to medical school likely to be greater than the opportunity cost of going to college? Why is the opportunity cost of a woman with a college education having a child greater than the opportunity cost of a woman with just a high school education having a child?

7. Bob likes to divide his recreational time between going to movies and listening to compact discs. He has 20 hours a week available for recreation; a movie takes two hours, and a CD takes one hour to listen to. Draw his "time-budget constraint" line. Bob also has a limited amount of income to spend on recreation. He has $60 a week to spend on recreational activities; a movie costs $7.50, and a CD costs $15. (He never likes to listen to the same CD twice.) Draw his budget constraint line. What is his opportunity set?

Appendix: Reading Graphs

Whether the old saying that a picture is worth a thousand words under- or overestimates the value of a picture, economists find graphs extremely useful.

For instance, look at Figure 2.5; it is a redrawn version of Figure 2.1, showing the budget constraint—the various combinations of CDs and DVDs that an individual, Michelle, can buy. More generally, a graph shows the rela-

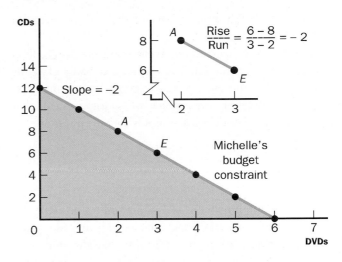

FIGURE 2.5 *Reading a Graph: The Budget Constraint*

Graphs can be used to show the relationship between two variables. This one shows the relationship between the variable on the vertical axis (the number of CDs) and the variable on the horizontal axis (the number of DVDs). The slope of a curve like the budget constraint gives the change in the number of CDs Michelle can purchase if she buys another DVD. The slope of the budget constraint is negative. A small portion of the graph has been blown up to illustrate how to calculate the curve's slope. (The jagged sections of the axes near the blown-up graph's origin indicate that the distance from the origin to the first value on each axis is not drawn to scale.)

tionship between two variables, here, the number of CDs and the number of DVDs that can be purchased. The budget constraint gives the maximum number of DVDs that she can purchase, given the number of CDs that she has bought.

In a graph, one variable (here, DVDs) is put on the horizontal axis and the other variable, on the vertical axis. We read a point such as *E* by looking across to the vertical axis and seeing that it corresponds to 6 CDs, and by looking down to the horizontal axis and seeing that is corresponds to 3 DVDs. Similarly, we read point *A* by looking across to the vertical axis and seeing that it corresponds to 8 CDs, and by looking down to the horizontal axis and seeing that it corresponds to 2 DVDs.

In the figure, each of the points from the table has been plotted, and then a curve has been drawn through those points. The "curve" turns out to be a straight line in this case, but we still use the more general term. The advantage of the curve over the individual points is that with it, we can read off from the graph points on the budget constraint that are not in the table.

Sometimes, of course, not every point on the graph is economically meaningful. You cannot buy half a DVD or half a CD. For the most part, we ignore these considerations when drawing our graphs; we simply pretend that any point on the budget constraint is actually possible.

Slope

In any diagram, the amount by which the value along the vertical axis increases from a change in a unit along the horizontal axis is called the *slope*, just like the slope of a mountain. Slope is sometimes described as "rise over run," meaning that the slope of a line can be calculated by dividing the change on the vertical axis (the "rise") by the change on the horizontal axis (the "run").

Look at Figure 2.5. As we move from *E* to *A,* increasing the number of CDs by 2, the number of DVDs purchased falls from *3* to *2.* For every two additional CDs bought, the feasible number of DVDs that can be purchased falls by 1. So the slope of the line is

$$\frac{\text{rise}}{\text{run}} = \frac{6-8}{3-2} = \frac{-2}{1} = -2.$$

When, as in Figure 2.5, the variable on the vertical axis falls when the variable on the horizontal axis increases, the curve, or line, is said to be *negatively sloped.* A budget constraint is always negatively sloped. But when we describe the slope of a budget constraint, we frequently omit the term "negative." We say the slope is 2, knowing that since we are describe the slope of a budget constraint, we should more formally say that the slope is negative 2. Alternatively, we sometimes say that the slope has an absolute value of 2.

Figure 2.6 shows the case of a curve that is *positively sloped.* The variable along the vertical axis, income, increases as schooling increases, giving the line its upward tilt from left to right.

In later discussions, we will encounter two special cases. A line that is very steep has a very large slope; that is, the increase in the vertical axis for every unit increase in the horizontal axis is very large. The extreme case is a perfectly vertical line, and we say then that the slope is infinite (Figure 2.7, panel A). At the other extreme is a flat, hori-

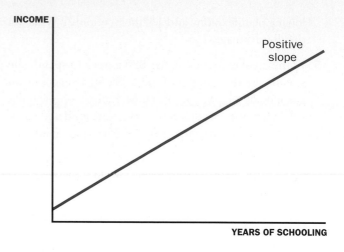

FIGURE 2.6   *Positively Sloped Curve*

Incomes increase with the number of years of schooling.

zontal line; since there is no increase in the vertical axis no matter how large the change along the horizontal, we say that the slope of such a curve is zero (panel B).

Figures 2.5 and 2.6 both show straight lines. Everywhere along the straight line, the slope is the same. This is not true in Figure 2.8, which repeats the production possibilities curve shown originally in Figure 2.3. Panel B of the figure blows up the area around point *E.* From the firgure, you can see that if the output of butter increases by 1 ton, the output of guns decreases by 1 million guns. Thus, the slope is

$$\frac{\text{rise}}{\text{run}} = \frac{69-70}{71-70} = -1$$

Now look at point *A,* where the economy is producing more butter. The area around *A* has been blown up in panel *C.* Here, we see that when we increase butter by 1 more unit, the reduction in guns is greater than before. The slope at *A* (again, millions of fewer guns produced per extra ton of butter) is

$$\frac{\text{rise}}{\text{run}} = \frac{38-40}{91-90} = -2.$$

With curves such as the production possibilities curve, the slope differs as we move along the curve.

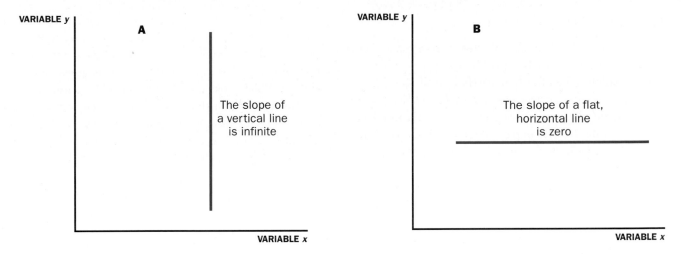

FIGURE 2.7 *Limiting Cases*

In panel A, the slope of a vertical line is infinite. In panel B, the slope of a horizontal line is zero.

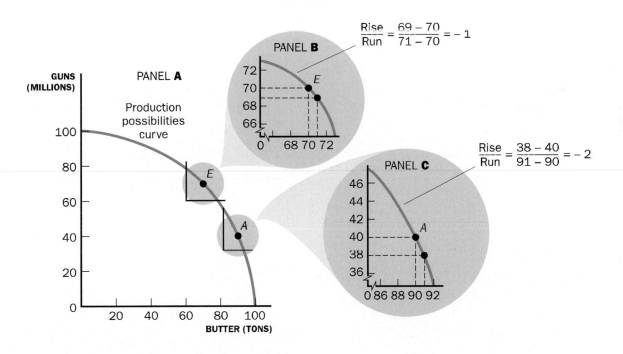

FIGURE 2.8 *The Guns and Butter Trade-off*

Panel A shows a trade-off between military spending ("guns") and civilian spending ("butter"), where society chooses point E. Panel B is an enlargement of the area around E, which focuses on the slope there, which also measures the marginal trade-offs society faces near that point. Similarly, panel C is an enlargement of the area around A and shows the marginal trade-offs society faces near that point.

Interpreting Curves

Look at Figure 2.9. Which of the two curves has a steeper slope? The one on the left appears to have a slope that has a larger absolute value. But look carefully at the axes. Notice that in panel A, the vertical axis is stretched relative to panel B. The same distance that represents 20 CDs in panel B represents only 10 CDs in panel A. In fact, both panels represent the same budget constraint. They have exactly the same slope.

This kind of cautionary tale also is important in looking at graphs of data. Compare, for instance, panels A and B of Figure 2.10. Both graphs show the level of passenger car production from 1980 to 1990. Which one exhibits more variability? Which looks more stable? Panel B appears to show that car production does not change much over time. But again, a closer look reveals that the axes have been stretched in panel A. The two curves are based on exactly the same data, and there is really no difference between them.

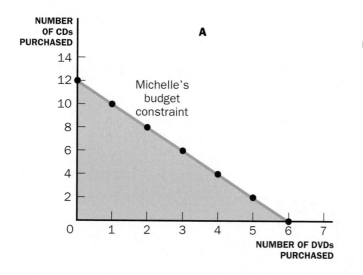
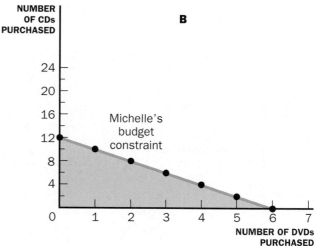

FIGURE 2.9 *Scaling and Slope*

Which of these two lines has the steeper slope? The units along the vertical axis have changed. The two curves have exactly the same slope.

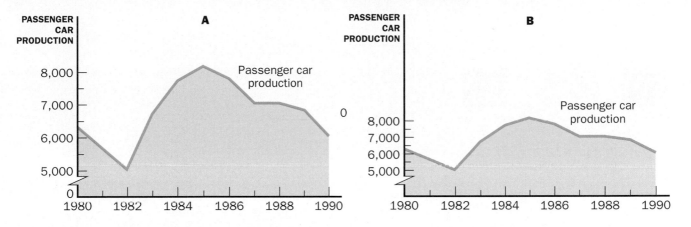

FIGURE 2.10   *Scaling and Graphs of Data*

Which of these two curves shows greater variability in the output of cars over time? The two curves plot the same data. The vertical scale has again been changed.

SOURCE: *Ward's Automotive Reports* (1991).

Chapter 3

Trade

Key Questions

1. Why is trade (exchange) mutually beneficial?

2. What are the similarities and differences between trade (exchange) between individuals within a country and trade between countries?

3. What determines what any particular country produces and sells on the international market? What is meant by comparative advantage, and why does it play such an important role?

4. What are the gains from specialization?

5. How valid is the argument, so often heard in political circles, that trade should be restricted?

*A*creature on another planet looking down at a developed modern economy on Earth might compare human activity to an enormous ant colony. Each ant seemingly has an assigned task. Some stand guard. Some feed the young. Some harvest food and others distribute it. Some shuffle paper, scribble notes in books, and type on computer keyboards at computer consoles. Others work in factories, tightening screws, running machines, and so on. How is all of this activity coordinated? No dictator or superintelligent computer is giving instructions. Yet somehow an immense amount is accomplished in a reasonably coordinated way. Understanding how a complex economy operates—how it is that certain individuals do one task, others do another, how information is communicated and decisions made—is a central objective of economics. We raised this issue in our discussion in Chapter 1 of the core concept of exchange. In this chapter we build on that discussion.

This chapter discusses the problem of economic interdependence at two levels: individuals and firms within a country, and countries within the world economic community. Many of the same principles apply at both levels.

The Benefits of Economic Interdependence

Economists often use the words *trade* and *exchange* interchangeably. When Chip goes to work, he exchanges, or trades his labor services for income. When Juanita purchases a new cell phone, she exchanges, or trades income for the product she chooses. The subject of international trade—the exchange of goods and services across national borders—is an extension of the basic principle of exchange that we presented in Chapter 1. We begin here where that discussion left off, probing more deeply into the benefits of trade. For now we focus on the exchange of goods that are already available in the economy. Later we will discuss how countries come to specialize in the production of particular goods.

The Gains from Trade

When individuals own different goods, have different desires, or both, there is an opportunity for trade that benefits all parties to the trade. Kids trading baseball cards learn the basic principles of exchange. One has two Ken Griffey Jr. cards, the other has two Barry Bonds cards. A trade will benefit both of them. The same lesson applies to countries. Nigeria has more oil than it can use, but it does not produce enough food to feed its populace. The United States has more wheat than Americans can consume, but needs oil. Trade can benefit both countries.

Voluntary trade involves only winners. If the trade would make a loser of any party, that party would choose not to trade. Thus, a fundamental consequence of voluntary exchange is that it benefits everyone involved.

"Feeling Jilted" in Trade

In spite of the seemingly persuasive argument that individuals only voluntarily engage in trade if they think they will be better off as a result, people often walk away from a deal believing they have been hurt. It is important to understand that when economists say that a voluntary trade makes the two traders better off, they do not mean that it makes them both happy.

Imagine, for example, that Frank brings an antique rocking chair to a flea market to sell. He is willing to sell it for $100 but hopes to sell it for $200. Helen comes to the flea market planning to buy such a chair, hoping to spend only $100, but willing to pay as much as $200. They argue and negotiate, eventually settle on a price of $125, and make the deal. But when they go home, they both complain. Frank complains the price was too low, and Helen that it was too high.

From an economist's point of view, such complaints are self-contradictory. If Frank *really* thought $125 was too low, he would not have sold at that price. If Helen *really* thought $125 was too high, she would not have paid the price. Economists argue that people reveal their preferences not by what they say, but by what they do. If one voluntarily agrees to make a deal, one also agrees that the deal is, if not perfect, at least better than the alternative of not making it.

Two common objections are made to this line of reasoning. Both involve Frank or Helen "taking advantage" of the other. The implication is that if a buyer or a seller can take advantage, the other party may be a loser rather than a winner.

The first objection is that either Frank or Helen may not really know what is being agreed to. Perhaps Helen recognizes the chair is an antique, but by neglecting to tell Frank, manages to buy it for only $125. Perhaps Frank knows the rockers fall off, but sells the chair without telling this to Helen, thus keeping the price high. In either case, lack of relevant information makes someone a loser after the trade.

The second objection concerns equitable division of the **gains from trade.** Since Helen would have been willing to pay as much as $200, anything she pays less than that is **surplus,** the term economists use for a gain from trade. Similarly, since Frank would have been willing to sell the chair for as little as $100, anything he receives more than that is also surplus. The total dollar value of the gain from the trade is $100—the difference between the maximum price Helen was willing to pay and the minimum price at which Frank was willing to sell. At a price of $125, $25 of the gain went to Frank, $75 to Helen. The second objection is that such a split is not fair.

Economists do not have much patience with these objections. Like most people, they favor making as much information public as possible, and they think vendors and customers should be made to stand behind their promises. But economists also point out that second thoughts and "If only I had known" are not relevant. If Frank sells his antique at a flea market instead of having it valued by reputable antique dealers, he has made a voluntary decision to save his time and energy. If Helen buys an antique at a flea market instead of going to a reputable dealer, she knows she is taking a risk.

The logic of free exchange, however, does not say that everyone must express happiness with the result. It simply says that when people choose to make a deal, they prefer making it to not making it. And if they prefer the deal, they are by definition better off *in their own minds* at the time the transaction takes place.

The objections to trade nonetheless carry an important message: most exchanges that happen in the real world are considerably more complicated than the Frank-Helen chair trade. They involve problems of information, estimating risks, and expectations about the future. These complications will be discussed throughout the book. So without going into too much detail at the moment, let's just say that if you are worried that you do not have the proper information to make a trade, shop around, get a guarantee or expert opinion, or buy insurance. If you choose to plunge ahead without these precautions, don't pretend you didn't have other choices. Like those who buy a ticket in a lottery, you know you are taking a chance.

Economic Relations as Exchanges

Individuals in our economy are involved in masses of voluntary trades. They "trade" their labor services (time and skills) to their employer for dollars. They then trade dollars with a multitude of merchants for goods (like gasoline and groceries) and services (like plumbing and hair styling). The employer trades the goods it produces for dollars, and trades those dollars for labor services. Even your savings account can be viewed as a trade: you give the bank $100 today in exchange for the bank's promise to give you $105 at the end of the year (your original deposit plus 5 percent interest).

Trade Between Countries

Why is it that people engage in complex sets of economic relations with others? The answer is that people are better off as a result of trading. Just as individuals *within* a country find it advantageous to trade with one another, so too do countries find trade advantageous. Just as it is impossible for any individual to be self-sufficient, it is impossible for a country to be self-reliant without sacrificing its standard of living. The United States has long been part of an international economic community. This participation has grown in recent decades, increasing the interdependence between the United States and its trading partners. How has this affected the three main markets in the U.S. economy?

Interdependence in the Product Market   Foreign-produced goods are commonplace in U.S. markets. In the 1990s, for instance, more than one-fourth of the cars sold in the United States were imported (**imports** are goods produced abroad but bought domestically), along with a third of apparel items, a third of the oil, and virtually all of the diamonds. Many of the materials essential for the U.S. economy must also be imported from abroad. At the same

time, U.S. farmers export almost two-fifths of the agricultural goods they produce (**exports** are goods produced domestically but sold abroad), including almost three-fourths of the wheat and one-third of the cotton.

Imports have grown in recent decades, not only in dollars, but also as a percentage of overall production. Exports have grown almost commensurately. Figure 3.1 shows how exports and imports have grown relative to the nation's total output: as a percentage of national output, both have more than doubled over the last twenty-five years. Smaller countries are typically even more dependent on international trade than the United States. Britain and Canada import one-fourth of their goods, France a fifth.

Earnings from abroad constitute a major source of income for some of our largest corporations; exports account for 45 percent of sales for Boeing, 20 percent for Hewlett-Packard, and 12 percent for Ford.

Interdependence in the Labor Market   International interdependence extends beyond simply the shipping of goods between countries. More than 99 percent of U.S. citizens either immigrated here from abroad or are descended from people who did. Though the flow of immigrants, relative to the size of the population, has slowed since its peak at the turn of the century, it is still substantial, numbering in the millions every year. Today many rural American areas are dependent upon foreign-born doctors and nurses. Half of the engineers currently receiving doctorates at American universities are foreign-born. The harvests of many crops are highly dependent on migrant laborers from Mexico.

The nations of Europe have increasingly recognized the benefits that result from this international movement of workers. One of the important provisions of the treaty establishing the European Union, an agreement among most of the countries within Western Europe, allows for the free flow of workers within the member countries.

Interdependence in the Capital Market   The United States has become a major borrower from abroad, but the country also invests heavily overseas. In 1997, for example, U.S. private investors owned approximately $4.8 trillion of assets (factories, businesses, building, loans, etc.) in foreign countries, while foreign investors owned $5.5 trillion of assets in the United States. American companies have sought out profitable opportunities abroad, where they can use their special skills and knowledge to earn high

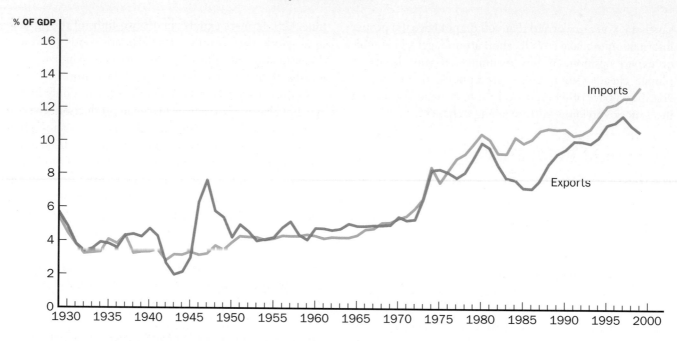

FIGURE 3.1   *International Trade*

Here, U.S. imports and exports are expressed as a fraction of a measure of the economy's total output, the gross domestic product (GDP). Notice that trade has increased over time, and that imports have exceeded exports since the mid-1970s.

SOURCE: *Economic Report of the President* (2001), Table B-1.

returns. They have established branches and built factories in Europe, Japan, Latin American, and elsewhere in the world.

Just as the nations of Western Europe have recognized the advantages that follow from the free flow of goods and labor among their countries, so too they have recognized the gains from the free flow of capital. Funds can be invested where they yield the highest returns. Knowledge and skills from one country can be combined with capital from another to produce goods that will be enjoyed by citizens of all countries. Though the process of liberalizing the flow of goods, labor, and capital among countries of the European Union has been going on for more than twenty years, 1992 marked the crucial date at which all remaining barriers were officially removed.

Multilateral Trade

Many of the examples to this point have emphasized two-way trade. Trade between two individuals or countries is called

bilateral trade. But exchange between two parties is often less advantageous than trade between several parties, called **multilateral trade.** Such trades are observed between sports teams. The New York Mets send a catcher to the St. Louis Cardinals, the Cardinals send a pitcher to the Los Angeles Dodgers, and the Dodgers send an outfielder to the Mets (see Figure 3.2A). No two of the teams were willing to make a two-way trade, but all can benefit from the three-way swap.

Countries function in a similar way. Japan has no domestic oil; it imports oil from Arabian countries. The Arabian countries want to sell their oil, but they want wheat and food, not the cars and television sets that Japan can provide. The United States can provide the missing link by buying cars and televisions from Japan and selling food to the Arab nations. Again, this three-way trade, shown in Figure 3.2B, offers gains that two-way trade cannot. The scores of nations active in the world economy create patterns far more complex than these simplified examples.

Figure 3.3 illustrates the construction of a Ford Escort in Europe, and dramatizes the importance of multilateral

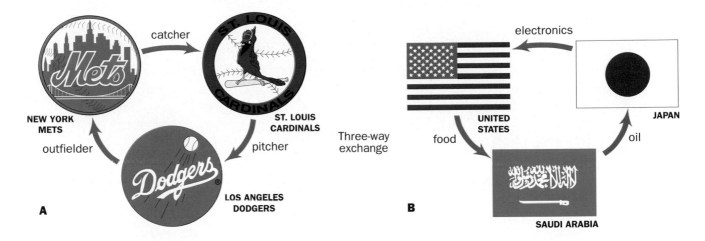

FIGURE 3.2 *Multilateral Exchange*

Panel A shows a multilateral, three-way trade between baseball teams. Notice that no two of the teams have the ingredients for a mutually beneficial exchange. Panel B illustrates exchange in international trade.

and interconnected trade relations. The parts that go into an Escort come from all over the world. Similar diagrams could be constructed for many of the components in the diagram: the aluminum alloys may contain bauxite from Jamaica, the chrome plate may use chromium from South Africa, the copper for wiring may come from Chile.

Multilateral trade means that trade between any two participants may not balance. In Figure 3.2B, the Arab countries send oil to Japan but get no goods (only yen) in return. No one would say that the Arab countries have an unfair trade policy with Japan. Yet some congressional representatives, newspaper columnists, and business executives complain that since the United States imports more from a particular country (often Japan) than it exports to that country, the trade balance is "unfair." A misguided popular cliché says that "trade is a two-way street." But trade in the world market involves hundreds of possible streets between nations. While there are legitimate reasons to be concerned with the overall U.S. trade deficit, there is no reason why U.S. exports and imports with any particular country should be balanced.

Comparative Advantage

We have so far focused on exchanges of existing goods. But clearly, most of what is exchanged must first be produced. Trade allows individuals and countries to concentrate on what they produce best.

Some countries are more efficient at producing almost all goods than are other countries. The possession of superior production skills is called having an **absolute advantage,** and these advanced countries are said to have an absolute advantage over the others. How can the countries with disadvantages successfully engage in trade? The answer lies in the principle of **comparative advantage,** which states that individuals and countries specialize in producing those goods in which they are *relatively,* not absolutely, more efficient.

To see what comparative advantage means, let's say that both the United States and Japan produce two goods, computers and wheat. The amount of labor needed to produce these goods is shown in Table 3.1. (These numbers are all hypothetical.) The United States is more efficient (spends fewer worker hours) at making both products. America can rightfully claim to have the most efficient computer industry in the world, and yet it imports computers from Japan. Why? The *relative* cost of making a computer (in terms of labor used) in Japan, relative to the cost of producing a ton of wheat, is low, compared with the United States. That is, in Japan, it takes 15 times as many hours (120/8) to produce a computer as a ton of wheat; in the United States, it takes 20 times as many hours (100/5) to produce a computer as a ton of wheat. While Japan has an absolute *dis*advantage in producing computers, it has a *comparative* advantage.

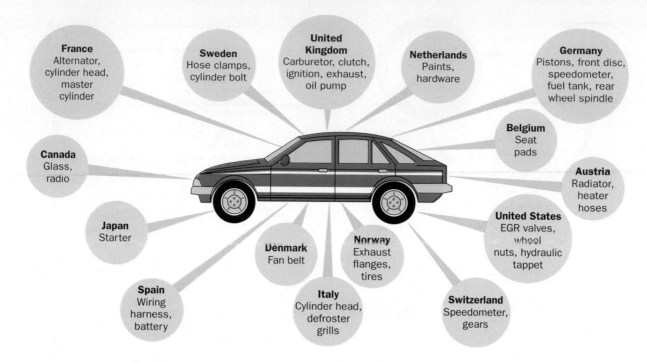

FIGURE 3.3 *The Making of a Modern Automobile*

The ingredients for a Ford Escort have been gathered from all over the world.

SOURCE: *World Development Report* (1990).

The principle of comparative advantage applies to individuals as well as countries. The president of a company might type faster than her secretary, but it still pays to have the secretary type her letters, because the president may have a comparative advantage at bringing in new clients, while the secretary has a comparative (though not absolute) advantage at typing.

TABLE 3.1

Labor Cost of Producing Computers and Wheat (worker hours)

	United States	Japan
Labor required to make a computer	100	120
Labor required to make a ton of wheat	5	8

Production Possibilities Schedules and Comparative Advantage   The easiest way to understand the comparative advantage of different countries is to use the production possibilities schedule first introduced in Chapter 2. Figure 3.4 depicts parts of hypothetical production possibilities schedules for two countries, China and the United States, producing two commodities, textiles (garments) and airplanes. In both schedules, point *E* represents the current level of production. Let us look at what happens if each country changes its production by 100 airplanes.

China has a comparative advantage in producing textiles. If it reduces its airplane production by 100, its textile production can be increased by 10,000 garments. This trade-off between airplanes and garments is called the **marginal rate of transformation.** By contrast, if the United States reduces its airplane production by 100 airplanes, its textile production can be increased by only 1,000 garments. Conversely, if it increases its airplane production by 100, it will have to reduce its garment production by only 1,000 gar-

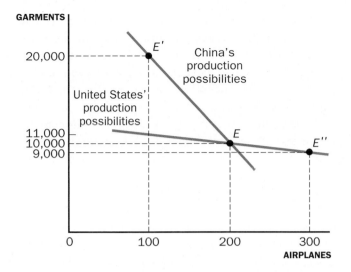

FIGURE 3.4   *Exploiting Comparative Advantage*

The production possibilities schedules for China and the United States, each manufacturing two commodities, textiles and airplanes, illustrate the trade-offs at different levels of production. Point *E* shows the current level of production for each country; *E'* and *E"* illustrate production decisions that better exploit each country's comparative advantage.

ments. We can now see why the world is better off if each country exploits its comparative advantage. If China moves from *E* to *E'* (decreasing airplane production by 100), 10,000 more garments can be produced. If the United States at the same time increases its airplane production by 100 from *E* to *E"*, it will produce only 1,000 fewer garments. In the new situation, the world production of airplanes is unchanged (100 + 300 = 200 + 200), but world production of garments has increased by 9,000 (20,000 + 9,000 is 9,000 more than 10,000 + 10,000). So long as the production trade-offs differ—that is, so long as the marginal rates of transformation differ—it pays for China to specialize increasingly in textiles, and the United States to specialize increasingly in airplanes. Notice that the analysis only requires knowledge about the production trade-offs. We do not need to know how much labor or capital is required in either country to produce either airplanes or garments.

Though it pays countries to increase the production and export of goods in which they have a comparative advantage and to import goods in which they have a comparative disadvantage, this may not lead to complete specialization. Thus the United States continues to be a major producer of textiles, in spite of heavy imports from the Far East. This does not violate the principle of comparative advantage: not all textiles require the same skill and expertise in manufacturing. Thus, while China may have a comparative advantage in inexpensive textiles, the United States may have a comparative advantage in higher-quality textiles. At the same time, the comparative advantage of other countries is so extreme in producing some goods that it does not pay for the United States to produce them at all: TV's, VCRs, and a host of other electronic gadgets, for example.

Comparative Advantage and Specialization

To see the benefits of specialization, consider the pencil. A tree, containing the right kind of wood, must be felled; it must be transported to a sawmill, and there cut into pieces that can be further processed into pencil casings. Then the graphite that runs through the pencil's center, the eraser at its tip, the metal that holds the two together must each be produced by specially trained people. The pencil is a simple tool. But to produce it by oneself would cost a fortune in money and an eternity in time.

Why Specialization Increases Productivity   Specialization increases productivity, thus enhancing the benefits of trade, for three reasons. First, specializing avoids the time it takes a worker to switch from one production task to another. Second, by repeating the same task, the worker becomes more skilled at it. And third, specialization creates a fertile environment for invention.

Dividing jobs so that each worker can practice and perfect a particular skill (called the **division of labor**) may increase productivity hundreds or thousands of times. Almost anyone who practices simple activities—like sewing on a button, shooting a basketball, or adding a column of numbers—will be quite a lot better at them than someone who has not practiced. Similarly, a country that specializes in producing sports cars may develop a comparative advantage in sports cars. With its relatively large scale of production, it can divide tasks into separate assignments for different people; as each becomes better at his own tasks, productivity is increased.

At the same time, the division of labor often leads to invention. As someone learns a particular job extremely well, she might figure out ways of doing it better—including inventing a machine to do it. Specialization and invention reinforce each other. A slight initial advantage in the production of some good leads to greater production of that good, thence to more invention, and thence to even greater production and further specialization.

Internet Connection

David Ricardo

The economist David Ricardo developed the theory of comparative advantage. Born in 1772, Ricardo was the third of seventeen children. He was a successful stockbroker before retiring at age forty-two to write about economics. The Virtual Economics Library at Biz/ed—a web site devoted to business and economics education—provides a brief biography of this famous economist and discusses his contributions to the theory of comparative advantage at http://www.bized.ac.uk/virtual/economy/library/economists/ricardo.htm.

Limits of Specialization   The extent of division of labor, or specialization, is limited by the size of the market. There is greater scope for specialization in mass-produced manufactured goods like picture frames than in custom-made items like the artwork that gets framed. That is one reason why the costs of production of mass-produced goods have declined so much. Similarly, there is greater scope for specialization in a big city than a small town. That is why small stores specializing in a particular food or type of clothing thrive in cities but are rare in smaller towns.

The very nature of specialization limits its benefits. Repetitive jobs can lead to bored and unproductive workers. And single-track specialization inhibits the new insights and ideas that can come from engaging in a variety of work activities.

What Determines Comparative Advantage?
Earlier we learned that comparative advantage determines the pattern of trade. But what determines comparative advantage? In the modern world, this turns out to be a complex matter.

Natural Endowments   In first laying down the principle of comparative advantage in the early 1800s, the great British economist David Ricardo used the example of Portugal's trade with Britain. In Ricardo's example, Portugal had an absolute advantage in producing both wool and wine. But it had a comparative advantage in producing wine, and Britain had a comparative advantage in producing wool. In this and other early examples, economists tended to assume that a nation's comparative advantage was determined largely by its **natural endowments.** Countries with soil and climate that are *relatively* better for grapes than for pasture will produce wine; countries with soil and climate that are relatively better for pasture than for grapes will produce sheep (and hence wool).

In the modern economy, natural endowments still count: countries that have an abundance of low-skilled labor relative to other resources, such as China, have a comparative advantage in producing goods like textiles, which require a lot of handwork. But in today's technological age nations can also act to *acquire* a comparative advantage.

Acquired Endowments   Japan has little in the way of natural resources, yet it is a major player in international trade, in part because it has **acquired endowments.** Japan's case underscores the principle that by saving and accumulating capital and building large factories, a nation can acquire a comparative advantage in goods, like steel, that require large amounts of capital in their production. And by devoting resources to education, a nation can develop a comparative advantage in those goods that require a skilled labor force. Thus, the resources—human and physical—that a country has managed to acquire for itself can also give rise to comparative advantage.

Superior Knowledge   In the modern economy, comparative advantage may come simply from expertise in using resources productively. Switzerland has a comparative advantage in watches because, over the years, the people of the country have accumulated superior knowledge and expertise in watch making. Belgium has a comparative advantage in fine lace; its workers have developed the requisite skills. A quirk of fate might have led Belgium to acquire a comparative advantage in watches and Switzerland in lace.

Although patterns of specialization sometimes occur as an accident of history, in modern economies they are more likely to be a consequence of deliberate decisions. The United States' strength in information technology is an example.

Specialization   Earlier we saw how comparative advantage leads to specialization. Specialization may also lead to

e-Insight

The United States' Comparative Advantage in the Internet Age

The United States holds a comparative advantage in information technology and Internet-based commerce. Large U.S. firms like Microsoft, Intel, and Sun Microsystems have led the surge in information technology over the last two decades, and Internet-based businesses like Amazon, Yahoo, and e-Bay have come to define the so-called new economy. How has the United States established itself as a leader in this field? Let's consider this question from the standpoint of the sources of comparative advantage described in this chapter.

The key to the United States' success in the information revolution has been its ability to innovate. U.S. firms have developed new types of computers and software, and new applications of these resources across various industries. This prowess in innovation derives from acquired endowments, superior knowledge, and specialization.

The human skills needed for innovation represent acquired endowments that have led to superior knowledge, some of which was acquired as a by-product of America's massive expenditures on defense-related research. Another aspect of acquired endowments that has played a major role is the distinctive set of *institutions* in the United States that are particularly well suited for promoting research. These institutions include a special set of financial institutions (venture capital firms) that are better able to supply capital to new and small enterprises, which have played a pivotal role in the new economy, and strong research universities, many of which have a close nexus to firms that can translate basic research into market applications. More broadly, both American labor and capital seem more able and willing to bear the high risks associated with new innovative enterprises, many of which may fold after a relatively short period of time. Americans may be more willing to bear these risks, partially because of the high levels of employment that have characterized the American economy for the last decade. Those who lose their job typically can get another one relatively quickly.

Partly as a result of these acquired advantages and superior knowledge, the United States has developed a relative specialization in high-tech industries; it has become, to a large extent, the world's research center.

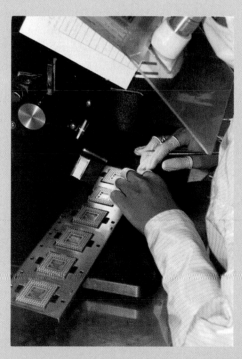

Intel's strength in computer chip production exemplifies the U.S. comparitive advantage in information technology.

comparative advantage. The Swiss make fine watches, and have a comparative advantage in that market based on years of unique experience. Such superior knowledge, however, does not explain why Britain, Germany, and the United States, which are at roughly the same level of technological expertise in building cars, all trade cars with one another. How can each country have a comparative advantage in making cars? The answer lies in specialization.

Both Britain and Germany may be better off if Britain specializes in producing sports cars and Germany in producing luxury cars, or conversely, because specialization increases productivity. Countries enhance, or simply develop, a comparative advantage by specializing just as individuals do. As a result, similar countries enjoy the advantages of specialization even when they specialize in different variations of basically similar products.

WRAP-UP

The Four Bases of Comparative Advantage

Natural endowments, which consist of geographical determinants such as land, natural resources, and climate

Acquired endowments, which are the physical capital and human skills a nation has developed

Superior knowledge, including technological advantages, which may be acquired either as an accident of history or through deliberate policies

Specialization, which may create comparative advantages between countries that are similar in all other respects

The Perceived Costs of International Interdependence

If the argument that voluntary trade must be mutually beneficial is so compelling, why has there been, from time to time, such strong antitrade sentiment in the United States and many other countries? This antitrade feeling is often labeled **protectionism,** because it calls for "protecting" the economy from the effects of trade. Those who favor protectionism raise a number of concerns. Some of the objections to international trade parallel the objections to trade among individuals noted earlier. Was the trade a fair deal? Was the seller in a stronger bargaining position? Such concerns, for individuals and countries, revolve around how the *surplus* associated with the gains from trade is divided. Weak countries may feel that they are being taken advantage of by stronger countries. Their weaker bargaining position may mean that the stronger countries get *more* of the gains from trade. But this does not contradict the basic premise: both parties gain from voluntary exchange. All countries—weak as well as strong—are better off as a result of voluntary exchange.

But an important difference exists between trade among individuals and trade among countries. Some individuals within a country benefit from trade and some lose. Since the trade as a whole is beneficial to the country, the gains to the winners exceed the losses to the losers. Thus, in principle, those who benefit within the country could more than compensate those who lose. In practice, however, those who lose remain losers and obviously oppose trade, using the argument that trade results in lost jobs and reduced wages. These concerns have become particularly acute as unskilled workers face competition with low-wage unskilled workers in Asia and Latin America: how can they compete without lowering their wages?

These concerns played a prominent role in the debate in 1993 over ratification of the North American Free Trade Agreement (NAFTA), which allows Mexican goods into the United States with no duties at all. Advocates of NAFTA pointed out that (1) more jobs would be created by the new export opportunities than would be lost through competition from Mexican firms; and (2) the jobs created paid higher wages, reflecting the benefits from specialization in areas where the United States had a comparative advantage.

Opponents of NAFTA, in particular, and trade, in general, are not swayed by these arguments, but instead stress the costs to workers and communities as particular industries shrink in response to foreign imports. The textile worker in North Carolina who loses his job as a result of imports of inexpensive clothing from China cannot instantly convert himself into a computer programmer in California or an aircraft engineer working for Boeing. But the fact is that jobs are being destroyed and created all the time, irrespective of trade. And over the long run, the economic incentive of the new jobs at Boeing may induce someone in the Midwest to leave his semi-skilled job and get the training that makes him eligible for one of the skilled jobs at Boeing. The vacancy created may be filled by someone who moves in from Kentucky, leaving a vacancy there for the laid-off textile worker in North Carolina.

Because of the practical complications and the very real costs of retraining and relocation, there is increasing recognition that government may need to play a role in facilitat-

Thinking Like an Economist

Exchange and the Globalization Controversy

In recent decades transportation and communication costs have come down markedly. So too have artificial barriers to the movements of goods and services—trade barriers like tariffs and quotas. The result is that the economies of the world are now more closely integrated than ever before.

From an economic perspective, this trend toward globalization would seem to offer a great benefit to the world. As we know, one of the core ideas of economics is that *voluntary exchange* is mutually beneficial to the parties involved. Yet, globalization has been a subject of great controversy. For instance, some critics of globalization see it as a one-sided process mainly benefiting rich countries and large multinational firms. Others on the opposite side of the debate see globalization as the best opportunity to increase the standards of living in poor countries. How do we make sense of this controversy from an economic perspective? A close look at the globalization controversy shows that some of the criticisms are misplaced, while others have merit.

Globalization no doubt has made us more aware of the huge inequalities around the world. Some workers in China, Africa, and India, for instance, earn less than a dollar a day working under conditions that appear inhumane by American standards. But, for the most part, globalization has not caused their misery; it has only brought it to global attention. Many of these workers have moved to jobs in seemingly awful factories—some run by multinational firms, others selling their goods to multinational firms—because their previous jobs were even worse or because they had no previous jobs. It may seem cruel for these corporations to exploit these workers, especially where working conditions could be improved at moderate expense. But even so, in many cases the workers have benefited from globalization.

Another economic aspect of globalization is that the *distribution* of its benefits may be highly uneven. For example, the owners of factories that make goods for multinational firms typically benefit more than the workers they employ.

Are the jobs of these Chinese workers a cost or benefit of globalization?

As a result, even if everyone is better off, an increase in inequality results. Critics attacking the issue from a normative stance—where social values about fairness play a role—may see increased inequality as the primary concern. In their view, the poor, who in some cases may benefit the least from globalization, are the very people who deserve to benefit more. But even if we agree with this contention, we have to recognize that it does not refute the basic economic principle about the benefits of voluntary exchange.

A further criticism of globalization maintains that some individuals are actually made worse off. Can this be? The answer is yes, and an example helps illustrate the point. The theory of comparative advantage says that countries should produce the goods that they are relatively good at producing. But with protection from foreign competition, firms may produce goods that are not part of the country's comparative advantage. The United States may produce cheap clothes, simply because of the limits put on importing inexpensive foreign-made clothes. Removing the protection may make the production of the inexpensive clothes unprofitable. The factory may have to shut down, and workers left unemployed. But in theory, this should not happen for long. If markets work well, some new enterprises will be created to take advantage of the country's comparative advantage. Resources get redeployed from where they are less productive to where they are more productive. And this increases the country's income. But this process of redeployment does not happen automatically, or necessarily quickly, and in the meanwhile, those who are pushed into unemployment often object to the removal of the protection.

Such problems are especially severe in developing countries, where there is a shortage of entrepreneurs and a short age of capital to start the new enterprises. In these poor countries, the problem of unemployment can be particularly severe, since there is no unemployment insurance system and no welfare system to fall back on. In many cases it may be true that the gains of those who benefit from freer trade more than offset the losses of those who suffer. Therefore, in principle, the gainers could compensate the losers so that everyone could be made better off. But in practice, the compensation is seldom paid. Thus, although a country may benefit from globalization, some of its citizens may suffer until the process of redeployment works itself out.

ing job movements. To the extent that such assistance increases the number of winners from trade, it should reduce opposition to trade.

While the perceived costs of economic interdependence cannot be ignored—especially when they become the subject of heated political debate—the fact that the country as a whole benefits from freer trade is one of the central tenets in which there is a consensus among the vast majority of economists. We can summarize this important point in the following way: *There are gains from voluntary exchanges. Whether between individuals or across national borders, all can gain from voluntary exchange. Trade allows parties to specialize in activities in which they have a comparative advantage.*

Review and Practice

Summary

1. The benefits of economic interdependence apply to individuals and firms within a country as well as to countries within the world. No individual and no country is self-sufficient.

2. Both individuals and countries gain from voluntary trade. There may be cases when there are only limited possibilities for bilateral trade (exchange between two parties), but the gains from multilateral trade (exchange between several parties) may be great.

3. The principle of comparative advantage asserts that countries should export the goods in which their production costs are *relatively* low.

4. Specialization tends to increase productivity for three reasons: specializing avoids the time it takes a worker to switch from one production task to another; workers who repeat a task become more skilled at it; specialization creates a fertile environment for invention.

5. A country's comparative advantage can arise from natural endowments, acquired endowments, superior knowledge, or specialization.

6. There is a basic difference between trade among individuals and trade among countries: with trade among countries, some individuals within the country may actually be worse off. Though free trade enhances national income, fears about job loss and wage reductions among low-skilled workers have led to demands for protection.

Key Terms

gains from trade
surplus
imports
exports
bilateral trade
multilateral trade
absolute advantage

comparative advantage
marginal rate of transformation
division of labor
natural endowments
acquired endowments
protectionism

Review Questions

1. Why are all voluntary trades mutually beneficial?

2. Describe a situation (hypothetical, if need be) where bilateral trade does not work but multilateral trade is possible.

3. What are some of the similarities of trade between individuals and trade between countries? What is a key way in which they differ?

4. Does a country with an absolute advantage in a product necessarily have a comparative advantage in that product? Can a country with an absolute disadvantage in a product have a comparative advantage in that product? Explain.

5. Why does specialization tend to increase productivity?

6. "A country's comparative advantage is dictated by its natural endowments." Discuss.

7. "If trade with a foreign country injures anyone in this country, the government should react by passing protectionist laws to limit or stop that particular trade." Comment.

Problems

1. Four players on a Little League baseball team discover that they have each been collecting baseball cards, and they agree to get together and trade. Is it possible for everyone to benefit from this agreement? Does the fact that one player starts off with many more cards than any of the others affect your answer?

2. Leaders in many less developed countries of Latin America and Africa have often argued that because they are so much poorer than the wealthy nations of the world, trade with the more developed economies of North America and Europe will injure them. They maintain that they must first become self-sufficient be-

fore they can benefit from trade. How might an economist respond to these claims?

3. If the United States changes its immigration quotas to allow many more unskilled workers into the country, who is likely to gain? Who is likely to lose? Consider the impact on consumers, on businesses that hire low-skilled labor, and on low-skilled labor in both the United States and the workers' countries of origin.

4. David Ricardo illustrated the principle of comparative advantage in terms of the trade between England and Portugal in wine (port) and wool. Suppose that in England it takes 120 laborers to produce a certain quantity of wine, while in Portugal it takes only 80 laborers to produce that same quantity. Similarly, in England it takes 100 laborers to produce a certain quantity of wool, while in Portugal it takes only 90. Draw the opportunity set for each country, assuming that each has 72,000 laborers. Assume that each country commits half its labor to each product in the absence of trade, and designate that point on your graph. Now describe a new production plan, with trade, that can benefit both countries.

5. Relate the comparative advantage of two countries to differences in the slope of their production possibilities schedules. In what sense might a small, poor country trading with a much larger, rich country be at a disadvantage? How might the differences affect how the gains from trade are divided.

6. In 1981, the U.S. government prodded Japanese automakers to limit the number of cars they would export to the United States. Who benefited from this protectionism in the United States and in Japan? Who was injured in the United States and in Japan? Consider companies that produce cars (and their workers) and consumers who buy cars.

7. For many years, an international agreement called the Multifiber Agreement has limited the amount of textiles that the developed economies of North America and Europe can buy from poor countries in Latin America and Asia. Textiles can be produced by relatively unskilled labor with a reasonably small amount of capital. Who benefits from the protectionism of the Multifiber Agreement, and who suffers?

8. Both the European Union and the United States produce cars and television shows. Assume the labor costs

(in worker hours) required for the production of cars and these shows are as follows:

	European Union	United States
Labor required to make a car	100	80
Labor required to produce a television show	600	400

Assume each region has 240,000 worker hours to divide between producing cars and television shows. Initially, assume workers are divided equally between producing cars and TV shows.

(a) What are the initial levels of production of cars and television shows in each region? What is total production in the two regions?

(b) Draw the production possibilities curves for the two regions.

(c) Which region has an absolute advantage in producing cars? Which region has an absolute advantage in producing television shows?

(d) Which region has a comparative advantage in producing cars? Which region has a comparative advantage in producing television shows?

(e) Starting with the initial levels of production, demonstrate how comparative advantage can be exploited to raise joint production of cars by 10 while leaving television show output unchanged.

The "New Economy" and the Old Economics?

It used to be that the only way you could buy recorded music was to go to a neighborhood music store or join a record club, which would send you an automatic selection each month or let you choose from its catalog. Today, you can shop for compact discs in stores ranging from music warehouses to drug stores, or you can shop on-line, listening to selections from the CD before you decide to buy it. You can even download music over the Internet. The market for recorded music provides just one example of how the new information technologies are changing the way people conduct business.

Many commentators argue that the tremendous growth in computer-related industries, communications, and Internet usage is fundamentally transforming the economy. Stories about the "new economy" often contrast the dynamic high-tech sectors with the "old economy" stalwarts that dominated in the past. Often commentators suggest the changes brought on by the new information technologies have rewritten the rules for how the economy operates. Can the basic principles of economics help us understand these transformations? The answer is yes. Chapter 1 introduced five core economic concepts—trade-offs, incentives, exchange, information, and distribution—each of which offers insights into the new economy.

Does information technology eliminate trade-offs? No. Changes in the way business is conducted and the technologies that are used can alter the trade-offs people face, but choices still need to be made. Even to incorporate new technologies requires that choices be made. For example, a firm planning to spend money on information technology equipment has other uses for those funds. It must weigh the benefits of the computers and software it needs to take advantage of the information technology revolution against the alternative investments it could make. New technologies can present us with new trade-offs. For instance, making on-line purchases saves time and the inconvenience of shopping, but the trade-off may be a loss of privacy. Even simply browsing the Web can allow others to collect personal information about your interests and shopping habits. Each individual has to decide if the convenience is worth the loss of privacy.

To noneconomists, the rapid growth of the Internet and the increase in business investment in information technologies, hardly calls for explanation, since they may view new technologies like the baseball diamond in the movie *Field of Dreams*—if technology firms invent it, households and business will buy it. But economists know that this is not the case—decision makers respond to *incentives*. An economist looks for the incentives to invest in new technologies. The new information technologies allow firms to do what they were doing before—keeping records, paying wages, sending out bills, keeping track of inventories—at a fraction of the cost previously incurred. And they allow firms to handle masses of information that they simply could not have managed before—allowing them to do things that were previously virtually impossible. For most firms, cutting costs and putting themselves ahead of their rivals provided the *incentives* for these huge investments.

An economist also looks at the role of *exchange* and the role of *information*, and here too the impact of information technologies has been profound. Many of the changes wrought by new technologies have affected the way goods are exchanged. On-line purchasing has become commonplace, and business-to-business (B2B) commerce has allowed firms to become more efficient. Many of these changes are based on the ability of information technologies to improve access to information. Numerous on-line services today can help you find the cheapest airfare, research colleges, locate a hotel, and buy car insurance. These services have lowered the cost of obtaining information.

Finally, the new technological revolution has affected the distribution of wealth and income in the economy. While hundreds of new information technology millionaires have been created, unskilled workers have been left behind. The new technologies require new skills, so the demand for unskilled workers has fallen, leading to a decline in their incomes. Households with low incomes also confront the "digital divide"—they are much less likely to own computers or have access to the Internet. Government programs aimed at making Internet access available to low-income households have been proposed. However, the huge drop in the cost of home computers means that cost may not be the impediment it once was. Instead, the skills needed to take advantage of the Internet may be the resource in short supply. Among African Americans, for instance, only 9 percent of those with less than a high school degree were on-line in January 2000 compared with 59 percent of African Americans with college degrees. For Hispanic Americans, the corresponding figures were 21 percent and 71 percent.

Economists are still debating whether there is in fact a new economy. After all, many previous technological changes also had major effects on the economy—just think of the railroads in the nineteenth century or the automobile in the twentieth century—yet we do not think of these as having created new economies. Even in California, a center of the high-tech industry, computer-related services accounted for just 2 percent of the state's total employment. In fact, Professor Robert J. Gordon at Northwestern University identifies four clusters of inventions that he believes played a greater role in boosting economic productivity than the information technology

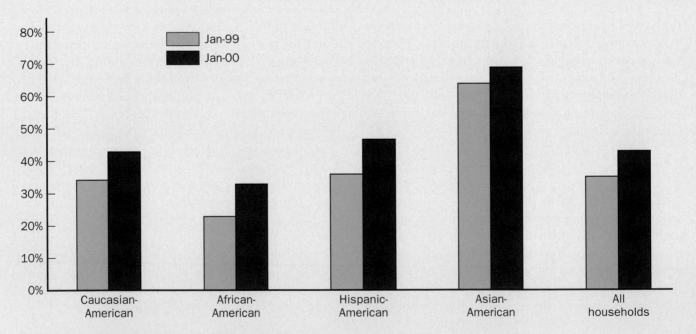

The Digital Divide: Percent of Households Online

revolution has played. These four are electricity; internal-combustion engines; the molecular advances that created petrochemicals, plastics, and pharmaceuticals; and the earlier communications revolution of the telephone, radio, movies and television.

Perhaps the information technology revolution will be even more far-reaching than these earlier technological revolutions. Only time will tell. What we can say, though, is that the core concepts of economics will help make sense of the new (and the old) economy.

Part 2

Perfect Markets

Chapter 4

Demand, Supply, and Price

Key Questions

1. What is meant by demand? Why do demand curves normally slope downward? On what variables, other than price, does the quantity demanded depend?

2. What is meant by supply? Why do supply curves normally slope upward? On what variables, other than price, does the quantity supplied depend?

3. Why do economists say that the equilibrium price occurs at the intersection of the demand and supply curves?

4. How do shifts in the demand and supply curves affect the equilibrium price?

*C*hoice in the face of scarcity, as we have seen, is the fundamental concern of economics. The **price** of a good or service is what must be given in exchange for the good. When the forces of supply and demand operate freely, price measures scarcity. As such, prices convey critical economic information. When the price of a resource used by a firm is high, the company has a greater incentive to economize on its use. When the price of a good that the firm produces is high, the company has a greater incentive to produce more of that good, and its customers have an incentive to economize on its use. In these ways and others, prices provide our economy with incentives to use scarce resources efficiently. This chapter describes how prices are determined in competitive market economies.

The Role of Prices

Prices are the way participants in the economy communicate with one another. Assume a drought hits the country, reducing drastically the supply of corn. Households will need to reduce their consumption of corn or there will not be enough to go around. But how will they know this? Suppose newspapers across the country ran an article informing people they would have to eat less corn because of a drought. What incentive would they have to pay attention to it? How would each family know how much it ought to reduce its consumption? As an alternative to the newspaper, consider the effect of an increase in the price of corn. The higher price conveys all the relevant information. It tells families corn is scarce at the same time as it provides incentives for them to consume less of it. Consumers do not need to know anything about why corn is scarce, nor do they need to be told by how much they should reduce their consumption of corn.

Price changes and differences present interesting problems and puzzles. In the early 1980s, while the price of an average house in Los Angeles went up by 41 percent, the price of a house in Milwaukee, Wisconsin, increased by only 4 percent. Why? During the same period, the price of computers fell dramatically, while the price of bread rose, but at a much slower rate than the price of housing in Los Angeles. Why? The "price" of labor is just the wage or salary that is paid. Why does a physician earn three times as much as a college professor, though the college professor may have performed better in the college courses they took together? Why did the average wage fall in the United States between 1973 and 1983? Why is the price of water, without which we cannot live, very low in most cases, but the price of diamonds, which we can surely live without, very high? The simple answer to all these questions is that in market economies like the United States, price is determined by supply and demand. Changes in prices are determined by changes in supply and demand.

Understanding the causes of changes in prices and being able to predict their occurrence is not just a matter of academic interest. One of the events that precipitated the French Revolution was the rise in the price of bread, for which the people blamed the government. Large price changes have also given rise to recent political turmoil in several countries, including Morocco, the Dominican Republic, Russia, and Indonesia.

Noneconomists see much more in prices than the impersonal forces of supply and demand. It was the landlord who raised the rent on the apartment; it was the oil company or the owner of the gas station who raised the price of gasoline. These people and companies *chose* to raise their prices, says the noneconomist, in moral indignation. True, replies the economist, but there must be some factor that made these people and companies believe that a higher price was not a good idea yesterday but is today. And economists point out that at a different time, these same impersonal forces can force the same landlords and oil companies to cut their prices. Economists see prices, then, as symptoms of underlying causes, and focus on the forces of demand and supply behind price changes.

Demand

Economists use the concept of **demand** to describe the quantity of a good or service that a household or firm chooses to buy at a given price. It is important to understand that economists are concerned not just with what people desire but with what they choose to buy given the spending limits imposed by their budget constraint and given the prices of various goods. In analyzing demand, the first question they ask is how the quantity of a good purchased by an individual changes as the price changes, keeping everything else constant.

The Individual Demand Curve

Think about what happens as the price of candy bars changes. At a price of $5.00, you might never buy one. At $3.00, you might buy one as a special treat. At $1.25, you might buy a few, and if the price declined to $.50, you might buy a lot. The table in Figure 4.1 summarizes the weekly demand of one individual, Roger, for candy bars at these different prices. We can see that the lower the price, the larger the quantity demanded. We can also draw a graph that shows the quantity Roger demands at each price. The quantity demanded is measured along the horizontal axis, and the price is measured along the vertical axis. The graph in Figure 4.1 plots the points.

A smooth curve can be drawn to connect the points. This curve is called the **demand curve.** The demand curve gives the quantity demanded at each price. Thus, if we want to know how many candy bars a week Roger will demand at a price of $1.00, we simply look along the vertical axis at the price $1.00, find the corresponding point *A* along the demand curve, and then read down the horizontal axis. At a price of $1.00, Roger buys 6 candy bars each week. Alternatively, if we want to know at what price he will

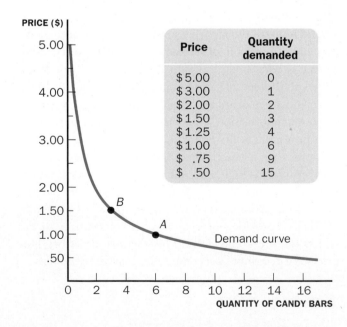

Price	Quantity demanded
$ 5.00	0
$ 3.00	1
$ 2.00	2
$ 1.50	3
$ 1.25	4
$ 1.00	6
$ .75	9
$ .50	15

FIGURE 4.1 *An Individual's Demand Curve*

This demand curve shows the quantity of candy bars that Roger consumes at each price. Notice that quantity demanded increases as the price falls, and the demand curve slopes down.

buy just 3 candy bars, we look along the horizontal axis at the quantity 3, find the corresponding point *B* along the demand curve, and then read across to the vertical axis. Roger will buy 3 candy bars at a price of $1.50.

As the price of candy bars increases, the quantity demanded decreases. This can be seen from the numbers in the table in Figure 4.1 and in the shape of the demand curve, which slopes downward from left to right. This relationship is typical of demand curves and makes common sense: the cheaper a good is (the lower down we look on the vertical axis), the more of it a person will buy (the farther right on the horizontal axis); the more expensive, the less a person will buy.

WRAP-UP

Demand Curve

The demand curve gives the quantity of the good demanded at each price.

The Market Demand Curve

Suppose there was a simple economy made up of two people, Roger and Jane. Figure 4.2 illustrates how to add up the demand curves of these two individuals to obtain a demand curve for the market as a whole. We "add" the de-

mand curves horizontally by taking, at each price, the quantities demanded by Roger and by Jane and adding the two together. Thus, in the figure, at the price of $.75, Roger demands 9 candy bars and Jane demands 11, so that the total market demand is 20 candy bars. The same principles apply no matter how many people there are in the economy. The **market demand curve** gives the total quantity of the good that will be demanded at each price. The table in Figure 4.3 summarizes the information for our example of candy bars; it gives the total quantity of candy bars demanded by everybody in the economy at various prices. If we had a table like the one in Figure 4.1 for each person in the economy, we would construct Figure 4.3 by adding up, at each price, the total quantity of candy bars purchased. Figure 4.3 tells us, for instance, that at a price of $3.00 per candy bar, the total market demand for candy bars is 1 million candy bars, and that lowering the price to $2.00 increases market demand to 3 million candy bars.

Figure 4.3 also depicts the same information in a graph. As with Figure 4.1, price lies along the vertical axis, but now the horizontal axis measures the quantity demanded by everyone in the economy. Joining the points in the figure together, we get the market demand curve. If we want to know what the total demand for candy bars will be when the price is $1.50 per candy bar, we look on the vertical axis at the price $1.50, find the corresponding point *A* along the demand curve, and read down to the horizontal axis; at that price, total demand is 4 million candy bars. If we want to know what the price of candy bars will be when the demand equals 20 million, we find 20 million along the horizontal

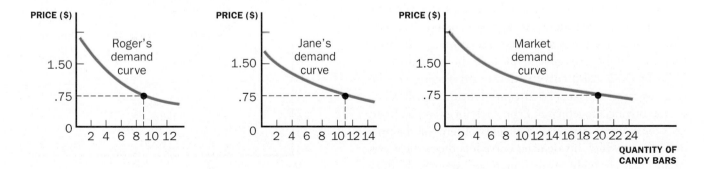

FIGURE 4.2   *Deriving the Market Demand Curve*

The market demand curve is constructed by adding up, at each price, the total of the quantities consumed by each individual. The curve here shows what market demand would be if there were only two consumers. Actual market demand, as depicted in Figure 4.3, is much larger because there are many consumers.

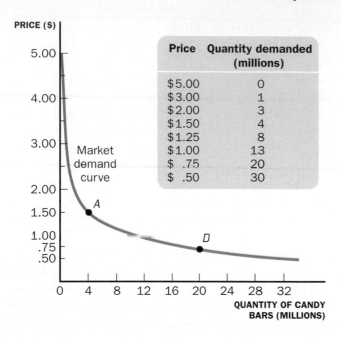

PRICE ($)

Price	Quantity demanded (millions)
$5.00	0
$3.00	1
$2.00	3
$1.50	4
$1.25	8
$1.00	13
$ .75	20
$ .50	30

QUANTITY OF CANDY BARS (MILLIONS)

FIGURE 4.3   *The Market Demand Curve*

The market demand curve shows the quantity of the good demanded by all consumers in the market at each price. The market demand curve is downward sloping, for two reasons: at a higher price, each consumer buys less, and at high-enough prices, some consumers decide not to buy at all—they exit the market.

axis, look up to find the corresponding point *B* along the market demand curve, and read across to the vertical axis; the price at which 20 million candy bars are demanded is $.75.

Notice that just as when the price of candy bars increases, the individual's demand decreases, so too when the price of candy bars increases, market demand decreases. Thus, the market demand curve also slopes downward from left to right. This general rule holds both because each individual's demand curve is downward sloping and because as the price is increased, some individuals will decide to stop buying altogether. In Figure 4.1, for example, Roger *exits the market*—consumes a quantity of zero—at the price of $5.00, at which his demand curve hits the vertical axis. At successively higher prices, more and more individuals exit the market.

Shifts in Demand Curves

When the price of a good increases, the demand for that good decreases—when everything else is held constant.

But in the real world, everything is not held constant. Any changes other than the price of the good in question shift the (whole) demand curve—that is, changes the amount that will be demanded at each price. How the demand curve for candy has shifted as Americans have become more weight conscious provides a good example. Figure 4.4 shows hypothetical demand curves for candy bars in 1960 and in 2000. We can see from the figure, for instance, that the demand for candy bars at a price of $.75 has decreased from 20 million candy bars (point E_{1960}, the original equilibrium) to 10 million (point E_{2000}), as people have reduced their "taste" for candy.

Sources of Shifts in Demand Curves

Two of the factors that shift the demand curve—changes in income and in the price of other goods—are specifically economic factors. As an individual's income increases, she normally purchases more of any good. Thus, rising incomes shift the demand curve to the right, as illustrated in Figure 4.5. At each price, she consumes more of the good.

Changes in the price of other goods, particularly closely related goods, will also shift the demand curve for a good. For example, when the price of margarine in-

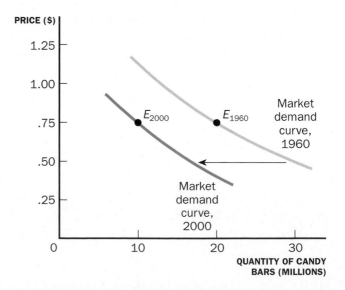

PRICE ($)

QUANTITY OF CANDY BARS (MILLIONS)

FIGURE 4.4   *Shifts in the Demand Curve*

A leftward shift in the demand curve means that a lesser amount will be demanded at every given market price.

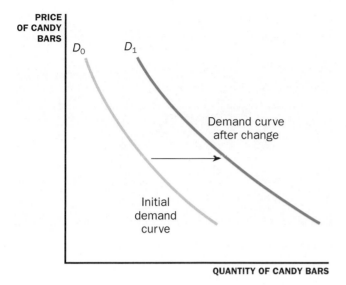

PRICE OF CANDY BARS

D_0 D_1

Demand curve after change

Initial demand curve

QUANTITY OF CANDY BARS

FIGURE 4.5 *A Right-ward Shift in the Demand Curve*

If, at each price, there is an increase in the quantity demanded, then the demand curve will have shifted to the right, as depicted. An increase in income, an increase in the price of a substitute, or a decrease in the price of a complement can cause a rightward shift in the demand curve.

creases, some individuals will substitute butter. Two goods are **substitutes** if an increase in the price of one *increases* the demand for the other. Butter and margarine are thus substitutes. When people choose between butter and margarine, one important factor is the relative price, that is, the ratio of the price of butter to the price of margarine. An increase in the price of butter and a decrease in the price of margarine increase the relative price of butter. Thus, both induce individuals to substitute margarine for butter.

Candy bars and granola bars can also be considered substitutes, as the two goods satisfy a similar need. Thus, an increase in the price of granola bars makes candy bars relatively more attractive, and hence leads to a rightward shift in the demand curve for candy bars. (At each price, the demand for candy is greater.)

Sometimes, however, an increase in a price of other goods has just the opposite effect. Consider an individual who takes sugar in her coffee. In deciding on how much coffee to demand, she is concerned with the price of a cup of coffee *with* sugar. If sugar becomes more expensive, she will demand less coffee. For this person, sugar and coffee

are **complements;** an increase in the price of one *decreases* the demand for the other. A price increase for sugar shifts the demand curve for coffee to the left: at each price, the demand for coffee is less. Similarly a *decrease* in the price of sugar shifts the demand curve for coffee to the right.

Noneconomic factors can also shift market demand curves. The major ones are changes in tastes and in the composition of the population. The candy example shown earlier was a change in taste. Other taste changes over the past decade in the United States include a shift from hard liquor to wine and from fatty meats to low-cholesterol foods. Each of these taste changes has shifted the whole demand curve of the goods in question.

Population changes that shift demand curves are often related to age. Young families with babies purchase disposable diapers. The demand for new houses and apartments is closely related to the number of new households, which in turn depends on the number of individuals of marriageable age. The U.S. population has been growing older, on average, both because life expectancies are increasing and because birthrates fell somewhat after the baby boom that followed World War II. So there has been a shift in demand away from diapers and new houses. Economists working for particular firms and industries spend considerable energy ascertaining population effects, called **demographic effects,** on the demand for the goods their firms sell.

Sometimes demand curves shift as the result of new information. The shifts in demand for alcohol and meat—and even more so for cigarettes—are related to improved consumer information about health risks.

WRAP-UP

Sources of Shifts in Market Demand Curves

A change in income
A change in the price of a substitute
A change in the price of a complement
A change in the composition of the population
A change in tastes
A change in information
A change in the availability of credit
A change in expectations

CASE IN POINT

Gasoline Prices and the Demand for SUVs

When demand for several products is intertwined, conditions affecting the price of one will affect the demand for the other. Changes in gasoline prices in the United States, for example, have affected the types of cars Americans buy.

Gasoline prices soared twice in the 1970s, once when the Organization of Petroleum Exporting Countries (OPEC) shut off the flow of oil to the United States in 1973 and again when the overthrow of the Shah of Iran in 1979 led to a disruption in oil supplies. The price of gasoline at the pump rose from $.35 a gallon in 1971 to $1.35 a gallon by 1981 (see Figure 4.6). In response to the price increases, Americans had to cut back demand. But how could they conserve on gasoline? The distance from home to office was not going to shrink, and people had to get to their jobs. One solution was for American drivers to replace their old cars with smaller cars that offered more miles to the gallon.

Low gas prices lead to higher demand for SUVs.

Analysts classify car sales according to car size, and usually the smaller the car, the better the gas mileage. Just after the first rise in gas prices, about 2.5 million large cars, 2.8 million compacts, and 2.3 million subcompacts were bought each year. By 1985, the proportions had shifted dramatically. About 1.5 million large cars were sold that year, representing a significant decline from the

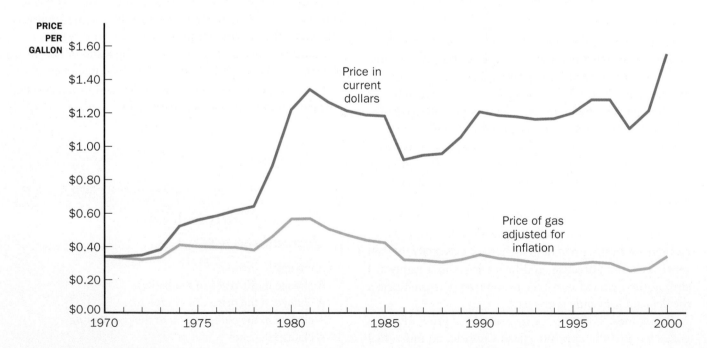

FIGURE 4.6   *U.S. Gasoline Prices*

Adjusted for inflation, gasoline prices in the 1990s were about the same as they had been before the price increases in the 1970s.

mid-1970s. The number of subcompacts sold was relatively unchanged at 2.2 million, but the number of compacts sold soared to 3.7 million.

The demand curve for any good (like cars) assumes that the price of complementary goods (like gasoline) is fixed. The rise in gasoline prices caused the demand curve for small cars to shift out to the right and the demand curve for large cars to shift back to the left.

By the late 1980s, the price of gasoline had fallen significantly from its peak in 1981, but then in the 1990s, gasoline prices again rose significantly. However, the prices of other goods were also rising over the thirty-year period shown in the figure. When gas prices are adjusted for inflation, the real price of gasoline—the price of gas *relative* to the prices of other goods—was lower in the 1990s than it had been *before* the big price increases of the 1970s (Figure 4.6). As a consequence, the demand curve for large cars shifted back to the right. This time, the change in demand was reflected in booming sales of sports utility vehicles, SUVs. The percentage of light-duty trucks (which include SUVs, minivans, and pickups) registered jumped from less than 20 percent 20 years ago to 46 percent in 1996.[1]

Changes in the availability of credit also can shift demand curves—for goods like cars and houses that people typically buy with the help of loans. When banks, for example, reduce the money available for consumer loans, the demand curves for cars and houses shift.

Finally, what people think will happen in the future can shift demand curves. If people think they may become unemployed, they will reduce their spending. In this case, economists say that their demand curve depends on expectations.

Shifts in a Demand Curve Versus Movements Along a Demand Curve

The distinction between changes that result from a *shift* in the demand curve and changes that result from a *movement along* the demand curve is crucial to understanding economics. A movement along a demand curve is simply the change in the

quantity demanded as the price changes. Figure 4.7A illustrates a movement along the demand curve from point *A* to point *B*; *given a demand curve,* at lower prices, more is consumed. Figure 4.7B illustrates a shift in the demand curve to the right; *at a given price,* more is consumed. Quantity again increases from Q_0 to Q_1, but now the price stays the same.

In practice, both effects are often present. Thus, in panel C of Figure 4.7, the movement from point *A* to point *C*—where the quantity demanded has been increased from Q_0 to Q_2—consists of two parts: a change in quantity demanded resulting from a shift in the demand curve (the increase in quantity from Q_0 to Q_1), and a movement along the demand curve due to a change in the price (the increase in quantity from Q_1 to Q_2).

Supply

Economists use the concept of **supply** to describe the quantity of a good or service that a household or firm would like to sell at a particular price. Supply in economics refers to such seemingly disparate choices as the number of candy bars a firm wants to sell and the number of hours a worker is willing to work. As with demand, the first question economists ask is how does the quantity supplied change when price changes, keeping everything else the same?

Figure 4.8 shows the number of candy bars that the Melt-in-the-Mouth Chocolate Company would like to sell, or supply to the market, at each price. As the price rises, so does the quantity supplied. Below $1.00, the firm finds it unprofitable to produce. At $2.00, it would like to sell 85,000 candy bars. At $5.00, it would like to sell 100,000.

Figure 4.8 (p. 76) also depicts these points in a graph. The curve drawn by connecting the points is called the **supply curve**. It shows the quantity that Melt-in-the-Mouth will supply at each price, holding all other factors constant. As with the demand curve, we put the price on the vertical axis and the quantity supplied on the horizontal axis. Thus, we can read point *A* on the curve as indicating that a price of $1.50, the firm would like to supply 70,000 candy bars.

In direct contrast to the demand curve, the typical supply curve slopes upward from left to right; at higher prices, firms will supply more.[2] This is because higher prices yield suppliers higher profits—giving them an incentive to produce more.

---

[1]P. S. Hu, S. D. Davis, and R. L. Schmoyer, *Registrations and Vehicle Miles of Travel for Light-Duty Vehicles 1985–1995* (publication ORNL-6936) (Oakridge, TN: Center for Transportation Analysis, February 1998), p. 1.

[2]Chapter 9 will describe some unusual situations where supply curves may not be upward sloping.

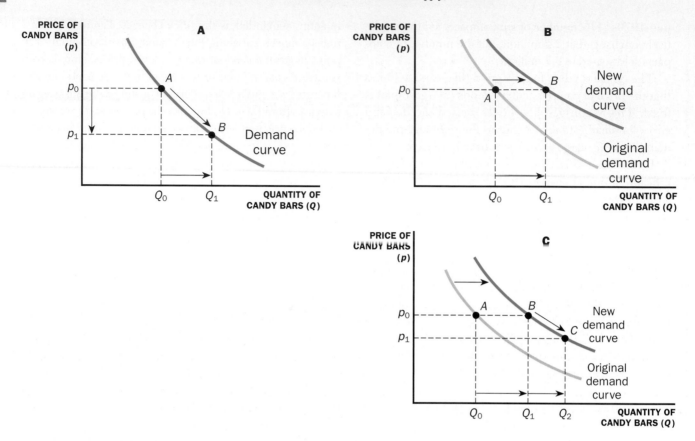

FIGURE 4.7   *Movement Along the Demand Curve Versus Shift in the Demand Curve*

Panel A shows an increase in quantity demanded caused by a lower price—a movement along a given demand curve. Panel B illustrates an increase in quantity demanded caused by a shift in the entire demand curve, so that a greater quantity is demanded at every market price. Panel C shows a combination of a shift in the demand curve (the movement from point *A* to *B*) and a movement along the demand curve (the movement from *B* to *C*).

e-Insight

The Demand for Computers and Information Technology

The demand for computers and other information technology products rose markedly during the 1980s and 1990s, as indicated in panel *A*. This increased demand oc-

curred for a simple reason: the *effective* price of computers fell enormously. Even though the average price of a personal computer remained relatively unchanged during this period, today's computer delivers much higher performance for the same price. Adjusting for this change in quality, between 1990 and 2000 the price of computers is estimated to have fallen an average of almost 18 percent per year (see panel B). At the lower price, we see a higher quantity demanded.

The demand for computers rose markedly during the 1980s and 1990s.

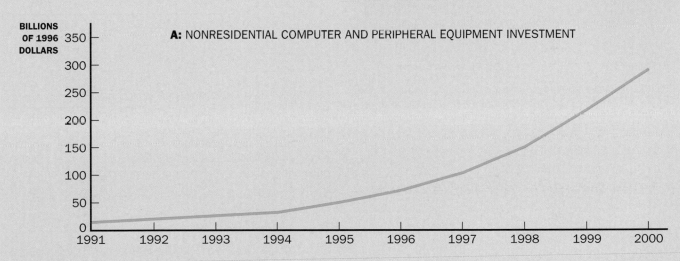

A: NONRESIDENTIAL COMPUTER AND PERIPHERAL EQUIPMENT INVESTMENT

BILLIONS OF 1996 DOLLARS

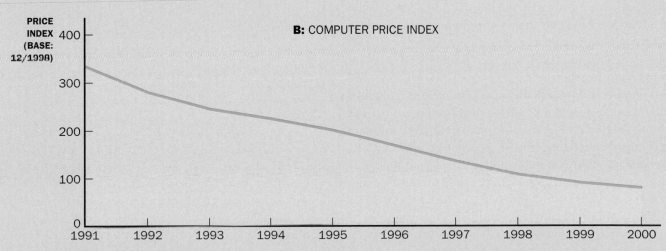

B: COMPUTER PRICE INDEX

PRICE INDEX (BASE: 12/1998)

SOURCE: *ERP(2001), Tables B-18, B-62.*

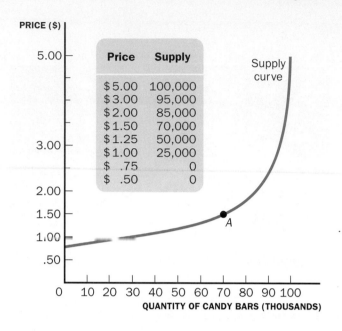

FIGURE 4.8   *One Firm's Supply Curve*

The supply curve shows the quantity of a good a firm is willing to produce at each price. Normally a firm is willing to produce more as the price increases, which is why the supply curve slopes upward.

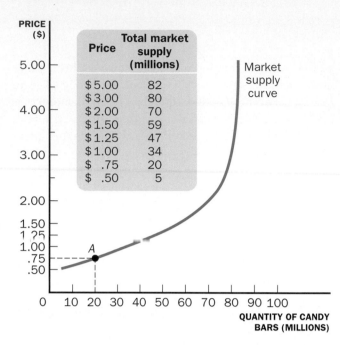

FIGURE 4.9   *The Market Supply Curve*

The market supply curve shows the quantity of a good all firms in the market are willing to supply at each price. The market supply curve is normally upward sloping, both because each firm is willing to supply more of the good at a higher price and because higher prices entice new firms to produce.

Market Supply

The *market supply* of a good is simply the total quantity that all the firms in the economy are willing to supply at a given price. Similarly, the market supply of labor is simply the total quantity of labor that all the households in the economy are willing to supply at a given wage. Figure 4.9 tells us, for instance, that at a price of $2.00, firms will supply 70 million candy bars, while at a price of $.50, they will supply only 5 million.

Figure 4.9 also shows the same information graphically. The curve joining the points in the figure is the **market supply curve.** The market supply curve gives the total quantity of a good that firms are willing to produce at each price. Thus, we read point *A* on the market supply curve as showing that at a price of $.75, the firms in the economy would like to sell 20 million candy bars.

As the price of candy bars increases, the quantity supplied increases, other things equal. The market supply curve slopes upward from left to right for two reasons: at higher prices, each firm in the market is willing to produce more; and at higher prices, more firms are willing to enter the market to produce the good.

WRAP-UP

Supply Curve

The supply curve gives the quantity of the good supplied at each price.

The market supply curve is calculated from the supply curves of the different firms in the same way that the market demand curve is calculated from the demand curves of the different households: at each price, we add horizontally the quantities that each of the firms is willing to produce.

Figure 4.10 shows how this is done in a market with only two producers At a price of $1.25, Melt-in-the-Mouth Chocolate produces 50,000 candy bars, while the Chocolates of Choice Company produces 40,000. So the market supply is 90,000 bars. The same principle applies to markets with many firms.

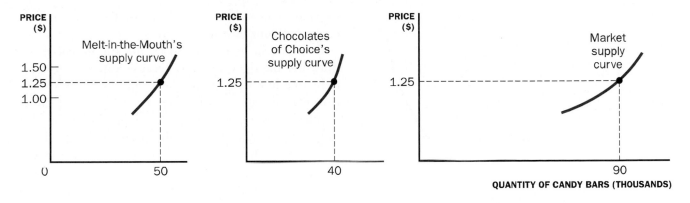

FIGURE 4.10   *Deriving the Market Supply Curve*

The market supply curve is constructed by adding up the quantity that each of the firms in the economy is willing to supply at each price. The figure here shows what market supply would be if there were only two producers. Actual market supply, as depicted in Figure 4.9, is much larger because there are many producers.

Shifts in Supply Curves

Just as demand curves can shift, supply curves too can shift, so that the quantity supplied at each price increases or decreases. Suppose a drought hits the breadbasket states of mid-America. Figure 4.11 illustrates the situation. The supply curve for wheat shifts to the left, which means that at each price of wheat, the quantity firms are willing to supply is smaller.

Sources of Shifts in Supply Curves

There are several sources of shifts in market supply curves, just as in the case of the market demand curves already discussed. One is changing prices of the inputs used to produce a good. Figure 4.12 shows that as corn

becomes less expensive, the supply curve for cornflakes shifts to the right. Producing cornflakes costs less, so at every price, firms are willing to supply a greater quantity. That is why the quantity supplied along the curve S_1 is greater than the quantity supplied, at the same price, along the curve S_0.

Another source of shifts is changes in technology. The technological improvements in the computer industry over

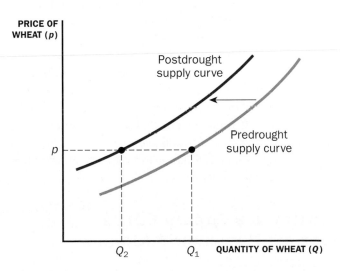

FIGURE 4.11   *Shifting the Supply Curve to the Left*

A drought or other disaster (among other possible factors) will cause the supply curve to shift to the left, so that at each price, a smaller quantity is supplied.

WRAP-UP

Sources of Shifts in Market Supply Curves

A change in the prices of inputs
A change in technology
A change in the natural environment
A change in the availability of credit
A change in expectations

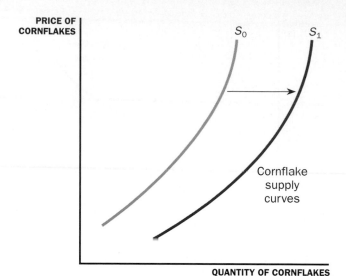

PRICE OF CORNFLAKES

S_0 S_1

Cornflake supply curves

QUANTITY OF CORNFLAKES

FIGURE 4.12   *Shifting the Supply Curve to the Right*

An improvement in technology or a reduction in input prices (among other possible factors) will cause the supply curve to shift to the right, so that at each price, a larger quantity is supplied.

the past two decades have led to a rightward shift in the market supply curve. Yet another source of shifts is nature. The supply curve for agricultural goods may shift to the right or left depending on weather conditions, insect infestations, or animal diseases.

Reduction in the availability of credit may curtail firms' ability to borrow to obtain inputs needed for production, and this too will induce a leftward shift in the supply curve. Finally, changed expectations can also lead to a shift in the supply curve. If firms believe that a new technology for making cars will become available in two years, they will discourage investment today, leading to a temporary leftward shift in the supply curve.

Shifts in a Supply Curve Versus Movements Along a Supply Curve

Distinguishing between a movement *along* a curve and a *shift* in the curve itself is just as important for supply curves as it is for demand curves. In Figure 4.13A, the price of candy bars has gone up, with a corresponding

increase in quantity supplied. Thus, there has been a movement along the supply curve.

By contrast, in Figure 4.13B, the supply curve has shifted to the right, perhaps because a new production technique has made it cheaper to produce candy bars. Now, even though the price does not change, the quantity supplied increases. The quantity supplied in the market can increase either because the price of the good has increased, so that for a *given supply curve*, the quantity produced is higher; or because the supply curve has shifted, so that at a *given price*, the quantity supplied has increased.

Law of Supply and Demand

This chapter began with the assertion that supply and demand work together to determine the market price in competitive markets. Figure 4.14 puts a market supply curve and a market demand curve on the same graph to show how this happens. The price actually paid and received in the market will be determined by the intersection of the two curves. This point is labeled E_0, for equilibrium, and the corresponding price ($.75) and quantity (20 million) are called, respectively, the **equilibrium price** and the **equilibrium quantity**.

Since the term **equilibrium** will recur throughout the book, it is important to understand the concept clearly. Equilibrium describes a situation where there are no forces (reasons) for change. No one has an incentive to change the result—the price or quantity consumed or produced in the case of supply and demand.

Physicists also speak of equilibrium in describing a weight hanging from a spring. Two forces are working on the weight. Gravity is pulling it down; the spring is pulling it up. When the weight is at rest, it is in equilibrium, with the two forces just offsetting each other. If one pulls the weight down a little bit, the force of the spring will be greater than the force of gravity, and the weight will spring up. In the absence of any further intrusions, the weight will bob back and forth and eventually reach its equilibrium position.

An economic equilibrium is established in the same way. At the equilibrium price, consumers get precisely the quantity of the good they are willing to buy at that price, and producers sell precisely the quantity they are willing to

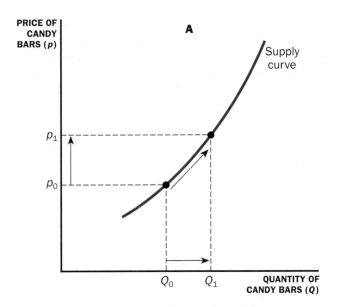

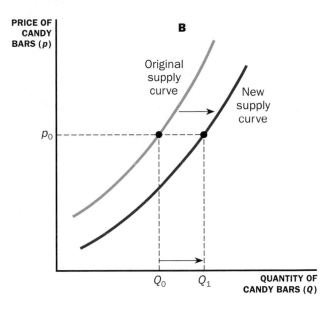

FIGURE 4.13   *Movement Along the Supply Curve Versus Shift in the
                Supply Curve*

Panel A shows an increase in quantity supplied caused by a higher price—a movement along a
given supply curve. Panel B illustrates an increase in quantity supplied caused by a shift in the
entire supply curve, so that a greater quantity is supplied at every market price.

sell at that price. The market clears. To emphasize this condition, economists sometimes refer to the equilibrium price as the **market clearing price.** In equilibrium, neither producers nor consumers have any incentive to change.

But consider the price of $1.00 in Figure 4.14. There is no equilibrium quantity here. First find $1.00 on the vertical axis. Now look across to find point *A* on the supply curve, and read down to the horizontal axis; point *A* tells you that a price of $1.00, firms want to supply 34 million candy bars. Now look at point *B* on the demand curve. Point *B* shows that at a price of $1.00 consumers only want to buy 13 million candy bars. Like the weight bobbing on a spring however, this market will work its way back to equilibrium in the following way. At a price of $1.00, there is **excess supply.** As producers discover that they cannot sell as much as they would like at this price, some of them will lower their prices slightly, hoping to take business from other producers. When one producer lowers prices, his competitors will have to respond, for fear that they will end up unable to sell their goods. As prices come down, consumers will also buy more, and so on until the market reaches the equilibrium price and quantity.

Similarly, assume that the price is lower than $.75, say $.50. At the lower price, there is **excess demand**: individuals want to buy 30 million candy bars (point *C*), while firms only want to produce 5 million (point *D*). Consumers unable to purchase all they want will offer to pay a bit more; other consumers, afraid of having to do without, will match these higher bids or raise them. As prices start to increase, suppliers will also have a greater incentive to produce more. Again the market will tend toward the equilibrium point.

To repeat for emphasis: at equilibrium, no purchaser and no supplier has an incentive to change the price or quantity. In competitive market economies actual prices tend to be the equilibrium prices, at which demand equals supply. This is called the **law of supply and demand.** Note: this law does not mean that at every moment of time the price is precisely at the intersection of the demand and supply curves. As with the example of the weight and the spring, the market may bounce around a little bit when it is in the process of adjusting. What the law of supply and demand does say is that when a market is out of equilibrium, there are predictable forces for change.

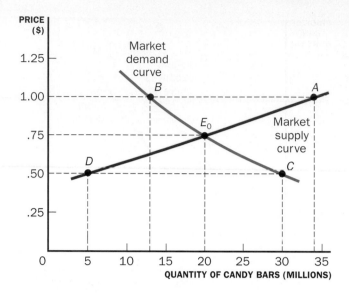

FIGURE 4.14   *Supply and Demand Equilibrium*

Equilibrium occurs at the intersection of the demand and supply curves, at point E_0. At any price above E_0, the quantity supplied will exceed the quantity demanded, the market will be out of equilibrium, and there will be excess supply. At any price below E_0, the quantity demanded will exceed the quantity supplied, the market will be out of equilibrium, and there will be excess demand.

Using Demand and Supply Curves

The concepts of demand and supply curves—and market equilibrium as the intersection of demand and supply curves—constitute the economist's basic model of demand and supply. This model has proved to be extremely useful. It helps explain why the price of some commodity is high, and that of some other commodity is low. It also helps *predict* the consequences of certain changes. Its predictions can then be tested against what actually happens. One of the reasons that the model is so useful is that it gives reasonably accurate predictions.

Figure 4.15 (p. 82) repeats the demand and supply curve for candy bars. Assume, now, however, that sugar becomes more expensive. As a result, at each price, the amount of candy firms are willing to supply is reduced. The supply curve shifts to the left, as in panel A. There will be a new equilibrium, at a higher price and a lower quantity of candy consumed.

Alternatively, assume that Americans become more health conscious, and as a result, at each price fewer candy

bars are consumed: the demand curve shifts to the left, as shown in panel B. Again, there will be a new equilibrium, at a lower price and a lower quantity of candy consumed.

This illustrates how changes in observed prices can be related either to shifts in the demand curve or to shifts in the supply curve. To take a different example, when the war in Kuwait interrupted the supply of oil from the Middle East in 1990, that was a shift in the supply curve. The model predicted the result: an increase in the price of oil. This increase was the natural process of the law of supply and demand.

Consensus on the Determination of Prices

The law of supply and demand plays such a prominent role in economics that there is a joke about teaching a parrot to be an economist simply by teaching it to say "supply and demand." That prices are determined by the law of supply and demand is one of the most long-standing and widely accepted ideas of economists. *In competitive markets, prices are determined by the law of supply and demand. Shifts in the demand and supply curves lead to changes in the equilibrium price. Similar principles apply to the labor and capital markets. The price for labor is the wage, and the price for capital is the interest rate.*

Price, Value, and Cost

Price, to an economist, is what is given in exchange for a good or service. Price, in this sense, is determined by the forces of supply and demand. Adam Smith, often thought of as the founder of modern economics, called our notion of price "value in exchange," and contrasted it to the notion of "value in use":

The things which have the greatest value in use have frequently little or no value in exchange; and, on the contrary, those which have the greatest value in exchange have frequently little or no value in use. Nothing is more useful than water, but it will purchase scarce any thing: scarce any thing can be had in exchange for it. A diamond, on the contrary, has scarce any value in use; but a very great quantity of other goods may frequently be had in exchange for it.[3]

---

[3] *The Wealth of Nations* (1776), Book One, Chapter IV.

Thinking Like an Economist

The Structure of Economic Models

Every economic model, including the model of how supply and demand determine the equilibrium price and quantity in a market, is constructed of three kinds of relationships: identities, behavioral relationships, and equilibrium relationships. Recognizing these component parts will help in understanding not only how economists think but also the source of their disagreements.

The market demand is equal to the sum of individual demands. This is an identity. An identity is a statement that is true simply because of the definition of the terms. In other words, market demand is *defined* to be the sum of the demands of all individuals. Similarly, it is an identity that market supply is equal to the sum of the supplies of all firms; the terms are defined in that way.

The demand curve represents a relationship between the price and the quantity demanded. Normally, as prices rise, the quantity of a good demanded decreases. This is a description of how individuals behave, and is called a behavioral relationship. The supply curve for each firm is also a behavioral relationship.

Economists may disagree over behavioral relationships. They may agree about the direction of the relationship but disagree about the strength of the connection. For any given product, does a change in price lead to a large change in the quantity supplied or a small one? But they may even disagree over the direction of the effect. As later chapters will discuss, in some special cases a higher price may actually lead to a *lower* quantity supplied.

Finally, an equilibrium relationship exists when there are no forces for change. In the supply and demand model, the equilibrium occurs when the quantity demanded is equal to the quantity supplied. An equilibrium relationship is not the same as an identity. It is possible for the economy to be out of equilibrium, at least for a time. Of course, being out of equilibrium implies that there are forces for change pushing toward equilibrium. But an identity must always hold true at all times, as a matter of definition.

Even when economists agree about what an equilibrium would look like, they often differ on whether the forces pushing the markets toward equilibrium are strong or weak, and thus on whether the economy is typically close to equilibrium or may stray rather far from it.

The law of supply and demand can help to explain the diamond-water paradox, and many similar examples where "value in use" is very different from "value in exchange." Figure 4.16 presents a demand and a supply curve for water. Individuals are willing to pay a high price for the water they need to live, as illustrated by point *A*, on the demand curve. But above some quantity, *B*, people will pay almost nothing more for additional water. In most of the inhabited parts of the world, water is readily available, so it gets supplied in plentiful quantities at low prices. Thus, the supply curve of water intersects the demand curve to the right of *B*, as in the figure—hence, the low equilibrium price. Of course, in the desert, the water supply may be very limited and the price, as a result, very high.

To an economist, the statements that the price of diamonds is high and the price of water is low are statements about supply and demand conditions. They say nothing about whether diamonds are "more important" or "better" than water. In Adam Smith's terms, they are not statements about value in use.

Price is related to the *marginal* value of an object, that is, the value of an additional unit of the object. Water has a low price not because the *total* value of water is low—it is obviously high, since we could not live without it—but because the marginal value, what we would be willing to pay to be able to drink one more glass of water a year, is low.

Just as economists take care to distinguish the words "price" and "value," they also distinguish the *price* of

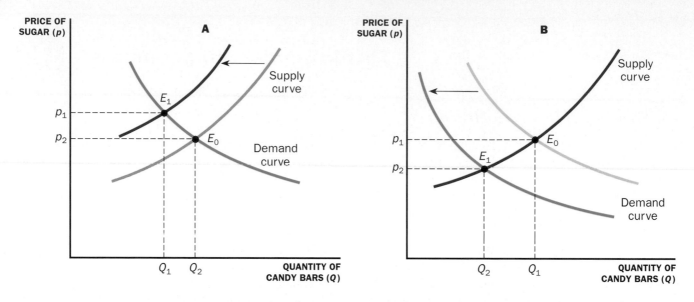

FIGURE 4.15   *Using Supply and Demand Curves to Predict Price Changes*

Initially the market for candy bars is in equilibrium at E_0. An increase in the cost of sugar shifts the supply curve to the left, as shown in panel A. At the new equilibrium, E_1, the price is higher and the quantity consumed is lower. A shift in taste away from candy results in a leftward shift in the demand curve as shown in panel B. At the new equilibrium, E_1, the price and the quantity consumed are lower.

Internet Connection

The Demand and Supply in the Oil Market

The U.S. Energy Information Administration (EIA) has a slide presentation at http://www.eia.doe.gov/emeu/25opec/anniversary.html that illustrates some of the major effects that the energy price increases during the 1970s had on the types of cars Americans bought and how they heated their homes.

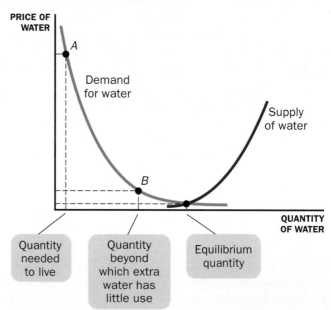

FIGURE 4.16   *Supply and Demand for Water*

Point *A* shows that people are willing to pay a relatively high price for the first few units of water. But to the right of *B*, people have plenty of water already and are not willing to pay much for an additional amount. The price of water will be determined at the point where the supply curve crosses the demand curve. In most cases, the resulting price is extremely low.

an object (what it sells for) from its *cost* (the expense of making the object). This is another crucial distinction in economics. The costs of producing a good affect the price at which firms are willing to supply that good. An increase in the costs of production will normally cause prices to rise. And in the competitive model, *in equilibrium*, the

Predicting the Effects of the Drought of 1988

For the midwestern United States, 1988 brought one of the worst droughts ever recorded. Corn production was 35 percent lower than had been expected before the drought; soybean production was down more than 20 percent, wheat was down more than 10 percent, and oats and barley were down more than 40 percent. As these events were developing, economists attempted to predict their consequences, using the basic laws of supply and demand that we have developed in this chapter.

The drought reduced the amount of any crop that would be supplied at any given price. The drought can be viewed as shifting the supply curve to the left. Predictably, with a given demand curve, the large shift of the supply curve resulted in much higher prices for these farm products: corn prices rose by 80 percent by the end of the summer, soybeans by almost 70 percent, and wheat by 50 percent.

Economists also used the supply and demand models to predict the effects on other products. Grain is a major input into cattle production. With cattle production less profitable, many farmers slaughtered their cattle sooner than they had originally planned. As a result, meat production rose slightly in 1988. The increased short-run supply resulted in a decrease in meat prices (adjusted for inflation). Grain is also a major input for the production of chicken. The supply curves for chickens and eggs shifted to the left, resulting in higher prices for these commodities. The higher prices of these agricultural goods resulted in a shift to the right of the demand curve for other foods which were substitutes. Thus, prices for foods, such as vegetables and fruits, whose supply was not affected by the midwestern drought, still increased—by 5 percent in July 1988 alone. ●

price of an object will normally equal its (marginal) cost of production (including the amount needed to pay a firm's owner to stay in business rather than seek some other form of employment). But there are important cases—as we will see in later chapters—where price does not equal cost.

In thinking about the relationship of price and cost, it is interesting to consider the case of a good in fixed supply, such as land. Normally, land is something that cannot be produced, so its cost of production can be considered infinite (though there are situations where land can be produced, as when Chicago filled in part of Lake Michigan to expand its lake shore). Yet there is still an equilibrium price of land—where the demand for land is equal to its (fixed) supply.

Review and Practice

Summary

1. An individual's demand curve gives the quantity demanded of a good at each possible price. It normally slopes down, which means that the person demands a greater quantity of the good at lower prices and a lesser quantity at higher prices.

2. The market demand curve gives the total quantity of a good demanded by all individuals in an economy at each price. As the price rises, demand falls, both because each person demands less of the good and because some people exit the market.

3. A firm's supply curve gives the amount of a good the firm is willing to supply at each price. It is normally upward sloping, which means that firms supply a greater quantity of the good at higher prices and a lesser quantity at lower prices.

4. The market supply curve gives the total quantity of a good that all firms in the economy are willing to produce at each price. As the price rises, supply rises, both because each firm supplies more of the good and because some additional firms enter the market.

5. The law of supply and demand says that in competitive markets, the equilibrium price is that price at which quantity demanded equals quantity supplied. It is represented on a graph by the intersection of the demand and supply curves.

6. A demand curve *only* shows the relationship between quantity demanded and price. Changes in tastes, in demographic factors, in income, in the prices of other goods, in information, in the availability of credit, or in

expectations are reflected in a shift of the entire demand curve.

7. A supply curve *only* shows the relationship between quantity supplied and price. Changes in factors such as technology, the prices of inputs, the natural environment, expectations, or the availability of credit are reflected in a shift of the entire supply curve.

8. It is important to distinguish movements along a demand curve from shifts in the demand curve, and movements along a supply curve from shifts in the supply curve.

Key Terms

price
demand
demand curve
market demand curve
substitutes
complements
demographic effects
supply
supply curve
market supply curve
equilibrium price
equilibrium quantity
equilibrium
market clearing price
excess supply
excess demand
law of supply and demand

Review Questions

1. Why does an individual's demand curve normally slope down? Why does a market demand curve normally slope down?

2. Why does a firm's supply curve normally slope up? Why does a market supply curve normally slope up?

3. What is the significance of the point where supply and demand curves intersect?

4. Explain why, if the price of a good is above the equilibrium price, the forces of supply and demand will tend to push the price toward equilibrium. Explain why, if the price of the good is below the equilibrium price, the market will tend to adjust toward equilibrium.

5. Name some factors that could shift the demand curve out to the right.

6. Name some factors that could shift the supply curve in to the left.

Problems

1. Imagine a company lunchroom that sells pizza by the slice. Using the following data, plot the points and graph the demand and supply curves. What is the equilibrium price and quantity? Find a price at which excess demand would exist and a price at which excess supply would exist, and plot them on your diagram.

Price per slice	Demand (number of slices)	Supply (number of slices)
$1	420	0
$2	210	100
$3	140	140
$4	105	160
$5	84	170

2. Suppose a severe drought hit the sugarcane crop. Predict how this would affect the equilibrium price and quantity in the market for sugar and the market for honey. Draw supply and demand diagrams to illustrate your answers.

3. Imagine that a new invention allows each mine worker to mine twice as much coal. Predict how this will affect the equilibrium price and quantity in the market for coal and the market for heating oil. Draw supply and demand diagrams to illustrate your answers.

4. Americans' tastes have shifted away from beef and toward chicken. Predict how this change affects the equilibrium price and quantity in the market for beef, the market for chicken, and the market for roadside hamburger stands. Draw supply and demand diagrams to illustrate your answer.

5. During the 1970s, the postwar baby boomers reached working age, and it became more acceptable for married women with children to work. Predict how this increase in the number of workers is likely to affect the equilibrium wage and quantity of employment. Draw supply and demand curves to illustrate your answer.

6. In 2001, Europeans became very concerned about what is called mad cow disease, and the dangers posed by eating contaminated meat. What would this concern do to the demand curve for beef? To the demand curves for chicken and fish? To the equilibrium price of beef, chicken, and fish?

Mad cow disease is spread by feeding cows food that contains parts from infected animals. Presumably the reason why cows are fed this food is that it is cheaper than relying exclusively on grain for their food. What is the consequence for the supply curve of beef of restricting feed to grain? What are the consequences for the price of beef (a) if the new restrictions fail to restore confidence in beef and (b) if the new restrictions succeed in restoring confidence so that the demand curve returns to its original position.

At about the same time in Europe, there was an outbreak of hoof and mouth disease, and to stop the spread of the disease, large numbers of cattle were killed. What does this do to the supply curve of beef? To the equilibrium price of beef?

7. Many advanced industrialized countries subsidize farmers. Assume that the effect of the subsidy is to shift the supply curve of agricultural products by farmers in the advanced industrialized countries to the right. Why might less developed countries be unhappy with such policies?

8. Farm output is extremely sensitive to the weather. In 1988, the midwestern region of the United States experienced one of the worst droughts ever recorded; corn production fell by 35 percent, wheat production by more than 10 percent, and oat and barley production by more than 40 percent. What do you suppose happened to the prices of these commodities?

These grains are an input into the production of cattle. The higher cost of grain led many ranchers to slaughter their cattle earlier. What do you think happened to the price of beef in the short run? In the intermediate run?

Why did the drought in the Midwest lead to increased prices for vegetables and fruits?

Chapter 5

Using Demand and Supply

Key Questions

1. What is meant by the concept of elasticity? Why does it play such an important role in predicting market outcomes?

2. What happens when market outcomes are interfered with, as when the government imposes price floors and ceilings? Why do such interferences give rise to shortages and surpluses?

The concepts of demand and supply are among the most useful in economics. The demand and supply framework explains why doctors are paid more than lawyers, or why the income of unskilled workers has increased less than that of skilled workers. It can also be used to predict what the demand for condominiums or disposable diapers will be fifteen years from now, or what will happen if the government increases the tax on cigarettes. Not only can we predict that prices will change, we can predict by how much they will change.

This chapter has two purposes. The first is to develop some of the concepts required to make these kinds of predictions, and to illustrate how the demand and supply framework can be used in a variety of contexts.

The second is to look at what happens when people interfere with the workings of competitive markets. Rents may seem too high for poor people to afford adequate housing. The price of corn may seem unfairly low, not adequate to compensate farmers for their work. Political pressure constantly develops for government to intervene on behalf of the group that has been disadvantaged by the market—whether it be poor people, farmers, or oil companies (which ask for government help when the price of oil falls). The second part of this chapter traces the consequences of political interventions into the workings of some markets.

Sensitivity to Price Changes: The Price Elasticity of Demand

If tomorrow supermarkets across the country were to cut the price of bread or milk by 5 percent, the quantity demanded of these items would not change much. If stores offered the same reduction on premium ice cream, however, demand would increase substantially. Why do price changes sometimes have small effects and at other times large ones? The answer lies in the shape of the demand and supply curves.

The demand for ice cream is more sensitive to price changes than is the demand for milk, and this is reflected in the shape of the demand curves, as illustrated in Figure 5.1. The demand curve for ice cream (panel A) is much flatter than the one for milk (panel B). When the demand curve is somewhat flat, a change in price, say from $2.00 a gallon to $2.10, has a large effect on the quantity consumed. In panel A, the demand for ice cream decreases from 100 million pints at a price of $2.00 a pint to 90 million pints at a price of $2.10 per pint.

By contrast, when the demand curve is steep, it means that a change in price has little effect on quantity. In panel B, the demand for milk decreases from 100 million gallons at $2.00 per gallon to 99 million gallons at $2.10 per gallon. But saying that the demand curve is steep or flat just pushes the question back a step: Why are some demand curves steeper than others?

The answer is that though substitutes exist for almost every good or service, substitution will be more difficult for some goods and services than for others. When substitution is difficult, an increase in the price of a good will not cause the quantity demanded to decrease by much, and a decrease in the price will not cause the quantity demanded to increase much. The typical consumer does not substitute milk for beer—or for anything else—even if milk becomes a good deal cheaper.

When substitution is easy, on the other hand, a fall in price may lead to a large increase in quantity demanded.

For instance, there are many good substitutes for ice cream, including sherbets and frozen yogurts. A price decrease for ice cream means that those close substitutes become relatively more expensive, and the demand for ice cream would thus increase significantly.

For many purposes, economists need to be precise about how steep or how flat the demand curve is. For precision they use the concept of the **price elasticity of demand** (for short, the price elasticity or the elasticity of demand). The price elasticity of demand is defined as the percentage change in the quantity demanded divided by the percentage change in price. In mathematical terms,

$$\text{elasticity of demand} = \frac{\text{percentage change in quantity demanded}}{\text{percentage change in price}}.$$

If the quantity demanded changes 8 percent in response to a 2 percent change in price, then the elasticity of demand is 4.

(Price elasticities of demand are really *negative* numbers; that is, when the price increases, quantities demanded are reduced. But the convention is to simply refer to the elasticity as a number with the understanding that it is negative.)

It is easiest to calculate the elasticity of demand when there is just a 1 percent change in price. Then the elasticity of demand is just the percent change in the quantity de-

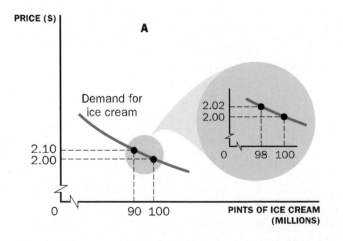

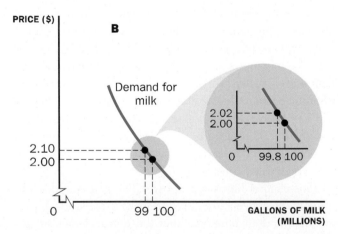

FIGURE 5.1   *Elastic Versus Inelastic Demand Curves*

Panel A shows a hypothetical demand curve for ice cream. Note that quantity demanded changes greatly with fairly small price changes, indicating that demand for ice cream is elastic. The telescoped portion of the demand curve shows that a 1 percent rise in price leads to a 2 percent fall in quantity demanded. Panel B shows a hypothetical demand curve for milk. Note that quantity demanded changes very little, regardless of changes in price, meaning that demand for milk is inelastic. The telescoped portion of the demand curve shows that a 1 percent rise in price leads to a .2 percent fall in quantity demanded.

manded. In the telescoped portion of Figure 5.1A, we see that increasing the price of ice cream from $2.00 a pint to $2.02—a 1 percent increase in price—reduces the demand from 100 million pints to 98 million, a 2 percent decline. So the price elasticity of demand for ice cream is 2.

By contrast, assume that the price of milk increases from $2.00 a gallon to $2.02 (again a 1 percent increase in price), as shown in the telescoped portion of Figure 5.1B. This reduces demand from 100 million gallons per year to 99.8 million. Demand has gone down by .2 percent, so the price elasticity of demand is therefore .2. Larger values for price elasticity indicate that demand is more sensitive to changes in price. Smaller values indicate that demand is less sensitive to price changes.

Price Elasticity and Revenues

The revenue received by a firm in selling a good is price times quantity. We write this in a simple equation. Letting R denote revenues, p price, and Q quantity:

$$R = pQ.$$

This means that when price goes up by 1 percent, whether revenues go up or down depends on the magnitude of the decrease in quantity. If quantity decreases by more than 1 percent, then total revenues decrease; by less than 1 percent, they increase.

We can express this result in terms of the concept of price elasticity. When the elasticity of demand is greater than unity, the change in quantity more than offsets the change in prices; we say that the demand for that good is **relatively elastic,** or *sensitive* to price changes, and revenues decrease as price increases and increase as price decreases.

In the case where the price elasticity is 1, the decrease in the quantity demanded just offsets the increase in the price, so price increases have no effect on revenues. This is called **unitary elasticity.** If the price elasticity is less than unity, then when the price of a good increases by 1 percent, the quantity demanded is reduced by less than 1 percent. Since there is not much reduction in demand, elasticities in this range, between 0 and 1, mean that price increases will increase revenues. And price decreases will decrease revenues. We say the demand for that good is **relatively inelastic,** or *insensitive* to price changes.

Business firms must pay attention to the price elasticity of demand for their products. Suppose a cement producer, the only one in town, is considering a 1 percent increase in price. The firm hires an economist to estimate the elasticity of demand so that the firm will know what will happen to sales when it raises its price. The economist tells the firm that its demand elasticity is 2. This means that if the price of cement rises by 1 percent, the quantity sold will decline by 2 percent.

The firm's executives will not be pleased by the findings. To see why, assume that initially the price of cement was $1,000 per ton, and 100,000 tons were sold. To calculate revenues, you multiply the price times the quantity sold. So initially revenues were $1,000 × 100,000 = $100 million. With a 1 percent increase, the price will be $1,010. If the elasticity of demand is 2, then a 1 percent price increase results in a 2 percent decrease in the quantity sold. With a 2 percent quantity decrease, sales are now 98,000 tons. Revenues are down to $98.98 million ($1,010 × 98,000), a fall of just slightly over 1 percent. Because of the high elasticity, this cement firm's price *increase* leads to a *decrease* in revenues.

The price elasticity of demand works the same way for price decreases. Suppose the cement producer decided to decrease the price of cement 1 percent, to $990. With an elasticity of demand of 2, sales would than increase 2 percent, to 102,000 tons. Thus, revenues would *increase* to $100,980,000 ($990 × 102,000), that is, by a bit less than 1 percent.

There are two extreme cases that deserve attention. One is that of a flat demand curve, a curve that is perfectly horizontal. We say that such a demand curve is perfectly elastic, or has **infinite elasticity,** since even a slight increase in the price results in demand dropping to zero. The other case is that of a steep demand curve, a curve that is perfectly vertical. We say that such a demand curve is perfectly inelastic, or has **zero elasticity,** since no matter what the change in price, demand remains the same. The basic modes of price elasticity, ranging from zero to infinite elasticity, are summarized in Table 5.1.

Price Elasticities in the U.S. Economy
The elasticity of demand for most foods is low (an increase in price will not affect demand much). The elasticity of demand for most luxuries, such as perfume, ski trips, and Mercedes cars, is high (an increase in price will lead to much less demand). Table 5.2 gives the elasticities of demand for some important goods. For example, the price elasticity of food and of tobacco is about .6, in contrast to the price elasticity for motor vehicles, which is 1.14. The

TABLE 5.1

Price Elasticity of Demand			
Elasticity	**Description**	**Effect on Quantity Demanded of 1% Increase in Price**	**Effect on Revenues of 1% Increase in Price**
Zero	Perfectly inelastic (vertical demand curve)	Zero	Increased by 1%
Between 0 and 1	Inelastic	Reduced by less than 1%	Increased by less than 1%
1	Unitary elasticity	Reduced by 1%	Unchanged
Greater than 1	Elastic	Reduced by more 1%	Reduced; the greater the elasticity, the more revenue is reduced
Infinite	Perfectly elastic (horizontal demand curve)	Reduced to zero	Reduced to zero

table also shows the price elasticities for broad groups of goods. It may be easy to substitute purchased meals for home-cooked food, but it is difficult to do without food. Thus, the price elasticity of purchased meals is 2.27, while the price elasticity of all food is much lower, at .58. More generally, goods for which it is easy to find substitutes will have high price elasticities; goods for which substitutes cannot easily be found will have low price elasticities.

Elasticity and Slope The elasticity of a curve is not the same as its slope. The best way to see the distinction is to look at the *linear* demand curve. The linear demand curve is a straight line, depicted in Figure 5.2. With a linear demand curve, the quantity demanded is related to the price by the equation

$$Q = a - bp.$$

If $a = 120$, and $b = 2$, at a price of 10, $Q = 100$; at a price of 11, $Q = 98$; at a price of 12, $Q = 96$, and so forth.

The demand curve also gives the price at which a particular quantity of the good will be demanded. Thus, we can rewrite the equation to read

$$p = \frac{a}{b} - \frac{Q}{b},$$

so that (with $a = 120$, $b = 2$ as before), at $Q = 100$, $p = 10$; at $Q = 99$, $p = 10.5$; at $Q = 98$, $p = 11$.

Slope gives the change along the vertical axis per unit change along the horizontal axis. Recall that when we draw the demand curve, we put price on the vertical axis and output on the horizontal axis.

$$\text{slope} = \frac{\text{change in price}}{\text{change in quantity}} = \frac{\Delta p}{\Delta Q},$$

where the symbol Δ—the Greek letter delta—signifies a change. Thus, ΔQ means the change in quantity and Δp means the change in price. Equivalently, slope is the change in price for a unit change in quantity. In our example, as we change quantity by 1, price changes by 1/2.

TABLE 5.2

Some Price Elasticities in the U.S. Economy

Industry	Elasticity
Elastic demands	
Purchased meals	2.27
Metals	1.52
Furniture, timber	1.25
Motor vehicles	1.14
Transportation	1.03
Inelastic demands	
Gas, electricity, water	.92
Oil	.91
Chemicals	.89
Beverages	.78
Tobacco	.61
Food	.58
Housing services	.55
Clothing	.49
Books, magazines, newspapers	.34
Meat	.2

SOURCES: Ahson Mansur and John Whalley, "Numerical Specification of Applied General Equilibrium Models: Estimation, Calibration, and Data," in Scarf and Shoven, eds., *Applied General Equilibrium Analysis* (New York: Cambridge University Press, 1984), p. 109; Hendrik S. Houthakker and Lester D. Taylor, *Consumer Demand in the United States: Analysis and Projections* (Cambridge: Harvard University Press, 1970).

More generally, the slope of the linear demand equation above is $1/b$.[1]

The elasticity, as we know, is given by

$$\text{elasticity} = \frac{\text{percentage change in quantity}}{\text{percentage change in price}}.$$

The percentage change in quantity is

$$\text{percentage change in quantity} = \frac{\text{change in quantity}}{\text{quantity}} = \frac{\Delta Q}{Q}.$$

Similarly,

$$\text{percentage change in price} = \frac{\text{change in price}}{\text{price}} = \frac{\Delta p}{p}.$$

We can now rewrite the expression for elasticity as

$$\text{elasticity} = \frac{\Delta Q/Q}{\Delta p/p} = \frac{\Delta Q}{\Delta p} \times \frac{p}{Q}$$

$$= b \times \frac{p}{Q}$$

$$= \frac{1}{\text{slope}} \times \frac{p}{Q}.$$

Everywhere along a linear demand curve, the slope is the same; but the elasticity is very high at low levels of output and very low at high levels of output.

The formula for elasticity has one other important implication, illustrated in Figure 5.3. Of two demand curves going through the same point, the flatter demand curve has the higher elasticity at the point of intersection. At the point where they intersect, p and Q (and therefore p/Q) are the same. Only the slopes differ. The one with the smaller slope has the greater elasticity.

Small Versus Large Price Changes

Often, economists are interested in what would happen if there is a large price change. For instance, if a 50 percent tax is imposed on cigarettes, what will happen to demand?

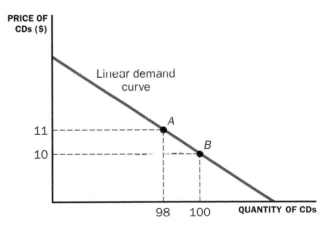

FIGURE 5.2   *Linear Demand Curve*

The linear demand curve is a straight line; it is represented algebraicly by the equation $Q = a - bp$. The slope of the demand curve is a constant. However, the elasticity varies with output. At low outputs (high prices) it is very high. At high outputs (low prices) it is very low.

---

[1] To see this, observe that at $Q + 1$, the price is

$$\frac{a}{b} - \frac{Q+1}{b}.$$

The change in price is

$$\frac{a}{b} - \frac{Q}{b} - \left(\frac{a}{b} - \frac{Q+1}{b}\right) = \frac{a}{b} - \frac{Q}{b} - \frac{a}{b} - \frac{Q+1}{b} = \frac{1}{b}.$$

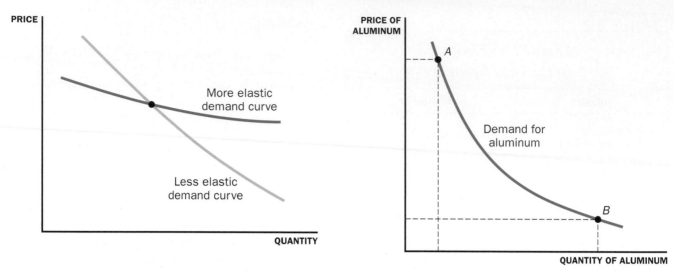

FIGURE 5.3   *Comparing Elasticities*

If two demand curves intersect, at the point of intersection the flatter demand curve has the greater price elasticity.

FIGURE 5.4   *Changing Elasticity Along a Demand Curve*

Near point *A*, where the price is high, the demand curve is quite steep and inelastic. In the area of the demand curve near *B*, the demand curve is very flat and elastic.

When price changes are small or moderate, we can *extrapolate.* That is, often we have information about the effect of a small price change. We then extrapolate, assuming that a slightly larger price change will have proportionately larger effects. For example, if a 1 percent change in price results in a 2 percent change in quantity, then a 3 percent change in price will probably result in an approximately 6 percent change in quantity.

With large price changes, however, such extrapolation becomes riskier. The reason is that *price elasticity is typically different at different points along the demand curve.*

The Determinants of the Elasticity of Demand

In our earlier discussion, we noted one of the important determinants of the elasticity of demand: the availability of substitutes. There are two important determinants of the degree of substitutability: the relative price of the good consumed and the length of time it takes to make an adjustment.

When the price of a commodity is low, and the consumption is high, a variety of substitutes exist. Figure 5.4 illustrates the case for aluminum. When the price of aluminum is low, it is used as a food wrap (aluminum foil), as

containers for canned goods, and in airplane frames because it is lightweight. As the price increases, customers seek out substitutes. At first, substitutes are easy to find, and the demand for the product is greatly reduced. For example, plastic wrap can be used instead of aluminum foil. As the price rises still further, tin is used instead of aluminum for cans. At very high prices, say near point *A,* aluminum is used only where its lightweight properties are essential, such as in airplane frames. At this point, it may take a *huge* price increase before some other material becomes an economical substitute.

A second important determinant of the elasticity of demand is time. Because it is always easier to find substitutes and to make other adjustments when you have a longer time to make them, the elasticity of demand is normally larger in the *long run*—in the period in which all adjustments can be made—than it is the *short run,* when at least some adjustments cannot be made. Figure 5.5 illustrates the difference in shape between short-run and long-run demand curves for gasoline.

The sharp increase in oil prices in the 1970s provides an outstanding example. The short-run price elasticity of gasoline was .2 (a 1 percent increase in price led to only a .2 percent decrease in quantity demanded), while the long-

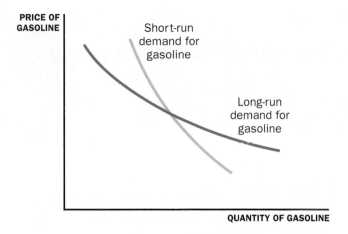

PRICE OF GASOLINE

Short-run demand for gasoline

Long-run demand for gasoline

QUANTITY OF GASOLINE

FIGURE 5.5 *Elasticity of Demand Over Time*

Demand curves tend to be inelastic in the short tun, when there is little time to adapt to price changes, but more elastic in the long run.

run elasticity was .7 or more; the short-run elasticity of fuel oil was .2, and the long-run elasticity was 1.2. In the short run, consumers were stuck with their old gas-guzzling cars, their drafty houses, and their old fuel-wasting habits. In the long run, however, consumer bought smaller cars, became used to houses with slightly lower temperatures, installed better insulation in their homes, and turned to alternative energy sources. The long-run demand curve was therefore much more elastic (flat) than the short-run curve. Indeed, the long-run elasticity turned out to be much larger than anticipated.

How long is the long run? There is no simple answer. It will vary from product to product. In some cases, adjustments can occur rapidly; in other cases, they are very gradual. As old gas guzzlers wore out, they were replaced with fuel-efficient compact cars. As furnaces wore out, they were replaced with more efficient ones. New homes are now constructed with more insulation, so that gradually, over time, the fraction of houses that are well insulated is increasing.

Some of these changes are reversible: in the 1990s, in response to low gas prices, fuel-efficient cars were replaced by gas-guzzling sport utility vehicles (SUVs). But when higher prices induce innovations—for example, manufacturers of cars discover ways of increasing mileage per gallon—then the benefits of those innovations remain even when prices subsequently fall.

The Price Elasticity of Supply

Supply curves normally slope upward. As with demand curves, they are steep in some cases and flat in others. The degree of steepness reflects sensitivity to price changes. A steep supply curve, like the one for oil in Figure 5.6A, means that a large change in price generates only a small change in the quantity firms want to supply. A flatter curve, like the one for chicken in Figure 5.6B, means that a small change in price generates a large change in supply. Economists have

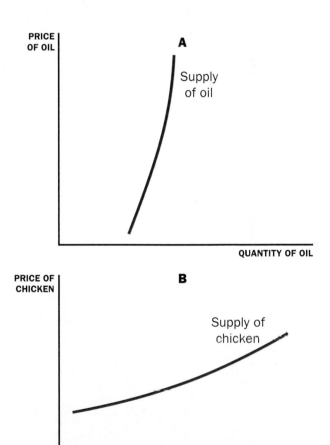

PRICE OF OIL

A

Supply of oil

QUANTITY OF OIL

PRICE OF CHICKEN

B

Supply of chicken

QUANTITY OF CHICKEN

FIGURE 5.6 *Differing Elasticities of Supply*

Panel A shows a supply curve for oil. It is inelastic: quantity supplied increases only a small amount with a rise in price. Panel B shows a supply curve for chicken. It is elastic: quantity supplied increases substantially with a rise in price.

International Perspective

Comparing Reactions to the Oil Price Shock of 2000

When gasoline prices soared in the fall of 2000, in response to the increase in oil prices, people in Great Britain and Europe took to the streets. Truckers blocked roads and entrances to refineries. There was a massive political outcry. One might have thought that given that Americans depend more on oil than Europeans do (Americans use far more gasoline per capita) and given that the *percentage* increase in prices in Europe was far smaller (since taxes constitute a far larger fraction of the total price), the outcry would be louder in the United States. But this brings home an important point: The consequences of the massive price increase depend not only on the level of consumption but also on consumers' ability to absorb the price increase. Europeans already had cut their use of oil down to low levels, because prices of gasoline are so high. Further cuts in consumption, accordingly, may be more difficult. Hence, the cost to consumers of a further increase in price may be far greater than when individuals can easily find ways to conserving on the use of oil.

For instance, Americans can easily conserve on gasoline by switching from high-consuming sports utility vehicles, many of which get as few as 15 miles to the gallon, to efficient diesel cars, which can get 50 miles to the gallon or more. Americans can conserve on fuel oil by keeping the temperature in their homes at 68 degrees rather than 72 degrees. But what are Europeans to do, when they already drive small, fuel-efficient cars and already keep their homes at colder temperatures?

These ideas can be related to demand curves. The elasticity of demand is the percentage reduction in the demand resulting from a 1 percent increase in the price. When the price is very low, the demand curve is very elastic; that is, the elasticity of demand is high because there are many ways of conserving on oil. When the price is very high, the demand curve is very inelastic; that is, the elasticity of demand is very low because all of the obvious ways of conserving on oil have already been employed.

Truckers in Newcastle, England protested high prices for fuel in September, 2000.

TABLE 5.3

Price Elasticity of Supply		
Elasticity	**Description**	**Effect on Quantity Supplied of 1% Increase in Price**
Zero	Perfectly inelastic (vertical supply curve)	Zero
Between 0 and 1	Inelastic	Increased by less than 1%
1	Unitary elasticity	Increased by 1%
Greater than 1	Elastic	Increased by more than 1%
Infinite	Perfectly elastic (horizontal supply curve)	Infinite increase

developed a precise way of representing the sensitivity of supply to prices in a way that parallels the one already introduced for demand. The **price elasticity of supply** is defined as the percentage change in quantity supplied divided by the percentage change in price (or the percentage change in quantity supplied corresponding to a price change of 1 percent).

$$\text{Elasticity of supply} = \frac{\text{percentage change in quantity supplied}}{\text{percentage change in price}}.$$

The elasticity of supply of oil is low—an increase in the price of oil will not have a significant effect on the total supply. The elasticity of supply of chicken is high, as President Nixon found out when he imposed price controls in August 1971. When the price of chicken was forced lower than the market equilibrium price, less than 10 percent lower, farmers found it was simply unprofitable to produce chickens and sell them at that price; there was a large decrease in the quantity supplied, and the result was huge shortages.

As is the case with demand, if a 1 percent increase in price results in more than a 1 percent increase in supply, we say the supply curve is elastic. If a 1 percent increase in price results in less than a 1 percent increase in supply, the supply curve is inelastic. In the extreme case of a vertical supply curve—where the amount supplied does not depend at all on price—the curve is said to be perfectly inelastic, or to have *zero* elasticity; and in the extreme case of a horizontal supply curve, the curve is said to be perfectly elastic, or to have *infinite* elasticity. Table 5.3 summarizes each of these cases.

Just as the demand elasticity differs at different points of the demand curve, so too does supply elasticity differ at different points of the supply curve. Figure 5.7 shows a typical supply curve in manufacturing. An example might be ball bearings. At very low prices, ball bearing plants are just covering their operating costs. Some plants shut down. In this situation, a small increase in price elicits a large increase in supply. The supply curve is relatively flat (elastic). But eventually, all machines in the plant will be used, and all three shifts of workers will be working. In this situation, it may be hard to increase supply further, so that the supply curve becomes close to vertical (inelastic). That is, however much the price increases, the supply will not change very much.

Short Run Versus Long Run Economists distinguish between the responsiveness of supply to price in the short run and in the long run, just as they do with demand. The long-run supply elasticity is greater than the short-run. We define the short-run supply curve as the supply response *given the current stock of machines* and *buildings.* The long-run supply curve assumes that firms can adjust the stock of machines and buildings.

Farm crops are a typical example of a good whose supply in the short run is not very sensitive to changes in price; that is, the supply curve is steep (inelastic). After farmers have done their spring planting, they are committed to a certain level of production. If the price of their crop goes up, they cannot go back and plant more. If the price falls, they are stuck with the

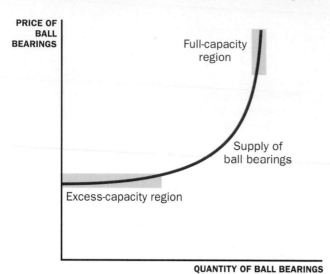

FIGURE 5.7   *Changing Elasticity Along a Supply Curve*

When output is low and many machines are idle, a small change in price can lead to a large increase in quantity produced, so the supply curve is flat and elastic. When output is high and all machines are working close to their limit, it takes a very large price change to induce even a small change in output; the supply curve is steep and inelastic.

crop they have. In this case, the supply curve is relatively close to vertical, as illustrated by the steeper curve in Figure 5.8.

The long-run supply curve for many crops, in contrast, is very flat (elastic). A relatively small change in price can lead to a large change in the quantity supplied. A small increase in the price of soybeans relative to the price of corn may induce many farmers to shift their planting from corn and other crops to soybeans, generating a large increase in the quantity of soybeans. This is illustrated in Figure 5.8 by the flatter curve.

Earlier, we noted the response of consumers to the marked increase in the price of oil in the 1970s. The long-run demand elasticity was much higher than the short-run. So too for supply. The higher prices drove firms, both in the United States and abroad in places like Canada, Mexico, and the North Sea off the coast of Great Britain, to explore for more oil. Though the alternative supplies could not be increased much in the short run (the short-run supply curve was inelastic, or steep), in the long run new supplies were found. Thus, the long-run supply elasticity was much higher (the supply curve was flatter) than the short-run supply elasticity.

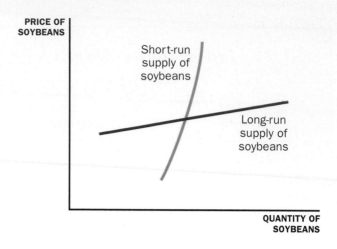

FIGURE 5.8   *Elasticity of Supply Over Time*

Supply curves may be inelastic in the short run and very elastic in the long run, as in the case of agricultural crops like soybeans.

WRAP-UP

Elasticity

Price elasticity of demand: the percentage change in the quantity of a good demanded as a result of a 1 percent increase (change) in the price charged. When elasticity is low, price changes have little effect on consumption. When elasticity is high, price changes have a large effect on consumption.

Price elasticity of supply: the percentage change in the quantity of a good supplied as a result of a 1 percent increase (change) in the price charged. When elasticity is low, price changes have little effect on supply. When elasticity is high, price changes have a large effect on supply.

Using Demand and Supply Elasticities

When the demand curve for a good such as wine shifts to the right—when, for instance, wine becomes more popular so that at each price the demand is greater—there is an increase in both the equilibrium price of wine and the quantity demanded, or consumed. Similarly, when the supply curve for a good such as corn shifts to the left—because, for instance, of a drought that hurt the year's crop so that at each price farmers supply less—there is an increase in the equilibrium price of corn and a decrease in quantity. Knowing that the shifts in the demand or supply curve will lead to an adjust-ment in both price *and* quantity is helpful, but it is even more useful to know whether most of the impact of a change will be on price or on quantity. For this, we have to consider the price elasticity of both the demand and supply curves.

Figure 5.9 illustrates the typical range of outcomes. If the supply curve is highly elastic (approaching the horizontal, as

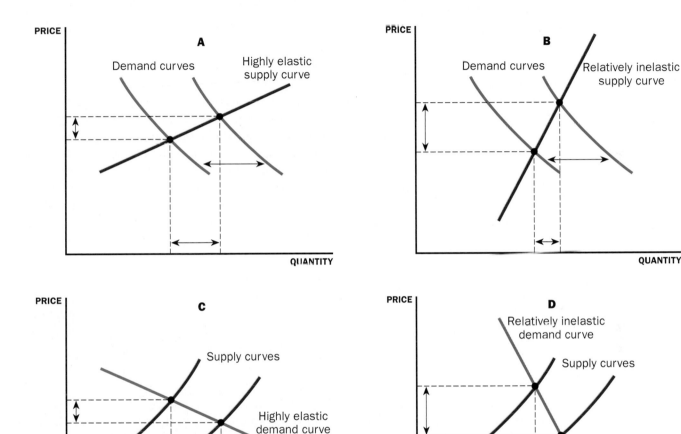

FIGURE 5.9 *Elasticity of Demand and Supply Curves: The Normal Cases*

Normally, shifts in the demand curve will be reflected in changes in both price and quantity, as seen in panels A and B. When the supply curve is highly elastic, shifts in the demand curve will result mainly in changes in quantities; if it is relatively inelastic, shifts in the demand curve will result mainly in price changes. Likewise, shifts in the supply curve will be reflected in changes in both price and quantity, as seen in panels C and D. If the demand curve is highly elastic, shifts in the supply curve will result mainly in changes in quantities; if it is relatively inelastic, shifts in the supply curve will result mainly in price changes.

in panel A), shifts in the demand curve will be reflected more in changes in quantity than in price. If the supply curve is *relatively* inelastic (approaching the vertical, as in panel B), shifts in the demand curve will be reflected more in changes in price than in quantity. If the demand curve is highly elastic (approaching the horizontal as in panel C), shifts in the supply curve will be reflected more in changes in quantity than in price. Finally, if the demand curve is *relatively* inelastic (approaching the vertical as in panel D), shifts in the supply curve will be reflected more in changes in price than in quantity.

The extreme cases can be easily seen by extending the graphs in Figure 5.9. If one tilts the supply curve in panel A to be completely flat (perfectly elastic), a shift in the demand curve will have no effect on price. If one tilts the supply curve in panel B to be vertical (perfectly inelastic), a shift in the demand curve will have no effect on quantity.

Long-Run Versus Short-Run Adjustments

Because demand and supply curves are likely to be less elastic (more vertical) in the short run than in the long run, shifts in the demand and supply curves are more likely to be reflected in price changes in the short run but in quantity changes in the long run. In fact, price increases in the short run provide the signals to firms to increase their production. Therefore, short-run price increases can be thought of as responsible for the output increases that occur in the long run.

Tax Policy and the Law of Supply and Demand

For many questions of public policy, understanding the law of supply and demand is vital. One of the important ways economists use this law is in projecting the effect of taxes. Assume that the tax on a pack of cigarettes is increased by 10 cents, that the tax is imposed on cigarette manufacturers, and that all the companies try to pass on the cost increase to consumers, by raising the price of a pack by 10 cents. At the higher price, fewer cigarettes will be consumed, with the decrease in demand depending on the price elasticity of demand. With lower demands, firms must reduce their price if demand is to equal supply; by

Thinking Like an Economist

Incentives and the Window Tax

The city of Bath in England predates the Roman occupation of the British Isles. It is located at a site where naturally heated springs occur, which is why the Romans built baths there. During the late eighteenth and early nineteenth centuries, the city became a popular watering hole for the well-to-do.

One of the striking features of the city is the beautiful brick used to build many of the buildings. But what also catches one's attention is the number of houses with windows that appear to have been bricked up. The explanation for the bricked-in windows provides an illustration of how taxation affects incentives and people's behavior.

In the eighteenth century, the city of Bath imposed taxes on houses, windows, and male servants, a set of taxes called the assessed taxes. People with more windows (and more male servants) presumably had larger houses and were wealthier. So the idea was that by basing the tax on the number of windows, the wealthy would pay more and the poor would pay less.

The effect of the tax was to raise the cost of having a window. Anyone in the process of building a new house would need to factor in the higher cost of a window and could design their house with fewer windows. It might seem that those people who already had lots of windows would be unable to avoid the tax. But this neglects how individuals are able to find ways of reducing their consumption of goods whose price has risen. People who already had houses with lots of windows could reduce their taxes by bricking up some of their windows. And this is what happened. The reduced demand for windows caused by the tax explains the blank walls that now fill window frames of many homes in Bath.

how much depends on the price elasticity of supply. The new equilibrium is depicted in Figure 5.10A.

For firms to produce the same amount as before, they must receive 10 cents more per pack (which they pass on to the government). Thus, the supply curve is shifted up by 10 cents. Since the demand for cigarettes is relatively inelastic, this shift will result in a large increase in price and a relatively small decrease in quantity demanded.

When a tax on producers results in consumers paying a higher price, economists say the tax is "passed on" or "shifted" to consumers. The fact that the consumer bears the tax (even though it is collected from the producers) does not mean that the producers are "powerful" or have conspired together. It simply reflects the system of supply and demand. Note, however, that the price did not rise the full 10 cents. Producers receive slightly lower after-tax prices and therefore bear a small fraction of the tax burden.

A tax imposed on a good for which the demand is very elastic leads to a different result. Assume, for instance, that the government decides to tax cheddar cheese (but not other cheeses). Since many cheeses are almost like cheddar, the demand curve for cheddar cheese is very elastic. In this case, as Figure 5.10B makes clear, most of the tax is ab-sorbed by the producer, who receives (net of tax) a lower price. Production of cheddar cheese is reduced drastically as a consequence.

Shortages and Surpluses

The law of supply and demand works so well in a developed modern economy, most of the time, that everyone can take it for granted. If you are willing to pay the "market price"—the prevailing price of the good, determined by the intersection of demand and supply—you can obtain almost any good or service. Similarly, if a seller of a good or service is willing to charge no more than the market price, he can always sell what he wants to.

When the price is set so that demand equals supply—so that any individual can get as much as she wants at that price, and any supplier can sell the amount he wants at that price—economists say that the market clears. But when the market does not clear, there are shortages or surpluses. To an economist, a **shortage** means that people would like to buy something, but they simply cannot find it for sale at the

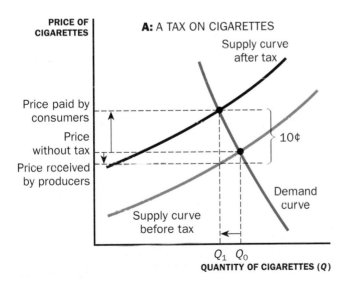

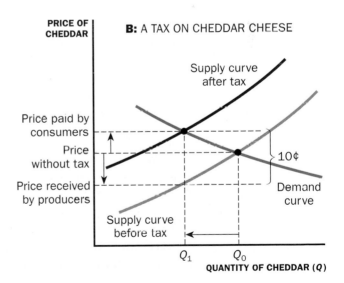

FIGURE 5.10   *Passing Along a Tax to Consumers*

A tax on the output of an industry shifts the supply curve up by the amount of the tax. Panel A shows that if the demand curve is relatively inelastic, as it is for cigarettes, then most of the tax will be passed on to consumers in higher prices. Panel B shows that if the demand curve is relatively elastic, as it is for cheddar cheese, then most of the tax cannot be passed along to consumers in higher prices, and must instead be absorbed by producers.

going price. A **surplus** means that sellers would like to sell their product, but they cannot sell as much of it as they would like at the going price. These cases where the market does not seem to be working are often the most forceful reminders of the importance of the law of supply and demand. The problem is that the "going price" is not the market equilibrium price.

Shortages and surpluses can be seen in the standard supply and demand diagram shown in Figure 5.11. In both panels A and B, the market equilibrium price is p^*. In panel A, the going price, p_1, is below p^*. At this price, demand exceeds supply; you can see this by reading down to the horizontal axis. Demand is Q_d; supply is Q_s. The gap between the two points is the "shortage." With the shortage, consumers scramble to get the limited supply available at the going price.

In panel B, the going price, p_1, is above p^*. At this price, demand is less than supply. Again we denote the demand by Q_d and the supply by Q_s. There is a surplus in the market of $Q_s - Q_d$. Now sellers are scrambling to find buyers.

At various times and for various goods, markets have not cleared. There have been shortages of apartments in New York; farm surpluses have plagued both Western Europe and the United States; in 1973, there was a shortage of gasoline, with cars lined up in long lines outside of gasoline stations. Unemployment is a type of surplus, when people who want to work find that they cannot sell their labor services at the going wage.

In some markets, like the stock market, the adjustment of prices to shifts in the demand and supply curves tends to be very rapid. In other cases, such as in the housing market, the adjustments tend to be sluggish. When price adjustments are sluggish, shortages or surpluses may appear as prices adjust. Houses tend not to sell quickly, for instance, during periods of decreased demand, which translate only slowly into lower housing prices.

When the market is not adjusting quickly toward equilibrium, economists say that prices are sticky. Even in these cases, the analysis of market equilibrium is useful. It indicates the direction of the changes—if the equilibrium price exceeds the current price, prices will tend to rise. Moreover, the rate at which prices fall or rise is often related to the gap, at the going price, between the quantity demanded and the quantity supplied.

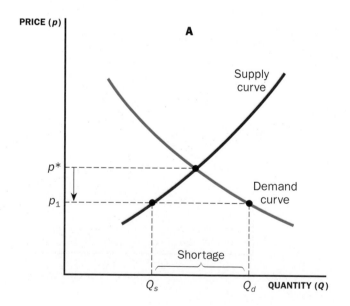

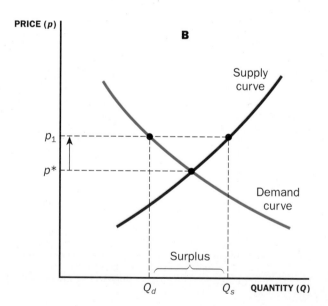

FIGURE 5.11   *Shortages and Surpluses*

In panel A, the actual price p_1 is below the market-clearing price p^*. At a price of p_1, quantity demanded exceeds quantity supplied, and a shortage exists. In panel B, the actual price p_1 is above the equilibrium price of p^*. In this case, quantity supplied exceeds quantity demanded, and there is a surplus, or glut, in the market.

Interfering with the Law of Supply and Demand

The law of supply and demand, which governs how prices are set, can produce results that some individuals or groups do not like. For example, a reduced supply of oil may lead to a higher equilibrium price for oil. The higher price is not a malfunction of the law of supply and demand, but this is little comfort to those who use gasoline to power their cars and oil to heat their homes. Low demand for unskilled labor may lead to very low wages for unskilled workers. An increase in the demand for apartments in New York City leads, in the short run (with an inelastic supply), to an increase in rents—to the delight of landlords, but the dismay of renters.

In each of these cases, pressure from those who did not like the outcome of market processes has led government to act. The price of oil and natural gas was, at one time, regulated; minimum wage laws set a minimum limit on what employers can pay, even if the workers are willing to work for less; and rent control laws limit what landlords can charge. The concerns behind these interferences with the market are understandable, but the agitation for government action is based on two errors.

First, someone (or some group) was assigned blame for the change: the oil price rises were blamed on the oil companies, low wages on the employer, and rent increases on the landlord. As already explained, economists emphasize the role of anonymous market forces in determining these prices. After all, if landlords or oil companies are basically the same people today as they were last week, there must be some reason why they started charging different prices this week. Sometimes the price increase is the result of producers colluding to raise prices. This was the case in 1973, when the oil-exporting countries got together to raise the price of oil. The more common situation, however, is illustrated by the increase in the price of oil in August 1990, after Iraq's invasion of Kuwait. There was no collusion this time. The higher price simply reflected the anticipated reduction in the supply of oil. People rushed to buy, increasing short-term demand and pushing up the equilibrium price.

The second error was to forget that as powerful as governments may be, they can no more repeal the law of supply and demand than they can repeal the law of gravity. When they interfere with its working, the forces of supply and demand will not be balanced. There will be either excess supply or excess demand. Shortages and surpluses create problems of their own, often worse than the original problem the government was supposed to resolve.

Two straightforward examples of government overruling the law of supply and demand are **price ceilings,** which impose a maximum price that can be charged for a product, and **price floors,** which impose a minimum price. Rent control laws are price ceilings, and minimum wage laws and agricultural price supports are price floors. A closer look at each will help highlight the perils of interfering with the law of supply and demand.

Price Ceilings

Price ceilings—setting a maximum charge—are always tempting to governments because they seem an easy way to assure that everyone will be able to afford a particular product. Thus, in the last couple of decades in the United States, price ceilings have been set for a wide range of goods, from chickens to oil to interest rates. In each case the result has been to create shortages at the controlled price. People want to buy more of a good than producers want to sell, because producers have no incentive to produce more of the good. Those who can buy at the cheaper price benefit; producers and those unable to buy suffer.

The effect of rent control laws—setting the maximum rent that a landlord can charge for a one-bedroom apartment, for example—is illustrated by Figure 5.12. In panel A, R^* is the market equilibrium rental rate, at which the demand for housing equals the supply. However, the local government is concerned that at R^*, many poor people cannot afford housing in the city, so it imposes a law that says that rents may be no higher than R_1. At R_1, there is an excess demand for apartments. While the motives behind the government action may well have been praiseworthy, the government has created an artificial scarcity.

The problems caused by rent control are likely to be worse in the long run than in the short run, because long-run supply curves are more elastic than short-run supply curves. In the short run, the quantity of apartments does not change much. But in the long run, the quantity of apartments can decline for several reasons, as landlords try to minimize the losses from rent control. Apartments may be abandoned as they deteriorate; they can be converted to condominiums and sold instead of rented; and apartment owners may not wish to construct new ones if they cannot charge enough in rent to cover their costs.

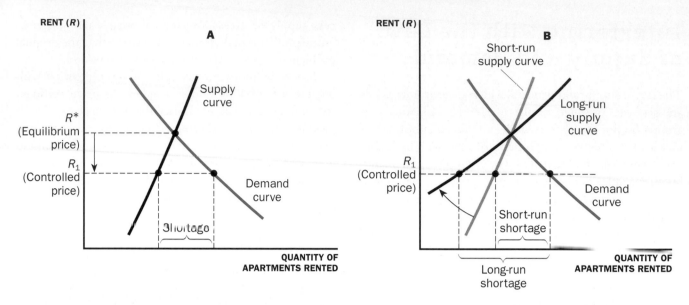

FIGURE 5.12   *A Price Ceiling: Rent Control*

Rent control laws limit the rents apartment owners may charge. If rents are held down to R_1, below the market-clearing level R^*, as in panel A, there will be excess demand for apartments. Panel B shows the long-run response. The supply of rental housing is more elastic in the long run, since landlords can refuse to build new apartment buildings, or they can sell existing apartments as condominiums. The price ceiling eventually leads to the quantity supplied being even farther below the quantity demanded.

Figure 5.12B illustrates how the housing shortages under rent control will increase over time. Rent control results in all *existing* renters being better off, at least as long as the landlord stays in the business. But the quantity of available rental housing will decrease, so that many would-be residents will be unable to find rental housing in the market. Since renters tend to be poorer than those who can buy a home, a shortage of rental housing will tend to hurt the poor most.

CASE IN POINT

Rent Control in New York City

New York City adopted rent control on a "temporary" basis during World War II. Half a century later, it is still in effect. Journalist William Tucker has been collecting stories of well-to-do New Yorkers who benefit from this situation. The minority leader in the state senate, for example, pays $1,800 a month for a *ten-room* apartment

overlooking Central Park. A newcomer pays $1,500 for a one-bedroom apartment in midtown Manhattan. A housing court judge who hears rent-control cases pays $93 a month for a two-bedroom apartment in a building where studio apartments (with no separate bedroom) rent for $1,200.

Of course, people who have been able to pay far below market value for decades tend to favor rent control. But since rent control is effectively a price ceiling, economists, looking to the law of supply and demand, would expect it to lead to problems and indeed it has.

For example, despite a serious shortage of housing in New York City, over 300,000 rental units have simply been abandoned. Almost no new rental housing is being built. Only about 2 percent of the apartments in New York are vacant at any time, as opposed to vacancy rates averaging 6 percent in East Coast cities, like Baltimore, that do not have rent control. When many people are struggling to obtain one of the few available apartments, poor people tend to lose out.

Even with rent control, the *average* rent in New York City is little different from that in some other large

Rent control is widespread in New York City.

cities, like Chicago. But in Chicago, a newcomer can find an apartment at something close to the average rent. In New York, newcomers often have to make special payments to secure an apartment, and then pay extraordinarily high rents that help to subsidize those who have been living there for a long time.

Attempting to provide moderate and low-cost housing is a worthy public goal. But the example of New York and other rent-controlled cities shows that even when the goal is worthy, the law of supply and demand does not simply fade away.[2] ●

Price Floors

Just as consumers try to get government to limit the prices they pay, sellers would like the government to put a floor on the prices they receive: a minimum wage for workers and a minimum price on wheat and other agricultural products for farmers. Both groups appeal to fairness. The price they are receiving is inadequate to cover the effort (and other resources) they are contributing.

In many countries, farmers, because of their political influence, have succeeded in persuading government to impose a floor on the prices of many agricultural products—a price which is above the market equilibrium, as illustrated in Figure 5.13. The consequences should be obvious: sup-

ply exceeds demand. To sustain the price, government has had to purchase and stockpile huge amounts of agricultural goods. The cost of supporting the price at these above-market levels has been in the billions—at the peak, in 1986, the government spent over $25 billion, or an average of more than $11,000 for every farmer.

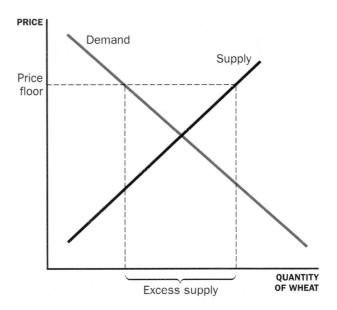

FIGURE 5.13 *Price Floors*

If the government imposes a price floor on, say, wheat—at a price in excess of the market equilibrium—there will be excess supply. Either the government will have to purchase the excess, putting it into storage or discarding it in some way, or it will have to limit production.

---

[2]William Tucker, "We All Pay for Others' Great Apartment Deals," *Newsday,* May 24, 1986; Tucker, "Moscow on the Hudson," *The American Spectator* (July 1986), pp. 19–21; Tucker, "Where Do the Homeless Come From?" *National Review,* September 25, 1987, pp. 32–43.

As government interferes with the law of supply and demand, it is led into a labyrinth of problems. To reduce supplies, it has imposed production limitations. Imposing limitations not only is administratively cumbersome but also impedes the adaptability of the market. This is because quotas are based on past production, but some areas should be expanding, and others contracting, in response to changed circumstances. The quota system does not allow this to happen easily. Worse still, wheat farmers have to keep producing wheat, lest they lose their quota. But this means that they cannot rotate their crops—and this is bad for the soil and the environment. To avoid the buildup of surpluses, exports are subsidized. But these subsidies have angered other countries, which view it as unfair competition. Our subsidies of wheat exports to Mexico have hurt our economic relations with Argentina. Even Mexico has viewed them with alarm, as they have interfered with Mexico's attempts to reform its agricultural sector.

Government is aware of these problems, but the political pressures to maintain high prices kept the price support program in place for a long time. The agricultural bill passed in 1996 is intended to lead to a phase-out of price supports for most major crops.

Alternative Solutions

Large changes in prices cause distress. It is natural to try to find scapegoats and to look to the government for a solution. Such situations call for compassion, and the economists' caution can seem coldhearted. But the fact remains that in competitive markets, price changes are simply the impersonal workings of the law of supply and demand; without price changes, there will be shortages and surpluses. The examples of government attempts to interfere with the workings of supply and demand provide an important cautionary tale: One ignores the workings of the law of supply and demand only at one's peril. This does not mean, however, that the government should simply ignore the distress caused by large price and wage changes. It only means that government must take care in addressing the problems; price controls, including price ceilings and floors, are unlikely to be effective instruments.

Later chapters will discuss ways in which the government can address dissatisfaction with the consequences of the law of supply and demand—by making use of the power of the market rather than trying to fight against it. For example, if the government is concerned with low wages paid to unskilled workers, it can try to increase the demand for these workers. A shift to the right in the demand curve will increase the wages these workers receive. The government can do this either by subsidizing firms that hire unskilled workers or by providing more training to these workers and thus increasing their productivity.

If the government wants to increase the supply of housing to the poor, it can provide housing subsidies for the poor, which will elicit a greater supply. If government wants to conserve on the use of gasoline, it can impose a tax on gasoline. Noneconomists often object that these sorts of economic incentives have other distasteful consequences, and sometimes they do. But government policies that take account of the law of supply and demand will tend to be more effective, with fewer unfortunate side effects, than policies that ignore the predictable economic consequences that follow from disregarding the law of supply and demand.

Internet Connection

Flawed Deregulation

The California electricity market became a major national news story in 2001 as Californians suffered rolling blackouts, a major utility declared bankruptcy, and the state government spent as much as $70 million per day to purchase electricity. Rising demand, shrinking supply, and a price ceiling on what utilities could charge consumers produced electricity shortages. Information on the California electric industry may be found at the California Public Utilities Commision Web site: http://www.cpuc.ca.gov. The University of California Energy Institute provides data on daily demand and supply curves for electricity in California at http://www.ucei.berkeley.edu/ucei/datamine/datamine.htm .

Review and Practice

Summary

1. The price elasticity of demand describes how sensitive the quantity demanded of a good is to changes in the price of the good. When demand is inelastic, an increase in the price has little effect on quantity demanded and the demand curve is steep; when demand is elastic, an increase in the price has a large effect on quantity demanded and the curve is flat. Demand for necessities is usually quite inelastic; demand for luxuries is elastic.

2. The price elasticity of supply describes how sensitive the quantity supplied of a good is to changes in the price of the good. If price changes do not induce much change in supply, the supply curve is very steep and is said to be inelastic. If the supply curve is very flat, indicating that price changes cause large changes in supply, supply is said to be elastic.

3. The extent to which a shift in the supply curve is reflected in price or quantity depends on the shape of the demand curve. The more elastic the demand, the more a given shift in the supply curve will be reflected in changes in equilibrium quantities and the less it will be reflected in changes in equilibrium prices. The more inelastic the demand, the more a given shift in the supply curve will be reflected in changes in equilibrium prices and the less it will be reflected in changes in equilibrium quantities.

4. Likewise, the extent to which a shift in the demand curve is reflected in price or quantity depends on the shape of the supply curve.

5. Demand and supply curves are likely to be more elastic in the long run than in the short run. Therefore a shift in the demand or supply curve is likely to have a larger price effect in the short run and a larger quantity effect in the long run.

6. Elasticities can be used to predict to what extent consumer prices rise when a tax is imposed on a good. If the demand curve for a good is very inelastic, consumers in effect have to pay the tax. If the demand curve is very elastic, the quantities produced and the price received by producers are likely to decline considerably.

7. Government regulations may prevent a market from moving toward its equilibrium price, leading to shortages or surpluses. Price ceilings lead to excess demand. Price floors lead to excess supply.

Key Terms

price elasticity of demand
relatively elastic
unitary elasticity
relatively inelastic
infinite elasticity
zero elasticity
price elasticity of supply
shortage
surplus
price ceilings
price floors

Review Questions

1. What is meant by the elasticity of demand and the elasticity of supply? Why do economists find these concepts useful?

2. Is the slope of a perfectly elastic demand or supply curve horizontal or vertical? Is the slope of a perfectly inelastic demand or supply curve horizontal or vertical? Explain.

3. If the elasticity of demand is unity, what happens to total revenue as the price increases? What if the demand for a product is very inelastic? What if it is very elastic?

4. Under what condition will a shift in the demand curve result mainly in a change in quantity? in price?

5. Under what condition will a shift in the supply curve result mainly in a change in price? in quantity?

6. Why do the elasticities of demand and supply tend to change from the short run to the long run?

7. Under what circumstances will a tax on a product be passed along to consumers?

8. Why do price ceilings tend to lead to shortages? Why do price floors tend to lead to surpluses?

Problems

1. Suppose the price elasticity of demand for gasoline is .2 in the short run and .7 in the long run. If the price of gasoline rises 28 percent, what effect on quantity demanded will this have in the short run? in the long run?

2. Imagine that the short-run price elasticity of supply for a farmer's corn is .3, while the long-run price elasticity is 2. If prices for corn fall 30 percent, what are the short-run and long-run changes in quantity supplied? What are the short- and long-run changes in quantity supplied if prices rise by 15 percent? What happens to the farmer's revenues in each of these situations?

3. Assume that the demand curve for hard liquor is highly inelastic and the supply curve for hard liquor is highly elastic. If the tastes of the drinking public shift away from hard liquor, will the effect be larger on price or on quantity? If the federal government decides to impose a tax on manufacturers of hard liquor, will the effects be larger on price or on quantity? What is the effect of an advertising program that succeeds in discouraging people from drinking? Draw diagrams to illustrate each of your answers.

4. Imagine that wages (the price of labor) are sticky in the labor market, that is, wages do not change in the short run, and that a supply of new workers enters that market. Will the market be in equilibrium in the short run? Why or why not? If not, explain the relationship you would expect to see between the quantity demanded and supplied, and draw a diagram to illustrate. Explain how sticky wages in the labor market affect unemployment.

5. For each of the following markets, explain whether you would expect prices in that market to be relatively sticky or not:

    (a) the stock market;

    (b) the market for autoworkers;

    (c) the housing market;

    (d) the market for cut flowers;

    (e) the market for pizza-delivery people.

6. Suppose a government wishes to assure that its citizens can afford adequate housing. Consider three ways of pursuing that goal. One method is to pass a law requiring that all rents be cut by one-fourth. A second method offers a subsidy to all builders of homes. A third provides a subsidy directly to renters equal to one-fourth of the rent they pay. Predict what effect each of these proposals would have on the price and quantity of rental housing in the short run and the long run.

7. In 1990, the U.S. government imposed a 10 percent tax on certain luxuries such as pleasure boats. Sales of pleasure boats fell by nearly 90 percent in southern Florida as prospective buyers bought boats in the Bahamas to avoid paying the tax. What does this imply about the size of the elasticity of demand?

8. Assume the elasticity of demand for oil is .7 and the initial quantity demanded is 100 million barrels a day. What is the impact of a 10 percent increase in the price of oil on the quantity of oil demanded? What happens to total expenditures? Assume that the United States initially imports 50 million barrels a day and that production remains unchanged. What happens to the level of imports and expenditures on imports?
   Assume that in the long run, the elasticity of demand increases to 1. How does this change your answers?

Chapter 6

The Consumption Decision

Key Questions

1. Where does the demand curve come from? Why is it normally downward sloping?

2. How does an increase in income shift the demand curve? How do changes in the prices of other goods shift the curve?

Ore than 100 million U.S. households taken together make an astounding number of spending choices every day. These decisions contribute to the overall demand for cars and bicycles, clothes and housing, and masses of other products available on the market. The members of each household also make decisions that affect how much income they will have to spend, like whether to work overtime or whether both partners in a marriage should work. They decide how much of their income to save. And they decide where to put the nest eggs they do save.

These four sets of decisions—about spending, working, saving, and investing—represent the basic economic choices facing the household. This chapter focuses on spending decisions and how these decisions are affected by taxes and other government policies. Later, in Chapter 9 we will tackle working and saving decisions.

These microeconomic decisions have macroeconomic consequences as well. Household decisions about whether to buy a car that is imported from Japan or one that is made in America will affect the U.S. trade deficit. Choices about how much one should work will affect overall levels of unemployment and production. Household decisions about saving and investment will affect the future growth of the economy.

The Basic Problem of Consumer Choice

The first basic problem facing a consumer is easy to state, though hard to resolve: What should he do with whatever (after-tax) income he has to spend? He must allocate (that is, divide) his available income among alternative goods. Should he buy compact discs, go to the movies, eat candy bars, or purchase sweaters? In the absence of scarcity the answer would be easy: have it all!

Chapter 2 provided the basic framework for economic decision making. The consumer defines his opportunity set, what is *possible* given the constraints he faces, and then chooses the most preferred point within this set. This chapter begins by reviewing how we define the opportunity set, and then asks how it changes—and how what the individual chooses changes—when incomes and prices change.

The Budget Constraint

The individual's opportunity set is defined by the budget constraint. If, after taxes, a person's weekly paycheck comes to $300 and he has no other income, this is his budget constraint. Total expenditures on food, clothing, rent, entertainment, travel, and all other categories cannot exceed $300 per week. (For now we ignore the possibilities that individuals may borrow money, or save money, or change their budget constraints by working longer or shorter hours.)

The line *BC* in Figure 6.1A shows a simplified individual budget constraint. A student, Fran, has a total of $300 each semester to spend on "fun" items. Figure 6.1 assumes that there are two goods, candy bars and compact discs. The simplified assumption of only two goods is an abstraction that highlights the main points of the analysis.

Let's say that a candy bar costs $1, while a compact disc costs $15. If Fran spent all her income on candy bars, she could purchase 300 candy bars (point *B* on the budget

constraint). If she spent all her income on CDs, she could buy 20 CDs (point *C* on the budget constraint). Fran can also choose any of the intermediate choices on line *BC*. For example, she could buy 10 CDs (for $150) and 150 candy bars (for $150), or 15 CDs ($225) and 75 candy bars ($75). Each combination of purchases along the budget constraint totals $300.

As we learned in Chapter 2, a budget constraint diagram has two important features. First, although any point in the shaded area of Figure 6.1A is feasible, only the points on the line *BC* are really relevant. This is because Fran is not consuming her entire budget if she is inside her budget constraint. Second, by looking along the budget constraint, we can see the trade-offs she faces—how many candy bars she has to give up to get 1 more CD, and vice versa. Look at points *F* and *A*. This part of the budget constraint is blown up in panel B. At point *A*, Fran has 10 CDs; at *F*, she has 11. At *F*, she has 135 candy bars; at *A*, 150. To get 1 more CD, she has to give up 15 candy bars.

These are her trade-offs, and they are determined by the relative prices of the two goods. If one good costs twice as much as another, to get 1 more unit of the costly good, we have to give up 2 units of the cheaper good. If, as here, one

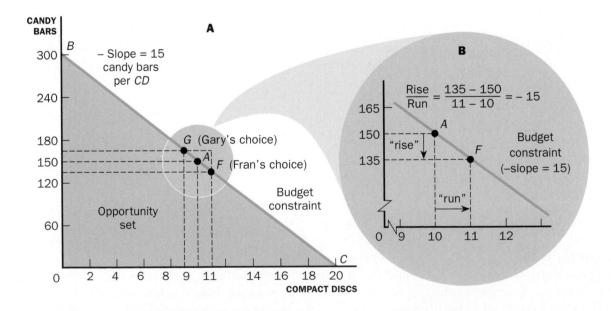

FIGURE 6.1   *An Individual's Budget Constraint*

Panel A is a budget constraint that shows the combinations of compact discs (at $15) and candy bars (at $1) that an individual could buy with $300. Fran chooses point *F*, with a relatively large number of CDs; Gary chooses point *G*, with a relatively large number of candy bars. Panel B shows that the trade-off of moving from 10 CDs to 11 (point *A* to *F*) is 15 candy bars.

good costs fifteen times as much as another, to get 1 more unit of the costly good, we have to give up 15 units of the less costly good.

The **slope** of the budget constraint also tells us what the trade-off is. The slope of a line measures how steep it is. As we move 1 unit along the horizontal axis (from 10 to 11 CDs), the slope measures the size of the change along the vertical axis. The slope is the rise (the movement up or down on the vertical axis) divided by the run (the corresponding horizontal movement). The slope of this budget constraint is thus 15.[1] It tells us how much of one good, at a given price, we need to give up if we want 1 more unit of the other good; it tells us, in other words, what the trade-off is.

Notice that the relative price of CDs to candy bars is 15; that is, a CD costs fifteen times as much as a candy bar. But we have just seen that the slope of the budget constraint is 15, and that the trade-off (the number of candy bars Fran has to give up to get 1 more CD) is 15. It is no accident that these three numbers—relative price, slope, and trade-off—are the same.

This two-product example was chosen because it is easy to illustrate with a graph. But this logic can cover any number of products. Income can be spent on one item or a combination of items. The budget constraint defines what a certain amount of income can buy, which depends on the prices of the items. Giving up some of one item would allow the purchase of more of another item or items.

Economists represent these choices by putting the purchases of the good upon which they are focusing attention, say CDs, on the horizontal axis and "all other goods" on the vertical axis. By definition, what is not spent on CDs is available to be spent on all other goods. Fran has $300 to spend altogether. A more realistic budget constraint for her is shown in Figure 6.2. The intersection of the budget constraint with the vertical axis, point *B*—where purchases of CDs are zero—is $300. If Fran spends nothing on CDs, she has $300 to spend on other goods. The budget constraint intersects the horizontal axis at 20 CDs (point *C*); if she spends all her income on CDs and CDs cost $15 each, she can buy 20. If Fran chooses a point such a *F*, she will buy 11 CDs, costing $165, and she will have $135 to spend on other goods ($300–$165). The distance 0*D* on the vertical axis measures what she spends on other goods; the distance *BD* measures what she spends on CDs.

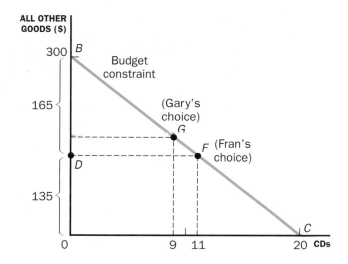

FIGURE 6.2 *Allocating a Budget Between a Single Good and all Others*

Some budget constraints show the choice between a particular good, in this case CDs, and all other goods. The other goods that might be purchased are collectively measured in money terms, as shown on the vertical axis.

Choosing a Point on the Budget Constraint: Individual Preferences

The budget constraint and a recognition of possible trade-offs is the starting point for the study of consumer behavior. The process of identifying the budget constraints and the trade-offs is the same for *any* two people. If a person walks into a store (that only accepts cash) with $300, any economist can tell you his budget constraint and the trade-offs he faces by looking at the money in his pocket and the prices on the shelves. What choice will he make? Economists narrow their predictions to points on his budget constraint; any individual will choose *some* point along the budget constraint. But the point actually chosen depends on the individual's preferences: Fran, who likes to listen to music, might choose point *F* in Figure 6.1, while Gary, who loves candy, might choose *G*.

Few people will choose either of the extreme points on the budget constraint, *B* or *C* in Figure 6.1, where only one of the goods is consumed. The reason for this is that the more you have of a good—say, the more CDs you have relative to another good such as candy—the less valuable is an additional unit of that good relative to additional

---

[1]We ignore the negative sign. See the appendix to Chapter 2 for a more detailed explanation of the slope of a line.

units of another good. At points near *C,* it seems safe to assume that to most individuals, an extra CD does not look as attractive as some candy bars. Certainly, at *B,* most people would be so full of candy bars that an extra CD would look preferable.

Where the individual's choice lies depends on how she values the two goods. Chapter 2 emphasized the idea that in making decisions, people look at the *margin;* they look at the extra costs and benefits. In this case, the choice at each point along the budget constraint is between 1 more CD and 15 more candy bars. If Gary and Fran choose different points along the budget constraint, it is because they value the marginal benefits (how much better off they feel with an *extra* CD) and the marginal costs (how much it hurts to give up 15 candy bars) differently. Gary chooses point *G* in Figure 6.1 because that is the point where, for him, the marginal benefit of an extra CD is just offset by what he has to give up to get the extra CD, which is 15 candy bars. When Fran, who loves listening to music, considers point *G,* she realizes that for her, at that point, CDs are more important and candy bars less important than they are for Gary. So she trades along the line until she has enough CDs and few enough candy bars that, for her, the marginal benefits of an extra CD and the marginal costs of 15 fewer candy bars are equal. This point, as we have supposed, is *F*.

The same reasoning holds for a budget constraint like the one shown in Figure 6.2. Here, Gary and Fran are choosing between CDs and all other goods, measured in dollar terms. Now in deciding to buy an extra CD, each one compares the marginal benefit of an extra CD with the marginal cost, what has to be given up in other goods. With CDs priced at $15, choosing to buy a CD means giving up $15 of other goods. For Gary, the marginal benefit of an extra CD equals the cost, $15, when he has only 9 CDs and can therefore spend $165 on other goods. For Fran, who has more of a taste for CDs, the marginal benefit of an extra CD does not equal this marginal cost until she reaches 11 CDs, with $135 to spend elsewhere. Thus, the price is a quantitative measure of the marginal benefit.

What Happens to Consumption When Income Changes?

When an individual's income increases, he has more to spend on consumption. Figure 6.3 shows the effect on the

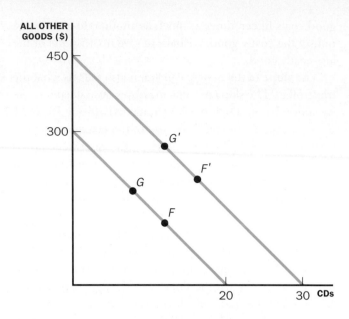

FIGURE 6.3   *The Effect on Consumption When Income Changes*

If the amount Gary and Fran have to spend on CDs and other goods rises from $300 to $450, the budget line shifts to the right. Because the price of CDs is still $15, the slope of the budget line does not change. The points Gary and Fran choose on the new budget line are *G'* and *F'*. With additional income, they both choose to buy more CDs *and* to spend more on other goods.

budget constraint of an increase in income. The original budget line is the same as that used in Figure 6.2. Gary and Fran have $300 to spend on CDs or other goods. If the total amount they have to spend increases to $450, the new budget line is farther to the right. Now, Gary and Fran could purchase 30 CDs if they spend the entire $450 on CDs, or they could spend it all on other goods. The budget line shows the combinations of CDs and other goods they can purchase for $450. Because the price of a CD has not changed, the slope of the new budget line is the same as that of the old budget line. Changes in income shift the budget line but do not alter its slope.

The new choices of Gary and Fran are at points *G'* and *F'*. Because they have more to spend, Gary and Fran each decide to purchase more CDs *and* more of other goods. This is typically the case; when people's incomes increase, they will buy a little more of many goods, although the consumption of some goods will increase more than that of others, and different individuals will spend their extra income in different ways. Jim may spend much of his extra income going to more concerts, while Maria may spend much of her extra income on computer software.

The **income elasticity of demand** (which parallels the price elasticity of demand presented in Chapter 5) measures how much consumption of a particular good increases with income:

$$\text{income elasticity of demand} = \frac{\text{percentage change in consumption}}{\text{percentage change in income}}.$$

The income elasticity of demand, in other words, is the percentage change in consumption that would result from a 1 percent increase in income. If the income elasticity of demand of a certain good is greater than 1, a 1 percent increase in an individual's income results in a more than 1 percent increase in expenditures on that good. That is, the amount he spends on that good increases more than proportionately with income. By definition, if the income elasticity of demand is less than 1, then a 1 percent increase in income results in a less than 1 percent increase in expenditures. In this case, the share of income a consumer spends on that good decreases with a rise in income.

As people's incomes increase, the types of goods they choose to buy also change. In particular, they have more money to spend on goods other than those required just to survive. For instance, while they may spend some of the extra income to buy better-quality food and other necessities, more money goes toward movies, more expensive automobiles, vacations, and other luxuries. Accordingly, poor individuals spend a larger percentage of their income on food and housing and a smaller percentage of their income on perfume. In other words, the income elasticity of necessities is less than one, and the income elasticity of luxuries is greater than one.

The consumption of some goods actually decreases as income increases and increases as income decreases. These goods are called **inferior goods**. They are in sharp contrast to **normal goods**, the consumption of which increases with income. In other words, goods for which the income elasticity is *negative* are, by definition, inferior, while all other goods are called normal. For instance, if Fran, who has been riding the bus to work, gets a large raise, she may find that she can afford a car. After buying the car, she will spend less on bus tokens. Thus, in this particular sense, bus rides represent an inferior good.

Figure 6.4 shows how typical families at different income levels spend their income. In the figure, we see that *on average*, the poorest 20 percent of the population spend more than 85 percent of their before tax income on housing. This contrasts with the richest 20 percent, who spend only a fifth of their income on housing. Similarly, the poorest 20 percent spend 35 percent of their before tax income on food, while the richest 20 percent spend less than a tenth. The total spending of the poorest 20 percent on food and housing adds up to more than 100 percent of their income; this is only possible because of government subsidies.

Information like that contained in Figure 6.4 is of great practical importance. For example, it helps determine how a tax will affect different groups. Anybody who consumes alcohol will be hurt by a tax on alcohol. But if the poor spend a larger fraction of their income on alcohol, as the figure suggests, they will bear a disproportionately large share of the tax.

WRAP-UP

Income Elasticity of Demand

The *income elasticity of demand* for a good is the percentage change in consumption that would result from a 1 percent increase in income.

When income elasticity of demand is *greater than 1,* a 1 percent increase in an individual's income results in a more than 1 percent increase in expenditures on the good.

When income elasticity of demand is *less than 1,* a 1 percent increase in an individual's income results in a less than 1 percent increase in expenditures on the good.

Normal goods have a positive income elasticity of demand.

Inferior goods have a negative income elasticity of demand.

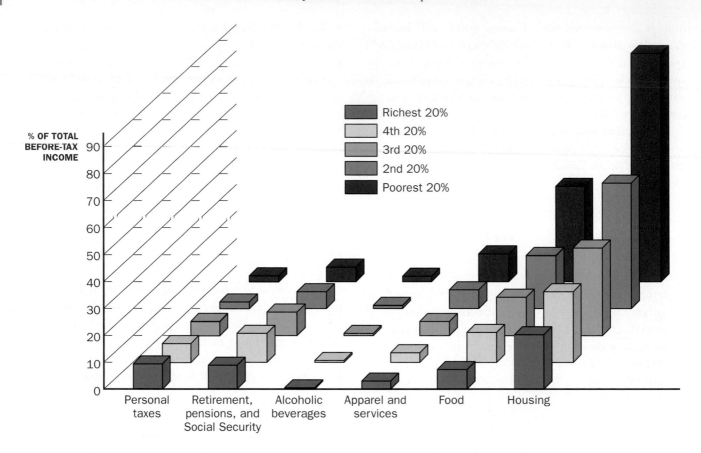

Richest 20%
4th 20%
3rd 20%
2nd 20%
Poorest 20%

Personal taxes | Retirement, pensions, and Social Security | Alcoholic beverages | Apparel and services | Food | Housing

FIGURE 6.4   *How Households of Different Incomes Spend Their Money*

The poor spend far higher proportions of their income on basic necessities like food and housing than do the rich.

SOURCE: *Consumer Expenditure Survey Data,* 1999.

CASE IN POINT

The Fate of the BTU Tax

Some of the differences in choices along a budget constraint reflect nothing more than differences in tastes— Fran likes CDs more than Gary. But some differences in choices are systematic, for instance representing differences in circumstances. Eleanor lives in New England and spends more on oil to heat her apartment than does Jim, who lives in Florida; Amy, who lives in Montana, 200 miles from the nearest town, buys more gas and spends more on cars than does someone from New York City.

Understanding such systematic determinants in how people spend their money helps us understand the markedly different responses in different regions of the country to government proposals to tax different goods. A case in point arose in 1993 after the Clinton administration took office with a pledge to reduce the huge federal deficit. Many policy analysts, both inside and outside government, favored a tax on energy. Most energy sources are relatively cheap in the United States compared to many other industrialized countries. Low energy prices lead Americans to consume high quantities of energy, thus increasing urban congestion, air pollution, and greenhouse gas emissions. A tax on energy would provide incentives to conserve energy—making such a tax an environmentally sound way of raising revenue.

Low energy prices in the United States lead Americans to consume high quantities of energy.

The administration proposed a BTU tax—named after the British Thermal Unit, a standard measure of energy. The intent was to levy the tax on the basis of energy used, treating all energy sources alike. The tax proposal generated immediate opposition from heavy energy users. Americans living in the Northeast, who needed to heat their homes for much of the year, claimed that the tax would hit them unfairly. The aluminum industry, a heavy user of energy, strongly opposed it along with other energy-intensive industries.

In an effort to make the tax more politically palatable—and increase the chance of passage through the Congress—policymakers whittled it down to a single-form-of-energy tax—on gasoline. The proposal turned into an increase in the gasoline tax from 14.1 cents to 20.6 cents per gallon. Americans in the West, who drive much longer distances in a typical day than people in other parts of the country, were up in arms. Politics dictated a reduction in the proposed gas tax. Congress finally passed, and the President signed, a mere 4.3 cents per gallon increase in the tax on gasoline, which raises only $5 billion a year more in federal revenue than before the gas tax increase. ●

A Closer Look at the Demand Curve

In Chapter 4, we saw the principal characteristic of the demand curve: When prices rise, the quantity of a good

demanded normally falls. Here, we take a closer look at why. This will help us understand why some goods respond more strongly to price changes, that is, have a greater price elasticity.

Let us return to our earlier example of Fran buying CDs in Figure 6.2. If the price of CDs rises from $15 to $20, Fran will face a new budget constraint. If she didn't buy any CDs, she would still have $300 to spend on other goods; but if she decided to spend all of her income on CDs, she could only buy 15 rather than 20. Figure 6.5 shows Fran's original budget constraint in light green and her new budget constraint in dark green.

The increase in the price of CDs has one obvious and important effect: Fran cannot continue to buy the same number of CDs and the same amount of other goods as she did before. Earlier, Fran bought 11 CDs. If she bought the same number of CDs, it would cost her $55 more, and she would have $55 less to spend on other goods. No matter what she does, Fran is worse off as a result of the price increase. It is *as if* she had less income to spend. When she has less income to spend, she reduces her expenditure on each good, including CDs. This part of the response to the higher price is called the **income effect**. An increase in income of about $55, or 18 percent ($55 out of $300), would

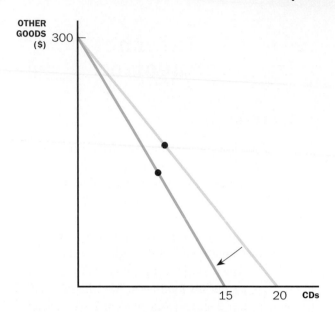

FIGURE 6.5   *Effect of Price Increase*

An increase in the price of CDs moves the budget constraint down as shown. Fran must cut back on the consumption of some goods. Here, using the black dots to mark her consumption points, we show her cutting back on the consumption of both CDs and other goods.

offset the price increase.[2] Assume the income elasticity is approximately 1; that is, with income reduced by 18 percent, she would reduce purchases of CDs by 18 percent, which is about 2 CDs. This part of the reduction of the demand of CDs, from 11 to 9, is the income effect.

The magnitude of the income effect depends on two factors: how important the commodity is to the individual—that is, how large a fraction of the individual's income is spent on the good—and how large the income elasticity is. Since, in most cases, individuals spend a relatively small fraction of their income on any particular good, the income effect is relatively small. But in the case of housing, for example, on which most individuals spend between a fourth and a third of their income on average, the income effect of an increase in the price of housing is significant.

Let us go back to Fran and the CDs. At the higher price, giving up one CD gets her more of other goods—more

candy bars, more movies, more tapes, more sweaters. The relative price of CDs, or the trade-off between CDs and other goods, has changed. At the higher price, she *substitutes* goods that are less expensive for the more expensive CDs. Not surprisingly, this effect is called the **substitution effect.** The magnitude of the substitution effect depends on how easily Fran can substitute other goods. If Fran still owns her tape player, and if the price of tapes remains unchanged, then the substitution effect might be large. She may drop the number of CDs she purchases to 2. But if Fran has no tape or MP3 player, if the only entertainment she likes is listening to music, and if she dislikes all the music played by the local radio stations, then the substitution effect may be small. She may drop the number of CDs she purchases only to 8.

Deriving Demand Curves

We can now see both how to derive the demand curve and why it has the shape it does. At each price, we draw the budget constraint and identify the point along the budget constraint that is chosen. In panel A of Figure 6.6, budget constraints are drawn for three different prices for CDs. If the price of a CD is $10, Fran purchases 15 CDs, indicated by point F_d. If the price rises to $15, the budget constraint shifts and Fran chooses to buy 11 CDs (point F). If the price is $30, Fran only buys 6 CDs (point F_i). As the price of CDs increases, Fran will purchase fewer CDs, as represented by points along successive budget constraints. Higher prices mean she is less well off, and therefore she decreases her purchases of all goods, including CDs. This is the income effect. The higher price of CDs *relative to other goods* means she will substitute other goods for CDs. This is the substitution effect.

Panel B plots the number of CDs purchased at each price. This is Fran's demand curve for CDs, and it is derived directly from the information panel A. Because Fran purchases more CDs as the price falls, the demand curve is downward sloping. The case illustrated in panel B is the normal case. As price falls, the quantity demanded increases through *both* the income effect and the substitution effect. For *inferior goods,* such as cheap cuts of meat and bus travel, the income effect goes in the opposite direction. As the price is lowered, the substitution effect leads to more consumption, but the income effect leads to less. The net effect can be either positive or negative. Generally, though, as individuals become better off, they typically reduce their consumption of these goods.

---

[2]Actually, it would slightly overcompensate. With the $55 increase, Fran could buy exactly the same bundle of goods as before, but as we shall shortly see, she will *choose* to reallocate her spending. The reallocation will make her better off.

Incentives, Income Effects, and Substitution Effects

Economists focus on incentives because they want to understand how choices are made. By using the concepts of income and substitution effects, economists are able to analyze the way that prices affect incentives, and therefore choices. The best way to understand income effects and substitution effects—and to begin thinking like an economist—is to use them, as the following example illustrates.

During the winter of 2001, the state of California was hit with an energy shortage. Under a partial deregulation of the electrical market, the state's major electrical utilities were required to buy electricity on the open market and sell to consumers at prices that were capped. As the cost of wholesale electricity rose sharply during early 2001, the price the utilities had to pay for electricity soared above what they were allowed to charge their customers. Demand outstripped supply.

When demand exceeds supply, two solutions are possible—increase supply or reduce demand. In a deregulated market system, the price of electricity would have risen, and the higher prices would have provided consumers with the incentive to conserve. A higher price for electricity reduces demand through two channels. As electricity prices rise relative to the prices of other goods that house-

holds purchase, each household has an incentive to economize on electricity. This is the *substitution effect*. But there is an income effect as well. Because electricity is more expensive, the household's real income is reduced—it has to spend more to obtain the same set of consumer goods (including electricity). With a reduced real income, the household cuts back its spending on all types of goods, including electricity. This is the *income effect*.

Because higher energy costs may have a disproportionate impact on low-income families, politicians are often reluctant to let energy prices rise. The solution is not to cap prices—keeping prices low simply reduces the incentives to all households to conserve a scarce resource. Instead, suppose the added energy costs for each household average $200. The income effect can be eliminated, while still allowing the substitution effect to do its job in reducing demand, by giving each household a refund of $200. On average, households' real income no longer falls—the impact of higher electricity prices is offset by the refund of $200. But the substitution effect still operates. In spending its income, a household faces a higher relative price of electricity. It faces an incentive to conserve on its use of electricity.

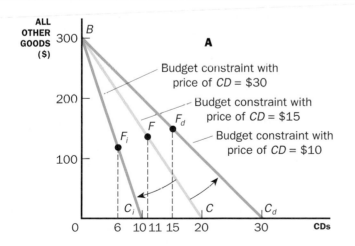
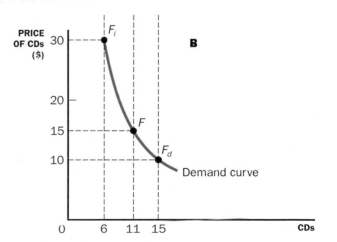

FIGURE 6.6 *Deriving Demand Curves from Shifting Budget Constraints*

In panel A, the budget constraint rotates down to the left as the price of CDs increases, leading Fran to change consumption from F to F_i. The budget constraint rotates to the right when the price of CDs decreases, and Fran moves from F to F_d. Panel B shows the corresponding demand curve for CDs, illustrating how the rising prices lead to a declining quantity consumed.

The Importance of Distinguishing Between Income and Substitution Effects

Distinguishing between the income and substitution effects of a change in price is important for two reasons.

Understanding Responses to Price Changes   First, the distinction improves our understanding of consumption responses to price changes. Thinking about the substitution effect helps us understand why some demand curves have a low price elasticity and others a high price elasticity. It also helps us understand why the price elasticity may well differ at different points along the demand curve. Recall from Chapter 5 that when an individual is consuming lots of one good, substitutes for the good are easy to find, and a small increase in price leads to a large reduction in the quantity demanded; but as consumption gets lower, it becomes increasingly difficult to find good substitutes.

Or consider the effect of an increase in the price of one good on the demand for *other* goods. There is always an income effect; the income effect, by itself, would lead to a reduced consumption of all commodities. But the substitution effect leads to *increased* consumption of substitute commodities. Thus, an increase in the price of Coke will lead to increased demand for Pepsi at each price; the demand curve for Pepsi shifts to the right, because the substitution effect outweighs the slight income effect.

Understanding Inefficiencies Associated with Taxes   A second reason to focus on income and substitution effects is to identify some of the inefficiencies associated with taxation. The purpose of a tax is to raise revenue so that the government can purchase goods; it represents a transfer of purchasing power from the household to the government. If the government is to obtain more resources, individuals have to consume less. Thus, any tax must have an income effect.

But beyond that, taxes often distort economic activity. The distortion caused by taxation is associated with the substitution effect. Take the window tax discussed earlier (Chapter 5, p. 98). It was intended to raise revenue. Instead, it led people to cover up their windows—a major distortion of the tax. Most of the distortions associated with modern taxes are somewhat more subtle. Take a tax on airline tickets or on telephone calls. Reducing consumption of things that are against society's interest can be a legitimate goal of taxation. But the government does not think flying or making telephone calls is a bad thing. The tax is levied to raise revenues. But it results in fewer air flights and telephone calls anyway— an unintentional consequence. Any tax leads to *some* reduction in consumption, through the income effect. But most taxes also change relative prices; so they have a substitution effect. It is the substitution effect that gives rise to the distortion. If the substitution effect is small, the distortion is small; if the substitution effect is large, the distortion is large.

WRAP-UP

Income and Substitution Effects and the Shape of Demand Curves

The *income effect* refers to a change in consumption arising from a change in the consumer's real income. When the price of a good you consume increases, your real income is reduced because you can no longer afford the same level of consumption. By the same logic, when the price of a good that you consume falls, your real income is increased.

The *substitution effect* refers to a change in consumption arising from a change in the relative prices of goods. When the price of a good you consume increases, that good becomes more expensive relative to other goods, inducing you to consume less of the expensive good and more of the other goods.

Normally, demand curves are downward sloping. This is because as the price is lowered, consumers are better off and so consume more of the good (the income effect); and the lower *relative* price induces a further increase in consumption (the substitution effect).

Utility and the Description of Preferences

We have seen that people choose a point along their budget constraint by weighing the benefits of consuming more of

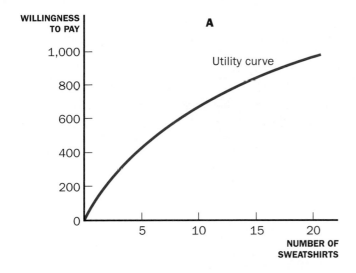

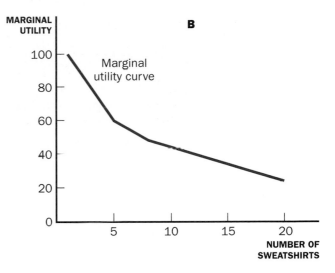

FIGURE 6.7   *Utility and Marginal Utility*

Panel A shows that utility increases continually with consumption but tends to level off as consumption climbs higher. Panel B explicitly shows marginal utility; notice that it declines as consumption increases.

one good against the costs—what they have to forgo of other goods. Economists refer to the benefits of consumption as the **utility** that individuals get from the combination of goods they consume. Presumably a person can tell you whether or not he prefers a certain combination of goods to another. Economists say that the preferred bundle of goods gives that individual a higher level of utility than the other bundle of goods he could have chosen. Similarly, economists say that the individual will choose the bundle of goods—within the budget constraint—that maximizes his utility.

In the nineteenth century, social scientists, including the British philosopher Jeremy Bentham, hoped that science would someday develop a machine that could actually measure utility. A scientist could simply hook up some electrodes to an individual's head and read off how "happy" she was. Most modern economists believe that there is no *unique* way to measure utility but that there are useful ways of measuring changes in how well-off a person is.

For our purposes, a simple way to measure utility will suffice: We ask how much an individual would be willing to pay to be in one situation rather than another. For example, if Joe likes chocolate ice cream more than vanilla, it stands to reason that he would be willing to pay more for a scoop of chocolate ice cream than for a scoop of vanilla. Or if Diane would rather live in California than in New Jersey, it stands to reason that she would be willing to pay more for the West Coast location.

Notice that how much a person is willing to pay is different from how much he *has* to pay. Just because Joe is willing to pay more for chocolate ice cream than for vanilla does not mean he will have to pay more. What he has to pay depends on market prices; what he is willing to pay reflects his preferences. Willingness to pay is a useful measure of utility, which is often helpful for purposes such as thinking about how an individual allocates his income along his budget constraint. But the hopes of nineteenth-century economists, that we could find some way of measuring utility that would allow us to compare how much utility Fran got from a bundle of goods with how much utility Gary obtained, are now viewed as pipe dreams.

Using willingness to pay as our measure of utility, we can construct a diagram like Figure 6.7A, which shows the level of utility Mary receives from sweatshirts as the number of sweatshirts she buys increases. This information is also given in Table 6.1. Here we assume that Mary is willing to pay $400 for 5 sweatshirts, $456 for 6 sweatshirts, $508 for 7 sweatshirts, and so on.[3] Thus, 5 sweatshirts give her a utility of 400, 6 a utility of 456, and 7 sweatshirts a utility of

---

[3]If these dollar amounts seem high relative to typical market prices, keep in mind that they reflect Mary's willingness to pay for sweatshirts, which is our measure of the utility she derives from them. Market prices may be lower.

TABLE 6.1

	Utility and Marginal Utility				
Number of sweatshirts	Mary's willingness to pay (utility)	Marginal utility	Number of pizzas	Mary's willingness to pay (utility)	Marginal utility
0	0	100	0	0	36
1	100	90	1	36	32
2	190	80	2	64	30
3	270	70	3	98	28
4	340	60	4	126	26
5	400	56	5	152	24
6	456	52	6	176	22
7	508	48	7	198	20
8	556	46	8	218	18
9	602	44	9	236	16
10	646	42	10	252	14
11	688	40	11	266	12
12	728	38	12	272	10
13	766	36	13	288	8
14	802	34	14	296	
15	836	32			
16	868	30			
17	898	28			
18	926	26			
19	952	24			
20	976				

508. Mary's willingness to pay increases with the number of sweatshirts, reflecting the fact that additional sweatshirts give her additional utility. The extra utility of an additional sweatshirt, measured here by the additional amount she is willing to pay, is the **marginal utility**. The numbers in the third column of Table 6.1 give the marginal (or extra) utility she received from her last sweatshirt. When Mary owns 5 sweatshirts, an additional sweatshirt yields her an additional or marginal utility of 56 (456–400); when she owns 6 sweatshirts, an additional one gives her a marginal utility of only 52 (508–456). Figure 6.7B traces the marginal utilities of each of these increments.[4]

As an individual's bundle of goods includes more and more of a good, each successive increment increases her utility less. This is the law of **diminishing marginal utility**. The first sweatshirt is very desirable, and additional ones are attractive as well. But each sweatshirt does not increase utility by as much as the one before, and at some

point, Mary may get almost no additional pleasure from adding to her sweatshirt wardrobe.

When Mary has a given budget and must choose between two goods that cost the same, say sweatshirts and pizza, each of which costs $15, she will make her choice so that the marginal utility of each good is the same. Table 6.1 shows Mary's willingness to pay (utility) for both sweatshirts and pizza. Suppose Mary has a $300 budget for sweatshirts and pizza. Look at what happens if she buys 20 sweatshirts with her money and no pizza. The marginal utility of the last sweatshirt is 24, and that of the first pizza is 36. If she switches $15 from sweatshirts to pizza, she loses a utility of 24 from the decreased sweatshirt, but gains 36 from her first pizza. It obviously pays for her to switch.

Now look at the situation when she has decreased her purchases of sweatshirts to 17 and increased purchases of pizza to 3. The marginal utility of the last sweatshirt is 30, and that of the last pizza is also 30. At this point, she will not want to switch anymore. If she buys another sweatshirt, she gains 28, but the *last* pizza, her 3rd, which she will have to give up, has a marginal utility of 30; she loses more than she gains. If she buys another pizza, she gains

---

[4]Since marginal utility is the extra utility from an extra unit of consumption, it is measured by the slope of the utility curve in panel A.

28, but the last sweatshirt (her 17th) gave her a marginal utility of 30; again, she loses in net. We can thus see that with her budget, she is best off when the marginal utility of the two goods is the same.

The same general principle applies when the prices of two goods differ. Assume that a sweatshirt costs twice as much as a pizza. So long as the marginal utility of sweatshirts is more than twice that of pizzas, it still pays for Mary to switch to sweatshirts. To get one more sweatshirt, she has to give up two pizzas, and we reason, as before, that she will adjust her consumption until she gets to the point where the marginal utilities of the two goods, *per dollar spent,* are equal. This is a general rule: In choosing between two goods, a consumer will adjust her choices to the point where the marginal utilities are proportional to the prices. Thus, the last unit purchased of a good that costs twice as much as another must generate twice the marginal utility as the last unit purchased of the other good; the last unit purchased of a good that costs three times as much must generate three times the marginal utility as the last unit purchased of the other good; and so on.

We can write this result simply as

$$\frac{MU_x}{P_x} = \frac{MU_y}{P_y},$$

where MU_x is the marginal utility of good x, MU_y is the marginal utility of good y, P_x is the price of good x, and P_y is the price of good y. The ratio of marginal utility to price should be the same for all goods. When this condition is met, Mary's consumption problem is solved—she has found the combination of the two goods that make her best off.

We have already seen that when the prices of sweatshirts and pizzas are the same, Mary is best off when she buys 17 sweatshirts and 3 pizzas. At that point, the marginal utility of the last sweatshirt purchased is the same as the marginal utility of the last pizza purchased. Suppose that the prices of the two goods are not the same. For example, let's suppose a pizza only costs $7.50, while sweatshirts continue to cost $15. Using the information in Table 6.1, we can see the combination of 17 sweatshirts and 3 pizzas is no longer the best one for Mary when the prices of the two goods differ. She could give up 1 sweatshirt, which reduces her utility by 30. With the $15 she saved, she can buy 2 more pizzas, for a gain in utility of 54. On net, her utility has gone up by 24, so it pays her to give up that last sweatshirt and buy more pizzas. Does it pay to give up more sweatshirts? Yes. By giving up a second sweatshirt, she reduces her utility by 32, but she gains 46 from the 2 additional pizzas she

can buy. Now look at Mary's situation if she buys 14 sweatshirts and 9 pizzas. By Mary giving up the last sweatshirt, her utility drops by 34, but by buying 2 more pizzas, going from 7 to 9, her utility gained 38. She is better off. Does it pay to reduce purchases of sweatshirts any more? No. Giving up 1 more sweatshirt leads to a loss in utility of 36 and the 2 extra pizzas only give a gain in utility of 30. She is best off with 14 sweatshirts and 9 pizzas. The marginal utility of the last sweatshirt is 36; the marginal utility of the last pizza is 18. Since sweatshirts cost twice as much as pizzas, the ratio of the marginal utility of each good to its price is the same, just as our formula said it should be.

In the example we have just analyzed, we assumed Mary's willingness to pay for sweatshirts—her measure of utility—does not depend on how many pizzas, or other goods, she has. This is seldom the case. The utility, and hence marginal utility, of sweatshirts will depend on the number of pizzas, books, and other goods she has. Thus, even when the price of sweatshirts remains the same, if the price of other goods changes, she will change her consumption of those other goods *and* sweatshirts. The same thing will happen if Mary's income changes.

WRAP-UP

Marginal Utility and Consumer Choice

Consumers allocate their income among different goods so that the marginal utility associated with the last unit purchased, per dollar spent, is the same for all goods.

Consumer Surplus

In Chapter 3, we learned that one of the basic principles of economics is that people are better off as a result of voluntary trade. The gains from trade apply whether we consider trade between individuals or trade between countries. Now that we have developed the fundamental ideas of consumer choice, we can use the demand curve to show how we can measure some of the gains that arise from economic exchange.

Assume you go into a store to buy a can of soda. The store charges you $.75. If you are particularly thirsty, you might be willing to pay as much as $1.25 for that can of soda. The difference between what you paid and what you would have been willing to pay is called **consumer surplus.** It provides a measure of how much you gained from the trade. In this example, you only had to pay $.75 for something for which you would have been willing to pay $1.25; the difference, or $.50, is your consumer surplus.

Earlier, we used the concept of marginal utility to determine Mary's choice of sweatshirts and pizzas. We can calculate from her demand curve the consumer surplus that Mary gets from buying pizza. To see how we do this, recall that Mary buys pizzas up to the point where the price is equal to the marginal utility of the last pizza she chooses to buy. Of course, she pays the same price for each of the pizzas she purchases. Suppose a pizza costs $10 and Mary buys 13. From the information in Table 6.1, we can see that the 13th pizza gives her a marginal utility of 10 and costs $10. But the 12th pizza she purchased also only cost her $10, yet it yielded a marginal utility of 12. Mary is getting a bargain; she would have been willing to pay more for the earlier pizzas. She would have been willing to pay $12 for the 12th pizza. The same is true for all the earlier pizzas. In fact, for her first pizza, she would have been willing to pay $36, for the second $32, and so on. She would have been willing to pay a total of $288 ($36 + $32 + $30 + $28 + $26 + $24 + $22 + $20 + $18 + $16 + $14 + $12 + $10) for the 13 pizzas. The difference between what she has to pay for 13 pizzas—$10 × 13 = $130—and what she would have been willing to pay, $288, is her consumer surplus. In the case, her surplus is $158.

Figure 6.8 shows Mary's demand curve for pizzas. If the price of pizzas is $36, she would purchase 1 pizza; if the price falls to $20, she would buy 8; and at a price of $10, she would buy 13. The total amount Mary would have been willing to pay for 13 pizzas is the total area under the demand curve between the vertical axis and 13, the combination of the blue and orange areas. This area is the sum of the willingness to pay for the 1st, 2nd, 3rd, and so on, up to 13 pizzas. The amount Mary actually has to pay is represented by the orange area—the price, $10, times the quantity, 13 pizzas. Her consumer surplus is the *difference,* the blue area above the price line and below the demand curve, over the range of the quantity purchased.

There is always some consumer surplus so long as the consumer has to pay only a fixed price for all the items she purchases. The fact that demand curves are downward sloping means that the previous units the consumer purchases are more valuable than the marginal units. She would have been willing to pay more for the earlier units than for the last unit, but she does not have to.

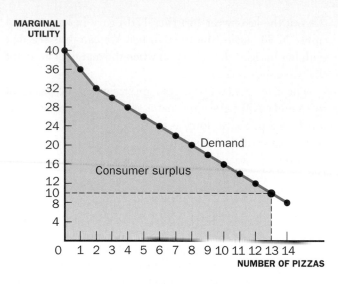

FIGURE 6.8   *Consumer Surplus*

The demand curve plots the amount Mary would be willing to pay for her 1st, 2nd, 3rd, and so on, pizza. The total amount she is willing to pay for 13 pizzas is the area under the demand curve up to the 13th pizza. The amount she actually has to pay is the *orange shaded* area. The consumer surplus is the difference between the two, the *blue shaded* area above the line and below the demand curve, over the range of the quantity purchased.

We can use the concept of consumer surplus to measure the effect on consumers of the type of agricultural price floor we analyzed in Chapter 5 using demand and supply. Figure 6.9 shows the demand and supply curves for wheat. For simplicity, supply is drawn as a vertical line (inelastic supply). In the absence of a price floor, the equilibrium

WRAP-UP

Consumer Surplus

Consumer surplus is the difference between what individuals would have been willing to spend to purchase a given amount of a good and what they actually had to spend. It is measured by the area under the demand curve, but above the price.

Consumer surplus provides a measure of the benefit to consumers of the market exchange for the good.

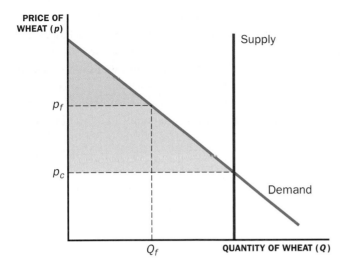

PRICE OF WHEAT (p)

Supply

p_f

p_c

Demand

Q_f **QUANTITY OF WHEAT (Q)**

FIGURE 6.9 *Consumer Surplus and a Price Floor*

The demand and supply of wheat are equal if the price is p_c. At this price, total consumer surplus is equal to the area between the demand curve, showing willingness to pay, and the market price, p_c. This is the sum of the blue and orange areas. With a price floor at p_f, the quantity demanded is only Q_f. At the price p_f, consumer surplus is the blue area. The orange area measures the fall in consumer surplus due to the price floor.

price will be p_c, and the consumer surplus is the total of the blue and orange areas. If the government imposes a price floor, at p_f, the quantity demanded is Q_f. Consumer surplus is equal to the blue area, the area under the demand curve from the vertical axis to the quantity purchased. The price floor reduces consumer surplus. The orange area measures the cost to consumers of the price floor.

Looking Beyond the Basic Model: How Well Do the Underlying Assumptions Match Reality?

In the market economy, "For whom are goods produced?" has a simple answer: Goods are produced for consumers. A

theory of consumer choice is, therefore, critical to understanding market economies. The model of budget constraints and individual preferences sketched in this chapter is the economist's basic model of consumer choice. It is a powerful one whose insights carry well beyond this course. Still, the model has been criticized. Four criticisms are summarized here. The first has no economic merit. The other three are somewhat relevant. The first criticism is that the model does not reflect the thought processes consumers really go through. This line of criticism is like criticizing the physicist's model of motion, which predicts with great precision how billiard balls will interact, simply because most pool players do not go through the equations before taking a shot. The appropriate question is whether the economic model of consumer choice can be used reliably to make predictions. By and large it can. Many businesses, for example, have found the model useful for predicting the demand for their products. And economists have used the model with remarkable success to predict consumer behavior in a variety of circumstances.

The second criticism questions the model's assumption that individuals know what they like, which is to say that they have well-defined preferences. This criticism has some merit. Having well-defined preferences means that if you gave someone a choice between two bundles of goods—one consisting of two apples, three oranges, and one pear and the other consisting of three apples, two oranges, and four pears—he could tell you quickly which he preferred. Furthermore, well-defined preferences imply that if you asked him tomorrow and the day after, he would give you the same answer. But in many cases, if you asked someone which of two things he preferred, he would say, "I don't know. Let me try them out." And what he likes may change from day to day. His preferences may, moreover, be affected by what others like. How else can we account for the frequent fads in foods and fashions as well as other aspects of our lives?

The third criticism has to do with the model's assumption that individuals know the prices of each good in the market. People often do not know prices. They know that there are bargains to be found, but they know it is costly to search for them. While we can talk meaningfully about the price of a bushel of wheat, what do we mean by the "price" of a couch or a house? If we are lucky and stumble onto a deal, we might find a leather couch for $1,000. If unlucky, even after searching all day, we may not find one for under $1,500. When we get the bargain leather couch home, if we are lucky, we will find it is even better than we thought. If unlucky, the couch will fall apart.

The final criticism points out that sometimes prices and preferences interact in a more complicated way than this chapter has depicted. People's attitudes toward a good can depend on its price. More expensive goods may have snob appeal. And when the quality of certain goods cannot easily be checked, individuals may judge quality by price. Because, on average, better (more durable) things are more costly, a cheap item is assumed to be of poor quality and an expensive item of good quality. In either case, demand curves will look quite different from those described in this chapter. Lowering the price for a good may actually lower the demand.

The fact that the basic economic model needs to be extended or modified for some goods in some instances does not deny its usefulness in the vast majority of situations where it provides just the information that businesses and governments need to making important decisions. Even in those instances where the model does not work so well, it provides a basic framework that allows us to enhance our understanding of the behavior of households. We will build on this framework in Part Three, and by asking which of the assumptions underlying the model seems inappropriate in each particular situation, we are guided in our search for a better model of consumption.

International Perspective

Spending Patterns Around the World

People in different countries spend their money in remarkably different ways. In the United States, people buy larger cars and spend more on gasoline than they do in other countries. In Paris, people spend more on restaurants than they do in the United States. Some of these differences reflect differences in circumstances; some are simply a matter of taste. Often the differences reflect a mixture—with politics thrown into the mix. Thus, Americans face lower prices of gasoline because there are lower taxes. The lower prices lead to more gas guzzlers and more consumption of gasoline. But one of the reasons why the United States has lower taxes on gasoline is that Americans value driving more, and this is partly due to differences in circumstances: More Americans live in sparsely populated areas where driving is the only way of getting around. The table below shows consumption patterns and relative prices in different countries. The first column gives the proportion of income that is spent on the good. The second shows the average prices at official exchange rates.

Americans spend more money on cars and gasoline than people in other countries.

	Education		Transportation and Communication		All Food	
	%	Price	%	Price	%	Price
Canada	21	88	9	301	14	61
France	8	83	12	258	22	59
Germany	10	89	7	355	14	66
Italy	17	84	8	234	23	65
Japan	22	72	13	258	12	101
U.K.	3	100	6	270	14	62
U.S.	6	74	8	374	13	54

SOURCE: World Bank, World Development Indicators.

Review and Practice

Summary

1. The amount of one good a person must use to purchase another good is determined by the relative prices of the two goods, and is illustrated by the slope of the budget constraint.

2. As a good becomes more expensive relative to other goods, an individual will substitute other goods for the higher-priced good. This is the substitution effect.

3. As the price of a good rises, a person's buying power is reduced. The response of this lower "real" income is the income effect. Consumption of a normal good rises as incomes rises. Thus, normally, when price rises, both the substitution and income effects lead to decreased consumption of that good.

4. When substitution is easy, demand curves tend to be elastic, or flat. If substitution is difficult, demand curves tend to be inelastic, or steep.

5. Economists sometimes describe the benefits of consumption by referring to the utility that people get from a combination of goods. The extra utility of consuming one more unit of a good is referred to as the marginal utility of that good.

Key Terms

slope
income elasticity of demand
inferior goods
normal goods
income effect
substitution effect
utility
marginal utility
diminishing marginal utility
consumer surplus

Review Questions

1. How is the slope of the budget constraint related to the relative prices of the goods on the horizontal and vertical axes?

2. How can the budget constraint appear the same even for individuals whose tastes and preferences differ dramatically?

3. Is the income elasticity of demand positive or negative for an inferior good?

4. If the price of a normal good increases, how will the income effect cause the quantity demanded of that good to change?

5. What is the substitution effect? Why do the substitution and income effects normally reinforce each other? Is this true for an inferior good?

6. Does a greater availability of substitutes make a demand curve more or less elastic? Explain.

7. Why does marginal utility tend to diminish?

8. What is meant by consumer surplus?

Problems

1. A student has an entertainment budget of $120 per term and spends it on either concert tickets at $10 apiece or movie tickets at $6 apiece. Suppose movie tickets decrease in price, first falling to $4, then $3, then $2. Graph the four budget constraints, with movies on the horizontal axis. If the student's demand for movies, D, is represented by the function $D = 60 - 10p$, where p is the price, graph both the demand curve for movies and the point she will choose on the budget line corresponding to each price.

2. Choose two normal goods and draw a budget constraint illustrating the trade-off between them. Show how the budget line shifts if income increases. Arbitrarily choose a point on the first budget line as the point a particular consumer will select. Now find two points on the new budget line such that the new preferred choice of the consumer must fall between these points.

3. DINKs are households with "double income, no kids," and such households are invading your neighborhood. You decide to take advantage of this influx by starting a gourmet take-out food store. You know that the price elasticity of demand for your food from DINKs is .5 and the income elasticity of demand is 1.5. From the standpoint of the quantity that you sell, which of the following changes will concern you the most?

(a) The number of DINKs in your neighborhood falls by 10 percent.

(b) The average income of DINKs falls by 5 percent.

4 Compare one relatively poor person, with an income of $10,000 per year, with a relatively wealthy person who has an income of $60,000 per year. Imagine that the poor person drinks 15 bottles of wine per year at an average price of $10 per bottle, while the wealthy person drinks 50 bottles of wine per year at an average price of $20 per bottle. If a tax of $1 per bottle is imposed on wine, who pays the greater amount? Who pays the greater amount as a percentage of income? If a tax equal to 10 percent of the value of the wine is imposed, who pays the greater amount? Who pays the greater amount as a percentage of income?

The income elasticity for alcoholic beverages is .62. Consider two people with incomes of $20,000 and $40,000. If all alcohol is taxed at the same rate, by what percentage more will the tax paid by the $40,000 earner be greater than that paid by the $20,000 earner? Why might some people think this unfair?

5. Consider two ways of encouraging local governments to build or expand public parks. One proposal is for the federal government to provide grants for public parks. A second proposal is for the government to agree to pay 25 percent of any expenditures for building or expansion. If the same amount of money would be spent on each program, which do you predict would be most effective in encouraging local parks? Explain your answer, using the ideas of income and substitution effects.

Appendix: Indifference Curves and the Consumption Decision[5]

This chapter explained the consumption decision in terms of the budget constraint facing the individual and the individual's choice of her most preferred point on the budget

---

[5]This appendix may be skipped without loss of understanding of later chapters.

constraint. Effects of changes in prices on the quantity demanded were analyzed in terms of income and substitution effects.

To facilitate a more rigorous analysis of choices and the consequences of changes in prices, economists have developed an extremely useful tool called **indifference curves**. Indifference curves give the combinations of goods among which an individual is indifferent or which yield the same level of utility. This appendix shows how indifference curves can be used to derive the demand curve and to separate more precisely changes in consumption into income and substitution effects.

Using Indifference Curves to Illustrate Consumer Choices

In this chapter solutions to consumer choice problems were characterized as having two stages: First, identify the opportunity set, and second, find the most preferred point in the opportunity set. For consumers with a given income to spend on goods, the budget constraint defines her opportunity set. Figure 6.10 repeats the budget constraint for Fran, who must divide her income between candy bars and CDs. In the chapter, we simply said that Fran would choose the most preferred point along the budget constraint. If she likes CDs a lot, she might choose point *B*; if she has a stronger preference for candy, she might choose point *A*.

The concept of the indifference curve can help us see which of these points she chooses.

The indifference curve shows the various combinations of goods that make a person equally happy. For example, in Figure 6.11, the indifference curve I_0 gives all those combinations of candy bars and compact discs that Fran finds just as attractive as 150 candy bars and 10 CDs (point *A* on the curve). At *B*, for instance, she has 12 CDs but only 130 candy bars—not so much candy, but in her mind the extra CDs make up for the loss. The fact that *B* and *A* are on the same indifference curve means that Fran is indifferent. That is, if you asked her whether she preferred *A* to *B* or *B* to *A*, she would answer that she couldn't care less.

Indifference curves simply reflect preferences between pairs of goods. Unlike demand curves, they have nothing to do with budget constraints or prices. The different com-

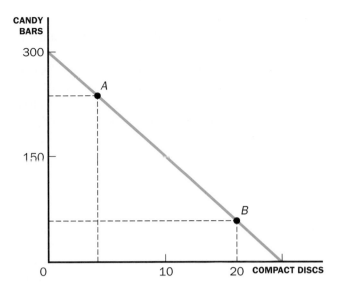

FIGURE 6.10   *Budget Constraint*

The budget constraint defines the opportunity set. Fran can choose any point on or below the budget constraint. If she has strong preferences for CDs, she might choose *B*; if she has strong preferences for candy bars, she might choose point *A*,

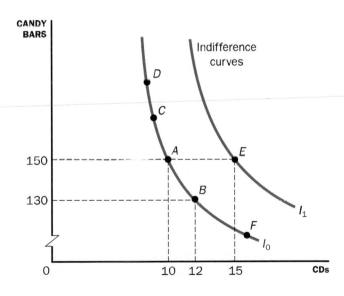

FIGURE 6.11   *Indifference Curves*

An indifference curve traces combinations of goods among which an individual is indifferent. Each reflects Fran's taste for CDs and for candy bars. She is just as well-off (has an identical amount of utility) at all points on the indifference curve I_0: *A*, *B*, *C*, *D*, or *F*.

binations of goods along the indifference curve cost different amounts of money. The indifference curves are drawn by asking an individual which he prefers: 10 candy bars and 2 CDs or 15 candy bars and 1 CD? or 11 candy bars and 2 CDs or 15 candy bars and 1 CD? or 12 candy bars and 2 CDs or 15 candy bars and 1 CD? When he answers, "I am indifferent between the two," the two points that represent those choices are on the same indifference curve.

Moving along the curve in one direction, Fran is willing to accept more CDs in exchange for fewer candy bars; moving in the other direction, she is willing to accept more candy bars in exchange for fewer CDs. Any point on the same indifference curve, by definition, makes her just as happy as any other—whether it is point *A* or *C* or an extreme point like *D*, where she has many candy bars and very few CDs, or *F*, where she has relatively few candy bars but more CDs.

However, if Fran were to receive the same number of candy bars but more CDs than at *A*—say 150 candy bars and 15 CDs (point *E*)—she would be better off on the principle that "more is better." The new indifference curve I_1 illustrates all those combinations of candy bars and CDs that make her just as well-off as the combination of 150 candy bars and 15 CDs.

Figure 6.11 shows two indifference curves for Fran. Because more is better, Fran (or any individual) will prefer a choice on an indifference curve that is higher than another. On the higher indifference curve, she can have more of both items. By definition, we can draw an indifference curve for *any* point in the space of an indifference curve diagram. Also by definition, indifference curves cannot cross, as Figure 6.12 makes clear. Assume that the indifference curves I_0 and I_1 cross at point *A*. That would mean that Fran is indifferent between *A* and all points on I_0, and between *A* and all points on I_1. In particular, she would be indifferent between *A* and *B*, between *A* and *C*, and accordingly between *B* and *C*. But *B* is clearly preferred to *C*; therefore, indifference curves cannot cross.

Indifference Curves and Marginal Rates of Substitution

The slope of the indifference curve measures the number of candy bars that the individual is willing to give up to get

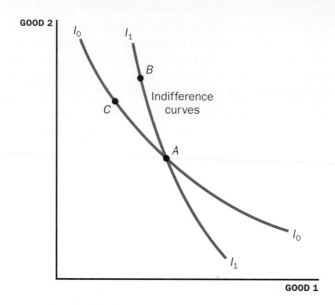

GOOD 2

I_0 I_1

B

Indifference
curves

C

A

I_0

I_1

GOOD 1

FIGURE 6.12   *Why Indifference Curves
Cannot Cross*

If two indifference curves crossed, a logical contradiction
would occur. If curves crossed at point A, then Fran would be
indifferent between A and B, between A and C, and therefore
between B and C. But since B involves higher consumption of
both goods than C, B is clearly preferred to C.

another compact disc. The technical term for the slope of
an indifference curve is the **marginal rate of substitution**.
The marginal rate of substitution tells us how much of one
good an individual is *willing* to give up in return for one
more unit of another. The concept is quite distinct from
the amount a consumer *must* give up, which is determined
by the budget constraint and relative prices.

If Fran's marginal rate of substitution of candy bars for
CDs is 15 to 1, this means that if she is given 1 more CD,
she is willing to give up 15 candy bars. If she only had to
give up 12 candy bars, she would be happier. If she had to
give up 20, she would say, "That's too much—having one
more CD isn't worth giving up twenty candy bars." Of
course, Gary could have quite different attitudes toward
CDs and candy bars. His marginal rate of substitution
might be 25 to 1. He would be willing to give up 25 candy
bars to get 1 more CD.

The marginal rate of substitution rises and falls according to how much of an item an individual already has. For
example, consider point F back in Figure 6.11, where Fran
has a lot of CDs and few candy bars. In this case, Fran al-

ready has bought all her favorite CDs; the marginal CD she
buys now will be something she likes but not something she
is wild over. In other words, because she already has a
large number of CDs, having an additional one is less important. She would rather have some candy bars instead.
Her marginal rate of substitution of candy bars for CDs at
F is very low; for the sake of illustration, let's say that she
would be willing to give up the marginal CD for only 10
candy bars. Her marginal rate of substitution is 10 to 1
(candy bars per CD).

The opposite situation prevails when Fran has lots of
candy bars and few CDs. Since she is eating several candy
bars almost every day, the chance to have more is just not
worth much to her. But since she has few CDs, she does
not yet own all of her favorites. The marginal value of another candy bar is relatively low, while the marginal value
of another CD is relatively high. Accordingly, in this situation, Fran might insist on getting 30 extra candy bars before she gives up 1 CD. Her marginal rate of substitution is
30 to 1 (candy bars per CD).

As we move along an indifference curve, we increase the
amount of one good (like CDs) that an individual has. In
Fran's case, she requires less and less of the other good
(candy bars) to compensate her for each one-unit decrease
in the quantity of the first good (CDs). This principle is
known as the **diminishing marginal rate of substitution**.
As a result of the principle of diminishing marginal rate of
substitution, the slope of the indifference curve becomes
flatter as we move from left to right along the curve.

Using Indifference Curves to Illustrate Choices

By definition, an individual does not care where he sits on
any *given* indifference curve. But he would prefer to be on
the highest indifference curve possible. What pins him down
is his budget constraint. As Figure 6.13 illustrates, the highest indifference curve that a person can attain is the one that
just touches the budget constraint—that is, the indifference
curve that is *tangent* to the budget constraint. The point of
tangency (labeled E) is the point the individual will choose.
Consider any other point on the budget constraint, say A.
The indifference curve through A is below the curve through

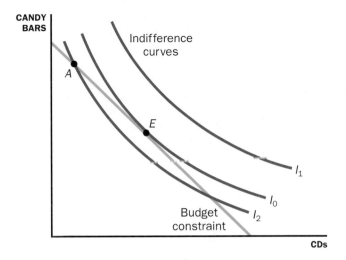

FIGURE 6.13 *Indifference Curves and the Budget Constraint*

The highest feasible indifference curve that can be reached is the one just tangent to the budget constraint, or indifference curve I_0 here. This individual's budget constraint does not permit her to reach I_1, nor would she want to choose point A, which would put her on I_2, since along I_2 she is worse off

E; the individual is better off at E than at A. But consider an indifference curve above I_0, for instance I_1. Since every point on I_1 lies above the budget constraint, there is no point on I_1 that the individual can purchase given his income.

When a curve is tangent to a line, the curve and line have the same slope at the point of tangency. Thus, the slope of the indifference curve equals the slope of the budget constraint at the point of tangency. The slope of the indifference curve is the marginal rate of substitution; the slope of the budget constraint is the relative price. This two-dimensional diagram therefore illustrates a basic principle of consumer choice: *individuals choose the point where the marginal rate of substitution equals the relative price.*

This principle makes sense. If the relative price of CDs and candy bars is 15 (CDs cost $15 and candy bars cost $1) and Fran's marginal rate of substitution is 20, Fran is willing to give up 20 candy bars to get 1 more CD, but only *has* to give up 15; it clearly pays her to buy more CDs and fewer candy bars. If her marginal rate of substitution is 10, she is willing to give up 1 CD for just 10 candy bars; but if she gives up 1 CD, she can get 15 candy bars. She will be better off buying more candy bars and fewer CDs. Thus, if the marginal rate of substitution exceeds the relative price,

Fran is better off if she buys more CDs; if it is less, she is better off if she buys fewer CDs. When the marginal rate of substitution *equals* the relative price, it does not pay for her to either increase or decrease her purchases.

Income Elasticity

Budget constraints and indifference curves show why, while goods normally have a positive income elasticity, some goods may have a negative income elasticity. As incomes increase, the budget constraint shifts out to the right in a parallel line, say from BC in Figure 6.14 to B_1C_1 to B_2C_2. The choices—the points of tangency with the indifference curves—are represented by the points E_0, E_1, and E_2. In panel A, we see the normal case, where as the budget constraint shifts out, more of both candy bars and CDs are consumed. But panel B illustrates the case of inferior goods. Potatoes are on the horizontal axis, and meat is on the vertical. As incomes rise, the points of tangency (E_1 and E_2) move to the left; potato consumption actually falls.

Using Indifference Curves to Derive Demand Curves

Indifference curves and budget constraints can be used to derive the demand curve, to show what happens when prices increase. The analysis consists of two steps.

First, we identify what happens to the budget constraint as, say, the price of CDs increases. We did this earlier in Figure 6.6, but now we can add indifference curves to the analysis. In the budget constraint drawn in Figure 6.15A, we find CDs on the horizontal axis and all other goods on the vertical axis. If Fran buys no CDs, she has $300 to spend on all other goods. At a CD price of $15, she can buy up to 20 CDs, producing the budget line running from point B to C. As the price of CDs increases, the budget constraint rotates in to become steeper. If she buys no CDs, she still has $300 to spend on other goods. But if she buys only CDs, the number of CDs she can buy falls as their price rises. If the price of CDs falls, the budget constraint rotates out to become flatter.

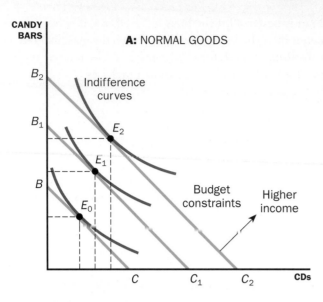

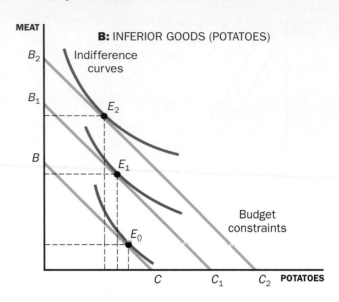

FIGURE 6.14   *Normal and Inferior Goods with Indifference Curves*

Panel A shows the case of two normal goods. An increase in income shifts the budget constraint out from BC to B_1C_1 to B_2C_2, and the consumption of both goods rises from E_0 to E_1 to E_2. Panel B shows the case of an inferior good. As the budget constraint shifts out, consumption of potatoes falls.

For each budget constraint, we find the point of tangency between the indifference curve and the budget constraint, the points labeled F_i, F, and F_d. This shows the point chosen along each budget constraint. Looking at the horizontal axis, we see, at each price, the quantity of CDs purchased. Panel B then plots these quantities for each price. At the price of \$15, Fran chooses 11 CDs; at a price of \$30, she chooses to buy only 6.

Substitution and Income Effects

Indifference curves also permit a precise definition of the substitution and income effects. Figure 6.16 plots some of Jeremy's indifference curves between CDs and candy bars. Jeremy's original budget constraint is line BC and his indifference curve is I_0; the point of tangency, the point he chooses, is point E_0. Suppose the price of candy increases. Now he can buy fewer candy bars, but the number of CDs he can buy, were he to spend all of his income on CDs, is unchanged. Thus, his budget constraint becomes flatter; it

is now line B_2C. While Jeremy originally chose point E_0 on the indifference curve I_0, now he chooses E_1 on the *lower* indifference curve I_1.

The price change has moved Jeremy's choice from E_0 to E_1 for two reasons: the substitution effect and the income effect. To see how this has happened, let's isolate the two effects. First, we focus on the substitution effect by asking what would happen to Jeremy's consumption if we changed relative prices but did not change how well-off he was. To keep him just as well-off as before the price change, we must keep him on the same indifference curve, I_0. Thus, the substitution effect is a movement along an indifference curve. As the price of candy rises, Jeremy, moving down the indifference curve, buys more CDs and fewer candy bars. The movement from E_0 to E_2 is the substitution effect. The budget constraint B_1C_1 represents the *new* prices, but it does not account for the income effect, by definition, since Jeremy is on the same indifference curve that he was on before.

To keep Jeremy on the same indifference curve when we increase the price of candy requires giving Jeremy more income. The line B_1C_1 is the budget constraint with the *new* prices that would leave Jeremy on the same indifference curve. Because prices are the same, the budget constraint

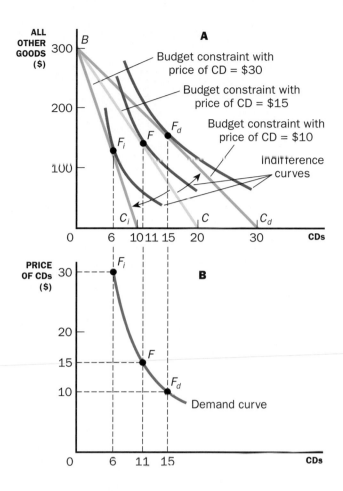

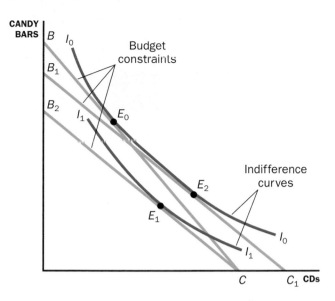

FIGURE 6.16 *Substitution and Income Effects with Indifference Curves*

As the price of candy bars increases, the budget constraint rotates down. The change of Jeremy's choice from E_0 to E_1 can be broken down into an income and a substitution effect. The line B_1C_1 shows the substitution effect, the change in the budget constraint that would occur if relative prices shifted but the level of utility remained the same. (Notice that Jeremy stays on the same indifference curve in this scenario.) The substitution effect alone causes a shift from E_0 to E_2. The shift in the budget constraint from B_1C_1 to B_2C shows the income effect, the change that results from changing the amount of income but leaving relative prices unchanged. The income effect alone causes a shift from E_2 to E_1.

FIGURE 6.15 *Deriving Demand Curves from Shifting Budget Constraints*

In panel A, the budget constraint rotates down to the left as the price of CDs increases, leading Fran to change consumption from F to F_i. The budget constraint rotates to the right when the price of CDs decreases, and Fran moves from F to F_d. Panel B shows the corresponding demand curve for CDs, illustrating how the rising prices lead to a decline in the quantity consumed.

B_1C_1 is paralleled to B_2C. We now need to take away the income that left Jeremy on the same indifference curve. We keep prices the same (at the new levels), and we take away income until we arrive at the new budget constraint B_2C, and the corresponding new equilibrium E_1. The movement from E_2 to E_1 is called the income effect, since only income is changed. We have thus broken down the movement from the old equilibrium, E_0, to the new one, E_1, into the movement from E_0 to E_2, the substitution effect, and the movement from E_2 to E_1, the income effect.

Chapter 7

The Firm's Costs

Key Questions

1. What do cost curves—curves relating costs to the level of production—look like in an economy where output depends on a single input to production?

2. What is the relationship between long-run and short-run cost curves?

3. What additional issues are raised when there are several inputs?

*T*he previous three chapters focused on the decisions of households and individuals. In this chapter, the focus shifts to the decisions of firms. Firms make decisions concerning what and how much to produce, and how to produce it, with the aim of maximizing their profits.

The basic competitive model is, once again, our starting point. Many firms, all making the same product, compete with one another to sell that product to well-informed customers, who recognize and act upon any price differences. Because customers are well informed about prices, all firms in a competitive market must accept the price set for their product by the forces of supply and demand in the market as a whole. Any firm trying to sell above that price will lose all its customers. Firms in competitive markets are, therefore, *price takers*. The classic example of competitive markets are agricultural markets—thousands of farmers, say, producing milk. A dairy farmer does not waste time wondering what price to set for the milk he has to sell. He knows he will get the "going price."

A firm does, however, have some control over its costs. The firm's total costs are affected by, among other things, its level of production, and its choice of inputs (how to produce

what it produces). Chapter 8 shows how a firm uses this relationship to choose the level of production that maximizes its profits. This chapter focuses on how firms minimize their costs and how costs are affected by the level of production.

Even though we talk in terms of "production" and "goods," it is important to bear in mind that only one-third of the U.S. economy consists of industries that produce goods in the conventional sense—manufacturing, mining, construction, and agriculture. The other two-thirds of the economy produces primarily services—industries like transportation, education, health care, wholesale and retail trade, and finance. The principles laid out here, however, apply equally to these other sectors.

Profits, Costs, and Factors of Production

A business that continually incurs losses over time will cease to exist because it will not have enough money to pay its bills. Businesses are under constant pressure to make money. The motivation of making as much money as possible—maximizing profits—provides a useful starting point for discussing the behavior of firms in competitive markets.

The definition of **profits** is simple:

$$\text{profits} = \text{revenues} - \text{costs}.$$

The **revenues** a business receives from selling its products are calculated as the quantity it sells of the product multiplied by the price of the product. A firm's *costs* are defined as the total expense of producing the good.

What the firm uses to produce the goods are called inputs or *factors of production*: labor, materials, and capital goods. The firm's total costs are simply the sum of the costs of these inputs. Labor costs are what the company pays for the workers it hires and the managers it employs to supervise the workers. The costs of materials include raw materials and intermediate goods. Intermediate goods are whatever supplies the company purchases from other firms—such as seeds, fertilizer, and gasoline for a farm; iron ore, coal, coke, limestone, and electric power for a steel company. The costs of capital goods include the cost of machinery and structures such as buildings and factories.

All firms work to keep their costs as low as possible. For given prices and levels of output, a firm maximizes its profits by finding the least costly way of producing its output. Thus, profit-maximizing firms are also cost-minimizing firms. Within limits, firms can vary the mix of labor, materials, and capital goods they use; and they will do so until they find the lowest cost method of producing a given quality and quantity of product. The simplest way of understanding how firms find the lowest cost point is to look at a firm with only two factors of production, one fixed (such as the amount of land a farmer has or the number of plants a manufacturer has) and one that varies with the level of production (such as the number of workers the firm hires). Not surprisingly, inputs that vary with the level of production are said to be variable.

Production with One Variable Input

A wheat farmer with a fixed amount of land who uses only labor to produce his crop is our example. The more labor he applies to the farm (his own time, plus the time of work-

ers that he hires), the greater the output. Labor is the single variable factor (input).

The relationship between the quantity of inputs used in production and the level of output is called the **production function.** Figure 7.1 shows the farmer's production function; the data supporting the figure are set forth in Table 7.1. The increase in output corresponding to a unit increase in any factor of production, labor in this case, is the **marginal product** of that factor. For example, when the number of hours worked per year rises from 8,000 to 9,000, output increases by 10,000 bushels, from 155,000 to 165,000. The marginal product of an extra 1,000 hours of labor is, according, 10,000 bushels. The marginal product is given in the last column of the table. Diagrammatically, it is given by the slope of the production function. The slope of a curve is the change along the vertical axis (the increase in output) from a unit increase along the horizontal axis (the increase in labor input).

Diminishing Returns   In the case of the wheat farmer, as more labor is added to a fixed amount of land, the

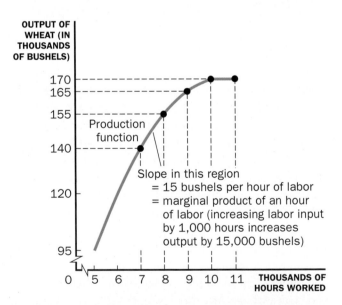

FIGURE 7.1   *Production Function with Diminishing Returns to an Input*

As the amount of the input (labor) increases, so does the output (wheat). But there are diminishing returns to labor; each increase in labor results in successively smaller increases in wheat output. Since the slope of the curve is the marginal product of labor, on the graph, this means the slope flattens out as the amount of labor increases.

TABLE 7.1

Level of Output with Different Amounts of Labor

Number of hours worked	Amount of wheat produced (bushels)	Marginal product (additional bushels produced by 1,000 additional hours of labor)
5,000	95,000	
6,000	120,000	25,000
7,000	140,000	20,000
8,000	155,000	15,000
9,000	165,000	10,000
10,000	170,000	5,000
11,000	170,000	0

marginal product of labor diminishes. This is another application of the concept of *diminishing returns,* which we originally encountered in Chapter 2. In the case of a firm's production function, diminishing returns implies that each additional unit of labor generates a smaller increase in output than the last. Increasing the number of hours worked from 7,000 to 8,000 raises output by 15,000 bushels, but increasing the hours worked from 8,000 to 9,000 raises output by only 10,000 bushels. Diminishing returns sets in with a vengeance at higher levels of input; moving from 10,000 to 11,000 hours worked adds nothing. Diagrammatically, diminishing returns are represented by the slope flattening out as the amount of labor increases. It is clear that with diminishing returns, increases in input lead to less than proportionate increases in output; doubling the input results in output that is less than twice as large.

WRAP-UP

Diminishing Returns

As more and more of one input is added, *while other inputs remain unchanged*, the marginal product of the added input diminishes.

Increasing Returns Although a production function with diminishing returns is an important case, other cases do occur. Figure 7.2 shows a production func-

tion where increasing an input (here, labor) raises output more than proportionately. A firm with this kind of production function has *increasing returns*. In the single-input case depicted, it is clear that the marginal product of the input increases with the amount produced; that is, when the firm is producing a lot, adding one more worker increases output by more than it does when the firm is producing little.

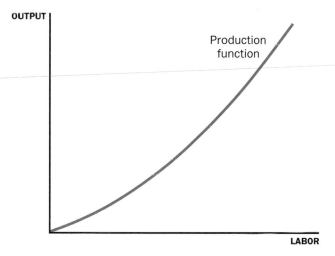

FIGURE 7.2   *Production Function with Increasing Returns to an Input*

As the amount of labor increases, so does output. But the returns to labor are increasing in this case; successive increases in labor result in successively larger increases in output. On the graph, this means the slope becomes steeper as the amount of labor increases.

Imagine a business that picks up garbage. If this business counts only one out of every five houses as customers, it will have a certain cost of production. But if the company can expand to picking up the garbage from two out of every five houses, while it will need more workers, the workers will be able to drive a shorter distance and pick up more garbage faster. Thus, a doubling of output can result from a less than doubling of labor. Many examples of increasing returns, like garbage collection, involve providing service to more people in a given area. Telephone companies and electric utilities are two other familiar instances.

Constant Returns

In between the cases of diminishing and increasing returns lies the case of *constant returns,* shown in Figure 7.3. Each additional unit of input increases output by the same amount, and the relationship between input and output is a straight line.

Types of Costs and Cost Curves

The production function is important to the firm because the inputs determine the cost of production. These costs are key determinants of the firm's profits and its decisions about how much to produce.

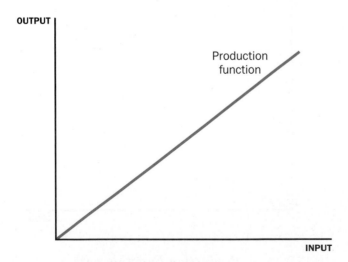

FIGURE 7.3 *Production Function with Constant Returns to an Input*

The marginal product of labor is constant, neither increasing nor diminishing as the firm expands production. On the graph, this means that the slope does not change.

Fixed and Variable Costs

Some costs associated with inputs do not vary as the firm changes the level of production. For instance, the firm may need to hire someone to run the personnel office and someone to supervise the workers, and the cost of these inputs do not change as production varies, within limits. These costs are called **fixed costs.** Whether the firm produces nothing or produces at maximum capacity, it antes up the same fixed costs. Figure 7.4 shows how costs depend on output. Panel A depicts fixed costs as a horizontal line—by definition, they do not depend on the level of output. As an example, consider a would-be farmer who has the opportunity to buy a farm and its equipment for $25,000. His fixed costs are $25,000.

Variable costs correspond to inputs that vary with the level of production. Any cost that the firm can change during the time period under study is a variable cost. To the extent that the costs of such items as labor and materials can go up or down as output does, these are variable costs. If our farmer has only one input to vary, labor, then his variable cost would be, say, $15 per hour for each worker. The variable costs corresponding to levels of output listed in Table 7.1 are shown in Table 7.2 and plotted in Figure 7.4B. As output increases, so do variable costs, so the curve slopes upward.

Total Costs

Table 7.2 also includes a column labeled "Total cost." **Total costs** are defined as the sum of fixed and variable costs, so this column is obtained by adding the farmer's fixed costs of $25,000 to the variable costs. Thus,

$$\text{total costs} = \text{total variable costs} + \text{fixed costs.}$$

The total cost curve, summarizing these points, is shown in Figure 7.4C.

Marginal Cost and the Marginal Cost Curve

Throughout this book we have emphasized that rational decision making depends on evaluating trade-offs in terms of marginal costs and benefits. Should Ann spend another hour at the party? To make the decision, she weighs the marginal cost—the other things she could do with an hour of her time—against the marginal benefit—the enjoyment she will experience from remaining at the party another hour. Firms apply this same logic in their

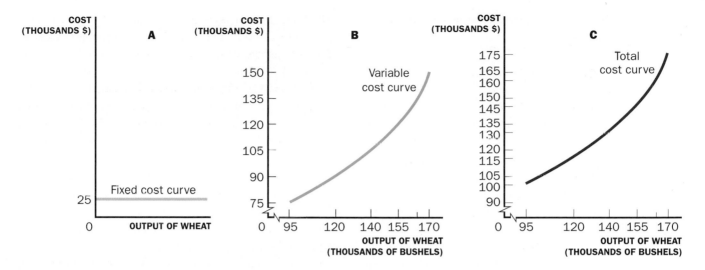

FIGURE 7.4   *Fixed, Variable, and Total Cost Curves*

Panel A shows a firm's fixed cost; by definition, fixed costs do not depend on the level of output. Panel B shows a firm's variable costs, which rise with the level of production. The increasing slope of the curve indicates that it costs more and more to produce at the margin, which is a sign of diminishing returns. Panel C shows a total cost curve. It has the same slope as the variable cost curve but is higher by the amount of the fixed costs.

decision making: They focus on marginal costs and benefits. Thus, one of the most important cost concepts is **marginal cost,** which we define here as the extra cost corresponding to each additional unit of production.

In the case of the wheat farmer's costs (see Table 7.2), as he increases labor input from 7,000 hours to 8,000

hours, output increases from 140,000 bushels to 155,000 bushels. Thus, the *marginal product* of the extra 1,000 hours of labor is 15,000 bushels. If the wage is $15 per hour, the cost of increasing output by 15,000 bushels is $15,000 ($15 × 1,000 extra hours). The marginal cost of the extra 15,000 bushels is $15,000. To determine the

TABLE 7.2

Cost of Producing Wheat

Output (bushels	Labor required (hours)	Total variable cost (at a wage of $15 per hour)	Total cost ($)	Marginal cost ($ per bushel)	Average cost ($ per bushel)	Average variable cost ($ per bushel)
95,000	5,000	75,000	100,000	—	1.05	.79
120,000	6,000	90,000	115,000	.60	.96	.75
140,000	7,000	105,000	130,000	.75	.93	.75
155,000	8,000	120,000	145,000	1.00	.94	.77
165,000	9,000	135,000	160,000	1.50	.97	.82
170,000	10,000	150,000	175,000	3.00	1.03	.88

marginal cost per bushel, we divide the change in cost (*C*) by the change in output (*Q*):

$$\frac{\Delta C}{\Delta Q} = \frac{\$15,000}{15,000} = \$1 \text{ per bushel.}$$

The *marginal cost curve* traces out the marginal cost for each additional unit of output. To derive the marginal cost curve using a graph, we start with the total cost curve. The marginal cost is the change in total cost (movements along the vertical axis) resulting from each unit increase in output (movements along the horizontal axis). This is shown in panel A of Figure 7.5. Panel B of Figure 7.5 shows this relationship in a different way. The slope of the line tangent to the total cost curve at Q_1 gives the marginal cost of Q_1. Thus, the marginal cost curve represents the slope of the total cost curve at each quantity of output.

Panel C of Figure 7.5 shows the marginal cost curve for the wheat farm example. Note that the curve is upward sloping, like the total cost curve, which reflects the fact that as more is produced, it becomes harder and harder to increase output further. This is an application of the familiar principle of diminishing marginal returns. In our wheat farm example, suppose the farmer is considering increasing production by 1,000 bushels. If his current level of output is 140,000 bushels, the marginal cost of this increase will be $1,000. But if his current level of output is 155,000 bushels, increasing production by 1,000 units will entail a marginal cost of $1,500. At the higher level of output, the marginal cost is greater because of diminishing marginal returns to labor.

Average Cost and the Average Cost Curve

A business firm also is concerned with its **average cost**. This is the total cost (*TC*) divided by output (*Q*), or

$$\text{average cost} = TC/Q.$$

The *average cost curve* gives average costs corresponding to different levels of output. Figure 7.6 shows the average cost curve for our wheat farm example (along with the marginal cost curve, for reasons indicated below). Working from the total cost curve (see Figure 7.4C and Table 7.2), we derive the average cost curve by dividing total costs (*TC*) by quantity (*Q*) at each level of output. Thus, since it takes 7,000 hours of labor to produce 140,000 bushels of wheat, and the wage is $15 per hour, the total cost is

$105,000, for an average cost of $0.93 per bushel ($105,000/140,000 bushels). When output increases to 155,000 bushels, costs increase to $145,000, for an average cost of $0.94 per bushel.

The typical average cost curve is U-shaped, like the one in Figure 7.6. To understand why, we need to think about the two parts of total costs—fixed costs and variable costs. Just to start production usually requires a significant expense on inputs. These fixed costs do not vary with the level of output. As output increases, these costs are spread over more units of output, so the average cost of each unit of output that is due to the firm's fixed costs will fall. If these were the only costs the firm faced, average costs would decline as output increases.

Firms also face variable costs. Because of diminishing returns, beyond some level of output the firm requires more and more labor to produce each additional unit of output. It may be almost impossible to increase output beyond some point. This is why the production function in Figure 7.1 flattens out as output rises and the total cost curve in Figure 7.4C becomes steeper as output increases.

Just as we defined average costs as total costs divided by output, we define **average variable costs** as total variable costs divided by output:

$$\text{average variable costs} = \frac{\text{total variable costs}}{\text{output}}.$$

Average variable costs increase with output as the law of diminishing returns sets in with strength. The final column of Table 7.2 gives the average variable costs associated with producing wheat. At low levels of output, the falling average fixed costs dominate, and average total costs decline. But once a high-enough level of output is achieved, rising average variable costs start to dominate and average total costs increase. This leads to the typical U-shape of the average cost curve, as shown in Figure 7.6.

Even if the average cost curve is U-shaped, the output at which average costs are lowest may be very great, so high that there is not enough demand to justify producing that much. Thus, when economists say that an industry has declining average costs, they mean that those costs are declining over the level of output that is likely to prevail in the market.

Relationship Between Average and Marginal Cost Curves

The relationship between average costs and marginal costs is reflected in Figure 7.6. The marginal cost curve intersects the average cost

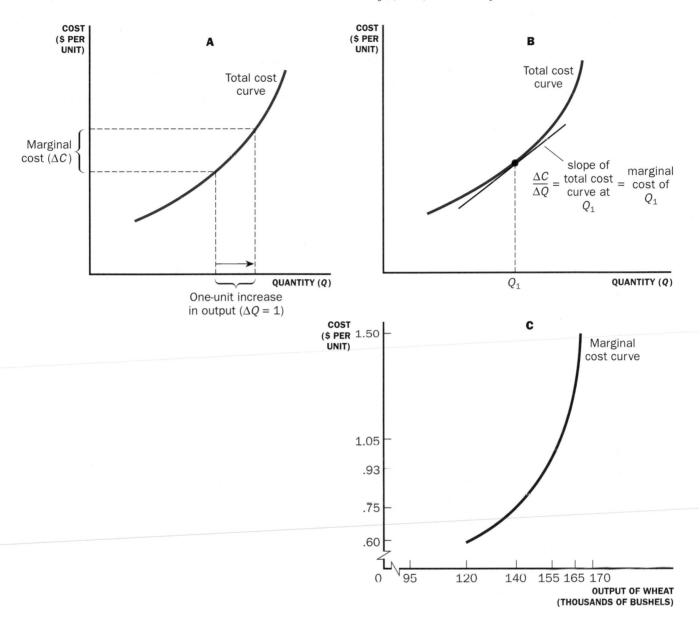

FIGURE 7.5 *Marginal Cost and the Marginal Cost Curve*

Marginal cost is the change in total cost resulting from a one-unit increase in output, as illustrated in panel A. Thus, marginal cost is the slope of the total cost curve at any given point ($\Delta C / \Delta Q$) (panel B). Panel C shows the marginal cost curve for the wheat farm example. Like the total cost curve, the marginal cost curve is upward sloping, reflecting diminishing marginal returns.

curve at the bottom of the U—the *minimum* average cost. To understand why the marginal cost curve will *always* intersect the average cost curve at its lowest point, consider the relationship between average and marginal costs. As long as the marginal cost is below the average cost, produc-

ing an extra unit of output will pull down average costs. Thus, everywhere the marginal cost is below the average cost, the average cost curve is declining. If the marginal cost is above the average cost, then producing an extra unit of output will raise average costs. So everywhere that the

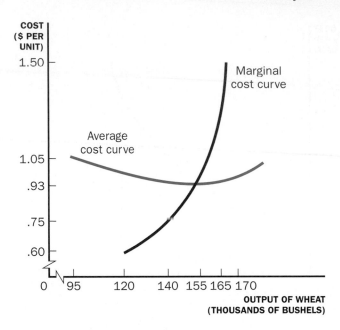

FIGURE 7.6   *Marginal and Average Cost Curves*

This figure shows the marginal cost curve and average cost curve for the wheat farm example of Table 7.2. With diminishing returns to an input, marginal costs increase with the level of output, giving the marginal cost curve its typical, upward-sloping shape. Average costs initially fall with increased output, as fixed costs are spread over a larger amount of output, and then begin to rise as diminishing returns to the variable input become increasingly important. Thus, the average cost curve is typically U-shaped. With a U-shaped average cost curve, the marginal cost curve will cross the average cost curve at its minimum.

marginal cost is above the average cost, the average cost curve must be rising.

The distinction between average and marginal costs is like the relationship between a student's grade point average (GPA) and her average grade in the next semester. How does the student increase her GPA? By getting grades higher than her GPA in the next semester. GPA is like average cost, and the next semester's grades are like marginal cost.

Changing Input Prices and Cost Curves

The costs curves shown thus far are based on the fixed prices of the inputs (factors) the firm uses. An increase in the price of a variable input like labor would shift the total, average, and marginal cost curves upward, as shown in Figure 7.7. An increase in fixed costs, such as an increase in the cost of the wheat farmer's land, shifts the total cost and

average cost curves upward. Since fixed costs do not vary with output (by definition), a change in fixed costs does not affect the marginal cost curve.

Example: Deborah's Web Consulting Business

A simple example illustrates these various cost concepts and relates them to the notions of opportunity costs introduced in Chapter 2.

Deborah tutors for the computer science department at her college, earning $5 per hour. She works a total of 20

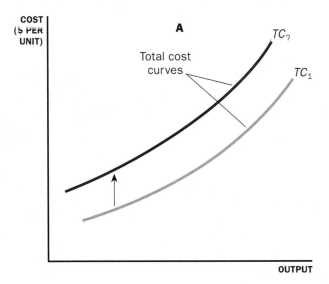

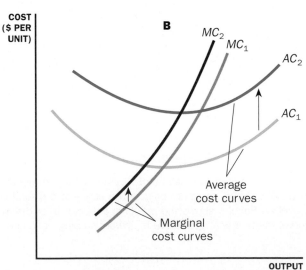

FIGURE 7.7   *How Changing Input Prices Affect Cost Curves*

An increase in the price of a variable factor shifts the total, average, and marginal cost curves upward.

TABLE 7.3

Deborah's Costs If She Works 10 Hours Doing Web Consulting			
	Fixed Costs	**Variable Costs**	**Total**
Sunk costs			
Software	$125.00		$125.00
Laptop lease	$ 60.00		$ 60.00
Opportunity costs			
Forgone earnings		$50.00	$ 50.00
Total	$185.00	$50.00	$235.00
Revenue			$200.00
Profit			$ (35.00)

TABLE 7.4

Deborah's Costs If She Works 20 Hours Doing Web Consulting			
	Fixed Costs	**Variable Costs**	**Total**
Sunk costs			
Software	$125.00		$125.00
Laptop lease	$ 60.00		$ 60.00
Opportunity costs			
Forgone earnings		$100.00	$100.00
Total	$185.00	$100.00	$285.00
Revenue			$400.00
Profit			$115.00

hours per week, which is the most she can devote to working while still maintaining good grades in her own courses. Recently, she decided to start her own business helping professors create Web pages for their classes. Deborah plans to charge $20 per hour for this service.

To get started, she had to purchase $125 worth of software, and she needed to obtain a faster laptop. A local computer store leased her the laptop she needs for $60 per month.

Tables 7.3 and 7.4 set out the costs Deborah faces in her first week of business if she works 10 hours for her new business (and continues to work 10 hours tutoring) and if she works 20 hours for her new business (and so quits tutoring completely).

Since Deborah has already purchased the software and leased the computer, these are fixed costs; they remain the same whether she decides to work 10 hours or 20 hours on her new business. These are also sunk costs; even if she decides to quit, she will be out the cost of the software and the first month's lease on the laptop.

What are her variable costs? For each additional hour she spends on her Web business, she works 1 hour less tutoring, losing the $5 she could have made by tutoring.

So her variable costs consist of the $5 per hour *opportunity cost.*

We can now calculate Deborah's profits for the week. If she works 10 hours, her revenue is $200 (10 hours × $20 per hour). Her total costs are $125 + $60 + $50 = $235. She suffers a loss of $35. If she works 20 hours, her revenue rises to $400, while her total costs rise only to $125 + 60 + $100 = $285. She makes a profit of $400 − $285 = $115. So she would be better off working the entire 20 hours she has available for her new business and quitting her tutoring job completely. Notice that since Deborah has $185 in sunk costs, she is better off consulting for 10 hours than closing up her business entirely. If she works 10 hours doing Web consulting, her revenues are $200, more than enough to cover her variable costs of $50.

Short-Run and Long-Run Cost Curves

Up to this point, we have referred to the distinction between inputs that are fixed (their cost does not vary with quantity produced) and inputs that are variable (their cost does depend on quantity produced). We have sidestepped the fact that inputs, and costs, may be fixed for some period of time, but if the time period is long enough, they can vary with production. Take the inputs of labor and machines, for example. In the short run, the supply of machines may be fixed. Output is then increased only by increasing labor. In the longer run, both machines and workers can be adjusted. The short-run cost curve, then, is the cost of production with a *given* stock of machines. The long-run cost curve is the cost of production when all factors are adjusted.[1]

---

[1]The distinction between short-run and long-run costs corresponds to the distinction between short-run and long-run supply curves introduced in Chapter 4. Chapter 8 will make clear the relationship. It is an exaggeration to think that only capital goods are fixed in the short run while all of labor is variable. In some cases, capital goods may easily be varied; a firm can, for instance, rent cars. And in some cases, as when a company has long-term contracts with its workers, it may be very difficult to vary labor in the short run.

Cost Concepts

Fixed costs:	Costs that do not depend on output
Variable costs:	Costs that depend on output
Total costs:	Total costs of producing output = fixed costs + variable costs
Marginal costs:	Extra cost of producing an extra unit
Average costs:	Total costs divided by output
Average variable costs:	Total variable costs divided by output

Short-Run Cost Curves

If we think of the number of machines as being fixed in the short run, and labor as the principal input that can be varied, our earlier analysis of production with a single variable factor provides a good description of short-run cost curves. Thus, short-run *average* cost curves are normally U-shaped.

Long-Run Cost Curves

Though short-run average cost curves for a given manufacturing facility are typically U-shaped, the long-run average cost curve may be different. As production grows, it will pay at some point to build a second plant, and then a third, a fourth, and so on. Panel A of Figure 7.8 shows the total costs of producing different levels of output, assuming that the firm builds one plant. This curve is marked TC_1. It also shows the total costs of producing different levels of output assuming the firm builds two plants (TC_2) and three plants (TC_3). How many plants will the company build? Clearly, the firm wishes to minimize the (total) costs of producing at any level of output. Thus, the *relevant* total cost curve is the lower boundary of the three curves, which is heavily shaded. Between 0 and Q_1, the firm produces using one plant; between Q_1 and Q_2, it uses two plants; and for outputs larger than Q_2, it uses three plants.

We can see the same results in panel B, using average cost curves. Obviously, if the firm minimizes the total costs of producing any particular output, it minimizes the average cost of producing that output. The figure shows the av-

International Perspective

Comparing Costs in Different Countries

The cost of producing a good differs in different countries. Part of the reason for this is the marked differences in the costs of inputs. In the United States, labor costs tend to be high. In many developing countries, the cost of capital is high. But an important source of differences in cost curves is differences in *knowledge* or *information*. Firms in some countries seem to be systematically more efficient than firms in others (just as some firms in the United States are more efficient than others). That is, the *quantity* of inputs required to produce any output is lower.

McKinsey, a large international consulting firm (http://www.mckinseyquarterly.com), has been comparing the efficiency of firms in the same industry in different countries and has found marked differences. In comparing the United States, Japan, and Germany, McKinsey consultants found that in four of the five industries they studied, capital was less efficient in Japan and Germany than it was in the United States. These differences in efficiency were traced to a number of different sources. For example, in the auto industry the use of more flexible assembly plant organizations and closer cooperation between suppliers and auto firms in both Japan and the United States gave them an edge over Germany in using inputs efficiently. In the telecommunications industry, U.S. firms have been more aggressive in offering cheap phone access and creating new products and services, including call waiting, toll-free numbers, and voice mail. As a result, Americans make many more calls per capita than do Japanese or German consumers. The resulting higher volume of calls has led to higher utilization of the wires and switches that make up the phone network, spreading the fixed cost of the network over a much larger volume of calls than in either Japan or Germany.

SOURCE: Raj Agrawal, Stephen Findley, Sean Greene, Kathryn Huang, Aly Jeddy, William Lewis, and Markus Petry, "Capital Productivity: Why the US Leads and Why It Matters," *McKinsey Quarterly* No. 3 (1996): 38–55.

Because of cheaper, more comprehensive phone services in the U.S., Americans make many more calls per capita than do Japanese or German consumers.

---

erage cost curves corresponding to the firm's producing with one, two, and three plants. The company chooses the number of plants that minimizes its average costs, given the level of output it plans to produce. Thus, if the firm plans to produce less than Q_1, it builds only one plant; AC_1 is less than AC_2 for all outputs less than Q_1. If the firm plans to produce between Q_1 and Q_2, it builds two plants, because AC_2 is, in this interval, less than either AC_1 or AC_3.

Similarly, for outputs greater than Q_2, the firm builds three plants.

In this case, the long-run average cost curve is the shaded bumpy curve in Figure 7.8B. When we draw a long-run average cost curve, we will typically ignore the bumps and draw a smooth curve. The bumps arise because we have ignored the many options the firm has besides building a new plant. If the firm is operating one

Internet Connection

Economic Definitions

Keeping the terms *average cost, marginal cost, variable cost, diminishing returns,* and *economics of scale* straight can be confusing. Investopedia provides an online dictionary of economic terms at http://www.investopedia.com/dictionary/ . Another useful source of economic definitions is the classroom page maintained by theShortrun.com (http:// (www.theshortrun.com/main.html).

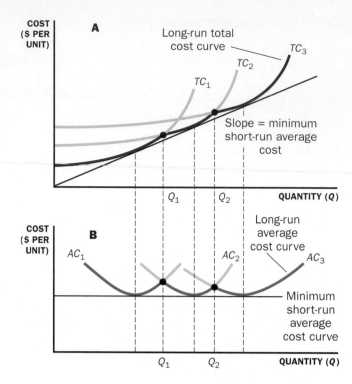

FIGURE 7.8   *Short-Run and Long-Run Cost Curves*

Panel A shows a series of short-run total cost curves, TC_1, TC_2, and TC_3, each representing a different level of fixed capital input. In the long run, a cost-minimizing firm can choose any of these, so the long-run total cost curve will be the lowest cost of producing any level of output, as shown by the heavily shaded lower boundary of the curves. Panel B shows a series of short-run average cost curves, AC_1, AC_2, and AC_3, each representing a different level of fixed capital input. In the long run, a cost-minimizing firm can choose any of these, so the long-run average cost curve will be the shaded lower boundary of the curves.

plant, it can expand its existing plant, say, by adding a new assembly line, rather than building a whole new plant. Or it can add new machines to its current plant. These types of adjustments would lead to series of total cost curves between TC_1 and TC_2 shown in the figure. When we take into account all the options the firm has to adjust its fixed costs, the bumps in the long-run average cost curve will become smaller and smaller, allowing us to ignore them in most cases.

We now need to ask whether long-run average cost curves are normally flat or slope upward or downward. To answer this question, we need to ask what happens when all inputs increase together. What happens, for example, if the firm doubles the number of plants it operates and doubles the labor it employs? If, when all of the inputs increase together and in proportion, output increases just in proportion, there are **constant returns to scale.** With inputs (and therefore costs) rising by the same proportion as output, average costs remain constant; the long-run average cost curve is flat. If output increases less than proportionately, there are **diminishing returns to scale.** Costs rise more than output, and average costs rise; the long-run average cost curve slopes upward. Finally, if output increases more than proportionately, there are **increasing returns to scale,** sometimes described as **economies of scale.** In this case, costs rise less than output, and average costs fall; the long-run average cost curve slopes downward.

Many economists argue that constant returns to scale are most prevalent in manufacturing; a firm can increase its production simply by replicating its plants. Then the long-run average cost curve is flat and long-run average costs equal minimal short-run average costs. When average cost is constant, the marginal costs of additional output must be equal to the average cost (otherwise average cost would be changing), so the long-run average cost curve and the long-run marginal cost curve are the same.

There are, however, also costs to running a firm—the overhead costs. The firm must bear these costs whether it operates 1, 2, or 100 plants. These overhead costs include not only the costs of the corporate headquarters, but also the basic costs of designing the original plant. Thus, we commonly think of the long-run average cost curve as slightly downward sloping, as in Figure 7.9A.

But sometimes small is beautiful, and big is bad. In these cases there are diminishing returns to scale. As the firm tries to grow, adding additional plants, it faces increasing managerial problems; it may have to add layer upon layer of management, and each of these layers increases its cost. When the firm is very small, the owner can watch all his workers. When the firm has grown to 10 employees, the owner can no longer supervise his workers efficiently; a new supervisor may be needed every time his firm hires 10 more workers. By the time the firm has grown to 100 workers, he has 10 supervisors. Now the owner spends most of his time looking after the supervisors, not the workers directly.

Eventually, the owner finds it difficult to keep tabs on the supervisors, so it becomes necessary to hire a manager for them. Notice that in this pattern, the number of supervisors and managers is a growing proportion of the workers in the firm. An organization with 10 workers requires only 1 supervisor; with 100 workers, it requires 10 supervisors and a manager; with 1,000 workers, 100 supervisors, 10 managers, and 1 supermanager. Besides the raw numbers of administrative people, decisions now must pass through a number of layers of bureaucracy, and communication will be slower.

Increasing returns to scale are possible in some industries, even for very large outputs. As the firm produces a higher output, it can take advantage of machines that are larger and more efficient than those used by smaller firms.

If there are increasing returns to scale, then the long-run average cost curve and the marginal cost curve will be downward sloping, as in Figure 7.9C.

Production with Many Factors

The basic principles of the case with only two factors—one fixed, one variable—apply also to firms producing many products with many different inputs. The only fundamental difference is that with many factors it becomes possible to produce the same output in several different ways. Cost minimization, therefore, involves weighing the costs of different mixes of inputs. (The analysis is somewhat more complicated, and is in the appendix to this chapter.)

Cost Minimization

There are usually several ways a good can be produced, using different quantities of various inputs. Table 7.5 illustrates two alternative ways of making car frames, one a highly automated process requiring little labor and the other a less automated process that uses more assembly-line workers. The table shows the daily wage and capital costs for each process. Each method produces the same quantity of output (say, 10,000 car frames per day). In this

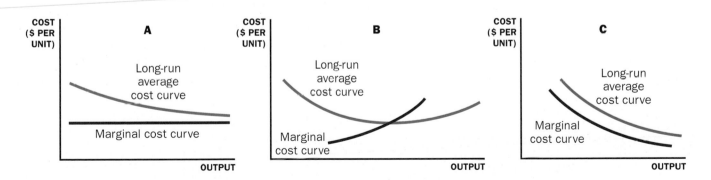

FIGURE 7.9 *Long-Run Average Costs*

Panel A shows that with overhead costs, long-run average costs may be declining, but they flatten out as output increases. In panel B, with managerial costs increasing with the scale of the firm, eventually average and marginal costs may start to rise. Panel C shows that if there are increasing returns to scale, long-run costs may be continuously falling.

The Firm's Costs: Key Ideas

1. Profits are equal to total revenues minus total costs.
2. Marginal cost is the extra cost of producing one more unit of output. Marginal cost is normally increasing at higher levels of output as diminishing returns sets in.
3. Average fixed costs decline as output increases, but average variable costs eventually rise. As a result, the average total cost curve is typically U-shaped.
4. The long-run average cost curve traces out the lower boundaries of the short-run average cost curve.
5. Returns to scale: There are economies of scale if doubling all inputs more than doubles output, and when there are economies of scale, the long-run average total cost curve slopes downward. There are diseconomies of scale if doubling all inputs less than

doubles output, and when there are diseconomies of scale, the long-run average total cost curve slopes upward. There are constant returns to scale if doubling all inputs doubles output; in that case, the long-run average total cost curve is flat.

Relationships between the cost curves

1. The marginal cost at output level Q is the slope of the total cost curve at output level Q.
2. The average cost curve is falling when the marginal cost is less than the average cost; the average cost curve is rising when the marginal cost is greater than the average cost. Consequently, the marginal cost curve always intersects the average cost curve at the point where average costs are at their minimum.

---

simple example, we assume all workers are identical (of equal skill) and hence get paid the same wage, and that all machines cost the same. As we can see from the table, the less automated process clearly costs more at the given costs of labor ($20 per worker per hour) and machines (rental costs equal $1,000 per day).

Although this table provides only two stark alternatives, it should be clear that in some cases the alternative possibilities for production will form a continuum, where the input of one increases a bit, the input of another falls a bit, and output remains the same. In other words, the firm can smoothly substitute one input for another. For instance, in

producing cars, different machines vary slightly in the degree of automation. Machines requiring less and less labor to run them cost more. When firms make their decisions about investment, they thus have a wide range of intermediate choices between the two described in the table.

The Principle of Substitution

One of the most important consequences of the principle of cost minimization in the case of multiple factors of production is that when the price of one input (say, labor) increases relative to that of other factors of production, the change in

TABLE 7.5

Costs of Production		
Inputs	More automated process	Less automated process
Labor	50 man hours @ $20 = $1,000	500 man hours @ $20 = $10,000
Machines	5 machines @ $1,000 = $5,000	2 machines @ $1,000 = $ 2,000
Total	$6,000	$12,000

CASE IN POINT

The Principle of Substitution and Global Warming

In the two hundred years since the beginning of the industrial revolution, there has been an enormous increase in the amount of carbon dioxide (CO_2) in the atmosphere, and concentrations continue to grow. There is an increasing consensus that the higher concentration of CO_2 and related gases (called greenhouse gases) will lead to global warming, with potentially significant impacts on the environment. Reflecting this consensus, the countries of the world signed an agreement in Rio de Janiero in 1992 to work towards limiting the growth of greenhouse gases, and in a subsequent meeting in 1997, in Kyoto, Japan, an effort was made to strengthen the international commitment to greenhouse gas reductions. But these political initiatives have yet to produce substantial reductions in greenhouse gases.

From an economic perspective, the principle of substitution is at the heart of the problem of greenhouse gas reductions. Slowing down the rate of increase in greenhouse gases entails using less energy, and substituting away from sources of energy that produce large amounts of greenhouse gases—like coal—towards sources of energy that produce less—like natural gas—or none at all—like hydroelectric power. With this objective in mind, in 1993 the Clinton administration proposed a carbon tax. This tax would have been levied on fuels in proportion to how much they contributed to greenhouse gases. Although the proposal never came to fruition, in part because it was adamantly opposed by powerful gas, coal, and oil interests, it remains a strong policy option should the prevention of global warming gain broader political momentum. ●

mated process will cost $17,000. Both processes rise in cost, but the less automated process rises less. It now becomes the less costly method. As a consequence, firms will switch from the more automated process to the less automated process. In this way, they are able to substitute away from the factor whose price has risen (machines in this case).

An increase in the price of any input shifts the cost function up. The amount by which the cost function shifts up depends on several factors, including how much of the input was being used in the first place and how easy it is to substitute other inputs. If the production process uses a great deal of the input, then the cost curve will shift up a lot. If there is a large increase in the price of an input, and the firm cannot easily substitute other inputs, then the cost curve will shift up more than it would if substitution of other inputs were easy.

In some cases, substitution is quick and easy; in other cases, it may take time and be difficult. When the price of oil increased fourfold in 1973 and doubled again in 1979, firms found many ways to economize on the use of oil. For instance, companies switched from oil to gas (and in the case of electric power companies, often to coal) as a source of energy. More energy-efficient cars and trucks were constructed, often using lighter materials like aluminum and plastics. These substitutions took time, but they did eventually occur.

The principle of substitution should serve as a warning to those who think they can raise prices without bearing any consequences. Argentina has almost a world monopoly on linseed oil. At one time, linseed oil was universally

relative prices causes firms to substitute cheaper inputs for the more costly factor. This is an illustration of the general *principle of substitution* we encountered in Chapter 4.

The principle of substitution can be illustrated using the information in Table 7.5. If the wage is $20 per hour and each machine costs $1,000, output can be produced at less cost by using the more automated process. But suppose the price of machines increases to $3,500 each. Then, the more automated process will cost $17,500, while the less auto-used for making high-quality paints. Since there was no competition, Argentina decided that it would raise the price of linseed oil and assumed everyone would have to pay it. But as the price increased, paint manufacturers learned to substitute other natural oils that could do almost as well.

Raising the price of labor (wages) provides another example. Unions in the auto and steel industries successfully demanded higher wages for their members during the boom periods of the 1960s and 1970s, and firms paid the higher wages. But at the same time, the firms redoubled their efforts to mechanize their production and to become less dependent on their labor force. Over time, these efforts were successful and led to a decline in employment in those industries.

WRAP-UP

The Principles of Substitution

An increase in the price of an input will lead the firm to substitute other inputs in its place.

Economies of Scope

Most firms produce more than one good. Deciding which goods to produce and in what quantities, and how to produce them are central problems facing firm managers. The problems would be fairly straightforward were it not for some important interrelations among the products. The production of one product may affect the costs of producing another.

In some cases, products are produced naturally together; we say they are **joint products.** Thus, a sheep farm naturally produces wool, lamb meat, and mutton. If more lambs are slaughtered for meat, there will be less wool and less mutton.

If it is less expensive to produce a set of goods together than separately, economists say that these are **economies of scope.** The concept of economies of scope helps us understand why certain sets of activities are often undertaken by the same firms. Issues of economies of scope have also played an important role in discussions of regulation over the past two decades. At the time of the breakup of AT&T, which previously had dominated both local and long-distance telephone service as well as research in telecommunications, some economists argued against the breakup on the grounds that there were important economies of scope among these activities.

Review and Practice

Summary

1. A firm's production function specifies the level of output resulting from any combination of inputs. The increase in output corresponding to a unit increase in any input is the marginal product of that input.

2. Short-run marginal cost curves are generally upward sloping, because diminishing returns to a factor of production imply that it will take ever increasing amounts of the input to produce a marginal unit of output.

3. The typical short-run average cost curve is U-shaped. With U-shaped average cost curves, the marginal and average cost curves will intersect at the minimum point of the average cost curve.

4. Economists often distinguish between short-run and long-run cost curves. In the short run, a firm is generally assumed not to be able to change its capital stock. In the long run, it can. Even if short-run average cost curves are U-shaped, long-run average cost curves can take on a variety of shapes. They can, for instance, be flat, continuously declining, or declining and then increasing.

5. When a number of different inputs can be varied, and the price of one input increases, the change in relative prices of inputs will encourage a firm to substitute relatively less expensive inputs; this is an application of the principle of substitution.

6. Economies of scope exist when it is less expensive to produce two products together than it would be to produce each one separately.

Key Terms

profits
revenues
production function
marginal product
fixed costs
variable costs
total costs
marginal cost
average cost
average variable costs
constant, diminishing, or increasing returns to scale
    (economies of scale)
joint products
economies of scope

Review Questions

1. What is a production function? When there is a single (variable) input, why does output normally increase less than in proportion to input? What are the alternative shapes that the relationship between input and output takes? What is the relationship between these shapes and the shape of the cost function?

2. What is meant by these various concepts of cost; total, average, average variable, marginal, and fixed? What are the relationships between these costs? What are short-run and long-run costs? What is the relationship between them?

3. Why are short-run average cost curves frequently U-shaped? With U-shaped average cost curves, what is the relationship between the average and marginal costs? If the average cost curve is U-shaped, what does the total cost curve look like?

4. What happens to average, marginal, and total costs when the price of an input rises?

5. If a firm has a number of variable inputs and the price of one of them rises, will the firm use more or less of this input? Why?

6. What are diminishing, constant, and increasing returns to scale? When might you expect each to occur? What is the relationship between these properties of the production function and the shape of the long-run average and total cost curves?

7. What are economies of scope, and how do they affect what a firm chooses to produce?

Problems

1. Tom and Dick, who own the Tom, Dick, and Hairy Barbershop, need to decide how many barbers to hire. The production function for their barbershop looks like this:

Number of barbers	Haircuts provided per day	Marginal product
0	0	
1	12	
2	36	
3	60	
4	72	
5	80	
6	84	

Calculate the marginal product of hiring additional barbers, and fill in the last column of the table. Over what range is the marginal product of labor increasing? constant? diminishing? Graph the production function. By looking at the graph, you should be able to tell at what point the average productivity of labor is highest. Calculate average productivity at each point to illustrate your answer.

2. The overhead costs of the Tom, Dick, and Hairy Barbershop are $160 per day, and the cost of paying a barber for a day is $80. With this information, and the information in problem #1, make up a table with column headings in this order: Output, Labor required, Total variable cost, Total cost, Marginal cost, Average variable cost, and Average cost. If the price of a haircut is $10 and the shop sells 80 per day, what is the daily profit?

3. Using the information in problems #1 and #2, draw the total cost curve for the Tom, Dick, and Hairy Barbershop on one graph. On a second graph, draw the marginal cost curve, the average cost curve, and the average variable cost curve. Do these curves have the shape you would expect? Do the minimum and average cost curves intersect at the point you expect?

4. Suppose a firm has the choice of two methods of producing: one method entails a fixed cost of $10 and a marginal cost of $2; the other entails a fixed cost of $20 and a marginal cost of $1. Draw the total and average cost

curves for both methods. At what levels of output will the firm use the low fixed-cost technology? At what levels of output will it use the high fixed-cost technology?

5. A firm produces cars using labor and capital. Assume that average labor productivity—total output divided by the number of workers—has increased in the last few months. Does that mean that workers are working harder? Or that the firm has become more efficient? Explain.

Appendix: Cost Minimization with Many Inputs

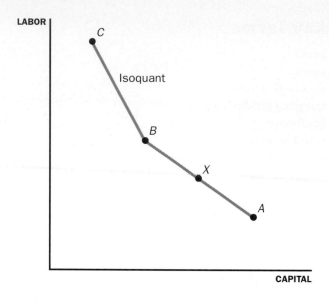

FIGURE 7.10   *Three Alternative Methods of Producing a Certain Amount*

Point *A* represents the inputs for a highly mechanized way of producing a certain number of car frames; point *C* represents a technique of production that uses a much less expensive machine, but more labor; point *B* represents a technique that is in between. By using different techniques in different proportions, the firm can use a combination of labor and capital on the line joining *A* and *B*, such as point *X*. The curve *ABC* is an isoquant.

This appendix shows how the basic principles of cost minimization can be applied to a firm's choice of the mix of inputs to use in production. To do this, we make use of a set of concepts and tools similar to those presented in the appendix to Chapter 6, in the analysis of how households make decisions about what mix of goods to purchase.

Isoquants

The alternative ways of producing a particular quantity of output can be graphically represented by **isoquants.** The first part of the term comes from the Greek word *iso,* meaning "same," while "quant" is just shorthand for quantity. Thus, isoquants illustrate the different combinations of inputs that produce the same quantity.

Consider this simple extension of the example of Table 7.5 on page 146. A firm can buy three different kinds of machines, each of which produces car frames. One is a highly mechanized machine that requires very little labor. Another is much less automated and requires considerably more labor. In between is another technique. These represent three different ways of producing the same quantity.

Assume the firm wishes to produce 10,000 car frames a day. It could do this by using highly mechanized machines, moderately mechanized machines, or nonmechanized machines. The total capital and labor requirements for each of these possibilities are represented in Figure 7.10. The horizontal axis shows the capital requirements, while the vertial axis shows the labor requirements. The labor and capital associated with the highly mechanized production process is shown by point *A*, the moderately mechanized by point *B*, and the low mechanized by point *C*.

If the firm wishes, it can produce half of its output on the highly mechanized machines and half on the moderately mechanized machines. If it chooses this option, its capital requirements will be halfway between the capital that would be required if it used only *A* or only *B*, and its labor requirements will also be halfway between. This halfway-between choice is illustrated by point *X*. By similar logic, the firm can achieve any combination of capital and labor requirements on the straight line joining *A* and *B* by changing the proportion of highly mechanized and moderately mechanized machines. And by changing the proportion of moderately mechanized and low-mechanized machines, it can achieve any combination of capital and labor requirements on the straight line joining *B* and *C*. The curve *ABC* is the isoquant. It gives all those combinations of capital and labor that can produce 10,000 automobile frames per day. All of these input combinations give the same output.

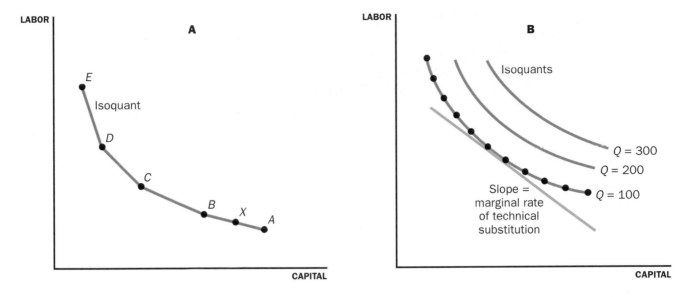

FIGURE 7.11   *Isoquants and the Marginal Rate of Substitution*

Panel A shows an isoquant defined with many alternative techniques of production. Panel B shows that as the number of production techniques increases, isoquants appear as a smooth curve. The slope of the isoquant tells how much of one input must be added to make up for the loss of a unit of the other input; this is the marginal rate of technical substitution.

Consider now what happens if many techniques are available instead of only three. The isoquant consists of points designating each of the techniques, and the short line segments connecting these points that represent combinations of two techniques, as shown in Figure 7.11A. When many, many production techniques are available, the isoquant looks much like a smooth curve, and economists often draw it that way, as in panel B.

Many different isoquants can be drawn, each representing one particular level of output, as in panel B. Higher isoquants represent higher levels of production; lower isoquants represent lower levels.[2] There is also a simple relationship between the production functions discussed earlier and isoquants. The production function gives the output corresponding to each level of inputs. The isoquant shows the levels of inputs that can yield a given level of output.

---

[2] Readers who have read the Chapter 6 appendix on indifference curves should recognize the similarities between isoquants and indifference curves: While indifference curves give those combinations of goods that yield the individual the same level of utility, the isoquant gives those combinations of goods (inputs) that yield the firm the same level of output.

Marginal Rate of Technical Substitution

The idea of marginal rate of substitution was introduced in the appendix to Chapter 6 to describe how individuals are willing to trade off less of one good for more of another. The concept is also useful in analyzing what technology firms will choose. In the case of firms, the marginal rate of substitution is defined not by individual preferences but by actual physical facts. If a firm reduces one input by a unit and then raises another input enough so that the final output remains the same, the amount of extra input required is called the **marginal rate of technical substitution.**

An example should help to clarify this idea. If a firm can reduce the amount of capital it uses by 1 machine, hire 2 more workers, and produce the same quantity, then it is possible for 2 workers to replace 1 machine. In this case, the marginal rate of technical substitution between workers and machines is 2/1. The marginal rate of technical substitution is just the slope of the isoquant, as Figure 7.11B shows diagrammatically: The slope simply tells how much of an increase in labor is needed to offset a one-unit decrease in capital to produce the same amount of output.[3]

Notice that the marginal rate of technical substitution and the slope of the isoquant change with the quantities of labor and capital involved. With fewer and fewer machines, it becomes increasingly difficult to substitute workers for machines. The marginal rate of technical substitution rises, and the slope of the isoquant becomes steeper and steeper. At the other end of the isoquant, with more and more machines, it becomes easier and easier to replace one of them. The marginal rate of technical substitution diminishes as the number of machines increases, and the slope of the isoquant becomes flatter. There is a **diminishing marginal rate of technical substitution** in production, just as there was a diminishing marginal rate of substitution in consumption.

The marginal rate of technical substitution can be calculated from the marginal products of labor and capital. If adding 1 more worker increases the output of automobile frames by 1, the marginal product of an extra worker in this industrial process is 1 (car frame). Let us also imagine that adding 1 machine leads to an increase in car output of, say, 2 a day. So in this industrial process, the marginal product of a machine is 2. In this example, adding 2 workers and reducing machine input by 1 leaves output unchanged. Thus, the marginal rate of technical substitution is 2/1. In general, the marginal rate of technical substitution is equal to the ratio of the marginal products.

The principle of diminishing returns explains why the marginal rate of technical substitution diminishes as a firm adds more and more machines. As it adds more machines, the marginal product of an additional machine diminishes. As the number of workers is reduced, the marginal product of an additional worker is increased. As workers are becoming more productive at the margin and machines are becoming less productive at the margin, it becomes increasingly easier to replace machines with additional workers.

Notice that calculating the marginal rate of substitution does not tell the firm whether it *should* substitute workers for machines, or machines for workers. The number itself only provides factual information about what the trade-off

would be, based on the technology available to the firm. To decide which combination of inputs should be chosen, the firm must also know the market prices of the various inputs.

Cost Minimization

Minimizing costs requires marginal decision making. Firms know the technology they are currently using and can consider changing it by trading off some inputs against others. To decide whether such a trade-off will reduce costs, they calculate the marginal rate of technical substitution and simply compare the market price of the input they are reducing with the price of the input they are increasing. If a firm can replace 1 machine with 2 workers and maintain the same output, and if a worker costs $12,000 a year and a machine costs $25,000 a year to rent, then by reducing machines by 1 and hiring 2 workers, the firm can reduce total costs. On the other hand, if a worker costs $13,000, it would pay to use 2 fewer workers (for a savings of $26,000) and rent 1 machine (for a cost of $25,000).

The only time that it would not pay the firm either to increase labor and reduce the number of machines or to decrease labor and increase the number of machines is when the marginal rate of technical substitution is equal to the relative price of the two factors. The reason for this is similar to the reason why individuals set their personal marginal rates of substitution equal to the ratio of market prices. The difference is that the individual's marginal rate of substitution is determined by individual preferences, while the firm's marginal rate of technical substitution is determined by technology.

Isocost Curves

The **isocost** curve gives those combinations of inputs that cost the same amount. The isocost curve is analogous to an individual's budget constraint, which gives those combinations of goods that cost the same amount. If a firm faces fixed prices for its inputs, the isocost curve is a straight line, whose slope indicates the relative prices; that is, if each worker costs, say, $50 per day, then if the firm reduces the labor used by one, it could spend $50 per day on renting more machines. If renting a machine for a day costs $100, then the firm can rent one more machine with the amount it would save by reducing the input of labor by two. There are, of course, many isocost lines, one for each level of expenditure. Lower isocost lines represent lower

---

[3] Again, readers who earlier studied indifference curves will recall that the slope of the indifference curve is also called the marginal rate of substitution; it tells us how much extra of one good is required when consumption of another good is reduced by one unit, if we wish to leave the individual at the same level of welfare—on his indifference curve.

expenditures on inputs. Cost along line C_1C_1 in Figure 7.12 are lower than costs along *CC*. The different isocost lines are parallel to one another, just as different household budget constraints representing different income levels are parallel.

Notice that all firms facing the same prices for inputs will have the same isocost lines. Similarly, different individuals with the same income face the same budget constraint, even when their preferences differ. However, the isoquant curves that describe each firm are based on the product the firm is making and the technology and knowledge available to the firm. Thus, isoquant curves will differ from firm to firm.

Isoquant curves and isocost lines can illuminate the behavior of a cost-minimizing firm. For example, any efficient profit-maximizing firm will wish to maximize the output it obtains from any given expenditure. Or to rephrase the same point, the firm must reach the highest possible isoquant, given a particular level of expenditure on inputs, represented by a particular isocost line. The highest possible isoquant will touch the isocost line at a single point; the two curves will be tangent.

The problem of cost minimization can be described in a different way. Consider a firm that has a desired level of output and wishes to minimize its cost. The firm chooses

an isoquant and then tries to find the point on the isoquant that is on the lowest possible isocost line. Again, the cost-minimizing firm will choose the point of tangency between the isocost line and the isoquant.

At the point of tangency, the slopes of the two curves are the same. The slope of the isoquant is the marginal rate of technical substitution. The slope of the isocost line is the relative price. Thus, *the marginal rate of technical substitution must equal the relative price.*

Applying the Diagrammatic Analysis

The isoquant/isocost diagram can be used to show how a change in relative prices affects the optimal mix of inputs. A change in relative prices changes the isocost line. In Figure 7.13, an increase in the wage makes the isocost curves flatter. *CC* is the original isocost curve that minimizes the costs of producing output Q_0 (that is, *CC* is tangent to the isoquant Q_0). C_1C_1 is the isocost line with the new higher wages that is tangent to the original isoquant. Obviously, to produce the same level of output will cost more if wages are increased. The figure also shows what this change in relative prices in the form of higher wages does to the cost-minimizing combination of inputs: As one would expect, the firm substitutes away from labor toward capital (from point E_0 to E_1).

Of course, the magnitude of the substitution will differ from industry to industry, depending on an industry's isoquant. In addition, substitution is likely to be much greater in the long run than in the short run, as machines wear out, firms try to find out how to conserve on the more expensive inputs, and so on. The figure represents these different possibilities for substitution. In panel A, the possibilities for substitution are very limited. The isoquant is very "curved." This figure illustrates a case where it is very difficult to substitute (at least in the short run) machines for labor (illustrated, perhaps, by the use of blast furnaces in producing steel). In panel B, substitution is very easy; the isoquant is very flat. This illustrates an opposite case; it is relatively easy for a firm to substitute machines for labor, say, by using robots.

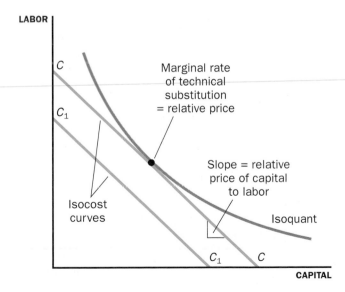

FIGURE 7.12 *Cost Minimization*

Cost-minimizing firms will wish to produce as much output as they can given a particular level of expenditure, so they will choose the highest isoquant they can reach with a given isocost curve, which will be the isoquant tangent to the isocost curve.

Deriving Cost Curves

The cost curves in this chapter represent the minimum cost of producing each level of output, at a particular level of input prices. Figure 7.14A shows the cost-minimizing

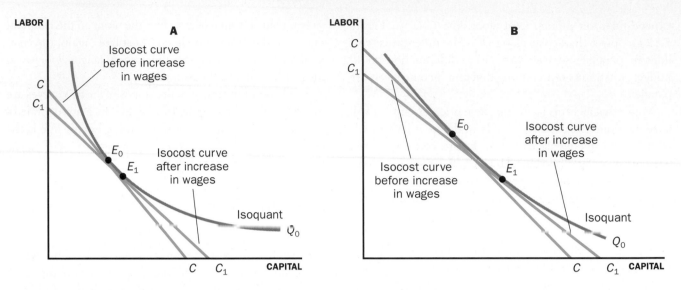

FIGURE 7.13   *Changing Factor Prices*

This firm has chosen the level of production associated with the isoquant shown, and the cost-minimizing combination of labor and capital for producing that amount is originally at E_0. But as wages rise, relative prices shift, and the cost-minimizing method of producing the given amount becomes E_1. In panel A, an increase in wages leads to little substitution. But in panel B, an increase in wages leads to a much larger amount of substitution.

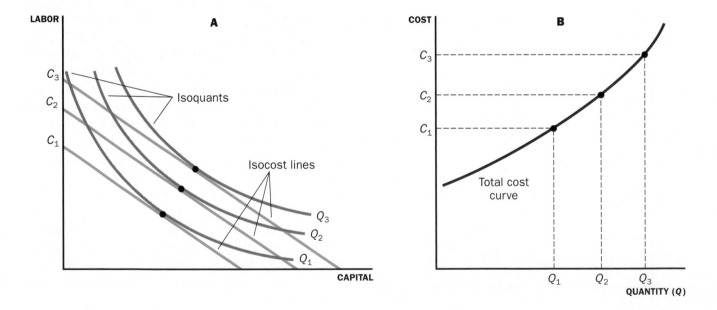

FIGURE 7.14   *Deriving the Total Cost Curve*

The total cost curve describes how total cost changes at different levels of output. Panel A shows three isoquants representing different levels of output, and three isocost curves tangent to those isoquants, representing the least-cost way of producing each of these amounts. Panel B plots the actual level of costs for each of these levels of output, producing the familiar total cost curve.

way of producing three different levels of output, Q_1, Q_2, and Q_3. Panel B then plots the actual level of costs associated with each of these levels of output. That is, the isocost curves tangent to the isoquants in panel A show the minimum level of costs associated with each output. Tracing out the costs associated with each level of output provides the total cost curve. And once we have the total cost curve, we know how to derive the marginal cost curve (the slope of the total cost curve) and the average cost curve (the slope of a line from the origin to the total cost curve).

Chapter 8

The Competitive Firm

1. What determines the level of output a firm will supply at any given price? How do we derive, in other words, the firm's supply curve?

2. What determines whether or when a firm will enter or exit a market?

3. How do the answers to these questions enable us to analyze the market supply curve, why it is upward sloping and why it may be more elastic than the supply curve of any single firm?

4. How do we reconcile economists' view that competition drives profits to zero with accountants' reports showing that most of the time most firms earn positive profits?

*C*hapter 4 described market equilibrium as the price at which the quantity demanded equals the quantity supplied—that is, where the demand and supply curves intersect. This basic model of supply and demand is the most fundamental building block in economics. In Chapter 6 we began to fill out the model by examining the underpinnings of demand, and we saw how consumption decisions determine the quantity of output households demand. In Chapter 7 we shifted our attention to the supply side of the market, looking in particular at the cost curves of the firm. In the present chapter we focus on the firm's revenues, and we examine how the aim of profit maximization guides the firm's decision of the quantity of goods to supply. Chapter 9 will show how these tools can be used to analyze not only the demand and supply of goods but also the demand and supply of *factors* like labor and capital

This chapter focuses on firms in highly competitive markets—that is, firms that take as given the prices they receive for the products they sell and the prices they pay for the inputs they purchase. Accordingly, economists sometimes refer to the principles developed here as the *theory of the competitive firm*.

Revenue

Consider the hypothetical example of the High Strung Violin Company, manufacturers of world-class violins. The company hires labor; it buys wood, utilities, and other materials; and it rents a building and machines. Its violins sell for $40,000 each. Last year the company sold 7 of them, for a gross revenue of $280,000. Table 8.1 gives a snapshot of the firm's financial health, its profit-and-loss statement for last year.

We see that High Strung's revenues were $280,000, and its costs were $175,000, so its profits were $105,000. If its costs had been $400,000 instead of $175,000, its profits would have been −$120,000. The firm would have made a negative profit, in other words, a loss.

The relationship between revenue and output is shown by the **revenue curve** in Figure 8.1. The horizontal axis measures the firm's output, while the vertical axis measures the revenues. When the price of a violin is $40,000 and the firm sells 9 violins, its revenue is $360,000; when it sells 10, revenue rises to $400,000.

TABLE 8.1

Profit-and-Loss Statement for the High Strung Violin Company

Gross revenue		$280,000
Costs		$175,000
Wages (including fringe benefits)	$150,000	
Purchases of wood and other materials	$ 15,000	
Utilities	$ 1,000	
Rent of building	$ 5,000	
Rent of machinery	$ 2,000	
Miscellaneous expenses	$ 2,000	
Profits		$105,000

The extra revenue that a firm receives from selling an extra unit is called its **marginal revenue.** Thus, $40,000 is the extra (or marginal) revenue from selling the tenth violin. It is no accident that the marginal revenue equals the price of the violin. A fundamental feature of competitive markets is that firms receive the same market price for each unit they sell, regardless of the number of units they sell. Thus, the extra revenue that firms in competitive markets receive from selling one more unit—the marginal revenue—is the same as the market price of the unit.

Costs

High Strung's costs increase as it expands its level of output. Total costs are given in column 1 of Table 8.2 and depicted diagrammatically in Figure 8.2A. Panel B shows the corresponding average and marginal costs. High Strung's average cost curve exhibits the typical U-shape that we associate with manufacturing firms.

Even before it builds its first violin, the company must spend $90,000. Space must be rented. Some employees

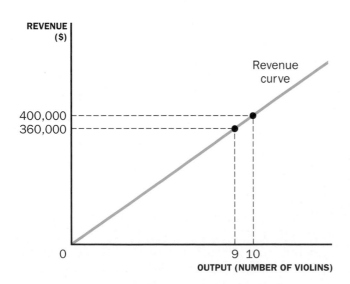

FIGURE 8.1   *The Revenue Curve*

The revenue curve shows a firm's revenues at each level of output. For the firm in a competitive industry, price does not change as more is produced, so the revenue curve is a straight line with a constant slope. In this example, the revenue of each additional violin is always $40,000.

Internet Connection

Firm's Profit and Loss Statements

Corporations issue annual reports each year, and these reports include their profit and loss statements. These statements are also called *income statements.* You can find the annual reports of many corporations on the Web. For example, you can find the Microsoft annual report at the Microsoft web page, http://www.microsoft.com , under "information for investors." Within the report, the income statement is found with the basic financial information. In 2001, Microsoft's net income was $7.3 billion on a total revenue of just under $25.3 billion. You can order copies of the annual reports from many corporations from the Public Record's Annual Report Service (PRARS), whose home page is http://www.prars.com/ .

TABLE 8.2

High Strung Violin Company's Costs of Production (thousands of dollars)

Output	(1) Total cost	(2) Average cost	(3) Marginal cost	(4) Total variable cost	(5) Average variable cost
0	90				
1	100	100	10	10	10
2	110	55	10	20	10
3	120	40	10	30	10
4	130	32.5	10	40	10
5	140	28	10	50	10
6	150	25	10	60	10
7	175	25	25	85	12.1
8	215	26.9	40	125	15.6
9	270	30	55	180	20
10	400	40	130	210	21

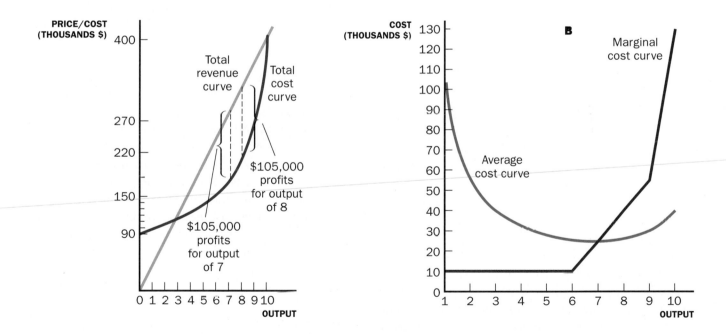

FIGURE 8.2   *Relating Revenues and Costs*

The firm's revenue and total cost curves can be diagrammed on the same graph, as in panel A. When total revenue exceeds total costs, the firm is making profits at that level of output. Profits, the difference between revenues and costs, are measured by the distance between the two curves; in this case, the highest level of profit is being made at a production level of 7 or 8. When total costs exceed total revenue, the firm is making losses at that level of output. When the two lines cross, the firm is making zero profits. The marginal and average cost curves for this company have their expected shape in panel B. Marginal costs are constant until a production level of 6, and then they begin to increase. The average cost curve is U-shaped.

will have to be hired. Equipment must be purchased. No matter how many or how few violins High Strung produces, its fixed costs will remain $90,000.

The *extra* cost of producing an additional violin, the marginal cost, is shown in column 3. Marginal cost is always associated with the additional cost of producing a *particular* unit of output. The marginal cost of increasing production from 1 to 2 violins, for example, is $10,000. Each additional violin costs $10,000 more until production reaches 6 violins. The extra (or marginal) cost of producing the seventh violin is $25,000. The marginal cost of producing the eighth violin is $40,000.

The High Strung Violin Company's average costs initially decline as its production increases, since the fixed costs can be divided among more units of production. But after 7 violins, average costs begin to increase, as the effect of the increasing average variable costs dominates the effect of the fixed costs.

Basic Conditions of Competitive Supply

In choosing how much to produce, a profit-maximizing firm will focus its decision at the margin. Having incurred the fixed cost of getting into this market, the decision is generally not the stark one of whether or not to produce, but whether to produce one more unit of a good or one less. For a firm in a competitive market, the answer to this problem is relatively simple: The company simply compares the marginal revenue it will receive by producing an extra unit—which is just the price of the good—with the extra cost of producing that unit, the marginal cost. As long as the marginal revenue exceeds the marginal cost, the firm will make additional profit by producing more. If marginal revenue is less than marginal cost, then producing an extra unit will cut profits, and the firm will reduce production. In short, the firm will produce to the point where the marginal cost equals marginal revenue, which in a competitive market is equal to price.

Figure 8.3 develops the graphical analysis underlying this principle. Panel A shows the firm's marginal cost curve. If the price of the good in a competitive market is p_1, the profit-maximizing level output will be Q_1. This is the level of output equating price and marginal cost. With an upward-sloping marginal cost curve, it is clear that the firm will produce more as price increases.

The marginal cost curve is upward sloping, just as the supply curves in Chapter 4 were upward sloping. This too is no accident: A firm's marginal cost curve is actually the same as its supply curve. The marginal cost curve shows the additional cost of producing one more unit at different levels of output. A competitive firm chooses to produce at the level of output where the cost of producing an additional unit (that is, the marginal cost) is equal to the market price. We can thus read from the marginal cost curve what the firm's supply will be at any price: It will be the quantity of output at which marginal cost equals that price.

Before we turn to panel B, look once more at Figure 8.2A, which shows total revenues as well as total costs of the High Strung Violin Company. We can see that profits—the gap between revenues and costs—are maximized at an output of either 7 or 8. If the price were just slightly lower than $40,000, profits would be maximized at 7, and if the price were just slightly higher than $40,000, profits would be maximized at 8.

The profit-maximizing level of output can also be seen in panel B of Figure 8.3, which shows the total revenue and total cost curves. Profits are the difference between revenues and costs. In panel B, profits are the distance between the total revenue curve and the total cost curves. The profit-maximizing firm will choose the output where that distance is greatest. This occurs at Q_1. Below Q_1, price (the slope of the revenue curve) exceeds marginal costs (the slope of the total cost curve) so profits increase as output increases; above Q_1, price is less than marginal cost, so profits decrease as output increases.

WRAP-UP

Equilibrium Output for Competitive Firms

In competitive markets, firms produce at the level where price equals marginal cost.

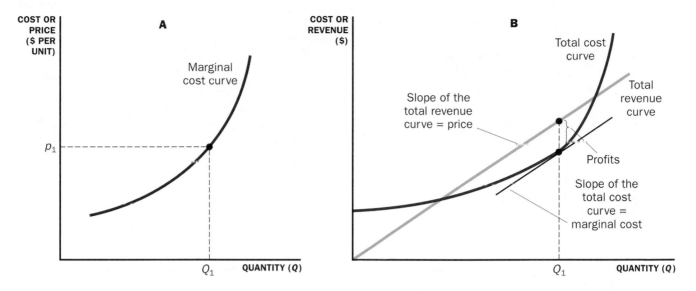

FIGURE 8.3   *The Profit-Maximizing Level of Output*

A competitive firm maximizes profits by setting output at the point where price equals marginal cost. In panel A, at the price of p_1, this quantity is Q_1. Panel B shows total revenue and total costs. Profits are maximized when the distance between the two curves is maximized, which is the point where the two lines are parallel (and thus have the same slope).

Entry, Exit, and Market Supply

We are now in a position to tackle the market supply curve. To do so, we need to know a little more about each firm's decision to produce. First let's consider a firm that is currently not producing. Under what circumstances should it incur the fixed costs of entering the industry? This is a relatively easy problem: the company simply looks at the average cost curve and the price. *If price exceeds minimum average costs, it pays the firm to enter.* This is because if it enters, it can sell the goods for more than the cost of producing them, thus making a profit.

Figure 8.4A shows the U-shaped average cost curve. Minimum average cost is c_{min}. If the price is less than c_{min}, then there is no level of output at which the firm could produce and make a profit. If the price is above c_{min}, then the firm will produce at the level of output at which price (p) equals marginal cost, Q^*. At Q^*, marginal costs exceeds average costs. (This is always true at output levels greater than that at which average costs are minimum.) Profit per unit is the difference between price and average costs.

Total profits are the product of profit per unit and the level of output (the shaded area in the figure).

Different companies may have different average cost curves. Some will have better management. Some will have a better location. Accordingly, firms will differ in their minimum average cost. As prices rise, additional firms will find it attractive to enter the market. Figure 8.4B shows the U-shaped average cost curves for three different firms. Firm 1's minimum average cost is AC_1, firm 2's minimum average cost is AC_2, and firm 3's minimum average cost is AC_3. Thus, firm 1 enters at the price p_1, firm 2 at the price p_2, and firm 3 at the price p_3.

Sunk Costs and Exit

The converse of the decision of a firm to enter the market is the decision of a firm already producing to exit the market. *Sunk costs* are costs that are not recoverable, even if a firm goes out of business. The High Strung Violin Company, for example, may have had an extensive television advertising campaign. The cost of this campaign is a sunk cost. There is no way this expenditure can be recouped even if production ceases. If there were no sunk costs, the decision to

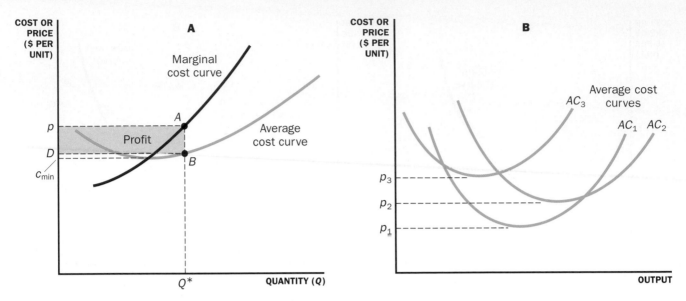

FIGURE 8.4   *Cost Curves, Profits, and Entry*

Panel A shows that if price is above the minimum of the average cost curve, profits will exist. Profits are measured by the area formed by the shaded rectangle, the profit per unit (price minus average cost, corresponding to the distance *AB*) times the output, Q^*. Thus, profits are the shaded rectangle, *ABDp*. Panel B shows average cost curves for three different firms. At price p_1, only one firm will enter the market. As price rises to p_2 and then to p_3, first the firm whose cost curve is AC_2 and then the firm whose cost curve is AC_3 will enter the market.

enter and the decision to exit would be mirror images of each other. Firms would exit the market when their average costs rose above the price. But if some costs remain even if a firm exits the market, the question facing that firm is whether it is better off continuing to produce or exiting.

Let us assume for simplicity that all fixed costs are sunk costs. A firm with no fixed costs has an average cost curve that is the same as its average variable cost curve. It will shut down as soon as the price falls below minimum average costs—the cost at the bottom of its U-shaped variable cost curve. But a firm *with* fixed costs has a different decision to make. Figure 8.5A depicts both the average variable cost curve and the average cost curve for such a case. As in the case with no sunk costs, the firm shuts down when price is below minimum average *variable* costs (costs that vary with the level of output), p_1. But if the price is *between* average variable costs and average costs, the firm will continue to produce, even though it will show a loss. It continues to produce because it would show an even bigger loss if it ceased operating. Since price exceeds average variable costs, the revenues it obtains exceed the additional costs it incurs from producing.

Different firms in an industry will have different average variable costs, and so will find it desirable to exit the market at different prices. Figure 8.5B shows the average variable cost curves for three different firms. Their cost curves differ; some may, for instance, have newer equipment than others. As the price falls, the firm with the highest minimum average variable costs finds it is no longer able to make money at the going price, and decides not to operate. Thus, firm 3 (represented by the curve AVC_3) shuts down as soon as the price falls below c_3, firm 2 shuts down as soon as the price falls below c_2, and firm 1 shuts down as soon as the price falls below c_1.

The Firm's Supply Curve

We can now draw the firm's supply curve. As Figure 8.6A shows, for a firm contemplating entering the market, supply is zero up to a critical price, equal to the minimum average cost. Thus, for prices below $c_{min} = p$, the firm produces zero output. For prices greater than $c_{min} = p$, the firm produces up to the point where price equals marginal cost, so the firm's supply curve coincides with the marginal cost curve. For a firm that has incurred sunk costs of entering the market

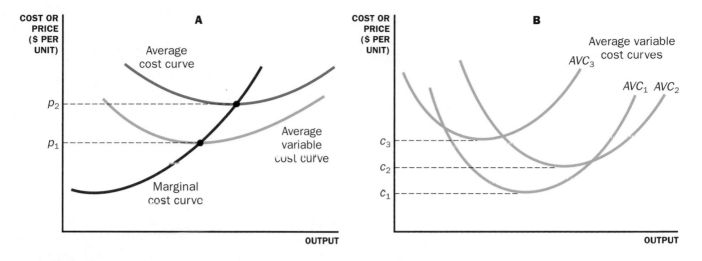

FIGURE 8.5 *Average Variable Costs and the Decision to Produce*

Panel A shows a firm's average variable cost curves. In the short run, firms will produce as long as price exceeds average variable costs. Thus, for prices between p_1 and p_2, the firm will continue to produce, even though it is recording a loss (price is less than average cost). Panel B shows that firms with different average variable cost curves will decide to shut down at different price levels. As price falls below c_3, the minimum average variable cost for firm 3, firm 3 shuts down; as price falls still lower, below c_2, firm 2 shuts down. Finally, when price falls below c_1, firm 1 shuts down.

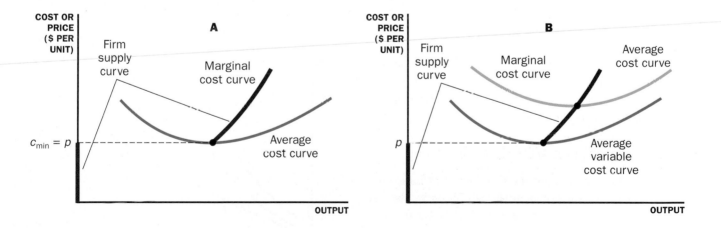

FIGURE 8.6 *The Supply Curve for a Firm*

Panel A shows that for a firm contemplating entering the market, supply is zero up to a critical price, equal to the firm's minimum average cost, after which the firm's supply curve coincides with the marginal cost curve. Panel B shows a firm that has already entered the market, incurring positive sunk costs; this firm will produce as long as price exceeds the minimum of the average variable cost curve.

e-Insight

The 2001 Recession: Cutbacks Versus Shutdowns

In late 2000, the economy seemed to slow down, and by early 2001 some parts of the economy were actually contracting. Many "dot com" firms that had been opened in the late 1990s were hit particularly hard. Some firms shut down, while others cut back. How do we explain the difference?

One sector that was hit particularly badly was publishers of magazines, which depend heavily on advertisements for revenues. Ad revenues for one magazine, *The Industry Standard,* that focused on the new economy fell by more than 60 percent. Publishing firms cut back on employment, but even the most adversely affected did not shut down. Why? The reason was simple: Though they were showing losses, their revenues exceeded their variable costs. Much of their costs were sunk costs that would not be recovered if they shut down. It paid them to continue publishing, even if at a scaled-back size.

On the other hand, many Internet companies (dot com's) did shut down. Some that had depended on advertising revenue did so because, even though their variable costs were low, their revenues were even lower. They could not cover their variable costs.

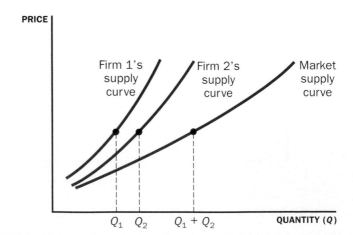

The online grocery service Webvan shut down during the economic slowdown of 2001.

(panel B), the supply curve coincides with the marginal cost curve so long as price exceeds the minimum value of average *variable* costs; when price is below the minimum value of average variable costs, the firm exits, so supply is again zero.

The Market Supply Curve

With this information about the cost curves of individual firms, we can derive the overall market supply curve. Back in Chapter 4, the market supply curve was defined as the sum of the amounts that each firm was willing to supply at any given price. Figure 8.7 provides a graphical description of the supply curve for a market with two firms. More generally, if the price rises, the firms already in the market (firms 1 and 2) will find it profitable to increase their output, and new firms (with higher average variable cost curves) will find it profitable to enter the market. Because higher prices induce more firms to enter a competitive market, the market supply

FIGURE 8.7   *The Market Supply Curve*

The market supply curve is derived by horizontally adding up the supply curves for each of the firms. More generally, as price rises, each firm produces more and new firms enter the market.

response to an increase in price is greater than if the number of firms were fixed. In the same way, as price falls, there are two market responses. The firms that still find it profitable to produce at the lower price will produce less, and the higher-cost firms will exit the market. In this way, the competitive market ensures that whatever the product, it is produced at the lowest possible price by the most efficient firms.

Long-Run Versus Short-Run Supply

As we saw in Chapter 7, in the short run the typical firm will have a U-shaped average cost curve, and a rising marginal cost curve at output levels above the lowest point of the U. But its long-run marginal cost curve is flatter. This is because adjustments to changes in market conditions take time, and some adjustments take longer than others. In the short run, you can add workers, work more shifts, and run the machines harder (or reduce the rate at which these things are done), but you are probably stuck with your existing plant and equipment. In the long run, you can acquire

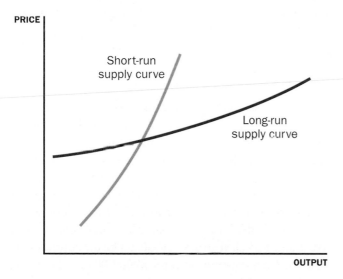

PRICE

Short-run supply curve

Long-run supply curve

OUTPUT

FIGURE 8.8 *Elasticity of Short-Run and Long-Run Supply Curves for a Firm*

Because there is a greater chance for a firm to adjust to changes in price in the long run, the price elasticity of the supply curve is greater in the long run than in the short run.

WRAP-UP

Adjustments in the Short Run and the Long Run

In the very short run, firms may be unable to adjust production at all; only the price changes.

In the short run, firms may be able to hire more labor and adjust other variable inputs.

In the long run, firms may be able to buy more machines, and firms may decide to enter or to exit.

The times required for these adjustments may vary from industry to industry.

more buildings and more machines (or sell them). Thus, the long-run supply curve for a firm is more elastic (flatter) than the short-run supply curve, as shown in Figure 8.8.

The same thing is true, only more so, for the industry—again because the number of firms is not fixed. Even if each firm can operate only one plant, the industry's output can be increased by 5 percent by increasing the number of firms by 5 percent. The extra costs of increasing output by 5 percent are approximately the same as the average costs. Accordingly, the long-run market supply curve is approximately horizontal. Under these conditions, even if the demand curve for the product shifts drastically, the market will supply much more of the product at pretty much the same price, as additional plants are constructed and additional firms enter the market.

Thus, the market supply curve is much more elastic in the long run than in the short run. Indeed, in the *very* short run, a firm may find it impossible to hire more skilled labor or to increase its capacity. Its supply curve, and the market supply curve, would be nearly vertical. In the short run machines and the number of firms are fixed, but labor and other inputs can be varied. Figure 8.9A shows the short-run supply curve. Contrast the short-run market supply curve with the long-run market supply curve. The short-run curve slopes up much more sharply. A shift in the demand curve has a larger effect on price and a smaller effect on quantity than it does in the long run. In the long run, the market supply curve may be horizontal. In this case, shifts in the demand curve have an effect *only* on quantity, as in panel B. Price remains at the level of minimum average costs; *competition leads to entry to the point where there are zero profits.*

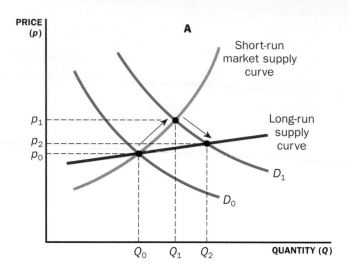
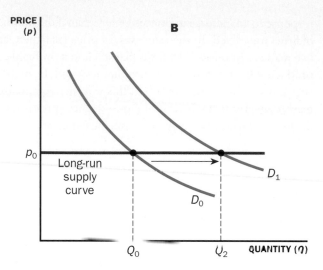

FIGURE 8.9   *Market Equilibrium in the Short Run and Long Run*

In panel A, the market equilibrium is originally at a price p_0 and an output Q_0. In the short run, a shift in the demand curve from D_0 to D_1 raises the price to p_1 and quantity to Q_1. In the long run, the supply elasticity is greater, so the increase in price is smaller—price is only p_2—and quantity is greater, Q_2. If supply is perfectly elastic in the long run, as shown in panel B, shifts in demand will only change the quantity produced in the long run, not the market price.

Again, it is worth asking, "How long is the long run?" that depends on the industry. It takes an electric power company years to change its capacity. For most other firms, buildings and equipment can be added, if not within months, certainly within a year or two. Recent improvements in technology, like computer-aided design and manufacturing, have made it possible for many companies to change what they are producing more rapidly, and thus have reduced the length of the long run and made supply curves more elastic than in the past.

Accounting Profits and Economic Profits

This chapter has shown how firms enter and exit markets in pursuit of profits. The result of this process is that competition among firms drives profits to zero. This leads to an apparent contradiction of the basic competitive model: If firms are profit maximizers, as we learned in Chapter 7, why would they ever choose to produce when there are no profits to be made? Moreover, how can it be true that profits are zero when firms in the real world routinely report making profits?

The answer is that accountants and economists think about profits differently in two important respects. The first is that economists take opportunity costs into account. The second has to do with the economic concept of rent. Both deserve a closer look.

Opportunity Costs

To begin to see how opportunity costs affect the economist's view of profits, consider a small firm in which the owner has invested $100,000. Assume the owner receives a small salary and devotes sixty hours a week to running the enterprise. An economist would argue that the owner ought to calculate his opportunity costs related to his investment of time and money into the business. The opportunity cost of his time is the best wage available to him if he worked sixty hours a week at an alternate job. The opportunity cost of his capital is the return that the $100,000 invested in this enterprise would produce in another investment. These are the true costs of the owner's time and capital investment. To calculate profits of the firm as the economist sees them, these opportunity costs have to be subtracted out.

One can easily imagine a business whose accountant reports a profit equal to 3 percent of the capital investment. An economist would note that if the investment capital had been put in a bank account, it would have earned at least 5 percent. Thus, the economist would say the business is operating at a loss. Failure to take into account opportunity costs means that reported profits often overstate true economic profits.

Taking opportunity costs into account is not always a simple matter; it is not always easy to determine the alternative uses of a firm's resources. Managerial time spent in expanding the firm in one direction, for example, might have been spent in controlling costs or expanding the firm in another direction. Land that is used for a golf course for the firm's employees might have been used for some other purpose, which could have saved more than enough money to buy golf club memberships for all employees who want them. In making decisions about resources like these, firms must constantly ask what price the resources might fetch in other uses.

Sometimes market data can provide appropriate prices for calculating opportunity costs. For example, the opportunity cost of giving huge offices to top executives can be gauged by the money those offices would bring if they were rented to some other company. But often the calculation is more difficult: How can, for example, a company measure the opportunity cost of the vice president who cannot be fired and will not retire for five years?

What about the costs associated with an expenditure already made, say on a building that is no longer really needed by the firm? The relevant opportunity cost of this building is not the original purchase or lease price, but instead the value of the building in alternate uses, such as the rent that could be earned if the building were rented to other firms.

The fundamental point is that you cannot use past expenditures to calculate opportunity costs. Consider a computer manufacturer that has purchased a parcel of land for $1 million an acre. It turns out, however, that the company made a mistake and the land is worth only $100,000 an acre. The firm now must choose between two different plants for producing new computers, one of which uses much more land than the other. In figuring opportunity costs, should the land be valued at the purchase price of $1 million an acre, or what the land could be sold for—$100,000 an acre? The answer can make a difference between whether or not the firm chooses to conserve on land. From an economics viewpoint, the answer to this valuation problem should be obvious: The firm should evaluate costs according to the *current* opportunity costs. The fact that the company made a mis-

take in purchasing the land should be irrelevant for the current decision.

Individuals and firms frequently do compound their economic errors, however, by continuing to focus on past expenditures. Business executives who were originally responsible for making a bad decision may be particularly reluctant to let bygones be bygones. Publicly announcing that the correct market price of land is $100,000 an acre, for example, would be equivalent to announcing that a major mistake had been made. Acknowledging such a mistake could jeopardize a business executive's future with the firm.

Economic Rent

A second difference between an economist's and an accountant's definition of profit concerns **economic rent.** Economic rent is the difference between the price that is actually paid and the price that would have to be paid in order for the good or service to be produced.

Although economic rent has far broader applications than its historic use to refer to payments made by farmers to their landlords for the use of their land, the example of rent for land use is still instructive. The critical characteristic of land in this regard is that its supply is inelastic. Higher payments for land (higher rents) will not elicit a greater supply. Even if landlords received virtually nothing for their land, the same land would be available. Many other factors of production have the same inelastic character. Even if you doubled his salary, Greg Maddux would not "produce" more pitches for the Atlanta Braves. The extra payments for this kind of rare talent fall into the economist's definition of rent. Anyone who is in the position to receive economic rents is fortunate indeed, because these "rents" are unrelated to effort. They are payments determined entirely by demand.

Firms earn economic rent to the extent that they are more efficient than other firms. We saw earlier that a firm is willing to produce at a price equal to its minimum average cost. Some firms might be more efficient than others, so their average cost curves are lower. Consider a market in which all firms except one have the same average cost curve, and the market price corresponds to the minimum average cost of these firms. The remaining firm is super-efficient, so its average costs are far below those of the other firms. The company would have been willing to produce at a lower price, at its minimum average cost. What it receives in excess of what is required to induce it

CASE IN POINT

Entering the Painting Business and Opportunity Costs

Individuals often forget to include opportunity costs when they are making important decisions. The following story illustrates this.

House painting is a summer business, for days that are hot and long, and with available low-skilled labor on vacation from high school and college. As a way of picking up some cash, Michael decided to start Presto Painters during the summer, after taking introductory economics.

Just getting started involved some substantial fixed costs. Michael ran the business out of his parents' home so he had no costs for office space. His fixed costs ended up looking like this:

Fixed costs	
Used van	$5,000
Paint and supplies	$2,000
Flyers and signs	$1,200
Business cards and estimate sheets	$ 500
Phone line and answering machine	$ 300
Total	$9,000

Michael went to work drumming up business. He took calls from potential customers and knocked on doors, made estimates of what he thought it would cost to paint someone's home, and then offered them a price. Of course, he was in direct competition with many other painters and had to meet the competition's price to get a job.

Michael found that the going rate for labor was $10 per hour. In the real world, labor is not the only variable input required for house painting. There are also costs from buying additional paint and brushes, but for the sake of simplicity, let's assume that he started off the summer with all the paint he needed. Thus, his variable costs were related to the labor he needed to hire.

Variable costs are also related to the amount of time it takes to paint a house, which varies depending on the quality of the labor you can find. The variable costs for Presto Painters were as follows:

Houses painted	Hours of labor hired	Payroll cost
5	100	$ 1,000
10	300	$ 3,000
15	600	$ 6,000
20	1,000	$10,000
25	1,500	$15,000
30	2,100	$21,000

to enter the market are rents—returns on the firm's superior capabilities.

Thus, when economists say that competition drives profits to zero, they are focusing on the facts that in competitive equilibrium, price equals marginal cost for every firm producing. A company will not increase profits by expanding production, and it will not pay for firms outside the industry to enter. We say that competition drives profits to zero at the margin.

In some cases, supplies of inputs are inelastic in the short run but elastic in the long run. An example is payment for the use of a building. In the short run, the supply of buildings does not depend on the return, and hence payments for the use of the building are rents, in the economist's sense. But in the long run, the supply of buildings does depend on the return—investors will not construct new buildings unless they receive a return equal to what they could obtain elsewhere. So the "rent" received by the building's owner is not really a rent, in the sense in which economists use the term.

The Theory of the Competitive Firm

We now have completed half of our description of the theory of the competitive firm. The firm takes as given the prices it

WRAP-UP

Accountants' versus Economists' Profits

Accounting profits: revenues minus expenditures

Economic profits: revenues minus rents minus economic costs (including opportunity costs of labor and capital)

Number of homes	Total cost	Average cost	Marginal cost (per house)
0	$ 9,000		
			$ 200
5	$10,000	$2,000	
			$ 400
10	$12,000	$1,200	
			$ 600
15	$15,000	$1,000	
			$ 800
20	$19,000	$ 950	
			$1,000
25	$24,000	$ 960	
			$1,200
30	$30,000	$1,000	

Given this information, Michael could calculate cost curves for Presto Painters (see above).

Based on his marginal and average cost curves, Michael figured that if market conditions allowed him to charge $1,000 or more for a typical house, then he could make a profit by painting at least 25 houses. Roughly speaking, that is how his summer worked out; painting 25 houses for $1,000 apiece. Thus, he earned $1,000 in profits.

Or so he thought. Nowhere on this list of costs did Michael consider the opportunity cost of his time. He was not getting paid $10 an hour for painting houses; he was out there stirring up business, hiring and organizing workers, taking calls from customers, dealing with complaints.

Imagine that Michael had an alternate job possibility waiting on tables. He could earn $6 per hour (including tips) and work 40-hour weeks during a 12-week summer vacation. Thus, he could have earned $2,880 during the summer with little stress or risk. If this opportunity cost is added to the fixed costs of running the business, then his apparent profit turns into a loss. Since Presto Painters did not cover Michael's opportunity cost *and* compensate him for the risk and aggravation of running his own business, he would have been financially better off sticking to the business of filling people's stomachs rather than painting their houses. ●

pays for the inputs it uses, including the wages it pays workers and the costs of capital goods. From this, it can calculate the costs of producing different levels of output. Taking the prices it receives for the goods it sells as given, the firm chooses the level of output to maximize its profits—that is, it sets price equal to marginal cost. From this, we can derive the supply curves that were used in Chapters 4 and 5. As prices increase, output increases; firms produce more, and more firms produce. Thus, supply curves are upward sloping.

But as the firm produces more, it will also demand more labor and more capital. Deriving firms' demand curves for labor and capital is our next task, which we take up in the following chapter.

Review and Practice

Summary

1. A revenue curve shows the relationship between a firm's total output and its revenue. For a competitive firm, the marginal revenue it receives from selling an additional unit of output is the price of that unit.

2. A firm in a competitive market will choose the level of output where the market price—the marginal revenue it receives from producing an extra unit—equals the marginal cost.

3. A firm will enter a market if the market price for a good exceeds its minimum average costs, since it can make a profit by selling the good for more than it costs to produce the good.

4. If the market price is below minimum average costs and a firm has no sunk costs, the firm will exit the market immediately. If the market price is below minimum average costs and a firm has sunk costs, it will continue to produce in the short run as long as the market price exceeds its minimum average variable costs.

5. For a firm contemplating entering a market, its supply is zero up to the point where price equals minimum average costs. Above that price, the supply curve is the same as the marginal cost curve.

6. The market supply curve is constructed by adding up the supply curves of all firms in an industry. As prices rise, more firms are willing to produce, and each firm is willing to produce more, so that the market supply curve is normally upward sloping.

7. The economist's and the accountant's concepts of profits differ in how they treat opportunity costs and economic rents.

Key Terms

revenue curve
marginal revenue
economic rent

Review Questions

1. In a competitive market, what rule determines the profit-maximizing level of output? What is the relationship between a firm's supply curve and its marginal cost curve?

2. What determines firms' decisions to enter a market? to exit a market? Explain the role of the average variable cost curve in determining whether firms will exit the market.

3. Why is the long run supply curve more elastic than the short run supply curve?

4. What is the relationship between the way accountants use the concept of profits and the way economists use that term?

Problems

1. The market price for painting a house in Centerville is $10,000. The Total Cover-up House-Painting Company has fixed costs of $4,000 for ladders, brushes, and so on, and the company's variable costs for house painting follow this pattern:

Output
(houses painted)   2   3   4   5   6   7   8   9   10
Variable cost
(in thousands of dollars) 26 32 36 42 50 60 72 86 102

Calculate the company's total costs, and graph the revenue curve and the total cost curve. Do the curves have the shape you expect? Over what range of production is the company making profits?

2. Calculate and graph the marginal cost, the average costs, and the average variable costs for the Total Cover-up House-Painting Company. Given the market price, at what level of output will this firm maximize profits? What profit (or loss) is it making at that level? At what price will the firm no longer make a profit? Assume its fixed costs are sunk; there is no market for used ladders, brushes, etc. At what price will the company shut down?

3. Draw a U-shaped average cost curve. On your diagram, designate at what price levels you would expect entry and at what price levels you would expect exit if all the fixed costs are sunk. What if only half the fixed costs are sunk? Explain your reasoning.

4. José is a skilled electrician at a local company, a job that pays $50,000 per year, but he is considering quitting to start his own business. He talks it over with an accountant, who helps him to draw up the following chart with their best predictions about costs and revenues.

Predicted annual costs		Predicted annual revenues
Basic wage	$20,000	$75,000
Rent of space	$12,000	
Rent of equipment	$18,000	
Utilities	$ 2,000	
Miscellaneous	$ 5,000	

The basic wage does seem a bit low, the accountant admits, but she tells José to remember that as owner of the business, José will get to keep any profits as well. From an economist's point of view, is the accountant's list of costs complete? From an economist's point of view, what are José's expected profits?

Chapter 9

Labor and Capital Markets

Key Questions

1. How can the basic tools introduced in Chapter 6 to analyze consumers' expenditures be applied to such important aspects of life as work, education, and saving?

2. What determines the number of hours an individual works, or whether she chooses to work or not?

3. How do income and substitution effects help us understand why labor supply may not be very responsive to changes in wages, or saving to changes in interest rates?

4. What determines the firm's demand for labor? What determines the firm's demand for capital?

5. How do the wage and interest rates ensure demand and supply balance in the labor and capital markets?

6. Why do economists think of education as an investment and refer to the result as human capital?

The previous three chapters examined demand and supply in the markets for goods and services. Choosing what goods to purchase, and how much to purchase, represents one of the basic decisions households face. How much money people have to spend depends on two other basic decisions: how much to work (and earn) and how much to save (or spend from savings). The decisions households make about work determine the economy's supply of labor. Their decisions about saving determine the economy's supply of funds in the capital market. Understanding the factors that influence these decisions will give us insight into the supply side of the economy's labor and capital markets.

Chapters 7 and 8 focused on the factors that affect the supply of goods and services. But just as firms must decide what to produce and how much to produce, they must also decide how much labor to hire and how many machines to buy. Their decisions determine the economy's demand for labor and the demand for funds in the capital market. Understanding the factors that influence these decisions will give us insight into the demand side of the economy's labor and capital markets.

In this chapter, we begin by focusing on the labor market. How can we use the approach of Chapter 6 to understand household decisions concerning how much to work? What determines the firm's demand for labor? We then turn to the capital market. Firms employ workers, but they also use capital—the tools, machinery, plants, office buildings, and computers that aid in production. A firm that wants to build a new plant may need to borrow funds to carry out construction. The funds available for firms to borrow come from household savings, so we will again use our model of the household to explain savings behavior.

The Labor Supply Decision

At one time, going to college was a full-time job. Students were supported by their families or by scholarships and loans, with few students holding down jobs. Today, most college students work to help pay their tuition and living expenses. In addition to deciding on which classes to take, students have to decide whether to work, and if they decide to work, they need to decide how many hours to work each week. Working more helps pay the bills, but it also takes time away from studies. It may even mean that it will take longer to graduate. Understanding the forces that affect decisions about how much to work—how much labor to supply to the market—is central to understanding how labor markets function.

The increase in student employment is just one of many changes in the pattern of labor supply that have taken place over the past half century. The average workweek has declined from 39 hours in 1959 to just under 35 hours in 1999. At the same time, the fraction of women in the labor force has increased enormously. In 1950, just 34 percent of women over the age of sixteen were in the labor force. Today, that figure is close to 60 percent. Many of the changes in American society in recent decades are reflections of the decisions individuals make about how much labor to supply.

The Choice Between Leisure and Consumption

Economists use the basic model of choice to help understand these patterns of labor supply. This is the model we used in Chapter 6 to examine the consumption decision. The decision about how much labor to supply is a choice between consumption, or income, and leisure. (*Leisure* to an economist means all the time an individual could potentially work for pay that is not actually spent working.) By

giving up leisure, a person receives additional income, and this allows her to increase consumption. By working less and giving up some consumption, a person obtains more leisure. An increase in income does not necessarily translate *immediately* into consumption; the individual has to decide whether to spend the extra income now or in the future. We will tackle that choice later in the chapter. Here, we assume the person spends all her income.

Even though the typical job seems to have a fixed time requirement, there are many ways in which people can influence how much labor they will supply. Many workers may not have discretion as to whether or not they will work full-time, but they have some choice in whether they will work overtime. In addition, many individuals moonlight, taking second jobs that provide them with additional income. Most of these jobs—like driving a taxi—provide considerable discretion in the number of hours worked. Hence, even when people have no choice about how much they work at their primary job, they still have choices. Further, the fact that jobs differ in their normal workweek means that a worker has some flexibility in choosing a job that allows her to work the number of hours she wishes. Finally,

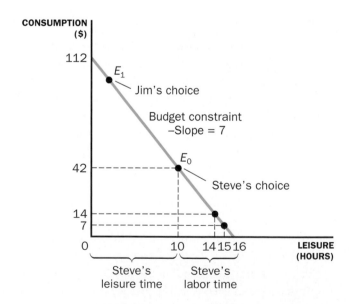

FIGURE 9.1   *A Budget Constraint Between Leisure and Income*

Individuals are willing to trade leisure for an increase in income, and thus in consumption. The budget constraint shows Steve choosing E_0, with 10 hours of daily leisure, 6 hours of work, and $42 in daily wages.

economists believe that social conventions concerning the "standard" workweek—the 40-hour week that has become the 35-hour week—respond over time to the attitudes (preferences) of workers.

We now apply the analysis of Chapter 6 to an individual's choice between work and leisure. Figure 9.1 shows the budget constraint of Steve, who earns an hourly wage of $7. Accordingly, for each hour less of leisure Steve enjoys—for each extra hour he works—he earns $7 more. That is, his consumption increases by $7. Underlying this budget constraint is his time constraint. He has only so many hours a day, say 16, to spend either working or at leisure. For each extra hour he works, he has 1 less hour of leisure. If he works 1 hour, his income is $7, if he works 2 hours, his income is $14, and so forth. If he works 16 hours—he has no leisure—his income is $7 \times 16 = 112. The trade-off between income and leisure given by his budget constraint is $7 per hour.

Steve will choose a point on the budget constraint according to his own preferences, just as a consumer chooses between two goods (see Chapter 6). Let's suppose that he chooses point E_0. At E_0 he has 10 hours of leisure, which means that he works 6 hours out of a total available time of 16 hours. His income is $42 per day.

In deciding which of the points along the budget constraint to choose, Steve balances out the marginal benefits of what he can buy with an additional hour's wage, with the marginal costs—the value of the hour's worth of leisure that he will have to forgo. Steve and his brother, Jim, assess the marginal benefits and marginal costs differently. Steve chooses point E_0, while his brother chooses point E_1. Jim values the material things in life more and leisure less.

For Steve, at E_0, the marginal benefit of the extra concert tickets or other goods he can buy with the money he earns from working an extra hour just offsets the marginal costs of that hour, the extra leisure he has to give up. At points to the left of E_0, Steve has less leisure (so the marginal value of leisure is greater) and he has more goods (so the marginal value of the extra goods he can get is lower). The marginal benefit of working less exceeds the marginal costs, and so he works less—he moves toward point E_0. Converse arguments apply to Steve's thinking about points to the right of E_0.

Thinking Like an Economist

Trade-offs

The relevant trade-off for the labor supply decision is that between consumption and leisure, as delineated in the budget constraint in Figure 9.1. To gain more consumption, you have to work more, and this means you have to give up leisure. To gain more leisure time, you have to give up consumption as you work fewer hours and earn less money.

Like all trade-offs, this one reflects an opportunity cost, a concept we introduced in Chapter 2 (p. 32). In the present case, the opportunity cost of an extra hour of leisure is the consumption you have to give up by working one hour less. Similarly, the opportunity cost of an extra $25 of consumption is the leisure time you have to give up to earn the extra $25.

Because the opportunity cost of leisure is the forgone consumption that must be given up, this opportunity cost depends on the wage you can earn. If your wage is $7 per hour, the opportunity cost of an hour of leisure is $7. If your wage is $25 per hour, the opportunity cost of an hour of leisure is $25. So the opportunity cost of leisure is greater for someone who earns a high wage than it is for someone who earns a lower wage.

Another key idea to remember is that economic decisions are determined by marginal trade-offs (see Chapter 2, p. 38). If you want to consume more, the benefit of the *extra* consumption must be weighed against the (opportunity) cost of the *diminished* leisure. Based on an individual's preferences for consumption and leisure, the worker chooses the point on the budget constraint where the marginal benefits and costs are equal.

We can apply the same kind of reasoning to see why the workaholic Jim chooses a point to the left of E_0. At E_0, Jim values goods more and leisure less. The marginal benefit of working more exceeds the marginal costs. At E_1, the marginal benefit of working an extra hour (the extra consumption) just offsets the marginal costs.

We can use this framework to derive a *labor supply curve* that shows the quantity of labor supplied at different wages. Changes in wages have both an income effect and a substitution effect. An increase in wages makes individuals better off. When individuals are better off, they purchase more of all goods. One of the "goods" they will want more of is leisure, so they work less. This is the income effect. But an increase in wages also changes the trade-offs. By giving up one more hour of leisure, the individual can get more goods. Because of this, individuals are willing to work more. This is the substitution effect.

When we looked at the case of a typical good in Chapter 6, we saw that the income and substitution effects reinforce each other. A higher price means that individuals are worse off—this income effect leads to reduced consumption of the good—and individuals substitute away from the good whose price has increased—the substitu-

tion effect also leads to reduced consumption of the good. *With labor supply, income and substitution effects work in opposite directions, so the net affect of an increase in wages is ambiguous.*

Figure 9.2A shows the normal case of an upward sloping labor supply curve where the substitution effect dominates. People choose to work more as the wage rises, trading off leisure for more income. Panel B illustrates the case of a backward-bending labor supply curve. At high wages, the income effect of further increases in wages outweighs the substitution effect, so that labor supply decreases. People choose to work less and enjoy more leisure. Doctors, dentists, and other high-income professionals who work only a four-day week may be evidence of a labor supply curve that is backward bending at high-income levels.

If income and substitution effects just balance each other, then labor supply will be relatively unaffected by wage changes. The evidence is that at least for men, the labor supply curve elasticity—the percentage increase in hours worked as a result of a 1 percent increase in wages—is positive but small. That is why, is spite of the huge increase in wages over the past fifty years, average hours worked, for men, has not changed much. For

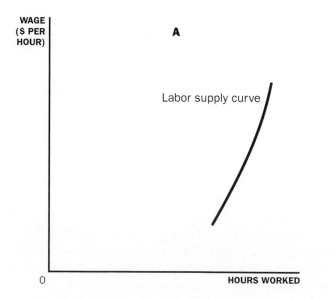

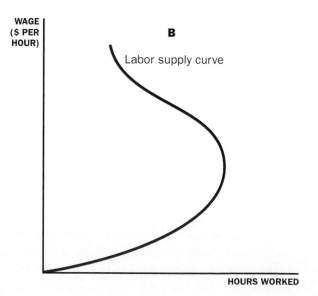

FIGURE 9.2   *The Labor Supply Curve*

Panel A shows the case where the substitution effect exceeds the income effect by just a bit, so increases in wages lead to only a small change in labor supply, and the labor supply curve is very steep. In panel B, the substitution effect dominates the income effect at low wages, so that the labor supply curve is upward sloping; and the income effect dominates the substitution effect at high wages, so that the labor supply is downward sloping over that range. Thus, the labor supply curve bends backward.

women, the evidence suggests a rise in wages increases labor supply.

So far, we have discussed the impact of a change in wages on labor supply while implicitly assuming that the prices of consumer goods remain unchanged. But in assessing the trade-off between leisure and consumption, an individual is concerned with the actual goods and services that can be purchased, not simply the number of dollars available to spend on consumption. If wages double, but so do the prices of all consumer goods, then the trade-off between leisure and consumption has not changed. If Jim's wage rises from $7 per hour to $14 per hour, but the price of a compact disc also doubles from $10.50 to $21.00, Jim must still give up an hour and a half of leisure to obtain one CD. What is important for labor supply decisions is the average dollar wage, called the **nominal wage,** corrected for changes in the prices of consumer goods. This corrected wage is called the **real wage.** Figure 9.3 shows how important it is to distinguish between nominal and real wages. Since 1980, the average nominal wage has risen by almost 100 percent, from $6.66 to $13.24 per hour. Yet the prices

of the things we buy have also risen, and when this is taken into account, the average real wage has remained virtually constant over the past twenty years.

WRAP-UP

Wage Changes and Labor Supply

Labor supply decisions depend on the real wage—the nominal wage corrected for the price of consumer goods.

As real wages rise, individuals become better off. This income effect induces them to work less. Offsetting this is the substitution effect—the higher return to working provides an incentive to work longer hours. Either effect may dominate. Thus, the quantity of labor supplied may increase or decrease with wage increases.

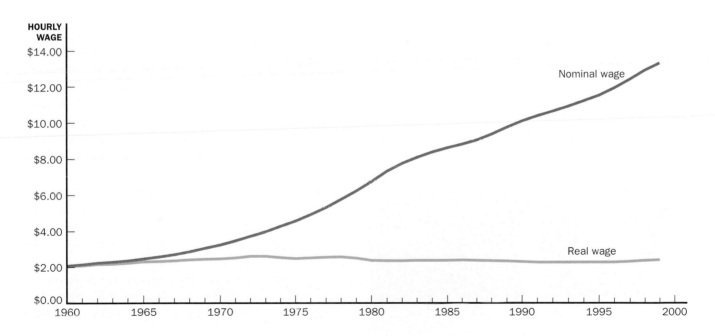

FIGURE 9.3   *The Nominal Wage and the Real Wage*

The average hourly wage in manufacturing has risen significantly over the past forty years. The nominal wage was 533 percent higher in 1999 than it was in 1960. What matters for labor supply decisions, though, is the real value of the wage—the amount of goods that can be purchased by working one hour. Because prices of goods have also risen, the average real wage in manufacturing has risen much less than the nominal wage. From 1960 to 1999, the real wage rose only 16 percent.

Labor Force Participation

The decision about how much labor to supply can be divided into two parts: whether to work and if so, how much to work. Traditionally for men, the question of whether to work has had an obvious answer. Unless they were very wealthy, they had to work to support themselves (and their families). Accordingly, the wage at which they decided to work rather than not to work was very low. For most men, a change in the wage still does not affect their decision of whether to work. It affects only their decision about how many hours to work, and even this effect is small.

The decision about *whether* to work is called the **labor force participation decision.** Figure 9.4 shows the labor supply curve for an individual—it shows how many hours the individual is willing to supply at each real wage. The minimum wage at which the individual is willing to work, W_R, is called the **reservation wage.** Below the reservation wage, the individual does not participate in the labor force. For men, the reservation wage traditionally has been very low.

Today, most women also work for pay. Women, however, have faced social expectations different from those facing men. Only a few decades ago, not only was there some question as to whether women should work, but also the social presumption was that working women would drop out of the labor market when they had children. And many mothers did not reenter the market even after their children were grown.

The increased quantity of labor supplied by women over the past fifty years can be viewed partly as a *movement* along the labor supply curve and partly as a *shift* in the

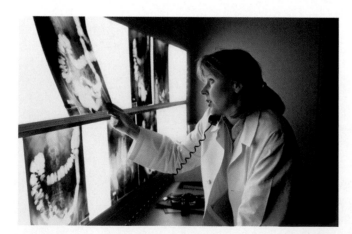

There has been a large increase in labor force participation by women over the past thirty years.

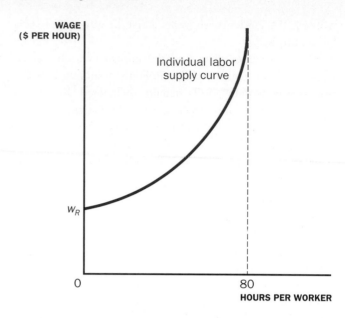

FIGURE 9.4   *The Labor Participation Decision*

The reservation wage W_R is the minimum wage at which an individual supplies labor.

curve. Job opportunities for women have increased enormously in the past thirty years, and relative wages have risen. Thus, the remuneration from working has increased; equivalently, the *opportunity cost* of being out of the labor force has gone up. For women already in the labor force, these wage increases have opposing income and substitution effects, just as they do for men. But for women who were not previously part of the labor force, only the substitution effect operates: if a woman was working zero hours, an increase in wages does not raise her income—there is no income effect. The substitution effect acts to draw more women into the labor force.[1] The aggregate effect of increased wages on the quantity of labor supplied by women represents a movement along the labor supply curve.

The labor supply curve for women also has shifted, increasing the labor supply at each value of the wage. Two changes have shifted the labor supply curve to the right

---

[1]It is important to note here that the labor force, as economists define it, includes not only those who have jobs but also those who are looking for jobs. It is also important to note that when we refer to "labor supply," we refer to "market" labor supply, that is, work for pay. Many people perform tasks at home that are comparable to those they perform at work; nonetheless, these are not included in the analysis of labor supply.

and contributed to the dramatic increase in labor force participation of women that is shown in Figure 9.5. Beginning around 1973, (real) wages stopped growing at the rate they had been increasing during the period following World War II (see Figure 9.3). Individuals and families had come to expect regular increases in their material standards of living. When these increases stopped, they felt the loss. This development encouraged many married women to take part-time or full-time jobs as a way of keeping the family income increasing or, in many cases, to prevent it from falling.

There also has been a change in attitudes, both on the part of women and on the part of employers, and today, the traditional perceptions about the role of women have changed significantly. Outright discrimination against women was barred by federal law in 1963; reduced discrimination made it more attractive for women to enter the labor force, as more careers were open to them. Enrollments of women in professional schools has increased dramatically, reflecting changing attitudes among men and women. Most women without small children participate in

the labor market, and many with children leave the labor force only for relatively short periods of time. These changes contributed to the shift in the labor supply curve for women and along with the effects of higher wages, led to the large increases in labor supply by women over the past thirty years.

Firms and the Demand for Labor

We have now examined the supply side of the labor market. It is time to turn to the demand side. What factors influence firms' decisions about how much labor to hire? Once we have examined these decisions, the basic law of supply and demand can be used to show how the wage is determined in the labor market. Labor is one of the primary inputs firms use in producing output. So our discussion begins by considering what determines a firm's demand for inputs.

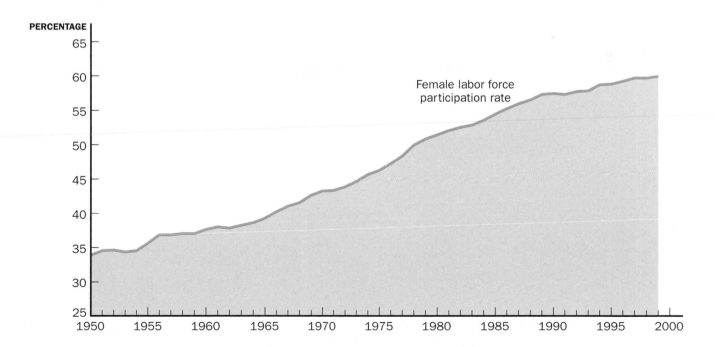

FIGURE 9.5   *Female Labor Force Participation*

Only one-third of all women were in the labor force in 1950. By 1999, 60 percent of all women were in the labor force.

SOURCE: *ERP* (2001), Table B-39.

Factor Demand

In the process of deciding how much of each good to supply and what is the lowest-cost method of producing those goods, firms also decide how much of various inputs they will use. This is called **factor demand.** It is sometimes called a *derived demand* because it flows from other decisions the profit-maximizing firm makes. In Chapter 7, the analysis of costs was broken up into two cases, one in which there was a single variable input, or factor of production, and one in which there were several factors. We proceed along similar lines here. Labor is used as our main example of an input. The same principles apply to any factor of production.

When there is only a single factor of production, say, labor, then the decision about how much to produce is the same as the decision about how much labor to hire. As soon as we know the price of the good, we can calculate the supply (output) from the marginal cost curve. As soon as we know the output the firm plans to produce, we know the labor required simply by looking at the production function, which gives the labor input required to produce any level of output. Thus, in Figure 9.6, at the price p_1, the output is Q_1 (panel A), and the labor required to produce that output (factor demand) is L_1 (panel B).

There is another way to derive the demand for a factor. If a firm hires one more worker, for example, the extra cost to the firm is the wage, w. The extra benefit of the worker is the extra revenue the firm receives from selling the output the worker produces. This is equal to the price of the good times the extra output. This extra output corresponding to the extra worker is the marginal product of labor. (Marginal products can be calculated for any other factor of production as well.) The price of the good thus produced times the marginal product of labor is referred to as the **value of the marginal product of labor.** The firm hires labor up to the point where the value of the marginal product (the marginal benefit to the firm) equals the price of labor, the wage (the marginal cost to the firm).

Using p for the price of the good, MPL for the marginal product of labor, and w for the wage of the worker, we can write this equilibrium condition as

$$\text{value of marginal product} = p \times MPL = w = \text{wage.}$$

From this equilibrium condition, we can derive the demand curve for labor. Figure 9.7 plots the value of the marginal product of labor for each level of labor. Since the marginal product of labor decreases as labor increases,

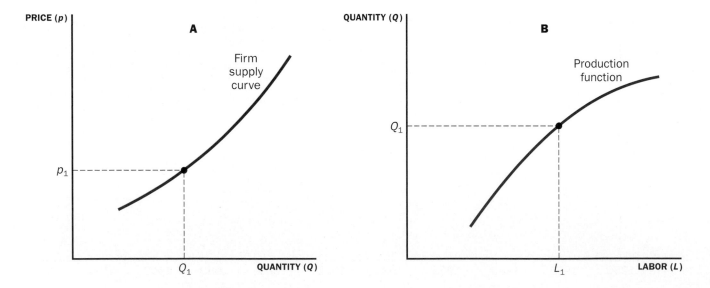

FIGURE 9.6   *The Demand for Labor*

The demand for labor can be calculated from the firm's supply curve and the production function. Panel A shows how the firm, given a market price p_1, chooses a level of output Q_1 from its supply curve. Panel B shows that to produce the output Q_1 requires L_1 units of labor. L_1 is the demand for labor.

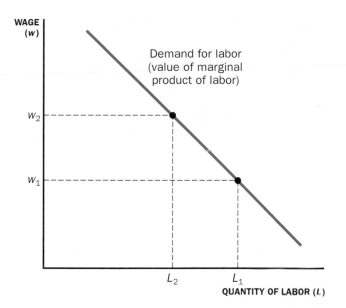

FIGURE 9.7 *The Demand Curve for Labor*

The value of the marginal product of labor declines with the level of employment. Since labor is hired up to the point where the wage equals the value of the marginal product, at wage w_1, employment is L_1, and at wage w_2, employment is L_2. The demand curve for labor thus traces out the values of the marginal product of labor at different levels of employment.

WRAP-UP

Factor Demand

A factor of production will be demanded up to the point where the value of the marginal product of that factor equals its price. In the case of labor, this is the same as saying the marginal product of labor equals the real product wage.

If we divide both sides of the equation giving the equilibrium condition by the price, we obtain the condition

$$MPL = w/p.$$

The wage divided by the price of the good being produced is defined as the **real product wage.** It measures what firms pay workers in terms of the goods the worker produces rather than in dollar terms. Thus, the firm hires workers up to the point where the real product wage equals the marginal product of labor.

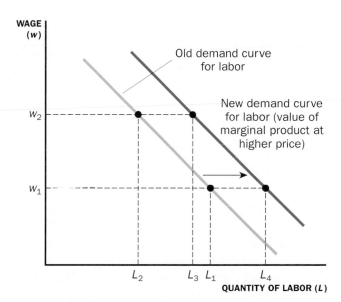

FIGURE 9.8 *Effect of Price Change on the Demand Curve for Labor*

An increase in the price received by a firm shifts the value of the marginal product of labor curve up, so that at each wage, the demand for labor is increased. At wage w_1, employment rises from L_1 to L_4; at wage w_2, employment rises from L_2 to L_3.

the value of the marginal product also decreases. When the wage is w_1, the value of the marginal product of labor equals the wage with a level of labor at L_1. This is the firm's demand for labor at a wage w_1. Thus, the curve giving the value of the marginal product of labor at each level of employment *is* the demand curve for labor.

It is easy to use this diagram to see the effect of an increase in the price of the good the firm produces. In Figure 9.8, the higher price increases the value of the marginal product of labor at each level of employment, and it immediately follows that at each wage, the demand for labor increases. The demand curve for labor shifts to the right.

Thus, the demand for labor depends on both the wage and the price the firm receives for the goods it sells. In fact, the demand for labor depends only on the ratio of the two, as we will now see.

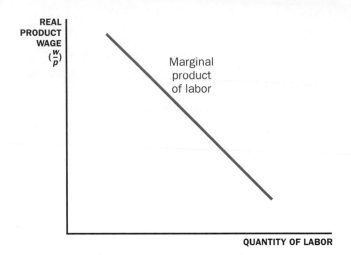

FIGURE 9.9   *The Firm's Demand Curve for Labor and the Real Product Wage*

Firms hire labor up to the point where the real product wage equals the marginal product of labor. As the real product wage increases, the demand for labor decreases.

This principle is illustrated in Figure 9.9, which shows the marginal product of labor. Because of diminishing returns, the marginal product diminishes as labor (and output) increases. As the real product wage increases, the demand for labor decreases.

From the Firm's Factor Demand to the Market's Factor Demand

Once we have derived the firm's demand curve for labor, we can derive the total market demand for labor. At a given set of prices, we simply add up the demand for labor by each firm at any particular wage rate. The total is the market demand at that wage. Since each firm reduces the amount of labor that it demands as the wage increases, the market demand curve is downward sloping. Figure 9.10 shows how we add up diagrammatically the demand curves for labor for two firms, High Speed Internet Services and Instant Access Web Providers. At a wage of w_1, High Speed demands 30 workers and Instant Access demands 30 workers, for a total demand of 60 workers. At a wage of w_2, High Speed demands 20 workers and Instant Access demands 10 workers, for a total demand of 30 workers.

Labor Supply, Demand, and the Equilibrium Wage

We have now discussed the factors that determine labor supply decisions and those that determine the demand for labor by firms. Households decide how much labor to supply to the marketplace, at each value of the wage. If the substitution effect dominates, higher real wages increase the quantity of labor supplied. Firms decide how much labor to demand at each value of the wage. At higher real wages, the quantity of labor firms demand is lower. The labor market is in equilibrium when the wage has adjusted to balance labor supply and labor demand. When the labor market is in equilibrium, the demand for labor equals the supply of labor. No worker who wishes to get a job (for which she is qualified) at the going market wage will fail to get one. No firm that wants to hire a worker at the going wage will fail to find a qualified employee. Adjustments in wages ensure that this will occur.

If demand and supply are not equal at the going market wage, the wage will adjust. If, at the going wage, the number of hours of labor households wish to supply is greater than the number of hours of labor firms wish to employ, those in the labor force without jobs will offer to work for less than the going wage. The process of competition will lead to lower wages, until eventually demand again equals supply. Likewise, if firms in the economy demand more labor at the going wage than is supplied, competition by firms to hire scarce labor services will bid the wage up until demand and supply are equal.

This basic model of the labor market makes clear predictions for the consequences of shifts in the demand and supply of labor. Consider first shifts in the supply curve of labor. This can occur because the total labor force grows, as more young people reach working age than there are old people retiring, because of new immigrants, or because of social changes such as the entry of more women into the labor force. The U.S. labor force expanded rapidly in the 1970s, for example, as the baby boomers entered the labor force and more and more women worked. An increase in the labor force shifts the supply curve of labor to the right; at each real wage, the total number of labor hours individuals wish to supply is greater. The equilibrium real wage falls. This fall in the price of labor indicates to firms that labor is less scarce than it was before, and so firms should economize less in the use of labor. Firms respond to the lower real wage by creating more jobs. Employment rises to absorb the increase in labor supply.

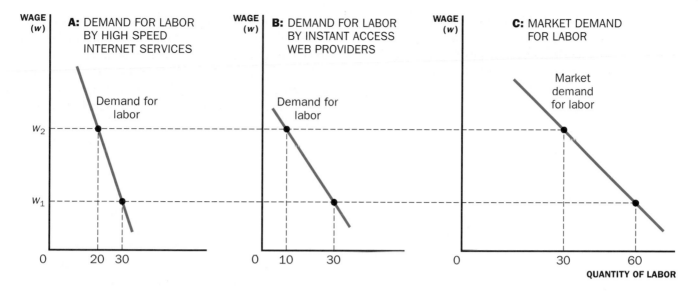

FIGURE 9.10 *The Market Demand Curve for Labor*

The market demand curve for labor at each wage is obtained by horizontally adding up the demand curves for labor of each individual firm. As the wage rises, at a fixed price of output, less labor is demanded.

Consider now the effects of a shift in the demand curve for labor. Suppose technological progress makes workers more productive, raising the marginal product of labor. At each wage, firms now wish to hire more labor, and the labor demand curve shifts to the right. Real wages rise to restore equilibrium in the labor market.

Over the past quarter century, increases in the American labor force have shifted the labor supply curve to the right. At the same time, increases in worker productivity have shifted the labor demand curve to the right as well. The basic model predicts that the total quantity of labor employed will rise, but real wages may fall (if supply shifts more than demand) or rise (if demand shifts more than supply). Average real wages in the United States have fallen slightly over this period (see Figure 9.3).

The Capital Market

At any given time, there are some people and companies who would like to borrow, so they can spend more than their current income. John has his first job and knows he needs a car for transportation; Chad is borrowing money to buy a new home; Jill needs to purchase kitchen equip-ment, tables, and chairs to open her new restaurant; Intel needs to build a new chip-assembly plant. Others would like to save, spending less than their current income. Julie is putting money aside for her children's college education and for her retirement; Bill is putting aside money to make a down payment on a house.

The basic tools we have developed to explain how households and firms make decisions about which goods to buy, which to produce, how much to work, and how many workers to hire can also be used to explain saving and borrowing decisions. When households save, spending less than they earn in income, they provide funds for those who want to spend more than their income. When an individual household puts its savings in a bank or invests it in the stock market, it might not think of itself as lending money, but that is exactly what it is doing. Firms who wish to buy new machines or build new factories or office buildings borrow the savings of the household sector. The **capital market,** or as it is also called, the **loanable funds market,** is the market in which the funds made available when households save are directed to those who wish to borrow, either to build a new home, to buy a new car, to build a new factory, or to install new machinery.

To understand the supply of saving to the loanable funds market, we will focus on households; even though many individual households borrow, households as a group typically save. This is not always the case, though: in 1999 U.S. households actually dissaved, spending more than they earned in income. We will focus on the firms as the major borrowers in the economy.

The Household Decision to Save

The assumption that individuals spend their money in a rational manner, thinking through the alternatives clearly, holds for the saving as well as the spending and working decisions. In making their saving decisions, individuals are making a decision about *when* to spend or consume. If they consume less today—that is, if they save more today—they can consume more tomorrow.

We use the budget constraint to analyze this choice. Instead of showing the choice between goods, the budget constraint now shows, as in Figure 9.11, the choice between spending in two time periods. The two time periods

here are "working years" and "retirement years." Consider the case of Joan. She faces the lifetime budget constraint depicted in the figure. The first period is represented on the horizontal axis, the second on the vertical axis. Her wages during her working life (the first period) are w. Thus, at one extreme, she could consume all of w in the first period (point C) and have nothing for her retirement. At the other extreme, she could consume nothing in the first period, save all of her income, and consume her savings, together with any accumulated interest she has earned on her savings, in the second period (point B). If we use r to denote the rate of interest, her consumption in the second period at point B is $w(1 + r)$. In between these extremes lies a straight line that defines the rest of her choices. She can choose any combination of first- and second-period consumption on this line. This is Joan's two-period budget constraint.

By postponing consumption—that is, by saving—Joan can increase the total amount of goods that she can obtain because she is paid interest on her savings. The cost, however, is that she must wait to enjoy the goods. But what is the relative price, the trade-off between future and current consumption? To put it another way, how much extra future consumption can she get if she gives up one unit of current consumption?

If Joan decides not to consume one more dollar today, she can take that dollar, put it in the bank, and get back at the end of the year that dollar plus interest. If the interest rate is 5 percent, for every dollar of consumption that Joan gives up today, she can get $1.05 of consumption next year. The relative price (of consumption today relative to consumption tomorrow) is thus 1 plus the interest rate. Because Joan must give up more than $1.00 of consumption in the second period to get an additional $1.00 worth of consumption today, current consumption is more expensive than future consumption. The opportunity cost of current consumption is the future consumption that is forgone, and this cost depends on the rate of interest.

Joan chooses among the points on this budget constraint according to her personal preferences. Consider, for example, point D, where Joan is consuming very little during her working life. Since she is spending very little in the present, any additional consumption now will have a high marginal value. She will be relatively eager to substitute present consumption for future consumption. At the other extreme, if she is consuming a great deal in the present, say at point F, additional consumption today will

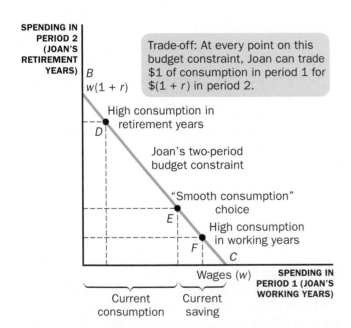

FIGURE 9.11 *The Two-Period Budget Constraint*

The two-period budget constraint *BC* describes the possible combinations of current and future consumption available. Wages not spent in period 1 become savings, which earn interest. As a result, forgoing a dollar of consumption today increases future consumption by more than a dollar.

have a relatively low marginal value, while future consumption will have a high marginal value. Hence, she will be relatively eager to save more for the future. She chooses a point in between, E, where consumption in the two periods is not too different. She has *smoothed* her consumption. That is, consumption in each of the two different periods is about the same. This kind of saving, motivated to smoothing consumption over one's lifetime and to provide for retirement, is called **life-cycle saving.** In Figure 9.11, the difference between the first-period income, w, and what she consumes in the first-period is her saving.

The Time Value of Money   Because you can earn interest on your savings, the cost of a dollar of current consumption is more than simply $1.00 of future consumption. As we learned in Chapter 2, calculating costs correctly is one of the basic steps in making rational decisions. But what if we are comparing costs that occur at different times, such as the cost of current versus future consumption? Or to take a more specific example, suppose one store advertises a car stereo system for $400 and another advertises it for $425 with no payment for a full year. How can we compare these two? If you have the $400 to spend today, is it cheaper to pay $400 right now for the stereo or pay $425 in one year?

To think about this comparison, what could you do with your $400 if you opted to buy from the store that lets you delay your payment. You might put the money in a bank. When you deposit money in a bank, you have loaned your money to the bank. In return, the bank pays you **interest.** If the interest rate is 5 percent per year, you will receive $420 in a year—the $20 is the interest payment, while the $400 is the repayment of the **principal,** the original amount you lent to the bank.

The interest rate is a price, and like other prices, it describes a trade-off. If the interest rate is 5 percent, by giving up $1.00 worth of consumption today, a saver can have $1.05 worth of consumption next year. Thus, the rate of interest tells us how much future consumption we can get by giving up $1.00 worth of current consumption. It tells us the relative price between the present and the future.

Because interest rates are normally positive, $1.00 today becomes more than a dollar in the future. This means that a dollar today is worth more than a dollar in the future. Economists call this the **time value of money.** The concept of **present discounted value** tells us precisely how to measure the time value of money. The present discounted value of $100 a year from now is what you would pay today for $100 a year from now. Suppose the interest rate is 5 percent. If you put $95.24 in the bank today, at the end of a year you will receive $4.76 in interest, which together with the original principal will total $100. Thus, $95.24 is the present discounted value of $100 one year from now, if the interest rate is 5 percent.

There is a simple formula for calculating the present discounted value of any amount to be received a year from now: just divide the amount by 1 plus the annual rate of interest. The annual rate of interest is often denoted by r.

To check this formula, consider the present discounted value of $100. According to the formula, it is $100/(1 + r)$. In other words, take the present discounted value, $100/(1 + r)$, and put it in a bank. At the end of the year you will have

$$\frac{\$100}{1+r} \times (1+r) = \$100,$$

confirming our conclusion that $100/(1 + r)$ today is worth the same as $100 one year from now.

We can now evaluate the two options for purchasing the stereo. To compare $400 today with $425 in one year, we need to calculate the present discounted value of $425. If the interest rate is 5 percent, the present discount value of $425 is $404.76. Since this is greater than $400, you are better off paying for the stereo today.

Present discounted values depend on the rate of interest. If the interest rate increases, the present discounted value of future amounts will decrease. If the interest rate rises to 10 percent, the present discounted value of $425 falls to $386.96. Now it is cheaper to postpone payment for the stereo. You can take your $400, put it in the bank, and earn 10 percent interest. In one year, you will have $440. After paying $425 for the stereo, you are left with $15 more than if you had paid for it immediately.

WRAP-UP

Present Discounted Value

Present discounted value of $1.00 next year = $1.00/(1 + interest rate).

The concept of present discounted value is important because so many decisions in economics are oriented to the future. Whether the decision is made by a person buying a car or a house or saving for retirement, or by a company building a factory or making an investment, the decision maker must be able to value money that will be received in one, two, five, or ten years in the future.

Inflation and the Real Rate of Interest

The interest rate, we have seen, is a price. It tells how many dollars next period we can get if we give up one dollar today. But except for misers like Scrooge who store money for its own sake, dollars are of value only because of the goods that can be bought with them. Because of inflation—the increase in prices over time—dollars in the future buy fewer goods than dollars today. Individuals want to know how much *consumption* they get tomorrow if they give up a dollar's worth of consumption today. The answer is given by the **real rate of interest.** This is distinguished from the **nominal rate of interest,** the rate one sees posted at one's bank and in the newspaper, which simply describes the number of dollars one gets next year in exchange for a dollar today. There is a simple relationship between the real interest rate and the nominal interest rate: The real interest rate equals the nominal interest rate minus the rate of inflation (the annual rate of change of prices on average). If the nominal interest rate is 10 percent and the rate of inflation is 6 percent, then the real interest rate is 4 percent. By saving a dollar today, you can increase the amount of goods that you get in one year's time by 4 percent.

Consider an individual who decides to deposit $1,000 in a savings account. At the end of the year, at a 10 percent interest rate, she will have $1,100. But prices meanwhile have risen by 6 percent. A good that cost $1,000 in the beginning of the year now costs $1,060. In terms of "purchasing power," she has only $40 extra to spend ($1,100 − $1,060)—4 percent more than she had at the beginning of the year.

WRAP-UP

Real Interest Rate

Real interest rate = nominal interest rate − rate of inflation.

Using the Model: Saving and the Interest Rate

We can use the budget constraint to understand how Joan's saving decision will be affected if the interest rate changes. Keep in mind two points as we apply this model, however. First, just as we saw earlier that the relevant wage for labor supply decisions is the real wage, the relevant interest rate for saving decisions is the real interest rate, that is, the interest rate adjusted for inflation. Also keep in mind that we have simplified the saving decision with our two-period model (current consumption on the one hand, future consumption on the other). In the real world, individuals usually earn interest on their savings year after year as they save for retirement. If you begin saving for retirement at the age of twenty-five, you might earn interest for forty years before reaching retirement. Typically, the interest is compounded each year (or month), which means that each year you earn interest on the interest paid in previous years. Compounding makes a huge difference over long periods of time. If you set aside $100 at 5 percent interest for forty years, you might think that each year you would earn $5 in interest (5% of $100) and that at the end of the forty years you would have your $100 plus $200 in interest (40 × $5), or $300 in total. In fact, because you earn interest for 39 years on the $5 of interest earned in year one, plus interest for 38 years on the interest earned in year two, and so on, you end up with much more than $300 after forty years. In fact, you will have $704!

To keep things simple in our model, to focus on the key factors important for understanding saving decisions, we will continue to distinguish current from future consumption and only apply interest once. This simplification captures the essential characteristic of the saving decision, the choice between consumption now and in the future.

When the interest rate increases, Joan's budget constraint changes. Her new budget constraint is shown in Figure 9.12A as line $B'C$. If she does not save, the interest rate has no effect on her consumption. She simply consumes her income during her working years, with nothing left over for retirement. But for all other choices, the higher interest rate allows her to get more consumption during her retirement years.

The increased interest rate has both an income effect and a substitution effect. Because Joan is a saver, higher interest rates make her better off. Because she is better off, she consumes more today; that is, she reduces her saving. This is the income effect. But her return to savings—to postpone consumption—is increased. For each dollar of consump-

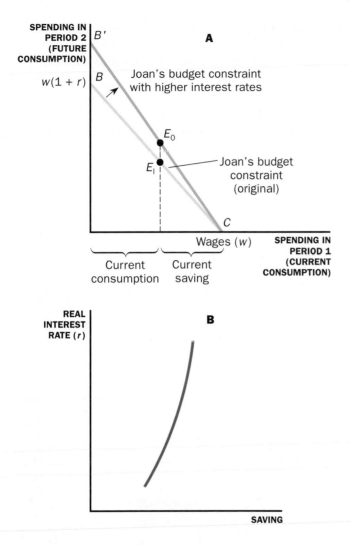

FIGURE 9.12 *Saving and the Interest Rate*

An increase in interest rates rotates the budget constraint out from *BC* to *B′C* (panel A). The fact that the individual is better off means that there is an income effect, leading to greater consumption in the present (and the future). Higher current consumption implies lower saving. However, the higher interest rate makes future consumption cheaper; the substitution effect, associated with the changed slope, leads to greater saving now (panel B). The saving function in panel B gives the level of saving at each level of the real interest rate. The curve depicted has the typical shape: increases in the real interest rate lead to slight increases in saving; the substitution effect slightly outweighs the income effect.

tion she postpones, she gets more consumption when she retires. The opportunity cost of current consumption is now higher. This induces her to consume less—to save

more. This is the substitution effect. Thus, the substitution and income effects work in opposite directions, and the *net* effect is ambiguous. Either may dominate. A higher interest rate may lead to more or less saving. In the case shown, current consumption— and hence saving—is unchanged.

What happens on *average* is a difficult empirical question. Most estimates indicate that the substitution effect outweighs the income effect, so that an increase in real interest rates has a slightly positive effect on the rate of savings.

Panel B of Figure 9.12 shows the saving function, which gives the level of saving for each level of the real interest rate. It is derived by finding the choices between consumption today and in the future for different real interest rates, represented by rotating the budget constraint. The curve depicted has the typical shape. Increases in the real interest rate lead to slight increases in saving; the substitution effect slightly outweighs the income effect. But the saving curve could be vertical; the income effect just outweighs the substitution effect. Or it can even be backward bending; the income effect slightly outweighs the substitution effect.

WRAP-UP

The Saving Decision

The saving decision is a decision of *when* to consume: today or tomorrow.

The slope of the budget constraint between consumption today and consumption tomorrow is determined by the rate of interest.

A principal motive of saving is to smooth consumption, so that consumption during working years and consumption during retirement years is about the same.

Other Factors Affecting Saving   We have now seen how individuals' decisions about saving can be looked at using the techniques of consumer choice analysis presented in Chapter 6. For saving, the two basic determinants are income and interest rates. As incomes rise, individuals want to consume more in their retirement, and hence must save more. As interest rates change, the income and substitution effects work in different directions, so the net effect is ambiguous.

The saving decision in the United States also involves an even more important determinant: Social Security. How much individuals need to save for their retirement depends on how large a check they get from the Social Security Administration when they retire. A generous Social Security system reduces the need to save for retirement. If this is the case, why have private pension programs grown at the same time that Social Security payments have become more generous? Two explanations are commonly put forward. First, as individuals' life spans have increased well beyond the normal retirement age, the need for retirement income has increased faster than has the generosity of Social Security. Second, with higher incomes, as we saw earlier in the chapter, individuals decide to enjoy more leisure, one form of which is earlier retirement. With earlier retirement, the need for retirement income increases.

Thinking Like an Economist

Wealth Distribution and Interest Rates

Government policies aimed at increasing the interest rate individuals receive, such as exempting certain forms of savings from taxation, are based on the belief that an increase in the interest rate on savings will significantly increase total (aggregate) saving in the economy. Though the impact of these provisions on the aggregate saving rate is debatable, the distributional impact is not. Since wealthy people save more, reducing taxes on interest—which increases the effective interest rate the saver receives—obviously benefits them more and increases the degree of income inequality. According to the Survey of Consumer Finances (1998), almost 82 percent of households with incomes of $100,000 or more during 1998 saved, and these families had an average net worth of $1.7 million. In contrast, less than 31 percent of households with incomes below $10,000 were able to save, and these families had an average net worth of just $40,000.

Low-income households save little and therefore enjoy little direct benefit from policies designed to increase the return to saving.

CASE IN POINT

Why is the U.S. Saving Rate So Low?

Between 1959 and 1992, the personal saving rate for U.S. households averaged 7.4 percent of disposable income (income after taxes). Since 1994, the saving rate has averaged only 4.5 percent, and by 2000, it had fallen just below 0 percent, meaning that households were spending down their accumulated savings (Figure 9.13). How come?

Economists have given several reasons for the low and falling saving rate among U.S. households. First, Social Security benefits are relatively generous, reducing the need for individuals to save for their retirement. Social Security benefits became much more generous in the 1970s. Second, it has become much easier to borrow for all kinds of purchases. In other words, the capital market in this country has improved its capacity to serve individual borrowers. Third, Americans prefer to consume now rather than later. Fourth, the need to save for a rainy day has been reduced in this country by the availability of better medical insurance, unemployment insurance, and so on. Fifth, the value of household wealth from investments in housing and corporate stocks in the United States rose dramatically through the 1980s and 1990s. As people saw their wealth rise, they spent more and saved less. Finally, there is the effect of the new economy. Increases in productivity as a result of new technologies led many to conclude that the economy would grow faster, leading to higher incomes in the future. The income effect of higher expected future income works to increase current consumption, reducing saving today.

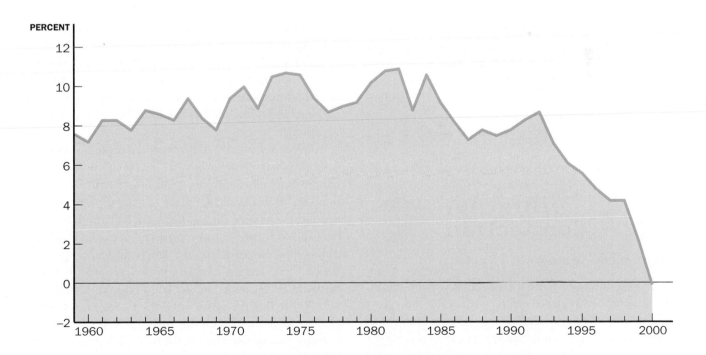

FIGURE 9.13 *U.S. Personal Saving Rate, 1980–2000*

Compared to earlier decades, U.S. households saved very little of their disposable income throughout the 1990s. In 2000 their spending exceeded their disposable income (saving rate was negative).

Aggregate Saving   The sum of the saving of all individuals in society is **aggregate saving.** At any time, some individuals are saving and others are spending their savings (or, as economists say, *dissaving*). Aggregate saving is the two activities taken together. The *aggregate saving rate* is aggregate saving divided by aggregate income. *Demographic* factors, that is, factors relating to population, in particular the rate of growth of the population, are important determinants of the aggregate saving rate. Retirees typically dissave. That is, they withdraw from savings accounts and cash in stocks and bonds if they have any (to supplement their main income sources, Social Security and interest on investments). There is considerable concern about the low aggregate saving rate in the United States (discussed further below). Our aging population is one reason for this. A more slowly growing population, like that of the United States, has a larger proportion of elderly and, on that account, a lower aggregate saving rate than faster-growing populations with higher birth rates.

Forms of Savings   To simplify our discussion, we have assumed that savings earns a single rate of interest, r. In fact, there are many different ways in which individuals can save, and these can differ in terms of the interest rate earned. For example, if you want to save, you can put money into a savings account at a bank. This earns interest and is very safe. The federal government insures savings accounts with balances up to $100,000. The tremendous boom in the stock market in the 1990s encouraged many

people to put some of their savings into stocks. Stocks earn a higher return on average than a savings account, but they are much riskier. The stock market can go down as well as up. Real estate also has been an attractive place to put savings, but it too is risky. We will postpone until Chapter 16 a fuller discussion of the various savings options that are available to households, keeping our focus in this chapter on the broad outlines of the capital market and the role played by the interest rate in affecting saving decisions.

Demand in the Capital Market

Our goal here is to understand how the supply of savings by households and the demand for saving by firms result in a market equilibrium. In the preceding sections we worked through the supply side of the market. Now we turn to demand. The demand side of the capital market is driven by firms who borrow the savings of households to fund their purchases of **capital goods**—the machines, tools, buildings, and other equipment used in the production process. We therefore begin our analysis with the demand for capital goods by firms.

Applying the same principle we used earlier to derive the demand for labor, we know that firms will demand capital (capital goods) up to the point where the value of the marginal product of capital is equal to the price. The marginal product of capital is just the additional output obtained if one more unit is employed. It is the extra output obtained by adding another machine. But what is the price of capital?

A quick answer is that the price of a piece of equipment is simply what it costs to buy it. If a new computer server to handle Internet orders costs the firm $20,000, isn't that the price of this particular piece of capital? The answer is no, and to see why more is involved, let's think about the decision of a new start-up company as it evaluates whether to buy this computer. To keep things simple, suppose Andrea and Bryan, the company founders, plan to sell the server after one year for $12,000. They can borrow the $20,000 to buy the server from their bank, and the bank charges them interest on this loan. Let's suppose for our example that the interest rate the bank charges is 5 percent. What has it cost them to use the equipment?

Andrea and Bryan pay $20,000 for the server. At the end of the year, they sell the server for $12,000, but they also have to repay the bank. Since the bank charged them 5 percent interest, at the end of the year they owe the bank

Internet Connection

Household Saving

The Federal Reserve Board conducts a survey of households every three years, called the Survey of Consumer Finances. Each one provides a wealth of information on household saving. The most recently available survey was conducted in 1998, and you can find it described at http://www.federalreserve.gov/pubs/oss/oss2/98/scf98home.html .

$21,000 (the $20,000 they borrowed plus $1,000 in interest). So the net cost of using the server is $21,000 − $12,000 = $9,000. A critical part of this cost is the interest Andrea and Bryan had to pay the bank. If the interest rate had been 10 percent, the cost of the computer would have been $10,000 ($20,000 + $2,000 − $12,000, since interest now totals $2,000). *The user cost of capital increases when the interest rate rises.*

The role of the interest rate would be exactly the same if Andrea and Bryan had not needed to borrow from the bank. Suppose they had savings of their own that they could use to purchase the computer. When they use their own savings to buy the computer, there is an opportunity cost associated with the purchase. Andrea and Bryan could have left their $20,000 in the bank. If the interest rate is 5 percent, they would have earned $1,000 in interest over the year. This opportunity cost must be included in calculating the cost of capital. So when the interest rate is 5 percent, the total cost of the server is $9,000, regardless of whether they borrow from the bank or use their own funds. An increase in the interest rate raises the cost (include opportunity costs) of using the server.

This simple example illustrates an important point—the user cost of capital will increase with the interest rate. At a higher interest rate, firms will demand less capital and will need to borrow less. At lower interest rates, firms will demand more capital and need to borrow more.

Figure 9.14 shows the demand for loanable funds in the capital market as a downward sloping relationship between the interest rate and the quantity of funds firms borrow. The figure also shows the supply of loanable funds as an upward sloping line; it is shown as a steep line because the income and substitution effects of a change in the interest rate have opposing effects on saving. The net effect, though, is some increase in saving as the interest rate increases. In the loanable funds, or capital market, the "price" is the interest rate, and the interest rate will adjust to bring supply and demand into balance. In the figure, the equilibrium interest rate is r^*.

We can now explain why the equilibrium interest rate is positive. If it were zero or negative, prospective borrowers would demand more funds than prospective savers would be willing to supply. Indeed, negative interest rates would mean that people could borrow to consume today and pay back less in the future, and that savers would receive less in the future than the amount they saved. Only at a positive interest rate can the demand for loans be equated to the supply.

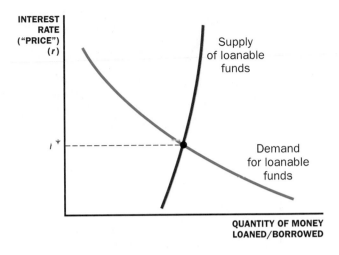

FIGURE 9.14   *Supply and Demand for Loanable Funds*

The amount of money loaned and borrowed is the quantity, and the interest rate is the price. At the equilibrium interest rate r^*, the supply of loanable funds equals the demand.

In our economy, borrowers and savers do not usually meet face to face. Instead, banks and other financial institutions serve as intermediaries, collecting savings from those who want to save and disbursing money to those who want to borrow. These intermediaries help make the market for loans work smoothly. For their services, the intermediaries charge fees, which can be measured as the difference between the interest rate they pay savers and the interest rate they charge borrowers.

New Technologies and the Demand for Capital   Modern economies have undergone tremendous changes as new computer and information technologies have transformed the ways goods are produced and sold. The development of new technologies has led firms to undertake investments in new equipment. To analyze the impact this change might have on the interest rate, we can use our model of the loanable funds market.

Figure 9.15 shows demand and supply as a function of the rate of interest. The new technology increases the marginal product of capital and increases firms' demand for capital at each rate of interest. To purchase this additional capital, firms borrow more. At each rate of interest, the demand for funds shifts to the right. The equilibrium rate of interest rises.

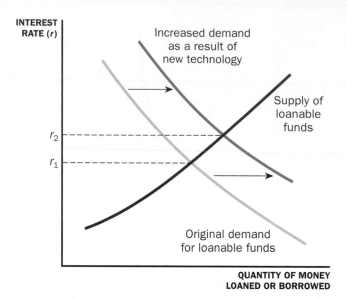

FIGURE 9.15   *The Effects of New Technologies that Increase the Demand for Capital*

If new technologies increase the demand for capital by firms, the demand for funds will shift to the right as firms attempt to borrow more to purchase new equipment. If the supply of funds from saving does not shift, the equilibrium interest rate rises from r_1 to r_2.

Education and Human Capital

Why go to college? Many answers spring to mind, but to tackle this question from an economic perspective, and to understand why educational choices are similar to saving decisions, let's focus on the costs and benefits of education.

Education is one of the most important determinants of workers' productivity. Staying in school longer, which usually means delaying entry into the labor force, increases expected annual income. On average, high school graduates earn more than those without high school degrees; those with some college earn more than those who only have a high school degree; those with a college degree earn more than those who started college but never finished. A student has lower income while in school but can expect to earn high incomes in the future. In addition, working *harder* in school, and giving up leisure, may result in better grades and skills, which in turn will result in higher wages in the fu-

ture. Thus, students face a trade-off between leisure and income today and income and consumption in the future.

Spending a year in college has its obvious costs—tuition, room, and board. But there are also opportunity costs, in particular the income that would have been received from a job. These opportunity costs are costs of going to school just as much as any direct tuition payments. Economists say that the investment in education produces **human capital,** making an analogy to the *physical capital* investments that businesses make in plant and equipment. Human capital is developed by formal schooling, on-the-job learning, and many other investments of time and money that parents make in their children, individuals make in themselves, and employers make in their employees.

The United States invests an enormous amount in human capital. In fact, the cumulative value of human capital is greater than that of physical capital. As much as two-thirds to three-fourths of all capital is human capital. This investment is financed both publicly and privately. Local, state, and federal governments spend about one-quarter of a trillion dollars a year on education. Government expenditures on primary and secondary education are the largest category of expenditure at the local and state levels, accounting for more than 20 percent of total expenditures.

The enormous increase in education in the past fifty years is illustrated in Table 9.1. Among those 65 and older, over 30 percent do not have a high school degree; of those 25–44 only one in eight has not received a high school degree. Similarly the percentage with at least a bachelor's degree is almost twice as high for those 25–44 in relation to those 65 and older.

This dental student improves his human capital by acquiring valuable skills and knowledge.

TABLE 9.1

Years of Schooling by Age			
Age group (in 1999)	% with less than high school degree	% with a high school degree but no bachelor's degree	% with at least a bachelor's degree
25–44	12	60	28
45–64	14	59	27
65 and older	32	53	15

Education and Economic Trade-offs

The production possibilities curve introduced in Chapter 2 can illustrate how decisions concerning investments in human capital are made. To accomplish this, we divide an individual's life into two periods: "youth" and "later working years." Figure 9.16 depicts the relationship between consumption in youth and in later life. As the individual gives up consumption in his youth, staying in school

e-Insight

Financing the New Economy

We have seen how the capital market links households who save with firms who invest, so that saving equals investment at the equilibrium interest rate. But how do firms actually get their hands on household saving? The answer is that financial intermediaries such as banks and investment companies perform the function of transferring funds between households and firms. Their job is to make sure that the households' money is well invested, so that the households can get back their money with a return.

Banks are perhaps the most important financial intermediary. In the nineteenth century, banks mainly lent money to firms to help finance their inventories. The inventories were held as collateral—that is, if the borrower defaulted on the loan, the lender could seize the inventories. Gradually, banks expanded their lending activities, for instance, to finance houses and commercial real estate, again with the buildings held as collateral. The past decade's revolution in information technology has presented special problems to these traditional forms of finance. Today firms invest heavily in software and new ideas. If the idea does not pan out, the firm may go bankrupt, but there is no collateral; there is little of value that the creditor can seize.

In the United States, financial markets have adapted, with a new form of financial institution—venture capital firms. Typically, the funds are provided by either wealthy private investors or institutions, such as universities, seeking high returns. The venture capital firms have developed expertise in assessing new ideas in the new economy—the most successful of the venture capital firms have an impressive record of picking winners. But they provide more than capital; they typically also provide managerial assistance and take an active role in oversight. After providing the initial capital that allows a firm to get established, the firm supported by the venture capital firms typically "goes public"—that is, it sells at least some of its shares on the market. It is at this point that they reap their gains.

While the first venture capital firms focused on Silicon Valley (the area surrounding Stanford University where much of the early development of computers occurred), more recently venture capital firms have ventured out into other areas of the country and into other sectors.

longer increases his expected future consumption because he can expect his income to go up. The curve has been drawn with a rounded shape. It shows diminishing returns: Spending more on education today (reducing consumption) raises future income, but each additional investment in education provides a smaller and smaller return.

Point *A* represents the case where Everett is a full-time student through four years of college, with little income until graduation (his youth) but with a high income in later life. Point *B* represents the consequences of dropping out of school after high school. When he does this, Everett has a higher income in his youth but a lower income in later life. Other possible points between *A* and *B* represent cases where Everett drops out of college after one or two years.

The Basic Competitive Model

We now have completed our description of the basic competitive model. Households make decisions about how much to consume and what goods to purchase. They decide how much labor to supply and how much to save. The firm in the competitive model takes the price it receives for the goods it sells as given. The firm also takes the prices of the inputs it uses, including the wages it pays workers and the cost of capital goods, as given. Given these prices, the firm chooses its outputs and inputs to maximize profits. Prices adjust to ensure that demand and supply are equal. In the labor market, wages bring demand and supply into balance; in the capital market, the interest rate is the "price" that adjusts to balance supply and demand.

We have now seen where the supply and demand curves that were introduced in Chapters 4 and 5 come from, and why they have the shapes they do. Whether it is the household's demand for goods, its supply of labor, or its savings decision, the effects of price changes on the household's choices can be analyzed in terms of income and substitution effects. We also learned that firms balance marginal cost and price in deciding on production levels, and they set the value of the marginal product equal to the price of an input in deciding on their demand for factors of production such as labor and capital. An increase in the real wage reduces the firm's demand for labor. An increase in the interest rate reduces the demand for capital. In the next chapter, we will put all these results together to yield a model of the complete economy.

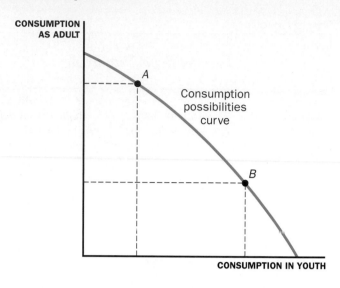

FIGURE 9.16 *Education and the Trade-Off Between Current and Future Consumption*

Point *A* represents a choice of a reduced consumption and better education in the present, with a higher consumption in the future. Point *B* represents the choice of higher consumption and less education now, with a lower level of consumption in the future.

Review and Practice

Summary

1. The decision about how to allocate time between work and leisure can be analyzed using the basic ideas of budget constraints and preferences. Individuals face a trade-off along a budget constraint between leisure and income. The amount of income a person can obtain by giving up leisure is determined by the wage rate.

2. In labor markets, the substitution and income effects of a change in wages work in opposite directions. An increase in wages makes people better off, and they wish to enjoy more leisure as well as more consumption; this is the income effect. But an increase in wages raises the opportunity cost of leisure and encourages more work; this is the substitution effect. The overall effect of a rise in wages will depend on whether the substitution or income effect is actually larger.

3. An upward-sloping labor supply curve represents a case where the substitution effect of higher wages outweighs the income effect. A relatively vertical labor supply curve represents a case where the substitution and income effects of higher wages are nearly equal. A backward-bending labor supply curve represents a case where the substitution effect dominates at low wages (labor supply increases as the wage increases), but the income effect dominates at high wages (labor supply decreases as the wage increases).

4. The basic model of choice between leisure and income also can be used to analyze decisions concerning labor force participation, including when to enter the labor force and when to retire.

5. The demand for labor arises from the firm's demand for the factors of production. To maximize profits, the firm will use labor up to the point where the value of the marginal product of labor equals the wage. This means the marginal product will equal the *real* wage.

6. In the basic competitive model, the real wage adjusts in labor markets to balance supply and demand.

7. The interest rate is determined in the capital market—also called the loanable funds market. The supply of loanable funds comes from savings, as some households and firms spend less than their income. The demand arises from those households and firms who spend more than their income.

8. In making a decision to save, people face a trade-off between current and future consumption. The amount of extra consumption an individual can obtain in the future by reducing present consumption is determined by the real rate of interest.

9. A dollar received in the future is worth less than a dollar received today. The present discounted value tells us how much a future dollar amount is worth today. The present discounted value of a future amount falls when the rate of interest rises.

10. The real interest rate adjusts to balance supply and demand in the capital market.

11. The interest rate is an important part of the cost of using capital. If the interest rate increases, the cost of using capital increases. Firm's demands for funds for investment fall as firms cut back on their purchases of capital goods.

12. Human capital adds to economic productivity just as physical capital does. It is developed by education, on-the-job learning, and investments of time and money that parents make in their children.

Key Terms

nominal wage
real wage
labor force participation decision
reservation wage
factor demand
value of the marginal product of labor
real product wage
capital market
loanable funds market
life-cycle saving
interest
principal
time value of money
present discounted value
real rate of interest
nominal rate of interest
aggregate saving
capital goods
human capital

Review Questions

1. How do people make choices about the amount of time to work, given their personal tastes and real wages in the market?

2. How will the income effect of a fall in wages affect hours worked? How will the substitution effect of a fall in wages affect hours worked? What does the labor supply curve look like if the income effect dominates the substitution effect? If the substitution effect dominates the income effect?

3. How does a choice to consume in the present determine the amount of consumption in the future?

4. What is the price of future consumption in terms of present consumption?

5. For savers, how will the income effect of a higher interest rate affect current saving? How will the substitution effect of a higher interest rate affect current savings?

6. What are some of the other factors, besides incomes and interest rates, that affect saving?

7. Describe how students invest time and money to acquire human capital.

Problems

1. Imagine that a wealthy relative dies and leaves you an inheritance in a trust fund that will provide you with $20,000 per year for the rest of your life. Draw a diagram to illustrate this shift in your budget constraint between leisure and consumption. After considering the ideas of income and substitution effects, decide whether this inheritance will cause you to work more or less.

2. Most individuals do not take a second job (moonlight), even if they could get one, for instance as a taxi driver. This is in spite of the fact that their "basic job" may require them to work only 37 hours a week. Most moonlighting jobs pay less per hour than the basic job. Draw a typical worker's budget constraint. Discuss the consequences of the kink in the budget constraint.

3. Under current economic conditions, let's say that an unskilled worker will be able to get a job at a wage of $5 per hour. Now assume the government decides that all people with a weekly income of less than $150 will be given a check from the government to bring them up to the $150 level. Draw one such worker's original budget constraint and the constraint with the welfare program. Will this welfare program be likely to cause a recipient who originally worked 30 hours to work less? How about a recipient who worked less than 30 hours? More than 30 hours? Explain how the government might reduce these negative effects by offering a wage subsidy that would increase the hourly wage to $6 per hour for each of the first 20 hours worked, and draw a revised budget constraint to illustrate.

4. This chapter focused on how interest rates affect savers. If an individual is a net debtor (that is, he owes money), what is the income effect of an increase in interest rates. Will an increase in the interest rates that he has to pay induce him to borrow more or less?

5. In the context of the life-cycle model of saving, explain whether you would expect each of the following situations to increase or decrease household saving.

a) More people retire before age 65.

b) There is an increase in life expectancy.

c) The government passes a law requiring private businesses to provide more lucrative pensions.

6. Explain how each of the following changes might affect people's saving.

a) Inheritance taxes are increased.

b) A government program allows college students to obtain student loans more easily.

c) The government promises to assist anyone injured by natural disasters like hurricanes, tornadoes, and earthquakes.

d) More couples decide against having children.

e) The economy does far worse than anyone was expecting in a given year.

7. Economists are fairly certain that a rise in the price of most goods will cause people to consume less of those goods, but they are not sure whether a rise in interest rates will cause people to save more. Use the ideas of substitution and income effects to explain why economists are confident of the conclusion in the first case but not in the second.

8. There is a negative relationship between a woman's real wage and her family size. Two possible explanations have been put forth. One is that women with higher real wages *choose* to have smaller families. Explain why this might be so. The second explanation is that larger family sizes might cause women to receive lower wages, for instance, because they have to accept jobs where they can be absent when their children are sick. What evidence might help you choose between these two explanations?

9. Suppose a new technology makes capital more productive, leading firms to want to borrow more at each rate of interest in order to purchase more capital. Using a supply-demand diagram of the loanable funds market, show what the likely effect on the equilibrium rate of interest would be.

10. Suppose younger households decide that they cannot rely on Social Security and must save more on their own for their retirement years. What is the likely effect

on the equilibrium rate of interest? Will the equilibrium amount of borrowing rise or fall?

11. We have all heard about winners of $10 million jackpot lotteries. The winner, however, does not get $10 million in cash on the spot, but rather typically gets a measly $500,000 for twenty years. Why is the present discounted value of the prize much less than $10 million? Calculate the present discounted value.

12. Consider an individual who is borrowing. Assume the nominal interest rate remains the same but the rate of inflation increases. What happens to the real interest rate? Why do you expect the individual to borrow more?

Appendix A: Indifference Curves and the Labor Supply and Saving Decisions[2]

This appendix investigates the labor supply and saving decisions using the indifference curve approach applied in the appendix to Chapter 6 to the consumption decision. Let's first look at the choice between leisure and consumption.

Figure 9.17 shows Tom's budget constraint between leisure and consumption. The slope of the budget constraint is the wage. The figure also shows two indifference curves; each gives the combination of leisure and consumption among which Tom is indifferent. As usual, since people prefer more of both consumption and leisure if that is possible, Tom will move to the highest indifference curve he can attain. This will be the one that is just tangent to the budget constraint.

The slope of the indifference curve is the marginal rate of substitution between leisure and consumption. It measures the amount of extra consumption Tom requires to compensate him for forgoing one additional hour of leisure. At the point of tangency between the indifference curve and the budget constraint, point *E*, both have the same slope. That is, the marginal rate of substitution equals the wage at this point.

---

[2]You will need to have read the appendix to Chapter 6 in order to follow this appendix.

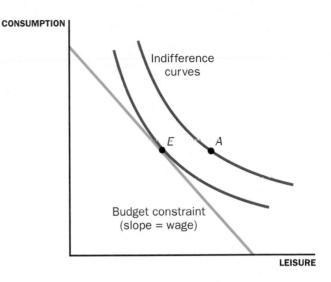

FIGURE 9.17   *Indifference Curves and Leisure-Income Choices*

An individual will choose the combination of leisure and income at *E*. Point *A* would be more desirable, but it is not feasible. Other points on the budget line or inside it are feasible, but they lie on lower indifference curves and are therefore not as desirable.

As in the appendix in Chapter 6, we can easily see why Tom chooses this point. Assume his marginal rate of substitution is $15 (dollars per hour), while his wage is $20 (dollars per hour). If he works an hour more—gives up an hour's worth of leisure—his consumption goes up by $20. But to compensate him for the forgone leisure, he only requires $15. Since he gets more than he requires by working, he clearly prefers to work more.

Deciding Whether to Work

Figure 9.18 shows how to use indifference curves to analyze how people decide whether to work or not. Consider a low-wage individual facing a welfare system in which there is a fixed level of benefits if one's income is below a threshold level. Benefits are cut off once income exceeds a certain level. The indifference curve I_0 is tangent to the budget constraint without welfare, and the point of tangency is E_0. The curve I_1 is the highest indifference curve consistent with the person receiving welfare.

The three possible cases are illustrated in panels A, B, and C. In panel A, the indifference curve through point E_0, I_0, is higher than the curve I_1. The individual chooses to work at E_0

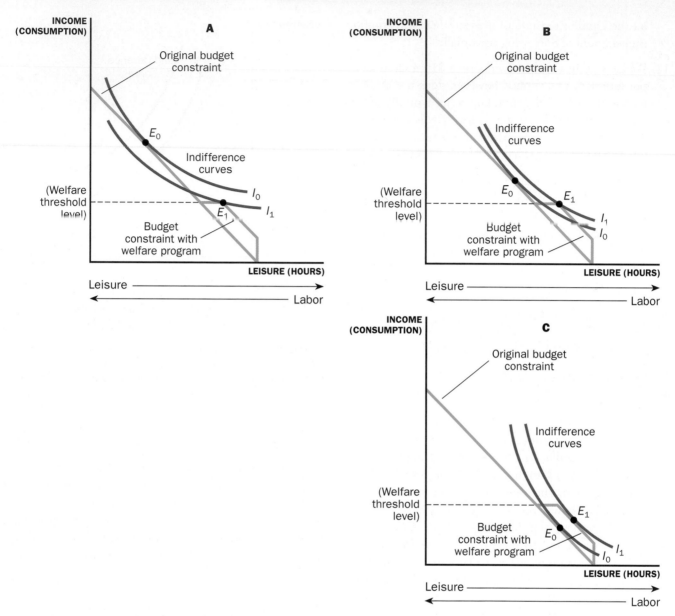

FIGURE 9.18 *Indifference Curves and Welfare Programs*

Panel A shows the case of an individual who chooses to work whether or not the welfare program exists. In panel B, before a welfare program is introduced, the individual is earning more than the welfare threshold. With the availability of welfare, this individual relies on welfare benefits to work less and move to a higher indifference curve. Panel C shows the case of someone who is earning less than the welfare threshold but would choose to work still less if the welfare program existed.

and is unaffected by the welfare program. In panels B and C, the person works sufficiently little to be eligible for welfare; that is, I_1 is higher than I_0, and so he chooses point E_1. In panel B, the individual realizes that if he works more, he will lose his welfare benefits. He earns just (little) enough to be eligible for welfare. In panel C, the welfare system has only an income effect. If the welfare benefits are large enough, the individual may choose not to work at all (at E_1 there is zero labor).

Deciding How Much to Save

The decision of how much to save is a decision about how much of lifetime income to consume now and how much to consume in the future. This trade-off is summarized in the two-period budget constraint introduced in the chapter, with present consumption measured along the horizontal axis and future consumption along the vertical axis. The slope of the budget constraint is $1 + r$, where r is the rate of interest, the extra consumption we get in the future from forgoing a unit of consumption today.

Figure 9.19 shows three indifference curves. The indifference curve through point A gives all the combinations of consumption today and consumption in the future among which the individual is indifferent (she would be just as well off, no better and no worse, at any point along the curve as at A). Since people generally prefer more to less consumption, they would rather be on a higher than a lower indifference curve. The highest indifference curve a person can attain is one that is tangent to the budget constraint. The point of tangency we denote by E. The individual would clearly prefer the indifference curve through A, but no point on that curve is attainable because the whole indifference curve is above the budget constraint. She could consume at F, but the indifference curve through F lies below that through E.

As we learned in the appendix to Chapter 6, the slope of the indifference curve at a certain point is the marginal rate of substitution at that point. In this case, it tells us how much future consumption a person requires to compensate him for a decrease in current consumption by 1 unit, to leave him just as well off. At the point of tangency, the slope of the indifference curve is equal to the slope of the budget constraint. The marginal rate of substitution at that point, E, equals $1 + r$. If the individual forgoes a unit of consumption, he gets $1 + r$ more units of consumption in the future, and this is exactly the amount he requires to compensate him for giving up current consumption. On the other hand, if the marginal rate of substitution is less than $1 + r$, it pays the individual to save more. To see why, assume $1 + r = 1.5$, while the person's marginal rate of substitution is 1.2. By reducing his consumption by a unit, he gets 1.5 more units in the future, but he would have been content getting only 1.2 units. He is better off saving more.

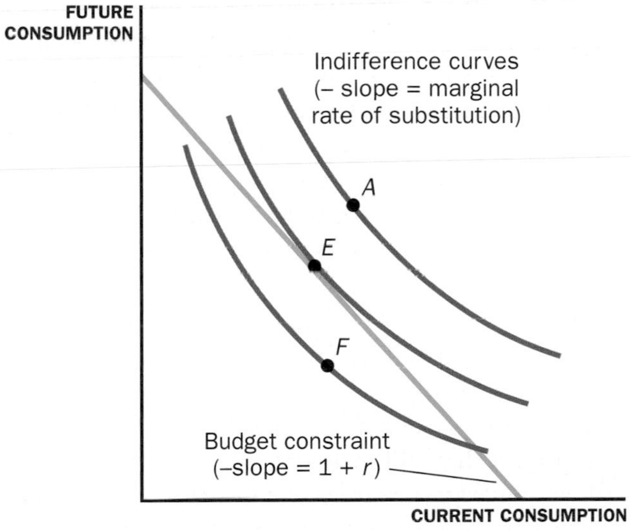

Changing the Interest Rate

With indifference curves and budget constraints, we can see the effect of an increase in the interest rate. Figure 9.20 shows the case of an individual, Maggie, who works while she is young and saves for her retirement. The vertical axis gives consumption during retirement years, the horizontal axis consumption during working years. An increase in the rate of interest rotates the budget constraint, moving it from BC to $B_2 C$. It is useful to break the change down into two steps. In the first, we ask what would have happened if the interest rate had changed but Maggie remained on the same indifference curve. This is represented by the movement of the budget constraint from BC to $B_1 C_1$. As a result of the increased interest rate, Maggie consumes less today—she saves more. This is the substitution effect, and it is seen in the movement from E_0 to E_2 in the figure.

In the second step we note that since Maggie is a saver, the increased interest rate makes her better off. To leave Maggie on the same indifference curve after the increase in

FIGURE 9.19 *Indifference Curves and Saving Behavior*

An individual will choose the combination of present and future consumption at *E*. Point *A* would be more desirable, but it is not feasible. Point *F* is feasible, but it lies on a lower indifference curve and is therefore less desirable.

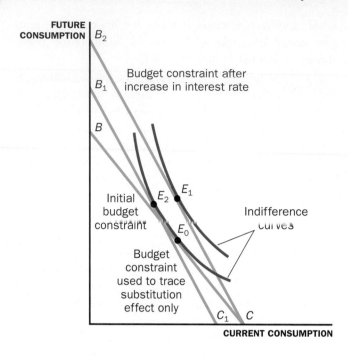

FIGURE 9.20   *Income and Substitution Effects of a Higher Interest Rate*

An increase in the interest rate rotates the budget constraint, moving it from BC to B_2C. The substitution effect describes what happens when relative prices are changed but Maggie remains on the same indifference curve; there is a shift in the budget line from BC to B_1C_1, and an increase in saving from E_0 to E_2. The income effect is the result of an outward shift of the budget line, keeping relative prices the same; the income effect is described by the shift from B_1C_1 to B_2C, and the increase in present consumption from E_2 to E_1.

the interest rate, we needed to reduce her income. Her true budget constraint, after the interest rate increase, is B_2C, parallel to B_1C_1. The two budget constraints have the same slope because the after-tax interest rates are the same. The movement from B_1C_1 to B_2C is the second step. It induces Maggie to increase her consumption from E_2 to E_1. At higher incomes and the same relative prices (interest rates), people consume more every period, which implies that they save less. The movement from E_2 to E_1 is the income effect.

Thus, the substitution effect leads her to save more, the income effect to save less, and the net effect is ambiguous. In this case, there is a slight increase in saving.

Appendix B: Calculating Present Discounted Value

In the text, we described how to calculate the present discounted value (PDV) of a dollar received a year from now. The present discounted value of a dollar received two years from now can be calculated in a similar way. But how much *today* is equivalent to, say, $100 two years from now? If I were given $PDV today and I put it in the bank, at the end of the year I would have PDV(1 + r)$. If I left it in the bank for another year, in the second year I would earn interest on the total amount in the bank at the end of the first year, $r \times PDV(1 + r)$. Therefore, at the end of the two-year period I would have:

$$PDV(1 + r) + [r \times PDV(1 + r)]$$
$$= PDV(1 + r)(1 + r)$$
$$= PDV(1 + r)^2.$$

Thus, the $PDV of $100 in two years is $100/(1 + r)^2$. If I put $100/(1 + r)^2$ in the bank today, I would have $100/(1 + r)^2 \times (1 + r)^2 = $100 in two years. In performing these calculations, we have taken account of the interest on the interest. This is called **compound interest.** (By contrast, **simple interest** does not take into account the interest you earn on interest you have previously earned.)

If the rate of interest is 10 percent and is compounded annually, $100 today is worth $110 a year from now and $121 (*not* $120) in two years' time. Thus, the present discounted value today of $121 two years from now is $100. Table 9.2 shows how to calculate the present discounted value of $100 received next year, two years from now, and three years from now.

We can now see how to calculate the value of an investment project that will yield a return over several years. We look at what the returns will be each year, adjust them to their present discounted values, and then add these values up. Table 9.3 shows how this is done for a project that yields $10,000 next year and $15,000 the year after, and that you plan to sell in the third year for $50,000. The second column of the table shows the return in each year. The third column shows the discount factor—what we multiply the return by to obtain the present discounted value of that year's return. The calculations assume an interest rate of 10 percent. The fourth column multiplies the return by the discount factor to obtain the present discounted value of that year's return. In the bottom row of the table, the present discounted values of each year's return have been added up to obtain the total present discounted value of the project. Notice that it is much smaller than the number we obtain simply by adding up the returns, which is the "undiscounted" yield of the project.

TABLE 9.2

Present Discounted Value of $100	
Year received	**Present discounted value**
Next year	$\frac{1}{1+r} \times 100 = \frac{100}{1+r}$
Two years from now	$\frac{1}{1+r} \times \frac{100}{1+r} = \frac{100}{(1+r)^2}$
Three years from now	$\frac{1}{1+r} \times \frac{100}{(1+r)^2} = \frac{100}{(1+r)^3}$

TABLE 9.3

Calculating Present Discounted Value of a Three-Year Project			
Year	**Return**	**Discount factor ($r = 0.10$)**	**Present discounted value ($r = 0.10$)**
1	$10,000	$\frac{1}{1.10}$	$ 9,091
2	$15,000	$\frac{1}{(1.10)^2} = \frac{1}{1.21}$	$12,397
3	$50,000	$\frac{1}{(1.10)^3} = \frac{1}{1.331}$	$37,566
Total	$75,000	—	$59,054

Chapter 10

The Efficiency of Competitive Markets

1. Why do so many economists believe that, by and large, reliance on private markets to solve society's basic economic problems is desirable? How do competitive markets result in economic efficiency?

2. If markets result in a distribution of income that society views as unacceptable, should the market be abandoned, or can government intervene in a more limited way to combine efficiency outcomes with acceptable distribution?

3. What is meant by the competitive equilibrium of the economy? Why is it that in competitive equilibrium, a disturbance to one market in the economy may have reverberations in other markets?

4. How do changes in one market affect other markets in the economy?

*I*n earlier chapters, we focused on the product market and saw that supply and demand come into balance at an equilibrium price and quantity. In equilibrium, the quantity of goods demanded by consumers equals the quantity supplied by firms. We have also seen that labor and capital markets achieve equilibrium in a similar way. In the labor market, labor supply and demand come into balance at an equilibrium wage; in equilibrium, the supply of labor by households equals the demand for labor by firms. In the capital market, equilibrium is achieved through adjustment in the interest rate; in equilibrium, the amount of savings supplied by households equals the amount of borrowing by firms. When all three markets are in equilibrium, the basic economic questions from Chapter 1— What gets produced? By whom? How? For whom?—are resolved through the interactions of households and firms in the marketplace. When all of the economy's central markets have achieved equilibrium in this way, economists say that the economy is in **general equilibrium.**

Understanding how markets provide answers to these basic economic questions is important. But we also are interested in evaluating whether markets do a good job.

When the assumptions of the basic competitive model hold, will the economy produce the right amounts of all the thousands and thousands of different goods and services? Will society's scarce resources be used *efficiently?* Once we evaluate how markets in our basic competitive model operate, we will be ready to extend the model in Part Three to deal with situations in which markets do not work perfectly, for instance, because competition is not perfect.

Competitive Markets and Economic Efficiency

The forces of demand and supply determine what is produced, how it is produced, and who receives the goods that are produced. To many people, relying on competitive markets seems like an undesirable way of addressing the fundamental economic questions. One often hears complaints about how markets result in too much of some goods being produced, or too few of others; that allowing markets free rein leads to inequalities in income and wealth; or that society's scarce resources could be used more efficiently if only the government would do something.

Economists have long been concerned with these issues. Are there circumstances in which markets do a good job in allocating society's scarce resources? Are there circumstances in which they don't? By and large, economists have concluded that *competitive* markets, the markets in our basic competitive model, make efficient use of society's scarce resources. This faith in markets can be traced back to Adam Smith's 1776 masterpiece, *The Wealth of Nations.* Smith argued that workers and producers, interested only in helping themselves and their families, were the basis of the success of the economy. As Smith put it,

> Man has almost constant occasion for the help of his brethren, and it is in vain for him to expect it from their benevolence only. He will be more likely to prevail if he can interest their self-love in his favor, and show them that it is for their own advantage to do for him what he requires of them. . . . It is not from the benevolence of the butcher, the brewer, or the baker, that we expect our dinner, but from their regard to their own interest. We . . . never talk to them of our necessities but of their advantage.[1]

In short, Smith argued that individuals pursuing their own self-interest would best promote the public interest. His insight was that individuals work hardest—and best—to help the overall economic production of the society when their efforts help themselves. Smith used the metaphor of the "invisible hand" to describe how self-interest led to social good: "He intends only his own gain, and he is in this as in many other cases led by an invisible hand to promote an end which was not part of his intention. . . . By pursuing his own interest he frequently promotes that of the society more effectually than when he really intends to promote it."[2]

This insight is one of the most fundamental in social science, and one that is not at all obvious. There is more to running an economy efficiently than just that individuals work hard. How do they know what to produce? How is it that the *uncoordinated* pursuit of self-interest then leads to efficiency? One of the most important achievements of

modern economic theory has been to establish in what sense and under what conditions the market is efficient.

Consumer and Producer Surplus

To evaluate the outcome in a competitive market, we can make use of Figure 10.1, which shows the market demand and supply curves for a market in equilibrium at a quantity Q_c and a price p_c. Can we measure the benefits that accrue to consumers and firms from participating in this market? From Chapter 6, we learned that consumer surplus provides a measure of the gain to consumers. The consumers who purchase the good will only do so if their willingness to pay is greater than the market price. The magnitude of

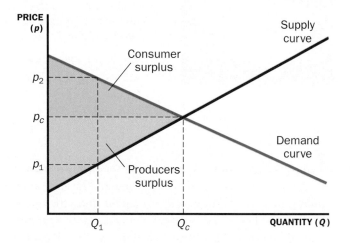

FIGURE 10.1   *The Competitive Market Equilibrium Maximizes Consumer and Producer Surplus*

When a competitive market is in equilibrium at the price p_c and quantity Q_c, at which demand and supply are equal, the sum of consumer surplus and producer surplus reaches its highest possible value. Consumer surplus is the blue area between the demand curve, showing willingness to pay, and the market price. Producer surplus is the purple area between the supply curve, showing marginal cost, and the market price. If quantity is Q_1, firms are willing to supply an additional unit at a price p_1, while consumers are willing to pay p_2. The value to consumers exceeds the cost to producers, and total surplus can be increased if production expands. At quantities above Q_c, surplus can be increased by reducing output. At the market equilibrium, p_c, and Q_c, the sum of consumer and producer surplus is maximized.

---

[1] *The Wealth of Nations* (1776), Book One, Chapter II.

[2] Ibid.

the *net* benefit they receive from, say, the *n*th unit of the good they purchase is the difference between what they have to pay for that good—the market price—and what they were willing to pay for that good, as reflected in the demand curve. Accordingly, the area shaded in blue measures the total consumer surplus.

Internet Connection

Digital Economist

The Digital Economist provides an on-line graphic demonstration of consumer surplus. You can test your understanding of how consumer surplus is calculated at http://www.digitaleconomist.com/cs_4010.html .

Firms also gain from participating in the market. As we learned in Chapter 8, the market supply curve reflects the marginal costs of producing the good. At the equilibrium quantity, Q_c, the marginal cost of producing the last unit of output is p_c, the equilibrium price. Just as the demand curve shows consumers' willingness to pay, the supply curve shows firms' willingness to produce; if the market price were p_1, firms would only be willing to produce the quantity Q_1. The supply curve has a positive slope, reflecting the fact that marginal cost rises as output increases. At an output of Q_1, the marginal cost of production is equal to p_1, so the marginal cost of producing Q_1 is less than the competitive equilibrium price p_c. Since the firm is able to sell all it produces at the competitive market price p_c, it sells all but the last (marginal) unit for more than its marginal cost production. The magnitude of the profit, the net benefit, firms receive from selling, say, the *n*th unit of the good is the difference between what they receive, the market price, and the price at which they would have been willing to produce the good, the marginal cost. The total gain to firms, called **producer surplus,** is the difference between the supply curve and the market price. The producer surplus is the purple area in the figure.

We measure the total gain to both consumers and producers by adding together consumer surplus and producer surplus. We can now state an important result: *The equilibrium price and quantity in a competitive market lead to the highest possible level of total surplus.* At quantities such as Q_1, which are below the market equilibrium quantity Q_c, consumers are willing to pay p_2 while firms are willing to sell at p_1. The value to consumers exceeds the cost to firms of producing an extra unit. Total surplus could be increased if the quantity were increased. At output levels greater than Q_c, the marginal cost exceeds what consumers are willing to pay for the last unit, and so total surplus would be increased by reducing output. At Q_c and p_c, the sum of consumer and producer surplus reaches its highest level.

Example: Efficiency Losses from Rent Control

In Chapter 5, the model of supply and demand was used to show how rent control could create an artificial scarcity in the market for rental housing. The concepts of consumer and producer surplus help illustrate how rent control interferes with economic efficiency.

Panel A of Figure 10.2 shows the supply and demand curves for rental apartments. The equilibrium rent at which supply equals demand is R^*. At this rent, the total surplus to renters and landlords is maximized. In panel A, the blue area is the consumer surplus—the value of apartments to renters in excess of the actual rent, R^*, they have to pay. The purple area is the surplus that goes to landlords.

Panel B illustrates what happens when the local government imposes a law that prevents rents from rising above R_1. A rental shortage results, as there will be an excess of demand over supply at the R_1. We can use this simple supply and demand model of the market for apartments to see what happens to consumer surplus and producer surplus. The blue area of panel B equals consumer surplus at the rent R_1. The purple area is the landlords' surplus. Comparing panels A and B, we can see that *total surplus is smaller as a result of rent control.* Total surplus has fallen by the area shown in green. The reduction in total surplus measures the inefficiency resulting from rent control.

Our analysis also highlights the distributional impact of policies such as rent control. Look again at panel B. Total surplus falls when the rent ceiling is R_1, but some individuals may be better off. While some consumers may be unable to find an apartment when rent control is imposed (notice that the equilibrium quantity falls from Q^* to Q_1), those who do find apartments at the rent R_1 gain—they would have been willing to pay more to get an apartment, but they only have to pay R_1. Renters who are fortunate

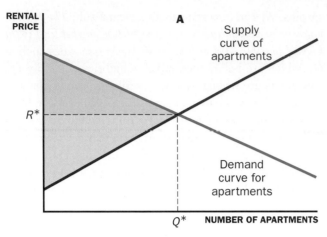

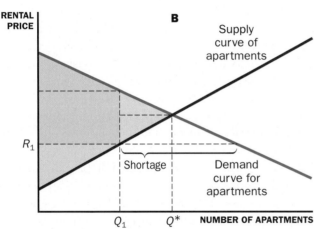

FIGURE 10.2   *The Effects of Rent Control*

Panel A of Figure 10.2 shows the supply and demand curves for rental apartments. The equilibrium rent at which supply equals demand is R^*. At this rent, the total surplus to renters and landlords is maximized. In panel A, the blue area is the consumer surplus—the value of apartments to renters in excess of the actual rent, R^*, they have to pay. The purple area is the surplus that goes to landlords.

enough to find a rent-controlled apartment gain, while landlords lose.

In the long run, the supply of apartments is more elastic. Low rents discourage the construction of new apartments and cause some landlords to remove units from the rental market (converting them to condominiums and selling them, for example). Consumer surplus falls as rent control leads to a decline in the quantity of apartments available for rent. Thus, the cost of rent control in terms of the inefficient allocation of resources and the distributional impact of rent

control can change in the long run. In general, the distributional impact is smaller in the long run, while the efficiency cost is greater. In the long run, landlords will put their money elsewhere—where they will get a normal return on their capital. The benefits to rent control will diminish, as the decreasing supply of rental apartments means that more and more of those who would like to get rent-controlled apartments simply will not find any available.

Taxes and Efficiency

Economists use the law of demand and supply to study the impact of taxes on consumers and producers. In Chapter 5 we learned that taxes imposed on producers can be passed on, or shifted, to consumers in the form of higher prices. There, two examples were contrasted. In the first, the law of supply and demand was used to study the impact of a tax on cigarette producers. When the demand for the taxed good is very inelastic, such as is the case with cigarettes, most of the burden of the tax is shifted to consumers. The second example involved a tax on one particular type of cheese, cheddar. In this case, the demand for the taxed good is very elastic, since close substitutes for cheddar cheese are available. When demand is elastic, most of the tax is borne by producers. Using the concepts of consumer surplus, producer surplus, and efficiency, we can gain additional insights into the effects of a tax.

Figure 10.3 shows the markets for cigarettes in panel A and the market for cheddar cheese in panel B. In each case, the equilibrium quantity without a tax is denoted by Q_0. The tax on the output of an industry paid by firms can be thought of as increasing the costs of production. This increase in cost shifts the supply curve up by the amount of the tax. Because the demand curve for cigarettes is relatively inelastic, the main impact of the tax is to raise the price to consumers. The price received by producers falls slightly, as does the quantity produced in the new equilibrium. In contrast, when the demand curve is relatively elastic, as shown in panel B for cheddar cheese, the effect is to cause a larger fall in the price producers receive and a smaller rise in the price paid by consumers.

The figure also shows what happens to consumer surplus when a good is taxed. In panel A, the entire blue area is equal to consumer surplus without the tax. After the tax, consumer surplus is only equal to the blue hatched area. Producer surplus is also reduced. It is equal to the entire purple region without the tax and the purple hatched area

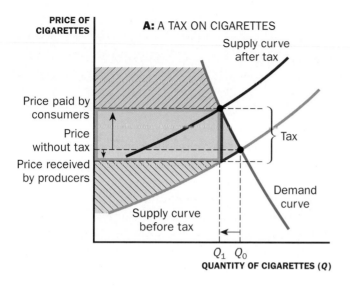

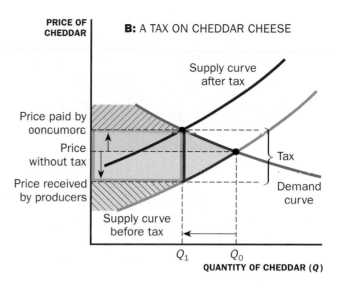

FIGURE 10.3 *Taxes and Efficiency*

A tax on the output of an industry shifts the supply curve up by the amount of the tax. Panel A shows that if the demand curve is relatively inelastic, as is the case with cigarettes, most of the tax is passed on to consumers. Both consumer surplus and producer surplus fall, but most of the tax burden falls on consumers. The area outlined in green is equal to the revenue the government collects from the tax. Consumer and producer surplus fall by more than the revenue collected by the government. The deadweight loss due to the tax is shown as the area outlined in red. Panel B repeats the analysis for a good whose demand curve is relatively elastic. More of the burden of the tax falls on producers, and the deadweight loss is larger.

with the tax. Because the demand curve for cigarettes is inelastic, the reduction in consumer surplus is greater than the reduction in producer surplus, reflecting the fact that the burden of the tax is shifted mainly to consumers in this case.

While both consumer surplus and producer surplus fall, not all of this is lost to society—after all, the government collects revenue from the tax on cigarettes, and this revenue is then available to spend on government services. The tax revenue that is collected equals the tax per unit of output times the quantity of output produced. The difference between the price consumers pay and the price received by producers is equal to the tax on each unit of output. So the tax revenues collected will equal the area outlined in green. When we add up consumer surplus, producer surplus, and the revenue collected by the government, we can see that this total is less than the total surplus without the tax—the efficiency cost of the tax is measured by the area outlined in red. This is called the **deadweight loss** caused by a tax. The cost to society of a tax is greater than the revenue actually collected by the government.

Panel B illustrates the situation for a market where the demand curve is relatively elastic. Here, the deadweight loss of the tax (the area outlined in red) is larger. Because consumers are more sensitive to price when the demand curve is elastic, the tax causes them to substitute away from the taxed good. The tax "distorts" consumers' choices more in this case, and the resulting efficiency loss is larger.

Efficiency

In the basic competitive model, with each consumer and each firm taking the market price as given, the equilibrium between demand and supply ensures the largest possible joint gain to consumers and firms. This is why most economists believe the basic competitive model provides an important benchmark for evaluating how well resources are allocated. Taxes on specific goods create efficiency losses, as does interfering with the law of supply and demand

Thinking Like an Economist

Exchange and Distribution

The concepts of consumer surplus and producer surplus remind us that *exchange* in competitive markets can benefit both buyers and sellers. The demand curve for a good shows the total willingness to pay for each unit of the good. Though consumers are willing to pay more for the marginal unit at lower quantities, all units are purchased at the market price, which reflects the value of the last unit purchased. Thus, the total utility of the units purchased by consumers is greater than the total cost to consumers. Similarly, the supply curve reflects the marginal cost of producing each unit of a good. The market equilibrium price will equal the marginal cost of the last unit produced. Because marginal cost increases as the firm produces more, the price the firm receives is greater than the marginal cost of producing every unit except the last.

Consumer surplus and producer surplus also remind us that exchange has *distributional effects*. The gains from exchange are not necessarily evenly distributed. If demand is relatively elastic while supply is inelastic, consumer surplus is small while producer surplus is large. If demand is relatively inelastic while supply is very elastic, consumer surplus is large while producer surplus is small.

---

through policies such as rent control. These policies may have desirable effects (a tax on cigarettes helps to reduce smoking, for instance), but these must be balanced against the inefficiencies they create. As we have seen before, trade-offs must be made.

If the conditions of the basic competitive model are satisfied, markets do a good job of allocating society's resources efficiently. But the benchmark provided by the basic competitive model is also useful because it helps us to understand how markets can fail when the basic assumptions of the model do not hold. In Part Three, we examine a number of factors that cause markets to be inefficient. But first, we need to examine more closely what economists mean when they talk about the efficiency of markets.

Pareto Efficiency

In everyday usage, we say something is efficient if it involves little waste. To economists, the concept of efficiency is related to concern with the well-being of those in the economy. When no one can be made better off without making someone else worse off, the allocation of resources is called **Pareto efficient,** after the great Italian economist and sociologist Vilfredo Pareto (1848–1923). Typically when economists refer to efficiency, Pareto efficiency is what they mean. Saying that a market is efficient is a compliment. In the same way that an efficient machine uses its inputs as productively as possible, an efficient market leaves no way of increasing output with the same level of inputs. The only way one person can be made better off is by taking resources away from another, thereby making the second person worse off.

It is easy to see how an allocation of resources might not be Pareto efficient. Assume the government is given the job of distributing chocolate and vanilla ice cream and pays no attention to people's preferences. Assume, moreover, that some individuals love chocolate and hate vanilla, while others love vanilla and hate chocolate. Some chocolate lovers will get vanilla ice cream, and some vanilla lovers will get chocolate ice cream. Clearly, this is Pareto inefficient. Allowing people to trade resources, in this case, ice cream, makes both groups better off.

There is a popular and misguided view that *all* economic changes represent nothing more than redistributions. Gains to one only subtract from another. Rent control is one example. In this view, the only effect of rent control is redistribution—landlords receive less and are worse off by the same amount that their tenants' rents are reduced (and the tenants are better off). In some countries, unions have expressed similar views and see wage increases as having no further consequences than redistributing income to workers from those who own or who manage firms. This view is mistaken because in each of these instances, there are consequences beyond the redistribution. Rent control that keeps rents below the level that clears the rental housing market does more than just take money out of the pocket of landlords and put it into the pocket of poor renters. It affects the amount of housing landlords are willing to supply. It results in inefficiencies. For those concerned about renters who cannot afford the going rate, there are better approaches that make the renters as well as the landlords better off than under rent control. Thus, with rent control, the economy is not Pareto efficient.

Conditions for the Pareto Efficiency of the Market Economy

For the economy to be Pareto efficient, it must meet the conditions of exchange efficiency, production efficiency, and product-mix efficiency. Considering each of these conditions separately shows us why the basic competitive model attains Pareto efficiency. (Recall the basic ingredients of that model: rational, perfectly informed households interacting with rational, profit-maximizing firms in competitive markets.)

Exchange Efficiency

Exchange efficiency requires that whatever the economy produces must be distributed among individuals in an efficient way. If I like chocolate ice cream and you like vanilla ice cream, exchange efficiency requires that I get the chocolate and you get the vanilla.

When there is exchange efficiency, there is no scope for further trade among individuals. Chapter 3 discussed the advantages of free exchange among individuals and nations. Any prohibition or restriction on trade results in exchange inefficiency. For instance, in war times, governments often ration scarce goods, like sugar. People are given coupons that allow them to buy, say, a pound of sugar a month. If sugar carries a price of $1 a pound, having $1 is not enough; you must also have the coupon. There is often considerable controversy about whether people should be allowed to sell their coupons, or trade their sugar coupons for, say, a butter coupon. If the government prohibits the sale or trading of coupons, then the economy will not be exchange efficient—it will not be Pareto efficient.

The price system ensures that exchange efficiency is attained. In deciding how much of a good to buy, people balance the marginal benefit they receive by buying an extra unit with the cost of that extra unit, its price. Hence, price can be thought of as a rough measure of the *marginal* benefit an individual receives from a good—that is, the benefit a person receives from one more unit of the good. For those who like chocolate ice cream a great deal and vanilla ice cream very little, this will entail consuming many more chocolate ice cream cones than vanilla ones. And conversely for the vanilla lover. Notice that no single individual or agency needs to know who is a chocolate and who is a vanilla lover for the goods to get to the right person. Not even the ice cream stores have to know individual preferences. Each consumer, by his own action, ensures that exchange efficiency is attained.

Notice too that if different individuals face *different* prices, then the economy will not, in general, be exchange efficient. This is because the difference in price opens up an opportunity for exchange. For example, Jim would love to fly to Hawaii but feels it is not worth it at the full fare offered. At the same time, Madeleine, whose mother is an airline executive and only has to pay half fares, is not keen on going to Hawaii but cannot pass up the good deal. Both can be made better off if they are allowed to make an exchange.

Production Efficiency

For an economy to be Pareto efficient, it must also be **production efficient.** That is, it must not be possible to produce more of some goods without producing less of other goods. In other words, Pareto efficiency requires that the economy operate along the production possibilities curve first introduced in Chapter 2.

Figure 10.4 shows the production possibilities curve for a simple economy that produces only two goods, SUVs and sedans. If the economy is at point *I*, inside the production possibilities curve, it cannot be Pareto efficient. Society could produce more of both SUVs and sedans, and by distributing them to different individuals, it could make people better off. Prices signal to firms the scarcity of each of the inputs they use. When all firms face the same prices of labor, capital goods, and other inputs, they will take the appropriate actions to economize on each of these inputs, ensuring that the economy operates along its production possibilities curve.

Product-mix Efficiency

The third condition for Pareto efficiency is **product-mix efficiency.** That is, the mix of goods produced by the economy must reflect

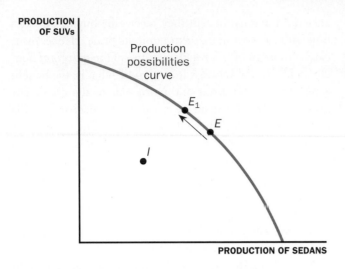

FIGURE 10.4   *The Production Possibilities Curve*

The production possibilities curve shows the maximum level of output of one good given the level of output of other goods. Production efficiency requires that the economy be on its production possibilities curve. Along the curve, the only way to increase production of one good (here, SUVs) is to decrease the production of other goods (sedans).

the preferences of those in the economy. The economy must produce along the production possibilities curve at a point that reflects the preferences of consumers. The price system again ensures that this condition will be satisfied. Both firms and households look at the trade-offs. Firms look at how many extra sedans they can produce if they reduce their production of SUVs. The result is given by the slope of the production possibilities curve, and is called the **marginal rate of transformation.** Firms compare this trade-off with the relative benefits of producing the two goods—given by the relative prices. Similarly, households look at the relative costs of SUVs and sedans—again given by the relative prices—and ask, given those trade-offs, whether they would like to consume more SUVs and fewer sedans or vice versa.

Changes in preferences are reflected quickly—through the operation of demand and supply curves—in changes in prices. These changes are then translated into changes in production by firms. Assume that the economy is initially producing at a point along the production possibilities curve, *E* in Figure 10.4. Consumers decide that they like SUVs more and sedans less. The increased demand for SUVs will result in the price of SUVs increasing, and this will lead to an

increased output of SUVs; at the same time, the decrease demand for sedans will result in the price of sedans falling, and this in turn will lead to a decreased output of sedans. The economy will move from *E* to a point such as E_1, where there are more SUVs and fewer sedans produced; the mix of goods produced in the economy will have changed to reflect the changed preferences of consumers.

Three Conditions for Pareto Efficiency

1. Exchange efficiency: Goods must be distributed among individuals in a way that means there are no gains from further trade.
2. Production efficiency: The economy must be on its production possibilities curve.
3. Product-mix efficiency: The economy must produce a mix of goods reflecting the preferences of consumers.

Competitive Markets and Pareto Efficiency

We now know that when economists say that market economies are efficient, or that the price system results in economic efficiency, they mean that the economy is Pareto efficient: no one can be made better off without making someone else worse off. We have also learned why competitive markets ensure that all three of the basic conditions for Pareto efficiency—exchange efficiency, production efficiency, and product-mix efficiency—are attained.

The argument that competitive markets ensure Pareto efficiency can be put somewhat loosely in another way: a rearrangement of resources can only benefit people who voluntarily agree to it. But in competitive equilibrium, people have already agreed to all the exchanges they are willing to make; no one wishes to produce more or less or to demand more or less, given the prices faced.

Pareto efficiency does *not* say that there are no ways to make one or many individuals better off. Obviously, resources could be taken from some and given to others, and the recipients would be better off. We have seen how, for

Thinking Like an Economist

Indirect Trade-offs and Air Safety for Children

General equilibrium analysis calls attention to the fact that trade-offs often exist across markets. The benefits of an action taken in one market may be offset by related costs that arise in another market. This same reasoning applies to government policies, as policymakers work to balance the costs and benefits of expenditure programs and regulations. Sometimes the costs of a policy arise through indirect repercussions of the initial policy. For instance, taking account of such indirect trade-offs was important to regulations related to air safety for children.

States require small children in cars to ride in specially designed safety seats. So why shouldn't small children traveling by plane be required to ride in safety seats as well? It seems clear that in at least a few cases, such seats would save a child's life in an airplane crash. Nevertheless, after considering the full potential consequences of requiring child safety seats in planes, the Federal Aviation Administration (FAA) argued against it.

On the benefit side, the FAA estimated that mandatory safety seats would save the life of one child in one airline crash every 10 years. But parents would have to pay as much as $185 to buy the safety seats themselves, in addition to paying for a regular airplane seat for the child. Now, children under two years old are allowed to sit in their parents' laps, avoiding the expense of an airline ticket. With those extra costs, the FAA estimated that 20 percent of the families who now fly with small children would either stay home or drive. The additional driving would lead to 9 additional highway deaths, 59 serious injuries, and 2,300 minor injuries over the same ten-year period, according to FAA estimates.

Even those who feel that saving an additional child's life has a value that cannot be reduced to a price tag, however high, must look beyond the market being regulated. Looking beyond airlines makes it clear that reducing airline deaths by requiring child safety seats for infants and toddlers is almost certain to cause even greater loss of life.

instance, government interventions with the market, such as rent control, do benefit some individuals—those who are lucky enough to get the rent-controlled apartments. But in the process, someone is made worse off.

Competitive Markets and Income Distribution

Efficiency is better than inefficiency, but it is not everything. In the competitive equilibrium, some individuals might be very rich, while others live in dire poverty. One person might have skills that are highly valued, while another does not. Competition may result in an efficient economy with a very unequal distribution of resources.

The law of supply and demand in a competitive economy determines how the available income will be divided up. It determines how much workers get paid for their labor and the return to owners of capital on their investments. By determining wages and the return to capital, the market thus determines the distribution of income.

Knowing how the distribution of income is determined is important, because it tells us how the nation's economic pie is divided: it provides the answer to the question, "For whom are goods produced?" While competitive markets produce economic *efficiency*—no one can be made better off without making someone else worse off—competitive markets may also produce distributions of income that seem, at least to some, morally repugnant. An economy where some individuals live in mansions while others barely eke out a living may be efficient, but that still hardly makes the situation desirable. Left to themselves, competitive markets may provide an answer to the question "For whom are goods produced?" that seems unacceptable.

This unacceptable response does not mean that the competitive market mechanism should be abandoned, at least not under the conditions assumed in our basic model, with perfectly informed, rational consumers and firms interacting in perfectly competitive markets. Even if society as a whole wishes to redistribute income, it should not dispense with competitive markets. Instead, *all* that is needed is to redistribute the wealth that people possess, and then leave the rest to the workings of a competitive market. With appropriate redistributions of wealth, the economy can achieve any desired distribution of income.

Of course, redistributing wealth is easier said than done, and as a practical matter, virtually all of the ways that the government engages in redistribution affect the workings of the market economy. Taxes on wages affect the labor market; taxes on capital, the capital market; taxes on luxuries, particular goods markets.

Perhaps the most important impact of government on the distribution of "wealth" is through education—in providing everyone a certain amount of human capital. By providing all individuals, regardless of the wealth of their parents, with a free basic education, government reduces the degree of inequality that otherwise would exist. Still, as we shall see in Chapter 16, the magnitude of inequality in the United States remains high—larger than in most other developed countries.

Frequently government interferences with the market are justified on the grounds that they increase equality. These government policies are often based on the widely held but mistaken (as we have already seen) view that all redistributions are just that, some individuals get more, others get less, but there are no further repercussions. We now know that changing relative prices to achieve redistribution—such as rent control—will have effects in addition to redistributing income. Such changes interfere with the economy's efficiency. One consequence of lower rents for apartments, for example, is that the return on capital invested in rental housing will fall, and as a result the economy will invest too little in rental housing. Because of this underinvestment, the economy is not efficient.

Thus, interventions in the economy justified on the grounds that they increase equality need to be treated with caution. To attain an efficient allocation of resources with the desired distribution of income, *if* the assumptions of the competitive model are satisfied by the economy, the *sole* role of the government is to redistribute initial wealth. Not only can one rely on the market mechanism thereafter, but interfering with the market may actually result in the economy not being Pareto efficient.

Both of the results just presented—that competitive markets are Pareto efficient and that every Pareto-efficient allocation, regardless of the desired distribution of income, can be obtained through the market mechanism—are *theorems*. That is, they are logical propositions that follow from basic definitions and assumptions, such as what is meant by a competitive economy and what is meant by Pareto efficiency. When these assumptions are not satisfied, market economies may not be Pareto efficient, and more extensive government interventions may be required to obtain Pareto-efficient allocations. Later chapters will explore these circumstance in greater detail.

Still, two important lessons emerge: There are costs associated with redistributions that entail interventions in market mechanisms, and those costs have to be weighed against the benefits; and redistributions can make use of the price mechanism, rather than try to override it. One cannot repeal the laws of supply and demand. Interventions like rent control can impose large costs. Some alternative forms of interventions, such as housing subsidies, may achieve comparable distributional objectives at less cost. If government cannot *costlessly* redistribute, it should look for efficient ways of redistributing—that is, ways that reduce the costs as much as possible. This is one of the main concerns of the branch of economics called the *economics of the public sector.*

General Equilibrium Analysis

In earlier chapters where we applied the idea of market equilibrium, we focused on one market at a time. The price of a good is determined when the demand for that good equals its supply. The wage rate is determined when the demand for labor equals its supply. The interest rate is determined when the demand for savings equals its supply. This kind of analysis is called **partial equilibrium analysis.** In analyzing what is going on in one market, we ignore what is going on in other markets. This is what we did earlier in this chapter when we analyzed the efficiency cost of rent control and the impact of a tax on cigarettes. In each case, we focused just on the demand and supply in the market for apartments and the market for cigarettes.

Interdependencies in the economy make partial equilibrium analysis overly simple, because demand and supply in one market depend on prices determined in other markets. For instance, the demand for skis depends on the price of ski tickets, ski boots, and possibly even airline tickets. Thus, the equilibrium price of skis will depend on the price of ski tickets, ski boots, and airline tickets. By the same token, the demand for ski tickets and ski boots will depend on the price of skis. **General equilibrium analysis** broadens the perspective, taking into account the interactions and interdependencies with the various parts of the economy.

The Basic Competitive Equilibrium Model

Economists view the entire economy as made up of numerous different markets, all interrelated. Individuals and firms interact in these different markets. In the labor market, for example, the supply of labor reflects the outcome of decisions by households as they determine the amount of labor they wish to supply. Households supply labor because they want to buy goods. Hence, their labor supply depends on both wages and *prices.* It also depends on other sources of income. If we assume, for simplicity, that households also have savings that yield a return, then we can see that the labor supply is connected to the product market and the capital market.

Equilibrium in the labor market requires that the demand for labor equal the supply. Normally, when we draw the demand curve for labor, we simply assume that p, the price of the good(s) being produced, and the interest rate (here, r) are kept fixed. We focus our attention solely on the wage rate, the price of labor. Given p and r, we look for the wage at which the demand and supply for labor are equal. This is a *partial equilibrium analysis* of the labor market. But in fact all markets are interrelated; the demand for

labor depends on the wage, on the interest rate, and on the price at which the firm sells its output.

The labor market is only one of the three markets, even in our highly simplified economy. There is also the market for capital to consider. In Chapter 9, we saw how households determine their saving, which in turn determines the available supply of capital. The supply of capital is affected, in general, by the return it yields (the interest rate r) plus the income individuals have from other sources, in particular from wages. Since the amount individuals are willing to save may depend on how well off they feel, and how well off they feel depends on the wage rate relative to prices, we can think of the supply of capital, too, as depending on wages, interest rates, and prices. In Chapter 9 we learned how to derive firms' demand for capital. This depends not just on the interest they must pay but also on the price at which goods can be sold, and the cost of other inputs such as labor.

Equilibrium in the capital market occurs at the point where the demand and supply for capital are equal. Again, partial equilibrium analysis of the capital market focuses on the return to capital, r, at which the demand and supply of capital are equal, but both the demand and supply depend on the wage rate and the price of goods as well.

Finally, there is the market for goods. Chapter 6 showed how to derive households' demand for goods. We can think of the household at first deciding on how much to spend (Chapter 9) and then deciding how to allocate what it spends over different goods (Chapter 6). Of course, with a single consumption good, the later problem no longer exists. In our simplified model, then, we can think of the demand for goods at any price as being determined by household income, which in turn depends on the wage and the interest rate.

Similarly, in Chapter 8, we analyzed how firms determine how much to produce. They set price equal to marginal cost, where marginal cost depends on wages and the interest rate. Equilibrium in the goods market requires that the demand for goods equal the supply of goods. Again, while in the simple partial equilibrium analysis we focus on how the demand and supply of goods depend on price, p, we know that the demand and supply of goods also depend on both the wage rate and the return to capital.

The labor market is said to be in equilibrium when the demand for labor equals the supply. The product market is in equilibrium when the demand for goods equals the supply. The capital market is in equilibrium when the demand for capital equals the supply. The economy as a whole is in equilibrium only when all markets clear simultaneously (demand equals supply in all markets). The general equilibrium for our simple economy occurs at a common wage rate, w, price, p, and interest rate, r, at which all three markets are in equilibrium.

WRAP-UP

Equilibrium in the Basic Competitive Model

The labor market clearing condition: The demand for labor must equal the supply.

The capital market clearing condition: The demand for capital must equal the supply.

The goods market clearing condition: The demand for goods must equal the supply.

In the basic equilibrium model, there is only a single good, but it is easy to extend the analysis to the more realistic case where there are many goods. The same web of interconnections exists between different goods and between different goods and different inputs. Recall from Chapter 4 that the demand curve depicts the quantity of a good—for instance, soda—demanded at each price; the supply curve shows the quantity of a good that firms supply at each price. But the demand curve for soda depends on the prices of other goods and the income levels of different consumers; similarly, the supply curve for soda depends on the prices of inputs, including the wage rate, the interest rate, and the price of sugar and other ingredients. Those prices, in turn, depend on supply and demand in their respective markets. The general equilibrium of the economy requires finding the prices for each good and for each input such that the demand for each good equals the supply, and the demand for each input equals the supply. *General equilibrium entails prices, wages, and returns to capital that ensure all markets for goods, labor, and capital (and other factors of production) clear.*

CASE IN POINT

The Labor Market and the Widening Wage Gap

A general equilibrium perspective can help us understand how changes in one market affect other markets. Often those repercussions on other markets feed back to cause further changes in the market originally affected. As a case in point, a general equilibrium analysis is needed to analyze how wages for skilled and unskilled workers are affected by changes in technology.

Those who have a college education are paid more on average than those who fail to complete high school. The average wage of workers with at least four years of college is two-thirds higher than that of workers whose education ended with a high school diploma. Because unskilled workers generally cannot perform the same jobs as skilled workers, it is useful to think about the wages of these two groups as determined in separate labor markets, as illustrated in Figure 10.5. Panel A shows the demand and supply curves of unskilled workers, and panel B those for skilled workers. The equilibrium wage for skilled workers is higher than that for unskilled workers.

What happens if a change in technology shifts the demand curve for skilled labor to the right, to DS_1, and the demand curve for unskilled labor to the left, to DU_1? The wages of unskilled workers will decrease from wu_0 to wu_1, and those of skilled workers will increase from ws_0 to ws_1. In the long run, this increased wage gap induces more people to acquire skills, so the supply of unskilled workers shifts to the left, and that of skilled workers shifts to the right. As a result, the wage of unskilled workers rises from wu_1 to wu_2, and that of skilled workers falls from ws_1 to ws_2. These long-run supply responses thus dampen the short-run movements in wages.

Over the past two decades, the ratio of wages of college graduates to high school graduates, and the ratio of wages of high school graduates to nongraduates has increased enormously. Indeed, the real wages (that is, wages adjusted for changes in the cost of living) of unskilled workers has fallen dramatically (by as much as 30 percent). Though there have been shifts in both demand and supply curves, the primary explanation of these shifts is a change in the relative demand for skilled labor, probably attributable largely to changes in technology.

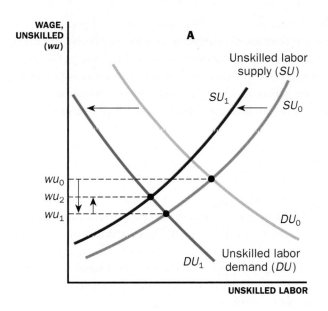

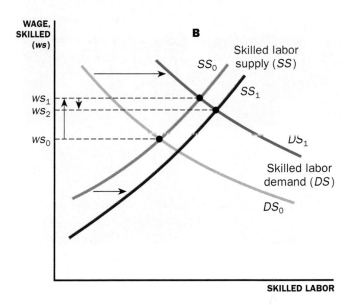

FIGURE 10.5   *The Market for Skilled and Unskilled Labor*

In panel A, new advanced technology shifts the demand curve for unskilled labor to the left, and reduces wages from wu_0 to wu_1. In panel B, the new technology shifts the demand curve for skilled labor out to the right, and thus raises wages from ws_0 to ws_1. Over time, this increased difference in wages may lead more individuals to obtain skills, shifting the supply curve for unskilled labor back to the left, raising wages for unskilled labor somewhat from wu_1 to wu_2, and shifting the supply curve for skilled labor to the right, reducing wages for skilled labor from ws_1 to ws_2.

While we can be fairly confident of the predicted shifts in long-run labor supply, how fast they will occur is less clear. At the same time that these supply shifts occur, there may be further shifts in the demand curves, exacerbating wage differences. The question is how long will it take for the wage gap to be reduced to the levels that prevailed in the 1960s? In the meantime, many worry about the social consequences of steadily increasing wage (and income) inequality. •

CASE IN POINT

The Minimum Wage and General Equilibrium

When the first minimum wage law was adopted by passage of the Fair Labor Standards Act of 1938, it had general equilibrium effects that altered the character of the country.

When enacted, the minimum wage law required that wages be no lower than 32.5 cents per hour. Because wages were much lower in the South than in the North, many more workers were affected there. For example, 44 percent of southern textile workers were paid below the minimum wage, but only 6 percent of northern textile workers were. African Americans in the South were particularly affected. Many lost their jobs and migrated North. The economy of the South, no longer able to pay low wages, adapted by seeking out investment, which over the years has helped make states like Texas and Florida among the fastest-growing in the country.

Gavin Wright, professor of economics at Stanford University, described the situation this way: "The overall effect of this history on black Americans is complex, mixed, and ironic. Displacement and suffering were severe. Yet in abolishing the low-wage South, the federal government also destroyed the nation's most powerful bastion of racism and white supremacy. The civil rights movement of the 1960s was able to use the South's hunger for capital inflows as an effective weapon in forcing desegregation. Similarly, migration

The effects of the first minimum wage were far reaching, including the migration of many African Americans to the North.

to the North allowed dramatic increases in incomes and educational opportunities for many blacks; yet the same migration channeled other blacks into the high-unemployment ghettos which if anything have worsened with the passage of time."[3]

A partial equilibrium analysis of the effects of enacting a minimum wage would only look at how the law affected labor markets. But for society as a whole, the effects of enacting such a law were far more momentous, touching on issues like racial desegregation and the growth of urban ghettos. ●

General Equilibrium over Time

A general equilibrium perspective focuses on the interrelationships among markets, including markets at different points in time. For example, the supply (and demand) for exhaustible natural resources like oil will depend on the price of oil today, but it will also depend on prices expected in the future. The role played by prices expected in the future is important for understanding how quickly the limited supply of a natural resource will be used.

Just as we did in Chapter 9 when we discussed household saving, we will simplify by considering just two periods, today and the future. Let's also assume that known reserves of oil are one billion barrels. The oil can be sold now or left in

[3]Gavin Wright, "The Economic Revolution in the American South," *Journal of Economic Perspectives* (Summer 1987) 1:161–78.

the ground and sold in the future period. Oil producers will want to compare the current price with the *present discounted* future price. If the current price is above the present discounted price, the oil producer will have an incentive to sell all one billion barrels today; if the present discounted future price is higher than the current price, the producer will have an incentive to save the oil and sell it in the future. In equilibrium, the oil producers must be indifferent between selling an extra barrel of oil today and saving it to sell in the future. This tells us that the current price and the present discounted future price must be equal.

The current price and the present discounted value of the future price will be equal, but how much oil will actually be produced today? To answer this question, we need to know the demand curves for oil today and in the future. In equilibrium, the quantity demanded today and in the future, when the current price and present discounted future price are equal, must equal the total reserves of one billion barrels.

Now suppose that new technologies or more fuel-efficient cars will reduce the demand for oil in the future at each price. The demand curve for oil in the future shifts to the left. This lowers the future price of oil. Whenever the present discounted future price falls, oil producers will want to sell more of their oil today. This increase in the supply of oil today lowers the current price of oil. The current price must adjust until it equals the present discounted future price, and total demand today and in the future equals one billion barrels. Because reduced demand in the future lowers the current price of oil, it leads to high current consumption of oil and an increase in the quantity of oil produced today.

When Partial Equilibrium Analysis Will Do

In the examples of the widening wage gap and the price of oil, general equilibrium analysis is clearly important. But can we ever focus on what goes on in a single market, without worrying about the reverberations in the rest of the economy? Are there circumstances in which partial equilibrium analysis will provide a fairly accurate answer to the effect of, say, a change in a tax? When will the sort of analysis we used earlier in this chapter to analyze the impact of a tax on cigarettes and cheddar cheese be sufficiently accurate?

Partial equilibrium analysis is adequate, for example, when the reverberations from the initial imposition of a tax are so dispersed that they can be ignored without distorting the analysis. Such is the case when individuals shift their demand away from the taxed good toward many, many other goods. Each of the prices of those goods changes only a very little. And the total demand for the factors of production (like capital and labor) changes only negligibly, so that the second round changes in the prices of different goods and inputs have only a slight effect on the demand and supply curve of the industry analyzed. In these circumstances, partial equilibrium analysis will provide a good approximation to what will actually happen.

Our earlier analysis of a tax on cigarettes provides an example where partial equilibrium analysis provides a good approximation. Since expenditures on cigarettes are a small proportion of anyone's income, an increase in their price will have a small effect on overall consumption patterns. While the reduced quantity demanded of cigarettes (and the indirect changed demand for other goods) will have a slight effect the total demand for labor, this effect is so small that it will have no noticeable effect on the wage rate. Similarly, the tax will have virtually no effect on the return to capital.

Under these circumstances, where more distant general equilibrium effects are likely to be so faint as to be indiscernible, a partial equilibrium analysis of a tax on cigarettes is appropriate.

Looking Beyond the Basic Model

This chapter has brought together the pieces of the basic competitive model. It has shown how the competitive equilibrium in an ideal economy is achieved. To the extent that conditions in the real world match the assumptions of the basic competitive model, there will be economic efficiency. Governments will have little role in the economy beyond establishing a legal framework within which to enforce market transactions.

What are the consequences when the underlying assumptions are not valid? Which of the assumptions are most suspect? What evidence do we have to assess either the validity of the model's underlying assumptions or its implications? The next part of this book is devoted to these questions, and to the role of government that emerges from the answers.

Review and Practice

Summary

1. General equilibrium in the basic competitive model occurs when wages, interest rates, and prices are such that demand is equal to supply in all labor, capital, and product markets. All markets clear.

2. The competitive equilibrium maximizes the sum of consumer and producer surplus.

3. Under the conditions of the basic competitive model, the economy's resource allocation is Pareto efficient; that is, no one can made better off without making someone worse off.

4. The distribution of income that emerges from competitive markets may possibly be very unequal. However, under the conditions of the basic competitive model, a redistribution of wealth can move the economy to a more equal allocation that is also Pareto efficient.

5. Changes in one market will have effects on other markets. To analyze the effects of a tax, for example, general equilibrium analysis takes into account the effects in all markets. But when the secondary repercussions of a change are small, partial equilibrium analysis, focusing on only one or a few markets, is sufficient.

Key Terms

general equilibrium
producer surplus
deadweight loss
Pareto efficient
exchange efficiency
production efficiency
product-mix efficiency
marginal rate of transformation
partial equilibrium analysis
general equilibrium analysis

Review Questions

1. How does the economy in general equilibrium answer the four basic economic questions: What is produced, and in what quantities? How are these goods

produced? For whom are they produced? Who decides how resources are allocated?

2. What is meant by Pareto efficiency? What is required for the economy to be Pareto efficient? If the conditions of the basic competitive model are satisfied, is the economy Pareto efficient?

3. What is the difference between partial and general equilibrium analysis? When is each one especially appropriate?

4. If the distribution of income in the economy is quite unequal, is it necessary to impose price controls or otherwise change prices in the competitive marketplace to make it more equal?

Problems

1. Decide whether partial equilibrium analysis would suffice in each of these cases, or whether it would be wise to undertake a general equilibrium analysis:

   (a) a tax on alcohol;

   (b) an increase in the Social Security tax;

   (c) a drought that affects farm production in the Midwestern states;

   (d) a rise in the price of crude oil;

   (e) a major airline going out of business.

   Explain your answers.

2. Explain how each of the following might interfere with exchange efficiency:

   (a) airlines that limit the number of seats they sell at a discount price;

   (b) doctors who charge poor patients less than rich patients;

   (c) firms that give volume discounts.

   In each case, what additional trades might be possible?

3. Assume that in the steel industry, given current production levels and technology, 1 machine costing $10,000 can replace 1 worker. Given current production levels and technology in the automobile industry, 1 machine costing $10,000 can replace 2 workers. Is

this economy Pareto efficient; that is, is it on its production possibilities curve? If not, explain how total output of both goods can be increased by shifting machines and labor between industries.

4. Consider three ways of helping poor people to buy food, clothing, and shelter. The first way is to pass laws setting price ceilings to keep these basic goods affordable. The second is to have the government distribute coupons that give poor people a discount when they buy these necessities. The third is for the government to distribute income to poor people. Which program is more likely to have a Pareto-efficient outcome? Describe why the other programs are not likely to be Pareto efficient.

5. Suppose the supply of rental apartments is completely inelastic in the short run. Show that imposing a ceiling on rents that is below the equilibrium rent does not cause any inefficiency by showing that total consumer and producer surplus is not reduced by the rent ceiling. If the supply of rental apartments is more elastic in the long run, explain why a ceiling on rents would reduce the total surplus.

6. If you do not know whether you would be able to get a rent-controlled apartment, under what circumstances might you nonetheless vote for rent control? Why would your enthusiasm for rent control wane over time?

Appendix: Pareto Efficiency and Competitive Markets

The concept of the marginal rate of substitution, introduced in the appendices to Chapters 6 and 9, can be used to see more clearly why competitive markets are Pareto efficient.

Exchange Efficiency

Exchange efficiency can be achieved only when all individuals have the same marginal rate of substitution, the amount of one good a person is willing to give up to get one unit of another. In competitive markets, individuals choose a mix of goods for which the marginal rate of substitution is equal to relative prices. Since all individuals face the same relative prices, they all have identical marginal rates of substitution, ensuring the exchange efficiency of the economy.

To see why exchange efficiency requires that all people have the same marginal rate of substitution, let's look at a simple example of Crusoe and Friday and their island economy. Assume that Crusoe's marginal rate of substitution between apples and oranges is 2; that is, he is willing to give up 2 apples for 1 extra orange. Friday's marginal rate of substitution between apples and oranges is 1; he is willing to give up 1 apple for 1 orange. Since their marginal rates of substitution are not equal, we can make one of them better off without making the other worse off (or we can make both of them better off). The allocation is not Pareto efficient.

To see how this is done, suppose we take 1 orange away from Friday and give it to Crusoe. Crusoe would then be willing to give up 2 apples, and be just as well off as before. If he gave up only 1½ apples to Friday, Friday would also be better off. Friday would have given up 1 orange in return for 1½ apples; he would have been willing to make the trade if he had received just 1 apple in return.

It is easy to see that Crusoe and Friday will continue to trade until their marginal rates of substitution are equal. As Friday gives up oranges for apples, his marginal rate of substitution increases; he insists on getting more and more apples for each orange he gives up. Similarly, as Crusoe gives up apples and gets more oranges, his marginal rate of substitution decreases; he is willing to give up fewer apples for each extra orange he gets. Eventually, the two will have identical marginal rates of substitution, at which point further trade will stop. Thus, the basic condition for exchange efficiency is that the marginal rates of substitution of all individuals must be the same.

Production Efficiency

The condition of production efficiency—when the economy is on its production possibilities curve—is very similar to the condition of exchange efficiency. An economy can only be productively efficient if the marginal rate of technical substitution between any two inputs in any two firms is the same. The marginal rate of technical substitution is the amount that one input can be reduced if another input is increased by one unit, while output remains constant (see appendix to Chapter 7).

Profit-maximizing firms in a competitive economy choose a mix of inputs such that the marginal rate of technical substitution of different inputs is equal to the relative prices of those inputs. If all firms face the same relative prices of inputs, their marginal rates of technical substitution will be the same, and production efficiency will result.

For example, consider a case involving the steel and auto industries. Assume that in steel, the marginal rate of technical substitution between capital expenditures and labor is $2,000; that is, if a company uses one more worker, it can save $2,000 on equipment (or equivalently, two $1,000 machines substitute for one worker). In the auto industry, the marginal rate of technical substitution is $1,000; one $1,000 machine substitutes for one worker. The marginal rates of technical substitution between inputs are not equal, which means that the economy is not productively efficient.

Consider a worker moving from the auto to the steel industry. If the steel industry keeps its output at the same level, the additional worker in that industry frees up two machines. One of those machines can be transferred to the auto industry, and production in that industry would stay at the same level. (We are assuming that in the auto industry one $1,000 machine substitutes for one worker.) But one machine is left over. It can be used in the steel industry, the auto industry, or both to increase production.

As we increase the number of workers in the steel industry, the marginal productivity of labor in that industry will diminish, while as we reduce workers in the automobile industry, the marginal productivity of labor in that industry will increase; conversely for machines. As a result, the marginal rates of technical substitution will shift in the two industries, so that they are closer. Spurred on by the profit motive of the individual companies in competitive markets, labor and capital will tend to move between companies until marginal rates of technical substitution are equated, and production efficiency is reached. Thus, production efficiency, which means that the economy is on its production possibilities curve, requires that the marginal rate of technical substitution between any two inputs be the same in all uses.

Product-mix Efficiency

This third condition of Pareto efficiency requires that the economy operate at the point along the production possibilities curve that reflects consumers' preferences. Look at a particular point on the production possibilities curve in Figure 10.4, say point *E*. The *marginal rate of transformation* tells us how many extra units of one good the economy can get if it gives up one unit of another good—how many extra cases of beer the economy can produce if it reduces production of potato chips by a ton, or how many extra cars the economy can get if it gives up one tank. The slope of the production possibilities curve is equal to the marginal rate of transformation. The slope tells us how much of one good, measured along the vertical axis, can be increased if the economy gives up one unit of the good along the horizontal axis.

Product-mix efficiency requires that consumers' marginal rate of substitution equal the marginal rate of transformation. To see why this is so, and how competitive economies ensure product-mix efficiency, consider an economy producing two fruits, apples and oranges. Assume that the marginal rate of substitution between apples and oranges is 2—that is, individuals are willing to give up 2 apples for an additional orange; while the marginal rate of transformation is 1—they only have to give up 1 apple to get an additional orange. Clearly, it pays firms to increase orange production and reduce apple production.

The competitive price system ensures that the economy satisfies the condition for product-mix efficiency. We know that consumers set the marginal rate of substitution equal to the relative price. In a similar way, profit-maximizing firms have an incentive to produce more of some goods and less of others according to the prices they can sell them for, until their marginal rate of transformation is equal to the relative price. If consumers and producers both face the same relative prices, the marginal rate of substitution will equal the marginal rate of transformation. Thus,

product-mix efficiency comes about when both consumers and firms face the same prices.

To see more clearly why competitive firms will set the marginal rate of transformation equal to relative prices, consider a firm that produces both apples and oranges. If the company reallocates labor from apples to oranges, apple production is reduced and orange production is increased. Assume apple production goes down by 2 cases and orange production goes up by 1 case. The marginal rate of transformation is 2. If a case of apples sells for $4 and a case of oranges sells for $10, the firm loses $8 on apple sales but gains $10 on orange sales. It is clearly profitable for the firm to make the switch. The firm will continue to switch resources from apples to oranges until the marginal rate of transformation equals the relative price. The same result will occur even if oranges and apples are produced by different firms.[4]

Thus, the basic condition for product-mix efficiency, that the marginal rate of substitution must equal the marginal rate of transformation, will be satisfied in competitive economies because firms set the marginal rate of transformation equal to relative prices, and consumers set their marginal rate of substitution equal to relative prices.

---

[4]The concept of product-mix efficiency can be illustrated by superimposing a family of indifference curves (Chapter 6, appendix) in the same diagram with the production possibilities curve. Assume, for simplicity, that all individuals are the same. The highest level of welfare that one representative individual can attain is represented by the tangency of her indifference curve with the production possibilities curve. The slopes of two curves that are tangent to each other are equal at the point of tangency. The slope of the indifference curve is the consumer's marginal rate of substitution; the slope of the production possibilities curve is the marginal rate of transformation. Thus, the tangency—and Pareto efficiency—requires that the marginal rate of substitution equal the marginal rate of transformation.

E-commerce

"We would do that *Harry Potter* promotion every week if we could. We lost money on every sale, but it's a small amount in the context of our revenues. That was actually one of our most effective marketing programs ever." Jeff Bezos, Amazon.com's founder and chief executive on its offer of free overnight delivery on all orders of *Harry Potter and the Goblet of Fire*

The old joke used to have the clueless businessman saying that he was losing money on every sale but making it up in volume. At times, the new world of e-commerce seems to have turned this joke into a respectable business plan as new companies post huge losses while trying to establish market share. In the process, these new businesses are changing the way the economy operates. Whether buying a car or car insurance, trading stocks, making airline reservations, or buying travel guides, you can do them all on-line, bringing the power of the Internet into the home, affecting the way people think about markets, how they make purchasing decisions, and how they gather information. Perhaps more than any other company, Amazon.com symbolizes the changing nature of commerce.

Despite all the hype, e-commerce involving consumer purchases from businesses, so-called B2C, for "business to consumers," is still small potatoes. In its first official estimate of on-line retail commerce, the U.S. Bureau of the Census found that B2C retail transactions reached $5.3 billion during the last quarter of 1999. This represents less than 1 percent of all retail sales during the same time period. Many new start-ups in the B2C sector have failed, while others, like Amazon.com, continue to expand by offering more and more products, turning into virtual on-line malls. During 2000, Amazon.com added new cars to its list of products.

So why the big interest in e-commerce if it is still so small? For one thing, the growth in e-commerce has been phenomenal. This way of making purchases will become increasingly important and is likely to produce major changes in the way people and firms interact. And much of

the growth in e-commerce reflects the growth of "business to business" commerce, known as B2B. These developments are affecting the way goods are bought and sold. Recall that exchange is a core concept in economics, and information technologies have expanded the whole notion of markets and exchange. Markets function differently too because of changes in the availability of information, another of our core concepts. For instance, it can be very easy to gather valuable price information over the Internet. And even when people do not make purchases over the Internet, they may gain information that they can put to use elsewhere. For example, a person may have better success negotiating a price with a local bricks-and-mortar car dealer because of information she gained accessing an Internet car dealer such as CarsDirect.com or Autobytel.com.

The chart shows one estimate of the worldwide growth in e-commerce over the next few years. While North America will continue to account for the bulk of e-commerce transactions, e-commerce is likely to grow phenomenally in Asia and Western Europe as well.

Jeff Bezos, CEO of Amazon.com

A second reason for the interest in e-commerce lies in its potential for transforming many of the ways business is conducted. B2B e-commerce is already having a major impact on the costs of doing business. Automating the process of ordering supplies is just one of the ways firms are able to lower their costs. Managers are better able to track the status of orders, and fewer mistakes are made when information on orders is collected over the Internet.

We have already learned how important a firm's costs are for determining how much it produces. Lowering costs can boost a firm's profits. But the basic competitive model tells us that these changes won't end with the increases in profitability. The lure of higher profits will entice new firms to enter the industry. This process shifts the industry supply curve to the right and results in a lower equilibrium price. The higher profits from lower costs disappear as firms are forced to lower prices. This means that consumers eventually gain from the reduction in costs obtained through B2B commerce. The basic competitive model contains a clear prediction for on-line businesses such as Amazon.com. If Amazon.com provides a combination of prices, convenience, and service that consumers prefer over traditional bricks and mortar retail stores, and that allow Amazon.com to earn high profits, then other firms will enter the field, pushing down prices and profit margins.

SOURCE: "Global eCommerce Approaches Hypergrowth," Matthew R. Sanders with Bruce D. Temkin, April 18, 2000 (<u>www.forrester.com</u>).

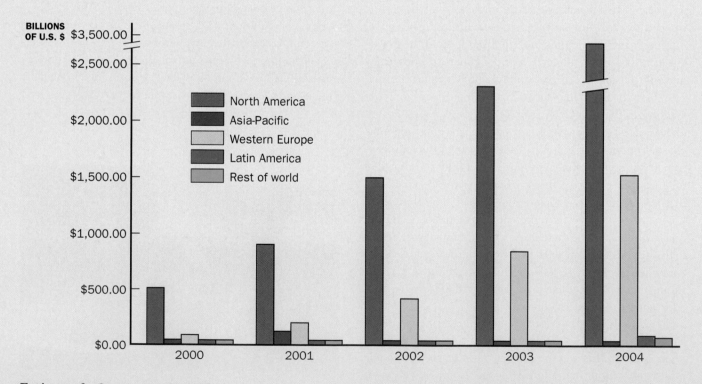

Estimated eCommerce Growth

Part 3

Imperfect Markets

Chapter 11

Introduction to Imperfect Markets

Key Questions

1. What are the key differences between modern economies and the economy described by the basic competitive model?

2. How are price and quantity determined when there is imperfect competition? How do price and quantity compare to the case of perfect competition? Is the market still efficient when there is imperfect competition?

3. Why is information different from other goods, such as hats or cameras? Why do markets for information often not work well? How does imperfect information affect the efficiency of markets?

4. How do externalities and public goods affect market efficiency?

*I*n the two centuries since Adam Smith enunciated the view that markets ensure economic efficiency, economists have investigated the basic competitive model with great care. Nothing they have discovered has shaken their belief that markets are, by and large, the most efficient way to coordinate an economy. However, economists have also found significant ways in which modern economics differ from that envisioned by the basic competitive model. These differences can cause markets to operate inefficiently, and they may provide a rationale for government involvement in the economy.

Before we can understand the role of government in the economy, we need to understand how the differences between modern economies and the world envisioned in our basic competitive model affect the way markets work. If competition is less than perfect, do markets still produce efficient outcomes? If they do not produce efficient outcomes, is too much produced or is too little produced? If people do not have enough information, say, about the quality of goods, will markets be efficient? And if the outcomes when information

is imperfect are not efficient, what can government do about it? What sorts of policies will improve the situation?

In this part of the book, we address these questions. We begin by outlining four important ways in which some markets may differ from the basic competitive model. These differences can help account for the important role that government plays in our economy. We examine how these differences affect the ability of private markets to efficiently use society's scarce resources. Subsequent chapters explore each of these differences in greater depth. By understanding when markets fail to produce efficient outcomes and why, we can greatly extend the range of insights that economics has to offer. These insights will provide the key to understanding some of the dissatisfactions with markets and some of the roles of public policy. And by going beyond the competitive model, we obtain insights into many of the economic changes associated with new technologies and the information revolution.

As we explore the economics of imperfect markets, the five key concepts introduced in Chapter 1—trade-offs, incentives, exchange, information, and distribution—continue to serve as guides to thinking like an economist. Individuals, firms, and government still face trade-offs when markets are imperfect. These trade-offs might differ from those faced in the world of the basic competitive model, and analyzing trade-offs when competition is imperfect or information is imperfect is an important step in any economic analysis. With trade-offs, choices must be made, and we must focus on incentives to understand these choices. Gaining an understanding of how market imperfections affect the outcome of market exchange will be especially critical. Information will take center stage in Chapter 14. Throughout, we will highlight how market imperfections affect not only the level but also the distribution of economic welfare. The basic concepts of economics do not apply just to the basic competitive model where competition is perfect and everyone has all the information they need. As economists have explored the role of imperfect competition and imperfect information in market economies, they have continued to find that these concepts provide the keys to thinking like an economist.

Extending the Basic Competitive Model

In Part Two, our understanding of markets and the role they play was aided by making several simplifying assumptions. We needed to focus on key factors that explain how markets work, without introducing all the details of actual markets. This is the general approach of theorizing in any field. If our objective had been to *describe* markets, detail would have been important so that we could obtain a good description of actual markets. Instead, our objective was to understand how prices and quantities are determined and to evaluate the nature of market outcomes. For that purpose, we needed to concentrate on the essence of markets, without being distracted by unnecessary detail.

The key assumptions in the basic competitive model include the following:

1. Firms and individuals take market prices as given—each is small relative to the market so that their decisions do not affect the market price.

2. Individuals and firms have perfect information about the quality and availability of goods, and about the prices of all goods.

3. Actions by an individual or firm do not directly affect other individuals or firms except through prices.

4. Goods are things that only the buyer can enjoy—if I buy and eat a slice of pizza, it is no longer available for you to eat; if you buy a bike, we both cannot use it at the same time.

There are many situations, however, in which we would like to analyze what happens if a firm has the power to set prices, or consumers are uninformed about the quality of different goods, or actions by one individual directly affect others (take secondhand smoke as an example), or there are goods we can all consume simultaneously (like national defense). We can extend our basic competitive model to deal with these cases. To extend the model, it will be helpful to begin by considering each of these assumptions in turn.

First, most markets are not as competitive as those envisioned by the basic model. In the competitive model discussed in Part Two, markets have so many buyers and sellers that no individual household or firm believes its actions will affect the market equilibrium price. The basic competitive model focuses on products like wheat or pig iron, which may be produced by different firms but are essentially identical and are perfect substitutes for one another. If a firm were to raise its price slightly above that of other firms, it loses all its customers. In that model, there is no room for brand names, yet it is hard to think of a consumer product without attaching a brand name to it. If Kodak raises the price of its film, it may lose some customers to other brands, but it won't lose all its customers. A Kodak enthusiast would probably pay slightly more for Kodak film than for Fuji film. Likewise in the consumer market for running shoes, if Nike charges slightly more than Adidas, it will not lose all its customers. By taking the market price as given, a firm in the competitive model does not need to consider how other firms would react when it considers changing the quantity it produces. However, when Kodak or Nike consider their production and pricing decisions, they must worry about how their rivals will react. In the real world, many firms spend enormous energies trying to anticipate the actions and reactions of rivals.

Second, buyers and sellers seldom have all the information that the basic competitive model assumes. In the basic competitive model, buyers know what they are buying, whether it is stocks or bonds, a house, a used car, or a refrigerator. Firms know the productivity of each worker they hire, and when workers go to work for a firm, they know exactly what is expected of them in return for the promised pay. Yet in most markets, participants do not have complete information. A buyer of a used car may not know the true condition of the car, a high school student choosing among colleges doesn't have complete information about the quality of the teachers or the actual availability of classes, and a firm hiring a new worker doesn't know precisely how productive he or she will be.

Third, in the basic competitive model, firms and consumers bear all the consequences of their actions. Whenever an individual or firm can take an action that directly affects others but for which it neither pays nor is paid compensation, economists say that an **externality** is present. (The effect of the action is "external" to the individual or firm.) Externalities are pervasive. A hiker who litters, a driver whose car emits pollution, a child who leaves a mess behind after he finishes playing, a person who smokes a cigarette in a crowded room, a student who talks during a lecture—all create externalities. In each case, the actor is not the only one who suffers the consequences of his action; others suffer them too. Externalities can be thought of as instances when the price system works imperfectly. The hiker is not "charged" for the litter she creates. The car owner does not pay for the pollution his car makes.

While these examples are of negative externalities, externalities also can be positive. A well-kept garden that provides a benefit to the neighbors is a positive externality; so is a hiker who picks up litter along a trail.

Fourth, in the basic competitive model, when one person consumes a good, it is not available for others to consume. If John buys a gallon of gas for his car, Sarah cannot also use that gallon of gas. But some goods, called **public goods,** are available for others to consume. They represent extreme cases of externalities. (Normally, we think of these as positive externalities—for example, all *benefit* from the provision of national defense. However, some individuals may dislike the public good, and they too cannot exclude themselves from the consequences. For them, the public good acts like a negative externality.) The consumption (or enjoyment) of a public good by one individual does not subtract from that of other individuals (consumption is said to be *nonrivalrous*). Public goods also have the property of *nonexcludability*—that is, it costs a great deal to exclude any individual from enjoying the benefits of a public good. The standard example of a public good is national defense. Once the United States is protected from attack, it costs nothing extra to protect each new baby from foreign invasion. Furthermore, it would be virtually impossible to exclude a newborn from the benefits of this protection.

Imperfect competition, imperfect information, externalities, and public goods all represent cases where the market will fail in its role of producing economic efficiency. Economists refer to these problems as **market failures** and have studied them closely. A market failure does not necessarily mean that a market fails to exist, only that it fails to produce efficient outcomes. When there is a market failure, government *may* be able to correct the market failure and improve economic efficiency. If we want to think about government policies to correct market failures, however, we first need to understand clearly how it is that market outcomes may be inefficient.

Many aspects of market economies cannot be well understood by the basic competitive model. For instance, in an economy with perfect information, there is no need—or role—for advertising. Innovation is at the heart of the modern economy and yet plays no role in the competitive model; indeed, since information is assumed to be perfect, there is no role for research.

Despite the presence of imperfect competition, imperfect information, externalities, and public goods, the basic competitive model continues to provide important and powerful insights. For that reason, most economists use the basic model as the starting point for building a richer, more complete model of the modern economy. This richer model is the focus of Part Three. In the next several chapters, we will examine how the introduction of imperfect competition, imperfect information, externalities, and public goods to the basic model increases the insights economics has to offer in understanding our economy.

Imperfect Competition and Market Structure

When economists look at markets, they look first at the **market structure,** that is, how the market is organized. The market structure that formed the basis of the competitive model of Part Two is called **perfect competition.** For example, there are so many wheat farmers (producers) that no individual farmer can realistically hope to move the price of wheat from that produced by the law of supply and demand.

Frequently, however, competition is not "perfect." Rather, it is limited. Economists group markets in which competition is limited into three broad structures. In the most extreme case, there is no competition. A single firm supplies the entire market. This is called **monopoly.** Your local electrical company may have a monopoly in supplying electricity in your area. In a recent court case, Microsoft was found to have a near monopoly in the market for personal computer operating systems. Since one would expect the profits of a monopolist to attract entry into the market, for the firm to maintain its monopoly position there must be some barrier to entry. In Chapter 12, we will learn what some of these barriers are.

In the second structure, several firms supply the market, so there is *some* competition. This is called **oligopoly.** The automobile industry is an example, with three main producers in the United States and a small number of foreign producers. The defining characteristic of oligopoly is that the small number of firms forces each to be concerned with how its rivals will react to any action it takes. If General Motors offers low-interest-rate financing, for instance, other companies may feel compelled to match the offer. Before making any such offer, General Motors will have to take this into account. By contrast, a monopolist has no rivals and considers only whether special offers help or hurt itself. And a firm facing perfect competition never needs to resort to any special offer—it can always sell as much as it wants at the market price.

In the third market structure, there are more firms than in an oligopoly but not enough for perfect competition. This is called **monopolistic competition.** An example is the market for laptop computers. IBM, Compaq, Toshiba, Sony, Gateway, Dell, and others produce their own brand of laptops. Each is slightly different from the others. But the laptops each makes are similar enough to those supplied by the other companies that there is considerable competition, so much so that profits may be driven down to zero. Even so, the laptops supplied by the different companies are different enough to make competition limited, so that the companies are not price takers. The degree of competition under monopolistic competition is greater than that of oligopoly. this is because monopolistic competition involves a sufficiently large number of firms that each firm can ignore the reactions of any rival. If one company lowers its price, it may gain a large number of customers. But the number of customers it takes away from any single rival is so small that none of the rivals is motivated to retaliate.

With both oligopolies and monopolistic competition, there is some competition, but it is more limited than under perfect competition. These in-between market structures are referred to as **imperfect competition.**

WRAP-UP

Alternative Market Structures

Perfect competition: Many, many firms, each believing that nothing it does will have any effect on the market price.

Monopoly: One firm.

Imperfect competition. Several firms, each aware that its sales depend on the price it charges and possibly other actions it takes, such as advertising. There are two special cases:

> *Oligopoly:* Sufficiently few firms that each must be concerned with how its rivals will respond to any action it undertakes.

> *Monopolistic competition:* Sufficiently many firms that each believes that its rivals will not change the price they charge should it lower its own price, and that profits may be driven down to zero.

Price and Quantity with Imperfect Competition

In the basic model of perfect competition, each firm took the market price as given. If one firm tried to raise its price, even slightly, it would lose all of its customers. When competition is imperfect, a firm will lose some but not all of its customers if it charges a slightly higher price. With imperfect competition, firms do not simply "take" the price as dictated to them by the market. They "make" the price. They are the *price makers*.

Whether a firm is a price taker or a price maker, it tries to maximize profits. In determining output, the firm will compare the extra, or **marginal revenue** that it will receive from producing an extra unit of output with the extra, or marginal cost of producing that extra unit. If marginal revenue exceeds marginal cost, it pays to expand output. Conversely, if marginal revenue is less than marginal cost, it pays to reduce output. Whether the firm operates in a market characterized by perfect or imperfect competition, it will produce at the output level at which marginal revenue equals marginal costs.

The essential difference between a firm facing perfect competition and one facing imperfect competition is in the relationship between marginal revenue and price. For a competitive firm, marginal revenue is just equal to the price. For instance, the marginal revenue received by a wheat farmer for one more bushel of wheat is just the price of a bushel of wheat. But with imperfect competition, a firm knows that the only way it can sell more is to lower its price. That is, it recognizes it faces a downward-sloping demand curve. By changing its price it will influence its sales. Marginal revenue is not equal to the present market price.

In the case of monopoly, for example, the firm controls the entire market, so a doubling of its output is a doubling of industry output, which will have a significant effect on price. If Alcoa, in the days when it had a monopoly on aluminum, had increased its production by 1 percent, the total supply of aluminum would have increased by 1 percent. Market prices would have fallen in response to a change in supply of even this magnitude.

How much the price must change as sales change will depend on whether the firm is a monopolist, a monopolistic competitive firm, or an oligopolist. If the firm is a monopolist, it controls the entire market, by definition, so the demand curve it faces is the market demand curve. By contrast, a firm such as PepsiCo will need to know how rivals like Coca-Cola will respond to any price change in order to determine how its sales will be affected if it changes its price. In either case, however, *marginal revenue will be less than price*. To sell more, the firm must lower its price, reducing the revenue it receives on all units that it produces.

To maximize profits, firms will set marginal cost equal to marginal revenue. When competition is imperfect, however, marginal revenue is less than price. As a consequence, the firm's profit-maximizing output level will be at a point where marginal cost is also less than price. The market price will be too high—it exceeds the cost of producing the last unit sold. Under conditions of perfect competition, producers would have an incentive to increase production when price exceeds marginal cost. Relative to the efficient outcome of perfect competition, imperfect competition leads to a market outcome that results in too little being produced at too high a price.

Government Policies

Because imperfect competition leads to an inefficient outcome, with too little produced at too high a price, government has taken an active role in promoting competition and in limiting the abuses of market power.

Antitrust laws are designed to break up monopolies, to prevent monopolies from forming, and to restrain firms from engaging in practices that restrict competition. For instance, before two large firms in an industry can merge, or before one can acquire another, they must seek government approval. The government will seek to determine whether the merger of the two firms will *significantly* reduce competition. The most recent highly publicized antitrust case involved the U.S. government and Microsoft, with the government arguing that Microsoft had a near monopoly in the market for operating systems and that it had abused that market power—not only was price above the competitive level, but also it had used its market power to deter and destroy rivals.

In some cases, the government may decide not to break up a firm even if it is a monopoly. It may believe, for instance, that it is more efficient for a single firm to provide the service. Such cases are called a **natural monopoly.** Typically the government establishes a regulatory body to oversee such a monopoly. Industries that have been characterized in the past as *regulated monopolies* include local cable TV, electrical utility, and telephone industries. The regulated monopoly firm normally must obtain the approval of the regulatory agency before it can raise the price it charges.

In Chapters 12 and 13 we will discuss some of the ways government attempts to limit the power of monopolies and promote competition. The policies government uses depend on the source of imperfect competition and the structure of the market.

Internet Connection

The Federal Trade Commission

The Federal Trade Commission (FTC) enforces consumer protection and antitrust laws and plays an important role in eliminating unfair or deceptive practices while ensuring that American markets function competitively. The FTC provides articles at http://www.ftc.gov/bcp/menu-internet.htm on what to watch out for in e-commerce and when making purchases or seeking information over the Internet.

International Perspective

Trade and Competition

The increasing globalization of the world economy means that firms face competition from both foreign and domestic rivals. Even a firm that is the sole domestic producer of a product may be unable to take advantage of its monopoly position because of competition from foreign producers. Government actions to open a country to trade, therefore, can help promote competition. New Zealand provides a case in point.

New Zealand had a long history of restricting imports to protect domestic firms. Since the New Zealand economy was small, many industries had only one firm. To prevent the problems created by these monopolies, the government developed numerous regulations. This created problems for consumers. For example, suppose you wanted to buy auto paint to touch up a scratch on your car. Because

New Zealand had a domestic paint producer, imports of paint were restricted. But because of the small size of the New Zealand market, the demand for any given type of paint was small. As a consequence, the New Zealand paint industry offered only a limited number of colors. If your car had an unusual color, you were out of luck.

In 1984, a Labor government was elected in New Zealand, and it implemented a new strategy for improving competition. The government realized that the regulatory structure that had limited the inefficiencies of monopoly could be eliminated, and competition could be increased simply by removing the many trade barriers that New Zealand had in place. It doesn't matter that only a single paint firm is located in New Zealand—that firm's market power will be limited if it must compete with foreign paint producers.

Imperfect Information

The model of perfect competition that was developed in Part Two assumed that market participants, whether consumers, firms, or the government, had *perfect information*. They had full information about the goods being bought and sold. Seldom do we actually approach this standard, and economists have gained new insights into how markets function by incorporating **imperfect information** into their models. Interestingly, economists' understanding of the importance of imperfect information occurred at almost the same time that new technologies improved the ability of firms and households to gather, process, and transmit information.

The Information Problem

The basic competitive model assumes that households and firms are well informed. This means that they know their opportunity set, or what is available and at what price. More strikingly, they know every characteristic of every good, including how long it will last. For some purchases, we do

have very good information, so the assumption of the basic model is a reasonable one. When I buy my favorite breakfast cereal at the grocery store, I know all I need to know.[1] Typically though, we must make decisions about what to buy with much less than perfect information.

The model also assumes that consumers know their preferences; that is, they know what they like. They know not only how many oranges they can trade for an apple but also how many oranges they want to trade. In the case of apples and oranges this may make sense. But how do students know how much they are going to enjoy, or even benefit from, a college education? How does an individual know whether she would like to be a doctor, a lawyer, or a writer? She gets some idea about what different professions are like by observing those who practice them, but her information is at best incomplete.

According to the basic model, firms too are perfectly well informed. They know the best available technology.

---

[1] Of course, to gain information about the cereal, I had to try it initially. So even in this example, the information was not automatically available. It is often only possible to gain information about a good by actually using it.

e-Insight

Information, Competition, and the Internet

The Internet is having a profound effect on consumer choices and on the nature of competition. One way it has done so is by providing consumers with easily accessible information at a low cost. For example, rather than pay a series of time-consuming visits to various car dealers when you want to shop for a car, you can now do your shopping from home through the Internet. Consumers can comparison shop using Web sites that provide car reviews and pricing information. They can even buy a car on-line and have it delivered to their doorstep. By increasing the information consumers have, many economists argue that the new information technologies will make the basic competitive model, with its assumption that consumers are fully informed, a *closer* approximation to actual markets.

The Internet also increases competition. Local retail stores must now compete against on-line sellers. Consumers can easily check prices at various on-line sellers, and there are even digital agents called "bots" that search

Internet sites for the best available deals. Because consumers can easily comparison shop on the Web, Internet sellers are forced to offer low prices.

In business-to-business (B2B) commerce, the sheer number of firms linked through the Internet allows larger pools of buyers and sellers to be brought together, creating new marketplaces and lower costs for many businesses. For instance, the major U.S. auto manufacturers are moving their purchasing operations on-line, forming a marketplace for parts and other items that is estimated to handle almost $250 billion of purchases each year. By increasing competition among parts suppliers, the auto manufacturers expect to gain significant cost savings. But some antitrust experts worry that to the extent that the U.S. auto manufacturers *cooperate* in purchasing, they may actually reduce competition among the buyers. Single buyers (called *monopsonists*) or limited competition among buyers are just as bad for economic efficiency as monopoly sellers or limited competition among sellers.

They know the productivity of each applicant for a job. They know precisely how hard every worker is working and how good a job each is doing. They know the prices at which inputs can be purchased from every possible supplier (and all the input's characteristics). And they know the prices at which they can sell the goods, not only today but in every possible circumstance in the future.

How Big a Problem?

That individuals and firms are not perfectly well informed is, by itself, not necessarily a telling criticism of the competitive model, just as the criticism that markets are not perfectly competitive does not cause us to discard the model. The relevant issues are as follows: Can the competitive model mislead us in these situations? Are there important economic phenomena that can be explained only by taking into account imperfect information? Are there important predictions of the model that are incorrect as a

result of the assumption concerning well-informed consumers and firms?

One benefit of this degree is that it conveys information about its recipient.

Increasingly, over the past two decades, economists have come to believe that the answer to these questions is yes. For example, college graduates may receive a higher income than high school graduates, not only because they have learned things in college that make them more productive but also because their college degree conveys valuable information to employers. Employers cannot easily learn in an interview which applicants for a job will be productive workers. They therefore use a college degree to help them identify those who are more productive. College graduates *are*, on average, more productive workers. But it is wrong to conclude from this that college has necessarily *increased* students' productivity. It may simply have enabled firms to sort more easily students who are more productive from the less productive.

How Prices Convey Information

The price system provides brilliant solutions for some information problems. We have seen how prices play an important role in coordinating production and communicating information about economic scarcity. Firms do not have to know what John or Julia likes, what their trade-offs are. The price tells the producer the marginal benefit of producing an extra unit of the good, and that is all the firm needs to know. Similarly, a firm does not need to know how much iron ore is left in Minnesota, the cost of refining iron ore, or a thousand other details. All it needs to know is the price of iron ore. This tells the company how scarce the resource is, and how much effort it should expend in conserving it. Prices and markets provide the basis of the economy's incentive system. But there are some information problems that markets do not handle, or do not handle well. And imperfect information sometimes inhibits the ability of markets to perform the tasks they perform so well when information is complete.

Markets for Information

Information has value; people are willing to pay for it. In this sense, we can consider information as a good similar to any other good. There is a market for information, with a price—just as there is a market for labor and a market for capital. Indeed, our economy is sometime referred to as an *information economy*. And every year, investors spend millions of dollars on newsletters that give them information about stocks, bonds, and other investment opportunities.

Magazines sell specialized information about hundreds of goods. The growth of the Internet has had a major impact in reducing the cost of all types of information.

However, even with all the new information technologies, the markets for information are far from perfect, and for good reasons. The most conspicuous one is that information is *not* just like any other good. When you buy a chair, the furniture dealer is happy to let you look at it, sit on it, and decide whether you like it. When you buy information, you cannot do the same. The seller can either say, "Trust me. I'll tell you what you need to know," or show you the information and say, "Here's what I know. If this is what you wanted to know, please pay me." You would rightfully be skeptical in the first scenario and might be unwilling to pay in the second. After you were given the information, what incentive would you have to pay?

In some cases, there is a basic credibility problem. You might think, if a stock tipster *really* knows that a stock's price is going to go up, why should he tell me, even if I pay him for the information? Why doesn't he go out and make his fortune with the information? Or is it that he really is not sure, and would just as soon have me risk my money rather than risk his?

Most important, even after the firm or consumer buys all the information he thinks is worth paying for, his information is still far from perfect. Some information is simply too costly to obtain relative to the benefit of having it. So imperfect information is a fact of life, and in Chapter 14 we will examine the ways it can affect economic behavior and the structure of markets.

Government Policies

The market inefficiencies resulting from imperfect information can take a number of forms, and we will discuss these in more detail in Chapter 14. Government concern for the consequences of ill-informed consumers has motivated a number of pieces of **consumer protection legislation.** For example, the Wheeler-Lea Act of 1938 made "deceptive" trade practices illegal and gave the Federal Trade Commission power to stop false and deceptive advertising. Truth-in-lending legislation requires lenders to disclose the true interest rate being charged. Truth-in-packaging legislation makes it less likely that consumers will be misled by what is printed on the package. And the Securities and Exchange Commission, which regulates the sale of stocks and bonds, requires firms selling these securities to disclose a considerable amount of information.

Yet much of this legislation is of only limited effectiveness. One problem occurs when consumers try to absorb and process the information. A cereal manufacturer may disclose not only what is required but also a host of other information, which may or may not be important. How are consumers to know what to pay attention to? They cannot absorb everything. Occasionally, as in the case of warnings about the dangers of smoking, government regulators, aware of these problems of information absorption, have required the disclosures to be of a specific form and lettering size to make them stand out. But this kind of intervention on a more massive scale would be, at the very least, extremely costly.

Another problem with outlawing deceptive advertising is the difficulty of drawing a clear line between persuasion and deception. Advertisers are good at walking along the edge of any line—a suggestive hint may do where an explicit claim might be called deceptive. Congress or the courts cannot be expected to draw a line between informative and noninformative advertising for all the economy's many products.

Most of the problems arising from imperfect information are not easily remedied. Firms will have imperfect information concerning potential employees, no matter what the government does. However, the government often must deal with the consequences. Imperfect information can lead to imperfect competition. In some markets, such as the health insurance market, the consequences are severe, and there has been considerable dissatisfaction with the way these markets work. Government has introduced a variety of interventions, but these clearly have not remedied the problems, and some question whether they have even improved matters.

Externalities

Even when there is perfect competition and information, the market may supply too much of some goods and too little of others. One of the reasons for this is externalities. Externalities arise whenever an individual or firm can take an action that directly affects others without paying for a harmful outcome or being paid for a beneficial one. When externalities are present, firms and individuals do not bear all the consequences of their action.

A common example of a negative externality is a factory that emits air pollution. The factory benefits from emitting the pollution, since the company can make its product more cheaply than if it put in pollution-control devices. When firms do not have to pay for the pollution they emit, society as a whole bears the negative costs of the pollution. If firms had to pay for their pollution, they would find ways to produce less of it, by adopting cleaner technologies, for instance. Government environmental regulations, which we will discuss in Chapter 21, are usually designed to ensure that firms bear the cost of the pollution they create.

When there are externalities, the market's allocation of goods will be inefficient. This happens because the producer fails to take into account "social costs" in deciding how much to produce. To put it another way, the price of a good such as steel, determined in competitive markets by the law of supply and demand, only reflects *private costs*, the costs actually faced by firms. If firms do not have to pay *all* the costs (including the costs of pollution), equilibrium prices will be lower and output higher than they would be if firms took social costs into account. When the production of a good such as steel entails a negative externality—like smoke and its effects on the air—the market level of production is too high.

The reason market outcomes are inefficient in the presence of externalities can be understood by considering an important characteristic of market outputs in the basic competitive model. There, the market price is equal to the value consumers place on the last unit of output and it is equal to the cost to firms of producing the last unit. This ensures that at the margin, the value of the last good produced is just sufficient to cover the costs of producing it. When an externality is present, this will not be true. If the price consumers pay does not fully reflect the costs of producing the good (a negative externality), consumers will demand too much of the good and too much will be produced. If there are social benefits in addition to the private benefits to consumers (a positive externality), too little will be produced.

Government Policies toward Externalities

Because externalities lead to market inefficiencies, they can justify a role for government intervention in markets. The government can prevent the overproduction of goods with negative externalities either by regulation (for instance, environmental regulations that restrict the levels of pollution) or by providing incentives (through imposing fees or fines for pollution).

When the production of a good involves positive externalities, the market level of production is too low, and the

Thinking Like an Economist

Incentives and the Environment

When economists think about environmental issues, they focus on the incentives individuals and firms face. If too much air pollution is produced, economists try to understand why firms and individuals have an incentive to engage in activities that generate excessive pollution. If too many fish are taken, depleting fishing stocks, economists ask, why don't fishermen have an incentive to preserve the fish stocks? In both of these examples, individuals and firms harm the environment because they do not have to bear the full cost of their actions. Take the case of fishermen. Each fisherman has to take into account the cost of operating his boat and the wages he needs to pay his crew. But he does not have to pay for the impact his fishing has on the total stock of fish. If he takes more fish, this reduces the stock available to other fishermen, but no individual fisherman has to account for this cost imposed on others. No one fisherman has an incentive to limit his own take to preserve the remaining fish stock.

In these, and many other cases of externalities, the source of the problem can be traced to the lack of property rights over valuable resources such as clean air or the stock of commercially valuable fish. When a valuable resource is not privately owned, individuals and firms do not need to pay a price to use the resource. If the stock of fish were privately owned, the owner would charge each fisherman a fee to take fish. When the cost to society of the resource is not reflected in what the user has to pay, there is no incentive to economize on its use. In some cases, it is easy to assign property rights. In the case of a small lake, the government

can auction off the exclusive right to fish to a single individual, who might extract the fish himself or might charge others for fishing. In either scenario, however, he would have an incentive to ensure that the resource is used efficiently. But in most cases, there is no reasonable or easy property rights solution: Who should be given the right to the air? Indeed, the inability of political leaders to address this question is at the center of the failure of attempts to reduce the greenhouse gas emissions that are leading to global warming. As an alternative to property rights solutions, governments can provide appropriate incentives by designing taxes to make users pay the full social costs of their activities, ensuring that individuals and firms face incentives to economize on all of society's scarce resources.

government can try to enlarge the supply. The rejuvenation of an apartment building in a decaying part of a city is an example of a positive externality; it will probably enhance the value of the buildings surrounding it. A government subsidy can lower the cost of rejuvenating buildings. In equilibrium there will be an increase in the number of buildings that are rejuvenated.

Public Goods

The final category of market failure arises in the presence of public goods. A *pure public good* is one where the marginal costs of providing it to an additional person are strictly zero and where it is impossible to exclude people from receiving the good. Many public goods that government provides are not *pure* public goods in this sense. The cost of an additional person using an uncrowded interstate highway is very, very small, but it is not zero, and it is possible, though relatively expensive, to exclude people from (or charge people for) using the highway.

Figure 11.1 compares examples of publicly provided goods against the strict definition of a pure public good. It shows ease of exclusion along the horizontal axis and the (marginal) cost of an additional individual using the good along the vertical axis. The lower left corner represents a pure public good. Of the major public expenditures, only national defense is close to a pure public good. Completely uncongested highways, to the extent they exist, are another example. The upper right corner represents a pure private good (health services or education), where the cost of exclusion is low and the marginal cost of an additional individual using the good is high.

Many goods are not purely public goods but have one or the other property to some degree. Fire protection is like a private good in that exclusion is relatively easy—individuals who refuse to contribute to the fire department could simply not be helped in the event of a fire. But fire protection is like a public good in that the marginal cost of covering an additional person is low. Most of the time, firefighters are not engaged in fighting fires but are waiting for calls. Protecting an additional individual has little extra cost. Only in the rare event when two fires break out simultaneously will there be a significant cost to extending fire protection to an additional person.

Sometimes the marginal cost of using a good to which access is easy (a good that possesses the property of nonexcludability) will be high. When an uncongested highway turns congested, the costs of using it rise dramatically, not in terms of wear and tear but in terms of the time lost by drivers using the road. It is costly to exclude by charging for road use—as a practical matter, this can only be done on toll roads, and ironically, the tollbooths often contribute to the congestion.[2]

Many of the goods that are publicly provided, such as education and health services, have high costs associated with providing the service to additional individuals. For most of these goods, exclusion is also relatively easy. In fact, many of these goods and services are provided privately in some countries, or provided both publicly and privately. Though they are provided publicly in this country, they are not *pure* public goods, in the technical sense in which the term is defined.

Private markets undersupply public goods. If a shipowner uses a port near which a lighthouse should be located, he could weigh the costs and benefits of constructing the lighthouse. But if there were one large shipowner and many smaller owners, it would not pay any one of the small owners to build the lighthouse; and the large shipowner, in deciding whether to construct the lighthouse, would only take into account the benefits she would receive, not the benefits to the small shipowners. If the costs of construction exceeded the benefits she alone would receive, she would not build the lighthouse. But if the benefits accruing to *all* the shipowners, large and small, were taken into account, those benefits might exceed the costs. It would then be desirable to build the lighthouse.

One can imagine a voluntary association of shipowners getting together to construct a lighthouse in this situation. But what happens if some small shipowner refuses to contribute, thinking that even if she does not contribute, the lighthouse will still be built anyway? This is the **free-rider** aspect of public goods; because it is difficult to preclude

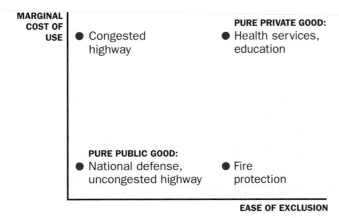

FIGURE 11.1   *Publicly Provided Goods*

Pure public goods are characterized by nonrivalrous consumption (the marginal cost of an additional individual enjoying the good is zero) and nonexcludability (the cost of excluding an individual from enjoying the good is prohibitively high). Goods provided by the public sector differ in the extent to which they have these two properties.

---

[2]New technologies will allow drivers to be charged for the toll without stopping at tollbooths. Scanners can identify cars as they pass, automatically billing the driver. Thus, new technologies can convert what was a public good into a private good.

anyone from using them, those who benefit from the goods have an incentive to avoid paying for them. Every shipowner has an incentive to "free ride" on the efforts of others. When too many decide to do this, the lighthouse will not be built.

Governments bring an important advantage to bear on the problem of public goods. They have the power to coerce citizens to pay for them. There might be *some* level of purchase of public goods—lighthouses, highways, parks, even police or fire services—in the absence of government intervention. But societies would be better off if the level of production were increased, and citizens were forced to pay for the increased level of public services through taxes.

Looking Ahead

We have now learned about four situations in which markets may fail to develop an efficient allocation of society's scarce resources. In each of these cases—imperfect competition, imperfect information, externalities, and public goods—a role for government exists. Government can employ a variety of policies to promote competition, address the problems created by externalities and imperfect information, and supply public goods.

In the next several chapters, we will study market failures in more detail, beginning, in Chapter 12, with the analysis of imperfect competition including the extreme case, that of a monopoly. Chapter 13 shows how public policy addresses the problems posed by imperfections of competition. Imperfect information is the focus of Chapter 14, while Chapter 15 examines how imperfect competition and imperfect information affect labor markets. Finally, Chapter 16 studies the role of the public sector in the economy.

Review and Practice

Summary

1. By and large, private markets allocate resources efficiently. However, in a number of areas they do not, as in the cases of imperfect competition, imperfect information, externalities, and public goods.

2. Economists identify four broad categories of market structure: perfect competition, monopoly, oligopoly, and monopolistic competition.

3. When competition is imperfect, the market will produce too little of a good and the market price will be too high.

4. The basic competitive model assumes that participants in the market have perfect information about the goods being bought and sold and their prices. However, information is often imperfect.

5. Individuals and firms produce too much of a good with a negative externality, such as air or water pollution, since they do not bear all the costs. They produce too little of a good with positive externalities since they cannot receive all the benefits.

6. Public goods are goods that cost little or nothing for an additional individual to enjoy, but to exclude an individual from enjoying them costs a great deal. National defense and lighthouses are two examples. Free markets underproduce public goods.

Key Terms

externality
public goods
market failures
market structure
perfect competition
monopoly
oligopoly
monopolistic competition
imperfect competition
marginal revenue
antitrust
natural monopoly
imperfect information
consumer protection legislation
free-rider

Review Questions

1. What is the difference between perfect competition and imperfect competition?

2. What does it mean when an economist says that monopoly output is "too little" or a monopoly price is "too high"? By what standard? Compared with what?

3. What role does information play in the basic competitive model? How does the market for information differ from the market for a good such as wheat?

4. What is an example of a positive externality? Of a negative externality? Why are goods with negative externalities often overproduced? Why are goods with positive externalities often underproduced? Give an example for each.

5. What sorts of policies can government use to address the problem of externalities?

6. What two characteristics define a public good? Give an example. Why will private markets not supply the efficient level of public goods?

Problems

1. Colleges and universities compete for students, and students shop for colleges. Is the market for college placements characterized by perfect competition? Does Harvard face a horizontal demand curve or a downward-sloping demand curve? Is the market for college placements characterized by perfect information? Describe how students' information about colleges might be imperfect. Describe how colleges' information about prospective students might be imperfect.

2. Each of the situations below involves an externality. Tell whether it is a positive or a negative externality, or both, and explain why a free market will overproduce or underproduce the good in question:

(a) a business performing research and development projects;

(b) a business that discharges waste into a nearby river;

(c) a concert given in the middle of a large city park;

(d) an individual who smokes cigarettes in a meeting.

3. When some activity causes a negative externality like pollution, would it be a good idea to ban the activity altogether? Why or why not? (Hint: Consider marginal costs and benefits.)

4. Do highways provide an example of a public good? Can you describe a situation in which the marginal costs of an additional driver on the highway might be high? How might society deal with this problem?

5. Many highways have designated car pool or high-occupancy lanes. Generally, only cars containing at least two people can use these lanes. Single drivers are fined heavily if they are caught using these lanes. With new technologies, it is possible to charge drivers using car pool lanes by recording identifying markings on the car and billing the owners. Would allowing single drivers to pay to use car pool lanes increase economic efficiency? Explain.

6. Group projects are often assigned in classes, with everyone in the group receiving the same grade for the project. Explain why a free-rider problem might arise in this situation.

Chapter 12

Monopoly, Monopolistic Competition, and Oligopoly

Key Questions

1. If there is only one firm in the market—a monopoly—how does it set its price and output? In what sense is the monopoly price too high?

2. What are the drawbacks of monopolies? Why do they lead to economic inefficiencies?

3. What factors limit competition? How do firms in an industry collude or act to restrict competition? How do monopolies and imperfectly competitive firms prevent other firms from entering their markets?

4. What are the characteristics of equilibrium in a market with imperfect competition, where barriers to entry are small enough that profits are driven to zero, yet there are few enough firms that each faces a downward-sloping demand curve?

5. In what ways do oligopolies differ from the other market structures—monopoly, perfect competition, and monopolistic competition?

6. What practices do firms in an oligopoly engage in that facilitate collusion and, in the absence of collusion, that restrict the force of competition?

*A*s we discussed in Chapter 11, many markets in our economy are not well described by the perfectly competitive model. For years, AT&T was the only long-distance telephone carrier. Kodak controlled the market for film, and Alcoa the market for aluminum. Some firms so dominated a product that their brand name became synonymous with the product, as with Kleenex and Jell-O. These firms did not simply take the market price as given: They recognized that their actions could affect the market price. And the power to affect prices will influence a firm's decision about how much to produce.

In some industries, such as the soft drink (Coca-Cola, Pepsi, and Canada Dry) or running shoe (Nike, Adidas, Reebok) industry, a handful of firms dominate the market, producing similar but not identical products. Other industries may include a large number of firms, with each producing a similar but slightly different product. When one firm raises its price a little—say, by 2 or 3 percent—it loses some customers, but it would not lose all customers as it would with perfect competition. If such a firm lowers its price by 2 or 3 percent, it gains additional customers but not the entire market.

Picking up where the discussion in Chapter 11 left off, this chapter explores markets where there is either limited competition or no competition at all. It explains why output in these markets is typically lower than it would be under more competitive conditions, and it identifies the various factors that limit competition.

241

Monopoly Output

Economists' concerns about monopolies and other forms of restricted competition stem mainly from the observation that the output, or supply, of firms within these market structures is less than that of firms faced with perfect competition, and prices are higher. To understand these concerns, we consider a monopolist that charges the same price to all its customers, and show how it decides on its level of output.

A monopolist, just like a competitive firm, will try to maximize profits. Both compare the marginal revenue of producing more with the marginal cost of doing so. The basic principle for output determination for both is the same. Each produces at the output level at which marginal revenue equals marginal cost. The key difference is in the marginal revenue each faces. When a competitive firm decides on its output level, it takes the market price as given. Such a firm faces a horizontal demand curve—it can sell as much as it wants at the market price. In contrast, the monopolist is the sole supplier to the market, so the demand curve facing a monopolist is the *market demand curve*. As we have already learned, market demand curves are downward sloping. The monopolist can only increase its sales by lowering its price.

Because the monopolist faces a downward-sloping demand curve, its marginal revenue is not equal to the market price. To understand why, we can break the marginal revenue a monopolist receives from producing one more unit into two separate components. First, the firm receives revenue from selling the additional output. This additional revenue is just the market price. But to sell more, the monopolist must reduce its price. Unless it does so, it cannot sell the extra output. Marginal revenue is the price it receives from the sale of the one additional unit *minus* the loss in revenue from the price reduction on all other units. Thus, for a monopolist, the marginal revenue for producing one extra unit is always less than the price received for that extra unit.

This can be represented by a simple equation:

$$\text{marginal revenue} = \text{net increase in revenue from selling one more unit}$$
$$= \text{price} + \Delta p \times Q,$$

where Δp represents the change in price and Q represents the initial quantity sold. For a competitive firm,

$\Delta p = 0$ since it can sell more without affecting the market price. So for a competitive firm, marginal revenue equals price. For a monopolist, Δp is negative—it must lower the price to sell more—so marginal revenue is less than the price.

Figure 12.1 shows the relationship between the demand curve and the marginal revenue of the monopolist. If the monopolist wants to sell the quantity Q_1, the market price must be p_1. Marginal revenue is less than price, so the marginal revenue curve lies below the demand curve. At the quantity Q_1, marginal revenue is MR_1, less than the price p_1.

Figure 12.2A shows the output decision of a competitive firm. Marginal revenue is just equal to the market price p^*. The competitive firm produces at Q^*, where marginal cost is equal to the market price. Panel B shows the output decision of a monopolist. Marginal revenue is always less than price. The monopolist produces an output of Q_m, since at that output level, marginal cost is equal to marginal revenue. Both the monopolist and the competitive firm maximize profits by producing where marginal cost equals marginal revenue. The differ-

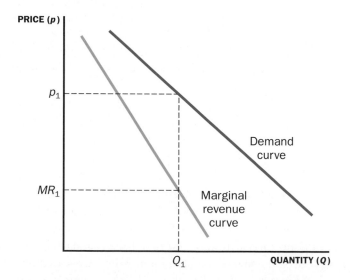

FIGURE 12.1   *Demand Curve and Marginal Revenue Curve for a Monopolist*

Because the monopolist faces a downward-sloping demand curve, marginal revenue is less than price. To sell an extra unit of output, the monopolist must accept a lower price on every unit sold. At the quantity Q_1, the market price is p_1 and the marginal revenue is MR_1.

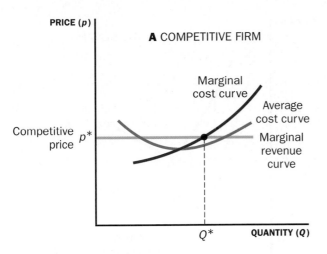

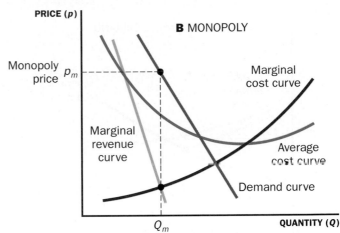

FIGURE 12.2 *Marginal Revenue Equals Marginal Cost*

A perfectly competitive firm gains or loses exactly the market price (p^*) when it changes the quantity produced by one unit. To maximize profits, the firm produces the quantity where marginal cost equals marginal revenue, which in the competitive case also equals price. Panel B shows the downward-sloping marginal revenue curve for a monopolist. A monopolist also chooses the level of quantity where marginal cost equals marginal revenue. In the monopolistic case, however, marginal revenue is lower than price.

ence is that for the monopolist, marginal revenue is less than price.

Note that with a monopolist, since marginal revenue is less than price and marginal revenue is equal to marginal cost, marginal cost is less than price. The price is what individuals are willing to pay for an extra unit of the product; it measures the marginal benefit to the consumer of an extra unit. Thus, the marginal benefit of an extra unit exceeds the marginal cost of producing that extra unit. This is the fundamental reason why monopolies reduce economic efficiency.

The extent to which output is curtailed depends on the magnitude of the difference between marginal revenue and price. This in turn depends on the shape of the demand curve. When demand curves are very elastic (relatively flat), prices do not fall much when output increases. As shown in Figure 12.3A, marginal revenue is not much less than price. The firm produces at Q_m, where marginal revenue equals marginal cost. Q_m is slightly less than the competitive output, Q_c, where price equals marginal cost. When demand curves are less elastic, as in panel B, prices may fall a considerable amount when output increases, and then the extra revenue the firm receives from producing an extra unit of output will be much less than the price received from selling that unit.

The larger the elasticity of demand, the smaller the discrepancy between marginal revenue and price. This can be seen simply by using the definitions of the elasticity of demand and marginal revenue:

$$\text{elasticity of demand} = -\frac{\text{change in market quantity}}{\text{market quantity}} \Big/ \frac{\text{change in price}}{\text{price}}$$

$$= -\frac{\Delta Q}{Q} \Big/ \frac{\Delta p}{p}.$$

If we consider a change in quantity by 1 (as we do when we calculate marginal revenue), so that $\Delta Q = 1$,

$$\text{elasticity of demand} = -\frac{1}{Q} \Big/ \frac{\Delta p}{p} = -\frac{p}{\Delta p \times Q}, \text{ and}$$

$$\text{marginal revenue} = \text{price} + \text{change in price} \times \text{quantity sold}$$

$$= p + (\Delta p \times Q)$$

$$= p\Big(1 + \frac{\Delta p \times Q}{p}\Big)$$

$$= p(1 - 1/\text{elasticity of demand}).$$

Hence, if the elasticity of demand is 2, marginal revenue is ½ of price. If the elasticity of demand is 10, marginal revenue is ⁹⁄₁₀ of price.

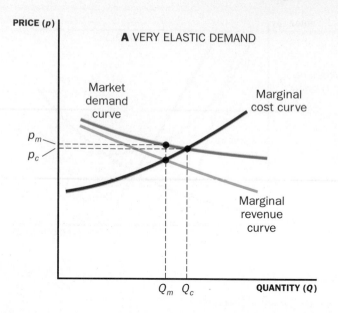

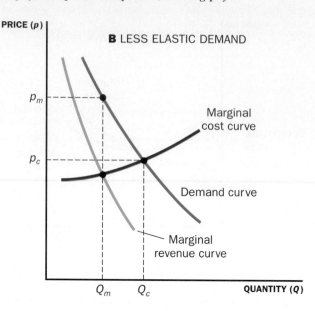

FIGURE 12.3   *Monopoly and the Elasticity of Demand*

In panel A, a monopoly faces a very elastic market demand, so prices do not fall much as output increases, and monopoly price is not much more than the competitive price. In panel B, a monopoly faces a less elastic market demand, so price falls quite a lot as output increases, and price is substantially above the competitive price.

WRAP-UP

The Firm's Supply Decision

All firms maximize profits at the point where marginal revenue (the revenue from selling an extra unit of the product) equals marginal cost. For a competitive firm, marginal revenue equals price. For a monopoly, marginal revenue is less than price.

An Example: The ABC-ment Company

Table 12.1 gives the demand curve facing the ABC-ment Company, which has a monopoly on the production of cement in its area. There is a particular price at which it can sell each level of output. As it lowers its price, it can sell more cement. Local builders will, for instance, use more cement and less wood and other materials in constructing a house.

For simplicity, we assume cement is sold in units of 1,000 cubic yards. At a price of $10,000 per unit (of 1,000 cubic

TABLE 12.1

Demand Curve Facing ABC-ment Company

Cubic yards (thousands)	Price	Total revenues	Marginal revenues	Total costs	Marginal costs
1	$10,000	$10,000		$15,000	
			$8,000		$2,000
2	$ 9,000	$18,000		$17,000	
			$6,000		$3,000
3	$ 8,000	$24,000		$20,000	
			$4,000		$4,000
4	$ 7,000	$28,000		$24,000	
			$2,000		$5,000
5	$ 6,000	$30,000		$29,000	
			0		$6,000
6	$ 5,000	$30,000		$35,000	

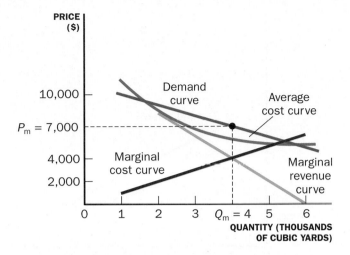

FIGURE 12.4 *Demand and Marginal Revenue*

At each level of output, the marginal revenue curve lies below the demand curve.

yards), the firm sells 1 unit, at a price of $9,000, it sells 2 units, and at a price of $8,000, 3 units. The third column of the table shows the total revenues at each of these levels of production. The total revenues are just price times quantity. The marginal revenue from producing an extra unit (of 1,000 cubic yards) is just the difference between, say, the revenues received at 3 units and 2 units or 2 units and 1 unit. Notice that in each case, the marginal revenue is less than the price.

Figure 12.4 shows the demand and marginal revenue curves, using data from Table 12.1. At each level of output, the marginal revenue curve lies below the demand curve. As can be seen from the table, not only does price decrease as output increases, but so does marginal revenue.

The output at which marginal revenue equal marginal cost—the output chosen by the profit-maximizing monopolist—is denoted by Q_m. In our example $Q_m = 4,000$ cubic yards. When the number of cubic yards increases from 3,000 to 4,000, the marginal revenue is $4,000, and so is the marginal cost. At this level of output, the price, p_m, is $7,000 (per 1,000 cubic yards), which is considerably in excess of marginal costs, $4,000. Total revenues, $28,000, are also in excess of total costs, $24,000.[1]

---

[1] In this example, the firm is indifferent between producing 3,000 or 4,000 cubic yards. If the marginal cost of producing the extra output exceeds $4,000 by a little, then it will produce 3,000 cubic yards; if the marginal cost is a little less than $4,000, then it will produce 4,000 cubic yards.

Monopoly Profits

Monopolists maximize their profits by setting marginal revenue equal to marginal cost. The total level of monopoly profits can be seen in two ways, as shown in Figure 12.5. Panel A shows total revenues and total costs (from Table 12.1) for each level of output of the ABC-ment Company. The difference between revenues and costs is profits—the distance between the two curves. This distance is maximized at the output $Q_m = 4,000$ cubic yards. We can see that at this level of output, profits are $4,000 ($28,000 − $24,000). Panel B calculates profits using the average cost diagram. Total profits are equal to the profit per unit multiplied by the number of units produced. The profit per unit is the difference between the unit price and the average cost, and total monopoly profits is the shaded area *ABCD*. Again, the sum is $4,000: ($7,000 − $6,000) × 4.

A monopolist enjoys an extra return because it has been able to reduce its output and increase its price from the level that would have prevailed under competition. This return is called a **pure profit.** Because these payments are not required to elicit greater effort or production on the part of the monopolist (in fact, they derive from the monopolist's *reducing* the output from what it would be under competition), they are also called **monopoly rents.**

Price Discrimination

The basic objective of monopolists is to maximize profits, and they accomplish this by setting marginal revenue equal to marginal cost, so price exceeds marginal cost. Monopolists can also engage in a variety of other practices to increase their profits. Among the most important is **price discrimination,** which means charging different prices to different customers or in different markets.

Figure 12.6 shows a monopolist setting marginal revenue equal to marginal cost in the United States and in Japan. The demand curves the firm faces in the two countries are different. Therefore, though marginal costs are the same, the firm will charge different prices for the same good in the two countries. (By contrast, in competitive markets, price equals marginal cost, so that regardless of the shape of the demand curves, price will be the same in the two markets, except for the different costs of delivering the good to each market.) With prices in the two countries differing, middlemen firms will enter the market, buying the product in the country with the low price and selling it in the other country. A company may attempt to thwart the middlemen—as many Japanese

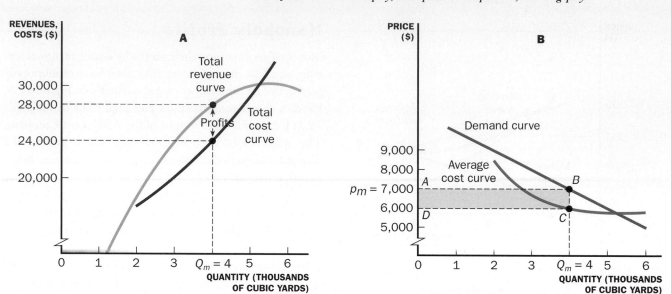

FIGURE 12.5   *Price Exceeding Average Cost Means Profit*

Panel A shows profits to be the distance between the total revenue and total cost curves, maximized at the output $Q_m = 4,000$ cubic yards. Profits occur when the market price is above average cost, as in panel B, so that the company is (on average) making a profit on each unit it sells. Monopoly profits are the area *ABCD*, which is average profit per unit times the number of units sold.

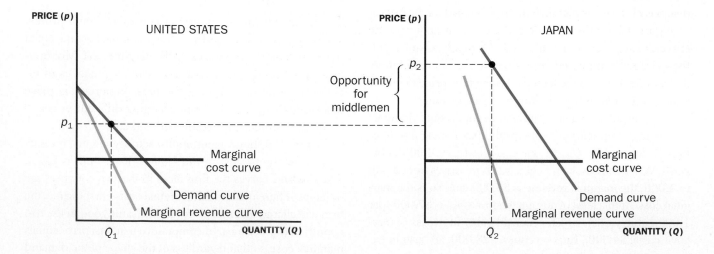

FIGURE 12.6   *Price Discrimination*

A monopolist who sells products in two different countries may find that the demand curve it faces in the two countries is different. Though it sets marginal revenue equal to the same marginal cost in both countries, it will charge different prices.

companies do—by, for instance, having distinct labels on the two products and refusing to provide service or honor any guarantees outside the country in which the good is originally delivered.

Within a country, a monopolist can also price discriminate *if* resale is difficult and *if* it can distinguish between buyers with high and those with low elasticities of demand. An electricity company can make its charge for each kilowatt hour depend on how much electricity the customer uses, because of restrictions on the retransmission of electricity. If the company worries that large customers faced with the same high prices that it charges small customers might install their own electric generators, or switch to some other energy source, it may charge them a lower price. An airline with a monopoly on a particular route might charge business customers a higher fare than vacationers. They do so knowing that business customers have no choice but to make the trip, while vacationers have many alternatives. They can travel elsewhere, on another day, or by car or train. Such business practices enable the monopolist to increase its profits relative to what they would be if it charged a single price in the market. Firms facing imperfect competition also engage in these practices, as we will see. Airlines again provide a telling example. Though the Robinson-Patman Act, which Congress passed in 1936, was designed to restrict price discrimination, it is only partially successful.

Economies of Scale and Natural Monopolies

The technology needed to produce a good can sometimes result in a market with only one or very few firms. For example, it would be inefficient to have two firms construct power lines on each street in a city, with one company delivering electricity to one house and another company to the house next door. Likewise, in most locales, there is only one gravel pit or concrete plant. These situations are called **natural monopolies.**

A natural monopoly occurs whenever the average costs of production for a single firm are declining up to levels of output beyond those likely to emerge in the market. When the average costs of production fall as the scale of production increases, we say there are economies of scale, a con-

cept first introduced in Chapter 7. In Figure 12.7, the demand curve facing a monopoly intersects the average cost curve at an output level at which average costs are still declining. At large enough outputs, average costs might start to increase, but that level of output is irrelevant to the actual market equilibrium. For instance, firms in the cement industry have U-shaped average cost curves, and the level of output at which costs are minimized is quite high. Accordingly, in smaller, isolated communities, there is a natural monopoly in cement.

A natural monopolist` is protected by the knowledge that it can undercut its rivals should they enter. Since entrants typically are smaller and average costs decline with size, their average costs are higher. Therefore, the monopolist feels relatively immune from the threat of entry. So long as it does not have to worry about entry, it acts like any other monopolist, setting marginal revenue equal to marginal cost.

In some cases, even when a market is occupied by a natural monopolist, there can still be competition *for the market.* Competition to be that single supplier is so keen that price is bid down to average cost, at p_r, where price equals average cost. If the firm were to charge a slightly higher price, another firm would enter the market, steal the entire

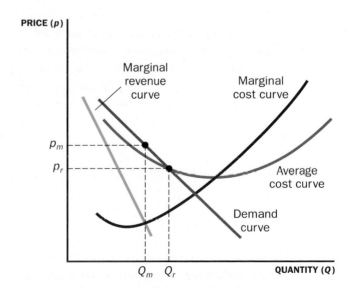

FIGURE 12.7 *Natural Monopoly*

In a natural monopoly, average cost curves are downward sloping in the relevant range of output. A firm can charge the monopoly price p_m. If the market is *contestable*, potential competition prevents the firm from charging a price higher than average costs. The equilibrium price is p_r.

International Perspective

South Africa, AIDS, and Price Discrimination

In perfectly competitive and well-functioning markets, goods cannot be sold at two different prices. Those who purchased the good at the low price could resell the good in the high-price market, making a pure profit. But in some markets, reselling the good is difficult; in others, governments assist in restraining the resale.

Research and testing account for the major cost of producing drugs. These are fixed costs. The drug manufacturers recoup these expenses by charging prices that are considerably in excess of the manufacturing costs. If they can price discriminate, the price they charge in each market will depend on the price elasticity *in that market*. But if they worry about resale, they may charge the same price in all markets.

Drug companies have developed some effective remedies against AIDS—not cures but treatments that can substantially prolong life. They charge $10,000 a year for treatment, a cost few in the developing countries can afford. The actual cost of manufacturing the drugs is much, much less. But the drug companies have been reluctant to sell the drugs at lower prices in these countries for two reasons. They worried that it would lower profits *in those countries,* and probably more importantly, they worried about resale, as it would lower profits in their own home markets (United States, Europe). But charging high prices in, say, South Africa, the country with perhaps the highest incidence of AIDS, in effect condemned millions in that country to a

premature death. Naturally, South Africa balked. It passed a law allowing the importation of drugs at lower prices, drugs possibly made by manufacturers that had ignored standard patent protections. The drug companies sued, saying it violated their basic economic rights. But protesters around the world argued that intellectual property rights must be designed to balance the rights of potential users and the rights of producers, that the benefits to the poor in Africa were significant in comparison with the loss in profits. In April 2001 they successfully pressured the drug companies to drop their suit against South Africa.

Protesters in South Africa objected to the high price of AIDS drugs.

market with its lower price, and still make a profit. Markets in which there is such fierce competition for the market are said to be *contestable*. Contestability requires that there be low or zero sunk costs. If there are significant sunk costs, a firm that entered the market could be undercut by the incumbent firm, which might lower price to marginal cost (since so long as price exceeds marginal cost, it makes a profit on the last unit sold). The lower prices that result are

sometimes referred to as a *price war,* and the result of a price war is that the entrant encounters a loss—at price equal to marginal cost, price is substantially below average cost. The entrant knows that even if it leaves, at this juncture, it loses its *sunk* costs. These costs are, by definition, the expenditures that are not recovered when the firm shuts down. But the potential entrant *anticipates* this, and therefore does not enter. Thus, there can be sustained *current* profits if a potential entrant believes those profits are like a mirage—that they are sure to disappear should it enter. In fact, sunk costs appear to be sufficiently important that few markets are close to perfectly contestable. Even in the airline industry, where sunk costs are relatively low—airlines can fly new planes into markets that seem profitable or out of markets that seem unprofitable—even the limited sunk costs act as a sufficiently large barrier to entry that there are sustained profits in certain routes, especially out of airline hubs (like American Airlines' hub in Dallas-Fort Worth). Just as most markets are not perfectly competitive, though there is some competition, most natural monopolies are not perfectly contestable, though the threat of competition (or potential competition) may limit the extent to which an incumbent monopolist exercises its monopoly power.

Whether a particular industry is a natural monopoly depends on the size of the output at which average costs are minimized relative to the size of the market.

The size of the market depends on transportation costs. If, somehow, the cost of transporting cement were lowered to close to zero, then there would be a national cement market. Many firms then would be competing against each other—the size of the national market is far larger than the output at which average costs are minimized. Globalization, the creation of global markets as a result of lower transportation costs, has increased the size of markets, introducing competition into markets that were natural monopolies.

The size of output at which costs are minimized depends in part on the magnitude of fixed costs. Since research is a fixed cost, as research has become more important in many industries, the size of output at which average costs are minimized is increased. At the same time, new technologies and business arrangements allow many firms to reduce their fixed costs. Today, firms need not have a personnel department for routine matters like paying checks; they can contract for these services as needed.

Because both technology and transportation costs can change over time, the status of an industry as a natural monopoly also can change. Long-distance telephone service used to be a natural monopoly. Telephone messages were transmitted over wires, and it would have been inefficient to install and use duplicate wires. As the demand for telephone services increased, and as alternative technologies like satellites developed, long-distance services ceased to be a natural monopoly. Today, a large number of firms compete to provide long-distance telephone service.

Assessing the Degree of Competition

In the real world, few industries match the extreme cases of monopoly and perfect competition. Usually industries have some degree of competition. This raises the question of how to assess the degree of competition in an industry.

One way to do this is to ask, What will happen if a firm in that industry raises its price? How much will sales of its product fall? In other words, what is the elasticity of demand for the firm's output? The lower the elasticity of demand—the less the quantity demanded falls when price is increased—the greater the firm's market power.

Two factors affect the elasticity of the demand curve facing a firm, and, therefore, its market power. The first is the number of firms in the industry—more generally, how concentrated is production within a few firms. The second is how different are the goods produced by the various firms in the industry.

Number of Firms in the Industry

Competition is likely to be greater when there are many firms in an industry (textiles, shoes) than when a few companies dominate (home refrigerators and freezers, greeting cards, soft drinks). Table 12.2 gives the percentage of output that is produced by the top four firms in a variety of industries ranging from breakfast cereals to furniture. The fraction of output produced by the top four firms in an industry is called the **four-firm concentration ratio,** one of several measures used to study industry concentration. When the four-firm percentage is high, as in the automobile or copper industry, companies have considerable market power. This is true even when they produce similar or identical products, as in the case of copper. When it is low, as in the case of furniture or women's clothes, market power is low; each firm faces a practically horizontal demand curve.[2]

---

[2]In both theory and practice, a critical issue in evaluating the extent of competition is defining the relevant market.

e-Insight

Network Externalities, the New Economy, and Monopoly Power

Network externalities arise whenever an individual benefits from an increase in the number of individuals that are part of the network. A telephone is not much use if there is no one at the other end of the line. The value of a telephone is increased as more people have telephones.

Assume there were two different telephone systems that do not interconnect. A new subscriber having to decide which network to sign up with is likely to choose the one with the larger number of subscribers. Thus, a firm that is initially in the lead will, over time, increase its dominance; it will be difficult for an entrant to make headway. And this in turn will enable it to exercise monopoly power. It can charge a price considerably in excess of its costs of production without worrying about a new entrant coming in and stealing its customers.

Government can limit the ability of this dominant firm to abuse its monopoly power by imposing restrictions, for example, by insisting that the dominant telephone network allow an entrant to interconnect, so that the subscribers in the new network can talk to the subscribers of the dominant network. It may be difficult, however, for the government to enforce effectively the restrictions, for example, because the dominant firm could provide low-quality interconnectivity but blame the problems on the entrant. That is why eventually, in the United States, the local telephone companies were separated from the dominant interstate and international telephone company (AT&T). The local telephone companies, it was hoped, would then provide equal access to AT&T and new entrants, like Sprint and MCI.

But the problem of network externalities is common in the new economy. If more people use the Windows operating system, then independent software developers will write more applications that work with Windows. If relatively few people use Apple's operating system (or Unix),

then it will not pay developers to write software that works on that operating system. But if there are many application programs that work on Windows, and few that work on Apple, customers will be induced to employ Windows. In fact, Windows has become the dominant operating system, with more than 90 percent of all personal computers using it.

But such market dominance almost invites abuse, and Microsoft evidently found it difficult to resist. This abuse can take a number of forms. Many in the software industry realized that Microsoft's market power would be reduced if they could develop a computer language that would allow programs to work on many alternative operating systems equally, or almost equally, effectively. Sun Microsystems developed Java to do just that. Had this effort been successful, it would have broken the network externality. Microsoft sought to frustrate these efforts, by developing a version of Java that was specifically adapted to Windows.

Another innovation that might have served as a platform for other applications and been applicable across operating systems was Netscape, the early entrant into Internet browsers. Microsoft sought to squash Netscape, not only by developing its own competing browser but also by delivering its browser free and insisting that computer manufacturers who purchased its operating system (to be installed on the computers they sell) *not* install Netscape as well. (This is called an *exclusionary practice.*) Note that in bundling the Internet browser with its operating system, so that everyone who purchased its operating system in effect got its Internet browser for free, it vastly undercut Netscape. In effect, it was supplying its browser at a zero price, a price that Netscape could only compete against because of the superiority of its product from the perspective of at least some users.

TABLE 12.2

Degree of Competition in Various Industries

	Market share of top 4 firms (percent)
Automobile, light truck and utility vehicles	88
Breakfast cereals	83
Cigarette manufacturing	99
Primary copper	95
Computers	45
Women's apparel manufacturing	13
Pharmaceuticals	32
Motorcycles, bicycles and parts	68
Furniture	11

SOURCE: *1997 Economic Census.*

Product Differentiation

The amount of competition also depends on the extent of differences between the products of an industry. In some industries, the goods produced are essentially identical, as in the case of agricultural goods such as wheat and corn. More typically, the firms in an industry with imperfect competition produce goods that are **imperfect substitutes**—goods sufficiently similar that they can be used for many of the same purposes, but different in ways that reflect consumer preferences. Kellogg's Corn Flakes and the store brand may look alike, but more people purchase the Kellogg's version, even though it is more expensive. Many of the goods people buy belong to clusters of imperfect substitutes: beverages (Coke, Pepsi, and store-brand colas), cars (Toyota Camry, Honda Accord, Ford Taurus, and other four-door sedans), clothing (Land's End, L.L. Bean, or Eddie Bauer), computers, cameras, telephone service, building materials, and many more. Economists refer to this phenomenon as **product differentiation.**

Because product differentiation is a source of market power, firms devote considerable effort to producing goods that are slightly different from those of their competitors. When goods are perfect substitutes, individuals will choose whichever is cheapest. In an imaginary world where all brands of cornflakes really are perfect substitutes for all consumers, they would all sell at the same price. By

contrast, if most consumers view the different brands as imperfect substitutes, the demand curve facing each firm will be downward sloping, which means that each firm has some degree of market power. Figure 12.8 shows this contrast graphically.

Equilibrium with Monopolistic Competition

In most industries there is some but limited competition. The number of firms in the industry is perhaps the most important determinant of the nature of competition. If the fixed costs are large—not so large as to result in a single firm but sufficiently large as to result in only two, three, or four firms—then there is a natural oligopoly. But before turning to the topic of oligopolies in the next section, we now consider the case where fixed costs are relatively small—sufficiently small that there are so many firms that profits are driven to zero, but sufficiently large that there is only a single firm producing any single product. However, the products produced are *close* but not perfect substitutes, and so each firm faces a downward-sloping demand curve. This is the case of monopolistic competition, first analyzed by Edward Chamberlin of Harvard University in 1933.

Figure 12.9 illustrates a market in which there is monopolistic competition. Assume initially that all firms are charging the same price, say p_1. If one firm were to charge a slightly lower price, it would steal some customers away from other stores. If there were twenty firms in the market, this price-cutting firm would attract more than one-twentieth of the total market demand. And if it should raise its price above that of its rivals, it would lose customers to them. Each firm assumes that the prices charged by other firms will remain unchanged as it changes its price or the quantity it produces. The demand curve facing each firm is thus the one shown in the figure.

In deciding how much to produce, the firm sets marginal revenue equal to marginal cost. The market equilibrium is (p_1, Q_1), with marginal revenue equaling marginal cost. In the equilibrium depicted in the figure, price exceeds average

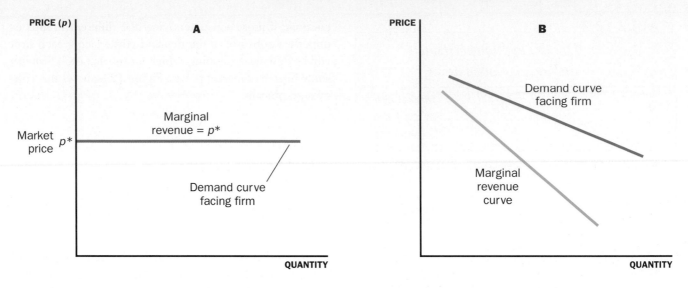

FIGURE 12.8 *Demand Curves with Perfect and Imperfect Competition*

Panel A shows the demand curve for a perfectly competitive firm: if it raises its price, all its customers will find substitutes. The marginal revenue curve for the firm is the same as its demand curve. Panel B shows the demand curve and marginal revenue curve facing a firm with only imperfect substitutes for its products.

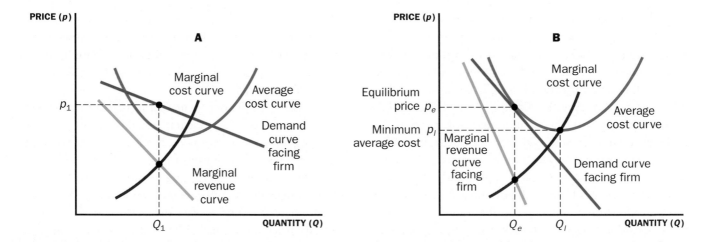

FIGURE 12.9 *Profit Maximizing for a Monopolistic Competitor*

A monopolistic competitor chooses the quantity it will produce by setting marginal revenue equal to marginal cost (Q_1), and then selling that quantity for the price given on its demand curve (p_1). In panel A, the price charged is above average cost, and the monopolistic competitor is making a profit, enticing other firms to enter the market. As firms enter, the share of the market demand of each firm is reduced, and the demand curve facing each firm shifts to the left. Entry continues until the demand curve just touches the average cost curve (panel B). When the firm produces Q_e, it just breaks even; there is no incentive for either entry or exit.

costs. One can think of this situation as a sort of minimonopoly, where each firm has a monopoly on its own brand name or its own store location.

But if existing firms are earning monopoly profits, there is an incentive for new competitors to enter the market until profits are driven to zero, as in the perfectly competitive model. *This is the vital distinction between monopolies and monopolistic competition.* In both cases, firms face downward-sloping demand curves. In both cases, they set marginal revenue equal to marginal cost. But in monopolistic competition, there are no barriers to entry. Entry continues so long as profits are positive. As firms enter, the share of the industry demand of each firm is reduced. The demand curve facing each firm thus shifts to the left, as depicted in panel B. This process continues until the demand curve just touches the average cost curve, at point (p_e, Q_e). At that point, profits are zero.

The figure also shows the firm's marginal revenue and marginal cost curves. As we have said, the firm sets its marginal revenue equal to its marginal cost. This occurs at exactly the level of output at which the demand curve is tangent to the average cost curve. This is because at any other point, average costs exceed price, so profits are negative. Only at this point are profits zero. Accordingly, this is the profit-maximizing output.

The monopolistic competition equilibrium has some interesting characteristics. Notice that in equilibrium, price and average costs exceed the minimum average costs at which the goods could be produced. *Less is produced at a higher price.* But there is a trade-off here. Whereas in the perfectly competitive market every product was a perfect substitute for every other one, in the world of monopolistic competition there is variety in the products available. People value variety and are willing to pay a higher price to obtain it. Thus, the fact that goods are sold at a price above the minimum average cost does not necessarily mean that the economy is inefficient.

The market may result in too little or too much product variety. There is a trade-off. Greater variety can only be obtained at greater cost and thus a higher price.

Oligopolies

In oligopolies there are just a few firms, so each worries about how its rivals will react to anything it does. This is true of the airline, cigarette, aluminum, and automobile industries, as well as a host of others.

If an oligopolist lowers its price, it worries that rivals will do the same and it will gain no competitive advantage. Worse still, a competitor may react to a price cut by engaging in a price war and cutting the price still further. Different oligopolies behave in quite different ways. The oligopolist is always torn between its desire to outwit competitors and the knowledge that by cooperating with other oligopolists to reduce output, it will earn a portion of the higher industry profits.

An oligopoly thus must think *strategically*. In deciding what to do, it faces four key questions: (1) Should it collude or compete? (2) If it cannot collude explicitly (because there are laws barring such behavior), how can it reduce the effectiveness of competition, for instance, through *restrictive practices*? (3) How can it deter entry? Like a monopolist, it knows that entry will erode profits. (4) How will rivals react to whatever it does? Will they, for instance, match price decreases? In the next four subsections, we take up each of these questions in turn.

Note the contrast with both competitive and monopolistic competitive models on the one hand and pure monopoly on the other. In the latter, there is no competition, hence no need to take actions to restrict competition; in the former, by assumption, there are so many competing firms that attempts to restrict competition are fruitless.

Collusion

In some cases, oligopolists try to *collude* to maximize their profits. In effect, they act jointly as if they were a monopoly, and split up the resulting profits. The prevalence of collusion was long ago noted by Adam Smith, the founder of modern economics: "People of the same trade seldom meet together, even for merriment and diversion, but the conversation ends in a conspiracy against the public, or in some contrivance to raise prices."[3] A group of companies that formally operate in collusion is called a **cartel.** The Organization of Petroleum Exporting Countries (OPEC), for instance, acts collusively to restrict the output of oil, to raise oil prices and hence the profits of member countries.

---

[3] *Wealth of Nations* (1776), Book One, Chapter 10, Part II.

In the late nineteenth century, two or more railroads ran between many major cities. When they competed vigorously, profits were low. So it did not take them long to discover that if they acted collusively, they could raise profits by raising prices.

In the steel industry at the turn of the century, Judge Elbert H. Gary, who headed the U.S. Steel Company, the largest of the steel firms, regularly presided over Sunday dinners for prominent members of his industry at which steel prices were set. But while cartels increase industry profits, it is hard to maintain the cooperative behavior required. We now look at three problems facing cartels.

Given the incentives to collude, it is not surprising that there have been several dramatic cases. In the 1950s, for instance, a cartel that included General Electric and Westinghouse colluded in setting the prices of electrical generators, and in the 1990s, the government uncovered price fixing by Archer Daniel Midland (ADM). But since firms today know that collusion is illegal, they go to great lengths to hide it, and it takes a committed and aggressive government to uncover and prosecute it.

The mere fact that collusion is illegal, however, inhibits collusion. At the high price—well in excess of the marginal cost of production—it pays each firm to cheat, to expand production. The members of the cartel cannot get together to discuss price fixing or restricting output. They typically must rely on *tacit collusion*—each restricting output with an understanding that the others will too. They cannot sign a contract that can be enforced in a court of law, simply because collusion to fix prices is illegal; hence they must rely on self-enforcement, which can be difficult and costly. The members of the cartel may try to discipline those that cheat. They may even incur losses in the short run, to punish the cheater, in the belief that the long-run gains from "cooperation" (that is, collusion) are worth the short-run sacrifice. For instance, if a firm cuts its price or expands its output *and the cheating is detected,* the other firms in the cartel may match, or even more than match, the price cuts or capacity expansions. The cheater ends up not only with lower profits than anticipated but also with lower profits than it would have obtained had it cooperated.

There are a variety of *facilitating practices* that make collusion easier, by making punishment for cheating easier. In some industries, there are cooperative arrangements—one firm, for instance, may draw upon the inventories of another, in the case of an unanticipated shortfall—and cheaters are excluded from these cooperative arrangements.

OPEC leaders met in Caracas, Venezuela, in September 2000.

Sometimes, policies that *seem* to be highly competitive actually have exactly the opposite effect. Consider the "meeting-the-competition clauses," in which some members of the oligopoly commit themselves to charging no more than any competitor. This sounds highly competitive. But think about it from the perspective of rival firms. Assume that one firm is selling for $100 an item that costs only $90 to produce, so it is making a $10 profit. Consider another firm that would like to steal some customers away. It would be willing to sell the item for $95, undercutting its rival. But then it reasons that if it cuts its price, it will not gain any customers, since its rival has already guaranteed to match the lower price. Further, the second firm knows that it will make less money on each sale to its current customers. Price cutting simply does not pay. Thus, a practice that seemingly is highly competitive in fact facilitates collusion.

Circumstances are always changing, and this necessitates changing outputs and prices. The cartel must coordinate these changes. The fact that collusion is illegal makes this coordination particularly difficult, all the more so since the interests of the members of the cartel may not coincide—some may find their costs lowered more than others and therefore want more of an output expansion than others. Were there to be perfect collusion, where industry profits were maximized, some might have to contract production and others expand it, with profits of some firms actually decreasing and others increasing. The gainers could, in principle, make payoffs to the losers and still be better off. However, these side payments are also illegal, and if they are to occur, they have to be done in subtle and hard-to-detect ways. While perfect coordination is seldom possible, some industries have found a partial solution by allowing one firm to play the role of the *price leader*. In the airline industry, American Airlines for a long time acted as a price leader. As it increased or decreased prices, others followed suit.

Using Game Theory to Model Collusion

In recent years economists have applied a branch of mathematics called **game theory** to study collusion among oligopolists. The basic aim of game theory is to understand strategic choices, that is, to understand how people or organizations behave when they expect their actions to influence the behavior of others. For instance, when executives at a major airline decide to change fares for flights on a certain route, they have to consider how their competitors might respond to the price change. And the competitors, when deciding how to respond, have to consider how the first airline might respond in turn to their actions. These are strategic decisions, just like the decisions typical of players in various sorts of games, like chess, football, or poker.

Using game theory, the economist views a situation as composed of participants in a game, with the rules of the game defining certain moves. The outcomes of the game what each participant receives—are referred to as its payoffs, and depend on what each player does. Each participant in the game chooses a strategy; he decides what moves to make. In games in which each player has the chance to make more than one move (there is more than one round, or period), moves can depend on what has happened in previous periods. Game theory begins with the assumption that each player in the game is rational and knows that his rival is rational. Each is trying to maximize his own payoff. The theory then tries to predict what each player will do. The answer depends on the rules of the game and the payoffs.

One example of such a game is called the **prisoner's dilemma.** Two prisoners, A and B, alleged to be conspirators in a crime, are put into separate rooms. A police officer goes into each room and makes a little speech: "Now here's the situation. If your partner confesses and you remain silent, you'll get five years in prison. But if your partner confesses and you confess also, you'll only get three years. On the other hand, perhaps your partner remains silent. If you're quiet also, we can only send you to prison for one year. But if your partner remains silent and you confess, we'll let you out in three months. So if your partner confesses, you are better off confessing, and if your partner doesn't confess, you are better off confessing. Why not confess?" This deal is offered to both prisoners.

Figure 12.10 shows the results of this deal. The upper left box, for example, shows the result if both A and B confess. The upper right box shows the result if prisoner A confesses but prisoner B remains silent. And so on.

From the combined standpoint of the two prisoners, the best option is clearly that they both remain silent and each serves one year. But the self-interest of each individual prisoner says that confession is best, whether his partner confesses or not. However, if they both follow their self-interest and confess, they both end up worse off, each serving three years. The prisoner's dilemma is a simple game in which both parties are made worse off by independently following their own self-interest. Both would be better off if they could get together to agree on a story, and to threaten the other if he deviated from the story.

The prisoner's dilemma game can be used to illustrate the problem of collusion among oligopolists. Let us work with the example of a *duopoly,* which is a market with two firms. Figure 12.11 shows the level of profits of each if both collude and restrict output (both get $1 billion), if neither restricts output (both get $.5 billion), or if one restricts output and the other does not (the one that does not gets $1.3 billion, the one that does gets $.4 billion). As each firm thinks through the consequences of restricting output, it observes that its profit is higher if it does not restrict output (does not collude), regardless of what the rival does. It thus pays neither to restrict output: They do not collude.

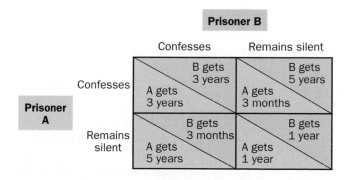

FIGURE 12.10 *The Prisoner's Dilemma*

Both prisoners would be better off if both remained silent, but their individual incentives lead each one to confess. From the standpoint of Prisoner A, confessing is the better strategy if Prisoner B confesses, and confessing is the better strategy if Prisoner B remains silent. The same holds for Prisoner B.

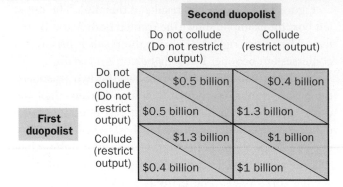

	Second duopolist	
First duopolist	Do not collude (Do not restrict output)	Collude (restrict output)
Do not collude (Do not restrict output)	$0.5 billion / $0.5 billion	$0.4 billion / $1.3 billion
Collude (restrict output)	$1.3 billion / $0.4 billion	$1 billion / $1 billion

FIGURE 12.11 *The Problem of Collusion as a Prisoner's Dilemma*

The payoffs for the duopolists delineate a prisoner's dilemma. Both firms would be better off if both colluded (restricted output), but their individual incentives lead each to not collude (not restrict output).

The central point is that even though the firms see that they could both be better off colluding, the individual incentive to cheat dictates the strategy each firm follows.

So far we have considered the prisoner's dilemma when each player makes only a single move to complete the game. But if firms interact over time, then they have additional ways to try to enforce their agreement. For example, suppose each oligopolist announces that it will refrain from cutting prices as long as its rival does. But if the rival cheats on the collusive agreement, then the first oligopolist will respond by increasing production and lowering prices. This strategy is called "tit for tat." If the rival firm believes this threat, especially after it has been carried out a few times, the rival may decide that it is more profitable to cooperate and keep production low rather than to cheat. In the real world, such simple strategies may play an important role in ensuring that firms do not compete too vigorously in markets where there are only three or four dominant firms.

The fact that such strategies are resorted to so commonly and are successful has been a puzzle to economists. The logic of game theory suggests that these strategies would not be effective.

Consider what happens if the two firms expect to compete in the same market over the next ten years, after which time a new product is expected to come along and shift the entire configuration of the industry. It will pay each firm to cheat in the tenth year, when there is no possibility of retaliation, because the industry will be completely altered in the next year. Now consider what happens in the ninth year. Both firms can figure out that it will not pay either one of them to cooperate in the tenth year. But if they are not going to cooperate in the tenth year anyway, then the *threat* of not cooperating in the future is completely ineffective. Hence in the ninth year, each firm will reason that it pays to cheat on the collusive agreement by producing more than the agreed-upon amount. Collusion breaks down in the ninth year. Reasoning backward through time, this logic will lead collusion to break down almost immediately. However, if there is no certain date at which the collusion will end, it is possible for collusion to carry on indefinitely. Whenever the firms contemplate cheating, each will compare the initial increase in profits from cheating with the future reduction in profits when the other firm retaliates. The firms therefore may decide to continue colluding.

Restrictive Practices

If members of an oligopoly could easily get together and collude, they would. Their joint profits would increase. Each of the members of the oligopoly would be better off than if they had competed. We have seen, however, that there are significant impediments to collusion. As a result, oligopolists typically resort to other ways of increasing profits. One approach is to restrict competition.

There are a number of practices firms engage in that restrict competition, called **restrictive practices.** Some of these practices were made illegal by the Federal Trade Commission Act of 1914. While these practices may not be quite as successful in increasing profits for the firms as the collusive arrangements discussed above, they do succeed in raising prices. In some cases, consumers may be even worse off than with outright collusion. Many restrictive practices are aimed at the wholesalers and retailers who sell a producer's goods. When one firm buys or sells another firm's products, the two companies are said to have a "vertical" relationship. Such restrictive practices are called *vertical restrictions,* as opposed to the price-fixing arrangements among producers or among wholesalers selling in the same market, which are referred to as *horizontal restrictions.*

One example of a vertical restriction is that of *exclusive territories,* in which a producer gives a wholesaler or retailer the exclusive right to sell a good within a certain region. Beer and soft drink producers, for instance, typically give their distributors exclusive territories. Coca-Cola manufactures its own syrup, which it then sells to bottlers who add the soda water. Coca-Cola gives these bottlers exclusive territories, so the supermarkets in a particular area can buy Coke from only one place. A store in Michigan cannot buy the soft drink from Coca-Cola bottlers in New Jersey, even if the price in New Jersey is lower. Indiana passed a law prohibiting exclusive territories for beer within the state. As a result, beer prices there are substantially lower (adjusting for other differences) than in other states.

Another example of restrictive practice is *exclusive dealing,* in which a producer insists that any firm selling its products not sell those of its rivals. When you go into an Exxon gas station, for instance, you can be sure you are buying gas refined by the Exxon Corporation, not Texaco or Mobil. Like most refiners, Exxon insists that stations that want to sell Exxon sell only its brand of gasoline.

A third example of a restrictive practice is *tie-ins,* in which a customer who buys one product must buy another. Mortgage companies, for example, used to insist that those who obtained mortgages from them purchase fire insurance as well. Nintendo designs its console so that it can only be used with Nintendo games. In effect, it forces a tie-in sale between the console and the computer games. In the early days of computers, IBM designed its computers so that they could only be used with IBM "peripherals," such as printers.

A final example of a restrictive practice is *resale price maintenance.* Under resale price maintenance, a producer insists that any retailer selling his product must sell it at the "list" price. Like exclusive territories, this practice is designed to reduce competitive pressures at the retail level.

Consequences of Restrictive Practices

Firms engaging in restrictive practices *claim* they are doing so not because they wish to restrict competition, but because they want to enhance economic efficiency. Exclusive territories, they argue provide companies with a better incentive to "cultivate" their territory. Exclusive dealing contracts, they say, provide incentives for firms to focus their attention on one producer's goods.

Regardless of these claims, restrictive practices often reduce economic efficiency. Exclusive territories for beer, for example, have limited the ability of very large firms, with stores in many different territories, to set up a central warehouse and distribute beer to their stores in a more efficient manner.

Regardless of whether they enhance or hurt efficiency, restrictive practices may lead to higher prices by limiting competitive pressures.

Some restrictive practices work by increasing the costs of, or otherwise impeding, one's rivals. In the 1980s, several major airlines developed computer reservation systems that they sold at very attractive prices to travel agents. If the primary goal of these systems had been to serve consumers, they would have been designed to display all the departures near the time the passenger desired. Instead, each airline's system provided a quick display for only its own flights—United's, for instance, focused on United flights—although with additional work, the travel agent could find out the flights of other airlines. Airlines benefited from these computer systems, not because they best met the needs of the consumer, but because they put competitors at a disadvantage and thereby reduced the effectiveness of competition.

An exclusive dealing contract between a producer and a distributor is another example of how one firm may benefit from hurting its rivals. The contract may force a rival producer to set up its own distribution system, at great cost. The already-existing distributor might have been able to undertake the distribution of the second product at relatively low incremental cost. The exclusive dealing contract increases total resources spent on distribution.

Courts have taken varying attitudes toward the legality of these and similar practices—in some circumstances ruling that they are illegal because they reduce competition, while in others allowing them, having been persuaded that they represent reasonable business practices.

WRAP-UP

Forms of Restrictive Practices

Exclusive territories
Exclusive dealing
Tie-ins
Resale price maintenance

Entry Deterrence

Oligopolists use restrictive practices to reduce competition and thereby increase profits. Another way to reduce competition is to prevent other firms from entering the market. This is called **entry deterrence.**

Entry deterrence seeks to limit the number of firms—the fewer the firms, presumably the weaker the competitive pressure. There are natural barriers to entry, such as the large fixed costs discussed earlier in the chapter. But typically these are not so large as to result in a single firm. When there are some natural barriers—so competition is limited—those in the market often try to supplement the natural barriers by *strategic barriers,* that is, acting in ways that make it unattractive for new firms to enter the market.

The issue of entry barriers is at the center of the theory of monopoly and oligopoly. In both cases, there are profits, and the basic question is, why don't new firms enter the market? What are the barriers to their entry? Thus, our discussion of entry deterrence applies to both monopolies and oligopolies.

Government Policies as Barriers to Entry.

Many early monopolies were established by governments. In the seventeenth century, the British government gave the East India Company a monopoly on trade with India. The salt monopoly in eighteenth-century France had the exclusive right to sell salt. Even today, governments grant certain monopoly franchises; for example, many governments grant monopolies for electric and telephone service within a locality.

The most important monopolies granted by government today, however, are patents. A patent gives inventors the exclusive right to produce or to license others to produce their discoveries for a limited period of time, currently seventeen years. The argument for patents is that without them, copycat firms would spring up with every new invention, inventors would make little money from their discoveries, and there would be no economic incentive to invent. The framers of the U.S. Constitution thought invention so important that they included a provision enabling the newly created federal government to grant patents.

Perhaps the best example of the use of patents to secure monopoly power is the case of Xerox. Until the 1970s, the Xerox company was almost synonymous with photocopying. The company had invented the photocopier and came to hold almost 1,700 closely interrelated patents on the photocopying process. Eventually the status of the patents was called into question when the Federal Trade Commission (FTC) charged that Xerox was purposely using its many patents to monopolize the photocopier market. Instead of using the patents to protect a new invention for a limited amount of time, the FTC argued, Xerox was making them part of a strategy to monopolize the market indefinitely. After several years of investigation and argument, a "consent order" was announced, and Xerox subsequently agreed to allow competitors to use its patents and even to give its competitors access to some future patents. This opened the market to a number of firms offering a variety of new photocopiers.

Single Ownership of an Essential Input

Another barrier to entry and source of monopoly power is a firm's exclusive ownership of something that is not producible. For example, an aluminum company might attempt to become a monopolist in aluminum by buying all the sources of bauxite, the essential ingredient. A single South African company, De Beers, has come close to monopolizing the world's supply of diamonds. There are, however, relatively few instances of such monopolies.

Information as a Barrier to Entry

Information can act as a barrier to entry. Consumers do not know and cannot easily assess the quality of a new product. It takes time and money to establish a reputation.

Imperfect information about the costs and responses of the incumbent firms too can act as a barrier to entry. Potential entrants may know that they can undercut the incumbent firm's current price, but they do not know how much the incumbent will (or can afford to) lower its price.

Market Strategies for Entry Deterrence

Some monopolies and oligopolies cannot be explained by any of the factors discussed so far. They are not the result of government policies and are not natural monopolies, nor can information problems explain a lack of entry. Many firms, whose original monopoly position may have been based on some technological innovation or patent, manage to maintain their dominant positions even after their patents expire, at least for a time. IBM, Kodak, and Polaroid are three examples. These firms maintained their dominant positions by the pursuit of market strategies that deterred other firms from entering the market.

Established firms often pursue a strategy to convince potential entrants that even though they are currently making high levels of profit, these profits will disappear should the new firm enter the market. These strategies are most likely to be effective if there are sunk costs, even if sunk costs are relatively small. Assume the incumbent firm has constant marginal costs and responds to entry of another firm by lowering the price to marginal cost. Then an entrant with even a small sunk cost, and with marginal costs equal to that of the incumbent, will know that once it enters, price will equal marginal costs, and it will not be able to recover its sunk costs. Hence, it will not enter. And the incumbent firm, knowing this, can charge a monopoly price with impunity, even though there are many firms that are equally efficient.

Two major forms of such **entry-deterring practices** are predatory pricing and excess capacity.

Predatory Pricing   If prices have fallen drastically in a certain market every time there has been entry in the past, then new firms may be reluctant to enter. An incumbent firm may deliberately lower its price below the new entrant's cost of production, in order to drive the new arrival out and discourage future entry. The incumbent also may lose money in the process, but it hopes to recoup the losses when the entrant leaves and it is free to raise prices to the monopoly level. This practice is called *predatory pricing* and is an illegal trade practice. However, shifting technologies and shifting demand often make it difficult to ascertain whether a firm has actually engaged in predatory pricing or simply lowered its price to meet the competition. Firms that lower their prices always claim that they were "forced" to do so by their competitors.

While allegations of predation are not uncommon, the courts have set high standards of proof. Thus, in one of the more recent cases, Liggett, a tobacco company that sells low-priced generic cigarettes that cut into name-brand sales, claimed that Brown & Williamson had engaged in predation. The charge was that B&W wanted Liggett to

Internet Connection

The Microsoft Case

In November 1999, a federal court judge ruled that Microsoft Corporation, makers of the Windows operating system, had a monopoly in the market for personal computer operating systems. This finding grew out of a case filed by the U.S. Justice Department and twenty states against Microsoft in 1998. By June 2000, the judge in the case, Thomas Penfield Jackson, had ruled that Microsoft be broken up into two separate companies, but Microsoft sucessfully appealed this ruling, and the two sides finally settled the case in 2001. The e-Case box on pages 340–341 provides a short history of the case and the economic and legal issues involved.

Another place to gain more information about the case is the Internet. New York University Professor Nicholas Economides maintains a Web page with all the latest information and analysis on the legal battles between Microsoft and the U.S. Department of Justice. The outcome of the Microsoft court battle will have major implications for the Internet, the personal computer industry, and high-technology industries in general. Professor Economides's Web site is http://raven.stern.nyu.edu/networks/ms/.

WRAP-UP

Entry Deterrence

Government policies: These include grants of monopoly (patents) and restrictions on entry (licensing).

Single ownership of an essential input: When a single firm owns the entire supply of a nonproducible input, entry is by definition precluded.

Information: Lack of technical information by potential competitors inhibits their entry; lack of information by consumers concerning the quality of a new entrant's product discourages consumers from switching to the new product, and thus inhibits entry.

Market strategies: These include actions such as predatory pricing and excess capacity aimed at convincing potential entrants that entry would be met with resistance, and thus would be unprofitable.

Thinking Like an Economist

Trade-offs, American Airlines, and Predation

Firms with market power like to keep it that way, as they can earn high profits by being the only, or dominant, firm in a market. One of the ways in which they do this is to be a *predator*. Like a predatory animal that eats up rivals, predatory firms lower their prices in an attempt to drive out competitors. A firm may find it can earn higher profits overall if it sacrifices some profit in the short run by cutting its prices to keep rivals out of its market.

This behavior is illegal. For instance, in 1999 the U.S. Justice Department accused American Airlines of predation. The Justice Department alleged that repeatedly, when a new, low-cost carrier entered a market, American Airlines would slash its prices and increase the number of flights, in an attempt to drive the entrant out of the market. As soon as it was successful, it would cut back on the number of flights and raise prices. While consumers benefited in the short run from the price war, in the long run they suffered from the lack of competition, with its high prices. Courts have the difficult task of trying to determine whether the lowering of prices is just a normal response to competition, or a predatory action intended to kill a firm entering the market.

One part of the test that is commonly employed asks, did the predatory firm give up profits today in the anticipation that it would earn back the profits later from its monopoly position? One test for that is to compare price and average variable cost. If price is below average variable cost, clearly the firm could not be maximizing its profits, because it would have been better off simply shutting down, ceasing production.

A more refined test looks at price in comparison with marginal cost. If price is less than marginal cost, a firm should contract production. The problem is that in many cases, marginal cost is hard to observe, and courts have had to rely on proxies. If the firm is operating at or near an efficient level of production, so that average total costs are minimized, then marginal cost equals average total costs. (Recall Figure 7.6.)

The American Airlines's case involved an expansion of output. In competitive markets, so long as the marginal cost curve is upward sloping, a lower price will be associated with lower output, since price must equal marginal cost. But predation occurs in markets that are not competitive. Still, it seemed peculiar that as a new entrant stole some of the demand facing American Airlines, it reacted by increasing supply. The Justice Department alleged that a closer look at American Airlines's behavior showed that it had given up profitable opportunities to drive out its rival. The additional revenue that it received from expanding its output was lower than the costs it incurred (including the opportunity cost associated with the profits the planes would have earned on alternative routes).

Predation cases present courts with difficult trade-offs involving the risk of finding an innocent party guilty versus the risk of finding a guilty party innocent. Consumers benefit from the lower prices in the first phase of predation. Courts worry that if firms that really were not engaged in predation are found guilty, it will stifle competition. But if predation is really occurring, competition in the long run is suppressed, and consumers will face higher prices and worse service. In most of the airline routes where the Justice Department alleged predation, after the entrant left, prices returned to high levels and service was cut back. As this book goes to press, the case remains in the courts.

raise its prices and thus shift demand back to B&W's name brands. B&W lowered prices on its brands as a warning to Liggett to do B&W's bidding. In the lower court a jury found in favor of Liggett. The Supreme Court reversed the lower court's judgment, however, in a 1993 decision.

Excess Capacity Another action firms can take to convince potential rivals that prices are likely to fall if they enter the market is to build up production facilities in excess of those currently needed. By building extra plants and equipment, even if they are rarely used, a firm poses an extra threat to potential entrants. A newcomer will look at this *excess capacity* and realize that the incumbent firm can increase production a great deal with minimal effort. The excess capacity serves as a signal that the incumbent is willing and able to engage in fierce price competition.

How Oligopolies Respond to Competition

In perfectly competitive markets, competitive behavior is clear and simple. Firms work to lower their costs of production. They can sell as much as they want at the going market price. They do not have to worry about clever marketing strategies, new products, or advertising. But these, and a host of other decisions, are the battlefields on which competition among oligopolists occurs. What an oligopolist will sell at any particular price, or what the market price will be if it produces a particular level of output, depends on what its rivals do. Thus, the actions of any oligopolist depend critically on its beliefs about how rivals will react. Economists have investigated the behavior of oligopolies under different assumptions concerning what each firm believes about what its rival will do.

Bertrand and Cournot Competition
Consider a duopoly. At one extreme is the case where firms believe that the rival will leave its price unchanged; an oligopolist can steal the entire market from its rival simply by undercutting it—it faces a horizontal demand curve up to the total market demand. Not surprisingly, in this case the equilibrium price will be the competitive price, even when there are only two firms. Each firm undercuts its rival, until the price equals the marginal cost of production. This kind of competition is called **Bertrand competition,** after the French economist, Joseph Bertand, who first studied it in 1883.

Alternatively, each firm might assume that its rival's output is fixed; to sell that output, the rival will lower its price as the firm increases its output. Because of this, the gain the firm gets from increasing output is lower. This form of competition is called **Cournot competition,** after Augustin Cournot, a French economist and engineer who first studied it in 1838. Typically, output is lower and prices are higher under Cournot competition than under Bertrand competition.

Kinked Demand Curves
Another hypothesis about how oligopolistic rivals may respond says that rivals match price cuts but do not respond to price increases. In this situation, an oligopolist believes that it will not gain much in sales if it lowers its price, because rivals will match the price cut, but it will lose considerably if it raises its price, since it will be undersold by rivals who do not change their prices. The demand curve facing such an oligopolist appears kinked, as in Figure 12.12. The curve is very steep below the current price, p_1, reflecting the fact that few sales are gained as price is lowered. But it is relatively flat above p_1, indicating that the firm loses many customers to its rivals, who refuse to match the price increases.

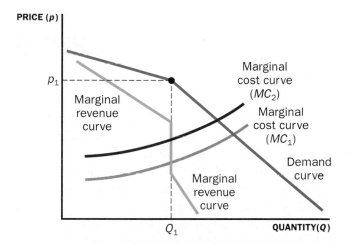

Figure 12.12 *A Kinked Demand Curve*

The demand curve facing a firm is relatively flat at price levels above the current level (p_1) showing that an oligopolist will lose a large amount of sales if it increases its price and rivals do not. However, the demand curve is relatively steep at prices below the current level, showing that the oligopolist will not gain much in sales if it lowers its price, since rivals will follow. The sharp drop in marginal revenue means that a firm may not change its level of price or output, even if marginal costs shift.

The figure also presents the marginal revenue curve, which has a sharp drop at the output level corresponding to the kink. Why does the marginal revenue curve have this shape, and what are the consequences? Consider what happens if the firm wants to increase output by one unit. It must lower its price by a considerable amount since, as it does so, its rivals will match that price. Accordingly, the marginal revenue it garners is small. If the firm contemplates cutting back on production by one unit, it needs to raise its price only a little since rivals will not change their prices. Thus, the loss in revenue from cutting back output by a unit is much greater than the gain in revenue from increasing output by a unit. With a flat demand curve, price and marginal revenue are close together.

The drop in the marginal revenue curve means that at the output at which the drop occurs, Q_1, extra revenue lost from cutting back production is much greater than the extra revenue gained from increasing production. This has one important implication. Small changes in marginal cost, from MC_1 to MC_2, have no effect on output or price. Thus, firms that believe they face a kinked demand curve have good reason to hesitate before changing their prices.

WRAP-UP

Competiton Among Oligopolists

Bertrand competition: Each firm sets its price believing its rivals will leave their own price unchanged in response to changes in the firm's price.

Cournot competition: Each firm believes its rivals will leave their output unchanged in response to changes in the firm's output.

Kinked demand curves: Each firm believes its rivals will match price cuts but not price increases.

The Importance of Imperfections in Competition

Many of the features of the modern economy—from frequent-flyer mileage awards to offers to match prices of competitors, from brand names to the billions spent every year on advertising—not only cannot be explained by the basic competitive model but also are inconsistent with it. They reflect the imperfections of competition that affect so many parts of the economy. Most economists agree that the extreme cases of monopoly (no competition) and perfect competition (where each firm has *no* effect on the market prices) are rare, and that most markets are characterized by some, but imperfect, competition.

Review and Practice

Summary

1. Both monopolists and firms facing perfect competition maximize their profits by producing at the quantity where marginal revenue is equal to marginal cost. However, marginal revenue for a perfect competitor is the same as the market price of an extra unit, while marginal revenue for a monopolist is less than the market price.

2. Since with a monopoly price exceeds marginal revenue, buyers pay more for the product than the marginal cost to produce it; there is less production in a monopoly than there would be if price were set equal to marginal cost.

3. Imperfect competition occurs when a relatively small number of firms dominate the market or when firms produce goods that are differentiated in ways that reflect consumer preferences.

4. An industry in which fixed costs are so large that only one firm can operate efficiently is called a natural monopoly. Even when there is only one firm (or a few), the threat of potential competition may be sufficiently strong that price is driven down to average costs; there are no monopoly profits. Such markets are said to be contestable. If, however, there are sunk costs, or other barriers to entry, markets will not be contestable, and monopoly profits can persist.

5. With monopolistic competition, barriers to entry are sufficiently weak that entry occurs until profits are driven to zero; there are few enough firms that each faces a downward-sloping demand curve, but a sufficiently large number of firms that each ignores rivals' reaction to what it does.

6. Oligopolists must choose whether to seek higher profits by colluding with rival firms or by competing. They must decide what their rivals will do in response to any action they take.

7. A group of firms that have an explicit and open agreement to collude is known as a cartel. While the gains from collusion can be significant, important limits are posed by the incentives to cheat and the necessity to rely on self-enforcement, and by the coordination problems arising out of the necessity to respond to changing economic circumstances. Although cartels are illegal under U.S. law, firms have tried to find tacit ways of facilitating collusion—for example, by using price leaders and "meeting-the-competition" pricing policies.

8. Even when they do not collude, firms attempt to restrict competition with practices like exclusive territories, exclusive dealing, tie-ins, and resale price maintenance. In some cases, a firm's profits may be increased by raising its rival's costs and making the rival a less effective competitor.

9. The nature of the equilibrium in oligopolies depends on beliefs about how rivals will respond. In Cournot competition, an oligopolist chooses its output under the assumption that its rivals' output levels are fixed. In Bertrand competition, each firm chooses the price of its product on the assumption that its rivals' prices are fixed. If rivals to an oligopolist match price cuts but do not match any price increases, then the oligopolist faces a kinked demand curve. A kinked demand curve will lead to a marginal revenue curve with a vertical segment, which implies that the firm will often not change its level of output or its price in response to small changes in costs.

Key Terms

pure profit or
  monopoly rents
price discrimination
four-firm concentration ratio
imperfect substitutes
product differentiation
natural monopoly
collusion
cartel

game theory
prisoner's dilemma
restrictive practices
entry deterrence
enter-deterring practices
Bertrand competition
Cournot competition

Review Questions

1. Why is price equal to marginal revenue for a perfectly competitive firm but not for a monopolist?

2. How should a monopoly choose its quantity of production to maximize profits? Explain why producing either less or more than the level of output at which marginal revenue equals marginal cost will reduce profits. Since a monopolist need not fear competition, what prevents it from raising its price as high as it wishes to make higher profits?

3. What are the primary sources of product differentiation?

4. Under what circumstances will price be equal to average costs, so that even though there is a single firm in the market, it earns no monopoly rents?

5. What is a natural monopoly?

6. Describe market equilibrium under monopolistic competition. Why does the price charged by the typical firm exceed the minimum average cost, even though there is entry?

7. What are the gains from collusion? Why is there an incentive for each member of a cartel to cheat, to produce more than the agreed upon amount? What is the "prisoner's dilemma" and how is it related to the problem of cheating? What are the other problems facing cartels?

8. Name some ways that firms might facilitate collusion, if explicit collusion is ruled out by law.

9. What are barriers to entry? How can firms try to deter entry?

10. Name and define three restrictive practices.

11. What are the different forms of competition among oligopolies? How do they relate to *expectations* concerning how rivals will respond?

Problems

1. Explain how it is possible that at a high enough level of output, if a monopoly produced and sold more, its revenue would actually decline.

2. Assume there is a single firm producing cigarettes, and the marginal cost of producing cigarettes is a constant. Suppose the government imposes a 10-cent tax on each pack of cigarettes. If the demand curve for cigarettes is linear (that is, $Q = a - bp$, where Q = output, p = price, and a and b are constants), will the price rise by more or less than the tax?

3. With what strategies might a furniture firm differentiate its products?

4. Suppose a gas station at a busy intersection is surrounded by many competitors, all of whom sell identical gas. Draw the demand curve the gas station faces, and draw its marginal and average cost curves. Explain the rule for maximizing profit in this situation. Now imagine that the gas station offers a new gasoline additive called zoomine, and begins an advertising campaign that says: "Get zoomine in your gasoline." No other station offers zoomine. Draw the demand curve faced by the station after this advertising campaign. Explain the rule for maximizing profit in this situation, and illustrate it with an appropriate diagram.

5. Explain how consumers may benefit from predatory pricing in the short run, but not in the long run.

6. Assume the demand curve for some commodity is linear
$Q = a - bp$.

   (a) Express how the price depends on the quantity produced.

   (b) What is the relationship between revenue and the quantity produced?

   (c) Assume that output increases slightly from Q to $(Q + \Delta Q)$. What happens to revenue? If ΔQ is a small number (much less than 1), then $(\Delta Q)^2$ is a *very* small number. Ignoring terms in $(\Delta Q)^2$, what is the relationship between marginal revenue and output?

   (d) Show that the expression for marginal revenue can be reexpressed as
$MR = 2p - \frac{a}{b}$

   (e) Assume that $b = 1$ and $a = 100$. Draw the demand and marginal revenue curves.

   (f) If the marginal cost is $1, what is the equilibrium competitive price and the monopoly price?

   (g) If the producer is required to pay a tax of $.10 per unit of output produced, what happens to the price under monopoly? under perfect competition?

7. How might cooperative agreements between firms—to share research information, share the costs of cleaning up pollution, or help avoid shortfalls of supplies—end up helping firms to collude in reducing quantity and raising price?

8. Explain why each of the following might serve to deter entry of a competitor:

   (a) Maintaining excess production capacity.

   (b) Promising customers that you will undercut any rival.

   (c) Selling your output at a price below that at which marginal revenue equals marginal cost. (Hint: Assume entrants are unsure about what your marginal costs are. Why would they be deterred from entering if they believed you have low marginal costs? Why might a lower price lead them to think that you had low marginal costs?)

   (d) Offering a discount to customers who sign up for long-term contracts.

9. Explain why frequent-flyer programs (in which airlines give credits for each mile traveled, with the credits being convertible into travel awards) might reduce competition among airlines. Put yourself in the role of consultant to one of the airlines in the days before any airline had such programs. Would you have recommended that the airline adopt the program? What would you have *assumed* about the responses of other airlines? Would this have been important to your assessment?

10. At various times, Nintendo has been accused of trying to stifle its competitors. Among the alleged practices have been (a) not allowing those who produce games for Nintendo to produce games for others; and (b) discouraging stores that sell Nintendo from selling competing games, for instance, by not fulfilling their orders

as quickly, especially in periods of shortages. Explain why these practices might increase Nintendo's profits.

11. Consider two oligopolists, with each choosing between a "high" and a "low" level of production. Given their choices of how much to produce, their profits will be:

Firm A

	High production	Low production
High production	A gets $2 million profit B gets $2 million profit	A gets $1 million profit B gets $5 million profit

Firm B

Low production	A gets $5 million profit B gets $1 million profit	A gets $4 million profit B gets $4 million profit

Explain how firm B will reason that it makes sense to produce the high amount, regardless of what firm A chooses. Then explain how firm A will reason that it makes sense to produce the high amount, regardless of what firm B chooses. How might collusion assist the two firms in this case.

12. Use the prisoner's dilemma analysis to describe what happens in the following two situations:

(a) Consider two rivals, say producers of cigarettes. If Benson and Hedges alone advertises, it diverts customers from Marlboro. If Marlboro along advertises, it diverts customers from Benson and Hedges. If they both advertise, they retain their customer base.

Are they genuinely unhappy with government regulations prohibiting advertising? In practice, they have complained quite bitterly about such government restrictions, including those aimed at children. Why?

(b) Consider two rivals, say producers of camera film, Fuji and Kodak. Consumers want a film that accurately reproduces colors and is not grainy. Assume that initially, they had products that were comparable. If one does R & D and improves its product, it will steal customers from its rival. If they both do R & D, and develop comparable products, then they will continue to share the market as before. Thus, the hypothetical pay-off matrix (in millions of dollars) appears as below (the profits in the case of research take into account the expenditures on research):

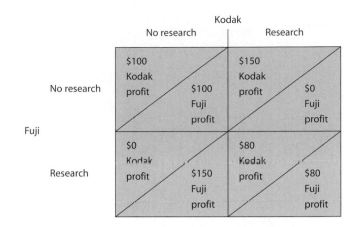

Explain why both will engage in research, even though their profits are lower. Could society be better off, even though profits are lower?

Appendix A: Monopsony

In any market, imperfections of competition can arise on either the buyer or the seller side. In this chapter, we have focused on imperfect competition among the sellers of goods. When there is a single buyer in a market, the buyer is called a **monopsonist.** Though monopsonies are relatively rare, they do exist. The government is a monopsonist in the market for a variety of high-technology defense systems.

In some labor markets, a single firm may be close to a monopsonist. In many markets, an employer may face an upward-sloping supply curve for labor, or at least labor with particular skills. Firms in one-company towns—like Gary, Indiana, which was founded and is dominated by U.S. Steel—particularly when they are geographically isolated, are most likely to face such upward-sloping supply curves for labor.

The consequences of monopsony are similar to those for monopoly. The basic rule remains: Produce at the point where marginal revenue equals marginal cost. The buyer firm is aware, however, that if it buys more units, it will have to pay a higher price. Then if the firm cannot price discriminate, the marginal cost of buying one more unit is not only what the company has to pay for the last unit, but also the higher price it must pay for all previously purchased units.

In the case of a labor market, Figure 12.13 illustrates the consequence. Chapter 9 showed that in competitive

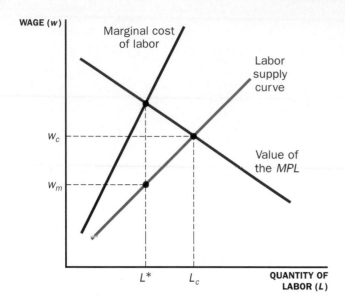

FIGURE 12.13 *Monopsony*

As a monopsonist buys more of an input, it must pay not only a higher price for the marginal unit but a higher price for all the units it buys; thus, the marginal cost of buying an input exceeds the price. The monopsonist sets the marginal cost of the input equal to the value of its marginal product at employment level L^*, and sets the wage at w_m. In a competitive labor market, a firm hires labor up to L_c, at wage w_c. Thus, a monopsonist hires less labor at a lower wage than competitive firms would.

markets, firms hire labor up to the point where the value of the marginal product of labor (the value of what an extra hour of labor would produce) equals the wage, the marginal cost of hiring an additional worker. The figure shows the curve that represents the value of the marginal product of labor *(MPL)*; it declines as the number of workers hired increases. The figure also shows the labor supply curve, which is upward sloping. From this, the firm can calculate the marginal cost of hiring an additional worker, the wage *plus* the increase in wage payments to all previously hired workers. Clearly, the marginal cost curve lies above the labor supply curve. The firm hires workers up to the point L^*, where the value of the marginal product of labor is equal to the marginal cost. Employment is lower than it would have been had the firm ignored the fact that as it hires more labor, the wage it pays increases.

Appendix B: Demand for Inputs Under Monopoly and Imperfect Competition

In Chapter 9, we saw that competitive firms hire labor up to the point where the value of the marginal product is equal to the wage. Similarly, any other factor of production is demanded up to the point where the value of its marginal product is equal to its price. From this, we could derive the demand curve for labor (or any other input).

A quite similar analysis applies with imperfect competition. A monopolist hires labor up to the point where the extra revenue it produces—what economists call the marginal revenue product—is equal to the wage. In competitive markets, the value of the marginal product is just equal to the price of the output times the marginal physical product, the extra quantity that is produced. In a monopoly, the marginal revenue product *(MRP)* is equal to the marginal revenue yielded by producing one more unit *(MR)* times the marginal physical product *(MPP): MRP = MR × MPP*.

The quantity of labor that will be hired is illustrated in Figure 12.14, which shows the marginal revenue product curve. It is downward sloping, for two reasons: the more that is produced, the smaller the marginal physical product (this is just the law of diminishing returns), and the more that is produced, the smaller the marginal revenue. The firm hires labor up to the point where the marginal revenue product equals the wage, point L_0. If the wage increases from w_0 to w_1, the amount of labor hired will fall, from L_0 to L_1. Thus, the demand curve for labor is downward sloping with imperfect competition, just as it is with perfect competition.

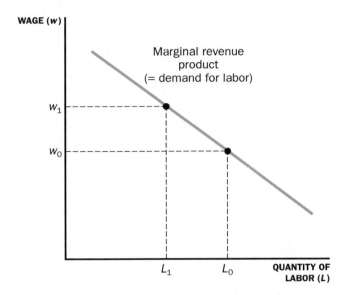

FIGURE 12.14 *Marginal Revenue Product Curve*

Firms hire labor up to the point where the marginal revenue product of an extra worker equals the marginal cost. In a competitive labor market, the marginal cost of labor is just the wage.

Chapter 13

Government Policies
Toward Competition

1. Why is government concerned with monopolies and imperfect competition? In what sense do markets with monopolies and imperfect competition result in inefficiency?

2. How have different governments attempted to address the problem posed by a natural monopoly?

3. How have governments used antitrust policies to break up monopolies, to impede the ability of any single firm to attain a dominant position in a market, and to outlaw practices designed to restrict competition?

*I*n the minds of most Americans, monopolies are not a good thing. They smell of income inequities and undemocratic concentrations of political power. To economists, however, the concern is economic efficiency. Motivated by both political and economic concerns, government has taken an active role in promoting competition and in limiting the abuses of market power. In this chapter, we review the economic effects of limited competition and look at government policies to reduce its negative effects.

The Drawbacks of Monopolies and Limited Competition

Four major sources of economic inefficiency result from monopolies and other imperfectly competitive industries: restricted output, managerial slack, insufficient attention to research and development, and rent-seeking behavior. The problems can be seen most simply in the context of mo-

nopolies (the focus here), but they also arise in imperfectly competitive markets.

Restricted Output

Monopolists, like competitive firms, are in business to make profits by producing the kinds of goods and services customers want. But monopolists can make profits in ways not available to competitive firms. One way is to drive up the price of a good by restricting output, as discussed in Chapters 11 and 12. They can, to use the popular term, gouge their customers. Consumers, by *choosing* to buy the monopolist's good, are revealing that they are better off than they would be without the product. But they are paying more than they would if the industry were competitive.

A monopolist who sets marginal revenue equal to marginal cost produces at a lower level of output than a corresponding competitive industry—an industry with the same demand curve and costs but in which there are many producers rather than one—where price equals marginal cost. Figure 13.1 shows that the monopoly output, Q_m, is smaller than the competitive output, Q_c, where the price

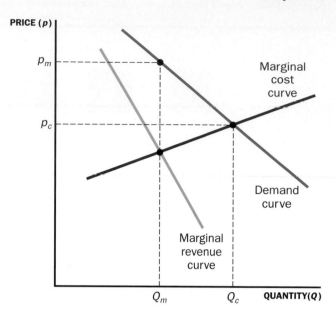

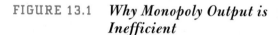

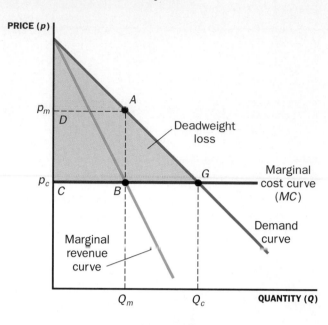

FIGURE 13.1 *Why Monopoly Output is Inefficient*

With perfect competition price is set equal to marginal cost, with output at quantity Q_c, and price p_c. A monopolist will set marginal revenue equal to marginal cost, and produce at quantity Q_m and price p_m, where the market price exceeds marginal cost.

FIGURE 13.2 *Measuring the Social Cost of Monopoly*

The higher, monopoly price removes some of the consumer surplus. Part of this loss (the rectangle *ABCD*) is simply a transfer of income from consumers to the monopolist; the remainder (the triangle *ABG*) is known as the deadweight loss of monopoly.

under competition, p_c, equals marginal cost. The price under monopoly, p_m, is higher than p_c.

The price of a good, by definition, measures how much an individual is willing to pay for an extra unit of a good. It measures, in other words, the marginal benefit of the good to the purchaser. With perfect competition, price equals marginal cost, so that in equilibrium the marginal benefit of an extra unit of a good to the individual (the price) is just equal to the marginal cost to the firm of producing it. At the monopolist's lower level of output, the marginal benefit of producing an extra unit—the price individuals are willing to pay for an extra unit—exceeds marginal cost.

By comparing the monopolist's production decision to the collective output decisions of firms in a competitive market, we can estimate the value of the loss to society when there is a monopoly. To simplify the analysis, in Figure 13.2 marginal cost is assumed to be constant, the horizontal line at the competitive price p_c. The monopolist produces an output of Q_m, at the point where marginal revenue equals marginal cost, and finds that it can charge p_m, the price on the demand curve corresponding to the output Q_m.

Two kinds of loss result, both related to the concept of consumer surplus introduced in Chapter 6. There we learned that the downward-sloping demand curve implies a bounty to most consumers. At points to the left of the intersection of the price line and demand curve, people are willing to pay more for the good than they have to. With competition, the consumer surplus in Figure 13.2 is the entire shaded area between the demand curve and the line at p_c.

The monopolist cuts into this surplus. First, it charges a higher price, p_m, than would be obtained in the competitive situation. This loss is measured by the rectangle *ABCD*, the extra price times the quantity actually produced and consumed. This loss to consumers is not a loss to society as a whole. It is a transfer of income as the higher price winds up as revenues for the monopoly. But second, it reduces the quantity produced. While production in a competitive market would be Q_c, with a monopoly it is the lower amount, Q_m. This second kind of loss is a complete loss to society, and is called the *dead weight loss* of a monopoly. Consumers lose the surplus to the right of Q_m, denoted by triangle *ABG*, with no resulting gain to the monopolist.

Some economists, such as Arnold Harberger of UCLA, have argued that these costs of monopoly are relatively small, amounting to perhaps 3 percent of the monopolist's output value. Others believe the losses from restricting output are higher. Whichever argument is right, output restriction is only one source of the inefficiencies monopolies introduce into the economy.

Managerial Slack

Chapter 7 argued that any company wants to minimize the cost of producing whatever level of output it chooses to produce. But in practice, companies already making a lot of money without much competition often lack the incentive to hold costs as low as possible. The lack of efficiency when firms are insulated from the pressures of competition is referred to as **managerial slack.**

In the absence of competition, it can be difficult to tell whether managers are being efficient. How much, for instance, should it cost for AT&T to put a call through from New York to Chicago? In the days when AT&T had a monopoly on long-distance telephone service, it might have claimed that its costs were as low as possible. However, not even trained engineers could really tell whether this was true. When competition developed for intercity telephone calls, shareholders in AT&T could compare its costs with those of Sprint, MCI, and other competitors and competition provided each company with an incentive to be as efficient as possible.

Reduced Research and Development

Competition motivates firms to develop new products and less expensive ways of producing goods. A monopoly, by contrast, may be willing to let the profits roll in, without aggressively encouraging technological progress.

Not all monopolists stand pat, of course. Bell Labs, the research division of AT&T, was a fountain of important innovations throughout the period during which AT&T was a virtual monopolist in telephone service. The laser and the transistor are but two of its innovations. But AT&T was also in a unique position. The prices it charged were set by government regulators, and those prices were set to encourage the expenditure of money on research. From this perspective, AT&T's research contribution was as much a consequence of government regulatory policy as of anything else.

In contrast to Bell Labs, the American automobile and steel industries are often blamed for falling behind foreign competition because of their technological complacence. By the end of World War II, these industries had attained a dominant position in the world. After enjoying high profits for many years, they lost a significant share of the market to foreign firms in the 1970s and 1980s. Foreign automobile and steel firms, for example, were able to undersell their U.S. counterparts during the 1980s, not only because they paid lower wages but also because their technological advances had made production processes more efficient.

More recently, there has been concern that firms with monopoly power not only engage in less innovation than they would under competition, but also seek actively to squash innovations by rivals that could reduce their market power. And even if they do not deliberately try to inhibit innovative activities of potential rivals, they may do so indirectly. Some of the most important inputs into the innovation process are prior innovations themselves, and by raising the "price" associated with these prior innovations (through their market power), monopolists reduce the incentives for follow-up innovations.

Rent Seeking

The final source of economic inefficiency under monopoly is the temptation for monopolists to expend resources in economically unproductive ways. A major example is devoting resources in obtaining or maintaining their monopoly position by deterring entry. Since the profits a monopolist receives are called monopoly rents, the attempt to acquire or maintain already existing rents by acquiring or maintaining a monopoly position in some industry is referred to as **rent seeking.**

Sometimes a firm's monopoly position is at least partly the result of government protection. Many less developed countries grant a company within their country a monopoly to produce a good, and they bar imports of that good from abroad. In these circumstances, firms will give money to lobbyists and politicians to maintain regulations that restrict competition so that they can keep their profits high. Such activities are socially wasteful. Real resources (including labor time) are used to win favorable rules, not to produce goods and services. There is thus legitimate concern that the willingness of governments to restrict competition will encourage firms to spend money on rent-seeking activities rather than on making a better product.

How much would a firm be willing to spend to gain and hold a monopoly position? The firm would be willing to spend up to the amount it would receive as monopoly profits. The waste from this rent-seeking activity can be much larger than the loss from the reduced output.

Further Drawbacks of Limited Competition

We saw in Chapter 12 that markets in which a few firms dominated were more prevalent than monopolies. Relative to monopolies, some of the inefficiencies discussed above are smaller under limited competition. Output is lower than under perfect competition but higher than under monopoly, for example. And competition to pro-duce new products (research and development) is often intense, as we shall see in Chapter 20. But other inefficiencies are worse in markets with limited competition than in monopoly markets. Firms under imperfect competition, for example, expend major resources on practices designed to deter entry, to reduce the force of competition, and to raise prices. Such expenditures may increase profits but they waste resources and make consumers worse off. Under imperfect competition firms may, for instance, maintain excess capacity to deter entry. A firm may gain a competitive advantage over its rival, not by lowering its own costs but by raising the rival's—for instance, by depriving it the use of existing distribution facilities. A firm may also spend money on uninformative (but persuasive) advertising.

e-Insight

Using the Internet to Enhance Price Discrimination

In 2000, on-line retailer Amazon.com conducted a marketing test that generated an immediate outcry of foul play from consumer advocates. Amazon.com offered different customers different prices on DVDs, and when the pricing strategy became public, it claimed that the prices were set randomly in an attempt to determine how consumers would respond to different prices. Analysts were skeptical, fearing that Amazon.com was using information about individual consumers collected from their previous purchases to fine-tune its prices. Customers from wealthier neighborhoods with a record of buying more expensive items might be receiving higher price quotes. Newspaper commentators accused Amazon.com of "unfair" pricing, and the marketing test was suspended.

Consumers have long accepted that airlines will offer different fares to travelers on the same flight, based on when tickets were purchased. Travelers who can plan in advance receive discount fares, while business travelers who need to get to a newly scheduled meeting will face much higher fares. The business traveler's demand is highly inelastic, so airlines can charge a higher price. People who can plan ahead and easily adjust travel dates and times will be more price sensitive—their demand curve is more elastic. By offering only price-sensitive customers lower fares, airlines can sell more seats without having to offer the same low price to everyone.

In imperfectly competitive markets, as we saw in Chapter 12, firms can try to boost profits through price discrimination—charging different prices to different consumers. The Internet is opening up new opportunities for this sales strategy. Here's an example of how it might work. Knowing that a blizzard is predicted for the weekend, early in the week you log onto a hardware site you have used before, to order extra lanterns, batteries, and candles. The Web site is programmed to check orders of emergency supplies from your zip code against a national weather database. Knowing that you are facing a blizzard, the hardware on-line retailer decides that your demand is inelastic, and raises the prices for purchase and delivery of the items you need.

By providing firms with more detailed information about their customers, the internet may open new possibilities for firms in imperfectly competitive markets to engage in price discrimination.

Policies Toward Natural Monopolies

If imperfect competition is as disadvantageous as the previous analysis has suggested, why not simply require that competition be perfect? To answer this question, we need to recall the reasons, discussed in Chapter 12, why competition is imperfect.

One reason is government-granted patents. Monopoly profits provide the return to inventors and innovators that is necessary to stimulate activities vital to a capitalist economy. We will discuss these issues more extensively in Chapter 20.

A second reason is that the cost of production may be lower if there is a single firm in the industry. This is the case with natural monopoly. In the case depicted in Figure 13.3, average costs are declining throughout the relevant levels of output, though marginal costs are constant. This is a case

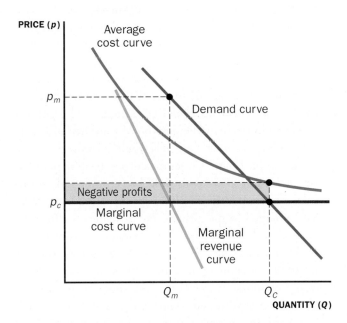

PRICE (p)

Average cost curve

p_m

Demand curve

Negative profits

p_c

Marginal cost curve

Marginal revenue curve

Q_m Q_c

QUANTITY (Q)

FIGURE 13.3 *A Problem with Regulating Natural Monopoly*

A natural monopoly will set marginal revenue equal to marginal cost, and produce at quantity Q_m and price p_m. In perfect competition, price would be equal to marginal cost, at Q_c and p_c. However, the perfectly competitive outcome is not possible in this case, since it would force the natural monopoly to produce at below its average cost, and thus to be making losses.

where there are very large fixed (overhead) costs. Natural monopolies present a difficult policy problem. Like any other firm, a natural monopolist will produce at the level where marginal revenue equals marginal cost, at Q_m, in Figure 13.3. At this level, it will charge a price of p_m, which is higher than the marginal cost at that point. Thus, it will produce less and charge more than it would if price were equal to marginal cost, as would be the case with perfect competition (the output level Q_c and the price p_c in the figure).

But in the case of natural monopoly, the very nature of the decreasing cost of technology precludes perfect competition. Indeed, consider what would happen if price were set equal to marginal cost. With a natural monopoly, average costs are declining, and marginal costs are below average costs. Hence, if price were equal to marginal cost, it would be less than average costs, and the firm would be losing money. Profits would be negative, as shown by the shaded area in the figure. If the government wanted a natural monopoly to produce at the point where marginal cost equaled price, it would have to subsidize the company to offset these losses. Taxes would have to be raised to generate the money for the subsidies, which imposes other economic costs. Moreover, the government would likely have a difficult time ascertaining the magnitude of the subsidy actually required. Managers and workers in such a firm have a way of exaggerating their estimates of the high wages and other costs they "need" to produce the required output.

Following are three different solutions governments have found to the problem of natural monopolies.

Public Ownership

In some foreign countries, government simply owns natural monopolies, such as electric power, gas, and water. There are problems with public ownership, however. Governments often are not particularly efficient as producers.

Managers often lack adequate incentives to cut costs and modernize vigorously, particularly given the fact that government is frequently willing to subsidize the industry when it loses money. In addition, public ownership brings with it a number of political pressures. Political pressure may affect where public utilities, for example, locate their plants—politicians like to see jobs created in their home districts—and whether they prune their labor force to increase efficiency. Publicly run firms may also be under pressure to provide some services at prices below marginal cost, and make up the deficit from revenues from other services, a practice referred to as **cross subsidization.** Thus, business customers of utilities are sometimes charged more, relative to the costs of serving them, than are households. There is in effect a hidden tax and a hidden subsidy; businesses are taxed to subsidize households. The same phenomenon can be seen in our most important public monopoly, the U.S. Postal Service. It charges the same price for delivering mail to small rural communities as it does to major cities, in spite of the large differences in costs. Small communities have their mail services subsidized by larger ones.

How much less efficient the government is as a producer than the private sector is difficult to determine. Efficiency comparisons between government-run telephone companies in Europe and America's private firms provided much of the motivation for the **privatization** movement—the movement to convert government enterprises into private firms. Britain sold its telephone services and some other utilities, Japan its telephones and railroads, France its banks and many other enterprises. Not all publicly run enterprises are less efficient than their private counterparts, however. For example, Canada has two major rail lines, one operated by the government and one private, which differ little in the efficiency with which they are run. This may be because competition between the two forces the government railroad to be as efficient as the private. Many of the publicly owned enterprises in France seem to run as efficiently as private firms. This may be because of the high prestige afforded to those who work in the French civil service, which allows them to recruit from among the most talented people in their country. There may also be less difference between government enterprises and large corporations—particularly when both are subjected to some market pressure and competition—than popular conceptions of inefficient government would suggest.

CASE IN POINT

Corporatizing the Air Traffic Control System

Everyday 66,000 planes fly across the country. With planes crisscrossing each other constantly in the sky, why are there not more collisions? The reason is the air traffic control system, currently run by the Federal Aviation Administration.

The system has not been kept up-to-date, however, because of budget pressure. It was one of the first government agencies to use computers on a large scale, and many of its original outdated computers are still in use. The failure to make long-run investments, combined with government restrictions on procurement and personnel, have increased the cost of running the air traffic control system, and throw into question its capacity to meet the needs of the future.

Other countries have faced similar problems and privatized the air traffic control system. There is a third alternative, between the two, called *corporatization,* entailing a government-owned corporation. The government would retain ownership, but the airlines and users along with government officials would be represented on the governing board. Under the corporatization plan, the air traffic control system would be run much like a private corporation. Its revenues would come from "user fees" charged to the airlines and airplanes that use the system, and a ticket tax. Like regular corporations it could borrow funds. Just as the government exercises safety supervision of private airlines, the government would continue to exercise safety supervision over the air traffic control system. The main difference between it and a private corporation would be that this "public" corporation could not sell shares. And its mandate would not be to maximize profits, but to provide the most efficient air traffic control services—for instance, minimizing unnecessary delay—at the lowest costs.

The major airlines were enthusiastic about the proposal. But supporters of general aviation—individually owned airplanes and corporate jets—were against it. Cross subsidization is the reason. General aviation currently pays little for the services of the air traffic control system. Corporatization would stimulate potential pressure to eliminate this subsidy. Partly as a result of the resistance of this interest group, the proposal stalled in Congress.

The problems of the government-run air traffic control system continue to mount—with increasing delays and increasing near-mishaps—as the system proves unable to keep up with the demands. ●

Regulation

Some countries leave the natural monopolies in the private sector but regulate them. This is generally the U.S. practice. Local utilities, for instance, remain private, but their rates are regulated by the states. Federal agencies regulate interstate telephone services and the prices that can be charged for interstate transport of natural gas.

The aim of regulation is to keep the price as low as possible, commensurate with the monopolist's need to obtain an adequate return on its investment. In other words, they try to keep price equal to average costs—where average costs include a "normal return" on what the firm's owners have invested in the firm. If the regulators are successful, the natural monopoly will earn no monopoly profits. Such a regulated output and price are shown in Figure 13.4 as Q_r and p_r.

Two criticisms have been leveled against regulation as a solution to the natural monopoly problem. The first is that regulations often take an inefficient form. The sources of inefficiency are several. The intent is to set prices so that firms obtain a "fair" return on their capital. But to make the highest level of profit, firms respond by increasing their amount of capital as much as possible, which can lead to too much investment. In addition, the structure of prices may be set so that some groups, often businesses, may be charged extra-high prices to make it possible to subsidize other groups. This problem of cross subsidies is no less a problem for natural monopolies if they are privately owned and regulated than it is if they are owned and operated by the government. Further, firms' incentives to innovate are weakened if every time they lower costs, regulated prices are reduced commensurately. Recently regulators have recognized that unless they reward innovation, it will not happen. They have agreed to allow the utilities to retain much of the increased profits they obtain from improved efficiency, at least for a few years.

The second criticism is that the regulators lose track of the public interest. The theory of **regulatory capture** argues

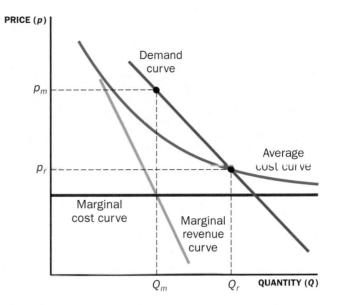

PRICE (p)

FIGURE 13.4 *Regulating Natural Monopoly*

Government regulators will often seek to choose the point on the market demand curve where the firm provides the greatest quantity at the lowest price consistent with the firm covering its costs. The point is the quantity Q_r and price p_r, where the demand curve intersects the average cost curve.

that regulators are pulled frequently into the camps of those they regulate. This could happen through bribery and corruption, but the much likelier way is that over time, employees of a regulated industry develop personal friendships with the regulators, who in turn come to rely on their expertise and judgment. Worse, regulatory agencies (of necessity) tend to hire from among those in the regulated industry. By the same token, regulators who demonstrate an "understanding" of the industry may be rewarded with good jobs in that industry after they leave government service.

Encouraging Competition

The final way government deals with the hard choices posed by natural monopolies is to encourage competition, even if imperfect. To understand this strategy, let us first review why competition may not be viable when average costs are declining over the relevant range of output.

If two firms divide the market between them, each faces higher average costs than if any one firm grabbed the whole market. As illustrated in Figure 13.5, Q_d denotes the output of each firm in the initial duopoly and AC_d its

International Perspective

The Darker Side of Privatization

In many countries around the world, the government used to own a large share of industry, and so privatization has had a marked impact on the economic landscape. One of the reasons for privatization is not only that government is inefficient but also that government enterprises provide a source of income and patronage for corrupt governments. Privatization, it was hoped, would reduce the scope for such corruption.

But privatization itself has turned out to be a major source of corruption, so much so that in many parts of the world privatization has come to be called *briberization.* By selling state assets at below market prices, those who are lucky enough to get control of these state assets win a huge bonanza. In Russia, it has made instant billionaires. And to be sure, those who control the privatization process get ample kickbacks.

The problem is that there are a host of technical details associated with conducting a sale of a large corporation. Potential buyers have to be certified—will they really come up with the cash they promise? The rules for conducting the sales have been written and implemented routinely in ways that serve the interests of some at the expense of others. As a result, the winners are not necessarily those best capable of managing the corporation, but are the most politically connected or are willing to bribe the most. This in turn has meant that the promised benefits of privatization—increased efficiency—often have not been realized. In many countries in the former Soviet Union and Eastern Europe, privatization more often has led to the stripping away of assets than to the creation of more efficient firms.

---

average costs. By undercutting its rival, a firm would be able to capture the entire market *and* have its average costs reduced. By the same token, a natural monopolist knows that it can charge a price above its average cost, AC_m, without worrying about entry. Rivals that might enter, trying to capture some of the profits, know that the natural monopolist has lower costs because of its larger scale of production, and so can always undercut them.

Even under these conditions, some economists have argued that a monopolist would not in fact charge higher than average costs, because a rival could enter any time and grab the whole market. (The zero profit equilibrium is shown in the figure at output Q_r and price $AC_r = p_r$.) On this argument, all that is required to keep prices low is potential competition. Potential competition forces prices down to p_r, where the demand curve intersects the average cost curve.

Most economists are not so optimistic about the effectiveness of potential, as opposed to actual, competition. Potential competition has not been able to keep airline prices down in those markets in which actual competition is limited to one or two carriers.

In the late 1970s and 1980s, many governments became convinced that competition, however imperfect, might be better than regulation, and began a process of deregulation. Deregulation focused on industries such as airlines, railroads, and trucking, where competition had a chance—there were, at most, limited increasing returns to scale. Government also sought to distinguish parts of an industry where competition might work from parts where competition was unlikely to be effective. In the telephone industry, for example, competition among several carriers was strong for long-distance telephone service, and there were few economies of scale in the production of telephone equipment. Accordingly, regulation of these parts of the industry was reduced or eliminated.

The virtues of competition have been borne out for the most part. Trucking—where the arguments for government regulation seemed most suspect—was perhaps the most unambiguous success story, with prices falling significantly. Railroads appear more financially sound than they did under regulation. But coal producers, who rely on railroads to ship their coal, complain that railroads have used their monopoly power to charge them much higher tariffs.

Airline deregulation has become more controversial in recent years. After its initial success—with new firms, lower fares, and more extensive routings—a rash of bankruptcies has reduced the number of airlines. Many air-

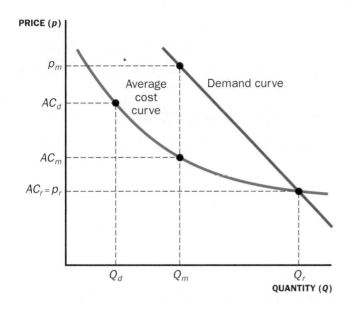

PRICE (*p*)

p_m

AC_d

AC_m

$AC_r = p_r$

Average cost curve

Demand curve

Q_d Q_m Q_r

QUANTITY (*Q*)

FIGURE 13.5 *Why Competition May Not Be Viable With Decreasing Average Costs*

If two firms share a market, each producing Q_d, one firm could double its output to Q_m, lower its cost, and undercut its rival. The larger firm has a cost advantage over the smaller competitor.

ports, including those at St. Louis, Atlanta, and Denver, are dominated by one or two carriers, and these communities often face extremely high fares. A pattern of discriminatory pricing has developed, with businessmen who cannot make reservations weeks in advance paying four or more times the fare for the same seat as a vacationer.

Deregulation has not yet extended to natural monopolies like water. But in the case of electricity a process for introducing some deregulation has begun.

WRAP-UP

Approaches to Natural Monopoly

Public ownership
Regulation
Encouraging competition

CASE IN POINT

California Electricity Deregulation

California was among the states in the forefront of electricity deregulation. Economists recognized that there were many potential suppliers of generating capacity and many potential retailers of electricity services. The only natural monopoly was in the transmission between the generators of electricity and the retailers. The old electricity companies integrated all of these functions. Breaking them up could lead to competition in all areas except transmission. Increased competition in the parts of the system where it is possible to structure competition would lead to greater efficiency and ultimately lower prices and better service—or so it was hoped.

In 2000, deregulation appeared to be a disaster, causing soaring electricity prices, shortages of generating capacity leading to brownouts and interrupted service, bankrupt electricity companies, and a massive government bailout. Clearly, things had not gone as planned. Not surprisingly, there was plenty of finger pointing. Critics blamed deregulation. Proponents said that even with deregulation, government had retained too large a role—it had put ceilings on the prices companies could charge consumers and prevented the use of long-term contracts. Well intentioned or not, these restrictions exposed the electricity companies to an impossible squeeze: high gas

Shasta Dam is a hydroelectric facility in California.

prices led to high wholesale prices for electricity that were greater than the controlled retail prices. The problem was not deregulation per se, but the way it was done. Critics countered that deregulation is extremely hard to do well. There were allegations that the firm that controlled the transmission of gas had used its monopoly power (under deregulation) to raise gas prices. Consumers would have been gouged one way or another. To be sure, the form of consumer protection provided in the California deregulation process was a recipe for disaster, but critics remained skeptical that, short of deregulation, there were any surefire ways to protect consumers. As this book goes to press, the controversy over California deregulation continues to rage. ●

Internet Connection

U.S. Department of Justice and Antitrust Laws

At http://www.usdoj.gov/atr/public/div_stats/1638.htm, the Department of Justice explains the role of antitrust laws and the role in preventing monopolies from depriving consumers of the benefits of competition.

Antitrust Policies

Only some of the failures of competition arise from natural monopolies. Other imperfections, as we have seen, are the result of sharp business practices to develop market power by deterring entry or promoting collusion. When encouraging competition does not work, government sometimes resorts to enforcing competition through antitrust policy.

As we will see, these policies have often been controversial. Consumer groups and injured businesses tend to support them, arguing that, without them, firms would focus more on competition-reducing strategies than on efficiently producing products that customers like. Many businesses, however, claim that such policies interfere with economic efficiency. For instance, even if the most efficient way to distribute its products is through exclusive territories for distributors, the firm might worry that such a contract might be illegal under *antitrust law,* the body of law designed to restrict anticompetitive practices. Government antitrust efforts have followed the ebb and flow of concern about competition versus concern about the efficiency costs of antitrust restrictions.

The U.S. government has been officially concerned about the negative consequences of imperfect competition since the late nineteenth century. Table 13.1 lists the major landmarks of antitrust policy. These take the form of legislation and relevant judicial decisions. They fall into two categories: (1) limiting market domination, and (2) curbing restrictive practices.

Limiting Market Domination

In this section, we look at how government tries to limit economic power. In the decades following the Civil War, entrepreneurs in several industries attempted to form **trusts.** These were organizations that controlled a market. One individual has a controlling interest in a firm, which in turn had a controlling interest in all the other firms in the industry. By adding more layers—firms that controlled firms that controlled firms, and so on—a relatively small ownership stake could be leveraged into enormous economic power.

A controlling interest need not be a majority interest when the shares of a company are widely held. An individual or group of individuals owning only 10 or 20 percent of the shares can frequently exercise control, since the rest of the shareholders will either split their votes or be apathetic about the outcome. Among the most famous of the nineteenth-century trusts was the oil industry trust, with Rockefeller and his partners eventually controlling 90 percent of oil sold in America between 1870 and 1899. In the early 1900s, Andrew Carnegie and J. P. Morgan merged many smaller steel companies to form U.S. Steel, which in its heyday sold 65 percent of all American steel.

Concern about these robber barons led to passage of the Sherman Antitrust Act of 1890, which outlaws "every contract, combination in the form of a trust or otherwise, or conspiracy in restraint of trade or commerce." Further, "every person who shall monopolize, or attempt to monopolize, or combine or conspire with any other person or persons, to monopolize any part of the trade or commerce among the several States, or with foreign nations, shall be

TABLE 13.1

Major Antitrust Legislation and Landmark Cases

Sherman Antitrust Act, 1890	Made acts in restraint of trade illegal.
Standard Oil and American Tobacco Cases, 1911	Broke up both firms (each of which accounted for more than 90% of their industry) into smaller companies.
Clayton Act, 1914	Outlawed unfair trade practices. Restricted mergers that would substantially reduce competition.
Establishment of the Federal Trade Commission, 1914	Established to investigate unfair practices and issue orders to "cease and desist."
Robinson-Patman Act, 1936	Strengthened provisions of the Clayton Act, outlawing price discrimination.
Alcoa Case, 1945	Alcoa, controlling 90% of the aluminum market, was found to be in violation of the Sherman Act.
Tobacco Case, 1946	The tobacco industry, a concentrated oligopoly, was found guilty of violation of the Sherman Act on the basis of tacit collusion.
Celler-Kefauver Antimerger Act, 1950	Placed further restrictions on mergers that would reduce competition.
Du Pont Cellophane Case, 1956	Broadened the definition of market. Ruled that a 20% market share was insufficient to establish market power.

deemed guilty of a misdemeanor." (A 1974 amendment made violations felonies.) Two important decisions based on the Sherman Act were the breakups of Standard Oil and American Tobacco in 1911, each of which had dominated their respective industries.

The Sherman Act was supplemented by the Clayton Act in 1914, which forbade any firm to acquire shares of a competing firm when that purchase would substantially reduce competition. The act also outlawed interlocking directorates (in which the same individuals serve as directors of several firms) among firms that were supposedly in competition. These antimerger provisions were further strengthened in 1950 by the Celler-Kefauver Antimerger Act.

The government does not care about absolute size itself. In the 1960s, huge firms called *conglomerates* were formed and brought together such disparate enterprises as a steel company, an oil company, and a company making films. For example, United Airlines bought Hertz rental cars and Westin Hotels. But while large, these conglomerates generally did not have a dominant position in any one market, and thus the antitrust laws were not concerned with them. The early antitrust laws were particularly concerned with **horizontal mergers,** with competition within a market. These are distinguished from **vertical mergers,** in which a firm buys a supplier or a distributor, amalgamating the various stages in the production process within a firm. Thus, Ford made its own steel, and General Motors bought out Fisher Body (the maker of GM's car bodies), as well as many of the specialized firms that produced batteries, spark plugs, and other components.

Under current court interpretations, market power *per se* (by itself) is also not the primary concern. To be convicted of an antitrust violation, one must show that the firm acquired its market position by anticompetitive practices or that it used its market power to engage in anticompetitive practices.

Thinking Like an Economist

Incentives and the Remedy to the Microsoft Monopoly Problem

In 2000, Judge Thomas Penfield Jackson found Microsoft guilty of violating U.S. antitrust laws. He then was faced with a difficult problem: what remedy to impose. Jackson was keenly aware of the *incentives* that Microsoft faced; its profitability depended on its ability to preserve its market power, and it therefore had strong incentives to squash innovations that might reduce that market power. For instance, Sun Microsystem had developed a language, Java, which would enable programmers to develop applications that would run not just on Microsoft's Windows operating system but on other operating systems as well. One of the reasons why Microsoft's operating system was so dominant was that rivals started with a marked disadvantage—no available applications could run on their operating system. Java would change all of that. It would result in real competition in the market for operating systems. Microsoft similarly worried that Netscape might serve as a platform through which competition in the operating system might be enhanced, and it sought to squash this threat by making its own browser, Internet Explorer, free, bundled with the Windows operating system. Microsoft had done what comes naturally to monopolists—it simply sought to maximize its long-run profits by reducing the threat of competition. The judge worried that no matter how he scolded Microsoft, or what fines he imposed, Microsoft had every incentive to continue these anticompetitive practices. Moreover, he was aware of how difficult it is sometimes to detect and prove anticompetitive behavior, and Microsoft had already demonstrated its willingness to face risks of antitrust prosecution. Hence, the only way to alter behavior was to alter incentives, and that entailed changing the structure of the enterprise. The Department of Justice proposed splitting Microsoft into two, with one company focusing on applications, and the other focusing on the operating system. The application company would have every incentive to ensure that its applications could be used on as many operating systems as possible. The hope was that Microsoft Word might then be written to work on alternative operating systems, like Linux, and if that were done, demand for these alternative operating systems would increase. And by restraining the operating system company from writing applications, it would at least prevent a repeat of what happened with Netscape and the browser market.

Some critics thought the judge, in approving the Justice Department's recommendations, went too far; others thought he did not go far enough. The former worried that there were important economies of scope—efficiencies that arose from the close interaction between those writing the operating system and those developing applications. These advantages, they contended, more than offset the disadvantages from the loss in competition. Moreover, they believed that Microsoft's monopoly power was temporary; within a few years, surely competition would erode its dominant position. Already, Linux was rapidly growing as an alternative operating system. They argued that Microsoft had achieved its dominant position by strong innovation, and it was wrong to punish this success now by breaking it up.

But critics on the other side said that at least a significant part of Microsoft's success was due to its ruthless business practices, and such behavior should not go unpunished. But there was more at stake: Microsoft represented a threat to innovation. Investment in innovation would be discouraged if investors believed that any innovation threatening Microsoft's competitive position would be squashed by Microsoft. This was the position of many Silicon Valley firms.

These critics worried that the Microsoft application company still might not write programs for other operating systems, that there might be sweetheart deals between the two companies, and argued that there were alternative ways in which Microsoft's incentives could be changed. For instance, some suggested limiting intellectual property protection—and requiring the disclosure of the code—for operating systems of a firm with a dominant position (like Microsoft) to, say, three to five years. This would mean that there would be a competitor to, say, Windows 2000—the freely available Windows 1995. Only if Windows 2000 were markedly better than Windows 1995 would people pay anything for it. This approach would enhance Microsoft's incentives to innovate. Meanwhile, application programmers would have an incentive to write programs that worked better and better with the freely available 1995 operating system. The hope was that out of this competition, consumers would benefit not only from lower prices but also from innovations, possibly leading to programs that crash less often and applications that are tailored better to the needs of particular groups of users, that run faster, and that even perform tasks currently not undertaken.

Defining Markets

The question of whether a firm dominates a market is usually phrased, "What is its size relative to the market?" The debate thus centers on what is the relevant market. We have learned that the extent to which a firm's demand curve is downward sloping, so it can raise prices without losing all its customers—its market power—is related to both the number of firms in the industry and the extent of product differentiation. The problem of defining markets for the purposes of antitrust enforcement is related to both factors.

Market Bounds   During the last quarter century, international trade has become ever more important to the United States and the world economy. This change has affected all aspects of economic analysis, including the extent of competition in many markets. Today, imports exceed 13 percent of national output—four times the level in the 1950s and 1960s.

Thus while the degree of concentration among domestic producers of automobiles has increased—three firms are responsible for more than 90 percent of all U.S. auto production—the industry has become more competitive in the 1980s and 1990s, as foreign competition has increased and as foreign companies such as Toyota and Honda have established plants in the United States. It used to be that American firms could increase their price without worrying about their consumers switching to Japanese or European imports, but no longer. Today, the degree of competition in a market must be assessed from a global viewpoint, rather than looking simply at how many firms produce a good in the United States.

Product Differentiation   While all firms that produce the same good and sell in the same location are clearly in the same market, when the goods produced by different firms are imperfect substitutes, the definitional problem is more ambiguous.

What is the market for beer? Those in the industry might claim that premium beers and discount beers are really two different markets, with relatively few customers crossing over from one to the other. In the early 1950s, Du Pont's cellophane had a virtual monopoly on the market for clear wrapping paper. In 1956, the company managed to fight off charges of monopoly by claiming that this market was part of a larger one for "wrapping materials." It claimed that brown paper was a good, though not perfect, substitute for cellophane, and in this broader market, Du Pont did not have a particularly large share (roughly 18 percent).

Legal Criteria   Today the courts look at two criteria for defining a market and market power. First, they consider the extent to which the change in prices for one product affects the demand for another. If an increase in the price of aluminum has a large positive effect on the demand for steel, then steel and aluminum may be considered to be in the same market—the market for metals. Second, if a firm can raise its price, say, by 5 percent, and lose only a relatively small fraction of its sales, then it is "large"—that is, it has market power. (In a perfectly competitive market, a firm that raises its price by 5 percent would lose all its customers, so this is a workable approach to measuring the degree of competitiveness in the market.)

Before one large company can acquire a competitor or merge with another, it must convince the government that the acquisition would not seriously interfere with competition. Thus, although Dr. Pepper made up only a small part of the soft drink market, the government was concerned that the proposed acquisition of Dr. Pepper by Coca-Cola would have a significantly adverse affect on competition in a market that was already highly concentrated.

Curbing Restrictive Practices

In addition to promoting competition by limiting the extent of concentration within an industry, the government works to limit restrictive practices. The history here begins with the 1914 Federal Trade Commission Act. The first ten words of the act read: "Unfair methods of competition in commerce are hereby declared unlawful." President Wilson defined the purpose of the new commission to "plead the voiceless consumer's case." Since then, a number of laws have been passed by Congress to make these general statements more specific.

Many of the restrictive practices targeted by the government involve the relations between a firm and its distributors and suppliers. Such practices include tying, exclusive dealing, and price discrimination. We have already encountered all three in Chapter 12. Tying requires a buyer to purchase additional items when she buys a product. Exclusive dealing is when a producer says to a firm that wants to sell its product, "If you want to sell my product, you cannot sell that of my rival." Price discrimination entails charging different customers different prices, when those price differences are not related to the costs of serving those customers. The Robinson-Patman Act of 1936 strengthened the provisions outlawing price discrimination, making it easier to convict firms engaged in the practice. Other practices discussed in Chapter 12 designed to deter entry or promote collusion are illegal as well.

The precise definition of an illegal restrictive practice has changed over time with varying court interpretations of the antitrust laws. Some practices are illegal *per se*—firms conspiring together to fix prices, for example. In 1961, General Electric, Westinghouse, and other producers of electrical equipment were found guilty of this practice. More recently, several huge price-fixing cases were prosecuted successfully, most notably against ADM (Archer Daniel Midland), involving lysine, citric acid, and high fructose corn syrup. The corporations paid more than $100 million in fines, and some of their officials went to prison. Today, however, for most practices a "rule of reason" prevails. Under a rule of reason, the practice is acceptable if it can be shown to be reasonable

business practice, designed to promote economic efficiency. The efficiency gains are balanced against the higher prices resulting from the reduced competition.

Thus, Budweiser beer delivers its product through distributors. In any area, there is only one distributor, and the distributors are not allowed to compete against one another. The New York attorney general has argued that this system, by restricting competition, raises prices. Anheuser-Busch has replied that the system of exclusive territories enhances the efficiency with which beer is delivered and is necessary to ensure that customers receive fresh beer. They have maintained that their distribution system satisfies the rule of reason, and thus far their view has been upheld by the courts.

During the 1980s, the view that markets are *normally* highly competitive, and that therefore one need have little concern about anticompetitive practices, began to have sway, especially among conservative judges appointed by presidents Ronald Reagan and George H. W. Bush. Ironically, at roughly the same time, research in economics was showing that under specific circumstances firms have strong incentives to engage in anticompetitve behavior. Nowhere was the conflict more apparent than in the area of predatory behavior—actions that a firm with market power takes to drive out entrants, to maintain its market power. For example, established airlines frequently not only match the prices of low-cost entrants, even if those prices are below their costs, but also expand capacity enormously, knowing that at comparable prices and availability, travelers will choose the established airline over the upstart. As soon as the upstart is driven out of the market, prices go up and capacity gets withdrawn. Economic theory has explained the circumstances under which it pays to engage in this kind of predatory activity. While one would not expect to see such activity in the wheat industry—what good would it do to drive out another wheat farmer—in the airline industry, entry is sufficiently hard, especially on certain routes, that driving out a newcomer may imply that the incumbent's market power would be preserved, at least long enough to compensate the incumbent for the losses it makes while driving out the newcomer. Moreover, the lesson—the losses incurred by the entrant—does not go unnoticed by other potential entrants in other markets served by the established airline. Thus, the predatory activity not only drives the entrant out of one market but also deters others from entering other markets.

Enforcing the Antitrust Laws

Today antitrust laws are on the books at both state and federal levels, and are enforced by both criminal and civil courts. The government takes action not only to break up existing monopolies but also to prevent firms from obtaining excessive market power.

The Federal Trade Commission (FTC) and the Antitrust Division of the Department of Justice are at the center of the government's efforts to promote competition. The FTC works like a law enforcement agency, investigating complaints it receives. It can provide advisory opinions on how an individual business should interpret the law, provide guidelines for entire industries, or even issue specific rules and regulations that businesses must follow. When necessary, the FTC enforces these decisions in court.

One interesting and controversial aspect of the antitrust laws is the use they make of *private* law enforcement. Any firm that believes it has been injured by the anticompetitive practices of another firm can sue, and if successful, can receive three times the dollar value of the damages and attorney fees incurred. The treble damage provision helps encourage private firms to call violations to the attention of the government. For example, MCI sued AT&T, claiming that the latter had used unfair trade practices to hurt MCI in its attempt to enter the long-distance telephone business. The jury estimated that MCI had, as a result of AT&T's activities, lost $600 million in profits, and ordered AT&T to pay triple that amount—$1.8 billion—in damages to MCI. The award was subsequently reduced on appeal to higher courts.

Two arguments favor private enforcement of antitrust laws. First, those who are injured by anticompetitive practices are in the best position to detect a violation of the law. Second, government may be lax in the enforcement of these laws because of the potential political influence of cartels and dominant firms.

On the other side of the argument are concerns about the rising costs of antitrust litigation—the number of private suits doubled between the 1960s and the 1970s. And many worry that businesses use the threat of an antitrust suit as a way of raising a rival's costs. Thus, Chrysler charged General Motors with an antitrust violation when GM proposed a joint venture with a Japanese firm, only to drop the action when it found a Japanese partner for its own joint venture.

WRAP-UP

Antitrust Policies

Objective: Ensure Competitive Marketplace
    Limit market domination
    Curb restrictive practices
Problems
    Defining markets
    Practices may *both* reduce competition *and* enhance efficiency
        Per se: practice is illegal (price fixing)
        Rule of reason: balance anticompetitive and efficiency effects
Enforcement
    Criminal
    Civil—private law enforcement, treble damages

CASE IN POINT

Coke and Pepsi Play Merger

Coca-Cola Company and PepsiCo, Inc., dominate the market for carbonated soft drinks. Early in 1986, each proposed to grow larger through acquisition. In January, PepsiCo proposed buying 7-Up, the fourth largest soft drink manufacturer, for $380 million. In February, Coca-Cola proposed buying Dr. Pepper, the third largest, for $470 million.

The mergers would have made the big even bigger. Coca-Cola and PepsiCo already held 39 percent and 28 percent of the market, respectively, while Dr. Pepper had 7 percent and 7-Up had 6 percent. The next largest firm in the market after 7-Up was R. J. Reynolds (known for Canada Dry and Sunkist), which held 5 percent of the soft drink market.

The Federal Trade Commission (FTC) announced that it would oppose the mergers. To assess the impact on competition, the government often uses in such cases what is called the Herfindahl-Hirschman index (HHI). The HHI is calculated by summing the squares of the market shares. If the industry consists of a single firm, then the HHI is $(100)^2 = 10,000$. If the industry consists of 1,000 firms, each with .1 percent of the market, then the HHI is $(.1)^2 \times 1,000 = 10$.

Thus, higher values of the HHI indicate less competitive industries.

Merger guidelines used by the federal government divide markets into three categories, with different policy recommendations. The divisions and policy recommendations are given in Table 13.2.

Before the mergers, a somewhat simplified HHI for the soft drink industry was (assuming that the 15 percent of the market not accounted for by the big five was divided equally among 15 small producers)

$$HHI = 39^2 + 28^2 + 7^2 + 6^2 + 5^2 + 15\,(1)^2$$
$$= 2{,}430.$$

If we plug in the 34 percent share that PepsiCo would have after acquiring 7-Up, the PepsiCo–7-Up merger would raise the HHI to 2,766. The two proposed mergers together would raise the HHI to 3,312.

With the announced FTC opposition to the merger, PepsiCo immediately gave up on purchasing 7-Up. Coca-Cola pushed ahead with its plan to buy Dr. Pepper until a federal judge ruled that it was a "stark, unvarnished" attempt to eliminate competition that "totally [lacked] any apparent redeeming feature."

The court case did bring a secret to the surface, however. The trial disclosed certain Coca-Cola company memos written after PepsiCo's offer for 7-Up had been made. In the memos, Coca-Cola executives expressed fear that the FTC might allow the PepsiCo merger, despite the merger guidelines. By announcing plans to buy Dr. Pepper, Coca-Cola hoped that the FTC would step in and block *both* mergers, as it did, thus preventing PepsiCo from using a merger to catch up in size to Coca-Cola. ●

SOURCES: Timothy K. Smith and Scott Kilman, "Coke to Acquire Dr. Pepper Co. for $470 Million," *Wall Street Journal*, February 21, 1986, p. 2; Andy Pasztor and Timothy K. Smith, "FTC Opposes Purchase Plans by Coke, Pepsi," *Wall Street Journal*, June 23, 1986, p. 2; Pasztor and Smith, "Coke Launched Dr. Pepper Bid to Scuttle Plans by PepsiCo, Documents indicate," *ibid.*, July 29, 1986, p. 3; Pasztor and Smith, "Coke's Plan to Buy Dr. Pepper is Blocked by U.S. Judge, Pending Decision by FTC, "*ibid.*, August 1, 1986, p. 3.

Review and Practice

Summary

1. Economists have identified four major problems resulting from monopolies and imperfect competition: restricted output; managerial slack; lack of incentives for technological progress; and wasteful rent-seeking expenditures.

2. Since for a natural monopoly average costs are declining over the range of market demand, a large firm can undercut its rivals. And since marginal cost for a natural monopoly lies below average cost, an attempt by regulators to require it to set price equal to marginal cost (as in the case of perfect competition) will force the firm to make losses.

3. Taking ownership of a natural monopoly allows the government to set price and quantity directly. But it also subjects an industry to political pressures and the potential inefficiencies of government operation.

4. In the United States, natural monopolies are regulated. Government regulators seek to keep prices as low and quantity as high as is consistent with the natural monopolist covering its costs. However, regulators are under political pressure to provide cross subsidies and are prone to being "captured" by the industry they are regulating.

5. In some cases, competition may be as effective as public ownership or government regulation at keeping prices low.

6. Antitrust policy is concerned with promoting competition, both by making it more difficult for any firm to

TABLE 13.2

Herfindahl-Hirschman Index	
Level of HHI	**Policy recommendation**
Less than 1,000, unconcentrated	Mergers allowed without government challenge
Between 1,000 and 1,800, moderately concentrated	Mergers challenged if they raise the industry HHI by more than 100 points
Above 1,800, concentrated	Mergers challenged if they raise the industry HHI by more than 50 points

dominate a market and by restricting practices that interfere with competition.

7. Under the "rule of reason," companies may seek to defend themselves from accusations of anticompetitive behavior by claiming that the behavior also leads to greater efficiency. In such cases, courts must often decide whether the potential efficiency benefits of restrictive practices outweighs their potential anticompetitive effects.

Key Terms

managerial slack
rent seeking
cross subsidization
privatization
regulatory capture
trusts
horizontal mergers
vertical mergers

Review Questions

1. What does it mean when an economist says that monopoly output is "too little" or a monopoly price is "too high"? By what standard? Compared with what?

2. Why might a monopoly lack incentives to hold costs as low as possible?

3. Why might a monopoly lack incentives to pursue research and development opportunities aggressively?

4. What might an economist regard as a socially wasteful way of spending monopoly profits?

5. Explain why the marginal cost curve of a natural monopoly lies below its average cost curve. What are the consequences of this?

6. If government regulators of a natural monopoly set price equal to marginal cost, what problem will inevitably arise? How might government ownership or regulation address this problem? What are the problems of each?

7. What is the regulatory capture hypothesis?

8. Explain the difference between a horizontal and a vertical merger.

9. Explain how the government uses antitrust policies to encourage competition, by making it more difficult for a firm to dominate a market and by curbing restrictive practices. What are some of the problems in implementing antitrust policy and some of the current controversies surrounding it?

Problems

1. Before deregulation of the telephone industry in 1984, AT&T provided both local and long-distance telephone service. A number of firms argued that they could provide long-distance service between major cities more cheaply than AT&T, but AT&T argued against allowing firms to enter only the long-distance market. If those other firms (which had no technological advantage) could actually have offered long distance service more cheaply, what does that imply about cross subsidies in AT&T's pricing of local and long-distance service? What would have happened if AT&T had been required to continue offering local service at the same price, but competition had been allowed in the long-distance market?

2. "The stories of $400 hammers and $1,000 toilet seats purchased by the Department of Defense prove that the private sector is more efficient than the public sector." Comment.

3. Explain the incentive problem involved if regulators assure that a natural monopoly will be able to cover its average costs.

4. Explain how some competition, even if not perfect, may be an improvement for consumers over an unregulated natural monopoly. Explain why such competition will not be as good for consumers as an extremely sophisticated regulator; and why it may be better than many real-world regulators.

5. Should greater efficiency be a defense against an accusation of an antitrust violation?

Chapter 14

Imperfect Information in the Product Market

Key Questions

1. When does the market price affect the quality of what is being sold? How does the fact that consumers believe price affects quality influence how firms behave?

2. When customers have trouble differentiating good from shoddy merchandise, what are the incentives firms have to produce good merchandise? What role does reputation play?

3. Why is it that, in the same market, identical or very similar goods will sell at different prices? How does the fact that search is costly affect the nature of competition?

4. How does advertising affect firms' demand curves and profits? Why may the firms in an industry be better off if they collectively agree not to advertise?

5. What has government done to address some of the problems resulting from imperfect information? Why do these efforts have only limited success?

*I*t was never any secret to economists that the real world did not match the model of perfect competition. Theories of monopoly and imperfect competition such as those covered in Chapters 12 and 13 have been put forth from Adam Smith's time to the present.

Another limitation of the model of perfect competition has recently attracted attention: its assumption of perfect information—that market participants have full information about the goods being bought and sold. By incorporating *imperfect information* into their models, economists have come a long way in closing the gap between the real world and the world depicted by the perfect competition, perfect information model of Part Two.

This chapter provides an overview of the major information problems of the product market, the ways in which market economies deal with them, and how the basic model of Part Two has to be modified as a result. In the following chapter, we will see how information problems affect labor markets (Chapter 15). We start our analysis of information problems by examining a market you may be familiar with—the used-car market.

The Market for Lemons and Adverse Selection

Have you ever wondered why a three-month-old used car sells for so much less—often 20 percent less—than a new car? Surely cars do not deteriorate that fast. The pleasure of owning a new car may be worth something, but in three months, even the car you buy new will be "used." But a couple of thousand dollars or more is a steep price to pay for this short-lived pleasure.

George Akerlof of the University of California at Berkeley has provided a simple explanation, based on imperfect information. Some cars are worse than others. They have hidden defects which become apparent to the owners only after they have owned the cars for a while. Such defective cars are called lemons. One thing after another goes wrong with them. While warranties may reduce the financial cost of having a lemon, they do not eliminate the bother—the time it takes to bring the car into the shop, the anxiety of knowing there is a good chance of a breakdown. The owners, of course, know they have a lemon and would like to pass it along to someone else. Those with the worst lemons are going to be the most willing to sell their car. At a high used-car price, they will be joined by owners of better-quality cars who want to sell their cars, say, to buy the latest model. As the price drops, more of the good used cars will be withdrawn from the market as the owners decide to keep them. And the average quality of the used cars for sale will *drop*. We say there is an **adverse selection** effect. The mix of those who elect to sell changes adversely as price falls.

Figure 14.1 shows the consequences of imperfect information for market equilibrium in the used-car market. Panel A depicts, for each price (measured along the horizontal axis), the average quality of used cars being sold in the market. As price increases, average quality increases. Panel B shows the supply curve of used cars. As price increases, the number of cars being sold in the market increases, for all the usual reasons. The demand curve is also shown. This curve has a peculiar shape: upward as well as downward sloping. The reason is that as price decreases, the average quality decreases. But demand depends not just on price but on quality—on the "value" being offered on the market. If, as price falls, quality deteriorates rapidly,

then quantity demanded will actually *fall* as price falls—consumers are getting less for their dollars. The equilibrium is depicted in panel B.

The situation just described is characterized by **asymmetric information** between sellers and buyers. That is, the seller of the used car has more information about the product than the buyer. Many markets are characterized by asymmetric information. One of the consequences of asymmetric information is that there may be relatively few buyers and sellers, far fewer than there would be with perfect information. Economists use the term **thin** to describe markets in which there are relatively few buyers and sellers. In some situations, a market may be so thin as to be essentially nonexistent. When there are important markets missing from an economy, it is said to have an **incomplete** set of markets. The used-car market, for example, is a thin one. Buyers may know that there are some legitimate sellers, those who for one reason or another always want to drive a new car. But mixed in with these are people who are trying to dump their lemons. The buyers cannot tell the lemons apart from the good cars. Rather than risk it, they simply do not buy. (Of course, the fact that demand is low drives down the price, increasing the proportion of lemons. It is a vicious cycle.)

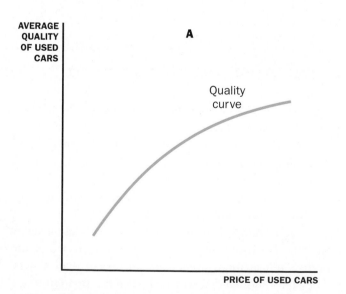

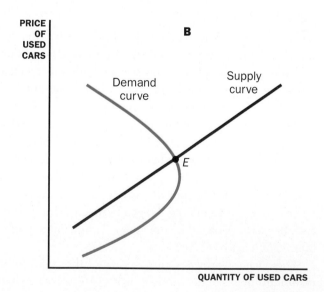

FIGURE 14.1   *A Market with Lemons*

Panel A shows the average quality of a used car increasing as the price increases. Panel B shows a typical upward-sloping supply curve, but a backward-bending demand curve. Demand bends back because buyers know that quality is lower at lower prices, and they thus choose to buy less as the price falls. Panel B shows the market equilibrium is at point *E*.

Signaling

If you have a good car and you want to sell it, you would like to persuade potential buyers that it is good. You could tell them that it is not a lemon, but why should they believe you? There is a simple principle: *actions speak louder than words*. What actions can you take that will convince buyers of the quality of your car?

The fact that Chrysler is willing to provide a five-year, fifty-thousand-mile warranty on its cars says something about the confidence Chrysler has in its product. The warranty is valuable, not only because it reduces the risks of having to spend a mint to repair the car, but also because the buyer believes that Chrysler would not have provided the warranty unless the chances of defects were low. Actions such as this are said to **signal** higher quality. A signal is effective if it differentiates goods—here between high-quality cars and low-quality cars. The cost to the producer of a five-year guarantee is much higher for a car that is likely to fall apart within five years than for a car that is unlikely to break down. Customers know this, and thus can infer that a firm willing to provide this warranty is selling high-quality cars.

When you go to a car dealer, you want to know that it will still be around if you have trouble. Some firms signal that they are not fly-by-nights by spending a great deal of money on their showroom. This indicates that it would be costly for them to just pack up and leave. (There are, of course, other reasons why they may spend money on a fancy showroom.)

Actions such as providing a better guarantee or a larger showroom are taken not just for the direct benefit that the consumer receives from them, but because those actions make consumers believe that the product is a better product or the firm is a better firm to deal with. In a sense, the desire to convey information "distorts" the decisions made relative to what they would have been in a perfect-information world. For example, if customers receive no direct benefit from the quality of the showroom, the cost of building and maintaining a luxurious showroom is a waste of resources.

Judging Quality by Price

There is still another clue that buyers use to judge the quality of what they are about to purchase. This is price. Consumers make inferences about the quality of goods based on the price charged. For example, they know that on average, if the price of a used car is low, the chance of getting a lemon is higher. Many if not most sellers know that buyers know this.

In markets with imperfect information, firms *set* their prices. And in setting their prices, they take into account what customers will think about the quality of the good being sold. Concerns about consumers (correctly or incorrectly) making inferences about quality impede the effectiveness of price competition. In the used-car example, we saw that as price rose, the average quality of cars on the market increased. But if firms think customers believe that cars being sold at a lower price are lemons—that the quality deteriorates more than the price declines—they will not lower the price because to do so would scare away customers who perceive that such "bargains" must be lemons. Under such circumstances, even if firms cannot sell all they would like at the going price, they will still not cut prices.

A situation can be sustained in which there is a seeming excess supply of goods. Imperfect information means that equilibrium will be achieved away from the intersection of supply and demand curves.

Information problems fascinate economists because they turn the basic competitive model upside down. Economists have long recognized that prices convey critical information about scarcity in a market economy. But only recently have the other informational roles of prices—and their consequences—become clear. Sellers will manipulate prices when they can to control the information conveyed. Buyers, for their part, see through these manipulations. And their concern that the seller is trying to pass off a lemon discourages trade. When information problems like these are severe, markets are thin or even nonexistent. Alternatively, price competition may be limited. Even when there is an excess supply of goods, firms may not cut their prices and the market may not clear.

WRAP-UP

Solutions to Adverse Selection Problems in Market Economies

Signaling
Judging quality by price

The Incentive Problem

We have seen throughout this book that providing incentives that motivate individuals to make the best choices is one of the central economic problems. The central problem of incentives, in turn, is that individuals do not bear the full consequences of their actions. The multi-billion-dollar collapse of the savings and loan associations in the 1980s—though fraud may have played a part—is attributable largely to incorrect incentives. Because S&L deposits were guaranteed by the government, depositors had no incentive to check on what the S&Ls were doing. For the same reason, the owners of many S&Ls had an incentive to take high risks. If they were successful, they kept the gains. If they failed, the government picked up the loss.

When there is a misalignment of incentives such as occurred in the S&Ls, we say there is a problem of **moral hazard.** The term originated in the insurance industry. Individuals who purchased insurance had an inadequate incentive to avoid the insured-against event—indeed, if they were insured for more than 100 percent of the loss, they would have an incentive to bring about the event. Doing so was considered immoral, hence the term. Today, economists think of these simply as incentive problems, with no moral overtones. Thus, an individual who has fire insurance has less of an incentive to avoid a fire. The benefit to him, for instance, of putting in a sprinkler system may not be worth the cost—though it would if he took into account the expected cost to the fire insurance company. That is why the fire insurance company is likely to require a sprinkler system, or to give a discount on the premium if an individual has one. It would then pay to have a sprinkler system installed.

In the basic competitive model of Part Two, private property and prices provide incentives. Individuals are rewarded for performing particular tasks. The incentive problem arises when individuals are not rewarded for what they do, or when they do not have to pay the full costs for what they do. In our economy, incentive problems are pervasive.

In product markets, firms must be given the incentive to produce quality products. Again, the incentive problem is an information problem. If customers could always tell the quality of the product they were getting, firms that produced higher-quality products would always be able to charge a higher price, and no company could get away with producing shoddy goods. Most of us have had the experience of going to a newly established restaurant, having a good meal, and then returning to find that the quality had deteriorated. Evidently something went wrong with incentives.

Market Solutions

In simple transactions, incentive problems can be solved by stipulating penalties and rewards. You would like a document typed. You sign a contract with someone to pay him $25 to deliver the typed document by tomorrow at 5:00 P.M. The contract stipulates that $.50 will be deducted for each typographical error, and $1.00 for every hour the paper is late. The contract has built-in incentives for the paper to be delivered on time and without errors.

But most transactions, even relatively simple ones, are more complicated than this one. The more complicated the transaction, the more difficult it is to solve the incentive problem. You want your grass mowed, and your neighbor's twelve-year-old son wants to mow it. You want him to take care of your power mower. When he sees a rock in the mower's path, he should pick it up. But what incentive does he have to take care of the mower? If you plan to charge him for repairs if the mower does hit a rock, how can you tell whether the rock was hidden by the grass? If he owned his own mower, he would have the appropriate incentives. That is why private property combined with the price system provides such an effective solution to the incentive problem. But your neighbor's son probably does not have the money to buy his own power mower. Then an incentive problem is inevitable. Either you let him use your lawn mower and bear the risk of his mistreating it. Or you lend him money to buy his own, in which case you bear the risk of his not paying you back.

Many private companies must hire people to run machinery worth hundreds or thousands of times more than a lawn mower. Every company would like its workers to exert effort and care, to communicate clearly with one another and take responsibility. Beyond private property and prices, the market economy has other partial solutions to these incentive problems, loosely categorized as contract solutions and reputation solutions.

Contract Solutions

When one party (firm) agrees to do something for another, it typically signs a contract, which specifies the conditions of the transaction. For example, a firm will agree to deliver a product of a particular quality at a certain time and place. There will normally be "escape" clauses. If there is a strike, if the weather is bad, and so on, the delivery can be postponed. These **contingency clauses** may also make the payment depend on the circumstances and manner in which the service is performed.

Contracts attempt to deal with incentive problems by specifying what each of the parties is to do in each situation. But no one can think of every contingency. And even if they could, it would take them a prohibitively long time to write down all the possibilities.

There are times when it would be extremely expensive for the supplier to comply with all the terms of the contract. He could make the promised delivery on time, but only at a very great cost; if the buyer would only accept a one-day delay, there would be great savings. To provide suppliers with the incentive to violate the terms only when it is really economically worthwhile, most contracts allow delivery delays, but with a penalty. The penalty gives the supplier the incentive to deliver in a timely, but not overly costly, way.

Sometimes the supplier may think it simply is not worth complying with the contract. If he violates the agreement, he is said to be in *breach* of the contract. When a contract has been breached, the parties usually wind up in court, and the legal system stipulates what damages the party breaking the contract must pay to the other side. Contracts, by stipulating what parties are supposed to do in a variety of circumstances, help resolve incentive problems. But no matter how complicated the contract, there will still be ambiguities and disputes. Contracts are incomplete and enforcement is costly, and thus they provide only a partial resolution of the incentive problem.

Reputation Solutions

Reputation plays an extremely important role in providing incentives in market economies. A reputation is a form of guarantee. Even though you may know that you cannot collect from this guarantee yourself—it is not a "money-back" guarantee—you know that the reputation of the person or company will suffer if it does not perform well. The incentive to maintain a reputation is what provides firms with an incentive to produce high-quality goods. It provides the contractor with an incentive to complete a house on or near the promised date.

For reputation to be an effective incentive mechanism, firms must lose something if their reputation suffers. The "something" is, of course, profits. For reputations to provide incentives, there must be profits to lose.

Thus, we see another way that markets with imperfect information differ from markets with perfect information.

In competitive markets with perfect information, competition drives price down to marginal cost. In markets in which quality is maintained as the result of a reputation mechanism, whether competitive or not, price must remain above marginal cost.

Why, in markets where reputation is important, doesn't competition lead to price cutting? If price is "too low," firms do not have an incentive to maintain their reputation. Consumers, knowing this, come to expect low-quality goods. This is another reason why cutting prices will not necessarily bring firms more customers. Most consumers, at one time or another, have encountered companies that tried to live off their reputation. For example, Head skis were the high-quality skis in the early 1970s. At high prices, of course, demand was limited. When the company lowered its price, sales increased. Consumers, knowing about the high quality, bought the skis thinking they were getting a bargain. But bargains are not so easy to come by. At the lower prices, profits were lower and Head had little incentive to maintain its reputation.

Reputation as a Barrier to Entry Competition is frequently very imperfect in markets where reputation is important. The necessity of establishing a reputation acts as an important barrier to entry and limits the degree of competition in these industries. Given a choice between purchasing the product of an established firm with a good reputation and the product of a newcomer with no reputation at the same price, consumers will normally choose the established firm's good. In choosing a new TV you may choose a Sony over an equally priced new brand with no track record for quality and reliability. The newcomer must offer a sufficiently low price, often accompanied with strong guarantees. In some cases, newcomers almost have

WRAP-UP

Solutions to Incentive Problems in Market Economies

Private property and prices
Contracts
Reputations

to give away their product in order to establish themselves. Entering a market thus becomes extremely expensive.

The Market for Health Insurance

The market for health insurance provides an illustration of the impact imperfect information can have. It is estimated that over 40 million Americans are without health insurance, and even those with insurance often feel dissatisfied with their coverage. Health insurance became one of the key campaign issues during the 1992 presidential election. While President Clinton's proposal for health care reform was ultimately rejected, health care has remained an important topic of debate. Understanding the problems with health care and the policy debates requires an understanding of the market for health insurance, a market in which information, or rather the lack of information, plays a major role.

The United States spends a larger fraction of its national income on health care but has a lower life expectancy and greater infant mortality than many other developed countries. Information problems and associated market failures are a large part of the reason. Moral hazard—the reduced incentive to economize on health care expenditures when a large fraction of the tab is picked up by insurance firms—is one source of market failure. Adverse selection—the attempt of each insurance firm to take the lowest-risk patients, leaving those with high medical costs to others—is another.

In the standard model, consumers are assumed to be well informed. But consumers go to the doctor for information, to find out what is wrong with them. Moreover, they typically must rely on the doctor's advice. Economists worry that under a fee-for-service system, where doctors are paid for each of the services they perform, there is an incentive to provide excessive care. Excessive means the marginal cost exceeds the marginal benefit to the patient. Making sure that health care dollars are used efficiently requires that the marginal benefits of a particular treatment, prescription, or procedure are balanced against the marginal costs. Consumers can be expected to balance marginal benefits and costs when they purchase most goods, but health care differs because consumers may lack the information needed to assess the potential benefits of care and because they typically bear only a small fraction of the marginal costs if covered by insurance.

Today, more and more doctors work in "managed care" organizations, or HMOs, where doctors are paid a flat fee up front. They then provide whatever care is needed and receive no extra income from doing extra procedures. On average, doctors working in managed care cost less and perform fewer surgeries, with no noticeable effect on patient health. Critics worry that with managed care, doctors have an incentive to underprovide care, since they receive no compensation at all for providing care at the margin. Newspaper accounts of managed care programs denying patients necessary care have galvanized legislators to enact a patients' bill of rights. But while admitting that there may be occasional abuses, advocates argue that any managed care organization that did so repeatedly would lose its patients. Reputations can provide effective discipline. When employers provide a level playing field between fee-for-service and managed care plans—contributing an equal amount for each and making employees pay for the extra costs if they choose the more expensive fee-for-service plans—more than half their employees, on average, choose the managed care plan. Evidently, the employees do not feel the benefits of the extra services provided under fee-for-service are worth the extra cost.

CASE IN POINT

Buying Health Insurance

Have you ever seen an advertisement for health insurance which stresses that no physical exam is required? What can economists, and the notion of adverse selection, tell us about who is likely to buy such insurance and whether it is a "good" deal?

Health insurance is designed to let individuals share the risks that are associated with health needs. To see how such insurance might work, let's suppose there is a medical condition that affects 1 person in 100. This condition can be treated through surgery, but the cost of the surgery is $50,000. Let's assume that the chances any one individual will need the surgery is the same for everyone. Without insurance, 99 of the 100 will not have to pay anything, but the unlucky person who turns out to need the surgery will have to pay $50,000. With insurance, 100 people could each contribute $500. Whoever ends up needing the operation has the surgery paid for by the insurance. The other 99 are "out" $500, but they have been insured against the much larger cost if they had turned out to be the one who needed the op-

will see this as a good deal—they will purchase the insurance. But the individuals at low risk will not think the insurance is worth $500 and they will not buy it. So the insurance company finds that only the bad risks buy the insurance—an example of adverse selection.

To continue our example, suppose 50 of our 100 individuals are in the high-risk group and buy the insurance. The insurance company collects $500 from each, for a total of $25,000, only half of what is needed to pay for an operation. So the insurance company has to charge $1,000 in order to break even. From the perspective of the likelihood of someone in the general population needing the operation (1 in 100), it looks like the insurance company is overcharging—$500 being the fair price. And at the premium of $1,000, the low-risk people find the insurance too unattractive. They see themselves as providing a large subsidy to the high-risk individuals. But if the insurance company cannot distinguish between high-risk and low-risk individuals, it will have to charge more because of the adverse selection effect. So if you think you are low risk for health problems, an insurance plan that does not require a medical exam is likely to be a bad deal. The adverse selection problem also explains why health and life insurance companies typically require medical exams—their incentive is to insure only healthy individuals, or at least to make sure that the premiums charged reflect the risks. ●

The Search Problem

A basic information problem is that consumers must find out what goods are available on the market, at what price, and where. Households must learn about job opportunities as well as opportunities for investing their savings. Firms, by the same token, have to figure out the demand curve they face, and where and at what price they can obtain inputs. Both sides of the market need, in other words, to find out about their opportunity sets.

In the basic competitive model of Part Two, a particular good sells for the same price everywhere. If we see what look like identical shoes selling for two different prices at two neighboring stores—$25 at one and $35 at the other—it must mean (in that model) that the stores are really selling different products. If the shoes are in fact identical, then what the customer must be getting is a combination

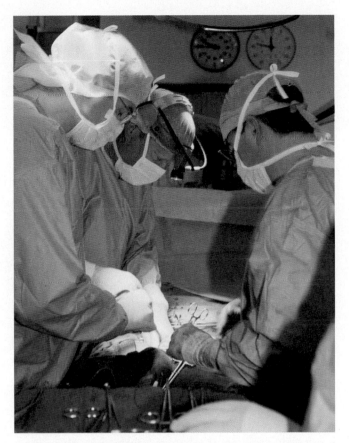

Health insurance is designed to let individuals share the risks of needing expensive health care, such as surgery.

eration. If all 100 were equally likely to need the operation, and the cost of the surgery is $50,000, then charging everyone $500 is the fair price for the insurance. A private company could offer this insurance since it will collect enough from selling the insurance to cover the amount it expects to have pay out.[1] Most people would probably find the option of paying $500 to avoid the much larger cost of the operation a good deal.

But suppose some people know that they are more likely to need the operation than others are. Perhaps, like heart disease, the likelihood an individual will need the surgery is higher if there is a family history of the disease. Suppose other individuals know they are extremely unlikely to need the surgery. Now, if an insurance company offers insurance for $500, all the individuals at high risk

---

[1] For simplicity, this ignores any administrative cost the insurance firm would have to include in the price charged to those who buy the insurance.

Thinking Like an Economist

Incentive and Information Problems in Health Care

The soaring costs of Medicare (the government program providing health insurance for the aged) have prompted a number of proposals from policy makers, among these a proposal to establish *medical savings accounts* (MSAs). MSAs, which were established by legislation passed in 1996, would encourage individuals to buy health insurance with large deductibles and co-payments. For instance, the insurance company would only pay 80 percent of the amount in excess of $1,000; in that case, there is a $1,000 deductible and a 20 percent co-payment. With such insurance, individuals have an *incentive* to economize on their use of health care, and the premium would, presumably, be considerably lower than the costs under the current system. Each individual would receive a check, representing the difference between what it costs the government under the old system and the premium under the new privately provided policies. Individuals could deposit this money in a tax-exempt MSA and use it to pay for the uninsured costs, deductible, and co-payments.

Sounds like a good system: improved incentives reduce costs for both government and individuals. But the problems of adverse selection and incentives are often intertwined, and critics say that adverse selection effects will dominate the incentive effects. The rich and healthy will take the MSA option, transferring to the standard option when their health deteriorates. Thus, the *apparent* cost under the new option will be lower, but mostly because of the adverse selection effect, not improved incentives. Meanwhile, the same adverse selection effect will drive up the average costs of those remaining under the standard option. Thus, the net costs to the government could actually increase. This problem could be rectified if there were some way of adjusting payments to reflect the health condition of the individual. Such "risk adjusters" have been discussed for several years, but so far, no one has devised a satisfactory method of making the appropriate risk adjustments. The problem is a lack of information—there is no way of ascertaining how risky each individual is.

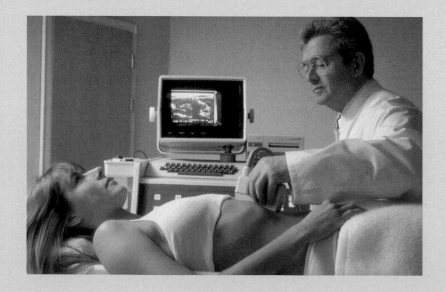

Information Technology and the New Economy

Perhaps the defining characteristic of the new economy is the role of information technologies. These new technologies allow the collection, analysis, and transmission of vast amounts of information—to a greater extent than anyone could have conceived even ten years ago. The new technologies no doubt will improve the flow of information in all markets, including product markets. Some have suggested that it will completely eliminate the need for middlemen such as retailers and wholesalers. Instead consumers will be able to deal directly with producers. Those claims are greatly exaggerated.

To be sure, in some markets information technologies will diminish the role of middlemen. Already, many consumers are buying computers, insurance, books, and airline tickets over the Internet. The Internet will make an enormous difference in the dissemination of prices about homogeneous products—a particular form of wheat, or steel, or a new Buick with power steering, leather seats, and so forth.

But the hardest choices often involve differences in quality and characteristics. In fact, most retailers see their job as searching among producers and making judgments about the quality of the goods different manufacturers produce. Retailers who establish a reputation do so on the basis of the quality they offer at a particular price range. Much of the relevant information concerning quality and characteristics cannot be conveyed easily over the Internet, so consumers need direct access to the product. For instance, without actually sitting in a driver's seat, how can an auto shopper detect whether the controls of a car feel right? The same point can be made for various other products. Thus, not only is it unlikely that information technology will make middlemen obsolete, but also it may make them even more competitive and efficient. They will be able to search the globe for the best prices, check out the producers to make sure they are reliable and that the quality is good, and thereby help create a truly global marketplace.

package, the shoes plus the service of having the shoes fitted. And the more expensive store is providing a higher-quality service.

In fact, however, essentially the same good may be sold at different stores for different prices. And you may not be able to account for the observed differences in prices by differences in other attributes, like the location of the store or the quality of the service provided. In these cases, we say there is **price dispersion.** If the act of finding out all prices were costless (or information perfect, as in the standard competitive model), consumers would search until they found the cheapest price. And no store charging more than the lowest price on the market would ever have any customers. But with costly information, a high-price store may still be able to keep some customers—and its higher profit per sale offsets its lower level of sales. Thus, price dispersion can persist.

Price dispersion, combined with variations in quality, means that households and firms must spend considerable

energies in searching. Workers search for a good job. Firms look for good workers. Consumers search for the lowest prices and best values. The process by which this kind of information is gathered is called **search.**

Search is an important, and costly, economic activity. Because it is costly, a search stops before you have *all* the relevant information. You know there are bargains out there to be found, but it is just too expensive to find them. You might worry that you will be disappointed the day or week after buying a new computer, if you find it for sale at 10 percent less. But in truth, there should be no regrets. There was a chance that you would not find a better buy, or that next week you would not even be able to buy it at the price offered today. You looked at these risks, the costs of further search, and the benefits of being able to get the computer today and use it now (compared with the benefits of waiting and the chance of finding it at a still lower price). After a careful balancing of the benefits and costs of further waiting, you decided to purchase now.

In Figure 14.2 the horizontal axis plots the time spent in searching, while the vertical axis measures the expected marginal benefit of searching. On the one hand, the expected marginal benefit of searching declines with the amount of search. In general, people search the best prospects first. As they search more and more, they look at less and less likely prospects. Say you are looking to buy a used car. You might first look in the newspaper, then go to local car dealers. Finally, you might drive the streets looking for cars with "for sale" signs. On the other hand, the marginal cost of additional search rises with increased search. This reflects the fact that the more time people spend in search, the less time they have to do other things. The opportunity cost of spending an extra hour searching thus increases. The amount of search chosen will be at the point where the expected marginal benefit just equals the marginal cost.

An increase in price (or quality) dispersion will normally increase the return to searching—there is a chance of picking up a really good bargain, and the difference between a good buy and a bad buy is larger. Thus, the expected marginal benefit curve shifts up, and the amount of search will increase from T_1 to T_2.

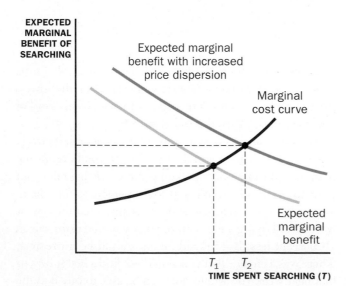

FIGURE 14.2   *Search*

Consumers search to the point where the expected marginal benefit of further search equals the marginal cost. Increased price dispersion increases the marginal benefit of search and thus leads to more search.

Search and Imperfect Competition

Firms know search is costly, and take advantage of that fact. They know they will not lose all their customers if they raise their prices. And if a store lowers its price slightly, it will not immediately attract *all* the customers from the other stores. Customers have to learn about the competitive price advantage, and this takes time. Moreover, even when people do hear of the lower price, they may worry about the quality of the goods being sold, the nature of the service, whether the goods will be in stock, and so on.

The fact that search is costly means that the demand curve facing a firm will be downward sloping. Competition is necessarily imperfect.

Consider, for instance, the demand for a portable CD player. When you walk into a store, you have some idea what it should sell for. The store asks $70 for it. You may know that somewhere you might be able to purchase it for $5 less. But is it worth the additional time, trouble, and gasoline to drive to the other stores that might have it, looking for a bargain? Some individuals are willing to pay the extra $5 simply to stop having to search. As the store raises its price to, say, $75, $80, or $85, some people who would have bought the CD player at $70 decide that it is worth continuing to shop around. The store, as it raises its price, loses some but not all of its customers. Thus, it faces a downward-sloping demand curve. If search were costless, everyone would go to the store selling the CD player at the lowest price, and any store charging more than that would have no sales. Markets in which search is costly are, accordingly, better described by the models of imperfect competition introduced in Chapters 12 and 13.

Search and the Labor Market

The economics of search—a comparison of the costs and benefits of search—has important applications in the labor market. New entrants into the labor market typically have much higher job turnover than older workers. While older workers typically stay with an employer for years, younger workers often leave after a period of a few weeks or months. How can we explain these differences?

To begin, contrast a job search for a sixty-year-old and a thirty-year-old. Even should the sixty-year-old find a better job, he is likely to enjoy the job for at most a few years. For the thirty-year-old, the marginal benefit of additional search is much greater: There is at least the *possibility* that he will stay with the new employer for two decades or more. Each worker evaluates the marginal benefit and the marginal cost of additional search, but their evaluations yield different answers.

Two other factors reinforce these outcomes. First, the younger worker is likely to be less informed both about her own preferences (what she likes and does not like) and about the job market. Moving from job to job provides additional information about both. Secondly, employers recognize this, so there is little stigma associated with a younger worker moving about. By contrast, employers worry that an older worker who is looking for a new job may know that he is about to be dismissed or demoted because of inadequate job performance. Excessive job mobility for an older worker is often interpreted as a "bad" signal.

Internet Connection

Job Search

The Internet's ability to disseminate information makes it a natural way for workers seeking new jobs and firms seeking new employees to exchange information. Several private companies have established sites for matching workers and jobs. One of the best known is Monster.com (http://www.monster.com). The Monster.com network consists of sites in over a dozen countries. In Canada, their address is http://www.monster.ca/, in France it is http://www.monster.fr/ , and in India it is http://www.monsterindia.com/. The U.S. government has also taken advantage of the Internet; all current job openings in the federal government are listed at http://www.usajobs.opm.gov/.

Search and Information Intermediaries

Some firms play an important role by gathering information and serving as intermediaries between producers and customers. These firms are part of the market for information discussed in the beginning of the chapter. One of the functions of good department stores, for example, is to economize on customers' search costs. The stores' buyers seek out literally hundreds of producers, looking for the best buys and the kinds of goods that their customers will like. Good department stores earn a reputation for the quality of their buyers. Customers still have a search problem—they may have to visit several department stores—but doing so is far less costly than if they had to search directly among producers. In addition magazines like *Consumer Reports* provide readers with detailed information on product quality and price, saving consumers considerable search cost. Today, numerous Internet sites allow consumers to compare prices offered by different on-line sellers, again helping to reduce search costs.

Advertising

Customers have an incentive to find out where the best buys are. Firms have a corresponding incentive to tell customers about the great deals they are providing. Companies may spend great sums on advertising to bring information about their products, prices, and locations to potential customers.

In the classic joke about advertising, an executive says, "We know half the money we spend on advertising is wasted, but we don't know which half." That joke says a lot about the economics of advertising. In the United States, many firms spend 2 percent, 3 percent, or more of their total revenues on advertising. Today, total expenditures on advertising are over $170 billion, with slightly more than half spent on national advertising. To add some perspective, these expenditures are only slightly less than spending on all federal, state, and local public assistance.

Advertising can serve the important economic function of providing information about what choices are available. When a new airline enters a market, it must convey that information to potential customers. When a new product is developed, that fact has to be made known. When a business is having a sale, it must let people know. A firm cannot just lower its price and wait for customers if it wants to be successful. Companies need to recruit new customers and convey information in an active way.

But not all advertising is designed to convey factual information about product prices or characteristics. Take the typical beer or car advertisement. It conveys almost no information about the product but seeks to convey an image, one with which potential buyers will identify. That these advertisements succeed in persuading individuals either to try a product or to stick with that product and not try another is a reminder that consumer behavior is much more complicated than the simple theories of competitive markets suggest. Few people decide to go out and buy a car or a new suit solely because they saw a TV ad. But decisions about what kinds of clothes to wear, what beer to drink, what car to drive, are affected by a variety of considerations, including how peers view them or how they see themselves. These views, in turn, can be affected by advertising.

To emphasize the different roles played by advertising, economists distinguish between *informative advertising* and *persuasive advertising.* The intent of the former is to provide consumers with information about the price of a good, where it may be acquired, or what its characteristics are. The intent of persuasive advertising is to make consumers feel good about the product. This can even take the form of providing "disinformation"—to confuse consumers into thinking there is a difference among goods when there really is not.

Advertising and Competition

Advertising is both a cause and a consequence of imperfect competition. In a perfectly competitive industry, where many producers make identical goods, it would not pay any single producer to advertise the merits of a good. You do not see advertisements for wheat or corn. If such advertising were successful, it would simply shift the demand curve for the product out. The total demand for wheat might increase, but this would have a negligible effect on the wheat grower who paid for the advertisement. If all the wheat farmers could get together, it might pay them to advertise as a group. In recent years, associations representing producers of milk, oranges, almonds, raisins, and beef have done just that.

If, however, advertising can create in consumers' minds the perception that products are different, then firms will face downward-sloping demand curves. There will be imperfect competition. If imperfect competition exists, advertising can be used to increase the demand for a firm's products.

Advertising and Profits

The objective of advertising is not only to change the slope of the demand curve—by creating the perception of product differences—but also to shift the demand curve out, as in Figure 14.3. The increase in advertising by one firm may divert customers away from rivals, or it may divert customers away from other products. Advertising a particular brand of cigarettes may be successful in inducing some smokers to switch brands and in inducing some nonsmokers to smoke.

The increase in profits from shifting the demand curve consists of two parts. First, the firm can sell the same quantity it sold before but at a higher price—p_3, rather than p_1. Profits then increase by the original quantity (Q_1) times the change in price (p_3–p_1), the rectangle *ABCD* in the figure. Second, by adjusting the quantity it sells, it can increase profits still further. This is because the advertising has shifted the firm's marginal revenue curve up. As usual, the imperfectly competitive firm sets marginal revenue equal to marginal cost, so it increases output from Q_1 to Q_2. The additional profits thus generated are measured by the area between the marginal revenue and marginal cost curves between Q_1 and Q_2. Marginal cost remains the same, so the

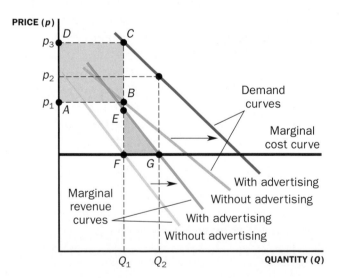

FIGURE 14.3   *How Advertising Can Shift the Demand Curve*

Successful advertising shifts the demand curve facing a firm. When the imperfect competitor equates its new marginal revenue with its old marginal cost, it will be able to raise both its price and its output.

second source of extra profits is the shaded area *EFG*. The net increase in profits is the area *ABCD* plus the area *EFG* minus the cost of advertising.

So far, in studying the effect of an increase in advertising on one firm's profits, we have assumed that other firms keep their level of advertising constant. The effect of advertising on both industry and firm profits is more problematical once the reactions of other firms in the industry are taken into account. To the extent that advertising diverts sales from one firm in an industry to another, advertising may, in equilibrium, have little effect on demand. For example, assume that Nike shoe ads divert customers from Reebok to Nike and vice versa for Reebok ads. Figure 14.4 shows the demand curve facing Reebok (1) before advertising, (2) when only Reebok advertises, and (3) when both companies advertise. The final demand curve is the same as the initial demand curve. Price and output are the same; profits are lower by the amount spent on advertising. We have here another example of a prisoner's dilemma. If the firms could cooperate and agree not to advertise, they would both be better off. But without such cooperation, it pays each to advertise, regardless of what the rival does. The government-mandated ban on cigarette advertising on radio and TV may have partially solved this prisoner's dilemma for the tobacco industry—in the name of health policy.

In practice, when all cigarette firms advertise, the ads do more than just cancel each other out. Some people who might not otherwise have smoked are persuaded to do so, and some smokers are induced to smoke more than they otherwise would have. But the shift in the demand curve facing a particular firm when all companies advertise is still much smaller than it is when only that firm advertises.

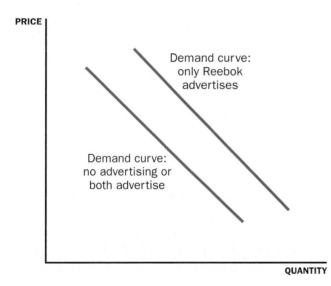

FIGURE 14.4 *How Advertising Can Cancel Other Advertising*

If only one company advertises, the demand curve for its product may shift out. But if both companies advertise, the resulting demand curve may be the same as it would if neither advertised.

WRAP-UP

Consequences of Imperfect Information

Adverse selection problems—quality may be affect by price
  Thin or nonexistent markets
  Signaling
  Markets may not clear
Incentive problems—weak or misdirected incentives
  Importance of contracts, with contingency clauses
  Reputations, with price exceeding marginal cost
Search problems
  Price dispersion
  Imperfect competition
Advertising
  To change slope of demand curve—create perception of product differences
  To shift demand curve

The Importance of Imperfect Information

The modern economy has sometimes been called "the information economy." This is partly because the major advances in computer technology have greatly enhanced the capacity to process information, and partly because such a large fraction of economic activity revolves around collecting, processing, and disseminating information. Personnel officers focus on finding out about potential employees; lending officers attempt to assess the likelihood of default of potential borrowers; market researchers try to determine

CASE IN POINT

Advertising Orange Juice

In the simple model of perfect competition, a new orange juice company would announce that its product was ready, match or beat the price prevailing in the market, and sell its product. When Procter and Gamble entered the orange juice business in 1983, it competed by setting the price for its Citrus Hill juice a little lower than the price for established competitors like Tropicana and Minute Maid, and by blanketing the country with Citrus Hill coupons. But Procter and Gamble evidently felt that something more was needed to get its product started. According to *Business Week,* it set an advertising and promotion budget of $75 to $100 million. (By comparison, only $2.5 billion worth of orange juice was being sold in a year by all existing companies.)

There are two lessons to be drawn from this and many similar episodes. First, by spending significant amounts of money on advertising, manufacturers demonstrate their belief that offering a lower price is not a sufficient way of competing. Second, manufacturers must believe that advertising helps to make people perceive their product as unique, even when, as in the case of orange juice, most consumers probably can barely distinguish the different brands. Companies are able to take advantage of such perceptions to earn higher profits.[2]

the potential market for some new product; large retail stores have buyers scouring the world for new suppliers of the clothes they sell. But no matter how much information we have, we seldom have as much as we would like.

Not only is information imperfect, but different people have different information. Information is asymmetric. The seller of a car knows more about his car's problems than the buyer. The worker may know more about his strengths and weaknesses than does the firm where he is interviewing for a job. The borrower may know more about some of the contingencies that may affect his ability to repay the loan than the lender. Because the parties to a transaction do not always have an incentive to be perfectly truthful, it may be difficult for the more informed party to convey convincingly what he knows to others.

[2]*Source: Business Week,* October 31, 1983.

In recent years, economists have come to agree that such imperfections of information fundamentally alter how individuals and markets behave. The fact that individuals and firms typically make decisions based on imperfect information affects the behavior of markets in various ways. Firms and individuals compensate for the scarcity of information. In many markets where problems of adverse selection and moral hazard arise, firms adjust prices to convey information about quality. Individuals and firms may attempt to signal information about their characteristics and work to establish a reputation.

Review and Practice

Summary

1. The basic competitive model assumes that participants in the market have perfect information about the goods being bought and sold and their prices. In the real world, information is often imperfect. Economists have modified the basic model to include a number of limitations on information.

2. A problem of adverse selection may arise when consumers cannot judge the true quality of a product. As the price of the good falls, the quality mix changes adversely, and the quantity demanded at a lower price may actually be lower than at a higher price.

3. Producers of high-quality products may attempt to signal that their product is better than those of competitors, for instance, by providing better warranties.

4. When consumers judge quality by price, there may be some price that offers the best value. Firms will have no incentive to cut prices below this "best value" price, even when, at this price, the amount they would be willing to supply exceeds demand. As a result, the market can settle in an equilibrium with an excess supply of goods.

5. When there is perfect information, private property and prices provide correct incentives to all market participants. When information is imperfect, two methods of helping provide correct incentives are contracts with contingency clauses, and reputations. For firms to have an incentive to maintain a reputation, there must be profits. The equilibrium price can exceed marginal cost. Reputation may serve as a barrier to entry.

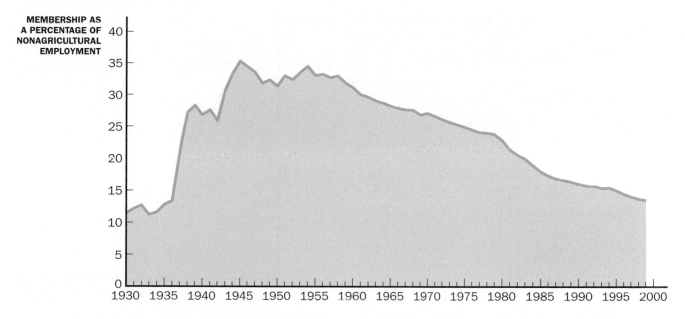

MEMBERSHIP AS A PERCENTAGE OF NONAGRICULTURAL EMPLOYMENT

FIGURE 15.1 *Unionization of the U.S. Labor Force*

The percentage of the U.S. labor force belonging to unions increased sharply in the 1930s and early 1940s but has been largely declining since 1950.

SOURCE: *Historical Statistics of the United States, Colonial Times to 1970, Employment and Earnings* (various issues).

during World War II, when the government encouraged unionization in all military plants. But since then, unions have had only limited success in recruiting new members, so the union share of nonagricultural employment has been falling. It fell below 20 percent in 1984, where it remains today. In fact, not only has the union share been declining, but also the actual number of unionized workers has been falling. Today there are about 17 million union members, 1 million less than there were in 1960.

These figures hide the even greater decline of unions in the private sector. In 1960 the percentage of union members working in the public sector was only 6 percent. Today it is more than 37 percent. Today only one out of ten nongovernment workers belongs to a union. Why the recent and continuing decline?

One explanation is that, whether as a result of union pressure or technological progress, working conditions for workers have improved enormously. Workers see less need for unions.

A second reason is related to the changing nature of the American economy. Unions have declined as the traditionally unionized sectors (like automobiles and steel) have weakened, and the service sector, in which unions have been and continue to be weak, has grown.

Third, unions may be less effective in competitive markets. When competition is limited, there are monopoly (or imperfect competition) profits or rents. Unions may be successful in obtaining for their workers a share in those rents. But when markets are competitive, firms cannot charge more than the market price for their goods, and if they are to survive, they simply cannot pay their workers more than the competitive wage.

In the late nineteenth and early twentieth centuries, for example, high wages in shoe and textile mills in New England drove plants to the nonunionized South. High wages also drive American firms to manufacture abroad. Unless unions manage to ensure that their workers are more productive than average, it is only when these sources of competition are restricted that unions can succeed in keeping their wages above average for long. In this view, the increased competition to which American industry was subjected in the 1970s and 1980s, both from abroad and from the deregulation of trucking, oil, airlines, banking, telephone service, and so on, led to a decline in the ability of unions in the private sector to garner higher wages for their workers.

A final explanation of the growth and decline of unions is the changing legal atmosphere. When laws support or encourage unions, unions prosper. When they do not, unions wither. Thus, the Wagner Act set the stage for the growth of unions in the 1930s. The Taft-Hartley Act paved the way for their decline in the post–World War II era.

Economic Effects

The source of union power is collective action. When workers join together in a union, they no longer negotiate as isolated individuals. The threat of a strike (or a work slowdown) poses many more difficulties for an employer than does the threat of any single employee quitting.

In the perfectly competitive model of labor markets, workers are price takers, facing a given market wage. But in situations where there is a downward-sloping demand curve for labor, as in Figure 15.2,[1] unions have some power to be price setters. As a result of this power, a worker at a given level of skill who works in a unionized establishment will be paid more than a comparable worker in a competitive industry. The firm would like to hire that lower-priced, nonunion worker, and the nonunionized worker could easily be induced to move, but the firm has a union contract that prevents it from doing so. But as the union raises the price of labor (the wage), firms will employ fewer workers. Higher wages are obtained at the expense of lower employment. In the figure, when wages rise from the competitive level w_c to w_m, employment is reduced from L_c to L_m.

Short-Run Gains at the Expense of Long-Run Losses
Sometimes unions can increase both employment and wages, at least for a time. They present the employer with, in effect, two alternatives: either pay a high wage *and* maintain an employment level above the labor demand curve for that wage, or go out of business. If the employer already has sunk costs in machines and buildings, he may concede to the union demands. In effect, the union takes away some of the employer's monopoly profits or return to capital. In competitive markets, where there are no monopoly profits, the higher wages can only

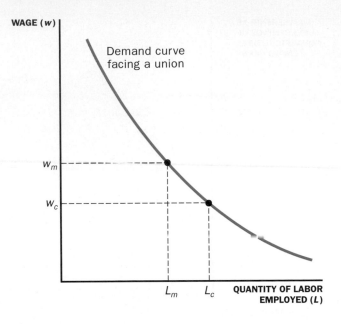

FIGURE 15.2   *The Union as a Monopoly Seller of Labor*

Unions can be viewed as sellers of labor, with market power. When they increase their wage demands, they reduce the demand for their members' labor services.

come out of employers' return to capital. But these employers will lose interest in investing in more capital. As capital wears out, the employer has less and less to lose from the union threat. As he refuses to invest more, jobs decrease. Even if the union makes short-run gains, they come at the expense of a long-run loss in jobs.

Effects on Nonunion Workers
The gains of today's union members not only may cost future jobs, but also may be at the expense of those in other sectors of the economy, for two reasons. First, the higher wages may well be passed on to consumers in the form of higher prices, particularly if product markets are not perfectly competitive. Second, the increased wages (and reduced employment) in the union sector drive down wages in the nonunionized sector, as the supply of nonunion labor increases. Some argue the opposite—that high union wages "pull up" wages in nonunion firms. The nonunion firms may, for instance, pay higher wages to reduce the likelihood of unionization. In particular sectors this effect is important, but most economists believe that the overall effect on nonunion workers is negative.

---

[1]Chapter 9 showed how the demand curve for labor is derived in competitive markets. Firms hire labor up to the point where the wage equals the value of the marginal product of labor. The derivation of the demand curve for labor in monopolies and imperfectly competitive markets follows along similar lines. Firms hire labor up to the point where the marginal revenue, the extra revenue they obtain from selling the extra output they produce from hiring an extra unit of labor, is equal to the wage.

Job Security and Innovation

The economy as a whole benefits from innovation, but particular groups are likely to suffer. In an innovative economy, those workers who are dislocated by new inventions are expected to learn new skills and seek out new jobs. Without labor shifting in response to changes in demand (resulting from either new technologies or changes in tastes), the economy will be inefficient.

Technological changes may threaten the job security unions seek for their members. As a result, unions have attempted to retard innovations that might decrease the demand for their members' labor services. Job transitions are necessary for economic efficiency, but they are costly and the costs are borne largely by the workers. Before the advent of unions and laws providing unemployment compensation, the human toll was considerable. Individuals could not buy insurance against these employment risks, but they could form unions, and union attempts to enhance job security were a response to this important problem. Today many countries are looking for ways of insulating workers against the risks of job transition without impeding the labor mobility that is so important for economic efficiency. For instance, the Swedish government has set up major programs to facilitate job transitions and job retraining.

Unions and Politics

We have seen that the fortunes of unions depend, to a large extent, on the legal environment in which they operate. Unions have also learned that what they cannot get at the bargaining table they may be able to obtain through the political process. For example, they have actively campaigned for higher minimum wages.

At the same time, unions have shown in their political stances that they recognize the economic forces that determine both the strength of their bargaining positions and, more generally, the level of wages. Thus, they have been active supporters of policies of high employment. They have sought to restrict imports from abroad (believing that this will increase the demand for American products and therefore the demand for labor). And historically they have been proponents of restrictions on immigration (recognizing that increases in the supply of labor lead to reductions in wages).

Finally, unions have been strong advocates, through the political process, of safer working conditions. Today, the Occupational Safety and Health Administration (OSHA) attempts to ensure that workers are not exposed to unnecessary hazards. OSHA seeks to make the kinds of episodes such as occurred in the asbestos industry, where workers were exposed to life-threatening risks, much less likely today.

Limits on Union Power

In the United States, no union has a monopoly on *all* workers. At most, a union has a monopoly on the workers currently working for a particular firm. Thus, the power of unions is partly attributable to the fact that a firm cannot easily replace its employees. When a union goes on strike, the firm may be able to hire some workers, but it is costly to bring in and train a whole new labor force. Indeed, most of the knowledge needed to train the new workers is in the hands of the union members. While one bushel of wheat may be very much like another, one worker is not very much like another. Workers outside the firm are not perfect substitutes for workers, particularly skilled ones, inside.

The Threat of Replacement

In the industries in which skills are easily transferable across firms, or where a union has not been successful in enlisting the support of most of the skilled workers, a firm can replace striking workers, and union power will be limited. Caterpillar, a manufacturer of tractors and road-making equipment, weathered a prolonged strike by the UAW beginning June 21, 1993. Eventually management announced that if workers did not return to their jobs, they would be replaced. The union caved in shortly after the firm made good on its threat.

In many cases, however, workers' skills are firm-specific. Just as, from the employers' perspective, workers outside the firm are not perfect substitutes for workers within, from the workers' perspective, one job is not a perfect substitute for another. Thus, there is often value both to workers and to firms in preserving ongoing employment relationships. The two parties are tied to each other in what is referred to as a *bargaining relationship*. The bargaining strengths of the two sides are affected by the fact that a firm, at a cost, can obtain other employees, and employees, at a cost, can get other jobs. The total amount by which the two sides together are better off continuing their relationship than ending it is referred to as the *bargaining surplus*. A large part of the negotiations between unions and management is about how to split this surplus.

The Threat of Unemployment

Unions have come to understand that in the long run, higher wages—other things being equal—mean lower levels of employment. When job opportunities in general are weak, concern about the employment consequences of union contracts increases.

This was evident in the early 1980s, as a deep recession threatened a number of union jobs, especially in the automobile industry, which also faced the threat of Japanese imports.

In the round of union negotiations that began in 1981, Ford Motor Company was the first auto company to settle with the UAW. In the new thirty-month contract, the UAW agreed to give up annual wage increases for two years, to defer what had been automatic increases in wages in response to increases in the cost of living, and to eliminate a number of paid personal holidays. The contract also provided for new employees to be paid at only 85 percent of the normal rate, thus creating a two-tier wage system. For its part, Ford offered a moratorium on closing any plants, a guarantee that extra profits arising during the term of the contract would be shared with workers, increased worker participation in decision making, and greater job security for workers. General Motors made a similar deal a few months later, and Chrysler was able to negotiate a better deal because of its even worse financial condition. The dollar value of the total concessions from the union was estimated at about $3 billion for the contract period. Similar wage cuts occurred in the airline and steel industries, among others.

The deal between Ford and the UAW set the pattern for auto labor contracts in the 1980s. Unions made wage concessions in return for job security. For example, in 1984, in return for wage concessions, GM agreed not to lay off for the next six years any worker with at least one year's seniority who was displaced by new technology. Instead, such workers would stay on at their full salary while they were retrained and relocated.

Wage Differentials

The basic competitive model suggests that if the goods being sold are the same, prices will also be the same. Wages are the price in the labor market; but even in the absence of unions, similar types of workers performing similar types of jobs are sometimes paid quite different wages. For example, some secretaries are paid twice as much as others. How can economists explain differences like these?

They begin by pointing to **compensating wage differentials.** Understanding compensating wage differentials begins with the observation that although different jobs may have the same title, they can be quite different. Some jobs are less pleasant, require more overtime, and are in a less convenient location. These are **nonpecuniary attributes** of a job. Other nonpecuniary attributes include the degree of autonomy provided the worker (that is, the closeness with which her actions are supervised) and the risk she must bear, whether in a physical sense or from the variability in income. Economists expect wages to adjust to reflect the attractiveness or unattractiveness of these nonpecuniary characteristics. Compensating wage differentials arise because firms have to compensate their workers for the negative aspects of a job.

Other differences are accounted for by differences in the productivity of workers. These are *productivity wage differentials.* Some workers are much more productive than others, even with the same experience and education.

Compensating and productivity wage differentials fall within the realm of the basic competitive model analysis. But other wage differentials are due to imperfect information. It takes time to search out different job opportunities. Just as one store may sell the same object for a higher price than another store, one firm may hire labor for a lower wage than another firm. The worker who accepts a lower-paying job simply because he did not know about the higher-paying one down the street faces an *information-based differential.*

Limited information has important implications for firms. First, in the standard competitive model, firms face a

---

WRAP-UP

Unions and Imperfect Competition in the Labor Market

Economic effects:

    Higher wages for union members, with fewer union jobs and lower wages for nonunion members

    Improved job security, sometimes at the expense of innovation and economic efficiency

    Minimum wages, restrictions on imports, improved working conditions, other gains achieved through the political process

Determinants of union power:

    Political and legal environment

    Economic environment: threat of replacement and unemployment

horizontal supply curve for labor. If they raise wages slightly above the "market" wage, they can obtain as much labor as they want. In practice, mobility is more limited. Even if workers at other firms knew about the higher wage offer, they might be reluctant to switch. They may worry that they are not well matched for the job, or that the employer is offering high wages because the work is unattractive.

Second, firms worry about the quality of their workforce. If an employer offers a higher wage to someone working for another firm, and the worker accepts, the employer might worry about the signal his action sends about the quality of the worker. Did the worker's current employer—who presumably knows a lot about the worker's productivity—fail to match the job offer because the worker's productivity does not warrant the higher wage? Does the worker's willingness to leave demonstrate a "lack of loyalty," or an "unsettled nature"—in which case, he may not stick with the new firm long enough to make his training worthwhile? These concerns again impede labor mobility—as employers prefer to keep their existing labor force even when there are lower-paid workers with similar credentials whom they might recruit at a lower wage.

There are a variety of other impediments to labor mobility, including the costs of moving from one city to another.

Different groups of individuals may differ in their mobility. For instance, older workers may be much more reluctant to move than younger workers. Sometimes, firms take advantage of these differences, to pay lower wages. Knowing that older workers will not leave even if wages fail to keep pace with inflation, employers may hold back raises from them. This provides a rationale for employers to engage in age discrimination in wage setting.

Discrimination

Discrimination is said to occur if two workers of seemingly similar *work-related* characteristics are treated differently. Paying higher wages to more educated workers is not discrimination, as long as the higher level of education is related to higher productivity. If older workers are less productive, then paying them lower wages is not discrimination. But if older workers are just as productive as younger workers, then taking advantage of their lower mobility *is* discrimination.

Forty years ago, there was open and outright discrimination in the labor market. Some employers simply refused to hire African Americans. Today much of the discrimination that occurs is more subtle. Firms seek to hire the best workers they can for each job at the lowest cost possible, operating with imperfect information. In making predictions about future performance, employers use whatever information they have available. On average, employers may have found that those receiving a degree from a well-established school are more productive than those receiving a degree from a less established college. Of the African Americans and Hispanics who have managed to get a college education, more may have gone to the less established schools. Screening the applicant pool to pick those with degrees from well-established colleges effectively screens out many African Americans and Hispanics. This more subtle form of discrimination is called **statistical discrimination.**

Some discrimination is neither old-fashioned prejudice nor statistical discrimination. Employers may just feel more comfortable dealing with people with whom they have dealt in the past. In a world in which there is so much uncertainty about who is a good worker, and in which a bad worker can do enormous damage, top management may rely on certain trusted employees for recommendations. And such judgments are inevitably affected by friendships and other ties. Many claim that if discrimination is to be eliminated, this form of discrimination, based on "old boy networks," has to be broken.

When firms pay lower wages to, say, women or minorities, it is called **wage discrimination.** Today, wage discrimination is perhaps less common than **job discrimination,** where disadvantaged groups have less access to better-paying jobs. Women are often said to face a "glass ceiling": they can climb up to middle management jobs but can't get beyond that to top management.

Some market forces tend to limit the extent of discrimination. If a woman is paid less than a man of comparable productivity, it pays a firm to hire the woman. Not to hire her costs the firm profits. To put it another way, the firm pays a price for discriminating. If there are enough firms that put profits above prejudice, then the wages of women will be bid up toward the level of men of comparable productivity.

Beginning in the 1960s, the government has taken an increasingly active stance in combatting discrimination. In 1964, Congress passed the Civil Rights Act, which prohibited employment discrimination and set up the Equal Employment Opportunity Commission to prosecute cases of discrimination. The reach of these laws was extended in 1975 when the government banned age discrimination.

Beyond this, the federal government has required its contractors to undertake **affirmative action.** They must actively seek out minorities and women for jobs, and actively seek to promote them to better-paying positions. In order to be effective, affirmative action has occasionally taken the form of quotas that specify that a certain number or fraction of positions be reserved for minorities or women. Critics claim that quotas are discriminatory—they imply that a minority individual would be chosen over a more qualified white male. One of the objectives of antidiscrimination laws was to discourage thinking in racial or gender terms. Courts have reaffirmed this, allowing quotas only in special circumstances such as redressing the effects of specific instances of past discrimination.

WRAP-UP

Explanations of Wage Differentials

Unions: Unions may succeed in obtaining higher wages for their workers.

Compensating differentials: Wage differences may correspond to differences in the nature of the job.

Productivity differentials: Wage differences may correspond to differences in the productivity between workers.

Information-based differentials: Wage differences may reflect the fact that workers do not have perfect information about the opportunities available in the market, and employers do not view all workers as perfect substitutes.

Imperfect labor mobility: Differentials will not be eliminated by individuals moving between jobs.

Discrimination: Wage differentials and hiring and promotion decisions can sometimes be traced to nothing more than racial or gender differences.

Motivating Workers

The discussion to this point has treated workers as if they were machines. Workers have a price—the wage—analogous to the price of machines. But even to the most profit-hungry and coldhearted employer, people are different from ma-

chines. They bring adaptability and a multitude of skills and experiences to a job. Most machines can only do one task, and even robots can only do what they are programmed to do. However, machines have one advantage over humans. Except when they break down, they do what they are told. But workers have to be motivated if they are to work hard and to exercise good judgment.

This can be viewed as an information problem. In the basic competitive model of Part Two, workers were paid to perform particular tasks. The employer knew perfectly whether the worker performed the agreed-upon task in the agreed-upon manner. If the worker failed to do so, he did not get paid. The pay was the only form of motivation required. But in reality, workers frequently have considerable discretion. Employers have limited information about what a worker is doing at each moment. So they have to motivate their workforce to exercise its abilities to the fullest.

To motivate workers, employers use both the carrot and the stick. They may reward workers for performing well by making pay and promotion depend on performance, and they may punish workers for shirking by firing them. Sometimes a worker is given considerable discretion and autonomy; sometimes he is monitored closely. The mix of carrots and sticks, autonomy and direct supervision, varies from job to job and industry to industry. It depends partly on how easy it is to supervise workers directly and how easy it is to compensate workers on the basis of performance.

Piece Rates and Incentives

When workers can be paid for exactly what they produce, with their pay increasing for higher productivity and falling for lower productivity, they will have appropriate incentives to work hard. The system of payment in which a worker is paid for each item produced or each task performed is called a **piece-rate system.** But relatively few Americans are paid largely, let alone exclusively, on a piece-rate system. Typically, even workers within a piece-rate system get a base pay *plus* additional pay, which increases the more they produce.

Why don't more employers enact a piece-rate system, if it would improve incentives? One major reason is that piece rates leave workers bearing considerable risk. A worker may have a bad week because of bad luck. For example, salesmen, who are often paid commissions on the basis of sales—a form of piece rate—may simply find the demand for their products lacking, no matter how hard they have worked.

A firm, by providing a certain amount of guaranteed pay, gives the worker a steady income and reduces the risk she must bear. But with lower piece-rate compensation, the worker has less incentive to work hard. There is thus a trade-off between risk and incentives. Compensation schemes must find some balance between offering security and offering incentives linked to worker performance. In many jobs, employers or managers achieve this balance by offering both a guaranteed minimum compensation (including fringe benefits) and bonuses that depend on performance.

A second reason more employers do not use piece-rate systems is a concern for quality. For workers on an assembly line, for example, the quantity produced may be easily measured, but quality cannot. If the workers' pay just depends on the number of items produced, the worker has an incentive to emphasize quantity over quality. The result may be less profitable for the firm than a lower level of higher-quality output.

In any case, most workers are engaged in a variety of tasks, only some of which can easily be defined and rewarded by means of a piece-rate system. For example, although employers would like experienced workers to train new workers, employees who are paid on a piece-rate system have little incentive to do this, or to help their co-workers in other ways. Similarly, when salesmen are paid on the basis of commissions, they have little incentive to provide information and service to potential customers whom they perceive as not likely to be immediate buyers. Even if providing information enhances the likelihood that a customer will return to the store to buy the good, there is a fair chance that some other salesperson will get the commission. To see this effect at work, visit a car dealer's showroom, make it clear that you are not going to buy a car that day, and see what service you get.

Efficiency Wages

When output is easily measured, then the carrot of basing pay at least partially on performance makes sense. And when effort is easily monitored, then using the stick of being fired for failure to exert adequate effort makes sense. But monitoring effort continuously is often expensive. An alternative is to monitor less frequently, and impose a big penalty if the worker is caught shirking. One way of imposing a big penalty is to pay above-market wages. Then, if a worker is fired, he suffers a big income loss. The higher the wage, the greater the penalty from being fired. Similarly, re-

warding workers with higher pay who are observed to be working hard whenever they are monitored provides incentives for workers to continue to work hard.

These are examples where higher wages help motivate workers and lead to increased productivity. There are additional reasons why it may pay a firm to pay high wages. High wages reduce labor turnover, lead to more loyalty and higher-quality work by employees, and enable the firm to attract more productive workers. For all of these reasons it may pay firms to pay high wages—higher than are absolutely necessary to recruit the desired number of workers. The theory that higher wages increase workers' net productivity, either by reducing labor turnover, by providing better incentives, or by enabling the firm to recruit a higher-quality labor force, is called the **efficiency wage theory.** While conventional theory emphasizes that increased productivity leads to higher wages, efficiency wage theory emphasizes that higher wages lead to increased productivity.

Efficiency wage theory provides an explanation for some wage differentials. In jobs where it is very costly to monitor workers on a day-to-day basis, or where the damage a worker can do is very great (where, for instance, by punching one wrong button the worker can destroy a machine), employers are more likely to rely on high wages to ensure that workers perform well.

These "wages of trust" may explain why wages in more capital-intensive industries (that require massive investments) are higher for workers with otherwise comparable skills than wages in industries using less capital. They may also explain why workers entrusted with the care of much cash (which they could abscond with) are paid higher wages than are other workers of comparable skills. It is not so much that they receive high wages because they are trustworthy, but that they become more trustworthy because they receive high wages—and the threat of losing those high wages encourages honest behavior.

Other Incentives

Other important incentives to increase job performance are enhanced promotion possibilities for those who perform well, with pay rising with promotions. But it is often hard to determine the difficulty of the task a worker is performing. One way to figure out who is performing well is to set up a contest among workers, with the winner receiving some valuable prize, like a cash bonus. Consider a firm trying to figure out how much to pay its sales force when it is promoting a new product. If a salesperson is successful, does that represent good salesmanship, or is the new product able to "sell itself"? All sales representatives are in roughly the same position. The representative who sells the most gets a bonus—and wins the contest.

At the top end of the corporate hierarchy, the top executives of America's largest firms are paid much higher average salaries than their counterparts in many other industrial economies, often running into the millions of dollars. Why is this? Economists continue to debate the issue. Some interpret these salaries as the payoffs of contests, others as reflecting the large contributions of these managers or as wages of trust. But some suspect that top managers have enough control over the firm to divert a considerable amount (though but a small fraction) of a firm's resources to their own betterment in the form of higher compensation.

Does minimum-wage legislation help or hurt low-income workers?

CASE IN POINT

Minimum Wages

Legislating a minimum wage below which it is illegal to hire workers has been sharply criticized by economists as hurting exactly the people it is designed to help—those at the bottom of the wage scale.

Critics base their reasoning on the traditional demand and supply model of Part Two. There, an increase in wages above the market equilibrium results in lower employment. Those who manage to get jobs are better off; those who are forced into unemployment are worse off. If the objective is to reduce poverty, the minimum wage, in this perspective, seems counterproductive.

But as this chapter has pointed out, markets for labor are different from markets for many other commodities. Workers have to be motivated to work hard. High wages lead to increased productivity, less absenteeism, and lower labor turnover. Presumably, rational firms would take this into account in their wage setting. Even so, if the government forces firms to pay higher wages through minimum wage legislation, the increased productivity may largely offset the increased wages, so that the employment effect may be very small.

In labor markets in which there is imperfect competition, minimum wages could actually lead to increased

employment. Because of imperfect mobility, firms face an upward-sloping supply schedule. Since all workers in a similar job have to be treated the same, the cost of hiring an additional worker may be high, above the wage it pays to its new employee. Not only must the firm raise the wage offered to the *new* worker, it must raise the wage paid to all existing workers. This discourages the firm from hiring additional employees. With a minimum wage, the cost of hiring an additional worker is just the minimum wage. Accordingly, the marginal cost of hiring an additional worker when there is a minimum wage may actually be lower than when there is not, in which case firms will actually hire more workers.

These perspectives are consistent with several recent empirical studies which have shown there to be negligible, or even positive, employment effects from a minimum wage.

Some economists have also pointed to broader, positive consequences of minimum wages: they induce firms to invest more in their workers, to increase their workers' productivity. Gavin Wright, a distinguished economic historian at Stanford University, has argued that minimum wages played a vital role in the transformation of the South. It was a region that had been vastly poorer than the North from the end of the Civil War to the Great Depression, with an economy largely based on very low wages. The minimum wage catalyzed changes which had dramatic effects on the South's economy, shifting the South away from low-wage industries to dynamic industries paying higher wages.

A further alleged advantage of raising the minimum wage is that it increases the incentives to work, by increasing the difference between what someone on welfare receives and what a worker gets. ●

In recent years, firms have explored the consequences of alternative ways of encouraging worker motivation and hence worker productivity. Some use teams. When pay depends on team performance, members of a team have an incentive to monitor and help one another. The Swedish automaker Volvo believes that such team arrangements have increased the productivity of its own workforce. Some firms have encouraged worker participation in decision making. Such participation may help both sides see that there is more to be gained by cooperation than by conflict. For instance, new ways of producing goods can make both the firm and the workers better off; if the company sells more goods, all share in the benefits.

Compensating Workers

We saw earlier that the wage a firm has to pay adjusts to take into account the nonpecuniary attributes. Some of these nonpecuniary attributes reflect decisions of the firm: The firm can try to make the workplace more attractive; it can try to make it safer; it can even try to lower the stress level of its employees. Some of these changes can affect the level of performance of workers. In making decisions concerning how to organize the workplace, firms take into account both the impact on productivity and how much the firm has to pay to recruit workers.

Today, much of the compensation a worker receives takes the form not of direct cash but of **fringe benefits,** such as health insurance, retirement pay, and life insurance. In recent years, fringe benefits have constituted an increasing share of total compensation.

Why do employers offer fringe benefits, rather than simply paying a straight salary to workers? One main reason involves the tax code; if employees are paid income and then purchase health insurance on their own, they must pay income tax on the money. But if the company buys the insurance for them, the fringe benefit is not counted as income. In addition, many employers use fringe benefits to offer an incentive for employees to stay with the company. For example, companies often require that the employee remain with the company for a period of several years before becoming eligible for the company pension plan. Such benefits show that employers are not eager to lose their long-term employees, and would rather offer some added benefits than go through the cost and trouble of hiring and training new workers. But why—other than for tax reasons—they should rely so heavily on rewarding these workers through better fringe benefits rather than through cash bonuses remains unclear.

e-Insight

Labor Markets and the Internet

One of the main *imperfections* in the labor market is that it is costly to search for a new job. Information is imperfect and is costly to acquire. Help-wanted ads play an important role in making the labor market work, but it is often not easy for individuals in one city to obtain on a regular and timely basis newspapers from other cities, to look at job opportunities there.

Employment agencies and government employment services have helped make the labor market work better. But the Internet promises a revolution in labor markets—or at least a vast improvement. Virtually without cost, individuals can see the help-wanted ads in newspapers in other cities. Employers can post help-wanted ads without cost and can provide far more complete descriptions both of the job and of the characteristics of the employees that they seek. Eighty percent of the world's largest 500 firms use Web sites for job recruitment and over 90 percent of American firms do. Existing employment agencies (including government-provided services) have used the Internet to extend their scope, and new firms have been created. Much of the relevant information—from the perspective of both the employer and the employee—will still be obtained by face-to-face contact, through an interview, and this process will remain costly. Still, by lowering search costs, the Internet holds out the promise of vastly increasing the efficiency of labor markets.

WRAP-UP

Ways of Motivating Workers

Piece rates, or pay based on measured output.

The threat of firing workers whose efforts or performance are deemed inadequate.

Efficiency wages, which introduce an extra cost to those dismissed for unsatisfactory performance.

Relative performance: promotions, contests.

Team rewards, pay based on team performance.

Fringe benefits, such as health insurance and retirement pay.

Review and Practice

Summary

1. The proportion of U.S. workers in unions has declined since the 1950s. Possible reasons include laws that have improved working conditions in general; the decline of manufacturing industries, where unions have traditionally been strong, relative to service industries; increased competition in the product market, providing firms with less latitude to pay above market wages; and a more anti-union atmosphere in the U.S. legal structure.

2. Union gains in wages are typically at the expense of lower employment, at least in the long run, and lower wages in the nonunion sector. Unions also have played an important role in enhancing job security, though sometimes at the expense of innovation. Some of the gains they have accomplished for workers have been through the political process, for instance, in pushing legislation that promotes occupational safety and health and the minimum wage.

3. Union power is limited by the ability of companies to bring in new, nonunion workers and by the threat of unemployment to union workers.

4. Explanations for wage differentials include compensating differentials (differences in the nature of jobs), productivity differentials (differences in productivity between workers), imperfect information (workers do not know all the job opportunities that are available), and discrimination.

5. Employers try to motivate workers and induce high levels of effort through a combination of direct supervision, incentives for doing well, and penalties for doing badly. They pay wages higher than workers could get elsewhere (efficiency wages), give promotions and bonuses, base pay on relative performance (contests), and grant team rewards.

Key Terms

union shops
right-to-work laws
compensating wage differentials
nonpecuniary attributes
statistical discrimination
wage discrimination
job discrimination
affirmative action
piece-rate system
efficiency wage theory
fringe benefits

Review Questions

1. Has the power of unions in the U.S. economy been shrinking or growing in the last few decades? Why? In what sector has union growth been largest? Why might this be so?

2. What effect will successful unions have on the level of wages paid by unionized companies? on the capital investment for those companies? What effect will they have on wages paid by nonunionized companies?

3. How might greater job security for union workers possibly lead them to become less efficient?

4. Does it make sense for a union to resist the introduction of an innovation in the short run? in the long run?

5. What are alternative explanations for wage differentials?

6. How do piece rates provide incentives to work hard? Why is there not a greater reliance on piece-rate systems?

7. What is efficiency wage theory?

Why Does the Government Intervene in the Economy?

There are three basic reasons why the government intervenes in the economy: (1) to improve economic efficiency by correcting market failures; (2) to pursue social values of fairness, or equity, by altering market outcomes; and (3) to pursue other social values by mandating the consumption of some goods, called merit goods, and prohibiting the consumption of other goods, called merit bads. The next three sections address each of these reasons for government participation in the economy.

Correcting Market Failures Chapter 11 described five sources of market failure in the economy: imperfect competition, imperfect information, externalities, public goods,

International Perspective

The Size of Government in Different Countries

The increase in central (federal) government expenditures during the twentieth century was dramatic, but expenditures in the United States are still among the smallest of any of the major industrialized economies when measured in proportion to the size of the economy. In Denmark, Sweden, and the United Kingdom, government expenditures are over one-third of GDP as compared to less than one fifth in the United States. Of the major industrialized countries, only Japan and Australia spend less than one third of GDP on the public sector. As a significant portion of U.S. federal expenditures goes to defense (about 3 percent of GDP), the relative size of nondefense expenditures is particularly low viewed from this international perspective.

In the United States, federal spending on nondefense public sector programs amounts to about 17 percent of GDP. In Sweden and the United Kingdom, this figure is 39 and 34 percent, respectively. The key difference is that Social Security and welfare programs are much larger in those countries relative to the United States.

These foreign comparisons prove different things to different people. Advocates of more government spending argue that the United States is out of step. Opponents of more government spending argue that all of these countries would do better to reduce public expenditures.

One factor to keep in mind is that the balance between federal government and local governments is quite different in these countries. In the United States, state and local government spending is about 12 percent of GDP, so total government expenditures in the United States are close to 31 percent, a figure more in line with other countries where local governments are much less important.

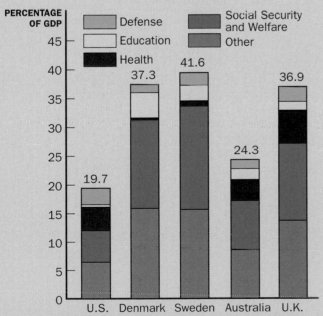

SOURCE: Government Finance Statistics Yearbook (2000) and ERP (2001).

and missing markets. Government programs are aimed at redressing each of these major categories of market failures. For instance, with imperfect competition, firms use their market power to raise prices and reduce output. Antitrust policies set by government attempt to maintain a competitive marketplace and restrain firms from abusing their market power. Firms produce too little of goods for which there are positive externalities (like research) and too much of goods for which there are negative externalities (such as those that generate pollution). Government subsidizes the former and taxes or otherwise regulates the latter. The market may not provide some goods for which the (marginal) value would seem to exceed the (marginal) costs. For example, workers might have wanted to purchase insurance against the risks of unemployment and the elderly might have attempted to purchase insurance against health risks, but before government provided these forms of **social insurance,** there was, at best, limited market provisions.[1] Similarly, individuals would have liked to own *annuities* that would pay them a certain amount every year after retirement, regardless of how long they live, payments that would increase with inflation; before Social Security (the government program that provides monthly payments upon retirement),[2] individuals could not obtain these annuities.

Equity and the Redistribution of Income   But even if markets were efficient, they would result in some individuals receiving too low of an income to survive at a standard of living that is viewed as acceptable. In the market, individuals' incomes are related to their ownership of assets and their productivity. Those with little education receive low wages. And even in the United States, most individuals have few assets: The bottom 80 percent of households by wealth own less than 20 percent of total wealth, and the average wealth of the bottom 40 percent of all households was just $1,100 in 1998. Particularly troubling is the fact that most low-wage individuals have no other assets to rely on. Income in the United States is highly unequal, with the

The lifetime prospects for a child born into a poor family are much bleaker than those of one born into a rich family.

top 5 percent of the population receiving 22 percent of the income, and the bottom 20 percent receiving just 4 percent of total income. Wealth is even more concentrated, with the top 5 percent of the population having 59 percent of the wealth, and the bottom 40 percent having only 0.2 percent. Some countries have even greater inequality, while others, such as many European countries, have somewhat less inequality.

There is concern about inequality for several reasons. High levels of inequality are often associated with a variety of social and political problems. And these problems often result in a climate that is adverse to investment. East Asia and Latin America illustrate the two extremes. Over the past thirty years, the countries of East Asia have grown very rapidly—at more than twice the rate of Latin America—and many economists believe that the greater degree of equality in East Asia provides at least part of the explanation. Many of the countries of Latin America, with high inequality, are plagued by urban violence and political unrest.

In most societies, there is a concern about *social justice* or *fairness*. It seems morally wrong for so much of society's

---

[1] Individuals still cannot buy annuities that increase with inflation, and until recently, the premiums for annuities were high relative to their benefits, reflecting in part high transaction costs. Whenever the government enters where the market has feared to tread, one needs to ask, why? In some cases, the government might face the same problems, e.g., associated with imperfections of information, that impair the market.

[2] In Europe, these are called *public pension programs*. The U.S. Social Security program also provides for disability payments.

goods to go to so few. Fairness, like beauty, however, is often in the eye of the beholder. Many of those with high incomes and wealth believe that they *deserve* it. Attitudes toward inequality differ markedly across countries and have changed over time. In the United States, inequalities that are a result of working hard are far more acceptable than inequalities that are a result of inheritance. Wealth that results from a brilliant innovation is more acceptable than wealth that results from the exercise of monopoly power or political influence (e.g., by the nineteenth-century "robber barons").

There is particular concern about two groups, the very poor and children. Especially troubling is the fact that even in the United States, supposedly the land of opportunity, the lifetime prospects of a child born in a poor family are much bleaker than those of one born in a rich family. That is one of the reasons why there is widespread support for high-quality public education; for Pell grants, which make a college education affordable to children from poor families; and for Project Head Start, which provides preschool education for poor children.

The government provides a variety of programs aimed at the very poor. These programs attempt to provide a basic *safety net,* to ensure that the very poor have a minimal level of income (through welfare programs), housing, food (through food stamps), and health (through Medicaid). Programs that take income from some people and *redistribute* it to others are called **transfer programs.** But there is a redistributive component to many government programs, such as education, and especially to social insurance programs. Low-wage individuals, for instance, get back more than they contribute to Social Security.

Merit Goods and Bads   Some government activities, however, neither correct market failures nor redistribute income. Rather, they attempt to impose social values on individuals, to force or encourage them to do more of some things and less of others. Governments try to discourage drug taking and encourage education. These are called **merit goods.** These merit goods (and bads) need to be distinguished from externalities: No one else may be harmed by someone taking marijuana, yet many governments make it illegal. Moderate drinking or smoking may have an adverse effect only on the individuals partaking, yet government still tries to discourage the consumption of alcohol and cigarettes through high taxes. These are instances in which the government interferes with the general principle of **consumer sovereignty,** which holds that individuals are the best judges of what is in their own interests and promotes their own well-being. The gov-

ernment acts *paternalistically,* that is, as if it were a father. Many economists believe that government should limit itself to acting this way with minors—few object to compulsory education requirements for children but question whether government should dictate what adults should or should not do, so long as it does not cause harm to others.

WRAP-UP

Reasons for Government Intervention in the Economy

To correct market failures: Market failures such as externalities provide a rationale for government intervention, with the goal of improving economic efficiency.

To pursue equity: Market outcomes, even when they are efficient, might fail to satisfy social standards of equity. Government may intervene to redistribute income.

Merit goods and bads: Sometimes government imposes social values, by mandating the consumption of merit goods (education) and prohibiting the consumption of merit bads (illicit drugs).

Equity-Efficiency Trade-offs

We have seen that government programs have multiple objectives. If the only task of the government were to address market failures, it would face difficult technical issues, for instance, how best to reduce pollution. But the hardest problems are those for which the government faces *trade-offs,* especially between improving the efficiency of the market and promoting equity. Equity—a sense of fairness—might suggest that the rich and wealthy contribute not only more to support the government but proportionately more (i.e., a larger fraction of their income). The United States has a **progressive** income tax system that is designed to do exactly that; tax rates for higher-income individuals are higher than those for lower-income individuals. (Conversely, tax systems in which the poor pay a higher proportion of their income to the government are **regressive**). But the inefficiencies associated with taxation arise from the **marginal tax rate,** the extra tax that an individual pays on the last dollar earned. If the marginal tax rate is high, incentives to work harder are reduced. Thus, if high-income individuals have a high income because their

The New Economy and Inequality

Income inequality in the United States has increased significantly over the past twenty years. One reason for this has been the increasing premium earned by skilled workers. The chart shows the average wage of college graduates relative to the wage of high school graduates. In 1980, college graduates received a wage that, on average, was 13 percent higher than that received by those with only a high school education; by 1990, that premium had increased to just over 70 percent. Over the 1990s, it continued to increase, rising to 75 percent in 1998.

The job skills demanded by the new, information-based economy are often cited as a major cause of the widening wage premium for skilled workers. In fact, two opposing forces have been at play. On the supply side, there has been a marked increase in the skills of the U.S. labor force. In 1980, only 20 percent of the work force had a college degree; by 1998, this fraction had risen to almost 30 percent. But at the same time that the supply of college educated workers was increasing, the new economy was generating an increasing demand for skilled labor. One way of interpreting the evidence on the increasing college wage premium is that, since 1980, increases in demand have outpaced increases in supply (at any given wage), and this has led to an increase in the skill premium.

Economists debate how much of the rise in the skill premium has been caused by the introduction of new computer-related technologies. According to a survey of human resource managers, new information technologies have led many organizations to decentralize decision making, and this has increased the demand for highly educated workers. And while the fraction of all workers who use computers at work rose dramatically, from 24 percent in 1984 to just over 50 percent in 1997, computer usage among college graduates is much higher, having risen from 41 percent in 1984 to 75 percent in 1997. Some economists believe that the wage premium associated with computer skills will erode over time. The current period is one of transition, in which these skills have not yet become widely disseminated, even among skilled workers.

The fact that the new economy values computer related skills so highly raises troubling issues for the future—a concern about what is sometimes called the *digital divide*. Children from middle class families grow up with computers in the home, become facile in using the computer, and have a big head start in the new economy. Children from poor families that cannot afford computers will be at a marked disadvantage. While (in 1998) only 20 percent of families with incomes below $25,000 used the Internet, 60 percent of those with incomes in excess of $75,000 did. There is thus the potential for a vicious circle, with children from poor families having less access to computers and therefore being condemned to earning lower incomes. Computers in schools may only partially redress the imbalance.

The digital divide within the United States may be far smaller than the digital divide between the poorest devel-

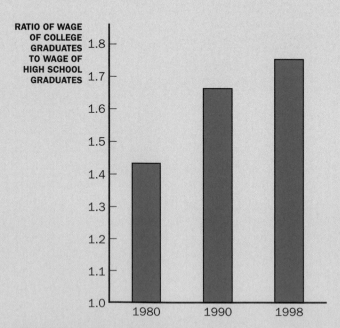

RATIO OF WAGE OF COLLEGE GRADUATES TO WAGE OF HIGH SCHOOL GRADUATES

The College Wage Premium

oping countries and the most advanced industrial countries. For some of the less developed countries, such as India and China, the new economy holds out the promise of narrowing the huge income gap that separates them from the more developed countries. Their access to the Internet puts them in touch with the knowledge base of the entire world. Programmers in Bangalore, India, can—and do—sell their services instantaneously to firms in California's Silicon Valley. But for other countries, such as many in sub-Saharan Africa, prospects are far bleaker. Unable to

afford extensive access to the new technologies, including the Internet, they may fall further and further behind. Japan has spearheaded a recent initiative of the G-7, the seven major industrialized countries, that is intended to reduce this global digital divide by providing greater access to the new technologies in the developing world. It is too soon to assess the success of this initiative.

source: Lawrence F. Katz, "Technological Change, Computerization, and the Wage Structure," Harvard University, Sept. 1999.

wages are high, and their wages are high because they are more productive, the effect of a progressive income tax is to discourage from work those who are the most productive. (What matters, of course, for *incentives* is the *marginal* tax rate. A tax system can be progressive in that the *average* tax rate paid by richer individuals increases with income, even if the highest-income individuals do not have the highest *marginal* tax rate. Such was the case in the United States between 1986 and 1993, when the richest individuals faced a marginal tax rate of 28 percent, but individuals with somewhat lower incomes faced a marginal tax rate in excess of 30 percent.)

While there are many instances in which governments face hard trade-offs, there are some in which equity and efficiency go together. Providing educational opportunities for the poor may be equitable and efficient, as the more efficient utilization of these human resources may also improve the efficiency of the economy. In many poor countries, there are large numbers of landless peasants who work under sharecropping contracts, in which the landlord gets one out of two dollars they earn. It is as if the sharecroppers face a 50 percent tax rate. Redistributing land to the poor may increase both efficiency and equity.

The U.S. Tax System in Practice

One out of every three dollars of total output of the U.S. economy goes to the government. Not surprisingly, there is

great concern about how the government raises its revenue. Nobody likes taxes, but taxes are necessary if the government is to provide public goods and services and if it is to redistribute income to create a "better" income distribution. At times, it seems that everybody wants more public services but to pay less for them. This can be done if the government improves its efficiency, and there have been significant increases in efficiency.

In 2000, the number of federal employees, for instance, was lower than it was thirty years earlier, even though the number of individuals served and the scope of government programs had vastly increased (state and local government in contrast, has grown by 85 percent over the past thirty years). But there is a limit to these improvements in efficiency, at least in the short run, and cutting taxes leads to either larger deficits or cutbacks in government programs. Voters have on numerous occasions voted against politicians who have promised tax cuts, largely because they believe that the benefits they receive from key government programs are worth the costs.

Characteristics of a Good Tax System

While the design of the tax system is a perennial subject of controversy—views of how to balance the equity-efficiency trade-off naturally differ markedly—there is broad consensus on the five *principles* of a good tax system.

Fairness   In most people's minds, the first criterion is fairness. But fairness is not always easy to define. In trying to define fairness, economists focus on two principles:

horizontal equity, which says that individuals who are in identical or similar situations should pay identical or similar taxes, and **vertical equity,** which says that people who are better off should pay more taxes.

Efficiency   The second criterion for a good tax system is efficiency. The tax system should interfere as little as possible with the way the economy allocates resources, and it should raise revenue with the least cost to taxpayers. Very high taxes may discourage work and saving, and therefore interfere with the efficiency of the economy. Taxes that select out particular goods to be taxed—such as excise taxes on perfume, boats, and airline tickets—discourage individuals from purchasing those goods, and therefore also interfere with efficiency.

The U.S. income tax system has many provisions that have the effect of encouraging some types of economic activity and discouraging others. For instance, the U.S. income tax allows certain child care payments to be taken as a credit against tax payments owed. The government thus subsidizes child care. Similarly, when firms spend money on R&D, their expenditures may reduce the amount they have to pay in taxes. Such arrangements are called **tax subsidies.** These subsidies cost the government money just as if the government paid out money directly for child care or research. Accordingly, the revenue lost from a tax subsidy is called a **tax expenditure.**

Sometimes, taxes can be used to improve economic efficiency or to advance broader social purposes: Taxes on pollution can improve the environment; taxes on cigarettes discourage smoking, leading to improved health. Such taxes are said to yield a "double dividend," improving overall efficiency or promoting social purposes and generating revenue at the same time.

Administrative Simplicity   The third criterion is administrative simplicity. It is costly—to the government and to those who must pay taxes—to collect taxes and administer a tax system. In addition to the costs of running the IRS, billions of hours are spent each year in filling out tax forms, hours that might be spent producing goods and services or enjoyed as additional leisure time. Billions of dollars are spent by taxpayers and by the IRS on accountants and lawyers in the annual ritual of preparing and processing tax forms. Finally, with a good tax system, it should be difficult to evade the taxes imposed.

Flexibility   The fourth criterion is flexibility. As economic circumstances change, it may be desirable to change tax rates. With a good tax system, it should be relatively easy to do this.

Transparency   The fifth criterion is transparency. A good tax system is one in which it can be ascertained what each person is paying in taxes. The principle of transparency is analogous to the principle of "truth in advertising." Taxpayers are consumers of public services. They should know what they (and others) are paying for the services they are getting.

WRAP-UP

Criteria for Evaluating a Tax System

Fairness
Efficiency
Administrative simplicity
Flexibility
Transparency

The Scope of the U.S. Tax System

The U.S. government raises tax revenues from a variety of sources. There are taxes on the earnings of individuals and corporations, known as **individual income taxes** and **corporation income taxes.** Real estate—buildings and land—is subject to taxation by most states; these taxes are known as **property taxes.** Large bequests and gifts are taxed, through **gift** and **estate taxes.** There are special provisions relating to the taxation of capital gains (the increase in value of an asset between the time an individual purchases it and the time she sells it). Furthermore, wage income is subject not only to the income tax, but also to the **payroll tax** (the tax levied on a company's payroll, half of which is deducted from employees' paychecks). Revenues from the payroll tax finance the Social Security (retirement income) and Medicare (medical care for the aged) programs.

There are also taxes on the purchase of specific goods and services, known as **excise taxes.** The two heaviest excise taxes are on alcohol and tobacco, also known as **sin taxes.** The excise taxes on air travel and gasoline are sometimes called **benefit taxes** because the proceeds go for benefits, like airports and roads, to those who purchase the good. Excise taxes on perfume, large cars, yachts, and expensive fur coats, targeted to the rich, are referred to as **luxury taxes.** Other excise taxes, such as the one on telephone services, have no particular justification other than raising revenue. Most states impose a general tax on purchases of goods and services, known as a **sales tax**, though typically a wide variety of items (such as food) are exempted.

As this list indicates, few transactions in our economy escape taxation. Figure 16.2 shows the relative importance of various taxes at the federal and the state/local levels. At the federal level (panel A), the single most important source of revenue is the tax on individuals' income (contributing almost half of total revenue), followed by the payroll tax. At the state/local levels (panel B), the sales tax is the most important revenue source.

Grading the U.S. Tax System

How well does the U.S. tax system fare, based on the five principles of a good tax system? Equally important, have the major changes in the tax laws over the past decade improved the tax system? During the past quarter century, the U.S. income tax system has undergone five major reforms, in 1981, 1986, 1993, 1997, and 2001. The announced intent of these reforms was to make the system more efficient, more fair, and administratively simpler. But each of the reforms faced trade-offs; some emphasized one more than the other, and each tended to undo what was widely viewed as the excesses of the previous reform. Meanwhile, a concern about soaring government expenditures put limits on the extent to which various social goals could be pursued through new programs. Hence, tax expenditures—such as tuition tax credits and deductions—were used to pursue these objectives in the tax bills of 1993, 1997, and 2001 inevitably greatly complicating the tax system.

Fairness   As noted, the U.S. federal income tax system is, overall, progressive. Low-income individuals are exempt from paying any income tax whatsoever. Beyond a certain level of income (depending on family size—for a family of four, the critical level in 2000 was $18,550), the tax rate is now 10 percent. This means that for each extra $100 an individual earns, he must pay an extra $10 of taxes; this is his *marginal tax rate*. At higher levels of income, the marginal tax rate increase further, eventually reaching 39.1 percent on incomes over $315,900 (for a family of four).

The **average tax rate** gives the ratio of taxes to taxable income. While there are big jumps in the marginal tax rate, the average tax rate increases smoothly. Figure 16.3 shows the 2000 marginal and average income tax rates for a typical family of four that did not itemize its deductions.

A SOURCES OF FEDERAL TAX REVENUE

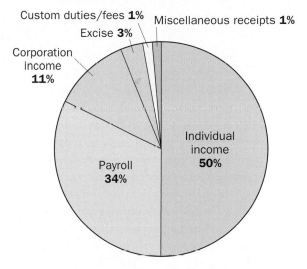

B SOURCES OF STATE AND LOCAL TAX REVENUE

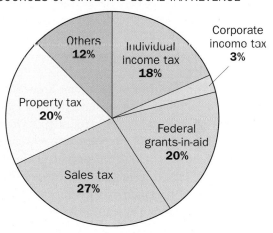

FIGURE 16.2   *The Importance of Various Taxes*

At the federal level, the largest share of taxes comes from the individual income tax, followed by the payroll tax and the corporate income tax, as shown in panel A. Sources of revenue at the state and local level are more fragmented, as seen in panel B, but include sales and property taxes, as well as revenue received from other levels of government.

SOURCE: Bureau of Economic Analysis, *National Income and Product Accounts, Table 3.2* http://www.bea.doc.gov/bea.

The income tax is only one of several income-related taxes that U.S. citizens pay. The payroll (Social Security) tax is another one that increases with income up to some level. An **earned-income tax credit** is designed to supplement the income of low-income workers with families; as a

Thinking Like an Economist

Incentives, Distribution, and the 2001 Bush Tax Cut

Proposals to change federal income taxes are always controversial, in part because they affect incentives—and that means some activities will be encouraged, others discouraged—and because they affect the distribution of income and wealth—some individuals and firms will be winners, others will be losers. The tax cut pushed by President G.W. Bush and passed by Congress as the Economic Growth and Tax Relief Reconciliation Act of 2001 was no exception. Most of the debate focused on whether the tax cut was skewed too heavily in favor of the rich and whether it would leave the government with too little revenue for new spending programs and Social Security and Medicare needs.

Critics of Bush's tax cut proposal attacked its fairness. As we have already noted, fairness is in the eye of the beholder, so it is not surprising that some argued the tax cut plan was not fair while others defended it as fair. Both sides agreed that most of the tax cut would go to benefit very high-income families. There were two reasons for this. First, part of the tax cut took the form of a reduction in the estate tax—the tax on large inheritances—and this part of the tax cut clearly benefited only the very wealthy. Second, for many American families, the payroll tax they pay on their wage income is much larger than the income tax they

pay. (Recall from Figure 16.2 that half of the federal government's tax revenues come from the income tax while another third comes from payroll taxes.) For example, a typical family of four with an income of $35,000 pays over $5,000 in payroll taxes for Social Security and Medicare and only about $2,500 in income taxes. For high-income families, however, the amount paid in income taxes is much larger than what they pay in payroll taxes. Thus, a cut in the income tax benefits high-income families more than lower income families. (A cut in payroll taxes would have the opposite effect.) Since most of the benefits from the tax cut went to the wealthy, many labeled it as unfair. Others argued that since the wealthy pay most of the income taxes, a tax cut that gives most of the dollar reduction to those who pay the most is fair.

The second area of debate centered on whether the country could afford a large tax cut. The 2001 tax bill reduced taxes by an estimated $1.35 trillion, although this reduction is spread out over the next ten years and most of the reductions occur in the second half of this ten-year period. When the tax cut was passed, opponents argued that it left too little of the government's projected surplus for Social Security reform and new spending needs. Proponents argued that the surplus should be returned to taxpayers and that there would still be enough money in the federal budget to meet critical spending needs.

At the time of the debate, the Congressional Budget Office (CBO) was projecting a surplus of $5.6 trillion dollars between 2002 and 2011. While this might make a $1.35 trillion tax cut look affordable, leaving over $4 trillion of the surplus for other uses, the CBO's projections hinged on a number of unrealistic assumptions. For one, the CBO assumed current government spending policies would remain unchanged. It is more reasonable to assume they will grow in line with growth in the population and the overall economy. Thus, Alan Auerbach of the University of California and William Gale of the Brookings Institution adjusted the CBO figures to take into account a more likely set of assumptions about future government spending and taxes. They found that if spending grows in line with growth in the economy, the CBO's ten year surplus figure needs to be reduced by about $1.3 trillion, leaving a smaller but still huge projected surplus of $4.3 trillion.[1] After subtracting the tax cut, there would be just under $3 trillion available for other uses. However, many analysts estimate that the U.S. government needs to set aside about $3 trillion over the next ten years to prepare for the huge increase in Social Security and Medicare costs as baby boomers retire. So after the tax cut and dealing with Social Security and Medicare, there would be nothing left of the surplus for any new spending programs.

Unfortunately, surplus projections are very sensitive to economic conditions and new developments. As the economy slowed down in 2001 and unemployment rose, projections for future tax revenue had to be adjusted downwards. When combined with the rise in spending in the wake of the terrorist attack on the United States in September 2001, talk of a surplus quickly evaporated. Indeed, some predicted the government would actually run a deficit in 2002.

---

[1] Alan Auerbach and William G. Gale, "Tax Cuts and the Budget," March 2001, unpublished working paper accessed at: http://elsa.berkeley.edu/users/auerbach/.

person's income increases beyond some level, the payments he *receives* under this program decrease.

To assess the overall progressiveness of the U.S. tax system, we have to look not only at federal taxes but at all taxes—including the corporation income tax and state and local taxes.

Many state and local taxes are regressive. This is because lower- and middle-income individuals spend a larger

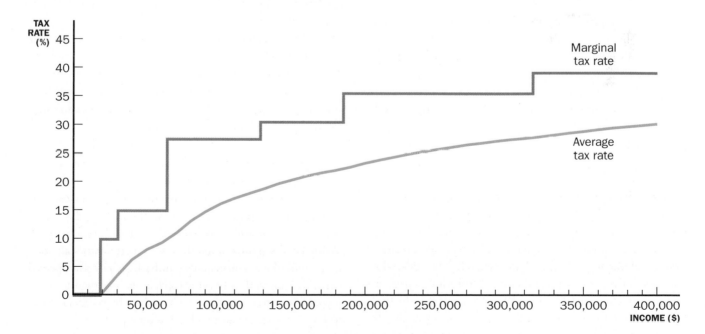

FIGURE 16.3 *Marginal and Average Federal Income Tax Rates*

Marginal tax rates change by jumps, as shown in the table, but average tax rates increase gradually.

SOURCE: Tax Relief Act of 2001.

fraction of their income on items that are subject to state sales taxes than do the rich. Our current *total* tax system—combining the slightly progressive federal tax system with the slightly regressive state and local tax system—is, in the judgment of most economists, only modestly progressive.

Tax changes in recent years have alternately decreased and increased the degree of progressivity. In 1981 and 1986, marginal tax rates on upper-income individuals, for instance, were brought down markedly, but in 1993, they were increased again, to levels that were still lower than they were in 1981. The tax cut passed by Congress in 2001 phases in lower marginal tax rates over a number of years. Prior to 1986, capital gains—the increases in the value of assets over time—were taxed at lower rates (varying from 40 to 50 percent of the "normal" rate) than were other forms of income. In 1986, this special treatment was abolished, but in 1997, it was restored. Earlier, we noted that wealth is heavily concentrated; not surprisingly, the rich benefited enormously. At the same time, other changes in the tax law helped those with lower incomes, especially those with children, and the 2001 tax changes reduced the marginal tax rate from 15 percent to 10 percent on the first $6,000 of taxable income ($12,000 for married couples).

Efficiency

Efficiency   In the area of efficiency, the U.S. tax system today, while considerably better than it was fifteen years ago, still has much room for improvement. The inefficiencies to which the tax system gives rise are related to two factors: the progressivity of the tax system and the extent to which different kinds of income and different expenditures are treated differently. The distortions in labor supply, for instance, are affected by the *marginal* tax rates, and the variations in those marginal tax rates discussed earlier have altered this distortion.

Similarly, the distortions associated with differential taxation have variously increased, decreased, and increased over time. As we noted, the 1981 tax law encouraged certain kinds of investment, the 1986 law created a more level playing field than had existed for decades, while changes in the tax law since then have introduced new distortions—some, such as for the oil and gas industries, largely reflect the influence of special interests while others, such as for education, reflect the use of the tax system to pursue social objectives.

Administrative Simplicity   Americans live in a complex society, and their tax laws reflect and contribute to this com-

plexity. As they have sought to make sure that the tax laws are fair and apply uniformly to all people in similar situations, the laws have become increasingly complex. High tax rates make it worthwhile for individuals and businesses to think hard about how to avoid taxes (legally, without going to jail). With high tax rates, it may pay a businessperson to devote almost as much energy to how he can avoid taxes as to how he can produce a better product. The tax law has evolved out of this constant battle between the government and taxpayers; as each new way of reducing taxes is discovered, the law is modified to close the loophole. Inevitably another hole is discovered, and another repair job is attempted. Today the federal tax law amounts to a multitude of volumes.

The objective of administrative simplicity seems to have been an elusive one. Many economists are convinced that the United States could have a tax system that is truly administratively simple, but to do so, other objectives would have to be given up. Some of the complexity derives from the attempt to have a progressive income tax and to tax the income from capital.

Flexibility   One of the weakest aspects of the U.S. tax system is its lack of flexibility. Any time a tax change is proposed, all of the issues discussed here are raised. There are debates about how different groups would be affected and about how efficiency is affected. Basic issues of values—how progressive should the tax system be?—are aired once again. Special-interest groups try to take the opportunity of any change in the tax law to get favorable treatment. It has turned out to be extremely difficult—and time consuming—to change the tax law.

Transparency   While the merits of transparency are widely preached, governments often do not want individuals to know how much they are really paying in taxes. They worry that if taxpayers really knew, there might be "sticker shock," that opposition to taxes might grow. It is easier for individuals to see how much they are paying with some taxes than with others. For instance, individuals pay sales taxes in dribs and drabs; they never get a clear view of their total payments. That may be one of the reasons why politicians seem to love the sales tax so much. Of all the parts of the tax system, the ultimate burden of corporation income tax is perhaps the least transparent. Although corporations write the check to the IRS, most economists agree that much of the burden of corporate taxes is shifted to individuals and households, through reduced wages and/or higher product prices.

Transfers

Earlier we noted the role of government in redistributing income. Very poor individuals receive more from the government than they contribute in taxes. This redistribution is carried out through five major public benefit programs for low-income Americans: welfare, Medicaid, food stamps, supplemental security income (SSI), and housing assistance. Until 1997, the program commonly known as "welfare" was AFDC (Aid to Families with Dependent Children). It provided cash assistance to poor families, mostly households with only one parent present. Since 1997 a new program, called TANF (Temporary Assistance to Needy Families), has performed the role of welfare. Medicaid provides health care to the poor. The food stamp program provides vouchers for the purchase of food. SSI provides cash assistance to the low-income elderly and disabled, to supplement their Social Security benefits. Housing assistance programs include public housing and rental vouchers. In addition to these five program areas, states and localities provide general assistance to those who fall between the cracks. Food stamps and SSI are federal programs (states can supplement SSI benefits). The other programs vary from state to state, with the federal government typically providing only broad program guidelines but footing much of the bill.

Our discussion here focuses on the most controversial program areas: welfare, housing, and social insurance.

Welfare

From 1935 until 1997, AFDC was the primary cash program in the U.S. welfare system. The program was a combination of federal and state programs. The states not only administered AFDC but also set benefit levels and had some discretion over rules. The federal government provided a fraction of the funds, which varied from approximately one half to three fourths, depending on the state's per capita income. Programs in which federal outlays depend on state expenditures are called **matching programs.** The federal matching subsidy presumably resulted in the states' providing higher levels of benefits than they would have if they had had to pay the full (marginal) costs themselves. States were given considerable discretion in determining the level of expenditures. Not surprisingly, there was considerable variation in the level of benefits provided by the states, with the highest benefits, in Alaska, being more than seven times the lowest benefits, in Mississippi.

Starting in 1997, TANF replaced AFDC. TANF represented a marked departure from the earlier system in two ways. First, it replaced the old system of matching grants with **block grants,** a fixed amount of money, with states given considerable discretion in how that money could be spent (including discretion in determining the eligibility of needy families and the benefits and services those families receive). Second, TANF focused on moving individuals from welfare to work. The states were given broad flexibility in the design and operation of their welfare-to-work programs, but the use of TANF funds had to be consistent with federal priorities of strong work requirements, time limits to receiving assistance, a reduction in welfare dependency, and the encouragement of two-parent families.

Housing

Public housing projects have been described as "warehouses of the poor," and the description has merit. By failing to integrate the poor more thoroughly into the communities in which they live, public housing projects help perpetuate the cycle of poverty. Moreover, many housing programs are inequitable. They provide generous benefits to those lucky enough to receive them, but many with the same income and family size get nothing. Worse still, providing a subsidy that is tied to a particular dwelling impedes labor mobility. Finally, the costs of public housing are high, and its quality is often much lower than housing of similar cost in the private sector.

WRAP-UP

Government Transfer Programs in the United States

Welfare: TANF (Temporary Assistance for Needy Families)

Medicaid: health care for the poor

Food stamps: vouchers for the purchase of food

Supplemental security income: cash assistance to the low-income elderly and disabled

Housing assistance: public housing and rental vouchers

All these drawbacks to public housing have led the government to reduce its role in directly supplying low-income housing and to turn increasingly to more market-based solutions. This is done by subsidizing the cost of housing for the poor through rental vouchers. As recipients use the vouchers, increasing demand for low-income housing, more builders are induced to provide housing for them. Vouchers have several other advantages. They allow for individuals to shop for their housing over broader areas, not just the inner cities, and they can be made "portable," so that individuals can relocate owing to job opportunities without losing their housing subsidy.

Social Insurance

Most Americans are neither rich nor poor. They belong to the "middle class." They have seen the poor get free medical care. They have heard about the rich hiring accountants to duck taxes by taking advantage of loopholes. They feel squeezed and unfairly treated. Some of this is a matter of perception. The middle class actually receives the benefits of many "hidden" loopholes that reduce their taxes. For instance, fringe benefits (health insurance, retirement funds), often representing between a quarter to a third of a person's salary, generally escape taxation. In addition, the United States has a variety of what are referred to as middle-class **entitlement programs,** so named because individuals do not have to demonstrate poverty to receive benefits. The most important of these are the social insurance programs. Social insurance programs are like private insurance, in that people nominally pay for their own protection through a tax on wage income, the payroll tax. But in other, important ways, they are *not* like private insurance, as we will see in the paragraphs that follow.

The Burden of Social Insurance Programs
The first myth about social insurance concerns who pays for it. Social Security is supported by a tax on wages, 50 percent paid by the employer, 50 percent by the employee. This division of the tax is entirely superficial; the consequences of the tax are essentially the same as they would be if the worker paid the entire tax.

Figure 16.4 uses demand and supply curves for labor to show this. Consider a payroll tax imposed on the employer based on what she pays her workers. The vertical axis measures the wage *received* by the employee. Since the cost of a worker is the wage received by the employee *plus* the tax, the tax shifts the demand curve down. In the new equilib-

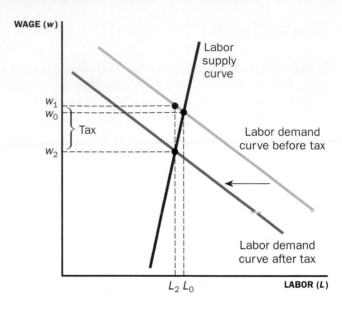

FIGURE 16.4   *The Incidence of Payroll Taxes*

The payroll tax introduces a wedge between the cost to an employer of an individual working an hour more (wage plus tax) and what the worker receives. The magnitude of the wedge does not depend on whether the tax is levied on the employer or employee. The tax leads to fewer workers being hired at the equilibrium wage, reduced from w_0 to w_2.

rium, workers' wages have fallen. The wage received by a worker is precisely the same as it would have been had the same tax been imposed on the worker directly. While normally the wage falls by less than the amount of the tax, the extent to which it falls depends on the elasticity of the demand and supply curves. The figure shows the "normal" case where the supply of labor is relatively inelastic, in which case wages fall almost by the full amount of the tax. Another view argues that, by and large, Social Security has relatively little impact on labor supply. This is because benefits increase with contributions (though the increase in benefits may not be *fully* commensurate with the increase in contributions); the program is largely a forced savings program. Indeed, most individuals are not forced to save more, or at least much more, than they otherwise would. As we note in the next paragraph, there is a redistributive aspect of the Social Security program. Accordingly some individuals receive back less than they contribute, and for them there is a disincentive effect not unlike the disincentive effects that would arise if a similar amount of redistribution occurred through the income tax system.

How Social Insurance is More than an Insurance Program The second myth about social insurance programs is that they have no redistribution effect. In any insurance program, some individuals receive back more than they contribute, some less. That, in a sense, is the whole purpose of insurance. No one knows whether she will be sick enough next year to need hospitalization. So people buy hospital insurance. Those who are lucky enough not to need hospitalization in effect help pay for the hospitalization of those who need it. But with private insurance, on average, the premiums (what you pay for the insurance) cover the costs of what you receive (including the costs of administration, which are often substantial). With the social insurance programs, however, there is often no close connection between the amount contributed and the amount received back. For instance, on average, single high-wage earners receive less back per dollar contributed than do low-wage families with a single earner. Thus, Social Security performs a redistributive as well as an insurance function.

To the extent that social insurance provides insurance that individuals want and the market has failed to provide, it performs an important economic function. To the extent that social insurance is popular because everyone believes someone else is picking up the tab, its role and function need to be reexamined. Social insurance is popular partly because it seems to benefit the majority of the population, the middle class. The problem facing the middle class, however, is that there are not enough "rich" people to pay for these programs, so the middle class must pay for them itself.

Designing Government Programs

Even when there is agreement about *what* the government should do, there is often disagreement about *how* it should do it. Consider, for instance, the problem of pollution. The government can tax those who pollute, it can regulate pollution, or it can subsidize actions that abate pollution. Or consider education. At the elementary and secondary level, the government provides free public education to all; it is a *producer*. But at the university level, the government makes different choices: Education is not free to all. Instead, state governments subsidize those who choose to go to state universities or colleges, and the federal government gives grants to low-income individuals to use for any university or college, public or private. A variety of considerations go into making these choices. The government often is an inefficient producer, and therefore providing educational *grants* may be a better way of ensuring that the poor have access to higher education than for the government to provide that education itself. But school *vouchers*—which individuals could use to purchase education in elementary or secondary private or public schools—are more controversial.

Government Failures

The choices of whether the government should intervene and *how* it should intervene thus depend on one's views of the efficiency and efficacy of government. One of the main rationales for government action we noted is to correct market failures. But proponents of a limited role for government argue that government often not only fails to correct the problems of the market but also makes matters worse. They argue that many of the problems facing the private sector—such as imperfect information—also plague the public sector. The public sector, they argue, has several additional problems, for instance, relating to incentives and commitments and budgetary constraints and processes.

The evidence on whether the government is inefficient is mixed actually. Government has long played an important role in the economy, and the list of commonly accepted successes is correspondingly long. The amazing increase in agricultural productivity over the past seventy-five years is generally attributed to the government's support of research and its dissemination of knowledge of new technologies to farmers. Key advances in computer technology and jet engines were the result of government support. The development of the important telecommunications sector has been based on government support—from Samuel Morse's first telegraph line between Baltimore and Washington in 1842 to the development of the Internet in the 1970s and 1980s. We are better able to breathe the air in our cities and to drink and swim in the water from our lakes and rivers, largely because of actions undertaken by government.

Critics of government point to a number of widely cited studies comparing the efficiency of the government and the private sector in similar activities—such as collecting garbage—to suggest that the public sector is systematically less efficient than the private sector. But there are two important caveats: First, much of the government activity is in areas where output is hard to measure, or the quality of an individual's contribution is hard to assess, and accordingly where the private sector too has a hard time designing effective incentive systems. Second, in several cases, public enterprises are every bit as efficient as private enterprises. For instance, in the United States, the administrative and transactions costs associated with Social Security are a much smaller percentage of the contributions than they are for privately provided annuities (insurance policies that pay a fixed amount every year in an individual's retirement). The government-run Canadian National Railroad appears to be as efficient as the privately run Canadian Pacific Railroad. And even the much maligned post office has managed to score productivity improvements in the past fifteen years that exceed the average for the U.S. economy. Some of the reasons cited for these successes are competition: The post office has to compete with private-sector competitors like Federal Express and UPS, and Canadian National Railroad had to compete with Canadian Pacific.

Still, failures of government are impressive, from public housing projects that rival the worst provided by any slumlord, to cost overruns on defense projects. And some of the government successes have had questionable side effects: The interstate highway system, while greatly reducing transportation time, contributed to the urban sprawl that plagues many of our cities. Given the frequency with which government failures occur, it is natural to ask, are there *systemic* reasons for these failures? Four major factors underlie systemic government failure: incentive problems, budgeting problems, information problems, and the nature of political decision making.

Incentives and Constraints

Unlike private organizations, government has the power of coercion. It can force people to pay taxes. It can prohibit people from paying less than the minimum wage if they engage in interstate commerce. And so on. But since this power carries with it enormous potential for abuse, certain procedures have been developed to protect the public against arbitrary use of government power. These procedures are called *due process*.

A good example to illustrate the potential incentive problems of due process procedures is the set of rules governing civil service employment. These rules are designed to ensure that there is no discrimination or other arbitrary treatment of government workers. But the rules are often inflexible and

make it difficult to pay comparable salaries to public officials who do their jobs as well as similarly qualified and dedicated persons in the private sector—or to offer them the same opportunities for rapid promotion. It is even more difficult for government to demote or fire incompetent and lazy workers. Thus, the public sector's ability to recruit and manage staff for maximum efficiency is typically limited.

In addition to the constraints of due process, the government has trouble making long-term commitments that are perceived to be binding. Any Congress can reverse decisions made by previous Congresses, though it may try to design both legislation and legislative rules in ways that make it more difficult to do so. Such limitations on the government's ability to make binding commitments can have major economic consequences. Take, for example, a government promise that it will pursue a policy of maintaining low inflation. The current government may convince investors of its commitment to keeping inflation low. But it has no control at all over what happens in the next election. Investors know that and make their own assessments of inflation risk, which may interfere with the effectiveness of what the government is trying to do today. The government today can make it more costly for future governments to increase the rate of inflation; for instance, it can issue short-term bonds, so that the interest cost to the government would rise quickly if inflation started to pick up.

Another factor that can undermine government efficiency, and lead to perverse decisions against the broad interests of society, is the political pressures inherent in the democratic process. A prime example here is legislators' concerns about the next election. These can lead to so-called pork barrel projects that create jobs in a pivotal legislator's home district but make no economic sense from a national perspective. In addition to the incentives to invest in projects that will aid the reelection chances of politicians, the enormous cost of running for office provides incentives for elected officials to pay particular attention to the views and needs of those who contribute to their campaign funds. Through this route, lobbyists, for example, can wield influence way out of proportion to the importance of the interests they represent.

Budgeting and Spending Procedures

The budgeting and spending constraints facing government decision makers differ from those of the private sector in three major ways. The first is the severity of the budget constraint facing public decision makers. Unlike a private firm, which faces the prospect of bankruptcy if enough of its ventures yield losses, a public enterprise can more easily turn to the government for budgetary help. This is the problem of *soft budget constraints.* Amtrak, for example, continues to make losses in its overall railroad operations, in spite of government promises to the contrary. A major reason for the continuing loss is a set of labor rules *imposed by the government* which require that workers be compensated if they are laid off or forced to relocate even a short distance. Soft budget constraints such as these weaken the incentives for public management to be efficient. There is nothing quite like the threat of bankruptcy to focus managerial attention.

The second budgetary difference between the private and public sectors—a factor that works in the opposite way from the soft budget constraints—is the annual appropriations process. This can force short-term spending constraints on the public sector that are not cost-effective in the long run. Limited investment flexibility is a particularly unfortunate fallout from the annual appropriations system.

The third budgetary constraint on government is the anti-efficiency effects of some of the procedures implemented to ensure strict cost control. No one likes to see public money wasted, least of all taxpayers or the congressional representatives who risk the taxpayers' wrath. Government has instituted detailed accounting, competitive bidding, and other procurement procedures to avoid waste and corruption. Yet these procedures can cost more than they save and not only because of the extra bureaucracy involved. When purchasing T-shirts, for example, the government in its efforts to ensure that the specifications were accurate and precise—so that bidders were competing to supply *exactly* the same product—created thirty pages of fine print documentation that prospective bidders had to follow carefully. These types of bureaucratic red tape reduce the supply of bidders willing to sell to the government and increase the cost to the government of goods and services. Procurement reforms

were enacted into law in the 1994 Federal Acquisitions Streamlining Act and are saving billions of dollars a year.

Imperfections of Information

Information problems plague government just as they plague the private sector. As a result, there are often adverse *unintended* (and often unforeseen) *consequences* of even well-intentioned programs. We already noted one example: The expansion of the superhighway system in the 1950s may have led to urban sprawl, weakened the inner cities, and increased air pollution (from increased driving); none of these effects were even widely discussed, let alone anticipated. Urban renewal programs, designed to increase the quality of housing, often led to a decrease in the supply of affordable housing for the poor, thus aggravating the housing problems they faced and even contributing to homelessness.

Collective Decision Making

A fourth important reason for public failures relates to how government decisions get made. Governments are not always consistent in their actions. This may not be surprising, given that government choices do not reflect the preferences of a single individual. More fundamentally, majority voting may not yield a determinate outcome even when only three people choose among only three alternatives, as was noted more than two hundred years ago by the Frenchman Marquis de Condorcet. This is referred to as the **voting paradox.** Consider the simple example of three people who want to go to a movie together. They have narrowed their choices down to three movies, which they rank as shown in Table 16.1.

When they compare each of the movies, they find that *Young and Romantic* is preferred over *Third and Goal to Go* by a two to one margin and *Third and Goal to Go* is

TABLE 16.1

Voting Preferences		
	Jessica's preferences	**Ralph's preferences**	**Brutus's preferences**
First choice:	*Young and Romantic*	*Third and Goal to Go*	*Automatic Avengers*
Second choice:	*Third and Goal to Go*	*Automatic Avengers*	*Young and Romantic*
Third choice:	*Automatic Avengers*	*Young and Romantic*	*Third and Goal to Go*

preferred to *Automatic Avengers,* also by a two to one margin. Taking this information alone, they might reason that —since *Young and Romantic* is preferred over *Third and Goal to Go* and *Third and Goal to Go* is preferred over *Automatic Avengers—Young and Romantic* is also preferred to *Automatic Avengers*. But when they put it to a vote, they find that *Automatic Avengers* is preferred to *Young and Romantic* by a two to one margin. There is no majority winner. Majority voting can compare any two of these choices but is incapable of ranking all three of them.

Nobel laureate Kenneth Arrow proved an even more remarkable result. All voting systems (two thirds majority, weighted majority, or any other), under some circumstances, yield the same kind of indecision. Inconsistencies are simply inherent in the decision-making process of any democratic government. The only way around this problem, to ensure that consistent choices are made, is to entrust a single individual with all decision. Such a system yields consistent choices but is hardly democratic!

Understanding how political processes work is one of the main subjects of *political science*. Economists have looked carefully at how political processes are affected by *incentives,* for example, the incentives of politicians, of political parties, of government bureaucrats, and of special interests to curry favor with these political actors to get favorable legislation. *Public choice* theory is a branch of political economics that analyzes the outcomes of political processes assuming that each of the participants acts rationally. James Buchanan of George Mason University received a Nobel Prize for his contributions in developing public choice theory. There is widespread understanding of how campaign contributions affect the behavior of politicians, and thus the outcomes of political processes, which is why so much attention has been focused on reforming campaign contribution laws.

Current and Recent Controversies in the Economics of the Public Sector

A significant fraction of the controversies in public policy revolve around the role of the government in the economy. In the following paragraphs, we describe three of the *major* controversies.

From How to Reduce the Deficit to How to Spend the Surplus

In 1981, President Reagan helped engineer a large tax cut. Some of his advisers promised, or at least hoped, that the reduction in tax rates would so stimulate the economy that total tax revenues would increase. All the statistical evidence suggested the contrary, and this evidence proved to be true. The result was that expenditures outpaced revenues, and the U.S. government accumulated its largest fiscal deficits in its history. At their worst, the deficits were in excess of 6 percent of the GDP. It proved difficult to undo the tax cuts or to cut back expenditures, especially since Reagan was committed to increasing defense expenditures and not cutting back Social Security. To have balanced the budget, keeping these items protected, would have necessitated huge and politically unacceptable cutbacks in other programs. When President Clinton took office in 1993, he managed both to cut back expenditures, mainly on defense (which the end of the Cold War made far easier), and to in-

WRAP-UP

Sources of Public Failures

Incentives and constraints
    Due process
    Constrained ability to make long-term commitments
    Political pressures
        Pork barrel projects
        Power of lobbyists who make campaign contributions
Budgeting and spending constraints
    Soft budget constraints
    Annual appropriations process
    Rigid procurement rules
Imperfect information
    Unforeseen changes in behavior resulting from government action
Problems in collective decision making

crease taxes, mainly on the upper 2 percent of the population. At the same time, the rate of growth of the U.S. economy picked up. Some believe this growth occurred partly because of the reduction in the deficit, which had been a drag on the economy, while others believe it was a result of the new computer technologies finally bearing fruit. In any case, within a few years, the huge deficit had turned into a surplus. The issue of how to cut the deficit was flipped around; now the political issue was how to spend the surplus. Three views dominated the discussion: Some wanted large tax cuts (often directed at the rich); others wanted to use the funds to reduce the debt, which had grown so much over the previous two decades; still others wanted to use the funds for an array of social programs—from financing Social Security and health care for the aged, to improving education for the poor.

Tax cuts won out in the first months of George W. Bush's presidency. During the 2000 election, Candidate Bush campaigned vigorously for tax cuts. By June 2001 President Bush was signing into law a new tax reform that provided extensive tax cuts over a ten-year period. At the same time, the slowing economy and the need for new spending in response to the September 11, 2001 terrorist attack on the United States have significantly reduced the size of projected surpluses. In fact, a deficit is now projected for 2002.

Social Security

Even though the U.S. budget showed a surplus by the end of the 1990s, there was concern that as the baby boomers (the large number of babies born in the years following World War II) reached retirement, the United States would once again face a fiscal problem. Projected expenditures on Social Security, for instance, exceeded revenues by so much that the huge surplus would be drained within a few decades. The surge in productivity in the United States that began in the mid-1990s, if maintained, would generate enough revenues to prolong the system's viability. Still, most young people had little confidence in the long-term sustainability of the program—surveys suggested that more believed in UFOs than that the program would be around (at least in its current form) for their own retirement. While there were numerous demands for reform, many politicians remained convincing that supporting any reforms represented political suicide—it was referred to as the third rail of American politics.

Among the most widely discussed reforms were those that would allow individuals to invest *part* of their Social Security contributions in privately managed investment accounts, referred to as *partial privatization*. The booming stock market of the 1990s led many to believe that they could do far better than the government, and those in the financial community saw a real bonanza for themselves.

Several countries have tried privatization, with mixed results. Private schemes tend to have high transactions costs—so large that even in the United Kingdom, with its well-functioning capital market, retirement benefits are whittled away by about 40 percent. By contrast, the U.S. Social Security Administration has an impressive record for efficiency and "customer" responsiveness. In Chile, enthusiasm for the privatized Social Security system waned when that country's stock market crashed. Critics of privatization argue that there are two reasons for the seemingly higher returns to private accounts. The first is risk. If many retired people invest in the stock market and it does crash, either there will be a government bailout, erasing all of the seeming savings from reform, or large numbers of individuals will be left destitute, not able to live comfortably in their retirement. The second is that the U.S. system is a pay-as-you-go system, where each generation partially pays for the retirement of the previous one. The proposed privatization reforms would convert the system into a fully funded system, where each individual has his own retirement account; his own contributions pay for his own retirement. But in moving from a *pay-as-you-go* system to a *fully funded* system, something will have to be done to those who have paid for their parents' retirement but for whom funds have not yet been put aside for their own. Their retirement would have to be financed by a supplementary tax—and this tax would imply that those in the current working generation would be no better off (and possibly worse off) than under a continuation of the pay-as-you-go system.

Critics of privatization argue that the present pay-as-you-go system should be retained, and that only smaller-scale reforms are necessary to correct particular problems.

Another problem is the need to bring benefits into line with revenues, but this too can be done largely through several minor reforms. The fact that individuals are living longer and the elderly are healthier means that there may not be much hardship in extending the retirement age (accompanying this change with better disability benefits for those aged who cannot work). One of the strengths of the Social Security program is that it protects individuals against inflation—few private investments provide effective inflation insurance. However, there is evidence that Social Security benefits actually increase more than in tandem with inflation. (One study suggested that current measures of inflation exceed "true" inflation by between 1 and 2 percent.) Lowering the inflation adjustment would save billions of dollars. These adjustments could be done gradually, with relatively little impact on those who are retired today or are nearing retirement, and with little if any effect on poverty among the aged. Yet the elderly are vocal and represent an active voting bloc, and groups claiming to represent them, such as AARP (American Association of Retired People), have so far been adamant in resisting any of these changes. Until some reforms are made, the fiscal position of the Social Security system will remain in doubt.

Health Care

There has long been dissatisfaction with certain aspects of the U.S. health care system, and yet it has been hard to reform. The United States spends a larger fraction of its GDP on medical care, but its health indicators (such as child mortality or life span) are lower than those in many other countries of comparable income. (One of the reasons for this is the high level of inequality in the United States compared with some other industrialized countries. Poverty and poor health are closely associated with each other, with low income leading to poor health and poor health leading to low income. Most other countries also do a better job than the United States in making sure that all citizens have access to health care.) Health care costs have been rising faster than the cost of living in general. The rising health care costs were a major reason for the soaring federal deficit in the 1980s. The federal government has two major problems: Medicaid, which provides health care for the poor, and Medicare, which provides health care for the aged. Both have become increasingly expensive.

Not only do Americans spend more, with seemingly poorer results, than do other countries, but also there is a greater sense of *insecurity*. In most advanced industrialized countries, everyone is guaranteed the right to a reasonably high level of health care; that is, there is effectively some form of comprehensive insurance. While most Americans receive health care coverage from their employers, many Americans are without insurance. For them a major illness can be a financial disaster. While most Americans do manage to receive health care in one way or another, it is

a major source of anxiety, especially for middle-income Americans who are too well off to receive Medicaid.

Health care is different from most other commodities in several respects. Most health care expenditures are paid by the government or insurance companies, not by individuals. Hence, individuals do not have the incentives to economize on health care expenditures. Individuals also are often not in a position to judge well the importance or quality of the services being provided. They must rely on the judgment of the physician. But under the standard fee-for-service system, the physician has an incentive to provide services, some of which may be of marginal value. To make matters worse, since individuals do not bear much of the cost, they have little incentive to check the value of the services; so long as the expected benefits exceed the costs they bear, they will wish the services to be performed. Moreover, medical malpractice suits mean that if a doctor fails to provide a service that may be of benefit, he can be sued. "Defensive medicine" has become a way of life for many doctors.

To correct these problems, there has been a massive increase in the use of an alternative system, called health maintenance organizations (HMOs), or managed care. Individuals pay a fixed annual amount and then pay nominal fees for each doctor's visit. The system is based on professional ethics; the family physician decides, for instance, on whether the services of a specialist are required. But while the fee-for-service system may have an incentive for excessive provision of services, there has been a worry that HMOs have an incentive not to supply services that are needed. In principle, an HMO that is excessively restrictive would lose customers to its competitors, but in practice, competition is limited. Thus, in the discussion of health care reform in 1993 and 1994, HMOs were widely bandied about as the solution to the country's soaring health care costs, but by the late 1990s, HMOs were viewed as part of the problem. They were criticized, for instance, for "drive-by deliveries"—requirements that mothers could stay in the hospital for only a day or two after a normal delivery.

The Clinton administration proposed a massive reform in 1993 that was defeated resoundingly the following year. Since then, the focus has been on more piecemeal reforms, for example, providing health care insurance for poor children. Another reform issue involved the many individuals who could not get insurance for preexisting conditions. This meant, for example, that if an employee or a member of the employee's family had an expensive disease that was covered under the employer's existing insurance policy, the employee could not change jobs without losing coverage. The Kennedy-Kassenbaum bill restricted the ability of insurance companies to impose these conditions. But even with these reforms, the number of individuals that are not covered by health insurance has continued to rise.

Five major issues remain on the reform agenda. The first is how to reduce the number of uninsured, such as through programs targeted at the unemployed and children. The second is how to improve the *quality* of coverage, especially for the aged, in particular by including a drug benefit in Medicare and developing a program for nursing home care. Today, many elderly rely on Medicaid for nursing home care, as family resources are drained or assets are transferred to children to gain eligibility. The third issue is how to contain costs in ways that are socially acceptable. In many countries, health care benefits are rationed to contain costs; that is, government programs only provide assistance to *some* of those who need it. For example, those over eighty-five years old may not be eligible for a hip replacement or must wait in line until all of those who are under eighty-five who need a hip replacement get one. Oregon has experimented with a program that limits the kinds of assistance it will provide for the poor. The attempt by HMOs to limit costs has been resoundingly criticized but there is no generally accepted alternative. The fourth issue, and perhaps the most debated reform in recent years, concerns the provision of drug benefits for the elderly under Medicare. As drugs have become increasingly important and increasingly expensive, the fact that Medicare does not cover most of these expenses is viewed as a serious flaw in the system.

Finally, medical care is only one of the factors affecting health status—and probably not the most important. Diet (too much fat is bad for health, fruits and vegetables are good), smoking, drinking, and environmental degradation have major effects. Expenditures in promoting better diet, discouraging smoking and drinking, and improving the environment may improve health status in general, and that of the poor in particular, better than increased expenditures on medical care. So far, government programs have focused mainly on discouraging smoking among the young.

Internet Connection

Policy Analysis

Washington, D.C., is home to many research groups that focus on government programs and policies. Among the better known are the Brookings Institution (http://www.brookings.org), the American Enterprise Institute (http://www.aei.org), and the Urban Institute (http://www.urban.org). These institutions post on their Web sites research and policy pieces dealing with major public sector issues and debates. Some, like the American Enterprise Institute, are associated with conservative views. Others, such as the Brookings Institution, tend to be associated with more liberal views. In any case, the best of these institutions provide thoughtful and careful analyses of major economic policy issues.

Concluding Remarks

The American economy as a mixed economy, in which the private sector is central but in which the government plays a vital role. The balance between the private and public sectors—what the government does and how it does it—though has remained, and will remain, a subject of constant discussion. As one set of problems gets resolved, new ones are posed. The central issue of the early 1990s, of how to reduce the deficit, was quickly been replaced by the issue of how to spend the surplus. Meanwhile, difficult problems, such as how to reform Social Security and Medicare, and what the government can do to reduce poverty, remain unsolved.

Review and Practice

Summary

1. Government plays a pervasive role in the economy, influencing the economy through taxes, expenditures, and a myriad of regulations that affect every aspect of economic life.

2. In the United States, federal government spending over the last fifty years has shifted away from defense and toward Social Security, health care, and welfare. These areas accounted for 57 percent of expenditures in 2000.

3. There are three basic reasons why the government intervenes in the economy: (1) to improve economic efficiency by correcting market failures; (2) to pursue social values of fairness by altering market outcomes; and (3) to pursue other social values by mandating the consumption of merit goods (such as education) and outlawing the consumption of merit bads (such as illicit drugs).

4. Sometimes government faces a trade-off between improving the efficiency of the economy and promoting equity. The U.S. income tax illustrates this trade-off. In the interest of equity, the system requires the wealthy to pay a greater share of the tax than the poor. On the other hand, the progressive income tax discourages from work those who are the most productive.

5. A tax system can be judged by five criteria: fairness, efficiency, administrative simplicity, flexibility, and transparency.

6. Government transfer programs alter the income distribution by transferring resources from those who are relatively wealthy to those who are relatively poor. In the United States, there are five major transfer programs: welfare, Medicaid, food stamps, supplemental security income, and housing assistance.

7. Social insurance programs, like Social Security and Medicare, are entitlement programs for everyone, regardless of income. But although everyone is entitled to benefits, some redistribution takes place, with some people getting back more than they contribute.

8. Just as markets may fail, attempts by the government to intervene in the economy may also fail. Four major factors underlie systematic government failure: incentive problems, budgeting problems, information problems, and the nature of political decision making.

9. Some of the most important areas of public policy debate regarding the economic role of government relate to the federal budget surplus, reform of the Social Security system, and reform of the U.S. health care system.

Key Terms

social insurance
transfer programs
merit goods
consumer sovereignty
progressive
regressive
marginal tax rate
horizontal equity
vertical equity
tax subsidies
tax expenditure
average tax rate
individual income taxes
corporation income taxes
property taxes
gift and estate taxes
payroll tax
excise taxes
sin taxes
benefit taxes
luxury taxes
sales tax
earned income tax credit
matching programs
block grants
entitlement programs
voting paradox

Review Questions

1. Name some of the ways government touches the lives of all citizens, both in and out of the economic sphere.

2. Explain the rationale for government intervention in the economy in connection with economic efficiency, equity, and the role of merit goods.

3. What are the five characteristics of a good tax system? How well does the U.S. tax system fare in terms of these criteria? What is the difference between horizontal equity and vertical equity? What is the difference between a progressive and a regressive tax?

4. How do tax and redistribution programs affect incentives? How do social insurance programs affect incentives? Describe some of the trade-offs involved.

5. How can redistribution take place through an entitlement program like Social Security, where all workers contribute and all retirees receive benefits?

6. What are some of the major controversies in the realm of policy and public sector economics?

7. In what ways do government enterprises face different constraints from those facing firms in the private sector? What effects do the differences have on incentives?

Problems

1. In each of the following areas, specify how the government is involved, either as a direct producer, a regulator, a purchaser of final goods and services distributed directly to individuals or used within government, or in some other role:

   (a) education

   (b) mail delivery

   (c) housing

   (d) air travel

   (e) national defense

   In each of these cases, think of ways that part of the public role could be provided by the private sector.

2. Assume that a country has a simple tax structure, in which all income over $10,000 is taxed at 20 percent.

Evaluate a proposal to increase the progressivity of the tax structure by requiring all those with incomes over $100,000 to pay a tax of 80 percent on income in excess of $100,000. Draw a high-wage earner's budget constraint. How does the surtax affect his budget constraint? What happens to his incentives to work? Is it possible that imposing the tax actually will reduce the tax revenues the government receives from the rich?

3. Imagine that Congress decided to fund an increase in Social Security benefits by increasing the payroll tax on employers. Would this prevent employees from being affected by the higher tax? Draw a diagram to illustrate your answer.

4. Consider an individual contemplating whether to quit her job and go on welfare. How might the fact that welfare is time limited affect her decision? Is it possible that time-limited welfare may not only lead people to leave welfare but also reduce the number who go on welfare?

5. The president is trying to decide which of three goals he should put at the top of his agenda—social security reform (s), a middle-class tax cut (m), and preserving the safety net for the poor (p). He puts the matter before his advisers in three separate meetings. Assume he has three advisers, and he takes a vote in each meeting. His political adviser's ranking is {m-s-p}, his economic adviser's ranking is {s-p-m}, and his health care adviser's ranking is {p-m-s}. What is the outcome?

Competition Policy in the Information Age—Microsoft Versus the Justice Department

On June 7, 2000, federal judge Thomas Penfield Jackson ordered that Microsoft Corporation, the computer software giant, be broken up into two separate companies. Some commentators applauded the order as a blow against a dangerous monopoly and a boon to competition that would ultimately benefit consumers. Critics claimed the court-ordered breakup, an antitrust measure used in 1984 against AT&T's telephone monopoly and in 1911 against Standard Oil's energy monopoly, was a misguided attempt to apply policies from the old economy to the new digital economy. E-commerce is changing the nature of markets and altering the landscape of competition. The Internet increases competition by lowering the cost of acquiring information. It allows consumers to comparison shop on-line, not just for consumer goods, but for insurance policies, mortgages, car loans, financial services—even financial aid packages from colleges. Businesses use the Internet to find low-cost suppliers and competitive shipping rates. At the same time, businesses are finding that it is no longer just plant and equipment that are the firm's key assets; increasingly, the value of the firm depends on employee's skills and ideas. These changes in the marketplace are forcing governments to rethink how policies designed to ensure competition should be applied in the information age.

To understand why the U.S. Department of Justice brought an antitrust case against Microsoft, we can use some of the basic principles we covered in Chapter 12. We learned there that monopolies can survive only if there are barriers that prevent potential competitors from entering an industry. In old-economy industries, such barriers frequently include legal barriers, economies of scale, predatory market strategies, and government policies. We also learned about a network externality—an externality that arises when the benefit to the user of a product rises as the number of users increases (see e-Insight box, p. 250). At the heart of the Justice Department's antitrust case against Microsoft was the argument that a network externality created a barrier to entry that allowed Microsoft to exercise monopoly power in the software industry.

To understand the Justice Department's argument, think about what makes an operating system like Microsoft's Windows valuable—having lots of applications that run on it. Once a system such as Windows dominates the market for operating systems, it is difficult for a competitor to enter. Few people will switch to a competing operating system—even if it is an improvement over Windows—if programmers have not already written many applications for the new operating

Judge Jackson

system. But applications companies won't find it profitable to write software to run on an operating system that few people use. With few applications to offer users, other operating systems cannot effectively compete. The Justice Department called this an "applications barrier to entry."

One of the most widely used software applications is Microsoft's Office, a suite of programs that includes the word processor Word and the spreadsheet program Excel. Users of non-Windows operating systems, such as Linux, would like to have access to these programs. However, Microsoft software developers have no incentive to adapt Microsoft Office to run on Linux. Writing Office for Linux would most likely just reduce Microsoft's own sales of the Windows operating system.

Judge Jackson's proposed solution was to split Microsoft into two separate companies, one controlling the Windows operating system and the other selling all other Microsoft products, including Microsoft Office. The rationale for such a breakup is grounded in a core concept of economics—incentives matter. Judge Jackson accepted the Justice Department's argument that competition in the software industry would increase only if the court changed Microsoft's incentives. If a new company were created to produce Microsoft applications, its profitability would no longer depend solely on Windows, which would be produced by a separate company. The Microsoft applications company could increase sales by helping to foster the growth of new operating systems, since it would no longer have to worry about taking business away from Windows.

Of course, Microsoft has disputed the finding that the "applications barrier to entry" protects its monopoly power.

The company has argued that the applications barrier is small or nonexistent, since many software application firms are writing programs for operating systems other than Windows. It claims that just a handful of applications is sufficient to meet the needs of almost all computer users—a word processor, a spreadsheet, an e-mail program, and an Internet browser—a proposition borne out by the popularity of bundled programs such as Microsoft Office or Lotus SmartSuite. Microsoft maintains that a competing operating system doesn't need to have hundreds of applications written for it to compete successfully. It needs just a few (but the right few).

The case against Microsoft illustrates how economic principles can guide the government's antitrust policies even in the new digital economy. Whether the government should pursue antitrust remedies depends on its assessment of whether barriers are, in practice, significant impediments to competition and whether the firm in question has used its market power to compete unfairly. In either new-economy or old-economy industries, antitrust policies are targeted at reducing barriers to promote competition that benefits consumers.

Microsoft appealed Judge Jackson's decision to the federal Appeals Court, and in June 2001, the Appeals Court threw out Judge Jackson's order breaking the company in two. The Appeals Court accepted Judge Jackson's ruling that Microsoft had engaged in anticompetitive practices, and it ordered a new judge to hear the case and decide on the appropriate punishment. The Justice Department and Microsoft eventually reached a settlement.

Part 4

Topics in Microeconomics

Chapter 17

A Student's Guide to Investing

Key Questions:

1. What are the principle alternatives available in which to invest savings?

2. What are the important characteristics of each?

3. Why do some assets yield a higher return than others?

4. Why are assets prices so volatile? How do expectations about the future affect prices today?

5. What is meant by an efficient market? Is it possible to "beat the market"?

6. What are the some of the basic ingredients in an intelligent investment strategy?

*T*he 1990s saw a tremendous rise in the value of the stock market. It seemed like almost every day some new company was going public, selling shares to the public, and creating new billionaires overnight. The ups and downs of the stock market are often taken as key signals of the economy's health. But what can economics tell us about the stock market and how it behaves? And what can economics tell us about how you should invest your money? Every decision to save is accompanied by a decision about what to do with the savings. They might go under the mattress, but usually savings are invested, for example, in bank accounts, the stock or bond market, or the real estate market. These financial opportunities can be thought of as enticements to defer consumption—to save. Broadly speaking, an **investment** is the purchase of an asset in the expectation of receiving a return. For the economy as a whole, **real investment** must be distinguished from **financial investment.** Real investment includes the purchase of new factories and machines—it is the investment that is part of aggregate expenditures. Financial investment is the purchase of financial assets such as stocks and bonds that are expected to generate income or to appreciate in value.

This chapter is about financial investment. It first takes up the major alternatives available to savers and discusses the characteristics of the different alternatives that are important to investors. From these characteristics, we can establish a simple theory to explain how the prices of financial assets like stocks and bonds are determined. We can use what we learn about the characteristics of investment alternatives and the theory of asset prices to develop some strategies for intelligent investing.

Investment Alternatives

Savers face a myriad of possibilities when it comes to investing savings. The choices they make depend on the amount of money they have to invest, motivations to save, willingness to bear risk, and characteristics like age and health. Of the seemingly endless array of places to put one's money, five are most important: bank deposits, including certificates of deposit (CDs); housing; bonds; stocks; and mutual funds. In making choices among them, investors focus on four characteristics: return, risk, liquidity, and tax liability.

345

Bank Deposits

As a student, your major savings are likely to be earnings from a summer job that will be spent during the next school year. If so, the decision about where to invest is generally uncomplicated. A *bank savings account* (or a similar account) offers three advantages: it pays you interest, it allows easy access to your money, and it offers security, because even if the bank itself goes broke the federal government, through the Federal Deposit Insurance Corporation, insures bank deposits of up to $100,000.

After leaving school, investment decisions become more difficult. You may want to put away some savings to make a down payment on a house. (With the average house selling for almost $250,000 a 20 percent down payment would be $50,000.) As savings increase, the value of a few extra percentage points of interest also increases. A **certificate of deposit (CD)**, in which you deposit money in a bank for a preset length of time, is as safe as an ordinary bank account and yields a slightly higher return. The drawback of a CD is that if you withdraw the money before the preset time has expired, you pay a penalty. The ease with which an investment can be turned into cash is called its **liquidity.** Perfectly liquid investments can be converted into cash speedily and without any loss in value. CDs are less liquid than standard savings accounts.

Housing

Two thirds of American households invest by owning their own homes. This investment is far riskier than putting money into a bank or a certificate of deposit. Home prices usually increase over time, but not always. In 1986, the price of housing in Houston declined by 11 percent, and in 1990, the price of housing in the Northeast and in the West declined by 6.8 percent and 3.5 percent, respectively. In addition, when prices do rise, the rate of increase is uncertain. Prices may be almost level for a number of years, and then shoot up by 20 percent in a single year. Note that while the bank may provide most of the funds for the purchase of a house, the owner bears the risk, since she is responsible for paying back the loan regardless of the market price of the house.

Housing as an investment has two other attributes—one attractive and one unattractive. On the positive side, real estate taxes, property taxes, and the interest on the mortgage are tax deductible, and the capital gains usually escape taxation altogether. On the negative side, housing is usually fairly illiquid. Houses differ from one another, and

it often takes considerable time to find someone who really likes your house; if you try to sell your house quickly, on average you will receive less than you would if you had two or three months in which to sell it. Moreover, the costs of selling a house are substantial, often more than 5 percent of the value of the house—in any case more than the costs of selling stocks and bonds.

Bonds

Bonds are a way for corporations and government to borrow. The borrower—whether it is a company, a state, a school district, or the U.S. government—promises to pay the lender (the purchaser of the bond, or investor) a fixed amount in a specified number of years. In addition, the borrower agrees to pay the lender each year a fixed return on the amount borrowed. Thus, if the interest rate on a ten-year bond is 10 percent, a $10,000 bond will pay the lender $1,000 every year, and $10,000 at the end of ten years. The period remaining until a loan or bond is to be paid in full is called its *maturity.* Bonds that mature within a few years are called *short-term bonds;* those that mature in more than ten years are called *long-term bonds.* A long-term government bond may have a maturity of twenty or even thirty years.

Bonds may seem relatively safe, because the investor knows what amounts will be paid. But consider a corporate bond that promises to pay $10,000 in ten years and pays $1,000 every year until then. Imagine that an investor buys the bond, collects interest for a couple of years, and then realizes that he needs cash and wants to sell the bond. There is no guarantee that he will get $10,000 for it. He may get more and he may get less. If the market interest rate has fallen to 5 percent since the original bond was issued, a new $10,000 bond now would pay only $500 a year. Clearly, the original bond, which pays $1,000 a year, is worth considerably more. Thus, a decline in the interest rate leads to a rise in the value of bonds; and by the same logic, a rise in the interest rate leads to a decline in the value of bonds. This uncertainty about market value is what makes long-term bonds risky.[1]

---

[1] The market price of the bond will equal the percent discounted value of what it pays. For instance, a 3-year bond that pays $10 per year each of 2 years and $110 at the end of the 3rd year has a value of

$$\frac{10}{1+r} + \frac{10}{(1+r)^2} + \frac{110}{(1+r)^3},$$

where r is the market rate of interest. We can see that as r goes up, the value of the bond goes down, and vice versa.

Even if the investor holds the bond to maturity, that is, until the date at which it pays the promised $10,000, there is still a risk, since he cannot know for sure what $10,000 will purchase ten years from now. If the general level of prices increases at a rate of 7 percent over these ten years, the real value of the $10,000 will be just one half what it would have been had prices remained stable during that decade.[2]

Because of the higher risk caused by these uncertainties, long-term bonds must compensate investors by paying higher returns, on average, than comparable short-term bonds. And because every corporation has at least a slight chance of going bankrupt, corporate bonds must compensate investors for the higher risk by paying higher returns than government bonds. The higher returns more than compensate for the additional bankruptcy risk, however, according to economic research. That is, if an investor purchases a very large number of good-quality corporate bonds, the likelihood that more than one or two will default is very small, and the overall return will be considerably higher than the return from purchasing government bonds of the same maturity (the same number of years until they come due).

Some corporate bonds are riskier than others—that is, there is a higher probability of default. These bonds must pay extremely high returns to induce investors to take a chance on them. When Chrysler looked on the verge of bankruptcy in 1980, Chrysler bonds were yielding returns of 23 percent. Obviously, the more a firm is in debt, the more likely it is to be unable to meet its commitments, and the riskier are its bonds. Especially risky bonds are called *junk bonds;* the yields on such bonds are much higher than those from a financially solid firm, but the investor must take into account the high probability of default.

Shares of Stock

You might also choose to invest in shares of corporate stock. When people buy shares in a firm, they literally own a fraction (a share) of the total firm. Thus, if the firm issues 1 million shares, an individual who owns 100 shares owns .01 percent of the firm. Investors choose stocks as investments for two reasons.

First, firms pay some fraction of their earnings—its receipts after paying workers, suppliers of materials, and all interest due on bank and other loans—directly to shareholders. These payments are called **dividends.** On average, firms distribute one third of earnings as dividends; the remainder, called **retained earnings,** is kept for investment in the company. The amount of a dividend, unlike the return on a bond, depends on a firm's earnings and on what proportion of those earnings it chooses to distribute to shareholders.

In addition to receiving dividends, those who invest in stocks hope to make money by choosing stocks that will appreciate in value, and then sell them at the higher price. The increase in the realized price of a share (or any other asset) is called a **capital gain.** (If the asset is sold at a price below that at which it was purchased, the investor realizes a *capital loss.*)

Shares of stock are risky for a number of reasons. First, the earnings of firms vary greatly. Even if firms do not vary their dividends, differences in profits will lead to differences in retained earnings, and these will be reflected in the value of the shares. In addition, the stock price of a company depends on the beliefs of investors as to, for instance, the prospects of the economy, the industry, and that particular firm. Loss of faith in any one could lead to a drop in the stock price. Thus, an individual who had to sell all his shares because of some medical emergency might find they had declined significantly in value. Even if the investor believes the shares will eventually return to a higher value, he may be unable to wait.

Shares of stock are riskier than bonds. This is because, when a firm goes bankrupt and must pay off its investors, the law requires bondholders to be paid off as fully as possible before shareholders receive any money at all. As a result, a bondholder in a bankrupt company is likely to be paid some share of her original investment, while a shareholder may receive nothing. Over the long run, shares of stock have yielded very high returns. While corporate bonds yielded on average an annual real rate of return of 2 percent in the period from 1926 to 1999, shares of stock yielded a real return of nearly 10 percent in the same period.

Mutual Funds

A **mutual fund** gathers funds from many different investors into a single large pool of funds, with which it can then purchase a large number of assets. A *money market* mutual fund invests its funds in CDs and comparably safe assets.

The advantage of a money market mutual fund is that you get higher rates of interest than on bank accounts and still enjoy liquidity. The fund managers know that most individuals will leave their money in the account, and some

---

[2]If prices rise at 7 percent a year, with compounding, the price level in 10 years is $(1.07)^{10}$ times the level it is today; $(1.07)^{10}$ is approximately equal to 2; prices have doubled.

will be adding money to the account as others pull money out. They are thus able to put a large proportion of the fund in certificates of deposits and still not have to pay the penalties for early withdrawal. In this way, money market mutual funds give investors the easy access to their funds associated with banks, while providing them the higher return associated with CDs.

Money market mutual funds may also invest their customers' money in short-term government bonds, called **treasury bills,** or **T-bills.** Treasury bills are available only in large denominations ($10,000 or more). They promise to repay a certain amount (their face value, say, $10,000) in a relatively short period, less than 90 or 180 days, and investors buy them at less than their face value. The difference between the amount paid and the face value becomes the return to the purchaser.

With most money market mutual funds, you can even write a limited number of checks a month against your account. The major disadvantage of mutual funds is that they are not guaranteed by the federal government, as bank accounts are. However, some money market funds invest only in government securities or government-insured securities, making them virtually as safe as bank accounts.

Other mutual funds invest in stocks and bonds. Typically, they buy stock or bonds in dozens, sometimes hundreds, of different companies. Investors recognize the advantage of **diversification**—of not putting all their eggs in the same basket. If you put all your savings into a single stock and that firm has a bad year, you'll suffer a large loss. If you own stock in two companies, losses in one company may offset gains in the other. Mutual funds, in effect, allow

much broader diversification. Of course, if the whole stock market does badly, a stock mutual fund will suffer too. When stocks go down, bonds often go up, so some mutual funds invest in both stocks and bonds. Others invest in risky ventures which, if successful, promise high returns; these are sometimes referred to as "growth" funds. There are many other specially designed mutual funds, and together they are enormously popular. For most investors, the first foray into the bond or stock market is through the purchase of a mutual fund.

Internet Connection

Index Funds

Many mutual funds are designed to follow the return of a market index, such as the Standard and Poor's (S&P) 500 index. Standard and Poor's Web site at http://www.spglobal.com provides the latest information on the performance of their indices. If you follow the links on the left side of the page, you will find a primer on the mathematics of calculating market indices.

Desirable Attributes of Investments

Table 17.1 sets forth the various investment opportunities we have described, with a list of their most important attributes. In surveying the broad range of investment opportunities available, individuals must balance their personal needs against what the different investment options have to offer. The ideal investment would have a high rate of return, be low risk, and be exempt from tax. Unfortunately, as economists always like to point out, investors face trade-offs. You can only expect to get more of one desirable property—say a higher expected return—at the expense of another, such as safety. To understand what is entailed in these trade-offs, we need to take a closer look at each of the principle attributes of investments.

Internet Connection

Returns on U.S. Treasury Securities

The Federal Reserve Bank of New York has a Web site that explains how to calculate returns on Treasury bonds. Its address is http://www.ny.frb.org/pihome/fedpoint/fed28.html.

TABLE 17.1

Alternative Investments and How They Fare

Investment	Expected returns	Risk	Tax advantages	Liquidity
Banking savings accounts	Low	Low	None	High
CDs (certificates of deposit)	Slightly higher than savings accounts	Low	None	Slightly less than savings accounts
Houses	High returns from mid-1970s to mid-1980s; in many areas, negative returns in late 1980s, early 1990s, high returns in late 1990s	Used to be thought safe; viewed to be somewhat riskier now	Many special tax advantages	Relatively illiquid; may take long time to find "good buyer"
Federal government long-term bonds	Normally slightly higher than T-bills	Uncertain market value next period; uncertain purchasing power in long run	Exempt from state income tax	Small charge for selling before maturity
Corporate bonds	Higher return than federal bonds	Risks of long-term federal bonds plus risk of default	None	Slightly less liquid than federal bonds (depends on corporation issuing bond)
Stocks stock	High	High	Capital gains receive tax preference if stocks held for more than 1 year	Those listed on major exchange are highly liquid; others may be highly illiquid
Mutual funds	Reflect assets in which funds are invested	Reflect assets in which funds are invested; reduced risk from diversification	Reflect assets in which funds are invested	Highly liquid
T-bills	About same as CDs	Low	Exempt from state income tax	Small charge for selling before maturity

Expected Returns

First on the list of desirable properties are high returns. As we have noted, returns have two components: the interest (on a bond), dividend payment (on a stock), or rent (on real estate), and the capital gain. For instance, if you buy some stock for $1,000, receive $150 in dividends during the year, and at the end of the year sell the stock for $1,200, your total return is $150 + $200 = $350 (a rate of return of 35 percent). If you sell the stock for only $900, your total

return is $150 − $100 = $50 (a rate of return of 5 percent). If you sell it for $800, your total return is a *negative* $50 (a rate of return of −5 percent).

Few assets offer guaranteed returns. If the stock market booms, a stock share might yield 20 percent, but if the market drops, the total return might be zero or even negative. To compare two alternative investment options, we apply the concept of **expected returns.** The expected return to an asset is the single number that combines the various possible returns per dollar invested with the chances that each of

e-Insight

Investing in the New Economy

Investors worry about risk. Risk can be reduced by *diversification,* that is by, "not putting all of your eggs in one basket." Dividing one's investments among a large number of securities lowers the risk because the value of some may go up when the value of others goes down. In spite of the distinct advantages of risk diversification, many individuals own relatively few securities. One of the reasons is that it is costly to buy and sell different stocks. As a result, individuals have increasingly turned to mutual funds. Mutual funds are financial intermediaries that buy large numbers of securities. Transactions costs are lowered because the securities are bought in bulk. But nothing is free in life. Mutual funds have to make a living, and they too charge transaction costs. These costs are substantially lower than if the individual tried to buy an equally diversified portfolio on his own, but they are substantial nonetheless. Mutual funds have significant tax disadvantages as well. For instance, you buy shares in a mutual fund, say, in January 2000. In February 2000, the mutual fund sells some shares that it purchased, say, 10 years ago, and records a large capital gain. Then the value of the fund decreases—perhaps because it was a high-technology fund, and technology shares plummeted in April 2000. At the end of the year you may think you have incurred a loss. But the IRS will still insist you pay a tax as if you had a capital gain, because you owned the mutual fund at the time the capital gain was realized. This may seem grossly unfair—you are worse off, yet you have to pay a tax as if you were better off—but that is the way the tax law works.

The new economy has opened up new possibilities for individuals to diversify without large transaction costs. At least one new economy firm (FOLIO*fn*) is offering to allow investors to trade large numbers of stock for a single monthly fee, *with no marginal costs.* This arrangement allows individuals to obtain a highly diversified portfolio, to avoid the transaction costs of mutual funds, and to avoid the tax disadvantages of mutual funds. Like all innovations, it will take time for it to penetrate throughout the economy, but if successful, it may revolutionize the way investors—especially small investors—invest their money.

CASE IN POINT

PG&E Employees Learn Why Diversification Is Important

In January 2001, Pacific Gas & Electric Company (PG&E), a major supplier of electricity to northern California, quite suddenly found itself facing bankruptcy. Under California's utility deregulation statues, PG&E was prohibited from raising prices to consumers but had to pay market prices for the electricity it purchased to deliver to consumers. When skyrocketing demand and energy shortages in the west led to record energy prices, PG&E quickly ran out of cash. Wall Street was equally quick to respond. PG&E's stock price plummeted from $31.64 on September 11 to $10.19 in January. The utility's bonds were downgraded to the lowest echelons of the "junk bond" range, indicating that Wall Street thought there was little chance that bondholders would be repaid or receive interest. PG&E suspended dividends on its stock, laid off workers, and hired bankruptcy lawyers to assess its options.

For some PG&E employees, the energy crisis that threatened to undermine the booming California economy carried a double threat. Workers were clearly in danger of losing jobs. But over 80 percent of PG&E's workers were also shareholders who owned stock through the company's retirement plan. PG&E for years had contributed stock one-for-one when employees purchased company stock for their individual 401(k) retirement accounts. Employees had the option of selling the PG&E stock and

A crowd protests rate hikes by the California utility PG&E, which were made in an effort to fend off bankruptcy.

replacing it with other assets, but not everyone took advantage of the chance to diversify. When PG&E stock lost two thirds of its value, these workers' 401(k) retirement plans followed suit. Though their pensions and 401(k) could not be seized by a bankruptcy court, workers whose 401(k) plans were heavily invested in PG&E stock had no protection from the risk that stock prices would nosedive.

Longtime employees who failed to diversify out of PG&E stock to obtain a more balanced portfolio saw their dreams of early retirement and a secure old age vanish. When asked why so many employees were overinvested in PG&E stock, one employee replied that people believed in the company that had provided a good living for them, and in some cases, their parents, for most of their lives. The sudden collapse of PG&E underscores the importance of diversification to minimize (though not avoid) the risk of holding individual stocks.[3] ●

---

[3]Based on an article by Jennifer Bjorhus, "PG&E's 'Family' Falling Apart," *San Jose Mercury News,* January 22, 2001, p. 1.

these various possibilities will occur. If there is a one in four chance (a 25 percent probability) a stock will yield a 20 percent return over the next year, a one in two chance (a 50 percent probability) the return will be 5 percent, and a one in four chance (a 25 percent probability) the return will be zero, the expected return on the stock is 7.5 percent (.25 times 20 percent + .5 times 5 percent + .25 times 0 percent).

An important first lesson in investment theory is as follows: *If there were no differences between assets other than the ways in which they produce returns (interest, dividends, etc.), then the expected returns to all assets would be the same.* Why? Suppose an asset offered an expected return of 10 percent while all others offered 6 percent. Investors, in trying to buy the higher-yielding asset, would bid more for the asset, pushing up its price. As the price rose, the expected return would decline. The upward pressure would continue until the expected return declined to match the level of all other investments.

In fact, the expected returns per dollar invested for different assets differ markedly from one another. This is because a number of other important attributes affect an asset's return. These include risk, tax considerations, and liquidity (the ease with which an asset can be sold).

Risk

Most of us do not like the risk that accompanies most future-oriented economic activity. We might spend a few dollars on some lottery tickets or occasionally play the slot machines at Las Vegas or Atlantic City, but for the most part we try to avoid or minimize risks. Economists refer to risk-avoidance behavior by saying individuals are *risk averse* and their behavior displays **risk aversion.**

A prime consideration for any investor, therefore, is the riskiness of any investment alternative. Bank accounts, in this regard, are safe. Since government deposit insurance came into play in the 1930s after the bank failures that occurred during the Great Depression, no one in the United States has lost money in an insured bank account. But investments in housing, stocks, and bonds and most other investments involve risk. The return may turn out to be substantially lower, or higher, than you expected.

Historically, stocks have yielded a higher average return than bonds, but stocks are riskier—prices on the stock market fluctuate, and they can do so quite dramatically. On the single day of October 19, 1987, stock prices on the New York Stock Exchange fell by 508 points, a drop in value of 23 percent.

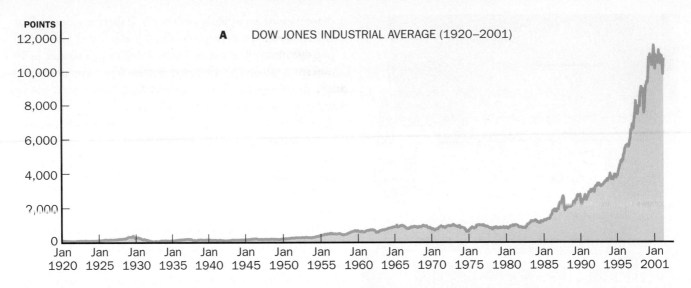

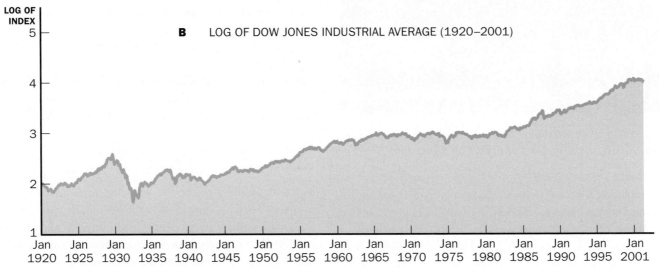

FIGURE 17.1   *Stock Market Indices*

Panel A shows the closing monthly value of the Dow Jones industrial average, an index of stock prices that is based on the prices of shares in major companies. Panel B plots the natural log of the Dow Jones index so that percentage changes in the level of stock prices can be seen more clearly. Panel C shows an index of prices on the Nasdaq market since 1984, while panel D shows the same index in natural log form.

Figure 17.1 shows two major indices of stock market prices. Panel A shows the closing daily value of the Dow Jones industrial average, an index of stock prices that is based on the prices of shares in major companies. Today, thirty companies are included in the index, which was revised in 1999 to include such firms as Microsoft and Intel. Because the index has grown so much since 1920, the 1929 stock market crash barely shows up in the figure. The index fell in value almost 13 percent on October 28, 1929, but this was a decline of only 38 points, well within the typical range of daily fluctuations in the market today. The largest one-day drop occurred on October 27, 1997, when the Dow Jones index lost 554 points.

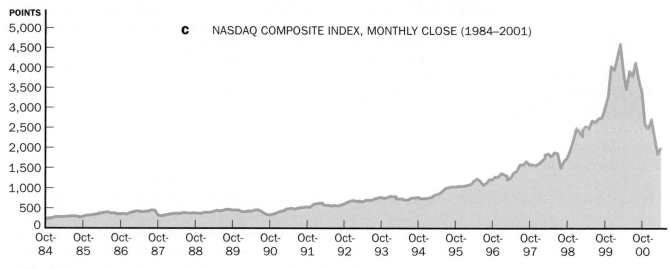

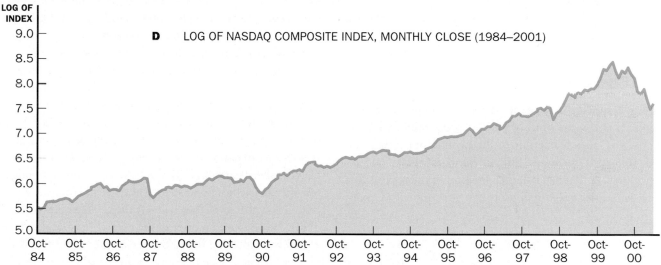

The percentage change in the level of stock prices can be seen more clearly by plotting the natural log of the Dow Jones index (panel B). The magnitude of the 1929 crash clearly stands out. What also stands out is the fact that the 1929 crash was not simply a one-day drop—three of the five biggest percentage daily declines over the 1900–2000 period occurred in late October and early November of 1929. The record for the largest percentage drop on a single day is held by December 12, 1914, when the market lost 24 percent of its value. Second is October 19, 1987, when the market fell 23 percent.

While the New York Stock Exchange is by far the largest stock market in the world, there are other markets, and in recent years the Nasdaq market has grown in importance. The Nasdaq stock market was created in 1971 and is heavily weighted toward the new technology companies.

The stocks of Microsoft and Intel, for example, are traded on the Nasdaq market, not the New York Stock Exchange. When Microsoft and Intel were added to the Dow Jones index in 1999, it represented the first time that companies traded on the Nasdaq market, and not the New York Stock Exchange, were included in the index. Panel C shows an index of prices on the Nasdaq market since 1984, while panel D shows the same index in natural log form.

The stock market decline between August 2000 and March 2001 shows up clearly in panel D. While both the Dow Jones index and the Nasdaq index show a tendency to rise over time—leading to capital gains from holding stock—both also show the ups and downs that occur over shorter periods. It is these fluctuations in value that make investing in stocks risky.

Risk can never be avoided completely, and it has been said that financial markets are the places where risk is bought and sold. We can see the effects of changes in risk in Figure 17.2. A reduction in the riskiness of an asset makes it more desirable, and this shifts the demand curve for the asset to the right. In the short run the supply of an asset is inelastic. Even in the longer run, supply is likely not to be perfectly elastic. Accordingly, as illustrated in the figure, the price of the asset goes up, from p_0 to p_1. Accompanying the increase in price is a reduction in the return per dollar invested.

An asset that is less risky will have a higher demand. The higher demand will lead to a higher price and lower return. Therefore, the expected return will be lower on assets that are safer. Economists say such desirable assets sell at a *premium,* while assets that are riskier sell at a *discount.* Still, market forces ensure that assets of comparable risk must yield the same expected returns.

Tax Considerations

The government is a silent partner in almost all investments. It is not the kind of partner you would ordinarily choose—it takes a fraction of the profits, but leaves you with almost all the losses. Still, investors must take into account the fact that a substantial fraction of the returns to a successful investment will go to the government as taxes.

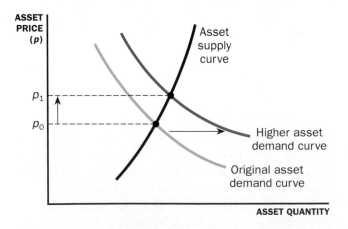

FIGURE 17.2   *Effects of Differences in Risk*

Lowering risk shifts the demand curve for the asset to the right, increasing the equilibrium price and lowering the average return.

Since different assets are treated differently in the tax code, tax considerations are obviously important in choosing a portfolio. After all, individuals care about after-tax returns, not before-tax returns. Investments that face relatively low tax rates are said to be *tax-favored.*

State and municipal bonds illustrate this point. These bonds yield a lower return than do corporate bonds of comparable risk and liquidity. So why do people buy them? The answer is that the interest on bonds issued by states and municipalities is generally exempt from federal tax. The higher your income, the more valuable this tax exemption is, because your tax savings are greater the higher your tax *rate.* The higher demand for these tax-exempt bonds from high-income investors drives up their price, which drives down the return received on the bonds. We can expect the return to decline to the point where the after-tax return for high-income individuals is at most only slightly higher than for an ordinary taxable bond of comparable risk.

Consider two bonds, identical in all respects except their tax treatment. Both promise to pay $110 next year, $10 of which is interest. The price of the taxable bond is $100. The equilibrium price for a municipal bond is greater than $100. This means that its average return, before tax, is less than 10 percent—less than the return on the taxable bond. If most investors have to pay 30 percent of any interest income in taxes, then the after-tax return is $7, not $10. They will be willing to buy the tax-exempt bond so long as its yield is at least 7 percent. Below that level, they will buy the taxable bond instead. Thus, the equilibrium price of the tax-exempt bond is $100 ÷ 1.07 = $102.80. That is, the tax-exempt bond yields the same return at a price of approximately $103 as the taxable bond does at $100.

Investing in housing, particularly a house to live in, is another tax-favored form of investment enjoyed by most Americans. You can deduct the interest payments on your mortgage and real estate taxes when you calculate your income for tax purposes. In addition, the capital gain from owning the house is not taxed until the house is sold. Even then, the capital gain (up to $500,000 for a married couple) from selling your house is not taxed at all. If the tax advantages of home ownership were ever withdrawn, we could expect housing prices to decline precipitously in the short run (in which supply is inelastic), as illustrated in Figure 17.3. It is not likely that tax preferences for housing will be suddenly removed, however, because most voters own houses, and politicians are loathe to anger such as a large number of their constituents.

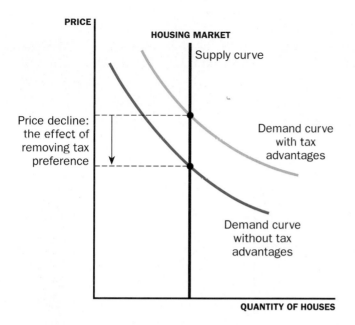

PRICE

HOUSING MARKET

Supply curve

Price decline:
the effect of
removing tax
preference

Demand curve
with tax
advantages

Demand curve
without tax
advantages

QUANTITY OF HOUSES

FIGURE 17.3   *Effect of Removing Tax
Preferences for Housing*

Removing tax preferences for housing will shift the demand
curve for housing down, and this will, in the short run (with
an inelastic housing supply), cause marked decreases in the
price of housing.

Liquidity

The fourth important attribute to consider is liquidity. An
asset is liquid if the costs of selling it are very low. A bank
account is completely liquid (except when the bank goes
bankrupt), because you can turn it into cash at virtually no
charge by writing a check. Corporate stock in a major company is fairly liquid, because the costs of selling at a well-
defined market price are relatively small.

In the basic competitive model, all assets are assumed
to be perfectly liquid. There is a well-defined price at
which anything can be bought and sold; any household
or firm can buy or sell as much as it wants at that price;
and the transaction is virtually without cost. But these assumptions are not always met. There are often significant
costs of selling or buying an asset. The costs of selling a
house, for instance, can be 5 percent or more of the value
of the house. At times, even municipal bonds have been
fairly illiquid. The prices at which such bonds could be
bought and sold have been known to differ by more than
20 percent.

Expectations and the
Market for Assets

Gardeners today would have been shocked at the price of
tulip bulbs in early seventeenth-century Holland, where
one bulb sold for the equivalent of $16,000 in today's dol-
lars. The golden age of tulips did not last long, however,
and in 1637, prices of bulbs fell by over 90 percent. Dramatic price swings for assets are not only curiosities of history. Between 1973 and 1980, the price of gold rose from
$98 to $613, or by 525 percent; then, from 1980 to 1985,
it fell to $318. Between 1977 and 1980, the price of farm
land in Iowa increased by 40 percent, only to fall by over
60 percent from 1980 to 1987. On October 19, 1987,
stock values on the U.S. stock market fell by one half trillion dollars, almost 25 percent. Even a major war would be
unlikely to destroy one fourth of the U.S. capital stock in a
single day. But there was no war or other external event to
explain the 1987 drop.

How can the basic demand and supply model explain
these huge price swings? If asset prices depend on the four
basic attributes of expected return, risk, tax treatment, and
liquidity, how can demand curves, or supply curves, shift
so dramatically as to cause these large price movements?

The answer lies in the critical role that expectations
play in the market for assets. Assets like gold, land, or
stocks are long-lived; they can be bought at one date and
sold at another. For this reason, the price individuals are
willing to pay for them today depends not only on today's
conditions—the immediate return or benefit—but also on
some expectation of what tomorrow's condition will be. In
particular, the demand for an asset will depend on what the
asset is expected to be worth in the future.

To see how expectations concerning future events affect
current prices, consider a hypothetical example. People suddenly realize that new smog-control devices will, ten years
from now, make certain parts of Los Angeles much more attractive places to live than they are today. As a result, future-
oriented individuals will think that ten years from now the
price of land in those areas will be much higher, say $1 mil-
lion an acre. But, they also think, nine years from now it will
already be recognized that in one short year an acre will be
worth $1 million. Hence, nine years from now investors will
be willing to pay almost $1 million for the land—even if, at
that date (nine years from now), the smog has not yet been
eliminated. But then, these same individuals think, eight

Thinking Like an Economist

The Distribution of Wealth and Ownership of Assets

The stock market boom of the 1990s generated large increases in wealth, but these gains were distributed unevenly among American families. Chart A shows median family net worth in 1998, classified by 1998 income. The median net worth of the 12.6 percent of families with income less than $10,000 was just $3,600. That means that half of the families in this income group had net worth less than $3,600. For the 8.6 percent of families with incomes over $100,000, median net worth was $510,800.

While poor families have less wealth than do high-income families, the types of financial and nonfinancial assets families hold also differ by income. Wealthy families are more likely to own stocks and bonds, to hold mutual funds, and to have retirement accounts. The value of holdings of nonfinancial assets—cars, homes, nonresidential property, and businesses—also varies widely by income. As the Chart B illustrates, high-income families tend to have greater holdings in cars, residential property, and other property than do families with lower incomes, but the biggest difference across income categories is in the ownership of businesses. The median value of business equity held by families with 1998 incomes greater than $100,000 was $230,000, compared with holdings of $56,000 for the next highest income group.

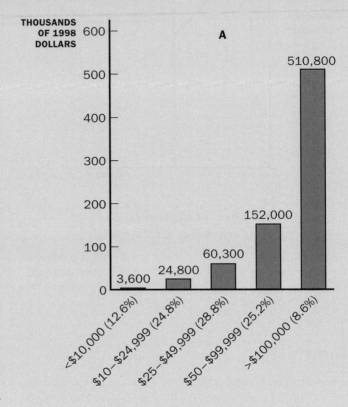

Median Family Net Worth by Income (1998)

years from now investors will realize that in one short year the price will rise to almost $1 million and will pay close to that amount. Working backward like this makes it apparent that if people are confident land is going to be much more valuable in ten years, its price rises today.

Thus, while changes in tastes or technology or incomes or the prices of other goods *today* could not account for some of the sharp changes in asset values described at the start of this section, changes in expectations concerning any of these variables in the future will have an effect *today* on the demand. Markets for assets are linked together over time. An event that is expected to happen in ten or fifteen or even fifty years can have a direct bearing on today's market.

To evaluate the effects of expected future prices on an asset's current price, the concept of present discounted value, introduced in Chapter 4, is important. Calculating the present discounted value allows us to measure and compare returns anticipated in the future. Demand today for an asset will depend on the present discounted value that it is expected to fetch when sold in the future.

Present discounted values can change for two reasons. First, they can change because of a change in the expected price of an asset at the time one expects to sell it. This type of change is illustrated in Figure 17.4. Such expectations of future prices can be quite volatile, and this helps to explain the volatility of asset prices. Investors in seventeenth-

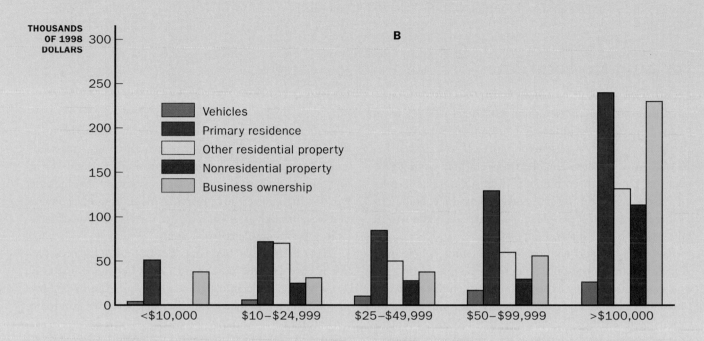

Median Family Holdings of Nonfinancial Assets, by Income

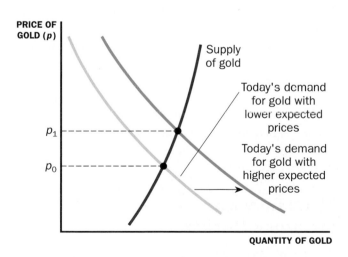

FIGURE 17.4 *How Expectations can Shift Demand*

Expectations that the price of an asset like gold will rise in the future can cause the demand curve to shift out to the right, thus raising the current price.

century Holland were willing to pay enormous prices for tulip bulbs because they expected to be able to sell the bulbs at even higher prices. Asset price increases that are based solely on the expectation that prices will be higher in the future—and not based on increases in the actual returns yielded by the asset—are called **asset price bubbles.** Prices continue to rise as long as everyone expects them to rise. Once people believe prices will not continue to rise, the current price crashes. The tremendous rise in stock prices in the United States during the 1990s led many to worry that it was a bubble that would eventually crash. Others pointed to increased productivity that promises higher corporate profits in the future—an increase in the actual returns that stocks can pay.

Second, present discounted values can change because the interest rate changes. An increase in the interest rate reduces the present discounted value of the dollars you expect to receive in the future. This is one reason why increases in the interest rate are often accompanied by drops in the prices of shares on the stock market, and vice versa. Smart investors thus try to forecast interest rates accurately. So-called Fed watchers try to anticipate changes in Federal Reserve policies that will affect the interest rate.

Forming Expectations

Changes in expectations about future returns or interest rates, then, can be reflected in large changes in asset prices today. How do individuals and firms form expectations? Partly by looking at past experience. If a company has steadily grown more valuable, investors may come to expect that pattern to continue. If every time inflation rates increase the Federal Reserve acts to slow the economy by raising interest rates, people come to expect inflation to be followed by higher interest rates.

Psychologists and economists have studied how individuals form expectations. Sometimes people are *myopic,* or short-sighted. They expect what is true today to be true tomorrow. The price of gold today is what it will be tomorrow. Sometimes they are *adaptive,* extrapolating events of the recent past into the future. If the price of gold today is 5 percent higher than it was last year, they expect its price next year to be 5 percent higher than it is today.

When people make full use of all relevant available data to form their expectations, economists say that their expectations are *rational.* While the price of gold rises during an inflationary period, the price of gold also goes down when inflation subsides. Thus, if a person knows that economic analysts are predicting lower inflation, he will not expect the gold price increases to continue. Even when individuals form their expectations rationally, they will not be right all the time. Sometimes they will be overly optimistic, sometimes overly pessimistic (although in making their decisions, they are aware of these possibilities). But the assumption of rational expectations is that on average they will be right.

The 1970s was a decade when adaptive expectations reigned. Many investors came to expect prices of assets such as land and housing to continue to rise rapidly. The more you invested, the more money you made. The idea that the price of a house or of land might fall seemed beyond belief—even though history is full of episodes (most recently in Japan during the 1990s) when such prices fell dramatically. The weak real estate markets of the 1980s in many regions reminded investors of the importance of incorporating historical data in forming expectations.

But in this, as in all types of fortune-telling, history never repeats itself exactly. Since the situation today is never precisely like past experience, it is never completely clear which facts will be the relevant ones. Even the best-informed experts are likely to disagree. When it comes to predicting the future, everyone's crystal ball is cloudy.

Efficient Market Theory

The demand for any asset depends on all four of the attributes just discussed—average return, risk, tax treatment, and liquidity. In a well-functioning market, there are no bargains to be had; you get what you pay for. If some asset yields a higher average return than most other investments, it is because that asset has a higher risk, is less liquid, or receives less favorable tax treatment.

That there are no bargains does not mean the investor's life is easy. He still must decide what he wants, just as he does when he goes into a grocery store. Figure 17.5 shows the kind of choices he faces. For simplicity, we ignore liquidity and tax considerations and focus only on average returns and risk. The figure shows the opportunity set in the way that is usual for this case. Because "risk" is bad, to get less risk we have to give up some average returns. That is why the trade-off has a positive slope. We can see that assets with greater risk have a higher average return. Point *A* represents a government T-bill—no risk but low return. Point *B* might represent a stock or mix of stocks of average riskiness; point *C,* one of high risk. A very risk-averse person might choose *A;* a less risk-averse person, *B;* a still less risk-averse person, *C.*

The theory that prices perfectly reflect the characteristics of assets—there are no bargains—is called the **efficient market theory.** Since much of the work on efficient market theory has been done on publicly traded stocks, our discussion centers on them. The lessons, however, can be applied to all asset prices.

Efficiency and the Stock Market

Most people do not think they can wander over to the racetrack and make a fortune. They are not so skeptical about the stock market. They believe that even if they themselves cannot sit down with the *Wall Street Journal* or browse an on-line broker's site and pick out all the best stocks, someone who studies the stock market for a living could do so. But economists startled the investment community in the

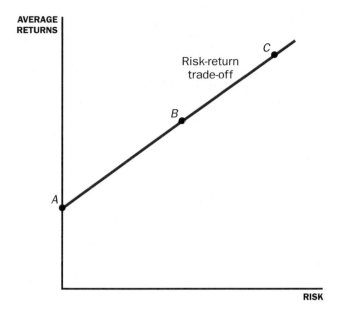

FIGURE 17.5 *The Risk-Return Trade-Off*

To get a higher expected return, an investor must accept more risk.

early 1960s by pointing out that choosing successful stocks is no easier—and no harder—than choosing the fastest horses.

The efficient market theory explains this discrepancy in views. When economists refer to an efficient market, they are referring to one in which relevant information is widely known and quickly distributed to all participants. To oversimplify a bit, they envision a stock market where all investors have access to *Barron's* and *Fortune* magazines or to one of the many Internet sites devoted to providing good information about businesses, and where government requires businesses to disclose certain information to the public. Thus, each stock's expected return, its risk, and its tax treatment, and so on will be fully known by all investors. Because participants have all the relevant information, asset prices will reflect it.

It turns out, however, that this broad dissemination of information is not only unrealistic but also unnecessary for the stock market to be efficient. Economists have shown that efficient markets do not require that *all* participants have information. If enough participants have information, prices will move as if the whole market had the information. All it takes is a few people knowledgeable enough to recognize a good deal (bad deal), and prices will quickly be bid up (or down) to levels that reflect complete information. And if

prices reflect complete information, even uninformed investors, purchasing at current prices, will reap the benefit; while they cannot beat the market, neither do they have to worry about being "cheated" by an overpriced security.

You cannot "beat" an efficient market any more than you can beat the track. You can only get lucky in it. All the research done by the many big brokerage houses and individual investors adds up to a market that is in some respects like a casino. This is the irony of the view, held by most economists, that the stock market is an efficient one. If you are trying to make money in an efficient stock market, it is not enough to choose companies that you expect will be successful in the future. If you expect a company to be successful and every one else also expects it to be successful, based on available information, then the price of the shares in that company will already be high. The only way to make abnormally high profits on stock purchases is to pick companies that will surprise the market by doing better than is generally expected. There are always such companies—the problem is identifying them before everyone else! When Microsoft shares first became available to the public in March 1986, they sold for $.19 a share—today, those shares are worth around $70 each. Early investors in technology stocks made enormous returns because technology firms did better than anyone initially expected. Because of the success of many of these companies, today when one "goes public"—sells shares to the public for the first time—the price often jumps immediately to a very high level. An investor buying the stock at the high market price can only expect to earn a normal level of profit.

The one exception is not really an exception because it involves trading with knowledge that other stock market participants do not have. *Inside traders* are individuals who buy and sell shares of companies for which they work. Studies show that their inside knowledge does in fact enable them to obtain above-average returns. Federal law requires inside traders to disclose when they buy and sell shares in their own company. People who may not have the inside knowledge but imitate the stock market behavior of the insiders also do slightly above average. The law also restricts the ability of insiders to share their information with outsiders and profit from their extra knowledge, and exacts penalties for violations. Ivan Boesky made untold millions trading on insider information in the 1980s and paid large fines and even served time in jail.

Because prices in an efficient market already reflect all available information, any price changes are a response to *unanticipated* news. If it was already known that something good was going to occur, for instance, some new computer model better than all previous computers was going to be unveiled, the price of the firm's stock would reflect this (it would be high) before the computer actually hit the market. You might not know precisely how much better than its competitors the new computer was, and hence you could not predict precisely by how much future earnings were likely to rise. You would make an estimate. The market will reflect the average of these estimates. When the new computer is introduced, there is some chance that it will be better than this average, in which case the price will rise further. But there is also a chance that it will not be quite as good as this average estimate, in which case the price will fall, even though the computer is in fact better than anything else on the market. In this case, the "surprise" is that the computer is not as good as the market anticipated.

Since tomorrow's news is, by definition, unanticipated, no one can predict whether it will cause the stock price to rise or fall. In an efficient stock market, prices will move unpredictably, depending on unexpected news. When a stock has an equal chance of rising or falling in value relative to the market as a whole, economists say that its price moves like a **random-walk.** Figure 17.6 shows a computer-generated random walk, giving an idea of how unpredictable such a path is.

Random walk conjures up the image of a drunk who rambles down the street with generally unstable—and unpredictable—movements.

So too with the stock market. Although there is an upward drift in the level of all stock prices, whether any particular stock will do better or worse than that average is unpredictable. If the stock market is indeed a random walk, it is virtually impossible for investors to beat the market. You can do just as well by throwing darts at the newspaper financial page as you can by carefully studying the prospects of each firm. The only way to do better than the market, on average, is to take greater risks; but taking greater risks means that there is also a larger chance of doing worse than the market.

The randomness of the market has one important consequence: *some* individuals are going to be successful. This is bad news for people who want to believe that their insights, rather than luck, are what has enabled them to beat the market.

Efficient Markets or Random Noise?

While most economists agree that there is little evidence individuals can consistently beat the market, even when they spend considerable money on information, there is controversy about how to interpret this finding. Some see it as evidence of the efficiency of the market, as we have seen. But some economists view it as evidence of nothing more than the market's randomness. Those who hold this view point out that there often seem to be large changes in stock market prices without any "news" of sufficient magnitude to account for these changes. For example, there are usually ten or fifteen days in the year when the stock market changes by more than 2 percent—a very large change for a single day—without any obvious news-related explanation.

The famous economist John Maynard Keynes compared predictions of the stock market to predictions of the winner of a beauty contest, where what one had to decide was not who was most beautiful, but who the judges would think was the most beautiful. If investors suddenly "lose confidence" in a particular stock or in the whole stock market, or if they believe others are losing confidence, share prices may fall dramatically.

Strategies for Intelligent Investing

So far, we have investigated major investment alternatives available to those who save, some of the important attributes of each, and the ways in which their prices reflect these attributes. If you are lucky enough (have enough money) to be considering some of these alternatives, keep in mind the following four simple rules. These rules will not tell you how to make a million by the time you are twenty-five, but they will enable you to avoid the worst pitfalls of investing.

1. *Know the attributes of each asset, and relate them to your personal situation.* Each asset has characteristic returns, risk, tax treatment, and liquidity. In making choices among different assets, your attitude toward each of these attributes should be *compared with the average at-*

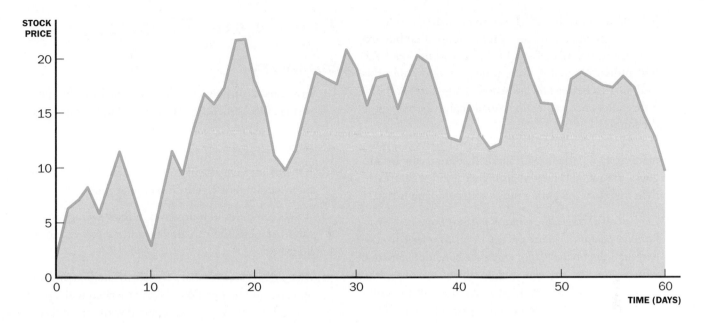

FIGURE 17.6   *A Computer-Generated Random Walk*

The series plotted here can be thought of as the closing price for a stock over 60 consecutive trading sessions. There is no predicting at the end of each day whether the stock will close higher or lower the next day.

titudes reflected in the marketplace. Most individuals prefer safer, tax-favored, more liquid assets. That is why those assets sell at a premium (and produce a correspondingly lower average return). Are you willing to pay the amount required by the market for the extra safety or extra liquidity? If you are less risk averse than average, you will find riskier assets attractive. You will not be willing to pay the higher price—and accept the lower return—for a safer asset. And if you are confident that you are not likely to need to sell an asset quickly, you will not be willing to pay the premium that more liquid assets require. If you are putting aside money for tuition next year, on the other hand, you probably will want to choose a relatively liquid asset.

2. *Give your financial portfolio a broad base.* In choosing among financial assets, you need to look not only at each asset separately but also at all of your assets together. A person's entire collection of assets is called her **portfolio.** (The portfolio also includes liabilities—what she owes—but they take us beyond the scope of this chapter.) This rule is seen most clearly in the case of

risk. One of the ways you reduce risk is by diversifying your investment portfolio. With a well-diversified portfolio, it is extremely unlikely that something will go wrong with all the assets simultaneously. An investor with a diversified portfolio must still worry about events like recessions or changes in the interest rate, which will tend to make all stocks go up or down. But events that affect primarily one firm will have a small impact on the overall portfolio.

Many mutual funds claim more than just diversification: they claim that their research and insight into markets enable them to pick winners. Our discussion of efficient markets casts doubt on these claims. Many mutual funds do no research, claim no insights, and do nothing more than provide portfolio diversification. These are called *index funds*. There are several measures of the average price of stocks in the market. For instance, the Standard & Poor's (S&P) 500 index is the average price of 500 stocks chosen to be representative of the market as a whole. Other indices track prices of various categories of stocks, such as transportation, utilities, or high technology. Index funds link their portfolio to these stock market indexes. Thus, there are a number of index funds that buy exactly the same mix of stocks that constitute the S&P 500 index. Naturally, these index funds do about as well as—no better and no worse than—the S&P 500 index, after accounting for a small charge for managing the fund.

Because the index funds have low expenses, particularly in comparison with funds that are trying to outguess the market, they yield higher average returns to their investors than other funds with comparable risk.

3. *Look at* all *of the risks you face, not just those in your financial portfolio.* Many people may be far less diversified than they believe. For example, consider someone who works for the one big company in town. She owns a house, has a good job, has stock in the company, money in the bank, and a pension plan. But if that single company goes broke, she will lose her job, the value of her stock will fall, the price of her house is likely to decline as the local economy suffers, and even the pension plan may not pay as much as expected.

4. *Think twice before you think you can beat the market!* Efficient market theory delivers an important message to the personal investor. If an investment adviser tells you of an opportunity that beats the others on all counts, don't believe him. The bond that will produce a higher than average return carries with it more risk. The bank account that has a higher interest rate has less liquidity. The dream house at an unbelievable price probably has a leaky roof. The tax-favored bond will have a lower return—and so on. Efficient market theory, as we have seen, says that information about these characteristics is built into the price of assets, and hence built in to the returns. Basically, investors can adjust the return to their portfolio only by adjusting the risk they face. Burton Malkiel, author of the best-selling book *A Random Walk Down Wall Street*, applies this theory to personal investment. "Every investor must decide the trade-off he or she is willing to make between eating well and sleeping well. The decision is up to you. High investment returns can be achieved only at the cost of substantial risk taking."[4]

---

[4]6th ed. (New York: Norton, 1995).

Review and Practice

Summary

1. Investment options for individuals include putting savings in a bank account of some kind or using them to buy real estate, bonds, or shares of stock or mutual funds.

2. Returns on investment can be received in four ways: interest, dividends, rent, and capital gains.

3. Assets can differ in four ways: in their average returns, their riskiness, their treatment under tax law, and their liquidity.

4. By holding assets that are widely diversified, individuals can avoid many of the risks associated with specific assets, but not the risks associated with the market as a whole.

5. Today's price of an asset is influenced by expectations of the asset's price in the future. Expectation of a higher price in the future will cause the asset's price to rise today.

6. Asset prices can be very volatile because of shifts in expectations about future returns.

7. The efficient market theory holds that all available information is fully reflected in the price of an asset. Accordingly, changes in price reflect only unanticipated events and, therefore, are random and unpredictable.

8. There are four rules for intelligent investors: (1) evaluate the characteristics of each asset and relate them to your personal situation; (2) give your financial portfolio a broad base; (3) look at all the risks you face, not just those in your financial portfolio; (4) think twice before believing you can beat the market.

Key Terms

investment
real investment
financial investment
certificate of deposit (CD)
liquidity
dividends
retained earnings

capital gain
mutual fund
Treasury bills (T-bills)
diversification
expected returns
risk aversion
asset price bubbles
efficient market theory
random walk
portfolio

Review Questions

1. Suppose an investor is considering two assets with identical expected rates of return. What three characteristics of the assets might help differentiate the choice between them?

2. List the principal alternative forms of investment that are available. What are the returns on each called? Rate them in terms of the characteristics described in question 1.

3. True or false: "Two assets must have equal expected returns." If we modify the statement to read "Two assets that are equally risky must have equal expected returns," is the statement true? Explain your answer.

4. If you found out that several company presidents were buying or selling stock in their own companies, would you want to copy their behavior? Why or why not?

5. What is the efficient market theory? What implications does it have for whether you can beat the market? Does it imply that all stocks must yield the same expected return?

6. Why do economists expect the market to be efficient?

7. What alternative interpretations are given to the observation that individuals cannot, even by spending considerable money on information, consistently beat the market?

8. List and explain the four rules for intelligent investing.

9. True or false: "A single mutual fund may be a more diversified investment than a portfolio of a dozen stocks." Explain.

Problems

1. Imagine a lottery where 1 million tickets are sold at $1 apiece, and the winning ticket receives a prize of $700,000. What is the expected return to buying a ticket in this lottery? Will a risk-averse person buy a ticket in this lottery?

2. Would you expect the rate of return on bonds to change with their length of maturity? Why or why not?

3. Why might a risk-averse investor put some money in junk bonds?

4. Would you predict that

   (a) the before-tax return on housing would be higher or lower than the before-tax return on other assets?

   (b) investors would be willing to pay more or less for a stock with a high return when the economy is booming and a low return when the economy is in a slump than they would pay for a stock with just the opposite pattern of returns?

   (c) an investment with low liquidity would sell at a premium or a discount compared with a similar investment with higher liquidity?

5. Imagine a short-term corporate $1,000 bond that promises to pay 8 percent interest over three years. This bond will pay $80 at the end of the first year and the second year, and $1,080 at the end of the third year. After one year, however, the market interest rate has increased to 12 percent. What will the bond be worth to an investor who is not too concerned about risk at that time? If the firm appears likely to go bankrupt, how will the expected return on this bond change?

6. Golfer Lee Trevino once said: "After losing two fortunes, I've learned. Now, when someone comes to me with a deal that's going to make me a million dollars, I say, 'Tell it to your mother.' Why would a stranger want to make me a million?" Explain how Trevino's perspective fits the efficient market theory.

Chapter 18

Trade Policy

Key Questions

1. Why and how do countries erect barriers to trade?

2. What is meant by fair trade laws? What is dumping, and why are economists often critical of antidumping laws?

3. Why are government subsidies to industries considered a barrier to trade? To what extent do countervailing duties correct this problem?

4. Why is protection so popular? Who are the winners and losers from free trade?

5. What are some of the institutions and agreements through which trade barriers have been reduced?

6. Why have international trade agreements become so controversial?

Go into any Gap or other clothing store and look at the labels: While some items are made in the U.S.A., others come from Hong Kong, Malaysia, China, Taiwan, the Philippines, or India. Today, Americans enjoy products produced around the world, and citizens in other countries travel in American jets, take American medicines, and watch American-made movies. In Chapter 3, we saw that there are gains for all countries when they produce and trade according to their comparative advantage.

In spite of the gains from trade, countries have imposed a variety of barriers to trade. Over the past fifty years, the United States has worked with other countries to lower these barriers to trade. This chapter explores both the barriers to trade and the major initiatives to remove these barriers.

Commerical Policy

Countries that have *no* barriers to trade are said to practice **free trade,** but most countries engage in some form of **protectionism**—that is, in one way or another they restrict the importation of goods. Policies directed at affecting either imports or exports are referred to as **commercial policies.** This and the next section take up the forms trade barriers take, their economic costs, and their economic and political rationale; the next section explores international attempts to reduce these trade barriers.

There are five major categories of trade barriers—tariffs, quotas, voluntary export restraints, other **nontariff barriers,** and a set of laws called "fair trade laws" that, by and large, actually serve to impede trade rather than promote fair trade.

Tariffs

Tariffs are simply a tax on imports. Since a tariff is a tax that is imposed only on foreign goods, it puts the foreign goods at a disadvantage. It discourages imports.

Figure 18.1 shows the effect of a tariff. The figure shows a downward-sloping demand curve for the product, and an upward-sloping domestic supply curve. For simplicity, we consider the case of a country sufficiently small that the price it pays for a good on the international market does

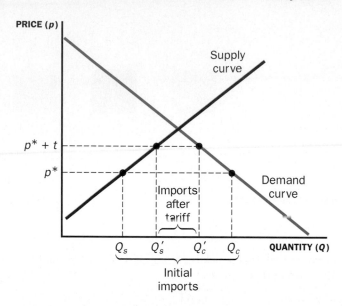

FIGURE 18.1   *Effect of Tariffs*

A small country faces a horizontal supply curve for a good at the international price, p^*. In the absence of tariffs, the price in the country will be p^*. The country will produce Q_s (the quantity along the supply curve corresponding to p^*), consume Q_c (the quantity along the demand curve corresponding to p^*), and import $Q_c - Q_s$. A tariff at the rate t increases the price in the country to $p^* + t$, lowers aggregate consumption to Q_c' (the quantity along the demand curve corresponding to $p^* + t$), and increases domestic production to Q_s' (the quantity along the supply curve corresponding to $p^* + t$). Domestic producers are better off, but consumers are worse off.

not depend on the quality purchased. In the absence of a tariff, the domestic price is equal to this international price, p^*. The country produces Q_s, consumes Q_c, and imports the difference, $Q_c - Q_s$. With a tariff, the price consumers have to pay is increased from p^* to $p^* + t$, where t is the tariff. Domestic production is increased (to Q_s')—producers are better off as a result. But consumers are worse off, as the price they pay is increased. Their consumption is reduced to Q_c'. Since production is increased and consumption reduced, imports are reduced; the domestic industry has been protected against foreign imports.

Quantifying the Losses to Society from Tariffs

We can quantify the net loss to society from imposing tariffs. The difference between the amount consumers are willing to pay and what they have to pay is called *consumer surplus*. For the last unit consumed, the

marginal benefit exactly equals the price paid, and so there is no consumer surplus. But for the first units consumed, individuals typically would be willing to pay far more—reflected in the fact that the demand curve is downward sloping in Figure 18.2. In the initial situation, the consumer surplus is given by triangle *ABC*, the area between the demand curve and the price line, p^*. After the price increase, it is given by the triangle *ADE*. The net loss is the trapezoid *BCED*.

But of this loss, the rectangle *BDHF* represents increased payments to producers (the increased price, *BD*, times the quantity that they produce), and *HFGE* is the tariff revenue of the government (imports, *HE*, × the tariff). Of the increased payments to domestic producers, some is the cost of expanding production. The rest represents a difference between price and the marginal cost of production—increased profits. This is the area *BIHD*. Thus, the societal loss is represented by two triangles, *EGC* and *HFI*. The triangle *EGC* is similar to the loss to consumers arising from a monopolist's raising his price. The triangle *HFI* is a waste of resources resulting from the fact that as the economy expands production because of the tariff, the cost of domestic production exceeds the costs of purchasing the good abroad.

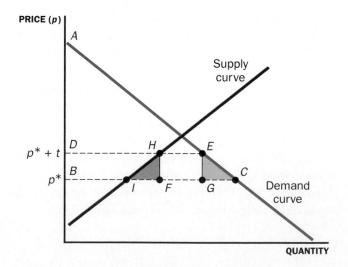

FIGURE 18.2   *Quantifying the Net Loss to Society from Imposing Tariffs*

The societal loss from imposing tariffs is represented by the two triangles, *EGC* and *HFI*.

Quotas

Rather than setting tariffs, many countries impose **quotas**—limits on the amount of foreign goods that can be imported. For instance, in the 1950s, the United States imposed a quota on the amount of oil that could be imported, and strict quotas still control imports of textiles.

Producers often prefer quotas. With limitations on the quantity imported, the domestic price increases above the international price. With quotas, domestic producers know precisely the magnitude of the foreign supply. If foreigners become more efficient or if exchange rates change in favor of foreigners, they still cannot sell any more. In that sense, quotas provide domestic producers with greater certainty than do tariffs, insulating them from the worst threats of competition.

Quotas and tariffs both succeed in raising the domestic price above the price at which the good could be obtained abroad. Both thus protect domestic producers. There is, however, one important difference: With quotas, those who are given permits to import get a profit by buying goods at the international price abroad and selling at the higher domestic price. The government is, in effect, giving away its tariff revenues. These profits are referred to as **quota rents.**

Voluntary Export Restraints

In recent years, international agreements have reduced the level of tariffs and restricted the use of quotas. Accordingly, countries have sought to protect themselves from the onslaught of foreign competition by other means. One that became popular in the 1980's was **voluntary export restraints** (VERs). Rather than limiting imports of automobiles, for example, the United States persuaded Japan to limit its exports.

There are two interpretations of why Japan might have been willing to go along with this VER. One is that they worried the United States might take stronger actions, like imposing quotas. From Japan's perspective, VERs are clearly preferable to quotas, because with VERs, the quota rents accrue to Japanese firms. A second interpretation is that VERs enable Japanese car producers to act collusively. It might have been in their self-interest to collude to reduce production and raise prices, but such collusion would have been illegal under antitrust laws. The VER "imposed" on the Japanese car producers output reductions they would have chosen themselves if they had been permitted to

under law. No wonder, then, that they agreed to go along! The cost to the American consumer of the Japanese VER was enormous. American consumers paid more than $100,000 in higher prices for every American job created.

Other Nontariff Barriers

VERs and quotas are the clearest nontariff barriers. But today they are probably not the most important. A host of regulations have the same effect of imposing barriers to trade. For instance, health-related regulations have been abused in ways that restrict trade. When, in 1996, Russia threatened to halt U.S. exports of chickens for failure to satisfy health regulations, U.S. chicken exporters were faced with a nontariff barrier. Various types of regulations have been used to establish nontariff barriers.

During the 1980s, as tariff barriers were being reduced, nontariff barriers increased. A study by the International Monetary Fund concluded that, whereas about one eighth of all U.S. imports were affected by protectionism in 1980, by the middle of the 1990s the figure had risen to one fourth. It is estimated that trade barriers (including nontariff barriers) may prevent consumers and business from buying as much as $110 billion in imports they would otherwise have purchased. Japan was particularly adversely affected by these actions. By the early 1990s, about 40 percent of Japan's exports to the United States were limited by some form of U.S. protectionism.

WRAP-UP

Comparison of Quotas and Tariffs

Both can be used to restrict imports by the same amount, with the same effect on consumers and domestic producers.

With quotas, the difference between domestic price and international price accrues to the importer, who enjoys a quota rent.

With tariffs, the difference accrues to government as tariff revenues.

VERs (voluntary export restraints) are equivalent to quotas, except that the quota rents are given to foreign producers.

"Fair Trade" Laws

Most people believe in competition. But most people believe that competition should be fair. When someone can undersell them, they suspect foul play. The government has imposed a variety of laws to ensure that there is effective and fair competition domestically. Laws have also been enacted by most countries to ensure "fair competition" in international trade. But most economists believe that in practice these are protectionist measures, reducing competition and restricting imports. To ensure fair competition, economists argue that the same laws which apply domestically should be extended internationally—that is, there should not be two standards of fairness, one applying domestically, one internationally. New Zealand and Australia, in their trade relations, have applied the same laws to trade between themselves that they do domestically. But elsewhere, progress has been limited.

The two most important "fair trade" laws apply to dumping and countervailing duties.

Antidumping Laws

Dumping refers to the sale of products overseas at prices that are below cost and lower than those in the home country. Normally, consumers greet discounted sales with enthusiasm. If Russia is willing to sell aluminum to the United States at low prices, why should we complain? One reason that might be of concern is predatory pricing. By selling below cost, the foreign companies hope to drive American firms out of business. Once they have established a monopoly position, they can raise prices. In such a case, American consumers gain only in the short run. In competitive markets, however, predation simply cannot occur, for in such markets, firms have no power to raise prices. In almost all of the cases where dumping has been found, markets are sufficiently competitive that predation is not of concern.

As administered, the antidumping laws are more frequently used as a protectionist tool. If dumping is discovered, a duty (tariff) is levied equal to the difference between the (calculated) cost of production and the price. Under the criteria employed, most American firms could be charged with dumping. Critics of the dumping laws worry that other countries will imitate American practices. If so, just as the international community has eliminated tariff barriers, a whole new set of trade barriers will have been erected.

Countervailing Duties

A second trade practice widely viewed as unfair is for governments to subsidize domestic firms' production or exports. For example, the government may give certain domestic industries tax breaks or pay a portion of the firms' costs. These subsidies give companies receiving them an unfair advantage. Trade is determined not on the basis of comparative advantage, but of relative subsidy levels.

The usual logic of economics seems to be reversed. If some foreign government wants to subsidize American consumers, why should they complain? Presumably, only if the subsidies are part of a policy of predation—if the subsidies are used to drive American firms out of business and establish a monopoly position, after which prices will be raised. Most foreign subsidies do not fall into this category.

Opposition to these subsidies arises from the companies who see their businesses hurt. While the gains to consumers outweigh the losses to businesses, the gain to each consumer is small, and consumers are not well organized. Producers, being far more organized, are able and willing to bring their case to Washington. In response, Congress has passed laws allowing the U.S. government to impose **countervailing duties,** that is, taxes that offset any advantage provided by these subsidies.

While governments preach against other countries providing subsidies, however, they engage in the practice themselves, most commonly in agriculture. At various times, the U.S. government has subsidized the export and production of wheat, pork, peaches, and a host of other commodities.

Political and Economic Rationale for Protection

Chapter 3 showed how free trade, by allowing each country to concentrate production where it has a comparative advantage, can make all countries better off. Why, in spite of this, is protection so popular? The basic reason is simple: protection raises prices. While the losses to consumers from higher prices exceed the gains to producers in higher

International Perspective

Surrogate Countries and Canadian Golf Carts

Question: How, if Canada did not produce golf carts, could the cost of Canadian golf carts be used to accuse Poland of dumping? Answer: The United States sometimes achieves wonders when its markets are at stake.

The standard criterion for judging whether a country is dumping is whether it is selling commodities on the U.S. market at prices below those for which it sells them at home or elsewhere, or at prices below the costs of production. For nonmarket economies, the Department of Commerce formulated a special criterion: Is the price below what it would have cost to produce the good in a "comparable" (or "surrogate") country.

The Department of Commerce, which is responsible for implementing the law, knows no shame. In a famous case involving Polish golf carts, it decided that the country most like Poland was Canada—at a time when Poland's per capita income was a fraction of Canada's. Even more surprising was the fact that Canada did not make comparable golf carts. Thus, the Commerce Department faced the question: What would it have cost

for Canada to produce these golf carts, had it chosen to do so? Not surprisingly, the resulting cost estimate was higher than the price the real golf carts were being sold for in the United States, and Poland was found guilty of dumping.

Similar charges have been made on similar grounds against Russian sales of natural resources. For years, Western countries had preached to the Soviet Union and the other socialist countries the virtues of the market. Beginning in 1989, with the demise of communism, former iron-curtain countries sought to transform their economies into market economies. Under the old regime, these countries had traded mainly with themselves, and generally engaged in barter. In the new era, they sought to enter international markets, like any other market economy.

Though the design and production quality of many of its manufactured goods made them unsuitable for Western markets, Russia had a wealth of natural resources—including uranium and aluminum—that it could produce on a competitive basis. Moreover, with the reduction of defense expenditures—good news from virtually every perspective—Russia's demand for many of these raw materials was greatly reduced.

American producers attempted to discourage Russian exports by filing, or threatening to file, dumping charges. Though Russia was probably not selling these commodities at prices below those prevailing at home or elsewhere, or at prices below the cost of production, the "surrogate" country criterion made the dumping charges a very real threat. Russia agreed to a cutback in aluminum production in 1994, to be matched by cutbacks in other countries.

To the Commerce and State Departments, this may have seemed a reasonable way to avoid trade conflict. But consumers paid a high price, in terms of higher prices for aluminum and products using aluminum.

profits, producers are well organized and consumers are not; hence producers' voices are heard more clearly in the political process than are consumers'.

There is an important check on firms' ability to use the political process to advance their special interests: the interests of exporters, who realize that if the United States closes off its markets to imports, other countries will reciprocate. Thus, exporting firms like Boeing have been at the forefront of advancing an international regime of freer and fairer trade through international agreements, of the kind that will be described in the next section.

But before turning to a review of these international agreements, we need to take a closer look at some of the other economic aspects of protection. While with free trade, the country as a whole may be better off, certain groups may actually be worse off. Those especially affected include displaced firms and workers, low-wage workers, and those in industries in which without free trade, competition is limited.

Displaced Firms and Workers

China has a comparative advantage in inexpensive textiles while the United States has a comparative advantage in manufacturing complex goods, like advanced telephone exchanges. If the United States starts to import textiles from China, U.S. textile manufacturers may be driven out of business, and their workers will have to find work elsewhere. More than offsetting these losses are the gains to the export industries. In principle, the gainers in those industries could more than compensate the losers, but such compensation is seldom made: hence, the opposition of the losers to opening trade.

Typically, economists shed few tears for the lost profits of the businesses who are hurt by opening trade. After all, that is just one of the risks that businesses face, and for which they are typically well compensated. New innovations destroy old businesses. But barring the door to new technologies—or cheaper products from abroad—is bad economics—and bad economic policy.

There is, however, often more sympathy toward workers affected by trade—though there is no reason why there should be greater concern for workers displaced by opening trade than for those displaced by new innovations. When the economy is running at close to full employment, workers who lose their jobs typically do find new employment. But they often go through a transition period of unemployment, and when they eventually do find a new job, there is a good chance that their wages will be lower (in the United States, in recent years, a worker who is successful in finding full-time employment experiences on average a 10 percent wage decline). While these particular laborers are worse off, workers as a whole are better off, because those who get newly created jobs in the export industries are paid far more (on average 13 to 15 percent more) than the average for the economy. Concern about the transitional costs borne by displaced workers has motivated Congress to pass laws for special assistance for these workers to help them find new jobs and obtain the requisite training.

Sensitivity to the problems of displaced workers is particularly strong when unemployment is high because those who lose a job cannot easily find alternative employment. To the auto workers in Detroit, it provides little solace that free trade has increased the demand for Boeing technicians in Seattle.

Responsibility for maintaining the overall level of employment lies with macroeconomic policy. Trade liberalization may cause pockets of unemployment, and labor market policies may be required to address the problem. But trade policy cannot and should not be blamed for persistent unemployment.

Beggar-Thy-Neighbor Policies

Nonetheless, worry about unemployment has provided the strongest motivation for protectionist policies. The argument is simple: If Americans do not buy foreign goods, they will spend the money at home, creating more jobs for Americans. Policies with this objective—to increase national output and employment by reducing imports—are called **beggar-thy-neighbor policies**, because the jobs gained in one country are at the expense of jobs lost in another. The critical fallacy in this reasoning is that if we do not buy goods from abroad, foreigners will not buy our goods. Thus, U.S. exports to other countries will fall in tandem with our imports from other countries. Everyone loses out on the benefits of specialization, and incomes fall.

The worst instances of these beggar-thy-neighbor policies occurred at the onset of the Great Depression, when, in 1930, the United States passed the Hawley-Smoot Tariff Act, raising tariffs on many products to a level which effectively prohibited many imports. Other countries retali-

Thinking Like an Economist

Distribution and Trade Liberalization

Trade liberalization may make a country as a whole better off, but it does not make everyone in the country better off. The gains to the winners are large enough that, in principle, any losers could be compensated, leaving everyone better off. But in practice, these compensations are seldom made. Thus, trade liberalization often entails trade-offs in balancing the gains to one group in the economy against the losses to another group. The problem is that in many situations, those who are adversely affected are among the poorest in the country. For example, in the United States trade liberalization threatens to force low-paid textile workers into unemployment. It is little comfort for the textile workers in South Carolina to know that new jobs are being created for aircraft engineers in Seattle or that all American consumers of textile products are now better off. In the United States, however, labor markets work reasonably well, and the laid off textile worker can eventually get a new job, though often at markedly reduced wages.

While low-wage textile workers in the United States are hurt by trade liberalization, low-wage textile workers in developing economies gain. Trade liberalization increases the demand for the textiles they produce, increasing the demand for their labor. Unfortunately, for those in developing countries who face increased competition as a result of trade liberalization, matters can be far bleaker. In many developing countries, unemployment is 15% or more, so the loss of a job is likely to have severe consequences.

In Mexico, those who produced goods for American car companies or other firms near the border of Texas have boomed since the North American Free Trade Agreement (NAFTA) was enacted. But in the south of Mexico, the poor have become even poorer. Highly subsidized American corn has depressed the prices received by Mexican farmers, even with their already low incomes and wages. To be sure, urban workers benefit, since they can buy corn for a lower price than they otherwise could.

When diverse groups are affected so differently, it is not clear whether trade liberalization is a good thing or not *in the absence of policies to address its distributional effects.* But it is not the role of economists to make that decision; in democracies, that is the role of the political processes. Society as a whole does benefit from trade liberalization, and the role of the economist is to point out this potential for gain. Economists also have a role to play in explaining who will be affected, and by how much.

---

ated. As U.S. imports declined, incomes in Europe and elsewhere in the world declined. As incomes declined and as these countries imposed retaliatory tariffs, they bought less from the United States. U.S. exports plummeted, contributing further to the economic downturn in the United States. With incomes in the United States plummeted further, U.S. imports declined even more, contributing still further to the decline abroad, which then fed further into the decline in U.S. exports. The downturn in international trade that was set off by the Hawley-Smoot Tariff Act, charted in Figure 18.3, is often pointed to as a major contributing factor in making the Great Depression as deep and severe as it was.

WRAP-UP

International Trade and Jobs

Restricting imports as a way of creating jobs tends to be counterproductive.

It is the responsibility of macroeconomic policy, not trade policy, to maintain the economy at full employment.

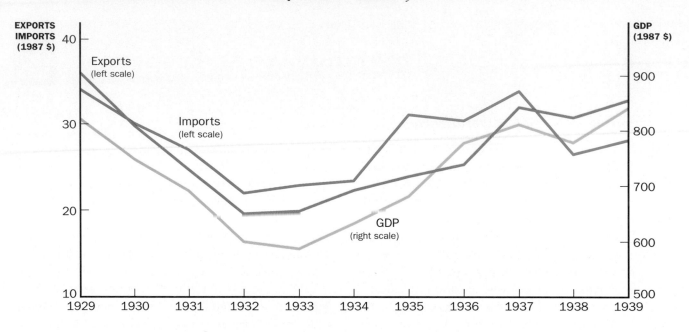

FIGURE 18.3   *The Decline in International Trade and the Great Depression*

U.S. exports and imports fell dramatically during the Great Depression. One contributing factor to the decline in trade was the Hawley-Smoot Tariff Act introduced in 1930.

Wages in Impacted Sectors

Beyond these short-run problems of transition and unemployment, there may be long-run problems facing workers in impacted sectors. The United States has a comparative advantage in producing goods such as airplanes and high-tech products that require highly skilled workers. As the United States exports more of these goods, the demand for these skilled workers increases in the United States, driving up the wage of skilled workers. Similarly, the United States has a comparative disadvantage in producing goods that require a high ratio of unskilled labor, such as lower-quality textiles. As imports compete against these U.S. industries and their production decreases, the demand for unskilled labor decreases. This drives down the wages of the unskilled workers.

These decreased wages for unskilled workers are often blamed on imports from third world countries like China, where wages are but a fraction of those in the United States. The consensus among economists who have looked closely at the matter is that international trade explains a relatively small part of the decline in wages—perhaps 20 percent. Nonetheless, those who see their meager livelihood being threatened are among the most ardent advocates of trade restrictions. Again, economists argue that the appropriate response is not to restrict trade but to increase skills: Not only are the workers receiving the skills better off, as their wages rise commensurate with the increase in their productivity, but also as more workers become skilled, the remaining supply of unskilled workers is reduced, and with a smaller supply of unskilled workers, the real wages of the remaining unskilled workers increases, offsetting the adverse effects of trade.

Increased Competition

International trade also has other adverse effects in industries where competition is limited. With limited competi-

WRAP-UP

Effects of Trade on Wages

International trade may lower wages of unskilled U.S. labor and those working in industries where competition is limited.

International trade raises wages of skilled U.S. workers.

tion, firms enjoy monopoly or oligopoly profits. Some of these extra profits are often passed on to workers. Particularly when those industries are unionized, workers may receive wages far higher than workers of comparable skill working elsewhere in the economy. International trade introduces more competition; with the increased competition, monopoly and oligopoly profits get competed away. Firms are forced to pay competitive wages—that is, the lowest wage that they can for workers with the given skill.

From the perspective of the overall economy, this competition that erodes market power and induces greater efficiency and responsiveness to consumers is one of the major virtues of free trade. From the perspective of those who see their higher wages and profits being competed away, it is one of its major vices.

The Infant Industry Argument

While job loss and decreased wages and profits from international competition provide much of the political motivation behind protection, economist have asked, are there any *legitimate* arguments for protection? That is, are there circumstances where protection may be in the *national* interest, and not just in the interests of those being protected? Two arguments have been put forward.

The first is the **infant industry argument.** Costs in new industries are often high, coming down as experience is gained. The infant industry argument is that, particularly in less developed countries, firms will never be able to get the experience required to produce efficiently unless they are protected from foreign competition.

Economists have traditionally responded to this argument skeptically. If it pays to enter the industry, eventually there will be profits. Thus, the firm should be willing to charge today a price below cost to gain the experience, because today's losses will be more than offset by the future profits. But more recently, the infant industry argument has found more favor. Firms can only operate at a loss if they can borrow funds. If capital markets do not work well, firms may not be able to borrow even if their eventual prospects are reasonable. This is a particular danger in less developed countries.

This may be a legitimate argument. But it is not an argument for protection. It is an argument for assistance, which can take the form of loans or direct subsidies. Economists argue for direct assistance rather than protection because the assistance is transparent. Everyone can see that it is a

subsidy to producers. Economists criticize protection because it is a hidden tax on consumers, with the proceeds transferred to producers. The lack of transparency encourages what is referred to as rent seeking[1]: Industries spend resources to persuade government to impose these hidden taxes that benefit themselves.

Strategic Trade Theory

Another argument for protection is that protection can give a country a strategic trade advantage over rivals by helping reduce domestic costs. There may be economies of scale: the larger the level of production, the lower the marginal costs. Protection ensures a large domestic sales base, and therefore a low marginal cost. The instances in which **strategic trade theory** might provide a rationale for protection appear relatively rare. Even then, they tend to be effective only when foreign governments do not retaliate by taking similar actions.

Debating Trade: Old Arguments Die Hard

In recent years, reducing trade barriers has risen high on the American political agenda in both Democratic and Republican administrations. But even so, critics of trade liberalization continue to make arguments that send shivers down the spines of economists. Many of these criticisms boil down to the view that exports are good and imports are bad, with the idea being that exports create jobs while imports destroy them. The basic economic point—that trade enables countries to increase productivity by specializing in their comparative advantage—is overlooked.

These debates have a long history. The belief that exports are good and imports are bad has captivated the minds of policy advocates for hundreds of years. This school of though, called *mercantilism,* was prevalent in Europe between 1500 and 1800. Mercantilism focused on building up the power and wealth of the state through aggressive pursuit of exports. Mercantilists also discouraged imports and

---

[1] *Rents* refer to payments to a factor of production that are in excess of what is required to elicit the supply of that factor. In the absence of entry, protection would result in higher prices, yielding returns to the industry that are above their competitive levels; these higher returns are rents. The irony is that typically, the higher returns do attract entry, and the additional entry dissipates the rents—though prices remain high.

thought that a country's strength was related to its store of gold and silver. Josiah Child, one of the better-known mercantilists, wrote in 1693: "Foreign trade produces riches, riches power; power preserves our trade and religion."

To have lots of products left over to export, the nation had to produce more than it consumed, so citizens were exhorted to work hard for low wages.

Adam Smith, the father of modern economics, recognized the fallacies in mercantilism. A country's wealth, he argued, was not measured by its gold and silver but by the productivity of its resources. Smith pointed out that even from the standpoint of national power, a nation's army does not run on gold and silver but on physical products like ships, food, clothing, and weapons.

The world has changed dramatically in the more than two centuries since Adam Smith formulated his attack on mercantilism. But the mercantilist spirit remains alive—and the criticisms of the new mercantilist arguments are direct descendants of Smith's analysis.

Modern mercantilists view exports as desirable today, not because they lead to the accumulation of gold but because they lead to job creation. By the same token, imports are viewed poorly, because they lead to both job loss and dependency on foreigners.

Some countries, such as Japan and Korea, have successfully pursued strong export-oriented policies; and most economists believe that these policies have contributed to their economic success. But the reason is quite different from that of the older mercantilist theories that focused on the accumulation of riches. Japan and Korea did accumulate capital rapidly, but this was because of their extraordinarily high saving rates. Their export-oriented policies were important because to be successful in international markets, their industries had to be efficient and adopt high standards of production. Their export-oriented policies helped their industries become more competitive and adopt advanced technologies.

Today, in the United States, we recognize that trade is important, not because it creates jobs—if the Federal Reserve Board does its job, the economy will operate at or close to full employment most of the time—but because it leads to higher standards of living, as Americans can specialize in producing those goods in which it has a comparative advantage, and because competition from abroad forces American firms to become more efficient. These are essentially the same reasons that Smith put forward for why, though protection may benefit businessmen, free trade would be beneficial for society as a whole.

International Cooperation

Recognizing both the temptation of shortsighted trade policy and the gains from trade, nations large and small have engaged since World War II in a variety of efforts to reduce trade barriers.

Gatt and the WTO

After World War II, the countries of the world realized that there was much to be gained from establishing an international economic order in which barriers to trade were reduced. They established the **General Agreement on Tariffs and Trade (GATT).** In 1995, this was replaced by the **World Trade Organization (WTO).**

GATT was founded on three guiding principles. The first was *reciprocity:* If one country lowered its tariffs, it could expect other countries in GATT to lower theirs. The second was *nondiscrimination:* No member of GATT could offer a special trade deal that favored only one or a few other countries. The third was *transparency:* Import quotas and other nontariff barriers to trade should be converted into tariffs, so their effective impact could be ascertained.

Reducing trade barriers has proceeded in a number of stages, called *rounds* (the Kennedy Round, completed in 1967, the Tokyo Round, completed in 1979, and most recently, the Uruguay Round, completed in 1993). Collectively, the rounds have reduced tariffs on industrial goods markedly. The average tariff on manufactured goods was 40 percent in 1947. By 1992, tariffs had been reduced to 5 percent, and the Uruguay Round reduced them still further.

The Uruguay Round was remarkable for two achievements. It began the process of extending the principles of free and fair trade to a number of much more difficult areas. There were, for instance, agreements to reduce agriculture subsidies, particularly export subsidies, and to ensure that intellectual property rights—patents and copyrights—were respected. Secondly, it created the WTO to help enforce the trade agreements. Previously, a country that believed that it was suffering from an "unfair trade" practice could bring a case to a GATT panel that would examine the evidence. Even if the panel was unanimous, however, in finding that an unfair trade practice had occurred, there was little in the way of effective enforcement. Under the WTO, a country injured by an unfair trade practice will be authorized to engage in retaliatory actions.

e-Insights

Trade Liberalization in IT and Financial Services

In recent years, there have been important trade agreements in information technology (IT) and financial services. This is a marked change from the past, in which trade agreements focused on traded goods, like cars, steel, and textiles. But the reaction in many developing countries to these two is distinctly different: while IT liberalization has been welcome, there is extensive opposition to financial services. Why the difference?

Economic theory says that unilateral liberalization—opening up one's market to cheaper goods of foreigners—is a good thing. Consumers benefit, and even if domestic producers are worse off, the gains of consumers more than offset the losses of producers. Unfortunately, however, producers often have a greater voice in the political process, and consumers cannot get together to compensate the producers for their losses. That is why countries often resist trade liberalization. But IT is different. Most developing countries do not have a large IT sector that would be hurt by liberalization. Instead, both producers and consumers in developing countries are purchasers of IT products, and both gain by having access to IT at lower prices.

Financial service liberalization is quite a different matter. The existing domestic banks in developing countries fear greater competition from foreign banks. It is not just that foreign banks are more efficient, depositors may feel safer putting their money in a large American or European bank than in a small domestic bank. But it is not just the domestic banks that are concerned about financial service liberalization. Many firms in developing countries worry that the foreign banks are more likely to lend to Coca-Cola and IBM than to small domestic firms, and there are some grounds for these worries. The government may worry that the foreign banks will be less subject to pressure from the government. Sometimes this pressure is part of corruption—the government puts pressure on the bank to lend to their friends. But sometimes this pressure can be part of economic policy—the government puts pressure on the bank to increase lending in an economic downturn and to contract lending when the economy is overheated. In developing countries, this "guidance" from the government may be an important tool for macroeconomic stability.

Today, as many countries liberalize their financial markets, they are asking, "how can they gain the advantages of the new competition without suffering the disadvantages?" Until they find effective ways of ensuring a flow of capital to small domestic businesses, banks in developing countries will find important allies in resisting financial market liberalization.

The Growing Protest Against the WTO

In December 1999, the WTO held a meeting in Seattle to launch a new round of trade negotiations. But thousands of protesters—some violent—dominated the stage. As this book goes to press, there is no agreement yet concerning a new round. What brought on such a vehement reaction? Old-fashioned protectionist sentiment played a role, but there were other important factors.

Some WTO critics believed that the agenda in previous rounds of trade negotiations had been set by the more advanced industrial countries—for their interests—and that the outcomes reflected their economic power. It was not only that they had gained the lion's share of the benefits but also that some poorer countries were actually worse off. The World Bank estimated that after the previous round of trade negotiations concluded in 1994, the poorest region in the world, sub-Saharan Africa, was actually worse off. While poorer countries were forced to cut their tariffs against goods produced in the more advanced industrial countries, the more advanced industrial countries continued to protect their agricultural sectors. While financial services had been opened up, industries with greater reliance on unskilled workers, like the construction and maritime industries, remained closed.

Thousands of protesters converged in Seattle to protest the WTO conference held there in December 1999.

CASE IN POINT

The Banana War

How can a dispute over bananas lead to unemployment among Scottish cashmere workers? The explanation lies in the spillover effect of the banana war between the United States and the European Union (EU). This dispute revolved around the claim by the United States that the EU was following discriminatory trade practices.

Beginning in 1993, the EU imposed a banana import tariff that favored banana producers in former European colonies in the Caribbean, Africa, and the Pacific over those in Latin America. The United States and five Latin American countries complained to the WTO. The United States claimed that EU banana import tariffs were harming the country. Since the United States does not produce bananas, one might reasonably ask how it could be harmed by the EU's policy on banana imports. While not a producer itself, the United States is home to two food distributors, Chiquita Brands and Dole, that do grow bananas in Central America. Even though Chiquita Brands has a larger share of the European market than do Caribbean banana producers, Chiquita strongly supported having the United States fight the EU policies.

The WTO ruled that the EU regime was in violation of GATT and ordered the EU to change its policies. The EU did, instituting a new banana import regime on January 1, 1999. However, the United States and Latin America banana producers argued that this new policy still effectively discriminated against them, and the dispute was sent to the WTO Dispute Settlement Body. The United States claimed victory in the banana war when, in April 1999, the Dispute Settlement Body accepted the results of the WTO arbitrators, agreeing that the new EU policies harmed the United States. This paved the way for the United States to impose sanctions against EU products. The WTO ruled that the United States could impose $191 million in sanctions against the EU. This amount was determined by estimating the economic damages to the United States resulting from the EU policies.

To retaliate against Europe, the United States imposed 100 percent tariffs on a range of European products, effectively doubling their prices in the United States. The list of goods hit by the punitive tariffs included Scottish cashmere, Italian cheese, and German coffee makers. The list was based on products that would bring maximum political pressures on the EU. The WTO ruling allowed the United States to impose these high tariffs until the EU revised its banana policy to eliminate discrimination against Latin American producers. The EU conceded defeat, and the banana war ended. ●

Environmental and human rights issues were two other prominent areas of intense debate. Environmentalists and human rights advocates wanted to use trade policy to help achieve their objectives. They worried that countries with bad environmental policies or inadequate labor rights would be able to undercut American firms, and this in turn would bring pressure within the United States to erode those standards here. The insistence on including clauses concerning labor and the environment by some was met with an equally adamant resistance by others, threatening to stall all efforts at trade liberalization. There was consensus on a few issues—for example, countries should not be allowed to export goods produced by child or prison labor. But beyond that, the debate raged on and it is likely to continue in the foreseeable future.

Regional Trading Blocs

GATT and WTO have made some progress in reducing trade barriers among all countries. But the difficulties of reaching agreements involving so many parties have made progress slow. In the meantime, many countries have formed **regional trade blocs,** agreeing with their more immediate neighbors not only to eliminate trade barriers but also to facilitate the flow of capital and labor. Perhaps the most important of these is the **European Union,** the successor to the *Common Market,* which now embraces most of Europe. The **North American Free Trade Agreement, NAFTA,** creates a free trade zone within North America that is, an area within which goods and services trade freely, without tariffs or other import restrictions. There are also many smaller free trade zones, such as those between New Zealand and Australia, and among groups of countries in Latin America and in Central America.

While the gains from internationally coordinated reductions in trade barriers are clear, the gains from regional trading blocs are more controversial. Reducing trade barriers within a region encourages trade by members of the trading bloc. Lowering barriers among the countries involved results in **trade creation.** But it also results in **trade diversion.** Trade is diverted away from countries that are not members of the bloc, who might, in fact, have a comparative advantage in the particular commodity. Under these conditions, the global net benefits will be positive if the trade creation exceeds the trade diversion. Typically, when trade blocs are formed, tariffs against outsiders are harmonized. If the external trade barrier are harmonized at the lowest common level (rather than at the average or highest levels) at the same time that internal trade barriers are lowered, it is more likely that the trade creation effects exceed the trade diversion effects.

Expanding regional trading blocs to cover investment flows raises particular anxieties, especially when the bloc includes countries with very different standards of living. In the NAFTA debate, Ross Perot used the metaphor of a giant sucking sound: Mexico would suck up huge amounts of investment that otherwise would have occurred in the United States. The accusation was not just that goods produced today in Mexico would cost Americans jobs. It was also that American firms would move down to Mexico, to take advantage of low-wage labor and that the capital that flowed down to Mexico would not be available for investment in the United States.

Such arguments are based on an important misconception. They fail to take account of the fact that capital markets are already global. The United States is not limited in its investment to savings in the United States. Capital will flow to good investment opportunities wherever they are. If there are good investment opportunities in the United States, capital will flow there, regardless of how much Americans invest in Mexico. Investment barriers impede this flow of capital to its highest productive use, thus lowering world economic efficiency.

The "Perot" argument is based on a "zero sum" view of the world—that what Mexico gains must come at the expense of the United States. Perot's argument is similar to the one that says when a country imports, it loses jobs: The gains to foreigners from their exports are at the expense of domestic firms, which otherwise would be creating these jobs. In Chapter 3, we saw what was wrong with this argument: The theory of comparative advantage says that when countries specialize in what they produce best, *both* countries are better off. Workers gain higher wages when they move into sectors where their productivity is highest; and consumers gain from the lower prices. So too with investment. When investment flows to where its return is highest, world output is increased. Since the return to capital is increased when it is efficiently allocated, saving rates may also increase, so that the overall supply of funds will be higher. Higher savings rate and more efficient use of available savings will combine to give a higher world economic growth rate.

But just as not everyone necessarily gains from trade according to comparative advantage, so too not everyone will necessarily gain from the flow of capital to Mexico. There will be some investment diversion from other countries to Mexico, as Mexico becomes more attractive to investors throughout the world because of its improved access to the huge American market. Most economist believe that the net effect on investment in the United States will be negligible, and could even be positive. Industries within the United States that see their opportunities expand by selling more to Mexico will invest more, more than offsetting the reduced investment from firms that decline in the face of competition from Mexican imports.

In fact, investment flows augment the gains from trade that would occur in their absence because there are important trade-investment links. American companies producing abroad tend to use more parts from America, just as French companies producing abroad tend to use more French parts. Thus, flows of investment often serve as a precursor to exports.

Trade-Offs Between Regional and International Agreements

The potential economic trade-off between increased trade within the region and the expense of reduced trade outside the region has led some economists, such as Jagdish Bhagwati of Columbia University, to oppose regional trade agreements. There is also concern about political trade-offs. Should the U.S. government spend the limited political resources it has to overcome protectionist antitrade sentiment focusing on regional or worldwide agreements? Recent U.S. governments have pursued a pragmatic policy. Their ultimate objective is to eliminate economic barriers everywhere, by means of international approaches coordinated through the WTO. At the same time, they are aggressively pursuing regional trade agreements involving broad removal of barriers within the Western Hemisphere and between the United States and the countries of the Pacific Rim. They view this as the most practical way to achieve economic integration. Agreements may be easier to obtain among a limited set of often similar partners than among all the countries of the world. This is especially true in relation to complicated issues such as investment and regulations. The U.S. government also believes that a successful regional strategy will bring to bear pressures that will hasten fully international agreements.

WRAP-UP

Areas of International Cooperation

Multilateral trade agreements—WTO
  Based on principles of reciprocity, nondiscrimination, and transparency;
  Uruguay Round extended trade liberalization to services and agricultural commodities and helped establish intellectual property rights.
Regional trade agreements—NAFTA, European Union
  Risk of trade diversion rather than trade creation;
  But may be better able to address complicated issues, such as those involving investment.

Review and Practice

Summary

1. Countries protect themselves in a variety of ways besides imposing tariffs. These nontariff barriers include quotas, voluntary export restraints, and regulatory barriers. Quotas and voluntary export restraints are now banned by international agreement. While in recent decades there have been huge reductions in tariff barriers, there has been some increase in nontariff barriers.

2. While all countries benefit from free trade, some groups within a country may be adversely affected. In the United States, unskilled workers and those in industries where, without trade, there is limited competition, may see their wages fall. Some workers may lose their jobs and may require assistance to find new ones.

3. Laws nominally intended to ensure fair trade—like anti-dumping and countervailing duty—often are used as protectionist measures.

4. Concern about imports is particularly strong when unemployment is high. But beggar-thy-neighbor policies, which attempt to protect jobs by limiting imports, tend to be counterproductive.

5. The WTO, which replaced the GATT, provides a framework within which trade barriers can be re-

duced. It is based on reciprocity, nondiscrimination, and transparency. The Uruguay Round of the GATT extended trade liberalization to new areas, including agriculture and intellectual property, and established the WTO.

6. Difficulties at arriving at trade agreements involving all of the nations of the world have resulted in broader regional agreements, including NAFTA. There is a risk that these regional agreements may give rise to trade diversion offsetting the benefits from trade creation.

Key Terms

free trade
protectionism
commercial policies
nontariff barriers
tariffs
quotas
quota rents
voluntary export restraints
dumping
countervailing duties
beggar-thy-neighbor policies
infant industry argument
strategic trade theory
General Agreement on Tariffs and Trade (GATT)
World Trade Organization (WTO)
regional trading blocs
European Union
North American Free Trade Agreement (NAFTA)
trade creation
trade diversion

Review Questions

1. What are the various ways in which countries seek to protect their industries against foreign imports?

2. How do tariffs and quotas differ?

3. Why are consumers worse off as a result of the imposition of a tariff?

4. What are the laws designed to ensure fair international trade? How have they worked in practice?

5. What are nontariff barriers to international trade?

6. How is it possible that while there are gains to free trade, some groups are adversely affected? Which are the groups in the United States that are most adversely affected?

7. What are beggar-thy-neighbor policies? What are their consequences?

8. What do GATT and the WTO do? What are their basic underlying principles? What have been GATT's achievements? What further advances were accomplished under the Uruguay Round?

9. What is NAFTA? What are the advantages of regional free trade agreements?

10. What is meant by trade diversion versus trade creation?

Problems

1. Suppose that Japanese products go out of fashion in the United States. How would this affect Japan's exports? What would happen to national income in Japan, on the assumption that the Japanese government did not undertake offsetting actions? What effect would this, in turn, have on U.S. exports? On U.S. national income, again on the assumption that the U.S. government did not undertake offsetting actions? Use the diagrammatic techniques learned in earlier chapters to answer these question.

2. Explain why, if the United States succeeded in getting Japan to remove some of its trade barriers, the exchange rate between the yen and the dollar might change, but the trade balance might not be affected much. Why would the removal of these trade barriers still be beneficial for the United States?

3. If you were a government intent on discouraging imports, how might you use regulatory policies to further your objectives?

4. If Mexican workers receive a third of the wages that U.S. workers do, why don't all American firms move down to Mexico?

5. If Mexico becomes a more attractive place to invest, is the United States helped or hurt?

6. Should the U.S. treat foreign-owned firms producing cars in the United States (like Mazda) differently from American firms? Should Ford, Chrysler, and GM be

allowed to form a research consortium, excluding these producers? Should the U.S. government give money to a research consortium that excludes these firms? Should they be eligible for research funds themselves on an equal basis?

7. How should the government prioritize its efforts on opening markets to U.S. firms? By the impact on U.S. workers? Impact on U.S. companies? Impact on U.S. investors? How would you prioritize the following four examples: (a) opening up the Japanese market to allow Toys-R-Us to open retail stores in Tokyo, selling toys made in China; (b) opening up the Japanese securities markets to ensure that Goldman Sachs and other U.S. investment firms can sell securities to Japanese pension funds; (c) opening up the Japanese car market to enhance the ability of GM, Ford, and Chrysler to sell U.S. cars in Japan; and (d) opening up the Chinese car market to enhance the ability of Toyota and Mazda to sell American-made cars to China?

Chapter 19

Strategic Behavior

Key Questions

1. How does game theory help us understand strategic behavior?

2. What is a dominant strategy? What is a Nash equilibrium?

3. What is rollback?

4. Why are reputations important? And how can they be maintained?

During the 2000 television season, viewers were enthralled by the show *Survivor*. Sixteen contestants were marooned on the island of Pulau Tiga, off the coast of Borneo, and at the end of each episode, the survivors voted to kick out one of their members. The last surviving contestant collected $1 million. By episode 13, the original group had been reduced to just three final contestants: Kelly, Rudy, and Rich. Based on a trial that involved answering questions about the thirteen previously evicted castaways, Kelly won immunity in the first round of voting that would reduce the group to the final pair. She still had to decide, though, whether to vote to oust Rudy or Rich. Assuming that Rudy votes against Rich and Rich votes against Rudy, Kelly's vote would decide who stays and who leaves. How should Kelly vote?

To know whom she should vote out in the first round, Kelly must think about how she would fare in the final round. Kelly must think backward from the end of the contest. Rudy seemed popular with the audience and with the other thirteen contestants who would get to vote for the final winner. So Kelly would reason that if the final contest comes down to her and Rudy, Rudy would prob-

ably win. On the other hand, Rich seemed to be very unpopular. So Kelly would reason that if it comes down to a choice between her and Rich, she would probably win. Her best chance would be to face off against Rich, not Rudy, in the final voting. Even if Kelly really dislikes Rich, her best strategy is to oust Rudy. As it turned out, that is exactly what happened. Rich and Kelly voted against Rudy. Unfortunately for Kelly, the voters ended up picking Rich over her, but her strategy was still the right one.

The participants in *Survivor* had to think strategically. They needed to think about how their rivals would respond to the decisions they themselves made. They had to consider how their situation would depend on who else survived and who didn't, and they had to use that information in deciding how to vote.

Thinking strategically doesn't just help in a made-up environment such as a television show. We all face situations that call for strategic thinking. Economists try to understand the choices individuals and firms make, and the reach of economics has been extended into many new areas by studying strategic behavior.

383

Economists study choices made by rational individuals and profit-maximizing firms. In the basic competitive model presented in the first two parts of this book, individuals and firms do not need to behave strategically. Consumers and firms can buy or sell as much as they want at the market price. A firm does not need to worry about how its rivals will react if it decides to produce more. Neither does a monopoly, but for a different reason: A monopoly has no rivals. In the basic competitive model and in a monopoly model, **strategic behavior**—decisions that take into account the possible reactions of others—plays no role.

Things were different in Chapter 12 when we studied oligopolies. With only a few firms in the industry, each firm needs to worry about how its rivals might react whenever it contemplates expanding production or cutting its price. Strategic behavior becomes important. When AMD considers cutting the prices of its various computer processor chips, it must try to assess how Intel will respond. If Intel reacts by also cutting prices, then AMD may not gain much market share. In this case, AMD's revenues will decline as a result of the lower prices. But if Intel keeps its prices unchanged, AMD may gain market share and its revenues might rise as it sells more chips.

Because oligopolies engage in strategic behavior, Chapter 12 used game theory—and the simple prisoner's dilemma game—to understand why it may be difficult for firms to collude. In this chapter, we return to the prisoner's dilemma and see how its basic insights can be applied to other areas of economics. The usefulness of game theory goes well beyond this simple game, however. In many situations, decisions and choices must take into account the potential reactions of others. You will learn more about game theory and how it helps us understand the choices individuals, firms, unions, and governments make. Game theory provides a framework for studying strategic behavior. Using this framework, economists have found that many examples of strategic behavior can be understood by relying on the core concepts of incentives and information.[1]

Review of the Prisoner's Dilemma

Let's very briefly recall the prisoner's dilemma game introduced in Chapter 12. Two prisoners, A and B, are alleged by the police to be conspirators in a crime. After being taken into custody, the two are separated. A police officer tells each, "Now here's the situation. If your partner confesses and you remain silent, you'll get five years in prison. But if your partner confesses and you confess also, you'll both get three years. On the other hand, if both you and your partner remain silent, we'll only be able to convict you of a lesser charge and you'll get one year in prison. But if your partner remains silent and you confess, we'll let you out in three months." This deal is offered to both prisoners.

Figure 19.1, which repeats a similar diagram from Chapter 12, shows the results of the deal the police have offered the prisoners. This type of table, showing the payoffs to each player, is called a **game table.** In Chapter 12, we saw that based on self-interest, each individual prisoner believes that confession is best, whether his partner confesses or not. By following their self-interest and confessing, they both end up worse off than if neither had confessed. The prisoner's dilemma is a simple game in which both parties are made worse off by independently following their own self-interest. Both would be better off if they could get together to agree on a story and to threaten the other if he deviates from the story.

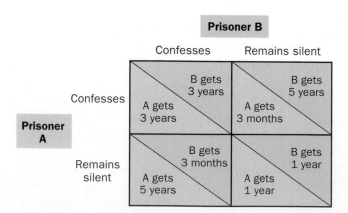

FIGURE 19.1 *Prisoner's Dilemma Game*

Each prisoner's dominant strategy is to confess.

---

[1]If you would like to learn even more about game theory, an accessible textbook is available: Avinash Dixit and Susan Skeath, *Games of Strategy* (New York: W.W. Norton, 1999).

This simple game has been widely applied in economics and in other fields such as international relations and political science. In Chapter 12, we used it to explain why two oligopolists would find it difficult to sustain an agreement to collude. We will discuss some further examples of the prisoner's dilemma and then consider other types of game situations. First, though, we will need to understand how we can analyze strategic situations to make predictions about how individuals and firms will behave.

Dominant Strategies

Behaving strategically means that each player must try to determine what the other player is likely to do. Will your accomplice confess or keep quiet? Will your rival match price reductions if you cut your prices? The decision one player makes depends on how he thinks the other player will respond.

In the basic prisoner's dilemma game, we assume that players reason along the following lines: "For each choice that I might make, what is the best choice for the other player to make?" In analyzing the prisoner's dilemma, we ask, "If prisoner A doesn't confess, what is the best strategy for prisoner B? If prisoner A confesses, what is the best strategy for prisoner B?" In both cases, we conclude that confessing is prisoner B's *best response*. If B's best response is to confess, no matter what prisoner A does, then A will conclude that B will confess, so A needs to decide what his best response is to prisoner B confessing. As we saw, prisoner A's best option is also to confess.

Confessing is the best strategy for each prisoner to follow, regardless of what the other player does. Such a strategy—one that works best no matter what the other player does—is called a **dominant strategy.** Recall that an objective of game theory is to predict what strategy each player will choose. When a player has a dominant strategy, that is the strategy we should predict a rational decision maker will choose.

Nash Equilibrium

It is easy to predict the outcome of a game—its equilibrium—if each player has a dominant strategy. Each will play his dominant strategy. Thus, in the prisoner's dilemma, the equilibrium is both players confessing. The situation is not quite so simple when only one player has a dominant strategy, or when neither player has one, and we will learn about such games later. To predict the equilib-rium outcomes in these more complex games, we need to look again at why confessing is the equilibrium in the prisoner's dilemma.

In the prisoner's dilemma, each prisoner confesses because this gives him the best, or *optimal* payoff—the least amount of time in prison—given what the other prisoner can be expected to do. The outcome is an equilibrium in the sense that neither prisoner would change his chosen strategy if offered the chance to do so at the end of the game. By confessing, both have played their best response. Such an equilibrium is called a **Nash equilibrium,** and it is the most fundamental idea for predicting the actions of players in a strategic game.

John Nash developed the notion that bears his name when he was just twenty-one years old and a graduate student in mathematics at Princeton University. Economists have found the concept of Nash equilibrium extremely useful for predicting the outcomes of games and understanding economic problems. In recognition of its importance, John Nash shared the 1994 Nobel Prize in economics. Nash is not an economist; he is a mathematician and the only winner of the Nobel Prize in economics whose life has been the subject of a best-selling biography. Published in 1998, *A Beautiful Mind* by Sylvia Nasar chronicles Nash's early mathematical brilliance, his struggle with mental illness, and his eventual recovery. Upon being informed he had won the Nobel Prize in economics, Nash commented that he hoped it would improve his credit rating.

The prisoner's dilemma arises in many contexts, both in economics and in other social sciences. The following examples provide some illustrations. Each example is sketched briefly.[2] We start with an example we analyzed in Chapter 12.

Example: Collusion   In Chapter 12, we studied an application of the prisoner's dilemma to the problem faced by two rivals who can benefit by colluding to restrict output. Colluding results in a higher price and therefore greater profits for each. The worst outcome for each occurs if both cheat on the agreement and expand output. This results in lower prices and profits. In this game, each firm has a dominant strategy—cheat on the agreement by expanding output. There is a unique Nash equilibrium in which the firms do not collude.

---

[2]You should test your understanding of each example by filling out a game table, identifying the dominant strategy for each player, and finding the Nash equilibrium.

Example: Politicians and Negative Ads

Why do politicians engage in negative advertising even though they all promise not to?

Consider the case of politicians A and B. If neither runs a negative campaign, the public thinks highly of both of them, but neither gains any advantage over the other. If both run negative campaign ads, the public thinks poorly of both, but again neither gains an advantage. Each is tarred by the other's ads. If politician A runs a clean campaign, politician B can gain an advantage by running a negative ad that tarnishes A's reputation. Conversely, A gains by running a negative ad if politician B runs a clean campaign.

Each politician will reason as follows. "If my opponent runs a negative ad, I'm better off if I also run negative ads. And if my opponent doesn't run a negative ad, then I can gain an advantage if I run negative ads. Either way, I'm better off if I run negative ads." Each politician has a dominant strategy, and there is a unique Nash equilibrium in which both run negative campaign ads, despite their promises not to.

Example: Military Spending

Two countries, A and B, are locked in a military balance. Each must decide whether to build a new generation of missiles. If neither builds the missile system, the military balance is preserved and each country will remain secure. If one builds the system while the other does not, one will gain a military advantage. If they both build the system, they each spend billions of dollars, but neither gains an advantage since each country now has the new missile system, and the military balance is preserved.

Each country reasons that if the other country fails to build the system, it can gain an advantage by going ahead and building the system. Both they also know that if one country builds the new missiles, the other will be worse off if it fails to also build the missile system. Each country has a dominant strategy—build the missile system. Both countries spend billions, only to find themselves left in the same military balance as before.

Example: Sports Owners and Player Salaries

Sports teams compete to hire the best players. Suppose there are just two teams, the Yankees and the Athletics. If both teams collude and keep salaries low, the owners make higher profits. If the Yankees owner instead offers high salaries while the Athletics owner does not, the Yankees will attract all the good players and will generate higher profits for the owner. Meanwhile, the Athletics end up with weaker players and have a poor season. Low attendance causes the owner to lose money. If the Athletics offer high salaries and the Yankees do not, the Athletics get all the good players and earn the higher profits, while the Yankees lose money. If both offer high salaries, neither team gets all the good players, but the owners earn lower profits because of their increased salary costs.

In a Nash equilibrium, both team owners offer players high salaries, and the owners are worse off than if they had been able to collude to keep salaries down.

WRAP-UP

The Prisoner's Dilemma

In the prisoner's dilemma, each player has a dominant strategy. There is a unique Nash equilibrium in which the players choose their dominant strategy. Yet the players are worse off in this Nash equilibrium than if they had chosen their alternative strategy. Applications of the prisoner's dilemma arise in many branches of economics, as well as in other social sciences and in everyday life.

Strategic Behavior in More General Games

In the prisoner's dilemma, players have a dominant strategy. In most games, however, this is not the case. What each player finds it best to do depends on what the other player does. This makes it harder to predict the outcome of a game. But we can often determine the outcome by thinking through the consequences from each player's perspective, just as we did in the prisoner's dilemma.

Games with Only One Dominant Strategy

To illustrate how we may be able to predict the outcome of a game even when one of the players does not have a dominant strategy, consider the situation of two firms deciding on whether to cut prices. Discounters Delux and Quality

International Perspective

Beggar-Thy-Neighbor Tariff Policies

During the international depression of the 1930s, many countries debated whether to impose restrictions on international trade. The argument made was that restricting imports from other countries would boost the demand for goods produced domestically. This in turn would allow domestic firms to expand employment and production. Such a policy would work by reducing the demand for goods produced in other countries, leading to fewer sales by foreign firms, who would then have to cut production and employment. The gains at home would come at the expense of foreign producers and workers, so these policies were often called "beggar-thy-neighbor" policies. The trade wars of the 1930s can be understood as another example of the prisoner's dilemma.

In 1930, the United States passed the Smoot-Hawley Tariff Act. This act raised tariffs on imported goods, making them more expensive for American consumers. By raising the price of foreign-produced goods relative to goods produced in America, the tariff provided an incentive for Americans to shift their demand to domestically produced goods. Other countries did not stand by idly while American tariffs reduced their market in the United States. They retaliated by raising their tariffs on goods produced in the United States. The result was that all countries suffered from the decline in world trade. By imposing tariffs that reduced trade, all countries lost the benefits of trade.

The outcome in the sort of trade war set off by the Smoot-Hawley Act can be illustrated in terms of a simple game. The diagram shows the payoffs to each of two countries that are deciding whether to impose trade restrictions. Payoffs to country A are shown below the diagonal line in each box. Payoffs to country B are given above the diagonal. The payoffs are defined as the gains (or losses) to a country's income relative to what they would be if neither imposed trade restrictions. The numbers are hypothetical and can be thought of as, say, tens of billions of dollars. Each country gains the most if it is the only one to impose

restrictions. Both are worse off if both impose restrictions and better off if neither imposes them.

Each country has a dominant strategy—impose trade sanctions. In the case of country A, for example, it would reason as follows: "If country B imposes trade restrictions, our country will be better off if we also impose restrictions. If country B does not impose restrictions, we are also better off if we impose restrictions. Therefore, we should impose trade restrictions regardless of what country B does." Country B would reason in exactly the same manner. Unfortunately, when they both impose restrictions, both are left worse off than if no restrictions had been imposed.

Another way to look at this situation is to recognize that both countries would be better off if they could cooperate and mutually agree not to impose trade restrictions. The problem is, there is no mechanism in our simple example that can make sure they cooperate. Just as in the collusion example discussed in Chapter 12, each player has an incentive to violate any voluntary agreement not to impose trade restrictions. One of the roles of international organizations such as the World Trade Organization (WTO) is to lay down rules designed to promote international trade and cooperation, to make it possible for them to make credible commitments not to raise tariffs or other barriers to trade.

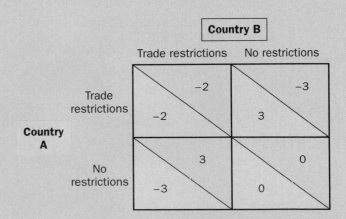

Brands compete with one another. Discounters Delux promises its customers the lowest prices; it would suffer a large loss of customers if it failed to offer the lowest prices. Quality Prices has higher costs and so would prefer not to cut prices. However, it risks losing some of its business if it does not match Discounters Delux's price reductions. The profits each expects to earn are shown in Figure 19.2. The payoffs to Discounters Delux are below the diagonal lines, while those of Quality Brands are above the diagonals.

Discounters Delux has a dominant strategy—reduce prices. It makes more in profits under this strategy, regardless of what Quality Brands does. Quality Brands, in contrast, does not have a dominant strategy. If Discounters Delux reduces prices, Quality Brand's best response is also to cut prices since otherwise it would lose too many sales. However, if Discounters Delux does not reduce prices, then Quality Brands is better off not reducing its prices.

Even though Quality Brands does not have a dominant strategy, we can predict the outcome if we reason as follows. Quality Brands knows that Discounters Delux will reduce prices since that is Discounters Delux's dominant strategy. So the fact that Quality Brands would find it best to keep prices high if Discounters Delux keeps its prices high is irrelevant. Quality Brands knows Discounters Delux will cut prices. Quality Brands's best strategy is also to cut prices. The outcome, or equilibrium, in this game will have both firms reducing their prices.

In this price-cutting game, each firm follows a strategy that is best for it, given that the other firm is playing its equilibrium strategy (cutting prices). Cutting prices is the unique Nash equilibrium. Given the other player's strategies, neither wants to change its strategy.

Internet Connection

The Zero Sum Game Solver

Games like *Survivor* have a fixed total payoff; the winner receives $1 million and the next few survivors receive smaller amounts. Nothing the contestants do can affect the total prize money available. If one contestant receives more, another receives less. Games like this are called *zero sum games.* When we think of games, we usually think of sports or chess, or perhaps gambling. These are all zero sum games. In sports, one team wins and the other loses. In gambling, every dollar you win is someone else's loss. While many people think that economic exchange is a zero sum game, you should understand by now that it is not—exchange can leave *both* parties better off. On the Web site of Professor David Levine at UCLA, you can find a program that will find the solution to any two-person, zero sum game. Invent a game yourself and find its solution at http://levine. sscnet.ucla.edu/Games/zerosum.htm.

Games Without Dominant Strategies

Both the prisoner's dilemma game and the price-cutting game have unique Nash equilibria. Often, however, a game will have more than one Nash equilibrium, as the following example illustrates.

Consider the situation of two friends who decide to study together. They both are enrolled in the same physics and economics classes, and both think that their performances on upcoming tests will be improved if they study together. However, John would prefer to spend the study

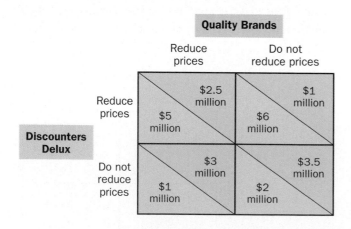

FIGURE 19.2 *Price-Cutting Game*

Discounters Delux has a dominant strategy, which is to reduce prices. Thus, the best response for Quality Brands is also to cut prices.

time focusing on physics, while Todd would rather devote the time to economics. The game table for this game is shown in Figure 19.3, with the payoffs expressed in the average grade for the two courses (the letter below the diagonal line in each box is the payoff to John).

Does either John or Todd have a dominant strategy? No. If John insists on studying physics, Todd is better off joining John in hitting the physics books than if he goes it alone in studying economics. On the other hand, if John is willing to study economics, then Todd's best response is obviously to study economics also. Similarly, John's best strategy is to study physics if that is what Todd also does, while John's best strategy is to study economics if Todd also studies economics. Neither player has a dominant strategy, one that is best regardless of what the other does.

Even though there are no dominant strategies in this game, there are two Nash equilibria—either both study physics or both study economics. If Todd pulls out Stiglitz and Walsh's economics textbook and starts reviewing the material on trade-offs and incentives, John's best strategy is to join him. Studying economics is John's best choice, given that Todd is studying economics. The same is true for Todd—given that John is studying economics, Todd's best strategy is to join him. So the lower-right box in the diagram is a Nash equilibrium. But it is not the only one. The upper-left box, where both end up studying physics, is also a Nash equilibrium. While the concept of a Nash equilibrium may not lead us to predict a *unique* equilibrium in a game, it can help eliminate some outcomes. Nei-

ther the upper-right nor lower-left box in the diagram is a Nash equilibrium. If Todd studies physics, studying economics is not John's best response.

Repeated Games

In the basic prisoner's dilemma game, each party makes only one decision. The game is played just a single time. The two players could do better if they could somehow cooperate and agree not to pick the dominant strategy. But when the game is actually played, each has an incentive to break any prior agreement and do what is in his own best interest. If the players or parties interact many times, then the strategies for each can become more complicated. There may be additional ways to try to enforce cooperation that would benefit both parties. Games that are played many times over by the same players are called **repeated games.**

To see how the nature of the game changes when it is repeated, let us consider the actions of two firms in a duopoly. Suppose each duopolist announces that it will refrain from cutting prices as long as its rival does. But if the rival cheats on the collusive agreement, then the first duopolist might respond by increasing production and lowering prices. Can this threat ensure that the two firms cooperate?

Consider what happens if the two firms expect to compete in the same market over the next ten years, after which time a new product is expected to come along and shift the entire configuration of the industry. It will pay each firm to

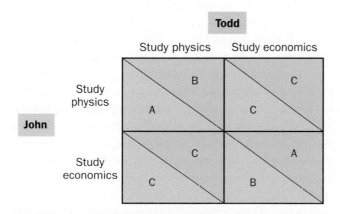

FIGURE 19.3 *The Study Game*

Neither player has a dominant strategy, but there are two Nash equilibria: both study physics or both study economics.

cheat in the tenth year, when there is no possibility of retaliation. Now consider what happens in the ninth year. Both firms can figure out that it will not pay either one of them to cooperate in the tenth year. But if they are not going to cooperate in the tenth year, then the threat of not cooperating in the future is completely ineffective. Hence, in the ninth year, each firm will reason that it pays to cheat on the collusive agreement by producing more than the agreed-upon amount. Collusion breaks down in the ninth year. Reasoning backward through time will lead to the breakdown of collusion almost immediately.

This example illustrates an important principle of strategic thinking: Think first about the end of the game and work backward from there to identify the best current choice. Making decisions in this way is called **backward induction,** or **rollback.** For each decision a player can make, she needs to work out her opponent's optimal response and what her own payoff will be in each case. Then, in the first stage of the game, she can adopt the strategy that gives her the highest payoff.

Rollback also applies to the various games considered earlier. To determine the behavior of each player, we assumed players would reason backward to determine what their best option was for each choice their opponent might make. For example, in the prisoner's dilemma, prisoner A reasoned, "Suppose my partner confesses, what is my best strategy? And if my partner does not confess, then what is my best strategy?" Each thought about the consequences of his opponent's choices and worked backward to determine what he should do.

Our analysis of collusion in a repeated game setting may seem too pessimistic about the ability of firms or individuals to cooperate. Certainly we see many situations in which individuals find ways to cooperate, trading a short-term gain to establish longer-term relationships that yield higher benefits. And firms do the same thing, offering services or providing higher-quality products that lower its immediate profits but contribute to higher profits in the future. In strategic games that do not have a finite end—for which there is always the possibility of another round—there are a variety of strategies that may allow players to cooperate to achieve better outcomes.

Reputations

Developing reputations can be useful when players are engaged in repeated interactions. A firm that relies on local customers for repeat business has more of an incentive to develop a reputation for good service than does one with little repeat business. A car mechanic might have an incentive to pad the bill or otherwise cheat a customer if he never expects to service the owner's car again, but the mechanic may do even better in the long run by gaining a reputation for good service and relying on repeat business from his customers.

Gaining a reputation is costly in the short run—the car mechanic must offer good service but initially he will not be able to charge any more than garages that do not care about their reputation. The lower profits in the short run are like an investment that will pay off in the future when the car mechanic has developed a reputation for good service and can charge more than garages that do not have such reputations.

Tit for Tat

Economists have set up laboratory experiments, much like those used in other sciences, to test how individuals actually behave in these different games. The advantage of this sort of **experimental economics** is that the researcher can change one aspect of the experiment at a time, to try to determine the crucial determinants of behavior. One set of experiments has looked at how individuals cooperate in situations like the prisoner's dilemma. These experiments tend to show that participants often evolve simple strategies that, although they may appear irrational in the short run, can be effective in inducing cooperation (collusion) as the game is repeated a number of times. One common strategy is "tit for tat." In the case of two oligopolists, one might threaten to increase output if the other does, even if doing so does not maximize its short-term profits. If the rival believes this threat, especially after it has been carried out a few times, the rival may decide that it is more profitable to cooperate and keep production

WRAP-UP

Rollback

When strategic interactions occur for a repeated but fixed number of times, the best approach is to start from the end of the game and work backward to determine the best strategy. Rollback helps the player focus on the future consequences of his current decision.

low rather than to cheat. In the real world, such simple strategies may play an important role in ensuring that firms do not compete too vigorously in markets where there are only three or four dominant firms.

Internet Connection

The Prisoner's Dilemma

You can play a repeated game version of the prisoner's dilemma against a computer at http://www.Princeton.edu/~mdaniels/PD/PD.html. Try a "tit for tat" strategy and see how the computer responds.

Institutions

In many situations, institutions ensure that a cooperative outcome is reached. International organizations such as the World Trade Organization (WTO) serve to enforce agreements that promote international trade. Member countries agree to abide by certain rules that forbid the type of trade restrictions and beggar-thy-neighbor policies that proved so disastrous during the 1930s. Professional sports leagues impose salary caps. These limit the ability of teams to boost salaries, and as the Minnesota Timberwolves and San Francisco 49ers recently discovered, violating the caps can lead to fines and other penalties. Deposit insurance eliminates the incentive that depositors have to withdraw funds when there are rumors of financial trouble at their bank, because depositors know their money is protected even if their bank fails.

CASE IN POINT

Banking Panics

Between 1930 and 1933, the United States suffered a massive financial panic that forced about nine thousand banks to fail. This disruption of the financial system contributed to the severity of the Great Depression, when unemployment reached levels as high as 25 per-

During the banking panics of the early 1930s, depositors rushed to banks to withdraw their savings.

cent of the labor force. As banks closed their doors, businesses that relied on bank credit to finance their inventories and investments were forced to cut back production and lay off workers. How can game theory help us understand why so many banks failed?

If you have a deposit in a commercial bank today, the federal government insures it (up to $100,000). That means that if your bank makes bad investments and goes bankrupt, the federal government will make sure that you receive all your money back. Before 1933, however, bank deposits were not insured. If your bank went bankrupt, you could lose everything—that is, unless you acted quickly at the first hint of trouble and withdrew your deposits before the bank ran out of cash. Banks lend out most of the money they receive as deposits, holding only a small fraction as cash to meet daily unpredictable fluctuations in deposits and withdrawals. If all depositors suddenly demand their money back, a bank would quickly run out of cash and be forced to close. And that's exactly what happened in the 1930s—depositors raced to be the first to withdraw their deposits. When they all demanded their deposits back, there simply was not enough money on hand to pay everyone. Banks were forced to shut their doors. Everyone would have been better off not trying to withdraw their deposits, since in that case the banks could have remained open.

The concept of Nash equilibrium can help us understand bank runs and financial panics. Consider a simple example of a bank with just two depositors, call them A and B. Each depositor must decide whether to try to withdraw her deposits at the bank or to leave them in the bank. Assume each has deposited $1,000 at the bank. The bank has used these funds to make loans and investments but keeps $200 on hand in its vault. If the bank's loans are repaid, the bank can pay an interest rate of 5 percent to its depositors.

If neither depositor tries to withdraw funds from the bank, let us assume they both will eventually receive the full value of their deposits plus the 5 percent interest (for a total of $1,050). If depositor A withdraws while depositor B does not, A can take out $200, all the cash the bank has on hand. The bank then must shut its doors, and depositor B receives nothing. The reverse happens if depositor B tries to withdraw its funds while A does not. If both try to withdraw their money, the most each can get is $100. The payoffs are shown in Figure 19.4.

Clearly both depositors are better off if neither tries to withdraw funds from the bank. In this case, they both would eventually receive $1,050. This is also a Nash equilibrium. If depositor A leaves her money in the bank, depositor B's best strategy is to do the same. Conversely, if depositor B leaves his money in the bank, depositor A's best strategy is to do the same. Each reasons as follows: "If the other leaves her deposits in the bank, my best strategy is also to leave my deposits in the bank."

So there is an equilibrium in which neither depositor trys to withdraw funds and the bank stays open.

Just as in the earlier example of the two friends deciding what to study, there are two Nash equilibria to the deposit-withdrawal game. The second Nash equilibrium occurs when both depositors try to withdraw their money and the bank fails. In this case, each reasons as follows: "If the other depositor tries to withdraw, I'm better off if I also try to withdraw. That way, at least I get $100, which is better than nothing." So there is an equilibrium in which each rushes to the bank, and the bank is unable to fully meet its obligations to the two depositors. The bank fails.

This example illustrates a situation in which there may be a good equilibrium—in this case, the one in which the bank remains open and the depositors eventually receive all their money plus interest—and a bad equilibrium—when the bank is forced to close. This situation should be contrasted with the prisoner's dilemma, where the only equilibrium was inferior to an alternative set of strategies (neither prisoner confesses) or the previous example of John and Todd, where one of the two equilibria was preferred by Todd and the other by John.

Financial panics can be thought of as a shift from the good to the bad equilibrium. This could happen if depositors start to worry about the financial soundness of the banking sector, even if such fears are unfounded. The simple argument illustrated by this game provides part of the rationale behind federal deposit insurance. With deposit insurance, each depositor is confident that her money is safe, regardless of what other depositors do. No depositor has an incentive to try to beat others by getting her money out first. ●

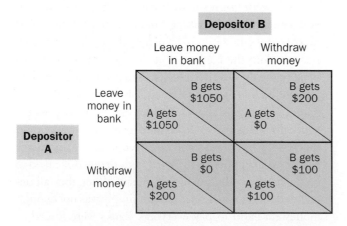

FIGURE 19.4 *Banking Panic as a Strategic Game*

Like the study game, this game has two Nash equilibria: both withdraw money or both leave money in the bank. The equilibrium in which both leave their money in the bank leaves both better off than if they both withdraw their money.

Sequential Moves

In the prisoner's dilemma, each player must make a choice without knowing what the other has done. The players move simultaneously. In many situations, however, one player must move first, and the second player then responds directly to the choice made by the first. This type of game is called a **sequential game,** since players take turns and each can observe what choices were made in earlier moves. In a sequential game, the player who moves first must consider how the second player will respond to each possible move he can make.

Sports offer many examples of strategic behavior. The situation a baseball manager faces in deciding whether to bring in a relief pitcher is a prime example of a sequential game. Conventional wisdom in baseball says that a left-handed batter does better against a right-handed pitcher, and a right-handed batter does better against a left-handed pitcher. Does that mean that if a right-handed batter is coming to the plate, the manager should bring in a right-handed pitcher? Not necessarily. Once a right-handed pitcher is brought in, the manager of the other team can send in a left-handed pinch hitter. So a manager considering a change of pitchers needs to think about how the opposing manager will respond to each of the possible pitching choices the first manager can make.

This example illustrates an important aspect of a sequential game. The player who moves first must think about how the second player will respond. Take the case of a firm facing the potential entry of a new rival into its market. Suppose a software firm, call it Redhat, is considering introducing a new operating system that will compete with Microsoft Windows. Redhat must decide whether to enter the business or stay out. If it enters, Microsoft must decide whether to peacefully compete or to wage a price war. Suppose that Redhat enters and Microsoft competes peacefully. Assume Microsoft will earn profits of $50 billion and Redhat $10 billion on its operating system. If instead Microsoft engages in a price war, assume both firms will lose money, with Microsoft losing $1 billion and Redhat losing $500 million. If Redhat decides not to enter, it earns $0, while Microsoft earns profits of $80 billion. Will Redhat enter? And will Microsoft engage in a price war?

We can use a **game tree** diagram to simplify this complex scenario. Game trees are the standard way to represent sequential games. Different branches on a game tree indicate the various outcomes that could occur, given all the alternative strategies the players could follow. For example, the entry game involving Microsoft and Redhat is represented by the game tree of Figure 19.5. At the end of each branch, the payoffs to Redhat and Microsoft are shown. The first number is Redhat's payoff; the second is Microsoft's.

Each node—the points where new branches split—represents a decision point for one of the players. In this game, Redhat moves first (node 1). Microsoft moves second after it has learned whether Redhat has entered or not. If Redhat decides to enter, we move along the upper branch of the game tree from node 1 to node 2. Microsoft

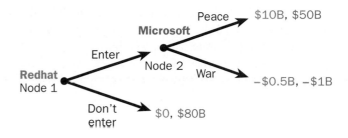

FIGURE 19.5 *Game Tree for a Sequential Game*

Redhat makes the first move. If Redhat decides to enter the market, Microsoft may then choose between peaceful coexistence or a price war. By reasoning backward from these options, we can see that Redhat will enter the market and Microsoft will choose to compete peacefully.

must then choose whether to compete peacefully or wage a price war. From node 2, we move along the upper branch if Microsoft competes peacefully, and the payoffs are $10 billion to Redhat and $50 billion to Microsoft, or we move along the lower branch if Microsoft wages a price war, in which case the payoffs are −$500 million and −$1 billion, respectively. If Redhat decides not to enter, we move along the lower branch from node 1. Here, there is nothing further Microsoft must decide, so the game ends and the players receive the payoffs shown ($0 for Redhat and $80 billion for Microsoft).

In deciding whether to enter, Redhat's managers will reason as follows: "If we enter, Microsoft can either wage a price war or compete peacefully. In the former case, it loses $1 billion, and in the latter case it makes $50 billion. Clearly once we enter it will be in Microsoft's best interest to compete peacefully, so we should enter."

This example again illustrates rollback. "Thinking strategically" requires that one think first about the end of the game, and work backward from there to determine the best current choice. Redhat asks itself what Microsoft will do if Redhat has entered. It works backward from there to determine if it should enter.

Using rollback is easy using a game tree. At each node that leads to an end to the game, determine the best strategy of the player who makes a decision at that node. Then work backward. At node 2, Microsoft's best strategy is to compete peacefully. It gets $50 billion that way, while it would lose $1 billion in a price war. Now work back to the previous node—node 1 where Redhat makes its decision.

From its analysis of Microsoft's options at node 2, Redhat knows that if it enters the market, Microsoft will compete peacefully, leaving Redhat with a $10 billion profit. Redhat's other option at node 1 is not to enter, which would leave it with profits of $0. Clearly, Redhat's best strategy is to enter.

Threats

We can add another aspect to this simple game by allowing Microsoft to decide whether to threaten Redhat with a price war before Redhat makes its decision on whether to enter the market. Microsoft might threaten a price war in the hope that this will discourage Redhat from entering. But will it really have any impact on Redhat's decision? No, because Redhat can again reason that if it does decide to enter, Microsoft's best response is to compete peacefully. The threat is not credible. By not credible, we mean that it will not be in the best interests of Microsoft to carry out its threat when the time comes to do so. The Nash equilibrium for this game involves Redhat entering and the two firms competing peacefully.

Things can be different when we think of the entry game as a repeated game. Suppose Microsoft is constantly

Thinking Like an Economist

Information and Thinking Strategically

Information plays a critical role in strategic behavior, but sometimes in surprising ways. Take the prisoner's dilemma, for example. Each prisoner must make a decision about whether to confess without knowing what the other prisoner has done. It might seem like the outcome would change if one prisoner could know in advance what the other had done. It turns out that providing this extra information does not change the prisoner's strategy—it is still best to confess. The reason is that confessing is a dominant strategy. Confessing is the best strategy for each prisoner, regardless of what the other did. So knowing for sure whether your partner confesses or remains silent does not change your strategy.

When a player does not have a dominant strategy, changing the information the player has is likely to alter the player's best strategy. Consider the case of an insurance company that offers health insurance. Suppose the insurance company can obtain information such as whether an individual smokes. Since smoking is associated with many health problems, the insurance company will offer different policies to smokers and nonsmokers, with smokers paying higher insurance premiums to reflect the likelihood they will incur higher medical bills. Now suppose a law is passed that forbids the insurance company from collecting such information. If the company offers just a single policy to everyone, it faces an adverse selection problem of the type we learned about in Chapter 14—those with the poorest health are the ones most likely to buy the insurance. But if the firm thinks strategically, it might reason along the following lines: "If we offer only one type of policy, we run the risk that only those with health problems will buy it and we will lose money. Instead, let's offer two different policies. One will have a high deductible, so that patients themselves have to pay a large amount for doctor visits and other services before insurance kicks in. The other policy will have a low deductible, with insurance paying for most medical services. We will charge more for the policy with the low deductible. The low-deductible policy will be more attractive to individuals who think they will need lots of medical services. It will be attractive to smokers. The policy with the high deductible will be more attractive to individuals who think they are less likely to need lots of medical care. It will be attractive to nonsmokers. By offering these separate policies, we can get individuals to reveal information about their health risks."

By thinking strategically, the insurance company is able to overcome some of the information problems it faces. By offering different policies, it is able to separate individuals into high- and low-risk groups.

faced with new entrants into its markets. It may be in Microsoft's long-term best interests to engage in an aggressive price war against a new competitor, even if this results in short-term losses for Microsoft. Doing so gains Microsoft the reputation of being a tough competitor and makes future threats more credible. A firm that behaves this way may sacrifice profits in the short run, but by keeping potential rivals out, it earners higher profits in the long run. Trading off short-term profits for long-term profits may make sense for the firm, but doing so may run afoul of the laws designed to restrict anticompetitive behavior.[3]

Time Inconsistency

Threats and promises are common components of strategic behavior. We have already discussed the case of a monopolist who threatens to wage a price war if another firm enters its market (our Redhat and Microsoft example). In that case, the firm that is considering entering the market understands that the existing firm's threat is not credible. Once the firm enters, the existing firm's best strategy is to compete peacefully. Because the potential entrant can use rollback to determine this, the initial threat is ineffective in deterring entry—it is not credible.

Now instead of looking at this problem from the perspective of the firm contemplating entrance into the market, consider the situation of the monopolist trying to protect its market. It makes sense to try to scare off potential rivals by making threats of a price war. But such a strategy is time inconsistent—when the time comes to actually carry out the threat, it is not in the best interest of the monopolist to do so. Because the potential rival knows this to be the case, it can ignore the threat. For the monopolist, announcing it will wage a price war is not a time-consistent strategy since the firm will not find it worthwhile to carry out the threat.

Time inconsistency arises in many contexts, usually in situations where one player's promise or threat is designed to influence the other player's actions. Consider the case of Sarah who has just graduated from high school. Her parents believe that holding down a summer job will help Sarah learn responsibility, so they offer to help pay her college tuition in the fall if she works during the summer. The implicit

threat is that they will not help with the tuition if Sarah loafs around over the summer and does not work.[4] But Sarah can see that such a threat is time inconsistent. If she hangs out at the beach with her friends all summer, the only choice her parents face in the fall is whether to help her pay for college. Since Sarah knows her parents want her to receive a college education, regardless of how lazy she is, she knows they will help pay for college even if she loafs all summer. Since she would rather loaf than work, she does not get a job. Her parents' threat, designed to force her to find a job, was ineffective because it was time inconsistent. Sarah knew they would never actually carry out the threat since doing so would not be their best strategy come the fall.

CASE IN POINT

Immigration Policy

At the end of 2000, Congressional Republicans and President Clinton were locked in a disagreement over a new immigration reform bill. At issue were provisions supported by Democrats and opposed by Republicans that would give amnesty to thousands of illegal immigrants. Debates over immigration policies are often contentious, and the concept of time inconsistency can help us understand why.

One objective of immigration policy is to deter illegal immigration. With this objective in mind, the best strategy for the government is to make it hard for illegal immigrants to obtain jobs or social services and to deport any that are caught. Tough policies are designed to deter illegal immigration by making it less attractive to potential illegal immigrants. Part of a deterrence policy would be a promise never to offer amnesty to illegal immigrants. A successful deterrent would reduce the number of individuals who enter the country illegally. Just as the monopolist's threat of a price war if a rival enters its market is designed to persuade the rival not to enter, laws that punish illegal immigrants or make immigration less attractive (e.g., by reducing employment opportunities) are designed to persuade potential illegal immigrants not to enter the country.

---

[3]See the discussion of predation in Chapter 12, *Thinking Like an Economist: Trade-offs, American Airlines, and Predation*, p. 260.

[4]This example is from Herb Taylor, "Time Inconsistency: A Potential Problem for Policymakers," Federal Reserve Bank of Philadelphia *Economic Review*, (March/April 1985): 3–12.

A border-control guard scans the horizon for illegal aliens crossing from Mexico to California.

But what if, despite the risks, people still decide to enter illegally? Even though the United States has laws that allow the deportation of illegal immigrants and impose fines on firms that hire them, many individuals enter the country illegally. These individuals find jobs, they pay taxes, and they put down roots. They become effective members of American society. Compassion argues for offering an amnesty that would allow them to become legal residents. Any earlier promise never to offer an amnesty is time inconsistent. And promises that "this will be the last amnesty" are also time inconsistent. Once enough illegal immigrants have established lives in the United States, there will be political support for an amnesty that recognizes their plight.

The 1986 Immigration Reform and Control Act (IRCA) illustrates the difficulties of balancing deterrence and compassion. IRCA established new sanctions against employers who hired illegal immigrants while at the same time it offered new means for aliens who had resided continuously in the United States since January 1, 1982 to gain permanent resident status. The government's best strategy is to forgive illegal immigrants who have established lives in the United States while at the same time promising penalties to discourage any future immigration. A potential immigrant may not be deterred, knowing that if he or she can stay in the country long enough without getting caught, there will be another amnesty offering an opportunity to gain permanent legal residency. If potential immigrants ignore the threatened penalties and enter the country, Congress will again be faced with dealing with a large population of illegal immigrants and will eventually decide to grant another amnesty.

Balancing deterrence and compassion is often difficult, and time inconsistency helps us to understand why. Because potential illegal immigrants will anticipate a future amnesty, the policies designed to deter them will not be effective. New penalties, and a promise that there will be no more amnesties in the future, compose a time-inconsistent policy. ●

Commitment

We have analyzed the situation faced by Sarah's parents at the end of the summer. At that point, it was too late to affect Sarah's summer activities, so the threat to not fund her college is no longer worth carrying out. Things would be different if her parents could somehow tie their hands in a way that would prevent them from paying for Sarah's tuition unless she actually worked during the summer. Being able to commit to undertake a future action may be necessary for threats or promises to be credible.

Military strategists commonly face the problem of making threats credible. During the Cold War, U.S. policy was that it would not rule out being the first to use nuclear weapons. This policy raised the possibility that if the Soviet Union invaded Western Europe, the United States would retaliate against the Soviet Union with nuclear weapons if necessary. Such retaliation would then lead the Soviet Union to launch a nuclear strike against the United States. A Soviet military planner using rollback might reason that if the Soviet Union invaded Europe, the U.S. government would be faced with the choice of either launching a nuclear attack on the Soviet Union and having millions of Americans killed in the ensuing nuclear war, or accepting a Soviet victory in Europe. Faced with that choice, the United States might decide to accept a Soviet victory. The U.S. threat to retaliate would not be credible. One argument for maintaining thousands of U.S. troops in Europe was that their loss in a Soviet invasion would force the U.S. military to launch a strike against the Soviet Union. By committing troops to Europe, the American threat was more credible.

In imperfectly competitive markets, there are many ways in which a firm may take concrete actions that deter rivals where threats alone would not be credible. This can be illustrated by a variant of the earlier example of Microsoft and Redhat. Consider a coffee company, let us call it Northwest Coffee, that opens a coffee store on every other corner of a city's downtown. To deter a potential rival, call it Pete's Coffee, from opening stores on the empty corners, Northwest Coffee might threaten a price war if a rival opens up competing stores. The game tree and payoffs are shown in Figure 19.6.

Just as in our earlier example, Pete's Coffee can use rollback to determine that if it enters, Northwest will find it more profitable to compete peacefully. Any threat by Northwest Coffee would not be credible.

Now let's change the game so that Northwest first decides whether to open on every *other* corner, or on *every* corner. The order of play now starts with Northwest's decision about how many stores to open. In the second stage of the game, Pete's Coffee must decide if it will enter. When it makes that decision, it knows whether Northwest has opened on every corner or only on every other corner. The game tree appears in Figure 19.7.

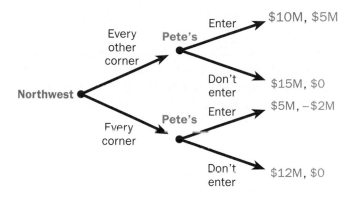

FIGURE 19.7 *Market Entry Game with Commitment*

Even though it costs more to operate stores on every street corner, Northwest will do so in order to prevent Pete's Coffee from entering the market. Opening stores on every street corner serves as a commitment mechanism.

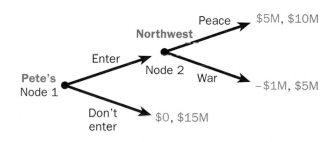

FIGURE 19.6 *Market Entry Game Without Commitment*

Northwest may threaten to wage a price war if Pete's Coffee enters the market, but such a threat lacks credibility.

First, notice that if Northwest opens on every other corner and Pete's Coffee enters, the payoffs—$10 million for Northwest Coffee and $5 million for Pete's Coffee—reflect the previous finding that Northwest will not wage a price war. Second, the new branches of the tree show the possible outcomes if Northwest opens on every corner. Because of the added costs, Northwest's profit is smaller when it opens the additional stores and Pete's Coffee stays out of the market ($12 million) than if it had only opened on every other corner and Pete's had stayed out ($15 million). If Northwest has a store on every corner and Pete's Coffee decides to enter the market, Northwest's profits fall

Thinking Like an Economist

Incentives and Strategic Behavior

Economists apply game theory to analyze behavior and choices in many situations. The situations are more complicated than the ones consumers and firms face in the basic competitive model. In that model, for instance, a firm did not need to worry about how rivals might respond to its actions. When studying situations in which strategic thinking is important, economists focus on incentives, just as they do when using the basic competitive model. To predict how consumers and firms will behave, to predict what choices they will make, economists look at incentives. Decision makers will evaluate the benefits and costs of different strategies and choose the one that gives them the best outcome.

to $5 million, while Pete's Coffee ends up losing $2 million.

We again use rollback to determine the equilibrium. Start from the Pete's Coffee decision node along the top branch (the branch followed if Northwest opens on every other corner). If it finds itself at this node, the best strategy is for Pete's Coffee to enter the market, earning $5 million. Now look at the Pete's Coffee decision node along the bottom branch (the branch followed if Northwest opens on every corner). Here, the best strategy is to not enter. That way, at least, it does not lose any money.

By applying rollback, we can now analyze Northwest Coffee's decision at the start of the game. Northwest knows that if it puts a store on every other corner, Pete's will enter and Northwest will earn $10 million. If it opens on every corner, Pete's will not enter, and Northwest will earn $12 million. Northwest's best strategy is to open a store on every corner. Even though the extra stores may look like they are lowering Northwest's profits from $15 million to $12 million, they are worth opening because they deter a potential rival. Northwest's extra stores are a more credible threat to a potential rival than is a threat to engage in a price war. Having stores open and in place serves as a commitment mechanism that deters potential rivals from entering. Northwest is worse off than if it opened fewer stores and Pete's stayed out of the market, but it is better off than if Pete's had entered.

Review and Practice

Summary

1. In perfectly competitive markets, firms and consumers can decide on how much to produce and how much to consume without taking into account how others might react. In imperfectly competitive markets, firms must take into account how their rivals will respond to the firm's production or pricing decisions. Firms must behave strategically in such situations. Individuals also face many situations in which they must behave strategically. Economists use game theory to predict how individuals and firms will behave.

2. In a Nash equilibrium, each player in a game is following a strategy that is best, given the strategies followed by the other players. A game may have a unique Nash equilibrium, or it may have several equilibria.

3. A dominant strategy is one that is best, regardless of what the other player chooses to do. Looking for dominant strategies can help predict behavior.

4. Rollback is crucial for strategic behavior. Thinking strategically means looking into the future to predict how others will behave, and then using that information to make decisions.

5. Strategic choices are often designed to influence the choice of others. Once those choices have been made, however, carrying out the initial strategy may no longer be best. When this is the case, the original strategy was time inconsistent.

Key Terms

strategic behavior
game table
dominant strategy
Nash equilibrium
repeated game
rollback (or backward induction)
experimental economics
sequential game
game tree
time inconsistency

Review Questions

1. Firms in perfectly competitive markets do not need to behave strategically. Why not? Why do oligopolists need to behave strategically? Does a monopolist need to behave strategically?

2. Professional sports leagues often have salary caps that limit the amount individual teams can pay players. Using the prisoner's dilemma game, explain why such a restriction might make the team owners better off.

3. What is a dominant strategy? Explain why each player in the prisoner's dilemma has a dominant strategy.

4. What is a Nash equilibrium? What is the unique Nash equilibrium in the prisoner's dilemma game? Can a game have more than one Nash equilibrium? Give an example.

5. In the prisoner's dilemma, each player has a dominant strategy and there is a unique Nash equilibrium in which the players choose their dominant strategy. Give an example of a game in which only one player has a dominant strategy. What is the Nash equilibrium?

6. This chapter opened with a discussion of the television show *Survivor*. What principle of strategic behavior did Kelly need to use?

7. What is a sequential game? Why does the player who moves first need to use backward induction?

8. An old parental saying, when punishing a child, is, "This hurts me more than it hurts you." Using the idea of a repeated game, explain why a parent might still punish the child even if doing so really did hurt the parent more than the child.

9. Why might threats and promises not be credible?

Problems

1. Consider two oligopolists, with each choosing between a "high" and a "low" level of production. Given their choices of how much to produce, their profits will be:

Explain how firm B will reason that it makes sense to produce the high amount, regardless of what firm A chooses. Then explain how firm A will reason that it makes sense to produce the high amount, regardless of what firm B chooses. How might collusion assist the two firms in this case?

2. Use the prisoner's dilemma analysis to describe what happens in the following two situations:

(a) Consider two rivals, say, producers of cigarettes. If Benson and Hedges alone advertises, it diverts customers from Marlboro. If Marlboro alone advertises, it diverts customers from Benson and Hedges. If they both advertise, they retain their customer base.

Are they genuinely unhappy with government regulations prohibiting advertising? In practice, cigarette firms have complained quite bitterly about such government restrictions, including those aimed at children. Why?

(b) Consider two rivals, say, producers of camera film, Fuji and Kodak. Consumers want a film that accurately reproduces colors and is not grainy. Assume that initially, the two firms had products that were comparable in quality. If one does research and improves its product, it will steal customers from its rivals. If they both do research, and develop comparable products, then they will continue to share the market as before. Thus, the hypothetical payoff matrix (in millions of dollars) appears below (the profits in the case of research take into account the expenditures on research):

Explain why both will engage in research, even though their profits are lower. Could society be better off, even though profits are lower?

3. Draw the game tree for the game discussed on pages 396-397 in which Microsoft moves first and decides whether to threaten a price war. Redhat then decides whether to enter, and finally, Microsoft decides whether to compete peacefully or wage the price war. Verify that Microsoft's decision at the first stage of the game has no effect on Redhat's strategy.

4. Suppose firm A is a monopolist. Firm A threatens a price war if any potential rival enters its market. Suppose firm B is contemplating entering. The game tree is as follows (firm B payoffs are shown first; firm A's are shown second):

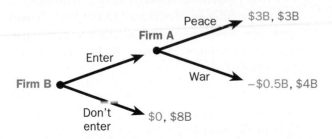

Should firm B enter? Is firm A's threat credible? Why? What makes this example different from the outcome in the Redhat-Microsoft example of the text?

5. "Tying one's hands" can be a way to commit credibly to a certain course of action. In the 1960s movie *Dr. Strangelove,* the Soviet Union deployed a doomsday device that could destroy the world and would be automatically triggered if the United States attacked. Explain how such a device could serve as a credible threat to deter a U.S. attack. In the movie, the Soviet Union did not inform the United States that the device had been deployed. Why was this a really bad strategy?

6. Suppose Quality Brands and Discounters Delux are involved in a repeated price-cutting game. Explain what a "tit for tat" strategy would be. Is a promise to "match any available price" a way for one firm to signal that it is playing "tit for rat"? Explain.

7. Restaurants often locate along major highways. Since most customers at such restaurants will not return, does the restaurant have an incentive to develop a reputation for good food? If reputations are important, will a restaurant that is part of a national chain (such as McDonalds or Burger King) or a locally owned restaurant have a greater incentive to offer good service?

8. How might a cultural or group norm or expectations about "correct" behavior, such as summarized in the old saying "honor among thieves," help enforce cooperation in the prisoner's dilemma?

Chapter 20

Technological Change

1. In what ways is the production of knowledge—including the knowledge of how to make new products and how to produce things more cheaply—different from the production of ordinary goods, like shoes and wheat?

2. Why is the patent system important in providing incentives to engage in research and development?

3. How may patents, as essential as they are for encouraging competition in research, at the same time reduce some aspects of competition?

4. How can government encourage technological progress?

*F*or much of the twentieth century, the United States has led in discovering and applying new technologies. Alexander Graham Bell and the telephone, the Wright brothers and the airplane, Thomas Edison and a host of electrical devices, for example, are all familiar early success stories. This tradition of innovation and invention continued as American inventors came up with products like the transistor and the laser. U.S. companies such as IBM, Eastman Kodak, and Xerox grew to become household names. More recently, Intel, Microsoft, and Genentech have experienced rapid growth and financial success based on their innovations.

The great strength of the market economy has been its ability to increase productivity, raise living standards, and innovate. Yet the basic competitive model on which we focused in Part Two simply *assumed* the state of technology as given. In fact, the huge changes in living standards that modern economies have experienced over the past two hundred years and the truly amazing differences between the economy in 1900 and the economy in 2000 are in large part due to technological change. We are not producing more of the same goods the economy produced in 1900. We are producing goods that the people of 1900 never dreamed of. Instead

of producing more horse-drawn carriages, we produce cars and airplanes. Instead of producing more horseshoes, we produce tires and jogging shoes. Key to the whole process of economic growth, then, is technological progress—thinking up new ways to do old things and new ways to do entirely new things. And this means that *ideas* are central to explaining economic growth. Indeed, economists estimate that as much as two thirds of all increases in productivity prior to 1973 were due to technological progress.

The current level of technological change has become so expected that it is hard to believe how different the view of reputable economists was in the early 1800s. Real wages of workers were little higher than they had been five hundred years earlier, when the bubonic plague killed a large part of the population of Europe and thereby created a scarcity of labor that raised real wages. After half a millennium of slow progress at best, Thomas Malthus, one of the greatest economists of that time, saw population expanding more rapidly than the capacity of the economy to support it. His prediction of declining living standards earned economics the nickname of "the dismal science." Today, many continue to predict that the world economy will be unable to grow faster than the population and that living standards must inevitably decline. Such predictions have been proved wrong over and over again by technological advances.

If we are to understand what determines the pace of innovation, we must go beyond the basic competitive model by recognizing two important factors. First, industries in which technological change is important are almost always imperfectly competitive. Second, the basic competitive model of Part Two assumed that individuals and firms receive all the benefits and pay all the costs of their actions, yet the basic research that leads to technological change can produce important **positive externalities.**

Since Tim Berners-Lee, Robert Cailliau, and their colleagues at the European particle physics center (CERN) in Geneva, Switzerland, invented the World Wide Web and hypertext formal language, or html, in 1990, programmers from around the world have been able to use and benefit from their ideas.[1] Alexander Graham Bell, Henry Ford, the Wright Brothers, and others were all rewarded for their inventions, some richly so. But these inventors reaped but a fraction of what society gained. The creation of these new products conferred benefits well beyond what consumers had to pay for them.

Links Between Technological Change and Imperfect Competition

In modern industrialized economies, often competition takes the form of trying to develop both new products and new ways of making existing products. Firms devote considerable resources to R & D—research (discovering new ideas, products, and processes) and development (perfecting, for instance, a new product to the point where it is brought to the market). In industries in which technological change and R & D are important, such as computer and drug industries, firms strive to earn profits by introducing new and better (at least in the eyes of consumers)

---

[1]For an interesting history of the Internet, see Janet Abbate's *Inventing the Internet* (Cambridge: MIT Press, 1999).

goods, or less costly methods of production. Only through such profits can the investment in R & D pay off.

Technological change and imperfect competition are inevitably linked for four major reasons. First, to make R & D expenditures pay, and therefore stimulate innovation, inventions are protected from competition by patents. Patents are specifically designed to limit competition. Second, industries where technological change is important typically have high fixed costs—costs that do not change as output increases. This implies decreasing average costs over a wide range of output, another characteristic that limits competition. Third, industries characterized by rapid technological change are also industries where the benefits of increasing experience in a new production technique can lead to rapidly decreasing costs. Finally, because banks are generally unwilling to lend funds to finance R & D, raising capital for new and small firms is difficult. All these make entry difficult, and reduce competition in the sense defined by the basic competitive model.

Patents and the Production of Ideas

If ideas are important for technological change, how are ideas produced? Can we use some of the basic ideas of economics to understand the production of ideas?

Most advances are a result of the deliberate allocation of resources to R & D. The typical large corporation may spend as much as 3 percent of its revenue on research. While many discoveries have occurred almost by accident (such as Fleming's discovery of penicillin), in the modern economy these are more the exception than the rule. In order for firms and individuals to have an incentive to allocate their valuable time and resources to research, they must reap a return. There are two ways they can do so—either by producing a product using the idea or by licensing the right to use the idea to others. In either case, however, the inventor has to prevent others from using the idea without paying. If rival firms could simply use the idea without paying, the inventing firm would have a hard time getting a return, because competition would drive the price down to the marginal cost of producing the product. But the cost of producing *ideas* is a fixed cost; once the idea is discovered and developed, it typically lowers the marginal cost of production. In short, for the inventor to obtain a return, she must be able to exclude users who do not pay. But some ideas are not very excludable. Once Henry Ford came up with the idea of

e-Insight

The New Economy and Innovation

The new economy sometimes has been characterized as an innovation in the process of innovation. Just as the industrial revolution represented a marked change in the way that goods are produced, the new economy represents a marked change in the way that ideas are produced and disseminated. There are many aspects of these changes.

While a century ago, inventors like Edison, Westinghouse, and the Wright brothers, working alone or with a few assistants, made major innovations that transformed

The Internet has both increased productivity and enabled new ideas to spread more quickly.

the economy, in the past hundred years the innovation process has been centered around large corporations, like DuPont and AT&T, with vast laboratories and research budgets in the hundreds of millions of dollars. In the new economy, once again it is small firms that seem to be playing a central role. Evidently, important innovations can occur at a far smaller scale—and then when they are successful, production can be quickly ramped up.

One of the reasons for this—and one of the reasons why the Internet has increased productivity—is that these innovations help markets work better. New firms can obtain from others many of the services that they previously had to provide for themselves, including significant portions of accounting and personnel services. And, at least in some cases, the Internet has markedly lowered the costs of marketing.

The new technologies, and especially the Internet, have enabled new ideas to be disseminated far more quickly than was previously the case. It used to take years, sometimes decades, for new ideas to spread from one part of the economy to another.

Another reason why productivity is being enhanced so much is that the new technologies have forced firms to rethink their core competencies, what they do and how they do it. When we think of innovations, we often think of dramatic inventions like the airplane or the automobile, but in practice, it is the small innovations that occur year after year that contribute the most, in total, to increases in productivity.

the modern assembly line, he might have kept it secret for a while by barring visitors to his factory, but certainly anyone who saw the assembly line could take the idea and set up a new factory. Most software companies do not make their source code public in order to exclude users who have not paid a licensing fee. The incentive to produce new ideas will be increased if inventors are able to exclude users who do not pay. This requires giving inventors property rights to ideas. If property rights are insecure—if a firm planning on

engaging in research is uncertain about whether it will be allowed to capture the benefits of any new ideas it produces—then fewer resources will be invested into research and the production of new ideas.

From society's point of view, however, there is another consideration. Producing a new idea may be very costly, but an idea only needs to be produced once. Your laptop embodies thousands of new ideas, but these ideas did not have to be reproduced each time a new laptop was produced. The screen, memory chips, and case did have to be produced for each laptop; they are examples of **rival goods**—the memory chips in your laptop cannot be in your roommate's laptop. But the design of the laptop only had to be produced once. Goods whose consumption or use by one person does not exclude consumption by other, are **nonrival goods** a concept we introduced in Chapter 11. If both you and your roommate are taking economics, both of you can use an idea like the law of supply and demand. If your roommate does her homework first, the idea is still available to you when you get around to studying. The marginal cost of *using* a nonrival good like an idea is zero. It does not cost anything to use the idea one more time. So from society's perspective, the idea should be freely available to anyone who wants to use it. After all, it costs nothing to let others use the idea.

Recall our definition of a pure public good from Chapter 11: A pure public good is one where the marginal cost of providing it to an additional person is strictly zero (it is nonrival) and where it is impossible to exclude people from receiving the good. Most types of knowledge come close to satisfying this definition, even though it is rarely entirely *impossible* to exclude consumption by others. Thus, we can think of knowledge, or an idea, as a public good. And like other public goods, there is a tension between providing incentives for its production, on the one hand, and ensuring it is widely used, on the other. Inventors need to secure property rights that allow them to benefit from their ideas; they need to be able to exclude users who do not pay. Yet, once an idea is invented, there is a zero marginal cost to producing it and so it should be freely available.

Societies address this tension through **patents.** The U.S. Constitution enables Congress to grant "for limited time to authors and inventors the exclusive right to their respective writing and discoveries." Economists refer to the output of this creative action as **intellectual property.** The "limited time" for inventors is currently seventeen years. During this period, other producers are precluded from producing the same good, or even making use of the invention in a product of their own, without the permission of the patent holder. A patent holder may allow others to use its patent (typically for a fee, called a **royalty**) or sell its product.

Thinking Like an Economist

Intellectual Property Rights and Distribution

As the importance of innovation in the economy has grown, so too has the importance of intellectual property rights. Hence, it was no surprise that the United States pushed for stronger intellectual property protection in the World Trade Organization's last round of trade negotiations, the so-called Uruguay Round, completed in 1994. Many developing countries objected to this initiative.

The key to understanding this dispute lies in the nature of intellectual property rights. How these rights are defined—for instance, the length of the patent—has significant distributional effects. Most of the production of new ideas occurs in the developed world; stronger intellectual property rights increases the incomes of those in the advanced industrialized countries but forces those in the developing world to pay higher prices. In the past, the latter often freely pirated books, copied CDs, and produced goods such as drugs that were covered by patents in the more advanced countries. Not surprisingly, many in these developing countries objected to stronger intellectual property rights protections. Two issues in particular grabbed popular attention.

The first concerned the patenting of drugs derived from plants and animals in the developing world. Developing countries argued that they deserved greater returns for preserving the biodiversity on which such drugs depend. The drug companies countered that they should reap returns from establishing the medicinal benefits of these drugs. Developing countries, on the other hand, maintain that many of these medicinal properties were already well known. All that the drug companies had done was to verify this information scientifically.

The second issue also concerned drugs. Previously, countries like South Africa had manufactured drugs, selling them at a fraction of the prices at which those goods were sold by the drug companies from the advanced industrial countries. Under the Uruguay Round agreement, people in developing countries would have to pay whatever the drug companies in the developed countries decided to charge. In the case of life-preserving AIDS drugs, this meant condemning thousands to a premature death, as few could afford the prices the drug companies insisted on charging. At first, the U.S. government backed the American drug companies, threatening trade retaliation if South Africa refused to comply. In the end, the international outrage was so great that the American government and the drug companies caved in and agreed to provide the drugs at cost.

The Trade-off Between Short-Term Efficiency and Innovation

The patent system grants the inventor a temporary monopoly, allowing her to appropriate some part of the returns on her inventive activity. In Chapter 12, we learned that, relative to a competitive market, a monopoly produces a lower level of output that sells at a higher price. In Chapter 10, we learned that competitive markets, with price equal to marginal cost, ensure economic efficiency. In our early analysis, we assumed the state of technology as given. We refer to this kind of economic efficiency as **static efficiency.**

But the overall efficiency of the economy requires balancing these short-term concerns with the long-term objectives of stimulating research and innovation. Firms will only innovate if they can reap a return on their investment, and that in turn requires some degree of monopoly power. An economy in which the balancing of short- and long-term concerns is appropriately done is said to have the property of **dynamic efficiency.**

A key provision of the patent law affecting the static efficiency versus the incentives for innovation necessary for dynamic efficiency is the *life of the patent.* If the life of a patent is short, then firms can appropriate the returns from their innovation for only a short time. There is less incentive to innovate than if the patent protection (and monopoly) lasted longer, but the economy has greater static efficiency. If the life of a patent is long, then there are large incentives to innovate, but the benefits of the innovation are limited. Consumers, in particular, must wait a long time before prices fall. The seventeen-year patent period is intended to strike a balance between the benefits to consumers and the return to investments in R & D.

An Example: The Sweet Melon Company

Figure 20.1 illustrates the effect of a patent owned by the Sweet Melon Company on a new, cheaper process for producing frozen watermelon juice. To make it simple, the marginal cost of production is constant in this example. Before the innovation, all producers face the same marginal cost of c_0. Sweet Melon's innovation reduces the marginal costs of production to c_1. Imagine that this industry is perfectly competitive before the innovation, so that price

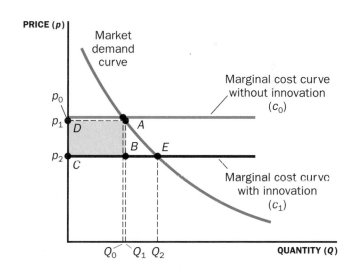

FIGURE 20.1   *Economic Effect of Patents*

Here, an innovation has reduced the marginal cost of production from c_0 to c_1. Before the innovation, the equilibrium price is p_0, which equals c_0. However, an innovator with a patent will drop the price to p_1, just below p_0, and sell the quantity Q_1. Total profits are the shaded area *ABCD*. When the patent expires, competitors reenter the market, price falls to p_2, which equals c_1, and profits drop to zero.

equals marginal cost, c_0. But now Sweet Melon is able to undercut its rivals. With patent protection, the firm sells the good for slightly less than p_0. Its rivals drop out of the market because at the new, lower price, they cannot break even. Sweet Melon now has the whole market. The company sells the quantity Q_1 at the price p_1, making a profit of AB on each sale. Total profits are shaded area $ABCD$ in the figure. The innovation pays off if the profits received exceed the cost of the research. (These profits may be thought of as "rents" associated with its superior technology.)

What happens when the patent expires? Other firms enter the industry, using the less expensive technology. Competition forces the price down to the now lower marginal costs, c_1, and output expands to Q_2. The new equilibrium is at E. Consumers are clearly better off. Static economic efficiency is enhanced, because price is now equal to marginal cost. But Sweet Melon reaps no further return from its expenditures on R & D.

If no patent were available, competitors would immediately copy the new juice-making process, and the price would drop to c_1 as soon as the innovation became available. Sweet Melon would receive absolutely no returns. (In practice, of course, imitation takes time, during which the company would be able to obtain *some* returns from the innovation.) If the patent were made permanent, consumers would benefit only a small amount from the innovation, since other companies could not compete. Output would remain at Q_1, slightly greater than the original output, and the price would remain high.

Breadth of Patent Protection

How broad a patent's coverage should be is as important as its duration. If an inventor comes up with a product quite similar to, but still slightly different from, one that has already been patented, can this inventor also get a patent for his variant? Or does the original patent cover "minor" variants? This issue became critical in the early days of the American automobile industry. Soon after Henry Ford's Model T had burst into the American marketplace—its sales rocketed from 58,000 in 1909 to 730,000 in 1916—Ford was challenged in court under a patent claim by George Baldwin Selden, who argued that his patent covered all self-propelled, gasoline-powered vehicles. Selden tried to force Ford and other pioneers of the automobile industry to pay royalties to him, but Ford successfully challenged the patent claim. Recently controversies have concerned patents in genetic engineering and superconductivity. Does a firm that decodes a fraction of a gene and establishes a use for that information, for example, get a patent? If so, does the patent cover the fraction in question or the whole gene?

The original innovators have every incentive to claim broad patent coverage, affecting their own product and those that are in any way related. Later entrants argue for narrow coverage, so that they will be allowed to produce variants and applications without paying royalties. As usual in economics, there is a trade-off. Broad coverage ensures that the first inventor reaps more of the returns of her innovation. But excessively broad coverage inhibits follow-on innovation, as others see their returns to further developing the idea squeezed by the royalties they must pay to the original inventor.

Trade Secrets

If patents protect the profits of innovation, why do many firms not bother to seek patent protection for their new products and processes? A major reason is that a firm cannot get a patent without disclosing the details of the new product or process—information that may be extremely helpful to its rivals in furthering their own R & D programs.

To prevent such disclosure, companies sometimes prefer to keep their own innovations a **trade secret.** A trade secret is simply an innovation or knowledge of a production process that a firm does not disclose to others. The formula for Coca-Cola, for example, is not protected by a patent. It is a trade secret. Trade secrets play an important role in metallurgy, where new alloys are usually not patented. Trade secrets have one major disadvantage over patents. If a rival firm *independently* discovers the same new process, say, for making an alloy, it can use the process without paying royalties, even though it was second on the scene.

Some of the returns to an invention come simply from being first in the market. Typically, the firm that first introduces a new product has a decided advantage over rivals, as it builds up customer loyalty and a reputation. Latecomers often have a hard time breaking in, even if there is no patent or trade secret protection.

Limitations to Patents

There are other limitations to the use of patents. Many of the most important ideas are not *patentable*—for instance, the basic mathematics behind the inner workings of computers, discovered by Alan Turing. Turing received no return on his innovation, which was of immense value. The *ideas* that led to the transistor or to the laser, the understandings of the underlying physics, also were not patentable.

What is patentable has changed over time. A recent new category of patents involves business applications. Thus, the *idea* of a mutual fund with certain distinctive characteristics might today be patentable, or that of an Internet firm providing a special type of auction. Some people believe that these new patents have provided much of the spur for the new economy. But many of these patents are being challenged: Are they sufficiently *novel* to deserve protection?

CASE IN POINT

Eli Whitney and the Cotton Gin

Obtaining a patent does not necessarily guarantee that the inventor will receive a return on her discovery. Others may "infringe" on her patent—that is, use the idea without paying for it—in which case the inventor will have to sue. One of the most famous examples of an inventor who found it difficult to enforce his patents is Eli Whitney and the cotton gin.

Late in the eighteenth century, the textile mills of England and the northern American states were up and humming, but there seemed to be a perpetual shortage of cotton. The kind of cotton grown in the southern United States could have filled the need, but someone had to find an inexpensive way to separate the seeds from the cotton. Eli Whitney invented the cotton gin to perform that task. Whitney did what an inventor is supposed to do. He applied for a patent and received one in 1794. He found a partner to put up the money and then started a business to make machines that would clean the seeds out of cotton. The cotton gin turned out to be a wonder, bringing prosperity to the American South. But Whitney received little of the benefit.

The problem was that Whitney's machine was both very effective and very simple. Cotton planters found it easy to copy the cotton gin and make a few minor changes. When Whitney sued in court for patent infringement, courts in cotton-growing states tended to find that his patent had not actually been infringed. Eventually, the states of South Carolina, North Carolina, Tennessee, and Georgia agreed to pay a lump sum to Whitney to purchase the rights to his invention. The amount paid, though, was barely enough to allow Whitney and his partner to recoup their expenses.

Whitney continued his lifelong career as an inventor, but he never bothered to patent an invention again. As he once wrote: "An invention can be so valuable as to be worthless to the inventor." Whitney's experience was extreme. Today patent laws provide essential protection for scientific firms engaged in producing new and better products. They may choose to share their new technology by selling their patent rights in return for royalties, which represent a substantial fraction of the revenues of some firms. ●

Whitney's cotton gin

R & D as a Fixed Cost

Patents and trade secrets are not the only reasons why industries in which technological change is important are generally not perfectly competitive. A second explanation is that R & D expenditures are fixed costs. That is, the cost of inventing something does not change according to how many times the idea is used in production.[2] The size of fixed costs helps determine how competitive an industry is. The larger the fixed costs relative to the size of the market, the more likely there will be few firms and limited competition.

Because expenditures on R & D are fixed costs, industries with large R & D expenditures face declining average

---

[2]R & D expenditures can themselves be varied. Differences in the expenditure level will affect when new products will be brought to market and whether a firm will beat its rivals in the competition for new products.

cost curves up to relatively high levels of output. We saw in Chapter 7 that firms typically have U-shaped average cost curves. The presence of fixed costs means that average costs initially decline as firms produce more, but for all the reasons discussed in Chapter 7, beyond some level of output average costs increase. When there are large fixed costs, large firms will have lower average costs than small firms and enjoy a competitive advantage (Figure 20.2). Industries with large fixed costs thus tend to have relatively few firms and limited competition. It is not surprising, therefore, that the chemical industry—where R & D is tremendously important—is highly concentrated.

Increased size also provides firms with greater incentives to undertake research. Suppose a small firm produces 1 million pens a year. If it discovers a better production technology that reduces its costs by $1 per pen, it saves $1 million a year. A large firm that makes the same discovery and produces 10 million pens a year will save $10 million a year. Thus, large firms have more incentive to engage in R & D, and as they do, they grow more than their smaller rivals do.

But while a large firm's R & D department may help the firm win a competitive advantage, it may also create managerial problems. Bright innovators can feel stifled in the bureaucratic environment of a large corporation, and they may also feel that they are inadequately compensated for their research efforts. In the computer industry, for example, many capable people have left the larger firms to start up new companies of their own.

Thus, size has both advantages and disadvantages when it comes to innovation. Important inventions and innovations, such as nylon, transistors, and the laser, have been produced by major corporations; on the other hand, small enterprises and individual inventors have produced Apple computers, Polaroid cameras, and Kodak film, all of which became major corporations as a result of their success. One objective of antitrust policies is to maintain an economic environment in which small, innovative firms can compete effectively against established giants.

Learning by Doing

Some increases in productivity occur not as a result of explicit expenditures on R & D, but as a by-product of actual production. As firms gain experience from production, their costs fall. This kind of technological change is called **learning by doing.** This systematic relationship between cumulative production experience and costs—often called the **learning curve**—was first discovered in the aircraft industry, where as more planes of a given type were produced, the costs of production fell dramatically.

This is the third reason why technological change and imperfect competition go together—because the marginal cost falls as the scale of production (and the experience accumulated) increases. The first firm to enter an industry has a particular advantage over other firms. Even if some of what the first company has learned spills over into other firms, not all of it does. Because of the knowledge the first firm has gained, its costs will be below those of potential rivals, and thus it can always undercut them. Since potential entrants know this, they are reluctant to enter industries where learning by doing has a significant impact on costs. By the same token, companies realize that if they can find a product that provides significant benefits from learning by doing, the profits they earn will be relatively secure. Hence, just as firms race to be the first to obtain a patent, so too they race to be the first to enter a product market in which there is a steep learning curve. This behavior is commonly displayed in the computer chip industry.

When learning by doing is important, firms will produce beyond the point where marginal revenue equals *current* marginal costs, because producing more today has an extra benefit. It reduces future costs of production.

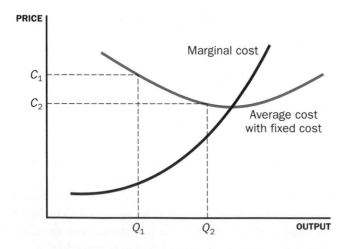

FIGURE 20.2   *Costs of Research and Development*

R & D costs are fixed costs—they do not vary with the scale of production. In industries that are R & D intensive, average costs will be declining over a wide range of outputs. Firms with low levels of output (Q_1) have higher average costs than those with higher output (Q_2).

How much extra a firm produces depends on the steepness of the learning curve.

Access to Capital Markets

Banks are generally unwilling to lend funds to finance R & D expenditures, because they are often very risky and these risks cannot be insured. When a bank makes a loan for a building, if the borrower defaults, the bank winds up with the building. If the bank lends for R & D and the research project fails, or a rival beats the firm to the patent office, the bank may wind up with nothing. Banks also often have a hard time judging the prospects of an R & D endeavor—inventors are always optimistic about their ideas. This difficulty is compounded because an inventor may be reluctant to disclose all the information about his idea, either to banks or to potential investors, lest some among them steal his idea and beat him either to the market or to the patent office.

For established firms in industries with limited competition and growing demand, financing their research expenditures presents no serious problem. They can pay for R & D out of their profits. That is why, for the economy as a whole, most R & D occurs in such firms. But raising capital is a problem for new and small firms, and also for firms in industries where intense competition limits the profits that any one company can earn. Thus, a firm's dominant position in an industry may be self-perpetuating. Its greater output means that it has more to gain from innovations that reduce the cost of production. And its greater profits give it more resources to expend on R & D.

Today much of the R & D in new and small companies is financed by venture capital firms. These firms raise capital, mainly from pension funds, insurance companies, and wealthy individuals, which they then invest in the most promising R & D ventures. Venture capital firms often demand, as compensation for their risk taking, a significant share of the new enterprise, and they usually keep close tabs on how their money is spent. They often specialize in particular areas, such as computer technology or biotechnology. In less glamorous industries, it is often difficult to find financing for R & D, because venture capital firms may be hesitant to invest in a higher-risk venture.

Schumpeterian Competition

While competition in markets in which innovation is important may not live up to the ideal of perfect competition discussed in Chapter 2, it still can be intense. Competition focuses on producing new products as much as on selling old products at lower prices. This kind of competition is often referred to as *Schumpeterian competition,* after the great economist of the early twentieth century, Joseph Schumpeter. Schumpeter began his career in Austria (serving from spring to October 1919 as Minister of Finance to the Emperor of the Austro-Hungarian Empire), and ended his career as a distinguished professor of economics at Harvard. His vision of the economy was markedly different from that of the competitive equilibrium model. That model focuses on equilibrium, a state of the world in which there is no change. He questioned the very concept of equilibrium. To him the economy was always in flux and the economist's role was to understand the forces driving those changes.

Schumpeter argued that the economy was characterized by a process of creative destruction. An innovator could, through his new product or lower costs of production, establish a dominant position in a market. But eventually, that dominant position would be destroyed, as a new innovator took his place.[3]

He worried that the giant corporations he saw being formed during his life would stifle innovation and end this process of creative destruction. His fears, so far, have been unfounded; indeed, many of the largest firms, like IBM, have not been able to manage the innovative process in a way that keeps up with upstart rivals.

Modern-day Schumpeterians often turn to biology to help them understand the process of change. They describe changes as *evolutionary.* They see a slow process of change, with many random elements, with firms that are the fittest—who, by luck or skill manage to discover new products or new ways of doing business that are better, in the particular environment, than their rivals—managing to survive and their practices spreading to other firms.

As respect for and understanding of the importance of innovation have grown, so too have the number of economists who think of themselves as Schumpeterians.

Basic Research As A Public Good

R & D expenditures on inventions or innovations almost always give rise to externalties. Externalities arise, as we

---

[3]We discussed this kind of competition—a succession of monopolies—in Chapter 13 under the topic of Schumpeterian competition.

Competition and Technological Change

HOW COMPETITION AFFECTS TECHNOLOGICAL CHANGE

Competition spurs R & D:	Competition impedes R & D:
A new innovation enables firms to enjoy profits (profits are driven to zero in standard markets).	Competitors may imitate, thus eroding returns from innovation.
Unless firms innovate, they will not survive.	Competition erodes the profits required to finance R & D.

HOW TECHNOLOGICAL CHANGE AFFECTS COMPETITION

R & D spurs competition:	R & D impedes competition:
R & D provides an alternative to prices as a way for firms to compete; it is one of the most important arenas for competition in modern economies.	Patents give a single firm a protected position for a number of years.
	The fixed costs of R & D give large firms an advantage, and mean that industries in which R & D is important may have few firms.
	Learning by doing gives a decided advantage to the first entrant into a market.
	Limited access to capital markets for financing R & D is a disadvantage to new and small firms.

learned in Chapter 11, whenever one individual's or firm's action produces costs or benefits to others. The total benefits produced by an R & D expenditure are referred to as its *social benefit*. Even with patents, inventors appropriate only a fraction of the social benefit of an invention. A firm that discovers a cheaper way of producing is likely to lower its price during the life of the patent to steal customers away from its rivals. This benefits consumers. After the patent expires, consumers benefit even more as rivals beat the price down further. And the benefits of an invention in one area spill over to other areas. The transistor, which revolutionized electronics, was invented at AT&T's Bell Laboratories. AT&T reaped the benefits from its direct application to telephone equipment. But the benefits in better radios, television sets, and other products accrued to others.

From society's viewpoint, a particularly valuable kind of R & D is **basic research.** Basic research is the kind of fundamental inquiry that produces a wide range of applications. Basic research in physics, for example, led to the ideas behind so many of the things we take for granted today—the laser, the transistor, atomic energy. The private returns to firms from any basic research they might undertake—which would dictate the amount of R & D spent on basic research in the absence of government intervention—are negligible in comparison to its social benefits. Indeed, the externalities flowing from basic research are so extreme that it can be considered a public good.

Public goods are defined by two properties. First, it is difficult to exclude anyone from the benefits of a public good. Basic research involves the discovery of underlying scientific principles or facts of nature. Such facts—like superconductivity, or even the fact that there exist certain materials that exhibit superconductivity at temperatures considerably above absolute zero—cannot be patented.

Second, the marginal cost of an additional individual enjoying a public good is zero. We say that consumption is nonrivalrous. An additional person being informed of a basic discovery does not detract from the knowledge that the original discoverer has, though it may reduce the profits the original discoverer can make out of the discovery. Indeed, sharing the fruits of basic research as soon as they are available can yield enormous benefits—as other researchers use this knowledge in their quest for innovations.

As with all public goods, private markets yield an undersupply of basic research. Accordingly the government supports basic research through the National Science Foundation, the National Institutes of Health, and other organizations. Some of the expenditures of the Department of Defense on R & D also go into basic research. Still, there is increasing concern among economists that expenditures on basic research are inadequate.

Figure 20.3 shows that support by the federal government for R & D, outside of defense, has not increased, as a percentage of the nation's output, over the last two decades. With the end of the Cold War, there has been an attempt to shift more of the federal government's support of R & D away from defense toward civilian or **dual-use** technologies (technologies that have both civilian and military use). Still, 55 percent of government R & D expenditures remain defense related. This explains why, while the United States devotes about the same proportion of its economy to R & D as do Japan and Germany, as shown in Figure 20.4, less of the total is spent in developing new products and processes to make American industry more competitive. And more is spent in developing better and more effective weapons. This may also partly explain why today foreigners are getting almost one out of every two patents granted by the U.S. Patent Office. (Inventors have the right to obtain a patent from a foreign country as well as their own.)

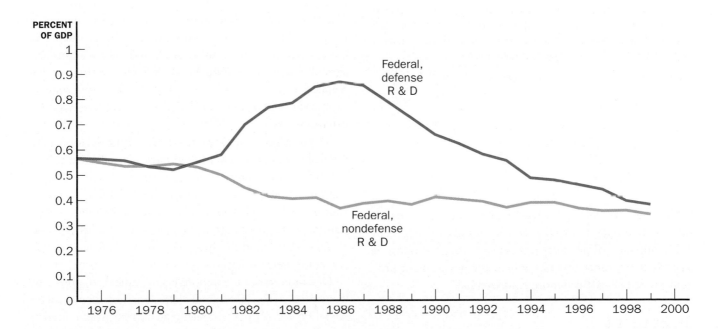

FIGURE 20.3   *Federal Expenditures on Research and Development*

The figure shows federal expenditures on R & D as a percentage of the nation's output. Expenditures on R & D for nondefense purposes have fallen since the 1970s, while expenditures on defense research increased during the 1980s and then declined dramatically during the 1990s.

SOURCE: *Statistical Abstract of the United States* (2000), Table 978, p. 603.

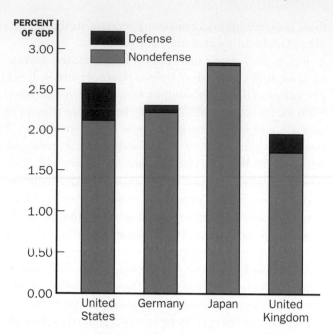

FIGURE 20.4   *Comparison of R & D Expenditures across Countries*

Total U.S. expenditures, as a percentage of the nation's output, are similar to those of other major industrialized countries. The difference lies in how these expenditures are allocated, with U.S. expenditures concentrated more heavily in defense than those of Germany or Japan.

SOURCE: *Science and Engineering Indicators*, 2000, NSF.

Government Promotion of Technological Progress

While there is widespread agreement that government should encourage innovative activity through the protection of intellectual property rights and through support of basic R & D, other ways by which the government promotes R & D have been more controversial.

Subsidies

One way in which government has sought to encourage new technologies is through subsidies. This approach has been criticized with the argument that the government has a bad record in picking what to subsidize. As evidence, they note that the Concorde, the supersonic airplane developed with the support of the French and British governments, has never been able to pay for itself. Closer to home, the government spent billions of dollars in an unsuccessful attempt to develop synthetic fuels. Broad-based subsidies, such as R & D tax credits, do not depend on government selection of particular projects, but are controversial due to their relatively high cost to the government. Critics claim that little additional research is generated per dollar of tax revenue lost.

But there are still supporters of more active involvement of government in R & D who claim there are large positive externalities associated with applied research, implying that the private sector underinvests in applied research. Policies aimed to support particular sectors of the economy are called **industrial policies,** even if those sectors are not industries as we conventionally think of them, such as agriculture.

Advocates of public support of applied R & D admit that government has not always picked winners. But they claim R & D is by its very nature risky, and a record of complete success cannot be expected. They also claim that, in fact, government's success record has been impressive. They point, for example, to the over 1,000 percent increase in the productivity of agriculture over the past century. This has resulted not only from research undertaken at the state agricultural colleges (which the federal government has helped for more than a century) but also from government-supported diffusion of knowledge, through the agricultural extension service.

Today telecommunications is one of the sectors at the forefront, and government has played an effective role in promoting this sector, sometimes referred to as the information superhighway. In 1842, the federal government supported Samuel Morse's first telegraph line, between Baltimore and Washington, More recently the federal government developed the Internet, which has linked people and computers throughout the world.

One indicator of the importance of federal support—and its success—is that virtually all of the American winners of the Nobel Prize in science and medicine have been supported by the federal government. The basic research of these scientists has spawned new industries, such as biotechnology, and has solidified America's technological leadership.

Advocates of a more active government role in promoting technology argue that the objective is not so much to pick winners as to identify areas where, in the absence of government support, there would be significant underinvestment, for instance because there are large externalities or spillovers. There is not a sharp demarcation between basic and applied research but rather a continuum, with many applied projects generating large knowledge spillovers. Substantial underinvestment is likely in sectors, such as agriculture, where there are a large number of small producers (in contrast to the chemical industry, for instance, where there are a few dominant firms). Well-designed government research programs serve as a complement to private sector efforts, rather than as a substitute for them. On average, increases in government expenditures are associated with increases, not decreases, in private research expenditures.

Advocates of government technology programs argue, further, that government should work in partnership with industry to increase the effectiveness of its R & D investment. They advocate requiring industry to put up money of its own and making competition for funds very broad. Technology programs of this sort were established when the Clinton administration took office in the early 1990s. Hundreds of partnership agreements between private firms and government-run laboratories were signed. It is too soon to assess the performance of these relatively recent efforts, but experience with earlier, similar programs has been encouraging. Even so, when the Bush administration came to power in 2001, it brought a new approach to technology policy, and the Clinton programs were drastically cut back. The Bush perspective is that a much larger share of R & D investment is best left strictly to the private sector. Defenders of the public programs argue that the existence of large technological spillovers justifies public support of R & D beyond basic research.

International Complications Subsidies have, however, raised the specter of unfair competition in the international arena. Countries facing competition from foreign firms with government subsidies often impose countervailing duties, that is, taxes on imports that are intended to offset the benefits of these subsidies. The concern is if, for instance, Europe and the United States become engaged in a contest to support some industry, the industry will benefit, but at the expense of the taxpayers in both countries. Thus, international agreements have tried to reduce the extent of subsidization. Broad-based R & D subsidies (such as through the tax system) are still permitted, but more narrowly focused subsidies are either prohibited or put into the category of questionable practices.

Protection

Firms in less developed countries often argue that they need to be insulated from competition from abroad in order to develop the knowledge base required to compete effectively in world markets. This is the **infant industry argument for protection.** Most economists are skeptical. They see this argument mainly as an attempt by rent-seeking firms who will use any excuse to insulate themselves from competition so they can raise prices and increase profits. The best way to learn to compete is to compete, not to be isolated from competition. If some help is needed to enable firms to catch up, it should be provided in the form of subsidies, the costs of which are explicit and obvious, unlike the hidden costs of higher prices that result from protection.

Relaxing Antitrust Policies

The antitrust policies explored in Chapter 13 were founded on the belief that government should push markets toward the model of perfect competition. But an increasing awareness of the importance of R & D in modern industrial economies has led some to argue for change.

A major argument for change is that cooperation aimed at sharing knowledge and coordinating research among firms in an industry has the effect of internalizing the externalities of R & D. But antitrust authorities long worried that cooperation in R & D could easily grow into cooperation in other areas, such as price setting, which would not serve the public interest. Public policy has tried to find an effective balance. In 1984, the National Cooperative Research Act was passed to allow some cooperative ventures. Ventures registered under the act are shielded from the risk of paying triple damages in a private antitrust suit but are not shielded from all antitrust risk. By the end of the 1980s, over a hundred such ventures had been registered. Among the best known are the Electric Power Research Institute, formed by electric power companies; Bell Communications Research, formed by local telephone companies; and Sematech.

Technological Change and the Basic Competitive Model

Basic competitive model	Industries in which technological change is important
Assumes fixed technology	The central question is what determines the pace of technological change. Related issues include what determines expenditure on R & D and how learning by doing affects the level of production.
Assumes perfect competition, with many firms in industry	Competition is not perfect; industries where technological change is important tend to have relatively few firms.
Perfect capital markets	Firms find it difficult to borrow to finance R & D expenditures.
No externalities	R & D confers benefits to those besides the inventor; even with patents, the inventor appropriates only a fraction of the social benefits of an invention.
No public goods	Basic research is a public good: the marginal cost of an additional person making use of a new idea is zero (nonrivalrous consumption), and it is often difficult to exclude others from enjoying the benefits of basic research.

Technological Change and Economic Growth

Living standards in the United States are far higher today than they were one hundred years ago. The reason is that productivity—the amount produced by the average worker per hour—has increased enormously. Underlying these increases is technological change. In the 1970s and 1980s the pace of growth in productivity in the United States slowed down markedly, from almost 3 percent to around 1 percent. In the latter half of the 1990s, it picked up again, by some measures to an even higher figure than in the earlier period. Some of the change has to do with changes in levels of investment in capital, but much of it has to do with the pace of innovation, and most of this innovation is the result of the deliberate allocation of resources to R & D. No wonder then that governments focus so much attention on the issue of how to create an economic environment that is conducive to innovation. While the *incentives* provided by intellectual property protection and government expenditures on basic research are important, several other features of the economy play an important role and have helped the United States maintain a dominant position. These features include financial markets (especially venture capital firms) that are willing to finance new ventures, and a labor force that is willing to take the risks associated with working for an upstart firm that has a large chance of failure. They also include a university system that has attracted the best scientists from around the world, and a close nexus between research universities and corporations.

Internet Connection

Competitiveness

The Council on Competitiveness is a nonprofit organization that focuses on the role of innovation and technological change in enhancing the international competitiveness of American firms. Their Web site (http://www.compete.org/) offers forums on issues related to technological innovation and national economic performance.

As the importance of innovation becomes increasingly recognized, increasing attention will be focused on how to further enhance the innovative environment.

Review and Practice

Summary

1. Ideas are different from the goods envisioned in the basic competitive model—they are nonrivalrous.

2. Industries in which technological change is important are almost necessarily imperfectly competitive. Patents are one way the government makes it difficult and costly for firms to copy the technological innovations of others. A firm with a patent will have a government-enforced monopoly. The expenditures on R & D are fixed costs; when they are large, there are likely to be few firms in the industry, and price competition is more likely to be limited.

3. Long-lived and broad patents reduce competition (at least in the short run), but provide greater incentives to innovate. Excessively broad patent coverage may discourage follow-on innovation.

4. Learning by doing, in which companies (or countries) that begin making a product first enjoy an advantage over all later entrants, may be a source of technological advantage.

5. Research and development generally provides positive externalities to consumers and other firms. But since the innovating firm cannot capture all the social benefits from its invention, it will tend to invest less than a socially optimal amount.

6. Basic research has both of the central properties of a public good: It is difficult to exclude others from the benefits of the research, and the marginal cost of an additional person making use of the new idea is zero.

7. A number of governmental policies encourage technological advance: patents; direct spending on research; tax incentives to encourage corporate R & D; temporary protection from technologically advanced foreign competitors; and relaxing antitrust laws to allow potential competitors to work together on research projects.

Key Terms

positive externalities
rival goods
nonrival goods
patent
intellectual property
royalty
static efficiency
dynamic efficiency
trade secret
learning by doing
learning curve
basic research
dual use
industrial policies
infant industry argument for protection

Review Questions

1. In what ways do industries in which technological change is important not satisfy the assumptions of the basic competitive model?

2. Why do governments grant patents, thereby conferring temporary monopoly rights? Explain the trade-off society faces in choosing whether to offer long-lived or short-lived patents, and whether to offer broad or narrow patents.

3. How does the existence of learning by doing provide an advantage to incumbent firms over prospective entrants?

4. Why might it be harder to raise capital for R & D than for other projects? How can established firms deal with this problem? What about start-up firms?

5. How do positive externalities arise from R & D? Why do externalities imply that there may be too little expenditure on research by private firms?

6. Explain how basic research can be thought of as a public good. Why is society likely to underinvest in basic research?

7. What are the arguments for and against industrial policies?

8. What possible trade-off does society face when it considers loosening its antitrust laws to encourage joint R & D ventures?

Problems

1. Imagine that Congress is considering a bill to reduce the current seventeen-year life of patents to eight years. What negative effects might this change have on the rate of innovation? What positive effect might it have for the economy?

2. Suppose that many years ago, one inventor received a patent for orange juice, and then another inventor came forward and requested a patent for lemonade. The first inventor maintained that the orange juice patent should be interpreted to cover all fruit juices, while the second inventor argued that the original patent included only one particular method of making one kind of juice. What trade-offs does society face in setting rules for deciding cases like these?

3. Although a patent ensures a monopoly on that particular invention for some time, it also requires that the inventor disclose the details of the invention. Under what conditions might a company (like Coca-Cola) prefer to use trade secrets rather than patents to protect its formulas?

4. Why might a company invest in R & D even if it does not believe it will be able to patent its discovery?

5. Learning by doing seems to be important in the semiconductor industry, where the United States and Japan are the main producers. Explain why U.S. and Japanese firms may race to try to bring out new generations of semiconductors. If learning by doing is important in the semiconductor industry, why might other nations try to use an infant industry strategy to develop their own semiconductor industry?

Chapter 21

Environmental Economics

Key Questions

1. Why do externalities such as pollution result in a market failure?

2. What alternatives can governments employ to remedy this market failure?

3. What market forces can lead to an efficient use of society's natural resources? What may impede markets from using scarce natural resources efficiently?

*A*mong the most contentious issues today is the impact of the economy on the environment. Usually, the discussion portrays economic activity and environmental concerns as diametrically opposed. Producing more goods and services generates more pollution, uses up more and more land, and contributes to global warming. It may seem that the fundamental perspective of economics—that of scarcity—hardly applies to things like pollution. After all, most people think we have too much pollution, not a scarcity of it. Yet the tools of economics can provide critical insights into the causes of environmental pollution, and these insights help to shape the ways government has tried to design policies to protect the environment.

The basic competitive model yielded the conclusion that markets would produce efficient outcomes. But we have seen, in Chapter 10 and again in Chapter 16, that there are situations in which markets fail to produce efficient outcomes. Government may have an economic role to play in these circumstances. This justification for government involvement in the market is known as the *market failure approach* to the role of government.

Many environmental problems are the result of a market failure. This failure arises because of the presence of externalities—costs and benefits of a transaction that are not fully reflected in the market price. In the previous chapter, we discussed innovations and the positive externalities that are often associated with innovative activity. Here, we shift our focus to negative externalities and the issues of environmental protection.

Negative Externalities and Oversupply

The basic competitive model assumes that the costs of producing a good and the benefits of selling it all accrue to the seller, and that the benefits of receiving the good and the costs of buying it all accrue to the buyer. This is often not the case. As was explained in Chapter 10, the extra costs and benefits not captured by the market transaction are called externalities.

Externalities can be either positive or negative, depending on whether individuals enjoy extra benefits they did not pay for or suffer extra costs they did not incur themselves. Goods for which there are positive externalities—such as research and development—will be undersupplied in the market. In deciding how much of the good to purchase, each individual or firm thinks only about the benefits it receives, not the benefits conferred upon others. By the same token, goods for which there are negative externalities, such as air and water pollution, will be oversupplied in the market. The fact that the market might not fully capture the costs and benefits of a trade provides a classic example of a market failure and a possible role for the public sector.

Figure 21.1A shows the demand and supply curves for a good, say, steel. Market equilibrium is the intersection of the curves, the point labeled *E*, with output Q_p and price p_p. Chapter 10 explained why, in the absence of externalities, the equilibrium *E* is efficient. The price reflects the marginal benefit individuals receive from an extra unit of steel (it measures their marginal willingness to pay for an extra unit). The price also reflects the marginal cost to the firm of producing an extra unit. At *E*, marginal benefits equal marginal costs.

Consider what happens if, in the production of steel, there is an externality—producers are polluting the air and water without penalty. The **social marginal cost**—the marginal cost borne by all individuals in the economy—will now exceed the **private marginal cost**—the marginal cost borne by the producer alone. Note that in a competitive industry, the supply curve corresponds to the horizontal sum of all producers' *private* marginal cost curves.

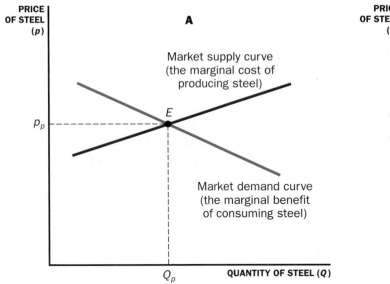

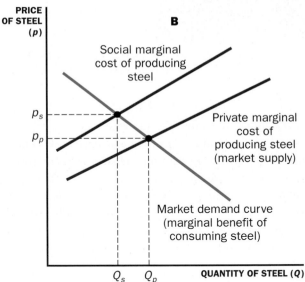

FIGURE 21.1   *How Negative Externalities Cause Oversupply*

In a perfectly competitive market, the market supply curve is the (horizontal) sum of the marginal cost curves of all firms, while market demand reflects how much the marginal consumer is willing to pay or how much the marginal unit is worth to any consumer. In panel A, the intersection or equilibrium, at quantity Q_p and price p_p, will be where private marginal cost is equal to the marginal benefit.

The private marginal cost includes just the costs actually paid by the producing firm. If there are broader costs to society as a whole, like pollution, then the social marginal costs will exceed the private costs. If the supplier is not required to take these additional costs into account (as in panel B), production will be at Q_p, greater than Q_s, where price equals social marginal cost, and the quantity produced will exceed the amount where marginal cost is equal to marginal benefit for society as a whole.

Panel B contrasts the two situations. It shows the social marginal cost curve for producing steel lying above the private marginal cost curve. Thus, with social marginal costs equated to social marginal benefits, the economically efficient level of production of steel will be lower, at Q_s, than it would be, at Q_p, if private costs were the only ones.

Thus, the level of production of steel, which generates negative externalities, will be too high in a free market. We can also ask, what about the level of expenditure on pollution abatement? Such expenditures confer a positive externality on others—the benefits of the equipment, the cleaner air, accrue mainly to others. Figure 21.2 shows a firm's demand curve for pollution-abatement equipment in the absence of government regulation. It is quite low, reflecting the fact that the firm itself derives little benefit. That is, the firm's marginal private benefit from expenditures on pollution-abatement equipment is small. The firm sets its marginal private benefit equal to the marginal cost of pollution abatement, which results in a level of expenditure on pollution abatement at E. The figure also depicts the marginal social benefit of pollution abatement, which is far greater than the marginal private benefit. Efficiency requires that the marginal social benefit equal the

marginal cost, point E'. Thus, economic efficiency requires greater expenditures on pollution abatement than there would be in the free market.

One of government's major economic roles is to correct the inefficiencies resulting from externalities. Among the many types of negative externalities, perhaps the most conspicuous are those that harm the environment.

Environmental Protection and Conservation: Examples

Freon gas, used as the propellant in aerosol cans and as a coolant in air conditioners, appears to have destroyed some of the ozone layer of the atmosphere—risking major climatic changes and possibly exposing individuals to radiation that may cause cancer. This is a worldwide externality. A major treaty signed by the nations of the world in early 1990 would eventually ban the use of this and related gases. The nature of the externality in this case was clear: The use of the gas anywhere could have disastrous effects on everyone.

Another major international treaty was signed in Rio de Janeiro in 1992. Since the beginning of the industrial revolution, enormous quantities of fossil fuels—coal, oil, and gas—have been burned. When they burn, they produce carbon dioxide (CO_2). Carbon dioxide is absorbed into the oceans and used by plants in photosynthesis. But the rate of emissions in recent decades has been far greater than the rate of absorption—so much so that the concentration of CO_2 in the atmosphere is 25 percent higher than it was at the beginning of the industrial revolution. Worse, in the next few decades, it is projected to double, or more, unless strong actions are taken. The United Nations convened an international panel of scientists to assess both the extent of these dramatic changes in the earth's atmosphere and their consequences. Their findings were alarming. These and other gases create a "greenhouse gas" effect, trapping radiation arriving at the earth, and leading to global warming. While the magnitude of the warming effect is likely to be small—only a few degrees—the potential harm is great: a partial melting of the earth's ice caps, a rise in sea levels, a flooding of low-lying countries such as Bangladesh, an increase in the spread of deserts.

At Rio, the developed countries agreed to restrain their level of emissions, returning them to their 1990 level by the year 2000. Since emissions increase with energy use, and energy use normally increases with economic growth, achieving this goal would require both substantial increases in energy

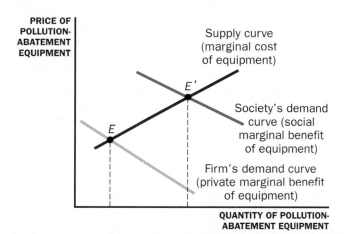

FIGURE 21.2 *How Positive Externalities Cause Undersupply*

The private marginal benefit includes just the benefits received by the firm, but since pollution-abatement equipment provides a positive externality, it will have a social marginal benefit that is higher. If the firm takes only its private benefit into account, it will operate at point E, using less equipment than at the point where marginal benefits are equal to marginal costs for society as a whole (E').

efficiency and switching from energy sources (such as coal) that produce high levels of emissions to those that produce little or none (such as hydroelectric power). In 2002, the United Nations will sponsor The World Summit on Sustainable Development (also called Rio + 10) to assess progress towards the goals established in Rio in 1992.

These are examples of global externalities. Most externalities are more local. Many of the world's cities are choking with smog, for example, caused largely by automobile exhausts. Many rivers, streams, and lakes are so polluted that they are unsafe to drink from or to swim in.

Policy Responses to Problems in the Environment

As the negative externalities associated with pollution and other environmental issues are increasingly recognized, the alternative ways government can curtail their bad effects have received considerable attention from economists and others. This section evaluates several of the major options.

International Perspective

Global Warming

Many environmental problems are local in nature. The pollution of a stream or a toxic waste site mainly impacts people in the neighborhood. But some environmental hazards affect the entire planet. As such, they require international cooperation. For instance, the Montreal Convention signed in 1990 limited the emissions of chemicals that had led to the depletion of ozone in the atmosphere. Ozone depletion was linked to a higher incidence of certain types of cancer caused by radiation normally blocked by the ozone layer. The agreement was remarkably successful: The use of these chemicals was phased out, with little cost to the economy, even ahead of schedule.

Today, the most serious global environmental problem is probably global warming, the increased temperature of the earth caused by the buildup of the so-called greenhouse gases, such as carbon dioxide, that trap the sun's energy just as a greenhouse does. The evidence of the buildup of these gases is strong, and there is mounting evidence about the consequences. A series of international panels of experts have concluded that the impacts are likely to be large and to have large consequences, including the melting of the polar ice cap and a rise in the sea level, inundating low-lying regions of the world. In 1992, at Rio de Janeiro an international convention was signed committing the world's governments to controlling the emission of greenhouse gases. In 1997, a further agreement, making the reductions binding, was signed in Kyoto. In 2001, President George W. Bush announced that although the United States had signed the agreement, it would not ratify it. The outrage from the rest of the world at this unilateral action by the United States was particularly strong because the United States is the largest polluter. The United States contends that it makes no sense for it to limit its emissions if others do not, and under the Kyoto agreement, the developing countries are not bound to reduce their emissions. Further, they point out that developing country emissions will soon exceed those of the developed countries. Moreover, President Bush has claimed that the cost is too great, relative to the risks imposed. But the developing countries retort that it is a matter of equity: On a per capita basis, their emissions are already much less than those of the United States. They note that the risks to the United States may be limited—some parts of the country might actually gain—but that we all share one planet, and the United States cannot or should not view the matter from its own selfish perspective. Many developing countries are desperately poor, and why should they make economic sacrifices when the United States claims that it cannot afford to do so. As this book goes to press, the world is deadlocked. Meanwhile, greenhouse gases continue to accumulate, and will probably make the process of controlling global warming more difficult in the future.

Property Rights Responses

Large-scale environmental degradation is a conspicuous form of negative externalities. Having identified them as market failures, what can the government do to improve matters? Some economists, led by Nobel laureate Ronald Coase of the University of Chicago Law School, argue that government should simply rearrange property rights. **Coase's theorem** says that with appropriately designed property rights, markets could take care of externalities without direct government intervention. Consider, for example, the case of a small lake in which anyone can fish without charge. Each fisherman ignores the fact that the more fish he takes out of the lake, the fewer fish there are for others to take out. If the government were to rearrange property rights and grant to a single individual the right to fish, then he would have every incentive to fish efficiently. There would be no externalities. He would take into account the long-term interests as well as the short-term ones. He would realize that if he fished too much this year, he would have fewer fish next year. If it were a large lake, he might let others do the fishing and charge them for each fish caught or regulate the amount of fish they could catch. But the prices he charged and the regulations he imposed would be designed to ensure that the lake was not overfished.

The point of this example is that the problem of overfishing is solved with only limited government intervention. All the government has to do is assign the property rights correctly.

This kind of problem arises repeatedly. The U.S. government leases public land to cattle ranchers. Since the ranchers only lease the land, they often impose a negative externality on future potential users by overgrazing the land, which leads to environmental damage like soil erosion. If the property rights were altered so that the land was sold to the ranchers, they would have reason to look after the land. In deciding on how many cattle to graze this year, they would take into account the effect on the pasture, and thus on the number of cattle they could graze next year.

Coase envisioned that once property rights were assigned, market solutions or bargaining among potential users would ensure efficient outcomes. Consider the conflict between smokers and nonsmokers over whether to allow smoking in a room. Smokers confer a negative externality on nonsmokers. Coase suggests a simple solution. Give the rights to the air to one individual, say, a smoker. He has the right to decide whether to allow smoking or not. For simplicity, assume that there are only two individuals in the room, one a smoker and the other a nonsmoker. If the value of fresh air to the nonsmoker exceeds the value of smoking to the smoker, the nonsmoker would offer the smoker enough money to compensate him not to smoke. Conversely, if the property rights were given to the nonsmoker, and if the value of smoking to the smoker exceeded the value of fresh air to the nonsmoker, then the smoker could compensate the nonsmoker.

Coase argued not only that assigning property rights ensures an efficient outcome but also that how the property rights are assigned affects only the distribution of income, not economic efficiency. Whether smoking would be allowed would depend simply on whether the value of smoking to smokers exceeded or was less than the value of fresh air to nonsmokers.

The appeal of Coase's theorem is that it assigns a minimal role to government. Government simply makes the property rights clear, and leaves the efficient outcome to private markets. Opportunities to apply the theorem are limited, however, because the costs of reaching an agreement may be high, particularly when large numbers of individuals are involved. Imagine the difficulties of assigning property rights to the atmosphere, and having all the individuals adversely affected by air pollution negotiating with all those contributing to it!

Today there is general agreement that while assigning property rights clearly may take care of some externality problems, most externalities, particularly those concerning the environment, require more active government intervention. Some forms this intervention might take include regulatory measures, financial penalties, subsidization of corrective measures, and creating a market for the externality.

Regulation

Government's first response to the need for intervention to address environmental externalities was to regulate. Electric utilities that burned high-sulfur coal would not be allowed to emit sulfur dioxide into the atmosphere. They would be required to install scrubbers, devices that removed the sulfur from the fumes. And cars would be required to have catalytic converters. This approach is sometimes called the **command and control approach.**

It quickly ran into problems. The same environmental benefits often could be achieved at much lower costs in ways that were not allowed by the regulations. This was partly because the regulations did not (and could not) allow for the myriad of variations in circumstances facing

Thinking Like an Economist

Environmental and Economic Trade-offs

In economics, what matters are *incentives,* not *intentions.* Often there are unintended consequences of well-intentioned acts. In 1973, Congress passed an important piece of legislation, the Endangered Species Act, intended to protect species that are threatened with extinction. If, for instance, a rare species, like the spotted owl, was discovered to nest in a tree on your property, you would not be allowed to cut down the tree. The act brought to the fore the point that we often think of private property in too simplistic a way: If I own something, I should be able to do with it what I like, *so long as I don't harm anyone else.* But there's the rub. What you do with your property does affect others. If you build a tall building on your property, blocking out the light that your neighbors receive, you are affecting them. If you build a dirty, noisy factory in a quiet residential neighborhood, you are affecting your neigh-

bors. That is why most cities have *zoning laws* restricting the use of land; there are residential zones and business zones and manufacturing zones. But society as a whole benefits from the preservation of endangered species; in that sense, destroying the habitat of an endangered species has repercussions that touch others beyond the owners of the land.

In 1993, a heated dispute arose over the spotted owl in the Pacific Northwest. Environmentalists, concerned over the spotted owl, had acted on a provision of the Endangered Species Act to halt logging, threatening the livelihood of hundreds of people in the area. In the region as a whole, there were new bases for economic growth, as, for instance, software and other high-tech industries moved in, attracted in part by the environment. But the loggers lacked the requisite skills to join in such developments. The end of logging would

different firms, and partly because the regulatory process is always slow (at best) in incorporating newly developing technologies. Worse still, the command and control approach failed to provide incentives for the development of new technologies to reduce environmental damage, since it often would not allow the technologies, even if they did a better job.[1]

Moreover, politics inevitably intrudes into the setting of regulations, resulting in higher than necessary costs. High-sulfur coal producers worried that the cost of scrubbers would put them at a competitive disadvantage relative to low-sulfur coal producers. (This is the correct market outcome from the viewpoint of economic efficiency because the social cost of high-sulfur coal—including the negative environmental impacts—was greater than that of the low-sulfur coal.) So they succeeded in getting Congress to mandate that low-sulfur coal also had to have unnecessary scrubbers. In another example, ethanol producers (domi-

nated by a single firm, ADM) succeeded in getting regulators to require a corn-based gasoline additive to reduce pollution rather than an oil-based one—even though the latter was cheaper and may be better environmentally.

Another reason economists are wary of regulations is that the costs they impose are often hidden. The rising costs of environmental regulation, now estimated to exceed $100 billion a year, have made the demand for better analysis when designing regulation almost irresistible. Such analysis should look at the cost and benefit of regulations, encouraging government to only undertake regulations where benefits exceed costs, and to focus on areas where environmental risks are greatest. These principles, supported by most economists, would seem to be unexceptional, and are in fact reflected in Executive Orders issued by both President Bush and President Clinton to guide the implementation of regulations. But some environmentalists take a "purist" stand. They argue that a child's health is not an issue for the cold calculus of costs and benefits. And they worry about "paralysis by analysis"—that the process of doing the cost-benefit analysis studies will effectively bring environmental regulation to a halt.

---

[1]On the other side, advocates argue that in some cases the tight regulations have "forced" development of new technologies to meet environmental standards that could not be met with existing technologies.

have presented them with bleak prospects. There seemed to be a clear *trade-off:* Which was more important, the livelihood of the loggers or the survival of the spotted owl? There was one way out of this box: If the value of preserving the spotted owl exceeded the economic damage to the loggers, those benefitting from preservation could pay off the loggers. Alternatively, the federal government might have used general tax revenues to compensate the loggers. But at the time, the government faced severe budgetary problems. A compromise was sought, whereby enough area was kept closed to protect the spotted owl's habitat while enough was kept open for logging to protect many of the jobs.

In other parts of the country, the Endangered Species Act gave rise to other problems. A development in Austin was stopped when it was discovered that the habitat of an endangered spider might be affected. People who worried that use of their land might be encumbered by a court injunction if they were found to have a habitat for an endangered species had an incentive to act before the injunction arrived: If you had a tree of the kind that the spotted owl might nest in, you would have an incentive to cut down the tree before the owl nested there. Some worried that these *unintended consequences* were so large that they undermined the very intent of the law.

Which is more important, the livelihood of loggers or the survival of the spotted owl?

Taxes and Subsidies

Most economists believe that taxes and subsidies provide a better way than regulation to encourage the behavior society wants. Taxes are the stick, while subsidies are the carrot. Both share the aim of adjusting private costs to account for social costs.

Panel A of Figure 21.3 shows the supply and demand curves for steel. If the production of steel generates a negative externality in the form of pollution, the social marginal cost of producing steel is higher than the private marginal cost. The market equilibrium leads to a production level of Q_p, which exceeds the socially optimal quantity Q_s. Panel B illustrates how a tax on the production of steel can lead to the socially optimal level of production. The tax, t, increases the firm's costs of producing steel, shifting up the market supply curve. The new market equilibrium is now at the socially optimal quantity Q_s. The equilibrium price is p_s; purchasers of steel pay a price that correctly reflects the social cost of producing steel. This ensures that the marginal benefits are set equal to the marginal costs. Steel-producing firms receive the market price less the tax, $p_s - t$, and this equals their private marginal cost of producing steel.

Taxes on pollution are similar to fines for violating regulations in one respect—they both increase the cost of and thereby discourage pollution. But taxes differ from regulation in a fundamental way. Regulations are a clumsy weapon. They penalize firms for polluting over a specific level, but polluters who stay just below that level get off scot-free. Pollution taxes can be set so that they reduce aggregate pollution by the same amount as a regulator would under a command and control system. But the economic effects are very different. Taxes add the cost of pollution to the costs a company has to cover to remain in business. As a result, companies have an incentive to reduce their pollution as far as possible and to find new, low-cost ways of reducing pollution or new production methods that are less polluting, rather than keeping it just below the legal standard. This is "efficient pollution abatement," with the producers who pollute less having their reward in lower costs.

Subsidies such as tax credits for pollution-abatement devices are an alternative way of providing incentives to reduce

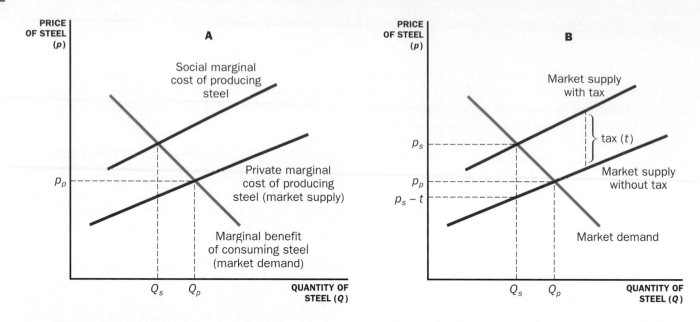

FIGURE 21.3   *Using a Tax in the Presence of a Negative Externality*

When production leads to a negative externality, such as pollution in the case of steel production, the firm's costs do not reflect the total social cost of production. The market equilibrium, before a tax is imposed, is at a price p_p and quantity Q_p (see panel A). The efficient level is at quantity Q_s. Panel B depicts the effects of imposing a tax on steel producers. The tax increases their costs, and the market supply curve shifts up. The new equilibrium price is p_s and the equilibrium quantity is Q_s.

International Perspective

Gasoline Taxes Around the World

Several externalities are associated with using an automobile: traffic congestion, air pollution contributing to smog, greenhouse gases that contribute to global warming, and social costs arising from accidents (like increased health care costs when accident victims receive emergency medical treatment they cannot afford).

Gasoline taxes discourage driving and can be justified because they reduce the negative externalities associated with using cars. Accordingly, the U.S. government and most European governments levy gasoline taxes. However, the taxes in Europe are typically $1 to $2 more than those in the United States. How do we explain the difference?

Because of the greater population density in Europe, some of the externalities, such as those associated with con-

gestion, are larger, and accordingly, a higher tax may be merited to align better the social and private costs of driving. But the major externality, the emissions of carbon dioxide leading to global warming, is a global environmental cost. By most calculations, if the social costs of global warming are taken into account, gasoline taxes in the United States are too low.

One interesting idea to reduce car usage that has recently received some attention is called *pay at the pump insurance.* Individuals would pay for their automobile liability insurance by an add-on charge when they purchase gasoline. Those who drive more would have to pay more. This would discourage driving and thus greenhouse gas emissions. New technologies would allow the charges levied at the pump to differ with different cars.

pollution. Subsidies are economically inefficient. Take the case of a steel firm. With subsidies, firms are not paying the full costs. Part of the costs are being picked up by the government. This allows producers to sell (and users to buy) steel at lower than its full cost of production, and it keeps steel and pollution production above the socially efficient level. Clearly, firms prefer subsidies to taxes.

The Marketable Permit Response

Still another approach to curbing pollution is **marketable permits.** Companies purchase (or are granted) a permit from the government that allows them to emit a certain amount of pollution. Again, the government can issue the amount of permits so that the company produces the same level of pollution that there would be under the command and control approach. However, companies are allowed to sell their permits. Thus, if a company cuts its pollution in half, it could sell some of its permits to another company that wants to expand production (and hence its emission of pollutants).

The incentive effects of marketable permits are very much like those of taxes. A market for pollution permits encourages development of the best possible antipollution devices, rather than keeping the pollution just under some government-set limit. If the government wishes to reduce pollution over time, the permits can be designed to reduce the amount of pollution they allow by a set amount each year. In the United States, this sort of shrinking marketable permit was used to reduce the amount of lead in gasoline during the early 1980s. Variants of this idea have recently been adopted to help control other forms of air pollution, such as sulfur dioxide.

CASE IN POINT

Reducing Acid Rain

Forests throughout the northeastern United States and Canada have been damaged by acid rain, rain polluted by sulfuric and nitric acids. These acids result from the reaction of sulfur dioxide (SO_2) and nitrogen oxides in the atmosphere. In the United States, coal-fired power plants in the Northeast and Midwest are the primary sources of the SO_2 that contributes to acid rain. The Clean Air Act Amendments of 1990 established programs to reduce the emissions of SO_2.

As part of this program, owners of pollution-producing plants are given permits, called *allowances*, that give them rights to emit a certain amount of SO_2. The critical aspect of the program is that these permits are tradable. A plant that has more permits than it needs can sell them to another plant that wishes to emit more than its allotted amount. A plant that finds the marginal cost of reducing SO_2 emissions to be greater than the price of a permit will choose to purchase a permit; a firm that finds the marginal cost of reducing emissions to be less than the price of a permit will want to sell a permit. As a consequence, the market price for permits will measure the marginal cost of reducing emissions.

A simple example illustrates how a system of tradable permits can reduce the total cost of lowering emissions. Consider the case of two plants that face different marginal costs of cutting back on their emissions of SO_2. For the sake of illustration, suppose the relevant cost data are those given below:

	Plant A		Plant B	
Reduction in emissions	Total Cost	Marginal Cost	Total Cost	Marginal Cost
0	$0	$0	$0	$0
1	$1	$1	$.5	$.5
2	$3	$2	$1.5	$1
3	$6	$3	$3	$1.5
4	$10	$4	$5	$2
5	$15	$5	$7.5	$2.5
6	$21	$6	$10.5	$3

In this example, plant B is able to reduce emissions at a lower cost than plant A.

Now suppose the goal is to reduce emissions by 6 units. One approach might be to require each plant to cut emissions by 3 units. In this case, the cost of reducing emissions would be $6 at plant A and $3 at plant B for a total cost of $9. However, the marginal cost of achieving the last reduction in emissions at plant A was $3, while plant B would be able to gain a further reduction (to 4) in its emissions at a marginal cost of only $2.

In forests throughout the northeastern United States and Canada, the effects of acid rain are easy to see.

Instead of requiring each plant to reduce its emissions by the same amount, suppose the same overall reduction of 6 units is achieved by having plant A cut emissions by 2 units and plant B by 4 units. The total cost is now only $3 + $5 or $8. We have achieved the same overall reduction in pollution more efficiently by having the plant that can cut emissions at a lower marginal cost (plant B) cut back the most.

If the two plants can participate in a market for permits, plant A would find it advantageous to purchase a permit from plant B. By only cutting back by 2 units instead of 3, plant A can reduce its costs by $3. Plant B, having sold a permit to plant A, must cut its emissions back further, from a reduction of 3 to a reduction of 4. This raises its costs by $2. As long as the price of a permit is between $2 and $3, both firms gain. Society gains by achieving the desired reduction in emissions at the least cost.

While the SO_2 tradable permit system has been in place only since the mid-1990s, the evidence is that it has achieved emission goals in a cost-effective manner.[2] ●

---

[2]See the articles by Schmalensee et al. and Stavins in the Summer 1998 issue of the *Journal of Economic Perspectives*.

Weighing the Alternative Approaches

Incentive programs, such as taxes or marketable permits, have an important advantage over direct controls, like regulations. The issue of pollution is not whether it should be allowed—after all, it is virtually impossible to eliminate all pollution in an industrial economy. Nor would it be efficient; the costs of doing so would far exceed the benefits. The real issue is how sharply pollution should be limited. The *marginal* benefits have to be weighed against the marginal costs. This is not done under regulation. If government ascertains the marginal social cost of pollution and sets charges or marketable permits accordingly, private firms will engage in pollution control up to the point at which the marginal cost of pollution control equals the marginal social return of pollution abatement (which is just the marginal cost of pollution). Each firm will have the correct marginal incentives.

Governments often prefer direct regulations because they believe that they can control the outcomes better. But such control can be illusory. If an unreachable standard is set, it is likely to be repealed. For example, as automobile companies have found the costs of various regulations to be prohibitive, they have repeatedly appealed for a delay in the enforcement of the regulations, often with considerable success.

It must also be kept in mind that choosing the socially efficient method of pollution abatement is the easy part of the policy problem. Figuring out the "right" level of pollution to aim for is much harder. Uncertainty about the consequences of pollution abounds and how to value certain options is an issue of hot debate. To what extent can envi-

Internet Connection

The National Center for Environmental Economics

The National Center for Environmental Economics (NCEE) conducts and supervises economic research on environmental issues. Their Web site is http://www.epa.gov/economics/.

ronmental degradation be reversed? How much value should be placed on the extinction of a species like the spotted owl, or the preservation of the Arctic wilderness? No matter what approach is chosen to externalities and the environment, such questions will remain controversial.

WRAP-UP

Solving the Problem of Externalities

Externalities, which occur when the extra costs and benefits of a transaction are not fully reflected in the market price, give rise to market failure. Four main solutions have been proposed and used:

1. The reassignment of property rights
2. Regulations that outlaw the negative externality
3. Tax and subsidy measures to encourage the behavior society wants
4. Marketable permits

Natural Resources

A recurrent theme among environmentalists is that our society is squandering its natural resources too rapidly. We are using up oil and energy resources at an alarming rate, hardwood timber forests that took hundreds of years to grow are being cut down, and supplies of vital resources like phosphorus are dwindling. There are repeated calls for government intervention to enhance the conservation of our scarce natural resources. Those who believe in the infallibility of markets reply, Nonsense! Prices give the same guidance to the use of natural resources that they give to any other resource, these people say. Prices measure scarcity, and send consumers and firms the right signals about how much effort to expend to conserve resources, so long as consumers and firms are well informed, and so long as there is not some other source of market failure.

There is, in fact, some truth in both positions. Prices, in general, do provide signals concerning the scarcity of resources, and *in the absence of market failures,* those signals lead to economic efficiency. We have seen some cases where a private market economy without government intervention will not be efficient—when there are negative externalities (pollution) or when a resource (like fish in the ocean) is not priced.

But what about a privately owned resource, like bauxite (from which aluminum is made) or copper? The owner of a bauxite mine has a clearly defined property right. Let's assume that he pays a tax appropriate to any pollution his mining operation causes. Thus, the price he charges will reflect both social and private costs. The question of resource depletion now boils down to the question of whether his bauxite is worth more to him in the market today or left in the ground for future extraction. The answer depends on what bauxite will be worth in the future, say, thirty years from now. If it is worth enough more thirty years from now (to compensate for waiting), he will keep the bauxite in the ground even though he may not be alive. That way he maximizes the value of his property, and he can enjoy his wise decision by selling the mine when he retires. The price at which he sells it should reflect the present discounted value of the bauxite.

If this miner and all other bauxite producers choose to bring the bauxite to market today, depleting the world's supply of bauxite, there are two possible reasons. Either, this is the socially efficient outcome—society values bauxite more highly today than it will tomorrow. Or, the miners have miscalculated the value of bauxite thirty years from now and underestimated future prices, though they have every incentive to get as accurate a forecast as they can. If they have indeed miscalculated, we might view the result as a market failure; but there would be no reason to expect a government bureaucracy to do any better than the firms at guessing future prices.

However, from society's viewpoint there are two plausible reasons why private owners may undervalue future benefits of a natural resource. First, in countries where property rights are not secure, owners of a resource may feel that if they do not sell it soon, there is a reasonable chance that the resources will be taken away from them. There may be a revolution, for example, in which the government will take over the resource with no or only partial compensation to the owners. Even in countries like the United States, where owners are not worried about government confiscating their property, increased regulations might make it more expensive to extract the resource in the future, or higher taxes might make it less attractive to sell the resource in the future. Second, individuals and firms often face limited borrowing opportunities and very high interest rates. In these circumstances, capital markets discount future returns at a high rate, far higher than society or the government would discount them.

Higher interest rates induce a more rapid depletion of resources. Suppose an oil company is deciding whether to extract some oil today or to wait until next year. For simplicity, assume there are no extraction costs, so the net return to selling the oil is just its price. If the price of a barrel of oil is the same today as a year from now, the firm's decision is simple. The firm will sell the oil today. But what if the price of oil is expected to go up 10 percent? Now the firm must compare the present discounted value of the oil sold a year from now with what it could receive today. To calculate the present discounted value, we simply divide next year's price by 1 plus the interest rate. If the interest rate is 10 percent, then a dollar a year from now is worth 10 percent less than a dollar today. So if the interest rate is less than 10 percent, it pays the firm to wait; if the interest rate is more than 10 percent, it pays the firm to extract the oil today. At higher interest rates, firms have a greater incentive to extract oil earlier.

Sometimes government has aggravated the waste of natural resources. In the United States, for example, much of the timber lies on government lands. The government, in making the land available, has paid less attention to concerns about economic efficiency than it has to the pleading of timber interest groups. Government policies aimed at restricting the import of foreign oil have also encouraged the use of domestic resources, a seemingly perverse policy of "drain America first." Government policies in keeping the price of water for farmers low has led to many negative outcomes: excessive use of water, draining water from underground basins built up over centuries, lowering the water table, and in some cases, leaching out the soil. In each of these cases, private property rights and market outcomes would have supplied solutions that almost everyone in society would regard as better than what happened.

Merit Goods and the Environment

In this chapter, we have explained how externalities provide a rationale for government intervention in the economy. To some people, how we treat the environment and the earth's natural resources is not just a matter of economic efficiency; it is a moral issue. They argue that the issue of allowing whaling should not be approached narrowly from the perspective of economic costs and benefits. This view reflects the principle of merit goods discussed in Chapter 16. The government becomes involved not just because markets have failed to produce efficient outcomes, but because government believes there are values that supersede those reflected in individual preferences, and it has the right and duty to impose those values on its citizens. It rejects the basic premise of *consumer sovereignty*, which holds that individuals are the best judges of their own welfare, and argues that in certain selected areas, there is a role for *paternalism*—government can make better choices in some matters than individuals.

e-Insight

Information and the Environment

In addition to regulation and taxation, some governments have sought to control pollution by requiring firms to disclose the type and level of toxic substances they are emitting into the air or water. Such information disclosure has proved to be extremely effective. Pressure brought by local communities, and worries on the part of firms about acquiring a bad reputation, have induced polluting firms to reduce their levels of emissions. In this effort, the Internet has proved to be an important ally. For instance, Environmental Defense, a not-for-profit environmental advocacy group, maintains an Internet site called *Scorecard* (www.scorecard.org) that provides a wide range of information on pollutants.

Review and Practice

Summary

1. Government may have a role in the economy when markets fail to produce an efficient outcome. When positive or negative externalities exist, markets will not provide an efficient outcome.

2. One way to deal with externalities is to assign clear-cut property rights.

3. Governments may deal with environmental externalities by imposing regulatory measures (the command and control approach), levying taxes and granting subsidies, or issuing marketable permits.

4. In a perfect market, natural resources are used up at an efficient rate. However, privately owned resources may be sold too soon, for two reasons. First, owners may fear that if they do not sell the resources soon, new government rules may prevent them from selling at all or, in any case, lower the return from selling it in the future. Second, interest rates facing owners may be high, so they may value future income less than society in general. High interest rates lead to a faster exploitation of natural resources.

Key Terms

social marginal cost
private marginal cost
Coase's theorem
command and control approach
marketable permits

Review Questions

1. Name several market failures. Why do economists see the existence of these market failures as a justification for government action?

2. Why will a free market produce too much of goods that have negative externalities, like pollution? Why will a free market produce too little of goods that have positive externalities, like pollution control?

3. What are the advantages and limitations of dealing with externalities by assigning property rights?

4. What are the advantages of marketable permits over command and control regulation? What are the advantages of using taxes for polluting rather than subsidies for pollution-abatement equipment?

5. How do markets work to allocate natural resources efficiently? In what cases will markets fail to give the correct signals for how quickly a resource like oil should be depleted?

Problems

1. Marple and Wolfe are two neighboring dormitories. Wolfe is considering giving a party with a very loud band, which will have a negative externality, a sort of sound pollution, for Marple. Imagine that the school administration decides that any dormitory has the right to prevent another dorm from hiring a band. If the band provides a negative externality, how might the residents of Wolfe apply the lessons of Coase's theorem to hire the band they want?

   Now imagine that the school administration decides that no dormitory can prevent another dorm from hiring a band, no matter how loud. If the band provides a negative externality, how might the residents of Marple apply the lessons of Coase's theorem to reduce the amount of time they have to listen to the band? How would your answer change if the band provided a positive externality?

2. The manufacture of trucks produces pollution of various kinds; for the purposes of this example, let's call it all "glop." Producing a truck creates one unit of glop, and glop has a cost to society of $3,000. Imagine that the supply of trucks is competitive, and market supply and demand are given by the following data:

Price (thousand $)	19	20	21	22	23	24	25
Quantity supplied	480	540	600	660	720	780	840
Quantity demanded	660	630	600	570	540	510	480

Graph the supply curve for the industry and the demand curve. What are equilibrium price and output? Now graph the social marginal cost curve. If the social cost of glop were taken into account, what would be the new equilibrium price and output?

If the government is concerned about the pollution emitted by truck plants, explain how it might deal with the externality through fines or taxes and through subsidies. Illustrate the effects of taxes and subsidies by drawing the appropriate supply and demand graphs. (Don't bother worrying about the exact units.) Why are economists likely to prefer fines to subsidies?

3. Consider a small lake with a certain number of fish. The more fish that one fisherman takes out, the fewer fish are available for others to take out. Use graphs depicting private and social costs and benefits to fishing to describe the equilibrium and the socially efficient level of fishing. Explain how a tax on fishing could achieve the efficient outcome. Explain how giving a single individual the property right to the fish in the lake might also be used to obtain an efficient outcome.

The more fish taken out this year, the less fish will be available next year. Explain why if there is a single owner for the lake, the fish will be efficiently extracted from it. Assume that anyone who wants to fish can do so. Would you expect that too many fish would be taken out this year?

4. Consider a crowded room with an equal number of smokers and nonsmokers. Each smoker would be willing to pay $1.00 to have the right to smoke. Each non-smoker would be willing to pay $.50 to have the room free from smoke. Assume there is a rule that says no smoking is allowed. Could everyone be made better off if smoking is allowed? How? If property rights to clean air are assigned to the nonsmokers, how might the efficient outcome be obtained? What difference does it make to the outcome whether there is initially a rule that smoking is allowed or that smoking is not allowed? What problems might you envision occurring if no smoking is allowed unless all the nonsmokers agree to allow it?

5. The following table gives the demand for water for two households, the Joneses and the Lopezes. Suppose these two households are the only ones in the market. Draw the individual demand curves for each household and the market demand curve. If the total quantity of water available is 80 units, what price would equate demand and supply?

Assume the local water authority has set the price at 3. Now suppose there is a water shortage, and the total quantity of water available falls to 60 units. Suppose the local water authority keeps the price unchanged and rations the available water supply, with each household receiving 30 units. What is the marginal benefit of an extra unit of water to the Joneses? To the Lopezes? Is the allocation of water between the two households efficient? Suppose the water authority let the price of water rise until market demand equated supply (60 units). How much would the Joneses consume? How much would the Lopezes consume? Is the allocation efficient?

Price	Demand by the Jones family	Demand by the Lopez family
2	50	40
3	45	35
4	40	30
5	35	25
6	30	20
7	25	15
8	20	10

e-Case

On-line Financial Services

In the not so distant past, everyone did their banking by walking or driving to the bank's branch office and standing in line for a teller. And they kept track of momentary stock market developments by going to the local stockbroker's office and watching an electronic sign board that provided a continuous stream of updated stock prices. Like the news boards in Times Square, the stock names and prices flowed in front of anxious investors' eyes in pretty much the same way information flowed out of a tickertape machine in the 1930s.

Now, hundreds of banks offer services on-line. Individuals can transfer money between accounts or pay their bills from the comfort of their home. Or they can log onto one of hundreds of different on-line Internet sites and obtain current prices for stocks, not just on the U.S. financial markets like the New York Stock Exchange or the Nasdaq, but on markets around the world. Traditional discount brokers like Charles Schwab and new Internet firms like E*TRADE allow you to easily, and cheaply, make trades on the world's major financial exchanges.

The new Web-based technologies that made such developments possible have clearly been important in transforming the financial scene. But not all firms automatically adopt the latest technologies—they do so only if the incentives are right. And the incentives to adopt new technologies are provided by the tremendous reduction in costs they allow.

The research firm Booz, Allen & Hamilton estimated the cost of carrying out a banking transaction using four competing technologies: a traditional full-service teller, a telephone, an ATM, and a personal computer. As the figure shows, new technologies have offered banks enormous cost savings. Banks have responded to these incentives by introducing on-line services and aggressively marketing them to induce customers to switch from costly traditional teller services to Internet banking.

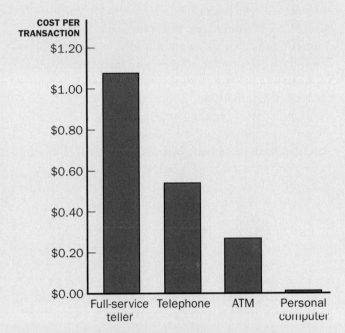

Cost of a Banking Transaction

Declining costs for financial transactions have affected more than just the banking sector. Individual investors can now trade shares on-line at a fraction of the cost charged by the full-service brokers that used to dominate the finance industry. A financial trade that formerly cost over $100 can now be executed for $29.95 or less. At least one Internet firm, FOLIO*fn*, even offers trading at zero marginal cost unlimited trading at a fixed monthly fee. Not surprisingly, at least not to anyone thinking like an economist, these lower costs have led to a huge increase in on-line trading.

In fact, on-line trading is often pointed to as one of the earliest and biggest Internet success stories. In the first quarter of 2000, the two largest on-line brokers, Charles Schwab and E*TRADE, were handling almost 450,000 trades daily. By the close of 2000, Gomez.com, an Internet firm that rates e-commerce businesses, listed more than sixty on-line brokerage firms. Among them were the on-line divisions of established brokers like Merrill Lynch Direct, Charles Schwab, and Morgan Stanley Dean Witter Online, and newcomers like National Discount Brokers, which boasted assets of $5 billion and 7,500 trades daily after only six years in business. Banks like Citicorp, Bank of America, and Wells Fargo have also entered the competition for on-line brokerage clients. In addition to stock trading, on-line firms offer services such as accounting and tax preparation help, financial planning, and retirement planning. Compared to stock trading, on-line banking is spreading at a snail's pace—while only about 3 percent of American families use on-line banking services, 16 percent of U.S. stock trades are now done on-line.

The costs of transactions in both stock trading and on-line banking have fallen, but these costs are not the only costs that have been reduced by Internet technologies. The Internet has vastly lowered the costs of acquiring information. Individual investors now have access to more information about a greater range of financial assets than ever before. Of course, not all that information is valuable. The Internet makes it cheap to spread both good information and misinformation. Information is more critical for investing decisions than it is for standard banking service. Declining transaction costs *and* information costs may explain why on-line stock trading has grown more rapidly than on-line banking.

As in so many other areas, the concepts of incentives, information, and distribution are relevant for studying the impact of the Internet.

Part 5

Introduction to Macroeconomics

Chapter 22

Macroeconomics and the Macroeconomy

Key Questions

1. What are the key topics studied in macroeconomics?

2. How did the Great Depression shape today's economy and the field of macroeconomics?

3. What are some of the legacies of the Great Depression?

4. What are some of the important macroeconomic trade-offs policymakers face?

The focus in this and the next three parts of this book is on *macroeconomics.* Macroeconomics is the study of the overall economy—not the study of employment levels and prices in a particular industry but the study of total employment and unemployment and the general level of prices throughout the whole economy. It is also concerned with the macroeconomic effects of government policies. Macroeconomics deals with the *aggregate* economy. To begin to get a sense of the field of macroeconomics, and how we got to the new economy, it is instructive to start with a brief history of the macroeconomy.

Imagine the world in 1929, nearly three quarters of a century ago. The stock market was booming, and no end to the good times was in sight. True, some commentators were saying the market was overvalued, that a crash was sure to come, but most investors were optimistic about the future. Unemployment was low, and the general level of prices was stable.

Only one year later, the world had changed forever. The stock market crash that occurred in October 1929 wiped out almost a quarter of the value of the New York stock market; similar crashes occurred in other countries. The Dow industrial average (the precursor of today's Dow Jones industrial average, a measure of stock market prices), which had hit a high of 381 in September 1929, fell to 41 in July 1932. Unemployment rose to previously unseen levels throughout the world economy. By 1933, one of every four workers in the United States was unemployed. The United States and other industrialized economies still had the same buildings, plants, and equipment as before, the same labor force was available and apparently willing to work, yet many of these physical and human resources lay idle. This time period, the 1930s, is now indelibly linked with hardship and depressed economic conditions and is commonly called the **Great Depression.**

Out of this catastrophe, macroeconomics was born. While the science of economics can be dated to the publication in 1776 of Adam Smith's *The Wealth of Nations,* the birth of macroeconomics as a separate branch within economics can be dated to the publication in 1936 of John Maynard Keynes's *The General Theory of Employment, Interest, and Prices.* Prior to Keynes's time, economists had studied the behavior of the entire economy and placed special emphasis on understanding the role of money and the general level of prices. But the modern field of macroeconomics, with its emphasis on understanding why economies experience episodes like the Great Depression and why employment and production grow and fluctuate over time, begins with Keynes. Our understanding of the forces influencing aggregate economies has evolved dramatically since Keynes wrote, but his work helped to define the field and has had lasting impacts (both good and bad) on economic policy.

Not just macroeconomics, but many of the government policies and programs we take for granted today grew out of the experience of the 1930s. Perhaps the most important is the general acceptance that governments are responsible for ensuring that periods like the Great Depression never reoccur. In the United States, the Employment Act of 1946 requires the federal government to cultivate "conditions under which there will be afforded useful employment opportunities . . . for those able, willing, and seeking to work, and to promote maximum employment, production, and purchasing power."

A second legacy of the Great Depression is the Social Security program that provides income support to millions of elderly. By affecting decisions about savings and retirement, this program has an important influence on the overall economy as well as on the lives of the millions of individuals who have paid taxes to support the program and who have received, or expect to receive, benefits from it. Today, the United States is engaged in a debate over how to ensure the continued financial health of Social Security.

A third legacy is our system of federal insurance for bank deposits. During the 1930s, thousands of banks were forced to close their doors as panicked depositors tried to withdraw their savings. Today, the federal government insures most deposits so that savers are protected even if their bank fails. Deposit insurance is one means by which the government helps to maintain financial stability. At the end of the 1990s, the financial crisis that started in Asia in 1997 and spread throughout the globe reminded governments of the importance of financial stability.

The impact these legacies of the Great Depression have had on the subsequent history of the United States and other major economies can teach us a great deal about economics and the economic way of thinking.

The Commitment to Full Employment and Growth

Before the Great Depression, the United States and other industrialized economies had gone through frequent periods of rapid economic growth followed by declines in production. These declines were often accompanied by financial panics in which banks were forced to close their doors, refusing to let depositors withdraw their funds.[1] The Roaring Twenties was one period associated with a booming economy. The 1990s was another such period, and as the twentieth century came to a close, the U.S. economy continued to enjoy high employment and rising incomes, even as much of the rest of the world was failing to generate enough jobs for those who wanted to work. Yet by early 2001, there were many signs that the economic boom in the United States was coming to an end.

When the Great Depression hit, it was not confined to the United States. Figure 22.1 shows that production declined in all the major industrial economies, with the United States and Germany being hit the hardest. We often think of the "global economy" and the close international linkages we have today as uniquely characteristic of the modern world, but the economies of Europe and North America were also linked in the 1920s, and economic crises took on a global dimension, just as they can today.

The world economy recovered slowly from the dramatic depths of the Great Depression. The United States produced less in 1936 than it had in 1929. And in 1937 another decline occurred, helping to solidify our view of the 1930s as an entire decade of hardship. Only with the increased production associated with the advent of World War II did incomes in the United States significantly surpass earlier levels and unemployment return to more normal levels (Figure 22.2). The massive increase in orders to factories for war materials stimulated firms to expand production and hire workers. By 1944, the unemployment rate had fallen to 1.2 percent of those willing to work.

The end of World War II brought new fears that the economy would lapse back into recession and that the hard times of the 1930s would return. The fear was that when the strong demand for production arising from the wartime needs of the government ended, firms would again be idle and the era of massive unemployment would return. Fortunately, while production declined from its wartime peaks, the economy did not return to the conditions of the Great Depression. The late 1940s saw strong growth in economic activity, in part fueled by household

---

[1]Each Christmas season, the movie *It's a Wonderful Life* is shown on television. A central event in the movie is the failure of the bank owned by the character played by Jimmy Stewart.

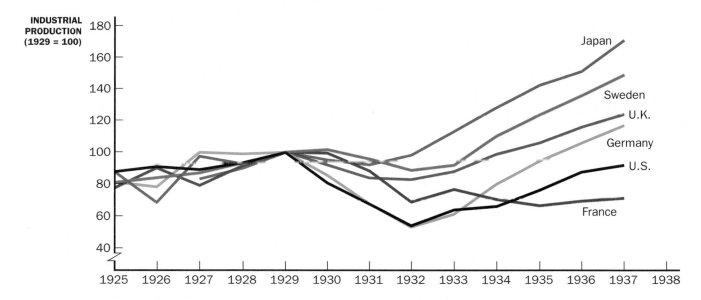

FIGURE 22.1 *Industrial Production*

The Great Depression was not limited to the United States. All industrial economies suffered declines in economic activity and production in the 1930s. The index of industrial production for each country is scaled so that all the indexes equal 100 for the year 1929. Sources: League of Nations, *World Production and Prices* (Geneva: League of Nations, 1936), Appendix II, p. 142; and *World Production and Prices* (Geneva: League of Nations, 1938), Table 1, p. 44.

spending as Americans moved to the suburbs, built homes, and had children. During the war years, few consumer goods had been available, purchases of some goods had been rationed, and households had been urged to save by buying war bonds to help finance the war effort. Americans wanted to enjoy the return of peace and prosperity by using the incomes they had earned during the war to buy new cars, homes, and appliances.

The shift from wartime production and the demands for military goods to peacetime production and the demands for civilian goods represented a tremendous change in what the economy produced. Assembly lines that had been producing tanks for the government shifted to producing automobiles for consumers. Construction boomed as it met the demand for new homes. Resources—workers and capital— had to be shifted from what they had been producing to meet the new needs and desires of Americans.

The end of the war also saw the government accepting responsibility for preventing a reoccurrence of the Great Depression. This was formalized when the U.S. Congress passed the Employment Act in 1946. Among its provisions was the establishment of the president's Council of Economic Advisors, a three-member committee of economists

who advise the president.[2] While economists have debated how much power the government actually has to influence macroeconomic developments, the voting public often shows that it expects the president to ensure continued economic growth, low inflation, and low unemployment.

Today, a slight rise in the unemployment rate brings demands for the government to do something to "get the economy moving again." And for good reason: In today's economy, when an extra 1 percent of the labor force becomes unemployed, incomes in the economy fall by about $160 billion. A commitment to maintaining full employment was absent in the 1930s, or at least there was much less agreement over whether the government could (as well as whether it should) stimulate the economy.

Along with responsibility comes accountability. Voters expect government to ensure the economy performs well, and macroeconomic conditions play an important role in determining the outcome of national elections. One simple measure of the economy's performance is the so-called misery

---

[2]Professor Stiglitz was chair of President Clinton's Council of Economic Advisors from 1995 to 1996.

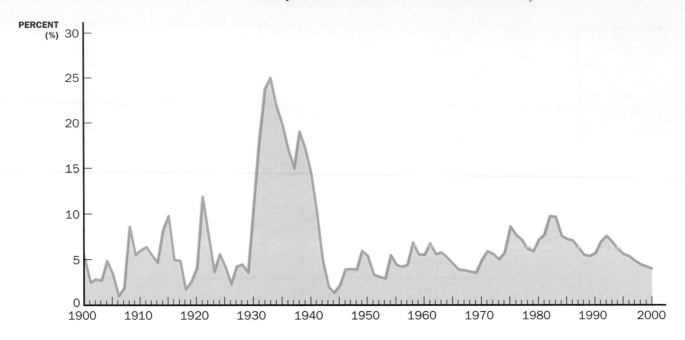

FIGURE 22.2   *Unemployment*

The proportion of the labor force unemployed and seeking jobs rose to 25 percent during the Great Depression. Since 1960, unemployment has fluctuated around an average of about 6 percent, but it has risen to almost 10 percent (in 1983) and fallen to as low as 3.5 percent (in 1969). After reaching 7.5 percent in 1992, the unemployment rate fell steadily over the rest of the 1990s and was at 4.0 percent in 2000, its lowest level since 1969. Source: *ERP* (2001), Table B-42.

index, the sum of the unemployment rate and the rate of inflation (the rate at which prices are rising). The misery index is shown in Figure 22.3. The figure also shows the vote share of the presidential candidate of the incumbent president's party. Increases in the misery index in 1979–1980 and 1990–1991 help to explain the poor showings of Presidents Carter and Bush in their reelection bids. Declines in the misery index during 1983–1984 and 1995–1996 helped to reelect Presidents Reagan and Clinton.

Getting the Country Moving Again

The attempts by government to pursue the goals established by the Employment Act have helped economists learn about how the economy operates.

The 1960s saw the first active use of government policy to try to reduce overall unemployment. During the 1960 presidential election, John F. Kennedy narrowly defeated Richard Nixon in what had been the closest presidential race in U.S. history until the Bush-Gore contest in 2000.

In part, Nixon's defeat was due to the slowdown in economic activity and rise in unemployment the country experienced in 1959. During the six years from 1958 through 1963, the unemployment rate averaged almost 6 percent; ten years before it had been 2.8 percent. Kennedy's Council of Economic Advisors proposed a policy based on the ideas of John Maynard Keynes that was designed to stimulate the economy and bring the unemployment rate down to 4 percent, a level that at the time was believed to be consistent with "full employment." The policy called for a major tax cut. Those who opposed the cut argued that it would be fiscally irresponsible and lead to a deficit, with the government spending more than it received in taxes. It was argued that inflation would rise and the cost of lower unemployment would be higher inflation. The government would need to decide how much inflation it was willing to tolerate to get unemployment down.

In what is perhaps the most famous macroeconomic policy experiment, the federal government did cut taxes in 1964. The unemployment rate subsequently fell; in fact, it fell below 4 percent, to as low as 3.5 percent by 1969. Un-

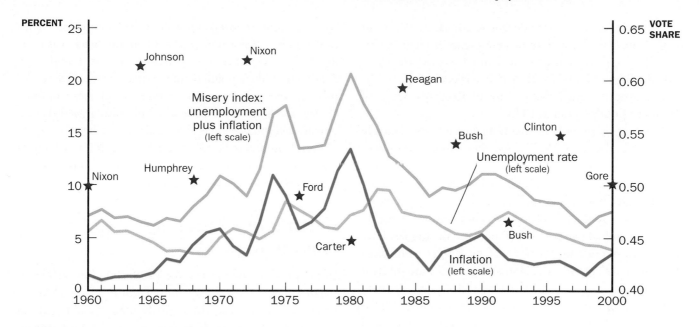

FIGURE 22.3 *The Misery Index*

Two important measures of the economy's performance are the unemployment rate and the inflation rate. The misery index adds the two together. The x's mark the vote share of the incumbent party's candidate in each presidential election. When the misery index is rising, the incumbent party tends to do poorly in the election.

fortunately, this fall in unemployment was accompanied by rising inflation; the general level of prices rose by only 1 percent in 1963, but by 1969 prices were rising at an annual rate of 6.2 percent. To some extent, policymakers at the time thought that higher inflation was simply the price to pay to maintain lower unemployment. They saw this as a trade-off; lower unemployment required accepting higher inflation, but inflation could always be reduced again, they believed, by letting average unemployment return to the levels of the late 1950s and early 1960s.

Stagflation

The U.S. economy in the 1970s faced very different problems than it had faced in the previous decade. During the first half of the 1970s, the unemployment rate averaged 5.4 percent, essentially the same level as before the Kennedy tax cut, yet as the unemployment rate rose from the low levels of the late 1960s, inflation remained high. The trade-off between unemployment and inflation that policymakers thought they faced seemed to have disappeared.

In the 1970s, the members of OPEC, the Organization of Petroleum Exporting Countries, were able to raise the world

price of oil significantly. This contributed to the general increase in prices in oil-importing countries, but it also caused changes in the behavior of households and firms as they faced higher energy prices. Consumers started buying small, more fuel-efficient automobiles. Many of these were produced in foreign countries, particularly Japan, since U.S. auto producers were slow to respond to changes in consumer demand. Firms needed to adjust their production techniques to conserve energy and adopt more energy-efficient equipment. They also needed to alter the products they made to respond to the demand by consumers for more energy-efficient goods.

The experience with rising inflation *and* rising unemployment in the 1970s was called **stagflation.** Numerous attempts to control inflation were made without success. In 1971, President Nixon imposed price and wage controls. These temporarily reduced inflation but failed to address the underlying causes. As soon as the controls were lifted, inflation reappeared.

The Conquest of Inflation

At the end of the 1970s, most industrial economies continued to suffer unacceptably high rates of inflation. The last big oil price increase of the decade occurred in 1979 and helped push inflation rates to new highs in many countries. The misery index in the United States reached a postwar high (Figure 22.3), and macroeconomic conditions played no small role in Ronald Reagan's defeat of President Jimmy Carter in 1980.

The turning point in the battle against inflation actually occurred in October 1979 when Paul Volker, President Carter's newly appointed chairman of the Federal Reserve System, shifted economic policy. Interest rates rose to record highs, but Volker's policies succeeded in getting inflation down. Reducing inflation was not without costs. By 1982, unemployment reached 10 percent, the highest level in the post–World War II era. President Reagan's ratings in the polls sunk to low levels. Many Democrats thought Reagan was sure to be defeated when new elections were held in 1984. But by then, the economy was expanding. Unemployment had fallen to 7.5 percent, yet inflation remained relatively low. With the macroeconomy improving, Reagan coasted to a landslide reelection victory.

Government Deficits and Trade Deficits

The last half of the 1980s and much of the 1990s were dominated by concern over two deficits. One was the federal government's budget deficit. The gap between what the federal government spent and what it collected in taxes reached $290 billion in 1992. When the government spends more than it receives in taxes, it must borrow, just as you would if you spent more than your income. The total amount the government owed rose from about $700 billion in 1980 to $3.7 trillion in 1997—that is $3,700,000,000,000, or about $13,500 for every man, woman, and child in the United States. Ours was not the only country showing an imbalance between government spending and tax revenues. Other countries faced the difficult task of balancing spending desires with available tax revenues. Germany, France, Italy, Japan, and the United Kingdom all had deficits in the second half of the 1990s that were larger, relative to the size of their economies, than the deficit of the U.S. federal government. Each government had to make trade-offs, deciding which expenditure programs to scale back or which taxes to increase.

The second deficit that became the focus of attention in the 1980s and 1990s was the trade deficit, the difference between what the United States purchases from other countries (our imports) and what we sell to other countries (our exports). Some argued that the trade deficit was costing American workers their jobs and that we should "Buy American." Others pointed out that trade provided access to new markets for American producers and more product choices for American consumers. They also argued that international capital markets allowed firms and the government to borrow from foreign lenders, increasing the availability of credit needed to build the new plants and equipment that contribute to future economic growth.

Getting the Economy Moving (Again)

In the presidential election of 1992, Bill Clinton's campaign slogan, "It's the economy, stupid!" struck a responsive cord among voters. After almost eight years of economic growth, the U.S. economy had stalled during the summer of 1990. The overall level of production in the economy declined throughout the rest of 1990 and into 1991. With firms producing less, they needed fewer workers; the unemployment rate rose. While the misery index remained well short of the peaks reached earlier, it was rising, and this was enough to sink President Bush's reelection bid. Strong economic growth in the second half of the 1990s, with low unemployment and low inflation, contributed significantly to President Clinton's reelection in 1996.

As the century ended, the United States was enjoying its strongest economic performance in decades. Unemployment had fallen to the lowest level since the 1970s, and inflation remained low. American workers were becoming more productive, perhaps owing to the computer and technological revolution that was changing the way the economy operates, and this was improving prospects for long-term growth in living standards.

Meanwhile, many other major economies were experiencing quite different macroeconomic conditions. Asia had been wracked by financial crises, rising unemployment, and stagnating growth, while many European countries found that their unemployment rates remained stubbornly high through most of the 1990s.

As the year 2000 ended, there were increasing signs that the United States economy was slowing down. Headlines were of firms reporting lower than expected profits and of high-tech firms scaling back operations or even going out of business. President-Elect Bush appeared to be inheriting a much weaker economy than commentators had been projecting just a few months earlier. The new administration entered amid concerns that the long expansion of the economy was finally coming to an end.

Social Security

A second legacy of the Great Depression, the **Social Security** system, emerged into the forefront of political debate in the late 1990s. As the federal budget began to show a surplus, with revenues exceeding expenditures, the question arose as to how much needs to be set aside to "save" Social Security. When Social Security was established in 1935, 50 percent of the elderly lived in poverty, life expectancy at age sixty-five was only 12.6 years, and the elderly constituted less than 10 percent of the adult population. Today, in 2001, the poverty rate for the elderly is close to 10 percent, a sixty-five-year-old can expect to live another 17.2 years, and the elderly make up over 20 percent of the adult population.

These changes have raised serious financial concerns about the ability of the Social Security system to remain solvent. As the post–World War II "baby-boom" generation ages, the costs of the Social Security program will rise significantly. The government has been setting aside funds to help meet these higher expenses, but current estimates suggest that without changes in the program or in the way it is financed, these funds will be exhausted before 2050.

Tough choices must be faced in addressing the problems of Social Security. Should current workers pay more taxes now to ensure that current benefit levels can be maintained in the future? Should benefits be reduced? Should people work longer? Should people be required to save more on their own for retirement? Should future workers pay higher taxes to support the retired?

Programs like Social Security affect the saving decisions of households, as well as the government's budget. If you know Social Security will provide you with income when you retire, you have less incentive to save for yourself. Savings provides the funds that can be used for building new plants and machinery that will raise future productivity. How Social Security is "saved" will have important effects on economic growth and future standards of living.

Internet Connection

Calculating Social Security Benefits

The Social Security Administration has an on-line calculator that lets people estimate the Social Security benefit they will receive at retirement. The calculator only works if you are over twenty-two and less than sixty-three years old and have some reportable income in the current year. For most college students, your current income is probably not a very good estimate of the incomes you will earn after graduation. So for fun, assume that upon graduation you will start a job earning $50,000 per year. Go to the Social Security quick calculator at http://www.ssa.gov/planners/calculators.htm to estimate your Social Security benefit.

Deposit Insurance

A third legacy of the Great Depression, federal deposit insurance, has contributed to the stability of the American financial system. Between 1930 and 1932, over nine thousand American banks failed as panicked depositors rushed to withdraw funds from their banks. Depositors worried that their banks would fail before they could withdraw their money, so each depositor had an incentive to rush to be the first to withdraw. With all depositors pulling out their funds, banks had to close their doors. Today, **deposit insurance** helps to maintain confidence in the banking system and avoid these panicked runs. Even if a bank fails, depositors do not risk losing their money.

Deposit insurance may make depositors feel safer, but it can actually make the banking system less safe. Think about the incentives bank owners face when deposits are insured. People are willing to put money in banks even if they only offer low interest rates because bank deposits are safe investments. Deposit insurance sees to that. If banks take the funds that have been deposited and invest in risky but high-return projects, they stand to make a profit. Normally, if a bank invested someone else's money in a risky project, it would have to offer an interest rate that is high enough to compensate for the risk. With deposit insurance, banks do not need to offer such a high rate because the depositors are not faced with any risk. If a risky project succeeds, banks make a big profit. If the project fails, the government bails out the depositors. There is an incentive for banks to take a chance on risky investments. For this reason, countries that provide deposit insurance usually also have in place a system of financial regulation that tries to make sure banks do not invest in projects that are too risky.

The financial sector plays a central role in modern economies by channeling the savings of millions of households to help finance the investment projects of thousands of firms. Today, the financial sector is truly global in character. When this sector functions well, it contributes to economic growth. When it fails—as occurred in the Great

Depression and during the financial crises experienced in Asia, Latin America, and Russia in the late 1990s—the results can be unemployment and hardships for millions.

A Look Ahead

This brief history of the macroeconomy sets the stage for our study of macroeconomics. Our first task, taken up in Chapter 23, is to understand the macroeconomic goals that governments try to achieve, and how economists measure the aggregate economy's performance in meeting these goals. How do we measure the aggregate output of the entire economy? How do we measure unemployment? How do we measure the general level of prices and inflation?

International Perspective

Financial Crises

In the United States, the savings and loan crisis of the 1980s occurred when regulations on what a savings and loan institution could invest in were relaxed. Many savings and loan institutions invested in risky projects that went bankrupt. Savings and loans in Texas were hit particularly hard, and the eventual cost to the government was over $150 billion. Despite this experience, most Americans probably view the type of wide-scale financial crises experienced during the 1930s as a thing of the past. But that is not the case in many other countries. In recent years, both economically developed and developing countries in many parts of the world have suffered from the effects of banking crises. These crises have contributed to economic and political disruptions, unemployment, and slower economic growth.

Among the high-income countries, Japan has suffered the most from its banking crisis. After enjoying spectacular economic growth for several decades after World War II, Japan has been mired in a decade-long recession, and its banking crisis is a major factor behind this stagnation. Japan has had particular difficulty dealing with its bank-

rupt banks, and the cost of bad loans has reached well over $1 trillion.

In the late 1990s, several developing countries also experienced financial crises. The most recent one, a severe financial and banking crisis in 1997, originated in Asia but then spread to affect countries around the world. This crisis started in Thailand and then moved on to Indonesia and Korea, before enveloping Russia and Brazil. Almost every developing country was affected before the crisis ended. Many countries saw aggregate income decline significantly—Indonesia's total income fell by 16 percent. As incomes fell and borrowers were unable to pay back loans, banks were weakened. When Indonesia closed down the first group of bankrupt banks, the government announced that more would be shut down but that depositors would not be insured. Not surprisingly, there was a run on the private banks—all depositors tried to pull their money out of the banks as quickly as possible. The already weak banking system was devastated, just as bank runs had devastated the American banking system in the 1930s.

Thinking Like an Economist

The Five Key Concepts

In Chapter 1 we introduced five key concepts that help you to think like an economist. These concepts were applied in studying the principles of microeconomics. They also provide insights into the principles of macroeconomics, as we will see over the next several chapters. The brief history of the macroeconomy, and the legacies of the Great Depression, provide ample illustrations of the importance of these concepts for understanding macroeconomics:

- *Trade-offs:* The debate over the Kennedy tax cut provides just one example of how macroeconomic policymakers must understand the trade-offs they face. One important trade-off is between inflation and unemployment. The Kennedy advisers thought they could gain lower average unemployment at the cost of higher average inflation. As it turned out, average inflation did rise, but unemployment fell only temporarily. A study of macroeconomics will help you understand why the fall in unemployment was not sustained.

- *Incentives:* The savings and loan crises of the 1980s can be traced to the incentives savings and loan institutions faced when their depositors were insured.

- *Exchange:* International trade between nations can bring benefits based on comparative advantage, but the balance between exports and imports is often an issue of concern, as the debate over the United States' huge trade deficit illustrates.

- *Information:* The Employment Act of 1946 established a commitment to full employment, but gauging how successful the economy has been requires information. The data that governments collect on employment, growth, and inflation provide the information economists use to monitor the macroeconomy.

- *Distribution:* The debate surrounding Social Security today is, in part, about distribution. Will future workers have to pay higher taxes to pay for the benefits enjoyed by the retired members of the baby-boom generation? Or will baby boomers bear the cost, perhaps by delaying retirement or receiving reduced benefits?

As you study macroeconomics, keep these five key concepts in mind. They offer insight into macroeconomics as well as microeconomics.

In Parts Six to Eight, we will learn about the factors that account for growth, inflation, and economic fluctuations. We also will learn how government policies affect the economy, and how these policies can be used to achieve macroeconomic goals. What happens to the aggregate economy depends not only on government policies but also on the individual decisions made by thousands of firms and millions of households. Microeconomics helps economists understand how firms and households make choices—what trade-offs they face, how they respond to incentives, the effects of information on their choices, and the role markets and exchange play in determining what is produced and how income is distributed. Macroeconomics helps economists understand how the choices of firms and households, together with government policies, affect the aggregate economy.

Review and Practice

Summary

1. Macroeconomics, a separate, distinct field within economics, grew out of the attempts to understand the worldwide depression of the 1930s.

2. Among the legacies of the Great Depression that continue to affect the macroeconomy are the commitment to full employment, Social Security, and deposit insurance.

3. The key concepts of trade-offs, incentives, exchange, information, and distribution help cast light on macroeconomic issues, just as they do in microeconomics.

Key Terms

Great Depression
stagflation
Social Security
deposit insurance

Review Questions

1. What trade-off between inflation and unemployment did Kennedy's Council of Economic Advisers believe they faced? What happened to unemployment and inflation after the 1964 tax cut?

2. What is stagflation? When has the United States experienced stagflation?

3. How does the Social Security program affect an individual's incentive to save? Why are people concerned about the financial future of Social Security?

4. How does deposit insurance affect the incentives faced by depositors? By banks?

Problems

1. Look at the front pages of a newspaper this week. What macroeconomic issues are in the news?

2. Give an example of a period during the last forty years when inflation and unemployment moved in opposite directions, one rising and the other falling. Give an exmple of a period during the last forty years when inflation and unemployment moved in the same direction, both rising or both falling.

3. Which two deficits were of concern in the 1980s and early 1990s? Which of these two deficits has turned into a surplus? Which one is still a deficit?

4. If bank depositors hear that their bank is in financial trouble, how are they likely to respond if they are covered by deposit insurance? How might they act if they do not have deposit insurance?

Chapter 23

Macroeconomic Goals and Measurement

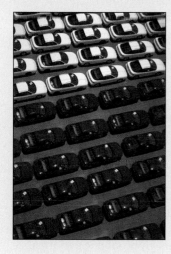

Key Questions

1. What are the main objectives of macroeconomic policy?

2. How are output, growth, unemployment, and inflation measured?

3. What are some of the central problems that arise in measuring these variables?

4. What are the costs of unemployment and inflation (or deflation)?

*M*acroeconomic policymakers focus on improving the health of the economy. The goals by which they gauge the health of the economy are high and sustainable rates of economic growth, low unemployment, and low inflation. To measure how well the economy is achieving these macroeconomic goals, economists need quantitative measures of its performance. For this reason, in this chapter we will discuss how output and growth, unemployment, and inflation are measured.

Understanding the yardsticks used to gauge the performance of the economy is important for judging how successful economies have been in achieving their policy goals. Many of the most common economic yardsticks—the unemployment rate, the consumer price index, and gross domestic product—are frequent topics of newspaper stories and televison news. They often figure prominently in political debates and presidential election campaigns. During the 2000 campaign, Vice President Al Gore emphasized the economy's strong performance over the previous eight years. In the 1992 presidential election campaign, two slogans that struck a responsive cord were "Jobs, Jobs, Jobs," and "It's the economy, stupid!" In the 1980 and 1984 elections, attention was given to the so-called misery index—the sum of the unemployment rate and the inflation rate. But how exactly do economists measure the performance of the economy? What exactly is the unemployment rate or the rate of inflation? And in studying these measures, do economists find patterns? Are good years regularly followed by lean years? Does inflation usually accompany periods of low unemployment? How does growth in the United States compare with growth in other countries? Are living standards in different countries converging? Economists look for patterns, and if they find patterns, they ask why.

In this chapter we will also discuss problems that affect the measurement of almost every economic variable. Some of our measures may suffer from bias. It is important to understand how such biases might arise so that we do not make errors in assessing economic conditions.

453

The Three Key Goals of Macroeconomic Performance

A key measure of the economy's performance is its rate of growth. *Economic growth* contributes to rising living standards, and it is therefore a fundamental macroeconomic goal. In early 2001, the U.S. economy was experiencing a degree of health seldom seen before, yet there was uncertainty about how much longer it would last. The economy had been growing for almost ten years, a record period of economic expansion, but signs were appearing that growth had slowed. During the 1960s, per capita income in the United States grew 3.07 percent per year; this growth rate fell to 2.19 percent in the 1970s, 2.07 percent in the 1980s, and 1.22 percent from 1990 to 1995. Growth increased again during the second half of the 1990s, jumping to 2.89 percent for the period from 1995 to 1999, which lead to more optimistic forecasts of future living standards. These differences in growth rates may seem small, but even such small differences can have a major impact on living standards as time goes by. Incomes double in just under twenty-five years at a growth rate of 3 percent; it takes more than forty-five years for incomes to double when the growth rate is 1.5 percent.

At the end of the 1990s, incomes in the United States grew rapidly. New technologies associated with computers and the explosive growth of the Internet—the new economy—are often cited as the sources of this increased growth. Whether this represents a temporary burst of growth, or a sustained period of more rapid income increases, remains to be seen. In contrast to the United States, many other countries have experienced slowdowns in economic growth, or even declines in total incomes, at the end of the 1990s. And slow economic growth is a critical problem for most developing economies. In comparing output in different countries, as well as comparing output within the same country over time, we have to adjust for differences in population. We do so by measuring *output per capita*, which simply is total output divided by the population count. Incomes must grow faster than the population if average living standards are to rise.

The *unemployment rate*, a basic measure of job opportunities and the health of the labor market, provides another measure of the economy's performance. In 2000, the U.S. unemployment rate averaged just 4.0 percent of the labor force. Unemployment this low had not been seen for thirty years. This rate still represented almost 6 million workers looking for jobs, but it is a far cry from the almost 11 million unemployed in 1983 (an unemployment rate of 9.6 percent) or even the 9.6 million in 1992 (an unemployment rate of 7.5 percent). A basic macroeconomic goal is to ensure full employment, so that all workers who seek work at current market wages can find jobs.

In addition to low unemployment, the United States in the 1990s also experienced another sign of economic health—low *inflation*. Inflation is the rate at which the general level of prices increases, and inflation was, again by historical standards, moderate, about 2 to 4 percent a year. Only twenty years earlier, inflation had hit double-digit levels (13.3 percent in 1979). Still, the U.S. experience has been tame compared with some countries. In Ukraine, the inflation rate reached 10,000 percent a year in the 1990s before falling to 40 percent a year in 1997.

Lack of growth, unemployment, and inflation are the three problems that macroeconomists are constantly trying to understand. Understanding them is the first step toward designing policies to improve macroeconomic performance and to achieve the goals of rapid growth, full employment, and low inflation. But the first step toward understanding them is to learn how we measure them.

WRAP-UP

Three Goals of Macroeconomic Policy

Rapid growth
Full employment
Low inflation

Measuring Output and Growth

To gauge the economy's success in raising the standard of living for its residents, we need to start by understanding how we measure the total output of the economy. We will learn later in this chapter that the aggregate income of the economy

TABLE 23.1

Calculating GDP				
	Prices and Quantities			
Year	**Price of PCs**	**Quantity of PCs**	**Price of CDs**	**Quantity of CDs**
1	$1,800.00	1.0 million	$15.00	50.0 million
2	$1,850.00	1.2 million	$17.00	45.0 million

GDP in year 1	= value of PCs + value of CDs
	= $1,800 × 1.0 million + $15 × 50.0 million
	= $2,550 million.

GDP in year 2	= value of PCs + value of CDs
	= $1,850 × 1.2 million + $17 × 45.0 million
	= $2,985 million.

is equal to the aggregate output of goods and services that the economy has produced. Thus, measuring output is our starting point for assessing the economy's performance.

Gross Domestic Product

The output of the economy consists of millions of different goods and services. We could report how much of each good or service the economy produced. This would yield a list that might include 1,362,478 hammers, 473,562,382 potatoes, 256,346 heart operations, and so forth. Such a list might be useful for some purposes, but it would not provide us with the information we want. If next year the number of hammers produced goes up by 5 percent, the potato crop yield goes down by 2 percent, and the number of heart operations performed rises by 7 percent, has the economy's total output gone up or down? And by how much?

We need a single number that summarizes the output of the economy. But how do we add up hammers, potatoes, heart operations, and the millions of other products produced in the economy? We do this by adding up the *money value* of all the *final* goods and services produced. By money value, we mean the dollar value of output. By final goods and services, we mean those goods and services sold for final usage and not those used to make other products. Since the money value of hammer production and the money value of heart operations are in the same units (dollars), we can add them together. The money value of final output is called the **gross domestic product,** or **GDP.** It is

the standard measure of the value of the output in an economy. It sums up the total money value of the final goods and services produced within a nation's borders within a specific period of time. GDP includes everything from buttons to air travel and from haircuts to barrels of oil. It makes no difference whether the production takes place in the private or public sector, or whether the goods and services are purchased by households, the government, or the foreign sector.[1]

Table 23.1 illustrates the calculation of GDP for a simple economy that produces just two goods, personal computers (PCs) and compact discs (CDs). The table shows the number of PCs and CDs produced in two different years, and the average prices at which they were sold. GDP in year 1 is

WRAP-UP

Gross Domestic Product

The total money value of all final goods and services produced for the marketplace within a nation's borders during a given period of time (usually a year).

---

[1]We use prices not only because they are a convenient way of making comparisons, but also because prices reflect how consumers value different goods. If the price of an orange is twice that of an apple, it means an orange is worth twice as much (at the margin) as an apple.

TABLE 23.2

Nominal and Real GDP

Real GDP (using year 1 as the base year):
    real GDP in year 1   = \$2,550 million
    real GDP in year 2   = \$1,800 × 1.2 million + \$15 × 45.0 million
                         = \$2,835 million.

Price index (GDP deflator) using year 1 as base year:
    GDP deflator, year 1 = 100
    GDP deflator, year 2 = 100 × (year 2 nominal GDP)/(year 2 real GDP)
                       = 100 × (2,985/2,835)
                       = 105.3.

Deflating nominal GDP: real GDP in year 2   = nominal GDP/price index
                                          = \$2,985/1.053 = \$2,835 billion.

found by multiplying the quantities of each good sold in year 1 by their price in year 1. This gives the money value of PC and CD production. Adding the resulting money values together gives us GDP for this economy. Using the data in the table, we calculate GDP to be \$2,550 million in year 1 and \$2,985 million in year 2. GDP grew by 17 percent—100(\$2,985–\$2,550)/\$2,550—from year 1 to year 2.

There is one problem with using money as a measure of the economy's output. The value of a dollar changes over time. Candy bars, books, movie tickets, hammers, and heart operations all cost more today than they did ten years ago. Another way of saying this is that a dollar does not buy as much as it did ten years ago. We do not want to be misled into believing the economy is producing more when, in fact, prices may simply have risen. In our example from Table 23.1, for instance, one of the reasons why GDP was higher in year 2 than in year 1 was that the prices of the two goods were higher. Even if output had remained unchanged in year 2 at 1.0 million PCs and 50.0 million CDs, GDP would have risen to \$2,700 million simply because prices rose.

To keep the comparisons of different years straight, economists adjust GDP for changes in the average level of prices. Unadjusted GDP is known as **nominal GDP;** that is what we calculated in Table 23.1. The term **real GDP** is used for the GDP numbers that have been adjusted for changes in the general level of prices. Real GDP gives a truer year-to-year measure of how much the economy actually produces. One way to think of real GDP is to ask, what would GDP be if all prices had remained unchanged? That is, from the example in Table 23.1, we could ask what GDP would have been in year 2 if prices had remained un-

changed from year 1. Table 23.2 gives us the answer. Real GDP in year 2 using year 1 prices is \$2,835 million. Since we are using the same prices to make this comparison, the measure of real GDP only changes if the quantities of the goods produced change. In this example, real GDP (\$2,835 million) is less than nominal GDP (\$2,985 million from Table 23.1), and this tells us that part of the increase in nominal GDP that we found in Table 23.1 reflected price increases. When we use year 1 prices to calculate real GDP in subsequent years, year 1 is called the *base year.*

When economists talk about adjusting nominal GDP for price changes to obtain a measure of real GDP, they say they "deflate" nominal GDP using a measure of the average level of prices called a *price index.* The price index for GDP is called the **GDP deflator.** As we have already seen, nominal GDP reflects changes in prices and quantities, while real GDP is a measure of how much quantities have changed. Real GDP can be defined by the equation

$$\text{real GDP} = \frac{\text{nominal GDP}}{\text{price index}}.$$

If nominal GDP has risen by 3 percent in the past year but prices have also risen by 3 percent, then real GDP would be unchanged. Since we have calculated nominal GDP and real GDP for the economy of Tables 23.1 and 23.2, we can determine that the price index must equal 1.053 (see Table 23.2). This is normally reported as 105.3 (so in the base year the price index is equal to 100), indicating that, for this example, prices rose by 5.3 percent from year 1 to year 2.

This approach encounters a problem when *relative* prices change dramatically. If the price of computers falls

Internet Connection

The Bureau of Economic Analysis

The home page of the Bureau of Economic Analysis can be found at http://www.bea.doc.gov. You can find the latest GDP data at this site.

rapidly as the output of computers increases—as has happened over the past two decades—then real output, using an earlier base year such as 1987, may be distorted. The large increases in computer production are valued at the high prices that existed earlier. This places a high value on computer output, and GDP will look like it is increasing very rapidly. When the base year used to calculate real GDP is changed—as it is periodically—the growth of the economy will appear to diminish suddenly; in the *new* base year, computer prices are lower so each computer "counts" for less in GDP. Of course, the growth of the economy did not really diminish; it was only that our previous yardstick distorted the picture.

To address this problem, the Bureau of Economic Analysis (BEA), the government agency in the Department of Commerce responsible for the GDP numbers, changed its approach in January 1996. It now provides a measure called the **chain-weighted real GDP.** This measure of the economy's output is designed to avoid some of the problems that arise when the prices of certain goods, such as computers, change greatly from the base year. The appendix to this chapter shows how the chain-weighted real GDP is calculated. The BEA currently uses 1996 prices as a base, so chain-weighted real GDP is also said to be measured in **chained 1996 dollars.**

Measuring GDP: The Value of Output

The general accounting system we use to measure GDP is called the National Income and Product Accounts (NIPA) and is produced by the Bureau of Economic Analysis. In the national income accounts, there are three approaches to measuring GDP (whether real or nominal), each of

which yields the same result. Two concentrate on output data. The third—relying on the fact that the value of output becomes income to someone—uses income figures to obtain a measure of output.

The Final Goods Approach On the face of it, measuring GDP is a straightforward task, albeit a massive one. One gathers together the dollar value of all goods and services sold in a country and then adds them up. Unfortunately, matters are not this simple, because it is first necessary to distinguish between final goods and intermediate goods. Final goods—like automobiles, books, bread, and shoes—are sold for final use by consumers, firms, the government, or foreigners. Intermediate goods are used to produce outputs—like coal used to make steel, silica used to make silicon computer chips, or apples used to make applesauce. A good such as an apple can be either a final good or an intermediate good, depending on how it is used. The *final goods approach* used to measure GDP adds up the total dollar value of goods and services produced, categorized by their ultimate users.

The reason why it is so important to distinguish between final and intermediate goods is that the value of the final goods *includes* the value of the intermediate goods that went into making the final goods. When Ford sells a truck for $15,000, that figure may include $150 worth of Uniroyal tires. It would be double counting to list both the value of the truck and the value of the tires on the truck in GDP. Likewise for steel, plastic, and other components that go into making the truck. In fact, cases where some intermediate goods are used to produce other intermediate goods could even lead to triple or quadruple counting.

The Components of GDP

One way of calculating the value of the final goods produced in the economy is to consider where those goods go. There are four possibilities. Some of the final goods are consumed by individuals—we call this aggregate *consumption* (and we include all consumption goods, regardless of where they are produced—we will see later how we correct for goods produced in other countries). Some are used by firms to build buildings and make machines—this is called aggregate *investment* (again, we include all investment goods that firms purchase, regardless of where they are produced). Some are purchased by government and are called *government purchases*. And some of the goods, called *exports*, go to other countries. If we did not import any goods (that is, buy goods produced in other countries), then GDP would simply consist of goods that went for private consumption, private investment, government purchases, or exports. But not all consumption, investment, or government purchases are produced in this country. For instance, many consumer electronics and automobiles that individuals purchase are produced in other countries. We, therefore, need a final step to calculate GDP using the final goods approach. We have to subtract the amount imported. Thus,

$$GDP = C + I + G + X - M,$$

where C is consumption, I is investment, G is government purchases, X is exports, and M is imports. The difference between exports and imports is referred to as *net exports*. This equation is an *identity;* that is, it is always true (by definition) that the GDP equals consumption plus investment plus government purchases plus net exports.

WRAP-UP

GDP equals consumption plus investment plus government purchases plus exports minus imports.

The final goods approach to calculating GDP in the United States can be illustrated using the figures for 2000. According to the *Bureau of Economic Analysis*,[2] the values for the components of GDP were as follows:

Category	Billions $
Consumption	$6,757.3
+ Investment	1,832.7
+ Government purchases	1,743.7
+ Exports	1,097.3
–Imports	1,468.0
= GDP	$9,963.1

By adding these components together, we find that the value of all final goods and services produced within the borders of the United States during 2000 was $9,963.1 billion.

[2]http:www.bea.doc.gov.

CASE IN POINT

Is Software a Final Good or an Intermediate Good?

Measuring output might seem straightforward when the economy produces cars and wheat and houses, but what happens when it produces ideas? The new technologies and the new economy they have created have forced the economists and statisticians at the Bureau of Economic Analysis to revise the National Income and Product Accounts. Updating and revising the accounts is nothing new; the bureau is always trying to improve its estimates of economic activity. However, the new economy has created some unique problems. One of the major changes in the *1999 Comprehensive Revision of the National Income and Product Accounts* (http://www.bea.doc.gov/bea/an/0899niw/maintext.html) dealt with the manner in which software is treated in GDP. Thinking about the correct way to measure the price and quantity of software highlights the differences between final and intermediate goods.

Prior to the new revisions, business and government expenditures on software were treated in an inconsistent manner. Software that was bundled in a product—a suite of office software programs such as a word processor and spreadsheet that was installed on a computer, for instance—was treated as a final good and included as an investment. After all, the computer is an investment good, and part of its value will represent the value of the software installed on it. If a business or government purchased the software separately to install on a computer, however, it was treated as an intermediate good. The same was true of software a business or the government produced itself. The costs a business incurred in producing software for its own use (so called own-account software) was treated as a business expense similar to any other intermediate good.

Under the new rules, all software expenditures are treated as investment spending. This reflects the fact that software is like other investment goods in that it produces a flow of services that lasts more than one year. In fact, the Bureau of Economic Activity estimates the average life of software is between three and five years. The effects of these new rules will be to raise GDP by the amount of software businesses and government agencies purchase and by the amount of own-account software they produce. These expenditures were not counted as part of GDP when they were viewed as intermediate goods. By treating them as a final good, GDP is increased by the amount spent on them.

How much difference does this make? The bureau estimates that the GDP figures for 1996 will be increased by $115 billion. This is a large number, but it represents a change in GDP of only about 1.5 percent.

The bureau will go back and revise GDP back to 1959 to incorporate this new treatment of software purchases. ●

The Value-Added Approach   A second way to calculate the value of GDP is to study the intermediate goods directly. The production of most items occurs in several stages. Consider the automobile. At one stage in its production, iron ore, coal, and limestone are mined. At a second stage, these raw materials are shipped to a steel mill. A third stage involves a steel company combining these ingredients to make steel. Finally, the steel and other inputs such as rubber and plastics are combined by the auto firm to make a car. The difference in value between what the automaker pays for intermediate goods and what it receives for the finished cars is called the firm's **value added.**

value added = firm's revenue − costs of intermediate goods.

GDP can be measured by calculating the value added at each stage of production.

GDP = sum of value added of all firms.

The Income Approach   The third method used to calculate GDP involves measuring the income generated by selling products, rather than the value of the products themselves. This is known as the **income approach.** Firms have four claims on their revenue. They must pay for labor they have hired, they must pay interest on any funds they have borrowed, they must pay for any intermediate goods they have purchased, and they must pay indirect taxes such as sales taxes to the government. Anything left over represents the firm's income. Some of the firm's income must be set aside to replace equipment worn out

during the production process (called *depreciation,* which we will discuss later), and the rest is the firm's profit.

revenue = wages + interest payments + cost of intermediate inputs + indirect taxes + depreciation + profits.

But we already know that the firm's value added is its revenue minus the cost of intermediate goods. Therefore,

value added = wages + interest payments + indirect taxes + depreciation + profits.

And since GDP is equal to the sum of the value added of all firms, it must also equal the sum of the value of all wage payments, interest payments, indirect taxes, depreciation, and profits for all firms:[3]

GDP = wages + interest payments + indirect taxes + depreciation + profits.

People receive income from wages, from capital, and from profits of the firms they own (or own shares in). And when firms spend to replace old equipment, this represents income for those who produce the new equipment. Thus, the right side of this identity is the total income of all individuals and the government revenue from indirect taxes. This is an extremely important result, one economists use frequently, so it is worth highlighting: *aggregate output equals aggregate income.*

Differences Between Individual Incomes and National Income   The notion of income used to calculate GDP differs slightly from the way individuals commonly perceive income, and it is important to be aware of the distinction.

First, people are likely to include in their view of income any capital gains they earn on assets. *Capital gains* are increases in the value of assets and accordingly do not represent current production (output) in any way. The national income accounts used to calculate GDP, which are designed to focus on the production of goods and services, do not include capital gains.

Second, profits that are retained by a firm are included in national income, but individuals may not perceive these

---

[3]This ignores a few small adjustments such as net income payments from the rest of the world and net subsidies to government enterprises.

retained profits as part of their own income. Again, this is because the GDP accounts measure the value of production, and profits are part of the value of production, whether these profits are actually distributed to the owners of the firm (its shareholders) or retained by the firm.

Comparison of the Final Goods and Income Approach   Earlier we learned how to break down the output of the economy into four categories—consumption, investment, government purchases, and net exports. We break down the income of the economy into three categories: payments to workers, consisting mainly of wages but also including the value of health and retirement benefits; payments to the owners of capital, including profits, interest, and rents; and taxes. Economists refer to the total payments to workers as *employee compensation*. As Table 23.3 shows, the value of GDP is the same whether it is calculated in output or income terms.

That the value of output is equal to the value of income—that GDP measured either way is identical—is no accident. It is a consequence of the circular flow of the economy. What each firm receives from selling its goods must go back somewhere else in the economy, as wages, profits, interest, rents, or taxes. In turn, the income of households flows back either to firms, in the form of consumption goods that households purchase or as saving, which eventually is used by firms to purchase investment goods such as plants and equipment, or to the government, in the form of taxes or newly issued government bonds. Similarly, the money spent by the government must have come from somewhere else in the economy—either from households or firms in the form of taxes, or through borrowing.

Potential GDP

Real GDP is a measure of how much the economy actually produces. But sometimes the economy is capable of producing more than it actually does. Workers may not be fully employed, and some plants and equipment may be operating at less than normal capacity. At other times, the economy may be producing more than would normally be sustainable. Firms may put on extra shifts, increase overtime, and delay maintenance in order to temporarily increase output. Another important macroeconomic measure of real output, **potential GDP,** indicates what the economy would produce if labor were fully employed at normal levels of overtime and plants and machines were used at normal rates of utilization. Real GDP will fall below potential GDP when the economy has above-normal levels of unemployed resources.

In some circumstances, real GDP can exceed potential GDP by a considerable amount. Even when the economy is operating at potential, some unused capacity remains. By fully utilizing this capacity, the economy's real GDP can temporally exceed potential. Individuals may be willing to temporarily put in extra overtime; other workers may take a second job when the labor market is particularly strong. This allows real GDP to be greater than

TABLE 23.3

Two Approaches to U.S. GDP, 2000			
Final Goods	**Billions of $**	**Income**	**Billions of $**
Consumption	6757.3	Employee compensation	5,638.2
Investment	1832.7	Profits, rents, interest, etc.	2,368.1
Government expenditures	1743.7	Indirect taxes	1,257.1
Net exports	−370.7	Depreciation	699.6
Total	**9,963.1**	**Total**	**9,963.1**

SOURCE: http://www.bea.doc.gov/bea/dn1.htm

would occur at more normal levels of utilization and work hours. One example when actual production can greatly exceed the economy's normal potential is when a country mobilizes for war. Figure 23.1 shows how real GDP and potential (real) GDP have increased over the past thirty years. Output does not grow smoothly; the jagged progression in the figure shows the effects of short-term fluctuations around an upward trend. Sometimes these fluctuations represent only a slowdown in real growth; sometimes output actually falls. The dips in real GDP from 1971 to 1973, from 1980 to 1981, and from 1990 to 1991 represent periods when U.S. economic output actually declined. A strong upward fluctuation is called a **boom,** and a downward one is called a **recession.** A severe recession is called a **depression.** The last depression, called the Great Depression because of its length and depth, began in 1929. The economy did not fully recover until World War II. While there is no technical definition of a boom, a recession is generally said to have occurred when real GDP falls for at least two consecutive quarters. (For statistical purposes, a year is divided into quarters, each of which is three months in length.)

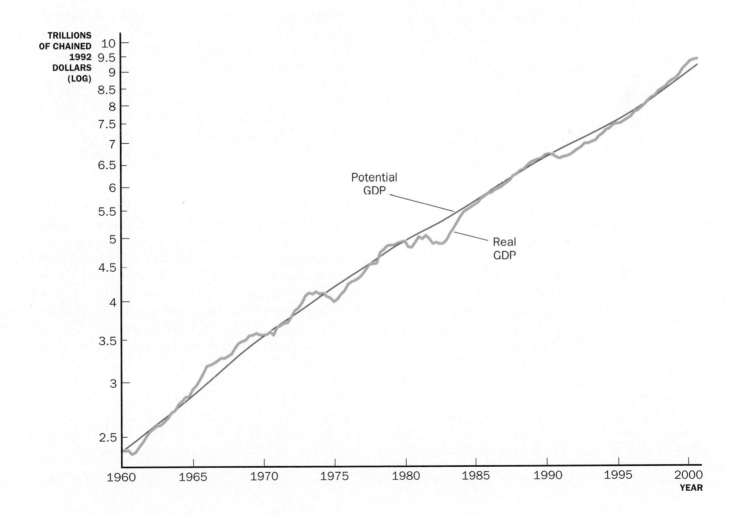

Figure 23.1 *Potential and Real GDP*

Potential GDP measures how much the economy could produce if it used all its resources at a normal level of overtime and capacity utilization. Real GDP shows what the economy actually produces. Notice that both have been growing over time.

SOURCE: Federal Reserve Board.

International Perspective

What Gets Measured in the GDP?

For sound economic reasons, Colombia includes the illegal coca leaf crop in its calculation of GDP.

In the United States, illegal activity is not counted as part of GDP. If we are trying to get a measure of market economic activity, excluding things like the drug trade means that GDP misses one type of output. For the United States, this omission is unlikely to have a major impact on the usefulness of our GDP statistics. But consider the case of a country in which illegal activity may be a major source of income. In this case, failing to count that income as part of GDP may give a misleading picture of the economy.

Columbia provides a case in point. Columbia is a major exporter of illegal drugs. Drugs are grown, processed, and transported. Each of these steps represents economic activity, yet the incomes generated directly by the trade in illegal drugs has been excluded from its GDP.

The Columbian government has begun to add income earned from illegal drug crops to GDP. It is estimated that treating drug crops like legal crops in calculating GDP may add as much as 1 percent to Columbia's GDP. The drug trade involves much more than just the growing of the crops—the processing and transporting of drugs are also huge businesses. But as of now, these parts of the drug trade are not included in Columbia's GDP. Including them would have an even bigger impact on the figures.

While adding even part of the value of drug-related income will raise Columbia's reported GDP, that does not mean the country's income is any higher—it simply means that more of it is being counted in the official statistics. This does highlight an important point, however. Often the exact definition of a statistic changes over time, or the methods used to collect the data change. Variables that have the same name for two different countries may not measure quite the same thing. This is important to keep in mind when making international comparisons of GDP, particularly when comparing economies that are quite different. If a particular type of economic activity, say, bread making, is done through markets in one economy and at home in another, bread consumption as measured in GDP will be higher in the former.

Robert Summers and Alan Heston carried out one of the best attempts to construct consistent international data on GDP. Their data, known as the Penn World Table, are available on the Web at http://pwt.econ.upenn.edu/.

In recessions the economy operates well below its potential. Unemployment is high and a large fraction of machines remain idle. Figure 23.2 shows the percentage of America's industrial capacity that was utilized for the past several decades. The figures vary from slightly more than 70 percent of industrial capacity in a recession to over 90 percent of industrial capacity in a boom. (Because some machines are being repaired and maintained, while others are idle because they are not suited for the economy's current structure, the economy never shows a 100 percent capacity utilization rate.) Low capacity utilization, like unemployment of workers, represents a waste of scarce economic resources.

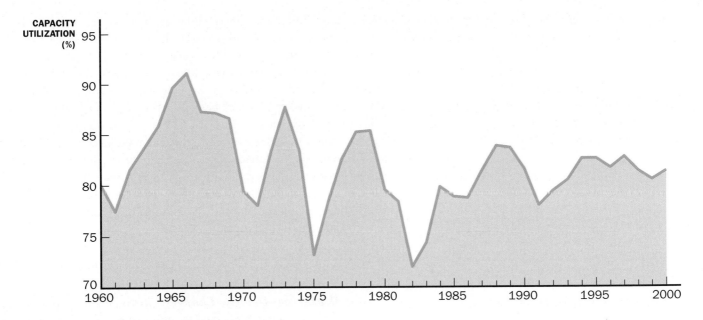

Figure 23.2 *Capacity Utilization*

Capacity utilization measures the fraction of machines and buildings that are actually in use. Notice that the figure fluctuates between about 70 and 90 percent as the economy moves between recessions and booms.

SOURCE: ERP (2001), Table B-54, and Federal Reserve Board.

Alternative Measures of Output

The U.S government has used GDP as its main statistical measure of output since 1991. Before then, **gross national product,** or **GNP,** was used. GNP is a measure of the incomes of residents of a country, including income they receive from abroad (wages, returns on investment, interest payments), but subtracting similar payments made to those abroad. By contrast, GDP ignores income received from or paid abroad. GDP is thus a measure of the goods and services actually produced *within* the country. The profits a Japanese auto manufacturer earns from producing cars in the United States is counted in the U.S. GDP since the value of the cars produced represents part of U.S. output even if the profits are paid to the firm's owners in Japan. And the earnings of IBM from its production in Europe are added to the U.S. GNP since IBM is an American corporation, but the earnings are not included in the U.S. GDP since they represent part of the value of production in Europe, not within the United States.

GDP has long been the standard measure of output used by most European countries because trade had traditionally been far more important than in the United States. As international trade became more important for the United States, it was natural for the country to switch from using GNP to using GDP. Besides, the switch made comparisons with the performance of other countries easier. The difference between GDP and GNP is small for the United States. In 2000, for example, GDP was $9,963.1 billion while GNP was $9,958.7 billion.

The treatment of machines and other capital goods (buildings) is another problem in measuring national output. As machines are used to produce output, they wear out. Worn-out machines are a cost of production that should be balanced against total output.

As an example, consider a firm that has a machine worth $1,000. It uses that machine, with $600 of labor, to produce $2,000 worth of output. Furthermore, assume that at the end of the year, the machine is completely worn out. The firm then has a *net* output of $400: $2,000 minus the labor costs *and* minus the value of the machine that has worn out.

The reduction in the value of the machines is called the machine's **depreciation.** Since machines wear out at all sorts of different rates, accounting for how much the machines in the economy have depreciated is an extremely difficult problem. The GDP figures take the easy road and make no allowance for depreciation. The term *gross* in "gross domestic product" should serve as a reminder that the statistic covers all production. Economists sometimes use a separate measure that includes the effects of depreciation, called **net domestic product,** or **NDP,** which subtracts an estimate of the value of depreciation from GDP:

$$NDP = GDP - depreciation.$$

The problem is that economists have little confidence in the estimates of depreciation. For this reason, they usually use the GDP figures as the measure of the economy's output. Since GDP, NDP, and GNP go up and down together, for most purposes it does not much matter which one we use as long as we are consistent.

WRAP-UP

Alternative Approaches to Measuring National Output

Measuring output of final goods
    Value of output:

        consumption + investment + government purchases + net exports

        Sum of value added in each stage of production

Measuring income
    employee compensation + profits, interest, rents + indirect taxes

Output = income

Problems in Measuring Output

In 1999, policymakers faced a growing controversy over whether the United States was entering a new era of rapid economic growth fueled by new information technologies. Growth, which had been markedly slower from 1973 to 1995 than it had been in the 1950s and 1960s, accelerated

after 1996. Productivity—how much an average worker produces per hour—had grown by about 1 percent per year from the mid-1970s until 1995. Then, after 1996 it began growing at over 2 percent per year. Many economists argued that the earlier period of slow growth might only be a statistical artifact, arising from well-known measurement problems. The rapid growth in recent years raises new issues: Can we attribute this increased growth to investment in computers and other new technologies? Does it represent a temporary boost that will shortly disappear? Or is the economy being fundamentally altered by new technologies in ways that will require us to rethink how we measure the economy's output?

Changes in the economy have made keeping track of output increasingly difficult. Yet the best-known measurement problems may actually understate the true growth in output

Measuring Quality Changes With many products, such as computers, quality improvements occur every year. GDP statisticians try to make adjustments for changes in quality. For example, when antipollution devices were first required in automobiles in the early 1970s, the price of cars rose. The national income accountants decided that the increased cost reflected a quality improvement and effectively added to real output; consumers were buying a better car. But in some sectors, such as the financial and health sectors and the computer industry, the adjustments may be inadequate. The real growth of GDP is accordingly understated, and because these sectors are expanding rapidly, the magnitude of the understatement may be larger today than it was thirty years ago.

Measuring Service Output Defining and measuring output in the service sector of the economy is increasingly complex and difficult. How should the value of automatic teller machines available twenty-four hours a day be measured? And what about services that are not sold, such as many government-produced services, or at least not sold directly? Imagine that state government employees become more efficient and are able to process car registrations faster. The state might be able to hire fewer workers to do the same job. But GDP statistics measure government output of car registrations by the costs of producing them, so if the state reduces its costs, measured GDP might go down, even though actual output—the number of car registrations in this case—is unchanged. The conventional GDP measure would understate the real growth of the economy.

Measuring Nonmarket Goods   Nonmarket goods and services, like housework done by family members, present similar problems. The statistics underestimate the true level of production in the economy because they ignore such activity. For example, if one spouse stays at home and cooks, the value of this production would not be counted in GDP because it does not represent a market activity. However, if that spouse leaves home to take a job and hires someone else to do the cleaning and cooking, then the production of both the spouse and the housekeeper would be measured in GDP.

If, in this way, more and more previously nonmarketed goods and services become part of the economy's measured output, then measured growth will overstate the actual growth in output.

While GDP is designed primarily to measure market economic activity, there are two important exceptions. GDP does include a measure of the value of owner-occupied housing and it includes the value of homegrown food consumed by farm families. In general though, nonmarket activity is not included since there are no prices that can be used to value the output.

Conclusions   Do these measurement problems mean that GDP is not a good measure of the economy's output? GDP provides our best estimate of the level of production for markets. And market activity is closely related to employment, another macroeconomic variable of interest. But changes in the nature of production, from growth in the underground economy to new technological innovations, can affect the ability of GDP to truly provide a good picture of the economy's performance.

Measuring the Standard of Living

GDP tells us something about the overall level of economic activity in a nation, the goods and services produced for the market. But it is only part of the measure of a society's overall well-being. Literacy rates (the percentage of the population that can read or write), infant mortality rates (the fraction of infants that die), and life expectancy are social indicators that are often employed to measure a nation's standard of living. Real GDP is not designed to measure these other important components of a nation's living standard. But at the same time, there is a strong connection between high levels of real GDP per capita and high levels of literacy, health, and

environmental quality. People in countries that are rich as measured by real GDP per capita are able to enjoy higher levels of health, life expectancy, education, clean water, and clean air than are people in poor countries.

A Green GDP   The national income accounts provide a measure of how much of the nation's plant and equipment depreciated during the year. It does not account for the depletion of natural resources or the deterioration in the environment that producing GDP may cause. Harvesting a hardwood forest may increase a country's GDP, but it decreases the country's assets. Hence, the output is not sustainable. A **green GDP** is a measure that would subtract the decrease in the natural resource base from the conventional GDP. Such a measure would better indicate whether an economic activity is adding to the nation's wealth or subtracting from it by using up natural resources. A measure of living standards, unlike a measure of goods and services produced for the marketplace, should include changes in the quality of the environment, as well as changes in such factors as health status and crime.

Green GDP takes account of exhausted natural resources, such as this clear-cut section of a National Forest.

Thinking Like an Economist

Information and the National Income and Product Accounts

Newspapers and TV news shows report the latest information about the economy. If new data show the economy slowing down or unemployment rising, policymakers face tough questions about whether there should be a change in macroeconomic policies. The stock market may boom or crash depending on whether the latest information leads people to think the Federal Reserve will lower or raise interest rates. The National Income and Product Accounts provide much of the basic information we need to monitor the health of the economy.

It has not always been this way. Before the birth of macroeconomics in the 1930s, countries did not have the type of data on their economy that we take for granted today. There had been earlier attempts to estimate national income in various countries, but these were carried out mainly by individual researchers or private organizations and not by governments themselves or on a regular basis. According to John Kendrick, Sir William Petty compiled the first estimates of national income for England in 1665. In the United States, George Tucker was the first to develop estimates of income and wealth, both by states and by industry. Tucker's estimates were published in 1843.

The 1930s saw a major growth in national accounting systems. By 1939, nine countries had instituted the regular provision of national income estimates. Part of this growth arose from the Great Depression and the need to obtain economic information for policy discussions that would allow the causes of the depression to be assessed. For example, a Senate hearing into the causes of the depression noted that U.S. estimates produced by the private National Bureau of Economic Research were available only after long delays. As a result, the Senate passed a resolution that called for the Department of Commerce to prepare national income estimates for 1929 to 1931. These estimates were then continued annually.

The 1930s also saw the spread of national income accounting because of the influence of John Maynard Keynes's *General Theory*. National expenditures—consumption, investment, and government purchases—played a central role in Keynes's theory. (We will examine their role in Part Seven, particularly Chapters 28 and 29.) Economists who wanted to test his theory and to develop policy recommendations needed information on these critical variables. The development of income accounts was furthered by the needs of governments during World War II to have information on the productive activity of the economy.

Many of the early advances in national income accounting took place in Great Britain. For example, in 1939 the British government charged two young economists, Richard Stone and James Meade, to complete a set of income and expenditure estimates for Great Britain.

Besides providing the information governments need to design macroeconomic policies and to assess the state of the economy, the national income accounts provide the data that economists use to test alternative theories of macroeconomics. In recognition of the fundamental contribution these accounts have played in improving our knowledge of both industrialized and developing economies, Sir Richard Stone received the Nobel Prize in economics in 1984. The Swedish Academy of Sciences cited Stone "for having made fundamental contributions to the development of systems of national accounts and hence greatly improved the basis for empirical economic analysis." (Earlier, in 1977, James Meade had won the Nobel Prize for his work on international trade and capital movements.)

SOURCE: John W. Kendrick, *Economic Accounts and Their Uses* (New York: McGraw-Hill, 1972).

Constructing a measure of a green GDP is difficult. Contrast the problem of measuring the value of auto production with the problem of measuring the value of the decline in the California sea otter population. In the former case, we can collect statistics on the number of cars produced and use the prices we observe in the marketplace to obtain a measure of the value of car production. While we may be able to measure the drop in the otter population, how do we value this decline? There is no market price that we can use. Unless we can use a common measure (say, dollars) to place a value on the change in the otter population, the change in old growth forests, the change in air quality, and the production of cars, we cannot add them up to obtain an overall measure of a green GDP. So developing an environmental measure of the economy's production is inherently difficult.

An alternative, proposed by the European Union's statistical office, Eurostat, simply reports changes in quantity. The change in the *number* of otters would be reported, as would the change in the *tons* of each component of air pollution. Unfortunately, if some measures improve and others worsen, how do we know whether things have improved or worsened overall? Unless the different changes can be combined, there is no way to really measure the change in the overall quality of the environment.

The United Nations System of Environmental and Economic Accounting combines traditional GDP measures with "satellite accounts" that focus on specific aspects of the environment and vary the method of accounting to reflect the types of information available. The United States recently used this approach to produce prototype accounts that incorporate environmental factors.

Unemployment

While growth is the central economic goal, when the economy goes into a downturn, unemployment becomes a source of immediate concern. To an economist, unemployment represents an underutilization of resources. People who are willing and able to work at current market wages are not being productively employed. To the unemployed individuals and their families, unemployment represents an economic hardship and changes in their way of life. If a person is unemployed for a long time, he will be unable to meet his current expenses—like utilities and rent—and will have to move to cheaper housing and reduce other aspects of his standard of living.

Unemployment not only costs individuals their paychecks but also can deal a powerful blow to their self-respect. Unemployed workers in today's urban America cannot fall back on farming or living off the land as they might have done in colonial times. Instead, they and their families may be forced to choose between poverty and the bitter taste of government or private charity. Many of these families break up under the strain.

Unemployment presents different problems for each age group of workers. For the young, having a job is necessary for developing job skills, whether they are technical skills or such basic work prerequisites as punctuality and responsibility. Persistent unemployment for them not only wastes valuable human resources today but also reduces the future productivity of the labor force. Such individuals fail to obtain critical on-the-job training that improves their skills, and to develop work habits that improve their on-the-job productivity. Furthermore, young people who remain unemployed for an extended period are especially prone to becoming alienated from society and turning to antisocial activities such as crime and drug abuse.

For the middle-aged or elderly worker, losing a job poses different problems. Despite federal and state prohibitions against age discrimination, employers are often hesitant to hire older workers. They may fear older workers are more likely than younger people to become sick or disabled. They may worry about being able to "teach old dogs new tricks." If older workers are unemployed for long periods of time, they may lose some of their skills. Even if the unemployed older worker succeeds in getting a job, these jobs often entail reduced wages and lower status than previous jobs and may make less than full use of the worker's skills. The toll of such changes is a heavy burden of stress on the dislocated workers and their families.

In addition to these personal losses, unemployment poses heavy costs for communities. If people in a town are thrown out of work—say, because a big employer closes down the facility or decides to move—everyone else in town is likely to suffer as well, since there is less income circulating to buy everything from cars and houses to gasoline and groceries. As more unemployment results in fewer people paying local taxes, the quality of schools, libraries, parks, and police can be threatened.

Unemployment also may reinforce racial divisions in a society as a whole. The rate of unemployment for African-Americans is generally more than twice that for whites. During the 1980s and early 1990s, among African-Americans between the ages of sixteen and nineteen who were just beginning to look for work, unemployment averaged 37 percent, nearly reaching 50 percent in the recession years of 1982 and 1983. By 2000, with overall unemployment at its lowest level in thirty years, all groups were benefiting from the strong labor market—unemployment for African-Americans was lower than at any time since separate statistics on black unemployment began being reported in 1971.

The Magnitude of the Problem

Living in the midst of the approximately 130 million people who get up and go to work every morning is a fluctuating group of several million healthy people who do not. During the 1991 recession, 8.5 million people were out of work, and one fourth of those people were jobless for fifteen weeks or more. In contrast, the number of unemployed dropped below 6 million in 1999, even though the total population was much larger than it had been in 1991. From the standpoint of the economy as a whole, the potential production of workers who cannot find jobs is a major loss. One calculation puts the loss in output from the high unemployment of the early 1980s at between $122 billion and $320 billion a year, for a per capita loss of between $500 and $1,300.[4] In other words, using the latter number, every man, woman, and child in the United States would have had (on average) an additional $1,300 to spend if the unemployed workers had been gainfully employed.

To calculate the loss from an increase in unemployment during a recession, we look at the output that could have been produced if those workers had remained employed. This lost output represents the *opportunity cost* of the higher unemployment. As we learned in Chapter 2, opportunity cost is an important concept in economics.

Unemployment Statistics

In the United States, unemployment data are collected by the Department of Labor, which surveys a representative mix of households every month. The survey takers ask each household whether a member of the household is currently employed, and if not, whether that member is currently seeking employment. The *labor force* is the total number of people employed or actively seeking employment. The **unemployment rate** is the ratio of the number seeking employment to the total labor force. If there are 127 million workers employed and 6 million say they are looking for a job but cannot find one, then the total labor force is 133 million, and the

$$\text{unemployment rate} = \frac{\text{number unemployed}}{\text{labor force}}$$

$$= \frac{\text{number unemployed}}{\text{number employed} + \text{number unemployed}}$$

$$= \frac{6 \text{ million}}{127 \text{ million} + 6 \text{ million}} = 4.5 \text{ percent.}$$

The unemployment rate does not include individuals who are not working but who also are not actively seeking a job. Such individuals are not counted as part of the labor force.

Figure 23.3 plots the unemployment rate for the United States since 1960. The figure illustrates two facts. First, unemployment is persistent; it has averaged just over 6 percent since 1960, and the lowest it has ever been was 3.5 percent (in 1969). Second, the level of unemployment can fluctuate dramatically. By the end of the 1990s, unemployment in the United States had fallen to levels not seen in thirty years, but as recently as 1983, the unemployment rate was nearly 10 percent. Fluctuations in unemployment were even more pronounced in earlier periods. In the worst days of the Great Depression of the 1930s, over one fourth of the U.S. labor force was unemployed. The unemployment rate among those who worked in manufacturing was even higher—at one point, one out of three workers in manufacturing had lost their jobs.

In recent years, unemployment in other countries often was worse than in the United States (Figure 23.4). In contrast to the 1960s, when U.S. unemployment rates exceeded those in other major industrialized economies, European unemployment rates rose dramatically during the 1980s and now exceed the rate in the United States. Japan historically has had very low levels of unemployment, but in 1999 the unemployment rate in Japan exceeded that of the United States for the first time. Unemployment in many developing countries is over 20 percent.

One problem with the unemployment measure is that, especially in a prolonged downturn, many individuals are *discouraged* from even looking for a job. Because they are not actively seeking employment, the statistics will not count them as unemployed and thus underestimate the number who would choose to work if a job were available. The fraction of the working-age population that is employed or seeking employment is called the **labor force participation rate.** Because of discouraged workers, the labor force participation rate tends to decline in recessions and rise in booms.

When the unemployment rate increases by more than a trivial amount, it is safe to conclude that the economy has slowed down. Some individuals have been laid off and have not found new jobs, and firms may have slowed down the pace at which they hire new workers.

---

[4]A. Blinder, *Hard Heads, Soft Hearts* (Reading, Mass.: Addison-Wesley, 1987).

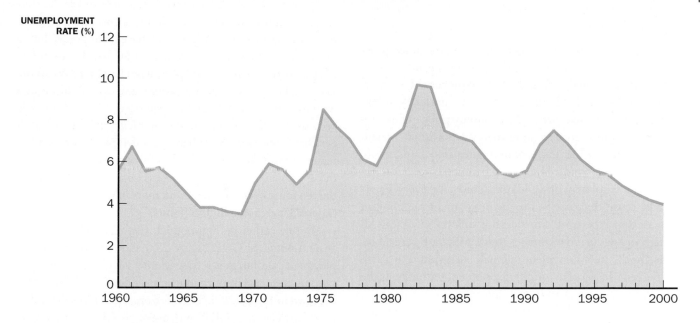

Figure 23.3 *Overall U.S. Unemployment Rate*

Unemployment in the United States rises during recessions and falls during booms. Between 1960 and 1999, it averaged about 6 percent. It reached a low of 3.5 percent in 1969 and a high of 9.7 percent in 1982.

SOURCE: *ERP* (2001), Table B-42.

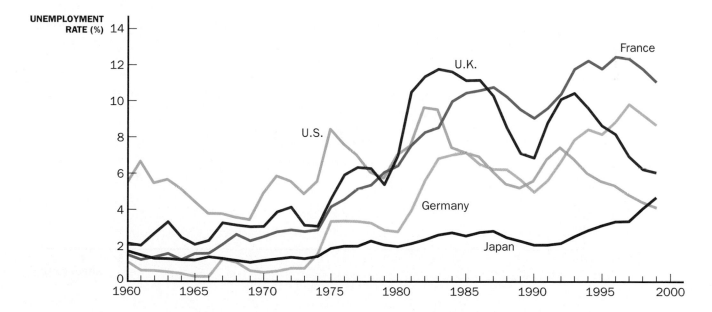

Figure 23.4 *Comparisons of International Unemployment*

In some developed countries, the unemployment rate has been higher than in the United States in recent years. Japan's unemployment averages much less than that in other countries.

SOURCE: *ERP* (2001), Table B-109.

Okun's Law

The connection between fluctuations in the unemployment rate and fluctuations in the economy's production is summarized by *Okun's law*. Arthur Okun served as chairman of the Council of Economic Advisors under President Johnson. He showed that as the economy pulls out of a recession, output increases more than proportionately with employment. And as the economy goes into a recession, output decreases more than proportionately with the reduction in employment. In Okun's study, for every 1 percentage point decrease in the unemployment rate, output increased by 3 percent. This result is called *Okun's law,* although today, current estimates predict that a 1 percent increase in the unemployment rate will correspond to a 2 to 2.5 percent decrease in output (a 2 percent reduction is the rule of thumb used elsewhere in this text).

This was a remarkable finding, for it seemed to run contrary to one of the basic principles of economics, the law of diminishing returns, which would have predicted that a 1 percentage point decrease in the unemployment rate would have less than a proportionate effect on output. The explana-

tion for Okun's law, however, is simple. Firms find it costly to hire and train workers. When they have a temporary lull in demand, they may not lay workers off for fear that once laid off, the workers will seek employment elsewhere. When demand picks up again, the firm would have to incur hiring and training costs as it rebuilds its workforce. Thus, firms will keep workers on the job but may not fully utilize them. This is called *labor hoarding*. Therefore, unemployment rises less than proportionately with the decline in production. Many of those who are employed in a recession are partially idle. As the economy heats up, they work more fully and thus the unexpected increase in output occurs.

We saw earlier, in Figure 23.1, that real GDP fluctuates around potential GDP. Figure 23.3 showed that the unemployment rate fluctuates too. Okun's law links the fluctuations in these two important macroeconomic variables. This is shown in Figure 23.5. The horizontal axis plots the difference between real GDP and potential GDP from Figure 23.1 (expressed in percentages); this is called the **output gap.** On the vertical axis is the unemployment rate from Figure 23.3. Each point represents the average value of the unemployment rate and the output gap for a single year.

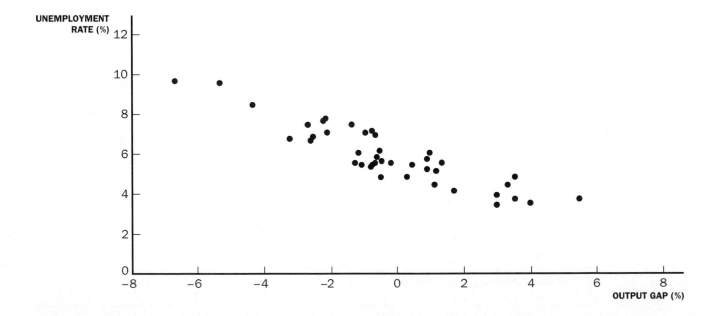

Figure 23.5   *Okun's Law: 1960–2000*

Okun's law related fluctuations in output relative to potential and fluctuations in the unemployment rate. For every 1 percentage point change in the unemployment rate, output changes approximately 2 percent relative to potential.

SOURCE: Unemployment: *ERP* (2001), Table B-42; output gap data from Figure 23.1.

When the output gap is zero, real GDP is equal to potential GDP. Figure 23.5 shows that during 1960–2000 (the period shown), the unemployment rate in the United States was usually around 6 percent when the output gap was zero. If real GDP falls below potential GDP, the output gap becomes negative and the unemployment rate rises above 6 percent. An output gap of –4 percent is associated with an unemployment rate of about 8 percent—the two-to-one ratio of Okun's law.

In Part Three of this volume, we will examine explanations for output fluctuations. It is important to remember, though, that fluctuations in real GDP are closely related to fluctuations in unemployment. Okun's law gives us a simple way to translate output fluctuations into their implications for the unemployment rate.

Forms of Unemployment

Even when output is equal to potential, unemployment is not zero. Figure 23.5 showed that unemployment typically has been around 6 percent when output equals potential. To understand why it has averaged 6 percent in the United States over the past forty years and why it fluctuates, economists distinguish between four different kinds of unemployment: seasonal, frictional, structural, and cyclical.

Right before Christmas, there is a huge demand for retail sales people to work in department stores and shopping malls across the country. In many parts of the country, construction slows down in the winter because of the climate. For the same reason, tourism often increases in the summer, as do the number of jobs that cater to tourists. The supply of labor also increases in the summer, as high school and college students enter the labor force on a temporary basis. Unemployment that varies predictably with the seasons is called **seasonal unemployment.** Since these movements in employment and unemployment reflect normal seasonal patterns, the unemployment rate reported on the news is adjusted according to the average amount of seasonal unemployment. These adjustments are called *seasonal adjustments*. Thus, if on average the unadjusted unemployment rate is normally .4 percent higher in the summer than at other times during the year, the seasonal-adjusted unemployment rate for July will be the measured unemployment rate minus .4 percent.

While workers in construction, agriculture, and tourism regularly face seasonal unemployment, other workers become unemployed as a part of a normal transition from one job to another. For example, if you graduate from college, you may spend a month looking for a job before finding one. During that month, you are counted as unemployed. This kind of unemployment is referred to as **frictional unemployment.** If people could move from one job to another instantaneously, there would be no frictional unemployment. In a dynamic economy such as in the United States, with some industries growing and others declining, there will always be movements from one job to another, and hence there will always be some frictional unemployment. Not all frictional unemployment represents wasted resources—time spent searching for a new job can be a valuable use of time.

Most individual bouts of unemployment are short-lived; the average person who loses a job is out of work for only about three months. However, about 10 percent of the jobless are unemployed for more than six months. This kind of long-term unemployment often results from structural factors in the economy and is called **structural unemployment.** Substantial structural unemployment is found quite often side by side with job vacancies, because the unemployed lack the skills required for the newly created jobs. For example, there may be vacancies for computer programmers while construction workers are unemployed. By the same token, there may be job shortages in parts of the economy that are expanding rapidly (as in the Sunbelt and Silicon Valley during the 1990s) and unemployment in areas that are suffering decline (as in Michigan during the period of a decline in the demand for U.S. cars).

Seasonal, frictional, and structural unemployment occur even when the economy is operating at its potential level of output. There is a fourth type of unemployment, however, that is associated with economic fluctuations when the economy falls below potential.

Unemployment that increases when the economy slows down and decreases when the economy goes into a boom is

WRAP-UP

Forms of Unemployment

Seasonal
Frictional
Structural
Cyclical

called **cyclical unemployment** and is one of the fundamental concerns of macroeconomics. Government policymakers are particularly interested in reducing both the frequency and the magnitude of this kind of unemployment, by reducing the frequency and magnitudes of recessions that give rise to it. Government also seeks to reduce its impact by providing unemployment compensation for those temporarily thrown out of work.

Inflation

In the 1920s, the years of silent pictures, a movie ticket cost a nickel. By the late 1940s, in the heyday of Hollywood, the price was up to $.50. By the 1960s, the price of a movie was $2.00, and now it is over $8.00. This steady rise is no anomaly. Most other goods undergo similar price increases over time. This increase in the general level of prices is called **inflation.** While unemployment tends to be concentrated in certain groups within the population, inflation affects everyone. Thus, it is not surprising that when inflation becomes high, it almost always rises to the top of the political agenda.

It is not inflation if the price of only one good goes up. It *is* inflation if the prices of *most* goods go up. The *inflation rate* is the rate at which the *general level* of prices increases. When inflation is positive—that is, the average price level is rising—a dollar buys less and less over time. Or, expressing it another way, it takes more and more dollars to purchase the same bundle of goods and service.

Measuring Inflation

If the prices of all goods and services rose by the same proportion, say, 5 percent, over a period of a year, then measuring inflation would be easy: the rate of inflation that year would be 5 percent. The difficulties arise from the fact that the prices of different goods rise at different rates, and the prices of some goods even decline. For example, since the period 1982–1984, which the United States uses as a base reference period, the prices of fruits and vegetables have risen by 212 percent, the price of medical care by 269 percent, and the price of housing by 175 percent, while the price of personal computers has fallen by 66 percent in just the last three years. To determine the change in the overall price level, economists calculate the *average* percentage increase in prices. But since some goods loom much larger in the typical

consumer's budget than others, this calculation must reflect the relative purchases of different goods. A change in the price of housing, for example, is much more important than a change in the price of pencils. If the price of pencils goes down by 5 percent but the price of housing goes up 5 percent, the overall measure of the price level should go up.

Economists have a straightforward way of reflecting the differing importance of different goods. They ask, what would it cost consumers to purchase the same bundle of goods this year that they bought last year? If, for example, it cost $22,000 in the year 2000 to buy what it cost consumers $20,000 to purchase in 1999, we say that prices, *on average*, rose by 10 percent. Such results are frequently expressed in the form of a *price index*, which, for ease of comparison, measures the price level in any given year relative to a common base year.

The price index for the base year is, by definition, set equal to 100. The price index for any other year is calculated by taking the ratio of the price level in that year to the price level in the base year and multiplying it by 100. For example, if 1999 is our base year and we want to know the price index for 2000, we first calculate the ratio of the cost of a certain bundle of goods in 2000 ($22,000) to the cost of the same bundle of goods in 1999 ($20,000), which is 1.1. The price index in 2000 is therefore $1.1 \times 100 = 110$. The index 110, using 1999 as a base, indicates that prices are 10 percent higher, on average, in 2000 than in 1999.

There are several different price indexes, each using a different bundle of goods. To track the movement of prices that are important to American households, the government collects price data on the bundle of goods that represent how the average household spends its income. This index is called the **consumer price index,** or **CPI.** To determine this bundle, the government, through the Bureau of Labor Statistics of the Department of Commerce, conducts a Consumer Expenditure Survey, which is updated once a decade or so. Currently the CPI is based on an expenditure survey conducted over the period 1993–1995.

To see how a price index like the CPI is constructed, we can calculate one for Bob, who spends all his income on rent, Big Macs, and CDs. Let's suppose his total expenditures during 1999 were $1,500 each month, of which $1,000 went for rent, $200 for 100 Big Macs (which cost $2 each), and $300 on 30 CDs (which cost $10 each). In 2000, his rent increases to $1,200, Big Macs go up in price to $2.25, while the price of a CD falls to $9. What has happened to Bob's price index? We want to know how much it costs, in year 2000, to

Internet Connection

Improving Our Measure of the CPI

The Bureau of Labor Statistics undertook a major revision of the consumer price index in 1998. Details of the changes can be found at http://stats.bls.gov/cpi1998.htm.

buy the same basket of goods Bob purchased in 1999. In 1999, these goods cost $1,500. In 2000, they cost $1,695: $1,200 for rent, $225 for 100 Big Macs, and $270 for 30 CDs. Bob's cost of living has increased. Setting the value of the index equal to 100 in the base year of 1999, Bob's price index in 2000 will equal $100 \times 1,695/1,500 = 113$.

The inflation rate is the percentage change in the price index. So if we look at Bob's price index, it rose from 100 to 113 between 1999 and 2000, an increase of 13 percent.

Inflation as measured by his price index was 13 percent in 2000. Now let's look at the actual CPI for the United States. The CPI in 1996 was 156.9, meaning the general level of consumer prices was 56.9 percent higher than it had been in the base years of 1982–1984. In 1997, the index rose to 160.5. The inflation rate in 1997 was the percentage change in the CPI from 1996 to 1997, or $100 \times (160.5 - 156.9)/156.9 = 2.29$ percent. In 1998 the CPI rose to 163, so the inflation rate for 1998 was $100 \times (163 - 160.5)/160.5 = 1.56$ percent. The CPI was 166.6 in 1999, so the inflation rate in that year was 2.21 percent.

Encapsulating the movements of masses of prices into a single index provides an easy way to look at price trends over time. The advantages of an index is that once there is an index number for a given year, we can compare it with any other year. The CPI for 1973 was 44, and for 1998 it was 163. Between those years, the index rose by 119, so the increase was

$$100 \times 119/44 = 270 \text{ percent.}$$

On average, prices rose 270 percent from 1973 to 1998. Figure 23.6 shows the CPI since 1913.

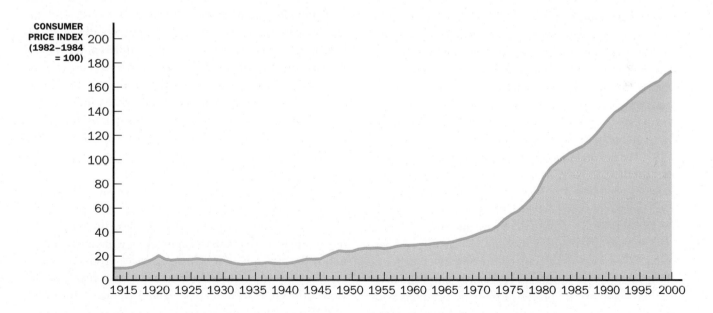

Figure 23.6 *The Consumer Price Index for 1913–2000*

Consumer prices have risen significantly since the early years of the twentieth century, with most of the increases occurring since 1970.

SOURCE: Bureau of Labor Statistics.

CASE IN POINT

The Price Index Makes a Difference

Price indexes increasingly have come to play an important role in recent economic debates. The Social Security benefits of the elderly increase with the cost of living index (the CPI), and tax brackets and tax exemptions also change with the index. If the index overstates the increases in the cost of living, the real benefits (purchasing power) of the elderly increase, and real inflation-adjusted tax revenues decrease. Both distortions increase the budget deficits of the government—the first by increasing outlays, the second by reducing the receipts of government.

By early 1994, it had become apparent that the price index the federal government used for adjusting both benefits and tax brackets was seriously flawed—overstating the rate of inflation by between .5 and 1.5 percent a year. The government made several changes to partly correct the errors in the index.

The upward bias stems from three problems. The first is the "fixed basket problem." The CPI is calculated by comparing how much it costs to purchase a particular market basket of goods that represents an average consumer's expenditure pattern. But expenditure patterns change steadily over time, while the market basket is revised only infrequently. For instance, in February 1998, the market basket was revised; it is now based on spending patterns in 1993–1995; previously it was based on 1982–1984 expenditure patterns. As people buy more of the goods that have become relatively less expensive (such as computers) and less of the goods that have become relatively more expensive, the index increasingly overweights goods whose prices have increased the most.

The second major problem is "quality adjustment." New products, which can do new and better things than older products, constantly enter the market. To compare the prices of the new products with the old, some quality adjustment must be made. If the price goes up by 10 percent but the product lasts longer and works better than the old one, in a real sense the price increase is less than 10 percent and may even represent a price reduction. Sometimes, the quality adjustments are easy; one machine can do what two machines did before. But usually the comparisons are difficult. If we measure the quality of computers by calculations per second, memory, and disk storage, the rate of decrease in computer prices is phenomenal. But even this does not fully reflect the quality improvements. We can do things with the computer now that were unimaginable twenty-five years ago at any price. And how do we treat a new drug that cures a previously incurable disease? The Bureau of Labor Statistics tries to make adjustments for quality. But the consensus is that these adjustments are imperfect and result in an overestimate in the inflation rate of anywhere between a few tenths of a percentage point to more than 1 percent.

The third problem is technical, having to do with the way the data are collected and the details of the calculations.

Many economists believe that the recent revisions will not fully eliminate the CPI bias. They argue that as a result, Social Security and taxes should be indexed to the CPI rate of inflation minus 1 or .5 percent. ●

Alternative Measures of Inflation The CPI provides one measure of inflation, based on what the average consumer pays. Other price indexes can be calculated using different market baskets. A different measure of prices is the **producer price index,** which measures the average level of prices of goods sold by producers. This index is useful because it gives us an idea of what will happen to consumer prices in the near future. Usually, if producers are receiving higher prices from their sales to wholesalers, eventually retailers will have to charge higher prices. This will be reflected in a higher CPI.

Earlier in this chapter we observed that real GDP is nominal GDP adjusted for the price level. The price index we used for calculating real GDP is called the *GDP deflator.* It represents a comparison between what it would cost to buy the total mix of goods and services produced within the country today and what it cost in a base year. In other words, the GDP deflator is a weighted average of the prices of different goods and services, where the weights represent the importance of the goods and services in GDP.

The goods and services whose prices go into the GDP deflator are different from those that go into the CPI. For example, households do not purchase Boeing 747s, so their price is not included in calculating the CPI, but the United

States produces these planes, so their price is included when we calculate the GDP deflator. Households purchase foreign goods, so their prices are factored into the CPI, but they are not included in the GDP deflator since GDP measures only production within the country's borders. Because of these differences we will obtain slightly different measures of inflation, depending on which price index we use.

Internet Connection

The Inflation Calculator

The Bureau of Labor Statistics has a handy inflation calculator that allows you to find out how much it costs today to purchase goods that cost $100 in some earlier year. For example, it takes $731 today to purchase goods you could have bought for $100 in 1949. Try it out at http://www.bls.gov/cpihome.htm.

The American Experience with Inflation

As we have learned, the inflation rate is the percentage increase in the price level from one year to the next. Figure 23.7 shows the inflation rate for the United States during the past century. Three interesting features stand out.

First, prices were relatively stable for much of the century, with the inflation rate under 5 percent except in three periods: around World War I, around World War II, and during the period 1973–1981. Indeed, from the start of the twentieth century until the early 1960s, the average inflation rate was only about 1 percent per year.

Second, prices can actually fall as well as rise. During the recession that followed World War I, prices fell by more than 15 percent, and during the Great Depression of the 1930s they fell by more than 30 percent. In fact, at the end of the nineteenth century, the concern was **deflation,** which is a steady *decline* in the price level. Borrowers at that time who were in debt and had not anticipated the fall in prices found that the dollars they had to pay back were worth far more than the dollars they had borrowed. They were as upset about this as investors (lenders) are when

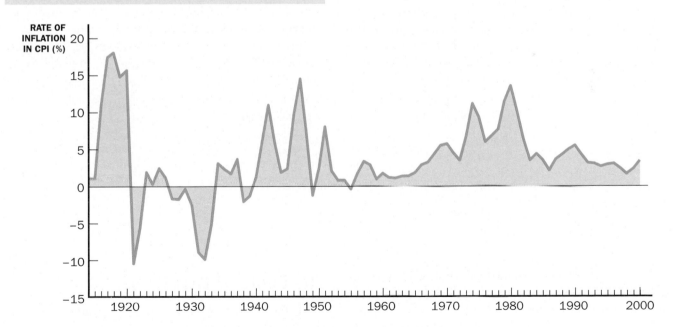

Figure 23.7 *The Inflation Rate*

The inflation rate is the percentage increase in the price level in a given year. Notice that inflation was low through most of the early part of the century, although it was high during both World Wars I and II. Inflation rose sharply in the 1970s, and then fell during the 1980s. It remained relatively low in the 1990s.

e-Insight

Measuring the Price and Quantity of Software

Measuring prices might seem easy—just go out to stores (or log on to e-commerce sites) and record the prices. Unfortunately, it is not that simple. A price index needs to measure how the price of an individual good or service changes over time, and this process is complicated because the quality of the good or service also can change over time. A car with air bags may cost more than a car without air bags, but that is partially because the two cars are not identical. In the case of something like air bags, the auto firm's cost of adding air bags can be used to estimate how much of price change is due to quality improvements (the addition of the air bags) and how much represents a change in the price of a car. Adjusting for quality changes is a particularly significant problem with many of the goods and services associated with the new economy, information technologies, and e-commerce.

Software provides an interesting case in point. Anyone who has used software for a number of years knows that today's programs have been improved in countless ways over the programs of the past. Word-processing software purchased for $100 today has many more features than a word-processing program purchased for $350 in 1985. A price index for software has to correct for these changes in quality.

The Bureau of Economic Analysis at the Department of Commerce tries to adjust for quality changes when it calculates its price index for software, but it does so only for prepackaged software, the type you might buy at the campus bookstore. This is only one type of software though. Many businesses develop specialized software for their own uses (called business own-account software), and the bureau bases the price index for this class of software on the cost of producing it. So if it costs the same to write a program today as it did ten years ago, the bureau assumes the programs are of equal quality. But this is unlikely—a programmer today can write in one hour a program that does much more than was possible ten years ago. Finally, the price of a third class of software—called custom software—is based on an average of the prices for business own-account software and prepackaged software. The price of prepackaged software gets a weight of 25 percent, with business own-account software prices receiving a weight of 75 percent. As with business own-account software, this method is likely to underestimate the quality improvements in custom software, and therefore overestimate the price index for constant-quality software. The Bureau of Economic Analysis treats software prices the way it does because, unfortunately, the detailed information needed to develop better measures of software prices and changes in the quality of software is not available.

SOURCE: Dale W. Jorgenson and Kevin J. Stiroh, "Raising the Speed Limit: U.S. Economic Growth in the Information Age," *Brookings Papers on Economic Activity*, 1 (2000): 61–211.

---

inflation makes the value of the dollars they get back from an investment or loan worth less than the value of the dollars they originally put in.

Finally, while prices have been stable over some periods and have fallen during others, there also have been periods of high inflation, when prices have increased rapidly. The most notable recent episode was in the late 1970s and early 1980s. In 1980 alone, consumer prices rose by more than 13 percent.

The Costs of Inflation

While the costs of unemployment are apparent—not only is there a loss in output, but also the misery of those who cannot secure gainful employment is palpable—the costs of inflation are more subtle.

People sense there is something wrong with the economy when there is high inflation. Workers worry that paychecks will not keep pace with increases in the price level, and thus their standard of living will be eroded. Investors worry that the dollars they receive in the future will be worth less than the dollars they invested, leaving them with less than enough to live comfortably in their old age.

When inflation is anticipated, many of its economic costs disappear. Workers who know that prices will be rising by 5 percent this year, for example, may negotiate wages that rise fast enough to offset inflation. Firms may be willing to agree to these larger wage increases since they anticipate being able to raise the prices of the goods they produce. Lenders know that the dollars they will be repaid will be worth less than the dollars they lent, so they take this into account when setting the interest rate they charge or when deciding whether to make a loan.

But even when inflation is not fully anticipated, workers and investors can immunize themselves against the effects of inflation by having wages and returns *indexed* to inflation. For instance, when wages are perfectly indexed, a 1 percent increase in the price level results in a 1 percent increase in wages, preserving the workers' purchasing power. In recent years, both Social Security payments and tax rates have been indexed. Many countries, including the United Kingdom, Canada, and New Zealand, sell indexed government bonds so that savers can put aside money knowing that the returns will not be affected by inflation.

Who Suffers From Inflation?

While indexing softens the effects of inflation, it is far from complete. So who suffers from inflation today? Many people may suffer a little because indexing does not fully protect them, but some are more likely to suffer than others. Among the groups most imperfectly protected are lenders, taxpayers, and holders of currency.

Lenders   Since most loans are not fully indexed, increases in inflation mean that the dollars that lenders receive back from borrowers are worth less than those they lent out. Many people put a large part of their retirement savings into bonds or other fixed-income securities. These people will suffer if an inflationary bout reduces the purchasing power of their savings. The extent to which they will suffer depends in large measure on whether the price changes were anticipated, as interest rates can adjust to completely compensate lenders for any inflation that was anticipated.

Taxpayers   Our tax system is only partially indexed, and inflation frequently hurts investors badly through the tax system. All returns to investment are taxed, including those that do nothing more than offset inflation. Consequently, real after-tax returns are often negative when inflation is high. Consider a rate of inflation of 10 percent and an asset that yields 12 percent before tax. If the individual has to pay a 33 percent tax on the return, the after-tax yield to the investor is only 9 percent—not even enough to compensate for inflation. The after-tax real return in this example is –1 percent.

Holders of Currency   Inflation also makes it expensive for people to hold currency because as prices rise, the currency loses its value. Since currency facilitates a variety of transactions, inflation interferes with the efficiency of the economy by discouraging the holding of currency. The fact that inflation takes away the real value of money means that inflation acts as a tax on holding money. Economists refer to this distortionary effect as an *inflation tax*.

This distortion is not as important in modern economies, where interest-paying checking accounts are frequently used instead of cash. As the rate of inflation increases, the interest rate paid on checking accounts normally increases as well. Even in Argentina in the 1970s, when prices were rising at 800 percent *a month*, bank accounts yielded more than this. Still, poorer individuals who do not have checking accounts—and therefore must hold much of what little wealth they have in the form of currency—are adversely affected. According to the Federal Reserve's 1998 Survey of Consumer Finances, almost 10 percent of American families do not have a checking, savings, or money market account. These families tend to have low incomes and little wealth.

The Economy

There are two costs of inflation to the economy as a whole. The first has to do with relative prices. Because price increases are never perfectly coordinated, increases in the rate of inflation lead to greater variability in relative prices. If the shoe industry makes price adjustments only every three months, then in the third month, right before its price increase, shoes may be relatively cheap, while right after the price increase, shoes may be relatively expensive. On the other hand, the prices of groceries might change continually throughout the three-month period. Therefore, the ratio of the price of groceries to the price of shoes will change continually. An average inflation rate of only 2 or 3 percent per year does not cause much of a problem. But when the average rate is 10 percent per month, inflation causes real distortions in how society allocates its resources. When inflation gets very high, individuals and firms tend to allocate considerable time and resources to avoid the costs of inflation and to take advantage of the discrepancies in prices charged by different sellers. Rather than carrying money, which quickly erodes in value, people rush to deposit their money in interest-bearing bank accounts.

The second economy-wide cost of inflation arises from the risk and uncertainty that inflation generates. If indexing were perfect, the uncertainty about the rate of inflation would be unimportant. But as indexing is not perfect, the resulting uncertainty makes it difficult to plan. People saving for their retirement cannot know how much to put aside if they do not know what a dollar will be worth in the future when they retire. Business firms borrowing money are uncertain about the price they will receive for the goods they produce. Firms are also hurt when they build wage increases into multiyear contracts to reflect *anticipated* inflation. If for any reason a firm finds that the prices it can charge have increased less rapidly than anticipated in the contract, the employer suffers.

Because of these economy-wide costs, countries that have experienced periods of very high inflation also tend to experience slower real economic growth.

It is clear that the costs of inflation are different, and undoubtedly lower, than they were before indexing was so extensive. Today, economists do not agree on the *magnitude* of the adverse effects of inflation. There is considerable evidence that high rates of inflation have strongly adverse effects on economic performance. But there is little evidence that the moderate rates of inflation the United States has experienced in recent years have any significant adverse effects.

The Costs of Deflation

Our focus has been on the costs of inflation—rising prices—since that has been the experience of the United States and most other countries over the past forty years. But inflation in many countries declined significantly during the 1980s, and falling prices—deflation—has become the concern in some countries. In Japan, for instance, prices have been falling over the past four years.

Many of the costs associated with inflation also make deflation costly. Variability in relative prices and increased uncertainty can arise when average prices are falling, just as they can when average prices are rising. And while inflation can hurt lenders, deflation can hurt borrowers. When prices are falling, the dollars a borrower must pay back are worth more than the dollars that were borrowed. In the United States, the 1870s and the 1930s were periods of declining prices. Borrowers, particularly farm families, were hard hit as the wages they earned or the prices they received for their crops fell. Many were forced to leave their farms. These periods have had a lasting impact on America's cultural history. L. Frank Baum's *The Wizard of Oz* originated, for example, as a political pamphlet on the dangers of the gold standard and in favor of raising the money supply by coining silver. (In Chapter 24, we will learn why a rise in the money supply—as occurred with the gold discoveries in South Africa in the 1880s—can lead to rising prices.) John Steinbeck's *The Grapes of Wrath* chronicles the hardships faced by Oklahoma farmers who were displaced during the 1930s.

Periods of deflation also have been associated with financial and banking crises. If firms that have borrowed loans are unable to repay them because of falling prices, they may be forced into bankruptcy. But this means the banks that have lent money will not be repaid, so they also may become bankrupt.

WRAP-UP

Real Costs of Inflation

Variability in relative prices
Resources devoted to mitigating the costs of inflation and taking advantage of price discrepancies
Increased uncertainty

CASE IN POINT

Hyperinflation in Germany in the 1920s

Following World War I, the victorious Allied nations required Germany to make substantial "reparations." But the sheer size of the reparations, combined with the wartime devastation of German industry, made payments nearly impossible. In *The Economic Consequences*

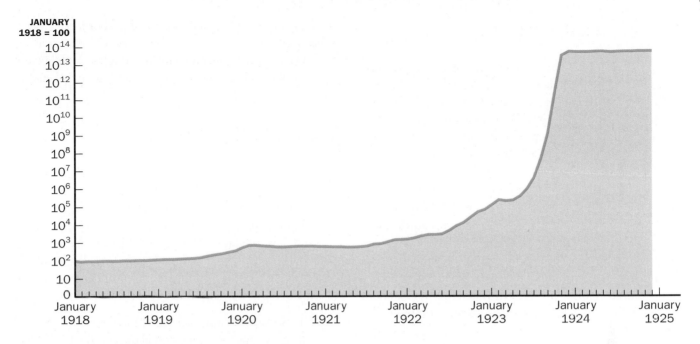

Figure 23.8   *Hyperinflation: Germany's Price Level (Log Scale)*

Inflation in Germany during the 1920s reached levels that may seem unbelievably high. At the end of 1923, prices were 36 billion times higher than they were two years earlier.

SOURCE: Thomas Sargent, "The Ends of Four Big Inflations," in R. Hall, ed., *Inflation, Causes and Effects* (Chicago: University of Chicago Press, 1982).

of the Peace, John Maynard Keynes, then an economic advisor to the British government, warned that the reparations were too large. To pay for some of Germany's financial obligations, the German government started printing money.

The resulting increase in both the amount of circulating currency and the price level can be seen in Figure 23.8. From December 1921 to December 1923, the average price level increased by a factor of 36 billion.[5] People made desperate attempts to spend their currency as soon as they received it, since the value of currency was declining so rapidly. One story Keynes often told was how Germans would buy two beers at once, even though one was likely to get warm, for fear that otherwise, when it came time to buy the second beer, the price would have risen.

At an annual inflation rate of 100 percent, money loses half its value every year. If you save $100 today, in five years it will have a buying power equal to only $3. It is possible for nominal interest rates to adjust even to very high inflation rates, but when those high inflation rates fluctuate in unanticipated ways, the effects can be disastrous.

Periods of hyperinflation create a massive redistribution of wealth. If an individual is smart or lucky enough to hold assets in a form such as foreign funds or land, then the hyperinflation will do little to reduce that person's real wealth. Those who cannot avail themselves of these "inflation-proof" assets will see their wealth fall. ●

---

[5]Thomas Sargent, "The Ends of Four Big Inflations," in R. Hall, ed., *Inflation, Causes and Effects* (Chicago: University of Chicago Press, 1982), pp. 74–75.

Flows and Stocks

GDP, GNP, and NDP are all measures of output *per year*. Rate measurements such as these are called **flows.** When a news reports says, "The quarterly GDP statistic, just released, shows that GDP was $8 trillion per year," it does not mean that $8 trillion of goods and services was produced during the quarter, a three-month period. Rather, it means that $2 trillion was produced during the quarter, so that if that rate were sustained for a whole year, the total value of goods and services produced would be $8 trillion.

Flow statistics need to be contrasted with **stock** statistics, which measure an item at a single point in time. Among the most important stocks is the capital stock—the total value of all the buildings and machines that underlie the economy's productive potential. The amount of money in your bank account is another example of a stock statistic.

The relationship between stocks and flows is simple. The stock of capital at the end of 2000, for example, consists of the stock of capital at the end of 1999 plus or minus the flows into or out of the stock during 2000. Investment is the flow into the stock of capital. Depreciation is the flow out of the capital stock.

Similarly, we can consider the *number* of unemployed individuals as a stock. This number at the end of 2000 consists of the number of unemployed at the end of 1999 plus or minus the flows into or out of the unemployment pool during 2000. Laid-off, fired, and resigned workers, as well as new workers entering the labor market to find a job, can be thought of as flows into the unemployment pool; new hires represent flows out of the unemployment pool.

Finally, a price index is a stock measure. We say the CPI was 166.6 in 1999. Inflation is a flow measure. We say that the inflation rate in 1999 was 2.2 percent *per year.*

A Look Ahead

In this chapter, we learned how output, unemployment, and inflation are measured. Each is associated with an important aspect of the economy's health. Now that we know how they are measured, we can turn to understanding how they are determined. In the next two parts of the book, we will address questions such as the following: Does the economy create enough new jobs as the labor force grows? What accounts for economic growth and changes in living standards? Why do unemployment and inflation fluctuate? Why is inflation high in some periods and low in others?

Review and Practice

Summary

1. The three central macroeconomic policy objectives of the government are high growth, low unemployment, and low inflation. Macroeconomics is the study of how these aggregate variables change as a result of household and business behavior, and how government policy may affect them.

2. Gross domestic product (GDP) is the typical way of measuring the value of national output. Real GDP adjusts nominal GDP for changes in the price level.

3. GDP can be calculated in three ways: the final goods approach, which adds the value of all final goods produced in the economy in a given year; the value-added approach, which adds the difference between firms' revenues and costs of intermediate goods; and the income approach, which adds together all income received by those in the economy. All three methods give the same answer.

4. Aggregate output in the economy is equal to aggregate income.

5. Unemployment imposes costs both on individuals and on society as a whole. Society loses what the unemployed workers could have contributed and what is needed to support them in other ways.

6. Seasonal unemployment, such as construction in areas with harsh winters, occurs regularly depending on the season. Frictional unemployment results from people being in transition between one job and another or as they first enter the labor market to search for work. Structural unemployment refers to the unemployment generated as the structure of the economy changes, with the new jobs being created having requirements different from the old jobs being lost. Cyclical unemployment increases or decreases as real output fluctuates around potential GDP.

7. Seasonal, frictional, and structural unemployment account for the positive unemployment rate even when the economy operates at potential GDP.

8. The inflation rate is the percentage increase of the price level from one year to the next. The U.S. inflation rate was low through most of the early part of the twentieth century, rose sharply in the 1970s and early 1980s, and then fell to lower levels in the rest of the 1980s and remained low throughout the 1990s. In different countries at different times, inflation has sometimes been very high, with prices increasing by factors of tens or hundreds in a given year.

9. The economy-wide costs of inflation are related to the distortions inflation creates in relative prices and in the increased risk and uncertainty it generates.

10. Economists distinguish between flows—such as output per year—and stocks—such as the stock of capital.

Key Terms

gross domestic product (GDP)
nominal GDP
real GDP
GDP deflator
chain-weighted real GDP
potential GDP
boom
recession
depression
value added
income approach
gross national product (GNP)
depreciation
net domestic product (NDP)
green GDP
unemployment rate
labor force participation rate
output gap
seasonal unemployment
frictional unemployment
structural unemployment
cyclical unemployment
inflation
consumer price index (CPI)
producer price index
deflation
flows
stocks

Review Questions

1. What are the three main goals of macroeconomic policy?

2. What is the difference between nominal GDP, real GDP, and potential GDP?

3. What is the difference between the final goods approach to measuring GDP, the value-added approach, and the income approach?

4. What is the difference between GDP, GNP, and NDP?

5. What is the difference between seasonal, frictional, structural, and cyclical unemployment?

6. When the prices of different goods change at different rates, how do we measure inflation?

7. Are all groups of people affected equally by inflation? Why or why not?

Problems

1. Geoffrey spends his allowance on three items: candy, magazines, and renting movie videos. He is currently receiving an allowance of $34 per month, which he is using to rent 4 movies at $3 dollars a piece, to buy 10 candy bars at $1 a piece, and to purchase 4 magazines at $3 a piece. In each of the following cases, calculate Geoffrey's price index for this basket of goods, with the current price level equal to 100:

   (a) The price of movies rises to $4.

   (b) The price of movies increases by $1 and the price of candy bars falls by $.20.

   (c) The prices of movies and magazines increase by $1 and the price of candy bars falls by $.20.

2. An increase in the consumer price index (CPI) will often affect different groups in different ways. Think about how different groups will purchase items like housing, travel, or education in the CPI basket, and explain why they will be affected differently by increases in components of the CPI. How would you calculate an "urban CPI" or a "rural CPI"?

3. Given the information below about the U.S. economy, how much did real GDP grow between 1980 and 1990? Between 1990 and 2000?

	1980	1985	1990	1995	2000
Nominal GDP (trillions)	$2.80	$4.21	$5.80	$7.40	$9.96
GDP deflator (1996 = 100)	57.0	73.7	86.5	98.1	106.9

4. Firms typically do not fire workers quickly as the economy goes into a recession—at least not in proportion to the reduction in their output. How might you expect output per worker and output per hour to change during the business cycle?

5. Suppose the Farsighted Forecasting Group, an organization of private economists, forecasts that the output gap will fall by 4 percent over the next year. Using Okun's law, determine how much the unemployment rate is likely to rise.

6. Using the following information on the CPI, calculate the rate of inflation in each year from 1997 to 2000.

	1996	1997	1998	1999	2000
CPI	156.9	160.5	163.0	166.6	172.2

7. War times are usually associated with inflation. Using the inflation calculator at http://www.bls.gov/cpihome.htm, determine what $100 in 1914 was worth in 1919. By how much did prices rise during World War I?

Appendix: The Chain-Weighted Measure of Real GDP

If you look up information on real GDP in 2000 for the United States, the units for real GDP will be "billions of chained 1996 dollars." In this appendix, we work through a simple example to illustrate what is meant by "chained dollars."

Table 23.4 provides the raw data from which we can calculate real GDP. This economy produces PCs and CDs. Average prices and quantities for each of three years are provided. The data for years 1 and 2 are the same as those in Table 23.1. Table 23.4 provides the values for nominal GDP in each of the three years.

In calculating real GDP, we use a constant set of prices so that our measure will reflect only changes in the quantities produced. If we use year 1 prices, for example, real GDP in year 2 would be $1,800 \times 1.2$ million PCs + 15×45.0 million CDs = $2,835 million. Since year 1 GDP at year 1 prices is $2,550 million, we would conclude that real GDP increased by ($2,835–$2,550)/$2,550 = 11.2 percent from year 1 to year 2.

As discussed in the text, when relative prices change, new goods are introduced, or quality is changed, there are problems with using prices from earlier years to value output. So in calculating real GDP in years 1 and 2, we also could have used year 2 prices. If we do so, real GDP in year 1 would be $1,850 \times 1.0$ million PCs + 17×45.0 million CDs = $2,700 million. Using year 2 prices, the increase in real GDP from year 1 to year 2 would be ($2,985–$2,700)/$2,700 = 10.6 percent.

To calculate the chain-weighted index for real GDP, we take the average of the two estimated increases, or 10.9 percent. Setting our index for real GDP in year 1 equal to 100, real GDP in year 2 would be 110.9.

We can calculate real GDP for year 3 in the same manner, using prices in year 2 and year 3. If we use year 2 prices, the increase in real GDP from year 2 to year 3 would be ($3,455–$2,985)/$2,985 = 15.7 percent. If we use year 3 prices instead, the increase is ($3,420– $2,970)/$2,970 = 15.2 percent. The average of the two estimated increases is 15.5 percent. Since our index for year 2 real GDP was 110.9, its value for year 3 will be 15.5 percent higher, or 128.0 (110.9 times 1.155).

TABLE 23.4

Calculating GDP

	Prices and Quantities			
Year	Price of PCs	Quantity of PCs	Price of CDs	Quantity of CDs
1	$1,800	1.0 million	$15.00	50.0 million
2	$1,850	1.2 million	$17.00	45.0 million
3	$1,800	1.5 million	$18.00	40.0 million

nominal GDP in year 1	= value of PCs + value of CDs = $1,800 × 1.0 million + $15 × 50.0 million = $2,550 million.
nominal GDP in year 2	= value of PCs + value of CDs = $1,850 × 1.2 million + $17 × 45.0 million = $2,985 million.
nominal GDP in year 3	= value of PCs + value of CDs = $1,800 × 1.5 million + $18 × 40.0 million = $3,420 billion.

Information Technology and the Macroeconomy

A distinctive feature of macroeconomics is its focus on *aggregate* measures of economic performance. Rather than looking at specific industries or sectors of the economy, like the auto industry or the housing sector, macroeconomists look at GDP, a measure of overall economic activity. Similarly, macroeconomists look at the consumer price index, a measure of the prices of thousands of different goods and services, rather than the individual prices of cars or houses. But this aggregate perspective raises some questions. What happens when the overall economy is really driven by just one sector, or when one sector is growing (or shrinking) in ways that are not typical of the rest of the economy? Can a macroeconomic perspective that ignores these differences give a misleading picture of the overall economy? The swings in the high-tech industry from boom to bust make these questions relevant for understanding the American economy in recent years. Did the rapid growth of the high-tech industry in the 1990s and then its contraction in 2001 distort our macroeconomic measures of overall economic performance?

Throughout the 1990s, the United States enjoyed a strong economic boom with rising incomes and low unemployment. At the same time, inflation remained low. There is no question that the high-tech industry was an important contributor to these developments. Production and employment in information technology (IT) sectors rose rapidly, and prices of IT goods like computers and cell phones fell dramatically. Our assessment of the U.S. economy might be skewed if favorable developments in the new economy were masking a stagnating old economy, or if price declines in IT were simply offsetting more significant inflation in the rest of the economy. If IT and non-IT sectors were experiencing quite different economic conditions, measures of the economy like GDP and overall inflation might paint a misleading picture of the economy's health.

A report by the U.S. Department of Commerce, *Digital Economy 2000* (http://www.esa.doc.gov/de2k.htm), provides some evidence on the contribution IT sectors have made to aggregate economic measures like GDP and overall inflation. The figure below shows that the share of IT production in total GDP grew during the second half of the 1990s, but even by 1999 it still accounted for less than 10 percent of the overall economy. However, when the Department of Commerce estimated how much of total income growth was pro-

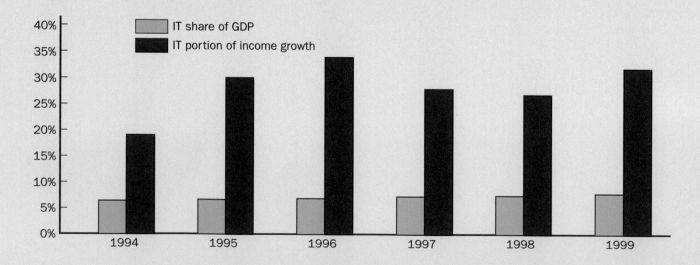

duced by the IT sector, it found that IT was contributing much more than 10 percent. In fact, between 1994 and 1999, IT accounted for almost 30 percent of income growth even though it accounted for only about 7 percent of GDP.

On the inflation front, IT also was having a noticeable impact on aggregate statistics. Between 1994 and 1998, prices in non-IT sectors rose at an average of 2.3 percent per year. Prices in the IT sector fell an average of 5.8 percent per year. These price declines in IT pulled down overall inflation during this period to just 1.8 percent per year (see figure below).

The macroeconomic perspective—a perspective that focuses on measures of overall economic performance—is useful for understanding such important economic topics as long-run growth and short-run fluctuations. In the case of fluctuations, for example, we will learn in Part Seven that there are periods when almost all industries experience economic expansions or when almost all industries are reducing production and employment. We also will learn that there are periods when almost all prices are rising rapidly. It makes sense, then, to focus on measures like GDP or overall inflation that provide good information on broad trends in the economy. But macroeconomists also must be alert to times when aggregate measures might be misleading. Whenever an economy is undergoing major transformations—the movement from agriculture to industry, the rise of the automobile, and now the growth of the IT sector—aggregate measures can sometimes mask very uneven experiences across different parts of the economy.

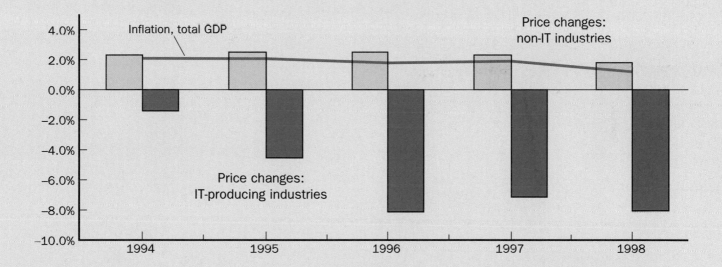

Part 6

Full-Employment Macroeconomics

Chapter 24

The Full-Employment Model

Key Questions

1. What forces in market economies operate to move the economy to full employment?

2. In an economy operating at full employment, what determines real wages, the level of output, and investment?

3. What role do interest rates and the capital market play in maintaining the economy at full employment?

4. What is the relationship between money, prices, and inflation in a full-employment economy?

*I*f we look at history in decades, the market economy has created jobs for almost all who seek them. In the 1980s, for example, the American labor force increased by 17 million people, and the number of people employed increased by 18 million. The 1990s saw the labor force grow almost 14 million, and the number of jobs grew by just under 15 million. This ability of the economy to create enough new jobs to employ millions of new workers as the labor force grows is the remarkable result of competitive markets. No government official can calculate where to place the millions of new workers who are expected to enter the labor force over the next decade. Indeed, anyone, from the president on down, who might have been asked where all the new entrants would find jobs in the last half of the 1990s would not have known the precise answer. That person might have pointed to particular parts of the economy that looked to be the most likely sources of job growth, but also might have said simply that on the basis of past experience, somehow, somewhere, the economy would create the jobs. The economic theories we explore in this and the next three chapters help explain this job growth.

Our focus here and in the next few chapters is on the long-run behavior of the economy. Our objective in this chapter is to understand how market economies manage to create the jobs needed to employ the new workers who enter the labor force. This process does not always occur smoothly—in some years job growth slows and unemployment rises, while in other years the opposite happens. But over the long run, jobs are created to employ those who want to work. To understand how this happens, we focus on the *aggregate* behavior of the economy—on movements in such macroeconomic variables as total output, interest rates, and average wages—when resources are fully employed. We show how competitive markets can help explain the vitality of the American economy.

Macroeconomic Equilibrium

The model we employ here is the basic competitive model described in earlier chapters. In it, large numbers of households and firms interact in the labor, product, and capital markets. Households supply labor to firms that use that labor to produce goods and services. Firms compensate workers by paying wages. Households use their income to purchase the goods and services firms produce. Households also save, and their saving finances firms' investments in the plant and equipment needed to undertake production. For the use of their funds, households earn interest and dividends from firms.

Two key lessons emerge from a study of macroeconomics. First, all markets are interrelated. What happens in one market will have an impact on other markets. The demand for labor, for instance, depends on the level of output in the product market. Second, wages, interest rates, and prices adjust to ensure demand equals supply in each market. One of our major assumptions in this part of the book will be that wages, interest rates, and prices adjust so that the labor, product, and capital markets are in equilibrium. That is, they all clear, with the quantity demanded equal to the quantity supplied.[1]

There are two ways to view this assumption. One way is to assume that wages, interest rates, and prices adjust rapidly so that a balance is always maintained between supply and demand in all markets. Alternatively, even if they do not adjust rapidly, we can view the assumption that markets clear as appropriate for understanding the long-run behavior of the economy, not how it operates year to year but how it behaves over decades. In either case, this assumption not only is a useful starting point for understanding how the macroeconomy operates, but also gives us powerful insights into some of the basic issues of macroeconomics.

We began the chapter with the observation that *somehow* the economy creates jobs for the millions of new entrants into the labor force each year. It has done this without any government official or private individual managing the whole process. The magic of the market—the adjustment of wages and prices equilibrating the labor market—guides this process, and the model we present here explains how this happens.

Our analysis differs in one important way from the kind of microeconomic analysis we have seen previously. In macroeconomics, we focus on aggregates—on the economy's total output, rather than the output of individual goods and services. We focus on total employment and on average wages. We also proceed as if there is a single good being produced using a single kind of labor. That is, we picture the economy as if all firms produce the same kind of commodity and all workers are identical. In looking at these aggregates, we ignore the richness of the microeconomic detail that captures the thousands of different products the economy produces and the many characteristics that differentiate one worker from another. The basic premise of macroeconomics is that we can learn a great deal about the aggregates—and gain insights into many important policy issues—without inquiring into these microeconomic details.

The Labor Market

Full employment in the labor market occurs when the demand for labor equals the supply of labor. No worker who wishes to get a job (for which she is qualified) at the going market wage will fail to get one. No firm that wants to hire a worker at the going wage will fail to find a qualified employee. Adjustments in wages ensure that this will occur. Of course, when economists say that there is full employment of the labor force—that the demand for labor is equal to the supply of labor—there are still always some workers who will be unemployed. As we learned in Chapter 23, this unemployment occurs as workers transition between jobs and new entrants to the labor force search for positions, as mismatches occur between the location or skill requirements of new jobs and those of the unemployed, and as unemployment in some sectors fluctuates to reflect normal seasonal patterns. These sources of unemployment are called *frictional, structural,* and *seasonal unemployment.* Even at full employment, the measured unemployment will be positive, owing to these sources.

In understanding how the economy reaches full employment, the relationship between nominal wages (w) and the price level (P) is very important. Workers earn

---

[1]What happens when markets do not clear is the topic of Part Seven and will be important for understanding short-run fluctuations in the economy.

wages, and they use those wages to buy goods and services. What matters to workers is how much their wages will buy. If a worker's wage goes from $6 per hour to $12 per hour but at the same time the prices of all the things the worker buys also double, the real value of the worker's wage has not changed. What matters to workers is their *real* wage, the nominal wage corrected for changes in the price level. Firms also will be concerned with the real wage, since what will matter to them is the cost of labor (the nominal wage) relative to the price firms receive for their output (the price level).

The real wage is obtained by dividing the nominal wage by the price level, or w/P. The real wage provides a measure of the purchasing power of wages. Nominal wages, the price level, and real wages over the past twenty years are shown in Figure 24.1. As the figure il-

lustrates, nominal wages have risen significantly over the past twenty years. But the prices of the goods and services workers buy also have risen. When we correct for the increases in the price level, the real wage actually declined during the first half of the 1990s and by 1999 was little changed from its value in 1980.

Figure 24.2 shows the aggregate labor market, with the real wage (w/P) on the vertical axis, the quantity of labor (L) on the horizontal axis, and the aggregate demand and supply curves for labor. With a given set of equipment and technology, the aggregate demand for labor depends on the wages firms must pay, the prices firms receive for the goods and services they produce, and the prices they have to pay for nonlabor inputs such as raw materials and equipment. With the prices of goods and inputs held constant, the aggregate labor demand curve traces out the quantity of labor

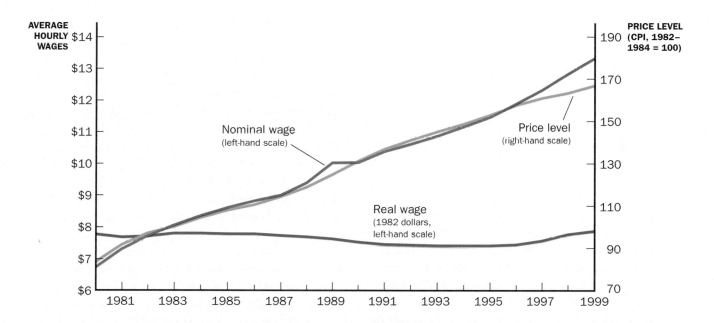

FIGURE 24.1 *Nominal Wages, the Price Level, and Real Wages*

The solid red line shows that nominal wages in the United States have risen significantly since 1980. The green line shows that the price level also has risen over this period. From 1980 to 1986, nominal wages and the price level rose at the same rate, so the real wage (shown by the blue line) remained constant. In the late 1980s, prices rose relative to nominal wages, and real wages declined. Only at the end of the 1990s have real wages risen as nominal wages rose relative to the price level.

SOURCE: *ERP* (2001), Tables B-47, B-60.

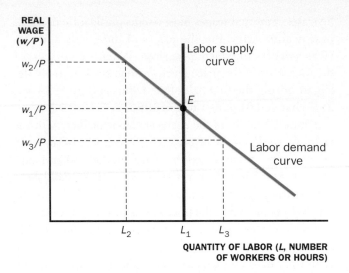

FIGURE 24.2   *Equilibrium in the Labor Market*

Equilibrium in the labor market is at the intersection of the aggregate demand and supply curves for labor. If the real wage is above w_1/P where demand equals supply, there will be unemployment, putting pressure on wages to fall as workers compete to offer their services. Below w_1/P there will be excess demand for labor, which will put pressure on wages to rise.

demanded by firms at different wages. At lower wages, the quantity of labor demand is greater. There are two reasons for this. First, as wages fall relative to the cost of machines, it pays firms to substitute workers for machines. Second, as wages fall, labor becomes relatively less expensive compared with the price of the goods firms produce (so at the old level of employment, the value of the marginal product of the last unit of labor hired would exceed the wage), and again firms will hire more workers. Thus, the demand curve for labor slopes down, as shown in the figure.

The two reasons for the negative slope of the aggregate labor demand curve stress the importance of wages relative to the costs of other inputs and the price of the output being produced. If wages fall *and all other prices in the economy also fall in proportion,* the demand for labor will not change. That is why we show the demand for labor as a function of the real wage, w/P.

The figure also shows an aggregate labor supply curve. To simplify matters, the labor supply curve is drawn as a vertical line—we assume that the labor supply is perfectly inelastic.[2] That is, either individuals are in the labor force, working a full (forty-hour) workweek, or they are not. In principle, workers might enter and exit the labor force as real wages go up or down, or they might reduce or increase the hours they work in response to such changes. When real wages rise, two factors are at work. First, higher wages mean the returns to working are greater. This should cause workers to want to work more hours—the opportunity cost of leisure is now higher, and the substitution effect works to induce individuals to work more as real wages rise. But higher wages mean that workers have higher income. With higher income, they will want to increase their consumption, including their consumption of leisure. So there is an income effect acting to reduce labor supply as real wages rise. The income and substitution effects act in opposite directions. In Figure 24.2, we assume they offset one another, so that as real wages change, labor supply remains constant.

One advantage of making the assumption that the number of hours worked per week is fixed is that we can put *either* the total number of hours worked per week (forty times the number of individuals in the labor force) or the number of workers hired on the horizontal axis of the figure. The demand and supply of hours (per week) is simply forty times the demand and supply of workers.

Basic supply and demand analysis implies that market equilibrium should occur at the intersection of the demand and supply curves, point E. The reason for this is straightforward. If the real wage happens to be above the equilibrium real wage w_1/P, say, at w_2/P, the demand for labor will be L_2, much less than the supply, L_1. There will be an excess supply of workers. Those in the labor force without jobs will offer to work for less than the going wage, bidding down the average wages of those already working. The process of competition will lead to lower wages, until eventually demand again equals supply at point E. Likewise, if the real wage is lower than w_1/P, say, at w_3/P, firms in the economy will demand more labor than is supplied. Competing with one another for scarce labor services, they will bid the wage up to w_1/P.

---

[2]Recall the definition of *elasticity* from Chapter 5: the percentage change in quantity divided by the percentage change in price. Thus, an inelastic labor supply means that a 1 percent increase in wages results in a small percentage increase in supply. A perfectly inelastic labor supply curve is vertical. That means that the labor supply does not change at all when real wages change.

Thinking Like an Economist

Incentives and Off-Setting Income and Substitution Effects

When prices change, economists try to understand how individuals will respond by thinking in terms of the income and substitution effects we introduced in Chapter 6. The substitution effect of a price increase is the reduction in demand caused by the changed trade-off as one now has to give up more of other goods in order to purchase the good whose price has risen. The income effect is the change in demand for a good whose price has risen that occurs because of the reduction in real income caused by the price increase. In many cases, these two effects act in the same direction, reinforcing each other. When the price of gasoline rises, the real income of car owners falls—it is more expensive to continue to purchase as much as before. Driving becomes more expensive and people have an increased incentive to substitute away from gas-guzzling cars and to drive less. Both the income and substitution effects lead us to predict that gas consumption will fall when its price rises.

In some cases, though, income and substitution effects can work in opposite directions, potentially offsetting each other. In macroeconomics, there are two important situations in which thinking about income and substitution effects helps us to understand why there may be little response to a change in a price. The first case involves saving and the real interest rate; this case was discussed in Chapter 9. The second one involves labor supply and the real wage. Earlier we said that the labor supply curve is inelastic; workers do not seem to alter their labor supply very much as real wages change. A rise in real wages does increase the incentive to work by changing the trade-off between work and other activities. This is the substitution effect. Taking a day off to go to the ballgame or the beach becomes more expensive if wages have increased. For individuals who are already working, an increase in the wage also raises their incomes. This increases their demand for goods and services and for leisure activities like going to the ballgame or the beach. This is the income effect of an increase in the real wage.

The substitution effect would lead to an increase in labor supply as the incentive to work rises with the real wage; the income effect would lead to a reduction in labor supply as workers "purchase" more leisure as the real wage rises. The net effect could go in either direction. As a reasonable approximation, we generally will draw the labor supply curve as vertical, assuming the income and substitution effects balance out.

Thinking in terms of income and substitution effects also can help us to understand why some groups may respond more strongly than others to wage changes. Consider a college student who currently is not working. If real wages increase, there is a substitution effect that might cause the student to enter the labor force since the return to taking a part-time job has risen. Because the individual was not working previously, there is no income effect to offset this substitution effect. So for individuals previously not in the labor force, only the substitution effect is at work, and we would expect to see a more elastic (and positive) labor supply response to real wage increases.

Shifts in the Demand and Supply of Labor

The full-employment model makes clear predictions for the consequences of shifts in the demand and supply of labor. First, let's consider shifts in the supply curve of labor. This can occur because there are more young people reaching working age than there are old people retiring, because of new immigrants, or because of social changes such as the entry of more women into the labor force. For example, the U.S. labor force expanded rapidly in the 1970s as the baby boomers entered the labor force and more and more women worked. The

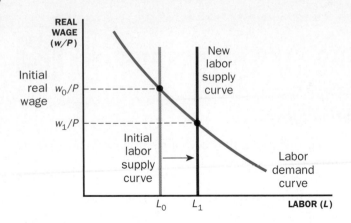

FIGURE 24.3 *Effects of a Shift in the Supply of Labor*

A shift of the supply curve to the right leads to a fall in real wages.

consequences of such a large shift in the labor supply curve are depicted in Figure 24.3. The supply curve of labor (shown here as vertical) shifts to the right. At each real wage, there are more individuals in the labor force. The equilibrium real wage falls. This fall in the price of labor indicates to firms that labor is less scarce than it was before, and so firms should economize less in the use of labor. Firms respond to the lower real wage by creating more jobs. Employment rises to absorb the increase in labor supply.

Now let's look at the effects of a shift in the demand curve for labor. First, consider the case of a decrease in investment leading to a reduction in the quantity of machines and equipment available for use by workers. This reduces the productivity of workers, thereby shifting the demand curve for labor to the left, as depicted in panel A of Figure 24.4. For a given real wage, firms want to hire fewer workers than before. The equilibrium real wage falls.

Panel B depicts the effects of technological progress on the demand for labor. Workers are more productive, and the labor demand curve shifts to the right. Real wages rise.

These examples suggest that increases in investment and improvements in technology lead to an increase in the demand for labor (a rightward shift in the labor demand curve). Although this is generally true, it may be the case that the demand for some types of labor, especially unskilled labor, actually declines with investment in new equipment and technology. At the same time, the demand for skilled workers may increase. In this case,

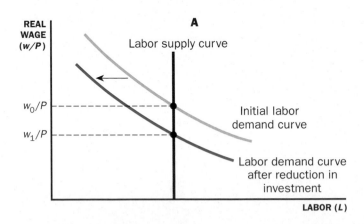

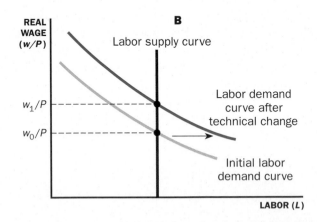

FIGURE 24.4 *Effects of Changes in Investment and Technology*

New investment or technological change shifts the demand curve for labor. Panel A shows the effects of a reduction in investment. Workers have fewer machines and equipment to work with, and the demand curve for labor shifts to the left, lowering real wages. Panel B shows an improvement in technology. The demand curve shifts to the right, as workers' marginal productivity increases, leading to higher real wages.

the labor market is really made up of two markets, that of skilled and that of unskilled workers. An increase in investment or technology may increase the demand for skilled workers, as in panel B, but decrease the demand for unskilled workers, as in panel A. This represents one case where a focus only on the aggregate labor market is not sufficient to understand an interesting macroeconomic phenomenon—the increase in wage inequality based on skill levels that has occurred in the United States in recent years.

WRAP-UP

Labor Market Equilibrium

Real wages adjust to equate labor demand with labor supply.

A rightward shift in labor supply lowers the real wage, inducing firms to create additional jobs equal to the increased labor supply.

Technological changes or new investment induce changes in the real wage so that all workers remain fully employed.

CASE IN POINT

Mass Migration in the Nineteenth Century

The nineteenth century provides a case study in how labor markets adjust to changes in labor supply. Between 1820 and 1920, 60 million emigrants left Europe for the New World (Argentina, Australia, Brazil, Canada, and the United States). About 36 million of these emigrated to the United States. This mass movement of people had a major impact on wages in both North America and Europe, just as our theory predicts.

Land was scarce and labor was abundant in Europe in 1850. As a consequence, wages were low. In North America, by contrast, land was abundant and labor was scarce. Consequently, wages were high.[3] In 1850, the average real wage in Europe was about half what it was in the New World. Real wages in Ireland, for instance, were 42 percent of the American level. This wage differential provided a powerful inducement for workers to migrate from Europe to areas offering higher living standards.

The mass migrations of the late nineteenth century shifted the North American labor supply curve to the right and the European labor supply curve to the left. Our theory predicts that wages adjust to balance the quantity of labor demanded and the quantity of labor supplied. Real wages needed to fall in the United States and rise in Europe in response to these shifts in labor supply.

Did this adjustment of wages occur? Irish real wages doubled between 1855 and 1913, with most of the increase occurring between 1860 and 1895. American wages also were rising during this period as a result of the industrialization of the economy. But Irish wages rose faster, closing the gap between what workers earned in Ireland and what workers earned in the United States. Just as the theory predicted, real wages adjusted in response to shifts in labor supply to bring the quantity demanded and the quantity supplied into balance in the labor market.[4] ●

---

[3]To help follow the discussion, you might find it useful to draw two supply and demand diagrams, one to represent the European labor market in 1850 and one to represent the North American labor market. Since our focus here is on labor supply and migration, draw the labor demand curves to be the same in both markets. For Europe, the labor supply curve is to the right of where it is for North America. The equilibrium real wage for this time period is higher in North America.

[4]For a discussion of the impact of mass migration during the late nineteenth century and other aspects of the globalization that occurred during this period, see K. H. O'Rourke and J. G. Williamson, *Globalization and History* (Cambridge: MIT Press, 1999).

International Perspective

Unemployment Comparisons

When wages and prices adjust to balance supply and demand in the labor market, the economy will operate at full employment. Even when supply and demand are equal in the labor market, the unemployment rate is still positive. Particularly in a dynamic labor market—with people entering and leaving the labor force, workers quitting to look for better jobs, new firms being created, often in new industries, and other firms shrinking—frictional unemployment and structural unemployment will be positive. There are also seasonal fluctuations in the unemployment rate, particularly in industries such as construction, where activity must slow in the winter as a result of the weather.

The unemployment rate is positive when the economy is at full employment. In the United States, the unemployment rate at full employment has varied over time, particularly in the face of demographic changes such as the entry of the baby boomers into the labor force. In the early 1990s, a typical estimate of the unemployment rate at full employment was around 6 percent, although many economists believe this rate fell during the late 1990s. Actual unemployment has fluctuated around this 6 percent figure—

the explanation for these fluctuations is the subject of Part Seven.

In other countries, unemployment has followed quite different patterns. In France, for example, the unemployment rate has risen steadily over the past twenty-five years, from below 3 percent in 1973–1974 to over 12 percent in 1996–1997. German unemployment has followed a similar pattern, although its average level has remained lower. The unemployment rates in the United Kingdom and Canada bear similarities to those in both France and the United States, with fluctuations (as in the United States) around a rising average level (as in France). The unemployment rate in Japan has been lower and more stable than in the other countries, but it rose significantly during the 1990s.

An important debate in countries such as France is whether the high unemployment rate is consistent with full employment. Has some change in the demographics of the labor force or the structure of the labor market led to increasing frictional and structural unemployment? Or does some other factor explain the rise in unemployment? For example, are wages failing to adjust to balance supply and demand?

The Product Market

Just as the real wage adjusts to ensure the demand for labor equals the supply, so too—in our full-employment model—adjustments will occur in the product and capital markets to ensure the demand for goods equals the economy's output when it is at full employment.

Aggregate Supply

At any point in time, the economy has a given capital stock (a set of machines, equipment, and buildings) that, together with labor and materials, produces output. If more workers are hired, output increases. The relationship between employment and output with a fixed amount of capital is called the **short-run aggregate production function,** depicted in Figure 24.5. The figure illustrates that as more workers are hired, output goes up, but at a diminishing rate. There are *diminishing returns to labor.* The most productive machines are used first; if more workers are hired, they are assigned to older and less productive machines.

We have been assuming here that there is a fixed supply of labor, reflected in the vertical labor supply curve. With this fixed supply of labor, the economy has a given

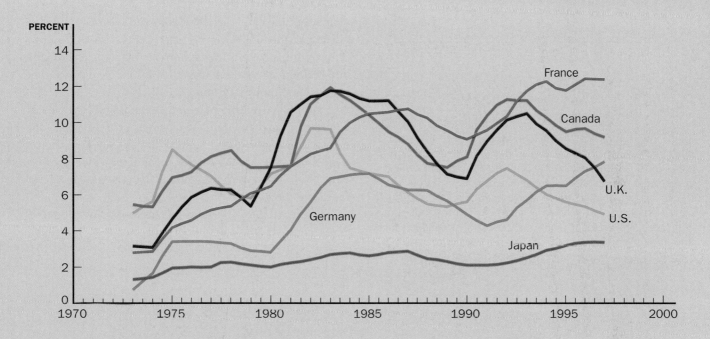

PERCENT

France

Canada

Germany

U.K.

U.S.

Japan

Civilian Unemployment Rates

productive capacity, also referred to as its **potential GDP** or the **full-employment level of output.** This level of output is also sometimes referred to as *aggregate supply*. It represents the amount of goods and services that firms are willing to produce, given their plant and equipment, when real wages adjust so that the labor market is in equilibrium. If labor market equilibrium leads to an employment level L^f, potential GDP will equal Y^f, as shown in Figure 24.5.

Potential GDP is the economy's level of output when the demand and supply in the labor market balance so that the economy is at full employment and firms are operating their plants and equipment at normal rates of utilization. The economy could produce more if firms operated plant and equipment more intensively, for example, by adding an extra shift or by deferring maintenance, or if they had workers put in more overtime hours. Wars provide examples when the economy operates above potential for sustained periods of time. At a war's end, production returns to levels consistent with normal rates of plant and equipment utilization, and weekly hours return to more normal levels.

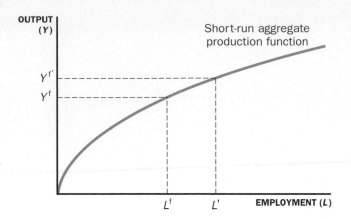

OUTPUT (Y)

Short-run aggregate production function

$Y^{f'}$

Y^f

L^f L' EMPLOYMENT (L)

FIGURE 24.5   *Short-Run Aggregate Production Function*

In the short run, with given technology and a given set of plant and equipment, as more labor is employed, output increases, but with diminishing returns. (Each successive increase in input results in smaller increases in output.) L^f is the full-employment level of employment, so Y^f is the full-employment level of output. An increase in the labor supply generates a movement along the short-run production function; the full-employment level of output will increase to $Y^{f'}$.

Demand and Equilibrium Output

If the product market is to be in equilibrium, then the supply of goods and services produced by firms in the economy must balance with the demand for the economy's goods and services. Firms will not continue to produce at the full employment level if their products go unsold. If the economy is to maintain full employment, the total level of demand in the economy must adjust to balance output at full employment. The capital market plays a critical role in achieving this balance. Examining its role reveals how the interrelation of markets plays a critical role in ensuring macroeconomic equilibrium.

A useful starting point in understanding how demand adjusts to equal full-employment output is to recall our earlier discussion of the circular flow of income. Figure 24.6 shows the circular flow of income for a closed economy. Notice that we have ignored the government sector for the moment.

The circular flow diagram illustrates the flow of goods and income that link the household, business, and finan-

e-Insight

Labor Markets and the Internet

One of the main *imperfections* in the labor market is that it is expensive, in terms of time and money, to search for a new job. Information is imperfect and is costly to acquire. Help-wanted ads play an important role in making the labor market work, but often it is not easy for individuals in one city to obtain on a regular and timely basis newspapers in other cities, to look at job opportunities there.

Employment agencies and government employment services have helped make the labor market work better. But the Internet promises a revolution—or at least a vast improvement—in labor markets. Virtually without cost, individuals can see the help-wanted ads in newspapers in other cities. Employers can costlessly post help-wanted ads and

provide far more complete descriptions of the job and of the characteristics of the employees that they seek. Eighty percent of the world's largest 500 firms use Web sites for job recruitment and over 90 percent of American firms do. Existing employment agencies (including government-provided services) have used the Internet to extend their scope, and new firms have been created. Much of the relevant information—from the perspective of both the employer and the employee—still will be obtained only by face-to-face contact, through an interview, and this process will remain costly. Still, by lowering search costs, the Internet holds out the promise of vastly increasing the efficiency of labor markets.

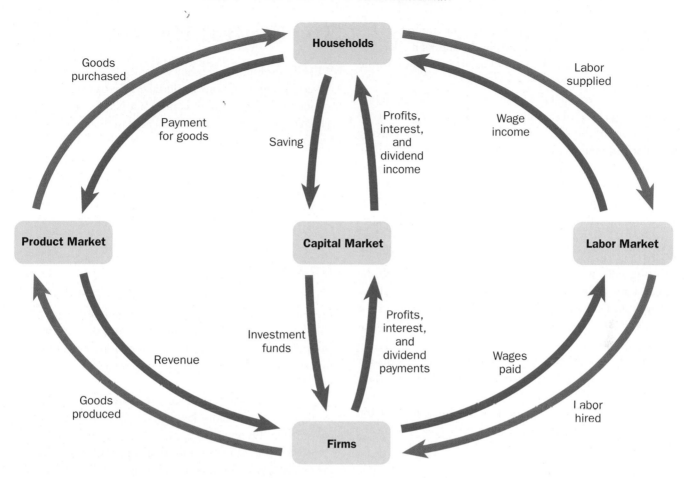

FIGURE 24.6 *The Circular Flow of Income*

The circular flow of income provides a summary picture of how the flows of commodities and payments link the household and firm sectors of the economy. Households provide resources, such as labor, to firms and receive income payments in return. They use this income to purchase goods and services in the product market. The revenue firms obtain from selling in the product market allows them to make the income payments to households for the labor and other resources firms have used. Saving from the household sector flows into the capital market, where it is available to firms who wish to borrow for investment projects.

cial sectors. In the diagram, the red lines indicate flows of real resources and goods and services; the blue lines represent the payments for those commodities. Households supply resources (labor, capital, land) to firms and in return receive payments for those resources. We have already learned in Chapter 23 that these income payments will equal the value of total production. This means that the household sector receives enough income to purchase all the goods and services firms have produced.

Of course, households do not choose to spend all their income on goods and services. They save part of their income. In our circular flow diagram, this is shown by the flow of saving to the financial capital market. Thus, household saving is a *leakage* out of the spending stream.

While households in the aggregate do not spend all their income, other sectors of the economy spend more than the incomes they receive. Firms, for example, may wish to invest in buildings, new plants, and equipment. To do so, they need to borrow funds in the capital market. Investment spending can be viewed as an *injection* into the spending stream.

We can now see that the total level of spending will balance with the level of output that has been produced if the leakages out of the spending stream in the form of saving are balanced by injections into the spending stream in the form of investment spending. If leakages are equal to injections, firms will find that total demand for goods and services will equal the amount they have produced. This does not mean that every firm will find it can sell all it has produced. Even in an economy producing at full employment, some firms will face weak demand and be left with unsold goods, while others will be unable to meet all the demand for their products. But in the aggregate, when leakages and injections are equal, the total demand for goods and services will equal the economy's total output at full employment.

What ensures that leakages equal injections? To answer this question, and to understand how injections and leakages are balanced to ensure the product market is in equilibrium at full-employment output, we must look at the role of the capital market.

WRAP-UP

Product Market Equilibrium

When the economy is at full employment, output is equal to potential GDP. This is the output that can be produced by the available labor force with the given set of plant and equipment at normal levels of weekly hours and capacity utilization.

Increases in the labor supply (rightward shifts in the labor supply curve), increases in the stock of plant and equipment as a result of new investment, and technological changes increase full-employment output.

When leakages at full employment equal injections, aggregate demand will equal full-employment output.

The Capital Market

When households save, they make funds available to borrowers. Whenever firms undertake investment, they need to borrow. The financial capital market is the market in which the supply of funds is allocated to those who wish to borrow. For this reason, it is also called the **loanable funds market.** Equilibrium in the capital market requires that saving (the supply of funds) equal investment (the demand for funds). Our analysis of each builds on the basic competitive model of Part Two.

Household Saving

The most important determinants of household saving are income and interest rates. Each year, families have to decide how much of their income to spend on current consumption and how much to save for future consumption, for retirement, for emergencies, to pay for their children's college education, or to buy a new car or new home. On average, families with higher incomes spend more *and* save more. Of course, before families can decide how much to consume and how much to save, they must pay any taxes they owe. What is relevant for consumption and saving decisions is how much income a household has after paying taxes; this is called their *disposable income.* When the government increases taxes, disposable income is reduced. Households typically will reduce both their consumption spending and their saving when disposable income falls.

In this chapter, we assume that the stock of plant and equipment, as well as the labor supply, is given. With wages and prices adjusting to ensure the labor market always clears, aggregate output is fixed at the full-employment level. We now make use of an important result from Chapter 23: national income equals aggregate output. The money used to purchase goods and services has to go into somebody's pockets, and thus becomes income to that person. If aggregate output is fixed, so is aggregate income. Since we are ignoring the government and taxes in this chapter (we will incorporate them into the analysis in the next chapter), aggregate disposable income will also be fixed at the full-employment level of output.

With income fixed, the level of saving will depend on the return households can earn on their savings—the *real* rate of interest. When households save, they set aside current income so that they will have more to spend in the future. What matters for saving decisions is the interest rate they can earn on their savings, corrected for changes in the prices of what they buy. The real interest rate is the correct measure of the return on savings because it takes into account changes in prices. Figure 24.7 shows two possibilities. In panel A, saving increases significantly with the real interest rate, while in panel B, saving responds only slightly to changes in the interest rate. Empirical studies suggest that at least for the United States, the saving curve looks more like the one in panel B than the one in panel A. For simplicity, in the rest of this chapter we will depict the saving curve as completely inelastic—that is, as a vertical straight line. In this case, changes in the real rate of interest do not lead to any change in saving.

But doesn't a higher real rate of interest provide a greater incentive to save? Yes, but keep in mind that a rise in the real rate of interest has an income effect, leading to less saving, and a substitution effect, leading to more saving. The two effects pull in opposite directions. The evidence suggests that they essentially offset each other. That is why household saving is not very sensitive to the interest rate and why we will often draw the saving curve as a vertical line.

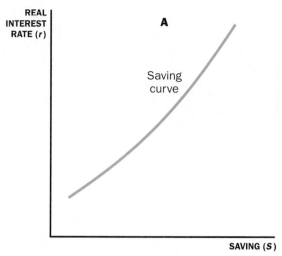

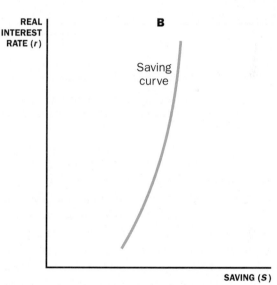

Investment

Economists use the word *investment* in two different ways. Households think of the stocks and bonds they buy as investments—**financial investments.** These financial investments provide the funds for firms to buy capital goods—machines and buildings. The purchases of new machines and buildings represent firms' investment, referred to as **capital goods investment** or simply as *investment. In macroeconomics, when we refer to investment, it is to physical investment in capital goods, not financial investment.*

Firms invest to increase their capacity to produce goods and services. They expect returns from the sales of this additional production to cover the costs of the additional workers and raw materials that were required to increase production, as well as the cost of the funds that financed the investment, leaving the firm with a profit.

There are two key determinants of investment: firms' expectations concerning future sales and profits, which for now we will assume to be fixed, and the real rate of interest. Many firms borrow to finance their investment. The cost of these funds—what they have to pay back to the financial sector for using the borrowed funds—is the interest rate. Since the firm pays back a debt with dollars

FIGURE 24.7 *Saving and the Real Interest Rate*

Different saving curves are shown in panels A and B. In panel A, saving increases with the real interest rate. In panel B, saving is only slightly sensitive to the interest rate (inelastic), a relationship in the United States that is supported by the empirical evidence.

whose purchasing power depends on inflation, the relevant cost is the real rate of interest.

The higher the real rate of interest, the fewer the investment projects that will be profitable—that is, the fewer the projects that will yield a return, after paying back interest on the borrowed funds, that is sufficient to compensate the firm for the risks undertaken. Even if the firm is flush with cash,

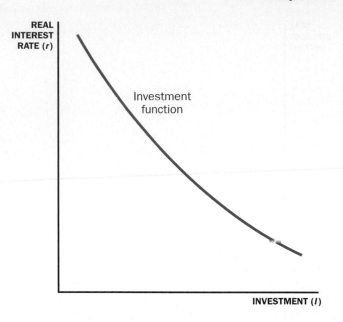

REAL INTEREST RATE (r)

Investment function

INVESTMENT (I)

FIGURE 24.8 *The Investment Function*

The investment function slopes downward to the right, tracing out the levels of real investment at different real interest rates. As the interest rate falls, investment increases.

the interest rate matters. The real interest rate then becomes the opportunity cost of the firm's money, what the firm could have obtained if instead of making an investment, it had simply decided to lend the funds to some other firm.

The **investment function** gives the level of (real) investment at each value of the real rate of interest. The investment function slopes downward to the right; investment increases as the real interest rate decreases. This is depicted in Figure 24.8, which shows the real interest rate on the vertical axis and the level of real investment on the horizontal axis.

WRAP-UP

Saving versus Investment

What we often call investing (putting money into a mutual fund, purchasing shares in the stock market) is actually *saving*—setting aside part of our income rather than spending it. These funds are then made available through the financial system to individuals and firms who wish to purchase capital goods such as plant and

equipment or build new office buildings, shopping malls, or homes.

Investment refers to these additions to the physical stock of capital in the economy. As the real interest rate rises, the cost of borrowing funds for these investment projects rises. As a result, fewer projects will look profitable, fewer households will buy a new car as car loan interest rates rise, and fewer homes will be constructed.

Investment declines as the real interest rate rises, while saving may rise as households reduce consumption to take advantage of higher rates of return on their savings.

Equilibrium in the Capital Market

The equilibrium real interest rate is the rate at which saving and investment balance, as depicted in Figure 24.9. Panels A and B show the effect of an increased demand for investment at each real interest rate. In panel A, both the equilibrium real interest rate and the equilibrium level of saving and investment are increased, while in panel B, only the equilibrium real interest rate is changed. Because panel B depicts saving as not sensitive to the real interest rate, and saving must equal investment, a shift in the investment function affects the equilibrium real interest rate but not the equilibrium levels of saving or investment. By contrast, a rightward shift in the savings curve results in a reduction in the real interest rate and an increase in equilibrium investment (panel C).

When the real interest rate adjusts to balance demand and supply in the capital market, saving will equal investment. We can express this same result by saying that when the capital market is in equilibrium, leakages from the spending stream equal injections. This was the condition that was needed to ensure the product market was in equilibrium. Therefore, the capital market plays a critical role in ensuring product market equilibrium.

We can use the national income relationships to demonstrate that if saving is equal to investment at the full-employment level of output, then aggregate demand equals aggregate supply. In our simplified model with no government and no foreign trade, there are two sources of demand, consumption (C) and investment (I):

$$\text{demand} = C + I.$$

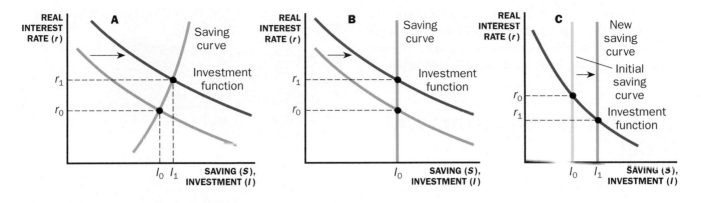

FIGURE 24.9 *Equilibrium in the Capital Market*

Equilibrium requires that the demand for funds (investment) equal the supply (saving). The level of desired investment decreases as the real interest rate increases.

We assume the economy is at full employment. In panel A, saving increases slightly with increases in the real interest rate. In panels B and C, saving is not interest sensitive, so the saving curve is a vertical line. The equilibrium level of investment is simply equal to the full-employment level of saving.

A shift in the investment function—so that at every real interest rate the demand for investment is increased—is depicted in panels A and B. In panel A, equilibrium investment is increased from I_0 to I_1, while in panel B, with inelastic saving, the only effect is to increase the equilibrium real interest rate from r_0 to r_1, leaving investment (and saving) unchanged.

Panel C shows a rightward shift in the saving curve. The level of saving increases at each real interest rate. In the new equilibrium in the capital market, the real interest rate has fallen from r_0 to r_1 and investment has increased from I_0 to I_1.

Y^f equals full-employment income, and full-employment incomes are either saved or consumed:

$$Y^f = C + S^f \text{ or } S^f = Y^f - C.$$

When desired investment (as reflected in the investment schedule) equals full-employment saving, S^f, we have

$$I = S^f.$$

Since from our second equation, full-employment saving is equal to full-employment income minus consumption:

$$I = S^f = Y^f - C.$$

Substituting the fourth equation back into the first equation gives

$$\text{demand} = C + I = C + (Y^f - C) = Y^f.$$

Thus, demand is equal to full-employment output when saving and investment balance. There is equilibrium in the product market at full-employment output.

WRAP-UP

Capital Market Equilibrium

In equilibrium, saving equals investment.

Increases in saving (shifts to the right in the saving curve) lead to lower real interest rates and higher levels of investment.

Shifts to the right in the investment function lead to higher real interest rates but unchanged or higher rates of investment. Equilibrium investment will be unchanged if the saving curve is vertical; equilibrium investment will rise if the saving curve has a positive slope.

Capital market equilibrium ensures that leakages equal injections at full-employment output. When saving is equal to investment at full employment, aggregate demand equals the economy's full-employment level of output.

The General Equilibrium Model

We can now describe the general equilibrium of the economy, the output level, the real wage, and real interest rate at which the labor, product, and capital markets all clear.

Start with the labor market. The real wage adjusts to ensure the demand for labor equals the supply of labor. This determines the equilibrium real wage and the level of employment that constitutes full employment. In the product market, the short-run aggregate production function then determines the level of output firms produce when the economy is at full employment. This output level is potential GDP, the output that the labor supply, working with the available capital stock, can produce when the economy is at full employment. Finally, the capital market balances leakages and injections in the circular flow of income. The real interest rate adjusts to ensure that at the full-employment level of output, saving is equal to investment. This also ensures that aggregate demand will equal aggregate supply at the full-employment level of output. The product market clears.

Using the General Equilibrium Model

The general equilibrium model is useful because it allows us to understand the effects of various changes in the economy—from the market in which these changes originate to all the other markets in the economy.

Consider the effects on the economy of the introduction of personal computers. By making workers more productive, personal computers increase the marginal product of workers. This increases the quantity of labor demanded at each real wage, causing a shift in the demand curve to the right. The equilibrium real wage increases, as shown in Figure 24.10, panel A.

Given the greater productivity of workers and the fixed supply of labor, full-employment output increases, as shown using the short-run aggregate production function in panel B. Product market equilibrium can only be maintained if aggregate demand also rises so that firms are able to sell the

Computer technology has increased the productivity of a wide range of workers.

new higher level of output they are producing. As we have seen, this will occur if the real interest rate adjusts to maintain saving equal to investment in the capital market. Investment at each level of the real interest rate may rise as firms take advantage of the available profit opportunities opened up by the new computer technology. At the same time, the increase in full-employment income leads to increases in both consumption and saving at each interest rate. The increases in investment and saving at each interest rate are represented by a rightward shift in both the investment and saving curves (panel C). In equilibrium, the real interest rate may either rise, fall, or stay the same (this is illustrated in panel C), depending on the relative magnitudes of the shifts. Whatever the impact on the real interest rate, we can conclude that equilibrium investment will rise.

We have focused here on the current effects of these changes, but there are important future effects as well. In the future, there will be more plant and equipment as a result of the higher level of investment. The economy's future capacity will increase, and this will contribute to future economic growth, a topic we will examine in Chapter 27. Thus, not only are all markets linked today, but also markets today are linked with markets in the future.

The basic full-employment model also can be used to examine the impact on the labor, product, and capital markets of the rise in labor force participation rates among women. The *labor force participation rate* is the fraction of a group that is in the labor force (either employed or seeking work). In 1970, the female labor force participation

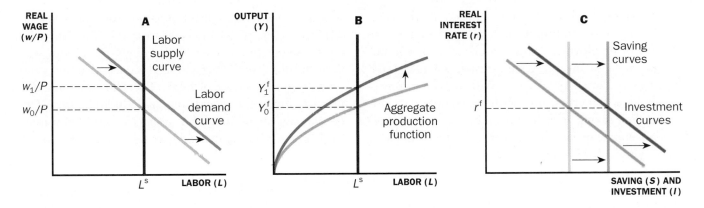

FIGURE 24.10 *Effects of Introducing Personal Computers into the Economy*

Panel A depicts the labor market. The labor supply curve is drawn as a vertical line at L^s. Personal computers increase the marginal product of workers, resulting in a rightward shift of the labor demand curve and an increase in the equilibrium real wage from w_0/P to w_1/P. Panel B depicts the aggregate production function; it shifts up due to the introduction of computers and the increased productivity of workers. Potential GDP increases from Y_0^f to Y_1^f. Panel C depicts the capital market. Investment increases as firms purchase personal computers, and saving increases as a result of increased income. Both the investment and saving curves shift to the right. There may be no net effect on the real interest rate (r_0) as shown here.

rate was 43 percent, compared to 80 percent for men. By 1999, the female rate had risen to 60 percent. The female population (sixteen years and older) in 1999 was about 108 million, of whom 65 million were in the labor force. If participation rates had remained at the level seen in 1970,

only 46 million women would be in the labor force. The rising participation rate among women has added almost 20 million additional workers to the U.S. economy.

The effects of this change are shown in Figure 24.11. The increased supply of workers shifts the labor supply

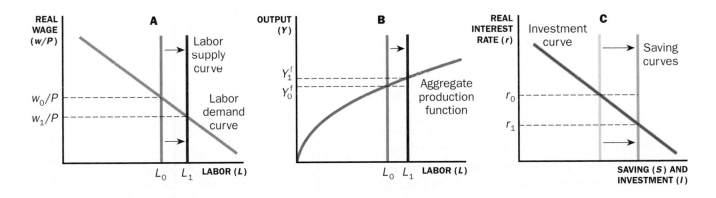

FIGURE 24.11 *Effects of an Increase in the Supply of Labor*

Panel A depicts the labor market. As more women enter the labor force, the labor supply curve shifts to the right, from L_0 to L_1. This results in a decrease in the equilibrium real wage from w_0/P to w_1/P and an increase in employment. Panel B depicts the aggregate production function; with employment higher, potential GDP rises from Y_0^f to Y_1^f. Panel C depicts the capital market. Saving increases as a result of increased income; the saving curve shifts to the right. The real interest rate falls, and in the new equilibrium, both saving and investment have increased.

curve to the right. As panel A shows, the equilibrium real wage falls, while equilibrium employment rises. Because the level of employment now associated with equilibrium in the labor market has increased, potential GDP rises; this is shown in panel B. With higher incomes, households will increase both their consumption spending and their saving at each level of the real rate of interest. This impact on the capital market is shown in panel C as a rightward shift in the saving curve. While equilibrium saving and investment rise, the equilibrium real interest rate falls.

We have used the full-employment model to analyze the impacts of two important changes in the economy: those associated with the introduction of a new technology (personal computers) and those associated with a change in the labor force. To focus on the effects each would have, we studied each change in isolation, assuming nothing else was changing. In fact, both effects have been at work over the last thirty years. Both have combined to expand employment and raise potential GDP. Since the introduction of new technologies tends to raise real wages, while the expansion in the labor supply tends to lower real wages, the combined effects on real wages could be to increase them, decrease them, or leave them unchanged.

sure the price level by using price indexes (see Chapter 23). The two most common ones are the GDP deflator and the consumer price index (CPI). The GDP deflator reflects the prices of all the goods and services that the economy produces as part of GDP. The CPI measures the prices of things households purchase. In 2000, the GDP deflator was about 107. This means that in 2000 it took $1.07 to purchase what could have been bought for $1.00 in the index base year. For the GDP deflator, the base year is 1996.

Because the price level tells us how much it costs to purchase goods and services, it is a measure of the value of money; if the price level rises, each dollar will buy less in terms of the goods and services that the economy produces. The value of money falls. If the price level falls, each dollar will buy more goods and services. The value of money rises.

Just as the value of other commodities is determined by the interaction of demand and supply, the value of money will depend on the demand for money and the supply of money. To understand what determines the price level, we will need to examine the factors that affect the demand for and supply of money.

Prices and Inflation

So far, our discussion has been entirely in *real* terms; real output, employment, real saving and investment, real wages, and the real rate of interest. At no time has the aggregate price level entered the discussion. This has one immediate implication: the economy's real equilibrium at full employment is independent of the level of prices! In Figure 24.12 we have plotted the economy's full-employment level of output Y^f against the price level. Since Y^f is determined by labor demand and labor supply (both of which depend on *real* wages) and the economy's aggregate production function (which depends on the state of technology and the capital stock), it will be the same regardless of the level of prices. Because full-employment output is independent of the price level, we have drawn a vertical line in Figure 24.12 at Y^f.

The price level simply tells us how many dollars (or euros in France or Germany, yen in Japan, pesos in Mexico) it takes to buy a basket of goods and services. We mea-

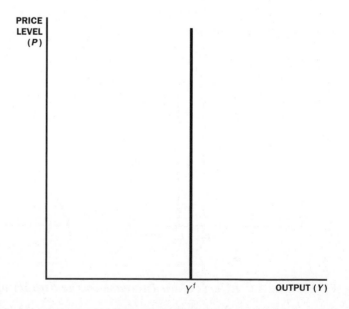

FIGURE 24.12 *The Aggregate Supply Curve*

The economy's potential GDP does not depend on the price level. This is illustrated by the vertical aggregate supply curve.

Money Demand and Supply

Money is a financial asset, just like stocks and bonds. But money differs from these other assets because we use it to carry out our day-to-day transactions. If you want to buy a cup of coffee, you cannot present the sales clerk with a share of Microsoft Corporation and expect change. In the United States, you have to present cash. Or you can pay with a credit card, but to pay for those credit purchases, you need to write a check at the end of the month. Cash and balances in checking accounts are the primary forms of money we use. The more transactions we engage in, or the higher the average value of these transactions, the more money we need to hold. Money we do not need for transactions is better used to purchase financial assets that earn interest. Increases in the dollar value of transactions increase the demand for money; decreases in the dollar value of transactions decrease the demand for money.

A useful simplifying assumption is that the amount of money individuals hold is proportional to the dollar value, or nominal value, of their income. As we learned in Chapter 23, we can express the nominal value of income as PY, the price level P times real income Y.[5] If nominal income in the economy rises, people hold, on average, more money. Nominal income can rise either because real incomes rise or because the price level rises. If real incomes rise, people typically will hold more money on average since they are likely to increase consumption and engage in more transactions. If total real income in the economy rises, money demand will rise. Money demand also rises if real income remains constant but the general level of prices changes. For example, if prices rise, each transaction involves more dollars. On average, individuals will need to hold more money to carry out their transactions.

If we use nominal GDP to measure the dollar value of transactions in the economy, the relationship between the amount of money individuals wish to hold and the dollar value of transactions is summarized by the **quantity equation of exchange:**

$$MV = PY.$$

In this equation, M is the quantity of money demanded, PY is nominal GDP (the price level P times real GDP Y), and

---

[5]Because output equals income, economists often use the letter Y to refer either to output or, as in the case here, to income.

V is **velocity**—the dollar value of transactions supported by each dollar of money holdings. While the quantity equation of exchange applies to the aggregate economy, we also can think of it in terms of an individual. For example, if Maria's nominal income is \$30,000 per year, and on average she keeps \$450 in cash or in her checking account, then the velocity of her money holdings is \$30,000/year ÷ \$450 = 66.67 per year. Velocity will depend on the methods available in the economy for carrying out transactions. If few purchases are made with money, V will be larger than if money is commonly used in making transactions. For instance, if each individual holds, on average, an amount of money equal to one week's income, then V would equal 52, while if each individual holds two weeks' worth of income as cash, V would equal 26. If innovations in the financial industry reduce the average amount of money Maria needs to hold, then velocity rises.

Since we are interested in the demand for money, we can rearrange the quantity equation to express the demand for money as

$$\text{money demand} = PY/V,$$

where PY is nominal GDP. The inverse of velocity, $1/V$, also has its own name—the Cambridge constant—after the formulation of money demand used by economists (including Keynes) at Cambridge University in the early twentieth century, and it is usually denoted by k. We can then write the demand for money as kPY. The Cambridge constant is equal to the fraction of nominal income held as money. If an individual, on average, holds two weeks' worth of income in the form of money, k is $1/26$.

The supply of money is affected by government policies, and one important role that governments play is in influencing the amount of money in circulation. This is done through *monetary policy*. In the United States, monetary policy is conducted by the Federal Reserve. How it conducts policy and how monetary policy affects the economy will be discussed at considerable length later in the book (in Chapters 25, 28, and 30 to 32). For now, we will assume that government determines the supply of money. Our focus will be on understanding the consequences for the economy if the government changes the supply of money.

Money Versus Wealth and Income We often say things like, "She has a lot of money," when we really mean that the person is wealthy or has a high income. The person in question may actually hold very little money, preferring to hold her wealth in the form of stocks, bonds, or real estate. Money is just one way individuals can hold their wealth. Since unlike other financial assets, money earns little or no interest, most people only hold what they need to carry out their everyday transactions.

Money differs from income too. For instance, suppose Maria earns $30,000 per year. It is very unlikely that she holds $30,000 in the form of money. By making some simple assumptions, we can estimate how much money, on average, Maria might hold. Assume that her monthly paycheck, after taxes and other deductions have been taken out, is $2,100. Assume also that she pays $1,000 in rent on the first of the month, puts $200 into a savings account, then spends the rest evenly throughout the month. In this case, her average money holdings during the month will equal $450, a far smaller figure than her income of $30,000 (or even her monthly take home pay of $2,100).[6] Income is the payment we receive from supplying labor, lending funds, owning capital, or owning land. It is a flow, measured over an interval of time (normally a year). Money is a stock; it is the value measured at a point in time of those financial assets used to carry out transactions.

The Price Level   If the money supply is set by the government through monetary policy, and the demand for money depends on the dollar value of transactions in the economy, how are money supply and money demand brought into balance in the full-employment model? The answer is that

the dollar value of transactions must adjust to ensure that money demand and money supply are equal.

We have already learned that when wages and prices adjust, output will be at the full-employment level that we have called Y^f. Nominal GDP is then equal to PY^f, and we can write the demand for money as

$$\text{demand for money} = P(Y^f/V),$$

which shows that the demand for money is proportional to the price level when velocity is constant. The demand for money is illustrated in panel A of Figure 24.13. Money demand increases with the general price level. An increase in the price level means that people need to hold, on average, more money in order to carry out their day-to-day transactions.[7] If the money supply is set at the level M_0 by the government, then money demand and money supply will be equal if the price level is equal to P_0. At that price level, the dollar value of transactions is such that individuals are willing to hold an amount of money just equal to the supply set by the government.

What happens if the supply of money increases? In panel A of Figure 24.13, the new money supply is M_1. At the initial price level P_0, individuals are holding more money than they want to. The easiest way to reduce the amount of money they are holding is to spend it. From the perspective of firms, increased spending by individuals provides a signal to increase prices. Faced with higher prices, workers demand high nominal wages. As prices rise, individuals need to hold more money to carry out their transactions. Equilibrium between demand and supply for money is restored when prices have risen enough to increase the quantity of money demanded by the same amount as the supply of money increased. Nominal wages will have risen by the same proportionate amount to maintain the real wage at the level that clears the labor market. In the figure, the new price level that ensures money demand is equal to

---

[6]After paying her rent and putting $200 into savings, Maria starts the month with $2,100 − $1,000 − $200 = $900, which she then spends over the course of the month. By the end of the month, her money holdings have fallen to zero, so her average holdings of money during the month are $900/2 = $450.

[7]We could write money demand as equal to bP where $b = kY^f$. Since k is a constant, the demand for money is simply proportional to the price level, for a given level of potential GDP. That is why we have represented money demand as a straight line through the origin in Figure 24.13.

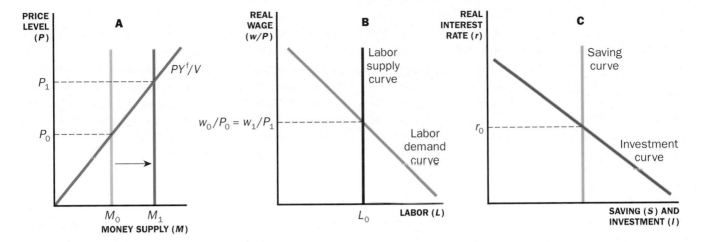

FIGURE 24.13 *The Neutrality of Money*

In panel A, the demand for money is equal to PY^f/V. If the nominal supply of money is M_0, the equilibrium price level is P_0. An increase in the money supply to M_1 leads to a rise in the price level to P_1. In panel B, the change in the price level from P_0 to P_1 does not affect the labor demand or supply curves, so the equilibrium real wage remains unchanged. The *nominal* wage increased from w_0 to w_1, where $w_1/P_1 = w_0/P_0$. Because equilibrium employment is unchanged, the increase in the money supply does not affect full-employment output. Finally, panel C shows that the investment and saving curves are also unaffected by the change in the price level. Equilibrium in the capital market continues to occur at an unchanged real rate of interest, r_0.

the new larger supply of money is P_1. At P_1, PY^f, the dollar value of transactions at full employment, has risen so that individuals now wish to hold the new stock of money, M_1. An increase in the money supply leads to an increase in the general level of prices and nominal wages.

In panel B we see the aggregate supply and demand curves for labor. In the labor market, the increase in the price level will be matched by an increase in the nominal wage, from w_0 to w_1. The *real* wage remains at its original level: $w_0/P_0 = w_1/P_1$. At this real wage, the demand for labor continues to equal the supply of labor. Thus, the effect on the labor market of an increase in the price level is simply a proportionate increase in the nominal wage. There are no real effects—the equilibrium real wage and the equilibrium level of employment, L_0, are unaffected.

In the capital market, real saving and investment depend on the real interest rate, which is not affected by the increase in the price level. Accordingly, in panel C, neither the saving curve nor the investment function shifts. At each real interest rate, *nominal* saving and investment increase by an amount exactly proportional to the increase in the money supply. Why? Because households

and firms must increase the dollar amount of saving and investment to maintain their real value, their value relative to the price level. With real saving and investment unchanged, panel C shows that the equilibrium real interest rate remains unchanged at r_0. Only the *nominal* levels of saving and investment change in proportion to the change in the price level.

We can say something more about how much the price level will increase if the money supply rises. If the money supply rises by 10 percent, the dollar value of transactions must rise by 10 percent to ensure that money demand increases by the same amount as the money supply. With full-employment output unaffected, this means the price level must rise by 10 percent, the same percentage amount as the money supply increased. The aggregate price level will move in proportion to changes in the money supply.

Most economists agree that in a full-employment economy, a one-time change in the money supply affects the price level but little else in the long run. In particular, it does not affect the quantity of goods and services produced or the number of workers employed. We can use an imaginary example to understand the point. Suppose that instantaneously, the entire supply of money in the economy was increased by a multiple of ten. In effect, we have tacked a zero onto the money supply. Stores, acting perfectly efficiently, and knowing that the money supply has multiplied by ten, would increase their prices tenfold. Thus, the actual amount of goods and services produced and consumed would be the same. There would be no real effect; the only difference would be the numbers on the bills, bank statements, and price tags.

The lesson is more general. A change in the supply of money accompanied by a proportionate change in the price level has no real effects on the economy. When changing the money supply has no real effect, we say that money is *neutral*. If the economy is at full employment and wages and prices are perfectly flexible, prices will change proportionally to any change in the money supply. Thus, the **neutrality of money** is a basic implication of the full-employment model.

The neutrality of money highlights the important distinction economists make between real and nominal phenomena. As we have seen here and in earlier chapters, in referring to a nominal variable such as nominal GDP or nominal wages, we mean the current money values of these variables—that is, the value *without* adjusting for changes in the price level. Our full-employment model with flexible wages and prices makes a perfect distinction between real and nominal phenomena. Relationships between real variables—which are the focus of the model—are completely independent of changes in nominal variables. This independence of real variables from changes in nominal variables is called the **classical dichotomy.**

Suppose instead of thinking about one-time changes in the level of the money supply, we think about what would happen if the money supply grows at 10 percent per year. Then, the price level and wages also would rise at 10 percent per year; the rate of inflation would be equal to the rate of growth of the money supply. Rapid money growth would be accompanied by high rates of inflation; low money growth would be accompanied by low rates of inflation. Figure 24.14 provides some evidence on this implication of the full-employment model. It shows average annual money supply growth rates and inflation rates for 110 countries for the period 1960–1990. Just as the full-employment model predicts, there is close to a one-for-one

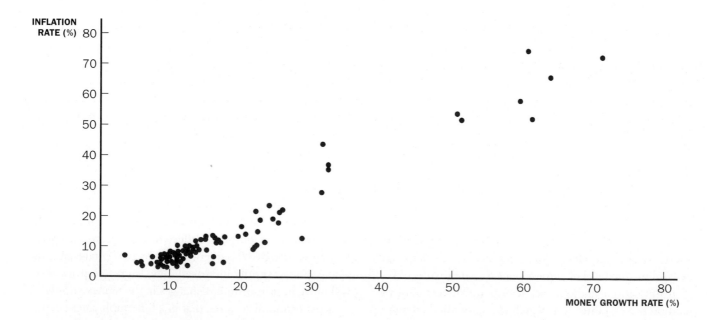

FIGURE 24.14 *Money Growth and Inflation*

Money growth and inflation are closely related, as this figure shows. Each dot represents the 1960–1990 average annual inflation rate and rate of money growth for a single country. In all, 110 countries are shown.

relationship between the growth rate of the money supply and the rate of inflation. Rapid money growth and high inflation go together; slow money growth and low inflation go together.

While the neutrality of money is a basic property of our full-employment model with flexible wages and prices, it is important to keep in mind the limitations of the model. If price increases themselves really had no real consequences, then inflation would not be a matter of much concern. But as we learned in Chapter 23, it is a concern. Later chapters will explore the more complicated effects of changes in the money supply and prices when the economy is not at full employment and wages and prices are not perfectly flexible.

Technological Change and the Price Level   Earlier in the chapter, we used the full-employment model to analyze the impact of technological change, such as the introduction of personal computers, on full-employment output, employment, the real wage, and the real interest rate. We can now complete our analysis by looking at how the price level would be affected by such a change.

A new technological innovation that makes workers more productive increases the quantity of labor demanded at each real wage. Consider the effects on the economy of the introduction of personal computers. By making workers more productive, personal computers increase the marginal product of workers. Figure 24.10 illustrated the impact of such a shift. In the new equilibrium, both real wages and employment are higher. Full-employment output is also higher. Armed with these results, we can investigate the consequences for the price level.

The demand for money is equal to PY^f/V. An increase in full-employment income Y^f increases the demand for money at each level of P. With higher output, more transactions are taking place, and individuals need to hold, on average, more money. In terms of Figure 24.13A, the demand for money curve would rotate down—at each P, the demand for money is higher. If the supply of money is kept fixed, the new equilibrium will occur at a lower price level. At the initial price level, individuals find they are holding less money than they would like to at the new higher level of income. To build up their money holdings, they cut back on spending. In response, firms cut prices. With prices lower, workers accept lower nominal wages (since they are concerned with their *real* wage). Equilibrium is restored at a lower price level and lower nominal wages. Thus, a technolog-

ical change that increases labor productivity will raise real wages and full-employment output, but it will lower the price level if the money supply is fixed.

WRAP-UP

Money and the Price Level

In the full-employment model, employment, the real wage, real output, and the real rate of interest are independent of the price level.

Changes in the nominal supply of money produce proportional changes in the price level, nominal wages, and the nominal value of output.

Money is neutral.

Looking Forward

In this chapter, we used the basic competitive model to analyze the economy at full employment. We have seen how real wages adjust to ensure that the demand for labor always equals the supply of labor. In an important illustration of the interrelated nature of markets, we learned that real interest rates, adjusting to balance saving and investment so that the capital market clears, also ensure that aggregate demand and supply are equal at the full-employment level of output. Finally, we introduced money and prices and learned that when prices and wages are flexible, money is neutral, and that the inflation rate will be determined by how fast the money supply grows.

The full-employment model provides important insights into the long-run behavior of the economy, helping us to understand how the economy responds to changes when prices and wages have had sufficient time to adjust to clear markets. In this chapter, we used a very simple model, one in which the only role of the government was to set the nominal supply of money. We now need to bring the government and open economy issues more fully into the analysis, and that will be the task of Chapter 26. In Chapter 27, we will use the full-employment model to examine long-run growth. Before turning to these tasks, however, we will examine the financial system and monetary policy in more detail in Chapter 25.

Review and Practice

Summary

1. Macroeconomic equilibrium focuses on equilibrium levels of aggregates: employment, output, saving, and investment. In a full-employment competitive equilibrium, each is determined by equating demand and supply. Full employment is attained as a result of flexible real wages.

2. The real wage equates the demand for labor with the supply of labor. Increases in labor supply at each real wage are reflected in lower real wages, which induce firms to create additional jobs to match the increases in supply.

3. The full-employment level of output is that level of output which the economy can produce with its given stock of plant and equipment, when labor is fully employed. It will increase with increases in the labor supply or as a result of new technologies.

4. The real interest rate (which takes into account inflation) equates investment and saving. The desired level of investment decreases with increases in the real rate of interest. Household saving depends on income and the real interest rate. When the economy is at full employment, the interest rate is the main variable of concern in determining saving. Saving increases slightly with increases in the real interest rate.

5. Shifts to the left in the saving curve lead to reduced investment and a higher real interest rate. Shifts to the left in the investment curve lead to unchanged or lower investment and lower real interest rates.

6. Shifts to the right in the saving curve lead to increased investment and a lower real interest rate. Shifts to the right in the investment curve lead to unchanged or higher investment and higher real interest rates.

7. When saving and investment are equal, the demand for goods and services will equal the level of output at full employment. The capital market balances leakages and injections in the circular flow of income.

8. All the markets in the economy are interlinked. Changes in one market have effects in all other markets.

9. The price level adjusts to equate the demand for money with the supply of money. In a full-employment economy with perfectly flexible wages and prices, money is neutral; increases in the money supply are simply reflected in increases in prices.

10. Even if all wages and prices are not completely flexible and adjust only slowly, they eventually will move to balance supply and demand. In this case, the full-employment model can give us important insights into the longer-run behavior of the economy.

Key Terms

short-run aggregate production function
potential GDP
full-employment level of output
loanable funds market
financial investments
capital goods investments
investment function
quantity equation of exchange
velocity
neutrality of money
classical dichotomy

Review Questions

1. How do competitive markets with flexible wages and prices ensure that labor is always fully employed? What induces firms to create just the right number of additional jobs to match an increase in the number of workers?

2. Describe the effects of shifts in the labor supply curve on equilibrium real wages and potential GDP (full-employment level of output).

3. What determines the economy's productive capacity or aggregate supply or potential GDP? How does aggregate supply increase when labor supply increases?

4. What is the investment curve? Why does investment decrease when the real interest rate increases? What role do expectations play in investment?

5. What determines the level of saving? Explain why, if taxes are fixed, disposable income in a full-employment

economy is fixed. Explain why saving may not be very sensitive to the real interest rate.

6. How are leakages and injections balanced? Why will demand and supply in the product market be equal if leakages and injections are equal?

7. Why will only the price level and money wages be affected by a change in the money supply in the full-employment economy? How is the rate of inflation related to the rate of growth of the money supply?

Problems

1. In the text, we assumed that the labor supply did not depend on the real wage. Assume that at higher real wages, more individuals wish to work. Trace through how each of the steps in the analysis has to be changed. (Show the equilibrium in the labor market. What happens to real wages, employment, GDP, and saving if the labor supply curve shifts to the right?)

2. An increase in capital resulting from an increase in investment allows a given number of workers to produce more. Show the effect on the short-run production function and the full-employment level of output.

3. Trace through how the effects of a change in one market—such as an increase in the supply of labor—have effects on other markets. How was it possible for there to be a large increase in the labor supply, such as occurred during the 1970s and the 1980s, and yet real wages changed relatively little?

4. The following table gives average hourly nominal wages in manufacturing and the price levels in the United States from 1994 to 1999.

Year	Nominal Wage	Price Level
1994	12.07	148.2
1995	12.37	152.4
1996	12.77	156.9
1997	13.17	160.5
1998	13.49	163.0
1999	13.91	166.6

(a) For each year, calculate the real wage.

(b) In what year did the nominal wage rise the most?

(c) In what year did the real wage rise the most?

(d) Did you get the same years for both (b) and (c)? If you didn't, what accounts for the difference?

5. Figure 24.10 showed the impact of personal computers on full-employment output, the real wage, and the real interest rate when the labor supply curve is vertical. Suppose instead that the labor supply curve is upward sloping. How does this change affect your conclusions about the impact of personal computers?

6. Suppose, due to the growth of consumer purchases over the Internet, individuals find they need less cash to carry out their transactions. If the demand for money is equal to kPY, this change can be thought of as leading to a fall in the value of k. If the money supply remains constant, what happens to the price level? What happens to nominal wages? To real wages? To employment?

7. Using the full-employment model, discuss the effect on employment, output, the real rate of interest, investment, and saving if households become more optimistic about the future and as a result reduce their current saving. (Be sure to distinguish between the impacts on the investment function and the saving curve and the impacts on the levels of saving and investment in the new equilibrium.)

8. Suppose personal computers increase labor productivity. If the government wants to keep the price level constant in the face of this technological change, should it increase the money supply, decrease it, or keep it unchanged?

Chapter 25

Money, Banking, and Credit

Key Questions

1. What are financial intermediaries? What do they do?

2. What is meant by the money supply, how is it measured, and how is it determined?

3. How do modern economies create money through the banking system? How do monetary authorities affect the creation of money and the availability of credit?

4. What is the Federal Reserve System?

5. What policy tools does the Federal Reserve use to affect the money supply and the nominal interest rate?

6. What factors are important in choosing between focusing on the nominal interest rate or on the money supply when conducting monetary policy?

*T*he capital market plays a critical function in the economy. It balances saving and investment at full employment, ensuring that demand and supply in the product market balance. This role of the capital market formed a central core of the full-employment model developed in Chapter 24. In that chapter, we also learned about the key relationship between the supply of money and the price level. In modern economies, banks are active participants in the capital market *and* are key to understanding how the supply of money is determined. In this chapter, we focus on the role of banks in the economy's financial market and on their role in affecting how monetary policy influences the economy.

In the United States, the Federal Reserve System, commonly called "the Fed," conducts monetary policy. In this chapter, we will discuss the Federal Reserve and the role of central banks in affecting the money supply and the nominal interest rate. The Fed, like other major central banks, has used its influence over the nominal interest rate to implement monetary policy. As it acts to affect the nominal interest rate, the Fed's policies influence the banking sector and lead to changes in the money supply.

While you might care about how much money you have because it provides a measure of how much you might be able to spend, macroeconomists focus on the supply of money in the economy because of its connection with the price level and inflation. Over the last fifty years, the general level of prices has risen significantly, as Figure 25.1 shows. The index of consumer prices has risen by more than 1,600 percent since 1913. Something that cost $1 in 1913 would cost over $17 today. A rising price level—inflation—is associated with growth in the supply of money. In the full-employment model presented in Chapter 24, faster money growth led directly to a higher rate of inflation. We did not explain in that chapter, however, how the growth rate of the money supply is determined, nor did we explain how government policy affects the money supply or even what the money supply is.

Money and prices go together, but there is also an interest rate that plays a key role in U.S. monetary policy. This interest rate is called the *federal funds interest rate*. In this chapter, we will explain what "federal funds" are, what determines supply and demand in the market for federal funds, and how the federal funds interest rate balances

515

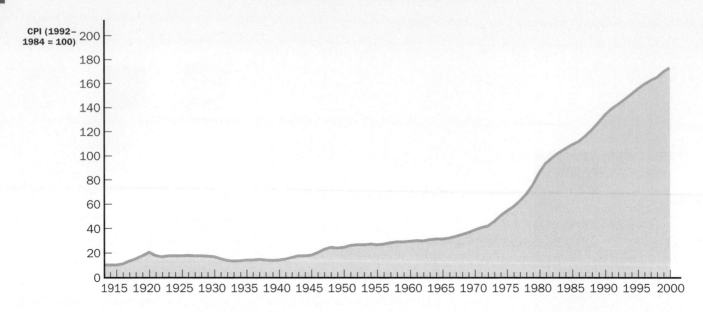

FIGURE 25.1   *The Consumer Price Index for 1913–2000*

Consumer prices have risen significantly since the early years of the twentieth century, with most of the increase occurring since 1970.

SOURCE: Bureau of Labor Statistics.

supply and demand. To do this, we begin by explaining the role financial institutions play and how banks create money. We focus on banks because they are key players in financial markets generally and the federal funds market in particular.

The Financial System in Modern Economies

The capital market is the market where the supply of funds is allocated to those who wish to borrow. In everyday language, we often refer to this as the country's financial market. Broadly speaking, a country's *financial system* includes all institutions involved in moving savings from households and firms whose income exceeds their expenditures and transferring it to other households and firms who would like to spend more than their current income allows.

The financial system in the United States not only allows consumers to buy cars, televisions, and computers even when they do not have the cash to do so, but also enables firms to invest in factories and new machines. Sometimes

money goes directly from, say, a household with some savings to a firm that needs some additional cash. For example, when Ben buys a bond from General Motors that promises to pay a fixed amount in 90 or 180 days (or in 5 or 15 years), he is lending money directly to the company.

But most funds flow through *financial intermediaries*. These are firms that stand between the savers, who have extra funds, and the borrowers, who need them. The most important of these financial intermediaries are banks, but there are many other groups of financial intermediaries as well, including life insurance companies, credit unions, and savings and loan associations. All are engaged in looking over potential borrowers, ascertaining who are good risks, and monitoring their investments and loans. The intermediaries take "deposits" from consumers and invest them. By putting funds into many different investments, they diversify and thus reduce risk. One investment might turn sour, but it is unlikely that many will. This provides the intermediary with a kind of safety it could not obtain if it put all "its eggs in one basket." Financial institutions differ in who the depositors are, where the funds are invested, and who owns the institution. Table 25.1 provides a glossary of the major types of financial intermediaries.

TABLE 25.1

A Glossary of Financial Intermediaries

A variety of financial intermediaries take funds from the public and lend them to borrowers or otherwise invest the funds. Of the many legal differences between these institutions, the principal ones relate to the kinds of loans or investments they make. The following list is ranked roughly by the asset size of each intermediary.

Commercial banks	Banks chartered by either the federal government (national banks) or a state (state banks) to receive deposits and make loans.	**Mutual funds**	Financial intermediaries that take funds from a group of investors and invest them. Major examples include stock mutual funds, which invest the funds in stocks; bond mutual funds, which invest in bonds; and money market mutual funds, which invest in liquid assets such as Treasury bills and certificates of deposit. Many mutual funds allow you to write checks against the fund.
Life insurance companies	Companies that collect premiums from policyholders out of which insurance payments are made.		
Savings and loan associations (S & L's, or "thrifts")	Institutions originally chartered to receive deposits for the purpose of making loans to finance home mortgages; in the early 1980s, they were given more latitude in the kinds of loans they could make.	**Institutional money market mutual funds**	Money market mutual fund accounts held by institutions.
		CMA™ accounts (cash management accounts)	Accounts at a brokerage firm (the name was given to the first such accounts, established by Merrill Lynch) that enable people to place stocks, bonds, and other assets into a single account, against which they can write checks.
Credit unions	Cooperative (not for profit) institutions, usually organized at a place of work or by a union, that take deposits from members and make loans to members.		

Financial intermediaries play an important role in our financial system. After all, few firms have the resources to undertake investments in new buildings, factories, or equipment without borrowing to do so. And in recent years, venture capitalists have played a critical role in providing the funding that allows new, high-tech firms to get started. For simplicity, our discussion in the rest of this chapter will focus on one very important group of financial intermediaries—commercial banks.

Traditionally, banks have been the most important way in which businesses raise capital. When the banking system collapses, as it did in the 1930s in the United States, firms cannot obtain funds to make their investments, consumers lose their deposits, and the entire economy suffers. For this reason, governments have developed banking regulations with the objective of ensuring greater financial stability. These regulations are designed to protect consumers. When banks go bankrupt, depositors stand to lose their life's savings, and the typical saver is not in a position to audit a bank's books to see whether it is really sound. During the Great Depression of the 1930s, hundreds of banks closed, leaving thousands destitute. Today, banks are regulated more tightly, and deposits are insured by the federal government, to limit the losses should a bankruptcy occur.

There is another reason why it is important to understand the role of banks. The actions of commercial banks affect the supply of money and therefore can have consequences for the overall level of prices in the economy. Because of this central role of banks, they play a critical role in the way monetary polices affect the economy.

While our focus will be on banks, it is important to recognize that there is a continuum of financial intermediaries that perform in varying ways the functions that banks perform. For instance, savings and loan associations (S & L's) accept deposits and make loans today in a way that is almost identical to that of banks.

Creating Money in Modern Economies

Banks have long played a key role in the financial sector. One reason for their importance is that they create money. Today's money supply is created not by a mint or a printing press but largely by the banking sector. The money supply not only consists of the cash we carry but also the deposits in checking accounts. The total level of deposits in the banking system is an important part of what we mean by the money supply. Whenever you deposit money to or withdraw money from your checking account, you are potentially having an impact on the quantity of money.

When you put $100 into the bank, the bank does not simply put it in a slot marked with your name and keep it there until you are ready to take it out. Instead, banks realize that not all their thousands of depositors will withdraw their money on any given day. Some people will withdraw their money in a week, some in two weeks, some not for a year or more. In the meantime, the bank can lend out the money deposited and charge interest on the loans it makes. The more money the bank can persuade people to deposit, the more it can lend out and the more money the bank will earn. To attract depositors, the bank pays interest on some of its deposits, effectively passing on (after taking its cut) the interest earned on its loans.

Money Is What Money Does

What do bank deposits and loans have to do with the total amount of money in the economy? When we talk about money, we often mean much more than just currency. Sometimes we talk about how much money someone makes, but that really refers to the individual's income. Or we say someone has a lot of money, but then we really mean the individual is wealthy, not that the person has lots of currency stashed away.

Economists define *money* by the functions it serves, and three functions are critical.

Money as a Medium of Exchange
Money's first function is to facilitate trade—the exchange of good and services. This is called the **medium of exchange** function of money. Trade that involves the direct exchange of goods without the use of money is called *barter*. For example, barter occurs when a mechanic fixes a plumber's car in exchange for plumbing work. Nations sometimes sign treaties phrased in barter terms; a certain amount of oil might be traded for a certain amount of machinery or weapons.

Barter works best in simple economies. For simple barter to work, however, there must be a *double-coincidence of wants*. That is, one individual must have what the other wants, and vice versa. If Helen has compact discs (CDs) and wants videos, and Joshua has videos and wants CDs, bartering will make them both better off. However, if Helen has CDs but Joshua does not want CDs, bartering for Joshua's videos will require that one or both of them search for people with other goods in hopes of putting together a multilateral exchange. Money provides a way to make multilateral exchanges much simpler. Helen sells her CDs for money and uses the money to buy Joshua's videos. Money is essential for the billions of exchanges that take place in a modern economy.

Money can be thought of as a social convention. People accept money in payment for what they sell because they know that others will accept money for what they want to buy. Any easily transportable and storable good, in principle, can be used as a medium of exchange, and different cultures have chosen widely different goods to use as money. South Sea Islanders once used cowry shells. In World War II prisoner-of-war camps and in many prisons today, cigarettes are a medium of exchange.

Today all developed countries use paper and metal coins produced by the government as currency. However, most business transactions do not involve the use of currency. Business transactions typically require the use of checks drawn on banks, credit cards whose balances are paid with checks, and funds wired from one bank to another. Since checking account balances are accepted as payment at most places, economists view checking account balances as money. Most people keep much more money in checking accounts than they do in their wallets, so economists' measure of the money supply is much larger than the amount of currency in circulation.

Money as a Store of Value
People will only exchange what they have for money if they believe they can later exchange money for things they need. For money to serve as a medium of exchange, it must hold its value. Economists call this second function of money the store of value function. Governments once feared that paper

money by itself would not hold its value unless it was backed by a commodity such as gold. People had confidence in paper money because they knew they could exchange their paper money at banks for gold.

Today, however, all major economies have *fiat money*—money that has value only because the government says it has value and because people are willing to accept it in exchange for goods. Dollar bills carry the message: "This note is legal tender for all debts, public and private." The term *legal tender* means that if you owe $100, you have fully discharged that debt if you pay with a hundred-dollar bill (or 100 one-dollar bills).

Money as a Unit of Account   Money serves a third critical function in the economy. It is a way of measuring the relative values of different goods and services. This is the **unit of account** function of money. If a laptop computer costs $1,800 and a desktop computer costs $900, then a laptop is worth twice as much as a desktop. People wishing to trade laptops for desktops will trade at the rate of one laptop for two desktops. Money provides a simple and convenient measure of relative market values.

Imagine how difficult it would be for firms to track their profitability without money. Their accounting ledgers would record how many items were sold or purchased, but firms would not know whether these transactions had left them better or worse off. Firms need to know the relative value of what they sell and what they purchase. Money provides the unit of account for measuring relative values.

We are now ready for the economic definition of **money.** Money is anything that is generally accepted as a medium of exchange, a store of value, and a unit of account. Money is, in other words, what it does.

CASE IN POINT

When Atlanta Printed Money

In the nineteenth and early twentieth centuries, in the rural South and West, there was often a shortage of cash for everyday transactions. Workers could not shop for food or clothing, bills were not paid, and the local economy lurched sideways or backward.

It was common in such cases for towns, private companies, and sometimes states to print their own currency, known politely as "scrip" and less politely as "soap wrappers," "shinplasters," "doololly," and many less printable names. The idea was that issuing scrip could keep the local economy going until official currency became available again, at which point people could cash in their scrip.

The last major issue of scrip in the United States came during the Great Depression of the early 1930s. Banks were crashing right and left, and bank runs were a daily occurrence. Remember, these were the days before deposits were insured. When President Franklin Roosevelt took office early in 1933, one of his first major actions was to declare a "bank holiday" for the week of March 6–12. He closed all the banks for a week to give everyone time to relax and get their bearings.

But these were also the days before checking accounts had become widespread, when workers were paid weekly, in cash. If firms could not get to the bank, they could not pay their workers. How could the local economy react to these sorts of financial disturbances?

Each area adapted in its own way. Let's consider Atlanta. The city issued about $2.5 million in scrip, in eight different issues made during the first half of the 1930s. One of the first payments was to schoolteachers, and the city made sure that Rich's, a prominent local department store, would take the scrip at full face value. Many other stores, however, would count the scrip only at 75 percent or less of face value. Notice that by taking scrip, which it would later turn in to the city for cash, stores were effectively loaning money to the city that issued the scrip.

Such stories of scrip may sound antiquated today (though in its 1992 financial crisis, California paid its workers with something akin to scrip). But they emphasize the fact that without something to serve as a medium of exchange, a yardstick for measurement, and a (short-term) store of value, an economy simply cannot function. Today the Federal Reserve acts to ensure that currency is available. But in the 1930s, issuing scrip was one thing a city could do on its own to cushion the ravages of the Great Depression. ●

SOURCE: William Roberds, "Lenders of the Next-to-Last Resort: Scrip Issue in Georgia During the Great Depression," *Economic Review of the Federal Reserve Bank of Atlanta* (September–October 1990), pp. 16–30.

Measuring the Money Supply

The quantity of money in an economy is called the *money supply*, a stock variable like the capital stock. Most of the other variables discussed in this chapter are stock variables as well, but they have important effects on the flow variables (like the level of economic activity, measured as dollars *per year*).

What should be included in the money supply? A variety of things serve some of the functions of money. For example, in a casino, gambling chips are a medium of exchange, and chips may even be accepted by nearby stores and restaurants. But no place outside the casino is obligated to take chips; they are neither a generally accepted medium of exchange nor a unit of account.

Economists' measure of money begins with the currency people carry around. Economists then expand the measure of money to include other items that serve the three functions of money. Checking accounts or **demand deposits** (so called because you can get your money back on demand) are part of the money supply, as are some other forms of bank accounts. But what are the limits? There is a continuum, running from items that everyone would agree should be called money, to items that work as money in many circumstances, to items that should never be considered part of the money supply.

Economists have developed several measures of the money supply to take account of this variety. The narrowest, called **M1,** is the total of currency, traveler's checks, and checking accounts. More simply, M1 is currency plus items that can be treated like currency throughout the banking system. In late 2000, M1 totaled $1.1 trillion.

A broader measure, **M2,** includes everything that is in M1, plus some items that are *almost* perfect substitutes for M1. Savings deposits of $100,000 or less are included. So are certificates of deposit (deposits put in the bank for fixed periods of time, between six months and five years); money market funds held by individuals; and eurodollars, U.S. dollars deposited in European banks. In late 2000, M2 totaled $4.9 trillion.

The common characteristic of assets in M2 is that they are *liquid*, or easily converted into M1. You cannot tell a store that the money needed to purchase a shirt is in your savings account. But if you have funds in a savings account, it is not hard to change these funds into either currency or a checking account, so that you can pay for the shirt with cash or a check.

A third measure of the money supply, **M3,** includes everything that is in M2 (including everything in M1) plus large-denomination savings accounts (over $100,000) and institutional money market mutual funds. M3 is nearly as liquid as M2. In late 2000, M3 totaled $6.5 trillion.

Table 25.2 provides a glossary of the financial assets used in the various definitions of money, and Figure 25.2 shows the relative magnitude of M1, M2, and M3. Figure 25.3 shows that the different measures grow at different rates, with swings in M1 growth being particularly erratic since the mid-1980s.

Recent changes in financial institutions, such as the growth of mutual funds, the extensive use of credit cards, and home equity loans, have made it more difficult to answer the question of what to include in the money supply. For instance, many people own shares in government-bond mutual funds that provide checkwriting privileges. When someone writes a check on a bond mutual fund, the mutual fund sells just the value of bonds required to transfer the amount of the check into the bank account of the check writer. The funds go into the bank account in a split second. Bond mutual funds with check-writing privileges function just like money, yet they are not included in the money supply, while money market mutual funds are. The introduction of electronic cash will further complicate the problem of measuring money.

CASE IN POINT

"Boggs Bills" and the Meaning of Money

J. S. Boggs is an artist who explores the social meaning of money. He starts by drawing a dollar, completely accurate except for some crucial details. The bill might say "In God We Rust" instead of "In God We Trust."

With the Boggs bill in hand, the artist sees if someone will accept it at face value in payment for actual goods or services. For example, he might offer a restaurant a $20 Boggs bill in exchange for a meal. If the restaurant accepts the bill and provides any change, Boggs notes the details of the transaction on the bill before turning it over. Boggs then sells the receipt and the change. An art dealer might purchase the receipt and change and then track down the restaurant and try to buy the Boggs bill. The dealer then resells the bill, the receipt, and the change. One such "transaction" sold for $420,000! The British Museum, the Museum of Modern Art, and the Smithsonian are among the museums holding Bogg's transaction pieces in their permanent collections.

TABLE 25.2

Glossary of Financial Terms

One of the problems in defining money is the wide variety of assets that are not directly used as a medium of exchange but can be readily converted into something that *could* be so used. Should they be included in the money supply? There is no right or wrong answer. Below are definitions of eight terms, some of which were defined in earlier chapters. Each of these assets serves, in progressively less satisfactory ways, the function of money.

Term	Definition	Term	Definition
Currency	One, five, ten, twenty, and hundred dollar bills; pennies, nickels, dimes, quarters, and half dollars.	**Certificates of deposit**	Money deposited in the bank for a fixed period of time (usually six months to five years), with a penalty for early withdrawal.
Traveler's checks	Checks issued by a bank or a firm such as American Express that you can convert into currency upon demand and are widely accepted.	**Money market accounts**	Another category of interest-bearing bank checking accounts, often paying higher interest rates but with restrictions on the number of checks that can be written.
Demand deposits, or checking accounts	Deposits that you can withdraw upon demand (that is, convert into currency upon demand), by writing a check.	**Money market mutual funds**	Mutual funds that invest in Treasury bills, certificates of deposit, and similar safe securities. You can usually write checks against such accounts.
Savings deposits	Deposits that technically you can withdraw only upon notice; in practice, banks allow withdrawal upon demand (without notice).	**Eurodollars**	U.S. dollar bank accounts in banks outside the United States (mainly in Europe).

Boggs bills illustrate the social nature of fiat money—anything can serve as money if others are willing to accept it as money. As Boggs puts it, "Nobody knows what a dollar is, what the word means, what holds the thing up, what it stands in for. And that's also what my work is about. Look at these things, I try to say. They're beautiful. But what the hell are they? What do they do? How do they do it?"

The Secret Service has taken a dim view of Boggs's efforts and has taken him to court. In its ruling against the artist, the U.S. Court of Appeals for the District of Columbia stated, "Art is supposed to imitate life, but when the subject matter is money, if it imitates life too closely it becomes counterfeiting." ●

Money and Credit

One of the key properties of money, as noted, is that it is the medium of exchange. However, many transactions today do not entail the use of any of the measures presented so far: M1, M2, or M3. They involve credit not money. In selling a suit of clothes or a piece of furniture or a car, stores often do not receive money. Rather, they receive a promise from you to pay money in the future. Credit is clearly tied to money; what you owe the store is measured in dollars. You want something today, and you will have the money for it tomorrow. The store wants you to buy today and is willing to wait until tomorrow or next week for the money. There is a mutually advantageous trade. But because the exchange is not *simultaneous,* the store must rely on your promise.

Promises, the saying goes, are made to be broken. But if they are broken too often, stores will not be able to trust buyers, and credit exchanges will not occur. There is therefore an incentive for the development of institutions, such as banks, to ascertain who is most likely to keep economic promises and to help ensure that once such a promise has been made it is kept.

When banks are involved, the store does not need to believe the word of the shopper. Rather, the shopper must convince the bank that he will in fact pay. Consider

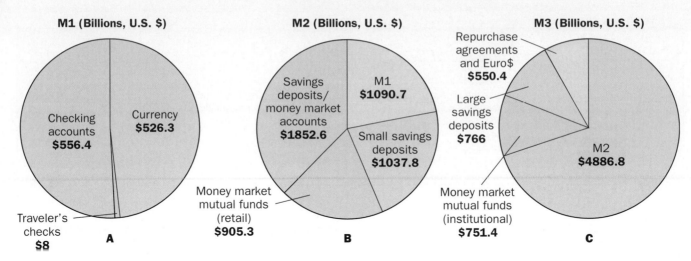

FIGURE 25.2   *The Measures of Money in 2000*

The money supply can be measured in many ways, including M1, M2, and M3.

SOURCE: *ERP* (2001), Tables B-67, B-68.

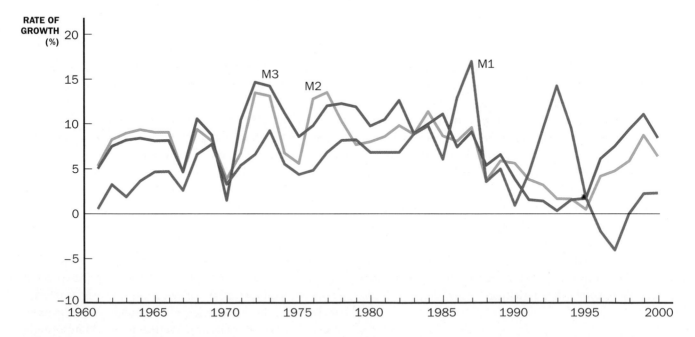

FIGURE 25.3   *Growth of the Money Supply*

It makes a difference which measure of the money supply is used. Different measures grew at different rates during the 1980s and 1990s.

SOURCE: *ERP* (2001), Table B-69.

Thinking Like an Economist

Exchange, Money, and the Internet

Imagine how difficult it would be to organize exchange without money. As individuals, we probably think about the value of money in terms of the wealth it represents. The cash we carry in our pockets has no intrinsic value—you cannot eat it, for instance—but it does represent value because it can be exchanged for things that are of direct utility to us—food, clothing, housing, and the thousands of goods and services we consume.

An economist naturally thinks of the benefits that are gained from voluntary exchange, and so thinks of the social benefits that money provides by reducing the costs of exchanging goods and services. The music store employee does not have to accept compact discs (CDs) for wages and then find a landlord who is willing to rent an apartment for CDs. Instead, wages are paid in money, and the landlord is happy to take money for rent, knowing that she can use the money to purchase the goods and services she wants. Thus, the role of money in helping to carry out transactions cheaply and efficiently is the most important service it provides.

The classic problem faced by barter systems—the need to find someone who has what you want and wants what you have—may be reduced by the ability of the Internet to match sellers and buyers. A number of companies have set up Web sites that arrange barter transactions. However, even with the information-processing capabilities of the Internet, these barter Web sites still rely on a form of money. Barter Systems, Inc. (http://www.bartersys.com) is typical. A seller receives "trade dollars," that then can be used to make purchases from other sellers. U.S. dollars are not used, but trade dollars serve just like a local currency to avoid the double coincidence of wants that makes barter inefficient.

---

a car purchase. Suppose the bank agrees to give Todd a loan, and he then buys the car. If he later breaks his promise and does not pay back the loan, the car dealer is protected. It is the bank that tries to force Todd to keep his commitment.

Modern economies have relied increasingly on credit as a basis of transactions. Banks have a long tradition of extending *lines of credit* to firms. This means that a bank agrees to lend money to a business automatically (up to some limit) as it is needed. With Visa and MasterCard and the variety of other national credit cards that came into widespread use in the 1970s and 1980s, lines of credit also have been extended to millions of consumers, who now can purchase goods even when they have no currency or checking balances on hand. Today, individuals also can get credit easily based on the equity in their homes (the difference between the value of the house and what they owe on their mortgage, which is the loan taken out to buy the house). This type of credit is called a *home equity loan.* When house prices increased rapidly in the 1980s and again in the 1990s, they provided a ready source of credit for millions of home owners.

These innovations make it easier for people to obtain credit. But they also have altered the way economists think about the role of money in the economy—blurring definitions that once seemed quite clear.

The Money Supply and the Bank's Balance Sheet

The banking system plays a critical role in the economy because demand deposits are an important component of the money stock, representing over 50 percent of M1 in 2000. Understanding what determines the money stock in a modern economy begins with a look at a typical bank's balance sheet.

Like any firm's balance sheet, a bank's balance sheet describes its assets and liabilities. The one thing to keep in mind, though, is that bankers see the world backward. Where else would loans be called "assets" and deposits be called "liabilities"? This is the perspective shown on the bank's balance sheet. *Assets* are what the bank owns, including what is owed to it by others. That is why the bank's loans appear as assets on its balance sheet. Liabilities are what it owes to others. We can think of the bank's

e-Insight

Electronic Cash

A TV ad shows a thirsty Italian gentleman who finds himself short of change for a soda trying to steal coins out of a fountain, while a young girl points her cellular phone at the same machine and retrieves a drink. The message? Cash is for old folks.

"Cold, hard cash" is becoming a rarity in the United States. Americans increasingly rely on credit cards and ATM cards for all but the smallest transactions. Credit card purchases are often an easy, if expensive, method of taking out a consumer loan. But even consumers who pay off their credit card balances every month enjoy the convenience of using cards instead of cash. They get complete records of their purchases every month, they do not have to write checks for recurring bills, and they collect benefits like air miles for their purchases. Such consumers choose automatic credit card payment for their phone bills, magazine subscriptions, and even their medical and dental bills. Cash is reserved for occasional purchases of small items at convenience stores. Soon even these "microtransactions" that still require cash may be taken over by electronic payment options. Seven U.S. financial powerhouses have contracted with Mondex USA to market electronic cash, and Visa is marketing its own version, VISA Cash. The companies involved are betting that the world is headed for marketplaces in which cash never changes hands.

Electronic cash cards are plastic "smart cards" that resemble the phone cards now widely used for long-distance calls. They contain microchips that enable users to transfer money from bank accounts to the cards at special ATMs or phones. The cards can then be used to make purchases at participating merchants. The purchases take place almost instantly, because, unlike credit card and ATM transactions, they do not require authorization over a phone line or verification of a password. Merchants are eager for this technology, as authorization charges and password verification are expensive, leading many stores to institute minimum purchase requirements for credit card or ATM card transactions. In a world of e-cash, consumers will never need to worry about minimum purchase requirements or about having the right change for a bus or a vending machine. The microchip in their e-cash card will communicate with the microchip at a store or vending machine, and if the chips have determined that there are no security issues, the transaction is complete.

For further discussion of the future of cash, see Kevin P. Sheehan, "Electronic Cash," *FDIC Banking Review* 11, no. 2 (1998), pp. 1–8.

This smart money card from Denmark's Danmønt system can be used to buy all sorts of goods.

depositors as having loaned money to the bank. That is why deposits are treated by the bank as liabilities.

Table 25.3 shows the balance sheet of a typical bank that we will call AmericaBank. Its assets are divided into three categories: loans outstanding, government bonds, and reserves.

Reserves are the deposits the bank has not used to make loans or buy government bonds. The cash a bank keeps in its vault to meet daily business needs is one part of the bank's reserves. There is another form reserves can take. In the United States, the Federal Reserve (the "Fed") acts as a bank for banks; private banks that are members of the Federal Reserve System can have accounts with the Fed, and the money the bank has in this account also is part of its reserves. The bank's riskiest assets are its loans outstanding. These consist of loans to business firms, real estate loans (mortgages), car loans, house-remodeling loans, and so on. Government bonds are more secure than loans to households or firms. Most banks' holdings of government bonds are typically concentrated in Treasury bills (or T-bills), short-term bonds maturing in thirty, sixty, or ninety days after the date of issue.[1] Most secure are the reserves that are held on deposit at the "banker's bank," the local Federal Reserve bank, and the cash in the vault.

The amount of money people need to set aside for emergencies depends (in part) on how easily they can borrow. The same is true for banks. If they can borrow easily from other banks to meet any shortfall of reserves, they need to keep very little in reserves. In the United States, the Federal Reserve Banks act as the banker's bank, lending money to other banks. (Banks do not, however, have an automatic right to borrow; the Fed must concur with the request. Many central banks use this discretionary power to elicit desired behavior.) But banks need to hold reserves for an additional reason other than caution. The Fed imposes reserve requirements on banks. Today, the amount of reserves banks hold is dictated more by regulations than by the banks' own perceptions of what is prudent. After all, holding T-bills is just as safe as holding reserves with the Fed—and yields higher returns. And the level of reserves required by the Fed is designed primarily from the perspective of controlling the money supply and thereby the level of economic activity. Table 25.4 shows the current reserve requirements. This sys-

TABLE 25.4

Required Reserves	
Type of deposit	**Minimum reserve required (percentage of deposits)**
Very large checking accounts (over $46.5 million)	10
Other checking accounts (under $46.5 million)	3
All other deposits	0
SOURCE: *Federal Reserve Bulletin* (1999).	

tem of banking, in which banks hold a fraction of the amount on deposit in reserves, is called a **fractional reserve system.**

The liability side of AmericaBank's balance sheet consists of two items: deposits and net worth. Deposits include checking accounts, which are technically known as demand deposits, and the variety of forms of savings accounts, which are technically known as time deposits. The bank's net worth is simply the difference between the value of its assets and the value of its liabilities. In other words, if the bank's assets were sold and its depositors paid off, what remained would equal the net worth of the bank.

Since net worth is *defined* as the difference between the value of the liabilities and the value of the assets, the numbers on both sides of the balance sheet always balance.

How Banks Create Money

As we have seen, the currency manufactured by the Treasury is a relatively small part of the money supply. Who creates the rest of the money? Banks.

To see how banks create money, let's consider all 9,500 U.S. banks as one huge superbank. Assume the Fed is requiring that reserves be 10 percent of deposits. Now suppose that a multi-multi-millionaire deposits $1 billion in currency in her account.

TABLE 25.3

AmericaBank Balance Sheet			
Assets		**Liabilities**	
Loans outstanding	$28 million	Deposits	$30 million
Government Bonds	$ 2 million		
Reserves	$ 3 million	Net worth	$ 3 million
Total	$33 million	Total	$33 million

---

[1]Long-term bonds are volatile in price, because their price changes with changes in interest rates. Banks typically hold short-term government bonds because the risk of such changes over a relatively short period of time is low, and banks wish to avoid risk.

The bank reasons as follows. It knows it must keep a reserve-to-deposit ratio of 1 to 10, and it has a long line of loan applicants. When the bank makes a loan, it does not actually give the borrower currency. It credits him with funds in his checking account. It does this by placing an entry into its books on both the left- and right-hand side of the ledger; there is a loan on the asset side and a deposit on the liability side. If it makes $9 billion worth of loans, its liabilities will have gone up to $10 billion (the $1 billion in currency originally deposited by the millionaire plus the $9 billion worth of loans). On the asset side, the bank takes the $1 billion in currency to the Fed and is credited with the amount, so that it now has $1 billion in reserves. Thus, its reserves have increased by $1 billion, its deposits by $10 billion; it has satisfied the reserve requirement.

This relationship between the change in reserves and the final change in deposits is called the **money multiplier.** We can reach the same result by a slower route, as shown in Table 25.5.

Money Multipliers with Many Banks

The money multiplier works just as well when there is more than one bank involved. Assume that Desktop Publishing and ComputerAmerica have their bank accounts in two separate banks, BankNational and BankUSA, respectively. When Desktop Publishing writes a check for $900 million to ComputerAmerica, $900 million is transferred from Bank National to BankUSA. Once that $900 million has been transferred, BankUSA will find that it can lend more than it could prevously. As a result of the $900 million increase in deposits, it can lend .9 × $900 = $810 million. Suppose it lends the $810 million to the NewTelephone Company, which uses the money to buy a machine for making telephone equipment from Equipment Manufacturing. If Equipment Manufacturing has its bank account at BankIllinois, after Equipment Manufacturing has been paid, BankIllinois will find that because its deposits have increased by $810 million, it can lend .9 × $810 = $729 million. The process continues until the new equilibrium is identical to the one described earlier in the superbank example, where there is a $10 billion increase in the money supply. The banking system as a whole will have expanded the money supply by a multiple of the initial deposit, equal to 1/reserve requirement.

In this example, there were no "leakages" outside the banking system. That is, no one decided to hold currency rather than put his money back into the bank, and whenever sellers were paid, they put what they received into the bank. With leakages, the increase in deposits and thus the increase in the money supply will be smaller. In the real world these leakages are large. After all, currency held by the public amounts to almost 50 percent of M1. The ratio of M1 to currency plus reserves held by the banking system is under 3, and for M2 the ratio is less than 10. Nevertheless, the increase in bank reserves will lead to some multiple increase in the money supply.

It should be clear that when there are many banks, no individual bank can create multiple deposits. Individual banks may not even be aware of the role they play in the process of multiple-deposit creation. All they see is that their deposits have increased and therefore they are able to make more loans.

The process of multiple-deposit creation may seem somewhat like a magician pulling rabbits out of a hat; it seems to make something out of nothing. But it is, in fact, a real physical process. Deposits are created by making entries in records; today electronic impulses create these records in computer files. The rules of deposit creation are rules specifying when one can make certain entries in these files. It is these rules—in particular, the fractional reserve requirements—that give rise to the system's ability to expand deposits by a multiple of the original deposit increase.

The money multiplier provides the link between the quantity of reserves in the banking system and the quantity of money. However, we have not yet explained where reserves come from. What determines the quantity of reserves, and therefore the money supply? To answer this question, we need to look more closely at the behavior of banks and the behavior of the Federal Reserve.

The Federal Reserve

We have already learned that the Federal Reserve serves as a bank for banks and that it sets the reserve requirement that determines the money multiplier. But the Fed's role in the economy extends well beyond just being a bank for banks. In fact, you have probably seen a recent news story about the Federal Reserve and whether its policy-making committee decided to raise its target interest rate, lower it, or leave it unchanged. The decisions of the Fed receive wide coverage in the press because of the role the Fed plays in affecting the level of nominal interest rates and general credit conditions in the economy.

TABLE 25.5

Superbank Balance Sheet

Before-deposit equilibrium

Assets		Liabilities	
Loans outstanding	$ 91 billion	Deposits	$100 billion
Government bonds	2 billion		
Reserves	10 billion	Net worth	3 billion
Total	103 billion	Total	103 billion

First round
(Add $1 billion deposits, $.9 billion loans)

Assets		Liabilities	
Loans outstanding	$91.9 billion	Deposits	$101 billion
Government bonds	2 billion		
Reserves	10.1 billion	Net worth	3 billion
Total	104 billion	Total	104 billion

Second round
(Add $.9 billion deposits, $.81 billion loans to previous round[a])

Assets		Liabilities	
Loans outstanding	$92.71 billion	Deposits	$101.9 billion
Government bonds	2 billion		
Reserves	10.19 billion	Net worth	3 billion
Total	104.9 billion	Total	104.9 billion

Third round
(Add $.81 billion deposits, $.73 billion loans to previous round[a])

Assets		Liabilities	
Loans outstanding	$ 93.44 billion	Deposits	$102.71 billion
Government bonds	2 billion		
Reserves	10.27 billion	Net worth	3 billion
Total	$105.71 billion	Total	105.71 billion

After-deposit equilibrium
(Add $10 billion new deposits, $9 billion new loans to original equilibrium)

Assets		Liabilities	
Loans outstanding	$ 100 billion	Deposits	$110 billion
Government bonds	2 billion		
Reserves	11 billion	Net worth	3 billion
Total	113 billion	Total	113 billion

[a]In each subsequent round, new deposits equal new loans of the previous round; new loans equal .9 × new deposits.

WRAP-UP

Money Multiplier

An increase in reserves by a dollar leads to an increase in total deposits by a multiple of the original increase.

The Federal Reserve is the **central bank** of the United States. A *central bank* is the government bank that oversees and monitors the rest of the banking system, serves as a bank for banks, and is responsible for the conduct of monetary policy. In Canada, the Bank of Canada is the central bank; in the United Kingdom it is the Bank of England; in the eleven-member European Monetary Union, it is the European Central Bank; and in Mexico, it is Banco de Mexico. A nation's central bank often plays an important role as a regulator of commercial banks. The Fed's most important role, however, arises from its responsibility for the conduct of monetary policy and the influence it has on the level of nominal interest rates and the supply of money.

The Federal Reserve was created by an act of Congress in 1913. In other countries, the central bank is a purely governmental institution, like the U.S. Treasury or the Environmental Protection Agency. When Congress set up the United States' central bank, however, it established a unique central bank that incorporates both public and private aspects. The Federal Reserve is overseen by a seven-member Board of Governors in Washington, D.C. Governors are appointed to fourteen-year terms (although the average length of service is about seven years). They are appointed by the president and are subject to confirmation by the Senate. The president appoints one of the governors to serve as chair (subject to Senate confirmation); the chair serves for four years and can be reappointed. The current chair is Alan Greenspan. Greenspan was originally appointed by President Ronald Reagan in 1987 and has since been reappointed by Presidents Bush and Clinton. Because the Fed chair plays a critical role in setting U.S. monetary policy, the chair is often described as the second most powerful person in the United States.

In addition to the Federal Reserve Board, the 1913 Federal Reserve Act established twelve regional Federal Reserve banks. The location of these regional Federal Reserve banks is shown in Figure 25.4. These banks are officially "owned" by the private commercial banks that are members of the Federal Reserve System (about 3,700 member banks in total). The directors of each regional Federal Reserve bank are appointed by the member banks and by the governors of the Federal Reserve Board. These directors, in turn, choose the presidents of the regional Federal Reserve banks.

The Federal Reserve Board of Governors in Washington, D.C. and the regional Federal Reserve banks collectively form the *Federal Reserve System*. The structure of the Federal Reserve System is depicted in Figure 25.5. The **Federal Open Market Committee,** or **FOMC,** is the monetary policy-making committee of the Fed. The name of the FOMC comes from the way the committee operates. The Fed engages in **open market operations**—so called because they involve the Fed entering the capital market directly, much as a private individual or firm would, to buy or sell government bonds.[2] Once the FOMC has set its policy targets, its operations are carried out by the Federal Reserve Bank of New York because of that bank's proximity to the huge capital markets in New York City.

The FOMC has twelve voting members. These include the governors appointed by the president and some of the regional bank presidents, who are appointed, in part, by private member banks. The seven governors of the Federal Reserve are all voting members of the FOMC. The president of the Federal Reserve Bank of New York is also a voting member of the FOMC. The remaining four votes rotate among the other eleven presidents of the regional Federal Reserve banks.

The Federal Funds Market

We usually think of banks lending to people to buy cars or homes, or to firms to build factories or stores or to finance their inventories. But banks also lend reserves to each other. If AmericaBank needs reserves and NationalBank has excess reserves, AmericaBank can borrow from NationalBank. Often, a bank needs funds on a very short-term

---

[2]We will discuss the exact role of open market operations later in this chapter.

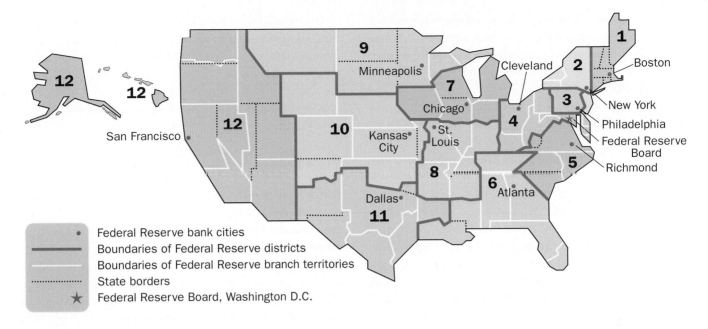

FIGURE 25.4 *Federal Reserve Districts*

The nation is divided into twelve Federal Reserve districts.

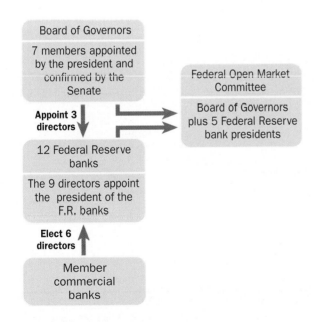

FIGURE 25.5 *The Structure of the Federal Reserve*

The Federal Reserve operates at both a national level and a district level. The president appoints the Board of Governors; the district level includes some directors appointed nationally and some from within the district; the Federal Open Market Committee includes the governors, appointed by the president, and representatives from the district banks.

Internet Connection

The Federal Reserve Banks and International Central Banks

Each of the regional Federal Reserve Banks maintains a Web site that contains a variety of useful information related to monetary policy and general economic conditions. The Web site of the Board of Governors of the Federal Reserve System provides links to all the regional banks, at http://www.federalreserve.gov.

The Bank for International Settlements in Basle, Switzerland, lists links to ninety-six central banks in countries around the world, from Albania to Zimbabwe. These can be found at http://www.bis.org/cbanks.htm.

basis, so AmericaBank might borrow from NationalBank for only one day, repaying the loan the next day. Banks borrow and lend reserves overnight in the **federal funds market.** The interest rate the borrowing bank pays is called the **federal funds rate.**

The federal funds rate plays a critical role in the economy because it is the rate the Federal Reserve most directly affects by its policy actions. The FOMC establishes a target for the federal funds rate. At each FOMC meeting, the members of the committee must decide whether to leave the federal funds rate target unchanged, raise it, or lower it. Though the FOMC decides on its *target* for the funds rate, the rate itself is determined by the interplay of demand and supply in the market for federal funds. This means that the federal funds rate can diverge from the Fed's target, but by influencing supply in the federal funds market, the Fed can keep these divergences very small. Figure 25.6 shows how closely the actual federal funds rate tracks the FOMC's target.

Understanding what the Fed does, and how it affects the economy, requires that we examine the factors that determine demand and supply in the federal funds market. We can then understand how the Fed is able to influence the market to make sure the equilibrium level of the federal funds rate is kept close to the target the FOMC has established.

The Demand for Reserves

Banks hold reserves for two reasons. First, they face the legal reserve requirement imposed by the Fed. Second, even if reserve requirements were zero (as they are in some countries), banks need to hold some reserves to meet their daily transaction needs. Deposits and withdrawals cannot be predicted perfectly each day, so a bank must make sure it has enough cash on hand in case withdrawals happen to exceed deposits. Similarly, when Desktop Publishing writes a check to ComputerAmerica on its account at

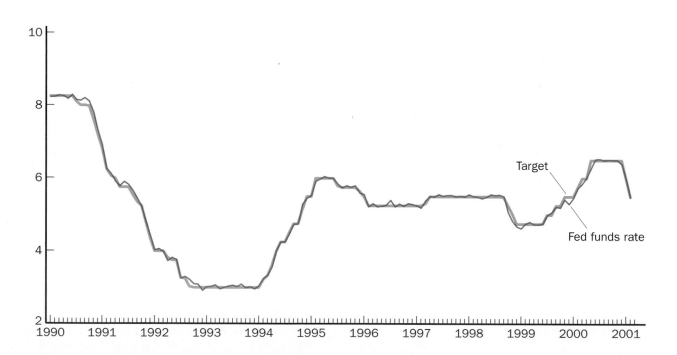

FIGURE 25.6 *The Federal Funds Rate and the FOMC's Target*

In recent years, the Federal Reserve has implemented monetary policy by setting a target for the federal funds rate. The actual funds rate is determined by supply and demand in the federal funds market. By controlling the supply of reserves, the Fed is able to keep the funds rate very close to its target.

SOURCES: *ERP* (2001), Table B-73, and Federal Reserve Board.

BankNational and ComputerAmerica deposits that check into its account with BankUSA, BankNational must have enough reserves to transfer to BankUSA to cover the check. Of course, BankNational will receive funds as it collects on checks it has received in deposits that are from accounts in other banks, but the daily balance of payments and receipts is unpredictable. BankNational needs to ensure it has access to reserves to make sure it can always settle its account. The reserves a bank holds over and above its required reserves are called **excess reserves.** Because reserves do not earn interest, banks try to keep excess reserves to a minimum. In 2000, for example, required reserves totaled $40 billion, while excess reserves were only just over $1 billion.

What happens if a bank discovers that it does not have enough reserves to meet its needs? It has two options. It can try to borrow reserves from the Fed. If the Fed agrees to lend reserves to the bank, the interest rate on the loan is called the **discount rate.** Unlike interest rates on other types of loans, the discount rate is not determined by conditions of demand and supply; the Fed simply sets the discount rate. In some countries, the discount rate is linked directly to market-determined rates of interest. If the discount rate is increased, banks find it more expensive to borrow from the Fed.

The second option a bank has is to borrow reserves from another bank. Just as some banks find themselves short of reserves, other banks may find they have larger reserve holdings than they need. Since the Fed does not pay interest to banks on reserve account balances, and vault cash also does not earn the bank any interest, a bank with more reserves than it needs will want to lend them out in the federal funds market. In this way, it can earn the federal funds interest rate on its extra reserves. The federal funds rate adjusts to balance supply and demand in the federal funds market.

The quantity of federal funds demanded will fall if the federal funds rate increases. A higher federal funds rate means that it is more costly to borrow reserves from other banks. Each bank has an incentive to take extra care to ensure it does not run short of reserves. Figure 25.7 shows the demand for federal funds as a downward-sloping function of the funds rate.

The position of the demand curve for reserves will depend on the lending opportunities banks face and on the general volume of transactions. Suppose, for example, that a new technological innovation causes firms to want to invest more money in new equipment. To finance this investment, firms try to borrow more from banks. With this increase in the quantity of bank loans demanded, interest rates on bank loans will rise. Any bank that was holding excess reserves will face a greater incentive to make additional loans since the interest that can be earned has risen (recall that reserves earn no interest). Other banks may not have an excess of reserves, but to take advantage of the higher returns on loans, they will try to borrow additional reserves in the federal funds market. At each level of the federal funds interest rate, the demand for reserves will be higher. Consequently, the demand curve for reserves shifts to the right.

Changes in the volume of transactions through the banking system also can shift the reserve demand curve. For example, as real incomes rise or as prices rise, the dollar volume of transactions in the economy will rise. Banks hold reserves because they cannot predict perfectly their daily flow of deposits and withdrawals. As these flows grow, banks will need to hold additional reserves.

The Supply of Reserves

The supply of reserves arises from two sources. First, some banks have borrowed reserves from the Fed. These reserves are called **borrowed reserves.** As the federal funds

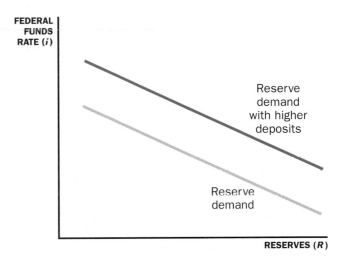

FIGURE 25.7 *The Demand for Reserves in the Federal Funds Market*

When the federal funds rate increases, it becomes more expensive to borrow reserves from other banks. Banks will turn to other sources (such as borrowing from the Fed) or adjust their balance sheets to reduce the chance that they will need to borrow in the fund market.

rate increases, it becomes more expensive to obtain funds from other banks in the federal funds market, and banks instead borrow more from the Fed. If the discount rate is increased, it becomes more expensive to borrow from the Fed and borrowed reserves fall. The main source of reserves, however, does not arise from borrowed reserves. In 2000, borrowed reserves accounted for only $400 million out of a total stock of reserves equal to about $40 billion. The difference between total reserves and borrowed reserves is called **nonborrowed reserves.** The supply of nonborrowed reserves is under the immediate control of the Fed, and it is by adjusting the supply of nonborrowed reserves that the Fed affects the funds rate.

Open Market Operations

The Fed alters the stock of nonborrowed reserves through the use of **open market operations.** Open market operations are the most important instrument the Fed uses to influence the economy. In open market operations, the Federal Reserve enters the market directly to buy or sell government securities (see A Day at the Trading Desk). Imagine that it buys $1 million of government bonds from a government bond dealer. The Fed pays the bond dealer with a $1 million check that the dealer deposits in its bank, AmericaBank, which credits the dealers account for $1 million. (Actually, this is all done electronically.) AmericaBank presents the check to the Fed, which credits the bank's reserve account with $1 million. AmericaBank now has $1 million of new deposits, matched by $1 million in new nonborrowed reserves,[3] and it can accordingly lend out an additional $900,000. The money multiplier goes to work, and the total expansion of the money supply will be equal to a multiple of the initial $1 million in deposits. And credit—the amount of outstanding loans—will also increase by a multiple of the initial increase in deposits.

The purchase of bonds by the Federal Reserve has quite a different effect from a purchase of the same bonds by a private citizen, Joe White. In the latter case, the dealer's deposit account goes up by $1 million but Joe's goes down by $1 million. The funds available in the banking system as a whole remain unchanged. The money multiplier goes to work only when funds from

---

[3]AmericaBank did not borrow the reserves under discussion but received them as payment from the Fed. So these constitute nonborrowed reserves.

"outside," in particular from the Federal Reserve, are changed.

The process works in reverse when the Federal Reserve sells some of the government securities it holds. If the Fed sells $1 million worth of bonds to a bond dealer, the dealer pays for them with a check drawn against its account at its bank, NationalBank. The Fed presents the check for payment to National Bank and deducts $1 million from NationalBank's reserve account. The total amount of nonborrowed reserves in the system has been reduced by $1 million. This change in reserves then has a multiplied impact on the money supply and bank credit.

You might be wondering where the Fed gets the money to purchase government securities in the first place, especially since purchases (or sales) on a given day might amount to over $1 billion rather than the $1 million in our example. When the Fed credited AmericaBank's reserve account for $1 million to settle the check it had used to purchase bonds, the Fed simply made an electronic entry in its bookkeeping system. In effect, it created the $1 million in reserves out of thin air! And when it sold government bonds and deducted $1 million from NationalBank's account, the reserves vanished into thin air!

Because the Fed, if it chooses, can always offset any change in borrowed reserves by adjusting the quantity of nonborrowed reserves, we can simplify the situation by treating the supply of *total reserves*, the sum of borrowed and nonborrowed reserves, as controlled directly by the Fed. In Figure 25.8, the stock of total reserves set by the Fed is shown as a vertical line, labeled TR_0. An open market sale decreases total reserves, shifting total reserve supply to TR_1.

Equilibrium in the Funds Market

We can now see how the Fed is able to affect the value of the funds rate through its control of the stock of total reserves. Figure 25.8 depicts the quantity of reserves demanded as depending negatively on the funds rate. Suppose the Fed's target for the federal funds rate is i_0. To achieve this target, the Fed must adjust the supply of reserves so that the quantity of reserves supplied and the quantity demanded are equal at i_0. The level of total reserves the Fed will need to supply is TR_0. With this level of total reserves, the supply curve for total reserves intersects the demand curve at the desired interest rate i_0.

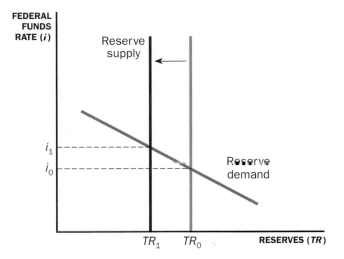

FIGURE 25.8   *The Supply of Reserves and Equilibrium in the Federal Funds Market*

The total supply of reserves consists of borrowed and non-borrowed reserves. The total reserves supply schedule is drawn as a vertical line. An open market sale decreases the total supply of reserves, shifting the reserve supply curve from TR_0 to TR_1.

The equilibrium federal funds rate is determined at the intersection of reserve demand and reserve supply. If the initial equilibrium funds rate is i_0 and the Fed wishes to increase the funds rate to i_1, it reduces the stock of nonborrowed reserves, shifting the supply schedule to the left until the equilibrium funds rate is i_1.

Now, assume the Fed decides to increase its target for the funds rate as it did in mid-2000. If the new target is i_1, the Fed engages in open market sales to reduce the supply of total reserves from TR_0 to TR_1. The supply curve for total reserves shifts to the left, and the new equilibrium funds rate is i_1, the target value the Fed wanted. The funds rate is determined by supply and demand in the funds market, but by adjusting the supply of reserves, the Fed is able to keep the funds rate equal to the target value it desires.

As conditions change in the economy, the quantity of reserves demanded at each funds rate may shift. If the Fed has not changed its target for the funds rate, the Fed has to adjust total reserves in response to any shifts in the demand curve for reserves. For instance, a change in bank deposits will shift the demand curve for reserves. The consequences of an increase in deposits that increases banks' demand for reserves is depicted in Figure 25.9. Initially, the funds market is in

equilibrium with the funds rate at i_0. If the Fed does nothing, a rightward shift in the demand for reserves will push the funds rate up to i_1. To prevent this from happening, and to keep the funds rate at its target value i_0, the Fed must increase the supply of nonborrowed reserves, through an open market purchase, shifting the total reserve supply curve to the right. In this way, the Fed can respond to shifts in reserve demand and keep the funds rate equal to its target.

The demand for reserves at each funds rate will also shift if the Fed changes the required reserve ratio. Suppose the Fed increases the reserve ratio. At each level of deposits, banks must now hold a higher level of reserves. The reserve demand curve shifts to the right. If the Fed keeps total reserves constant, the equilibrium funds rate rises. If the Fed wishes to prevent the funds rate from changing, it would need to engage in an open market purchase to increase the total reserve supply.

These shifts in the reserve demand curve illustrate another important consequence of a monetary policy that

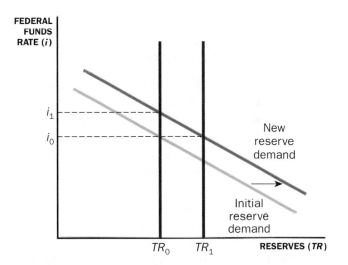

FIGURE 25.9   *The Effect of an Increase in the Quantity of Reserves Demanded*

Suppose the demand curve for reserves shifts rightward. If the Fed leaves the stock of nonborrowed reserves unchanged, the funds rate rises to i_1 where reserve demand and reserve supply are again equal. If the Fed wishes to keep the funds rate at i_0, it increases nonborrowed reserves in order to shift the supply schedule to the right by an amount equal to the shift in demand. Total reserves rise from TR_0 to TR_1.

targets the funds rate. The rightward shift of the reserve demand curve shown in Figure 25.9 led to an equal shift in reserve supply to keep the funds rate from changing. While the funds rate remained constant, the *quantity of reserves* rose, from TR_0 to TR_1. Through the money multiplier process, this increase in reserves can support an increase in the stock of money.

When monetary policy is implemented through control of the federal funds rate, shifts in the quantity of reserves demanded are accommodated automatically. If banks' demand for reserves at each federal funds rate were to increase, the Fed would automatically allow the supply of reserves to increase so that the funds rate would not change.

This highlights one of the chief dangers of a policy that tries to prevent the nominal interest rate from adjusting. Suppose prices begin to rise. The rise in prices increases the dollar volume of transactions in the economy. The increased demand for reserves by banks increases reserve demand at each funds rate. If the Fed tries to keep the funds rate from rising, it automatically increases reserve supply. As a result, the money supply automatically adjusts to changes in inflation. Such a policy can fuel an ongoing inflation, ensuring that the money supply grows at the rate prices are rising.

Discount Rate Changes

The supply and demand model of the funds market also can be used to analyze the effects of a change in the Fed's discount rate. When the Fed increases the discount rate, banks find it more expensive to borrow reserves from the Fed. As a consequence, borrowed reserves fall at each funds rate. Whether this affects the equilibrium federal funds rate depends on what happens to total reserve supply.

If the Fed raises the discount rate and keeps the quantity of nonborrowed reserves fixed, banks borrow fewer reserves from the Fed and the supply of total reserves (borrowed plus nonborrowed) falls. This is depicted in Figure 25.10. If there is no other change, the funds rate rises to i_1, the new point of equilibrium between demand and supply. If the Fed wants to keep the funds rate from changing, it must increase the supply of nonborrowed reserves to offset the fall in borrowed reserves. In this case, it could prevent the supply of total reserves from changing and keep the funds rate at i_0.

The discount rate is the only interest rate that the Fed directly sets. All other interest rates are set in the market, by the forces of supply and demand. But under a policy of setting a target for the funds rate, the discount rate does not

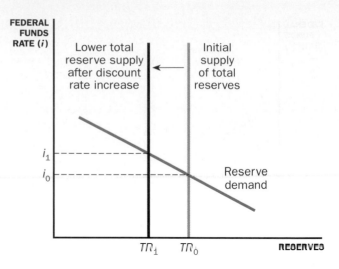

FIGURE 25.10 *Changes in the Discount Rate*

The impact of a rise in the discount rate is shown for when the stock of nonborrowed reserves is held constant. The higher cost of borrowing from the Fed reduces the amount of reserves banks borrow; total reserve supply shifts left. The equilibrium funds rate rises.

If the Fed wanted to increase the discount rate without changing its target for the funds rate, it could increase nonborrowed reserves, leaving total reserves constant. In this case, the funds rate would not change.

play an important role in monetary policy. Generally, if the Fed has increased the funds rate, it will also eventually raise the discount rate. Otherwise, the gap between the funds rate and the discount rate would become too large, leading banks to be tempted to borrow excessively from the Fed. If the Fed has reduced the funds rate, it will also eventually reduce the discount rate. Sometimes the Fed uses changes in the discount rate as a signal of its intentions. When the Fed lowers its funds rate target *and* the discount rate together, the market knows the Fed is serious about lowering market interest rates and making credit more available in the economy. When it raises the funds rate target and the discount rate, the market knows the Fed is serious about raising market interest rates and restricting credit.

The Money Stock

We began our discussion of the banking system by explaining how the level of deposits is linked to the stock of reserves through the money multiplier. We then examined the federal funds market and showed how the stock of reserves and the funds rate are determined by equilibrium in the federal funds market. Federal Reserve policy actions, chiefly open market operations, allow the Fed to exercise close control over the funds rate. The Fed adjusts nonborrowed reserves to keep the funds rate equal to the target level set by the FOMC. As the supply of reserves changes, the money multiplier tells us how the quantity of money will be affected.

CASE IN POINT

A Day at the Trading Desk

Open market operations by the Fed are conducted at the Trading Desk at the Federal Reserve Bank of New York. A typical workday for the Trading Desk personnel involves gathering information about reserve market conditions, evaluating this information to assess the level of reserves required to keep the funds rate at the target value set by the FOMC, and engaging in actual open market operations to affect the level of nonborrowed reserves.

Around 7 A.M., staff at the Trading Desk begin the process of collecting information about financial developments. Information about factors that may affect reserves arrives from other Federal Reserve Banks and is used to develop projections of nonborrowed and borrowed reserve levels.

As financial market activity begins in the United States, the staff talk with the primary dealers on government security markets and with the managers of reserve positions for the largest banks. This provides the Trading Desk personnel with information about the likely demand and supply conditions in the federal funds market. If the demand for reserves, at the current funds rate, exceeds the current supply, the funds rate will rise unless the Trading Desk increases reserve supply. If supply at the current funds rate exceeds demand, the funds rate will fall unless the Trading Desk acts to reduce the supply of reserves.

Reserve conditions also can be affected by the net cash flow of the U.S. Treasury. The Treasury has cash accounts with the Federal Reserve. If tax payments exceed government expenditures on a particular day, there will be a net flow of funds into the Treasury accounts at the Fed and a corresponding fall in funds held by the banking sector. This decline in total reserves in the banking sector pushes up the funds rate unless offsetting open market operations are undertaken. Treasury balances with the Fed are fairly stable from year to year, but they can fluctuate greatly on a daily basis.

Once all this information is collected, the staff at the Trading Desk decide on its program for open market operations. A conference call then takes place between the Trading Desk, Federal Reserve Board staff in Washington, D.C., and one of the four regional Federal Reserve Bank presidents (other than New York) currently serving as a voting member of the FOMC. This call, which lasts about fifteen minutes, reviews the plans formulated by the Trading Desk personnel and the information about financial conditions on which they are based. A member of the Federal Reserve Board staff then prepares a brief summary report that is distributed to all the Federal Reserve governors and Federal Reserve Bank presidents.

The next step in the process is the actual execution of open market operations, and this takes place between 9:20 and 9:40 A.M. (EST) each day, with a die used to randomly choose the exact minute. The Trading Desk staff informs dealers of the exact details of the operation. Is the Trading Desk buying or selling? How much? Does the sale or purchase involve a repurchase (or resale) at a later date? (If the Trading Desk forecasts a change in reserve conditions that is expected to be temporary, it uses what are known as *repurchases* or *RPs*, transactions that involve, for example, a combined sale of a government security and an agreement to repurchase it at a future day, perhaps the next day.)

The last major activity of the day is a telephone conference call at 3:15 P.M. with representatives of the government security market dealer firms. The interchange of information helps keep the Trading Desk staff informed of the dealers' perceptions of financial market developments.

For an excellent and detailed discussion of how monetary policy is conducted in the United States, see Ann-Marie Meulendyke, *U.S. Monetary Policy and Financial Markets* (New York: Federal Reserve Bank of New York, 1998). ●

cut back on their lending and firms may postpone investment plans.

WRAP-UP

Instruments of Monetary Policy

1. *Reserve requirements*: the required ratio of reserves to deposits. The Fed can change the reserve requirement, the amount banks must hold as reserves. Increasing the reserve ratio forces banks to hold a larger fraction of deposits as reserves. This shifts the demand curve for reserves to the right and increases the equilibrium funds rate if nonborrowed reserves are held constant.

2. *Discount rate*: the rate the Fed charges member banks on borrowed reserves. An increase in the discount rate raises the opportunity cost of borrowing from the Fed. Banks reduce their borrowing, and if the supply of nonborrowed reserves is fixed, total reserve supply (borrowed plus nonborrowed) falls. The equilibrium funds rate rises.

3. *Open market operations*: purchases and sales of Treasury bills by the Fed. When the Fed buys government bonds from the public, the stock of nonborrowed reserves is increased. This increase in the total supply of reserves reduces the equilibrium funds rate. When the Fed sells government bonds to the public, the stock of nonborrowed reserves falls.

Selecting the Appropriate Instrument

Of its three instruments available to implement monetary policy, the Federal Reserve uses open market operations most frequently. Changes in the discount rate and in reserve requirements are blunt tools compared with the fine-tuning that open market operations make possible. Thus, changes in reserve requirements and in the discount rate are used primarily to announce major shifts in monetary policy and occur infrequently. Such changes can be quite effective in signaling tighter conditions (that is, changes that entail higher interest rates and reduced credit availability) or looser conditions (that is, changes that have the reverse effects). Banks foreseeing a tightening of credit may

Monetary Policy Operating Procedures

The actual manner in which a central bank implements monetary policy is often called the monetary authority's **operating procedures**. In the case of the Fed, the federal funds rate is the key interest rate the Fed uses to implement monetary policy. Based on its policy goals and assessment of the economy, the FOMC sets a target for the funds rate. The *Trading Desk* at the Federal Reserve Bank of New York conducts the actual open market operations required to keep the funds rate equal to the target established by the FOMC. Implementing monetary policy in this fashion is often called an *interest rate operating procedure*.

An interest rate procedure is not the only way monetary policy can be implemented, and over the course of the last twenty-five years, the Fed has changed its operating procedures several times. The basic alternative to an interest rate procedure is a *money supply operating procedure* that focuses on controlling a quantity—either a reserve quantity such as total reserves or a monetary aggregate such as M1. Rather than letting reserve supply adjust automatically to achieve an interest rate target, the Fed could decide on a target for the money supply or the quantity of reserves, letting the funds rate adjust automatically to clear the federal funds market.

Under a money supply procedure, just as with an interest rate procedure, monetary policy discussions start with an assessment of the state of the economy and what changes in policy are needed, if any, to achieve the goals of the policy. Once the path for the money supply consistent with the goals of policy is determined, open market operations are conducted to supply a level of reserves that leads to the desired level of the money stock.

During the 1970s, many economists argued that the Fed should focus on controlling the money supply. There were two reasons behind this argument. First, inflation was the primary policy problem at the time. Our full-employment model showed that the average rate of inflation and the average rate of money growth are related; if the monetary authority controls money growth, it can control inflation. Second, there appeared to be a tight link between a measure of the money supply such as M1 and total dollar GDP. By controlling M1, the argument went, the Fed could control total aggregate income.

The Choice of an Operating Procedure

What difference does it make whether the central bank implements monetary policy by setting a target for the nominal interest rate or by controlling the money supply? And why have many central banks switched from money supply operating procedures to interest rate operating procedures over the last fifteen years?

The chief reason why central banks have come to focus less on the money supply is that financial markets have gone through tremendous changes in recent years. Much of this is the result of financial innovations—the development of new financial instruments such as checkable money funds—and financial market deregulation. These changes in financial markets have had a profound effect on the relationship between money and economic activity.

We can use the concept of velocity, introduced in Chapter 24, to examine the relationship between money and aggregate income. The velocity of money is formally defined as the ratio of nominal GDP to the money supply. It provides a measure of the speed with which money circulates in the economy. If Y represents the real output of the economy and P represents the price level, PY is equal to nominal GDP (which, as we know, equals nominal aggregate income). Using the symbol V to denote velocity and M as the money supply,

$$MV = PY.$$

This equation is referred to as the *equation of exchange.*

In 2000, nominal income was $9.96 trillion per year and M1 was $1.1 trillion. (Notice the units—income is a flow, M1 is a stock.) In this case, velocity was 9.05 per year. If producing one dollar of output required only one transaction, the average dollar would have to circulate 9.05 times every year to produce output (income) of $9.96 trillion.

Let's use this equation of exchange to look at what happens when the money supply increases. We can rewrite the equation of exchange as

$$M = PY/V.$$

Now suppose you are the head of the Fed and you control the supply of money. What value for M should you set? Suppose we let Y^f denote full-employment output and let P^* be the price level associated with your desired target. Further, suppose V is a constant. Then your policy decision is straightforward. Just set the money supply equal to P^*Y^f/V. If velocity remained constant at its 2000 level of 9.05, and nominal income was expected to grow by 4 percent between 2000 and 2001, how much would the money supply need to increase? If nominal income increases 4 percent, it will be $1.04 \times \$9.96$ trillion = $10.36 trillion. At a velocity of 9.05, M1 would need to be $1.14 trillion to support this level of spending. If V is not a constant, the problem becomes more complicated, since you will have to forecast velocity. During the 1960s and 1970s, velocity was very predictable. It was not constant, but it seemed to grow at a relatively constant rate (Figure 25.11).

Because of these arguments, the Fed shifted its policy focus in late 1979 toward controlling the money supply. Unfortunately, as Figure 25.11 shows, just as the Fed shifted to a money supply–oriented policy, velocity became much more unstable and difficult to predict. With velocity harder to predict, it became more difficult to conduct policy using the money supply. As a consequence, in the 1980s the Fed shifted back to using the nominal interest rate as its instrument for implementing monetary policy.

Economists attribute the instability in velocity to two factors—deregulation and financial innovation. Before deregulation of the financial sector, banks could not pay interest on demand deposits. The opportunity cost of holding funds in checking accounts was the interest income individuals could have earned by investing in interest-earning assets. Particularly during the 1970s, when nominal interest rates were high due to inflation, this opportunity cost was large. People only held enough in their checking accounts to meet their needs for transactions. This meant that M1 was closely related to spending. After deregulation, accounts that were part of the money supply now paid interest, reducing the opportunity cost of holding money. The supply of money was now less closely related to spending as people now could use these accounts to hold their savings balances.

Financial innovation during the last twenty years has led to new types of accounts and new ways of making payments. For example, you can pay your phone bill directly from a money market account over the Internet now, so the connection between traditional definitions of the money supply and spending has broken down.

Inflation, Money Supply, and the Nominal Rate of Interest

While unstable velocity has led most central banks to implement monetary policy by setting a target interest rate, such policies can lead to problems when inflation rises as it did in the late 1960s. The full-employment model tells us

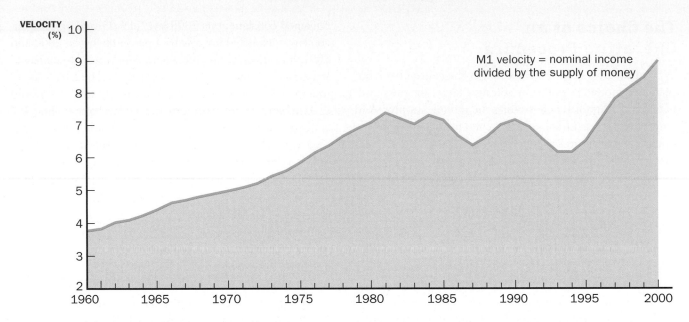

FIGURE 25.11 *The Velocity of Money*

Velocity is defined as the ratio of nominal GDP to the money supply. Before 1980, velocity grew fairly steadily, making it easy to predict the relationship between M1 and aggregate expenditures. After 1980, velocity became much more unstable and difficult to predict.

SOURCE: Federal Reserve Board for M1; Bureau of Economic Analysis, Department of Commerce, for nominal GDP.

that increases in the money supply provide the fuel for inflation. Under an interest rate policy, an initial increase in inflation can lead to automatic increases in the money supply that allow the inflation to continue.

Suppose prices have been stable in the economy—an inflation rate of zero. Then, suppose inflation rises to 5 percent. (In Part Seven we will discuss factors that might lead to an increase in inflation, but for now let's just suppose inflation has increased.) The demand for money will rise as the dollar value of transactions increases as prices rise. A sandwich that costs $5.00 one year will cost 5 percent more, or $5.25 after one year, $5.51 after two years, and $8.14 after 10 years. People will want to hold, on average, about 5 percent more money each year, both as cash for everyday transactions and in their checking accounts.

As prices rise, the dollar value of transactions in the economy increases. The increase in the volume of transactions through the banking system means that banks will need to hold more reserves to balance their payment flows. This increase in the demand for reserves at each value of the funds rate means the reserve demand curve shifts to the

right. If the Fed keeps its target for the funds rate unchanged, the Fed will need to increase the supply of reserves over time, allowing the money supply to rise with the increased demand for money. From our money multiplier analysis, we know that by allowing the supply of reserves to increase, the Fed also ensures that the quantity of money increases. *When the monetary authority tries to keep the nominal interest rate constant, the quantity of money automatically increases as prices rise. Inflation causes the money supply to automatically increase, further fueling and sustaining the inflation.*

In the full-employment model, we assumed that government controlled the supply of money directly. With full-employment output determined by such factors as labor supply, the capital stock, and the economy's technology, changes in the money supply led to proportional changes in the price level (see Chapter 24). When the central bank adjusts the reserve supply to achieve an interest rate target, the supply of money adjusts in line with prices. To prevent inflation from continuing, the central bank must raise its target interest rate to prevent an ongoing expansion of the money supply. This is why, when inflation rose to high levels in the 1970s, central banks shifted from interest rate operating procedures to procedures that focused more directly on controlling the money supply.

Interest Rates and Credit Conditions

Monetary policy affects the macroeconomy by altering interest rates and credit conditions, which influence the spending decisions of millions of households and firms. How can such major effects be caused by a change in the interest rate banks charge each other for overnight loans? The answer to this question is found by considering one of the basic concepts in economics—opportunity cost.

Recall from the balance sheet of AmericaBank (Table 25.3) that its assets consisted of loans, government bonds, and reserves. Its liabilities were deposits and net worth. Now suppose the Fed decides to make an open market purchase, and for simplicity, assume it purchases $1 billion from AmericaBank. The bank now has $1 billion more in reserves while its holdings of government bonds are now $1 billion less. There is an opportunity cost to holding additional reserves. Since the bank does not earn any interest on reserve holdings, it will want to use the funds to make additional loans on which it expects to earn a positive return. As a consequence, the supply of loans increases. To induce additional borrowing, the bank will need to reduce the interest rate it charges on its loans. So the injection of additional reserves into the banking system reduces the federal funds rate *and* it leads to reductions in interest rates on bank lending.

But suppose the bank decides not to increase lending, instead using its extra $1 billion in reserves to buy government bonds. The extra demand for bonds will cause their price to rise, and this means the rate of return on bonds falls. With bond yields lower, making additional loans starts to look more profitable. Loan supply shifts out, and the interest rate on loans falls.

We have reached an important conclusion: *When the federal funds rate falls, other interest rates in the economy also decline. When the funds rate increases, other interest rates rise.* Figure 25.12 illustrates how the general level of interest rates tends to follow the pattern of the funds rate. It is

because all interest rates tend to move together in response to monetary policy actions that we could simplify in our earlier discussion and talk about *the* nominal rate of interest, as if there were only one interest rate in the economy.

An equally important point to recognize is that money policy actions, in addition to affecting nominal interest rates, also affect the quantity of money and credit. Open market operations alter the supply of reserves. We have seen how, through the money multiplier process, changes in reserves alter the quantity of bank deposits and the money supply. From the balance sheet of the banking sector (Table 25.5), we also learned that an increase in reserves and deposits will produce an increase in bank lending.

The Stability of the U.S. Banking System

The fractional reserve system explains how banks create money. It also explains how, without the Fed, banks can get into trouble. Well-managed banks, even before the advent of the Fed and its reserve requirements, kept reserves equal to some average expectation of day-to-day needs. A bank could get into trouble in a hurry if one day's needs exceeded its reserves.

If (for good reasons or bad) many depositors lose confidence in a bank at the same time, they will attempt to withdraw their funds all at once. The bank simply will not have the money available, since most of the money will have been lent out in loans that cannot be called in instantaneously. This situation is called a *bank run*. Bank runs were as common in nineteenth-century America as they were in the old Western movies, where customers in a small town would line up at the bank while it paid out what reserves it had on a first-come, first-served basis until there was no more left. Such a run could quickly drive even a healthy bank out of business. If a rumor spread that a bank was in trouble and a few savers ran to the bank to clean out their accounts, then other investors would feel they were foolish not to run down to the bank themselves and withdraw their deposits. One vicious rumor could result in a healthy bank shutting down, and the panic setting off a run on other banks, thus destabilizing the banking system and the whole economy.

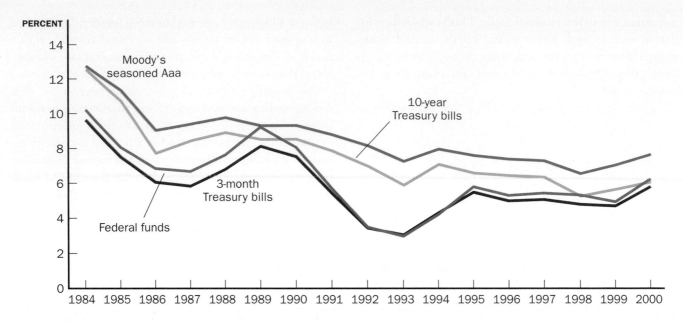

FIGURE 25.12 *Market Interest Rates*

When the federal funds rate changes, other interest rates tend to change also. Longer-term rates such as the interest rate on ten-year government bonds or on Aaa corporate bonds fluctuate less than short-term rates like the federal funds rate and the three-month Treasury bill rate.

SOURCES: *ERP* (2001), Table B-73, and Federal Reserve Board.

Reducing the Threat of Bank Runs

Bank runs and panics have periodically afflicted the American banking system. In fact, one reason the Fed was set up in 1913 was to make them less likely. The last major panic occurred in the midst of the Great Depression in 1933. Since then, the modern banking system has evolved a variety of safe-guards that have ended the threat of bank runs for most banks. There are four levels of protection.

First, the Fed acts as a "lender of last resort." If a bank faces a run, it can turn to the Fed to borrow funds, to tide it over. Knowing that the bank could meet its obligations means, of course, that there is no need to run to the bank. The Fed lends money when a bank faces a liquidity problem; that is, it has a temporary shortage of funds, but its assets still exceed its liabilities. It is, in other words, solvent. The objective of the next two measures is to reduce the likelihood that banks face problems of illiquidity or insolvency.

Second, the Fed sets reserve requirements. Even bank executives who might like to live recklessly, getting along on minimal reserves, are unable to do so.

The third level of protection is provided by the owners of the bank. Most banks are started by investors who put up a certain amount of money in exchange for a share of ownership. The net worth of the firm—the difference between the bank's assets and its liabilities—is this initial investment, augmented or decreased over time by the bank's profits or losses. If the bank makes bad investment decisions, then these shareholders can be forced to bear the cost. This cushion provided by shareholders not only protects depositors but also encourages the bank to be more prudent in its loans. If the bank makes bad loans, the owners risk their entire investment. But if the owners' net worth in the bank is too small, the owners may see themselves in a "Heads I win, tails you lose" situation. If risky investments turn out well, the extra profits accrue to the bank; if they turn out badly, the bank goes bankrupt, but since the owners have little at stake, they have little to lose. To protect against this danger, the government requires banks to maintain certain ratios of net worth to deposits. These are called *capital requirements*. Capital requirements protect against insolvency; they mean that if the bank invests badly and many of its loans default, the bank will still be able to pay back depositors. (By contrast, reserves and the ability to borrow from the Fed protect against illiquidity; they ensure that if depositors want cash, they can get it.) On occasion a bank will make so many bad loans that its net worth shrinks to the point where it can no longer satisfy the capital requirements.

As a fourth and final backstop, the government introduced the Federal Deposit Insurance Corporation (FDIC) in 1933. Since then, federal banks and savings and loans have had to purchase insurance, which ensures that depositors can get all their money back, up to $100,000 per account. Since deposits are guaranteed by the federal government, depositors fearing the collapse of a bank have no need to rush to the bank. The deposit insurance thus not only protects depositors but also has an enormous impact in increasing the stability of the banking system. Simply because it exists, the threat against which it insures is much less likely to occur. It is as if life insurance somehow prolonged life.

Deposit insurance has an offsetting disadvantage, however. Depositors no longer have any incentive to monitor banks, to make sure that banks are investing their funds safely. Regardless of what the bank does with their funds, the funds are protected. Thus—to the extent that capital requirements fail to provide banks with appropriate incentives to make good loans—bank regulators must assume the full responsibility of ensuring the safety and soundness of banks.

Review and Practice

Summary

1. The Federal Reserve is the central bank of the United States. Its policy actions affect the money supply and nominal interest rates.

2. Money is anything that is generally accepted in a given society as a medium of exchange, store of value, and unit of account.

3. There are many ways of measuring the money supply. The most common measures in the United States are M1, M2, and M3. All include both currency and demand deposits (checking accounts). M2 and M3 differ from M1 in that they also include assets that are close substitutes to currency and checking accounts.

4. Financial intermediaries, which include banks, savings and loans institutions, mutual funds, insurance companies, and others, all form the link between savers who have extra funds and borrowers who desire extra funds.

5. Government is involved with the banking industry for two reasons. First, by regulating the activities banks can undertake and providing deposit insurance, government tries to protect depositors and ensure the stability of the financial system. Second, by influencing the willingness of banks to make loans, government attempts to influence the level of investment and overall economic activity.

6. By making loans, banks can create an increase in the supply of money that is a multiple of any initial increase in the bank's deposits. If every bank loans all the money it can and every dollar lent is spent to buy goods, purchased from other firms who deposit the checks in their accounts, the money multiplier is 1 over the reserve requirement imposed by the Fed. In practice, the multiplier is considerably smaller.

7. The federal funds rate, the interest rate on overnight interbank loans, adjusts to balance the supply and demand for reserves.

8. The Federal Reserve can affect the market for reserves by changing the reserve requirement, by changing the discount rate, or by conducting open market operations.

9. The chief tool of the Fed is open market operations. These affect the supply of reserves and allow the Fed to achieve the target for the federal funds rate set by the FOMC.

10. Under a money supply operating procedure, open market operations can be used to achieve a target for the money supply. Because the linkages between money and nominal GDP summarized in velocity have become less predictable in recent years, most central banks implement policy by setting the nominal interest rate, an interest rate operating procedure.

11. Changes in reserve supply affect interest rates, the money supply, and the availability of credit. Interest rates tend to move with the federal funds rate, owing to its effect on banks' opportunity costs.

12. The reserve requirement, capital requirements, the Fed's acting as lender of last resort, and deposit insurance have made bank runs rare.

Key Terms

medium of exchange
store of value
unit of account
money
demand deposits
M1
M2
M3
fractional reserve system
money multiplier
Federal Open Market Committee, or FOMC
open market operations
federal funds
federal funds rate
excess reserves
discount rate
borrowed reserves
nonborrowed reserves
operating procedures

Review Questions

1. What is the name of the committee that sets monetary policy for the United States? Who are the members of this committee?

2. What are the three characteristics that define "money"?

3. What are the differences between M1, M2, and M3?

4. What are the two main reasons for government involvement in the banking system?

5. What are the three instruments of the Federal Reserve?

6. Why do nonborrowed reserves fall if the Fed engages in an open market sale? Why do they rise if the Fed engages in an open market purchase?

7. Why do borrowed reserves fall if the Fed raises the discount rate? Why do they rise if the federal funds rate increases?

8. Why does the Fed increase the supply of reserves when prices rise if it is targeting the federal funds rate? What would happen to the funds rate if prices rose and the Fed held the supply of reserves fixed?

9. Why did the instability of velocity lead the Fed to switch to focus on the funds rate?

Problems

1. Identify which of money's three traits each of the following assets shares, and which trait each does not share:

   (a) A house

   (b) A day pass for an amusement park

   (c) German marks held by a resident of Dallas, Texas

   (d) A painting

   (e) Gold

2. Down Home Savings has the following assets and liabilities: $6 million in government bonds and reserves; $40 million in deposits; $36 million in outstanding loans. Draw up a balance sheet for the bank. What is its net worth?

3. While gardening in his backyard, Bob finds a mason jar containing $100,000 in currency. After he deposits the money in his bank, where the reserve requirement is 5 percent, how much will the money supply eventually increase? Suppose Bob decides to keep $5,000 of his find as cash and only deposits $95,000 in his bank. How much will the money supply increase?

4. Why is it that the money supply changes when the Fed sells government bonds to a bank but the money supply does not change if a large corporation sells government bonds to a bank?

5. Using a supply and demand diagram of the federal funds market, show how an increase in reserve requirements would affect the equilibrium federal funds rate.

6. Suppose the economy's income falls, reducing the demand for money. If the Fed keeps its target for the funds rate constant, what happens to reserve demand and the supply of reserves? If instead the Fed keeps

the supply of reserves constant, what would happen to the funds rate?

7. In 1999, there was broad concern about the Y2K computer problem. Banks and the Fed predicted that many people would want to hold additional cash in case there were financial problems on January 1, 2000. Use the money multiplier analysis to predict what would happen to deposits and the money supply if people increased their holding of cash and the Fed kept total reserves fixed. What would be the consequences for interest rates?

Now suppose instead of keeping reserves fixed, the Fed attempted to keep the fed funds rate constant. What would be the consequences for the money supply of the increased demand for cash?

8. Figure 25.11 showed that velocity rose through the 1960s and 1970s and again in the late 1990s. Discuss how greater use of credit cards, the introduction of ATM machines, and the growth of Internet commerce might affect velocity.

9. Does money growth cause inflation or inflation cause money growth? Discuss. How does your answer depend on the behavior of the Fed?

Chapter 26

Government Finance and the Open Economy at Full-Employment

Key Questions

1. How does the government affect the economy's full-employment equilibrium?

2. What are the consequences of fiscal deficits and surpluses?

3. What gave rise to the huge trade deficits of the 1980s and 1990s? What are their consequences?

4. How are trade deficits and international capital flows related?

*P*olitical news stories are filled with debates over government spending and tax policies. Since 1998, the U.S. federal government has collected more in taxes than it has spent, and Al Gore and George W. Bush spent most of the 2000 presidential election debating what to do with these excess tax revenues. Should they be used to finance additional government spending? Or should taxes be cut? In early 2001, Congress took up the debate over President Bush's tax cut plan, eventually approving a large cut.

The government's budget situation was quite different before 1998. During the 1980s and through most of the 1990s, the U.S. government consistently spent more than it raised in tax revenues, borrowing to cover this deficit. The ballooning budget deficit emerged as a major national issue, and by the 1992 presidential election, public opinion polls were persistently ranking the huge deficits among the central problems facing the country.

During this same period, the gap between the value of U.S. exports and the value of its imports widened. Each year, the United States imported billions more than it exported, and this led to concerns that U.S. jobs were being lost as a result of the flood of goods entering the country. While the decade of the 1990s ended with the budget deficit problem apparently solved, the imbalance between exports and imports continued to worsen. Imports exceeded exports by a record $371 billion in 2000. Associated with the gap between exports and imports was a flow of foreign savings into the United States as foreigners purchased factories, land, and U.S. financial assets. These flows of savings from one country to another play a major role in linking together the global economy.

In this chapter, we extend the full-employment model developed in Chapter 24 to include the government and the foreign sector. This will allow us to understand how government decisions about taxes and spending affect the full-employment economy. By using the model to understand the consequences of changes in the federal budget, we will gain insights into the origins of the gap between exports and imports. We will learn how this gap is related to international capital flows and how it might be affected by various policies.

Extending the Basic Full-Employment Model

The basic full-employment model ignored the role of the government and treated the economy as a **closed economy,** one not linked to the rest of the world through trade or capital flows. A closed economy is a useful starting point for a study of macroeconomics, since it allows us to focus on a few key aspects of the economy. But in reality, the government plays a major role in all economies, and the United States has an **open economy,** one that is linked through international financial markets and trade with other economies. Major macroeconomic policy issues often center around the impact of government spending and taxation decisions and the impact of international trade. To address these important policy issues, we need to extend the basic full-employment model.

Adding the Government

Introducing government into the analysis affects both the product market and the capital market. In the product market, the government affects the economy in two ways. First, the government purchases goods and services produced by firms. These purchases affect demand in the product market. Second, taxes subtract from demand in the product market because they reduce disposable income, lowering consumption spending.[1] In the capital market, governments affect the economy if they need to borrow to cover deficits when spending exceeds tax revenues or if they repay government debt when tax revenues exceed spending.

Figure 26.1 shows the circular flow of income when the government sector is added to our model. Households pay taxes to the government sector. These payments, just like household saving, represent a leakage from the spending stream. The government sector's purchases of goods and services represent an injection into the spending stream similar to investment spending. If tax revenues fall short of government expenditures, the government has a **fiscal deficit,** and it will need to borrow in the capital market to cover the difference. If the government runs a **fiscal surplus,** so that its tax revenues exceed its expenditures, then the government, like the household sector, will be a net saver and will represent a source of saving for the economy.

The Government and the Capital Market

Focusing on the capital market makes the effects of the government on the general equilibrium clear. In Chapter 24, we examined a simplified economy, one with no government and no trade with other countries (a *closed* economy). There, we saw that at the equilibrium real interest rate, saving was equal to investment. Now let's see how equilibrium in the capital market, and the real interest rate, are affected when we bring government into the picture. If government expenditures (G) exceed tax revenues (T), the government must borrow to obtain the funds necessary to finance its expenditures.[2] This means the government will compete with private borrowers for the saving of the private sector. Less saving is available for private investment.

When the government runs a deficit, private saving (S_p) now has two purposes—to finance private investment (I) and to finance the government's deficit ($G - T$). Equilibrium in the capital market occurs when private saving is equal to investment plus the deficit, or

$$(S_p) = I + (G - T).$$

Alternatively, we can think of the deficit as *negative public government saving* (S_g):

$$G - T = -S_g.$$

From this perspective, the first equation can be rewritten as

$$S_p = I - S_g,$$

or

$$S_p + S_g = I.$$

---

[1]Governments also can affect the economy as a producer of goods. In the U.S. economy, the government is not a major producer of goods and services and so we will neglect that aspect of the government in our analysis. Government production is, however, very important in some areas of the economy, education being a prime example.

[2]It used to be that some governments simply printed money to pay for the difference. Today, within the developed countries, printing money to finance deficits is more the exception than the rule.

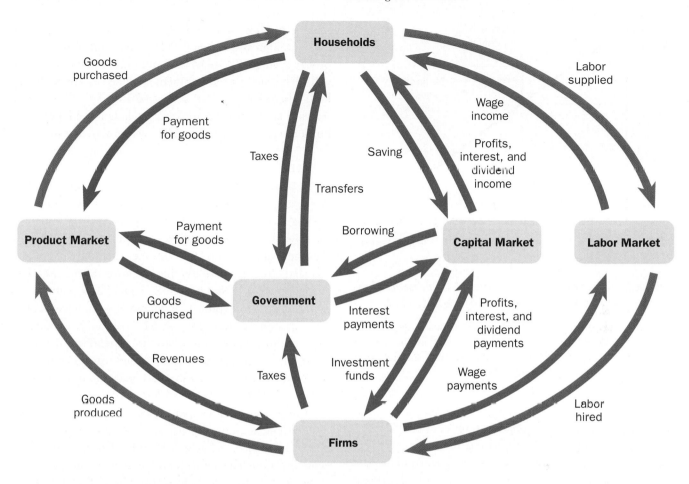

FIGURE 26.1 *Government and the Circular Flow of Income*

The government purchases goods and services in the product market and receives tax revenues from households and firms. It also makes transfer payments such as Social Security benefits to households. Government purchases represent an injection into the spending flow, while taxes (net of transfers) represent a leakage. If government expenditures exceed revenues, the government will need to borrow in the capital market. If government revenues exceed expenditures, the government surplus adds to the supply of funds in the capital market. When the capital market is in equilibrium, leakages will again balance injections, and demand and supply in the product market will be equal.

The left side is called **national saving,** the combined saving of the private (households and businesses) and public (government) sectors. In chapter 6 we learned that private saving is equal to $Y - T - C$. Public saving is equal to $T - G$. Adding these together tells us that national saving is equal to $Y - C - G$. When the capital market in a closed economy is in equilibrium, *national saving equals investment*.

The effect in the capital market of a government deficit is illustrated in Figure 26.2. The investment schedule is downward sloping. Saving is assumed to be infinitely inelastic and so is drawn as a vertical line. The initial level of national saving is S_0. The capital market is in equilibrium when the real rate of interest is r_0. Now suppose the government increases expenditures without increasing taxes so that the government needs to borrow an amount equal to its deficit, $G - T$, the excess of spending over revenue. The increase in the government deficit reduces national saving, so the saving schedule is now shifted to the left, to S_1. It is shifted to the left by the amount the government has borrowed. Equilibrium

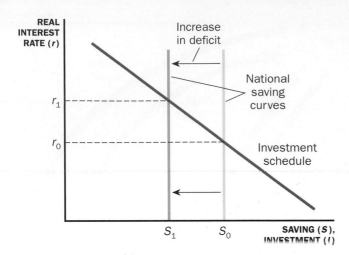

FIGURE 26.2   *Effects of Increased Government Deficit on the Capital Market*

An increased government deficit (reduced public saving) reduces national saving. With a leftward shift in the saving curve, the equilibrium level of real interest rates is higher and the equilibrium level of investment is lower.

in the capital market now occurs at a higher real interest rate (r_1). The higher real interest rate reduces private investment spending. As a consequence, government borrowing has crowded out an equal amount of private investment.

When the government has a budget surplus, the opposite effects occur. With a surplus, public saving is positive. A cut in government expenditures without a corresponding reduction in taxes increases the surplus and shifts the national saving schedule to the right. As a result, the equilibrium real interest rate falls and private investment rises.

The Effects of Changes in Taxes   While we have focused on changes in expenditures, the same analysis allows us to understand how the economy would be affected by a tax cut not balanced by a cut in government expenditures. The tax cut increases households' disposable income. To make the example concrete, suppose taxes are reduced by $100 billion. As a result, disposable income rises by the full $100 billion that households no longer need to pay to the government as taxes. They will use this additional disposable income to increase their current consumption spending and to increase their

saving.[3] For example, aggregate consumption might rise by $90 billion and saving by $10 billion. If this is the case, private saving will rise by $10 billion, but national saving will fall because the government's deficit rises by $100 billion. Therefore, national saving falls by $90 billion. The leftward shift in the savings curve leads to a higher equilibrium real interest rate and a lower level of investment.

Balanced Budget Changes in Expenditures and Taxes   The previous examples considered cases in which expenditures or taxes were changed, leading to changes in public saving. But what happens if the government changes *both* expenditures and taxes by the same amount so that public saving remains unchanged? Suppose initially that the government has a balanced budget so that revenues match expenditures. In 1998, for example, both U.S. federal government receipts and expenditures were roughly $1.7 trillion. Now suppose that the government increases its expenditures, say, by $100 billion. To pay for these expenditures, suppose the government increases taxes by an equal amount. We would describe this as a *balanced budget change in taxes and expenditures*. Since both expenditures and revenues increase by the same amount, the government's overall budget remains in balance. What will be the effect on the macroeconomy of such a balanced budget increase in spending?

Since taxes have risen by $100 billion, the private sector's disposable income—income after paying taxes—has been reduced by $100 billion. When disposable income falls, households typically adjust by reducing both their consumption and their saving. For example, to pay the additional $100 billion in taxes, total consumption might fall by $90 billion and saving by $10 billion. The reduction in consumption and saving totals $100 billion, the amount households needed to pay the higher taxes.

The reduction in disposable income from the tax increase reduces private saving. Since public saving is unchanged (remember, expenditures and taxes were increased by the same amount), national saving falls. In the capital market, the national saving curve shifts to the left. With an unchanged investment schedule, the equilibrium real inter-

---

[3]This does not mean every household will use some of the tax cut to increase their saving. Many households might decide to spend the entire amount. Others might decide to save it all. But when we add up over all the households in the economy, both aggregate consumption and aggregate saving will have increased.

est rate rises and the equilibrium investment level falls. This is an important conclusion. Equal changes in government revenues and expenditures—balanced budget changes in taxes and expenditures—affect investment and the real interest rate. A balanced budget *increase* in taxes and expenditures will *reduce* consumption and investment and *raise* the real interest rate. A balanced budget *decrease* in taxes and expenditures will *increase* consumption and investment and *lower* the real interest rate.

A balanced budget change in expenditures and taxes changes the composition of output between private (consumption and investment) and public (government purchases) uses. We think of total output as a pie to be divided among various uses. A balanced budget change does not alter the total size of the pie; we assume that the economy remains at full employment so that output remains at its full-employment level. The effect of government is simply to change how the pie is divided. If government expenditures and taxes increase, private sector spending on consumption and investment shrinks—it is **crowded out**—to make room for increased public sector spending. Crowding out occurs even if the government increases taxes enough to fully pay for the increased expenditures, as individuals adjust to higher taxes in part by reducing private saving.

In this example, the total pie—full-employment output—was treated as fixed. It is important to understand why this is the case. In Chapter 24 we learned that full employment output depends on the economy's capital stock, its technology, and the level of employment that occurs when demand and supply balance in the labor market. None of these factors is likely to be affected directly by changes in general government expenditures or taxes. So full-employment output, potential GDP, will remain unchanged. Government expenditures can have an impact on *future* income levels and growth—for example, increased government purchases that lower private sector investment will reduce the amount of capital the economy has in the future, reducing full-employment income in the future. When we discuss economic growth and productivity in Chapter 27, we will consider some types of government expenditures and taxes that might affect the discovery of new technologies, the productivity of capital, and the demand for labor by firms. When we deal with these policies, we will need to investigate their impact on potential GDP.

Increased government expenditures, even when matched by taxes, crowd out private investment. It is easy to quantify the effect. Assume the government increases its expenditures by $100 billion and increases taxes on individuals by $100 billion. With higher taxes, individuals have lower income, and so—at any interest rate—they save less. For simplicity, assume that for each extra hundred dollars of after-tax income, individuals save ten dollars and that saving is completely insensitive to the interest rate. Thus, the increased $100 billion in taxes reduces saving by $10 billion. Then, if saving equals investment, and saving is reduced by $10 billion, investment must also fall by $10 billion. In the new equilibrium, aggregate output is unchanged (at the full-employment level); government expenditures increase by $100 billion, offset by a reduction of consumption of $90 billion and of investment by $10 billion.

If saving has a slightly positive elasticity to changes in interest rate, then as interest rates rise, there will be increased saving. Thus, investment will fall by less, and consumption by more, than when saving is totally insensitive to the interest rate.

Government Deficits and Surpluses

In 1981, federal taxes were cut in the United States, but expenditures on defense and social programs (medical, income security, and Social Security) increased. Figure 26.3 shows the resulting increase in the federal deficit. In twelve years, from 1981 to 1992, the deficit more than quadrupled, from $60 billion to $280 billion. Even after adjustment for inflation, the increase in the real deficit was dramatic, as panel B shows. These represented the first major peacetime deficits in the country's history.

When the government spends more than it receives in revenues, it must borrow to finance its deficit. The government *debt* is the accumulative amount the government owes. The *deficit* represents the additional borrowing in a given year, while the accumulated amount the government owes (the debt) is a result of all the borrowing it has done in the past. Panel A of Figure 26.4 shows the U.S. federal debt. The deficits of the 1980s and 1990s pushed the federal debt to record levels. The economy has grown enormously over the almost fifty years shown in the figure, so a better measure of the debt is obtained by expressing the size of this debt as a percentage of GDP. As panel B shows, the debt today is smaller relative to the size of the economy than it was immediately following World War II.

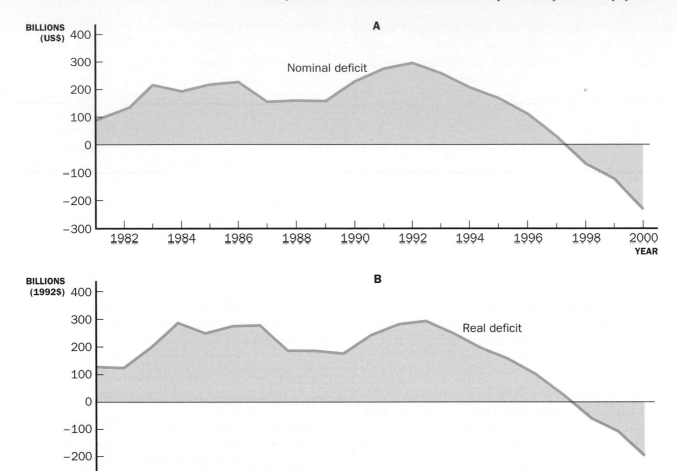

FIGURE 26.3 *The Federal Deficit*

No matter how it is measured, federal borrowing increased dramatically during the 1980s and early 1990s. Panel A shows the nominal deficit; panel B is the real deficit, the deficit adjusted for inflation.

SOURCE: *ERP* (2001), Table B-78.

Ricardian Equivalence

Will deficits caused by tax cuts always have the effects we have just discussed? Some economists, most notably Robert Barro of Harvard University, argue that deficits will not raise real interest rates or lower investment. Barro bases his argument on an analysis David Ricardo, an eighteenth-century English economist, originally developed. Ricardo noted that when the government cuts taxes and runs a deficit, it must borrow to finance its expenditures. The gov-

ernment will need to raise taxes in the future to pay back what it has borrowed. If households correctly perceive that a tax cut today means higher taxes in the future, they will save all the tax cut in order to ensure they have the resources needed to pay the higher taxes in the future. Barro argues that even if current taxpayers expect that higher taxes will occur long in the future, after they are no longer alive, they care enough about their children that they will save any tax cut and pass it to their children in the form of a bequest, so that their children will have the wealth that is

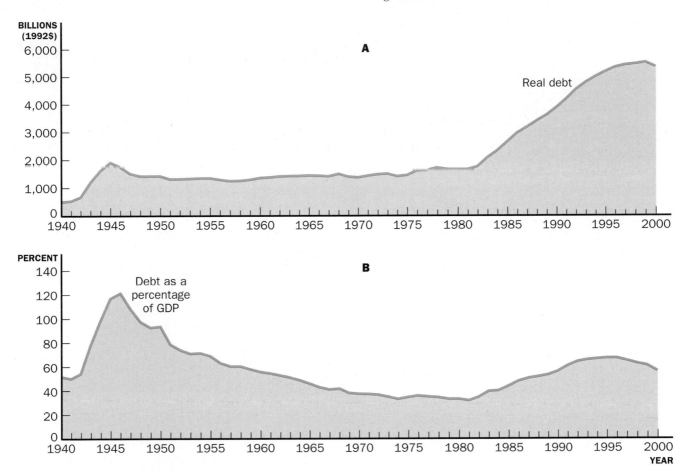

FIGURE 26.4 *The Real Federal Debt and Debt Relative to GDP*

The federal debt fell dramatically after World War II and rose rapidly after 1982 (panel A). Expressing the debt relative to GDP (panel B) shows that the debt reached a peak relative to the size of the economy immediately after World War II, rose between 1982 and 1996, and has declined since.

SOURCE: *ERP* (2001), Tables B-78, B-79.

needed to pay the higher taxes. As a result, private saving rises by the full amount of the tax cut. When private saving increases by the same amount public saving has fallen, national saving is unchanged. The equilibrium real interest is unaffected, as is investment. While Ricardo ultimately rejected this view, it does highlight an important fact. Governments must pay for their expenditures; if they do not raise enough tax revenues today, they will have to raise more revenue in the future. Borrowing is equivalent to taxing, in this view, hence, the name *Ricardian equivalence*.

Most economists follow Ricardo and reject Ricardian equivalence, arguing that the evidence does not support Barro's theoretical claim. Increased government deficits may lead to slightly higher household saving, but far too little to offset the deficit increase.

Leakages and Injections

We have focused our discussion of government deficits on the capital market. Recall, however, that when the capital market is in equilibrium, balancing national saving and investment, leakages and injections in the circular flow of income also will be balanced. This result holds just as it did in Chapter 24 when we ignored the government sector.

International Perspective

Deficits and Debt in Other Countries

The United States was not alone in experiencing large deficits and growing government debt during the 1980s and 1990s. In fact, most other major economies witnessed the same pattern of deficits in the 1980s. And while the United States had balanced its budget by the end of the 1990s and was actually running a fiscal surplus, other major industrialized economies were still running sizable government deficits at that time (panel A). The debt to GDP ratios were similar in most of these countries, with the exception of Italy, which had a much larger debt to GDP ratio (panel B).

One lesson we can take from this international comparison is that in searching for explanations for the fiscal deficits in the United States, we will need to go beyond explanations that focus solely on developments in this country. We need to ask whether broader forces can account for the simultaneous development of fiscal deficits in many countries during the 1980s.

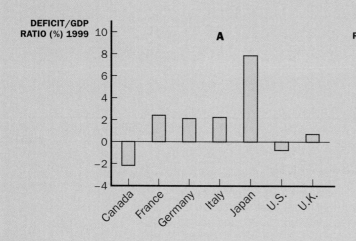
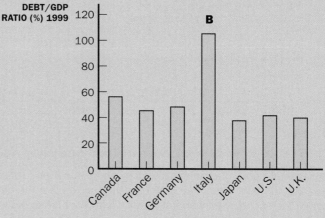

International Comparisons

Many European countries and Canada have had higher deficits to GDP (panel A) and debt to GDP ratios (panel B) than the United States.

SOURCE: OECD, *Economic Outlook* (December 1998), Annex Tables 30, 35.

Leakages now consist of household saving and taxes. Injections consist of investment and government expenditures. By adjusting to ensure that national saving equals investment, real interest rates also ensure that leakages from the spending flow equal injections at full-employment output. The total demand for the goods and services produced by firms will balance the total output that is produced at full employment.

Adding Government   When we incorporate the government into our model, there are now three sources of

Thinking Like an Economist

Distribution, Deficits, and Intergenerational Transfers

If you borrow money to buy a car, you can enjoy the car now and pay for it in the future. Rather than paying for it all right now, borrowing allows you to spread the payments out over a longer time period. The same is true for governments when they borrow. Instead of raising enough taxes right now to pay for all of its expenditures, the government can borrow and raise taxes in the future to repay its debt. But this raises an issue of distribution. Let's suppose the government borrows $20 billion today, uses the money to reduce the current level of taxes, and then plans to raise taxes in fifty years to repay the money that it has borrowed. In fifty years, most of today's taxpayers who benefited from the tax reduction will have died, while many of those who will pay the higher taxes to repay the debt were not even born when the money was borrowed. Does this mean government borrowing results in a transfer between generations, from future taxpayers to today's?

Believers in Ricardian equivalence say the answer is no. Those future taxpayers are the children of today's taxpayers. Rather than spend the tax cut, today's taxpayers can save it and simply pass it on to their children in the form of a larger inheritance. The children would then have the extra wealth they need to pay the higher taxes they will face. They will not have to reduce their own consumption spending to pay for the tax cut enjoyed by their parents.

Most economists do not believe that private saving increases in this way when taxes are cut. Instead, when people find their disposable incomes have risen as a result of a tax cut, they increase their consumption spending. They may save some of the tax cut, but private saving does not increase enough to offset the government's dissaving (deficit). As a consequence, national saving falls. In the capital market, the saving curve shifts to the left. The equilibrium real interest rate rises, and investment falls. Lower investment means less capital is built, and future generations inherit a smaller stock of capital. The distribution of wealth between generations is affected—current taxpayers have been able to consume more, while future generations will have less capital and therefore lower incomes.

---

aggregate demand: consumption (C), investment (I), and government purchases (G):

$$\text{demand} = C + I + G.$$

At full employment, households receive a total income of Y^{f} plus any transfers from the government, TF. This income is used for consumption (C), to pay taxes (TX), or to save (S):

$$Y^{\mathrm{f}} + TF = C + S^{\mathrm{f}} + TX \text{ or } S^{\mathrm{f}} = Y^{\mathrm{f}} - C - T,$$

where we use the superscript to remind us that this is the level of saving and consumption at Y^{f}, and T to denote taxes minus transfers ($TX - TF$). When the capital market is in equilibrium, desired investment (as reflected in the in-

vestment schedule) plus the government deficit ($G + TF - TX = G - T$) equals full employment saving:

$$S^{\mathrm{f}} = I + (G - T).$$

Then from the second equation,

$$Y^{\mathrm{f}} - C - T = S^{\mathrm{f}} = I + (G - T) \text{ or } I = Y^{\mathrm{f}} - C - G.$$

Substituting the fourth equation back into the first equation gives

$$\text{demand} = C + I + G = C + (Y^{\mathrm{f}} - C - G) + G = Y^{\mathrm{f}}.$$

Thus, aggregate demand equals full-employment output, and the product market is in equilibrium at full employment.

Projecting Fiscal Budget Surpluses

As the 1990s closed, the fiscal budget outlook in the United States took a turn that few would have predicted even five years earlier. After fifteen years during which huge federal budget deficits overwhelmed every discussion of policy, the United States actually achieved a budget surplus in 1998, and both the Clinton administration and the Congressional Budget Office (CBO) were projecting huge budget surpluses for the foreseeable future. The debates during the 2000 presidential campaign focused on alternative proposals for dealing with the projected surpluses, and President George W. Bush made a major tax cut his first priority on taking office.

Debates about future surpluses often sound as if the surpluses are a reality rather than simply a *projection*. Past experience shows that such projections can change dramatically as economic conditions or fiscal policies change.

Figure 26.5 illustrates a dramatic change in the budget outlook at the end of the 1990s. Each line shows the projected path of the deficit or surplus made by the CBO at the time indicated next to each line. Each projection starts from the actual deficit at the time of the projection, represented by the points on the red line. In January 1997, the actual budget deficit of $107 billion in 1996 was projected to grow to $124 billion in 1997 and swell to $278 billion by 2007. The CBO's projection for the 1997 deficit turned out to be off by over $100 billion—the projected $124 billion deficit turned into an actual deficit of just $22 billion. This was the first evidence that the budget outlook was about to take a huge swing.

The real change in the outlook for the federal budget shows up in the CBO's 1998 report. Rather than a continuation of budget deficits, the CBO projected a balanced budget through the year 2000, with rising surpluses thereafter. Looking further out, the CBO reports for January 1997 and January 1998 showed enormous revisions. The 2007 projection shifted from a deficit of $278 billion to a projected surplus of $129 billion, a swing of over $400 billion!

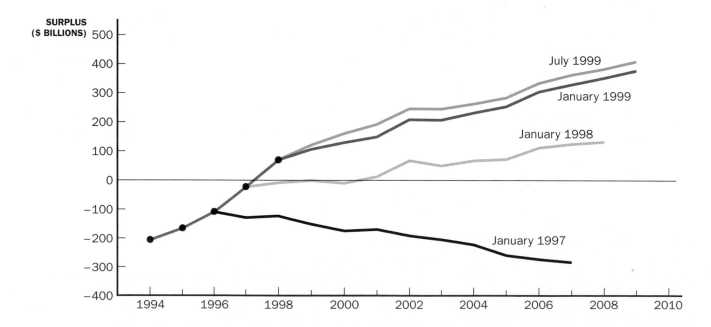

FIGURE 26.5 *Changing Budget Projections*

The federal budget outlook changed dramatically at the end of the 1990s. Each line shows the projected path of the federal deficit or surplus made by the CBO for the period indicated next to each line.

The two primary recent changes affecting the budget projections were the Balanced Budget and Taxpayer Relief Act of 1997 and the continued strong growth of the U.S. economy between 1997 and 2000. But by their very nature, these budget projections are likely to be wrong. The current projected surpluses are triggering changes in spending and revenue policies, changes that mean actual surpluses will be much smaller than current projections show. ●

SOURCE: Carl E. Walsh, "Projecting Budget Surpluses," Federal Reserve Bank of San Francisco, *Economic Letter,* No. 99–27, September 10, 1999.

WRAP-UP

Government Deficits and Surplus

Government expenditures and taxes affect the capital market.

Increases in taxes reduce disposable income, and this shifts the private saving curve to the left. The equilibrium real interest rate is higher and investment is lower.

When the government spends more than it receives in revenue, it must borrow in order to finance its deficit. The deficit reduces national saving, leading to higher real interest rates and lower private investment.

A surplus has the opposite effect. When the government spends less than it receives in revenue, it raises national saving, increasing the funds available to private borrowers. This leads to lower real interest rates and higher private investment.

The Open Economy

Globalization and the increasing integration of the world economy are topics encountered in the news all the time. Whether at our local auto dealer, computer store, or grocery store, we encounter goods produced in many other countries. Trade in goods and services is not the only way in which modern economies are linked. Financial markets are global in nature. News reports of financial crises in other countries can affect the U.S. stock market. To under-

stand the macroeconomic implications of being part of a world economy, we need to extend our full-employment model to incorporate international trade and finance. In doing so, we turn from the analysis of a closed economy and focus on an open economy. An *open economy* is one whose households and firms trade with other countries and borrow from and lend to other countries. The basic lessons learned from the study of the closed economy continue to guide our analysis of the open economy.

International trade affects the product market because net exports represent a demand for what the economy produces. More importantly, an open economy has access to international sources of funds for financing domestic investment or for financing government deficits. The saving schedule depicted so far is the domestic source of funds. If the demand for funds for investment exceeds domestic national saving, firms (and governments) in an open economy can borrow abroad. To understand the role that international trade and international flows of financial capital play, we can again start our analysis with the capital market.

The Capital Market in the Open Economy

Because households and firms in an open economy can borrow or lend abroad, foreign borrowing and lending must be accounted for when we look at equilibrium in the capital market. The money coming into the United States to buy investments—to be deposited in U.S. banks, to buy U.S. government bonds, or to be lent directly to Americans for any reason—is called **capital inflows.** U.S. dollars going to other countries for similar purposes are called **capital outflows.** In the closed economy, equilibrium occurred when national saving and investment were equal. In the open economy, investment can be financed *either* from domestic sources of saving or by borrowing abroad, essentially making use of foreign sources of saving, thus:

$$\text{national saving } (S_\text{p} + S_\text{g}) + \text{foreign borrowing } (\textit{NCF}) = \text{investment.}$$

We have denoted net foreign borrowing by *NCF,* which stands for **net capital inflows** (the inflows minus the outflows). If net capital inflows are positive, it means the domestic economy is borrowing more from foreigners than it is lending to foreigners. In 1999, for example, national saving in the United States totaled $1.41 trillion (of which private saving was $1.34 trillion and government saving was $65 billion), while private investment was $1.65 trillion. The difference between investment and national saving was $240 billion, which was financed by a net capital inflow. Because this investment was financed by foreign borrowing, it represents the amount that foreigners have invested in the United States, and so it is also called *net foreign investment*.

When the capital market in an open economy is in equilibrium, *national saving plus net foreign investment equals private investment*. National saving plus capital flows from abroad can be thought of as the "sources" of funds, and investment can be thought of as the "use" of these funds.

The Capital Market in the Small Open Economy

Capital market equilibrium requires that national saving plus net foreign investment equal private investment, but the implications this has for the economy will depend on how the supply curve of funds from both domestic and foreign sources depends on the real interest rate. A country with a small open economy like Switzerland faces an essentially horizontal supply curve of funds at a given real interest rate. If borrowers in Switzerland were to pay a slightly higher interest rate than that paid in other countries, those with financial capital to lend would divert their funds to Switzerland. If Switzerland were to pay slightly less than the interest rate available in other countries (adjusted for risk), it would not obtain financial capital. Those who have financial investments in Switzerland can take their funds and invest them abroad to earn higher interest rates. These flows of international financial capital play an important role in the global economy. For a small country, the interest rate is determined by the international capital market. Effectively, such a country takes the interest rate as fixed. This is shown in Figure 26.6, where the interest rate is fixed at r^*. A fixed interest rate, in turn, means that the level of investment is fixed, at I^* in Figure 26.6 Any shortfall between the level of domestic national saving and the level of domestic investment is funded by borrowing from abroad. A reduction in the amount of domestic saving increases the amount of foreign borrowing (B_1) but leaves investment unaffected.

This result contrasts with our earlier result for a closed economy, one in which there is no foreign borrowing or lending. There, we noted that lower national saving (a shift to the left in the saving curve) results in less investment. There is a similar contrast in the effect of an increase in government expenditures matched by an increase in taxes. In a closed economy, increased taxes reduce household and thus na-

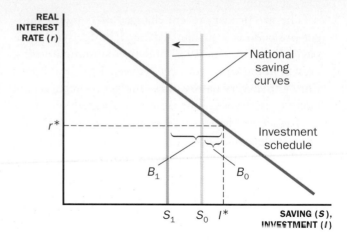

FIGURE 26.6 *Supply of Saving in a Small Open Economy*

In a small open economy, the real interest rate, r^*, is determined by the international capital market. That in turn determines the level of investment, I^*. In the figure, saving is assumed to be fixed, unaffected by the interest rate. If domestic national saving equals S_0, the shortfall, B_0, is made up by borrowing from abroad. A reduction in national saving to S_1, caused, for example, by an increase in the government's deficit, leads to increased international borrowing, B_1, but leaves investment unchanged.

tional saving, and hence, reduce investment (see Figure 26.2). In a small open economy, investment is unchanged. The fall in domestic national saving is fully offset by increased borrowing from abroad (resulting in a capital *inflow*).

We showed earlier that in a closed economy, an increase in government expenditures not matched by an increase in taxes reduces investment and raises the real interest rate. Again, the situation is different in a small open economy. An increase in the government's deficit in a small open economy reduces national saving, and the saving schedule shifts to the left, but this just leads to an increase in foreign borrowing. Domestic investment is left unchanged.

Though investment is unaffected, the increased foreign borrowing has consequences for the future. Foreigners who have lent funds must be repaid. Income used to repay foreign borrowing is not available for raising domestic standards of living. Access to foreign funds alleviates the need for investment to fall when national saving falls, but the effects of foreign borrowing on future standards of living are much the same as the effects of a lower level of investment. These effects will be discussed more fully in Chapter 34.

WRAP-UP

Government Finance in a Small Open Economy

In a closed economy, an increase in government expenditures not accompanied by an increase in taxes (or a decrease in taxes not accompanied by a corresponding decrease in government expenditures) results in higher interest rates and decreased investment.

In a small open economy, interest rates and investment remain unchanged but foreign borrowing increases.

The U.S. Economy

The United States has an open economy. Trade is important; in 2000 exports totaled $1.1 trillion, about 11 percent of GDP. Capital flows are also important. The United States has been a net borrower from abroad every year since 1981. But this country is such a large part of the world economy that—unlike a small country like Switzerland—changes in U.S. saving affect the international interest rate, with global ramifications. The U.S. economy represents about one fourth of world output and one fifth of world saving. A shift to the left in the U.S. saving curve (implying less national saving at each real interest rate) raises real interest rates in the world and leads to less investment in the United States. When real interest rates in the world rise, investment also falls in other open economies as well. Because the full impact is spread throughout the world, the effect on U.S. investment is far less than it would be if the United States were a closed economy.

The discussion so far also has assumed that the world's capital markets are fully integrated. However, this is far from the case. Individuals know more about what is going on in their own country than what is going on abroad. American investors require a slightly higher return on foreign investments to compensate for this increased risk. In recent years, with the greater flow of information, the magnitude of this risk premium—the extra return they must earn—has decreased. But it is still the case that financial capital does not flow perfectly freely, so that interest rates are not equalized and a decrease in U.S. saving is not made up fully by an increased flow of capital from abroad.

How much does U.S. investment decrease as a result of a shift to the left of the U.S. saving curve by, say, $1 billion? Early estimates, for the decades immediately following World War II, suggested that U.S. investment would fall by $800 million to $1 billion—by almost the full amount of the change in saving. Current estimates indicate that the effect would be much smaller, somewhere between $350 and $500 million. This provides one example of the effect of an increasingly integrated world economy.

Similar effects occur if the U.S. investment schedule shifts to the right. Many economists have argued that this type of shift occurred in the 1990s as firms increased investment at each interest rate to take advantage of new technologies. In a closed economy, such a shift would raise the real interest rate, and investment would be constrained by the availability of domestic saving. But in today's integrated world economy, an investment boom in the United States can be financed by capital inflows. A rightward shift in the U.S. investment schedule raises world interest rates, but the capital inflow results in more investment than occurs when investment must be financed solely from domestic saving.

WRAP-UP

Open Economy Investment

The United States is a large open economy. Reductions in the U.S. national saving rate are reflected in increases in the real interest rate internationally (and therefore in the United States also) and reduced levels of investment. But the effects on investment in the United States are smaller than would be the case if the economy were closed.

The Basic Trade Identity

The capital market balances saving and investment, but in doing so it balances leakages and injections from the spending stream. Earlier, we showed how this was the case when the government was added to the basic full-employment model. The same continues to hold true for an open economy.

Reexamination of the connection between capital market equilibrium and aggregate spending in an open economy reveals an important relationship between net capital flows and the balance between exports and imports.

When the capital market is in equilibrium, desired investment (as reflected in the investment schedule) equals private saving plus government saving plus net capital inflows (NCF):

$$S_p + S_g + NCF = I.$$

Households receive a total income of Y^f, plus any transfers, and private saving is income minus consumption and taxes, $S_p = Y^f - C - T$. Since government saving is $T - G$, capital market equilibrium implies

$$Y^f - C - T + (T - G) + NCF = I.$$

When an economy engages in international trade, there are four sources of aggregate demand: consumption, investment, government purchases, and net exports (NX). In equilibrium, $Y = C + I + G + NX$. If we substitute this into the previous equation to eliminate Y, we find that $NX + NCF = 0$. In words, net exports plus net capital inflows equal zero. If net capital inflows are positive, net exports must be negative (imports exceed exports). If net capital inflows are negative (the case in a country such as Japan that lends more abroad than it borrows), net exports must be positive (exports exceed imports). The level of foreign borrowing that bridges the difference between national saving and investment is intimately related to the balance between exports and imports. The **trade deficit** is the difference between imports and exports in any given year. The high net capital flow into the United States and the large U.S. trade deficit are not separate phenomena.

To understand better the relationship between foreign borrowing and the trade deficit, we first need to see the links between trade flows and capital flows. Let's trace what happens when an American buys a German car. It seems like a simple matter: the buyer pays American dollars to a dealer. The dealer buys the car—in dollars—from an importer. The importer buys the car from the German manufacturer, who wants to be paid in German marks (or euros). For the importer, this is no problem. He goes to a bank, say, in Germany, and exchanges his dollars for marks. But the bank will not hold onto those dollars. It will sell them either to someone wanting to purchase U.S.

goods or to someone wanting to invest in a dollar-denominated asset.

As we have seen, every dollar an American spends to buy a foreign import eventually comes back, either to buy American exports or to buy an investment in the United States. We can express this relationship by a simple equation:

$$\text{imports into the United States} = \\ \text{exports} + \text{net capital inflows}.$$

Subtracting exports from both sides, we obtain the basic trade identity:

$$\text{trade deficit} = \text{imports} - \text{exports} = \\ \text{net capital inflows}.$$

Thus, a trade deficit and a net inflow of foreign capital are two ways of saying the same thing. This can be put yet another way: the only way that American consumers and businesses can import more from abroad than they export abroad is if foreigners are willing to make up the difference by lending to or investing in the United States.

In a world of multilateral trade, the accounts between any particular country and the United States do not have to balance. Assume Japan and Europe are in trade balance and the United States and Europe are in trade balance, but Japanese investors like to put their money into Europe and Europeans like to invest in the United States. Europe will have a zero net capital inflow, with a positive capital inflow from Japan offset by a negative outflow to the United States. In this situation, the U.S. trade deficit with Japan is offset by a capital inflow from Europe. But what must be true for any country is that total imports minus total exports (the trade deficit) equals total net capital inflows.

The basic trade identity can describe a capital outflow as well as a capital inflow. In the 1950s, the United States had a substantial trade surplus, as the country exported more than it imported. Europe and Japan did not receive enough dollars from selling exports to the United States to buy the imports they desired, and they borrowed the difference from American households and firms. There was a net capital outflow from the United States that gradually accumulated. Japan now exports more than it imports, with the difference equal to its capital outflow.

The basic trade identity implies that if public saving and investment are unchanged and private saving falls, capital flows from abroad must increase and foreigners must end up holding more American assets. But the identity does not specify which assets they will hold. They may buy government bonds or they may buy U.S. companies.

CASE IN POINT

The Trade Deficit

At the same time that the fiscal budget deficit in the United States was exploding in the 1980s, so too was the trade deficit. From about $20 million a year from 1977 to 1982, it soared (in nominal terms) to $142 billion in 1987. It then fell to $20 billion in 1991 before ballooning again in the late 1990s, reaching $371 billion (almost 4 percent of GDP) in 2000.

Figure 26.7 shows the trade and federal budget deficits. The two have often moved together. This is no accident; we have noted already that for an open economy, an increase in the government's deficit results in increased foreign borrowing. But it is important to note that while the trade and fiscal deficits often move together, they are certainly not mechanically linked together. During the late

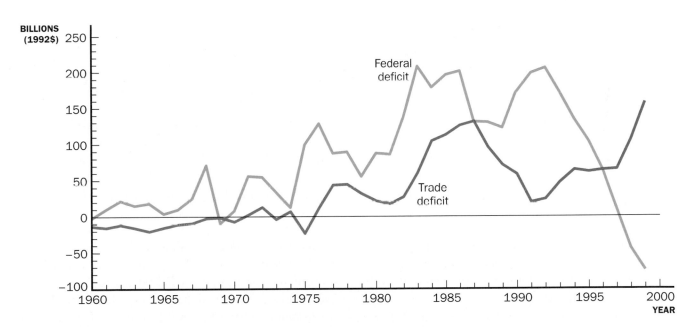

FIGURE 26.7 *The U.S. Fiscal Deficit and Trade Deficit*

Increases in government deficits in the 1980s were accompanied by increases in foreign borrowing. During the last few years, the fiscal deficit has fallen while foreign borrowing has increased.

SOURCES: *Survey of Current Business* (Bureau of Economic Analysis [BEA], Department of Commerce); and *ERP* (1999).

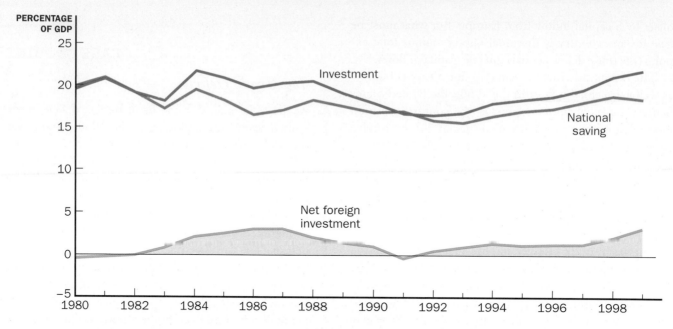

FIGURE 26.8   *National Saving, Investment, and Net Foreign Investment*

During the 1980s, the large federal budget deficits reduced national saving. To finance the high level of private investment, the United States had a large capital inflow. This was reflected in the large trade deficit. In the 1990s, the budget deficit was eliminated, and government became a net saver. However, private saving declined, and investment rose at the end of the decade. Investment continued to exceed national saving. Since the capital inflow is equal to the trade deficit, the United States continues to run a trade deficit.

1990s, for example, the U.S. fiscal deficit fell dramatically while the trade deficit widened significantly. The reason is straightforward—net capital flows reflect the difference between national saving and investment. Looking at Figure 26.7, we can see that the fiscal deficit has been reduced. Despite this, the trade deficit has continued to grow. The reason is that the other two factors at work—private saving and investment—have moved to offset the reduction in the fiscal deficit. Figure 26.8 shows domestic investment, national saving, and net foreign borrowing as a percentage of the GDP. By the late 1990s, the U.S. economy was experiencing a record-setting economic boom, increasing the attractiveness of this country as a place to invest. At the same time, the household saving rate actually turned negative. Yet even though the U.S. private saving rate fell to record lows in the late 1990s, the rise in government saving increased total national saving. Still, the increase in national saving was less than the increase in investment. The net effect has been a rise in foreign borrowing (and a larger trade deficit). ●

Exchange Rates

If a country borrows more (or less) from abroad, what ensures that net exports adjust? The answer is the **exchange rate.** The exchange rate tells how much of one currency can be bought with a given amount of another currency. For instance, in 2000, one dollar could be exchanged for approximately 107 Japanese yen. That is, with $1 you could buy 107 yen. Exchange rates may change rapidly. In August 1998, a dollar could buy 144 yen. But in January 1999, it could buy only 113 yen. This represents a 21 percent fall in the value of the dollar relative to the yen in just five months. When the dollar becomes less valuable relative to another currency, we say the dollar has **depreciated.** When the dollar becomes more valuable relative to other currencies, we say the dollar has **appreciated.** When the dollar-yen exchange rate fell from 144 to 113 in 1998, the dollar depreciated relative to the yen and the yen appreciated relative to the dollar. Since the United States trades with many countries, it is often useful to measure the value of the dollar relative to an average of other currencies. A

High-Tech Exports and Imports

The United States has emerged as the international leader in many aspects of the new information and computer revolution. The Silicon Valley in northern California, home to such firms as Intel, Apple, Sun Microsystems, and Google, has become synonymous with new, information-based industries and the new economy. With American firms at the leading edge of the new economy, one might naturally think that the United States is a major exporter of computer-related products. The figure shows the amount, in millions of dollars, of computer-related products exported from and imported to the United States in 2000. It is not surprising that the United States is a net importer of audio and video equipment (imports exceed exports). Asian companies such as Sony have long dominated this

market. But the United States also imports more computer equipment and semiconductors and other electronic components than it exports.

The figure illustrates two important aspects of trade. First, for many categories like "computer equipment," the United States is both an exporter *and* an importer. This is very common. The United States produces cars for export, and it imports cars from Asia and Europe. The United States produces semiconductors for exports and imports semiconductors. One must look at product categories that are more narrowly defined to see the specific composition of U.S. exports and imports. In the area of telecommunications equipment, for instance, the top three U.S. exports in 1999 were radio transceivers,

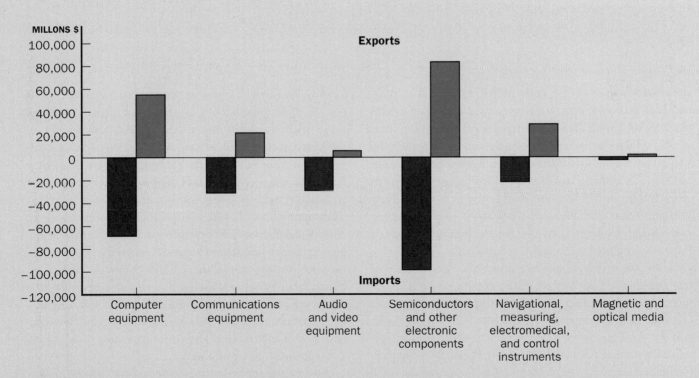

U.S. Exports and Imports of Selected Manufactured Goods, 2000

miscellaneous radio parts, and telephonic apparatus. The top three U.S. imports were cellular phones, radio transceivers, and cordless telephones.

Second, trade reflects both microeconomic and macroeconomic factors. The United States leads the world in computing technologies, but this does not necessarily mean it will be a net exporter of the computers. We learned in this chapter that the overall balance between exports and imports reflects the balance between a country's national saving and investment. If national saving is less than investment, borrowing from foreigners must finance the difference. The basic trade identity tells us that when the United States is a net borrower from foreigners, it also must have a trade deficit. Imports will exceed exports. The overall U.S. trade deficit grew from $89.3 billion in 1997 to $371 billion in 2000 as strong domestic investment exceeded national saving. Mirroring this deterioration of the overall trade balance, U.S. exports of computer equipment rose from $56 billion in 1997 to $83 billion in 2000, yet imports rose even more, so that net exports of computer equipment fell from -$12 billion in 1997 to -$15 billion in 2000.

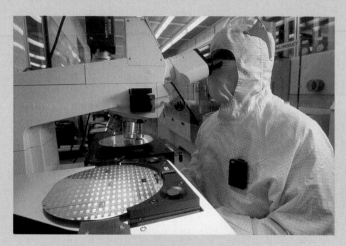

Many foreign-made computers are powered by American-made computer chips, such as the chips being manufactured here.

standard measure of the value of the dollar is the *trade-weighted exchange rate*: an average of the exchange rates between the dollar and the currencies of our trading partners in which the average reflects the amount of trade the United States does with the other countries. So, for example, the U.S. dollar–Canadian dollar exchange rate is given more weight in the measure than is the U.S. dollar–New Zealand dollar exchange rate since the United States engages in much more trade with Canada. Figure 26.9 shows the trade-weighted value of the U.S. dollar.

Thus, the exchange rate is a price—the relative price of two currencies. Like any price, the exchange rate is determined by the laws of supply and demand. For simplicity, let's continue to focus on the exchange rate between the dollar and the yen (ignoring the fact that in the world trading system, all exchange rates are interlinked). Figure 26.10 depicts the market for dollars in terms of the exchange rate with the yen. The exchange rate in yen per dollar is on the vertical axis, and the quantity of U.S. dollars is on the horizontal axis. The supply curve for dollars represents the quantity of dollars supplied by U.S. residents to purchase Japanese goods and to make investments in Japan. At higher exchange rates—when the dollar buys more yen—Americans will supply larger quantities of dollars. A Japanese good that costs 1,000 yen costs $10 when the exchange rate is 100 but only $6.67 when the exchange rate rises to 150. Americans will wish to buy more Japanese goods as the exchange rate rises. The supply curve of dollars thus slopes upward to the right. The demand curve for dollars represents the dollars demanded by the Japanese to purchase American products and to make investments in the United States. At higher exchange rates—when it takes more yen to buy one dollar—the Japanese demand lower quantities of dollars, resulting in a demand curve that slopes downward to the right. The equilibrium exchange rate, e_e, lies at the intersection of the supply and demand curves for dollars.

Now we can see how the exchange rate connects the flow of capital and goods between countries. We continue with the case of the United States and Japan. Suppose the United States wants to borrow more from Japan. Higher

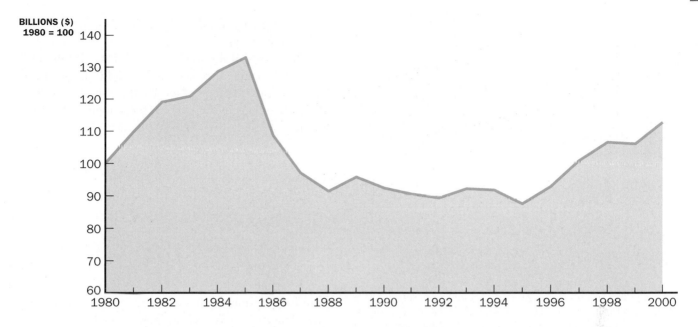

FIGURE 26.9 *The Trade-Weighted Real Value of the U.S. Dollar*

The figure shows an index of the average exchange rate of the U.S. dollar against the other major currencies, weighted by the value of trade and adjusted for the consumer price index.

SOURCE: Federal Reserve Board.

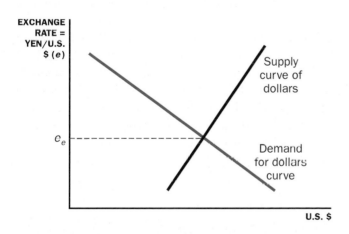

FIGURE 26.10 *Equilibrium in the Market for Dollars*

The exchange rate is the relative price of two currencies. The equilibrium exchange rate, e_e, occurs at the intersection of the supply and demand curves for dollars.

U.S. interest rates will attract more Japanese investment to the United States. Japanese demand for dollars increases at each exchange rate, shifting the demand curve for dollars to the right, as depicted in Figure 26.11. The higher U.S. interest rates also will make Japanese investments relatively less attractive to American investors, who will therefore increase their investments at home. Americans will be willing to supply few dollars at each exchange rate, shifting the supply curve for dollars to the left. These shifts in the supply and demand curves for dollars cause the exchange rate to rise from e_0 to e_1—the dollar appreciates and the yen depreciates.[4] Since the dollar can now buy more Japanese products, U.S. imports increase (Japanese exports increase). Since the yen can now buy fewer U.S. products, U.S. exports fall. Changes in the exchange rate thus ensure that the trade deficit moves in tandem with foreign borrowing.

Is the Trade Deficit a Problem?

So far, our discussion has shown the relationship between the trade deficit and the international capital flows that

---

[4]Later, in Chapter 34, we will see that matters are somewhat more complicated. Investors have to take into account expectations concerning future changes in the exchange rates as well.

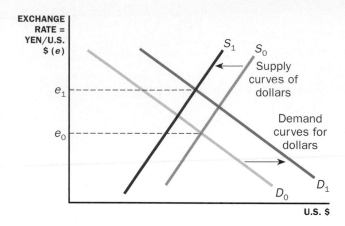

FIGURE 26.11 *Exchange Rate Effects of Increased Foreign Borrowing*

The equilibrium exchange rate is e_0 before the increase in U.S. borrowing from Japan. Higher interest rates in the United States attract Japanese investment to the United States, shifting the demand curve for U.S. dollars to the right. At the same time, more Americans decide to invest in their own country rather than abroad, shifting the dollar supply curve to the left. The equilibrium exchange rate rises from e_0 to e_1. At the higher exchange rate, the dollar buys more yen, so U.S. imports of Japanese products increase. Conversely, U.S. goods are now more expensive for the Japanese, so U.S. exports decrease.

reflect differences between national saving and investment. But we have not said anything about whether a trade deficit is good or bad. Certainly much of the popular discussion about the U.S.'s huge trade deficit suggests that it is a major problem.

Trade deficits mean the country is borrowing from abroad. Just like borrowing from any other source, borrowing can be sensible or not depending on the reason for borrowing.

In its first century, this country borrowed heavily from abroad. For most of the twentieth century, the United States loaned more money to foreign countries and investors than it borrowed. This pattern is typical. In the early stages of economic development, countries borrow to build up their economies, and they repay the loans with a portion of their economic gains. More mature economies typically lend capital.

The enormous U.S. trade deficits in the 1980s reversed this pattern. Just as when the government borrows year after year, the cumulative budget deficits lead to a high level of government debt, when the country borrows from abroad year after year, the cumulative trade deficits (cumulative capital inflows) also lead to a high level of debt to foreigners.

The effects of the trade deficits of the 1980s were to convert the United States from the world's largest creditor nation at the beginning of the 1980s to the world's largest debtor nation by the end of the 1980s. Figure 26.12 shows the net international position of the United States—the value of all American-owned assets abroad plus what others owe Americans minus the value of all assets within the United States owned by foreigners and what Americans owe foreigners. In the mid-1980s, the United States became a net debtor nation. As a result, the U.S. economy will have to pay interest, dividends, and profits to foreign investors each year, spending more dollars abroad for these payments than it is receiving.

But is this good or bad? Suppose you borrow a large sum from a bank. In the future, unless you used the borrowed funds to make an investment that yielded a return at least equal to the interest you had to pay the bank, you would be unable to consume as much as you would otherwise, for the simple reason that you must pay the bank interest as well as principle. The same applies to foreign borrowing. During the 1980s, the large trade deficits were caused by the large fiscal budget deficits that reduced national saving. Because the foreign borrowing was not being used to finance investment spending that would boost future income, the concern was that the large trade deficits represented a future burden on the economy. In contrast, the trade deficit in the late 1990s *is* a reflection of strong investment spending. As long as these investments raise future income, the country will have the additional resources necessary to repay foreign borrowers without reducing consumption.

Looking Ahead

In this chapter we used the full-employment model to analyze the effects of fiscal deficits and surpluses, the role of foreign borrowing in open economies, and the connection between capital flows and trade deficits. The full-employment model assumes that wages, interest rates, prices, and exchange rates adjust rapidly to ensure that demand and supply are equal in all markets. With the labor market in equilibrium, the economy produces its full-employment level of output. The real rate of interest, and equilibrium saving and investment, are determined

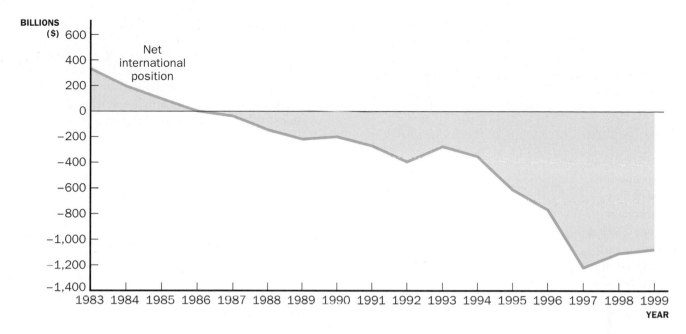

FIGURE 26.12 *The United States Becomes a Debtor Nation*

The United States was a large creditor nation in the beginning of the 1980s; that is, American-held foreign assets exceeded foreign-held U.S. assets. By the 1990s, it had become a large debtor nation.

SOURCE: *Survey of Current Business* (Bureau of Economic Analysis, Department of Commerce, July 2000), Table 3.

in the capital market. In the open economy, capital flows serve to close any gap between national saving and investment. These capital flows equal the trade balance. A capital inflow implies a trade deficit; a capital outflow implies a trade surplus. The exchange rate adjusts to achieve the necessary trade balance.

While we have extended the full-employment model to incorporate government and international trade, we have ignored one of the most important of all macroeconomic phenomena—economic growth. In Chapter 27, we turn to this important topic.

Review and Practice

Summary

1. In the full-employment model, an increase in government expenditures matched by taxes reduces disposable income. This reduces both consumption and

saving at full-employment output. The saving curve shifts to the left, investment declines, and the real interest rate rises. Consumption and investment are crowded out.

2. Equal changes in government revenues and expenditures—balanced budget changes in taxes and expenditures—do not affect full-employment output or employment. Balanced budget changes do affect the composition of output.

3. When the government runs a deficit or surplus, the capital market is affected. If there is a fiscal deficit, the government must borrow in the capital market to finance the deficit.

4. In an open economy, investment can be financed from domestic national saving or foreign borrowing. In a small open economy, shifts in the saving curve will not affect the international real interest rate or the level of domestic investment. Shifts in the saving curve will affect the level of foreign borrowing.

5. The trade deficit must equal capital inflows. When domestic investment exceeds national saving in an open economy, the difference is equal to foreign borrowing (a capital inflow), and the economy will have a trade deficit.

Key Terms

closed economy
open economy
fiscal deficit
fiscal surplus
national saving
crowding out
net capital flows
capital inflows
capital outflows
trade deficit
exchange rate
depreciation
appreciation

Review Questions

1. What happened to the size of the budget deficits in the 1980s? What is the relationship between the deficit and the level of the debt?

2. What are the consequences of an increased deficit for private investment in an open economy and in a closed economy?

3. What happened to the trade deficit during the 1980s? How did the foreign indebtedness of the U.S. economy change during the 1980s? What is the relationship between these two changes?

4. What is the relationship between the trade deficit and an inflow of foreign capital?

5. What is the relationship between the trade deficit and the fiscal deficit?

6. What is the exchange rate? How is it determined? What role do adjustments in the exchange rate play in ensuring that capital inflows equal the trade deficit?

7. What is the saving-investment identity for an open economy?

Problems

1. Suppose households save 5 percent of their disposable income. If the government increases expenditures and taxes by $100 billion, by how much will saving decline? By how much will consumption decline? What happens to investment? (Assume a closed economy.)

2. Redo question 1 but assume households save 10 percent of their disposable income. What happens to consumption and investment? Why does investment decline more with a higher saving rate?

3. Suppose a certain country has private saving of 6 percent of GDP, foreign borrowing of 1 percent of GDP, and a balanced budget. What is its level of investment? If the budget deficit is 1.5 percent of GDP, how does your answer change?

4. Why does it make a difference if a country borrows abroad to finance the expansion of its railroads, or to finance increased Social Security benefits for the elderly?

5. The primary deficit is defined as the difference between government expenditures *excluding interest payments* and tax revenues; it represents what the deficit would have been, had the government not inherited any debt. The table below shows the primary deficit over time. (A negative deficit means the government is running a surplus.) Discuss why the concept of a primary deficit may or may not be useful or relevant.

Year	Primary deficit	Actual deficit
1980	21.3	73.8
1985	82.8	212.3
1990	37.2	221.4
1995	−68.4	163.8

6. U.S. foreign indebtedness is greater than that of Mexico, Brazil, and Argentina combined. But does this necessarily mean that the United States has a larger debt problem than those countries? Why or why not? Can you think of a situation in which an individual with debts of larger value may actually have less of a debt problem?

7. If Congress were to pass a law prohibiting foreigners from buying U.S. Treasury bills, would this prevent government borrowing from leading to capital inflows? Discuss.

8. Japan had large trade surpluses during the 1980s. Would this cause Japan to be a borrower or a lender in international capital markets?

9. If a nation borrowed $50 billion from abroad one year and its imports were worth $800 billion, what would be the value of its exports? How does the answer change if, instead of borrowing, the nation loaned $100 billion abroad?

10. Since other countries benefit from exporting their products to the United States, why shouldn't the U.S. government charge them for the privilege of selling in the United States?

11. If the U.S. investment schedule shifts to the right and world interest rates rise, what is the effect on private investment in other countries? What is the effect on the U.S. national saving?

Chapter 27

Growth and Productivity

Key Questions

1. What are the principle determinants of growth in the economy?

2. What accounts for changes in the economy's growth rate?

3. Do living standards in different countries tend to converge to become similar?

4. Are there policies available to the government that might stimulate economic growth?

5. Are there limits to economic growth?

*T*he changes that have taken place in the U.S. standard of living during the past century are hard to comprehend. In 1900, the average American's level of consumption was little higher than the average citizen's in Mexico or the Philippines today. Life expectancy was low, in part because diseases like smallpox, diphtheria, typhoid fever, and whooping cough were still common. People were fifteen times more likely to catch measles in 1900 than they are today. The abundance of land meant that relatively few Americans were starving, but luxuries were scarce. People worked as long as they could, and when they could no longer work, they became the responsibility of their children; there was no easy retirement. Most of the goods that people consume today—from CDs to cellular phones to frozen pizzas—could not even be conceived of in 1900.

During the nineteenth century, the standards of living in England and a few other European countries were perhaps slightly higher than that of the United States. These countries' living standards were the highest in the world, but even within Europe, there were famines. During the most famous of these, the Irish potato famine of 1845–1848, more than a tenth of the population died, and more than

another tenth migrated to the United States. For those living in Asia, Africa, and Latin America, as the vast majority of people did then and do now, life was even harder.

The tremendous improvements to our standards of living are the fruits of economic growth—our ability to produce more of the things that provide for our material standard of living. To analyze the factors that account for economic growth, we can use the insights provided by the full-employment model that we have used in the last three chapters. The full-employment model provides what we can think of as a snapshot of the economy. We assumed the economy's capital stock—its plant and equipment—was fixed, and we assumed the labor force was fixed. Now we look at the economy through a sequence of snapshots through time so that we obtain a movie of the economy. In this way, we can capture the changes that occur over time. At each point in time, the full-employment model shows how real wages and the real interest rate adjust to ensure the economy produces at potential GDP. Over time, new investment leads to more machines and buildings, population growth and immigration lead to increases in the labor force, and innovation and research and development generate technological changes that alter what the economy produces and how it produces it.

Higher standards of living are reflected not only in higher incomes and longer life expectancies but also in shorter working hours and higher levels of education. Improved education is both a benefit and a cause of higher living standards. Table 27.1 compares the United States in 1900 and 1998, indicating stark contrasts in living standards. Underlying all of these differences is an increase in the output produced for each hour worked, what we identified in Chapter 5 as productivity. One major goal of this chapter is to understand what causes productivity to increase.

The rate of growth of total output in the economy can be expressed as the sum of two factors: the rate of increase in the number of hours worked, and the rate of increase in the output per hour worked (the productivity of the labor force):

$$\text{growth rate of output} = \text{growth rate of hours worked} + \text{growth rate of productivity.}$$

The first term—growth in total hours worked—occurs because the labor force is growing or workers are, on average, working longer. The second term—growth in productivity—is the key to rising living standards.

Figure 27.1 shows average growth rates for the U.S. GDP by decades. Two important points stand out. First, overall growth has declined since the 1960s. Second, this decline is attributable to a decline in productivity growth. The fall in

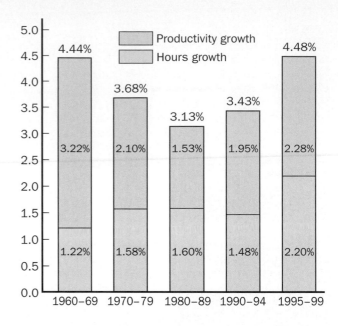

FIGURE 27.1   *Output Growth*

The growth rate of total output is equal to the growth rate in the number of hours worked plus the growth rate of productivity. Total growth slowed during the 1970s through the first half of the 1990s, with the decline accounted for by the decline in the growth rate of productivity. Productivity growth increased markedly during the second half of the 1990s.

SOURCE: *ERP* (2001), Table B-50.

TABLE 27.1

The United States in 1900 and 1998		
	1900	**1998**
Population	76 million	270 million
Life expectancy	47 years	76 years[a]
GDP (in 1998 dollars)	$492 billion	$8,760 billion
GDP per capita (in 1998 dollars)	$6,470	$32,440
Average hours worked each week in manufacturing	59	42
Average hourly wage in manufacturing (1998 dollars)	$5.15	$13.49
Number of telephones	1.3 million	>200 million
% of those age 5–19 enrolled in school	51 percent	92 percent[b]

[a]1997 figure.

[b]1995 figure.

SOURCES: *ERP* (1999); *Statistical Abstract of the United States* (1999).

Rate of growth of output = rate of increase in the number of hours worked + the rate of increase in the output per hour worked

$$g_Q = g_H + g_P,$$

where

g_Q = rate of growth of output
g_H = rate of growth of hours
g_P = rate of increase in productivity (output per hour).

the growth rate of productivity—the "productivity slowdown"—began in 1973. Figure 27.2 shows the sharp drop in productivity growth in the early 1970s, a drop that was reversed at the end of the 1990s. The productivity slowdown was not just an American phenomenon—all the industrialized economies have grown more slowly since 1973. This suggests that to explain why productivity fell after 1973, we cannot simply look at factors in the United States.

If we are interested in the economy's ability to provide material goods and services to its residents, then we should focus on the growth rate of output per capita. The growth rate of output per capita depends on the growth in the number of hours worked per capita plus the growth rate of productivity. Figure 27.3 shows that during the 1960s, the average number of hours individuals worked declined (a negative growth rate). Despite this, real per capita income grew rapidly due to productivity increases. During the 1980s, a significant portion of the growth in per capita incomes was due to increases in the average number of hours worked. In part, this reflects the increases in the labor force as more women took on full-time careers. As a result, the average number of hours worked increased.

Since 1996, productivity growth in the United States has risen dramatically. Whether this faster productivity growth will be sustained will be important for determining our future standard of living. One other factor is important to keep in mind: since 1870, the average rate of growth of per capita income in the United States has been 1.8 percent per year. That means that the 1960s might have been unusual and that the decline in productivity growth during 1973–1995 was simply a return to more normal times.

Explaining Productivity

For almost a century, the United States has been at the center of the technological advances that have changed the world. The telegraph, telephone, laser, transistor, airplane, assembly line, jet engine, atomic energy, memory chips… the list of U.S. technological achievements goes on and on. Beyond these path-breaking developments are countless smaller improvements: new as well as better products, and less expensive ways of making old products. The country has reaped a huge reward from these productivity-enhancing changes—it is through these productivity increases that rising standards of living are possible. That is why the productivity slowdown in the 1970s shown in Figure 27.2 was cause for concern and why the speedup in the 1990s was so exciting.

Does it make a difference if the average rate of productivity growth rises from about 2 percent to 3 percent? In fact, it makes a great deal of difference because the differences compound over time. Consider this simple calculation. Two countries start out equally wealthy, but one grows at 2 percent a year while the other grows at 3 percent per year. The difference in productivity would be barely perceptible for a few years. But after thirty years, the slower-growing country would be only three fourths as wealthy as the faster-growing one. America's slower growth compared with the growth of other developed economies explains why many countries have almost caught up to the United States, as shown in Figure 27.4 (p. 574).

One way to grasp the importance of even small differences in growth rates is to compare how long it takes for income to double. To do this, we can make use of the *rule of seventy*—dividing the growth rate into 70 will tell us the approximate number of years needed for income to double.[1]

---

[1]In case you are wondering where the rule of seventy comes from, it is based on the use of logarithms. If income starts out at Y_0 and the growth rate is g (where 2 percent per year is expressed as .02), then after n years, income will be equal to $(1 + g)^n Y_0$. This will have doubled, so that it equals $2Y_0$, when $(1 + g)^n = 2$. Taking natural logs of both sides and solving for n gives $n = \ln(2)/\ln(1 + g)$. Now we use two approximations. First, since $\ln(2) = .693$, we approximate it by using .70. And since g is a small number, such as .02 or .04, $\ln(1 + g)$ is approximately equal to g. So this gives us $n = .70/g$.

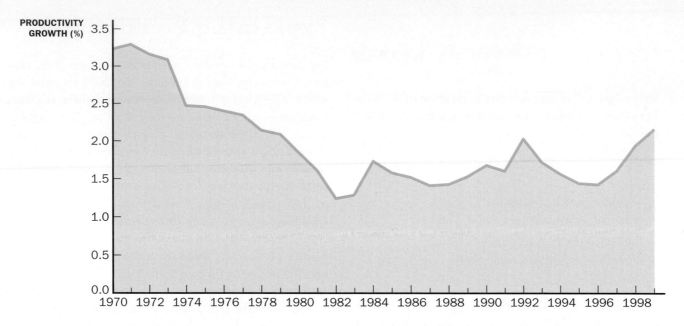

FIGURE 27.2 *U.S. Productivity Trends*

The rate of productivity growth dropped sharply in the 1970s. (The figure shows for each year the average growth rate of productivity over a decade ending in that year.) Productivity growth increased sharply at the end of the 1990s.

SOURCE: *ERP* (2001), Table B-50.

For example, if an economy grows at 5 percent per year, income will double in 14 years (70/5 = 14).

Average annual growth rate	Number of years for income to double
1 percent	70
2 percent	35
3 percent	23
4 percent	18
5 percent	14
6 percent	12
7 percent	10
8 percent	9

The difference between growing at 3 percent per year instead of 2 percent may sound small, but as the table shows, the difference compounds over time. The slower-growing economy would have incomes 20 percent lower after only twenty-five years.

Lower growth in productivity means that, on average, people will have less of everything—smaller houses, poorer health care, less travel, and fewer government services than otherwise. When output growth is sustained through in-

Internet Connection

How Fast Is Economic Growth?

Measuring the rise in per capita income is one way to assess economic growth and rising living standards, but another way is to ask how many hours a typical worker must work in order to purchase some specific good. For example, in 1895, the average worker needed to work 44 hours to earn the income necessary to purchase a set of dishes—today, it takes only about 3.6 hours. Brad de Long, a professor at University of California, Berkeley, provides further examples at http://www.j-bradford-delong.net/Comments/ FRBSF June11.html as he addresses the question, How fast is economic growth?

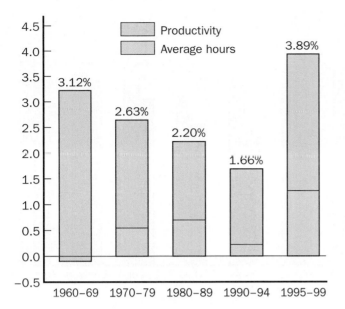

FIGURE 27.3 *Per Capita Output Growth*

The growth rate of output per capita depends on productivity growth and the growth in the average number of hours worked per capita. During the 1960s, rapid growth in per capita incomes occurred even as the average number of hours worked per capita declined. In the 1980s, labor force participation of women increased, raising the average number of hours worked per capita. Despite this increase in hours, per capita income grew more slowly than in the 1960s because of the decline in productivity growth. In the late 1990s, productivity growth increased markedly.

SOURCE: *ERP* (2001), Tables B-47, B-50, B-2, and B-34.

To understand what may have contributed to these fluctuations in productivity, we need to understand what causes increases in output per hour in the first place. There are four key factors: saving and investment; education and the quality of the labor force; reallocating resources from low- to high-productivity sectors of the economy; and technological change. The insights from the full-employment model can help us to understand how changes in each of these factors affect the economy and lead to changes in living standards. The following sections discuss each factor in turn.

Saving and Investment

Workers today are much more productive than they were one hundred or even twenty years ago. One important reason for this is that they have more and better machines to work with. American textile workers can produce far more than textile workers in India, partly because of differences in the equipment they use. Many textile workers in India still use handlooms, similar to those used in America two hundred years ago.

Higher levels of investment relative to GDP result in more capital per worker. Economists call this **capital deepening**. As capital per worker increases, output per worker increases. We can illustrate this using the concept of the aggregate production function that was introduced in Chapter 24. There, we used it to relate employment to output, when the amount of capital was fixed. When we focus on growth, with the labor force and the capital stock growing over time,

creases in the number of hours worked rather than through productivity increases—when families sustain income increases only by having both spouses working, for instance—the reduced leisure puts strains on families and means that focusing only on the income increases would exaggerate the rise in living standards.

The critical role productivity growth plays in improving living standards accounts for the attention that has been given to an apparent speedup in productivity growth at the end of the 1990s. It is too early to tell whether this represents the reversal of the slow productivity growth experienced since the 1970s or whether it is only a short-lived phenomena, but many commentators are heralding the arrival of a "new economy." They argue that the tremendous advances in computer and informational technologies in recent years will contribute to higher productivity growth and rising standards of living.

Modern textile manufacturing bears little resemblance to the traditional hand loom.

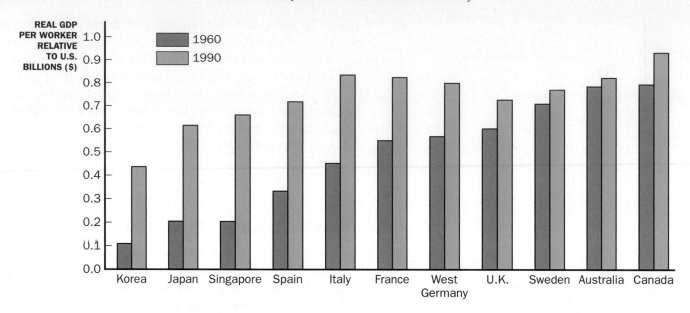

FIGURE 27.4 *Levels of GDP per Capita*

The United States still leads the world in GDP per worker, although because of its lower average growth rate, other developed countries have been drawing closer.

SOURCE: Penn World Tables at http://www.pwt.econ.upenn.edu .

it becomes more useful to express the aggregate production function in terms of output *per worker*. As each worker has more capital to work with, output per worker rises. But because of diminishing returns, output per worker rises less and less as capital per worker increases. This is illustrated in

Figure 27.5. Increasing capital per worker from k_0 to k_1, capital deepening, raises output per worker from y_0 to y_1.

In Chapters 24 and 26 we discussed the relationship between saving and investment. In a closed economy, saving equals investment, as illustrated in Figure 27.6. In the fig-

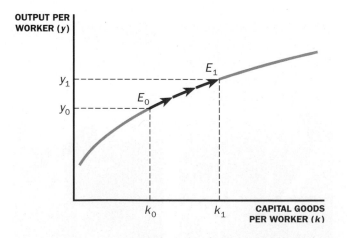

FIGURE 27.5 *Investment and Productivity*

An increase in the investment rate (the ratio of investment to GDP) results in capital deepening. As capital per worker increases, output per worker increases.

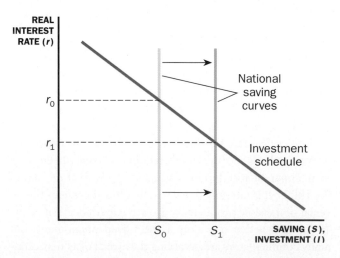

FIGURE 27.6 *Saving and Investment*

Higher saving rates lead to lower real interest rates and higher investment.

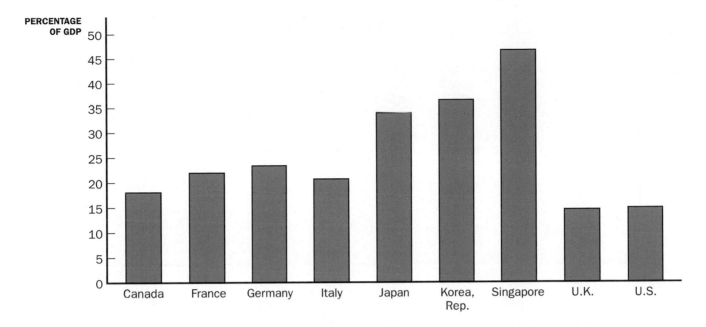

FIGURE 27.7 *Saving Rates in Developed Economies*

During the 1980s and 1990s, the U.S. saving rate was significantly lower than those in many other industrialized economies.

SOURCE: *World Development Indicators* (Washington, D.C.: World Bank, 2000).

ure, we assume that saving does not depend on the real interest rate. A rise in saving (a shift in the saving curve to the right) leads to lower real interest rates, and lower real interest rates lead to higher investment.

In an open economy, matters are more complicated. Domestic saving need not equal investment, because a country can finance investment by borrowing from abroad. But even though the U.S. economy is open, U.S. saving and investment tend to move together (recall Figure 26.8), with a reduction in national saving of $100 leading to a reduction of investment of between $35 and $50.

Figure 27.7 compares the saving rates in developed countries. Both in relation to other countries and historically, U.S. saving rates in recent years have been low. For example, the U.S. saving rate has been significantly less than that of Japan. Because of its adverse effects on investment, the low saving rate may underlie some of the slowdown in U.S. productivity growth that occurred from the mid-1970s to the mid-1990s.

Why is the United States Saving Rate So Low?

To see why the U.S. saving rate is so low, it is useful to break down saving into three components: personal (or household) saving, business saving, and government saving (the fiscal surplus). Figure 27.8 shows how each of these as well as total national saving has changed over time. The figure makes clear that the low level during the 1980s and the first half of the 1990s was largely attributable to the huge government deficits and declines in the household saving rate. Beginning in 1993, the federal government succeeded in reducing the deficit, from almost 5 percent of GDP to a small surplus in 1999. At the same time, state and local governments were running large surpluses so that total government saving turned positive. The household saving rate has, however, continued to decline, moderating the overall increase in national saving. Here we focus on the factors affecting household saving.

We can use the basic framework for consumer choice introduced earlier (Chapter 6) to analyze the determination of saving. Prices (here, the interest rate) and preferences affect the desire for consumption in the future versus consumption today. People save for future needs—for retirement (life-cycle savings); to buy a home, pay for their children's college education, or meet certain other needs (target savings); for emergencies, for periods in which their incomes may be low, say, because they are laid off, or in

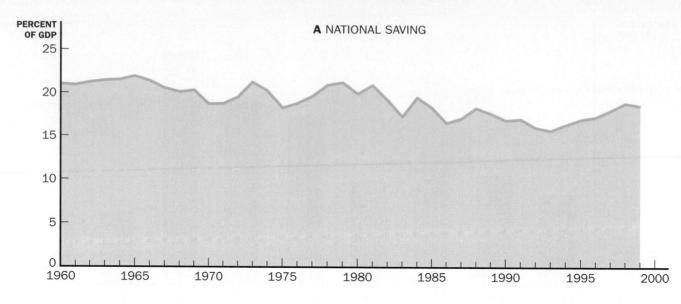

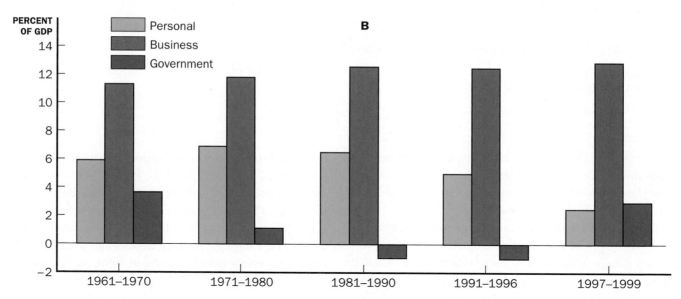

FIGURE 27.8   *United States Saving*

Saving can come from households, businesses, or government. During the 1980s, total national saving was low, and the most significant decline arose from government saving. The federal budget improved after 1993, but personal saving has continued to fall.

SOURCE: *ERP* (2001), Table B-32.

which their needs are high, or because they require medical attention (precautionary savings); and to leave something to their children (bequest savings).

During the past two decades, virtually all of the motives and incentives for saving changed in a way to discourage saving. Improved Social Security (particularly during the 1970s) reduced the need for private savings for retirement; improved capital markets and insurance, provided by both government and employers, meant that people did not have to save as much for emergencies; improved capital markets also meant people did not have to save as much for a down payment on a house; and improved government student-loan programs meant that parents did not have to save as much for their children's education.

But one change should have stimulated saving. An increase in the real after-tax return. In the 1980s, taxes on the return to capital, particularly for upper-income levels, plummeted—from 70 percent in 1980 to 28 percent in 1986—and real after-tax returns soared. Nevertheless, saving fell. By the logic of income and substitution effects, this should not come as too much of a surprise.[2] The effect of a change in real after-tax interest rates on saving, while positive, is probably small. In fact, we drew Figure 27.6 on the assumption that saving was unaffected by the interest rate (so the saving curve was vertical).

But the changes discussed so far, by themselves, do not seem to account fully for the low level of saving in the United States. Accordingly, economists have looked elsewhere for an explanation.

The **life-cycle theory of savings** emphasizes that saving will differ in different parts of an individual's life. People in the age group of forty-five to sixty-five typically are high savers; no longer facing the burden of children, they recognize the necessity of setting aside money for their retirement. The percentage of the population in this group was low in the mid-1970s, but beginning in the mid-1990s it began to grow as the baby-boom generation entered their fifties. This should provide an impetus for an increased personal saving rate, although it does not yet appear to have done so.

Some economists argued that the huge increase in real estate prices in the 1980s meant that more individuals were saving in the form of home equity. This form of saving is not recorded in the national income accounts. Though the explanation seemed plausible at the time, it suggested that when real estate prices leveled out, or fell, as they did in the late 1980s and early 1990s, saving would increase; it did not.

More recently, the tremendous rise in stock prices has increased household wealth. As a consequence, households may feel there is less need to save out of their current income. From the perspective of individual households, their wealth is rising just as if they had saved more themselves. As their wealth rises, households may choose to consume more. This could be one factor accounting for the continued low saving rate in the United States. The stock market decline in 2000 may lead people to increase their saving rate.

---

[2]Although the *substitution* effect leads to increased saving, the *income* effect results in reduced saving. While on theoretical grounds the *net* effect is ambiguous, the evidence supports a small positive effect.

Finally, some economists attribute the decline in saving rates to a change in values: the "Now" generation wants its consumption now and puts less income aside for its children.

WRAP-UP

Explanations for Low Saving Rates

Improved Social Security
Improved insurance markets
Improved capital markets
Rising stock prices
Changes in values: less future-oriented behavior

Policies to Stimulate Saving and Investment   Government has only limited tools to stimulate saving and investment. A government surplus adds to national saving and in a closed (or not perfectly open) economy, leads to increased investment. However, the relationship between the government's surplus (or deficit) and overall investment in the economy can depend on the nature of government spending. Increased government investment in **infrastructure**—roads, bridges, airports, and other public capital projects that help the private sector perform more effectively—can raise overall investment (private plus public) even though it may reduce the government surplus.

When the economy is at full employment, investment subsidies have little or no effect on aggregate investment in a closed economy. Since the saving rate is relatively insensitive to interest rates, an upward shift in the investment function as a result of government subsidies leads to higher interest rates and relatively little change in saving and investment. In an open economy, investment subsidies induce more investment and more borrowing from abroad. If the subsidies lower the before-subsidy marginal return to investment to the point where it is below the cost of capital from abroad, the country (at the margin) is actually worse off as a result of the additional investment. GDP—what is produced in the United States—increases, but GNP—netting out what has to be paid to foreign lenders (so what Americans can actually spend)—actually decreases.

GDP can be increased if saving can be increased (and consumption reduced). The apparent unresponsiveness of the saving rate to the real interest rate has made most economists skeptical about the potential use of tax policy to encourage saving. There is some evidence that IRAs (individual retirement accounts) have had some effect, largely because banks and other financial institutions have used them as a basis of advertising campaigns to obtain deposits.

Why Saving and Investment Is Not the Whole Story

As important as saving and investment rates are in explaining the growth rate of productivity, they are not the whole story. As we have seen, capital accumulation leads to increases in output per worker—in productivity (see Figure 27.5). However, this effect is limited to the shortrun. After an increase in the rate of saving and investment, the economy eventually reaches a new ratio of capital to worker. This is capital deepening. At the new high level of capital to worker, the economy is indeed operating at a higher level of productivity, but the productivity *increase* has run its course. This is illustrated in Figure 27.9. Three segments of the growth path are evident. The first segment *(AB)* represents the economy's growth before the increase in the rate of saving and investment. The steep segment that follows *(BC)* represents the period of capital accumulation arising from the increase in the rate of saving and investment; as capital per worker increases, so do productivity and the growth rate of the economy. But once the new, higher level of capital per worker is reached, the economy resumes its original growth rate, represented by the third segment *(CD)*.

This analysis may suggest that repeated increases in the rate of saving and investment, generating continuous capital deepening, will result in a long-run increase in the rate of productivity increase and therefore a long-run increase in the rate of economic growth. This is *not* the case because of the law of diminishing returns, which says that as the amount of capital goods per worker continues to increase, successive increments of capital increase output per worker by less and less. Eventually, further increases in capital per worker will yield almost no increase in output per worker. Figure 27.10 shows that as the economy increases capital per worker from k_2 to k_3, the increase in output per worker is much smaller than when the economy increases capital per worker by a similar amount from k_1 to k_2.

Yet in fact, productivity growth did not diminish during periods of rapid capital accumulation. Figure 27.11 shows productivity growth in the United States in twenty-year periods since 1880. Productivity growth actually in-

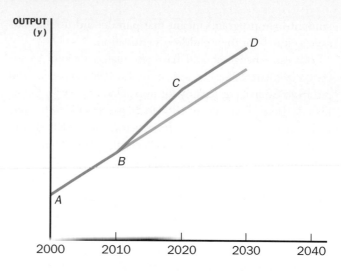

FIGURE 27.9 *Short-Run and Long-Run Effects of Capital Deepening*

Capital deepening increases output per worker (productivity) and therefore economic growth, but the effects on the rate of growth of productivity (as opposed to the level of productivity) are limited to the short run. The graph shows three segments of a hypothetical growth path. *AB* represents the economy's growth before an increase in saving and investment. *BC*, the steep segment, represents the period of capital accumulation resulting from the increase in saving and investment. When the new, higher level of capital per worker is reached, the economy resumes its original growth rate, represented by segment *CD*. Note that while *CD* is parallel to the original path (the growth rates are the same), the *level* of output is higher on the new path.

creased from 1900 to 1970 during a period of enormous accumulation of capital goods. Similar patterns have been observed elsewhere. Japan, for example, has had steadily increasing productivity growth along with large increases in capital goods per worker for the past quarter century.

The reason why productivity growth can continue over long periods is that capital deepening is not the only, or even the primary, source of productivity increases. If we are to understand why productivity has increased, we need to look at the other sources, to which we now turn.

Higher Quality of the Labor Force

A second major source of productivity growth, which today is even more important than increased capital per

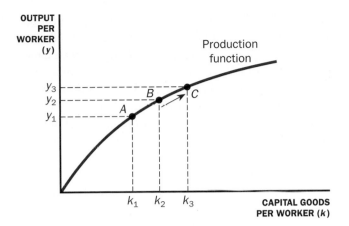

FIGURE 27.10 *Diminishing Returns to Capital*

With a given production function, the increase in capital goods per worker from k_2 to k_3 would result in a smaller increase in productivity than the corresponding increase from k_1 to k_2.

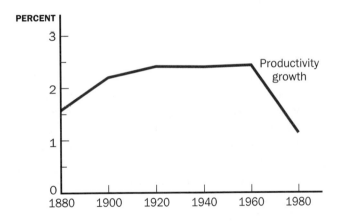

FIGURE 27.11 *Long-Run U.S. Productivity Growth*

Productivity growth increased sharply during the first part of the twentieth century, a period of rapid capital goods accumulation, before declining in the 1970s.

SOURCE: Angus Maddison, *Dynamic Forces in Capitalist Development* (Oxford: Oxford University Press, 1991).

worker, is a higher-quality labor force. Running a modern industrial economy requires a well-educated labor force. In addition, an economy on the cutting edge of technological change needs trained engineers and scientists to discover and shape those innovations.

Spending money on education and training improves workers' skills and productivity. These expenditures are investments—just like investments in machines and buildings. And just as expenditures on plant and equipment result in physical capital, we say that expenditures on education result in **human capital.** Thus, increases in human capital are one of the major sources of economic growth.

One nationally representative survey found that establishments with more educated work forces had significantly higher productivity: increasing years of education by 10 percent increased productivity by 8.6 percent. Indeed, returns to education have increased markedly—even as the number of educated has increased: by 1994 the median full-time worker with at least a bachelor's degree earned 74 percent more per week than one with only a high school diploma—up from 36 percent in 1979. Though some of this difference may be attributed to the fact that those who graduate from college are more able (and hence would have earned higher incomes even if they had not gone on to college), even accounting for factors such as family background or high school performance, the returns to education appear significant. Just a year of college has been estimated to increase earnings by 5 to 10 percent, or more.

The Strengths of the U.S. Educational System

In recent years, there have been significant increases at least in the "quantity" of education in the United States. More students are finishing high school. The drop-out rate fell from 14.1 to 11 percent between 1973 and 1993. More high school students are attending and completing college. The percentage of high school graduates enrolling in college after graduation increased from 49 percent in 1980 to 62 percent in 1993. As the new, more highly educated workers have replaced older workers, the share of the work force with a college degree has risen, from 21 percent in 1976 to 29 percent in 1997.[3] And enrollment in graduate schools has increased even more than undergraduate enrollment.

A particular strength of America's educational system has been its egalitarianism. While other countries have made decisions on whether a particular child is suitable for a college education at early ages (sometimes as young as eleven), in the United States such decisions are made

[3]Data are from the Bureau of Labor Statistics and U.S. Census Bureau's *Current Population Survey.*

much later, and students typically get repeated chances. Early sorting, based on test scores, gives a distinct advantage to children with more educated parents.

Another great strength is the U.S. system of community colleges and state universities, many of which provide a high-quality education to those who cannot afford to go to private schools or who may not have performed well in high school. In many countries, such students are precluded from further education. (Ironically, while in many respects the American educational system is more egalitarian than those of other developed countries, in one respect it is less so. Most European countries charge virtually no tuition to students who are admitted to their universities, and some actually pay all or part of students' living costs.)

Still another strength is America's universities, which number among the greatest in the world. Students from virtually every country come to the United States to study, as both undergraduate and graduate students. The discoveries and innovations flowing out of the universities' research laboratories have been an important basis of America's technological superiority.

Symptoms of a U.S. Human Capital Problem
While there is great strength within the U.S. educational system, there are also problems. The concern is that while on quantitative measures the U.S. system looks good, with high levels of expenditure and high levels of enrollment, the quality of U.S. education is low. On a number of standardized tests, particularly in areas of science and mathematics, American students perform below students from many other countries—even countries that have until recently been classified as less developed, such as Korea and Taiwan. Of course, standardized tests are imperfect and limited; one of the many problems with them is that they do not measure creativity. But the tests do measure success in certain objectives of education, such as mastery of basic skills. The poor performance of American students is thus disturbing.

Similarly, while the United States remains unique in the large fraction of its youth that goes to college, a smaller proportion of U.S. college students choose to study science and engineering, in comparison to students from some other countries, such as Japan and Korea. Evidence suggests that the fraction of the work force that is composed of engineers and scientists is a major determinant of rapid economic growth.

Finally, a significant fraction of America's population is deprived of the opportunity to realize their full potential.

The role of family background in determining educational achievement has increasingly been recognized. Children who grow up in poverty are less likely to attain an education commensurate with their ability. Yet the number of children in poverty has increased markedly in recent decades, from 15 percent in 1970 to 21 percent in 1992. With the flight to the suburbs that began in the 1950s, and with increasing violence and drugs in inner-city high schools, those left in inner cities are less likely to get a quality education. Moreover, a college education has become less affordable for children from poor families. Tuitions at public and private colleges and universities have increased at rates far exceeding increases in the cost of living; real incomes of poorer families have fallen; and the real value of government grant and loan programs (such as Pell grants) has declined. Not surprisingly, the gap between the fraction of children from poor families and rich families going on to higher education has increased.

Reallocating Resources from Low- to High-Productivity Sectors

During the past century, the United States has evolved from an agricultural economy to an industrial economy to a service economy. Figure 27.12 shows this dramatic structural change. The service sector, broadly defined, includes not only traditional services such as those provided by barbers and waiters but also the more sophisticated services provided by doctors and lawyers, educational institutions, and computer programmers, among others. The medical sector alone has grown to the point where it accounted for about 15 percent of GDP in 2000.

The movement out of agriculture and into industry explains some of the productivity increase in the early part of the twentieth century. While the level of productivity in agriculture was increasing rapidly, it remained lower than that in industry. Thus, as workers shifted out of low-productivity jobs in agriculture into high-productivity jobs in manufacturing, average productivity in the economy increased. With almost all labor now out of agriculture—and with agricultural productivity increased to the point where incomes in that sector are comparable to those in the rest of the economy—this kind of shift can no longer be a source of overall productivity growth. But there remain other opportunities. Productivity in the telecommunications industry, other high-tech sectors, and export sectors is substantially higher

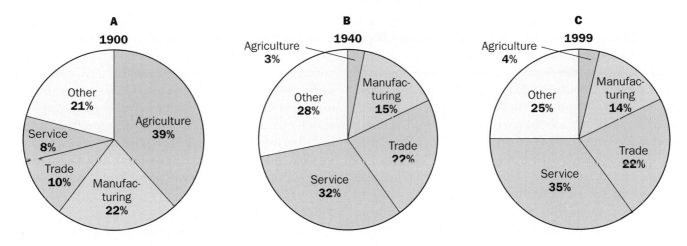

FIGURE 27.12 *Sectoral Shifts*

Employment in the U.S. economy shifted from agriculture to manufacturing in the first half of the twentieth century, and from manufacturing to services in the second half.

SOURCE: *ERP* (2001), Tables B-36, B-46.

than that in other parts of the economy. Telecommunications deregulation in the 1990s will facilitate the movement of resources into that sector. Rapid innovation in computer technology is having an impact in all sectors of the economy. And recent international trade agreements will open up new opportunities for export growth. These changes should contribute to the overall increase in productivity.

Technological Change and the Role of Ideas

While capital—both physical and human—is important for explaining the huge changes in living standards over the past two hundred years, just having more machines or better educated workers cannot account for the truly amazing differences between the economy in 1900 and the economy in 2000. We are not producing more of the same goods the economy produced in 1900; we are producing goods that the people of 1900 never dreamed of. Instead of using more machines to produce more horse-drawn carriages, we produce cars and airplanes. Instead of producing more horseshoes, we produce tires and jogging shoes. Key to the whole growth process, then, is technological progress—thinking up new ways to do old things and new ways to do entirely new things. And this means that *ideas* are central to explaining economic growth. Indeed, economists estimate that as much as two thirds of all

increases in productivity prior to 1973 were due to technological progress.

Investment increases the economy's stock of physical capital, and education leads to increases in human capital, but what leads to technological progress? To understand the economics of technological progress, we need to start by considering how ideas are different from goods like a laptop computer or a piece of chocolate cake. These goods are *rivalrous*; if I eat that piece of chocolate cake, you can't. But ideas are different. If both you and your roommate are taking economics, both of you can use an idea like the law of supply and demand. If your roommate does her homework first, the idea is still available to you when you get around to studying. When Tim Berners-Lee, Robert Cailliau, and their colleagues at the European particle physics center (CERN) in Geneva, Switzerland, invented the World Wide Web and hypertext format language, or html, in 1990, programmers from around the world could use their ideas. If you use html to construct a Web page, the idea of html is still also available to others—it is *nonrivalrous*. This is a key property of ideas. An idea is not used up once the first person uses it; it is still available to others.

One of the major differences between the economy today and in 1900 is the routine nature of the change brought about by new ideas. This technological progress comes about through the activities of thousands of entrepreneurs and innovators, particularly in the computer industry, and the thousands of scientists and engineers engaged in large-scale research projects in the business, government, and university sectors. Much of modern research is centered in huge laboratories, employing thousands of people. While the government runs some of these—such as the Brookhaven, Argonne, and Lawrence laboratories that carry out research in basic physics—many are private, like Bell Labs (part of AT&T), where the transistor and the laser were developed. Indeed, most major firms spend about 3 percent of their gross revenues on research and development (R & D).

The current level of technological progress has become so expected that it is hard to believe how different the view of reputable economists was in the early 1800s. Real wages of workers were little higher than they had been five hundred years earlier, when the bubonic plague killed a large part of the population of Europe and thereby created a scarcity of labor that raised real wages. After half a millennium of slow progress at best, Thomas Malthus, one of the greatest economists of that time, saw population expanding more rapidly than the capacity of the economy to support it. His prediction of declining living standards earned economics the nickname of "the dismal science." Today, many continue to predict that the world economy will be unable to grow faster than the population and that living standards must inevitably decline. Such predictions have been proved wrong over and over again by technological advances. The role of technological change on the economy's aggregate production is depicted in Figure 27.13.

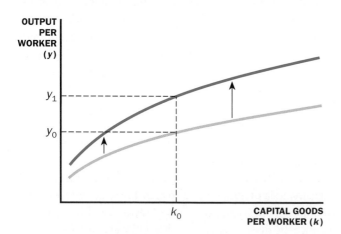

FIGURE 27.13 *Technological Change and Output per Worker*

Improvements in knowledge and technology shift up the production function; at each level of capital per worker, higher levels of output per worker can be achieved.

Improved technology allows the economy to achieve more output per worker at each level of capital per worker.

As we learned in Chapter 23, many of the new information technologies, and their applications in service industries such as finance and health, have made it increasingly difficult to measure the economy's output. In fact, one of the explanations for the apparently slow productivity growth measured in the last two decades, at the same time that tremendous innovation and technological changes have been taking place, is that GDP measures understate the true level of output.

The Production of Ideas   If ideas are important for economic growth, how are ideas produced? Can we use some of the basic ideas of economics to understand the production of ideas?

To start, think about the incentives that face a potential inventor. The incentives will be greatest if the inventor can charge a fee to anyone who uses her new idea. She must be able to exclude users who do not pay. But some ideas are not very excludable. Once Henry Ford came up with the idea of the modern assembly line, he might have kept it secret for a while by barring visitors to his factory, but certainly anyone who saw the assembly line could take the idea and set up a new factory. Most software companies do not make their source code public in order to exclude users who have not paid a licensing fee. The incentive to produce new ideas will be increased if inventors are able to exclude users who do not pay. This requires giving inventors property rights to ideas. If property rights are insecure, if a firm planning on engaging in research is uncertain about whether it will be allowed to capture the benefits of any new ideas it produces, then fewer resources will be invested into research and the production of new ideas.

From society's point of view, however, there is another consideration. Producing a new idea may be very costly, but an idea only needs to be produced once. Your laptop embodies thousands of new ideas, but these ideas did not have to be reproduced each time a new laptop was produced. The screen, memory chips, and case did have to be produced for each laptop; they are examples of rivalrous goods—the memory chips in your laptop cannot be in your roommate's laptop. But the design of the laptop only had to be produced once. The marginal cost of a nonrivalrous good like an idea is zero. It does not cost anything to use the idea one more time. So from society's perspective, the idea should be freely available to anyone who wants to use it. After all, it costs nothing to let others use the idea.

There is a tension, then, between providing incentives for the production of new ideas and ensuring they are widely used. Inventors need secure property rights that allow them to benefit from their ideas; they need to be able to exclude users who do not pay. Yet, once an idea is invented, there is a zero marginal cost to producing it and so it should be freely available.

Society addresses this tension through patent laws. By getting a patent, the inventor is given the exclusive rights to the invention. Other users have to pay to use it, and this allows the inventor to capture some of the benefits of her idea. But in the United States, patents expire after seventeen years and then the idea is freely available. In this way, society increases the incentive to produce new ideas, but at the same time the ideas eventually become available to everyone.

Expenditures on R & D   A major determinant of the pace of technological progress is the level of expenditure on R & D. These expenditures are a form of investment—expenditures today that yield returns in the future.

While overall expenditures on R & D, as a percentage of GDP, are relatively high in the United States—only in Japan are they higher—much of this has been for defense purposes. Government nondefense R & D in the United States plays a relatively small role. Over the last fifteen years, federal expenditures on nondefense R & D have actually fallen.

The high rates of return on R & D expenditures support the view that there is underinvestment in research. Some estimates put the private returns at over 25 percent, and since many of the returns accrue to firms other than those undertaking the research, social returns are estimated to be even higher. High risk and limitations on the

WRAP-UP

Factors Contributing to Productivity Growth

Saving and investment (capital accumulation)
Improved quality of the labor force
Reallocation of labor from low-productivity to high-productivity sectors
Technological progress

ability to borrow to finance R & D provide part of the explanation for the seeming underinvestment in R & D.

Total Factor Productivity: Measuring the Sources of Growth

In an advanced economy like the U.S. one, reallocation of resources from low- to high-productivity sectors is not viewed as a major source of further growth. That leaves saving and investment, human capital, and technology as the three sources of growth in productivity. But how important is each? Can we assess the relative contribution each has made to productivity growth? To answer this question, economists use a methodology called **total factor productivity analysis** in which they attempt to determine the change in total output that can be "attributed" to increases in the stock of capital (both human and physical) and increases in the supply of labor. Any output growth that cannot be attributed to capital or labor is attributed to technological change.

Suppose the share of capital in output—the amount of output attributable to capital (the total returns earned by capital divided by GDP)—is 20 percent. If the growth of capital is 10 percent, then the share of capital in output (20 percent) multiplied by capital growth (10 percent) gives us the amount that capital contributes to the growth of total output (2 percent in this example).[4]

---

[4]To see this, consider the change in output ΔQ "attributable" to an increase in capital of ΔK, if r is the return to capital:

$$\Delta Q = r\Delta K.$$

The percentage increase in Q is just

$$\Delta Q/Q = r\Delta K/Q.$$

Multiplying the numerator and denominator of the expression on the right side by K, we obtain

$$\Delta Q/Q = r(\Delta K/K)(K/Q) = r(K/Q)(\Delta K/K).$$

rK/Q is just the share of capital income in total GDP (rK is the total return to capital and Q is total output). Hence, the percentage increase in output attributable to the increase in K is the percentage increase in capital times the share of capital.

This same logic applies to labor. But capital and labor do not account for all of growth. The part that cannot be explained by increases in capital or labor is called the *increase in total factor productivity* (TFP). The rate of TFP increase is calculated as follows:

$$TFP = g_Q - (S_K \times g_K) - (S_L \times g_L),$$

where S_K = share of capital in GDP, S_L = share of labor in GDP, g_Q = rate of growth of output, g_K = rate of growth of capital, and g_L = rate of growth of labor.

The increase in TFP reflects the increasing efficiency with which an economy's resources are used. Some of this is the result of R & D, but at least prior to 1973, much of the increase could not be easily explained. The part that could not be explained was referred to as the *residual*—the part of growth that was "left over" after all the systematic sources of growth were taken into account. New production techniques such as replaceable parts in the nineteenth century, the assembly line in the early twentieth century, and just-in-time inventory management techniques in recent years are all examples of technological advances that bear little relationship to R & D expenditures, and thus form part of this "residual."

The equation for TFP can be rearranged in the equivalent form

$$g_Q = (S_K \times g_K) + (S_L \times g_L) + TFP.$$

In this form, the growth rate of output is accounted for by the contribution of capital, $S_K \times g_K$; the contribution of growth in labor input, $S_L \times g_L$; and TFP. Figure 27.14 uses this methodology to analyze the sources of increases in productivity for four different time periods—1959–1973, 1973–1990, 1990–1995, and 1995–1998.

Several conclusions emerge from the chart. First, the overall rate of growth was much higher before 1973 than it was during the period from 1973 to 1995. Second, between 1973 and 1995, almost all of the growth in output can be explained by increases in the inputs of capital and labor, while before 1973 and after 1995, there was a large residual (TFP). It is the decrease in TFP that appears to account for most of the growth slowdown in the 1970s and 1980s. Third, the decline in productivity after 1973 was accounted for, in part, by a decline in the contribution of capital, but since 1995, increases in capital, together with increases in TFP, have accounted for the increase in the

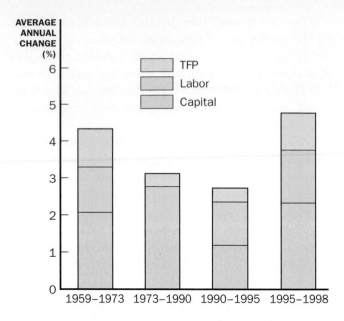

FIGURE 27.14 *Growth Accounting*

Over half the decline in growth between 1973 and 1990 is left unexplained after accounting for changes in the growth rates of capital and labor. The end of the 1990s saw an increase in TFP growth, returning it to levels similar to those seen in the 1959–1973 period. Increases in capital also account for the faster growth experienced during the second half of the 1990s.

SOURCE: Dale W. Jorgensen and Kevin J. Stiroh, "Raising the Speed Limit: U.S. Economic Growth in the Information Age," *Brookings Papers on Economic Activity,* 1 (2000): 125–211.

growth rate of output. Output grows because of increases in the factors of production such as labor and capital and because of increases in TFP—the ability to get more output from a given amount of labor and capital. The rapid growth at the end of the decade of the 1990s represented a return to the high growth rates of the 1950s and 1960s after two decades of slow productivity growth during the 1970s and 1980s.

These results, especially the fact that the unusually high growth rates in the 1960s cannot be explained easily, pose major problems for those involved in long-term forecasting. Was the rapid growth in the 1959–1973 period an aberration? Or were the 1970s and 1980s an aberration, with the late 1990s representing a return to the higher growth rates of earlier decades as fundamentally new technologies, such as computers, become more widely used?

CASE IN POINT

Calculating Total Factor Productivity in the 1990s

Between 1995 and 1998, private domestic output in the United States grew by 20 percent, or 4.7 percent per year. Dale Jorgensen and Kevin Stiroh[5] in 2000 estimated that average labor productivity grew by 2.3 percent per year over this period—each hour of labor input produces more output than previously. The accounting used earlier to explain the contribution of various factors to economic growth also can be used to explain the sources of this growth in labor productivity.

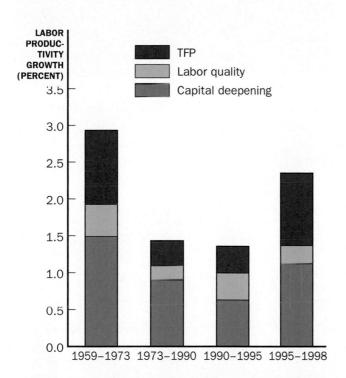

FIGURE 27.15 *Sources of Labor Productivity Growth*

Growth in labor productivity is due to capital deepening, increases in labor quality, and increases in total factor productivity. During the late 1990s, increases in labor productivity growth were due to increases in the contributions of capital deepening and total factor productivity.

SOURCE: Dale W. Jorgensen and Kevin J. Stiroh, "Raising the Speed Limit: U.S. Economic Growth in the Information Age," *Brookings Papers on Economic Activity,* 1 (2000): 125–211.

One of the reasons why labor might become more productive is because of capital deepening—when there is more capital per worker, each worker is able to produce more output. Thus, growth in capital per worker will cause labor productivity to grow. According to Jorgensen and Stiroh, capital deepening accounted for 1.1 percentage points, or about 48 percent, of the 2.3 percent growth rate of labor productivity. Figure 27.15 shows that labor productivity growth increased during the second half of the 1990s, and part of this increased growth can be accounted for by capital deepening. This source of labor productivity growth is, however, still less today than it was in the 1959–1973 period when capital deepening accounted for over 50 percent of the growth in labor productivity.

A second source of labor productivity growth arises from increases in the *quality* of labor. Labor quality can increase through education or through shifts in the composition of the labor force. For instance, in the early 1970s, the baby-boom generation entered the workforce. This shifted the composition—there were now more younger and relatively inexperienced workers in the labor force. Such a shift acts to reduce labor productivity. In the 1990s, as these baby boomers gained more work experience and training, the overall quality of the labor force increased, and this contributed to rising labor productivity. In the second half of the 1990s, however, increases in labor quality accounted for only 10 percent of the total growth in labor productivity.

The final source of labor productivity growth is due to increases in TFP. As the figure shows, TFP has increased significantly over the levels experienced between 1973 and 1995. ●

Are There Limits to Economic Growth?

In the early 1800s, the famous British economist Thomas Malthus envisioned the future as one in which the ever-increasing labor force would push wages down to the subsistence level, or even lower. Any technological progress

[5]Dale W. Jorgensen and Kevin J. Stiroh, "Raising the Speed Limit: U.S. Economic Growth in the Information Age," *Brookings Papers on Economic Activity,* 1 (2000): 125–211.

e-Insight

Computers and Increased Productivity Growth

If the recent increases in productivity growth are due to new information and computer technologies, then we might expect that all the major industrialized economies would be benefiting from them. Chart A shows average labor productivity growth for seven advanced economies, a group of countries known as the "group of seven," or the G-7 for short. As the chart shows, only the United States has seen labor productivity increase in recent years. For all the other members of the group, productivity growth was higher from 1980 to 1995 than it has been since. Since the new information and computer technologies are available to all these countries, why hasn't growth increased in all of them? Does this mean the new technologies are not the source of America's increased productivity growth?

One explanation for the acceleration in U.S. productivity growth that has not been matched in these other indus-

Physicians can now make virtual house calls using time-saving technology.

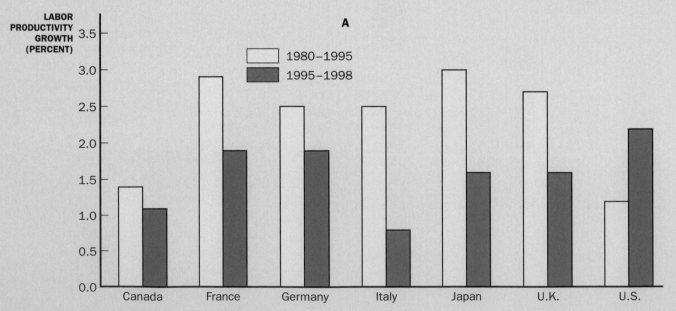

Productivity Growth in the G-7 Countries

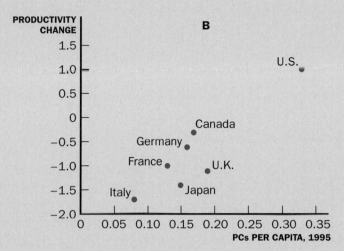

PRODUCTIVITY CHANGE vs **PCs PER CAPITA, 1995**

PCs and Productivity Growth

countries. For example, the Organization for Economic Cooperation and Development (OECD) estimated that in 1995 the number of personal computers (PCs) per capita was almost twice as high in the United States than in Canada and 75 percent higher than in the United Kingdom. As shown in the Chart B, the change in productivity growth between the 1980–1995 and 1995–1998 periods does appear to be associated with the adoption of computers. The United States, with the most PCs per capita in 1995, experienced the biggest increase in growth, while Italy, with the fewest PCs per capita in 1995, had the largest growth slowdown. While this association between PCs and productivity growth cannot prove whether the adoption of computers has helped *cause* America's growth speedup, it is suggestive.

SOURCE: Casey Cornwell and Bharat Trehan, "Information Technology and Productivity," Federal Reserve Bank of San Francisco *Economic Letter*, No. 2000-34, Nov. 10, 2000.

trialized economies may be that the United States has been more successful in adopting new technologies throughout the economy and has done so more quickly than other

that occurred would, in his view, raise wages only temporarily. As the labor supply increased, wages would eventually fall back to the subsistence level.

Over the past century, there has been a decrease in the rate of population growth, a phenomenon perhaps as remarkable as the increase in the rate of technological progress. One might have expected improved medicine and health conditions to cause a population explosion, but the spread of birth control and family planning has had the opposite effect, at least in the more developed countries. Today family size has decreased to the point where in many countries population growth (apart from migration) has almost halted. Those who worry about the limits to growth today believe that *exhaustible* natural resources—like oil, natural gas, phosphorus, or potassium—may pose a limit to economic growth as they are used up in the ordinary course of production.

Most economists do not share this fear, believing that markets do provide incentives for wise use of most resources—that as any good becomes more scarce and its price rises, the search for substitutes will be stimulated. Thus, the rise in the price of oil led to smaller, more efficient cars, cooler but better insulated houses, and a search for alterna-

tive sources of energy like geothermal and synthetic fuels, all of which resulted in a decline in the consumption of oil.

Still, there is one area in which the price system does not work well—the area of externalities. Without government intervention, for example, producers have no incentive to worry about air and water pollution. And in our globally connected world, what one country does results in externalities for others. Cutting down the rain forest in Brazil, for example, may have worldwide climatic consequences. The less developed countries feel that they can ill afford the costs of pollution control, when they can barely pay the price of any industrialization. Most economists do not believe that we face an either/or choice. We do not have to abandon growth to preserve our environment. Nevertheless, a sensitivity to the quality of our environment may affect how we go about growing. This sensitivity is building a new consensus in favor of **sustainable development,** that is, growth not based simply on the exploitation of natural resources and the environment in a way that cannot be sustained. In many cases, policies can be devised that improve economic efficiency, and thus promote economic growth, at the same time that they decrease adverse environmental

International Perspective

Growth Convergence

A handful of the world's economies enjoy standards of living that are unimaginable when compared to the experiences of most of the world's population. The rich countries of Western Europe, North America, New Zealand, and Australia have been joined in recent decades by a few countries in Asia that have managed to grow fast enough to significantly raise per capita income. But these countries account for only a small fraction of the world's population. About three fourths of the world's people live in less developed countries (LDCs).

Other developed economies have tended to grow more rapidly than the U.S. economy during the past forty years. While the United States has the highest level of per capita income, these other countries are closing the gap. Concern is often expressed that the United States will eventually fall behind as other countries continue to grow faster. An alternative perspective, however, is that countries will tend to converge. As those with lower per capita income levels catch up to the U.S. level, their growth rates will also start

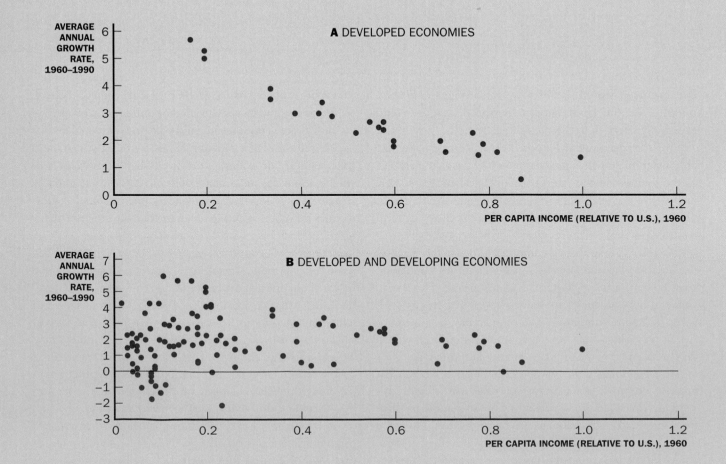

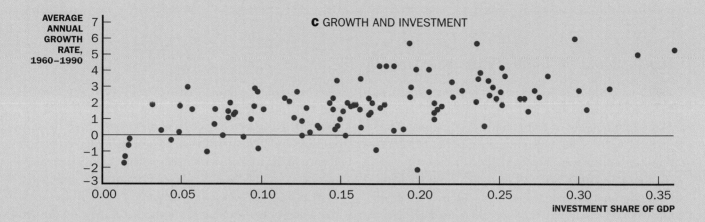

to slow down. Once economies have converged, per capita income will tend to grow at similar rates.

One reason why we might expect this type of convergence has to do with capital deepening and diminishing returns to capital. Workers in the United States are highly productive because American workers have, on average, high levels of capital to work with. However, as we illustrated in Figure 27.10, output per worker rises less when more capital is added if the amount of capital per worker is already high. Countries that have lower levels of capital per worker will experience larger increases in output per worker, and hence, output growth, when they increase capital per worker. As a result, we would expect countries that start out with less capital per worker and lower levels of output per worker to grow faster than countries that start out richer.

The figure provides some evidence for this hypothesis. The horizontal axis gives each country's per capita income level in 1960, measured relative to the U.S. level. In panels A and B, the vertical axis gives the country's average growth rate from 1960 to 1990. In panel A, only developed economies are shown. Here, strong evidence of convergence is apparent. In part, this may simply reflect the fact that any poor country in 1960 that is classified as developed in 1990, by definition, must have grown rapidly. Singapore, Hong Kong, and Japan, for example, had very low levels of per capita income in 1960 but had high growth rates and are now classified as developed. Panel B shows that when many more countries are added to the picture, including countries in Latin America, Africa, and South Asia, no evidence of convergence seems apparent.

In our earlier discussions, investment was highlighted as one of the major sources of productivity growth. Panel C, with investment share of GDP on the horizontal axis, illustrates that growth rates are positively related to investment rates.

effects. These include elimination of energy subsidies and certain agricultural subsidies that induce farmers to use excessive amounts of fertilizers and pesticides.

Review and Practice

Summary

1. The United States experienced a marked slowdown in the rate of productivity growth in the early 1970s, compared with the preceding two decades. The late 1990s saw a remarkable increase in productivity growth. Even seemingly small changes in the rate of increase in productivity will have powerful effects on the standard of living over a generation or two.

2. There are four major sources of productivity growth: increases in the accumulation of capital goods (investment); a higher quality of the labor force; greater efficiency in allocating resources; and technological change. Since 1973 almost all of the increase in productivity can be attributed to increases in capital,

Thinking Like an Economist

Trade-offs and the Costs of Economic Growth

Faith in the virtues of economic progress is widespread. Few openly embrace the alternative of economic stagnation and lower standards of living. Yet not everyone benefits from changes in technology, and there may be environmental and other costs associated with growth.

In the early 1800s, English workmen destroyed labor-saving machinery rather than see it take over their jobs. They were referred to as *Luddites,* after their leader Neil Ludd, whose role may have been largely mythical. Concerns about workers thrown out of their jobs as a result of some innovations are no less real today.

What needs to be kept in mind, and has already been stressed earlier in this book, is that technological progress *creates* jobs as it destroys them. Of course, it can be hard to retrain workers in declining industries to gain the skills necessary for new jobs, so middle-aged or older workers who lose jobs may have real difficulty in getting another one that is as good.

Not surprisingly, technical progress frequently meets with resistance. While there is growing acceptance that such resistance is futile—change will eventually come—and that the benefits of economic progress exceed the costs, there is also recognition of the role of government in assisting individuals who are displaced by technological change in their transition to alternative employment. Such assistance can be thought of as a form of insurance. Most workers face the possibility that their jobs will be made technologically obsolete. Knowing that if they are thrown out of work for this reason they will be at least partially protected adds to a sense of security, something most workers value highly.

An important cost of economic growth can be the toll growth puts on the environment. As we noted in Chapter 23, a Green GDP measure might give a different picture of growth as it would include the economic costs to the environment of producing more goods and services. Accounting for all the costs, as well as the benefits, of growth would provide a clearer picture of the trade-offs growth can involve.

improvements in human capital, and expenditures on research and development. In recent years, the relative role of human capital has increased and the role of physical capital has decreased.

3. The rate of saving in the United States has declined in recent years. Some of the reasons are improved government retirement programs, more extensive insurance coverage and greater ease in borrowing, and changes in social attitudes.

4. Increases in human capital—improved education—are a major source of productivity increases. There are large returns to investments in education. While the U.S. educational system has important strengths, there are serious concerns about the quality of education American students are receiving in preparation for the labor force and about the number of scientists and engineers being trained.

5. The twentieth century was marked by shifts in the U.S. economy from an agricultural base to an industrial base and then to a service base. Some economists think that the potential for technological progress is less in the service sector than in the industrial sector, and this accounts for part of the change in productivity growth.

6. Improvements in technology, partly as a result of expenditures on research and development (R & D), are a major source of increases in productivity. Government supports R & D through both direct spending and tax incentives, though direct support for R & D that is not defense related has actually declined during the past quarter century.

7. Some of the changes in the rate of growth of the economy are a result of changes in the rate of growth of the labor force. This is partly a result of demographics—changes in the number of children born in different years—and partly a result of decisions to participate in the labor force.

8. There has long been concern that certain natural resources (like oil) will run out someday, causing economic growth to halt. However, most economists would argue that the price of resources will increase as they become more scarce, and this will encourage both greater conservation and a search for substitutes.

9. Sustainable development requires growth strategies that use resources and the environment in ways that do not jeopardize future potential growth.

Key Terms

capital deepening
life-cycle theory of savings
infrastructure
human capital
total factor productivity analysis
sustainable development

Review Questions

1. True or false: "Since growth-oriented policies might have an effect of only a percent or two per year, they are not worth worrying much about." Explain.

2. What are the four possible sources of productivity growth?

3. What are the components of overall U.S. saving, and how did they change in the 1980s?

4. What are some reasons for the decrease in the saving rate in recent years?

5. Will government policies to raise the rate of return on savings, such as exempting interest from taxes, necessarily lead to much increased savings?

6. What is the link between changes in the capital stock (investment) and the rate of growth of productivity in the short run? What is the link between changes in the capital stock and the *level* of productivity (output per worker) in the long run? What is meant by capital deepening?

7. What policies might the government use to increase investment in R & D?

8. What is total factor productivity and how is it measured?

9. Are there limits to economic growth? What was Malthus's view? Is growth limited by exhaustible resources?

10. What are some of the concerns about limits to economic growth? How have they been overcome in the past?

Problems

1. Will the following changes increase or decrease the rate of household saving?

   (a) The proportion of people in the 45- to 64-year age bracket increases.

   (b) Government programs provide secure retirement benefits.

   (c) Credit cards become much more prevalent.

   (d) The proportion of people in the 21- to 45-year age bracket increases.

   (e) Government programs to guarantee student loans are enacted.

2. Explain how the following factors would increase or decrease the average productivity of labor:

   (a) Successful reforms of the educational system

   (b) The entry of new workers into the economy

   (c) Earlier retirement

   (d) Increased investment

3. Explain why a rapid influx of workers might result in a lower output per worker (a reduction in productivity). Would the effect on productivity depend on the skill level of the new workers?

4. Explain, using supply and demand diagrams, how a technological change such as computerization could lead to lower wages of unskilled workers and higher wages of skilled workers.

5. Using the model of Chapter 24, discuss the effect on the level of investment for an open economy of (a) an increased government deficit; (b) an increased government expenditure, financed by taxes on households that reduce their disposable income; (c) an investment tax credit. How will such policies affect future living standards of those living in the country?

6. Calculate the growth rate in the number of hours worked per capita, total output, and output per capita from the following information:

   Growth rate in number of hours worked = 1.5 percent

   Growth rate of the population   = 1.2 percent

   Growth rate of productivity   = 2.3 percent

   What happens to the growth rates of total output and per capita output if the growth rate of productivity rises to 3.3 percent? What happens to the growth rates of total output and per capita output if the growth rate of the population rises to 2.0 percent?

7. The table below gives growth rates for the United States for various time periods. Using these data, calculate the growth rate of average hours worked per capita for each decade.

	1960–1969	1970–1979	1980–1989	1990–1998
Total output	4.19%	3.17%	2.69%	2.57%
Output per capita	2.88%	2.12%	1.75%	1.58%
Productivity	3.19%	2.04%	1.23%	1.26%
Total hours	1.00%	1.13%	1.46%	1.31%

8. Assume investments in human capital yield a return of 15 percent, private investments yield a total return of 10 percent, and public investments in research yield a return of 25 percent. Assume the deficit is $100 billion per year, and the government wishes to eliminate it. What will be the impact on economic growth of a deficit reduction package which consists of reducing Medicare expenditures by $50 billion, education expenditures by $40 billion, and research expenditures by $10 billion?

e-Case

Raising the Speed Limit

Technological change has been key to long-term economic growth, and the pace of technological growth puts limits on how fast the economy can grow. The revolution in information technology has had the effect, according to many economists, of "raising the speed limit" on growth. The acceleration of growth during the 1990s is hard to miss—from 1990 to 1995, real output in the private sector of the U.S. economy grew at an average annual rate of 2.7 percent, but from 1995 to 1999 it grew at an average annual rate of 4.7 percent. An increase of this magnitude will have profound effects on living standards if it can be sustained. Over twenty years, an extra 2 percent growth per year translates into incomes that are 50 percent higher. Quite naturally, economists are actively debating whether the speed limit really has been raised. Will this increase in the growth rate be sustained? And how much of any increase is the result of information technologies? Are we really in a "new economy"?

In Chapter 27, we learned that economic growth is due to (1) increases in inputs (more capital or labor), (2) improvements in the quality of those inputs (e.g., better educated workers), (3) increases in technology that allow more output to be produced from a given level of inputs, or (4) reallocation of resources to high-productivity sectors. Dale Jorgensen of Harvard University and Kevin Stiroh of the Federal Reserve Bank of New York estimated the contributions that increases in inputs and technology have made to the growth of private sector output (they excluded the government sector). The chart shows what they found. Each column shows the sources of economic growth for different periods, with the total height of the column measuring average output growth during that period. Two interesting facts emerge.

First, the increase in growth from the first half to the second half of the 1990s reflects increased growth in both inputs *and* technology (what economists call *total factor productivity*). Both labor and noncomputer capital grew more rapidly, but the increased growth attributed to

investment in computers and software and to total factor productivity stands out. Second, total growth at the end of the 1990s was similar though slightly higher than the average experienced in the period 1959–1973, but the sources of growth changed significantly. Compared to that earlier period of rapid growth, the economy of 1995–1999 got some of its higher growth from faster growth in labor and much more from computers and software. What this evidence cannot answer is whether the new technologies have permanently raised the speed limit, or whether growth will recede to the low rates of the 1973–1995 period once everyone works with a computer and shops on-line.

One way to assess whether the economy's speed limit has been raised is to consider each of the sources of growth

that contributed to the rapid growth in 1995–1999 and forecast how that component might change. For example, part of the increased growth can be traced to faster growth in labor. There are two reasons to expect this component to be less important to the future. First, part of the 1990s employment growth was due to falling rates of unemployment. Falling unemployment adds to economic growth as more workers find jobs and contribute to the economy's output. But increased growth from this source cannot permanently raise the speed limit for the simple reason that

the unemployment rate cannot fall forever. Second, the U.S. labor force is aging, and the growth rate of labor will fall as baby boomers reach retirement age and leave the labor force.

Growth in the capital stock is likely to be a continued source of high growth in output. As the prices of information technology equipment continue to fall, firms will make further investments in information technology capital. As long as productivity continues to grow rapidly in that sector, capital growth will help to sustain faster overall growth.

Finally, what about technology? The acceleration in growth due to total factor productivity revealed in the chart is largely a reflection of high rates of productivity growth in information technology–producing sectors of the economy such as the semiconductor industry. Whether this will continue is hard to predict.

So what is the speed limit? According to Jorgenson and Stiroh, the best guess for the next few years is that labor will contribute about 1.06 percentage points, capital will add about the same amount, 1.07 percentage points, while technology (total factor productivity) will add another 1.22 percentage points. Adding these together yields a speed limit of 3.35 percent for GDP growth. While this might not sound like a lot more than the 2.7 percent growth the economy averaged during the first half of the 1990s, it can make a significant difference in living standards if sustained for several years.

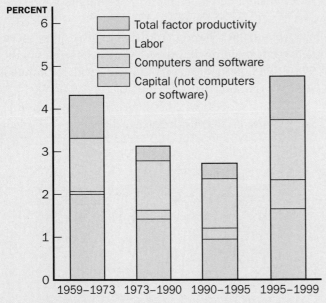

PERCENT

Sources of Economic Growth

SOURCE: Dale W. Jorgenson and Kevin J. Stiroh, "Raising the Speed Limit: U.S. Economic Growth in the Information Age," *Brookings Papers on Economic Activity*, 1 (2000):125–211.

Part 7

Macroeconomic Fluctuations

Chapter 28

Introduction to Macroeconomic Fluctuations

Key Questions

1. Can the full-employment model explain unemployment fluctuations?

2. Why might unemployment result if wages fail to adjust in response to shifts in the aggregate demand and supply curves for labor?

3. What are the key differences between the full-employment model and a model that can explain fluctuations?

4. What are the key concepts that economists use to analyze aggregate output and employment in the short run when wages and prices are slow to adjust?

*T*he theory of full-employment macroeconomics laid out in Part Two offers important insights. We used the model to explore the effects of fiscal deficits on interest rates and exchange rates, the impact of changes in the supply of labor on the economy, the sources of economic growth, and the role of monetary policy in affecting inflation. What was absent was an explanation for the fluctuations in real economic activity and employment that also characterize market economies. Why did unemployment in the United States reach nearly 11 percent in November and December of 1982 and fall to 3.9 percent in April 2000? Why did real GDP decline in 1990? Why was inflation over 10 percent in 1979 and under 3 percent in 1999?

Over the long run, as we have seen in Part Two, the economy has managed to create jobs to keep pace with the increasing number of workers. But we also learned in Chapter 24 that the unemployment rate is never zero in a dynamic market economy. Some firms and industries are shrinking—jobs are being lost—at the same time that new jobs are being created. Workers voluntarily quit jobs to relocate or look for better positions. In the United States, it is estimated that 8 to 10 percent of workers—over ten million

workers—leave their jobs each quarter, either by quitting or by being laid off. Unemployment also varies seasonally. We call these normal patterns in unemployment structural, frictional, and seasonal unemployment. But in addition to these normal levels of unemployment, there are times when the unemployment rate becomes much higher than usual, with the economy experiencing periods of slow job growth and rising unemployment. Labor markets seem not to clear—the demand for labor is less than the supply. At other times, unemployment drops to unusually low levels, plant and equipment operate at high rates of utilization, and the economy booms. We call the fluctuations of the unemployment rate around its normal level *cyclical unemployment*. Understanding these fluctuations in the economy is the primary focus of Part Seven.

The key to understanding cyclical unemployment is the recognition of two important "facts" about modern economies. First, prices and wages do not always adjust quickly. This means that the demand for labor and the supply of labor will not always balance—the economy can depart from full employment. Second, while wages and prices do not adjust quickly, they eventually do adjust in

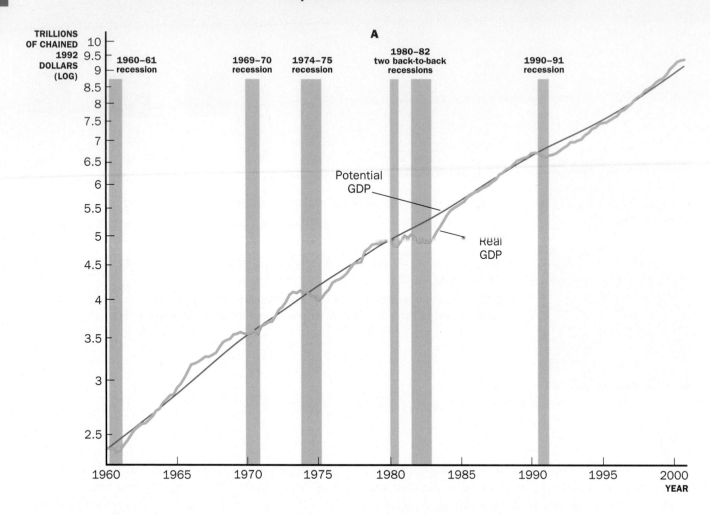

response to demand and supply. As they do, markets will be brought back into balance. This includes the labor market. Given enough time, wages will normally adjust to restore full employment.

In this and the next five chapters, we will study how the economy behaves when prices and wages have not adjusted to balance demand and supply in the labor market. This allows us to understand the causes of cyclical unemployment, why the economy experiences fluctuations, and how monetary and fiscal policy affect inflation and cyclical unemployment. We begin in this chapter by discussing why the full-employment model of Part Two cannot explain the fluctuations in unemployment that modern economies experience. To explain fluctuations we need to go beyond the full-employment model in several important ways. Four key concepts will guide our discussion of economic fluctuations and help us understand both their causes and the role of government policies. The most critical key concepts are

that both wages and prices fail to respond quickly to shifts in labor demand and supply. Because of its importance, the chapter concludes with an appendix that provides a more complete discussion of some of the explanations for the failure of wages and prices to adjust rapidly.

Economic Fluctuations

All industrialized market economies experience fluctuations in the general level of economic activity. Panel A of Figure 28.1 shows the fluctuations in U.S. GDP over the past forty years. A smooth "trend line" has been drawn through the plotted line, tracing out a hypothetical path the economy would have taken had it grown smoothly throughout this forty-year period. This trend line provides an estimate of the path of potential output, the output the economy would pro-

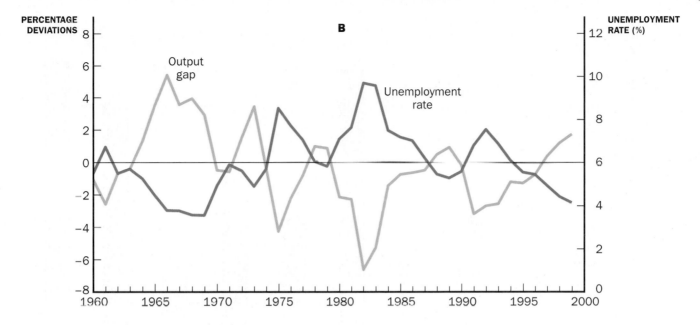

FIGURE 28.1 *Economic Fluctuations: Output*

Panel A shows how real GDP from 1960 to 2000 has moved above and below a long-term trend line. Panel B compares the deviations of GDP from its long-term trend with the unemployment rate. Notice that when real GDP is above its long-term trend, unemployment tends to be low, and when real GDP is below its long-term trend, unemployment tends to be high. The relationship between fluctuations in real GDP and fluctuations in unemployment is one we have seen before in Okun's law.

SOURCE: Federal Reserve Board.

duce if full employment were always maintained. The economy is sometimes above the trend line and sometimes below. The shaded bars in the figure mark out economic **recessions**, periods during which output declines significantly. During the almost forty-year period shown in the figure, there were six recessions; the last recession was in the period 1990–1991. Panel B shows the percentage by which the economy has been above or below the trend line. The percentage deviation between actual GDP and potential GDP is called the **output gap**. The figure also shows the unemployment rate. When output grows relative to potential (so the output gap rises), the unemployment rate falls; when output falls relative to potential (so the output gap declines), the unemployment rate rises.

Since 1960, the unemployment rate has averaged just a little above 6 percent of the civilian labor force. But during recessions, it rises much higher. In 1982 and 1983, for example, the unemployment rate exceeded 9 percent for over eighteen months. Perhaps the difference between 6 per-

cent unemployment and 9 percent sounds small, but with a U.S. labor force of over 110 million at the time of the 1982 recession, that 3 percentage points translated into more than 3 million additional workers unemployed.

Economic **expansions** are periods in which output grows. To describe the point when the economy moves from an expansion to a recession or from a recession to an

WRAP-UP

Economic Fluctuations

Recessions: periods of significant decline in real GDP.
Expansions: periods in which real GDP grows.
Output gap: the percentage deviation of real GDP from potential.

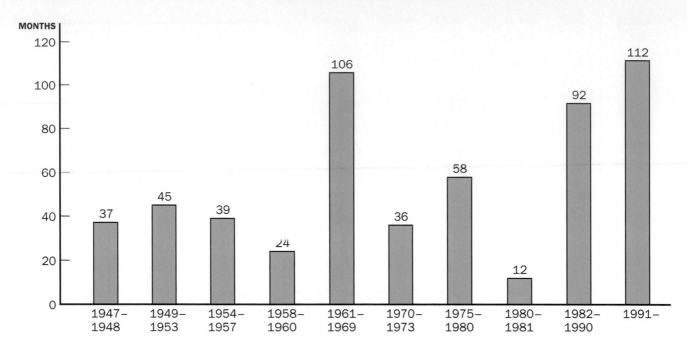

Figure 28.2   *The Duration of Economic Expansions*

Over the past fifty-four years, there has been a high variability in the duration of economic expansions. The average was 56 months; the shortest, 12 months; and the longest completed expansion, 106 months. The expansion that began in 1991 has lasted more than 112 months.

SOURCE: NBER Business Cycle Reference Dates (http://www.nber.org/cycles.html).

expansion, economists use the terms *peaks* and *troughs*. A high point in output is called a *peak*; a low point is called a *trough*. These fluctuations in economic activity are called *business cycles*, although the cycles themselves differ in both their length and their severity. Since World War II, the length of time between recessions has varied significantly, as Figure 28.2 shows. The average duration of expansions from World War II to the present was fifty-six months, the shortest was twelve months, and the longest was the expansion that began in 1991.

Figure 28.3 provides a close-up of real GDP since 1980. The three recessions that occurred during this twenty-year period can be seen clearly. The troughs were in 1980, 1982, and 1991. The peaks were in 1981 and 1990. The expansion that peaked in 1981 was unusually short and weak, making the whole period from 1980 to 1982 one of weak economy growth. This period in the early 1980s was associated with Federal Reserve Chairman Paul Volcker's actions to reduce inflation. Since 1982, however, the United States has experienced over two hun-

dred months of expansion broken only by one recession in 1990–1991 that lasted just eight months. The 1990–1991 recession, and the slow recovery that followed it, played a major role in the 1992 presidential election between George H. W. Bush and Bill Clinton.[1]

Cyclical unemployment reflects unused labor resources. Idle factories and underutilized plant and equipment also accompany periods of high unemployment. Figure 28.4 illustrates this by showing a measure of capacity utilization in the manufacturing sector of the economy. There is a cost to the economy if its labor and capital resources are not fully employed. The output that could have been produced with these productive resources is the opportunity cost of cyclical unemployment. These costs can be very large.

Because of the costs, and the individual hardships, caused by high levels of cyclical unemployment, most governments

---

[1]One of Clinton's election slogans, designed to call attention to the recession, was "It's the economy, stupid!"

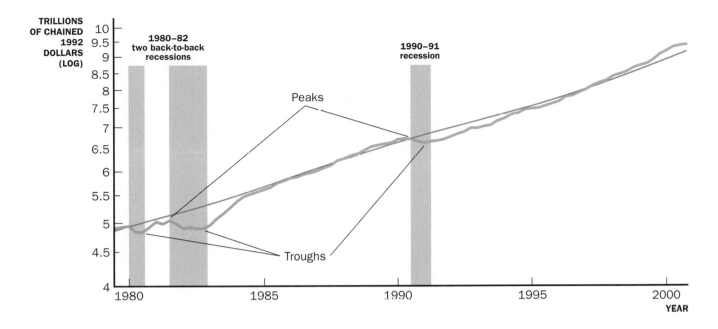

Figure 28.3 *Peaks and Troughs Since 1980*

There have been three economic recessions since 1980. The economy reached a peak in January 1980 and entered a recession that lasted until July 1980, when the trough was reached. The next peak was in July 1981, making this the shortest expansion in U.S. history. The trough of the 1981–1982 recession came in November 1982. The economy then entered a long expansion, with the peak occurring in July 1990. Since the trough in March 1991, the U.S. economy has experienced its longest expansion on record.

Internet Connection

Dating Business Cycle Peaks and Troughs

Almost all the data that economists use to study the economy are produced by the government. In the United States, the Bureau of Labor Statistics and the Department of Commerce collect many of the data economists use, such as the statistics on unemployment and GDP. The widely accepted dates for the peaks and troughs of business cycles, however, are determined by the members of the Business Cycle Dating Committee of the National Bureau of Economic Research (NBER), a private, nonprofit research organization. The NBER publishes business cycle dates going back to 1854. You can find the entire list of dates at the NBER's Web site (http://www.nber.org/cycles.html). The NBER defines a recession as "a recurring period of decline in total output, income, employment, and trade, usually lasting from six months to a year, and marked by widespread contractions in many sectors of the economy." In popular usage, the economy is usually considered to be in a recession if real GDP declines for two consecutive quarters.

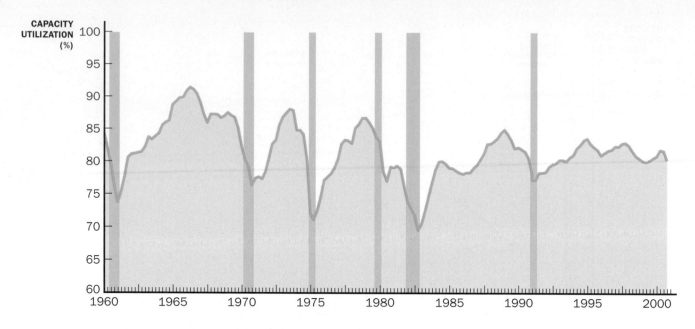

FIGURE 28.4   *Capacity Utilization Rate*

The shaded bars are business cycle recessions. Plant and equipment utilization falls during recessions. Just as unemployment rises during recessions, capacity utilization falls. Recessions are associated with unused labor *and* capital.

SOURCE: Federal Reserve Board.

Thinking Like an Economist

Employment Fluctuations and Trade-offs

We measure the cost of cyclical unemployment by the output that could have been produced if full employment had been maintained. This represents the *opportunity cost* to society of *cyclical* unemployment. Not all unemployment represents an opportunity cost, either to the individual worker or to society. A worker who voluntarily quits a job to look for another is classified as unemployed, but the decision to quit reveals that the value of the worker's time spent searching for a job is worth more than the income the worker loses.

To measure the cost of employment fluctuations, we need to take into account the trade-offs individuals face. For some individuals, the value of time spent in leisure activities and other nonmarket activities (taking care of children, for example) is greater than the real wage that could be earned from working.

Parents face a trade-off between working hours and leisure time with their children.

attempt to manage macroeconomic policies to reduce its occurrence. In the United States, the Employment Act of 1946 and the Full Employment and Balanced Growth Act of 1978 (often called the Humphrey-Hawkins Act) reflect the commitment of the federal government to take responsibility for maintaining full employment. The Humphrey-Hawkins Act mandates the federal government to ". . . promote full-employment and production, increased real income, balanced growth, a balanced Federal budget, adequate productivity growth, proper attention to national priorities, achievement of an improved trade balance . . . and reasonable price stability." How governments try to achieve these goals, and how successful they have been, are among the topics we will discuss in the next few chapters.

CASE IN POINT

Estimating the Output Costs of a Recession

Panel B in Figure 28.1 made use of a measure, the output gap, of the percentage deviation between GDP and the long-run trend of the economy. The output gap provides a useful means of measuring the extent of a recession. For example, the gap reached –8 percent during the 1982 recession, while it fell to only –3.4 percent in the recession of 1991. This concurs with most observers' views that the recession of 1982 was a much more severe recession. We saw an earlier use of the output gap measure in Chapter 23 when we learned about Okun's law. Okun's law says that the unemployment rate rises above the full-employment level by 1 percentage point for every 2 percentage point decline in the output gap. Based on Okun's law, an 8 percent output gap such as the United States experienced in the 1982 recession would translate into an unemployment rate about 4 percentage points above the full-employment rate. Since most estimates at the time placed the unemployment rate at full employment around 6 percent, this is consistent with 1982's 9.7 percent unemployment rate (6 percent plus 4 percent yields a total unemployment rate of 10 percent, just slightly above the actual average for 1982).

During the recession in the early 1990s, the unemployment rate reached 7.5 percent in 1992. Most estimates of frictional and structural unemployment at the time suggested that full employment corresponded to an unemployment rate of about 6 percent. We can use this information, together with Okun's law, to estimate the output cost of the cyclical unemployment in 1992.

Step 1: We estimate cyclical unemployment as the difference between the actual unemployment rate (7.5 percent) and the rate estimated to correspond to full employment (6 percent), or 1.5 percent.

Step 2: Okun's law tells us that the percentage gap between actual output and full-employment output is about twice the level of cyclical unemployment. So the lost output was roughly $2 \times 1.5 = 3$ percent of real GDP.

Step 3: In 1992, real GDP was $6.2 trillion, and 3 percent of this is $186 billion. This is the value of the output lost in 1992 due to the recession.

To provide some perspective, in 1992 the total real value of expenditures by the federal government for all nondefense programs was only $152 billion. ●

Are "Cycles" Regular?

Calling fluctuations in economic activity "business cycles" may suggest a regular pattern to these fluctuations. But business cycles follow irregular patterns, and predicting when an expansion will end and a recession will begin is often difficult. One reason is that there is little evidence that expansions die of old age—an economic downturn is almost as likely to occur after three years of an expansion as after five years. In contrast, not only do economic downturns tend to be much shorter than expansions, but also the longer they last, the more likely they are to end. The reason for this is partly that the longer the recession lasts, the stronger the pressures are on the government to take action to stimulate the economy.

The Wage-Employment Puzzle

It is difficult to reconcile economic fluctuations, and the associated changes in employment and wages, with the full-employment model. We can start to understand why by considering an economy at full employment. The real wage is at the level that clears the labor market. Labor demand and supply are equal. If the demand for labor curve and the supply of

Thinking Like an Economist

Information and Measuring the Business Cycle

Designing macroeconomic policy requires accurate information about the economy. Economists' views concerning the severity of business cycles and whether the economy has become more stable are affected by the quality of their information.

While some recessions are more severe than others, most economists have accepted the view that recessions since World War II have been, on average, milder than the recessions the United States experienced earlier in the century. Christina Romer of the University of California, Berkeley, has argued against this view. She has noted that the macroeconomic data now available to economists are vastly better than the data that were available to measure macroeconomic performance in the early decades of the twentieth century. She has argued that in large measure the apparent decline in the severity of business cycles reflects improvements in our ability to measure fluctuations in the economy. However, most economists believe that better data do not explain the whole story. Economists do measure the economy better today than was possible before World War II, but changes in the economy and improvements in economic policymaking have helped to make business cycles less severe.

Even though the quality of economic data has improved, accurately gauging the behavior of the economy is still difficult. Policy must be based on preliminary measures of GDP that later may be revised significantly as more complete information becomes available. A good example is provided by the recession of 1974. Preliminary data on real GDP indicated that output declined between the third and fourth quarters at just over a 9 percent annual rate. Such a decline would suggest an economic downturn similar to that experienced in the Great Depression. The final estimates for real GDP, however, showed that output declined at only a 1.6 percent annual rate, suggesting a much milder recession.

Measuring fluctuations is also complicated by the fact that economists have to estimate variables such as full-employment output or the unemployment rate at full employment. Some have argued that full employment now corresponds to an unemployment rate of 4.5 percent, not the 6 percent level previously associated with full employment. If this lower value were used to measure the severity of the 1991 recession, the estimate of cyclical unemployment in 1991 would be much higher.

---

labor curve do not shift, the real wage will remain constant at the value w_0/P as shown in panel A of Figure 28.5.

Now consider what happens if the labor demand curve shifts to the left. If we apply the full-employment model to the labor market, we would predict that when the demand for labor goes down, as in a recession, the real wage also falls, as illustrated in panel B of Figure 28.5. A leftward shift in the demand for labor results in lower real wages. If the supply of labor is relatively unresponsive to real wage changes (that is, the labor supply curve is inelastic), as depicted by the steepness of the line in panel B, the reduction in the real wage is large and the fall in employment is small.

In the real world, it does not seem to happen this way. In the Great Depression of the 1930s, for example, when the demand for labor fell drastically, real wages in manufactur-

ing actually rose. One estimate shows that while unemployment increased from 5.5 percent in 1929 to 22 percent in 1934, real wages *rose* by more than 20 percent.[2] In the early 1980s, a much more recent example, real wages again rose as the unemployment rate increased from below 6 percent to over 10 percent.

Figure 28.6 shows the real wage and unemployment rates during the 1980s and 1990s. Real wages have not been affected very much by changes in unemployment. There are three possible explanations. The first is that the supply curve

---

[2]Nominal wages did fall during the depression, but prices fell more so that the real wage actually rose. Between 1929 and 1933, the average nominal wage fell by over 20 percent before recovering in 1934.

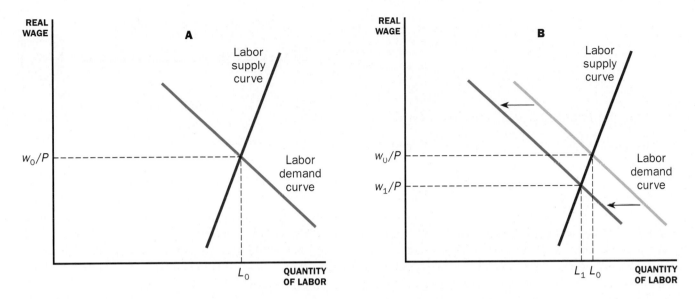

FIGURE 28.5 *Changes in the Demand for Labor and Real Wages*

Panel A shows the labor market in equilibrium at full employment. The real wage is equal to w_0/P and employment is equal to L_0. In panel B, the demand for labor curve has shifted to the left. Traditional theory predicts that when such a shift occurs, the real wage will fall to w_1/P. Full employment is maintained, although the level of employment in equilibrium declines to L_1. If the labor supply curve had been completely inelastic (vertical), the real wage would have fallen with no change in employment.

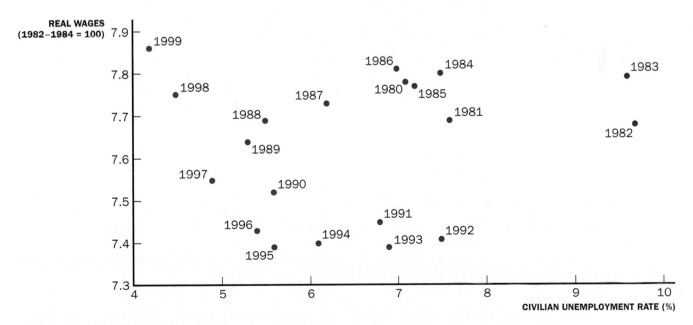

FIGURE 28.6 *Real Wages and Unemployment*

When real wages and unemployment are plotted on a graph, no pattern emerges. Apparently there may be large changes in unemployment with relatively small changes in real wages.

SOURCE: *ERP* (2001), Tables B-47, B-42.

International Perspective

Is There an International Business Cycle?

All modern economies experience business cycle fluctuations. The Great Depression of the 1930s, for instance, affected economies around the world. It truly was an international depression. Evidence of an international business cycle—that is, a common pattern shared by many countries—can also be found in more recent history. The oil price increases that occurred in 1973, for example, had global effects and led to recessions in most industrial economies. This can be seen for Canada, Japan, the United Kingdom, and the United States in the first figure, which is based on a measure of output gaps from the World Economic Outlook of the International Monetary Fund (IMF). Output gaps became negative (GDP fell below potential GDP) in 1973–1974 for all four countries. All four experienced rising output gaps between 1975 and 1979, and all suffered recessions in the early 1980s.

The situation in the 1990s was different, with individual countries having experienced different business cycles.

The figure for the period 1985–1999 shows that while the United States, Canada, and the United Kingdom experienced recessions in 1990–1991, Japan continued to expand. Then, through the rest of the 1990s, the economies of the first three countries were expanding while Japan suffered a prolonged recession, interrupted only by a brief expansion in 1996. In 1999, the output gap fell in the United Kingdom, while it continued to rise in both the United States and Canada.

Business cycles are common to all modern economies, but their frequency, timing, and severity differ across countries. Because we are part of a global economy, developments in the United States are affected by economic conditions in other countries. In the next few chapters we will be learning how economic activity abroad can affect economic activity and employment in this country.

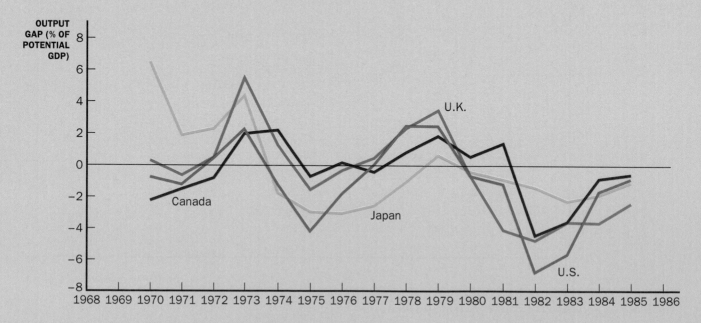

International Business Cycles 1970–1985

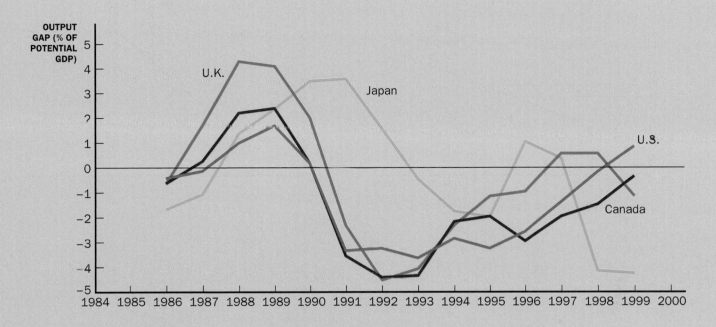

OUTPUT GAP (% OF POTENTIAL GDP)

International Business Cycles: 1985–1999

for labor is nearly horizontal and the demand curve for labor has shifted, as shown in Figure 28.7, panel A. In this case, the labor market has moved along the labor supply curve to a new point of equilibrium. Almost all economists reject this interpretation because of the extensive evidence suggesting that the labor supply curve is relatively inelastic (steep), not flat.

The second possible interpretation is that there are shifts in the labor supply curve that just offset the shifts in the labor demand curve, as depicted in panel B. The shifting demand and supply curves trace out a pattern of changing employment with little change in the real wage. Again, the labor market winds up at an equilibrium point with lower employment and little change in the real wage. In this view, a recession is due to a decreased willingness to supply labor—in other words, an increased demand for leisure. As we learned in Chapter 27, there have been marked changes in labor force participation, as women and baby boomers have entered the workforce. But most economists do not see any persuasive evidence that the supply curve for labor shifts much as the economy goes into or comes out of a recession, let alone to the extent required in panel B. And they see no reason why shifts in the demand curve for labor would normally be offset by shifts in the supply curve.

The third interpretation is that there has been a shift in the demand curve for labor, with no matching shift in the supply curve *and no corresponding change in the real wage*, depicted in panel C of Figure 28.7. The labor market is stuck in disequilibrium; demand does not equal supply. At the real wage w_0/P, the amount of labor that workers would like to supply remains at L_0. But as the demand for labor shifts, the number of workers hired at w_0/P falls from L_0 to L_1. The difference, $L_0 - L_1$, is the level of cyclical unemployment. People are willing to work *at the going wage*, but the work is not there. The same argument holds even if there is a slight shift in the labor supply curve and a slight change in the real wage. The adjustment in the real wage is too small to align demand with supply.

Nominal Versus Real Wages

When we discuss the labor market, it is important to keep in mind the distinction between the real wage and the money, or *nominal*, wage. The nominal wage is the wage expressed in dollars. In 1999, the average hourly wage in the private sector was $13.24. The real wage is a measure of the purchasing power of this $13.24. What happens to the real wage as the

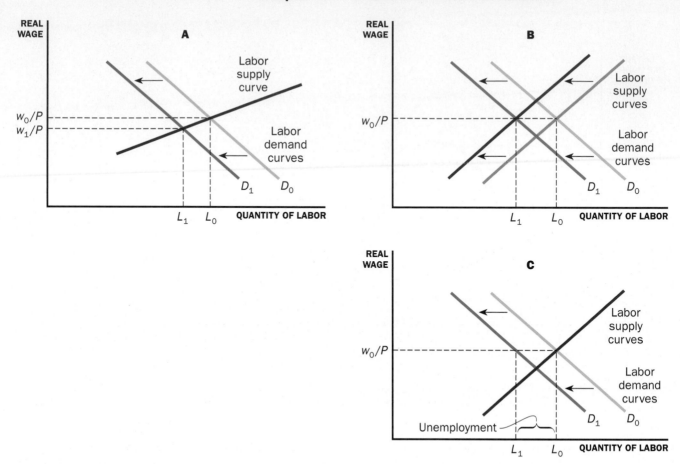

FIGURE 28.7   *Why Wages Do Not Fall When Demand Shifts*

Panel A shows a very elastic labor supply curve. A leftward shift in demand for labor from D_0 to D_1 will decrease employment while having little affect on real wages. Panel B shows a shift in both supply and demand curves. Although the shift in demand for labor from D_0 to D_1 would reduce wages by itself, it is offset by a shift in the supply of labor from S_0 to S_1, leaving the real wage unchanged. In panel C, the demand for labor shifts from D_0 to D_1, but real wages do not fall for some reason. Unemployment results.

nominal wage changes depends on how prices are changing. Even if the real wage is constant, the *nominal* wage may be changing. When the general level of prices is rising, the nominal wage will need to rise at the same rate as prices to keep the real wage constant. If prices have been rising at 3 percent per year, the nominal wage also must rise by 3 percent per year simply to maintain a constant real wage. If nominal wages rise only 2 percent, then even though wages have gone up, workers' real wages have fallen. They will be unable to purchase as many goods and services as before. If the inflation rate rises from 3 percent to 5 percent, nominal wages must rise by 5 percent per year to keep the real wage con-

stant. When economies experience ongoing inflation, the wage- and price-setting decisions of workers and firms will reflect their expectations of inflation. Because individuals care about the purchasing power of their income, and firms care about the real costs of labor, nominal wages will rise to reflect expected increases in prices. The higher the rate of inflation, the faster nominal wages will rise.

Both labor demand and labor supply depend on real wages, and *it is the failure of the real wage to adjust when the labor demand curve shifts to the left that leads to increases in unemployment.* But why don't real wages adjust quickly? Since the real wage is the nominal wage relative to the prices of goods and services, the failure of the real wage to adjust can be traced to slow adjustment of both nominal wages and many prices.

The Slow Adjustment of Nominal Wages

There are several reasons why nominal wages adjust slowly, and we will briefly mention three. These are discussed more fully in the appendix to the chapter. The appendix also explains why prices, like wages, may adjust slowly to shifts in demand and supply.

First, some wages may be set by union contracts that typically last for a fixed period—three years is common. If the contract is signed just before an economic downturn, it may be more than two years before any wage adjustment can occur, even if workers agree to one at that time. Average union wages adjust slowly to changes in unemployment, since different contracts expire in different months and different years. Similar rigidities may come about even in the absence of a union or an explicit labor contract. This is because the relations between employers and employees are governed by a host of implicit understandings developed over time. These implicit understandings are referred to as an **implicit labor contract**. Although most workers are not covered by explicit contracts, it is common for wages or salaries to be adjusted only once a year, again contributing to the sluggish adjustment of nominal wages.

Second, even when labor demand falls short of labor supply, wages may not fall enough to eliminate cyclical unemployment. Firms want to pay the wage that minimizes their total labor costs, called the **efficiency wage**. *If paying higher wages leads to higher worker productivity, firms may find they make more profits by paying a real wage higher than the one at which the labor market would clear.* When Henry Ford opened his automobile plant in 1914, he paid his workers more than double the going wage. He wanted his workers to work hard. He knew that his new technique of production—the assembly line—when combined with motivated workers would increase his profits. Productivity can depend on the wage for several reasons. If a firm cuts its wages, its best workers are the ones most likely to leave to find another job. Paying above average wages creates an incentive for workers to work hard and remain with the firm—losing a job at a high-paying firm is costly to the worker both because the worker will be unemployed while searching for a new job and because any new job is likely to be at a firm paying average wages. Finally, when a firm cuts wages, workers are more likely to quit to look for another job—the firm's *labor turnover rate* rises and the firm faces the increased costs of hiring and training new workers.

Third, cutting wages may be a risky strategy for a firm that wants to reduce its labor force. Whether the wage cut succeeds in getting workers to quit will depend on what other firms do—are other firms also cutting wages? The firm may face less uncertainty by simply laying off the workers it does not need.

To summarize, when sluggish nominal wages prevent the real wage from adjusting to maintain labor market equilibrium, shifts in labor demand will result in fluctuations in cyclical unemployment, as we illustrated in Figure 28.7, panel C. Such shifts can occur fairly rapidly, mainly because of changes in output. Wages fail to fall enough to restore equilibrium (where labor demand equals labor supply) when labor demand shifts downward, resulting in a rise in cyclical unemployment. The slow adjustment of real wages can be traced to the slow adjustment of both nominal wages and prices.

WRAP-UP

Cyclical Unemployment

Cyclical unemployment typically is generated by shifts in the aggregate demand curve for labor when real wages fail to adjust. The shifts in the aggregate demand curve for labor often arise from changes in aggregate output.

Understanding Macroeconomic Fluctuations: Key Concepts

We have argued that the full-employment model of Part Two cannot explain cyclical unemployment. To understand

e-Insight

Cyclical and Structural Productivity

Productivity growth is the key to economic growth and rising standards of living, and the information technologies we associate with the "new economy" have contributed significantly to the rapid productivity growth the United States enjoyed between 1995 and 2000. When productivity growth first rose in 1995, few commentators thought this heralded a new period of sustained rapid growth. By 2000, most were convinced that the economy's average, or *structural*, rate of productivity growth had risen. One reason why it can take several years to discover changes in structural productivity growth is the influence the business cycle has on productivity.

When the economy goes through recessions and booms, GDP and employment fluctuate. Measures of productivity such as output per hour—real GDP divided by the total number of hours worked—will be affected as GDP and employment change over the business cycle. This can make it difficult to measure whether changes in productivity represent changes in the structural growth rate or whether they are simply due to business cycle fluctuations.

The best way to understand how the business cycle affects productivity is to visualize what happens in a small firm as the economy enters a recession. Let's call the firm YourPlace.com, and suppose it offers specialized Internet consulting and troubleshooting services to other businesses. YourPlace.com employs 20 people: the owner, an accountant, a sales manager, 16 computer service technicians who actually visit the clients' sites and provide the consulting services, and a person who manages and coordinates the technicians' schedules. Suppose initially that YourPlace.com has 96 clients, with each service technician responsible for 6 clients. When the economy starts to go into a recession, YourPlace.com finds that the demand for its business services falls. Some of its clients may have gone bankrupt, while others may have scaled back their contracts with firms like YourPlace.com as a cost-saving measure. Suppose YourPlace.com loses 12 clients. In response, YourPlace.com lays off 2 technicians. Even though business has fallen, it still needs the scheduler to handle its remaining 14 technicians, and it still needs its sales manager and its accountant. While YourPlace.com has seen its business fall by 12.5 percent (from 96 to 84 clients), its workforce fell by only 10 percent (from 20 to 18 employ-

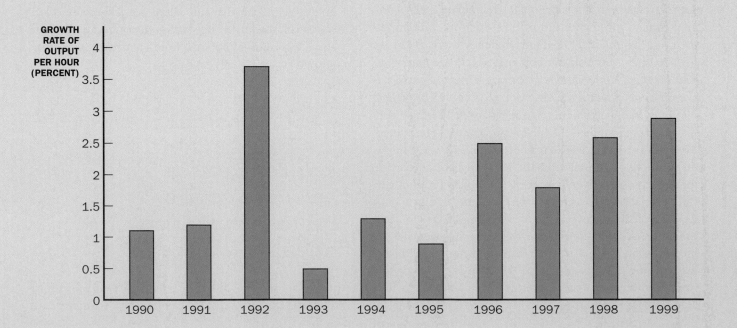

ees). This means that labor productivity goes down—in our example, the firm is producing 12.5 percent less but its employment has fallen by only 10 percent. (For simplicity, we are measuring the firm's output as proportional to the number of clients it has.)

When the economy comes out of the recession, the firm can hire new technical staff as it adds new clients. It does not need to add a new accountant or sales manager or scheduler. So its output will increase more (in percentage terms) than its employment. Labor productivity rises.

Labor productivity falls as the economy goes into a recession; it rises when the economy comes out of a recession. This is often called the *cyclical* component to productivity. These cyclical fluctuations in productivity can make it hard to discern changes in structural productivity. And this is why it took some time before it was clear that the U.S. structural growth rate of productivity had risen in the 1990s. When productivity first increased, the economy was recovering from the 1990–1991 recession. In 1992, productivity grew by 3.7 percent, well above estimates for the growth rate of structural productivity. This rise in productivity growth did not signal any change in structural productivity growth but was instead a normal cyclical effect; productivity growth always increases when the economy comes out of a recession.

Normally, once the recovery is well underway, productivity growth tends to settle in at the economy's structural growth rate. And after the initial spurt in productivity growth in 1992, the normal pattern seemed to be occurring. The chart on the previous page shows that productivity growth (output per hour) slowed significantly in 1993. That is what made the increase in productivity growth starting in 1996 so unusual. By 1999, it was clear that the rise in productivity growth was not related to any cyclical factors and that it appeared to be a sustained increase. The higher productivity growth rate represented a change in structural productivity growth rather than a temporary change resulting from cyclical factors.

At the beginning of 2001, the U.S. economy seemed to be slowing down, and economists were forecasting a recession. Productivity growth will slow if the economy enters a recession. If this happens, the decline in productivity will be due to cyclical factors. It will not mean that information technologies have not raised the structural growth rate of productivity.

economic fluctuations, and how government policies can affect the economy, economists have developed a basic model that differs from the full-employment model in several critical respects. Some of these differences reflect behavior we observe around us, such as the slow adjustment of wages. Other differences reflect simplifying assumptions about how individuals, firms, or economic policymakers behave. Fortunately, this model for understanding economic fluctuations shares many features with the full-employment model of Part Two. And an important implication of the model of fluctuations is that once wages and prices have had enough time to adjust, the economy returns to full employment, where the model of Part Two holds sway.

We can identify four fundamental ideas that will help us understand economic fluctuations. Each will be discussed briefly in turn, giving an overview of the model of fluctuations. Each is developed in more detail in the chapters that follow.

Sticky Wages

Our first key concept is one we have already discussed: the fundamental explanation for cyclical unemployment is that wages do not adjust quickly enough when either the demand or the supply curve for labor shifts. *At least for a while, and sometimes for extended periods of time*, the demand for labor at market wages can differ from the supply of labor. Because this is such a key assumption in macroeconomics, we will discuss some of the reasons for the slow adjustment of wages later in this chapter.

When wages (and prices) have had enough time to adjust, supply and demand will balance in all markets, including the labor market. Once this has happened, the level of employment, potential output, the real rate of interest, and the price level are determined, as the full-employment model of Part Two showed. Because it takes time for wages to fully adjust, we often refer to the full-employment model as describing the economy in the long run. The **long run** is a length of time sufficient to allow wages and prices to fully adjust to equilibrate supply and demand.

When wages adjust sluggishly, the basic price mechanism that operates to balance labor supply and demand cannot function effectively. In the **short run**—the period during which wages have failed to keep demand and supply in balance—the level of employment can diverge from the full-employment level, and wages will not respond quickly enough to move the economy back to full employment.

Fundamentals of Fluctuations 1

Sticky Wages

In the short run, shifts in the labor supply and demand curves often result in labor surpluses (high unemployment) or shortages (very low unemployment). This occurs because nominal wages tend to adjust slowly.

Sticky Prices

Like nominal wages, many prices are also sticky. And just as shifts in labor demand lead to fluctuations in unemployment when wages fail to adjust, shifts in product demand will lead to fluctuations in production. When demand for a firm's product falls, the firm might respond by lowering its price or by reducing production. Our analysis of economic fluctuations is based on a fundamental insight: *in the short run, firms adjust production and employment in response to demand.* They adjust production, not prices, initially. This is the second key concept in understanding fluctuations.

This concept, like our first one, captures an important aspect of actual behavior. When demand at retail stores rises in December because of the holiday season, for example, stores could respond by raising prices and keeping sales relatively constant. Instead, they keep the prices constant and satisfy the greater demand with increased sales. In some markets, prices do respond quickly to shifts in demand; competitive markets such as those for agricultural products usually are characterized by rapid price adjustments. In many markets, both price and production adjust. If an automobile company sees demand fall, it may offer rebates or other price reductions to spur demand, but it will

also scale back production, perhaps closing an assembly line and laying off workers. Most markets, particularly those characterized by imperfect competition, experience adjustments in production as demand shifts. In the appendix to this chapter we will discuss some of the reasons why firms respond to demand shifts by changing production levels rather than prices.

Fundamentals of Fluctuations 2

Sticky Prices

In the short run, shifts in the demand curves facing firms lead firms to adjust production and employment. This occurs because the prices of many goods and services tend to adjust slowly.

Inflation Adjustment

In the short run, wages and prices are sticky. Changes in demand cause fluctuations in output and employment. But in macroeconomics, we also are interested in understanding the factors that determine inflation, and our third key concept provides a link between unemployment and inflation.

The adjustment of inflation turns out to be one of the keys to understanding how economies return eventually to full employment. But it is important to avoid two common confusions involving the distinctions between levels versus rates of change on the one hand, and sticky versus constant on the other.

Levels Versus Rates of Change In macroeconomics, it is very important to understand the difference between the *price level* and the *inflation rate.* The price level is an index number that measures overall prices relative to a base year (see Chapter 23 if you need to review how price indexes are constructed). In 2000, when the base period was 1982–1984, the consumer price index (CPI) was equal to 172.2. Since the CPI is equal to 100 in the base period, this means that from 1982–1984 to 2000 the prices of the goods and services in the CPI had risen 72.2 percent. The price level in 2000 was higher than it was in 1982–1984.

The inflation rate tells us how fast the price level is rising. In 2000, the CPI inflation rate was 3.4 percent. That means that the price level in 2000 was 3.4 percent higher than it had been in the previous year. A higher inflation rate means the price level is rising faster. A lower inflation rate means the price level is rising more slowly. A negative inflation rate (deflation) would mean that prices are falling.

A higher price level does not mean inflation is higher. For example, the price level was much higher in 2000 than it was in 1982, but the inflation rate was lower. Inflation in 1982 was 6.2 percent, compared to only 3.4 percent in 2000. Prices were at a higher level in 2000 but they were rising more slowly than they were in 1982.

Most discussions in macroeconomics focus on the rate of inflation, and many countries have explicit policy objectives that call for keeping inflation low and stable. For that reason, we will also focus on inflation and the factors that determine it. To understand what causes inflation to adjust, however, we draw upon the evidence that wages and prices adjust slowly to shifts in demand and supply.

Sticky Versus Constant   If wages and prices are "sticky," how can we be talking about inflation since that, by definition, means wages and prices are changing? When speaking about sticky wages and prices, economists mean that wages and prices fail to adjust rapidly in the face of shifts in supply and demand. Let's use a simple example. A union and a firm sign a labor contract that will last for three years. The contract calls for wages to rise, say, 3 percent each year. If something happens in year 2 of the contract that reduces the firm's demand for labor, instead of falling to rebalance labor supply with the new, lower demand for labor, wages will continue to rise at 3 percent per year, as called for in the contract. The firm will lay off workers and employment falls. The wage did not adjust to keep demand and supply equal.

Over time, wages (and prices) do adjust to balance demand and supply. In our example, when the labor contract comes up for renewal, if the firm's demand for labor is still low, the new contract will probably call for only 2 percent wage growth. The *rate of wage inflation* is lower.

What Causes Inflation to Adjust?
The law of supply and demand tells us that whenever supply and demand are out of balance in a market, there will be pressures for the price in that market to adjust. The same applies for the aggregate economy. The balance between labor demand and supply, as reflected in unemployment, will be an important factor influencing how wages change. As cyclical unemployment falls—that is, labor markets be-

come *tight*—firms must boost the wages they pay to attract new workers and retain their existing workforce. In unionized sectors, a tight labor market increases the bargaining power of unions, enabling them to negotiate larger wage increases. So in tight labor markets, wages rise more rapidly. Conversely, increases in cyclical unemployment will reduce wage and price inflation.

This connection between cyclical unemployment and inflation means that the economy faces a trade-off. When the economy experiences a business cycle expansion and enjoys lower unemployment, inflation is likely to start to rise. To lower inflation typically requires a period of high cyclical unemployment. This means that policymakers face a short-run trade-off: if inflation is too high, the cost of lowering it will be temporarily high unemployment. Of course, cyclical unemployment is not the only factor that affects inflation. In Chapter 31 we will discuss the additional factors.

Fundamentals of Fluctuations — 3

Short-Run Inflation-Unemployment Trade-off

In the short run, there is a trade-off between low unemployment and stable inflation. This trade-off occurs because low unemployment causes nominal wages to increase faster than productivity. This increase in wages raises firms' labor costs and causes prices to rise faster (inflation to increase). High cyclical unemployment tends to reduce wage increases and leads to a decrease in inflation.

Inflation, Monetary Policy, and Spending

We have just set out three of the key concepts we will use as we explore the way the economy behaves in the short run. These will help us start to understand economic fluctuations, but they also open up new questions. For example, if firms respond to shifts in demand by adjusting production and employment, what explains the level of demand? And what can cause it to shift? And is spending, like cyclical unemployment, also related to that other important macroeconomic variable, inflation?

The answer to the third question is yes. As inflation starts to rise, government policies, and particularly monetary policy, act to reduce aggregate spending. Governments try to keep inflation stable, and if it starts to rise, they need to slow the economy down to moderate the increase in inflation. This is a consequence of our third key concept. Reducing inflation in the short run requires a rise in cyclical unemployment. So when inflation rises, governments (actually their central banks responsible for conducting monetary policy) take actions to reduce aggregate spending. Why? Because our second key concept tells us that firms react to a fall in demand by reducing production. When production falls, cyclical unemployment rises, acting to moderate the initial rise in inflation. Increases in inflation lead to reductions in aggregate spending and output. Decreases in inflation reverse the process and lead to increases in spending and output.

Fundamentals of Fluctuations

Inflation, Monetary Policy, and Spending

In the short run, increases in inflation lead to a reduction in aggregate spending. This occurs because higher inflation pushes up the real rate of interest, and spending (mainly investment spending) falls when the real interest rate rises. This relationship depends critically on the way the central bank reacts to inflation.

This relationship between inflation and aggregate spending depends in part on the way monetary policy is conducted. The behavior of the economy, as it experiences disturbances, will depend on what policy responses occur, just as it depends on how firms and households respond to changing economic conditions. If we want to understand how the economy operates, how it adjusts when world oil prices jump or there is a financial crisis in Asia, we will need to incorporate the way government acts.

In understanding short-run fluctuations in the economy, the role of the Federal Reserve and its decisions regarding monetary policy are particularly important. In Chapter 25, we explained the basic tools of the Fed and discussed how the Fed can influence the nominal interest rate and the money supply. We also learned (see Chapter 24) that it is the real interest rate that affects households' saving decisions and firms' investment decisions. The real interest rate is the nominal interest rate adjusted for inflation. *In the long run*, at full employment, the real interest rate balances national saving and investment. *In the short run*, when the economy can fluctuate around full employment, the Fed is able to affect the real interest rate by influencing the nominal interest rate.

Like many other central banks, the Fed reacts to changes in inflation. If inflation rises, the Fed undertakes policies that result in a higher real interest rate. A decline in inflation results in a lower real interest rate. This type of monetary policy in reaction to inflation is most explicit in countries where the central bank follows a policy of trying to keep in-

CASE IN POINT

Inflation Targeting

During the 1990s, many central banks adopted policies that are described as *inflation targeting*. Under inflation targeting, the central bank strives to achieve a low and stable rate of inflation. In some countries, such as the United Kingdom, New Zealand, Canada, and Sweden, the government or the central bank formally announces a target for the inflation rate. In England, for example, the target is 2.5 percent. We will learn more about inflation targeting in later chapters, but inflation-targeting policies illustrate our four key concepts.

The basics of an inflation-targeting policy are simple. The central bank wants to keep the inflation rate equal to its targeted value. If inflation rises above target, the central bank tries to push up the real interest rate. Doing so acts to reduce aggregate spending (key concept 4). Because wages and prices are sticky, this reduction in spending causes firms to cut back production, leading to a rise in unemployment (key concepts 1 and 2). Higher cyclical unemployment moderates inflation (key concept 3) and helps bring the inflation rate back on target. The process works in reverse when inflation falls below the central bank's target. In this case, the central bank tries to lower the real interest rate. This increases aggregate spending, and the increase in demand leads firms to increase production. With production increased, labor demand increases, and the subsequent decrease in cyclical unemployment and increased spending strengthen pressures for prices to rise. This helps to keep inflation on target. ●

Fundamentals of Short-run Fluctuations in Output, Employment, and Inflation

1. *Sticky wages*: Wages do not adjust rapidly to shifts in labor supply and labor demand. As a result, the labor market may not always be in equilibrium (Chapter 28).

2. *Sticky prices*: When the labor market does not clear, shifts in the demand for goods and services in the product market lead firms to adjust production rather than simply change prices (Chapters 28, 29).

3. *Short-run inflation–unemployment trade-off*: A fall in cyclical unemployment leads to an increase in inflation—increases in cyclical unemployment reduce inflation. This implies there is a trade-off in the short run between lower unemployment and higher inflation (Chapters 30, 31).

4. *Inflation, monetary policy, and spending*: As inflation rises, the real rate of interest increases to reduce aggregate spending. When inflation falls, the real interest rate also falls, boosting aggregate spending. The slope and position of this relationship depend importantly on monetary policy (Chapters 30, 32).

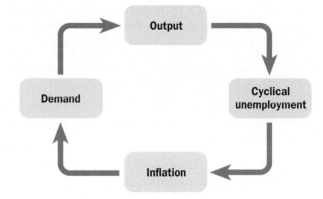

FIGURE 28.8 *Aggregate Demand and Inflation*

The four fundamental keys to understanding short-run fluctuations serve to link together demand, output, cyclical unemployment, and inflation. The next three chapters examine these links.

flation equal to a target value—so-called inflation-targeting policy regimes. Fortunately, a wide range of monetary policy behaviors, and not just inflation targeting, is consistent with a negative relationship between inflation and spending. This link between inflation, monetary policy, and aggregate spending is our fourth key concept. We will focus on it in Chapter 30. As with the other key concepts, we will need to understand what changes lead to shifts in the relationship between inflation and spending, as well as what changes lead to movements along a given relationship.

Linking the Four Key Concepts

The four key concepts work together to explain how output and inflation are determined when the economy is not at full employment. Figure 28.8 shows how. We can start at any

one of the boxes and use the key concepts to travel around the circle. For example, let's suppose something causes demand to drop. It might be a financial crisis in Asia or Latin America that reduces sales of U.S. goods in those countries. The drop in demand causes U.S. firms to scale back production—output falls. With production now at lower levels, firms do not need as many workers, so layoffs occur and cyclical unemployment rises. Wages fail to adjust quickly enough to keep the economy at full employment. High cyclical unemployment leads to slower wage growth, and inflation declines. In the face of a decline in inflation, the Fed lowers interest rates. By helping to boost some types of spending, lower interest rates help offset some of the initial drop in demand that started the process.

Over the next few chapters, we will examine each of these links in detail, learning about how they operate and about the causes of economic fluctuations.

Review and Practice

Summary

1. Economies experience recessions and booms in which output fluctuates around its full-employment

level. Recessions are periods in which real GDP declines, and booms are when real GDP increases. The fluctuations in output are called business cycles.

2. If wages and prices do not adjust quickly enough to ensure markets are always in equilibrium, where demand and supply are balanced, the economy may experience fluctuations in cyclical unemployment.

3. To explain cyclical unemployment, we need to explain why the aggregate labor market does not clear. If real wages do not adjust to shifts in the aggregate supply or demand for labor, and either the demand curve for labor shifts to the left or the supply curve for labor shifts to the right, then the quantity of labor supplied will exceed the quantity demanded at the prevailing wage and there will be cyclical unemployment.

4. Wages may be slow to adjust because of union contracts and implicit contracts that lead to infrequent wage changes. Firms minimize total labor costs by paying the efficiency wage. Cutting wages may raise costs by lowering productivity, causing the best workers to leave, or leading to higher labor turnover costs.

5. The labor market and the aggregate production function are key determinants of the economy's full-employment output, but in the short run, firms adjust production in response to fluctuations in demand. Thus, aggregate demand plays a critical role in determining the short-run equilibrium level of output.

6. Our model of fluctuations will be built around four key components: (1) wages are sticky; (2) prices are sticky; (3) there is a trade-off between inflation and cyclical unemployment in the short run; and (4) inflation and aggregate spending are linked by monetary policy.

Key Terms

recessions
output gap
expansions
implicit labor contract
efficiency wage
sticky wages
long run
short run
sticky prices
short-run inflation–unemployment trade-off

Review Questions

1. If the labor market always clears, would there be any unemployment? Any cyclical unemployment? What does it mean for the labor market "not to clear"? What gives rise to cyclical unemployment?

2. If the labor market always clears, what factors can cause fluctuations in the level of employment?

3. What inferences can you draw from the following two facts?

   (a) The labor supply curve is relatively inelastic.

   (b) Large variations in employment coexist with relatively small variations in real wages.

4. What might shift the aggregate demand curve for labor?

5. What are the four key concepts that help explain economic fluctuations?

6. If cyclical unemployment increases, what would you expect to happen to inflation? If cyclical unemployment falls, what would be the effect on inflation?

7. If inflation falls, why will aggregate expenditures rise? If inflation rises, why will aggregate expenditures fall?

8. What are some explanations for sticky wages?

9. Give three reasons why productivity may depend on the level of wages paid.

10. How does an efficiency wage differ from a wage that clears the labor market?

Problems

1. In the 1970s, a large number of new workers entered the U.S. economy from two main sources. The baby-boom generation grew to adulthood and the proportion of women working increased substantially. If wages adjust, what effect will these factors have on the equilibrium level of wages and quantity of labor? If wages do not adjust, how does your answer change? In which case will unemployment exist? Draw a diagram to explain your answer. What is the effect of the increased labor supply on the product market? Illustrate your answer diagrammatically.

2. Soon after Iraq invaded Kuwait in August 1990, many firms feared that a recession would occur. Anticipating

a lack of demand for their goods, they began cutting back on production. If wages adjust, what will happen to the equilibrium level of wages and employment? If wages do not adjust, how does your answer change? In which case will unemployment exist?

3. While for the most part, macroeconomics focuses on aggregate employment, ignoring distinctions among different categories of workers, it sometimes focuses on broad categories, such as skilled and unskilled workers. Assume, for simplicity, that there are just these two categories, and that for the most part, they cannot be substituted for each other.

   (a) Draw demand and supply curves for skilled and unskilled workers, marking the initial equilibrium in each market.

   (b) Assume now that there is a technological change which increases the demand for skilled labor at each wage, while it shifts the demand curve for unskilled labor to the left. If wages do not adjust, can there be vacancies of one type of labor at the same time there is unemployment of another type?

4. In 1996, Congress passed legislation increasing the minimum wage in two steps from $4.25 per hour to $5.15 per hour. Explain why efficiency wage theory suggests that the effect on employment may be relatively small.

5. Would you be more or less likely to observe implicit contracts in industries where most workers hold their jobs for only a short time? What about industries where most workers hold jobs a long time? Explain.

6. Go to the National Bureau of Economic Research's Web site (http://www.nber.org/cycles.html) and find the Business Cycle Reference Data for all peaks and troughs since 1854. What has been the average length of recessions since 1854? Since 1945? What has been the average length of expansions since 1854? Since 1945?

7. In the Case in Point on page 253, the cost of cyclical unemployment was estimated for 1992 by assuming that the unemployment rate associated with full employment was 6 percent. Suppose the 7.5 percent un-

employment rate in 1992 was caused, in part, by a rise in the unemployment rate that corresponds to full employment. Specifically, suppose changes in the age structure of the workforce meant that full employment in 1992 was actually associated with an unemployment rate of 6.5 percent rather than the 6 percent figure used earlier. Recalculate the output costs of the recession. Explain why they are lower.

Appendix: Explanations of Wage and Price Stickiness

How do we explain the apparent fact that real wages do not fall in the face of a shift in the demand for labor curve? Why don't real wages fall enough to eliminate unemployment quickly? Why does a shift in demand lead firms to cut production rather than simply lower prices? These questions are fundamental to macroeconomics. Three explanations are important for the current discussion. First, firms may not be allowed to adjust wages quickly, because of union pressure or government legislation. Second, it may not pay the firm to reduce wage levels, even if the supply curve for labor changes. Third, the firm may face greater risks and uncertainty if it adjusts to shifts in demand by cutting wages or lowering prices.

Wage Stickiness

Contracts and Government Regulation

One reason why real wages may not decline as employment declines is that contracts and regulations keep them from doing so. In effect, there are wage floors, like the price floors we encountered in Chapter 5.

Union Contracts   Labor union power explains sluggish wage adjustment in some industries. Economists do not agree about whether unions can obtain higher wages for their members over the long run than would be the case in a competitive labor market. But there is little doubt that unions slow the pace of wage adjustments. Because union contracts last for extending periods, wages cannot adjust quickly as economic conditions change. As contracts expire and are renegotiated, wages can change to reflect changes in demand and supply conditions. But in countries such as the United States, only a small fraction of all contracts are renegotiated each year. Different contracts expire at different times. This delays the adjustment of overall wage levels in the economy.

Union contracts, however, cannot provide the full explanation for sluggish wages in the United States. There was high unemployment before unions became important, and there has been high unemployment in the recent past, despite the steady decline in the number of unionized workers over the past thirty years.

Implicit Contract Theory

Union contract–style wage stickiness may come about even in the absence of a union or an explicit labor contract because of implicit contract-like understandings between employers and employees.

Workers are generally risk averse. Many have fixed financial commitments like monthly rent or car payments. They do not want their incomes to fluctuate with every change in the demand and supply of labor. Firms can bear these market fluctuations more easily. First, the owners of firms tend to be wealthier, with a larger cushion for adjusting to variations in income. Second, in the event of a temporary shortfall of funds, companies can borrow more easily.

Given that firms are less vulnerable to economic fluctuations than individual workers, it pays companies to provide at least some indirect "insurance" to their workers. Workers will be willing to work for a dependable firm that pays a steady wage, even if that wage is somewhat lower on average than the highly varying wages they could get elsewhere. Such a firm provides a form of insurance to its workers through an implicit contract, an understanding that the wages will not vary with the month-to-month, or even year-to-year, fluctuations in the labor market. It is called an implicit contract because it is an understanding, not a formal or explicit contract. In these circumstances, the wage workers receive can be thought of as consisting of two parts: the "market" wage (the wage the worker could receive elsewhere) plus an adjustment for the implicit insurance component. When the market wage is relatively low, the wage received by the worker may be higher than the market wage. The worker is receiving a benefit on the implicit insurance

policy. When the market wage is high, the wage received by the worker may be lower than the market wage. The difference is the premium the worker pays for wage stability.

For many industries in which long-term employment relations are common, implicit contract theory provides a convincing explanation of why wages for existing employees do not vary much. But even in the deepest recession, the labor market is like a revolving door, with people quitting jobs and some firms hiring new workers. Implicit contract theory does not explain why employers do not pay new employees lower wages than they pay to their existing workforce. If the wages paid to new employees fell sufficiently, presumably there would be no unemployment. However, such *two-tiered wage systems* remain relatively uncommon.

Insider-Outsider Theory

Seeking an explanation for why firms faced with recessionary conditions do not pay lower wages to new employees, economists have devised what is known as the *insider-outsider theory*. Insiders in this case are those with jobs at a particular firm. Outsiders are people who want jobs at that firm.

The insider-outsider theory focuses on the importance of training costs. Each firm needs a labor force trained in the special ways that it operates. Most of the training is done by current employees, the insiders. The insiders recognize that by training new employees, outsiders, they are reducing their bargaining position with the firm. The company can promise to continue to pay them higher wages than the newcomers, but the insiders know this promise can be broken. In future bargaining situations, the employer can use the availability of the lower-wage workers to exert downward pressure on the wages of the other employees. Knowing this, the insiders refuse to cooperate with training the outsiders, unless the new employees' interests are made coincidental with their own. The firm can accomplish this only by offering similar pay. This results in wage stickiness.

Minimum Wages

A minimum wage set by the government may result in unemployment. The minimum wage is a government-enacted price floor. To the extent that workers would accept and firms would offer wages below the minimum if they were allowed to, the minimum wage keeps the demand for labor from equaling supply. Most workers in the United States earn considerably more than the minimum wage, so minimum-wage legislation has little effect on unemployment for these workers. However, many economists believe that minimum-wage legislation probably does contribute *somewhat* to the unemployment of unskilled workers, including teenagers just entering the labor force.

Efficiency Wage Theory

Even in a world without contracts, explicit or implicit, real wages may not fall enough to eliminate unemployment. The employer wants to pay the efficiency wage—the wage at which total labor costs are minimized. Cutting wages may not reduce labor costs if labor productivity depends on the wage the firm pays.

Why Does Productivity Depend on Wages?

Economists have identified three main reasons why firms may benefit if they pay high wages. First, wages may affect the quality of the firm's workforce. It is all too common for companies to discover after a wage cut that they have lost their best workers. Indeed, this is the reason frequently given by firms for not cutting wages. This is an example of adverse selection: the average quality of the firm's workforce is affected adversely by a lowering of the wage.[3]

Second, the level of effort workers put in may depend on the wage. Any firm that raises wages above the market-clearing level creates an incentive for its workers to work hard for two reasons. First, any worker who gets fired will now expect to have to take the lower wage being offered by other firms. Second, if many firms offer wages higher than the market-clearing level, the unemployment that results means a worker who is fired may have to remain unemployed for a time before finding another job. Higher wages also may lead to higher levels of worker morale; if workers think the firm is treating them well, they will be more likely to work hard, boosting productivity.

Finally, wages may affect the rate at which workers quit, called the *labor turnover rate*. The lower the wages a firm offers, the more likely its workers will find another job, either because the other job offers higher wages or for some other reason. The firm may save on its direct labor costs by paying lower wages, but if it experiences more turnover, it will face higher training and hiring costs as it replaces workers who quit. Its labor costs might actual rise if it lowered wages.

Each of these reasons suggests that productivity depends not just on the wage paid but also on the wage paid relative to that paid by other firms and on the unemployment rate. The wage paid by other firms matters because if other firms pay a lower wage, a firm will find that it does not have to pay quite as high a wage to keep its best workers, to elicit a high level of effort, and to reduce turnover. The unemployment rate also matters because as it increases, a firm will again find that it can pay a lower wage without losing workers. Workers know that if they quit or are fired when unemployment is high, they will face greater difficulty in finding a new job.

Risk and Uncertainty

If a firm wants to reduce its workforce, it could reduce wages and let workers quit. But there are risks involved in this strategy. Other firms may leave their wages unchanged and try to attract the firm's best employees. Or other firms may respond by lowering wages in a corresponding manner, so the firm finds that its workers do not quit. In the one case, the firm reduces its labor force as it desired, but does so by losing its best workers. In the second case, it has not achieved the desired employment reduction. The effects of cutting wages are uncertain and depend on how workers and other firms respond.

WRAP-UP

Alternative Explanations of Slow Wage Adjustment

1. Unions with explicit contracts and employees with implicit contracts prevent rapid wage adjustment. Insider-outsider theory explains why firms do not pay newly hired workers a lower wage. Minimum wages explain why wages for very low-skilled workers do not fall.

2. Efficiency wage theory suggests that it is profitable for firms to pay above-market wages. This is because real wages affect the quality of the labor force, labor turnover rates, and the level of effort exerted by workers.

3. Firms face risk and imperfect information about the consequences of wage changes. Adjusting employment directly may involve less uncertainty.

---

[3]It should be clear that we have now moved away from the assumption that all workers are identical.

If the firm wants to avoid risk, it may decide to reduce employment by not hiring new workers as older workers leave or retire or by simply firing workers. The uncertainty associated with adjusting wages may be much more than that associated with adjusting employment levels directly.

Price Stickiness

When real wages fail to keep labor demand and labor supply in balance, shifts in the labor demand curve result in cyclical unemployment. These labor demand shifts arise predominantly from shifts in output. When production declines, firms need fewer workers. This means that to understand cyclical unemployment, we must understand what causes changes in output. In the short run, variation in the demand for goods and services plays the key role in affecting changes in output and therefore, the demand for labor. This was the second of our four key concepts. If a firm experiences a decrease in demand, as in Figure 28.9, it can respond by either decreasing its price or decreasing the quantity it produces. If a firm experiences an increase in demand, it can respond by either increasing its price or increasing production, since even in economic booms, firms normally have some spare capacity to expand production.[4] *In the short run, firms typically adjust production in response to changes in demand rather than adjust prices.* Economists have identified two key reasons why firms may respond by adjusting production rather than by adjusting prices.[5]

The Role of Costs

The first explanation for slow price adjustment emphasizes the implications of sluggish wage adjustment. Labor costs

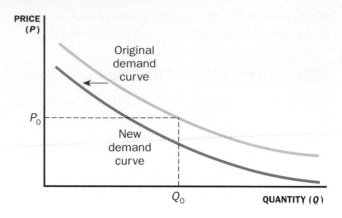

FIGURE 28.9   *Adjustment Costs*

Shifts in the demand curve facing a firm necessitate adjustments in either prices charged or quantity produced. How the firm adjusts depends in part on the costs of adjusting each and the risks associated. If the costs or risks of adjusting prices are high, and of adjusting quantities are low, then the firm will leave prices unchanged and will lower the quantity: there will be price stickiness.

are, for most businesses, the major component of their costs of production. In competitive markets, prices move in tandem with marginal costs, and changes in wages translate into changes in the marginal costs of production. Some firms, at least in the short run, use a simpler rule of thumb in setting prices—they set price as a given markup over costs (e.g., 120 percent of costs). In this case, prices adjust slowly to changes in demand because wages adjust slowly.

Risk and Uncertainty

Risk and imperfect information provide important reasons for slow price adjustment just as they did for wage adjustments. In perfectly competitive markets, firms simply take prices as given, but with imperfect competition, firms have some control over the price of the goods they produce. But firms face a great deal of uncertainty about the consequences of price changes. When a firm lowers its price, whether sales increase or not depends on how other firms in the industry respond and on how its customers respond. If rivals respond by lowering their prices, the firm may fail to gain market share, and its profits simply plummet with the decline in prices. If rivals fail to respond, the firm may gain a competitive advantage. Customers may

---

[4]Recall from Figure 28.4 that capacity utilization in manufacturing rarely has exceeded 90 percent.

[5]In some cases, these explanations seem to explain too much—they suggest that in some situations, prices and wages will not adjust at all to, say, small changes in demand or costs. But the economy consists of many firms in different circumstances. Some may be in a situation where they do not respond at all, while others may respond fully. The *average* for the economy will reflect a slow response.

think this is just the first of several price cuts and decide to postpone purchases until prices get still lower. Thus, a decrease in prices might even result in lower sales.

The uncertainty associated with changing prices is often much more than that associated with changing output and employment. When a firm cuts back on production, provided it does not cut back too drastically, its only risk is that its inventories will be depleted below normal levels if sales turn out to be stronger than expected. In this case, it can simply increase production next period to replace the lost inventories. If production costs do not change much over time, there is accordingly little extra risk to cutting back production.

Since firms like to avoid risks, they try to avoid making large changes in prices (and wages, as discussed earlier). They would rather accept somewhat larger changes in quantities—in the amount produced and in employment. As a result, prices are sticky.

WRAP-UP

Sources of Price Stickiness

1. When firms set price as a markup over costs, sluggish wage adjustment translates into sluggish price adjustment.

2. The risks associated with adjusting price may be greater than the risks of adjusting production.

Chapter 29

Aggregate Expenditures and Income

Key Questions

1. What are the components of aggregate expenditures?

2. What determines the aggregate level of expenditures in the economy?

3. How do consumption and net exports change as income changes?

4. If government purchases (or investment or exports) rise by $1 billion, why do total aggregate expenditures rise by more than $1 billion?

5. How does the rate of interest affect the exchange rate and net exports?

6. How does the interest rate affect aggregate expenditures?

*I*n Chapter 28 we learned that recessions and booms can result from shifts in the demand for the goods and services the economy produces. When demand falls, firms scale back production. As production falls, firms need fewer workers—workers are laid off and firms hire fewer new workers. Wages and prices fail to adjust quickly enough to ensure that the economy always remains at full employment. The unemployment rate rises. When demand increases, firms expand production and the economy expands—employment increases and the unemployment rate falls.

The task of this chapter is to explain what determines the level of demand at each value of the real rate of interest, what causes it to change, and why it can be so volatile. We will do so in four steps. First, we will study the relationship between equilibrium output and aggregate expenditures. *Aggregate expenditures* are the total spending by households, firms, government, and the foreign sector on the goods and services the economy produces. Changes in spending affect the level of production and income, and these changes in turn have further effects on spending. Second, we will discuss the major factors that affect the

three components of private expenditures—consumption, investment, and net exports. Third, we will explain how government spending affects the economy's equilibrium. Fourth, we will explain why total aggregate expenditures in the economy vary with the real rate of interest.

Income-Expenditure Analysis

Aggregate expenditures have four components: consumption, investment, government purchases, and net exports.[1] We can think of aggregate expenditures as the total expenditures in the four parts of the economy: households on consumption, firms on investment goods,

---

[1]Since our objective is to explain *real* GDP and employment, our focus continues to be on *real* consumption, *real* investment, *real* government purchases, and *real* net exports.

the government on public goods, and foreigners on net exports. We already have seen that total income (output) is equal to the sum of consumption, investment, government purchases, and net exports. Income depends on spending, but spending also depends on income. When income rises, for example, households will increase their consumption spending. This spending then becomes income for the producers of the goods and services households buy. Understanding the implications of this two-way relationship is critically important for understanding why the economy experiences fluctuations in production and employment.

The key to solving for the equilibrium level of output and the equilibrium level of aggregate demand is the **aggregate expenditures schedule.** The aggregate expenditures schedule traces out the relationship, at a fixed real interest rate, between aggregate expenditures and national income—the aggregate income of everyone in the economy. It is depicted in Figure 29.1, where the vertical axis measures aggregate expenditures and the horizontal axis measures national income.

The aggregate expenditures schedule has three critical properties. First, it is upward sloping—as national income goes up, so do aggregate expenditures. Changes in other variables (like interest rates, tax rates, and exchange rates) cause the aggregate expenditures schedule to shift up or down, and they may even alter its slope. Later in this chapter we will examine why expenditures increase with income and how the aggregate expenditures schedule is shifted by changes in other variables.

Second, as income increases by $1 billion, aggregate expenditures increase by less than $1 billion. The reason for this is that consumers save some of their additional income. If a household's income increases by $1,000, its consumption might rise by $900 and its saving by $100. The same applies to aggregate expenditures; they will rise less than the increase in income. Figure 29.1 also shows a line through the origin at a 45-degree angle. The slope of this line is unity. All along this line, a change in the horizontal axis (income) is matched by an equal change in the vertical axis (aggregate expenditures). By contrast, the aggregate expenditures schedule is flatter than the 45-degree line since aggregate expenditures increase less than dollar for dollar with increased income.

Third, at very low levels of national income, aggregate expenditures will exceed income. Households, for example,

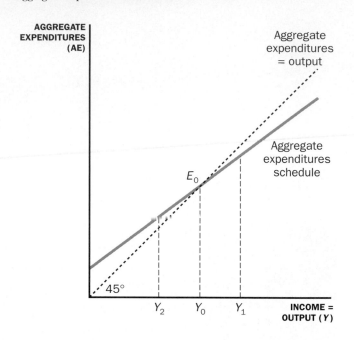

FIGURE 29.1   *The Aggregate Expenditures Schedule and Income-Expenditure Analysis*

The aggregate expenditures schedule gives the sum of consumption, investment, government purchases, and net exports at each level of national income. Aggregate expenditures increase with income. Equilibrium occurs at the intersection of the aggregate expenditures schedule and the 45-degree line, where aggregate expenditures equal income (at point E_0). At outputs greater than Y_0, such as Y_1, aggregate expenditures are less than output (remember, income equals output). Goods that are being produced are not being sold; there are unintended inventory accumulations. The reverse is true for outputs less than Y_0, such as Y_2.

ple, will use up their savings to maintain consumption if aggregate income were to fall to dramatically lower levels.

The facts that (1) the aggregate expenditures schedule slopes up, (2) the aggregate expenditures schedule is flatter than the 45-degree line through the origin, and (3) aggregate expenditures are greater than income at very low income levels imply that the aggregate expenditures schedule intersects the 45-degree line, as seen in Figure 29.1.

This brings us to our central questions: What determines the (short-run) equilibrium level of aggregate expenditures? Where on the schedule in Figure 29.1 will the economy find itself? To answer these questions, our analysis needs two more concepts.

The National Income-Output Identity

National income is equal to national output (as explained in Chapter 23). This reflects the fact that when a good or service is purchased, the money that is paid must eventually wind up as someone's income—as wages, in the pockets of the workers in the firm that produced the good (or to workers who produced the intermediate goods that were used in the production of the final good); as interest payments, in the pockets of those who loaned the firm money; or as profits, in the pockets of the owners of the firm. For simplicity, we will assume that the residents of the country neither receive money (net) from abroad nor make payments (net) to abroad so GNP and GDP coincide.[2] If Y is used to represent national income, this identity can be written as

$$\text{GDP} = \text{national income} = Y.$$

This identity allows us to interpret the horizontal axis in Figure 29.1 in two different ways. We can say the aggregate expenditures schedule gives the level of expenditures at each level of national income. We also can say it gives the level of expenditures at each level of national output.

Equilibrium Output

Normally, firms will produce only what they believe they can sell. This means that the total output produced by all firms will equal the total demand for output. In equilibrium, aggregate expenditures, which we will denote by AE, must equal aggregate output (GDP). Since aggregate output also equals national income (Y), we have the simple equation

$$AE = \text{GDP} = Y.$$

In Figure 29.1, the 45-degree line through the origin is labeled "Aggregate expenditures = output." All points on the 45-degree line have the property that aggregate expenditures, measured on the vertical axis, equal aggregate out-

put, measured on the horizontal axis. Only points on this 45-degree line satisfy the equilibrium requirement that aggregate expenditures equal output.

Equilibrium lies at the point on the aggregate expenditures schedule that also satisfies the "Aggregate expenditures = output" condition. That point is at E_0 in the figure, where the aggregate expenditures schedule intersects the 45-degree line. The corresponding equilibrium value of aggregate output, for given inflation and interest rates, is denoted Y_0.

The analysis that determines equilibrium output by relating income (output) to aggregate expenditures is called **income-expenditure analysis.** We can see that Y_0 is the equilibrium in two ways. The first way is to note that it is the only point that satisfies the two conditions for equilibrium. In equilibrium, everything produced must be purchased. Thus, aggregate expenditures must be equal to output, as represented by the 45-degree line. In equilibrium, the level of aggregate expenditures also must be what households, firms, government, and the foreign sector want to spend in total at that level of national income (output), as represented by the aggregate expenditures schedule. Only point E_0 is consistent with both conditions.

The second way is to consider what happens at a level of income, Y_1, in excess of Y_0. At that point, the aggregate expenditures schedule lies below the 45-degree line. What households, firms, government, and the foreign sector would like to spend at that level of national income, as reflected in the aggregate expenditures schedule, is less than national income (output). More goods are being produced than what individuals want to buy. Some of the goods, like strawberries, cannot be stored. They simply spoil. The goods that can be stored go into inventories. Since firms find they cannot sell all the goods they produced, the income level Y_1 is not the equilibrium level of output. Firms will respond by cutting back production until national income falls to Y_0. At Y_2, the aggregate expenditures schedule lies above the 45-degree line. Households, firms, government, and the foreign sector are spending more than national income. They are purchasing more than what is being produced. This is possible (temporarily) because firms can sell out of inventories. When firms find they are selling more than they are currently producing, they respond by increasing production. Aggregate output rises until equilibrium is restored at Y_0.

---

[2]You should review pages 457 to 463 in Chapter 23 if you have forgotten the distinction between GNP and GDP.

Shifts in the Aggregate Expenditures Schedule

The aggregate expenditures schedule can shift through a variety of changes in the economy that lead households, firms, the government, and the foreign sector to decide, at each level of income, to spend more or less. Figure 29.2 shows what happens if the level of aggregate expenditures increases at each level of national income by the amount S. The new aggregate expenditures schedule is denoted AE_1. Equilibrium output increases from Y_0 to Y_1. The increase in equilibrium output *is greater than the amount S*; how much output increases depends on the slope of the aggregate expenditures schedule.

To understand why, think about an economy that is initially in equilibrium at the output level Y_0 in Figure 29.2. At this level of income, the amount households, firms, the government, and the foreign sector wish to purchase (given

by the AE_0 schedule) is exactly equal to Y_0, the amount of output firms are producing. Now planned spending increases at each level of income, represented by the shift of the aggregate expenditures schedule to AE_1. If firms continued to produce Y_0, demand would exceed output; inventories would decline and this would signal to firms that they should increase production.

As output rises, households find that their incomes have risen. This leads them to increase their spending. Consequently, aggregate expenditures end up increasing by more than the initial amount S that the aggregate expenditures schedule shifted up. If the aggregate expenditures schedule is steep, rising income increases spending significantly, and the final increase in equilibrium output will be large. If the schedule is flatter, rising income has a smaller impact on spending, and the final increase in equilibrium output will be smaller. In Figure 29.3, the aggregate expenditures schedule shifts up by the same amount as it did in Figure 29.2, but the aggregate expenditures schedule is flatter and as a result, equilibrium output rises by less.

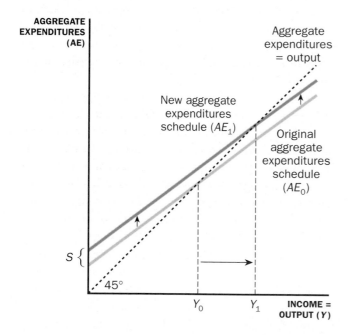

FIGURE 29.2   *Effect of a Shift in the Aggregate Expenditures Schedule*

An upward shift in the aggregate expenditures schedule results in an increase in the equilibrium level of output. The magnitude of the increase in equilibrium output from a given upward shift in the aggregate expenditures schedule is greater than the magnitude of the upward shift; that is, $Y_1 - Y_0$ exceeds S, the magnitude of the shift.

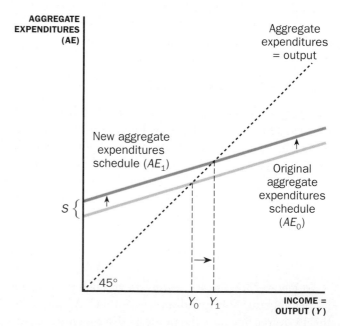

FIGURE 29.3   *The Importance of the Slope of the Aggregate Expenditures Schedule*

The flatter the aggregate expenditures schedule, the smaller the magnitude of the increase in output resulting from a given upward shift in the schedule.

Mathematical Formulation

We can describe the equilibrium using simple algebra. The aggregate expenditures equation can be written as

$$AE = A + bY,$$

where A is the vertical intercept of the aggregate expenditures schedule (the value of AE when $Y = 0$); and b is the slope of the schedule (an increase in Y of \$1 increases AE by \$$b$). The fact that the slope is positive but less than 45 degrees implies that b is between 0 and 1. Equilibrium requires that aggregate expenditures equal income, which, under our simplifying assumptions, equals Y:

$$Y = AE.$$

Substituting the second equation into the first equation yields

$$Y = A + bY,$$

which can be solved for Y:

$$Y = A/(1-b).$$

An upward shift in the aggregate expenditures schedule corresponds to an increase in A, say, to $A + 1$. Then Y increases from $A/(1-b)$ to $(A+1)/(1-b)$, or by $1/(1-b)$. Since b is less than 1, $1/(1-b)$ is greater than 1. If $b = .9$, then $1-b = .1$ and $1/(1-b) = 10$. In this case, an upward shift in the aggregate expenditures schedule by \$1 increases GDP by \$10. The factor $1/(1-b)$ is called the **multiplier.** The multiplier tells us how much total aggregate expenditures and output increase when the aggregate expenditures schedule shifts by \$1, for a given level of real interest rates.

As we will learn in the next few chapters, changes in aggregate demand also will have effects on interest rates, net exports, and inflation, and these changes will act to reduce the ultimate effect of shifts in the aggregate expenditures schedule on equilibrium output. When we have incorporated these additional adjustments into our analysis, as we will do over the next three chapters, the change in equilibrium output per dollar change in the AE schedule is closer to 1.5 to 2 in the short run and close to 0 in the longer run as wages and prices have time to completely adjust.

Income-Expenditure Analysis

1. Equilibrium output is at the point where the aggregate expenditures schedule equals output (income).

2. Upward shifts in the aggregate expenditures schedule result in increases in equilibrium output, for a given level of real interest rates. Downward shifts in the aggregate expenditures schedule result in decreases in equilibrium output, for a given level of real interest rates.

3. The changes in equilibrium output are larger than the initial shift in the aggregate expenditures schedule. How much larger depends on the slope of the aggregate expenditures schedule. The steeper the slope, the greater the change.

A Look Forward

We have just learned two of the central principles of macroeconomics: (1) shifts in the aggregate expenditures schedule determine changes in the equilibrium output of the economy, for a given value of the real interest rate, and (2) the magnitude of these changes is greater than the magnitude of the shift up or down in the aggregate expenditures schedule. We also have learned that the magnitude of the change in output increases with the slope of the aggregate expenditures schedule. The remainder of this chapter explores three critical questions. First, why does the aggregate expenditures schedule have a positive slope and what determines that slope? Second, what factors lead to shifts in the aggregate expenditures schedule? And third, how do changes in interest rates affect the aggregate expenditures schedule? This last question is important because, as we have learned, the interest rate plays a critical role in the full-employment model and because interest rates and credit conditions are important for understanding how monetary policy affects the economy.

To address these questions, we will take a closer look at each of the four components of aggregate spending: (1) consumption: purchases by households of goods and services, such as food, television sets, and clothes; (2) investment: purchases of capital goods, machinery, and buildings by firms to help them produce goods and services; (3) government purchases, both of goods and services bought for current use (government consumption) and of goods and services like buildings and roads bought for the future benefits they produce (public investment); and (4) net exports. We say *net exports*, because to determine the total purchases of goods and services produced domestically (and therefore included in GDP), we must subtract from the value of goods sold abroad (exports) the value of the goods and services purchased by U.S. households, businesses, and the government that were produced abroad (imports).

Consumption

Consumption is by far the largest component of aggregate expenditures. In the United States, consumer expenditures represent about 67 percent of total expenditures. Figure 29.4 shows real consumption and real GDP in the

United States since 1960. The figure, in addition to showing that consumption is a large fraction of GDP, also shows that the two tend to move together. In 2000, real GDP was $9.32 trillion and real consumption was $6.29 trillion (in 1996 dollars).

The close connection between the two should not be surprising. GDP is total output in the economy, but remember that national output is also equal to national income. And the most important determinant of consumption is income. On average, families with higher incomes spend more.

Aggregate consumption is the sum of the consumption of all the households in the economy. Just as when a typical family's income rises, its consumption increases, when total income in the economy rises, aggregate consumption rises. It is the **aggregate consumption function,** the relationship between aggregate consumption and aggregate income, that is important for macroeconomics. The measure of income that is important is disposable income, or what households have after paying taxes. Figure 29.5 plots aggregate real U.S. consumption against aggregate real U.S. disposable income; the close relationship is quite apparent.

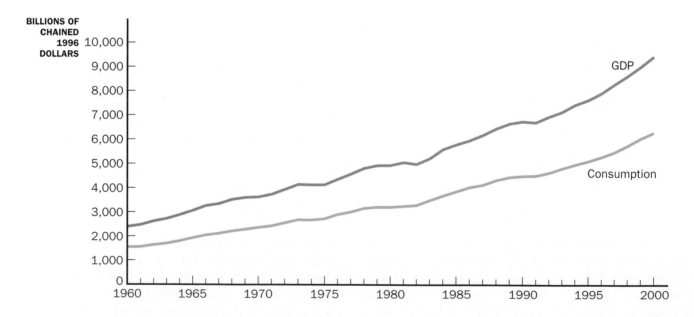

FIGURE 29.4 *Consumption and GDP*

Real consumption spending is the largest component of aggregate expenditures. It moves closely with total real income in the economy.

SOURCES: *ERP* (2001), Table B-2, and Federal Reserve Board.

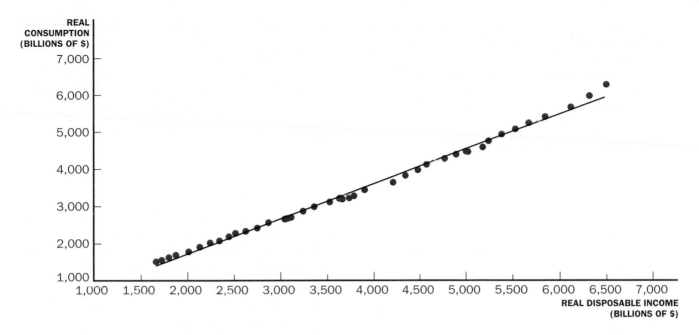

FIGURE 29.5   *Consumption and Disposable Income from 1960 to 2000*

The chief factor that determines household consumption spending is disposable income, the income available after taxes. From 1960 to 2000, there was a remarkably close relationship between real disposable income and real consumption in the United States. The black line shows the relationship predicted by a very simple linear consumption function. While the "fit" is very good, there are periods when consumption has risen above or fallen below the level predicted by the linear consumption function.

SOURCES: *ERP* (2001), Tables B-2, B-31, and Federal Reserve Board.

The Marginal Propensity to Consume

The amount by which consumption changes as income changes is called the **marginal propensity to consume** (*MPC*). For example, if a household's income rises by $2,000 per year and its consumption spending rises by $1,600 per year, the marginal propensity to consume is found by taking the change in consumption and dividing it by the change in income, or 1,600/2,000 = 0.8. Since our interest is in the aggregate behavior of the economy, we are most interested in the change in aggregate consumption as aggregate income changes. The aggregate marginal propensity to consume can be thought of as an average of all the individual marginal propensities to consume of the millions of households in the economy. The aggregate marginal propensity to consume is equal to the slope of the aggregate consumption function.

The aggregate marginal propensity to consume conveys important information. Since consumption is a large fraction of total aggregate expenditures, the upward slope of the aggregate expenditures schedule shown in Figure 29.1 is closely related to the marginal propensity to consume. As aggregate income rises, households increase their consumption spending. If the marginal propensity to consume is high, then the aggregate expenditures schedule will be steep, as the rise in aggregate income causes a large increase in consumption spending. If the marginal propensity to consume is small, the aggregate expenditures schedule will be flatter.

The Marginal Propensity to Consume and the Simple Multiplier

As Figure 29.5 suggested, consumption (C) is closely related to national income. Suppose the relationship between the two is

$$C = a + MPC \times Y,$$

where *MPC* is the marginal propensity to consume and *a* is an intercept term (equal to the value of consumption if income were zero). If the other components of aggregate expenditures (in a closed economy, investment, I, and government purchases, G) are equal to a fixed amount denoted by A, then total aggregate expenditures will be

$$AE = C + I + G = a + MPC \times Y + A.$$

In equilibrium, aggregate expenditures equal output, so

$$AE = Y.$$

Combining these last two equations, we have

$$Y = a + MPC \times Y + A,$$

or

$$Y = (a + A)/(1 - MPC).$$

As a numerical example, let $a = \$2$ trillion, $A = \$3$ trillion, and $MPC = .8$. If we substitute these values into the expression for equilibrium output, we get $Y = \$25$ trillion. If any of the components of A change by $\$1$, equilibrium output changes by $1/(1 - MPC)$. For example, suppose A increases to $\$3.5$ trillion. Equilibrium output rises to $\$27.5$ trillion. The multiplier is equal to the change in output ($\$2.5$ trillion) per dollar change in A ($\$.5$ trillion), or 5. This also can be found directly as $1/(1 - MPC)$. Since MPC is the marginal propensity to consume, the multiplier will be larger if the MPC is larger.

The Marginal Propensity to Save

Individuals have to either spend or save each dollar of disposable income. The definition "disposable income = consumption plus saving" tells us that when disposable income rises by a dollar, if consumption rises by 90 cents, saving must rise by 10 cents. The higher level of saving stemming from an extra dollar of income is called the **marginal propensity to save** (MPS). Since the extra dollar is either spent or saved, the marginal propensity to consume and the marginal propensity to save must always sum to one:

$$MPC + MPS = 1.$$

This relationship holds both for the individual households in the economy and for the aggregate economy. If the

aggregate MPC is .9, the aggregate MPS must be .1. This means that if the MPS is large, the aggregate expenditures schedule will be flatter.

The Multiplier, the Marginal Propensity to Save, and the Capital Market

In Chapter 24, we learned how the capital market plays an important role in ensuring that saving and investment are balanced at full-employment output. If we ignore the government and the foreign sector, aggregate expenditures will equal consumption plus investment, or $AE = C + I$. Equilibrium requires that $C + I$ equal output, or $Y = C + I$. Subtracting C from both sides of this equilibrium condition yields $Y - C = I$. But income minus consumption ($Y - C$) is just saving (S), so an equivalent expression for equilibrium is $S = I$.

Figure 29.6 illustrates the determination of equilibrium output graphically in terms of saving and investment. The upward-sloping line shows desired saving at each level of total income. The slope of this line is just the marginal propensity to save. If investment is equal to a fixed amount, I_0, equilibrium output will be equal to Y_0. At this income level, desired saving is equal to investment spending.

Now suppose investment increases to I_1. Equilibrium output rises to Y_1. Since the slope of the savings line is the

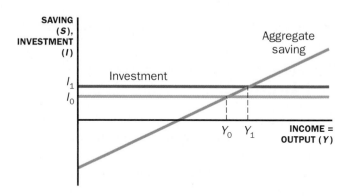

FIGURE 29.6 *Saving, Investment, and Equilibrium Income*

As incomes increase, the amount individuals desire to save increases. The amount by which saving increases as the result of a $\$1$ increase in income—the slope of the saving function—is called the *marginal propensity to save*. In equilibrium, saving equals desired investment. Thus, equilibrium occurs at the intersection of the saving function and the level of investment. At an investment level of I_0, equilibrium output is Y_0.

A shift in investment from I_0 to I_1 leads to an increase in equilibrium output from Y_0 to Y_1; the increase in output is a multiple of the original increase in investment.

marginal propensity to save, we can see from the graph that the marginal propensity to save will equal the change in investment $(I_1 - I_0)$ over the change in output $(Y_1 - Y_0)$, the rise over the run. But this means the multiplier, which is the change in output over the change in investment, must equal $1/MPS$. Finally, since the MPS is $1 - MPC$, we also have that the multiplier is $1/(1 - MPC)$.

When we studied the economy at full employment, we assumed that the real interest rate would adjust to ensure saving and investment balance. In this chapter, we no longer assume output is at its full-employment level, and so far we have treated the interest rate as fixed. In this case, Figure 29.6 shows how the level of output will need to adjust to bring saving and investment into balance.

Taxes and the Slope of the Aggregate Expenditures Schedule

Consumption spending by households depends on their disposable income, both its current level and the level expected in the future. Disposable income is the amount of income households have to spend after paying taxes. For a given level of total income, an increase in taxes reduces disposable income and leads to a fall in consumption. Tax increases, therefore, shift the aggregate expenditures schedule down. Tax decreases shift it up.

Taxes have a second effect on the aggregate expenditures schedule. The government's tax revenues typically go up when income rises and fall when income declines. Personal income taxes, for instance, are related to income. Individuals with higher incomes generally pay more in taxes. As total national income rises, tax revenues rise. This implies that disposable income will increase by less than the increase in total income. The same process works in reverse if income falls. As total income declines, so do taxes. Since people pay less in taxes, disposable income declines less than total income. For example, if the average tax rate on the last dollar of income earned (the marginal tax rate) is 30 percent, then a $1 fall in income reduces taxes by $.30; disposable income only falls by $.70.

What does this imply for the slope of the aggregate expenditures schedule? Because changes in total income lead to smaller changes in disposable income when taxes vary with income, the changes in consumption spending also will be smaller. If the marginal propensity to consume out of disposable income is .9 and the marginal tax rate is 30 percent, a $1 increase in total national income will re-

sult in an increase of consumption spending of $.63. Of the $1 increase in total income, $.30 cents must be paid in taxes, so disposable income rises by only $.70. With a marginal propensity to consume of .9, consumption rises by .9 times the $.70 increase in disposable income, or by $.63. A rise in total income leads to a smaller rise in spending. This means that the aggregate expenditures schedule is flatter if marginal tax rates are high. As we have already learned, a flatter schedule means the multiplier will be smaller.

Taxes that increase with income are an example of an *automatic stabilizer*. By reducing the multiplier, they make the economy more stable. A shift down in the aggregate expenditures schedule results in a smaller drop in total output. A shift up results in a smaller rise in output. These effects occur automatically because tax revenues change automatically as income changes. Automatic stabilizers will be discussed more fully in Chapter 32.

Putting Government into the Equation
When we add government purchases and taxes, then consumption depends on disposable income:

$$C = a + MPC \times Y_d,$$

where Y_d is disposable income. The equation for aggregate expenditures becomes

$$AE = C + I + G = a + MPC \times Y_d + G.$$

For simplicity, we assume a given fraction, t, of income is paid in taxes, so

$$Y_d = (1 - t)Y.$$

Hence, in equilibrium, with aggregate expenditures equaling income,

$$AE = Y = a + MPC(1 - t)Y + G$$

or

$$Y = (a + G)/[1 - (1 - t)MPC].$$

The multiplier is equal to

$$1/[1 - (1 - t)MPC].$$

If $MPC = .8$ and $t = .25$, the multiplier is 2.5. By contrast, the multiplier without taxes would be 5, twice as large.

The reason that the multiplier is larger without taxes is simple. Without taxes, every dollar of extra income translates into $.80 of extra spending. With taxes, when income goes up by $1, disposable income rises by $.75 and consumption increases by only $.8 \times .75 = \$.60$.

Internet Connection

Japan and the Keynesian Cross

Diagrams such as those we saw in Figures 29.1 to 29.3 are often called *Keynesian cross* diagrams. Equilibrium occurs where the aggregate expenditures schedule crosses the 45-degree line. Economist Paul Krugman of Princeton University uses the Keynesian cross to explain Japan's recent economic problem at http://www.pkarchive.org/japan/scurve.html.

Shifts in the Consumption Function

The simple consumption function relating consumption to disposable income, often called the *Keynesian consumption function*, is a good starting point for understanding consumption, as Figure 29.5 illustrates. Income varies from year to year, and so does consumption. Figure 29.5 shows that the relationship is remarkably close to a linear one. Still, consumption has often diverged from the predictions of the simple Keynesian consumption function—at the end of the 1990s, for instance, consumption spending was higher than the Keynesian consumption function would predict. Understanding the factors, in addition to income, that can influence consumption is important since consumption is the largest component of aggregate expenditures. Changes in these factors will shift the consumption function and the aggregate expenditures schedule.

Future-Oriented Consumption Behavior

In the decades after Keynes's time, many economists questioned his notion that current consumption spending depends primarily on current income. They argued that individuals, in making consumption decisions, take into account both their current income *and* the income they expect to receive in the future.

Nobel laureate Franco Modigliani, for instance, emphasized that people save for retirement. He called this motive *life-cycle saving*, to convey the notion that individuals will save during their working years so that they will not have to curtail consumption after they retire. Milton Friedman, also a Nobel laureate, emphasized how the future affects consumption today by pointing out that people save in good years to carry them through bad years. His view is called the *permanent income hypothesis*. Permanent income is just a person's expected average lifetime income. Both Modigliani and Friedman stressed that individuals generally try to stabilize their consumption, using savings to smooth consumption so that it does not fluctuate dramatically from year to year. They also stressed that individuals will be forward looking, basing current consumption decisions on their expectations about future income.

These future-oriented theories of saving and consumption have several important implications. One implication is that changes in expectations about future income will affect current consumption, even if current income has not changed. If households become more pessimistic about future income prospects, as seemed to occur in 1990, current consumption will decline even if current income has not changed. Such a change will cause the aggregate expenditures schedule to shift down.

Another implication is that one-time or temporary income changes may have only a small effect on current consumption. Consider a person who receives a windfall gain in income in one year—perhaps she wins $1 million in the state lottery. If the marginal propensity to consume is .9, the Keynesian consumption function predicts she will consume $900,000 of the winnings that year. The future-oriented consumption theories suggest that the lucky winner will spread the extra income over a lifetime of consumption. Similarly, if the government temporarily lowers taxes for one year, the future-oriented consumption theories predict that taxpayers will not dramatically increase consumption in that year but will spread the extra consumption the one-year tax reduction allows over their lifetimes. Thus, future-oriented consumption theories predict that *temporary* tax changes will be much less effective in stimulating consumption (and shifting the aggregate expenditures schedule) than the Keynesian model predicts.

Finally, the future-oriented consumption theories have an important implication for the multiplier. Since the relationship between current consumption and current income is weaker than in the Keynesian model, changes in aggregate income that households expect to be only temporary will cause little change in consumption spending. Thus, the marginal propensity to consume is likely to be much smaller than the Keynesian consumption function would suggest. The aggregate expenditures schedule is flatter, and the multiplier is smaller.

Wealth and Capital Gains The future-oriented consumption theories suggest that consumption will be affected by changes in household wealth. Wealthier people consume more (at each level of current income). Just as changes in individuals' wealth will affect their consumption choices, so will changes in aggregate wealth affect aggregate consumption.

The distinction between income and wealth as a determinant of consumption is important. It corresponds to the distinction between flows and stocks. Flows are measured as "rates." Both income and consumption are flow variables; they are measured as dollars *per year*. Wealth is a stock variable. It is measured simply by the total value ("dollars") of one's assets.[3] Future-oriented theories emphasize that there is no reason why an individual's current consumption should be related to current income. What individuals consume should be related to how well off they are, and that is better measured by their wealth.[4]

An individual's wealth changes when the value of assets rises or falls. These changes are called *capital gains* or *losses*. When stock market prices or real estate prices rise and people expect this change to last for a long time, individuals who own these assets will increase their consumption. They will do so because their overall wealth has risen, even if they do not immediately receive any increased income from the rise in asset prices.

There is some evidence to support this view. Many economists believe the stock market crash of 1929 contributed to the Great Depression by causing a downward shift in the consumption function. On the other hand, when the stock market fell by 22 percent on a single day in October 1987, consumption did not decline sharply in the way one might have expected. One reason for this is that individuals respond to changes only slowly, and in 1987 their consumption had not yet fully adjusted to the increases in stock prices that had occurred during the preceding few years. A prolonged and persistent decline in the stock market, however, might have an extremely depressing effect on consumption. The prolonged rise in stock prices during the 1990s was probably a major cause of the decline in the U.S. household saving rate. Individuals felt wealthier and increased their consumption spending faster than incomes rose. In 1999, the saving rate for U.S. households was actually negative.

Reconciling Consumption Theory with Facts

The permanent income and life-cycle saving hypotheses contain large elements of truth. Families do save for their retirement, and they do smooth their consumption between good years and bad. Even so, household spending appears to be more dependent on current income than either future-oriented theory would suggest. There are two reasons for this: durable goods and credit rationing.

Durable Goods Goods such as cars, refrigerators, and furniture are called *durable goods*. Purchasing a durable good is like an investment decision, because such goods are bought for the services they provide over a number of years. Decisions to postpone purchasing a durable good have quite different consequences from decisions not to buy food or some other nondurable good. If you do not buy strawberries today, you will have to do without them. But not buying a durable good often does not mean you will do without. It simply means you may have to make do with the services provided by an older durable good. The costs of postponing the purchase of a new car are often quite low; you can make do with your old car a little bit longer.

When a household's income is temporarily low, rather than borrowing to purchase a durable like a new car, the household simply postpones the purchase. Figure 29.7

---

[3]Other stock variables in macroeconomics include the capital stock and level of employment; other flow variables include the interest rate and investment.

[4]Future-oriented theories take an expansive view of what should be included in wealth. For example, they include *human capital*, the present discounted value of future wage income, in measuring an individual's wealth. (See Chapter 9 for a definition of present discounted value.)

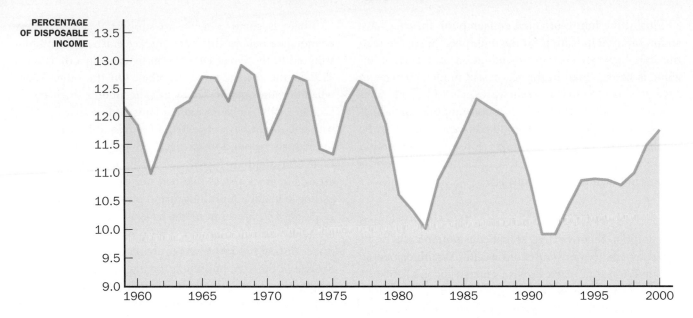

FIGURE 29.7   *Variability in Purchases of Durable Goods*

The consumption of durable goods fluctuates considerably from year to year, much more than consumption as a whole.

SOURCES: *ERP* (2001), Tables B-8, B-16, and Federal Reserve Board.

traces the purchases of durable goods as a percentage of disposable income since 1960. These fluctuations in purchases help account for why current household spending moves closely with changes in current income. Variations in the consumption of nondurable goods and the services provided by durable goods—hence, variations in true consumption—are much smaller.

Households often borrow to purchase durable goods. This is particularly true for cars and homes.[5] Purchases of durable goods will be affected by the cost of borrowing. This cost is measured by the interest rate on the loan. If interest rates rise, it becomes more costly to take out a loan to buy a car or a mortgage to buy a house. At each level of income, a rise in the rate of interest will reduce household spending and shift the aggregate expenditures schedule down.

Credit Rationing   Empirical studies show that even nondurable consumption expenditures seem more depen-

dent on current income than the future-oriented theories suggest. These theories, in particular the permanent income hypothesis, assume that when individuals have a bad year, they can maintain consumption at a steady level. The theories assume, in other words, either that people have a large stock of savings to draw upon while income is temporarily low or that they can easily borrow.

For many people, neither of these conditions is true. Most individuals, even in the United States, have few liquid assets upon which they can draw. They may have considerable savings tied up in a pension plan or in the form of equity in their house, but neither of these can be drawn upon easily to maintain consumption when income temporarily falls. Moreover, it is precisely in times of need, when a person is unemployed or a business is doing badly, that banks are least forthcoming with funds. (As the saying goes, banks only lend to those who don't need the money!)

Credit rationing occurs when people are unable to borrow funds at the market rate of interest because of the risks associated with lending to them. Many people experience credit rationing. For those who do, cutting back on consumption spending when income declines is not a matter of choice. For those individuals, consumption depends heavily on current income. When households face credit rationing,

---

[5]In the GDP accounts, household purchases of new homes are classified as part of investment spending rather than as part of consumption spending. This reflects the fact that buying a home is an investment decision that is more like the purchase of a new building by a firm than it is like the purchase of food, movie tickets, or other nondurable goods.

purchases of durable goods will depend on both the cost of credit (the interest rate) and the availability of credit.

Macroeconomic Implications of Consumption Theories

The Keynesian theory of consumption, with its emphasis on the importance of current income, and the future-oriented theories, with their emphasis on future expected income and wealth, provide important insights that help to explain consumption.

First, total consumer expenditures (spending on both nondurable and durable goods) will move closely with current income. Purchases of durable goods and credit rationing help to account for this close connection. Since the aggregate expenditures schedule that we used to determine equilibrium output depends on total consumption expenditures, it is the relationship between current income and current consumption, summarized in the marginal propensity to consume, that is an important determinant of the slope of the aggregate expenditures schedule.

Second, households in the aggregate are likely to adjust consumption less in response to income changes that are viewed as temporary than they would to changes viewed as permanent. One way to express this is that the marginal propensity to consume out of permanent income is larger than the marginal propensity to consume out of temporary income. This has important implications for macroeconomic policies. For instance, a one-year tax cut is likely to have a much smaller impact on consumption than a tax cut that is expected to remain in place for a much longer period of time.

Third, the future-oriented consumption theories point to a number of factors that will shift the consumption function and therefore also shift the aggregate expenditures schedule. Most importantly, changes in household wealth or household expectations about future income will affect current consumption even if current income has not changed. When households become more pessimistic about future income prospects, current consumption falls. When they become more optimistic, current consumption rises. For that reason, measures such as the University of Michigan's Survey of Consumer Confidence are often used to gauge whether households are likely to increase or decrease consumption spending.

Finally, because households typically borrow to purchase durable goods such as cars and homes, household spending, and therefore the aggregate expenditures schedule, will be affected by changes in the rate of interest. An in-

crease in the rate of interest, for example, would reduce spending at each level of current income, shifting the aggregate expenditures schedule down.

WRAP-UP

Approaches to Consumption Determination

1. *Keynesian consumption function*: stresses the dependence of consumption on current income.

2. *Future-oriented consumption theories*: stress the dependence of consumption on total lifetime expected income and the role of savings in smoothing consumption.

   a. *Life-cycle theory*: stresses the importance of saving for retirement.

   b. *Permanent income theory*: stresses the role of savings in smoothing consumption between good and bad years.

   c. Implications:

      i. Consumption is not very dependent on temporary changes in income; the multiplier is small.

      ii. Consumption is sensitive to capital gains and losses.

3. Two factors that explain why spending seems to be more dependent on current income than future-oriented theories predict:

   a. Durable goods

   b. Credit constraints

4. Purchases of durables may depend on the rate of interest.

Investment

Variations in investment spending are probably the principal cause of shifts in aggregate expenditures. Just how volatile

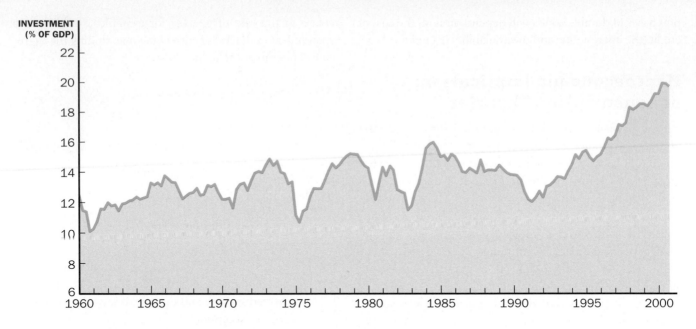

FIGURE 29.8   *The Variability of Investment*

The share of investment in GDP has varied greatly in recent years.

SOURCES: *ERP* (2001), Table B-2, and Federal Reserve Board.

investment is can be seen in Figure 29.8. In recent years, investment has varied from just over 10 to almost 20 percent of GDP.

The investment relevant for aggregate expenditures includes three broad categories. The first is firms' purchases of new capital goods (everything from buildings and machinery to cash registers, computers, and desks). These make up **plant and equipment investment.** Firms also invest in inventories (**inventory investment**) as they store their output in anticipation of sales or store the raw materials they will need to produce more goods. The third investment category consists of households' purchases of new homes, called **residential investment.**

The purchases of previously owned capital goods or houses do not count because they are not purchases of current production. Recall from Chapter 5 that GDP consists of total final goods and services *produced* in the current year. We exclude from investment any purchases of capital goods or houses that were built in earlier years. If one person buys a home built ten years ago, the individual might view this as an investment. But for the seller it is a "disinvestment"—so the transaction simply changes who owns the economy's assets and does not represent new investment.

We restrict our focus in this discussion to business investment, which includes two of the three major investment categories: plant and equipment, and inventories. The third category, household purchases of new homes, is best analyzed as a very long-lived durable good, using the same principles governing the demand for durable goods developed earlier in this chapter.

Investment in Plant and Equipment

To undertake investment, firms must believe that the expected future returns will be large enough to compensate them for the risks of the investment. Moreover, firms are aware that a dollar in the future is worth less than a dollar today; if they had the dollar today, they could put it in a bank and get back the dollar *with interest* next year. As the interest rate rises, future dollars are worth less relative to today's dollars. This means that there will be fewer investment projects with future returns large enough to offset the forgone interest. To put it another way, think of a firm as having to borrow money for the investment project. Higher interest rates increase the cost of undertaking the project. Fewer projects will have an expected return that is high enough to pay these higher interest costs and still yield a profit. Thus, higher interest rates lead to lower levels of investment. The relationship between interest rates and investment is demonstrated in the investment schedule introduced in Chapter 24. It is depicted as the downward-sloping curve in Figure 29.9. Of course, what matters for investment is the *real interest rate*, the cost of funds after taking into account the effect of inflation. If the *nominal* interest rate increases but expected inflation increases in an offsetting way, firms' investment will be unaffected. (The real interest rate is the nominal interest rate minus the expected rate of inflation.)

In addition to the cost of borrowing, the availability of funds also can affect investment. Particularly during recessions, many firms *claim* they cannot borrow as much as they would like. When they cannot borrow, they must resort to *retained earnings*—their profits less what they pay out to shareholders in dividends—to finance their investment projects.

For instance, in the 1992 economic downturn, many builders claimed that they could not obtain funds to continue their construction activities. Banks simply would not lend to them. At that time, many banks had been hurt badly by high defaults on existing loans. These losses made banks less willing to bear the risks of lending. Bankers also said that bank regulators prohibited them from making many loans that previously would have been approved. However, some banks—and many economists— argued that the issue was not banks' willingness to make loans. The problems were a shortage of good borrowers and an unwillingness of many borrowers to pay an interest rate commensurate with banks' perceptions of the riskiness of the loans.

Variability in Plant and Equipment Investment

Investment decisions must be based on expectations about future returns. Predicting the future is always difficult. There may be *technological risks*—the firm might be using a new technology that could prove unreliable. In most cases, there are *market risks*. Will there be a market for the new product? At what price will it sell? What will labor costs be in the future? What about the prices of energy and other inputs? Firms must base investment decisions on educated guesses, recognizing that there is often great uncertainty.

The risks associated with investment spending are the primary reason why investment is so volatile. Changes in expectations about the future may swing sharply. Fluctuations in current economic conditions may lead to large fluctuations in investment spending. When sales are up today, firms may expect future sales to be high and perhaps even increasing. With high and increasing sales, firms will want to have more capital—that is, they will want to invest more. If sales dip, firms may decide to scale back or even cancel their plans for new capital—so investment falls. Changes in current output, therefore, will shift the investment schedule. For instance, when the economy goes into a recession, the investment schedule typically shifts to the left, as depicted in Figure 29.9. Expectations of future profits decrease, risks appear larger, and the ability and willingness to bear risks are reduced. Moreover, firms that are not able to borrow have to use retained earnings to finance investment and have fewer funds available for investment when a recession lowers current sales. And banks may be less willing to make loans. Under these circumstances, even large declines in real interest rates may be unable to generate much additional investment.

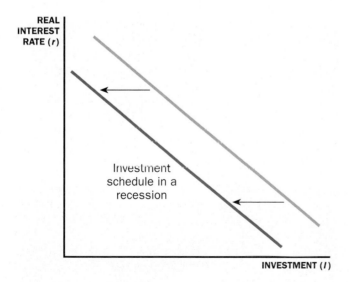

FIGURE 29.9 *The Investment Schedule*

At higher real interest rates, firms are willing to invest less. As the economy enters a recession, expectations of profits decrease, the ability to share risks decreases, and the availability of financing decreases. This leads to a shift in the investment schedule to the left.

Inventory Investment

One of the most volatile components of investment is inventories—materials that are held in storage awaiting use in production or for sale to customers. Inventories are typically very large. In 1998, for example, the value of inventories in retail industries was $335 billion, compared to the value of monthly final retail sales of business of only $229 billion. In other words, there was $1.46 worth of goods and services in inventory for every $1 of goods sold each month.

Inventory investment is equal to the change in the stock of goods in inventory. Firms hold inventories of intermediate goods used as inputs in production; this helps facilitate production by ensuring parts are available when they are needed. Similarly, stores hold inventories so that customers can obtain the goods they want without wait-

ing; otherwise, stores risk losing customers. Finally, gearing up a production facility and then closing it down as sales fluctuate can be costly, so firms find it profitable to produce at a more constant rate, adding to inventories when sales weaken and selling out of inventories when sales strengthen.

Inventory investment is the most volatile component of aggregate expenditures. One reason for this variability may again be the risk-averse behavior of firms and the impact of the availability of credit. When the economy enters a recession, firms often find that their net worth is decreased. They are less willing to make any kind of investment, including inventory investment. Where possible, they would like to "disinvest," or convert their assets tied up as inventories back into cash. By far, the easiest kind of disinvestment is to sell off inventories. When a business faces credit rationing, it may be forced to sell off its inventories to raise the

e-Insight

Investment in the New Economy

Investment is a key component of aggregate expenditures. In the old economy, investment conjured up an image of the construction of a new factory or office building, or the purchase of new equipment like a harvester or a metal stamping machine. Factories, office buildings, and equipment are part of the economy's capital stock, and the capital stock grows as firms and individuals undertake investment.

Increasingly, private investment spending has been on information-processing equipment and software. From just over 14 percent of total private fixed investment in 1980, this category had grown to represent almost 27 percent of total private investment by 1999. Computers and software are two of the major forms this investment has taken. As the chart shows, investments in computers and software have grown as a fraction of total private fixed investment. The growth in investment in software has been particularly dramatic. From only about 2 percent of total investment in 1980, software now represents over 11 percent of all investment spending.

In the new economy, computers and software are not the only types of capital that have grown in importance. Capital

Increasingly, private investment spending has been on information-processing equipment and software.

requisite capital. And even if it is not yet forced to sell off its inventories, it may fear future credit rationing and in anticipation, seek to reduce its inventories.

Often, as the economy goes into a recession, or simply slows down, inventories build up "involuntarily." Retail stores, for instance, make orders based on expected sales; if the sales fail to materialize, the store holds the unsold merchandise as inventories. This unintended inventory accumulation can feed back quickly into production, as stores reduce their factory orders in response to their larger than desired inventories. Lower orders lead quickly to cutbacks in production. The cutbacks in production as firms try to restore inventories to normal size relative to sales are referred to as *inventory corrections*. Cyclical variabilities induced by inventories are called *inventory cycles*.

WRAP-UP

Determinants of Investment

1. Investment spending will depend negatively on the real interest rate.

2. Shifts in the investment schedule can be caused by changes in credit availability, changes in risk, or changes in expectations about future returns.

3. Fluctuations in current economic conditions can affect current investment by altering firms' expectations about future sales.

is increasingly *intangible*. The ability of firms to compete depends increasingly on their ability to innovate. A firm's organizational practices, its research capabilities, its reputation, and its human resources are critical to its success in a rapidly changing business environment. One measure of these intangible assets is provided by the relationship between the firm's market value and the cost of replacing its tangible capital (its plants, equipment, and structures). This ratio has risen markedly for U.S. firms, one more indication of the importance of intangibles in the new economy.

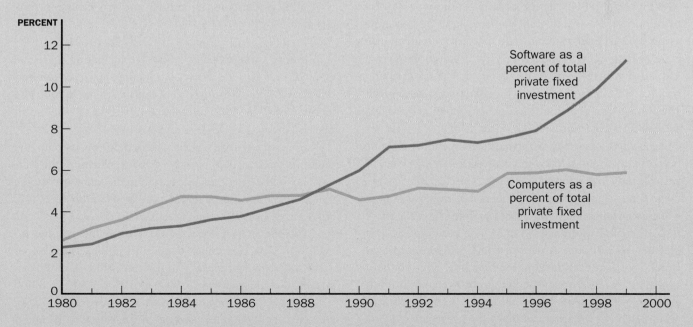

Investment in Computers and Software

Macroeconomic Implications of Investment

Three important macroeconomic implications result from this discussion of investment spending. First, we have identified another reason for the positive slope of the aggregate expenditures schedule: as current output rises, firms will increase investment spending, whereas if current output falls, they will scale back investment plans. So the positive slope of the schedule arises because as income increases, both consumption and investment expenditures will rise.

Second, investment depends on the real interest rate; at each level of income, a rise in the real interest rate will lower investment. A higher real interest rate lowers total aggregate expenditures, shifting the aggregate expenditures schedule down. A reduction in the real interest rate will shift the schedule up.

Third, changing perceptions of risk or of future economic conditions, as well as changes in credit availability, affect investment expenditures. These factors help account for the volatility of investment, and they can be added to our list of factors that shift the aggregate expenditures schedule.

Government Purchases

The third component of aggregate expenditures is government purchases. At this point in our analysis, it is useful to assume government purchases do not vary with income but instead are simply fixed, say, at $1,000 billion. Earlier, we learned that taxes vary with income, so the government's revenue will rise and fall as income fluctuates. Because the government can borrow (run a deficit) when tax revenues are less than expenditures, and repay its debt when tax revenues exceed expenditures, government spending does not need to move in lockstep with tax revenues. In later chapters we will study in greater detail the role of fiscal policy, government expenditures, and tax policies. For now, though, we will assume government purchases are fixed (in real terms).

Government purchases (G) are one component of aggregate expenditures. An increase in G will raise aggregate expenditures at each level of total income. This shifts the aggregate expenditures schedule up by the amount of the increase in G. This is shown in Figure 29.10. Equilibrium again occurs at the intersection of the aggregate expenditures schedule and the 45-degree line.

Calculating Equilibrium Output: An Example

Suppose we have the following information on a closed economy. Each row gives the level of output (Y) in the first column and the levels of taxes (T), consumption (C), investment (I), and government purchases (G) at that level of output. Investment and government purchases are assumed to be the same, regardless of the level of output, but both taxes and consumption rise with income.

Y	T	C	I	G
1,000	200	1,000	1,200	1,200
2,000	450	1,600	1,200	1,200
3,000	700	2,200	1,200	1,200
4,000	950	2,800	1,200	1,200
5,000	1,200	3,400	1,200	1,200
6,000	1,450	4,000	1,200	1,200
7,000	**1,700**	**4,600**	**1,200**	**1,200**
8,000	1,950	5,200	1,200	1,200
9,000	2,200	5,800	1,200	1,200
10,000	2,450	6,400	1,200	1,200
11,000	2,700	7,000	1,200	1,200
12,000	2,950	7,600	1,200	1,200
13,000	3,200	8,200	1,200	1,200

Equilibrium output occurs at the point where Y is equal to $C + I + G$. Using the information in the table, we can add up C, I, and G. If we do this, we find that equilibrium output is 7,000. At this output level, consumption is 4,600, investment is 1,200, and government purchases are 1,200, so $C + I + G = 4,600 + 1,200 + 1,200 = 7,000 = Y$.

Suppose G increases to 1,600. Recalculating aggregate expenditures ($C + I + G$) at each income level, we can find that the new equilibrium level of output will be 8,000. The increase of G by 400 increased Y by 1,000, so the multiplier is 2.5.

We also know that when taxes depend on income, the multiplier is equal to $1/(1 - (1 - t)MPC)$, where t is the marginal tax rate. Using the information in the table, we can see that as income rises by 1,000, say, from 7,000 to 8,000, taxes increase by 250, one fourth as much. So $t = .25$. As total income increases by 1,000, disposable income increases by 750. How much does consumption rise? It goes up by 600. For example, as Y goes from 7,000 to 8,000, disposable income goes from $7,000 - 1,700 = 5,300$, to $8,000 - 1,950 = 6,050$. Consumption rises from 4,600 to 5,200, an increase of 600. The marginal propensity to consume is the increase in C per dollar increase in disposable income,

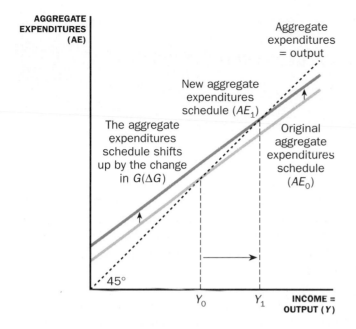

FIGURE 29.10 *The Effect of an Increase in Government Purchases*

Government purchases (*G*) are one of the components of aggregate expenditures. An increase in government purchases shifts the aggregate expenditures schedule up by the amount of the increase. Because of the multiplier effect, the increase in equilibrium output, $Y_1 - Y_0$, is greater than the increase in government purchases, ΔG.

or $600/750 = .8$. Using these values, we can calculate the multiplier to be $1/(1 - (1 - .25) \times .8) = 1/(1 - .75 \times 8) = 1/(1 - .6) = 1/.4 = 2.5$, exactly the same value we found directly by finding the new equilibrium after an increase in *G*.

The Effects of International Trade

The analysis so far has ignored the important role of international trade. This is appropriate for a closed economy, an economy that neither imports nor exports, but not for an open economy, one actively engaged in international trade. Today, the United States and other industrialized economies are very much open economies.

The effect of exports and imports on aggregate expenditures is straightforward. Recall that what we are concerned

with here is total purchases of *domestically* produced output. GDP is the sum of the total output of final goods and services produced within a given geographic area in a year. Consequently, exports of U.S.-produced goods to other countries represent an additional component of aggregate expenditures, just like consumption, investment, and government expenditures. However, some of what households, firms, and the government purchase are goods made abroad. To get the total demand for domestically produced goods, we must subtract the value of imports from the total. The net effect of international trade on aggregate expenditures is measured by net exports, exports minus imports.

Just as we did when discussing the other components of aggregate expenditures, we need to ask whether net exports depend on income (and if so, how), and we need to ask what factors might shift net exports at each level of income.

Imports

When households' incomes rise, they buy not only more American-made consumer goods but also more goods from abroad. We can draw an **import function** in much the same way that we illustrated the relationship between disposable income and consumption with the consumption function. The import function shows the levels of imports corresponding to different levels of income. For simplicity, we assume that imports are bought by consumers and that disposable income determines the level of imports. The import function is depicted in Figure 29.11.

Imports increase with income. The **marginal propensity to import** gives the amount of each extra dollar of income that is spent on imports. If the marginal propensity

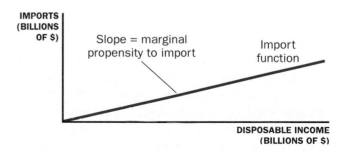

FIGURE 29.11 *The Import Function*

Imports increase steadily as disposable income rises. The slope of the import function is equal to the marginal propensity to import.

Thinking Like an Economist

Incentives and the Real After-Tax Rate of Interest

In other chapters we have emphasized that real values determine incentives. Thus, decisions to save and invest respond to real interest rates. So far, deriving the real interest rate from the nominal interest rate has been straightforward: subtract the rate of inflation from the nominal interest rate. But for simplicity we have ignored another important factor, the effect of taxation. In the absence of taxes on interest income, a nominal interest rate of 2 percent and 0 percent inflation yields the same real return as a nominal interest rate of 6 percent and 4 percent inflation. If nominal interest income is taxed, the relationship between the nominal interest rate, inflation, and the real interest rate is more complicated.

Suppose that nominal interest income is taxed at a 25 percent rate. If inflation is 0 percent and the nominal interest rate is 2 percent, the *after-tax* nominal return would be the 2 percent return minus the taxes (.25 × 2 percent = .5 percent), leaving an after-tax nominal return of 1.5 percent. With 0 percent inflation, this is also the real return.

Now consider the situation when inflation rises to 4 percent. If the nominal interest rate were to rise to 6 percent, the after-tax return would be 6 percent minus taxes (.25 × 6 per-

cent = 1.5), leaving a nominal after-tax return of 4.5 percent. Since inflation was 4 percent, the *real after-tax* return is only .5 percent! Even though the nominal interest rate rose by the same amount as inflation rose, the real after-tax return fell.

To maintain the same 1.5 percent real after-tax return that was obtained with 0 percent inflation, the nominal interest rate would need to rise to 7.33 percent when inflation increases to 4 percent. With a nominal return of 7.33 percent, the nominal after-tax return would be 5.5 percent, and the real after-tax return would be 1.5 percent. The nominal interest rate must rise more than one for one with increases in inflation in order to maintain the same real return. In this example, if inflation increases 4 percent, the nominal interest rate must rise 5.33 percent.

The relationship would be different if countries designed their tax systems to tax real returns rather than nominal returns. In this case with 4 percent inflation, a nominal interest rate of 6 percent would yield a real before-tax return of 2 percent and an after-tax return of 1.5 percent, the same after-tax return as was earned with 0 percent inflation and a 2 percent nominal interest rate.

---

to import is .1, then imports rise by $100 if income rises by $1,000 ($100 is .1 × $1,000). The marginal propensity to import is given by the slope of the import function.

Imports also depend on the relative cost of foreign and domestically produced goods. If the price of a Toyota 4-Runner produced in Japan rises relative to the cost of an American-produced Ford Explorer, consumers in the aggregate purchase fewer 4-Runners and more Explorers.

The relative price of goods produced abroad and goods produced domestically is affected by the exchange rate. If the dollar rises in value, foreign goods become less expensive. Households tend to increase their purchases of goods produced abroad and imports rise. One reason for the big drop in U.S. net exports in the mid-1980s was because the

value of the dollar rose significantly. As foreign goods became less expensive, imports rose. Changes in the exchange rate affect imports at each level of income. A rise in the value of the dollar shifts the import function up; a fall in the value of the dollar shifts the import function down.

Exports

What foreigners buy from the United States depends on their income; it does not depend directly on income in the United States. Exports also may depend on other factors such as the marketing efforts of American firms and the prices of American goods relative to foreign goods. To simplify, we will assume that income in other countries does not depend on what happens in the United States. Exports, like government purchases, will not vary with U.S. income.

Exports minus imports (net exports) is sometimes referred to as the *balance of trade*. As incomes increase, imports rise while exports remain unchanged. This means that net exports fall as income rises. This fact helps to explain the decline in U.S. net exports in the last half of the 1990s (Figure 29.12). With the U.S. economy booming, and many other countries in recession, our imports rose significantly, reducing net exports.

Changes in the exchange rate affect exports for the same reason that imports depend on the exchange rate. If the dollar rises in value, U.S. goods become relatively more expensive. Foreigners buy fewer American goods, and exports will fall. Since this change in exchange rate makes foreign goods relatively cheaper, our imports rise, so net exports fall. Conversely, a fall in the value of the dollar will stimulate exports and reduce imports, leading to an increase in net exports.

Macroeconomic Implications of Net Exports

Net exports affect the aggregate expenditures schedule in two ways. First, net exports alter the slope of the schedule. As incomes rise, imports also rise, and this acts to reduce the net increase in expenditures on domestically produced goods and services. While aggregate expenditures rise with income because of the increases in consumption and investment, the slope of the schedule will be flatter in an open economy. If the marginal propensity to import is small, the slope of the aggregate expenditures schedule is reduced only slightly; if the marginal propensity to import is large, as it might be in a very open economy, the slope of the schedule will be reduced significantly.

Second, factors such as exchange rates and income developments in other countries can affect net exports and lead to shifts in the aggregate expenditures schedule. A recession in Europe will reduce U.S. exports and shift the aggregate

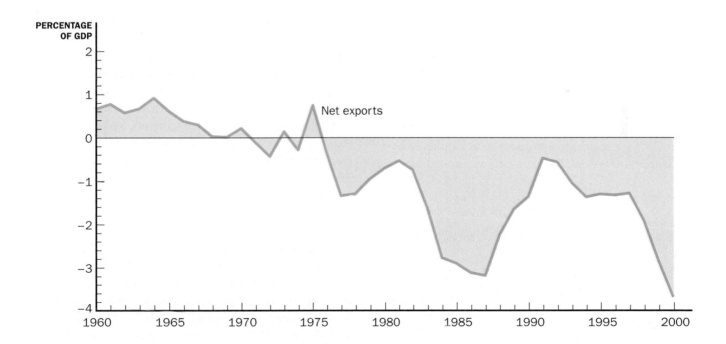

FIGURE 29.12 *Net Exports as a Percentage of GDP*

In the 1980s, the U.S. trade deficit deteriorated because of falling national saving due to the federal budget deficit (see Chapter 25). During the last few years, strong growth in U.S. incomes, together with recessions in many countries we trade with, has caused U.S. exports to fall and imports to rise, producing a fall in net exports.

SOURCES: *ERP* (2001), Table B-103, and Bureau of Economic Analysis, Department of Commerce.

expenditures schedule for the United States down. In the absence of any other change, equilibrium output in the United States will fall. In the late 1990s, the financial crises and subsequent recessions in many Asian economies raised the concern that the resulting fall in U.S. exports would lead to a recession here. The drop in exports shifted the aggregate expenditures schedule for the United States down. Fortunately, not everything else remained unchanged, and this country continued to enjoy an economic boom. This illustrates an important point—we often use our theoretical models to illustrate what would happen if one factor changed, holding other things constant. This approach is useful in that it allows us to understand clearly the effects of changes in each factor. In the real world, many of the things we assumed constant are also changing, and we need to use our models to analyze simultaneous changes in many factors.

Putting International Trade into the Equation

When we add exports (X) and imports (M), aggregate expenditures are given by

$$AE = C + I + G + X - M.$$

Imports are related to disposable income by the import function

$$M = MPI \times Y_{\mathrm{d}},$$

where MPI is the marginal propensity to import. Exports are assumed to be fixed. Hence, aggregate expenditures are

$$AE = a + MPC \times (1 - t) \times Y + I + G + X - MPI \times (1 - t) \times Y.$$

Since aggregate expenditures equal income, in equilibrium,

$$Y = (a + I + G + X)/[1 - (1 - t)(MPC - MPI)],$$

so the multiplier is

$$1/[1 - (1 - t)(MPC - MPI)].$$

If $t = .25$, $MPC = .8$, and $MPI = .1$, the multiplier is

$$1/[1 - .75(.8 - .1)] = 2.1.$$

This is smaller than the value we found earlier in the absence of trade (2.5).

Aggregate Expenditures and the Real Interest Rate

Our discussion of the components of aggregate expenditures has highlighted a number of factors in addition to national income that affect expenditures. Expectations about future income, wealth, the real interest rate, and the exchange rate can alter aggregate expenditures at each level of national income. One of the critical factors affecting the aggregate expenditures schedule is the real rate of interest, as this constitutes a key channel through which monetary policy affects economic activity. Changes in the real interest rate affect investment spending and household purchases of new homes and durable goods like automobiles. They also affect the exchange rate and net exports.

The Real Interest Rate and Net Exports

In today's open, international economy, one of the most important ways that interest rate changes affect the level of economic activity is by affecting the exchange rate. If U.S. interest rates fall, and the decrease is not matched by other countries, the lower yields on financial assets in the United States make these assets less attractive to both foreigners and Americans. The demand for dollars will fall as investors shift their money out of American assets and into foreign assets. This decreased demand for dollars lowers the dollar exchange rate—one dollar will now buy fewer yen, or euros, or pounds, than before. A lower value of the dollar makes American goods less expensive abroad—and foreign goods more expensive here. Exports will rise and imports fall. For example, between August 1998 and January 1999, the yen-dollar exchange rate fell from 145 yen per dollar to 113, a fall of approximately 22 percent. To a Japanese consumer, a $100 American-made shirt fell in price by 22 percent, from 14,500 yen to 11,300 yen. And to an American consumer, the price of Japanese goods increased by 28 percent.[6] A CD player that sold in Japan for 25,000 yen—and cost 25,000 yen/145 = $172—would now cost Americans 25,000

---

[6]It might seem that the price of Japanese goods to Americans should increase by the same 22 percent that prices faced by Japanese consumers fell. The reason for the difference is the fact that the cost of 1 yen to a holder of dollars goes from 1/145 to 1/113, a rise of 28 percent. The cost of a dollar to a holder of yen goes from 145 to 113, a fall of 22 percent.

yen/113 = $221. (In practice, the changes were somewhat less dramatic, since in the short run, exporters and importers "absorb" some of the variation in exchange rates to reduce the variability of prices faced by consumers.) As exports increase and imports decrease, *net* exports increase.

WRAP-UP

The Real Interest Rate and Equilibrium-Output

An increase in the real interest rate reduces investment spending and household purchases of durables and new homes. It also raises the value of the dollar and lowers net exports. This shifts the aggregate expenditures schedule down.

The Real Interest Rate and the Aggregate Expenditures Schedule

Each of the aggregate expenditures schedules used in this chapter was drawn for a given real rate of interest. A change in the real rate of interest shifts the schedule. It does so through two channels. First, changes in the real rate of interest affect investment spending. A decrease in the real rate, for instance, raises investment spending as firms find it less costly to borrow to undertake investment projects and as credit becomes more available. Second, the exchange rate responds to interest rate changes. A change in the exchange rate alters the relative price of foreign and domestic goods, leading to changes in net exports. If a fall in interest rates lowers the exchange rate, net exports will rise. The increase in net exports reinforces the effect of a lower real rate of interest on investment. These changes shift the aggregate expenditures schedule upward. The new level of equilibrium output is higher.

The effect of a change in the real rate of interest on the aggregate expenditures schedule is depicted in panel A of Figure 29.13. At the initial real interest rate r_0, the aggregate expenditures schedule is $AE(r_0)$. This schedule crosses the 45-degree line at a level of output equal to Y_0. If the real interest rate falls to r_1, the aggregate expenditures schedule shifts up to $AE(r_1)$ as investment and net exports increase at each level of national income. Equilibrium output rises to Y_1. A lower real interest rate leads to higher equilibrium output. This negative relationship between the real interest rate and output is shown in panel B of the figure.

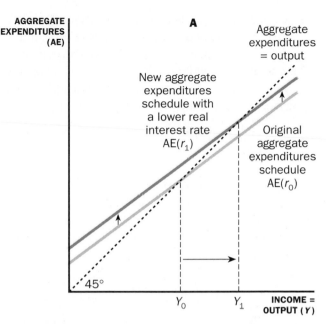

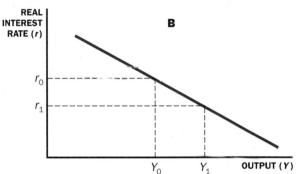

FIGURE 29.13 *Deriving the Relationship Between the Real Interest Rate and Equilibrium Output*

Panel A shows the effect of a decrease in the real interest rate from r_0 to r_1 on the aggregate expenditures schedule. It increases equilibrium output from Y_0 to Y_1. Panel B traces out the equilibruim values of aggregate expenditures (and output) corresponding to different real interest rates.

Review and Practice

Summary

1. Income-expenditure analysis shows how the equilibrium level of output in the economy is determined when firms produce to meet demand.

2. Equilibrium output is determined by the intersection of the 45-degree line and the aggregate expenditures schedule. The aggregate expenditures schedule shows the level of expenditures at each level of national income, while the 45-degree line represents the points where aggregate expenditures equal output.

3. Shifts in the aggregate expenditures schedule give rise to changes in equilibrium output. The magnitude of the increase in output resulting from an upward shift in the schedule depends on the slope of the schedule. Much of macroeconomic analysis focuses on what determines the slope of the schedule, what causes shifts in the schedule, and how government policies affect the schedule.

4. Aggregate expenditures are the sum of consumption, investment, government purchases, and net exports.

5. Consumption increases as disposable income increases, and the relationship between consumption and income is called the consumption function. The amount by which consumption increases when disposable income increases by a dollar is called the marginal propensity to consume.

6. The multiplier is the factor by which a change in investment or government purchases must be multiplied to get the resulting change in national output. The multiplier is larger if the marginal propensity to consume is large.

7. If tax revenues rise with income, the aggregate expenditures schedule is flattened and the multiplier is reduced. Taxes act as an automatic stabilizer. Increases in government purchases shift the schedule up.

8. Imports increase with income. The relationship between imports and income is called the import function; its slope is the marginal propensity to import. Exports are determined by factors in other countries. Trade reduces the multiplier, because as income increases, some of it goes to purchase foreign rather than domestic goods. Both imports and exports depend on the exchange rate. A fall in the value of the dollar increases exports and reduces imports; this increase in net exports shifts the aggregate expenditures schedule up.

9. Changes in the real interest rate affect investment, the exchange rate, and net exports. A rise in the real interest rate reduces investment and net exports, leading to a downward shift in the aggregate expenditures sched-

ule. Consequently, the level of output consistent with equilibrium falls as the real interest rate rises.

Key Terms

aggregate expenditures schedule
income-expenditure analysis
multiplier
aggregate consumption function
marginal propensity to consume
marginal propensity to save
plant and equipment investment
inventory investment
residential investment
import function
marginal propensity to import

Review Questions

1. What is the aggregate expenditures schedule? What are the components of aggregate expenditures?

2. If output is determined by aggregate expenditures, explain how the equilibrium level of output is determined. Why are points on the aggregate expenditures schedule above the 45-degree line not sustainable? Why are points on the aggregate expenditures schedule below the 45-degree line not sustainable?

3. What is the consumption function? What determines its slope? What is the import function? What determines its slope?

4. What factors might cause shifts in the aggregate expenditures schedule? List at least four.

5. How is the multiplier affected by the marginal propensity to consume? By the marginal tax rate? By the marginal propensity to import?

6. What is the relationship between the exchange rate and net exports? What is the relationship between the interest rate and the exchange rate?

7. Why does an increase in the real rate of interest lower equilibrium output?

Problems

1. In the economy of Consumerland, national income and consumption are related in this way:

National income	$1,500	$1,600	$1,700	$1,800	$1,900
Consumption	$1,325	$1,420	$1,515	$1,610	$1,705

Calculate national saving at each level of national income. What is the marginal propensity to consume in Consumerland? What is the marginal propensity to save? If national income rose to $2,000, what do you predict consumption and saving would be?

2. To the economy of Consumerland, add the fact that investment will be $180 at every level of output. Graph the consumption function and the aggregate expenditures schedule for this simple economy (no government or net exports). What determines the slope of the aggregate expenditures schedule? What is the equilibrium output?

3. Calculate the effect of a one-dollar increase in investment on output for each of the following economies:

(a) A simple consumption and investment economy where the *MPC* is .9

(b) An economy with government but no foreign trade, where the *MPC* is .9 and the tax rate is .3

(c) An economy with an *MPC* of .9, a tax rate of .3, and a marginal propensity to import of .1

4. If at each level of disposable income, saving increases, what does this imply about what has happened to the consumption function? What will be the consequences for the equilibrium level of output?

5. Under which theory of consumption would a temporary tax cut be predicted to have the largest effect on consumption? Under which theory would a perma-

nent rise in Social Security benefits have the largest immediate impact on consumption?

6. Which theory of consumption predicts that aggregate saving will depend on the proportion of retired and young people in the population? What is the relationship? Which theories predict consumption will not vary a great deal according to whether the economy is in a boom or a recession? Why?

7. If the government made it easier for people to borrow money, perhaps by enacting programs to help them get loans, would you expect consumption spending to become more or less sensitive to current income? Why? How is the marginal propensity to consume affected? How is the multiplier affected?

8. Suppose an eighty-year-old and a twenty-year-old each receive lottery winnings of $1 million. According to future-oriented consumption theories, which one will increase consumption the most? Why?

9. Suppose the consumption function is given by $C = a + bY_d$ where a and b are constants (b is the marginal propensity to consume), and Y_d is disposable income, equal to $Y - T$. Taxes vary with income and are equal to $t_0 + tY$ where t_0 and t are constants (t is the marginal tax rate).

(a) What is the effect on consumption of a $1 change in total income?

(b) What is the effect on saving of a $1 change in total income?

(c) Show how the saving line in Figure 29.6 is affected by the tax rate t.

Chapter 30

Aggregate Demand and Inflation

Chairman Greenspan

Key Questions

1. How is equilibrium in the capital market affected when output and employment fluctuate?

2. What is a monetary policy rule? How does the central bank's policy rule depend on inflation?

3. What is the aggregate demand–inflation, or ADI, curve? How does it depend on monetary and fiscal policy?

4. What causes the ADI curve to shift?

5. What happens to GDP when the ADI curve shifts? What happens to inflation when the economy is not at full employment?

6. If cyclical unemployment rises, what forces might move the economy back to full employment?

*E*very six weeks, the members of the Federal Open Market Committee (FOMC), the policy-making committee of the Federal Reserve, gather in Washington, D.C. They come from across the nation to discuss the state of the economy and to make decisions that can determine the outlook for inflation and unemployment in the United States over the next several years. Stock markets can rise or fall in anticipation of decisions by the FOMC. On April 14, 2000, when the government released the latest figures suggesting inflation was rising, the Dow Jones industrial average fell 616 points, its largest one-day point loss ever, as investors feared the FOMC would raise interest rates. Nine months later on January 3, 2001, the Dow jumped 300 points and the Nasdaq 325 points when the FOMC cut interest rates. Investors know that if the economy booms and inflation rises, the Fed will increase interest rates; if the economy slows and inflation falls, the Fed will lower interest rates. These decisions by the FOMC affect the cost of credit for major corporations as well as for small family businesses. They affect the cost of car loans, student loans, and home mortgages. The importance of the FOMC for everyone in the economy has spawned a whole industry of "Fed watchers" who try to predict what the FOMC will do. Since 1986, the chair of the Federal Reserve has been Alan Greenspan, and Fed watchers have followed closely every speech and statement Greenspan makes for clues about future policy actions.

Macroeconomists want to understand the factors that determine GDP and inflation, and for that reason, macroeconomists must incorporate the Fed's behavior into their models. In Chapter 29, we learned that the economy's level of output (GDP) and employment is determined in the short run by the level of aggregate expenditure. We also learned that aggregate expenditures depend on the real rate of interest. We now need to bring inflation back into the picture so that we can understand the linkages between inflation, the real interest rate, and aggregate expenditures. Monetary policy plays a critical role in this story. This should not be surprising, since we learned in Chapter 25 that when the economy is at full employment, the average inflation rate is determined by monetary policy. In the United States, monetary policy is the responsibility of the Federal Reserve, our central bank.

651

Like central banks in many other countries, the Fed is concerned with keeping inflation low and stable. If aggregate expenditures rise relative to the economy's full-employment output, inflation will rise as firms, facing strong demand, can boost prices and as low unemployment leads to wage increases in excess of productivity gains that push up firms' costs. If output falls relative to potential, inflation will moderate. To keep inflation stable, central banks act to reduce output when inflation starts to rise and increase output when inflation falls.

In the previous two chapters, we focused on the first two of the four key concepts that will be used to understand short-run economic fluctuations—wages and prices do not adjust fast enough to keep the economy always at full employment. As a result, unemployment and output can fluctuate around the full-employment level, and equilibrium occurs where output equals aggregate expenditures. In this chapter, we bring into our analysis the third and fourth key concepts—there is a short-run trade-off between inflation and unemployment, and increases in inflation reduce aggregate spending. Doing so allows us to bring inflation into the picture. By the end of this chapter, you will have a simple framework that can be used to understand many important macroeconomic debates.

The Real Interest Rate and the Capital Market

In Chapter 29, we examined the components of aggregate expenditures—consumption, investment, government purchases, and net exports—and their determinants. We learned that the real interest rate is one of the main factors that influences aggregate expenditures. To simplify the analysis in this and the next two chapters, we will focus on the case of a closed economy. This allows us to ignore net exports and exchange rates. Despite the growing importance of international trade, the vast bulk of goods and services purchased in the United States are produced in the United States. Imports represent about 13 percent of GDP, while exports total about 11 percent. These are sizable fractions, and they have grown significantly during the past decade. However, we can still gain important insights into macroeconomics by initially restricting our focus to a closed economy. In Chapter 33 we will discuss how the lessons learned from a study of a closed economy need to be modified when we deal with an open economy.

In a closed economy, a higher real interest rate lowers aggregate expenditures through two primary channels: (1) higher interest rates reduce the profitability of investment, leading businesses to scale back investment projects; and (2) higher interest rates on consumer loans and mortgages cause households to reduce purchases of new homes and consumer durables such as automobiles.

When we discuss interest rates and monetary policy, it is natural to start with the capital market. We have already seen, in Chapter 24, how the real rate of interest balances saving and investment when the economy is at full employment. When the economy is not at full employment, saving and investment must still balance to ensure the capital market is in equilibrium. Saving and investment depend on both the real interest rate and the level of output. Figure 30.1 shows capital market equilibrium for two different levels of output. When the economy is producing at full employment, as we assumed in Part Two, the saving and investment schedules are given by S^f and I^f. (For simplicity, we have assumed saving does not vary with the real interest rate—that is why it is drawn as a vertical line.) The equilibrium real rate of interest is r_0. If output in the economy is less than its full-employment level, household income will be lower, and households will save less at each value of the real interest rate. This is shown by the saving schedule S_1, to the left of S^f. The leftward shift in the saving schedule occurs because the marginal propensity to consume is less than one—a one dollar decline in income reduces consumption by less than a dollar, which means that saving is also reduced. If there is no change in the investment schedule, the capital market will again be in equilibrium at an income level below full employment when the real interest rate rises to r_1.

However, investment will not remain the same if GDP drops. When output falls and the economy enters a recession, the investment schedule also will be affected. Declines in production lead to higher unemployment of labor *and* lower utilization of plant and equipment. This reduces the need for new investment, and firms are less likely to invest when the business outlook is bleak. The leftward shift in the investment schedule is depicted by the investment schedule I_1 in Figure 30.1. In this case, the equilibrium real interest rate is r_2. Depending on the relative shifts of the savings and investment schedules, the new equilibrium real interest rate may be greater or less than r_0.

When the economy is at full employment, equilibrium in the capital market determines the full-employment real

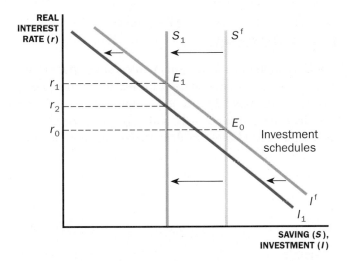

FIGURE 30.1 *Capital Market Equilibrium at Different Income and Interest Rates*

A fall in income from Y^f to Y_1 will shift the savings line to the left, from S^f to S_1. If the investment schedule remains unchanged, capital market equilibrium will occur at a higher real interest rate, r_1, and lower level of real income. A decline in output, however, is likely to shift the investment schedule to the left as firms reduce planned investment spending at each value of the real rate of interest. If the new investment schedule is I_1, the equilibrium real rate of interest is r_2.

interest rate. When output and the real interest rate depart from their full-employment values, what determines their values? To answer this question, we turn now to the connection between inflation, spending, and monetary policy.

The Aggregate Demand—Inflation Curve

The effect that inflation has on aggregate expenditures, and hence on equilibrium output, depends critically on monetary policy. In Chapter 28, we listed the effect inflation has on aggregate expenditures as the fourth key concept for understanding short-run fluctuations of the economy. Now we need to explore this relationship in more detail. Monetary policy plays an important role in determining how changes in inflation affect aggregate expenditures, so we need to focus on Fed policy.

The Fed's Policy Rule

The key idea is that the Fed is concerned about inflation, and it knows that as unemployment falls, inflation tends to rise (our third key concept). As inflation rises, the Fed acts to reduce aggregate expenditures since this will slow the economy down and lessen any upward pressure on inflation. The Fed can affect aggregate expenditures by influencing the real interest rate. An increase in the real interest rate, for example, will reduce investment spending. As inflation falls, the Fed acts to lower the real interest rate to boost aggregate expenditures. These changes in aggregate expenditures affect the economy's equilibrium level of output.

The Fed's concern with inflation is illustrated by the frequent warnings Greenspan gives. For example, in testifying before the Committee on Banking and Financial Services of the U.S. House of Representatives on July 22, 1999, Greenspan said, "The already shrunken pool of job-seekers and considerable strength of aggregate demand suggest that the Federal Reserve will need to be especially alert to inflation risks. Should . . . demand growth persist or strengthen, the economy could overheat. That would engender inflationary pressures and put the sustainability of this unprecedented period of remarkable growth in jeopardy. . . . If new data suggest it is likely that the pace of cost and price increases will be picking up, the Federal Reserve will have to act promptly and forcefully. . . ." [1] Shortly after issuing this warning, the Federal Reserve raised its target for the federal funds rate, the key nominal interest rate it uses to implement monetary policy.

The Fed's systematic reaction to the economy is called a **monetary policy rule.** A policy rule is a description of how the Fed moves the interest rate in response to economic conditions. We will assume a very simple policy rule, one in which the Fed reacts to the rate of inflation. In actuality, the Fed does not react only to inflation—for example, a financial crisis might cause the Fed to lower interest rates even though inflation has not changed, or the Fed might be concerned that economic growth is slowing. For instance, on January 3, 2001, the FOMC cut its interest rate target. In explaining its actions, the FOMC stated that "these actions were taken in light of further weakening of sales and production, and in

---

[1] The complete text of Greenspan's most recent testimony before Congress can be found at http://www.federalreserve.gov/boarddocs/testimony/2001/.

the context of lower consumer confidence, tight conditions in some segments of financial markets, and high energy prices sapping household and business purchasing power. Moreover, inflation pressures remain contained."

When the Fed responds to other such factors, the policy rule linking the interest rate to inflation changes. A given policy rule reflects the adjustment of interest rates to inflation; a change in the policy rule occurs when, at a given level of inflation, the Fed sets a different interest rate than before, as it did in January 2001. The Fed follows a policy rule of raising the real interest rate when inflation rises because of the effect output has on inflation. If inflation starts to rise and the Fed wants to counteract this increase, it must reduce output, increasing cyclical unemployment. It does so because higher cyclical unemployment reduces inflation. When GDP falls below potential, inflation slows, and the Fed can act to reduce the real interest rate, increasing aggregate expenditures and moving the economy back toward full employment.

This chain of linkages from inflation to monetary policy to aggregate expenditures raises a question. How does the Fed actually affect the real interest rate? In Chapter 25 we studied the instruments of the Fed and saw how the Fed was able to closely control the *nominal* interest rate by affecting the supply of reserves in the federal funds market. It is important to keep in mind that the Fed directly controls reserve supply; by adjusting reserve supply it can exercise close control over the nominal interest rate. But to influence aggregate expenditures, it must affect the real interest rate. The real interest rate is the nominal interest rate adjusted for inflation. This means the Fed must move the nominal interest rate in the same direction as inflation, but by more. For instance, if inflation rises by 1 percentage point, say, from 3 to 4 percent, the Fed must increase the nominal interest by *more* than 1 percentage point to increase the real interest rate. Only then can it affect the real rate of interest. For now, we will simplify our analysis by postponing discussion of the details of the linkage between Fed actions and the real interest rate until Chapter 32.[2]

---

[2] These details will be critical, however, so we will need to return to them. We have already seen from the full-employment model that the economy's full-employment real interest rate does not depend on monetary policy (see Chapter 24). This means that the Fed's actions affect the real interest rate only in the short run when the economy can fluctuate around full employment.

Inflation and Aggregate Expenditures

Our discussion of the Fed's policy rule leads to the following conclusion: As inflation rises, the real interest rate rises, and aggregate expenditures and output fall; as inflation falls, the real interest rate falls, and aggregate expenditures and output rise. This means that inflation and output move in opposite directions; they have a negative relationship. This can be summarized in the following set of linkages:

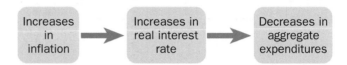

This negative relationship between inflation and spending is called the **aggregate demand–inflation curve,** or the ADI curve, and is shown in Figure 30.2. Output (GDP) is on the horizontal axis; inflation is on the vertical axis. The ADI curve in Figure 30.2 shows that equilibrium output will equal

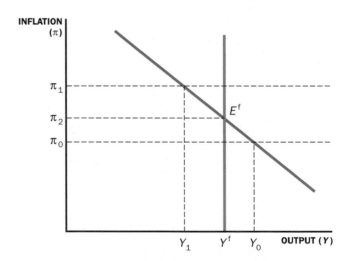

FIGURE 30.2   *Equilibrium Output and the ADI Curve*

For each rate of inflation, the ADI curve shows the economy's equilibrium level of output. If inflation is π_0, an output level of Y_0 is consistent with equilibrium; at Y_0, aggregate expenditures equal output. At a higher inflation rate such as π_1, the real interest rate is higher, aggregate expenditures are lower, and the equilibrium level of output is only Y_1. The vertical line at Y^f denotes full-employment output.

Y_0 if the rate of inflation is equal to π_0. At this output and inflation combination, aggregate expenditures equal output.

Now suppose the inflation rate rises to π_1. This rise in inflation leads the Fed to boost the nominal interest rate enough to raise the real rate of interest. This higher real interest rate leads firms to scale back investment spending. Fewer projects look profitable now that the real interest rate is higher, and firms may find it more difficult to raise funds to finance their investment projects. Households, seeing that they face higher interest rates for car loans and home mortgages, also reduce their spending. Some households may decide they can no longer afford the new car they had planned to buy; other households may opt for a less expensive car than before. As a result of all these individual decisions by firms and households, total aggregate expenditures fall. Through the multiplier process, equilibrium GDP declines. This is why the slope of the ADI curve is negative.

WRAP-UP

The Aggregate Demand–Inflation (ADI) Curve

shows for each value of inflation, the level of equilibrium output determined by income-expenditure analysis. Higher rates of inflation are associated with a lower level of equilibrium output because real interest rates increase, as a result of monetary policy actions, and reduce aggregate expenditures.

What Determines the Slope of the ADI Curve?

When we use a demand and supply framework to analyze how price and quantity are determined, both the positions and the slopes of the demand and supply curves are important. If demand is inelastic, for example, and responds only a little to changes in price, then a shift in the supply curve will have a large impact on the equilibrium price and only a small impact on the equilibrium quantity. Similarly, the adjustment of inflation and output to economic disturbances also will depend on whether the ADI curve is relatively flat or relatively steep. Changes in inflation cause large changes

in aggregate demand when the ADI curve is relatively flat. Changes in inflation result in only small changes in aggregate demand when the ADI curve is relatively steep.

The slope of the ADI curve in the closed economy is determined by two factors. First, it depends on how the central bank adjusts interest rates as inflation changes—that is, it depends on the monetary policy rule. If the central bank responds more strongly to inflation, a change in inflation will result in a larger change in the real rate of interest. A given change in inflation then leads to a larger fall in aggregate expenditures, making the ADI curve relatively flat. In contrast, if the reaction of the central bank to changes in inflation is weaker, the real interest rate rises by a smaller amount and aggregate expenditures decline less. As a result, the ADI curve will be relatively steep.

The second factor that affects the slope of the ADI curve is the impact the real interest rate has on the decisions households and firms make about how much to spend on consumption and investment. For example, if investment spending is very sensitive to the real interest rate, then the ADI curve will be quite flat. In other words, a given change in the real interest rate caused by inflation leads to a large change in aggregate expenditures. If investment and household spending do not respond much to changes in the real interest rate, the ADI curve will be steep.

What Can Shift the ADI Curve?

An ADI curve shows for each value of the rate of inflation, the equilibrium level of output. Movements in GDP caused by changes in inflation represent movements along a given ADI curve. Changes in inflation lead to changes in the real interest rate, which in turn produces changes in aggregate expenditures and output. Changes in any other factor that, for a given inflation rate, affects aggregate expenditures will *shift* the ADI curve. A primary example of a factor that will shift the curve is fiscal policy.

Fiscal Policy A change in government purchases or taxes alters the level of aggregate expenditures, and therefore output, for a given rate of inflation. An increase in government purchases, for example, raises aggregate expenditures at each level of the inflation rate; for every value of inflation, total expenditures, and therefore GDP, are higher, and this leads to an increase in equilibrium output. This effect of a rise in government purchases is shown in

International Perspective

How Do Other Central Banks React to Inflation?

The way the central bank reacts to inflation is a critical factor determining the slope of the ADI curve. One implication of this is that ADI curves in different countries may have different slopes because the central banks in those countries do not all react to inflation in the same way. Countries where the central bank responds strongly to inflation, pushing up interest rates at the slightest hint of inflation and cutting interest rates whenever inflation falls below target, will have flatter ADI curves than will countries with central banks that react more weakly to changes in inflation.

Economists Rich Clarida of Columbia and Jorgi Galí and Mark Gertler of New York University estimated how various central banks respond to inflation. For the Federal Reserve, the German Bundesbank, and the Bank of Japan, they find strong evidence consistent with the type of policy rule we have used to represent monetary policy. When inflation increases, these central banks raise nominal interest rates. If inflation rises by 1 percentage point, they raise the nominal interest rate by more than 1 percentage point to ensure the real interest rate rises. When inflation falls, they reduce the nominal interest rate more than one for one so that the real interest rate falls.

Clarida, Galí, and Gertler found that while the responses to inflation by these three central banks were similar, there were some differences. Of the three, the Bank of Japan responded the most strongly to changes in inflation. The Bundesbank showed the weakest reaction to inflation. From what we have learned about the factors that affect the slope of the ADI curve, these differences in policy rules among Germany, Japan, and the United States mean that the slopes of each country's ADI curve will differ. The strong response to inflation in Japan should produce a flatter ADI curve for that country than in Germany. However, we also learned that the policy rule is not the only factor that affects the ADI slope, so we also would need to know how sensitive spending is in each country to changes in the real interest rate before we could make a final prediction about how the ADI slopes might differ.

It is important to remember that policy rules describe how the central bank behaves. And these can change over time. In the United States, the Fed reacted much less strongly to inflation in the 1960s and 1970s, for example, than it has during the past fifteen years. And Germany is a member of the European monetary union, so its monetary policy is now conducted not by the Bundesbank but by the European Central Bank.

SOURCE: R. Clarida, J. Galí, and M. Gertler, "Monetary Policy Rules in Practice: Some International Evidence," *European Economic Review* 42, No. 6 (1998): 1033–1067.

Figure 30.3. The increase causes a rightward shift in the ADI curve. If the initial level of inflation was π_0, the initial level of output was Y_0. After the increase in government purchases, equilibrium output increases from Y_0 to Y_1. At the inflation rate π_0, output is now Y_1.

Changes in the Monetary Policy Rule

The position of the ADI curve also depends on monetary policy. We have already learned how the slope of the ADI curve is affected by the policy rule that describes how the central bank adjusts the real interest rate in response to changes in inflation. The slope of the ADI curve has built into it this automatic reaction by the central bank to changes in inflation. But we also can investigate what would happen if, at each rate of inflation, the central bank changed interest rates, that is, if the policy rule were to shift. For example, suppose the Fed decides to cut interest rates for a given rate of inflation. The Fed did just that in 2001 when it was concerned that the U.S. economy was heading into a recession. How will such an interest rate cut affect the ADI curve?

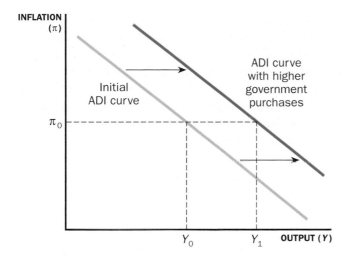

FIGURE 30.3 *The Effect of Government Purchases on Aggregate Expenditures and the ADI Curve*

An increase in government purchases raises aggregate expenditures at each value of the real rate of interest. This increase in aggregate expenditures increases equilibrium output. At the initial inflation rate π_0, this change represents an increase in output from Y_0 to Y_1. The rise in government purchases causes the ADI curve to shift to the right, as shown.

To answer this question, we need to work out the effects of the policy change on the real interest and then determine the impact on aggregate expenditures. Doing so will tell us whether equilibrium GDP has increased or decreased. Since we are holding the rate of inflation constant, if GDP has increased, the ADI curve has shifted to the right; if GDP has decreased, the ADI curve has shifted to the left.

We can now determine how the ADI curve is affected by the Fed's decision to cut interest rates at a given rate of inflation. First of all, this decision lowers the real rate of interest. We know that this in turn will boost aggregate expenditures by lowering the cost of credit to households and firms. The rise in aggregate expenditures leads to an increase in equilibrium GDP. Hence, we can conclude that the ADI curve shifts to the right when, at each rate of inflation, the Fed cuts nominal interest rates.

We could run through this argument in reverse to determine what happens to the ADI curve when the Fed raises interest rates at each rate of inflation. Since each rate of inflation now leads, through the actions of monetary policy, to a higher real interest rate, aggregate expenditures will

become lower. The fall in aggregate expenditures at each value of inflation lowers equilibrium GDP. This would shift the ADI curve to the left.

Other Factors That Can Shift the ADI Curve

While fiscal policy and monetary policy are key factors that can shift the ADI curve, similar effects occur if there are shifts in investment or consumption behavior at each value of the real interest rate. For example, the stock market boom of the 1990s boosted consumption spending for given levels of income and the real interest rate. This type of wealth effect on consumption spending increases total aggregate expenditures and the equilibrium level of output. Increased optimism about the future can lead to an increase in consumption and investment spending, increasing aggregate expenditures. For a given level of the real interest rate, equilibrium output would be higher, and this is represented by a rightward shift of the ADI curve.

If households and firms become more pessimistic about the future and scale back their spending, or if wealth falls due to a stock market collapse, for example, aggregate expenditures would fall at each level of the real interest rate. This results in a leftward shift in the ADI curve.

WRAP-UP

Factors That Shift the Aggregate Demand–Inflation (ADI) Curve

Factors that increase aggregate expenditures at each rate of inflation (and shift the ADI curve to the right) include

    Increases in government purchases,

    Decreases in taxes,

    Increase in wealth,

    Increase in business or household optimism, and

    A cut in interest rates at each rate of inflation.

Factors that decrease aggregate expenditures at each rate of inflation (and shift the ADI curve to the left) include

    Decreases in government purchases,

    Increases in taxes,

    Decrease in wealth,

    Increase in business or household pessimism, and

    An increase in interest rates at each rate of inflation.

Example of Factors That Have Shifted the ADI Curve

Over the last forty years, the ADI curve has been shifted by fiscal and monetary policy actions, as well as by changes in spending behavior by households and firms. Among the major factors that produced shifts in the ADI curve were

- The increase in government purchases associated with the Vietnam War in the 1960s;

- The increase in interest rates that resulted from the major shift in Fed policy in 1979, which was designed to bring inflation down from the high levels reached in the 1970s;

- The drop in consumption as households became more pessimistic at the time Iraq invaded Kuwait in 1990;

- The increase in consumer spending due to the wealth effects of the stock market boom of the late 1990s; and

- The increase in investment spending associated with the introduction of new information technologies in the 1990s.

For each of these examples, be sure that you can explain whether the ADI curve shifted to the left or right and why it did so.

Using the ADI Curve

We have now learned about one of the key components of the theory of economic fluctuations, the ADI curve. In the short run, firms adjust production in response to changes in demand at each level of inflation. That means that *the economy's short-run equilibrium GDP will be determined by the level of aggregate expenditures*. In Figure 30.2, the economy's equilibrium level of GDP will be Y_0 if the inflation rate is equal to π_0. If inflation is higher, say, at π_1, equilibrium output will be lower, at Y_1.

Figure 30.2 includes a vertical line at the economy's full-employment level of output, denoted as Y^f. The vertical line at Y^f is called the **long-run aggregate supply curve.** As we know from Chapter 24, full-employment output, or potential GDP, is determined by the level of employment that occurs when labor demand and labor

supply are balanced and by the economy's stock of capital and its current level of technology. Full-employment output *does not depend on the rate of inflation*. For this reason, we have drawn the long-run aggregate supply curve as a vertical line at Y^f. In the long run, the full-employment model tells us that wages adjust to ensure the labor market clears and that the economy produces at full employment. At point E^f in the figure, the economy is at full employment with an inflation rate of π_2. At that point, the labor market is in equilibrium, and the level of aggregate expenditures is equal to the level of output produced at full employment. In the short run, however, wages and prices do not respond quickly enough to keep the labor market always in equilibrium at full employment. Employment and output fluctuate around their full-employment levels.

There are some markets in which prices do adjust rapidly—the stock market, or the market for gold and other commodities like wheat or oil—display rapid price movements as adjustments occur in response to shifts in demand and supply curves. But for most goods and services, whether sold by producers, wholesalers, or retailers, there is considerable rigidity in the adjustment of the rate at which wages and prices change. For now, we will assume that the inflation rate adjusts slowly in our short-run analysis of the product market and equilibrium output.

Output Effects of a Shift in the ADI Curve

Consider what happens in the short run if the ADI curve shifts to the left, as depicted in Figure 30.4 by the shift from ADI_0 to ADI_1. Suppose that the economy starts out with an inflation rate equal to π_0. We have drawn a horizontal line at this initial inflation rate, and we have labeled it the IA_0 (for inflation adjustment) curve. The initial equilibrium is at point E_0. A leftward shift in the ADI curve like that shown in the figure occurred in mid-1990 when American households became more pessimistic about the future and scaled back their consumption spending. Similarly, when Japan's financial sector collapsed in the early 1990s, households and firms reduced their spending. When the ADI curve shifts to ADI_1, the new equilibrium is at point E_1, where ADI_1 crosses the IA_0 line. At the inflation rate π_0, output falls from Y^f to Y_1 as firms will produce only the quantity they can sell. One result of the reduced output will be a decrease in the demand for labor. Because wages do not adjust quickly, this decrease in the demand

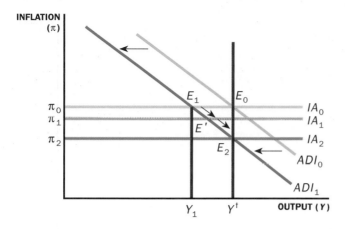

FIGURE 30.4 *A Recession Caused by a Shift in Aggregate Demand*

The full-employment level of output, Y^f, is given by the vertical long-run aggregate supply curve. The aggregate demand inflation curve ADI_0 intersects the long-run aggregate supply curve at the initial inflation rate π_0. If the aggregate demand inflation curve shifts to the left (to ADI_1), the economy will fall below the full-employment level of output. Equilibrium output will be given by the new ADI curve at the inflation rate π_0. The short run equilibrium output level is Y_1. Eventually, if the ADI curve remained at ADI_1, inflation would decline and the economy would move down the ADI curve until full employment is restored at E_2 at an inflation rate π_2.

for labor leads to a fall in employment and a rise in cyclical unemployment. The economy enters a recession.

This is not the end of the story, however. At point E_1, output is below potential, and there is cyclical unemployment. Because of the decline in production and the slack in the labor market, wages and prices increase more slowly, so inflation falls. With higher unemployment, workers must settle for smaller wage increases, and firms are less able to pass along cost increases by increasing their prices. This impact of cyclical unemployment on inflation was set out in Chapter 28 as the third of our four key concepts. We can represent the fall in inflation that occurs when the equilibrium is at E_1, with output below the full-employment level, by shifting the inflation adjustment line down, to IA_1. If the ADI curve remains in its new position (ADI_1), the economy will move down along the ADI curve as inflation falls. Equilibrium output rises because as inflation declines, the Fed cuts the interest rate. As a consequence, the real interest rate falls, helping to boost aggregate expenditures. This increases equilibrium output, so GDP rises. This represents a movement along ADI_1 to E'.

This process of adjustment continues, with inflation declining as long as GDP is below potential. The inflation adjustment curve continues to shift downward, and the economy moves back toward the full-employment equilibrium at E_2. Cyclical unemployment eventually will be eliminated, and the economy will have a lower rate of inflation, π_2. Even though this process restores full employment, in the short run, a period that may span a year or more, the economy will operate below capacity and at less than full employment.

CASE IN POINT

The Volcker Disinflation

In 1979 and 1980, there was widespread agreement that something should be done to halt inflation. At the time, inflation was at a postwar high and appeared to be moving even higher. The position of the economy was

Paul Volcker, former chairman, Federal Reserve Board

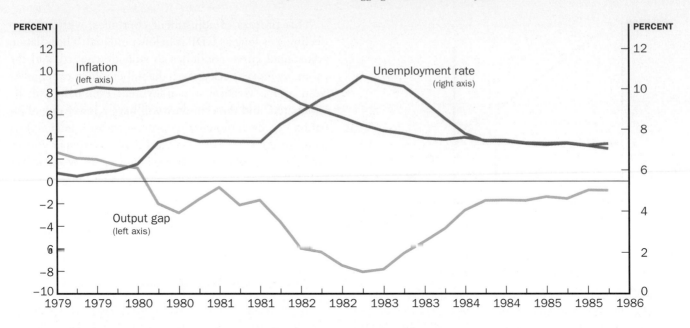

FIGURE 30.5   *The Output Gap, Unemployment Rate, and Inflation Rate in the 1980s*

Beginning in the late 1970s and early 1980s, the Federal Reserve Board, worried about runaway inflation, acted to restrict credit and thus consumption and investment. The decrease in aggregate demand beginning in late 1979 raised unemployment and lowered output below potential. The effects were so strong that they more than offset the increased expansionary effects from the 1981 tax cut. Inflation gradually declined. By 1985, the economy was back at full employment but with a lower rate of inflation.

SOURCES: Unemployment, *ERP* (2001), Table B-35; inflation, *ERP* (2001), Table B-64; output gap, Federal Reserve Board.

at a point such as E_0 in Figure 30.4—the economy was at full employment (the unemployment rate was 5.8 percent in 1979, about equal to estimates of full employment at the time), but the inflation rate was very high (over 8 percent in 1979 as measured by the GDP price deflator).

Paul Volcker, chair of the Federal Reserve Board at the time, pushed through a sharp increase in interest rates in order to choke off inflation. This represented a major shift in the monetary policy rule. As a result of the higher real interest rates caused by the Fed's actions, firms cut back their investments, and households cut back their purchases of items like new cars and homes. Interestingly, at the same time that the Fed was taking actions to restrict aggregate spending, fiscal policy was stimulating the economy. President Reagan cut taxes without cutting government expenditures by an offset-

ting amount. But the contractionary impact of monetary policy more than offset the expansionary effect of lower taxes, and the ADI curve shifted to the left, as shown in Figure 30.4.

Figure 30.5 shows the results of this shift in monetary policy. Output declined below potential GDP and the unemployment rate briefly hit a post–World War II high of 11 percent. However, the recession did succeed in curbing inflation, which fell from around 9 percent in 1980 to just 3.2 percent in 1983.[3] As the economy moved to its new equilibrium at point E_2 in Figure 30.4, unemployment fell and full-employment output was restored. ●

---

[3]The peak rate of inflation in 1980 was even higher if measured by the consumer price index (CPI), reaching 13 percent in 1980.

Thinking Like an Economist

Tough Trade-Offs

The Volcker policy to control inflation in late 1979 provides a graphic illustration of the trade-offs policymakers are often forced to make. Inflation had risen to unacceptable levels in the United States, but the only way the Federal Reserve could bring it down was to create a recession. It had to make a trade-off. The Federal Reserve could continue to let inflation remain at high levels, accepting the distortions that involved. Or it could act to lower inflation, knowing that the cost would be an increase in cyclical unemployment, with all the hardships that creates for the unemployed.

In weighing the costs of higher cyclical unemployment against the benefits of lower inflation, our model of fluctuations has an important implication. The rise in cyclical unemployment would be temporary. Eventually, the economy would return to full employment. That may not be much comfort to the workers who lost their jobs during the recessions in 1980 and 1982, but it was an important fact for policymakers to keep in mind. In assessing trade-offs, we need to know whether the consequences of one action are likely to be permanent or only temporary. If the Federal Reserve policymakers had believed its disinflation policies would lead to permanently higher unemployment, they might have made a different choice.

In April 1980, the federal funds rate peaked at over 17.5 percent (for comparison, in March 2001 the federal funds rate stood at 5 percent). Just two years earlier, in 1978, it had been only 6.89 percent. Of course, what matters for spending decisions is the real interest rate, so we need to adjust the federal funds rate for inflation. During 1978, inflation averaged almost 9 percent, while in 1980 it was over 12 percent. Between 1978 and 1980, the real federal funds rate swung from a negative 2.11 percent (6.89 percent minus 9 percent inflation) to a positive 5.5 percent (17.5 percent minus 12 percent inflation). This rise in the real interest rate reduced aggregate expenditures, as we learned it would in Chapter 29.

The Federal Reserve's policy actions in 1979 and 1980 eventually did succeed in bringing inflation down. But cyclical unemployment rose significantly during the disinflation. From an average of 6 percent of the labor force in 1978–1979, the unemployment rate averaged 8.5 percent over 1980–1983.

In Chapter 31, we will learn more about the short-run trade-off between inflation and unemployment.

Sometimes policy makers have accepted the closing of factories, and the resulting higher cyclical unemployment, in pursuit of lower inflation.

An Expansionary Shift in the ADI Curve

Figure 30.6 illustrates a different scenario, one in which the ADI curve has shifted to the right. This type of shift is caused by a positive shock to spending; perhaps firms have been more optimistic about the future and have increased investment spending on plant and equipment. Or perhaps the government has increased its purchases or cut taxes. In response to an increase in demand, firms

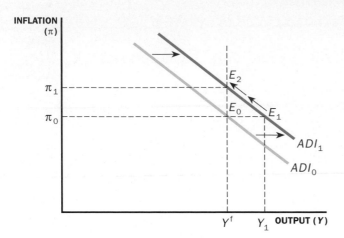

FIGURE 30.6   *A Boom Caused by a Shift in Aggregate Demand*

If the aggregate demand curve shifts to the right (from ADI_0 to ADI_1), firms will increase production. Output and employment rise, and the new short-run equilibrium level of output is Y_1. Eventually, wages and prices will start rising more rapidly and the economy will move up the aggregate demand curve toward the full-employment equilibrium at point E_2, where output has returned to Y^f but inflation is now higher at π_1.

expand production. They hire more workers, average weekly hours rise as workers work more, and unemployment falls. Firms utilize their plant and equipment more intensively, perhaps adding extra shifts or delaying maintenance in order to keep production lines running at top speed. These adjustments allow output to rise above levels associated with normal conditions. Output rises above Y^f, moving the economy to E_1; the new equilibrium level of output is now Y_1.

Just as in the case of a recession caused by a drop in spending, the boom caused by the increased spending does not last forever. To attract and retain workers, firms are willing to increase wages more rapidly, and firms can push up prices with less fear of losing markets. As inflation rises, the Fed boosts interest rates. As it does so, the economy's equilibrium level of output will tend to fall back toward the full-employment level. The economy moves up the ADI curve from point E_1 toward point E_2 in Figure 30.6. Eventually, output will return to Y^f at point E_2 with a higher rate of inflation.

The Kennedy Tax Cut

In 1963, the unemployment rate in the United States seemed to be stuck at an unacceptably high level, 5.5 percent. Ten years before it had been 2.8 percent. President Kennedy's economic advisors believed that a cut in the individual income tax would cause households to consume more. This increased consumption would lead to a rightward shift in the ADI curve. An increase in aggregate expenditures, Kennedy's advisors believed, would result in increased output and a lower unemployment rate, not higher inflation. They believed that there would not be higher inflation because the economy had excess capacity—productive workers and machines were lying idle. As a result, the shift in the ADI curve would be translated into increases in output, as shown in Figure 30.6.

Increases in output, as we have learned, imply increases in employment. The predictions of the Kennedy advisors turned out to be correct. Unemployment fell to 4.4 percent in 1965 and stayed under 4 percent for the rest of the 1960s. In addition, real GDP grew at the remarkable rate of 5.5 percent from 1964 to 1966, while inflation initially remained at low levels. Figure 30.7 shows these developments. Output was below potential in 1962 and 1963, but the output gap was shrinking and the unemployment rate was falling. The tax cut boosted the economy and pushed output above potential by 1965.

With the economy operating above potential, we would predict that wages and prices would start to rise more rapidly. This is just what happened. Throughout the late 1960s, inflation rose. Eventually, the economy fell back toward potential GDP, just as the analysis illustrated in Figure 30.6 predicted. By the end of 1970, unemployment was back above 5.5 percent. Inflation, which had averaged 1.3 percent in 1963, averaged 5.7 percent in 1970.

Macroeconomic Policy and Shifts in the ADI Curve

Our examples have illustrated the effects on aggregate demand and output in the short run. For each example, we assumed the economy started out at full employment.

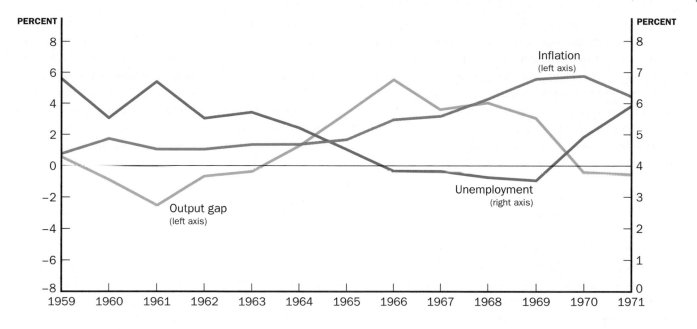

FIGURE 30.7 *The Output Gap, Unemployment Rate, and Inflation Rate in the 1960s*

The increase in aggregate demand during the 1960s lowered unemployment. As the economy continued to expand above full-employment GDP, the rate of inflation increased. By the end of the decade, the economy was back at full employment but with a higher rate of inflation.

SOURCES: Unemployment, *ERP* (2001), Table B-35; inflation, *ERP* (2001), Table B-64; output gap, Federal Reserve Board.

Tracing through the effects of the disturbance on output and employment in the short run is a useful way of focusing on the effects of a single disturbance to the economy. More commonly, however, we want to use our macroeconomic model to analyze how policy might help maintain the economy at full employment. In Figure 30.4, the initial leftward shift in the ADI curve pushed the economy into a recession, with output at E_1, below the economy's full-employment output at point E_0. If the aggregate demand curve remains at ADI_1, inflation will eventually fall and the economy will reach full employment at point E_2 with an inflation rate of π_2. If inflation adjusts slowly, it may take a long time for full employment to be restored. An expansionary fiscal or monetary policy that shifts the aggregate demand curve to the right would push the short-run equilibrium output level closer to full employment. If the ADI curve is shifted all the way to ADI_0, full employment is restored at the original rate of inflation, π_0.

Shifts in the Inflation Adjustment Curve

So far, we have focused on the impact of shifts in the ADI curve on the economy. Such a focus is natural in that aggregate expenditures determine output (and employment) in the short run, and inflation typically adjusts relatively slowly. But economies also experience disturbances that directly affect inflation. Two of the most important are changes in energy prices and shifts in potential GDP.

Changes in Energy Prices

For a given level of cyclical unemployment, inflation can be affected by shocks that alter firms' costs of production. For example, during the 1970s, oil prices increased dramatically. By raising the price of energy, the increase in oil prices pushed up the costs of production for firms. In response to the increase in their costs, firms raised prices, leading to a jump in the inflation rate. An increase in labor productivity relative to wages such as America experienced in the 1990s would work in the opposite manner, lowering production costs and moderating the rate of inflation.

We can analyze the consequences of an inflation shock such as the oil price increase using the ADI and inflation adjustment curves. To do so, suppose the economy is initially at full employment with an inflation rate equal to π_0. This is shown as point E_0 in Figure 30.8. The inflation shock causes inflation to increase to π_1, as shown by the upward shift in the inflation adjustment curve to IA_1. The new equilibrium is at E_1. Inflation is higher, and because the rise in inflation leads to a higher real interest rate and lower aggregate spending, output has fallen. Economic disturbances that shift the inflation adjustment curve—inflation shocks— are often also called **supply shocks.**

The economy will not remain at point E_1, however. Over time, cyclical unemployment leads to a decline in inflation. As inflation falls, the inflation adjustment curve shifts back

down. Output starts to rise as the real interest rate falls, and cyclical unemployment declines as full employment is restored. Eventually, the equilibrium returns to point E_0, with the inflation rate and output back at their initial values.

While the graphic analysis is useful in helping to keep track of how inflation and output move in response to various economic disturbances, it is important to understand *why* the economy adjusts as it does. In the case of an oil price shock, the initial impact on the inflation rate leads the central bank to boost interest rates. It is the resulting increase in the real interest rate that reduces aggregate expenditures (a movement along the ADI curve). This suggests that the decline in output after an oil price shock (or any other shock that shifts the inflation adjustment curve in the short run) will depend on how monetary policy responds. Does the central bank aggressively raise interest rates as inflation rises? Or does it respond very little? These questions deal with critical issues faced by monetary policymakers, and we will be considering them in Chapter 32.

CASE IN POINT

Oil Price Shocks of the 1970s

The Arab-Israeli War in 1973 led the Organization of Petroleum Exporting Countries (OPEC) to restrict oil exports to Western industrialized economies and to raise the price of oil sharply. The fuel and utilities component of the consumer price index jumped over 16 percent in 1973. Overall inflation as measured by the GDP deflator rose from 4.14 percent in 1972 to 5.23 percent in 1973 to 8.58 percent in 1974 as the impact of higher oil prices raised the prices of goods and services throughout the economy.

The jump in inflation resulting from the oil price increases shifted the inflation adjustment curve up, as illustrated in Figure 30.8. Our model of fluctuations predicts that output declines after such an inflation shock, and this is just what happened. Unemployment, which had averaged 4.9 percent in 1973, had risen to 8.5 percent by 1975 as the economy entered a recession. Figure 30.9 shows the path of the output gap, unemployment rate, and inflation rate from 1972 until 1977. The high level of cyclical unemployment during the recession put downward pressure on inflation. As inflation declined during

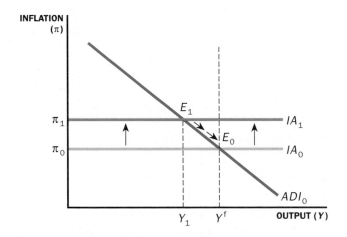

FIGURE 30.8   *The Impact of an Inflation Shock*

The increase in the cost of production at each level of output increases the inflation rate, shifting the inflation adjustment curve up, from IA_0 to IA_1. The short-run equilibrium is at the point of intersection between the inflation adjustment and ADI curves. The upward shift in the inflation adjustment curve moves the economy to E_1, where output has fallen to Y_1. If there are no further inflation shocks, inflation declines since output is below its full-employment level. Eventually, full employment and an inflation rate of π_0 are restored.

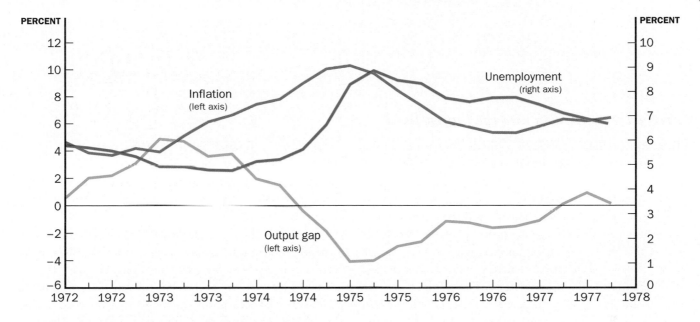

FIGURE 30.9 *The 1973 Oil Price Shock*

In 1972, the U.S. economy was expanding, with output rising above potential (the output gap was positive) and unemployment declining. In 1973, OPEC sharply raised the price of oil. This inflation shock pushed up U.S. inflation and sent the economy into a recession. The output gap fell and unemployment rose. After peaking in 1975, inflation started to decline. As Figure 30.8 indicated, falling inflation was associated with a rise in output and fall in unemployment as output returned to potential. A second oil price shock hit the economy in 1979.

1976, falling from 9.0 percent in 1975 to 5.7 percent in 1976, output recovered and unemployment began to decline, eventually reaching 5.8 percent in 1979, a level close to most estimates of full employment. ●

A Shift in Potential GDP

Changes in the economy's potential GDP can shift the inflation adjustment curve. Potential GDP might shift because of productivity changes or because of labor market changes that increase the level of employment associated with full employment, leading to higher output at full employment. Many of the recent discussions about the new economy and the impact of information technologies in boosting productivity can be thought of as arguing that potential GDP has risen.

Consider what happens if there is a productivity increase that boosts full-employment GDP. In Figure 30.10, the initial equilibrium is at E_0. The increase in potential GDP shifts the vertical long-run aggregate supply curve to the right, from the old level of potential output (Y_0^f) to the new, higher value (Y_1^f). If there is no change in the ADI

curve, equilibrium output remains at point E_0 at the initial inflation rate π_0.

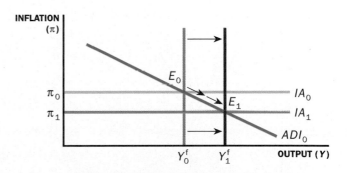

FIGURE 30.10 *The Impact of an Increase in Potential GDP*

If potential GDP increases, the long-run aggregate supply curve shifts to the right, from Y_0^f to Y_1^f. Initially, equilibrium output remains at the point where the inflation adjustment line at the current inflation rate π_0 intersects with the ADI curve (point E_0). Eventually, the economy achieves its new, higher level of potential GDP at the inflation rate π_1.

e-Insight

Productivity Growth and the Punch Bowl

To prevent inflation from rising, the Fed must not let the economy overheat—if output rises above potential, the tight labor market will lead wages to rise in excess of productivity growth. As firms face increasing labor costs, they will boost their prices, and inflation will rise. Sometimes it seems that just when the good times of low unemployment arrive, the Fed starts raising interest rates to slow things down. An old adage about monetary policy is that the job of the Fed is to take the punch bowl away just when the party really gets going. Increases in productivity growth brought on by new technologies will let the Fed leave the punch bowl out a bit longer during booms.

The Fed's actions have to do with the relationship between wage increases, productivity, and inflation. As long as wages do not increase faster than productivity, firms' costs of production will not rise. The reason is simple—firms may have to pay more to their workers but their

workers are producing more. The labor costs of producing each unit of output—unit labor costs—do not increase when wages rise at the same rate as productivity. The faster productivity grows, the faster wages can rise without fueling price increases.

Sometimes the Fed is criticized for raising interest rates whenever wages start to rise. It is not wage increases themselves that concern the Fed, however. The Fed is concerned with inflation, and as long as wage increases are in line with increases in productivity, they do not increase firms' costs or contribute to inflation. So the Fed looks at unit labor costs to determine if wage increases are inflationary or not. As the chart illustrates, during the early 1980s, wage increases far outstripped increases in productivity, causing unit labor costs to rise rapidly. The opposite has occurred during the 1990s. While wages started rising faster in the late 1990s, so did productivity.

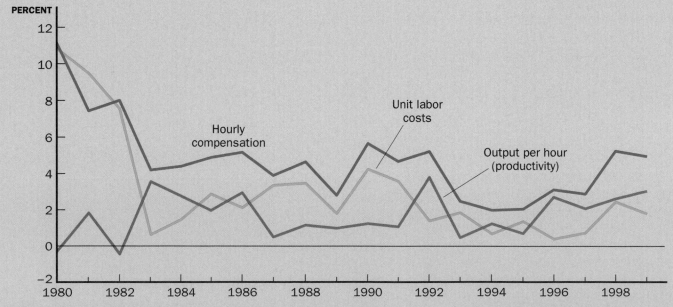

Labor Compensation, Productivity, and Cost

The years 1999 and 2000 illustrate the difficulties the Fed faces as it makes its policy decisions. If the recent increases in productivity growth are heralds of a new economy in which productivity growth will remain strong, then wages can rise much faster than previously without causing concerns of igniting a new bout of inflation. If the increased productivity growth is only temporary, however, then faster wage growth will start to push up unit labor costs and prices. Information and computer technologies are transforming the economy, and if these changes lead to sustained increases in productivity growth, workers' real wages will rise faster than they did during the previous quarter century. But when wages grow faster than productivity, even the new economy will discover that the Fed will have to put away the punch bowl to keep inflation under control.

The economy will not remain at E_0, however. At an output equal to the old level of potential GDP, Y_0^f, firms now have excess capacity—the increase in productivity means they could produce more than previously with the same resources. This places downward pressure on inflation. As inflation declines, the real interest rate also falls, leading to an increase in aggregate expenditures and equilibrium output (this is a movement along the ADI curve). Eventually the economy will reach point E_1, with output now at the new, higher level of potential GDP and inflation lower than initially.

In Figure 30.10, the ADI curve was held fixed. But if potential output rises, there may be a direct impact on the ADI curve as well. Higher potential output means total incomes in the economy are higher. Households will want to increase their consumption spending when their real incomes are expected to rise, and this can lead to a rightward shift in the ADI curve. As a consequence, the economy may move to a higher level of output with very little change in inflation.

CASE IN POINT

The 1990s

Now that we have a complete model for understanding how the economy adjusts, we can use it to analyze the U.S. economy at the end of the 1990s. Figure 30.11 shows the unemployment rate, the output gap, and the inflation rate since 1990. The recession of 1990–1991 shows up clearly in the path of the unemployment rate, which rose from 5.3 percent of the labor force in 1989 to 7.5 percent in 1992. This recession was caused by demand factors that shifted the ADI curve to the left. Both consumption and investment spending dropped, as people became more pessimistic about the future at the time of the Gulf War.

Our model predicts that a drop in aggregate expenditures will lead to an increase in unemployment and a decline in inflation. Output will eventually return to potential (see Figure 30.4), so unemployment should return to its full employment level, but inflation will remain lower. In the late 1980s and early 1990s, estimates of the unemployment rate at full employment placed it in the 5.5 to 6 percent range. As Figure 30.11 shows, by 1996 the unemployment rate had returned to its pre-recession level. And inflation remained at a level lower than its pre-recession value.

From 1996 to the end of the 1990s, the economy continued to expand, and both unemployment *and* inflation continued to fall. Economic output displayed strong growth and the growth rate of productivity increased. These developments were consistent with a supply shock that lowered the unemployment rate at full employment and shifted the inflation adjustment curve down, as illustrated in Figure 30.10. As our model predicted, this resulted in lower unemployment and lower inflation. The prime candidate for such a favorable supply shock is the new computer and information technologies that have transformed so many parts of the American economy.

As the 1990s ended, the Fed was concerned that the booming economy would eventually lead to higher inflation. To counteract this, the Fed raised interest rates several times in 1999 and 2000. These interest rate hikes were designed to slow the economy by reducing demand, and by the end of 2000, there were signs the economy's strong growth was weakening. However, by December 2000, economic conditions seemed to be weakening much more quickly than had been expected. As a consequence, the Fed's concerns shifted; it now needed to focus on preventing the economy from entering a recession. In a dramatic action on January 3, 2001, the committee cut the target for the federal funds rate by a full half percentage point, from 6.5 percent to 6 percent. The decision to lower the funds rate caught most commentators by surprise, since the move was taken between regularly scheduled FOMC meetings. The Fed cut its target for the federal funds rate several times more during 2001, bringing the rate down to 2.50 percent by the end of October. ●

WRAP-UP

Factors That Shift the Inflation Adjustment Curve

Energy prices: an increase in energy prices raises the cost of production at a given level of the output gap. This shifts the inflation adjustment curve upward.

Potential GDP: an increase in potential output reduces the output gap and lowers inflation at each level of output. This shifts the inflation adjustment curve downward.

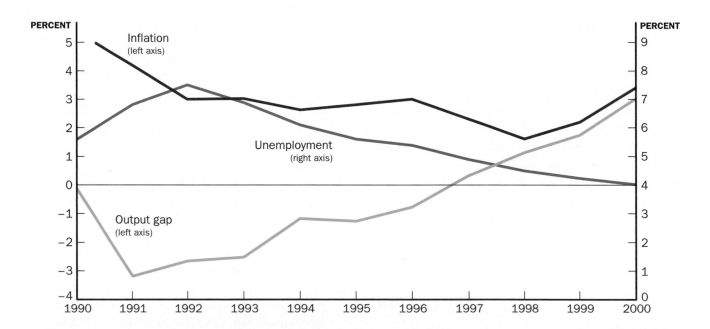

FIGURE 30.11 *The Boom of the 1990s*

The U.S. economy began the 1990s recovering from the recession of 1990–1991. Steady growth throughout the decade reduced the output gap and led to a significant reduction in unemployment. Inflation remained stable despite the decline in unemployment.

SOURCES: Unemployment, *ERP* (2001), Table B-35; inflation, *ERP* (2001), Table B-64; output gap, Federal Reserve Board.

Review and Practice

Summary

1. Aggregate demand will be negatively related to inflation. As inflation increases, the central bank raises interest rates, thus reducing aggregate expenditures. This negative relationship is called the aggregate demand–inflation, or ADI curve.

2. At a given rate of inflation, the economy's equilibrium level of output is given by the ADI curve.

3. Changes in fiscal policy, private investment, consumption spending, or monetary policy at a given rate of inflation shift the ADI curve.

4. The slope of the ADI curve depends on the central bank's behavior. If it increases interest rates by a lot when inflation rises, the impact on aggregate demand will be large and the ADI curve will be relatively flat. If the bank responds less to inflation changes, the ADI curve will be steeper.

5. The slope of the ADI curve also depends on the responsiveness of investment to interest rate changes. If increases in the real interest rate have a large impact on investment and spending, the ADI curve will be relatively flat.

6. If GDP is below the full-employment level, inflation will fall, shifting the inflation adjustment line down and increasing equilibrium output. This process continues until full employment is restored.

7. If GDP is above the full-employment level, inflation will rise, shifting the inflation adjustment curve up and decreasing equilibrium output. Eventually full employment is restored.

8. Once inflation has adjusted, the economy will be at full employment. Shifts in the ADI curve affect GDP in the short run, but in the long run such shifts only affect the inflation rate.

Key Terms

monetary policy rule
aggregate demand–inflation curve
long-run aggregate supply curve
supply shocks

Review Questions

1. How can the capital market be in equilibrium at different levels of aggregate output? If income is below the full-employment level, can we say whether the interest rate that balances saving and investment will be higher or lower than the equilibrium rate at full employment?

2. If the inflation rate is slow to adjust and is initially above a level at which aggregate expenditures equal long-run aggregate supply, what will be the level of output? What will happen if the aggregate demand–inflation (ADI) curve shifts to the left? To the right? If the long-run aggregate supply curve shifts to the left? To the right?

3. How does the slope of the ADI curve depend on monetary policy?

4. If investment is not very sensitive to changes in real interest rates, will the ADI curve be relatively flat or steep? Explain why.

5. If current output is below potential GDP, what will happen to the inflation rate? How does inflation adjustment move the economy back to full employment?

6. Use the ADI curve and long-run aggregate supply framework to describe some of the major episodes of the post–World War II period.

Problems

1. Use the ADI curve and the long-run aggregate supply framework to describe how the economy would respond to a productivity shock that increases full-employment output. If there is no impact on the ADI curve, what will happen to output in the short run?

2. Suppose that as a result of the Fed's policy, the relationship between the real rate of interest and the inflation rate is given by the following table (all numbers are annual percentages):

Inflation	0	2	4	6	8	10
Real interest rate	3	4	5	6	7	8

The relationship between aggregate expenditures and the real interest rate is given by the following table (expenditures are in trillions of 1996 dollars):

Real interest rate	3	4	5	6	7	8
Aggregate Expenditures	8.3	8	7.7	7.4	7.1	6.8

Plot the ADI curve. If inflation is 4 percent, what is the level of aggregate expenditures? Suppose investment now becomes more sensitive to interest rate changes. How would this affect the ADI curve?

3. Draw an ADI curve. As we move up and to the left on a given ADI curve, the real rate of interest increases. Explain why.

4. In 1994, the Fed raised interest rates in a "preemptive strike" against inflation. If you were in the position of the Fed at the time, with unemployment approaching 6 percent and other indicators suggesting the economy was close to full employment but showing no strong signs of rising inflation, would you have raised interest rates? Why or why not?

Chapter 31

Inflation and Unemployment

Key Questions

1. Does inflation tend to increase if unemployment gets too low? Does it decrease if unemployment gets too high?

2. Is there a trade-off between inflation and unemployment? Is a recession necessary to reduce inflation?

3. How do expectations about inflation affect the level of inflation associated with a given level of output?

4. Why is the trade-off between inflation and output only a short-run trade-off?

During the 1970s, the most pressing macroeconomic policy issue facing industrialized economies was inflation. Despite repeated attempts to reduce it, inflation remained stubbornly high throughout the decade. Figure 31.1 shows the inflation rates for the United States, Japan, and Western Europe. All display roughly similar patterns. Inflation had remained relatively low during the 1960s, but it jumped to much higher levels in the following decade. And as if high inflation were not bad enough, many economies suffered from "stagflation"—high inflation *and* high unemployment.

To understand how governments might control inflation, we need to understand what causes inflation. How do we explain why some countries have higher rates of inflation than others? What are the costs of reducing inflation? Why do the United States and most other industrialized economies have lower inflation rates today than they did twenty years ago? And why do some countries continue to suffer from high rates of inflation?

We have already learned about the costs of inflation in Chapter 23. Many of these costs are associated with *variability* in inflation rates. Countries that experience high av-

erage inflation also experience greater inflation variability than do countries with low average inflation. It is this unpredictable variability of inflation that can impose large costs on the economy. When inflation turns out to be higher than anticipated, lenders lose as the dollars they receive are worth less than the dollars they loaned; borrowers gain since the dollars they repay are worth less than the dollars they borrowed. Conversely, if inflation turns out to be lower than anticipated, borrowers lose and lenders gain. The possibility of these unanticipated gains and losses increases uncertainty and the general level of risk in the economy. We also learned in Chapter 23 that inflation imposes further costs on the economy as individuals devote resources to trying to avoid the costs of inflation.

If inflation disrupts the economy, why don't governments simply get rid of it? The answer is that normally, inflation can be reduced only at a cost—only if the unemployment rate is allowed to increase temporarily. This short-run trade-off between inflation and unemployment is one of the key concepts we use to understand macroeconomic developments. This chapter looks at this short-run trade-off. Most economists believe that in the

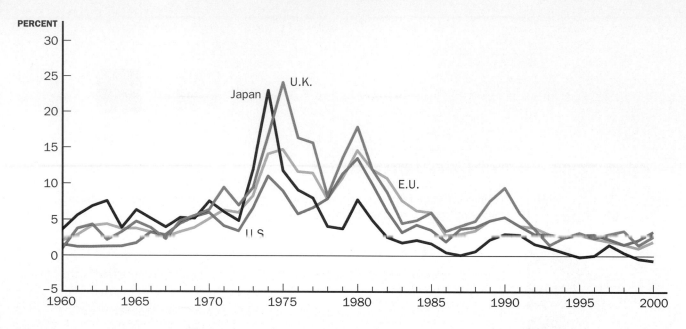

FIGURE 31.1 *Inflation Among the Major Industrialized Economies*

The general pattern of inflation in the United States, Japan, United Kingdom (U.K.), and European Union (E.U.) during the past forty years has been quite similar. Average inflation rose dramatically in the early 1970s, rose again in the late 1970s, and declined in the early 1980s.

SOURCE: International Financial Statistics (March 2001).

long run, there is no trade-off—the full-employment model shows that once real wages have adjusted, the economy will be at full employment, no matter what the rate of inflation might be.

If we look at Figure 31.1 again, we can see that the inflation rate is almost always positive. That is, prices have been rising. The only exception occurred in Japan in the 1990s. In the other countries, prices have risen in every year shown in the figure. In some years, particularly in the 1970s, prices rose rapidly—the inflation rate was high. In other years, particularly the 1990s, prices rose more slowly—the inflation rate was low.

If we were to examine longer historical episodes, we would find periods of falling prices similar to Japan's recent experience. The United States at the end of the nineteenth century and during the Great Depression of the 1930s also saw general prices falling. Periods of declining prices normally have been associated with depressed economic conditions.

The key assumption we have made so far in our study of the short run is that wages and prices do not adjust rapidly enough to keep labor and product markets in equilibrium at full employment. But wages and prices eventually do adjust, and in Chapter 30 we assumed that inflation rises and falls as the economy moves above or below potential GDP. The adjustment of inflation played a critical role in eventually moving the economy to full employment.

In this chapter, we will examine the foundations of inflation adjustment in more detail. Three factors are important for explaining how inflation varies over time. First, while wages do not adjust quickly to keep demand equal to supply, they do respond over time whenever demand does not equal supply. We summarized this as the third fundamental concept needed to understand short-run economic fluctuations. Increases in cyclical unemployment lead to lower inflation. Second, wages and prices depend on workers' and firms' expectations about inflation. For example, if workers expect prices to rise faster, they will demand higher wage increases. An increase in *expected* inflation leads to an increase in *actual* inflation. Third, economies occasionally experience inflation shocks, increases in costs such as the dramatic rise in oil prices of the 1970s. We will see that increases in inflation expectations or inflation shocks that boost actual inflation force policymakers to make difficult trade-offs.

Price and Wage Stickiness

In Chapter 28, we provided several reasons to account for the slow adjustment of wages and prices. Wages may adjust slowly because of contracts. These may be explicit wage contracts in unionized sectors of the economy, or implicit contracts under which wages might be adjusted infrequently, say, only once each year. Efficiency wage theory implies that the real wage that maximizes the firm's profits might not fall when there is an excess supply of labor because firms might want to retain their best workers. There also may be legal constraints, such as minimum wage legislation, that prevent money wages from falling in the face of high unemployment.

In the product market, prices may be slow to adjust as demand and supply shift. For instance, firms may face greater risks if they adjust prices rather than production. The effect of any price change will depend on how the firm's rivals respond and on how customers react. These contingencies may make the uncertainty associated with changing prices greater than those from simply adjusting production levels. Firms may be slow to raise prices unless they think their competitors will also be changing prices, for fear that they will lose sales. Firms may find it preferable to adjust production levels instead.

Short-Run Inflation Adjustment

The fact that wages and prices do not adjust fast enough to keep the economy always at full employment does not mean they remain constant. Wages and prices do adjust in response to demand and supply pressures, and they will rise faster if workers and firms expect higher inflation. Prices also will be affected by shocks that change the costs of production. These three factors—demand and supply pressures, expectations, and inflation shocks—will be the keys to understanding inflation. We will discuss each in turn.

Demand and Supply Pressures

The framework for thinking about how demand and supply pressures influence the rate of change of wages is summarized in a famous relationship called the **Phillips curve.** A.W. Phillips was a New Zealander who taught economics in England during the 1950s. He examined data from England on unemployment and the rate of increases in money wages. He found a negative relationship between the two and this relationship is known as the *Phillips curve.* At higher unemployment rates, money wages rose more slowly. At lower unemployment rates, money wages rose faster. The relationship he found is shown in Figure 31.2.

The logic behind the Phillips curve is straightforward. If unemployment is low, firms have greater difficulty hiring workers. This puts upward pressure on wages as firms attempt to attract workers by paying more. If unions and firms negotiate over wages, the union will be in a

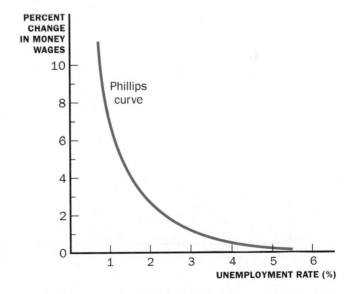

FIGURE 31.2 *The Original Phillips Curve*

The Phillips curve shows that the rate of wage growth rises as the unemployment rate falls. The curve shown here is the one Phillips plotted in 1958 for the British economy.

stronger bargaining position, better able to get larger wage increases, if labor markets are "tight." At low unemployment rates, workers are more likely to decide it is a good time to look for another job. Firms that do not keep pace with wage increases elsewhere may discover that their best workers are leaving. If workers believe it is easier to find another job, they may worry less about being fired. As a consequence, they may not work as hard. To maintain worker productivity, firms will need to raise wages more rapidly. In contrast, if unemployment is high, there will be little upward pressure on real wages. Money wages will increase more slowly or even decrease for some workers.

From Wages to Prices   The Phillips curve relates unemployment to the rate at which wages are changing. The bigger the imbalance between labor demand and labor supply, the faster money wages will change.

The link between the rate at which wages are changing and the rate at which prices are changing—the rate of inflation—is direct. Labor costs are, for most businesses, the major component of their costs of production. In com-

petitive markets, prices will move in tandem with marginal costs, and an increase in wages will translate directly into an increase in the marginal costs of production. Some firms, at least in the short run, use a simpler rule of thumb in setting prices—they set price as a given markup over costs (e.g., 120 percent of costs). If firms set prices as a markup over their costs, then changes in the rate at which wages are changing will translate directly into changes in the rate of inflation. Figure 31.3 shows the close historical relationship between the two.

Because they move together, we can replace the rate of nominal wage increase on the vertical axis of the Phillips curve with the rate of inflation. Even though Phillips originally studied the behavior of unemployment and wages, it is more common today to see Phillips curves that have the inflation rate on the vertical axis. We will adopt this practice from now on when we talk about the Phillips curve.

The Phillips Curve and Cyclical Unemployment   The relation between inflation and unemployment that Phillips found for the United Kingdom also has been found for other countries. Figure 31.4

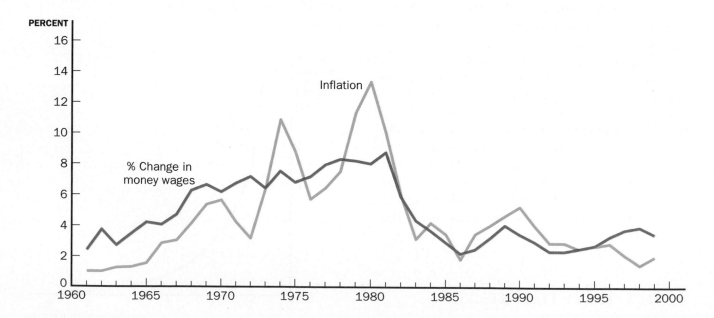

FIGURE 31.3   *The Rate of Wage Increase and Inflation Move Together*

The original Phillips curve related the rate of wage increase to the rate of unemployment. Because the rate of increase in money wages moves closely with the overall rate of inflation, we also use the Phillips curve to relate inflation to the rate of cyclical unemployment.

SOURCE: *ERP* (2001), Tables B-47, B-64.

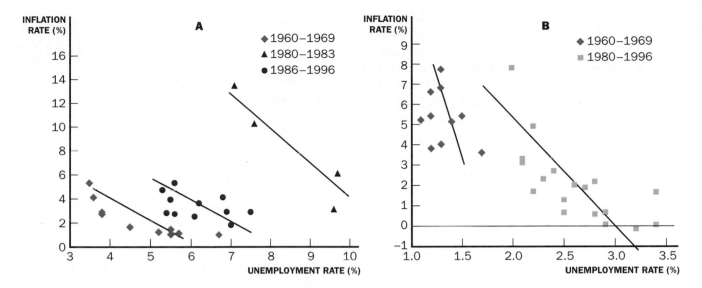

FIGURE 31.4   *The Phillips Curve for the United States and Japan*

Panel A depicts the Phillips curve relationship for the United States in the 1960s, the early 1980s, and 1986–1996. Notice that the Phillips curve has shifted over time. Panel B plots the Phillips curve for Japan for 1960–1969 and 1980–1996.

shows inflation and unemployment for the United States and Japan during different periods. Two characteristics stand out. First, the unemployment rate is always positive. In the United States, it has never fallen below 3.5 percent. Second, the Phillips curve seems to shift. The relationship between unemployment and inflation is not stable, and understanding the reason for these shifts is a primary objective of this chapter. Economists' understanding of both characteristics is based on the concept of the natural rate of unemployment and on the role of expectations.

The Natural Rate of Unemployment

There are reasons why unemployment is always positive. Not every worker is qualified to do every job. There may be unemployment of autoworkers and excess demand for computer programmers. Similarly, there may be unemployment in Detroit and vacancies in Seattle. But unemployed workers in Detroit cannot simply walk into jobs making airplanes in Seattle. In Chapter 23, we referred to this type of unemployment as structural. By the same token, there will always be some workers moving between jobs. This latter type of unemployment is referred to as frictional unemployment. Structural and frictional unemployment account for positive unemployment even at full employment. The unemployment rate that occurs at full employment, when the economy is producing at potential output, usually is called the **natural rate of unemployment.**

The pressures on wages that lead to increases or decreases in inflation are produced by *cyclical* unemployment, fluctuations in total unemployment around the natural rate. When output is below potential so that cyclical unemployment is positive, total unemployment exceeds the natural rate of unemployment. Labor markets are slack, and wages rise more slowly. When output rises above potential output, total unemployment falls below the natural rate, labor markets are tight, and wages rise more rapidly. When the actual unemployment rate equals the natural rate, cyclical unemployment is zero. It is cyclical unemployment, not the total level of unemployment, that best measures the inflationary pressures in the economy.

To summarize, when output rises above potential, unemployment falls below the natural rate and inflation increases. When output falls below potential, unemployment rises above the natural rate and inflation decreases. The resulting relationship between output and inflation is called the **short-run inflation adjustment curve** (SRIA Curve). It is shown as the solid line in Figure 31.5. In the figure, Y^f is the economy's potential level of output. If actual output rises above potential, say, to Y_1, unemployment falls below the natural rate and wages rise more rapidly. This increases the costs of production for firms, and prices rise more rapidly. The inflation rate increases to π_1.

In Chapter 30, we combined the aggregate demand–inflation (ADI) curve with an inflation adjustment line. We drew the inflation adjustment line as a horizontal line at the economy's current rate of inflation. If equilibrium output rose above or fell below full-employment output, we shifted the inflation adjustment line to reflect the way inflation would change over time. The horizontal line provided a starting point for understanding the way fluctuations in the economy can cause inflation to rise or fall. Now we can use the discussion of the Phillips curve to elaborate on the relationship between output and inflation, recognizing that the inflation adjustment line should have a positive slope. As output expands and unemployment falls below the natural rate, inflation will rise. That is why the SRIA curve in Figure 31.5 is drawn with a positive slope, rather than as a horizontal line.

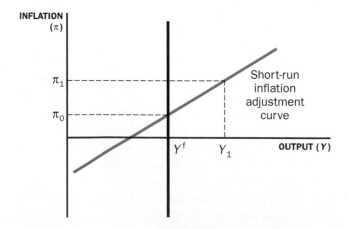

FIGURE 31.5 *The Inflation Adjustment Curve*

Increases in output above potential lead to higher inflation. Y^f is potential output. If the economy expands from Y^f to Y_1 inflation rises from π_0 to π_1. The expansion in output causes unemployment to fall below the natural rate. This leads wages to increase faster, and inflation rises.

WRAP-UP

Inflation and Cyclical Unemployment

The *natural rate of unemployment* is the unemployment rate when the economy is at potential GDP and cyclical unemployment is zero.

The *short-run inflation adjustment (SRIA) curve*, shows the rate of inflation at each level of output relative to potential GDP, for a given expected rate of inflation.

The SRIA curve has a positive slope. If output increases above potential, inflation increases. If output falls below potential, inflation falls.

The Role of Expectations: Shifts in the Short-Run Inflation Adjustment Curve

Figure 31.4 illustrated a second characteristic of the relationship between unemployment and inflation—the relationship does not seem to be stable. It has shifted over time. While the relationship between cyclical unemployment and inflation was stable in the 1960s, the stability disappeared in the 1970s. The U.S. economy experienced high unemployment *and* high inflation. *Stagflation* was the term coined to describe this undesirable situation. High inflation occurred while output was below potential. At other times, output was above potential, yet inflation was low. The SRIA curve is not stable.

There is a simple explanation for why the SRIA curve is unstable: the level of cyclical unemployment is not the only factor that affects wages. For one thing, expectations of inflation also matter.

At any given rate of cyclical unemployment, the rate at which wages increase depends on expectations about inflation. Take the case of a union contract. If workers and firms expect that inflation will be 3 percent per year over the life of the contract, then the nominal wage called for in the contract will rise 3 percent per year even if the negotiated real wage remains constant. Employers are willing to let the nominal wage increase, because they believe they will be able to sell what they produce at higher prices.

If unemployment is low, output is above potential, and people are expecting inflation, wages may rise even faster than is necessary simply to offset expected inflation. With low unemployment and output above potential, workers face better job prospects and are more likely to quit to take better jobs, while firms will find it harder to hire replacements. Wages will rise faster as firms try to prevent their existing workers from leaving and to attract new workers. If an inflation rate of 3 percent is expected, nominal wages might rise at 5 percent per year (3 percent to compensate for increases in the cost of living and 2 percent because labor markets are tight). If workers and firms expect a much higher rate of inflation, say, 10 percent, then low unemployment may lead money wages to rise at 12 percent per year (10 percent to compensate for the rising cost of living, plus 2 percent because labor markets are tight).

Because expectations of inflation affect actual inflation, the SRIA curve shows the relationship between output (relative to potential) and inflation, *for a given expected rate of inflation*. This is represented diagrammatically in Figure 31.6. The position of the SRIA curve depends on the level of expected inflation. Because it includes inflationary expectations, we refer to it as the *expectations-augmented SRIA curve*.

To better understand the role of the natural rate of unemployment, consider how expectations about inflation are affected by both recent experience and anticipated changes in policy and economic conditions. Take the simple case of **adaptive expectations**[1]—that is, expectations that respond or adapt to recent experience. Assume the economy is initially in a situation where prices have been stable for an extended period of time. Given this historical experience, workers and firms expect zero inflation. The SRIA curve is represented in Figure 31.6 by the curve labeled "Expected inflation = 0." Suppose the government reduces unemployment below the natural rate by expanding output above potential (where actual inflation equals expected inflation). In the short run, the actual inflation rate rises to π_1. With actual inflation now positive, workers and firms will not continue to expect zero inflation. They

will come to expect positive inflation. If they now expect inflation to be π_1, the expectations-augmented SRIA curve shifts up, so there will be a higher rate of inflation at each level of output. The new SRIA curve is labeled "Expected inflation = π_1" in Figure 31.6. If the government continues to maintain output above Y^f, inflation will rise to π_2. Now workers and firms will start to expect inflation at the rate π_2, and this higher expected inflation will be incorporated into wage- and price-setting behavior. The expectations-

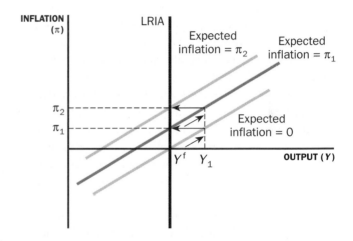

FIGURE 31.6 *Short-Run Inflation Adjustment Curves and Inflation Expectations*

Increases in output above potential lead to higher inflation for a given expected rate of inflation. Suppose expected inflation initially is equal to zero and the economy is at potential output Y^f. The SRIA curve is labeled "Expected inflation = 0." If the government, through monetary or fiscal policy, decides to "buy" more output and lower unemployment by increasing output to Y_1, inflation rises. When output increases, the unemployment rate will be below the level associated with full employment, and inflation will increase to π_1. If workers and firms now expect an inflation rate of π_1, the SRIA curve shifts up, increasing the inflation rate associated with any given output. Only when output has returned to potential will actual and expected inflation be equal (at an inflation rate of π_1 in the figure). If the government were to attempt to expand output to Y_1 again, it could only do so by moving up the new, higher SRIA curve to an inflation rate of π_2, This shifts the curve up again as expectations adjust to the new, higher rate of inflation. Inflation will be stable only when output is equal to potential. The only output level that can be sustained with a fixed rate of inflation is Y^f. The long-run inflation adjustment (LRIA) curve is a vertical line at potential GDP.

---

[1]Expectations are called *adaptive* if they respond to recent experience. Adaptive expectations are also called *backward-looking* since they respond to actual past experience. *Forward-looking expectations* respond to anticipated future developments.

augmented SRIA curve shifts up again as shown in Figure 31.6 by the curve labeled "Expected inflation = π_2." Inflation rises further.

If the government attempts to maintain output above potential (the unemployment rate below the natural rate), inflation will continue to increase. As expectations adapt to each successive increase in the inflation rate, inflation increases still more. Accordingly, the natural rate of unemployment is also commonly called the **nonaccelerating inflation rate of unemployment,** or **NAIRU** for short.[2] The curve stabilizes when actual inflation equals expected inflation. This occurs whenever output is equal to potential output (and so unemployment is equal to the NAIRU). This is an important property—actual and expected inflation coincide when cyclical unemployment is zero and the economy is at potential.

We can now understand why the data on unemployment and inflation for the United States and Japan shown in Figure 31.4 seemed to shift over time. The 1960–1969 period was one of low average inflation. The data from this period show the negatively sloped relationship between inflation and unemployment that is implied by the SRIA curve. Both inflation and expected inflation were much higher during 1980–1983. The SRIA curve in that period shifted up, as can be seen in Figure 31.4. Finally, the period since 1984 has seen much lower inflation and reductions in inflationary expectations. Declines in expected inflation have shifted the SRIA curve again, this time in, toward the origin, as our analysis predicts.

The recognition that the SRIA curve shifts as inflationary expectations change brings us to an important conclusion: *When output remains above potential (the unemployment rate remains below the NAIRU), the rate of inflation increases; when it remains below potential (the unemployment rate remains above the NAIRU), inflation decreases. An economy cannot keep its unemployment rate below the NAIRU without facing ever-increasing rates of inflation.* Because the inflation rate remains stable only when the economy is at full employment, the **long-run inflation adjustment (LRIA)**

curve is a vertical line at full-employment GDP, as shown in Figure 31.6. An economy cannot *permanently* lower its unemployment rate below the NAIRU without facing higher and higher inflation. It cannot "buy" higher output and lower unemployment by accepting a slightly higher (but stable) inflation rate.

An important implication of this conclusion is a consensus belief about macroeconomic policy: governments should not try to use macroeconomic policies to maintain the unemployment rate below the NAIRU or output above potential. Expansionary policies will temporarily lower unemployment and boost income, but eventually unemployment returns to the NAIRU. Thus, the policy question is whether the *temporary* fall in unemployment is worth the potential cost of higher inflation.

A key issue is how fast the expectations-augmented SRIA curve shifts up when output is above potential. The answer depends in part on the economy's recent inflationary experience. If inflation has been high and volatile, everyone will be sensitized to inflation, inflationary expectations may respond quickly, and the expectations-augmented SRIA curve shifts quickly. Recent experience in the United States, where inflation has been low and stable, suggests a rather sluggish response; if the unemployment rate is kept below the NAIRU by 2 percentage points for one year, then the inflation rate will increase by about 1 to 2 percentage points. Conversely, to bring down the inflation rate by 1 to 2 percentage points requires keeping the unemployment rate *above* the NAIRU by 2 percentage points for one year (or by 4 percentage points for six months). The amount by which the unemployment rate must be kept above the NAIRU for one year to bring inflation down by 1 percentage point is called the **sacrifice ratio.** Recent estimates for the United States suggest that the sacrifice ratio is in the 1 to 2 range. Because the sacrifice ratio will depend on how quickly expectations adjust, the cost of reducing inflation can vary significantly at different times.

A second key issue is identifying the NAIRU and potential GDP in a dynamic economy. At one time, economists thought the NAIRU was around 6 percent. Unemployment rates below that level were expected to lead to increases in the inflation rate. Yet when the unemployment rate fell below 6 percent in 1995 and below 5 percent in 1997 without causing inflation to rise, economists needed to reassess their estimates of the NAIRU. We will discuss shifts in the NAIRU later in this chapter.

---

[2]If unemployment is below the natural rate, the inflation rate keeps increasing. Since the inflation rate is the rate of change in the price level, it is really the price level that is accelerating. So while the natural rate of unemployment should probably be called the "nonaccelerating price level rate of unemployment," the name NAIRU has become standard.

Thinking Like an Economist

Distributional Effects of Inflation and Unemployment

Inflation and cyclical unemployment impose macroeconomic costs on the economy. Each does so by affecting the lives of millions of individuals. However, not everyone is affected equally. Even when cyclical unemployment reaches very high levels, as it did during the 1982 recession, only a small fraction of the total labor force bears the direct hardship of losing a job, and the burden does not fall evenly on different groups in the population. For example, unemployment rates differ significantly by race and age in the United States. Even during the long expansion of the 1990s, unemployment rates for blacks remained about double the overall rate and more than double the rate for whites (see figure). Young workers experience much higher rates of unemployment than do older workers. For young black workers, the unemployment rate exceeded 25 percent in 1999. The overall labor force has not experienced that level of unemployment since the Great Depression of the 1930s.

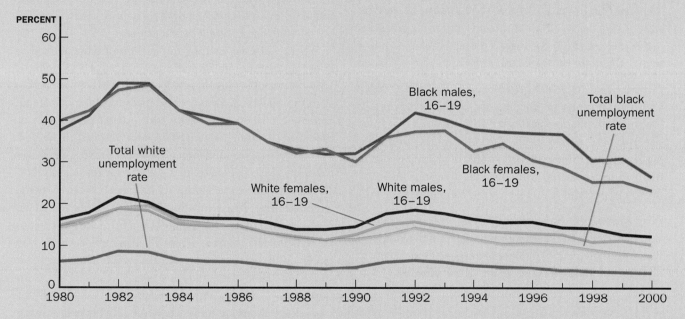

Unemployment Rates

The figure shows two recessionary periods—the early 1980s and the early 1990s. All unemployment rates rise during recessions and fall during expansions. And as Christina and David Romer of the University of California, Berkeley, recently documented, increases in unemployment are positively related to increases in the fraction of the population living in poverty.

The other macroeconomic problem—inflation—also has effects on the distribution of well-being in the econ-

omy, although the effects on the poorest households seem to be small. As we learned in Chapter 23, inflation, particularly if it is unexpected, redistributes wealth from creditors to debtors. Those who have borrowed funds are able to repay in dollars whose value has fallen as a result of inflation. Romer and Romer found, however, that inflation has little actual effect on the financial conditions of the poorest households. The reason for this is straightforward: the poor have few financial assets or liabilities.

Many other countries have experienced much greater variation in inflation than the United States has. In Brazil, for example, the inflation rate averaged over 80 percent per year between 1970 and 1990, while in Mexico it averaged over 30 percent per year. The evidence obtained from a comparison across countries suggests that low inflation and stable economic conditions provide the most favorable environment for creating and sustaining improved economic conditions for the poor.

SOURCE: Christina Romer and David Romer, "Monetary Policy and the Well-being of the Poor," Federal Reserve Bank of Kansas City, *Economic Review*, 84 (1999): 21–49.

WRAP-UP

Basics of Inflation Adjustment

Short-run inflation adjustment (SRIA) curve: shows the relationship between inflation and output *for given inflation expectations*; the higher output is relative to potential, the higher the inflation rate.

Expectations-augmented SRIA curve: the SRIA curve with expectations of inflation explicitly incorporated. The level of inflation associated with any level of output depends on expectations concerning inflation; the higher the inflationary expectations, the higher the level of inflation associated with any level of output. As inflationary expectations increase, the SRIA curve shifts up.

Long-run inflation adjustment (LRIA) curve: the relationship between the inflation rate and output in the long run, with full adjustment of inflationary expectations. There is no long-run trade-off between output and inflation.

Rational Expectations In the example given above, the expectations-augmented SRIA curve shifts up gradually over time, as market participants experience higher inflation rates and build those expectations into their wage bargains. Their expectations are assumed to *adapt* to what they actually experience.

In path-breaking work done in the 1970s that earned him the Nobel Prize in 1995, Robert Lucas suggested that the upward shift in the expectations-augmented SRIA curve could occur much more rapidly. Market participants did not have to wait until inflation actually occurred to build it into their expectations. They could *rationally anticipate* it. If, for instance, the government tried to stimulate the economy to lower unemployment below the NAIRU, workers and firms would rationally anticipate that inflation would rise. They would adjust their wage- and price-setting behavior in light of their expectations of higher inflation. These expectations, based on an understanding of the structure of the economy, are referred to as **rational expectations.**

There is one very strong implication of rational expectations. Assume the government announced it was going to keep the unemployment rate below the NAIRU by expanding aggregate spending. Workers and firms would anticipate the increased inflation, and this would instantaneously shift up the expectations-augmented SRIA curve. Indeed, in this case, the vertical long-run inflation adjustment curve applies even in a relatively short time span, possibly even less than a year.

How quickly expectations adjust depends on economic circumstances. When inflation has been stable for an extended period of time, households and firms are likely to take the inflation rate as given. They will change expectations only gradually. But in economies that have experienced high and variable inflation rates, households and firms realize the importance of forming accurate predictions of inflation. In this case, expectations are more likely to be highly responsive to changes in government policy that affect inflation.

There is one curious aspect of highly responsive expectations. The government cannot reduce unemployment below the NAIRU level without causing inflation to increase rapidly. But the government may be able to reduce the inflation rate at little cost. If firms and households believe that the government will reduce inflation, inflationary expectations can be brought down almost overnight. This produces a downward shift in the expectations-augmented SRIA curve. The trick is for the government to convince others that it will succeed in getting inflation down. It may be difficult to establish such credibility, particularly if the government has a history of failing to control

International Perspective

Output Sacrifice Ratios

We have defined the *sacrifice ratio* as the unemployment rate in excess of the NAIRU that is required to reduce inflation by 1 percentage point. Cyclical unemployment is associated with a level of output that is below the economy's potential GDP. An alternative measure of the sacrifice ratio, therefore, looks at the costs of reducing inflation in terms of the lost output experienced. We can call this the *output sacrifice ratio*.

The output costs of reducing inflation depend on a variety of factors that can change over time. If expectations respond quickly to a drop in inflation, the expectations-augmented SRIA curve shifts down quickly, bringing a faster reduction in actual inflation. A given reduction in inflation can be achieved after a shorter period of high cyclical unemployment. For given expectations of inflation, how quickly inflation responds to a rise in cyclical unemployment will depend on the rigidity of wage- and price-setting behavior. If labor market conditions translate

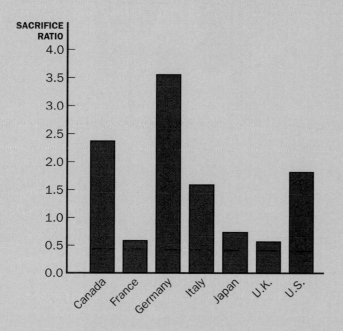

Output Sacrifice Ratios in the 1980s

quickly into changes in wage and price inflation, then even a slight rise in cyclical unemployment may have a large impact in reducing inflation—the sacrifice ratio will be small.

Most industrialized economies experienced recessions in the early 1980s as inflation was reduced from the high levels it had reached in the 1970s. The chart shows the wide variation in the estimated output costs per percentage point reduction in inflation.

Germany, Canada, and the United States seem to have suffered the greatest cost in reducing inflation, with France, Japan, and the United Kingdom experiencing much smaller output costs. In looking at a large number of countries, the evidence suggests that output sacrifice ratios are larger in countries with relatively rigid wages. When wages are more flexible, they can adjust to bring the economy back to full employment more quickly.

The output sacrifice ratios in the chart were estimated from experiences in the early 1980s. In Germany, inflation was reduced by 6 percentage points over a six-year period. Canada reduced inflation by nearly 8 percentage points over a four-year period, while inflation fell almost 9 percentage points in the United States over a four-year period. These reductions in inflation pale in comparison to the declines in inflation experienced by several European countries after World War I. From June 1921 to June 1924, the index of German wholesale prices rose from 1,370 to 115,900,000,000,000. Something that cost 1 mark in June 1921 cost over 84 billion marks two years later, an average *monthly* inflation rate of 185 percent. Hungary, Poland, and Czechoslovakia experienced similar extreme inflations—called hyperinflations—in the early 1920s. Most of these countries eventually brought inflation to a halt very rapidly, yet Tom Sargent of Stanford University has argued that the sacrifice ratios were quite small. These inflation rates were accompanied by rapid growth in the money supply, consistent with the full-employment model of Chapter 24. But why was money growth so high? The governments of these countries were printing money to pay for government expenditures. The inflation rates were eventually halted by instituting major fiscal reforms that reduced the need to print money to finance government expenditures. These reforms led to a rapid decline in inflation expectations, allowing actual inflation to fall dramatically without, Sargent has argued, the high output costs that might have been expected.

SOURCES: The estimated output sacrifice ratios in the chart are from L. Ball, "What Determines the Sacrifice Ratio?" in N. G. Mankiw, ed., *Monetary Policy* (Cambridge: Harvard University Press, 1994), Table 5.1. Thomas J. Sargent, "The Ends of Four Big Inflations," in R. Hall, ed., *Inflation, Causes and Effects* (Chicago: University of Chicago Press, 1982).

inflation. The "price" of a lack of credibility can be high—running the economy at a high unemployment rate over an extended period of time to reduce inflation.

In addition to emphasizing the importance of credibility, the assumption of rational expectations has other interesting implications. For example, if the Fed raises its interest rate target whenever inflation increases, individuals will come to anticipate these policy changes. As a result, prices in financial markets often adjust *before* the Fed actually changes its interest rate target. On the day the FOMC meets and issues its policy decision, financial prices only adjust further if the FOMC's decision turns out to differ from what the market was expecting. The interest rate cut by the Fed in March 2001 provides an interesting example of this phenomenon. The Fed cut its target for the federal funds rate from 5.5 percent to 5 percent, yet stock prices fell. The investors were anticipating an even larger cut, from 5.5 to 4.75 percent. Stock prices had already adjusted to this lower expected level of interest rates. When the Fed cut rates less than anticipated, it was as if they had increased the rate from 4.75 percent to 5 percent, so stock prices declined.

Milton Friedman, Nobel Laureate, 1976

CASE IN POINT

Nobel Views on Inflation and Unemployment

Our understanding of the shifting relationship between unemployment and inflation owes much to the contributions of Milton Friedman and Robert Lucas, the 1976 and 1995 winners of the Nobel Prize in economics. Friedman

and Lucas are two of the giants of monetary economics. Friedman is most widely known for his emphasis on the role of monetary policy as a force in shaping the course of inflation and business cycles. He is best known outside the field of economics for his advocacy of free markets. Lucas is probably unfamiliar to most noneconomists, but like Friedman, he too has made fundamental contributions to the study of money, inflation, and business cycles.

During the 1960s, most economists believed that a stable Phillips curve allowed lower average unemployment rates to be achieved if one were willing to accept a

Robert Lucas, Nobel Laureate, 1995

permanently higher (but stable) rate of inflation. Friedman argued that such a trade-off could not persist. Expanding the economy to lower unemployment would lead to increases in nominal wages as firms attempt to attract additional workers. Firms would be willing to pay higher nominal wages if they expected prices for their output to be higher in the future due to the economic expansion. Workers would recognize that inflation had increased, and would therefore demand more rapid wage increases. Inflation would not stabilize at a higher level but would continue to increase. Inflation would only remain stable when the economy returned to its natural rate of unemployment.

Most economists have followed Friedman in accepting that there is no long-run trade-off that would permanently allow lower unemployment to be traded for higher inflation. Part of the reason for this acceptance is due to the contributions of Lucas. Lucas demonstrated the striking implications of assuming individuals formed their expectations rationally. He stressed the forward-looking nature of expectations. Expectations of

a future economic expansion could immediately raise expectations of inflation, shifting up the Phillips curve. Inflation would rise without even a temporary decline in unemployment.

This chapter has shown how experiences with inflation lead individuals to revise their expectations concerning inflation, and this shifts the short-run Phillips curve. But Lucas stressed that workers, in their wage bargains, and firms in their price-setting behavior can also be forward looking—they can anticipate inflation and thereby shift the short-run Phillips curve even before the inflation is actually experienced. For instance, if the government were to announce that it was going to change its target for inflation, many individuals might adjust their inflation expectations.

These expectations-driven shifts can be both good news and bad news for the economy. On the one hand, inflation can pick up quite quickly—the economy can even have an unemployment rate above the NAIRU, but expectations that future inflation will be higher can push up inflation immediately. The good news is that inflation can be brought down quite quickly as well, without a period of painful unemployment. Brazil, Israel, and Ghana all succeeded in bringing down inflation in this manner.

Friedman argued that the growing evidence the vintage Phillips curve for the 1960s was unstable was instrumental in forcing the profession to adjust its thinking. As Friedman put it, "The drastic change that has occurred in accepted professional views was produced primarily by the scientific response to experience that contradicted a tentatively accepted hypothesis—precisely the classical process for the revision of a scientific hypothesis."[3]

The insights of Friedman and Lucas continue to guide developments in macroeconomics. Their work on the links between inflation and unemployment has influenced the course of economic theory *and* the most practical of policy discussions. For example, Lucas's theory of rational expectations emphasizes the role of credibility in the conduct of monetary policy. This emphasis continues to have a major impact on policy discussions. ●

---

[3]Milton Friedman, "Nobel Lecture: Inflation and Unemployment," *Journal of Political Economy* 185 (1977): 451–472

Shifts in the NAIRU

Though the *concept* of the natural rate of unemployment, or NAIRU, is now well accepted, economists do differ in their estimates of what the critical level of unemployment is below which inflation increases. That is because the NAIRU itself may vary over time and our estimates of it are quite imprecise. In the late 1980s, most economists thought the NAIRU was around 6 percent or slightly higher. As the unemployment rate fell to 5.6 percent in 1995, then to 5.4 percent in 1996, and eventually to 3.9 percent in 2000 without evidence that inflation was increasing, more and more economists believed the NAIRU had decreased. Today, few economists believe the evidence is strong enough to yield a precise value for the NAIRU; the best that can be done is to identify a range of plausible values. President Clinton's Council of Economic Advisors, in its annual report issued in February 1999, suggested that the NAIRU was somewhere in a range centered at 5.3 percent.

Some of the changes in the NAIRU are predictable. There is always some frictional unemployment, people moving from job to job. Such movements are more common among new entrants into the labor force; in the 1970s, there were many new entrants as the baby boomers reached working age and as more women entered the labor force. As a result, the NAIRU increased. In the 1990s, these trends reversed themselves, partially accounting for the decline in the NAIRU. Government policies to help workers move quickly from one job to another may lower the NAIRU. Similarly, competitive

pressures have increased, and unionization has decreased, so that wages more frequently fall and are slower to rise. This too has helped lower the NAIRU. Policies designed to lower the NAIRU are discussed in Chapter 35.

CASE IN POINT

The Baby Boomers and the NAIRU

The NAIRU or natural rate of unemployment is not a constant. One reason it changes is because the demographics of the labor force change over time. The prime example of the role of demographics is provided by the effect of the baby boomers on the NAIRU.

We have focused on the overall unemployment rate, the fraction of the total civilian labor force that is unemployed. However, not all groups in the labor force experience the same unemployment rate. Teenagers, for example, have much higher unemployment rates than older workers. At the end of 2000, while the overall unemployment rate averaged only 4 percent, the rate for females sixteen to nineteen years old was 11 percent and for teenage males it was over 13 percent. In contrast, the unemployment rates for older workers were much lower.

These differences in the unemployment experiences of different age groups have important implications for the total unemployment rate when the age distribution of the population is changing. The total unemployment rate is equal to a weighted average of the unemployment rates of different age groups. The weight placed on the unemployment rate of teenagers, say, will equal the number of teenagers in the labor force as a fraction of the total labor force. So if teenage workers represent 6 percent of the total labor force, as they did in 2000, the teenage unemployment rate will receive a weight of .06 (6 percent) in calculating the overall unemployment rate.

Because teenagers experience higher rates of unemployment, a change in the age distribution can alter the overall unemployment rate. This is exactly what happened in the 1960s when the post–World War II baby-boom generation started entering the labor force. This boosted the NAIRU; the same labor market conditions resulted in a higher measured overall unemployment rate because there were more young workers than previously. One recent estimate concluded that the baby boomers added 1.8 percent to the unemployment rate between 1959 and 1980. As boomers aged, they entered periods of life typically associated with low unemployment rates. This has cut almost 1.5 percent off the overall unemployment rate since 1980. ●

Shifts in Potential GDP

The inflation adjustment curve relates inflation to the state of the economy, measured by a comparison of actual output with potential output, the output gap. Positive output gaps—output levels above potential—accompany unemployment rates below the NAIRU. Negative output gaps—output levels below potential—accompany unemployment rates above the NAIRU. Just as measuring cyclical unemployment is difficult because the NAIRU can shift, measuring the output gap is also difficult because the economy's potential output level can shift.

Figure 31.7 shows the impact of an increase in potential output on the inflation adjustment curve. Initially, the

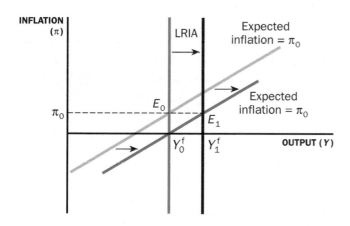

FIGURE 31.7 *The Position of Both the SRIA and the LRIA Curve Will Shift if Potential GDP Shifts*

An increase in the economy's potential GDP will shift the SRIA *and* LRIA curves. In the figure, the economy is initially at point F_0 at full employment (output equals potential) and an inflation rate of π_0 that is fully incorporated into expectations. If potential output rises from Y_0^f to Y_1^f, the new LRIA curve is a vertical line at Y_1^f. The SRIA curve goes through the point E_1 where expected inflation and actual inflation are equal and output is at the new level of potential GDP.

economy's potential GDP is Y_0^f. The LRIA curve is a vertical line through Y_0^f. If inflationary expectations are equal to π_0, the SRIA curve is positively sloped and goes through the point E_0. Many economists have argued that the new information technologies have increased productivity and raised the economy's potential GDP. If potential increases to Y_1^f, the new LRIA curve is now a vertical line at Y_1^f. Since actual inflation and expected inflation are equal when the economy is at potential, the SRIA curve also shifts to the right, going through the point E_1.

Many commentators have argued that the advent of new information technologies in the 1990s has significantly increased potential GDP. This has allowed output to expand without leading to an increase in inflation. Rather than moving up a fixed SRIA curve as output expanded in the 1990s, with an associated increase in inflation, the rise in potential GDP shifted the SRIA and LRIA curves to the right. If this is the correct analysis of recent economic developments, then the long economic boom of the 1990s did not risk a renewed increase in inflation. An alternative interpretation, though, is that temporary factors have kept inflation low, and that the SRIA curve has not permanently shifted to the right. Temporary shifts in the SRIA curve—often called inflation shocks—have been important in the past.

Inflation Shocks

During 1973 and again in 1979, there were major increases in the price of oil. In 1973, supplies of oil to the United States were disrupted by the oil embargo imposed by the Organization of Petroleum Exporting Countries (OPEC) as a result of the 1973 Arab-Israeli War. If you look back at Figure 31.1, the sharp increases in inflation caused by these oil price increases are clearly visible. As this experience suggests, there are factors in addition to cyclical unemployment and expectations that influence inflation, the factors we have already discussed.

The basic relationship between output and inflation that we summarized in the inflation adjustment curve started with the Phillips curve relationship between cyclical unemployment and wage increases. We then argued that wages and prices move in tandem, so the SRIA curve linked cyclical unemployment and inflation. While Figure 31.3 showed that wages and prices generally move together, it also showed that inflation exceeded wage increases at the time of the oil price shocks. The oil price changes altered the relationship between wages and prices.

The reason is straightforward. Wages are a large part of the costs that firms face. But firms have other important costs too, and the cost of the energy involved in producing is one of them. For a given increase in wages, prices will rise more as the increases in these other costs rise. The oil price increases of the 1970s increased inflation relative to wages, as shown in Figure 31.3. Such events are called **inflation shocks,** and they produce temporary shifts in the SRIA curve. For given inflation expectations and output, a positive inflation shock increases the actual rate of inflation.

Some economists have argued that the late 1990s were a repeat of the 1970s but in reverse. That is, the United States was again hit by an inflation shock, but this time, it was a negative shock that temporarily shifted the SRIA curve down. Inflation was lower at each level of output. Or, equivalently, we can say that inflation was lower at each level of cyclical unemployment. Two pieces of evidence are consistent with this story. First, if we again look back to Figure 31.3, we see that just as the positive inflation shocks of the 1970s pushed inflation above wage increases, during the 1990s inflation fell below the rate of wage increases. Second, at the end of the 1990s, unemployment was at levels not seen for thirty years. In April 2000, for example, the overall jobless rate fell to 3.9 percent, the lowest level since 1970. Despite this evidence of tight labor markets, inflation had not increased, as the SRIA curve would imply should happen. This too might indicate that the economy was experiencing a negative inflation shock.

Combining the Aggregate Demand–Inflation and Inflation Adjustment Curves

The SRIA curve summarizes the impact of cyclical unemployment and the output gap—the difference between output and potential GDP—on inflation for given inflation expectations. The aggregate demand–inflation (ADI) curve developed in Chapter 30 summarizes the short-run impact of inflation on real interest rates, aggregate expenditures, and equilibrium output. Putting the two together allows us to understand the factors that determine both output *and* inflation in the short run.

Factors That Affect Inflation

Changes in output relative to potential (the output gap): An increase in output relative to potential increases inflation; a decrease reduces inflation. Changes in the output gap represent movements along a given SRIA curve.

Changes in expected inflation: An increase in expected inflation shifts the SRIA curve up; a decrease shifts it down.

Inflation shocks: Changes in the marginal cost of production from sources other than wages shift the SRIA curve. An oil price increase shifts the curve up; an oil price decrease shifts it down.

These three determinants of inflation—output relative to full employment, expectations, and inflation shocks—are shown schematically below. Each plays a critical role in explaining actual inflation.

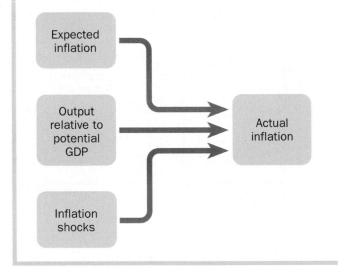

Equilibrium in the short run occurs where the ADI and SRIA curves intersect. Figure 31. 8 adds the ADI curve to Figure 31.7. The initial SRIA curve is drawn for an expected inflation rate equal to π_0. The situation depicted is one in which the short-run equilibrium occurs at point E_1 with output equal to Y_1 and inflation equal to π_1. Two aspects of this short-run equilibrium are important to note. First, the economy is producing at an output level above potential (Y^f). Second, the inflation rate π_1 is greater than people had expected.

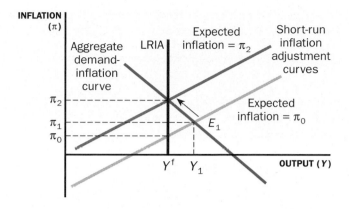

FIGURE 31.8 *Combining the ADI and SRIA Curves*

The economy's short-run equilibrium is at the point where the ADI and SRIA curves intersect, at point E_1 in the figure. At E_1 output is above potential and inflation exceeds expected inflation. As people revised upwards their expectations of inflation, the SRIA curve shifts up. Eventually, output returns to Y^f at an inflation rate equal to π_2. At that point, output is equal to potential and inflation is equal to expected inflation.

The economy will not remain at point E_1, however, because inflation is now higher than people had expected. Inflation expectations will rise. As we learned in this chapter, a rise in inflation expectations causes the SRIA curve to shift up. As the SRIA curve shifts up, the economy's equilibrium moves along the ADI curve, as

shown by the arrow. Inflation continues to rise and output falls. This movement along the ADI curve involves rising interest rates. As inflation expectations rise, so does actual inflation. In response to rising inflation, the Fed raises interest rates and aggregate expenditures fall. Equilibrium output declines toward the full-employment level. Eventually, full-employment output is reached at an inflation rate of π_2. At this point, equilibrium output is equal to Y^f (so the economy is on its ADI curve) and both actual inflation and expected inflation are equal to π_2 (so the economy is on its LRIA curve).

Review and Practice

Summary

1. Prices and wages may be slow to adjust for several reasons. Firms may face large adjustment costs. Firms may adjust output and employment rather than prices and wages because the uncertainties associated with changing prices and wages may be greater. Contracts may restrict the flexibility of wages to adjust, or minimum wage legislation may prevent money wages from being cut.

2. *Other things being equal*, in the short run, higher unemployment is associated with lower inflation. This relationship is called the Phillips curve.

e-Insight

A New Trade-off?

Low unemployment and low inflation are two of the major goals of macroeconomic policy, and America's success in achieving these was one of the most commented-on aspects of the American economy from the mid-1990s through 2000. In the early 1990s, most economists placed the NAIRU at around 6 percent. If unemployment were to fall below this level, inflation was expected to

rise. Unemployment did fall below 6 percent at the end of 1994, and it kept falling, reaching a low of 3.9 percent in April 2000. Yet inflation did not rise. In fact, from 1994 to 1998 it fell from an annual rate of 2 percent to just over 1 percent (measured by the GDP price index). As the chart illustrates, the 1990s was a period of falling unemployment *and* falling inflation.

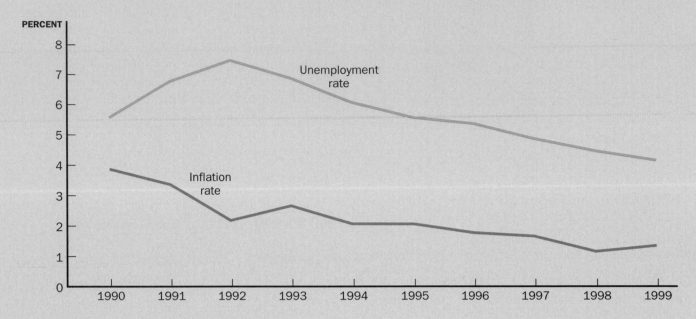

Unemployment and Inflation in the 1990s

In discussing the relationship between inflation and unemployment, we have emphasized the basic trade-off between unemployment and inflation that policymakers face in the short run. The experience of the 1990s led many commentators to argue that this trade-off had been altered—low unemployment no longer produces increased inflation. And the new information economy is the chief factor pointed to as being responsible for this favorable change. Does this mean the balancing act policymakers must deal with—posed between the dangers of higher inflation on the one hand and higher unemployment on the other—is no longer of relevance in the new economy?

Unfortunately, while the new technologies that are affecting the economy have many beneficial aspects, they will not eliminate the inflation-unemployment trade-off. This trade-off arises from the connection between labor markets and the prices firms set for the goods they produce. As unemployment falls and labor markets tighten, firms will find it harder to attract and hire the workers they need. They will have an incentive to offer higher wages to get the workers they want and to retain their current workforce. If these wage increases exceed any growth in labor productivity, firms will find their costs rising. Faced with increased costs, they will start to raise prices. As long as wage increases do not exceed productivity growth, low unemployment and low inflation can coexist. As discussed in *e*-Insights: Pro-

ductivity Growth and the Punch Bowl (in Chapter 30), the rapid productivity growth experienced in recent years has allowed the economy to enjoy much lower unemployment without increases in inflation. Expressed differently, the productivity gains have lowered the NAIRU. However, this does not mean there is no longer an inflation-unemployment trade-off. If unemployment drops below the new NAIRU, growth in wages will outpace productivity growth and inflation will start to rise.

Finally, the ADI-SRIA model of this chapter is consistent with periods of declining inflation and unemployment. Shifts in the SRIA curve cause inflation and unemployment to move in the same direction. The oil price shocks of the 1970s serve as an example of an adverse inflation shock that shifted the SRIA curve to the left, boosting inflation and lowering the output gap (leading to a rise in unemployment). The rapid productivity growth of the 1990s can be viewed in part as a favorable inflation shock, shifting the SRIA curve to the right. The behavior of inflation and unemployment that the economy experiences is determined by both the ADI and the SRIA curve. Because monetary and fiscal policies act primarily on the ADI curve, policies that shift the ADI to the left will lower inflation while leading to increased unemployment; policies that shift the ADI curve to the right will result in higher inflation and lower unemployment. This is the trade-off policymakers face.

3. *Other things being equal*, lower output is associated with lower inflation. This relationship is called the inflation adjustment curve.

4. The level of inflation associated with any particular level of cyclical unemployment or output gap will increase as expectations of inflation increase. As a result, if the government attempts to maintain unemployment at too low a rate, the inflation rate will continually increase, as each increase in inflation is built into individuals' expectations. The expectations-augmented inflation adjustment curve reflects the effects of inflationary expectations.

5. The unemployment rate at which inflation is stable—at which actual inflation is equal to expected inflation—is called the nonaccelerating inflation rate of unemployment (NAIRU). We can express this in an equivalent way by saying inflation is stable when the output gap is zero.

6. The NAIRU can change because of changes in the structure of the labor force or increasing competition in labor and product markets.

7. With rational expectations, changes in policy translate directly into inflation expectations; the expectations-augmented inflation adjustment curve can shift up immediately upon the announcement of a credible policy change.

8. Inflation shocks such as oil price fluctuations will affect inflation, for given levels of output and inflationary expectations. A sharp rise in oil prices, for example, shifts the SRIA curve up.

Key Terms

Phillips curve
natural rate of unemployment
short-run inflation adjustment curve
adaptive expectations
nonaccelerating inflation rate of unemployment (NAIRU)
sacrifice ratio
long-run inflation adjustment curve
rational expectations
inflation shocks

Review Questions

1. Why is there a trade-off between cyclical unemployment and inflation in the short run?

2. What role do changes in expectations play in shifting the SRIA curve? What difference does it make whether expectations are adaptive or rational?

3. What is the NAIRU? Why, if unemployment is kept below the NAIRU, will the rate of inflation rise? What is the long-run trade-off between unemployment and inflation?

4. What factors affect the NAIRU?

5. What is an example of an inflation shock? How does a positive inflation shock affect the inflation adjustment curve?

Problems

1. Jennifer earns $40,000 per year, but her wages are not indexed to inflation. If over a period of three years inflation is at 5 percent and Jennifer receives raises of 2 percent every year, how much has the actual buying power of her income changed over that time?

2. The sacrifice ratio measures the number of "unemployment years" required to bring down the inflation rate by 1 percent. Thus, if the sacrifice ratio is 2, one can bring down the inflation rate by 1 percent by increasing the unemployment rate by 2 percent for one year, or 1 percent for two years. If the sacrifice ratio is 1, how much would unemployment need to increase to reduce inflation by 2 percent in one year? If the inflation reduction is spread over two years, how much would the unemployment rate need to increase?

3. What would be the effect on the inflation adjustment curve of an announcement that OPEC—the cartel of oil-producing countries—had fallen apart, and thus the price of oil was expected to fall dramatically?

4. While playing around with old economic data in your spare time, you find that in 1963 the unemployment rate was 5.7 percent and the inflation rate was 1.6 percent; in 1972, the unemployment rate was 5.6 percent and the inflation rate was 3.4 percent; in 1979, unemployment was 5.8 percent and inflation was 31.3 percent; in 1988, unemployment was 5.5 percent and inflation was 4.4 percent; in 1996, unemployment was 5.4 percent and inflation was 3.3 percent. Does this evidence necessarily

imply anything about the shape of the SRIA curve? What about the LRIA curve? How might you interpret these data?

5. A simple form of adaptive expectations has expectations equal to inflation in the previous year. If inflation in year t is written as π_t, then expected inflation in year t would be π_{t-1}. Suppose we write the Phillips curve relationship between unemployment and inflation as

$$\pi_t = \pi_{t-1} - .5 \times (U_t - U^*),$$

where U_t is the unemployment rate for year t and U^* is the NAIRU. Assume $U^* = 5$ percent. Suppose initially in year 1 the inflation rate is 4 percent per year and the unemployment rate is 5 percent (i.e., $U_1 = U^* = 5$ percent). Now suppose in year 2 the unemployment rate falls to 4 percent and remains there. Complete the next four rows of the table. What is the inflation rate in year 7?

Year	Unemployment	Expected Inflation	Inflation
1	5 percent	4 percent	4 percent
2	4 percent	4 percent	4.5 percent
3	4 percent	4.5 percent	5 percent
4			
5			
6			
7			

6. Return to the situation of year 1 in the previous problem. By how much would unemployment need to rise to lower inflation in year 2 to 3 percent? Suppose unemployment is kept at this higher level. What happens to inflation in year 3? In year 4? How many years does it take to get inflation down to zero? Make a table like the one in the previous problem to show your results.

7. Suppose the Phillips curve in Problem 6 is replaced by

$$\pi_t = \pi_{t-1} - (U_t - U^*).$$

Redo Problem 6 with this new Phillips curve. What can you conclude about the impact of the Phillips curve slope on the effects of a decline in unemployment?

8. The relationship between the output gap and unemployment summarized in Okun's law takes the form

$$U_t - U^* = .5 \times (Y_t - Y^f)/Y^f,$$

where $(Y_t - Y^f)/Y^f$ is the percentage gap between output at time t and full-employment output. Use this expression for Okun's law and the Phillips curve from Problem 8 to derive the inflation adjustment curve linking inflation and the output gap.

9. The United States at the end of the 1990s witnessed rapid growth in real income and historically low rates of unemployment. Suppose two hypotheses for this decline are offered. The first is that productivity has increased owing to new technologies and that the NAIRU has fallen. The second is that the economy has been in a cyclical boom and unemployment has fallen well below the NAIRU. How might you distinguish between these two hypotheses? Do they have different implications for inflation?

10. Suppose people expect higher inflation in the future. What are the short-run effects of this change in expectations on unemployment and actual inflation? How can monetary policy maintain the economy at full employment? If policy succeeds in maintaining full employment, what happens to inflation?

11. Using the ADI-SRIA framework, show how the economy adjusts to a negative aggregate demand shock in the short run and in the long run.

12. If individuals based their expectations of inflation on inflation in the recent past, we can write the SRIA schedule as

$$\pi_t = \pi^{t-1} + a \times (Y_t - Y^f),$$

where a is a constant, $\pi(t)$ is inflation at time t, $Y(t)$ is output at time t, and Y^f is potential output. Suppose the ADI curve is given by

$$Y_t = A - b \times \pi_t.$$

Assume that initially output is equal to potential and inflation is 8 percent. If $A = 116$, $Y^f = 100$, $a = .25$, and $b = 2$, fill in the rest of the following table to show how the economy would respond if A falls by 5.

Period	Inflation	Expected Inflation	Output
0	8 percent	8 percent	100
1	7.17 percent	8 percent	96.67
2			
3			
4			
5			

Use an ADI-SRIA graph to explain why output and inflation behave in the way you calculated.

13. Using a spreadsheet program, repeat Problem 12 but calculate inflation, expected inflation, and output for twenty periods. Does output return to Y^f? What is the new long-run equilibrium rate of inflation? Plot output and inflation on the vertical axis, with the time period on the horizontal axis, to show how they move over time.

Chapter 32

The Role of
Macroeconomic Policy

TAX RELIEF FOR AMERICA

Key Questions

1. How do automatic stabilizers affect the government's budget? How can we measure activist changes in fiscal policy?

2. Do central banks respond only to inflation? How is the central bank's policy rule affected by the economy's equilibrium real interest rate at full employment and by the central bank's target for inflation?

3. What is the credit channel of monetary policy?

4. How do monetary and fiscal policies differ in their impacts on the economy?

*E*conomic policy debates have always been at the core of macroeconomics. After all, macroeconomics began as an attempt to understand the causes of the Great Depression of the 1930s and to formulate government policies that might end the depression. Much of the decade of the 1990s was dominated by the debate over the huge federal government deficits and the impact deficits might have on economic growth. At the beginning of the twenty-first century, the debate shifted to focus on how to spend the surpluses now being projected for the federal government, how to maintain the longest boom in U.S. history, and how to prevent a resurgence of inflation.

Economies are constantly experiencing economic disturbances. During the 1990s alone, the U.S. economy was affected by financial crises in Europe, Asia, and Latin America, by oil price increases, by large swings in the federal budget, by a stock market boom, and by new technologies that transformed many sectors of the economy. These factors have the potential to create recessions or booms. In the face of disturbances, policymakers must try to ensure the economy continues to operate at potential output while keeping inflation low and stable.

In thinking about macroeconomic policy, we need to distinguish between the role of policy as an automatic stabilizer, adjusting routinely to offset fluctuations in the economy, and the more active role of policy as a means to achieve macroeconomic goals. There are aspects of both fiscal and monetary policies that fit these two roles.

In this chapter, we will examine the role of both monetary and fiscal policy in affecting the economy in the short run. Chapters 30 and 31 provided a framework for understanding the impact government actions have on the economy. In those chapters, the analysis treated policy in isolation—explaining how a change in fiscal or monetary policy can affect the economy. But macroeconomic policy decisions are not made in isolation—governments use monetary and fiscal policies to try to stabilize the economy, and this role of policy is the topic of the present chapter.

Fiscal Policy

Fiscal policy is defined as changes in government expenditures and taxes that are designed to achieve macroeconomic policy goals. In earlier chapters, we learned about the consequences of changes in fiscal policy. The full-employment model was useful for assessing the impact of budget deficits and surpluses on the real interest rate, investment, and growth. The model of short-run fluctuations provided a framework for analyzing how unemployment and inflation would be affected by swings in fiscal policy. These models give insights into the effects of fiscal policy, but we now need to use those insights to focus on how fiscal policy can contribute to the macroeconomic goals of full employment, low and stable inflation, and economic growth.

Automatic Stabilizers

One way that fiscal policy contributes to these macroeconomic goals is by serving as an **automatic stabilizer.** Automatic stabilizers are expenditures that automatically increase or taxes that automatically decrease when economic conditions worsen. They therefore tend to stabilize aggregate expenditures automatically. As incomes rise, individuals and businesses will have to pay more in taxes to local and state governments and the federal government. This acts to limit spending increases and keep overall aggregate spending more stable. For example, suppose the marginal tax rate is 30 percent—that is, for each additional dollar you earn, you have to pay 30 cents in taxes. When your income goes up by $1,000, your disposable income—what you have left after paying taxes—only increases by $700. Three hundred dollars of your increased income must go to pay taxes. If the marginal propensity to consume is .8, you increase your spending by .8 × $700, or $560. This is significantly less than if you had gotten to keep the entire $1,000. Without the increased tax bite, you would have increased your spending by .8 × $1,000, or $800. Because taxes rise and fall with income, they help to reduce swings in spending and, as a result, make the economy more stable.

Taxes are not the only form of fiscal automatic stabilizers. Many transfer payments, such as unemployment benefits, adjust automatically as economic conditions change. When unemployment rises, the payment of unemployment benefits automatically increases. This helps provide income support to those without employment. As a consequence, they are not forced to reduce their consumption spending to the extent they would in the absence of these benefits. By limiting the decline in spending, automatic stabilizers make the economy more stable.

Automatic stabilizers influence the slope of the aggregate demand–inflation (ADI) curve that we introduced in Chapter 30. For example, the impact that an increase in inflation which leads to a rise in the real interest rate has on aggregate spending will depend on the tax system. As spending and income fall in reaction to the increased cost of credit, tax payments also fall. This decrease in tax payments cushions the decline in disposable income and household consumption spending. It acts to limit the extent to which spending, and therefore aggregate income, decline when inflation increases. As a consequence, an economy in which automatic fiscal stabilizers are important will have a steeper ADI curve than one without fiscal stabilizers.

The impact of automatic stabilizers on the ADI curve and the way spending shocks affect the short-run equilibrium are illustrated in Figure 32.1. The figure combines the ADI curve and the short-run inflation adjustment curve—the economy's short-run equilibrium is where the two intersect.[1] Two sets of ADI curves are shown, reflecting how an economy with strong fiscal automatic stabilizers might differ from an economy with much weaker automatic stabilizers. For ease of comparison, the two ADI curves intersect the long-run inflation adjustment line at the same inflation rate. The economy with the stronger automatic stabilizers has the steeper ADI curve (the solid green one in the figure). A change in inflation leads, through its impact on the real interest rate, to a smaller change in output because of the automatic stabilizers. For example, when inflation rises and the central bank boosts the real interest rate, spending falls and equilibrium income declines, but when automatic stabilizers kick in—tax payments decline and government spending, particularly transfer spending, increases automatically—the decline in spending and output is cushioned. The economy lacking automatic stabilizers will suffer a bigger decline in output, and this means that such an economy has a flatter ADI curve, such as the blue one in the figure.

Automatic stabilizers also reduce the effect on the economy of shocks to the GDP. A fall in government purchases shifts the ADI curve to the left, but the size of this shift is reduced by automatic stabilizers. Recent research estimated that the federal tax system offsets about 8 percent of

---

[1]Notice that we have drawn the short-run inflation adjustment curve with a positive slope as implied from the discussion of the Phillips curve in Chapter 31.

Monetary Policy

Monetary policy affects the level of nominal interest rates, the money supply, and average inflation in the economy. Decisions the Federal Reserve makes about interest rates are a major focus of news reports and financial market participants. Speeches by Alan Greenspan, the chair of the Federal Reserve Board, are examined closely for hints of possible interest rate changes, and speculation can reach a fever pitch when the Federal Open Market Committee (FOMC)—the policy-making committee of the Federal Reserve—meets to decide on policy.

Some aspects of monetary policy are like automatic stabilizers, working to keep the economy more stable. But like fiscal policy, monetary policy also has been used more actively to achieve macroeconomic goals.

We already have incorporated one aspect of the Fed's behavior in the ADI curve. As inflation increases, the Fed, like central banks in other major industrialized economies, raises the nominal interest rate. And the nominal rate is raised enough so that the real interest rate rises. This normal reaction works exactly like an automatic stabilizer. If the economy expands above potential and inflation starts to rise, the Fed acts to produce a higher real interest rate. This curtails aggregate spending and serves to stabilize the economy at its potential. A critical issue in the design of good monetary policy is determining how much to raise the nominal interest rate in response to an increase in inflation. The strength of this response plays an important role in affecting the slope of the ADI curve.

Behind The ADI Curve—The Role of Monetary Policy

When the ADI curve was introduced, we explained that as inflation increases in the short run, the Fed raises the real rate of interest. This lowers aggregate expenditures and equilibrium output. Now it is time to take a closer look at the role of monetary policy in affecting the shape and position of the ADI curve.

Conducting Monetary Policy The FOMC meets approximately every six weeks to decide on monetary policy. In their discussions, FOMC members consider economic conditions for the economy as a whole. At the same time, the regional bank presidents report on conditions in their districts. The Fed, like the central banks in most other industrial economies, conducts monetary policy by setting a target for a nominal interest rate. At the close of each FOMC meeting, a vote is taken on whether to raise, lower, or leave unchanged this interest rate target. The interest rate the Fed targets is called the *federal funds rate*, or "the funds rate" for short. It is the rate on overnight loans among banks. When the Fed changes its target, it issues a press release that announces the change.[3] Occasionally, the FOMC will change its target between meetings, as it did on January 3, 2001, in the face of mounting evidence that the economy was slowing down and an interest rate cut was necessary.

Internet Connection

The Beige Book

The summary of economic conditions for each meeting of the FOMC is contained in what is known as the *Beige Book*. You can see the latest *Beige Book* at the Fed's Web site: http://www.federalreserve.gov/policy.htm .

While the Fed sets a target for the funds rate, its actual value is determined by supply and demand in financial markets, and as a consequence, it can fluctuate above or below the target set by the Fed. Figure 32.4 shows the Fed's target for the funds rate (green), the actual funds rate (red), and the prime interest rate (blue), the interest rate banks charge their best customers on loans. Two facts stand out. First, the actual funds rate is almost indistinguishable in the figure from the Fed's target. The Fed is able to keep the funds rate very close to the target it sets. In Chapter 25, we explained exactly how the Fed is able to do this using open market operations, and the implications of open market operations for the supply of reserves and the money supply. Now our focus is on the consequences of

---

[3]You can read the Fed's press releases at http://www.federalreserve.gov/pressreleases.htm .

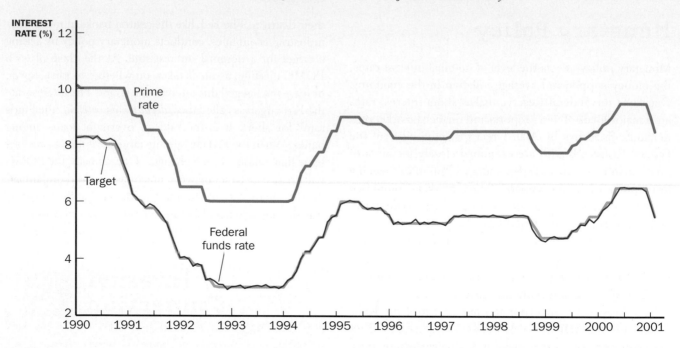

FIGURE 32.4 *The Fed's Target, the Funds Rate, and the Prime Rate*

The actual funds rate is determined by supply and demand, but as the figure shows, the actual funds rate closely follows the target set by the Fed. The prime interest rate is the rate banks charge on loans to their best business customers. It also moves closely with changes in the Fed's target for the funds rate.

changes in interest rates for the economy and on the factors the Fed looks at in setting its target.

The second fact revealed by the figure is the way the prime interest rate moves in tandem with the funds rate. The prime rate is always higher, reflecting the greater risk of business loans. But whenever the funds rate is raised or lowered, the prime rate also rises or falls. If an increase in the funds rate increases the real interest rate, borrowing will become more costly, raising the real cost of auto loans, mortgage interest rates, and commercial loans to firms. As credit becomes more costly, households and firms will scale back their spending plans.

Because changes in the funds rate affect the entire range of market interest rates, we simplified the discussion in previous chapters by assuming that the Fed sets the level of nominal interest rates. In Chapter 25, we learned that setting a target for the interest rate is not the only way monetary policy can be implemented. For example, between 1979 and 1985, the Fed often focused more closely on various measures of the money supply rather than the funds rate. Since 1985, however, the Fed has implemented mone-

tary policy by setting a target for the funds rate. Because this is the way the Fed actually behaves, we treat the interest rate as the main tool of monetary policy. What we need to examine now is *why* the Fed decides to raise or lower market interest rates. And to do that, we must examine the goals of monetary policy.

CASE IN POINT

The Fed's Domestic Policy Directive

After each FOMC meeting, any policy decisions are conveyed to the Federal Reserve Bank of New York for implementation. In recent years, these directives have specified the average value for the federal funds rate that the FOMC believes is consistent with its policy objectives. The following is taken from the minutes of the January 30/31, 2001, meeting of the FOMC:

At the conclusion of this discussion, the Committee voted to authorize and direct the Federal Reserve Bank of New York, until it was instructed otherwise, to execute transactions in the System Account in accordance with the following domestic policy directive:

> The Federal Open Market Committee seeks monetary and financial conditions that will foster price stability and promote sustainable growth in output. To further its long-run objectives, the Committee in the immediate future seeks conditions in reserve markets consistent with reducing the federal funds rate to an average of around 5-1/2 percent.

The minutes of an FOMC meeting are not released until after the following FOMC meeting. However, immediately after each meeting, the FOMC issues a press release that summarizes any monetary policy actions taken during the meeting and provides an indication of the FOMC's assessment of economic conditions. The press release from the January 30/31, 2001, meeting stated,

> The Federal Open Market Committee at its meeting today decided to lower its target for the federal funds rate by 50 basis points to 5-1/2 percent.[4] In a related action, the Board of Governors approved a 50 basis point reduction in the discount rate to 5 percent.
>
> Consumer and business confidence has eroded further, exacerbated by rising energy costs that continue to drain consumer purchasing power and press on business profit margins. Partly as a consequence, retail sales and business spending on capital equipment have weakened appreciably. In response, manufacturing production has been cut back sharply, with new technologies appearing to have accelerated the response of production and demand to potential excesses in the stock of inventories and capital equipment.
>
> Taken together, and with inflation contained, these circumstances have called for a rapid and forceful response of monetary policy. The longer-term advances in technology and accompanying gains in productivity, however, exhibit few signs of abating and these gains, along with the lower interest rates, should support growth of the economy over time.

New York Stock Exchange traders listen to the results of a recent FOMC meeting.

> Nonetheless, the Committee continues to believe that against the background of its long-run goals of price stability and sustainable economic growth and of the information currently available, the risks are weighted mainly toward conditions that may generate economic weakness in the foreseeable future.

Real Interest Rates and Nominal Interest Rates

To understand the links between the Fed's decisions and real output and inflation, we must start by recalling an important distinction between *real interest rates* and *nominal interest rates*. The nominal, or market, interest rate gives the percentage rate of return on a deposit, loan, or financial asset *without taking into account the effects of inflation*. When prices are rising, the value of a dollar is falling since each dollar will buy fewer and fewer goods and services over time. The dollars a borrower repays are worth less than the dollars that were borrowed. When prices are falling, the value of a dollar is rising since each dollar will buy more and more goods and services over time. The dollars a borrower repays are then worth more than the dollars that were borrowed. The nominal interest rate as a measure of the cost of a loan or the rate of return on a financial asset fails to correct for these changes in the value of money.

The real rate of interest is the percentage return on a deposit, loan, or other financial asset *after the effects of*

---

[4]A basis point is a hundredth of a percent, so a 50 basis point decrease is a .50 percentage decrease, in this case, from 6.00 percent to 5.50 percent.

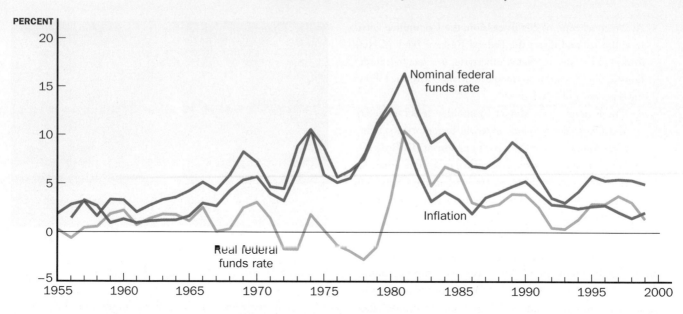

FIGURE 32.5 *Nominal and Real Federal Funds Rate*

The nominal federal funds rate is the market interest rate most directly influenced by Federal Reserve policy. By changing the nominal funds rate, monetary policy influences the economy. The major channel through which policy has its effects is through the real federal funds (interest) rate. The real rate is the market rate adjusted for inflation. During the 1970s, the funds rate was high, but so was inflation. Consequently, the real interest rate was low, and even negative.

inflation are taken into account. It represents the change in the real purchasing power that the lender receives. If the market rate of interest is 6 percent and inflation is 2 percent, the real interest rate is 4 percent; 2 percentage points of the 6 percent nominal interest rate represent compensation for the falling value of the dollar. The relationship between the real rate of interest, the nominal rate of interest, and inflation is given by[5]

nominal rate of interest = real rate of interest + inflation.

Figure 32.5 shows the nominal federal funds rate, the inflation rate, and the nominal funds rate minus the inflation rate as a measure of the real interest rate. Two points are worth noting. First, the level of nominal and real interest rates can differ significantly. In the 1970s, for instance, the nominal funds rate was high, yet the real rate was negative for most of the decade. In the 1990s, the nominal funds rate was lower than it had been in the 1970s, yet the

real rate was higher. Second, the average level of the funds rate moves closely with inflation. Periods of high inflation typically are associated with a high nominal rate; periods of low inflation typically are associated with a low nominal interest rate.

From the definition of the nominal interest rate, it is easy to understand why nominal interest rates are high when inflation is high. Both borrowers and lenders care about the real interest rate since that determines the purchasing power they must give up to borrow or the purchasing power they receive by making the loan. If inflation rises, lenders demand, and borrowers are willing to pay, a higher market interest rate. And a market interest rate of 10 percent with inflation equal to 6 percent represents the same real interest rate as a market rate of 5 percent with inflation of 1 percent. The interest rates we hear reported in the news or read in the newspaper are nominal interest rates that are not adjusted to take into account changes in the value of money. Economic decisions—decisions about how much to consume or save, whether to invest in a new plant, or whether to buy a new home—are based on real interest rates.

---

[5]We are ignoring taxes on interest income here.

Thinking Like an Economist

Real Values Matter for Incentives

Economists believe that to understand how individuals and firms behave, we should assume they make rational decisions. In making decisions, individuals and firms respond to incentives. But for decisions to be affected, a change in incentives has to be a *real* change—it has to reflect an actual change in the trade-offs the decision maker faces. This means that a worker will be concerned with how much her wages can purchase—the real value of wages, not simply their amount in terms of dollars. If a worker's nominal wage rises by 10 percent but prices also rise by 10 percent, the worker's incentive to supply labor is unaffected. Supplying an extra hour of labor increases the worker's nominal income by more than before, but it yields the worker the same real income as it did before prices and wages rose. The incentive to work is unchanged.

Similarly, households and firms will base decisions about borrowing and investing on the *real* costs of borrowing and the *real* returns to investing. In deciding whether to borrow to finance a car, for example, you must weigh the consumption of other goods and services that must be given up in order to purchase the car. If the interest rate on the car loan is 15 percent, but you expect prices and your nominal income to be rising at 5 percent owing to inflation, then each year the dollars you use to pay the interest on your loan are worth 5 percent less than the year before. The effective real interest rate on the loan is 10 percent. Now suppose that when you took out the car loan, inflation had been zero rather than 5 percent per year. Your incentive to borrow would be unaffected if the interest rate on the loan falls to 10 percent. You pay fewer dollars each year at a 10 percent interest rate, but those dollars are worth more since there is no inflation. Your real cost is the same, so the incentives to borrow are also unchanged.

Economic decisions are based on the real interest rate, not the nominal interest rate. Changes in the real interest rate alter the incentives individuals face.

The Central Bank Policy Rule

In setting its nominal interest rate target, the Fed attempts to influence the level of aggregate expenditures. When inflation rises, or when the Fed expects inflation to rise, the Fed raises the nominal interest rate. But because the spending plans of households and firms depend on the real interest rate, the Fed must raise the nominal interest rate enough to ensure that the real interest rate rises. When it does so, aggregate expenditures fall, lowering equilibrium output and reducing the upward pressure on prices. Similarly, if the economy is entering a recession and inflation is falling, the Fed will reduce the nominal interest rate to lower the real interest rate, stimulate aggregate expenditures, expand output, and moderate the recession. This type of behavior leads to a positive relationship between inflation and the real interest rate: an increase in inflation causes the Fed to raise the nominal interest rate, and it boosts the nominal rate enough to raise the real rate of interest.

This relationship between inflation, the nominal interest rate set by the central bank, and the real interest rate is important in accounting for the slope of the ADI curve. We illustrate the connection between inflation and the nominal interest rate the central bank sets in panel A of Figure 32.6. The real interest rate is the nominal rate minus inflation, so the nominal interest rate must rise by more than a one-to-one ratio with increases in inflation to ensure the real interest rate increases.[6] This means that the slope of the line in the figure is greater than 1. If the inflation rate increases from π_0 to π_1, the nominal interest rate is raised from i_0 to i_1. The change in the nominal interest rate, i_1 to i_0, is greater than the change in the rate of inflation, π_1 to π_0.

---

[6]If nominal interest income is taxed, the nominal rate will need to rise by more than a one-to-one ratio with inflation to ensure that the real, after-tax interest rate rises.

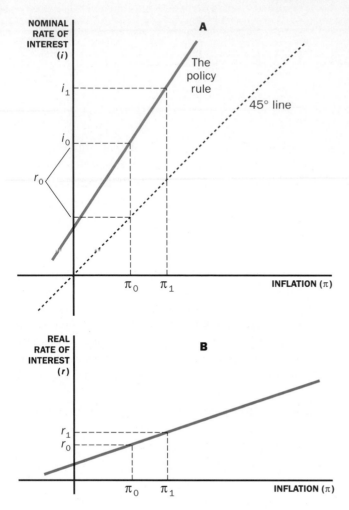

Figure 32.6   *Interest Rates and Inflation: The Fed's Policy Rule*

To ensure that the real interest rate increases when inflation rises, the Fed must raise the nominal interest rate by more than a one-to-one ratio with an increase in inflation. In panel A, at an inflation rate of π_0, the central bank sets the nominal rate equal to i_0; the real rate of interest is $r_0 = i_0 - \pi_0$. If inflation increases to π_1, the nominal interest rate increases to i_1. This increase is greater than the increase in inflation, so the real rate, shown in panel B, increases as inflation rises.

The relationship between inflation and the interest rate set by the central bank is an example of a **monetary policy rule**. A monetary policy rule is the systematic relationship between the central bank's setting of policy and the variables that it reacts to, such as inflation, cyclical unemployment, or the output gap. We have assumed that the policy rule takes a very simple form—the central bank changes the

nominal interest rate in response to changes in inflation. We will discuss later in this chapter how the central bank may respond to other macroeconomic variables, such as unemployment. With the type of policy rule we are assuming, one that captures important aspects of actual Fed behavior over the last fifteen years, the real rate of interest increases as inflation rises. This ensures that an increase in inflation leads to an increase in the real rate of interest (and a decline in aggregate spending) as shown in panel B. Conversely, a fall in inflation leads to a decline in the real interest rate.

Because the Fed sets a target for the nominal federal funds rate, we have discussed monetary policy in terms of its effects on interest rates. The relationships shown in Figure 32.6 also would arise if the central bank instead adopted a policy that focused on achieving a target for the money supply. As we learned in Chapter 25, as prices rise faster with an increase in the inflation rate, individuals will want to hold more money to carry out transactions. The demand for money, including bank deposits, rises. Banks will need to hold more reserves—at each level of the federal funds rate, the demand for reserves shifts up. If the Fed holds reserve supply constant, the federal funds rate will rise. So the policy rule represented in Figure 32.6 would arise under a policy focused on the control of the money supply. Since the Fed sets policy in terms of the nominal interest rate (as do most other major central banks), we will continue to discuss monetary policy in terms of the Fed's target for the nominal interest rate. As we discussed in Chapter 25, however, the Fed must use open market operations to affect interest rates, and these operations have implications for reserve supply and the money supply.

The policy rule in Figure 32.6 illustrates how the Fed responds to inflation. If the Fed reacts to other factors, the policy rule will shift. For example, suppose at a given rate of inflation the Fed decides to lower interest rates. It might do this if it was trying to offset the effects of a contractionary shift in fiscal policy. This decision would shift the entire policy rule downward; at each rate of inflation, the nominal (and real) interest rate would be lower.

Do Central Banks Only Respond to Inflation? We have assumed that the central bank adjusts policy when inflation changes. This assumption is a convenient simplification, one that captures an important aspect of how many major central banks conduct policy today. It helps explain why the Fed did not initially raise interest rates as the unemployment rate fell to very low levels in the late 1990s—as long as inflation seemed stable, the Fed did not alter its policy.

But few central banks (if any!) react *only* to inflation. The goals of monetary policy include low, stable inflation *and* overall economic stability and growth. If the economy enters a recession, central banks normally lower interest rates to help stimulate aggregate expenditures and moderate the rise in unemployment as the Fed did in 2001.

So whether the central bank lowers interest rates when inflation declines or lowers rates when unemployment rises will usually, but not always, amount to the same thing. In fact, because of the time it takes for changes in monetary policy to affect output and inflation, central banks often respond to their forecasts of *future* inflation. If the current level of unemployment or the size of the output gap helps to forecast future inflation, then even central banks that focus narrowly on inflation objectives will want to adjust interest rates in response to changes in unemployment.

Any policy change the Fed does make does not affect the economy overnight. If the change in policy results in a higher real interest rate, firms may cancel investment plans and households may reduce auto purchases, but these effects take some time to occur. Because of these lags between a policy action and its impact on aggregate spending and inflation, the Fed must be forward looking. It must set policy today based on its forecast of future economic conditions. This is one reason why making policy decisions can be difficult—no one has a crystal ball that can predict the future. It also means that the Fed must react to *expected* inflation, not simply current inflation. For example, in 1999 and 2000 the Fed raised its target for the funds rate even though inflation was still low. The FOMC members believed that without the shift in policy, inflation would eventually rise. They were reacting to their expectations about future inflation.

CASE IN POINT

The Interest Rate Cut of January 3, 2001

The effects of the interest rate increases engineered by the Fed during 1999 and the first part of 2000 started to make themselves felt by the end of 2000. And when the signals of a slowdown in economic activity started appearing, they seemed to indicate the economy might be headed toward a recession. On January 3, 2001, for instance, new figures on auto sales by U.S. domestic manufacturers were down by almost 8 percent from the levels of a year earlier. Chrysler announced that it would be temporarily shutting down five of its twelve North American factories for two weeks, putting as many as 30,000 workers on temporary furloughs. The day before, the National Association of Purchasing Management released their index of activity in the manufacturing sector during December—it had fallen to its lowest level since the last recession in 1991. Declines in the stock market during the last few months of 2000 also had created concerns that households would become more pessimistic about the economy and scale back their spending.

Faced with growing evidence that the chances of a recession were rising, the FOMC cut its federal funds rate target from 6.5 percent to 6 percent on January 3, 2001. By cutting interest rates, the FOMC hoped to stimulate investment and consumption spending. A boost to spending would help counter the slowdown in economic activity. The interest rate cut was consistent with the FOMC's desire to stabilize the economy at full employment while keeping inflation low and stable. During early 2000, it looked like the economic expansion would rekindle inflation, so the FOMC had hiked up interest rates. Once the evidence was clear that these rate increases were slowing the economy down, the FOMC wanted to ensure that the economy experienced a "soft" landing—with growth brought down to a sustainable rate without causing a recession. As signs mounted that the economy might be slowing, the FOMC cut interest rates again in late January and in March 2001. As this is being written in 2001, it is too early to know whether the FOMC has managed to avoid a "hard" landing. If the FOMC succeeded, the economy will continue to grow, albeit at a slower rate than experienced in the late 1990s.

A central bank that cared only about the rate of inflation might not have acted as the FOMC did in early 2001. If the FOMC focused solely on inflation, it would have cut the federal funds rate only if it thought inflation was getting too low. In fact, as the decision at the January meeting shows, the Federal Reserve is concerned not just with inflation but with maintaining overall economic stability. ●

The Dot-com Bubble and Macroeconomic Stability

Just think if in June 1996 you had invested $20,000 in a little known and fledgling new company called Yahoo. It would have been a risky decision; Yahoo was offering a free service to users of the Internet—something that most Americans still knew little about. A share of stock in Yahoo was selling for $2.09.

It would have been a great investment decision. As the year 2000 dawned, each share of Yahoo's stock was worth $176.50 and your $20,000 investment would have been worth $1,688,995! This represented a 255 percent annual return. A year later, in January 2001, things would have looked a bit different. You would no longer be a millionaire, since your Yahoo stock had plunged until it was worth only $262,010, a fall of 84 percent. Each of your shares would have been selling for just $27.38.

The experiences of Yahoo were mirrored by hundreds of other dot-com firms that had begun in the 1980s and 1990s as small start-ups and then saw their share prices break all records for growth as investors clamored for

shares in their companies when they "went public." Thousands of dot-com millionaires, and quite a few billionaires, were created, and millions of Americans who had never before thought of investing in stocks started speculating in the market. Fluctuations in the New York Stock Exchange or the Nasdaq exchange became part of daily conversations. But just as quickly, it seemed, the high-flying days ended during 2000. Dot-com start-ups started going bankrupt, and the technology heavy Nasdaq index, after reaching a peak at just over 5,000 in March 2000, had fallen to 2,291.46 by New Years Day in 2001. By March 2001, it was below 2,000.

The stock market affects macroeconomic conditions and in turn is influenced by economic conditions. Several times during the 1990s, the stock market was feared to be a source of instability in the economy. For example, consumption spending was fueled by soaring stock prices in the mid-1990s, which concerned the Federal Reserve for two reasons. First, increased consumption spending in an

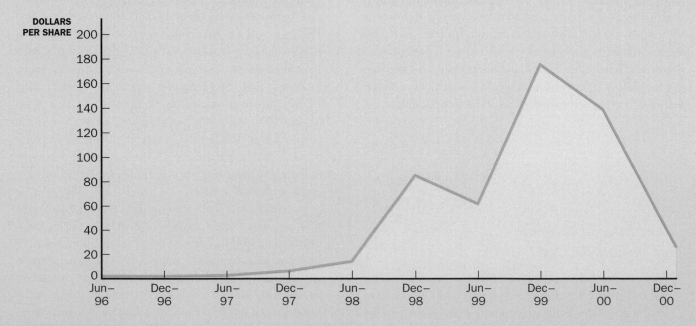

The Price of Yahoo's Stock

economy already experiencing a strong expansion threatened to overheat the economy and lead to a resurgence of inflation. Second, many feared the stock market boom was based on unrealistic expectations about the value of the new dot-com businesses. Although many of these firms had yet to actually earn profits, investors were bidding their stock prices higher and higher in expectation of future profitability. If expectations were to become less optimistic, the stock market might collapse suddenly, leading to spending cutbacks by households as they saw their wealth fall.

The stock market boom generated by dot-com businesses represented a major source of uncertainty for the Federal Reserve. Was the boom based on realistic expectations of the value of new economy firms? Or was it simply so much "irrational exuberance," as Federal Reserve Chair Greenspan labeled it in a widely quoted speech in December 1996? Did it reflect the fundamental soundness of the new economy, or was it setting the economy up for an inevitable market crash, much as had occurred in 1929? When the market slumped in the fall of 1998, the Fed cut interest rates, and this helped to restore optimism to the market. During the summer of 2000, the market drifted downward as the Fed boosted interest rates to slow the economy and head off a possible increase in inflation. Many economists have argued that the Fed should act to tighten monetary policy whenever a stock market boom seems based simply on expectations of continued unrealistic increases in stock prices—a so-called speculative bubble. Yet the new economy has made it more difficult to judge whether stock prices are "reasonable." With so many changes affecting the economy, and the constant emergence of new firms producing totally new products, judging whether the stock market is reflecting the fundamental reality of the new economy or simply irrational exuberance is a difficult task.

The Position of the Policy Rule

We can say more about the position of the monetary policy rule by asking what nominal interest rate the Fed would want to target if the economy were at full employment. Recall from Chapter 24 that the full-employment model made an important prediction about the real interest rate: when the economy is at full employment, the real interest rate must balance saving and investment in the capital market. Neither saving, investment, nor full-employment output depend on the inflation rate or on monetary policy. Consequently, monetary policy cannot influence the real interest rate that balances saving and investment at full employment.

This implication of the full-employment model has important consequences for monetary policy and the relationship between the nominal interest rate and inflation. Suppose, for instance, that the equilibrium real interest rate when the economy is at full employment is 2 percent. A central bank that could control the real interest rate directly would want to set it equal to 2 percent to keep the economy at full employment. Central banks, however, affect the nominal rate of interest, so the question we must ask is, What nominal interest rate will the central bank wish to set when the economy is at full employment?

The answer to this question depends on the average rate of inflation the central bank would like to achieve. Suppose the central bank wants to keep inflation equal to 1 percent. When the economy is at full employment and inflation is 1 percent, the nominal interest rate must be 3 percent. Why? The nominal interest rate is equal to the real interest rate plus inflation, so if inflation is equal to the desired target of 1 percent, a *nominal* interest rate equal to the full-employment equilibrium real interest rate (2 percent) plus the desired inflation rate (1 percent) would be consistent with full employment. If inflation is on target, the Fed will set the nominal rate equal to 3 percent, the real interest rate will be 2 percent, and aggregate demand will equal full-employment output. Figure 32.7 shows the policy rule for this example (the line labelled AA); when inflation is equal to 1 percent, the policy rule shows that the central bank sets the nominal interest rate equal to 3 percent.

If inflation rises above target, the policy rule in Figure 32.7 shows that the real interest rate increases. This helps to reduce output and inflation so that inflation returns to its target level. If inflation falls below target, the real interest rate is reduced, stimulating output and bringing inflation back on target.

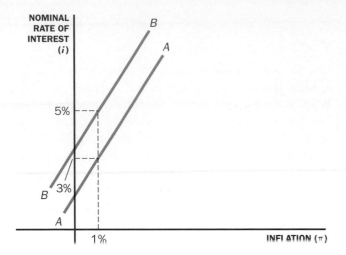

FIGURE 32.7 *The Monetary Policy Rule and the Equilibrium Real Interest Rate at Full Employment*

The central bank's policy rule needs to be consistent with the economy's equilibrium real interest rate at full employment and the central bank's target inflation rate. If the equilibrium real interest rate at full employment is 2 percent and the central bank's inflation target is 1 percent, then the nominal interest rate must be 3 percent when inflation is equal to its target, as shown by the policy rule line *AA*.

If the equilibrium real interest rate at full employment rises to 4 percent, the central bank must set the nominal rate equal to 5 percent when inflation is on target. The entire policy line shifts up to *BB*.

Shifts in the Full-Employment Real Interest Rate and the Policy Rule

In Chapter 24 we learned that the equilibrium real interest rate at full employment can change. An increase in the fiscal deficit, for example, leads to a higher real interest rate at full employment. If households reduce their saving at the full-employment level of income, the real interest rate will rise. Continuing with the previous example, suppose the equilibrium real interest rate at full employment rises from 2 percent to 4 percent. Now, when inflation is on target (equal to 1 percent), the central bank must set the nominal interest rate at 5 percent. So when inflation is 1 percent, the nominal rate will be 5 percent. As illustrated in Figure 32.6, when the equilibrium full-employment real interest rate rises, the central bank must shift its policy rule up.

If the equilibrium full-employment real interest rate falls, as might happen if households decide to save more at full-employment income or the government's deficit falls, the central bank must shift its policy rule down.

These shifts in the policy rule as the full-employment equilibrium real interest rate changes are not automatic—the Fed must make an explicit decision to alter its policy rule. If it fails to, the economy can be affected adversely. Some of the policy errors of the last forty years arose when the Fed did not adjust its policy rule when the full-employment equilibrium real interest rate changed.

The 1960s provide an example. The expansion in government spending associated with the Vietnam War and the War on Poverty, and the increased consumption resulting from the 1964 tax cut, pushed the economy above potential output by the end of the 1960s, leading inflation to start to rise. Figure 32.8 illustrates this situation. The initial equilibrium, at full employment, is labeled as E_0. The fiscal expansion shifted the ADI curve to the right. The economy's new, short-run equilibrium is at E_1. As we learned in Chapter 30, the inflation adjustment curve shifts up when the public comes to expect higher inflation. Eventually, full employment is restored at E_2, with a higher rate of inflation.

What did the Fed need to do if it wanted to prevent inflation from rising? The fiscal expansion raised the full-employment equilibrium real interest rate. In response, the Fed should have shifted its policy rule. At each inflation rate, it should have set a higher interest rate. This would have counteracted the rightward shift in the ADI curve so that full employment would have been restored at E_0, with both output *and* inflation returning to their original levels.

Shifts in the Inflation Target and the Policy Rule

Monetary policy plays a critical role in determining inflation. Many countries have established explicit targets for inflation that their central bank is then responsible for achieving. For example, the Bank of England has a target inflation rate of 2.5 percent. Other countries, such as New Zealand and Canada, have target ranges for inflation; in New Zealand, it is 0 to 3 percent. The central banks of Sweden, Australia, Israel, and the Czech Republic are also inflation targeters. In the European Monetary Union, the European Central Bank has considered using an inflation-targeting strategy. Under inflation targeting, the central bank establishes, and usually publicly announces, a target for the inflation rate. Other countries, like the United States, have not set explicit targets for the inflation rate. In the United States, the Federal Reserve describes price stability as its objective, but its behavior seems consistent with a target for inflation of 1 to 3 percent.

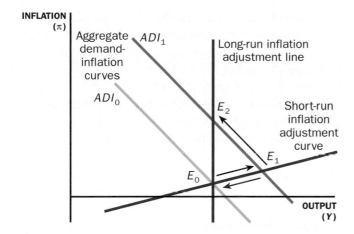

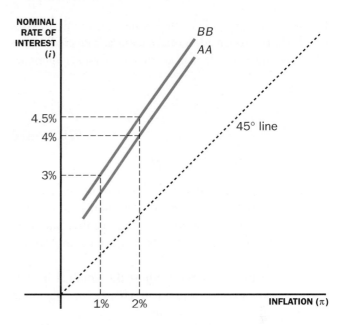

FIGURE 32.8 *A Fiscal Expansion When the Fed's Policy Rule Does Not Adjust and When It Does*

The figure illustrates the consequences if the Fed fails to adjust its policy rule when the equilibrium real interest rate at full employment changes. A fiscal expansion shifts the ADI curve from ADI_0 to ADI_1. In the short run, equilibrium output and inflation rise, and the new equilibrium is at E_1. As the public adjusts to expect higher inflation, the short-run inflation adjustment curve shifts up. If the Fed does not adjust its policy rule, the economy eventually returns to full employment at E_2 with higher inflation. The black arrows show the path the economy takes. To prevent the fiscal expansion from leaving inflation higher, the Fed must raise interest rates at a given rate of inflation. This shift in the Fed's policy rule is necessary because a fiscal expansion raises the real interest rate that balances the capital market at full employment. If the Fed's policy rule shifts, the ADI curve is shifted back to ADI_0 and the economy returns to full employment and inflation returns to its initial level at E_0 along the red arrow.

The position of the monetary policy rule linking interest rates and inflation depends on the central bank's target for inflation. Suppose the central bank decides to lower its inflation target from 2 percent to 1 percent. And for purposes of illustration, let's assume the full-employment equilibrium real interest rate is 2 percent. Figure 32.9 depicts the initial policy rule, the one for a target inflation rate of 2 percent, as *AA*. When inflation is equal to the target, the nominal interest rate is 4 percent (the 2 percent real interest rate plus 2 percent inflation). What happens to the policy rule when the inflation target is reduced to 1 percent? With the new target for inflation equal to 1 percent, the nominal interest rate at full employment falls from 4 percent to 3 percent (the 2 percent real interest rate plus the target inflation rate of 1 percent). The policy rule shifts

Figure 32.9 *The Effect of a Shift in the Inflation Target on the Central Bank's Policy Rule*

The position of the monetary policy rule depends on the central bank's target for inflation. Policy rule *AA* is based on an inflation target of 2 percent and an equilibrium real interest rate of 2 percent at full employment. If the central bank reduces its inflation target to 1 percent, the policy rule shifts up. At a given inflation rate, the central bank now sets nominal interest rates higher.

up to *BB*, as illustrated. At each rate of inflation, the nominal rate is now set at a higher value.

Does this shift in the policy rule succeed in lowering inflation? It does. If the economy initially has 2 percent inflation, the Fed now increases the nominal interest rate in line with the new policy rule *BB*. As shown in Figure 32.9, the nominal rate rises to 4.5 percent. Since inflation is still equal to 2 percent, this represents a rise in the real interest rate from 2 percent to 2.5 percent. As we have learned, a rise in the real interest rate causes output to decline in the short run. This puts downward pressure on inflation. The economy suffers an increase in cyclical unemployment, but eventually full employment is restored with a lower rate of inflation.

Other Channels of Monetary Policy

Our discussion has emphasized the important role of interest rates in explaining how monetary policy affects aggregate demand. Monetary policy often is thought to affect aggregate demand through additional channels. The credit channel and the portfolio channel are two of the most important.

WRAP-UP

The Monetary Policy Rule

A monetary policy rule describes how the central bank adjusts its policy in response to economic conditions. Inflation is one of the major factors central banks respond to, but central banks also react to unemployment and real GDP.

The central bank must adjust the nominal interest rate more than one for one with changes in inflation in order to stabilize the economy.

If the central bank has a target for the rate of inflation, the policy rule the central bank adopts will set the nominal interest rate equal to the real interest rate at full employment plus the inflation target when inflation is equal to the target rate.

Shifts in the real interest rate at full employment or the central bank's inflation target will shift the monetary policy rule.

The Credit Channel   Monetary policy affects aggregate demand through credit markets and the banking system. In Chapter 25 we examined in detail the linkages between the Fed's actions and the banking system. Moves by the Fed to raise real interest rates reduce the supply of lending that the banking system can undertake. A reduction in the supply of credit will increase the equilibrium interest rate at which credit is made available, while decreasing the equilibrium level of lending.

At times, banks may ration the amount of credit they make available. Typically they simply do not lend to everyone willing to borrow at the interest rates they charge. At times, they may not even extend loans to all those deemed "credit worthy" who would like loans. The direct effect of monetary policy on credit availability and therefore aggregate spending is called the **credit channel.** If the demand for loans exceeds the supply of credit, banks could raise the interest rate they charge, but they may worry that by doing so, the individuals and firms that are the best risks—

those most likely to repay the loan—will go elsewhere or decide it is not worth borrowing at such interest rates. If interest rates—like other prices—remain fixed, a shift in the loan supply curve has an even larger effect than when interest rates adjust, as Figure 32.10 illustrates.

Even when credit is not being rationed, banks respond to a situation of tighter credit by adjusting the terms of the loan contract other than the interest rate. They may, for instance, require more collateral on a business loan or a larger down payment on a home to qualify for a mortgage.

In any case, the decrease in the availability of credit (the shift in the loan supply curve to the left) results in lower investment, either because interest rates are higher (making it less attractive to undertake investment projects), because other terms of the loan contract are adjusted to make borrowing less attractive, or because funds required to undertake investments simply are not available.

The credit channel and bank lending received a great deal of attention during the 1990–1991 recession in the United States, particularly in the New England states. Many argued that firms were unable to borrow because

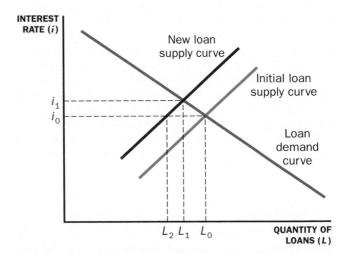

FIGURE 32.10 *Effect of Monetary Policy Viewed Through the Impact on Credit Availability*

Restrictive monetary policy reduces the supply of loans available at any interest rate. Thus, the equilibrium interest rate increases (from i_0 to i_1) and the quantity of loans made is reduced (from L_0 to L_1). In some circumstances, interest rates appear to be rigid and do not adjust. There will then be credit rationing, with the demand for loans exceeding the supply. In that case, the decrease in loans may be even greater (to L_2).

banks were curtailing lending. More recently, the economic recession in Japan has been worsened by the banking crisis the country has suffered. With many banks insolvent, lending has been severely reduced. An earlier example is provided by the Great Depression in the United States. Between 1929 and 1933, the number of U.S. banks fell by half because of failures and mergers. This banking collapse disrupted the credit system and contributed to the severity of the depression.

Why the Credit Channel May Be Less Effective in an Open Economy The credit channel may be much weaker in an open economy. One of the ways monetary policy may affect the economy is through its impact on the availability of credit. Restrictive monetary policy raises interest rates and reduces the availability of credit. But if American firms can borrow from foreign sources, then restricting credit from American banks simply induces borrowers to seek funds elsewhere. To be sure, not everyone has access to foreign banks. But the thousands of multinational firms do. If enough of these firms switch their borrowing abroad, it frees up funds so American banks can continue their lending to those who do not have access to foreign banks.

The Portfolio Channel

Monetary policy also can affect aggregate spending by affecting the stock market. A cut in interest rates initiated by the Fed lowers the return on interest-bearing bonds. Because of lower bond returns, individual investors will turn to stocks. As the demand for stocks increases, their prices rise. This effect can be quite pronounced, with the stock market reacting strongly even to hints that the Fed might change interest rates. Higher stock prices can lead to increases in consumption spending, since households are wealthier. Investment also can be stimulated; at the higher stock prices, more firms believe it is a good time to issue new shares, to raise additional capital, and to finance new investments. These effects are often described as a **portfolio channel** since they arise as individuals shift their portfolios between stocks and bonds.

For our purposes, the key point is that moves by the Fed to lower interest rates will raise aggregate spending. Whether this occurs only through the standard real interest rate and exchange rate channels, or whether credit channels and portfolio effects are also present, the important result is that aggregate spending will increase.

WRAP-UP

Other Channels of Monetary Policy

Monetary policy affects credit availability. The impact of reduced credit availability on aggregate spending is called the credit channel of monetary policy.

Changes in interest rates affect the stock market. The impact of changes in the stock market on aggregate spending is called the portfolio channel of monetary policy.

Interactions Between Monetary and Fiscal Policies

So far, we have treated monetary and fiscal policies as if they were two distinct policies. In the United States, fiscal policy is the responsibility of Congress and the president, while monetary policy is the responsibility of the Federal Reserve. This makes it convenient to discuss them separately. In fact, what is important for the economy is the net impact of both types of policies and the important interactions between them. Consider the earlier discussion of a fiscal stimulus. If the Fed simultaneously raises interest rates, monetary policy may partially or totally offset the expansionary effect of fiscal policy. The two are pulling in opposite directions. This happened in the early 1980s, when restrictive monetary policy more than offset expansionary fiscal policy and the economy went into a major recession.

We also have seen how a change in fiscal policy may require the Fed to alter its policy rule. If one of the goals of monetary policy is to maintain a low and stable inflation rate at full employment, then the central bank will need to offset the effects fiscal policy might otherwise have on inflation.

Both fiscal policy and monetary policy can be used to expand aggregate demand and increase output in the short run. Both types of policies can be used to dampen aggregate demand when inflation threatens to increase. But these two policies do more than just affect aggregate demand. Because they have different implications for investment, they can have different longer-run effects on the economy. A monetary expansion lowers real interest rates, stimulating investment. In contrast, a fiscal expansion reduces national saving and results in a higher real interest rate and lower investment. Using fiscal policy to stimulate the economy, by reducing private investment, may have harmful effects on future potential output.

The different effects fiscal and monetary policies have on interest rates and investment are just some of the ways these two types of policies differ. In Chapter 33, we will discuss a number of other differences that are important for evaluating these two policies.

Review and Practice

Summary

1. The actual fiscal deficit increases in a recession as tax revenues decline. This provides an important automatic stabilizer. To measure discretionary shifts in fiscal policy, economists look at the full-employment budget deficit.

2. The ADI curve depends on the monetary policy rule used by the central bank. The slope of the policy rule affects the slope of the ADI curve, while shifts in the policy rule are reflected in shifts in the ADI curve.

3. If the central bank wants to keep inflation stable, it must adjust its policy rule whenever the equilibrium full-employment real interest rate changes. The policy rule must be shifted up if the full-employment real interest rate increases, leading to a higher nominal interest rate at each inflation rate.

4. The monetary policy rule shifts if the central bank alters its target for inflation. If it reduces its inflation target, the policy rule shifts up, leading to a higher nominal interest rate at each rate of inflation.

5. Both fiscal and monetary policies can affect aggregate demand and output in the short run. They have different effects on the interest rate. A fiscal expansion raises the real interest rate; a monetary expansion lowers the real interest rate. Consequently, investment will be higher in the short run if monetary policy is used to stimulate the economy.

Key Terms

automatic stabilizer
full-employment deficit
monetary policy rule
credit channel
portfolio channel

Review Questions

1. What are automatic stabilizers and how do they affect the economy?

2. What happens to the government surplus when the economy goes into a recession? What happens to the full-employment surplus when the economy goes into a recession?

3. In the 1990s, the federal government's surplus rose dramatically. How would you determine if this resulted from the economic expansion of the 1990s or from discretionary changes in expenditures and taxes?

4. How does the slope of the aggregate demand–inflation (ADI) curve depend on the monetary policy rule?

5. If the central bank wants to keep inflation equal to its target, how must the monetary policy rule shift if the equilibrium full-employment real interest rate falls?

6. How does the monetary policy rule shift if the central bank's target for inflation is reduced? How does this affect the ADI curve?

7. Compare the effects of monetary and fiscal policies on the level of investment and the composition of output.

8. What happens to the nominal interest rate if the rate of inflation increases? Why does it matter if the nominal rate rises more or less than the increase in inflation?

9. In addition to the effects of monetary policy on aggregate demand that operate through the real interest rate, what other channels are there through which monetary policy may affect aggregate expenditures?

Problems

1. Why would the economy be more or less stable if there were no automatic stabilizers?

2. In 1999, the actual federal government surplus was larger than the full-employment surplus. Does this mean the economy was in a recession or a boom in 1999?

3. In recent years, many central banks have placed increased emphasis on controlling inflation. Suppose the central bank of the nation of Economica decides that it will move interest rates sharply whenever inflation differs from its desired target of 1 percent. Previously, policymakers in Economica had adjusted interest rates only slightly in response to inflation.

   (a) How will this switch in policy affect the central bank's monetary policy rule?

   (b) How will it affect the slope of the ADI curve?

   (c) Suppose Economica suffers an inflation shock that increases inflation. Use a graph to illustrate how output and inflation respond under the old and new policy rules.

4. Assume that the economy is currently at the NAIRU with an inflation rate of 2 percent. The government embarks on a major new expenditure program that increases aggregate expenditures (assume that full-employment output and the NAIRU are unaffected).

   (a) If the central bank's policy rule remains unchanged, what will be the short-run and long-run effects on output and inflation of this change in fiscal policy? What will be the long-run effects on the real interest rate at full employment?

   (b) Suppose the central bank's policy rule adjusts to reflect the change in the full employment real interest rate. Will this alter the short-run or long-run effects of the fiscal expansion?

5. In late 2000, there were signs the U.S. economy might be heading into a recession. Some argued that the rise in energy prices during 2000 was the cause of the economic slowdown. Others pointed to the decline in the stock market and argued that this decline in wealth would reduce consumption spending. Assume the economy is initially at full employment.

   (a) Using the ADI-SRIA framework, explain how a rise in energy prices would affect output and inflation in the short run.

   (b) Using the ADI-SRIA framework, explain how a fall in stock prices would affect output and inflation in the short run.

   (c) Suppose you are chair of the Federal Reserve Board. If your *only* concern is keeping inflation stable, would you raise or lower interest rates if you believe energy prices are the cause of the slowdown? Would you raise or lower interest rates if you believe the stock market decline is the cause of the slowdown?

   (d) Suppose you are chair of the Federal Reserve Board. If your *only* concern is keeping unemployment stable, would you raise or lower interest rates if you believe energy prices are the cause of the slowdown? Would you raise or lower interest rates if you believe the stock market decline is the cause of the slowdown?

Chapter 33

Policy in the Open Economy

Key Questions

1. What new factors influence the slope of the ADI curve in an open economy?

2. How do foreign economic events affect the U.S. economy?

3. How does a fiscal expansion affect the exchange rate and net exports? How does an expansionary monetary policy affect them?

4. Is fiscal policy more or less effective in an open economy?

5. Is monetary policy more or less effective in an open economy?

*M*odern economies are open economies. They are actively engaged in international trade and linked to international financial markets. The increasing "globalization" of the world's economies, and what it means for individual countries and their citizens, are sources of often strident political debate. Because it is part of the global economy, the United States is affected by, and in turn affects, international economic developments. A financial crisis abroad can affect the value of the dollar and U.S. exports and imports. U.S. budget surpluses influence interest rates and net exports. Exchange rate movements can affect U.S. inflation and influence decisions by the Federal Reserve.

The United States and other countries are linked by exchanges of goods and services and of financial assets. In 2000, the United States exported $1 trillion worth of goods and services. Exports as a percentage of total GDP equaled almost 12 percent; in 1970, they totaled only 5 percent. Imports of goods and services in 2000 exceeded $1.4 trillion. But these exchanges of goods and services are not the only international trades that take place. Trade also occurs in financial capital: a British firm borrows money in the U.S. capital market, interest is paid to Japanese investors who own U.S. government bonds, and U.S. investors are holding Korean government debt. Financial linkages also have grown tremendously over recent decades. It is estimated that foreign-owned assets in the United States grew from $142 billion in 1990 to over $500 billion in 1999. International flows of goods and capital have important implications for the macroeconomy.

The previous three chapters focused on a closed economy. We ignored international trade and financial linkages. We did this to simplify the analysis, but now it is time to add back the international dimension to see if any of the basic conclusions we reached in the earlier chapters need to be altered. Fortunately, the basic linkages between inflation, interest rates, and output operate in much the same manner as before. But there are new linkages as well, and international factors can be a source of economic fluctuations at home.

The aggregate demand–inflation (ADI) curve and the short-run inflation adjustment (SRIA) curve form the core framework used to understand economic fluctuations. Our main objective in this chapter will be to see how international trade in goods and in financial assets affects these two key relationships. Our focus will be on economies like the U.S. economy that have a flexible exchange rate, determined by the interplay of supply and demand in the foreign exchange market. In Chapter 26, we discussed the basic properties of the foreign exchange market. In Chapter 34, we will discuss other types of exchange systems.

The ADI Curve and the Open Economy

In the closed economy, the components of aggregate spending are consumption, investment, and government purchases. In the open economy, we must add net exports to this list. Just as an increase in government purchases leads firms to expand production and employment, an increase in net exports has the same impact. If foreigners purchase more U.S.-produced goods and services, U.S. exports rise. The firms producing these goods increase production and employment. If U.S. residents switch from buying goods produced in the United States to buying more foreign goods—buying Olympus cameras rather than Kodak ones or Heineken beer rather than Bud—U.S. firms see demand drop and they respond by cutting back production and employment. The impact of exports and imports on domestic aggregate demand is measured by *net exports*—exports minus imports.

The ADI curve developed in Chapter 30 summarized the relationship between aggregate demand and inflation in a closed economy. Increases in inflation lead to increases in the real interest rate, and this reduces household and business spending on consumption and investment. This connection between inflation and demand continues to hold in an open economy like the U.S. economy—changes in inflation continue to result in interest rate changes through the actions of monetary policy. But these interest rate changes now affect the exchange rate—the value of the dollar relative to other currencies such as the euro, the yen, or the peso—and net exports. Understanding how they do so is our next task.

Inflation, the Interest Rate, and the Exchange Rate

How does an increase in inflation affect the exchange rate? When inflation increases, monetary policy responds to cause the real interest rate to increase. The impact of infla-

tion on the real interest rate depends on the central bank's monetary policy rule, as we learned in Chapter 32. International investors constantly seek out the most attractive financial investments around the globe, so when interest rates rise in the United States, they sell financial assets in other countries in order to invest in this country and take advantage of the higher interest rates available. As they do so, exchange rates are affected.

If interest rates in the United States rise relative to the rates of return available in other countries, international investors, rather than lending funds in the capital markets of Japan or Europe, will lend their funds in U.S. capital markets to take advantage of the higher interest rates. But borrowers in the U.S. capital market want to borrow dollars, not yen or euros. So international investors need to buy dollars in the foreign exchange market if they want to lend those dollars to U.S. borrowers.[1] As international investors buy dollars, the price of dollars rises, just as a rightward shift in the demand curve for any other good would cause its price to rise.

While this discussion has focused on the demand for dollars by foreign investors, the supply of dollars in the foreign exchange market will also be affected. With U.S. interest rates higher, U.S. investors will be less likely to buy foreign securities, and this reduces the supply of dollars in the foreign exchange market. Again, the result is to raise the value of the dollar as demand increases and supply decreases.

When the dollar rises in value relative to other currencies, we say that the dollar **appreciates**. The rise is called an **appreciation**. When it falls in value relative to other currencies, we say that it **depreciates**. The fall is called a **depreciation**. Figure 33.1 shows the value of the dollar relative to the currencies of our trading partners over the past twenty-five years. During the 1980s there was a pronounced swing in the exchange rate. During the early 1980s, the dollar appreciated significantly. It became cheaper for U.S. residents to buy foreign goods such as Volvos, BMWs, and Sony electronics. Americans traveling abroad got more when they exchanged their dollars, lowering the cost of foreign travel. Of course, U.S. firms found it more difficult to sell abroad as their higher prices made them less competitive. After peaking in 1985, the dollar depreciated throughout the rest of the 1980s. By the end of the decade, its value was below the level it had been in 1980. The second half of the 1990s saw an appreciation of the dollar.

---

[1]See Chapter 25 for a discussion of the foreign exchange market.

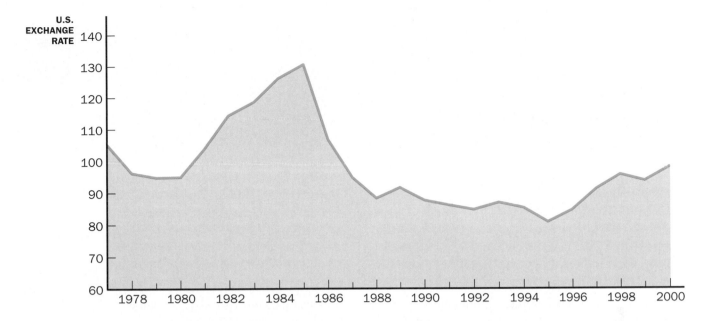

FIGURE 33.1   *The Trade-Weighted Exchange Rate*

The trade-weighted exchange rate is the value of the dollar measured against other currencies, where each currency is weighted according to the volume of trade with the United States. Thus, the Canadian dollar receives a larger weight than the Swedish kroner since the United States trades more with Canada than with Sweden. The dollar appreciated in the early 1980s and then depreciated in the late 1980s. The second half of the 1990s also saw a dollar appreciation.

SOURCE: Federal Reserve Board.

Our discussion took as its starting point a rise in U.S. interest rates. While this leads to an appreciation of the dollar, from the perspective of other countries, a rise in U.S. interest rates causes their currencies to depreciate. For example, if U.S. interest rates rise relative to interest rates in Canada, the Canadian dollar will depreciate, falling in value relative to the U.S. dollar. To take another example, in June 2000, the European Central Bank boosted interest rates. Because higher returns could now be earned on European financial assets, investors sold off some holdings of dollar assets in order to invest in euro assets. But to do this, they needed to use their dollars to buy euros. This increased demand for euros pushed up the price of euros in terms of dollars—that is, the exchange rate changed and euros appreciated relative to dollars.

Two points are worth noting. First, the value of the dollar is affected by changes in interest rates in other countries. This is just one example of the ways in which international economic developments can affect the U.S. economy. Second, our examples of how interest rates affect exchange rates are based on interest rates in one country changing relative to interest rates in other countries. This is what causes investors to shift funds in pursuit of higher returns. If the Fed raises the interest rate in the United States, and other countries respond by increasing their interest rates, the dollar will not appreciate.

The Exchange Rate and Aggregate Expenditures

Changes in the value of the dollar affect net exports. As the dollar appreciates, U.S. exports fall and imports rise. With dollars more expensive, foreigners find that U.S. goods cost more in terms of their own currencies. Faced with this increase in cost, foreigners will buy fewer goods produced in the United States. And conversely, foreign goods are now cheaper for Americans to purchase since dollars buy more now in terms of other currencies. U.S. imports rise as Americans buy more goods produced abroad.

The fall in exports and rise in imports means that U.S. *net* exports fall. And that means the total demand for U.S.

Thinking Like an Economist

Incentives and the Real Exchange Rate

Whether it is real GDP, real consumption, real interest rates, or real exchange rates, economists focus on *real* variables. In the case of real GDP, economists focus on a measure of production and correct for changes in the general level of prices. In the case of the real interest rate, saving and investment decisions are based on interest rates corrected for changes in price levels. Similarly, when dealing with exchange rates, economists distinguish between the *nominal* exchange rate—how many euros or pesos one dollar can buy—and the **real exchange rate**—the nominal exchange rate adjusted for changes in the relative price levels in different countries. It is the relative price of domestic and foreign goods that affects the incentives we face in choosing between goods produced in different countries. The real exchange rate is the relative price that affects net exports.

To understand why we need to adjust for relative prices in different countries, take the example of an Italian bike that sells for 1,430 euros in Italy. An American consumer

trying to decide between the Italian bike and an American-made bike that sells for $1,200 needs to know the exchange rate between lira and dollars. Let's suppose it is 1.1 euro to the dollar. That means it would take $1,300, each buying 1.1 euro, to obtain the 1,430 euro needed to buy the bike. So the consumer needs to compare the features of the U.S.-built bike for $1,200 with the Italian bike for $1,300 and decide which is the best buy. The U.S. bike costs 8 percent less than the Italian bike. To make this price comparison, we needed to know three things—the dollar price of the U.S. bike, the euro price of the Italian bike, and the nominal exchange rate.

Now suppose prices are rising an average of 2 percent per year in the United States and 5 percent in Italy. If nothing else changes, the price of the U.S. bike would rise to $1,224 and the Italian bike to 1,502 euros after a year. If the nominal exchange rate is still 1.1 euro to the dollar, the dollar price of the Italian bike would be $1,365. The U.S.

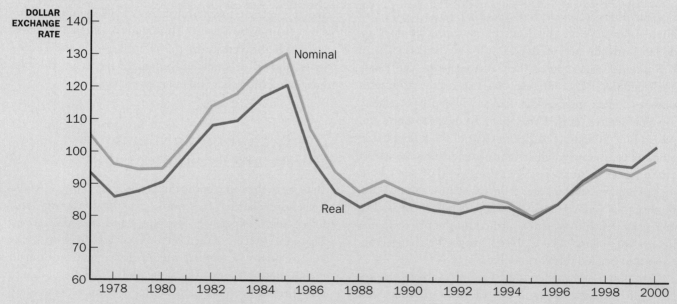

U.S. Real and Nominal Exchange Rates

bike now costs about 10 percent less than the Italian bike. Even though the *nominal* exchange rate has not changed, the relative price of the two bikes has changed. The U.S. bike is now relatively cheaper, so consumers are likely to buy more U.S. bikes and fewer Italian bikes. If the euro falls to 1.13 euros to the dollar, then the relative price of the two bikes remains unchanged.

This example illustrates why we need to adjust for changes in the price levels to determine whether a change in the nominal exchange rate will affect net exports. If the change simply reflects differences in the price levels in different countries, the relative price of domestic and foreign goods will not change, and net exports will not be affected. This was the case in our example when the nominal exchange rate rose from 1.1 euro to the dollar to 1.13 euro. The figure shows the nominal and real value of the dollar. As is evident, the nominal and real exchange rates move together closely. So in practice, when the nominal exchange rate rises or falls, the real exchange rate usually moves in a similar fashion. But when two countries have very different inflation rates, distinguishing between the nominal exchange rate and the real exchange rate can be very important.

SOURCE: Federal Reserve Board.

goods and services (consumption plus private investment plus government purchases plus net exports) falls. As firms producing for the export market see their sales decline, and consumers shift their spending toward imported goods, total production and employment in the U.S. decline.

What this means is that when we take into account the fact that modern economies are open economies, the ADI curve continues to have a negative slope. Just as in our earlier analysis, a rise in inflation leads the central bank to boost the real interest rate, and this increase reduces private spending, particularly investment spending. In addition, as the interest rate rises, the dollar appreciates, and this reduces net exports. So equilibrium output falls when inflation rises because investment spending *and* net exports fall. A movement along a given ADI curve now involves changes in both interest rate and exchange rate.

The Slope of the ADI Curve The slope of the ADI curve will depend on the effect of the real interest rate on the exchange rate and net exports. If exports and imports are very sensitive to changes in the exchange rate, then the ADI curve will be flatter than when they are less sensitive. A rise in inflation leads, through the response of monetary policy, to an increase in the interest rate. This causes the value of the dollar to rise, making domestic goods relatively more expensive. Households and firms will substitute away from domestically produced goods, increasing their purchases of foreign goods. Imports rise. Foreigners will buy fewer U.S. goods since they are now

more expensive. If the substitution effects are large, the rise in inflation causes a larger decline in domestic aggregate demand. If the substitution effects are small, the decline in domestic aggregate expenditures will be smaller. In this case, the larger the effects of changes in exchange rates are on net exports, the flatter the ADI curve will be.

Net Exports and Shifts in the ADI Curve

While net exports depend on the real exchange rate, they also can be affected by other factors. For instance, U.S. exports to other countries will be affected by the level of income in other countries. If incomes in Mexico rise, Mexicans will buy more goods and services, including more U.S.-produced goods. So U.S. exports to Mexico will rise when incomes in Mexico rise. And similarly, if Mexico suffers a recession, U.S. exports to Mexico will fall.

Shifts in net exports at a given real exchange rate, as might be caused by income fluctuations among our trading partners, cause the ADI curve to shift, just as shifts in government purchases do. A case in point occurred in the late 1990s. Financial crises in several Asian and Latin American economies led to severe recessions in many of these countries. As incomes fell, households and firms cut back spending. As a consequence, the demand for U.S.-produced goods fell, lowering U.S. exports. At the same time, the financial crises reduced the value of many Asian currencies relative to the dollar. This rise in the value of the dollar also acted to reduce U.S. net exports. At a given rate of inflation, total demand for U.S. goods fell, shifting the ADI curve to the left.

If this shift in net exports were the only factor affecting the U.S. economy at the time, the impact would have been to push the United States into a recession. As the ADI curve shifts left, equilibrium output declines. In the short run, the economy will find itself operating below potential output. Cyclical unemployment rises, and inflation declines. Inflation expectations decline as individuals and firms adjust to lower inflation, and the inflation adjustment curve shifts down. The decline in inflation leads the Fed to lower interest rates, helping to spur investment spending. Lower interest rates act to reduce the value of the dollar, and this works to revive net exports. Eventually, although it may take an appreciable period of time, the economy returns to full employment.

The United States did not experience a recession in the 1990s—the decade was actually one of the strongest periods of growth in the twentieth century. So what happened? Is our model wrong? Two things happened to prevent the Asian financial crisis from creating a recession in the United States. First, domestic consumption and investment spending remained very strong in the United States. The growth in these components of demand served to offset the drop in net exports. The second development was the Fed's response. As problems in Asia developed during 1995, the Fed cut the federal funds rate. The Fed's target for the funds rate fell from 6 percent in 1995 to 5.25 percent in February 1996. This is a good example of the type of stabilization policy discussed in Chapter 32. To offset a potential leftward shift in the ADI curve due to a drop in net exports, the Fed cut the interest rate to boost investment spending.

Foreign Interest Rates and Shifts in the ADI Curve

A recession in the rest of the world is just one example of the type of foreign economic development that can have a direct impact on the U.S. economy. Policy actions by foreign governments also have the potential to affect interest rates and exchange rates. If the European Central Bank, for example, decides to raise interest rates in Europe, euro assets become more attractive, and the euro appreciates in value relative to the dollar. This appreciation makes European goods more expensive for Americans to buy, and it makes American goods cheaper for Europeans to buy. The appreciating euro increases U.S. net ex-

ports as our exports rise and our imports fall. For a given inflation rate in the United States, this increase in demand for U.S. output means the ADI curve has shifted to the right. In the short run, U.S. output and inflation rise.

This discussion can be summarized in two points: First, the ADI curve is downward sloping in the open economy, just as it was for the closed economy. There is a new channel from inflation to spending, however, and this affects the slope of the ADI curve—as inflation rises, and the real interest rate rises, the value of the domestic currency rises and this appreciation reduces net exports. Second, international developments—booms or recessions abroad or changes in foreign interest rates—can have a direct impact on the U.S. economy by shifting the ADI curve.

WRAP-UP

International Factors That Affect the Slope of the ADI Curve

When monetary policy increases interest rates in response to a rise in inflation, the dollar appreciates. An appreciation reduces net exports, one of the components of aggregate spending. A rise in inflation leads to a fall in investment and net exports.

When monetary policy decreases interest rates in response to a fall in inflation, the dollar depreciates. A depreciation increases net exports, one of the components of aggregate spending. A fall in inflation leads to an increase in investment and net exports.

International Factors That Shift the ADI Curve

Factors that increase aggregate expenditures at each rate of inflation (and shift the ADI curve to the right) include

> Economic booms abroad
> A rise in interest rates abroad

Factors that decrease aggregate expenditures at each rate of inflation (and shift the ADI curve to the left) include

> Economic recessions abroad
> A fall in interest rates abroad

The Exchange Rate and the Inflation Adjustment Curve

Because net exports are one of the components of aggregate spending, fluctuations in net exports can affect the equilibrium level of output. Fluctuations in output around potential output in turn will affect inflation. The impact of output on inflation for given expectations of inflation was summarized in the inflation adjustment curve discussed in Chapter 31. The inflation adjustment curve was the second key component of the model of fluctuations. But changes in the exchange rate also can have a more direct impact on inflation. The relationship between the output gap, expected inflation, and actual inflation is affected by international factors, just as the ADI curve is.

Imported Inputs

In Chapter 31, we discussed how the SRIA curve shifts when the prices of imported goods such as oil rise. The economic fluctuations and much of the high inflation of the 1970s can be traced to the huge jumps in the price of imported oil. The prices in dollars that American firms must pay for imported goods depend both on the prices charged by the foreign producers of these goods *and* on the value of the dollar. If the dollar falls in value (depreciates), it costs more to buy foreign goods, just as if the foreign producers had raised their prices. Firms face increased costs for inputs when the value of the dollar falls, and if firms set prices as a markup over costs, prices will rise. As a consequence, inflation rises temporarily. For a given output gap and inflation expectations, changes in the exchange rate can shift the SRIA curve.

Consumer Price Inflation and the Exchange Rate

The competitiveness of U.S. firms on world markets depends on the prices of the goods they produce, the prices of foreign goods that they compete against, and the nominal exchange rate, the three factors that combine to determine the real exchange rate. When we go beyond individual goods (such as the bikes in our earlier example—see Thinking Like an Economist, page 720) and look at measures for the aggregate economy, the prices of U.S.-produced goods and services are measured by a price index like the GDP deflator introduced in Chapter 23. The GDP price index includes prices of all the goods and services produced in the United States.

But for most consumers, a more relevant price index for measuring changes in the cost of living is the consumer price index (CPI), which is an index of the prices of goods and services that households purchase. Since households do not buy jumbo jet airplanes, their prices are not included, although the cost of air travel would be. The price of French cheese is not included in the U.S. GDP price index since the U.S. does not produce French cheese. But U.S. households buy French cheese, so their price is included in the CPI. Because the CPI includes both domestically produced and foreign-produced goods, it is affected by changes in the exchange rate.

If the dollar appreciates, the dollar prices of foreign goods will fall. Since the CPI includes foreign consumer goods, while the GDP price index does not, the CPI will fall relative to the GDP index. When the dollar depreciates, the opposite will occur—the CPI index will rise relative to the GDP index. Fluctuations in the exchange rate are one reason for the differences in reported inflation rates, differences that depend on which price index is used to measure inflation.

Comparing Monetary and Fiscal Policies in the Open Economy

In today's open economy, policymakers designing macroeconomic policies must take into account the effects of the exchange rate. In a closed economy, expansionary monetary policy affects aggregate expenditures in the short run through lower interest rates and an increase in available credit, while expansionary fiscal policy eventually crowds out private investment. In the open economy, we have already seen how the effects of changes in exchange rates, and their impact on net exports, lead to new channels that come into play when we analyze macroeconomic policy. In an open economy, the relative effectiveness of monetary and fiscal policies changes—monetary policy becomes more effective in the short run while fiscal policy becomes less so.

Monetary Policy with Flexible Exchange Rates

When discretionary monetary policy actions are undertaken, their impact on the economy is reinforced by the exchange rate. Suppose the Fed decides to raise interest rates in the United States. And suppose Japan, the European Monetary Union, and other countries do not match the interest rate increase. The higher yields on U.S. bonds make them more attractive to both foreign and U.S. investors. The resulting demand for U.S. dollars leads the dollar to appreciate.

The dollar appreciation discourages exports and encourages imports. The ADI curve shifts to the left. Thus, monetary policy succeeds in dampening aggregate demand both through the interest rate effect on private investment spending—the channel that operates in a closed economy—and through the effect the exchange rate has on net exports. This impact on net exports reinforces the effect on investment, strengthening monetary policy's impact on aggregate expenditures and output.

When monetary policy expands the economy by lowering interest rates, the exchange rate depreciates and this depreciation encourages exports and discourages imports. The improvement in net exports is part of the overall impact of monetary policy in expanding aggregate expenditures. For small economies in which net exports are a large fraction of total spending, these exchange rate effects are the main channels of monetary policy.

Although monetary policy may be more effective in the short run in an open economy, one of our key earlier conclusions continues to hold—as wages and prices eventually adjust, the economy returns to full employment. So even in an open economy, the long-run effect of monetary policy is on inflation, not on output or unemployment. But in the short run, monetary policy can help stabilize employment around its full-employment level.

Fiscal Policy with Flexible Exchange Rates

While changes in the exchange rate tend to reinforce the impact of monetary policy, they act to reduce the impact of fiscal policy. The reason again can be traced to the way interest rates move. We have already learned that a fiscal expansion that shifts the ADI curve to the right increases output and inflation. If the SRIA curve is relatively flat, the initial impact will be primarily on output, with only a small rise in inflation. As inflation starts to rise, the central bank

will act to raise interest rates. Since central banks try to react if they forecast future increases in inflation, interest rates are likely to rise even if initially there is little actual increase in inflation. Also, a fiscal expansion raises the equilibrium full-employment real interest rate. As we learned in Chapter 32, a central bank that desires to maintain a stable inflation rate will shift its monetary policy rule when the equilibrium full-employment real interest rate changes. In the case of a fiscal expansion, this will lead to higher interest rates.

Internet Connection

Foreign Exchange Rates

The Universal Currency Converter at http://www.xe.com/ucc/ allows you to find out how much $1 is worth in any of more than seventy other currencies, from the Algerian dinar to the Zambian kwacha. Historical series on U.S. dollar exchange rates with many countries are provided by the Federal Reserve at http://www.federalreserve.gov/releases/H10/hist/.

As interest rates increase, the exchange rate will appreciate and this in turn will dampen net exports. Any decline in net exports works to offset the original fiscal stimulus to aggregate expenditures. As a consequence, the exchange rate adjustment limits the impact of fiscal policy on expenditures. In the long run, as the economy returns to full employment, an increase in the government's deficit crowds out private investment and net exports, as the full-employment model of Chapter 24 explains.

Exchange rates, unlike wages and prices, adjust very rapidly, but that does not mean that exports and imports adjust as quickly. For instance, German and Japanese automakers responded very slowly to changes in the exchange rate that occurred in the 1980s; they changed the prices they charged in the United States only gradually, so automobile imports decreased slowly as the dollar depreciated. A change in government expenditures may have an immediate impact on aggregate expenditures, while the offsetting movements in net exports may occur much later.

e-Insight

New Technology and the Integration of World Financial Markets

New information technologies are leading to tremendous reductions in the costs of carrying out transactions. This is particularly true in financial markets. Today, you can search the Web for low-cost brokers and trade in financial stocks and bonds in markets in New York, London, Frankfurt, or Tokyo, right from your home computer.

The increased integration of world financial markets alters the impact that fiscal policy has on the economy. To see how it does so, imagine a world in which shifting investment funds from one country to another was prohibitively expensive. Economists describe such a world as one in which transaction costs are very high. High transaction costs will limit opportunities to take advantage of high returns in other countries. If you consider investing in the United Kingdom, you first need to sell your dollars to buy pounds. (The currency of the United Kingdom is the pound.) Buying pounds will involve a transaction fee. Next, you need to buy a U.K. financial asset such as a bond with your pounds. This also will involve a transaction fee. Finally, when your investment pays interest to you in pounds, you have to convert those pounds back into dollars. Again, you have to pay a transaction fee. As an investor, you need to evaluate the return you can earn from investing in a foreign country by taking into account the interest rate you could earn, any change in the exchange rate you expect, *and* the transaction costs you will have to pay.

Even though U.K. interest rates might be higher than interest rates in the United States, the difference may not be enough to compensate for the transaction fees you will have to pay if you try to shift your investments to the United Kingdom. If you do not shift your investments, you do not need to buy pounds. The rise in U.K. interest rates does not increase the demand for pounds, and the value of the pound does not rise.

In this imaginary world, an expansionary fiscal policy in the United Kingdom leads to a rise in U.K. interest rates, but this rise in interest rates does not lead to an appreciation of the pound.

Now consider what happens in today's world with its lower transaction costs. Again, assume there is an expansionary fiscal policy in the United Kingdom. As interest rates start to rise in the United Kingdom, the higher returns attract international investors. These investors buy pounds so they can shift their investments into U.K. assets. As a result, the value of the pound rises. This, however, increases the price of U.K. exports on world markets and lowers the price of imported goods to U.K. consumers. The United Kingdom's net exports decline. Because net exports are one of components of aggregate expenditures, the fall in net exports offsets the initial expansionary fiscal policy. The closer integration of world financial markets as transaction costs fall makes exchange rates more sensitive to interest rate movements and reduces the impact fiscal policy can have on the economy.

Policy Coordination

Net exports provide one of the channels through which economic conditions in one country affect others. Interest rates provide another linkage. Because of these linkages, the major industrialized economies of North America, Europe, and Asia meet regularly to discuss global economic conditions and often try to coordinate macroeconomic policies. The meetings of the Group of Seven, or G-7, consisting of the United States, Canada, Japan, Germany, France, Italy, and the United Kingdom, provide a forum for discussions of international economic developments. In recent years, these discussions included such topics as the ongoing Japanese recession and policies to end it, the emerging market economies and the Russian economy, the role of international organizations such as the International Monetary Fund and the World Bank, and the debt burden of developing nations.

WRAP-UP

Policy in an Open Economy

In an open economy, monetary policy is strengthened because it may affect the real exchange rate and through the exchange rate, the level of aggregate expenditures. This effect reinforces the impact of monetary policy on aggregate expenditures through interest rates and credit availability.

In an open economy, fiscal policy is dampened because it may affect the real exchange rate and through the exchange rate, the level of net exports. The change in exchange rates caused by a fiscal expansion reduces net exports, offsetting some of the impact of the fiscal expansion.

The argument that countries may gain from coordinating their macroeconomic policies is best illustrated with an example. Suppose two countries are in recessions. Each contemplates using expansionary fiscal policy to try to speed its return to full employment. Each realizes, however, that if it expands fiscal policy while the other country does not, its currency will appreciate. This has a detrimental impact on the net exports of the country undertaking the fiscal expansion and negates some of the effect desired from the policy action. But suppose both countries could agree to undertake fiscal expansions. As their economies expand, interest rates in *both* countries will rise, so the exchange rate can remain at its initial level—the fiscal expansions are not offset by the exchange rate movement.

Conclusions

The U.S. economy is part of the global economic system—we export goods to countries around the globe, and we import the goods these countries produce. At the same time, American savers lend funds abroad, just as foreign investors lend in U.S. capital markets. These linkages bring many benefits to the United States, but they also introduce new channels through which macroeconomic policies affect the economy and they introduce new factors that can lead to economic fluctuations.

Among the most important are the effects of economic fluctuations abroad on net exports and the effects of foreign interest rates on exchange rates. The exchange rate consequences of monetary and fiscal policies play an important role in determining the overall impact of these policies on the economy.

CASE IN POINT

Engine of Growth or Source of the Flu?

The globalization of the world economy means that economic developments in an economy like that of the United States both affect and are affected by economic developments in other countries. Because the U.S. economy is the world's largest, fluctuations in the U.S. economy often can have major effects on other economies. During the past five years, the U.S. economy has gone from being viewed as the engine of growth for many other countries to the economy that when it sneezes, gives everyone else the flu. Our basic model can help to understand these two views.

During the late 1990s, the U.S. economy was growing rapidly. As incomes grew, American households and firms increased their purchases of goods produced in other countries. Imports of European cars, Finnish cell phones, and Japanese audio equipment soared. From the perspective of the countries sending all these goods to the United States, their increased exports to this country reflected a shift in the demand for the things they produce. In other words, their ADI curves shifted to the right. As we have previously learned, the short-run effect of such a shift is to increase real output. Since this expansionary shift was the result of the U.S. expansion, America was described as "the engine of growth."

At the end of 2000, signs were mounting that the U.S. economy was slowing down. No longer was this country an engine of growth. Instead, the concern in other countries was that the slowdown in the United States would lead to reduced sales to this country. For economies dependent on the United States as the major market for their exports, even a modest slowdown in the U.S. economy could have major repercussions. Hence, the fear was that if the United States sneezed, other countries might catch the flu of a recession.

The linkage we just described is one of the ways the economies of different countries interact. As economic conditions change in the United States, the value of the dollar also will be affected, and this can either offset or amplify the impact of the U.S. economy on other countries. As the U.S. economy expanded rapidly in the late 1990s, the Fed became worried about the possibility that inflation would rise. So beginning in 1998, the Fed raised interest rates. As U.S. interest rates rose relative to interest rates in other countries, the dollar rose in value. Because prices are sticky, this increase in the nominal value of the dollar also represented a real appreciation of the dollar. As a consequence, U.S. goods became more expensive relative to foreign goods. So even though the interest rate hikes worked to reduce growth in the United States, the impact on foreign countries is not clear-cut—slower U.S. growth, by itself, reduces U.S. demand for goods in other countries, but the stronger dollar increases the demand for foreign goods. Because of the adjustment of exchange rates, the linkages between economies are often not as simple as such phrases as "the engine of growth" might suggest. ●

As the U.S. economy grew rapidly in the late 1990s, imports of cell phones made by the Finnish company Nokia soared, helping boost Finland's real output.

International Perspective

Is a Strong Dollar Good for the United States?

Politicians and news commentators frequently interpret the "strength" of a currency as a reflection of the underlying health of the economy. And concerns are often expressed when the value of a currency falls. The experience with the euro provides a case in point. The euro came into existence on January 1, 1999, when eleven European countries joined together to form a monetary union. The exchange rate between the euro, the currency of the monetary union, and the dollar was initially $1.16 in January 1999. That is, it took $1.16 to purchase one euro. Over the next seventeen months, the euro declined in value. By May

2000, you could buy one euro for only $.91. The fall in the euro was accompanied by great concern, as some suggested the weakness of the euro was a sign that the monetary union was a failure.

But is a strong currency really good for an economy? Does the United States benefit if the dollar is strong? And critically, should policymakers take action to prevent the dollar from weakening? To answer these questions, we can focus on the role exchange rates play in helping to stabilize the macroeconomy and on how different sectors of the economy are affected.

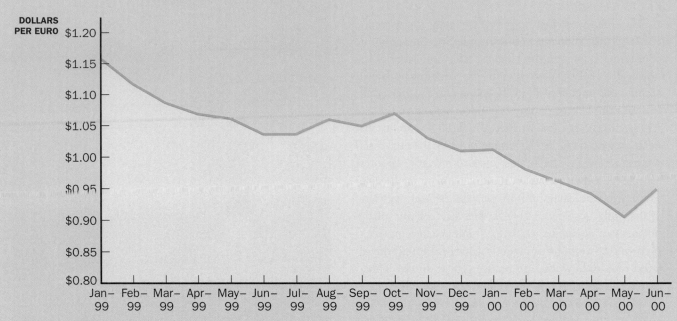

DOLLARS PER EURO

The Euro-Dollar Exchange Rate

Movements in the exchange rate serve to offset fluctuations in aggregate expenditures. In this way, they help stabilize the economy. For instance, at the end of the 1990s, European economies were in recession. As the euro fell in value, it made European goods cheaper on world markets. This increased Europe's exports. The fall in the euro made imported goods more expensive for Europeans to buy. This decreased Europe's imports. The falling euro boosts Europe's net exports, helping to end the recession. If the European Central Bank had increased the interest rate to try to prevent the weakening of the euro, it would have made Europe's recovery from recession more difficult.

A weak currency will boost exports and reduce imports. A strong currency has the opposite effect. So if you buy lots of imported goods, you benefit from a strong dollar. But if you are a business that sells abroad, your sales suffer from a strong dollar. If you work for a company that competes against foreign imports, your company is hurt by a strong dollar. Farmers may see world demand for American wheat fall when the dollar appreciates, while consumers enjoy lower prices for imported electronic goods. There are winners and losers from exchange rate movements, so apart from its affect on macroeconomic stability, there are no grounds for always preferring a strong dollar.

U.S. wheat farmers can be hurt by a strong dollar, which makes U.S. exports such as wheat more expensive on world markets.

Review and Practice

Summary

1. In the open economy, net exports are a component of aggregate spending. Both imports and exports depend on the real exchange rate. A lower real exchange rate increases exports and reduces imports.

2. Changes in the real interest rate affect investment, the exchange rate, and net exports. A rise in the real interest rate reduces domestic investment and net exports, leading to a downward shift in aggregate expenditures.

3. The ADI curve in an open economy has a negative slope—the level of output consistent with equilibrium falls as inflation rises. The ADI curve can shift if incomes abroad fluctuate or if foreign interest rates rise or fall relative to the U.S. interest rate.

4. Exchange rate movements can have a temporary but direct effect on U.S. inflation. If the dollar depreciates, the prices of imported inputs rise, and firms may pass this through in the form of higher prices.

5. Exchange rate movements can directly affect the CPI measure of inflation, because the CPI includes the prices of imported goods purchased by households.

6. Monetary policy is more effective in an open economy— changes in interest rates affect private investment, but they also cause reinforcing changes in net exports through the exchange rate channel.

7. Fiscal policy is less effective in an open economy—the exchange rate causes net exports to offset the initial fiscal action.

Key Terms

real exchange rate
appreciate/appreciation
depreciate/depreciation

Review Questions

1. What is the relationship between the interest rate and the exchange rate? What is the relationship between the exchange rate and net exports?

2. As we move up and to the left on a given ADI curve, what happens to the value of the domestic currency and net exports?

3. If firms import a lot of raw materials, what impact would a depreciation in the dollar have on the SRIA curve?

4. How does a fiscal expansion affect the real exchange rate and net exports?

5. How does a monetary policy expansion affect the real exchange rate and net exports?

6. If the United States raises its interest rate, and Canada does not, will the Canadian dollar appreciate or depreciate? If Canada follows the United States and also raises its interest rate, what will happen to the value of the Canadian dollar?

Problems

1. Explain how U.S. net exports would be affected by each of the following:

   (a) An economic expansion in Western Europe

   (b) Financial crises in Asia and Latin America that cause the U.S. dollar to appreciate

   (c) An interest rate increase by the European Central Bank

2. Using the information in the table below, calculate the real exchange rate between the nations of Nordamer and Sudamer (the nominal exchange rate is the number of Nordamer dollars that can be purchased with one Sudamer dollar):

	Price level in Nordamer	Price level in Sudamer	Nominal exchange rate
Year 1	100	100	1
Year 2	110	100	1.1
Year 3	121	100	1.21
Year 4	133	100	1.33

   (a) Has the Sudamer dollar appreciated or depreciated in nominal terms?

   (b) Has the real exchange rate appreciated or depreciated?

(c) Have Nordamer goods become less expensive for Sudamers to buy? Explain.

3. Suppose a fall in net exports due to a recession among our major trading partners causes a recession in the United States.

   (a) If fiscal policy is used to stimulate the economy and return it to full employment, what happens to the real interest rate, investment, and future output?

   (b) If monetary policy is used to stimulate the economy and return it to full employment, what happens to the real interest rate, investment, and future output?

4. The United States is a major export market for Canadian goods. Use the ADI and inflation adjustment framework to illustrate how Canadian output and inflation will be affected by the Fed increasing interest rates.

5. Suppose the U.S. economy is in a recession. The government is considering using expansionary fiscal or monetary policy to help get the economy back to full employment. Which type of policy will result in a higher level of net exports?

6. True or False: "A contractionary monetary policy hurts export industries; a fiscal contraction helps export industries." Explain why fiscal and monetary policies might have different effects on industries that produce a lot of goods for export.

Has the Business Cycle Changed?

At the beginning of 2001, there were signs that the economic expansion that began in April 1991 was coming to an end. In December 1998, this record-setting boom became the longest peacetime expansion since World War II, surpassing the record previously held by the 1982–1990 expansion. In January 2000, it tied the period of growth associated with the Vietnam War as the longest expansion on record since we began to track business cycles in 1854. This long period of economic growth has prompted some to argue that the types of business cycles and economic fluctuations we studied in Part Seven are no longer relevant for new, technology-based economies. The business cycle is dead—long live never-ending growth!

Extended periods of expansion always lead to speculation that the conventional business cycle is dead. In 1969, for example, a book titled *Is the Business Cycle Obsolete?* was published just as the 1961–1969 boom came to an end and the economy entered a recession. With two record-setting expansions in a row, though the current one may be over, it is not surprising that the notion of regular business cycles is being questioned again. The current favorite hypothesis is that a new economy has emerged in which our old understanding of business cycle forces is no longer relevant.

While few economists believe we have seen the end of business cycles, the nature of business cycles is changing. In fact, business cycles have been evolving ever since economists first started studying them. Changes in business cycles reflect real transformations in the U.S. economy such as those caused by information technologies and other technological developments. But the modifications also reflect changes in our ability to measure economic developments, as well as variations in the way policymakers have responded to changing economic conditions.

One important aspect of the business cycle that is changing is the length and frequency of recessions. While the Great Depression was not the longest period of economic decline (that record belongs to the recession of 1873–1879), it does appear to represent a watershed. No recession since has lasted even half as long as the 1929–1933 contraction. It is not just that recessions have been shorter on average in the post–World War II era, they have *all* been much shorter. Of the nineteen recessions before the Great Depression, only three lasted less than a year; of the eleven recessions since the Great Depression, only three have lasted more than a year.

Expansions have also changed. Of the twenty-one that occurred prior to World War II, only three lasted more than three years. In contrast, of the ten expansions since, only three have lasted less than three years. Even if the wartime expansions associated with the Korean and Vietnam Wars are ignored, post–World War II expansions have averaged fifty-two months, compared to an average of only twenty-four months for pre–World War II peacetime expansions. So economic booms have gotten longer and recessions have gotten shorter, and this change was evident even before the arrival of the new economy.

A simple comparison of how long expansions and recessions last, however, cannot tell us about the severity of recessions or the strength of booms. This is better measured by the decline in output that occurs in a recession or the growth that occurs in an expansion. Most studies that have examined the volatility of economic activity concluded that output has been somewhat more stable in the post–World War II era.

However, comparing the business cycle over time is difficult. For one thing, the quality of economic data has improved tremendously over the past one hundred years. Data from the nineteenth century and the early twentieth century were less reliable, and this can make the economy in earlier periods look more unstable. In addition, earlier data on economic output provided only partial coverage of the economy. For example, better statistics were available on industrial output than on services. Since services tend to fluctuate less over a business cycle, the earlier data undoubtedly exaggerated the extent of fluctuations in the economy as a whole.

This last point is directly relevant to our thoughts about the impact of the new economy, for two reasons. First, just as in earlier days it was often easier to measure how many tons of steel were produced than it was to measure the value of the output produced by doctors, bankers, and lawyers, today some argue that output is inherently harder to measure when, increasingly, it is new ideas that the economy is producing.

Second, the post–World War II era has seen a shift away from manufacturing industries toward services. Service industries generally have been less sensitive to cycles than manufacturing industries have been. In fact, some service industries may actually see demand rise during a recession. Auto repair shops, for example, might see business pick up as households postpone the purchase of new cars and continue to use older cars that need more maintenance. As service industries have grown as a share of total GDP, the overall economy has become less sensitive to fluctuations. The transformation of the economy away from the production of manufactured goods toward one that produces more services has led to a more stable econ-

omy. Whether the transformation to an economy that produces "ideas" and new technologies will lead to further stability is uncertain.

If the spread of information technologies does make the economy more stable, it may be due to the impact of new technologies on old industries more than the growth of the computer and high-tech industries themselves. For example, inventory investment is the most volatile component of aggregate spending. Today, new computer-aided methods of tracking inventories and adjusting orders provide firms with better information. And this allows them to manage their inventories better, helping to make total aggregate spending more stable.

The chart shows the ratio of inventories to sales in the manufacturing sector. During the 1970s and 1980s, manufacturing firms held, on average, about $1.76 worth of goods in inventory for every $1 of sales. As the chart illustrates, new inventory-management techniques allowed manufacturers to reduce the inventories they held, and by 1998, the inventory-sales ratio had fallen to just $1.38 in inventories for every $1 of sales.

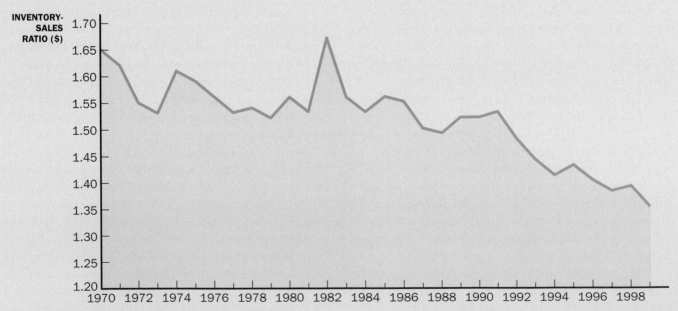

Inventory-Sales Ratio: Manufacturing

SOURCE: *ERP* (2001), Table B-57.

While the U.S. economy has enjoyed two consecutive record expansions, a longer historical perspective does help to remind us that business cycles are unlikely to be gone for good. Despite talk of the new economy, all economies experience ups and downs that are reflected in swings in unemployment, capacity utilization, and overall economic output. Though changes in the structure of the economy may alter the extent of these fluctuations, they are unlikely to eliminate them.

In addition, the business cycles are not independent of policy decisions. The economy may not have changed fundamentally; perhaps we have simply benefited from good economic policy. With less successful policies, recessions could become more frequent and longer again. The Great Depression, for example, was prolonged by, among other things, poor economic and monetary policy decisions, and the recessions of the early 1980s were the price of policy mistakes in the 1970s that allowed inflation to rise significantly. Thus, one reason why business cycles can change, even if the underlying economy or sources of disturbances has not, is that policymakers do a better (or worse) job of stabilizing the economy.

Part 8

Topics in Macroeconomics

The International Financial System

Key Questions

1. What determines the exchange rate? How does monetary policy affect the exchange rate?

2. Increasingly, we are living in a world in which all economies are interrelated. How does this fact affect the ability to achieve the goals of domestic macroeconomic policies?

3. Why do currency and exchange rate crises occur? What are their effects?

Every day, U.S. exporters receive payments from their sales in foreign countries that they need to convert to dollars, while U.S. importers need foreign currencies to pay their foreign suppliers. Foreign investors wishing to purchase American assets need to buy dollars, while others may be selling American assets, switching their investments into a different country. A foreign multinational corporation expanding its American operations needs to purchase dollars to carry out its investment plans. All these transactions involve one or more currencies and give rise to a huge volume of daily foreign currency trading—about $1.5 trillion every day.

The international financial system that has developed to carry out these trades, and that allows Americans to invest in Brazilian stocks or Ford to buy Volvo, Japanese investors to buy U.S. Treasury bonds or Toyota to build assembly plants in Tennessee, links together the members of the global economy. In economies that are open to trade and capital flows, international factors can play a critical role in affecting the macroeconomy. This point was driven home in the late 1990s by the financial crises in many Asian countries, only the most recent in a recurring string of international financial crises.

Opening a country's financial markets to foreign investors can have many benefits. The most important is that domestic investment is no longer constrained by domestic saving. There are potential costs as well, though, as speculative capital flows can constrain the flexibility of domestic policymakers. In this chapter we will trace the role of capital flows and exchange rates in macroeconomic equilibrium.

Determining the Exchange Rate

The starting point for understanding the international financial system is the *foreign exchange market*. This is the market in which currencies of different countries are bought or sold. Just as with the other markets we have studied, the foreign exchange market does not have a single physical location. Instead, it involves thousands of currency traders at computer terminals around the globe, buying and selling different currencies. Most trading is heavily concentrated, though, in the three major centers of London, New York, and Tokyo. London is the largest of the three, accounting for over 30 percent of the world foreign exchange trading with a daily trading volume of over $600 billion.

The *exchange rate* is the rate at which one currency can be traded for another. If the dollar-yen exchange rate is 115, it means that $1 will exchange for 115 yen. Systems in which exchange rates are determined by the law of supply and demand, without government interference, are called **flexible** or **floating exchange rate systems.** We have already had a brief look, in Chapter 26, at how exchange rates are determined by supply and demand in the foreign exchange market. Governments often intervene in foreign exchange markets, and later in this chapter we will look at the different forms this intervention takes. But first we need to understand what determines the exchange rate in flexible exchange rate systems.

Consider a world consisting of only two countries, America and another country consisting of the members of the European Monetary Union we will call Europa, whose currency is the euro. Americans and Europans exchange dollars for euros. There are three reasons why Europans might want dollars, and might therefore supply euros to the foreign exchange market: to buy American goods (American exports, or imports into Europa), to make investments in the United States, or for speculative purposes—that is, if Europans think the dollar is going to become more valuable relative to the euro, they might want to hold dollars in order to reap that increase in value, called a capital gain. Similarly, there are three reasons why Americans might want euros, and might accordingly sup-

ply dollars to the foreign exchange market: to buy Europan goods, to make investments in Europa, and for speculative purposes, if they think that the euro is going to become more valuable relative to the dollar. The question is, how many euros will an American get in exchange for a dollar, or equivalently, how many dollars will a Europan get in exchange for euros? The exchange rate can be thought of as nothing more than the *relative price* of dollars and euros.

In competitive markets, prices are determined by demand and supply. We can view the exchange rate in this two-country example as being determined from the perspective of either the demand and supply of dollars or the demand and supply of euros. The two are equivalent. The Europan supply of euros on the foreign exchange market is equivalent to Europans' demand for dollars. The U.S. supply of dollars is equivalent to Americans' demand for euros.

The three reasons why Europans might want dollars and Americans might want euros are the three main factors that determine the exchange rate. The first factor is the demand and supply of exports and imports, to which we now turn.

Exchange Rates with No Borrowing

Figure 34.1A shows a demand and supply diagram for U.S. dollars. The vertical axis is the exchange rate, the "price" of dollars, expressed in this example as euro/ dollar. When the exchange rate is two euros to the dollar, the dollar is very expensive; when it is a half a euro to the dollar, the dollar is relatively cheap. The figure shows a

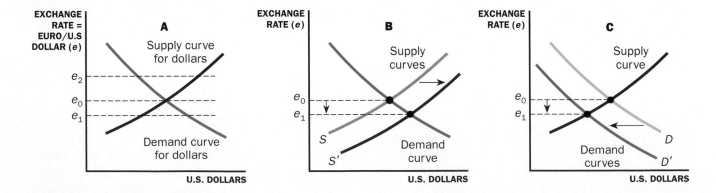

FIGURE 34.1   *The Exchange Rate*

In equilibrium, the exchange rate is determined where the demand for dollars equals the supply, as in panel A. A rightward shift in the supply curve of dollars (panel B) or a leftward shift in the demand curve for dollars (panel C) results in a lower exchange rate; that is, the dollar depreciates.

downward-sloping demand curve and an upward-sloping supply curve, and the intersection represents the equilibrium exchange rate. A rightward shift in the supply curve (panel B) or a leftward shift in the demand curve (panel C) leads to a depreciation of the dollar. The value of the dollar relative to euros is then lower.

While thinking about exchange rates in terms of demand and supply is helpful, it pushes the question back still one more step. Why do demand and supply curves for foreign exchange have the shape they do? What might cause them to shift and thus the exchange rate to change?

Exports and Imports

Suppose Europa was a country that trusted no one and that no one trusted. No Europan would be able to borrow abroad, because potential lenders would fear that the loan would not be repaid. Similarly, the country would refuse to loan out any money to foreigners.

When U.S. producers sell products in Europa, they receive euros, and they want to convert those euros immediately into dollars. After all, if they do not convert the euros into dollars, they will have to deposit them in a bank or investment in Europa—they will have to *lend* the euros to Europa—and they do not trust Europa enough to do that. Similarly, when producers from Europa sell in the United States, they receive U.S. dollars, and they want to exchange those dollars immediately into euros. In short, this situation has parties who want to trade euros for dollars and parties who want to trade dollars for euros. Clearly, there are possibilities for mutually beneficial exchange. At a low exchange rate, like e_1 in Figure 34.2, the demand for dollars exceeds the supply. At a high exchange rate, like e_2, the supply of dollars exceeds the demand. The point at which the demand for dollars equals the supply is the equilibrium exchange rate. In the figure, this point is e_0.

We can also see how the exchange rate is determined by focusing directly on exports and imports. In the absence of borrowing or lending, the value of exports must equal the value of imports. Americans might like to import more from Europa than they export, but unless they sell goods to Europa, they will not have the money (the euros) with which to buy Europan goods. And since Europans are skeptical about whether Americans will repay any loans, they will not deliver the goods without receiving the money first. There are no credit sales.

At a high value of the dollar, U.S. exports will be low. Europans must give up a lot of their currency to buy Amer-

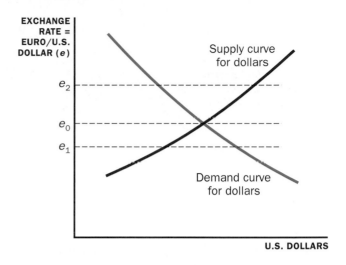

FIGURE 34.2 *The Equilibrium Exchange Rate*

At the exchange rate e_2 supply exceeds demand. At e_1, demand exceeds supply. At e_0 equilibrium is achieved.

ican goods. Europans' demand for imports will translate directly into a supply of dollars. A high value of the dollar is equivalent to a low value of the foreign currency (here, euros). From the perspective of Americans, foreign goods are cheap, and Americans will want to buy them. Their demand for imports will be high. To buy these goods, they have to pay the Europans in their own currency, euros. So American importers supply dollars to be exchanged for euros on the foreign exchange market.

Figure 34.3A and B shows how imports increase and exports decrease as the exchange rate increases (as the dollar becomes "more expensive"). The exchange rate at which exports equal imports is the equilibrium exchange rate. In the U.S.-Europa example, a decrease in the exchange rate has one of two causes: either a reduction in the demand for U.S. exports *at any exchange rate,* which will translate into a leftward shift in the demand curve for dollars, or an increased U.S. demand for imports *at any exchange rate,* which will translate into a rightward shift in the supply of dollars. These are illustrated in panel C.

The model of trade without foreign lending or borrowing made more sense a few decades ago, when international financial markets were not widely developed and so exchange rates were shaped primarily by the supply and demand for imports and exports. Today we need to look beyond exports and imports to capital markets.

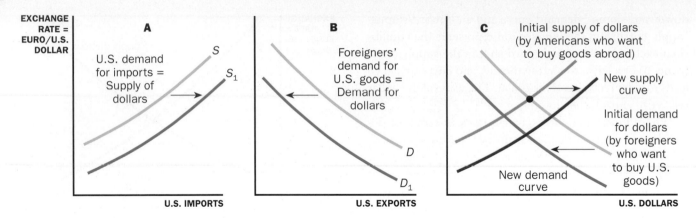

FIGURE 34.3   *Equilibrium Exchange Rate with No Borrowing and Lending*

The supply of dollars is determined by the U.S. demand for imported goods (panel A), and the demand for dollars is determined by foreigners' demand for U.S. goods (panel B). Panel C shows that a change in tastes that causes Americans to import more goods at any exchange rate shifts the supply curve of dollars to the right and results in a lower exchange rate. A shift in tastes that causes foreigners to import fewer goods (the United States to export fewer goods) at any exchange rate shifts the demand curve for dollars to the left and also results in a lower exchange rate.

Foreign Borrowing and Lending

In the world of the previous section, there is never a trade deficit. The values of exports and imports, when compared by using the exchange rate, are always the same. This means that the problem of trade deficits will never arise. *A trade deficit can only occur if foreign borrowing and lending are possible.*

Today there is a massive amount of international borrowing and lending, and this is the second factor that determines the exchange rate. Capital markets today, the markets in which funds are borrowed and lent, are global. Investors in Japan, Europe, and the United States, constantly seeking to maximize their returns, will shift their funds from Japan or Europe to the United States if returns there are highest. When investors respond quickly and shift their funds in response to slight differences in expected returns, economists say that capital is **perfectly mobile.** In today's world, capital is highly but not perfectly mobile. American investors may still feel slightly more comfortable keeping their money within the United States than sending it abroad; they may feel relatively uninformed about changes in economic conditions or tax conditions that could quickly and adversely affect their investments.

Foreign investors may feel the same way about keeping their funds within their own country. The more stable the political and economic environment of the world, the more mobile capital becomes across countries.

Determining the exchange rate becomes considerably more complicated when foreign borrowing and lending are introduced. Now the equilibrium exchange rate is not just a matter of balancing imports and exports as they occur; it is affected by borrowing and lending decisions as well. Figure 34.2 can be modified to incorporate these effects. Foreigners who want to invest in the United States will want dollars to make their purchases of American assets. This increases the demand for dollars. On the other hand, some Americans may want to make investments abroad. They want to sell dollars to get foreign currency with which to make these investments. How these investments affect the exchange rate depends on whether foreigners want to invest more in the United States than Americans want to invest abroad.

Figure 34.4 shows the demand and supply curves for dollars both with and without foreign borrowing and lending. Some Americans want to invest abroad, and hence the supply of dollars at any exchange rate is greater than it would have been without foreign investment; and some foreigners want to invest in the United States, and so the demand for dollars is greater than it otherwise would have been. In this

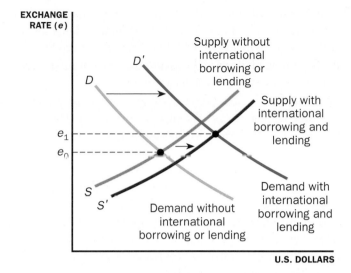

FIGURE 34.4 *Equilibrium Exchange Rate with Borrowing and Lending*

When Americans want to invest abroad and foreigners want to invest in the United States, the supply of and demand for dollars are greater than they otherwise would have been. In the figure, more foreigners want to invest in the United States than Americans want to invest abroad, so the demand curve for dollars shifts more to the right than does the supply curve for dollars. As a result, the exchange rate increases.

example, however, the amount foreigners want to invest in the United States is much greater than the amount Americans want to invest abroad. The demand curve for dollars shifts more to the right than does the supply curve for dollars. As a result, the dollar appreciates.

Normally, if investments in the United States become more attractive, Americans will decide to leave more of their wealth at home rather than investing abroad. Then the supply of dollars will shift to the left, as in Figure 34.5. At the same time, foreigners will decide to invest more in the United states, shifting the demand for dollars to the right. Both of these effects work to increase the value of the dollar relative to other currencies.

This helps to explain what caused the changes in the exchange rate in the 1980s. In the early part of the decade, foreign investment in the United States surged, which resulted in an appreciation of the dollar, lower exports, and higher imports. The increase in foreign investment continued through the mid-1980s and then declined, and the dollar fell in the late 1980s.

At the end of the 1990s, as the U.S. economy boomed while other economies were suffering recessions, investing in the United States became more attractive. This helped to boost the value of the dollar. The importance of foreign borrowing and lending for exchange markets is clear when one recognizes that the world volume of exports in 1997 was $6.6 trillion, or roughly $25 billion per day, compared to an average foreign exchange trading volume of $1.5 *trillion* per day.

Speculation

The third factor that is important in determining the exchange rate today is speculation. The demand for any asset depends on beliefs about what that asset could be sold for in the future; it depends on expectations. Money in any country is an asset. If Americans believe that the Japanese yen is going to increase in value relative to the dollar, they may want to hold Japanese yen. For instance, consider what happens if the current exchange rate is 200 yen to the dollar and investors believe that the yen is going

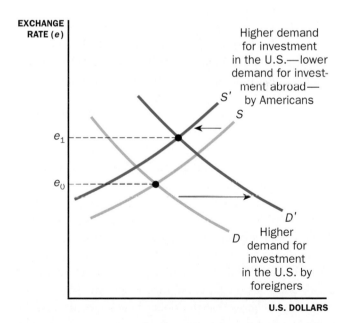

FIGURE 34.5 *Increased Attractiveness of Investing in the United States*

As some Americans decide not to invest abroad, the supply curve of dollars shifts to the left. As more foreigners wish to invest in the United States, the demand curve shifts to the right. Both shifts serve to increase the equilibrium exchange rate.

to appreciate, so that by the end of the month it will be worth 100 to the dollar. They believe, in other words, that if they took $1,000 and bought 200,000 yen (each dollar is exchanged for 200 yen), at the end of the month they could exchange the yen back for $2,000. By holding yen for a month, they would earn a phenomenal 100 percent return. American investors with such a belief will want to hold more yen today. This is how expectations about future changes in exchange rates are translated *immediately* into increased exchange rates *today*.

Demanding currency for the possible gains from the appreciation of the currency is called *foreign exchange speculation.* With speculation, exchange rates in the market depend not only on the demand and supply for exports and imports and investment today but also on expectations concerning those factors in the future.

Expectations

Expectations about changes in the exchange rate in fact play a role in all overseas investments. Consider the Japanese investor who is planning to convert his yen into dollars and invest it in the United States. He will want to bring his profits back to Japan, and he may even decide eventually to sell his investment and bring his money back home. In either case, he will have to convert his dollars back into yen at some later date. The question is, how many yen will he get for his dollars? If he believes that the dollar is going to become weaker, then he believes that he will get fewer yen when he exchanges his dollars in the foreign exchange market. If he thinks that the dollar will become stronger in the future, investment in the United States appears more attractive.

American investors thinking about investing abroad will be equally concerned about changes in exchange rates. But for Americans, expectations that the dollar will become *weaker* in the future make investment abroad more attractive.

Now let's suppose our Japanese investor is thinking about buying a U.S. Treasury bill. He will not want to put his money in a T-bill that yields a 10 percent return, even if bonds issued by the Japanese government yield only 5 percent, if he believes that the dollar is going to decrease in value by more than 5 percent during the year. To see why this is so, suppose he has 300,000 yen to invest, and assume the current exchange rate is 300 yen to the dollar. If he invests the 300,000 yen in a Japanese government bond, he will have 315,000 at the end of the year. But if he takes the 300,000 yen to his banker, his banker will give him 1,000. With that $1,000, he buys a Treasury bill. At the end of the year, he has $1,100. He now takes this $1,100 back to his

banker, who tells him that because the dollar has depreciated in value, each dollar is worth, say, 250 yen. Thus, at the end of the year, he has only 275,000 yen, fewer yen than at the beginning of the year. The Japanese investor's expected returns can be summed up in a formula:

$$\text{rate of return in yen} = \text{dollar interest rate} - \text{expected rate of depreciation of dollars.}$$

With perfect capital mobility, investors shift funds to whichever country appears to offer the highest expected rate of return. This process ensures that expected returns are closely linked across different countries. Changes in expected yields on the investment in one country can lead to changes in interest rates and exchange rates in other countries. To see why, consider the case of our Japanese investor. If he had expected the dollar to depreciate in value from 300 yen to 250 yen, a fall of 17 percent, his expected return from buying the U.S. Treasury bill would have been the dollar interest rate of 10 percent minus the expected depreciation of the dollar of 17 percent, for a total expected return of –7 percent. Clearly he would be much better off with the 5 percent yield on a Japanese government bond. The lower expected return on U.S. financial assets shifts the demand curve for dollars to the left at each exchange rate as the demand for financial investment in the United States falls. The dollar falls in value, and this process continues as long as expected returns are lower in the United States than elsewhere.

The situation would be exactly reversed if expected returns were higher in the United States than elsewhere. Now foreign investors would wish to take advantage of the higher expected U.S. returns. The demand for dollars shifts to the right and the dollar rises in value.

Whenever expected returns differ across countries, the attempts by investors to take advantage of these differences by shifting their funds from one country to another cause exchange rates to adjust. In equilibrium, with perfect capital markets, expected returns would have to be equal in different countries. From the perspective of our Japanese investor, we can express this requirement for equilibrium as

$$\text{rate of return on yen assets (expressed in yen)} = \text{rate of return on dollar assets expressed in yen} = \text{dollar interest rate} - \text{expected rate of depreciation of the dollar.}$$

This condition for equilibrium with perfect capital mobility is known as the **interest rate parity condition.**

The interest rate parity condition has a couple of important implications. First, if interest rates are lower in one country, then interest parity tells us that investors must expect the currency of that country to rise in value (appreciate). For instance, suppose the interest rate in Europa is 8 percent while in the United States it is 5 percent. This is consistent with exchange market equilibrium and perfect capital mobility only if investors expect the dollar to rise at a 3 percent rate relative to the euro.

Second, the role of speculation in the foreign exchange market can introduce a source of instability. Suppose investors suddenly decide the euro is going to fall in value. Each investor will want to sell euros before they fall, but as all investors try to do this, the collapsing demand for euros pushes its value down. So expectations that the euro would depreciate become self-fulfilling. This process plays an important role in currency crises, a topic we will return to later.

The interest rate parity condition assumes perfect capital mobility. As we noted earlier, international financial capital is highly mobile but not perfectly mobile, so we would not expect interest parity to hold exactly. If expected returns in the United States were slightly lower than those in Japan, American residents might still prefer to keep their money at home. For countries with restrictions on capital flows or that are not well integrated into the global financial market, the parity condition would not be relevant. For the major industrialized economies, however, interest parity can help us understand how economic developments in global financial markets affect macroeconomic conditions in different countries.

Interest Rate Parity and Inflation   Interest rate parity provides an important link between nominal interest rates in different countries and expectations about exchange rate movements. In earlier chapters, we learned that the nominal interest rate in a country is affected by its rate of inflation. Nominal interest rates will be high in a country with high inflation and low in a country with low inflation. When countries have different inflation rates, their nominal interest rates will differ. The interest rate parity condition, however, tells us that differences in nominal interest rates also reflect how investors expect the exchange rate to change.

If two countries differ in their rates of inflation, over the long run there will be changes in the exchange rate that offset the inflation differences. For example, if the rate of inflation in the United States is 2 percent and there is no inflation in Japan, the dollar is becoming less valuable—each year people can purchase 2 percent fewer goods with a dollar bill—while the value of the yen is unchanged. Just as the dollar buys fewer goods each year, it will also buy fewer yen; the dollar will depreciate 2 percent against the yen each year.

In a world of perfect capital mobility, interest rates would have to adjust quickly to reflect differences in inflation rates and changing exchange rates. If the interest rate in Japan is 3 percent, the interest rate in the United States should be 5 percent; the extra 2 percent reflects the depreciation associated with the higher inflation rate in the United States. Notice that if this is the case, the *real* interest rate in Japan and the United States is the same (3 percent).

WRAP-UP

What Determines the Exchange Rate?

The U.S. exchange rate today is determined by the supply and demand for dollars. Foreigners' demand for U.S. dollars and Americans' supply of dollars are determined by

1. Underlying trade factors: the demand for U.S. goods (U.S. exports) and Americans' demand for foreign goods (U.S. imports);

2. Underlying investment factors: the returns to investments in the United States and abroad; and

3. Speculation based on expectations concerning future changes in the exchange rate.

A shift in tastes or an increase in income in the United States that increases demand for foreign goods will lead to a depreciation of the dollar.

Improved attractiveness of investment in the United States will lead to an appreciation of the dollar.

The interest rate parity condition tells us that with perfect capital mobility, the dollar interest rate minus the expected rate of depreciation of the dollar is equal to the foreign interest rate. Higher inflation in the United States leads to higher nominal interest rates and an expected depreciation of the dollar.

Moreover, a Japanese investor will be indifferent between investing in the United States or Japan; his expected *real* return is the same, even though he earns a higher *nominal* return in the United States.

These adjustments in interest rates and exchange rates offset the effects of inflation. As a result, Americans find that Japanese products become no more or less attractive over time as prices of American goods rise at the 2 percent rate of inflation while prices of Japanese goods also rise at a 2 percent rate because of the falling value of the dollar in relation to the yen. Similarly, Japanese consumers find that American goods become no more or less attractive over time.

Like the real wage and the real interest rate, economists use the term **real exchange rate** to indicate the exchange rate adjusted for changes in the relative price levels in two countries. That is, if the inflation rate is 2 percent higher in the United States than in Japan, and the nominal exchange rate has changed so that the dollar is worth 2 percent less relative to the yen, the real exchange rate has remained unchanged. The changes in the nominal exchange rate are those required to offset the changes in relative price levels as U.S. prices rise faster than Japanes prices. Similarly, in spite of differences in nominal returns, investors find real returns to be the same.

Exchange Rate Management

As the link between monetary policy and exchange rates has become increasingly clear, central banks in many countries have attempted to "manage" the exchange rate. In some cases, they have simply tried to smooth out day-to-day fluctuations in the foreign exchange market. In other cases, they have tried to move the exchange rate permanently higher or lower.

Fixed Exchange Rate System

The United States has had a flexible exchange rate for three decades. However, prior to 1971, the United States and most other countries had a **fixed exchange rate system,** in which exchange rates were pegged at a particular level. Changes in exchange rates only occurred as the result of explicit government decisions. Many countries currently have a fixed exchange rate system. The creation of the Eu-

ropean Monetary Union on January 1, 1999, involved permanently fixing the exchange rates between the currencies of the members of the union. Often smaller countries will decide to fix their exchange rate relative to an important trading partner. Three questions arise: How does a country "fix" its exchange rate? What are the consequences of fixed exchange rates for monetary policy? And what are the pros and cons of a fixed exchange rate system?

Fixing the Exchange Rate   Let's suppose the government of Mexico has decided to fix the exchange rate between the peso and the dollar at 9 pesos to the dollar. Figure 34.6 depicts the foreign exchange market for dollars and pesos. As drawn in the figure, the market equilibrium exchange rate (e^*) is below the pegged rate (e_f). Without some sort of government intervention, the peso will depreciate until the exchange rate reaches e^*. At the pegged rate e_f, the supply of pesos exceeds the demand for pesos. To keep the exchange rate from falling, the Mexican government would need to shift the demand curve for pesos to the right, as shown in the figure. It can do this by buying pesos, and to buy pesos, it would sell dollars, other foreign currencies, or gold that it holds.

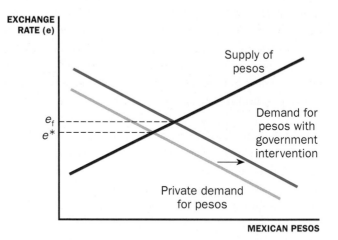

FIGURE 34.6   *Government Intervention in a Fixed Exchange Rate System*

If the "fixed" rate for pesos under the fixed exchange rate system, e_f, exceeds the market equilibrium rate, e^*, then sustaining the fixed exchange rate requires government intervention. The government enters the foreign exchange market demanding pesos (supplying dollars or other foreign currencies) to the point where the equilibrium exchange rate is equal to the pegged rate.

Thinking Like an Economist

Interest Rate Parity and Incentives

Whenever expected returns on different assets are different (after adjusting for differences in risk), economists see a profit opportunity. By selling the lower-yielding assets and buying the higher-yielding one, investors can increase their total return. Investors have an *incentive* to adjust their portfolios to take advantage of the opportunity offered by the higher-yieling assets. This idea—that investors seek out the highest returns—lies at the heart of the interest parity condition.

When expected returns differ in, say, Canada and the United States, investors have an incentive to sell their holdings in the country with the lower return and invest in the country with the higher return. For example, suppose the interest rate in Canada is 8 percent and in the United States it is 5 percent. Further, suppose investors do not expect any change in the Canadian-U.S. exchange rate. In this case, there is a strong incentive to sell financial assets in the United States and invest in the high-yielding Canadian assets. As investors try to take advantage of the high Canadian interest rates by buying Canadian assets, they first need to buy Canadian dollars. This increased demand for Canadian dollars causes their value to rise—the Canadian dollar appreciates. As it rises, investors may start to worry that it is overvalued and likely to eventually fall in value, perhaps back to its earlier value. Now, the 8 percent interest rate in Canada starts to look less attractive. If the Canadian dollar is expected to fall by, say, 2 percent, then investing in Canadian financial assets will yield a return of only 6 percent (an 8 percent interest rate minus the 2 percent depreciation). This is still better than the 5 percent return in the United States, but the incentive to shift funds to Canada is now smaller than it was initially. As investors continue to respond to the incentive offered by the higher expected returns in Canada, the Canadian dollar will continue to appreciate. In this example, once investors believe the value of the Canadian dollar is so high that it is likely to depreciate in the future by 3 percent, there is no longer any incentive to shift funds out of the United States and into Canada.

With perfect capital markets, any difference in expected returns is quickly eliminated as investors respond to the incentives offered by these differences. So if you look at the major industrial economies—countries whose financial markets are closely linked—and see interest rates higher in one country than another, you can conclude that investors must believe the currency of the country with the higher interest rate is going to depreciate.

Just as we discussed earlier how speculation might be destabilizing, it also can be stabilizing. If the exchange rate falls to e^* but investors are convinced the government plans to intervene to bring it back to e_f, then foreign speculators will believe that if they buy pesos now, their value will rise when the government intervenes. They can expect to earn large profits by buying pesos. But this shifts the demand curve for pesos to the right, helping to drive the equilibrium exchange rate back to e_f.

Problems can arise when investors believe the equilibrium exchange rate is far different from the pegged rate. Recall that the way the Mexican government attempted to sustain the exchange rate was by buying pesos and selling its holdings of dollars, other currencies, or gold. But if the government has insufficient resources and investors believe the government will be unable to, or unwilling to, sustain the exchange rate at e_f, the results can be disastrous. Once investors believe the pegged rate will be abandoned, and the exchange rate will fall, they expect a capital loss on their peso holdings. Their best bet is to try to unload pesos before the pegged rate is abandoned. The supply curve shifts to the right, widening the gap between the pegged rate and the equilibrium exchang rate. To sustain the pegged rate, the government now has to shift the demand curve even further to the right than before, using up even more of its holdings of dollars, other currencies, or gold. The gap between supply and demand at the original pegged rate becomes enormous. Eventually, the government may be forced to abandon the pegged rate, letting the exchange rate fall and validating the speculators who dumped pesos.

When the government announces there will be a new, lower exchange rate under a fixed exchange rate system, it is said to **devalue** the currency.

Monetary Policy Under a Fixed Exchange Rate System

One cost of a fixed exchange rate system is the loss of one of the key tools of macroeconomic policy—monetary policy.

Adopting a fixed exchange rate system has important implications for a country's ability to use monetary policy. To understand why, recall first that monetary policy affects aggregate expenditures, and therefore output and inflation, by influencing the interest rate and credit conditions. With this in mind, suppose Canada decides to fix the Canadian dollar–U.S. dollar exchange rate. With a high degree of capital mobility between Canada and the United States, the interest parity condition links the Canadian interest rate, the U.S. interest rate, and the rate at which the exchange rate is expected to change. Under a fixed exchange rate system, the exchange rate is fixed, so people will not expect it to change. In this circumstance, the interest parity condition becomes

$$\text{Canadian interest rate} = \text{U.S. interest rate.}$$

To maintain a fixed exchange rate, the Bank of Canada (Canada's central bank) must ensure that it keeps the Canadian interest rate equal to the U.S. interest rate. If the Bank of Canada tries to reduce interest rates slightly, perhaps in an attempt to stimulate Canadian investment spending if Canada is in a recession, foreign investors will sell Canadian dollars as they take their capital out of the country to earn higher yields in the United States. To defend the pegged currency rate and prevent the exchange rate from changing, the Bank of Canada would have to push interest rates back up. Similarly, any attempt to raise interest rates would attract a capital inflow that would push the value of the currency up. To keep the exchange rate at its pegged rate, the central bank would have to lower interest rates back down. *In a small open economy under a fixed exchange rate system with perfect capital mobility, the central bank must keep the interest rate equal to the foreign interest rate. The country cannot run an independent monetary policy.*

This result can help us understand three important issues. First, it helps to explain why the European economies decided to adopt a common currency once they integrated their economies and fixed their exchange rates. No individual country in the monetary union can run an independent monetary policy, so the members of the union have given up their own national currencies and delegated monetary policy for the entire union to the European Central Bank.

Second, it helps us to understand why in 1992 the United Kingdom dropped out of the European Monetary System, a system of fixed exchange rates that preceded the European Monetary Union. The United Kingdom was in a recession, and many economists argued for interest rate cuts to help expand aggregate expenditures. As long as the United Kingdom wanted to maintain its fixed exchange rate, it could not cut interest rates. Because speculators thought the country might drop out of the European Monetary System and cut interest rates, they expected the pound to depreciate. This shifted the demand curve for pounds to the left, and to offset this downward pressure on the pound exchange rate, the Bank of England had to keep its interest rates higher than those in Germany just when domestic factors called for interest rate cuts. Finally, the system collapsed; the United Kingdom dropped out of the European Monetary System, cut its interest rates, and let the pound depreciate against the other European currencies.

Third, the loss of monetary control under a fixed exchange rate system explains why countries that have experienced high inflation rates often decide to fix their exchange rate as part of a disinflation policy. In fact, while the loss of an independent monetary policy is one of the chief arguments against a fixed exchange rate system, paradoxically it is also one of the chief arguments in favor of a fixed exchange rate system for countries that have a history of high inflation and bad monetary policy.

Pegging the nominal exchange rate forces a high-inflation country to bring its own inflation rate down. If it does not, its exports will become more and more expensive as its price level rises faster than that of other countries (a real appreciation). As its net exports decline, the demand for its currency, at the fixed exchange rate, falls. To maintain the fixed exchange rate, the central bank must raise interest rates. Doing so reduces aggregate expenditures, reducing output, and finally inflation.

One of the attractions of the European Monetary System of fixed exchange rates for countries like Italy was that it linked their monetary policy with that of Germany, a low-inflation country. Before the creation of the European Monetary Union, Italy's inflation rate was higher than Germany's. Maintaining a fixed nominal exchange rate with Germany forced Italy to bring down inflation by reducing net exports from Italy, reducing aggregate expenditures, output, and eventually inflation.

Reducing Exchange Rate Volatility A major argument for a fixed exchange rate system is that it reduces risks from exchange rate volatility. Many economists have been concerned with the high degree of volatility in exchange rate markets. Exchange rates have fluctuated greatly, both on a day-to-day and on a longer-term basis, as illustrated in Figure 34.7. The Japanese yen went from 94 yen to the dollar in 1995 to 131 yen in 1998, and back to 107 yen in 2000. The dollar has had single-day declines of more than 1 percent against the German mark (February 18, 1985), and more than 1 percent against the Japanese yen (October 14, 1987). This may not seem like a lot, but if there were a 1 percent decline every business day for a year, it would mean that the exchange rate would have declined by more than 240 percent within a year. Many of these gyrations, particu-

larly the ones that happen from day to day, cannot be explained by any correspondingly large changes in the economy. They only seem explainable in terms of large shifts in expectations.

As was noted above, dollars or yen are assets. That is why the value of the exchange rate today depends on what investors expect the exchange rate will be next year. Thus, the stability of the exchange rate depends on the stability of the expectiations of investors. For instance, when the dollar is lower, foreign investors might expect it to rise again. In that case, as the value of the dollar declines, the expected return to holding dollars increases because investors believe that it is likely to appreciate and that they will benefit from a capital gain when the dollar does appreciate. In this case, expectations help stabilize the market, since foreign investors may help to limit any decline in the dollar by buying it as it falls.

But if as the dollar depreciates foreign investors expect further depreciation, then their willingness to invest in America may actually decrease as the dollar falls in value. In that case, an initial decline in the value of the dollar in effect shifts the demand curve for dollars down, leading to further decreases in the value of the dollar.

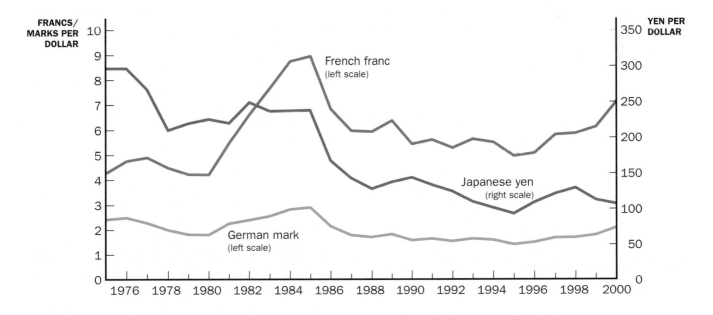

FIGURE 34.7   *Volatility of Exchange Rates*

During the 1980s and 1990s, exchange rates exhibited considerable volatility.

SOURCE: Federal Reserve Board.

Whatever their cause and whatever the nature of expectations concerning future movements, huge swings in exchange rates add to the risk of doing business in the world market and thus discourage businesses and countries from pursuing their comparative advantages. If the exchange rate appreciates greatly, exporters suddenly find that the market for their goods has dried up, unless they drastically cut prices; either way, profits are dramatically reduced. Even American firms that produce only for the American market face huge risks as a result of exchange rate fluctuations. Shoe manufacturers may find the American market flooded with cheap Brazilian shoes if the dollar appreciates relative to the Brazilian real; again, they either lose sales or must cut their prices, and in either case, profits fall.

There are ways that exporting and importing firms can mitigate the effects of foreign exchange risks in the short run, say, the next three to six months. Consider an American firm that exports abroad. It has a contract to deliver so many ball bearings to France at so many francs per ball bearing. But it pays its workers in dollars, not francs. If the franc depreciates, when the firm takes the francs it receives and converts them into dollars, its revenues will fall short of the dollars it has already paid to workers. It can insure itself by making a contract (with either a bank or a dealer in the foreign exchange market) for the future delivery or sale of those francs at a price agreed upon today. It can thus avoid the risk of a change in the foreign exchange rate. However, firms cannot easily buy or sell foreign exchange for delivery two or three years into the future. Since many investment projects have a planning horizon of years or even decades, investors are exposed to foreign exchange risks against which they cannot get insurance. But even firms that do not buy or sell in foreign markets are exposed to risks from foreign exchange rate fluctuations: American firms cannot buy insurance against the longer-term risk that the American market will be flooded with cheap imports as a result of an appreciation of the U.S. dollar. These risks are reduced if the exchange rate is fixed.

Flexible Exchange Rate Systems

Today, while most governments do not peg the exchange rate at a particular value, they do frequently intervene in the foreign exchange markets, buying and selling in an attempt to reduce day-to-day variability in exchange rates. Rather than let the exchange rate freely *float* as demand and supply vary, as would occur under a flexible exchange rate system, governments intervene. Economists sometimes refer to this as a *"dirty float"* system.

CASE IN POINT

The European Monetary Union

On January 1, 1999, eleven Western European countries joined a common monetary union, the European Monetary Union (EMU), in which they permanently fixed the exchange rates between their currencies.[1] They also introduced a new currency, the euro, that will eventually replace the existing national currencies in these countries. Starting in 2002, French francs, German marks, and Italian lira will be replaced by the euro in everyday transactions. Monetary policy for the EMU is conducted by the European Central Bank (ECB) rather than the central banks of the individual member countries.

The EMU itself follows a flexible exchange rate system in that the value of the euro can fluctuate against the dollar, the pound, and the yen. For example, a country such as Italy has a fixed exchange rate relative to the other members of the monetary union and a flexible exchange rate relative to nonmembers. This is similar to the situation of an American state. Both California and Massachusetts use U.S. dollars, so they have a fixed exchange rate relative to each other, but they both have a flexible exchange rate relative to the Canadian dollar, the yen, or the euro.

The primary economic reason for the EMU was the belief that a common currency will further the economic integration of Europe and promote economic trade and growth within Europe. Imagine if all fifty states in the United States had their own currencies and their values were constantly changing relative to one another. If you had a business in California and wanted to sell goods in Massachusetts, you would need to worry about the exchange rate between the currency of California and that of Massachusetts. Extra risk and uncer-

---

[1]The eleven countries are Austria, Belgium, Germany, Finland, France, Ireland, Italy, Luxembourg, the Netherlands, Portugal, and Spain. Greece joined the European Monetary Union in 2000.

European Monetary Union, Frankfurt, Germany

tainty would be added to your business problems. The advantages the United States has gained from allowing unrestricted trade among the states would be reduced. Europe hopes to enjoy similar gains from a common currency as it promotes greater economic integration and increased trade. ●

Stabilizing the Exchange Rate   Given the costs of exchange rate instability, there have been demands that the government should actively try to stabilize the exchange rate. What producers are particularly concerned with is stabilizing the real exchange rate, so that if inflation in the United States is higher than in foreign countries, American exporters can still sell their goods abroad. As

Figure 34.8 shows, there have been large movements in real exchange rates, just as there have been in nominal exchange rates.

There are three requirements facing any government program to stabilize the (real) exchange rate. First, the government must choose what the exchange rate should be. Second, it must have a mechanism for keeping the real exchange rate at that value. For example, if the dollar seems to be climbing too high against the yen, a plan might propose that the Fed sell dollars and buy yen, thus pushing up the demand for yen and increasing the supply of dollars. Producers in the United States may be delighted by this move; demand for exports will increase, as will demand for goods that compete closely with imports. But producers in Japan will feel just the opposite. If the Japanese government, responding to these pressures, were to intervene simultaneously and start selling yen and buying dollars, the two efforts would offset each other. In effect, it would be as if the U.S. government sold dollars in exchange for yen directly to the Japanese government, with private markets unaffected.

This brings up a third requirement of exchange-rate-stabilization proposals: there must be some degree of cooperation among countries. This is particularly true in the modern world economy, where no single country is dominant. There are several big players—Japan, the European Monetary Union, and the United States—and setting exchange rates requires these governments to work together.

International Cooperation   Following World War II, the major countries, including Britain, France, and the United States, recognized their economic interdependence and the importance of orderly foreign exchange markets for the conduct of international trade. In a famous 1944 meeting at Bretton Woods, New Hampshire, at which Keynes was a leader, they signed an agreement that called for fixed exchange rates between countries and that set up the *International Monetary Fund (IMF)*. Just as the Federal Reserve was set up as a central or banker's bank, providing a source that U.S. banks could borrow from in times of need, the IMF was to serve as the bank for the various central banks of the world. In the United States, a bank could borrow from the Fed in the case of a bank run, and the knowledge that a bank could do so was supposed to reduce the likelihood of a run. Likewise, a central bank could borrow from the IMF, and this was supposed to protect the country against runs on its currency and help it maintain the agreed-upon exchange rate.

International Perspective

Global Financial Crises

The decade of the 1990s witnessed three global financial crises. The first occurred in 1992, forcing the United Kingdom, Italy, and Sweden to abandon pegged exchange rates and leading several other members of the European Monetary System (EMS) to devalue their currencies. The second occurred in 1994 with the collapse of the Mexican peso. The collapse raised concerns among speculators about the financial health of other Latin American countries, and their currencies also came under pressure. This process, by which concerns about one country spread to others, is called *contagion*. Because the 1994–1995 crisis was centered in Latin America, the fallout from the Mexican crisis has been called the *tequila effect*.

The third crisis of the 1990s was set off in mid-1997 when speculators began selling the Thai currency, the baht. In June, the Thai government stopped fixing the value of the baht and it immediately devalued. As investors continued to shift into safer currencies, such as the dollar,

the Thai economy continued to suffer. Between June 1997 and December 1998, the Thai stock market lost almost half its value—as if the Dow Jones average in the United States had fallen from 11,000 to 5,500. As stock prices and other asset prices fell, banks that had loaned money with the inflated asset values as collateral were threatened.

Initially, no one expected what seemed to be an isolated event in Thailand to lead to a global financial crisis. It did because investors' assessments of the risks of investing in emerging market economies like Thailand's changed. Investors started pulling funds out of Indonesia, Malaysia, and the Philippines. As these countries were forced to let their currencies depreciate, Singapore and Taiwan stopped fixing the value of their currencies out of concerns that their exports would otherwise be at a competitive disadvantage. With investments in emerging markets looking more risky, investors wanted out. They started selling holdings in other Southeast Asian economies. The Hong Kong stock market

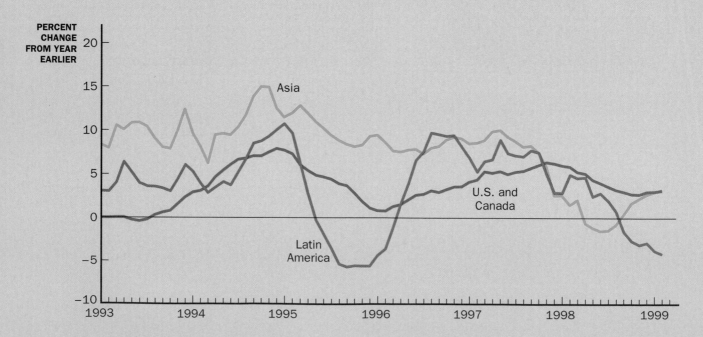

World Industrial Production

fell 23 percent in just four days in October 1997. Even the U.S. market was hit by fears of a crisis. The Dow Jones industrial average dropped 554 points on October 27, 1997, at that time the largest one-day point loss ever. In Asia, selling pressure spread from Thailand, to Indonesia, to South Korea, Taiwan, and Malaysia before jumping across the globe to hit Russia and Brazil.

As speculators withdrew capital, the governments of the affected countries faced difficult choices. One option was to simply let their currencies depreciate. Unfortunately, in many of these countries, domestic banks and firms had borrowed heavily from foreign sources; a devaluation would make it more difficult to repay these loans because it raises the domestic currency value that must be repaid. De-

valuation would threaten the solvency of the banking sector of these countries. The second option was to prevent a devaluation by raising interest rates high enough to halt the capital outflow. But this would severely constrict investment, cut aggregate expenditures, and lead to output declines and increases in unemployment.

The devastating economic consequences of financial crises are clear from the declines in production in Latin America during 1995 and 1996 and the declines in Asia in 1998 and 1999. The chart illustrates the very high rates of economic growth experienced in Asia throughout most of the 1990s. These growth rates started falling in Asia in mid-1997, turning negative in 1998.

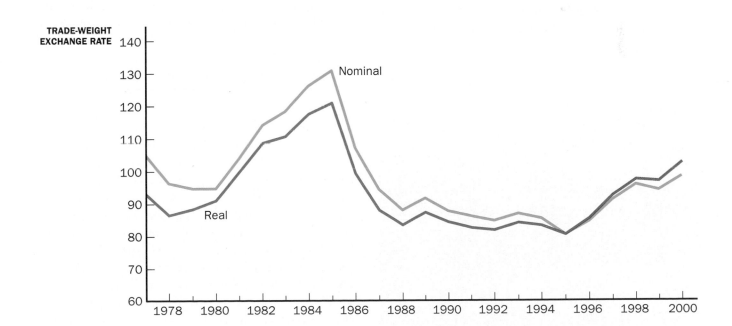

FIGURE 34.8 *Volatility of Nominal and Real Exchange Rates*

Both the nominal and real exchange rates for the United States fluctuated considerably over the 1980s. The figure shows the trade-weighted value of the dollar relative to other currencies, unadjusted (nominal) and adjusted (real) for price level changes in the United States and abroad.

SOURCE: *ERP* (1999), Table B-110.

CASE IN POINT

Currency Boards and Dollarization

Currency crises in Latin America and Asia have increased interest in new forms of monetary reform that could avoid future crises. Two suggestions that have figured prominently in discussions are a **currency board** and **dollarization.**

Under a currency board, the exchange rate between the local currency and, say, the dollar is fixed by law. The central bank holds enough foreign currency to back all the domestic currency and reserves it has issued. This makes a run on the currency unlikely—the central bank always has enough dollars to pay off anyone who shows up wanting to exchange the domestic currency for dollars. Since there is never any fear the country will run out of reserves, investors do not have to panic and try to get their funds out before the pegged rate is abandoned.

Argentina has operated with a currency board since 1991. Because Argentina had a history of high inflation, a currency board was viewed as a means of establishing a credible, low-inflation environment by tying the Argentinean currency to the U.S. dollar. The disadvantages of

a currency board are two. First, exchange rate adjustments can help ensure macroeconomic stability when two countries face different economic disturbances. For example, a recession in Argentina might be lessened by an exchange rate depreciation that spurs exports. A currency board, like other fixed exchange rate systems, eliminates the ability to conduct an independent monetary policy. If a country has a history of bad monetary policy, however, such a limitation may be desirable. Second, under a currency board the central bank cannot create reserves in the event of a domestic banking crisis—it can no longer serve as the lender of last resort.

A more extreme solution to exchange rate volatility and currency crises is to simply abandon the domestic currency and use the U.S. dollar, a policy called *dollarization.* Ecuador *dollarized* in 2000; the Ecuador currency, the sucre, is no longer used for transactions and all prices are quoted in U.S. dollars. By eliminating the possiblity of exchange rate changes and tying itself to Federal Reserve policy, it is argued, countries can benefit from the effects of reduced risk and lower uncertainty. Like other fixed exchange rate systems, dollarization removes monetary policy from a country's control—in this case, giving it to the Fed. The potential drawback is that the Fed bases its policy decisions on U.S. economic conditions and would be unlikely to alter monetary policy if a country that had switched to dollars were to experience a domestic economic or financial crisis. ●

Ecuadorians read about their country's switch to the U.S. dollar as the new official currency.

In the years after World War II, the countries of the world tried to maintain exchange rates within fairly narrow bands. To do this required governments' buying and selling money and gold out of their reserves. To keep the dollar at the desired level, the United States would have to buy dollars and sell German marks, Japanese yen, and whatever other currencies were gaining strength against the dollar. During the first two decades after the war, the American economy dominated the world scene, and it was easy for the United States to take on the responsiblity of stabilizing exchange rates—buying and selling dollars, foreign currencies, and gold to do so. Everyone wanted American goods, and the United States exported much more than it imported. The Fed accumulated vast amounts of foreign currency. Thus, if it looked like the demand for marks at the fixed exchange rate exceeded the supply, the Fed would simply sell some of the marks out of its horde.

But what happens when the Fed runs out of its reserves, when it has no more marks or yen to sell?

If the demand for dollars is weak, the dollar's exchange rate will not be able to be sustained at the desired value. Foreign central banks could intervene. The German Bundesbank might, for instance, buy dollars and sell marks, and the increased demand for dollars would allow the exchange rate to be maintained. But the German bank might not want to do this. If it believes that the dollar cannot be sustained at the pegged value, then the Germans will be left holding dollars that are about to decrease in value. This seems like bad business. Why should they pay the price for America's problems?

Although the Fed could borrow from the IMF, this may only postpone the eventual day of reckoning. Try as they might, governments cannot support forever an exchange rate that differs from the one that would have emerged without government intervention in the market. Under the Bretton Woods system, Britian, France, and other countries found from time to time that they simply had to devalue their currencies.

The end of the system of fixed exchange rates can probably be dated to 1971, when the United States, which had been the pillar of the system, found it increasingly difficult to support the value of the dollar. The United States (with the rest of the world quickly following) switched to a system of flexible exchange rates. Advocates of flexible exchange rates say that it is better to have frequent small changes in response to market forces rather than the large, disruptive changes that characterize a fixed exchange rate regime. Even with flexible exchange rates, however, there are still heavy doses of government intervention, requiring continuing cooperation among the countries of the world. Every year there is an economic summit of the leaders of the major industrialized countries, and one of the topics frequently discussed is exchange rate management. The United States has been concerned with not only the volatility of the dollar but also its level.

Especially in the mid-1980s when the dollar was flying high, it was often argued that the dollar was overvalued, making it difficult for the United States to export and for American producers to compete with foreign imports. Most of the leaders of the other countries have been only mildly sympathetic. They believe that in the long run the exchange rate is determined by basic economic forces. Most economists share this view. The high value of the dollar in the mid-1980s was caused by the huge flow of capital to the United States; this in turn was caused by the high interest rates paid in the United States, which in turn was related to the huge amount of borrowing on the part of the federal government.

Can Governments Stabilize Exchange Rates?

Some economists are skeptical about the ability of government to stabilize the exchange rate even in the short run. If the current exchange rate between the peso and the dollar is 10 pesos to the dollar, and if the market knows that the exchange rate must change in the near future to 12 pesos to the dollar, it will be futile for the Mexican government to try to maintain the current exchange rate in the short run. Mexican investors, believing that there will be a devaluation of the peso, know the return to holding assets in dollars will be enormous. By converting their pesos to dollars and holding them for the short period until the peso is devalued, they obtain a large return.

There will be what is referred to as a *run* on the peso, as those holding assets denominated in pesos seek to sell them now. This run will be too large for the Mexican government to stop by buying pesos and selling dollars. There are more private individuals willing to sell pesos and buy dollars than the Mexican government has resources to cope with. The government may be successful in postponing the fall of the peso for a few days, but to do

e-Insight

Capital Flows in the New Economy

International capital flows played a major role in financing the investment boom the United States experienced between 1995 and 2000. The figure shows the dramatic rise since 1992 in private domestic investment as a percentage of GDP. The strong growth in the U.S. economy and the need for firms to invest in the new technologies is reflected in the rising share of GDP that represents investment in information-processing equipment such as computers and in software.

National saving in the United States has been insufficient to finance this investment boom. Instead, the gap between domestic investment and national saving is financed by a capital inflow. This capital flow is shown in green in the figure. The basic trade identity discussed in Chapter 26 showed that the gap between national saving and domestic investment is equal to the trade deficit, and the growing gap between U.S. saving and investment after 1998 was reflected in a rise in the trade deficit from $90 billion in 1997 to $370 billion in 2000.

It is the international financial system that has channeled saving from the rest of the world into investment in America. Without a well-functioning international financial system, the low level of national saving in the United States would have restricted America's ability to invest in new technologies.

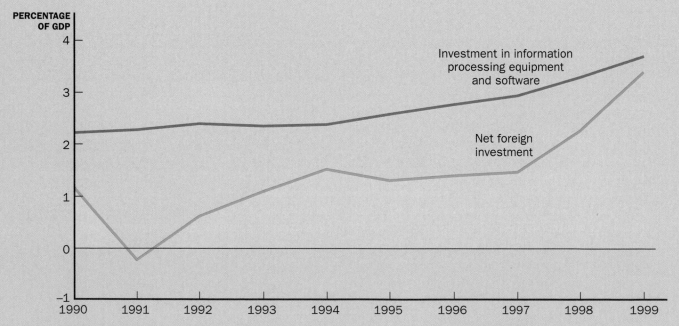

Investment in Information Processing Equipment and Software and the Capital Inflow

so it may pay a huge price. It would have obtained the capital gain on the dollars it held if it did not sell dollars for pesos. Instead, the capital gain is earned by private individuals. If the government spends $1 billion trying to support the peso and the peso goes down 20 percent (as in our example), the cost of the short-run support is more than $200 million.

Critics of government stabilization programs make several points. First, they stress the difficulties in determining the equilibrium exchange rate that is supposed to be stabilized. Is there any reason, they ask, to believe that government bureaucrats are in a better position to make judgments about the equilibrium exchange rate than the thousands of investors who buy and sell foreign exchange every day? If the government makes mistakes, as it is almost bound to do, it can actually contribute to destabilizing the exchange rate rather than stabilizing it.

Exchange rates often need to change. For example, if one economy grows faster than another or has higher inflation than another, the exchange rate will have to adjust to compensate. How will a scheme for stabilizing exchange rates let them adjust naturally while controlling them at the same time?

Second, critics of government stabilization programs question whether international economic cooperation is achievable. Running domestic economic policy is difficult enough. For example, will a country take steps to raise its exchange rate and thus hurt its exporters to keep a political agreement with foreign countries?

Thus, there are serious questions about whether stabilizing the currency is possible either economically or politically.

Review and Practice

Summary

1. Exchange rates are determined by the forces of supply and demand. The demand and supply for dollars are determined by exports and imports, foreigners' demand for investment in the United States and Americans' demand for investment abroad, and by speculators, whose demands for various currencies are based on expectations concerning changes in exchange rates.

2. Interest rate parity is the condition for equilibrium with perfect capital mobility. If interest rates in one country

are higher, then investors must expect the currency of that country to depreciate. If the country's interest rates are lower than those available in other countries, investors must expect its currency to appreciate.

3. In an open economy, government monetary policy is likely to have stronger effeects on aggregate expenditures. If the Fed raises interest rates, capital can flow in from abroad and this pushes the exchange rate up, reducing exports and increasing exports.

4. Under fixed exchange rate systems, the government must intervene in the foreign exchange market to ensure that demand and supply balance at the pegged rate. This means that monetary policy must be used to peg the exchange rate and cannot be used to address other macroeconomic goals.

5. It may not be possible for the government to stabilize exchange rates effectively. It is difficult to determine the equilibrium exchange rate that is supposed to be stabilized, and international coordination may not be achievable.

Key Terms

flexible or floating exchange rate system
perfectly mobile capital
interest rate parity condition
real exchange rates
fixed exchange rate system
devaluation
currency board
dollarization

Review Questions

1. Name three factors that cause exchange rates to shift.

2. How does monetary policy affect output in an open economy under a flexible exchange rate system?

3. If the European Central Bank raises interest rates in Europe while the Fed leaves U.S. interest rates unchanged, would you expect the dollar to appreciate or depreciate?

4. Why are expectations concerning changes in the exchage rate important? How do relative rates of inflation affect those expectations?

5. What are the costs of exchange rate instability? How might the government attempt to reduce instability in exchange rates? Why is international cooperation important? What problems result from government attempts to stabilize the exchange rate at a level that is not the equilibrium level?

6. Can a country run an independent monetary policy to achieve domestic economic policy goals if it is committed to maintaining a fixed exchange rate?

7. Under a fixed exchange rate system, when will speculation by foreign investors be stabilizing? When will it be destabilizing?

Problems

1. Tell whether each of the economic actors in the following list would be suppliers or demanders in the foreign exchange market for U.S. dollars:

   (a) An American tourist in Europe

   (b) A Japanese firm exporting to the United States

   (c) A British investor who wants to buy U.S. stocks

   (d) A Brazilian tourist in the United States

   (e) A German firm importing from the United States

   (f) A U.S. investor who wants to buy real estate in Australia

2. Explain whether each of the following changes would tend to appreciate or depreciate the U.S. dollar, using supply and demand curves for the foreign exchange market to illustrate your answers:

   (a) Higher interest rates in Japan

   (b) Faster economic growth in Germany

   (c) A higher U.S. rate of inflation

   (d) A tight U.S. monetary policy

   (e) An expansionary U.S. fiscal policy

3. Suppose that at the start of 2001, a U.S. investor put $10,000 into a one-year euro investment. If the exchange rate was 1.5 euros per dollar, how much would $10,000 be in euros? Over the course of the year, the euro investment paid 10 percent interest. But when the investor switched back to dollars at the end of the year, the exchange rate was 2 euros per dollar. Did the change in the exchange rate earn the investor more or less money? How much? How does your analysis change if the exchange rate had fallen to 1 euro per dollar?

4. If the government wanted to reduce the trade deficit by altering the exchange rate, what sort of monetary policy should it employ? Explain.

5. If the government succeeds in raising the exchange rate, who benefits and who is injured?

6. Suppose inflation in the United States is 2 percent and in Mexico it is 5 percent. Explain how these differences in inflation will affect the long-run behavior of the exchange rate between the peso and the dollar.

7. Suppose Americans go on a "Buy American" campaign that reduces imports. Use a supply and demand model of the foreign exchange market to show how this would affect the value of the dollar. Does the change in the exchange rate act to increase the reduction in imports or does it partially offset the initial reduction in imports? Explain.

8. Suppose the interest rate in Japan is 2 percent and you expect the yen to appreciate against the euro by 4 percent over the next year. What would the nominal interest rate in the European Union have to be according to the interest parity condition?

Chapter 35

Controversies in
Macroeconomic Policy

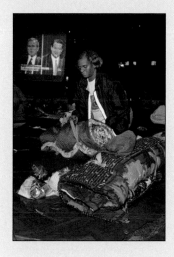

Key Questions

1. What are the key issues facing policymakers as they decide whether to stimulate or dampen the economy? What are the costs of inflation? Of unemployment?

2. Why do some economists believe the government should not intervene to stabilize the economy? Why do they believe that such intervention is unnecessary, ineffective, and more likely to do harm than good? And why do other economists believe that intervention can be helpful?

3. What are the fundamental trade-offs that policymakers face? How does policy affect these trade-offs?

T he model of economic fluctuations we developed in Part Three provides us with the tools to analyze many important macroeconomic policy debates. We have learned how monetary and fiscal policies affect the economy, and we have learned how economic disturbances can lead to fluctuations in output, employment, and inflation. Much of our analysis represented positive economics—we asked what the impact of a policy action would be without asking whether the policy was good or bad. Now we need to apply the tools we have learned to questions of normative economics: What are good policies? How should policies be designed and implemented? What sorts of policy-making institutions seem to produce good policies?

Making macroeconomic policy can be like walking on a tightrope. Lean too far one way, and unemployment increases. Lean too far the other way, and inflation rises. Sometimes, the worst of both worlds—high unemployment and high inflation—occurs, facing those making policy with difficult choices. Slowing the economy down to reduce inflation will make unemployment worse, while expanding the economy to reduce unemployment risks making inflation worse. Fortunately, periods of low unemployment and low inflation

also can occur, as witnessed in the 1990s. But when the goals of macroeconomic policy cannot be achieved simultaneously, tough trade-offs must be faced.

After briefly reviewing the basic goals of macroeconomic policy, we will address some fundamental questions: Should the government intervene to stabilize the economy? If it should, then how? With monetary or fiscal policy? What are the trade-offs that must be faced? And how are they affected by policy choices?

The Impact of Inflation and Unemployment

The goals of macroeconomic policy in the United States are spelled out in the Full-Employment and Balanced Growth Act of 1978, more commonly known as the Humphrey-Hawkins Act. This Act directs the federal government to "...promote full-employment and production, increased real income, balanced growth, a balanced Federal budget, adequate productivity growth, proper attention to national priorities, achievement of an improved trade balance . . . and reasonable price stability." The Humphrey-Hawkins Act sets specific "interim" goals for unemployment (4 percent) and inflation (3 percent). These were ambitious macroeconomic goals. In 1978, actual unemployment was 6.1 percent while inflation was 9 percent. Over the next five years, unemployment averaged just under 8 percent, twice the interim goal of 4 percent, and inflation averaged 8.5 percent. Neither of the basic objectives of macroeconomic policy—low unemployment and low inflation—was achieved.

At other times, the economy has achieved its goals, enjoying low unemployment and high growth with low inflation. In 2000, for instance, unemployment averaged 4 percent while inflation was only 3.3 percent. Our basic model predicts that the economy tends to return to full employment, but inflation can be high or low. Policymakers should aim to stabilize the economy around full employment (i.e., stabilize output around potential GDP) while maintaining an average inflation rate that is low and stable. Yet even when average inflation is low, policymakers must continually face trade-offs. Consider the situation faced by the Federal Reserve in 2000. Unemployment, which in 1998 and 1999 had fallen to its lowest levels in almost thirty years, continued to remain well below previous estimates of the nonaccelerating inflation rate of unemployment (NAIRU). Was it only a matter of time before inflation increased? Or had the NAIRU fallen, allowing lower rates of unemployment to be sustained without fear of inflation? If the Fed raised interest rates too soon, it might hasten the end of the boom unnecessarily; if it waited too long, inflation might increase. The Fed did raise interest rates in 2000, and by the end of the year, there were signs the economy was slowing. In 2001, the Fed reversed course and cut interest rates as it moved to forestall a recession.

Chapter 13 clarified the nature of the short-run unemployment-inflation trade-off. Today, the focus is not so much on trading a little more inflation for a temporary lowering of the unemployment rate. Governments realize that they cannot permanently run the economy at a rate lower than the NAIRU; attempting to do so eventually will lead to unacceptable levels of inflation. Temporarily low unemployment in the near term may have to be "given back" in higher unemployment later to bring inflation back down. As a result, the debate focuses more on how to maintain full employment with low average inflation and on the risks policymakers face. Will an emphasis on maintaining a stable (and low) rate of inflation lead to greater fluctuations in unemployment and output? Will attempts to stabilize unemployment inevitably cause more inflation instability? And if there is uncertainty about the value of the NAIRU, how aggressive or conservative should policy be? How willing should policymakers be to risk an increase in inflation, at the cost of failing to use the economy's resources as fully as they might be in the short run? In assessing these risks, economists must continually evaluate the costs of inflation and unemployment. Not surprisingly, those who worry more about unemployment and its costs argue for policies that move aggressively to stimulate production and employment, while those who worry more about the costs of inflation argue for aggressive policies to keep inflation in check.

Different Views of the Trade-off

Key to understanding these different positions is the recognition that unemployment and inflation affect different groups. Low-wage workers and other disadvantaged groups are the most likely to benefit from low unemployment policies and are the most likely to bear the costs of high unemployment if inflation increases and must then be reduced. Since these workers have little savings, they bear little of the direct costs of inflation. The costs of *unanticipated* increases in inflation are typically borne most by those who hold long-term bonds—who see the value of these bonds decrease as the nominal interest rate rises, as happens when inflation increases. Workers also may suffer from unanticipated increases in inflation if their pension funds are invested in long-term bonds.

Because the costs of unemployment and inflation are not borne equally by all, it is not surprising that different groups hold different positions in policy debates. Making economic policy—an exercise in normative economics—requires both an understanding of how the economy operates (the role of positive economics) and a set of values to guide choices when trade-offs are present. Very often, economists reach different policy conclusions even when they share the same model of the economy. This is to be expected since different economists will evaluate the relative costs and benefits of policies differently. But perhaps an even more fundamental question splits many economists: Should governments even attempt to intervene to stabilize the macroeconomy, or will such attempts simply worsen economic performance?

Thinking Like an Economist

Trade-offs and Choices

When economists analyze the decisions of individual households making consumption purchases, they focus on two aspects. First, what are the choices available to the household? These are defined by the household's income and the prices of the different goods it could purchase. With limited income, buying more of one thing means buying less of something else—the household faces trade-offs. Second, what are the preferences of the household? Faced with the same choices, different individuals will make different choices because their preferences—what they like to do or enjoy consuming—differ.

Economists use this same perspective to analyze actions by economic policymakers. First, they focus on the trade-offs. In the case of cyclical unemployment and inflation, they ask what the short-run trade-offs are—if unemployment is reduced slightly, how much will inflation rise over the next year, say? And they need to understand the long-run trade-offs. Will the reduction in unemployment be only temporary? Once the policymakers understand the trade-offs, they can assess the costs and benefits of the different options and choose the actual policies they want to implement. A policymaker who believes inflation is very costly will make different choices than one who assesses inflation costs as being lower. Even if there is agreement over the way the economy behaves, differences in preferences will lead to differences in policy recommendations.

The Non-Interventionist Perspective

Those who share the view that government should not intervene to stabilize the economy differ in their reasons. Some believe that the economy is efficient, so that there is little the government can add. Others believe that government action is ineffective, while still others argue that governments do have significant effects, but often these simply make matters worse. We now take a closer look at each of these perspectives.

Real Business Cycle Theory: Intervention Is Unnecessary

Intervention is clearly unnecessary if the economy always operates efficiently at full employment. Real business cycle theorists, led by Ed Prescott of the University of Minnesota, attribute the economy's fluctuations to exogenous shocks, such as the 1973 and 1979 oil price increases, or to shifts in the economy's underlying productivity, such as what may have occurred in the late 1990s. More importantly, these theorists believe that markets adjust quickly—prices and wages are sufficiently flexible that full employment will be restored quickly—and certainly more quickly than it would take government to recognize a problem, take actions, and have an effect. According to real business cycle theorists, the fluctuations we observe are not signs that output is deviating from potential; instead, they argue that potential GDP fluctuates, with wages and prices adjusting to ensure all markets clear. If the economy experiences a temporary decrease in productivity, output declines, firms hire fewer workers, and wages fall, inducing households to supply less labor. Measured unemployment may rise, but this reflects the economy's efficient response to the change in productivity.

Since the economy is at full employment, government need worry only about keeping inflation low and stable. The central bank just needs to set a low target for inflation and ensure that it is achieved.

New Classical Macroeconomics: Intervention Is Ineffective

Some noninterventionists, while not claiming all fluctuations are efficient, still argue that the government cannot affect output even in the short run. If the government attempts

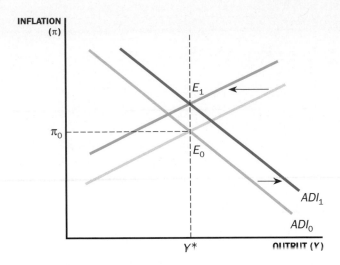

FIGURE 35.1   *Policy Ineffectiveness*

Some economists have argued that any anticipated policy will have little impact on output. If monetary policy shifts the ADI curve to the left, as depicted in the figure, the public will immediately expect higher inflation, shifting the SRIA curve up. The economy moves from its initial equilibrium at E_0 to a new equilibrium at E_1; output and employment have not been affected, but inflation is higher.

to expand the economy, shifting the aggregate demand-inflation (ADI) curve to the right (Figure 35.1), all market participants recognize that this will lead to higher inflation. So price- and wage-setting behavior and expectations adjust immediately in anticipation of the higher inflation, and the short-run inflation adjustment (SRIA) curve shifts up, leaving the economy with higher inflation and no expansion in real output. In Figure 35.1, the equilibrium jumps immediately from point E_0 to E_1 when the ADI curve shifts out.

The new classical view also argues that inflation can be reduced without leading to higher unemployment. Suppose that the economy starts out at E_1 in Figure 35.1. By reducing its inflation target to π_0, the monetary authority shifts the ADI curve to the right. If market participants are convinced that the inflation target has been reduced, they will immediately adjust their wage and price behavior, the SRIA curve shifts down immediately, and the economy jumps to E_0, with lower inflation achieved at no cost.

The new classical economists, led by Robert Lucas of the University of Chicago, strongly advance the view that predictable and systematic macroeconomic policies are largely ineffective in influencing real output and employment.

Intervention Is Counterproductive

Faith in markets is one thing; faith in the government to improve on markets is another. Some noninterventionists accept that government policies can affect the economy, and they may see shortcomings in markets, but they have little confidence in the ability of governments to improve macroeconomic performance. Indeed, some hold the view that intervention is counterproductive, for two reasons.

First, they recognize that there are important *lags* that make policy making difficult. It takes time for the government to recognize a problem—lags in getting data, revisions in preliminary data, and the often conflicting information available mean that policymakers face great uncertainty as they try to assess the state of the economy. Is this month's rise in new claims for unemployment insurance a signal that the economy is starting to head into a recession? Or is it just a transitory fluctuation likely to be reversed the following month? Once a problem is recognized, it takes time to take action. The Federal Open Meeting Committee (FOMC) of the Federal Reserve meets frequently, but fiscal policy actions may require congressional approval which can easily take many months to secure. Finally, once a policy action is taken, there are lags before it has an impact on the economy. Interest rate changes by the Fed, for example, take six months or more to have significant effects on output and even longer before inflation is affected.

Because of these lags, by the time the policy effects are fully realized, the action may no longer be appropriate. Expansionary policies may finally take effect just as the economy is already recovering, pushing it into an inflationary situation. Or contractionary policies designed to slow inflation might affect the economy just as it is starting to enter a recession, worsening the subsequent rise in unemployment.

Lags by themselves would not be a problem if the government could accurately forecast. But everyone, including government economists, sees the future with a cloudy crystal ball, and as a result, governments risk taking the wrong action. The problem is compounded by our uncertain knowledge about the lengths of the lags. Nobel Prize–winning economist Milton Friedman, formerly at the University of Chicago, and now at Stanford's Hoover Institution, argued that the lags were long and variable, making it extremely difficult to conduct successful policies. In recent years, governments have become more sensitized to the problem of timing. One of the reasons given for former

President George H. W. Bush's reluctance to take strong actions to stimulate the economy in the midst of the economic downturn in 1991 was a worry that, given the shallowness of the recession, the economy might quickly recover on its own, making any extra government spending or tax reductions unnecessary and potentially harmful.

Second, critics of strong interventionist policies argue that there are systematic political reasons why interventionists are often misguided. Politicians want the economy to expand before an election. They might boost government spending to overheat the economy, with gains in employment showing up before the election but the costs, in terms of higher inflation, showing up only after the election. In recent years, many countries have attempted to reduce the influence of elected politicians on monetary policy for just this reason.

Rules Versus Discretion

Critics of intervention claim that historically, whether because of political motivations or simply because of the lags described earlier, government has actually exacerbated the economy's fluctuations. When the government attempts to dampen a boom, its policies reducing demand take effect just as the economy is weakening, reinforcing the downward movement. Conversely, when the government attempts to stimulate the economy, the increase in demand kicks in as the economy is strengthening on its own, thereby igniting inflation. Thus, critics of government action such as Milton Friedman conclude that better outcomes would result if policies were based on simple **rules** rather than the **discretion** of the government policymakers. A policy rule specifies the automatic adjustment of policy in response to macroeconomic conditions. Discretionary policies are explicit policy decisions that are taken in light of economic conditions. In Chapter 30 we used a monetary policy rule linking inflation to the Federal Reserve's target for the federal funds interest rate to construct our ADI curve. Friedman proposed that the government should expand the money supply at a constant rate, rather than actively use monetary policy to respond to economic events in the hopes of stabilizing the economy. According to Friedman and others, by sticking to rules, the government would eliminate a major source of uncertainty and instability in the economy—uncertainty about future government policies.

A second argument for rules stresses the importance of commitment. A government might promise to keep inflation low. But as an election nears, the government might be tempted to try to expand the economy a bit to improve its reelection chances, even though this will lead to lower unemployment only temporarily while leaving the economy with higher inflation. Knowing the government will face this temptation, individuals will not believe the initial promise to refrain. Individuals will anticipate higher inflation in the future. As we learned in Chapter 31, a rise in inflation expectations increases current inflation. The inability to commit to a low-inflation policy means the economy may end up with higher than desired inflation without even a temporary gain of lower unemployment.

The problem of whether a government will actually carry out a promised course of action is called the problem of **dynamic inconsistency.** This problem arises in many contexts. A city may promise to keep taxes low in order to attract a new shopping mall. Once the mall is built, however, the city may find it an irresistible source of tax revenues, despite earlier promises. Anticipating this, the developers may decide not to build the mall in the first place. In 1981, new legislation gave special tax breaks to the real estate industry. These breaks were intended (by the legislators) to be permanent. A real estate boom resulted. The boom was partially attributed to builders' rushing to take advantage of the tax break that they believed would be repealed eventually. They were right; the tax advantages were repealed in 1986. Outcomes would have been different had the government made a commitment not to change its behavior.

As another example of dynamic inconsistency, consider the case of a final exam. The purpose of a final is to provide students with an incentive to study the course material, so the teacher almost always thinks it is good policy to announce there will be a final exam. When the time for the exam comes, however, it is too late for the teacher to influence whether students studied or not—the only thing the teacher has to look forward to is grading all those exams. So it makes sense to cancel the exam. But if students anticipate this, they will not study, and announcing that there will be an exam no longer has its desired effect of getting students to study. Few teachers cancel final exams because they know if they do it once, their future students will not prepare for an exam they expect to be cancelled. The teacher has a *reputation* to protect. Similarly, governments may refrain from breaking their promises in order to maintain a reputation for doing what they promise. The desire to maintain a good reputation can help governments fulfill their promises.

The Interventionist Perspective

The case for intervention is based on two key beliefs. First, economic fluctuations are not simply the efficient response of the market to shifts in productivity, as the real business cycle theorists argue. Instead, wages do not adjust quickly enough to maintain a balance between labor supply and labor demand, so declines in aggregate expenditures lead to cyclical unemployment. Second, the period of excessive unemployment can persist for a long time. In contrast, the underlying assumption of the noninterventionists is that markets adjust quickly and so cyclical unemployment is a short-term affair at most. While the process of wage and price adjustment eventually may bring the economy back to full employment, interventionists believe this adjustment can be speeded up by appropriate policy interventions. As a practical matter, democratic governments face enormous political pressures to intervene if the economy enters a deep recession. Interventionists believe that macroeconomic policies can do more than simply help stimulate the economy if a deep recession occurs; these policies can help ensure that deep recessions are avoided and help stabilize the overall economy.

Today, the leading school of thought among economists who believe that government can and should design policies to stabilize the economy is called *New Keynesianism*. These economists share Lord Keynes's view that unemployment may be persistent and that though market forces may restore the economy to full employment, these forces often work so slowly that government action is required. The new Keynesian theories differ from older Keynesian analysis in their emphasis on microeconomics—they share, for instance, with many real business cycle and new classical economists the view that theories of aggregate behavior should be based on theories of the individual households and firms that make up the economy—and in their emphasis on the important role expectations about the future play. But they also have identified a variety of reasons, such as costs of adjustment and imperfections of information, why markets do not adjust quickly to disturbances.

Moreover, they agree that while there are forces that enable the economy to dampen and absorb exogenous shocks, there are also endogenous forces that sometimes amplify shocks and make them more persistent.[1] Noninterventionists stress the former forces. As firms cut back on production in response to a drop in export demand, wages and prices decline. The real interest rate also falls, lowering the cost of credit. This encourages households to decide it is a good time to purchase durable goods and new houses, while firms may increase their investment spending. These decisions help raise aggregate expenditures, offsetting the contractionary impact of the export decline.

WRAP-UP

Schools of Thought on Macroeconomic Policy

Noninterventionists

Real business cycle theorists believe fluctuations in economic activity are due to exogenous shocks and that markets respond quickly and efficiently. Government intervention has no useful role to play.

New classical economists think that the scope for government intervention is limited because wages and prices adjust quickly and because the private sector will adjust in anticipation of policies in ways that offset the impacts of the policies.

Others believe that even though markets adjust slowly, discretionary macroeconomic policies make matters worse rather than better because of the long and uncertain lags in determining the need for policy actions, in implementing policy changes, and in affecting the economy.

Interventionists

New Keynesian economists generally accept that policies can have no long-run effect on GDP or the NAIRU because wages, prices, and expectations eventually adjust, but they think markets respond slowly, so periods of cyclical unemployment can persist. Discretionary macroeconomic policy can be effective, and governments should design built-in stabilizers that can help to make the economy less volatile.

---

[1] *Exogenous* economic disturbances are disturbances that originate outside the economy such as wars or developments in other countries. *Endogenous* forces are those properties of the economy that tend to generate or exacerbate fluctuations.

By contrast, New Keynesian economists emphasize the forces within the economy that amplify fluctuations and help make those fluctuations persist. An initial economic slowdown might lead to an increase in bankruptcies that raises perceptions about the risks of making new loans. Banks might then curtail lending or limit credit availability, forcing households and firms to cut back on spending. The initial slowdown might then lead to an amplified fall in aggregate demand, output, and employment.

New Keynesian economists agree that adjustments in interest rates, wages, and prices may *partially* offset destabilizing influences—lower interest rates providing greater impetus for firms to invest during a recession, for instance—these adjustments are simply too weak to ensure cyclical unemployment is minimized.

Policies to Improve Economic Performance

While academic economists often debate *whether* government should intervene, most actual policy debates center around *when* and *how* to intervene. There are three sets of policies designed to improve the economy's macroeconomic performance.

One class of government policies works to automatically stabilize the economy. Automatic stabilizers (discussed in Chapter 32) that cause tax revenues to fall when the economy enters a recession are primary examples. Systematic monetary policies that lower interest rates when the economy slows are another example.

Discretionary policies are explicit policy actions taken in light of economic conditions and designed to affect macroeconomic equilibrium. A government spending bill designed to increase government purchases in a recession or a reduction in the central bank's inflation target as part of a disinflation would be examples of discretionary policies.

The distinction between automatic policy responses and discretionary policy actions is not always a clear one. Most press coverage of Federal Reserve decisions treats them as discretionary actions: Should interest rates be changed? If so, when? By how much? In fact, there is evidence that during the past fifteen years the Fed has acted systematically to adjust interest rates in response to inflation. This type of behavior underlies its policy rule and the ADI curve. Because the Fed acts systematically, interest rate adjustments by the Fed have an effect similar to that of fiscal automatic stabilizers. But because the exact timing of interest rate changes as well as the size of a particular change are left to the FOMC, the policy actions share characteristics of discretionary policies.

A third class of policies focuses on the microeconomy. These policies aim at affecting the job skills of workers or the microeconomic structure of the labor market and are designed to lower the NAIRU so the economy can attain a lower average level of unemployment.

WRAP-UP

Policies to Improve Economic Performance

1. Automatic stabilizers help stabilize the economy.
2. Discretionary policies reflect explicit policy actions taken in light of economic conditions.
3. Microeconomic policies are designed to lower the NAIRU.

Inflation-Unemployment Trade-Offs

Economists focus on trade-offs: If we want more of one thing, what do we have to give up? Can we have lower average unemployment if we are willing to accept higher average inflation? Does maintaining low and stable inflation mean that output and unemployment will be less stable? Chapters 31 and 32 provided the analytical basis for addressing these questions. Clearly, we would like to have both low (and stable) inflation and low (and stable) unemployment. But what are the trade-offs policymakers must face? Economists' understanding of the trade-offs has evolved over time.

The Old Inflation-Unemployment Trade-off

In the years immediately following the discovery of the Phillips curve, most economists thought that there was a trade-off between the *average* level of unemployment and the *average* rate of inflation. Economists who thought the costs of inflation were high argued for low inflation and a high unemployment rate, while those who thought the benefits of low inflation paled in comparison with the costs of high unemployment argued for lower unemployment rates and higher inflation. Thus, disagreements about policy largely hinged on disagreements about the relative *costs* of inflation and unemployment.

Attempts in the 1960s to exploit this trade-off by reducing unemployment to much lower levels led, as expected, to higher inflation. But as unemployment fell and inflation rose, individuals began to expect that inflation would be higher. Rather than remaining stable at a new higher level, the inflation rate continued to increase as long as unemployment remained below the economy's NAIRU. The economy ended up back at the same levels of unemployment as before but with higher inflation rates. As the unemployment rate and inflation rate increased together in the 1970s, economists became more aware of the importance of inflationary expectations. Any sustained rate of inflation would come to be expected, shifting the SRIA curve. A consensus developed that the economy could not enjoy a sustained level of unemployment below the natural rate, or NAIRU.

That experience convinced most policymakers that no trade-off exists between average rates of inflation and unemployment. As we learned in Part Two, the average level of the unemployment rate and the rate of real economic growth are determined by such fundamentals as technological change, population growth, labor market institutions, and the skills of the workforce. These factors are unrelated to the economy's average rate of inflation, so allowing average inflation to rise brings no long-run benefit in the form of faster growth or lower average unemployment. The choice facing policymakers appeared to be a simple one—the economy could operate at the NAIRU with low inflation, or it could operate at the NAIRU with high inflation. Given this choice, low inflation clearly was to be preferred to high inflation.

There still remain three important elements of disagreement. First, while there was general agreement that the long-run Phillips curve (long-run inflation adjustment, or LRIA curve) was vertical, some economists believe the SRIA curve is relatively flat so that in the short run—a period that might last for a fairly extended period of time—the economy can experience lower unemployment with only moderate increases in inflation. Others worry that with rational expectations, even short periods of low unemployment will quickly

lead to higher inflationary expectations, shifting the SRIA curve up and leading to higher inflation. In fact, the evidence suggests that inflation responds with a long lag to declines in the unemployment rate. At least for countries with moderate rates of inflation, there is substantial inflation inertia.

The second disagreement concerns the costs of disinflation—the name given to reducing the inflation rate. Assume policymakers make a mistake and push the unemployment rate below the NAIRU. Inflation initially increases only slightly. What would it take to reduce inflation? Clearly, the economy would have to operate for a while at a higher level of unemployment—at a level above the NAIRU. Those who advocate a cautious policy—making sure that inflation is kept low and stable—worry that the costs of reducing inflation are very high. In particular, they look to the experience of the 1970s and 1980s. To wring the inflationary expectations of the 1970s (when inflation hit double-digit levels) out of the economy, the United States had to go through a deep recession with unemployment reaching 10 percent. Similar experiences were common in most industrialized economies as inflation was brought down from the high levels of the 1970s. Any gain in output and employment while unemployment is below the NAIRU is simply matched by the loss in employment and output needed to "kill" inflation.

The third disagreement centers on the value for the NAIRU. Is it 6 percent or 5 percent, or perhaps even lower? As unemployment in the United States fell in the 1990s to levels below most previous estimates of the NAIRU, disagreements arose over whether inflation would soon start rising or whether the NAIRU had actually fallen. The NAIRU cannot be observed directly; it must be estimated, and most estimates of it are imprecise. Overestimating or underestimating the NAIRU can lead to policy problems. If policymakers believe the NAIRU is 6 percent when it is really 5 percent, they will try to slow the economy down whenever unemployment dips below 6 percent, running the risk of slowing economic growth prematurely. If policymakers believe the NAIRU is 5 percent when it is really 6 percent, they may act too slowly to head off inflation, risking an increase in expected inflation that will make subsequent moves to reduce inflation more costly.

The New Trade-off: Output Stability–Inflation Stability

In recent years, economists have focused on a new trade-off. Economists such as John Taylor of Stanford University have argued that attempts to stabilize fluctuations in output and employment will cause inflation to fluctuate more. And attempts to stabilize fluctuations in inflation will cause output and employment to fluctuate more.

Taylor has summarized the current thinking on policy trade-offs in the form of two propositions:

The *first* proposition, about which there is now little disagreement, is that there is no *long-run* tradeoff between the rate of inflation and the rate of unemployment.

The *second* proposition, and there is more disagreement here, is that there is a *short-run* tradeoff between inflation and unemployment. I think that the short-run tradeoff is best described in terms of a tradeoff between the *variability* of inflation and the *variability* of unemployment; that is, in terms of the short-run fluctuations in the variables rather than their levels over time.[2]

Taylor suggests that if policymakers focus too much on keeping inflation stable, undesirable fluctuations in output will occur. If policymakers focus too much on keeping unemployment equal to the NAIRU, undesirable fluctuations in inflation will occur. One important aspect of this trade-off is that it focuses on *stabilizing* the economy through macroeconomic policies rather than on attempting to achieve outcomes (such as an unemployment rate below the NAIRU) that cannot be sustained. Later in this chapter we will see how the trade-off between output stabilization and inflation stabilization is affected by the policy rule followed by the central bank.

Implementing Macroeconomic Policies

So far, our discussion has focused on the goals of macroeconomic policies and on the trade-offs policymakers face. But even when there is agreement about the objectives, there may be disagreements about how best to achieve those objectives. Should fiscal policy be limited to auto-

matic stabilizers? Should monetary policy take the lead in actively attempting to stabilize the economy?

Fiscal Policy

Discretionary fiscal policy has played little role in the United States in recent decades, and the chief reason for this is the lags inherent in the fiscal policy process. It takes time before the government recognizes that a fiscal expansion or a contraction might be needed. Then, Congress must approve the necessary expenditure or tax changes. This process can take as much as a year to accomplish, and the final expenditure or tax bill that Congress passes may bear little resemblance to the original proposal. Once the bill is passed, more time may pass before aggregate expenditures are affected significantly. A new investment tax credit, for instance, may cause firms to plan more investment projects, but there are delays before actual expenditures on these projects take place. By this time, the economy may be in a quite different stage of the business cycle than it was when the need for policy action was originally recognized.

These policy lags have meant that at least for the United States, the main role of fiscal policy in helping stabilize the economy operates through automatic stabilizers. As the economy enters a recession, tax revenues decline automatically as falling incomes reduce people's taxes. Some government expenditure programs, such as unemployment insurance, increase automatically as incomes and employment fall. These responses help to stabilize household disposable income and household consumption spending.

This discussion has focused on the practical difficulties of using discretionary fiscal policy to "fine-tune" the economy, ensuring it always remains at full employment. Suppose, however, that the economy is in a serious recession with high unemployment that is expected to persist for some time. In this case, is a more active use of fiscal policy warranted? Is it worth reducing the surplus (or increasing a deficit) to get out of a recession?

Is It Worth Incurring a Deficit or Reducing the Surplus to Get out of a Recession?

If the government is running a deficit, spending more than it collects in revenue, an increase in government expenditures,

---

[2]John Taylor, "How Should Monetary Policy Respond to Shocks While Maintaining Long-Run Price Stability?—Conceptual Issues," in *Achieving Price Stability* (Federal Reserve Bank of Kansas City, 1996), pp. 11–95.

or a tax cut, will worsen the fiscal deficit. This was the situation through most of the 1980s and 1990s in the United States, and deficits continue to be problems in many countries. The presence of deficits has led many countries to place limits on fiscal policy. In 1997 the U. S. Congress agreed to a self-imposed constraint that it would not increase expenditures (over agreed-upon levels) unless there was also an agreement to increase taxes by a corresponding amount.[3] Such action is unlikely, given that raising taxes is politically so unpopular. Similarly, the 1991 Maastricht Treaty that guided the formation of a single currency (the euro) for the European Monetary Union[4] required that countries reduce their deficits to 3 percent of GDP by 1997 if they wanted to qualify to join the common currency. Achieving this goal required expenditure cuts and tax increases, leaving little room for expansionary fiscal policies to stimulate the economy.

Those concerned with increasing a deficit to stimulate the economy point out that even if a fiscal stimulus makes us better off now, future generations are saddled with more government debt, making them worse off. However, if the government increases its expenditures by spending more on investment rather than current consumption—increasing spending on infrastructure, human capital, or research—future generations may actually be better off, provided the return on those investments exceeds the interest rate. Estimated returns to government investment in many of these areas are very high. Most estimates put the return on investment in research in excess of 20 percent, and estimates of the return on investment in education exceed the interest rate. Of course, under these conditions, the government should expand investment spending even if the economy is not in a recession.

The situation in the United States is quite different in 2001. The federal government is running a surplus. Given current expenditure and tax policies, the federal government is projected to continue to run a surplus. In Chapter 26 we learned how a fiscal surplus adds to national saving and contributes to lower interest rates and higher private investment. The changing fiscal situation in the United States has allowed more flexibility in the use of fiscal policy to stimulate the economy in 2001 as a recession threatens.

---

[3] As projections in 1999 began showing large future surpluses, Congress started to ignore these self-imposed constraints.

[4] The euro came into existence on January 1, 1999.

Monetary Policy

Monetary policy has become the primary tool in the United States for reducing short-run macroeconomic fluctuations and ensuring low inflation. The Federal Reserve implements monetary policy, and the Fed's policy-making committee, the Federal Open Market Committee (FOMC), meets frequently. As a consequence, monetary policy decisions can be made quickly. Although the FOMC meets every six weeks, it can hold telephone conferences between its regularly scheduled meetings if necessary. In January 2001, as new information suggested that the economy was slowing down, the FOMC decided not to wait until its next regular meeting and instead immediately cut its federal funds interest rate target by a half percent.

The time it takes for policymakers to recognize a change in economic conditions and to implement a policy action is called the *inside lag* of policy. This lag is generally viewed as much shorter for monetary policy than it is for fiscal policy.

Even though a decision to change monetary policy can be made quickly, lags are still important for monetary policy. Actions by the Fed can take a long time to affect economic activity and inflation. While changes in government expenditures directly affect aggregate expenditures, monetary policy works through interest rate, credit, and exchange rate channels to affect aggregate expenditures. As a consequence, the lag between a change in the federal funds rate and unemployment or inflation is very long. Interest rate cuts often take twelve to eighteen months to have their maximum impact on the economy.

The lag between a change in policy and its impact on the economy is called the *outside lag* of policy. Both monetary policy and fiscal policy affect aggregate expenditures.

WRAP-UP

Policy Lags

Inside lag: the time required to recognize a need for a change in policy and to implement the policy change. The inside lag is shorter for monetary policy.

Outside lag: the time required for the change in policy to affect the economy. The outside lag is normally shorter for fiscal policy.

Since government purchases are a component of aggregate expenditures, a change in government expenditures has a direct and immediate impact on aggregate expenditures. In contrast, it may take several months for a change in interest rates brought about by monetary policy to affect actual spending plans of households and firms. For this reason, the outside lag is generally viewed as much shorter for fiscal policy than it is for monetary policy.

Monetary and Fiscal Policy and the Composition of Output

There are major differences between monetary and fiscal policy in their effects on the composition of output. Assume, first, that we could use either monetary or fiscal policy to stimulate the economy to the same extent. If we use monetary policy, we lower the real interest rate, stimulating investment. Thus, future levels of income will be higher. Using monetary policy, governments can pursue both a high-growth and a full-employment strategy. If we use fiscal policy to shift out the ADI curve, interest rates will rise as inflation increases. This will lower private investment spending. If government purchases were for current consumption, future incomes will be lower.

Figure 35.2 contrasts the composition of GDP under alternative policies, assuming part of the fiscal stimulus comes from tax cuts and part from increases in purchases. In comparing the two panels in the figure, investment and net exports are larger when monetary policy is used to ex-

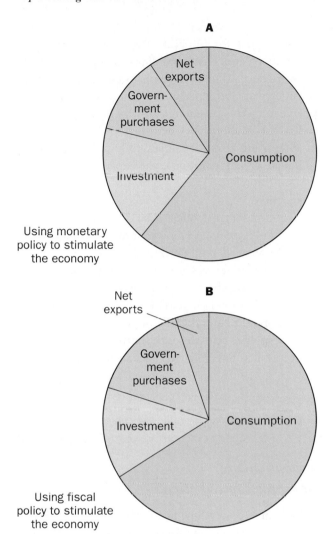

FIGURE 35.2 *Comparison of the Effects of Monetary and Fiscal Policies*

The share of investment is highest when monetary policy alone is used to restore full employment, and lowest when increased government purchases alone are used.

pand the economy in the short run. In contrast, panel B shows that consumption and government purchases are larger with a fiscal expansion, with investment and net exports correspondingly smaller. While either fiscal or monetary policy may be able to restore the economy to full employment, they have different effects on investment and future economic growth.

These differences become less clear if government purchases are for investment purposes. A substantial portion—

Internet Connection

The Economic Report of the President

Every February, the president's Council of Economic Advisors issues the *Economic Report of the President.* This report contains a discussion of the state of the economy and developments in fiscal policy. Each year, the report provides chapters on issues of current policy debate. The latest report can be found at http://w3.access.gpo.gov/eop/.

in recent years, approximately 16 percent—of government expenditures goes for physical investments, such as the construction of roads and buildings. Additionally, large amounts are devoted to investments in people (investment in human capital) and in technology, both of which potentially serve to increase economic growth. If the government stimulates the economy by increasing public investment rather than using monetary policy to lower interest rates and stimulate private investment, the impact on growth will depend on the relative rates of return of these two forms of investment.

Fiscal and monetary policies also differ in their impact on exports and imports. A monetary expansion that lowers interest rates also will tend to cause the currency to depreciate as the lower returns lead foreign investors to seek higher returns elsewhere.[5] A depreciation decreases imports (by making foreign goods more expensive) and increases exports. In contrast, a fiscal expansion that causes interest rates to rise also causes the currency to appreciate. Net exports fall as foreign goods become less expensive.

WRAP-UP

Implementing Macroeconomic Policies

In the United States, long inside lags are involved when discretionary changes in fiscal policy are made. Consequently, the major role of fiscal policy in stabilizing the economy has operated through automatic stabilizers.

Monetary policy has short inside lags but long outside lags.

Fiscal policy and monetary policy have different effects on the economy. Expansionary fiscal policy raises the real interest rate and causes an appreciation that crowds out private investment spending and net exports. Expansionary monetary policy lowers the real interest rate and causes a depreciation that stimulates private investment spending and net exports.

Designing Monetary Policy

Compared to our global financial system today, the financial structure of the country was vastly different in 1913. Reflecting those differences, the role of the Fed has evolved over time. As originally laid out in the 1913 Federal Reserve Act, Congress intended that the Fed should prevent financial panics and bank runs. Only in the post–World War II era, after the experience of the Great Depression, have governments recognized a responsibility for preventing economic fluctuations. Accordingly, today the Fed's goal in conducting monetary policy is to promote low inflation, general economic stability, and sustainable economic growth.

An important lesson from the full-employment model examined in Part Two is that monetary policy is the chief determinant of inflation. Central banks, through their policies that affect reserve supply and the money supply, can control the *average* rate of inflation. This does not mean that inflation can be closely controlled on a month-to-month basis, or even year to year, but a central bank can exercise considerable control over the average level of inflation that the economy experiences over longer time periods. For this reason, in recent years most central banks have accepted that one of their primary responsibilities is to maintain low average inflation.

Monetary policy also can have important effects on two other macroeconomic goals—low (and stable) unemployment and economic growth. However, according to the full-employment model, neither the economy's potential GDP nor the unemployment rate at full employment depend on the money supply. Potential GDP and the unemployment rate at full employment depend on household decisions about how much labor to supply in the marketplace, firms' decisions about how many workers to hire, and the economy's capital stock and technology. None of these factors depend on the absolute level of prices or the number of green (or other colored) pieces of paper that make up the money supply.

This implication of the full-employment model is important. If full employment corresponds to an unemployment rate of, say, 5 percent, then the Fed cannot push the unemployment rate down to 4 percent and keep it there.[6]

---

[5]See Chapter 33 to review why the interest rate affects the exchange rate.

[6]Full employment occurs when labor demand and labor supply balance so that cyclical unemployment is zero. The unemployment rate is still positive at full employment because of frictional, seasonal, and structural unemployment.

It can do so temporarily, but as wages and prices adjust to restore labor market equilibrium, unemployment will return to 5 percent. We discussed the mechanisms that ensure the economy returns to full employment in detail in Chapters 31 and 32. If monetary policy cannot succeed in keeping the unemployment rate below its full-employment level, the appropriate goals of monetary policy are to contribute to economic stability by helping to ensure full employment is maintained and by keeping inflation low. In this way, monetary policy contributes to the overall stability of the economy, ensuring the economy can experience sustainable economic growth.

How can the Fed achieve the goals of full employment and low inflation? It can do so by pursuing two types of policies. First, the Fed can engage in **countercyclical policies**—policies designed to keep the economy at full employment by smoothing out fluctuations in the economy. If a recession begins, the Fed can try to stimulate the economy to move unemployment quickly back to its full-employment level. Second, the Fed can focus on keeping the average inflation rate at low levels.

During the 1990s, central banks in many countries (including Canada, New Zealand, Mexico, England, Israel, and Sweden) adopted **inflation targeting** as a framework for carrying out monetary policy. Inflation targeting policies are designed to stabilize the economy through countercyclical policies while ensuring that average inflation remains low. As might be expected of any policy adopted by a number of countries, the exact meaning of inflation targeting has varied greatly. It generally involves the central bank defining its policy goals solely in terms of keeping the inflation rate within a narrow range around a low average level. For example, New Zealand, which was the first to use inflation targeting to guide monetary policy, set a target for inflation of 0 to 2 percent. Under a law passed in 1989, the governor of the Reserve Bank of New Zealand (New Zealand's "Alan Greenspan") could be fired if inflation went above 2 percent.[7]

Many economists have expressed concern that by focusing only on inflation, the other important goals of economic policy—low unemployment and sustained economic growth—will be ignored. When wages and prices are slow to adjust, monetary policy has important effects on unemployment and growth, at least in the short run. Since monetary policy can affect these important macroeconomic variables, central banks also should be concerned with helping to maintain full employment and prevent recessions.

CASE IN POINT

Fed Policy Statements— Balancing Policy Goals

In 1999, the U.S. economy continued to expand and unemployment remained at historically low levels. The Fed was concerned that this strong growth would lead to higher inflation. The chief uncertainty was whether the low unemployment reflected a fall in the NAIRU. If the NAIRU had fallen, then unemployment could remain low without a risk of inflation increasing. If, however, the NAIRU had not fallen, then a continuation of actual unemployment below the NAIRU would lead to a buildup in inflationary pressures over time. In this case, the Fed would want to raise interest rates to gradually slow the economy down, letting unemployment return to the NAIRU while maintaining low inflation.

During the summer, the Fed began to lean toward increasing interest rates. At their May meeting, the FOMC members decided not to change interest rates, but they provided a clear signal that they were likely to raise rates soon. After their meeting (on May 19, 1999), the Fed released the following statement:

> While the FOMC did not take action today to alter the stance of monetary policy, the committee was concerned about the potential for a buildup of inflationary imbalances that could undermine the favorable performance of the economy and therefore adopted a directive that is tilted towards the possibility of a firming in the stance of monetary policy. Trend increases in costs and core prices have generally remained quite subdued. But domestic financial markets have recovered and foreign economic prospects have improved since the easing of monetary policy last fall. Against the background of already-tight domestic labor markets and ongoing strength in demand in excess of productivity gains, the committee recognizes the need to be alert to developments over the coming

[7]In 1998, the target range was widened to 0 to 3 percent.

months that might indicate that financial conditions may no longer be consistent with containing inflation.

By the time of their next meeting (on June 30), the FOMC members decided it was time to boost interest rates. After their meeting, they issued the following statement:

> The Federal Open Market Committee today voted to raise its target for the Federal Funds rate 25 basis points to 5 percent.[8] Last fall the committee reduced interest rates to counter a significant seizing-up of financial markets in the United States. Since then, much of the financial strain has eased, foreign economies have firmed and economic activity in the United States has moved forward at a brisk pace. Accordingly, the full degree of adjustment is judged no longer necessary.
>
> Labor markets have continued to tighten over recent quarters, but strengthening productivity growth has contained inflationary pressures. Owing to the uncertain resolution of the balance of conflicting forces in the economy going forward, the F.O.M.C. has chosen to adopt a directive that included no predilection about near-term policy actions. The committee, nonetheless, recognizes that in the current dynamic environment it must be especially alert to the emergence, or potential emergence, of inflationary forces that could undermine economic growth.

The Fed continued to increase the funds rate target through early 2000. By December 2000, there were signs the economy was slowing quickly, and a change in policy was needed to prevent it from heading into a recession. Acting between its normally scheduled meetings, the FOMC cut the funds rate target by half a percentage point on January 3, 2001. After the action, the FOMC released the following statement:

> The Federal Open Market Committee decided today to lower its target for the federal funds rate by 50 basis points to 6 percent.
>
> These actions were taken in light of further weakening of the sales and production, and in the context of lower consumer confidence, tight conditions in some segments of financial markets and high energy prices sapping household and business purchasing power. Moreover, inflation pressures remain contained. . . . ●

Inflation Targeting and Policy Trade-offs

We can use the ADI–inflation adjustment model of the economy to understand the implications of inflation targeting. Figure 35.3A shows two monetary policy rules. For both, the central bank's target for the inflation rate is π^T and the full-employment equilibrium real interest rate is r^*. When the economy is at full employment and inflation is on target, the nominal interest rate set by the central bank will be $i^* = r^* + \pi^T$. The policy rule labeled A is steeper than the one labeled B. If policy is set using the rule labeled by A, a rise in inflation leads the central bank to boost interest rates by a larger amount than it would when using the rule given by B. Panel B shows the ADI curves under the two different policy rules, ADI_A and ADI_B. Also shown are the SRIA and LRIA curves. The full-employment equilibrium is at point E_0.

Suppose the economy is hit by a temporary inflation shock that shifts the SRIA curve up, as shown in panel B. An oil price increase or a rise in inflationary expectations would have this effect. If the central bank's behavior is described by the policy rule A, the economy moves to a new short-run equilibrium at point E_A. If the central bank's behavior is described by the policy rule B, the economy moves to a new short-run equilibrium at point E_B. Under policy rule A, output declines more and inflation increases less in the face of the disturbance than occurs under policy rule B. In the face of shifts in the SRIA curve, the economy will experience more stable inflation and less stable output and employment under policy rule A than under policy rule B. If the central bank responds less aggressively to inflation (as under rule B), it lets inflation fluctuate more but succeeds in keeping output and employment more stable. This is the trade-off between output stability and inflation stability that the central bank faces.

In practice, because of the lags between a change in interest rates and their effects on the economy, central banks must be forward looking, adjusting interest rates based on expectations about future inflation. By responding aggressively to changes in expected inflation (a steep policy rule), monetary policy will limit inflation fluctuations, but the cost will be greater instability in real output and employment when the inflation adjustment curve shifts. By responding less aggressively, monetary policy

---

[8]A basis point is a hundreth of a percent, so a 25 basis point increase is a .25 percent increase, in this case, from 4.75 percent to 5 percent.

International Perspective

Central Bank Mandates

The formal policy goals of the Fed have evolved over time. In fact, the 1913 Federal Reserve Act that created the Federal Reserve System did not establish any specific macroeconomic goals for the Fed. Instead, the chief hope was that the Fed would ensure an end to the financial crises that the United States had suffered periodically. The Great Depression of the 1930s and the high inflation rates experienced during the 1970s affected what we now consider to be the goals of monetary policy. A 1977 amendment to the Federal Reserve Act provides that the Fed "shall maintain long run growth of the monetary and credit aggregates commensurate with the economy's long run potential to increase production, so as to promote effectively the goals of maximum employment, stable prices, and moderate long-term interest rates." (See "The Goals of U.S. Monetary Policy," by John Judd and Glenn Rudebusch at http://www.frbsf.org/econrsrch/wklyltr/wklyltr99/el99-04.html.) These goals involve measures of economic performance that are based both on the behavior of *real* economic activity (full employment, increased real income, growth, trade balance) and on the behavior of the general level of prices (stable prices).

Until recently, most other countries were similar to the United States in listing goals such as high employment, high growth, and low inflation or stable prices as the objectives to be pursued by monetary policy. While there has been little debate in the United States over the legislated goals assigned to the Fed, this has not been the case in other countries. The high inflation rates of the 1970s led many countries to rethink the goals of monetary policy. They have revised their laws to assign their central bank a more focused objective. Usually, this involves establishing

low inflation or price stability as the primary, or in some cases, the sole objective of monetary policy. New Zealand was the first country to move in this direction. After the country suffered years of poor inflation performance, the legislation governing New Zealand's central bank (the Reserve Bank of New Zealand) was revised in 1989. The new legislation states, "The primary function of the Bank is to formulate and implement monetary policy directed to the economic objective of achieving and maintaining stability in the general level of prices." Goals such as high employment or growth are not mentioned.

Monetary policy for the member countries of the European Monetary Union is conducted by the European Central Bank, which came into existence January 1, 1999. As in New Zealand, the governing legislation for the bank specifies that price stability is the primary objective of monetary policy. Again, unlike the case in the United States, unemployment considerations are not explicitly named among the policy objectives of the European Central Bank.

The full-employment model implies that monetary policy plays an important role in determining the average rate of inflation, but monetary policy can do little about the economy's average rate of unemployment. From this perspective, it is perhaps not surprising that many countries have established low inflation or stable prices as the central bank's primary policy objective. In the short run, however, monetary policy actions can have important effects on real economic activity and employment. In Chapter 32 we saw how the actions of the central bank affect the achievement of the twin goals of maintaining low (and stable) inflation and maintaining full employment.

will cause inflation to fluctuate more when the inflation adjustment curve shifts, but output and employment will be more stable.

Price Level Targeting

The 1977 amendment to the Federal Reserve Act established "stable prices," not

stable inflation, as one of the Fed's goals. Under a policy of keeping inflation at a low rate, say, 2 percent per year, the average level of prices continues to rise from year to year. If the price level rises more rapidly in one year, a policy of inflation targeting aims to reduce the inflation rate back to its target level. In contrast, a policy of **price level targeting**

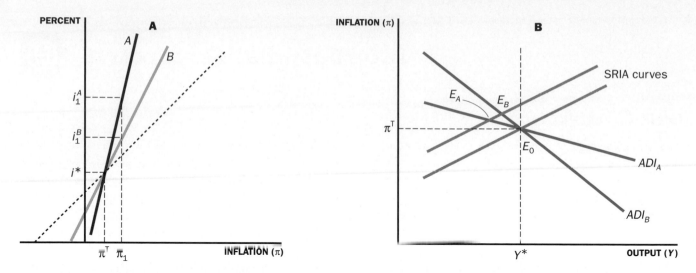

FIGURE 35.3   *The Policy Rule and Fluctuations*

The way the central bank responds to inflation affects the slope of the ADI curve, and this in turn has important effects on how the economy responds to disturbances. Panel A shows two policy rules. Under rule *A*, changes in inflation lead to larger changes in the real interest rate than is the case under rule *B*. If inflation rises from π^T to π_1, the nominal interest rate is increased to i_1^A under rule *A* and only to i_1^B under rule *B*. Since as a result the real interest rate changes more under rule *A*, a change in inflation has a bigger impact on aggregate demand than with rule *B*. As a consequence, the ADI curve with rule *A* is flatter than the one under rule *B* (see panel B). An inflation shock that shifts the SRIA curve up, as in Panel B, leads to a bigger fall in output and a smaller rise in inflation under rule *A*. Output will vary more and inflation less with rule *A* than with rule *B*.

would try to cause prices to actually fall to bring the average level of prices back to its targeted level.

The difference between inflation targeting and price level targeting is illustrated in Figure 35.4. The figure assumes the target inflation rate is zero but that in period 2 a temporary shock pushes inflation up to 2 percent for one period, as depicted by the orange line in panel A. Under inflation targeting, the inflation rate is brought back to zero. For simplicity, it is assumed that this occurs in period 3. Panel B shows what happens to the price level. It jumps to a higher level in period 2 and then remains permanently higher. Policy brings inflation back to zero but no attempt is made to return prices to their initial level.

The green lines in the figure illustrate what happens under price level targeting. The inflation shock pushes the price level higher but now policy acts to return the price level to its initial level. This requires a *deflation*—prices must actually fall.

Few central banks have adopted price level targeting. The deflation needed to get the price level back on target after a positive inflation shock would require a costly recession and a period of high unemployment.[9]

Deflation and a Zero Nominal Interest Rate

During the 1970s and early 1980s, inflation seemed an intractable problem. Most countries succeeded in eventually reducing inflation, but only at the cost of significant increases in unemployment. Today, the situation is quite different. The average inflation rate in the United States was just over 3 percent in 2000.

In many countries, concern over inflation has been replaced by worries that prices will fall—deflation. In Japan, prices fell at a 2 percent rate during 1998 and 1999. Japan also has been suffering its worst recession of the postwar era. The last significant deflation in the United States occurred in the 1930s during the Great Depression.

[9]While no central bank has adopted price level targeting as a formal policy, the appendix to this chapter shows how our basic model can be modified to deal with the case of a price level target.

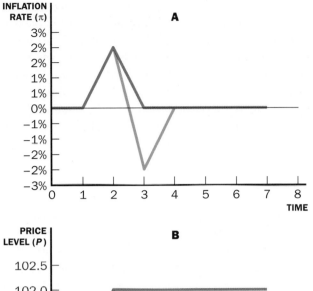

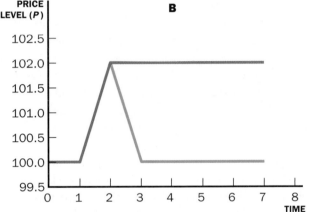

FIGURE 35.4 *Inflation Targeting Versus Price Level Targeting*

The orange line in panel A shows the rate of inflation as initially equal to zero. In period 2, there is a positive inflation disturbance, and inflation jumps to 2 percent. Under a policy of inflation targeting, the central bank tries to bring inflation back down to zero (shown in the figure as occurring in period 3). The behavior of the price level under this policy is shown in panel B. The temporary increase in inflation leaves the price level permanently higher than before.

Under a policy of price level targeting, the central bank would try to bring the price level back to its initial value, as shown by the green line in panel B. For the price level to fall, inflation must be negative, as shown in panel A by the green line.

Monetary policy faces a new problem in stimulating the economy when prices are falling during a recession. To stimulate the economy, the central bank should lower interest rates. Suppose the real interest rate needed to restore full employment is 1 percent, and suppose due to falling prices people expected deflation to continue at 2 percent.

What nominal interest rate will the central bank need to target to achieve a real interest rate of 1 percent? The real rate is the nominal interest rate minus expected inflation, so

1 percent = required nominal interest rate – (–2 percent),

since the expected rate of inflation is –2 percent—that is, an expected deflation. If we rearrange this equation, the necessary nominal interest rate would be

required nominal rate = 1 percent – 2 percent = –1 percent!

So a *negative* nominal interest rate would be necessary. But here is where the problem arises. Nominal interest rates cannot be less than zero. A negative nominal interest rate means you could borrow $100 today, pay back the $100 in a year, and receive an interest payment from the lender! If the nominal rate were –1 percent, after one year you would receive $1 from the lender. If this were the case, everyone would try to borrow as much as they could. After all, if you could borrow $1 billion and just put it under your bed for a year, you would receive 1 percent, or $10 million from the lender. Since everyone would try to borrow, and no one would want to lend, supply and demand would not balance in the capital market. A negative nominal interest rate cannot be an equilibrium.

The central bank can push the nominal interest rate down to zero but no lower. This means that if the public expects a 2 percent deflation, the real interest rate cannot go below 2 percent, and this might not be low enough to get the economy out of its recession. This is the situation the Bank of Japan faced at the end of the 1990s. Nominal interest rates were down to zero. Because the Bank of Japan continued to indicate its real concern was ensuring that inflation did not reappear, people continued to expect falling prices, and the real interest rate remained too high.

Faced with this situation, what can a monetary authority do? For one thing, it could announce that its target for inflation is higher. Suppose it announces that it will aim for 0 to 2 percent inflation. If this causes people to start expecting some inflation, say, 1 percent, the real rate of interest falls from 2 percent to –1 percent (zero nominal rate –1 percent expected inflation). The promise to deliver some inflation helps stimulate the economy.

Deflations often have been associated with tough times, times of economic stagnation and high unemployment. When prices fall, the dollars a borrower must repay are worth more than the dollars that were borrowed. Just as unexpected inflation redistributes wealth from lenders to borrowers, an unexpected deflation benefits lenders at the expense of borrowers. During the 1870s and the 1930s, falling wages and prices for farm products hit borrowers hard, particularly farm families. Periods of deflation also have been associated with financial and banking crises. As the prices they receive for their products fall, many firms are unable to repay their loans. If they are forced into bankruptcy, the banks that have loaned money will not be repaid, so they may also become bankrupt, leading to further disruptions in credit and economic activity.

Credibility   Notions of credibility and reputation play a large role in discussions of monetary policy. It is easy to see why when we think about the problem of disinflation. As we have learned, policies to reduce inflation cause output to decline and unemployment to rise. Eventually, the economy returns to full employment with lower inflation, but the cost, in terms of cyclical unemployment, of reducing inflation can be quite significant. Many economists have argued that the cost of disinflation will be much smaller if the central bank announces in advance its plans to reduce inflation and if the central bank has credibility. If people expect lower inflation, the SRIA curve shifts down quickly, reducing the extent to which unemployment must exceed the NAIRU to get inflation down.

Central banks with a reputation for delivering on their promises will have an easier time reducing inflation should it ever get too high. Many advocates of inflation targeting argue that setting explicit inflation goals, and meeting them, will build credibility for a central bank. It then will be better able to help stabilize the economy at full employment. Should unemployment fall below the NAIRU, people will know that the monetary authority will keep inflation from getting out of control. Inflation expectations will remain stable, and actual inflation will not increase much. In contrast, if people are not sure about the monetary authority's commitment to low inflation, an economic expansion will raise concerns about higher future inflation. Inflation expectations will rise and actual inflation will start to increase more quickly.

Demand Versus Supply Disturbances and Policy Trade-offs

Our discussion of inflation targeting and the interaction between fiscal and monetary policy illustrates an important insight. When the economy experiences disturbances that shift the inflation adjustment curve—such as oil price increases, temporary shifts in productivity, or shifts in inflation expectations—policymakers face a critical trade-off. They can try to keep output and employment stable, but this causes inflation to fluctuate more (see Figure 35.3). Alternatively, policymakers can try to keep inflation stable, but this leads to bigger swings in output and employment. Even though they would like to keep the economy stable at full employment and low inflation, policymakers must choose which goal to focus on—they cannot achieve both their goals.

Policymakers do not face this same fundamental trade-off when the economy experiences disturbances that shift the ADI curve—such as shifts in fiscal policy, changes in spending decisions by households or firms, or economic fluctuations in other countries that affect net exports. If the ADI curve shifts to the left, threatening a recession, policymakers should engage in expansionary policies to offset the disturbance and keep the economy at full employment. In doing so, inflation also remains stable. By offsetting disturbances that affect aggregate expenditures, policymakers can succeed in stabilizing both employment *and* inflation. It is not necessary to trade off one goal for another.

This does not mean that making policy decisions is easy in the face of demand disturbances. The problem of lags and the difficulties of forecasting still apply. An example is provided by the Asian financial crisis of the late 1990s. This was widely predicted to reduce U.S. net exports and slow the U.S. economy down. The impact on U.S. output and inflation could be minimized if the Fed adopted a more expansionary policy. But the Fed had to decide how much more. Should the nominal interest rate be cut by 1 percent? 2 percent? And when? If fiscal policy turns more contractionary, the full-employment real rate of interest falls, but by how much? And how quickly will the fiscal contraction lead to a decline in spending? In principle, the central bank can offset the impacts of shifts in aggregate demand, such as fiscal policy, and keep both employment and inflation stable. In practice, policymakers do not have the ability to "fine-tune" the economy to this extent. The key lesson, though, is that the choices between policy goals that are faced when supply shocks occur are much tougher than when demand shocks occur.

Hysteresis

We now need to examine a fundamental assumption of our analysis that plays a critical role in our discussions of policy.

e-Insight

e-Time and Macroeconomic Policy

As the U.S. economy boomed during the late 1990s, economists speculated on how the business cycle would be affected. There has been less discussion of the impact the new information-based economy will have on macroeconomic policy. Policymakers will be affected if the economy now responds more rapidly to changing conditions.

Because fluctuations in inventory investment have been a major factor in several previous business cycles, the new information technologies that allow firms to manage inventories better may serve to limit future fluctuations. In past business cycles, a slowdown in sales caused inventories to build up, as decisions about production could not be based on real-time sales information. The rising level of unsold inventories then triggered large cuts in production. Today, with virtually instantaneous information on sales, production, and inventories, managers can fine-tune their production levels, avoiding the types of fluctuations seen in the past. New technologies provide managers with information more rapidly, and this speeds their responses to changing economic conditions.

If businesses are able to respond more quickly to changing economic conditions, policymakers may have less time to react and may find themselves unable to anticipate economic developments in time to adjust policy. Because there is a lag between changes in policy and their effect on the economy, policymakers need to be forward looking. In the case of monetary policy, the Federal Reserve would like to raise interest rates *before* inflation increases and lower rates *before* economic growth slows. If economic adjustments occur more quickly now, it may be harder for policymakers to react in time. Just such a situation occurred at the end of 2000. The sudden slowing of the U.S. economy caught policymakers by surprise. The Federal Reserve reacted with a half point interest rate cut on January 3, 2001, *after* the slowdown began.

In the past, interest rate cuts by the Fed have taken twelve to eighteen months to have their peak impact on the economy. While the new economy may give the Fed less time to react, it remains to be seen whether it also shortens the lag between changes in policy and their impact on the economy.

Instantaneous computer tracking enables managers to avoid both inventory shortages and unnecessary inventory build-ups.

That assumption was that the NAIRU either is constant or depends on such factors as the age structure of the population or the structure of the labor market. Most importantly, the NAIRU does not change as the economy experiences recessions and booms. This is a reasonable assumption for the United States. Unemployment rises during recessions but then returns to more normal levels. Unemployment falls during booms but again eventually returns to more normal levels.

Unemployment seems to behave differently in Europe. There, the disinflations of the early 1980s led to large unemployment increases, just as they did in the United States, but then unemployment remained high. Figure 35.5 illustrates this by showing how unemployment in the United States, France, Germany, and Italy has evolved since 1973. For each country, the unemployment rate is scaled by its 1973 value so that for each country it starts out equal to zero. Unemployment in the United States has fluctuated up and down since 1973 but has stayed around the same basic level. In contrast, unemployment rates in Europe have fluctuated since 1973 but have also drifted up over time. There is little evidence for these countries that unemployment tends to return to a relative constant NAIRU.

Some economists have argued that the European case illustrates *hysteresis*: the history of the unemployment rate matters for its current equilibrium level. In this case, the natural rate, or NAIRU, depends on the actual unemployment rate. In the view of these economists, high unemployment, as occurred during the disinflations of the 1980s, increases the NAIRU. Rather than return to its previous level, unemployment increases and remains high.

One explanation for this phenomenon is that when workers are unemployed for long periods of time, their job skills deteriorate—they lose their skills and work habits. They become less employable. What started out as cyclical unemployment becomes structural, boosting the NAIRU. Another explanation focuses on the policies instituted to deal with unemployment. As a response to the high unemployment in the 1980s, some countries increased unemployment benefits to reduce the hardships of the unemployed. By making unemployment benefits more generous, these policies lowered the incentives of the unemployed to find work. The unemployed put less downward pressure on wages as a result, and the NAIRU increased.

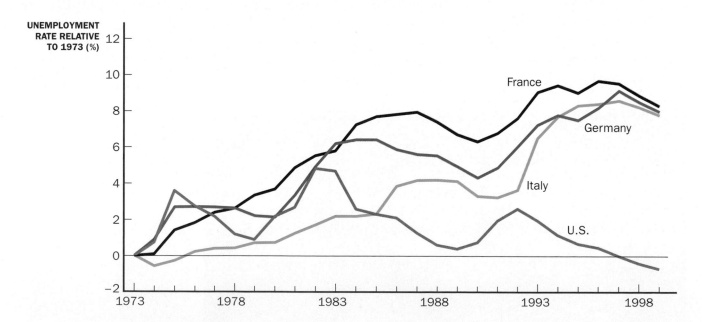

FIGURE 35.5   *Comparison of International Unemployment Rates*

The figure shows the behavior of unemployment in the United States, France, Germany, and Italy. In each case, the unemployment rate is expressed relative to its 1973 value, so for each country the plot starts out equal to zero in 1973. In the United States, unemployment has fluctuated around a relatively constant level. In contrast, European economies have seen rising unemployment rates, particularly since the 1980s.

Theories of hysteresis have important policy implications for Europe. If the natural rate is independent of actual unemployment, as the U.S. experience suggests, then using monetary or fiscal policy to lower unemployment would eventually generate increased inflation. On the other hand, if the natural rate does adjust to actual unemployment, then a monetary or fiscal expansion in Europe could lower actual unemployment and bring the natural rate down. By helping to bring the long-term unemployed back into the workforce, an economic boom might reverse the process and lower the natural rate of unemployment.

Structural Policies

Most macroeconomic policy discussions take as given the basic microeconomic structure of the economy and are carried out in the context of the existing policy-making institutions. For instance, the NAIRU is treated as fixed, or at least not affected by monetary or fiscal policies. Governments have tried to lower the NAIRU through policies that focus on the microeconomic structure of labor markets. Similarly, commentators speculate on the likely decisions of the FOMC, not on whether the institutional structure of the Fed should be changed. In many countries, however, central banks have undergone reforms that have altered their structure or goals. These types of institutional changes can affect the macroeconomic performance of the economy.

Reducing the NAIRU

Governments have tried to lower the NAIRU in several ways. The most important have involved increasing labor mobility, increasing job skills, and increasing the competitiveness of the economy. The aim is to lower the NAIRU by addressing the problems of frictional and structural unemployment.

Increasing Labor Mobility By reducing the time it takes for people to move from job to job, the government can reduce frictional unemployment and thus lower the average level of unemployment. Policies that facilitate labor mobility include one-stop job centers that enable individuals to ascertain quickly any vacancies for which they might be suited.

Some government policies, particularly in Europe, probably have reduced labor mobility—and thus increased the NAIRU. There is concern that legislation intended to increase workers' job security (by making it more difficult for employers to fire workers) has had the unintended consequence of making employers more reluctant to hire new workers. This impedes the process of job transition. Changing these laws may lower the NAIRU.

Increasing Workers' Skills Structural unemployment can arise when unemployed workers do not have the skills needed for the new jobs being created. Expanding demand for computer engineers will not help reduce unemployment among those with only a high school degree. A central part of Sweden's active labor market policies involves training programs that provide those who have lost their jobs with the skills employers are looking for. By helping to equip workers with the skills needed in today's labor force, government programs can help to reduce the economy's average unemployment rate.

Changing Institutions: Central Bank Independence

In recent years, many countries have changed their central banking institutions. Most of these reforms have altered the relationship between the policymakers responsible for monetary policy and the rest of the government or have clarified the goals monetary policy should pursue.

When the Federal Reserve conducts monetary policy, it enjoys a high degree of independence. Neither the president nor Congress can directly influence the policy decisions of the Fed. This independence from political pressures is the result of several aspects of the Fed's structure. For example, once appointed, the chair of the Fed is theoretically fully independent of the president and Congress. Although the chair must report to Congress on the Fed's policies and actions, the Fed's budget is not dependent on Congress.[10] So the Congress and the president cannot even threaten to reduce the Fed's funding.

Most central banks enjoy much less independence than the Fed. In a number of countries, however, reforms in

---

[10]The Fed's funding comes from the profits it earns, chiefly the interest it receives on its holdings of government debt. In 2000, its net income was $29.9 billion. The Fed returned $25.3 billion of this to the U.S. Treasury.

recent years have been designed to insulate their central banks from direct political influences. Support for such reforms comes from evidence that countries with independent central banks have experienced lower average inflation than have countries with more politically dependent central banks. Institutional reforms are viewed as important components of policies designed to maintain low inflation. Examples of countries that have given their central banks more independence include New Zealand, Mexico, Chile, Japan, and the United Kingdom. Perhaps the most independent central bank in the world is the new European Central Bank. This central bank is responsible for the conduct of monetary policy for the members of the European Monetary Union that came into existence on January 1, 1999.

Some economists have worried that insulating monetary policy from direct political influence will cause the central bank to focus too much on keeping inflation stable and not enough on helping to maintain full employment. There is little evidence to support this argument. While average inflation is lower in countries with independent central banks, neither average growth nor output fluctuations appear to be worse in these countries.

Does this mean that countries that have not yet given their central banks more independence should do so immediately? Not necessarily. There are several reasons for questioning the role of independence. First, the empirical evidence on inflation and central bank independence can be questioned. Germany had very low average inflation and the Bundesbank, Germany's central bank, had a high level of independence. Was it this independence that explains Germany's excellent inflation record? Or did the hyperinflation Germany suffered after World War I create a public consensus on the importance of low inflation? With strong public support for low inflation, Germany may have maintained low inflation even if politicians had had a more direct say in monetary policy. Simply transferring Germany's policy institutions to another country without also transferring the same level of public support for low inflation might fail to replicate Germany's experience with inflation.

Second, a fundamental principle in democracies is that those making important policy decisions should be answerable to the public. They should be *accountable*. Typically, we hold policymakers accountable through the election process. Officials who fail to deliver good macroeconomic policies are voted out of office. Central bankers with too much independence may not be accountable, failing to react sufficiently during a recession because they place excessive weight on inflation objectives. In the United States, the Fed has a great deal of independence in conducting policy, but accountability is enforced through two mechanisms. First, the chair of the Board of Governors is appointed by the president, subject to Senate confirmation, and while members of the Board of Governors have fourteen year terms, the chair's term of office is only four years. Second, the Fed chair must appear before Congress to explain Fed policy, and Congress can change the Federal Reserve Act. This provides a role for politicians to press the Fed on policy issues while still allowing the Fed independence in the actual conduct of policy.

A somewhat different solution to the issue of central bank independence was chosen by the Labour party in England after its 1997 election landslide. Before 1997, the Bank of England needed the government's approval before it could change interest rates. Under the new policy arrangement, the government sets a target for the rate of inflation, and the bank is responsible for achieving the target. In doing so, the bank is free to raise or lower interest rates. This type of arrangement, in which the elected government establishes the goals of monetary policy while the central bank is then free to set its policy instruments to achieve these goals, is often described as involving "goal dependence" and "instrument independence." In contrast, the Fed has both goal independence and instrument independence.

The European Central Bank was set up to enjoy a high degree of independence. The treaty establishing the bank defined price stability as the primary objective of monetary policy but left it to the bank to decide what price index to use in measuring inflation and how that translates into an explicit inflation target. The charter of the European Central Bank forbids it from taking instructions from any of the member governments, and members of the governing board are appointed for long (eight-year) nonrenewable terms. Some economists have argued that the European Central Bank has too much independence and too little accountability.

The long-term effect of these recent changes in central banking remains to be seen. As our model suggests, low inflation is consistent with full employment, so there is no fundamental inconsistency between full employment and low average inflation. The real trade-off is likely to be between inflation stability and employment stability. Central banks that focus solely on controlling inflation may impose real costs on the economy if output and employment become more unstable.

Review and Practice

Summary

1. Those who criticize active policy intervention to stabilize the economy argue that markets adjust quickly, so that unemployment is only short-lived. Attempts by government to intervene are not only unnecessary but also largely ineffective since they are offset by actions of the private sector. And to the extent that they do have effects, such policies often exacerbate fluctuations because of long lags and limited and imperfect information.

2. Most governments believe they should attempt to stabilize the economy and that without government intervention there may be long periods of high unemployment. While policymakers recognize that there are long lags and that policy is made with imperfect information (so that at times policy actions will be ill-timed or counterproductive), they also believe that on average, policy can be and has been stabilizing.

3. Critics of discretionary policy believe government should tie its hands, using fixed rules. Discretionary policies may be time inconsistent, leading to worse outcomes than occur when government follows predictable rules. Critics of fixed rules argue that this represents giving up on an important set of instruments and that fixed rules never work well because they fail to respond to the ever-changing structure of the economy.

4. Current policy discussions recognize that the economy cannot be kept at an unemployment rate below the NAIRU for long. The debate is over the following: (a) What is the NAIRU level and have changes in the structure of the economy lowered it? (b) What are the risks and rewards of exploiting the short-run trade-off between inflation and unemployment to gain a temporary reduction in unemployment at the potential cost of unemployment above the NAIRU later on? (c) How should the relative costs of fluctuations in inflation and fluctuations in output and employment be balanced?

5. Aggregate supply shocks require policymakers to balance the goals of full employment and stable inflation. Achieving one goal requires that the other be sacrificed. In the face of aggregate demand shocks, there is no inherent conflict between these goals.

6. In the face of disturbances such as oil price changes or shifts in inflationary expectations, policymakers face a trade-off between stabilizing unemployment and stabilizing inflation. If the central bank adjusts interest rates more aggressively to changes in inflation, it can make inflation more stable, but output and employment will fluctuate more.

7. Institutional changes may improve economic performance. Microeconomic policies may help to lower the NAIRU. Many countries have tried changing their policy-making institutions in an attempt to achieve better outcomes.

Key Terms

rules
discretion
dynamic inconsistency
countercyclical policies
inflation targeting
price level targeting

Review Questions

1. How do inflation and unemployment affect different groups differently, and how do these differences affect views concerning macroeconomic policy?

2. Why do some economists argue that interventions to reduce economic fluctuations are either ineffective or counterproductive?

3. Why do some economists argue that interventions to reduce economic fluctuations are effective and productive?

4. What trade-off between average unemployment and average inflation do policymakers face? What trade-off between fluctuations in unemployment and fluctuations in inflation do policymakers face?

5. What sorts of policies might the government take to lower the NAIRU?

6. What is meant by a dynamically inconsistent policy? Give at least two examples of policies that are dynamically inconsistent.

7. What is the difference between a policy of inflation targeting and a policy of price level targeting?

Problems

1. If you were in the position of the Fed in early 2001, with unemployment around 4 percent and inflation low, but with signs the economy was starting to slow, would you have lowered interest rates? Why or why not? Does your answer depend on whether your estimate of the NAIRU is 4 percent or 6 percent?

2. "If expectations adjust quickly to changes in economic circumstances, including changes in economic policy, then it is easy to start an inflationary episode. But under the same conditions, it is also easy to stop inflation." Discuss. If true, what implications might this finding have for economic policy?

3. Use the aggregate demand-inflation and inflation adjustment curves to explain the short-run and long-run effect on inflation and output of each of the following events:

    (a) An increase in business confidence

    (b) The development of new technologies that increase productivity

    (c) An increase in government purchases

    (d) An increase in inflation expectations

4. Assume that two members of the FOMC agree that the Fed's goals are to maintain full employment while ensuring low inflation, but one member (call this member W) believes the costs of unemployment make it a much more pressing problem than inflation, while the other (member H) holds the opposite beliefs. For each of the following disturbances, will member W want the Fed to raise or lower interest rates? What about H? In which cases will the two agree? In which cases will they disagree?

    (a) An increase in business confidence

    (b) The development of new technologies that increase productivity

    (c) An increase in government purchases

    (d) An increase in inflation expectations

5. Suppose a fall in net exports due to a recession among our major trading partners causes a recession in the United States.

    (a) If fiscal policy is used to stimulate the economy and return it to full employment, what happens to the real interest rate, investment, and future output?

    (b) If monetary policy is used to stimulate the economy and return it to full employment, what happens to the real interest rate, investment, and future output?

6. Suppose the economy is at full employment but inflation is viewed as too high. Consider the following two scenarios:

    (a) The central bank has great credibility. The central bank announces a policy of disinflation, and the public believes the announcement. Inflationary expectations fall immediately.

    (b) The central bank has no credibility. The central bank announces a policy of disinflation but the public is skeptical that the bank will actually follow through with it. The public's inflationary expectations only fall if they see actual inflation coming down.

    Discuss the likely unemployment consequences of reducing inflation in each of these two scenarios. In which case will the sacrifice ratio (the unemployment cost of reducing inflation) be highest? Explain why.

7. In parliamentary governments, such as the United Kingdom, the prime minister can announce a change in taxation or expenditure and implement the change almost immediately. How might this fact affect the balance between the use of monetary and fiscal policies for short-run stabilization?

Appendix: Price Level Targeting

Almost all central banks focus on inflation, not the price level, and they implement monetary policy through their control of a nominal interest rate. Some economists have advocated forms of price level targeting in which the central bank would try to keep the price level constant rather than simply keep inflation low. Although this type of price level targeting is not practiced by any central bank, many traditional textbooks treat central banks as if their chief concern were the level of prices. The approach we have followed—one that focuses on inflation and the policy response to inflation—can be modified easily to deal with the case of a central bank that targets the price level.

Under a policy of targeting the price level, the central bank will increase the nominal interest rate whenever the price level rises and lower the nominal interest rate whenever the price level falls. The objective in either case is to affect the real interest rate and aggregate expenditures. Rather than the negative relationship between inflation and aggregate expenditures represented by our ADI curve, a policy of price level targeting will lead to a negative relationship between the price level and aggregate expenditures. This relationship, shown in Figure 35.6, is usually called an "aggregate demand curve."

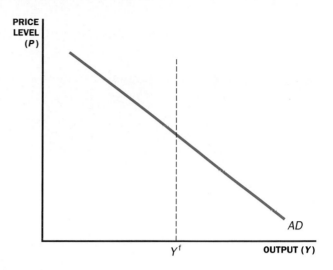

FIGURE 35.6 *The Aggregate Demand Curve*

If the central bank adjusts the interest rate whenever the price level deviates from its target level, the ADI curve is replaced with a relationship between the price level *(P)* and aggregate expenditures called the aggregate demand (AD) curve. If *P* increases, the central bank increases the interest rate, leading to a reduction in aggregate expenditures. Changes in fiscal policy or shocks to consumption, investment, or net exports shift the aggregate demand curve in the same way they would shift the ADI curve. An increase in government purchases, for instance, shifts the AD curve to the right.

Chapter 36

Government Fiscal Policy, Deficits, and Surpluses

Key Questions

1. What does the U.S. federal government spend its budget on? Where do its tax revenues come from?

2. Is government debt a burden?

3. How should future surpluses be used? What are the economic consequences of proposed alternatives?

4. What are the long-term problems the United States and other industrialized countries face that may affect future budgets?

*B*eginning in 1998, the U.S. federal government started to take in more tax revenue than it was spending, running fiscal surpluses. These surpluses represented a major turnaround in the government's budget situation. Between 1981 and 1998, the federal government spent more money than it collected in taxes, running large fiscal deficits. Just as you would have to do if you spent more than your income allowed, the government had to borrow. As the government borrowed more each year to cover its expenditures, the amount it owed—the government's debt—ballooned. Interest payments on this debt rose from $53 billion in 1980 to $244 billion in 1997, almost as much as the entire budget of the Department of Defense. Beginning in 1993, the deficit was finally reduced not only as a percentage of GDP but also in absolute terms—with the debt to GDP ratio leveling off and finally beginning to decline. The Balanced Budget and Taxpayer Relief Act of 1997 extended the caps on spending that had already helped close the deficit gap. Finally, the budget recorded a surplus in 1998 for the first time since 1969. With large surpluses now projected for the next ten years, the debate has shifted from how to reduce the deficit to how to use the surplus.

In this chapter we will discuss briefly the composition of government spending and taxes before we review the origins of the deficit problem, how the deficit problem was solved, and the debate about the consequences of government deficits and surpluses. We then will discuss the outlook for the budget, the debate over how surpluses should be used, and some of the long-term budgetary problems facing the United States and other industrialized countries.

The Composition of Spending and Taxes

In 2000, the U.S. federal government spent almost $1.8 trillion on everything from pencils to jetfighters, from AIDS research to Social Security benefits. Total spending can be divided into two basic types: **discretionary spending** and **nondiscretionary spending**. Discretionary expenditures—which include expenditures on the military, government operations, and most education and training programs—are decided on an annual basis. Each year, Congress and the president have the *discretion* to change their levels. Nondiscretionary spending has two components. First, the government makes interest payments on the national debt. Second, the government pays for **entitlements** that arise when the law specifies certain benefits, such as Social Security, Medicare, and food stamps, to which individuals who meet certain criteria are *entitled*, and expenditures are then determined simply by the cost of those entitlements.

Panel A of Figure 36.1 shows the composition of federal spending in 2000 by major category. Health, Medicare, Social Security and income security, and net interest are largely nondiscretionary expenditures, and in 2000 they constituted over 69 percent of all spending. Panel B shows the same categories of spending in 1980. Comparing panels A and B shows how the composition of government spending has changed since 1980. Defense spending has shrunk as a proportion of total spending, while the proportion of spending represented by Social Security has remained roughly constant. The major changes have been in two areas. First, health costs have risen dramatically, increasing from 9 percent of the budget in 1980 to 20 percent by 2000. Second, interest payments have risen from 9 to 12 percent of total spending, reflecting the large increase during the 1980s and 1990s in what the government owes.

The sources of the government's income have changed only slightly since 1980. As shown in Figure 36.2, individual income tax payments represent just under half of the federal government's receipts.

Factors Affecting the U.S. Budget

A good way to pose the question of what caused the budget deficit to soar in the 1980s and 1990s and to turn into surpluses at the end of the 1990s is to look at the changes in expenditures and revenues as a percentage of GDP. Figure 36.3 shows outlays, receipts, and the deficit, each expressed as a percentage of GDP. Also shown are projections for future outlays and receipts.

The deficit grew in the mid-1970s and again in the early 1980s as tax revenues were cut by the recessions of 1975, 1980, and 1981. As the economy recovered from reces-

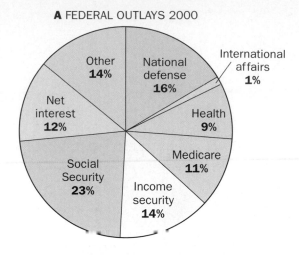

A FEDERAL OUTLAYS 2000

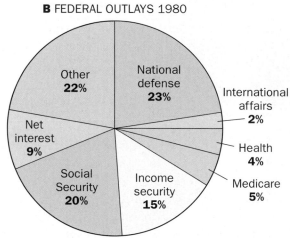

B FEDERAL OUTLAYS 1980

FIGURE 36.1   *The Composition of Government Spending*

The composition of the federal budget has changed over the last two decades. Net interest, health, and Medicare are now a much larger share of total spending than they were earlier.

sions, and income and tax revenues grew, the deficit shrank. The big change in the deficit picture occurred with the 1981 tax cut. Revenues as a percentage of GDP dropped sharply, opening a wide gap between expenditures and revenues. The fall in the deficit, and the development of a surplus as the 1990s ended reflected declines in government spending as a percentage of GDP and an increase in revenues. As the figure also illustrates, the projections for large surpluses in the future are based on the assumption that revenues will remain at historically high levels while outlays will continue to decline relative to GDP.

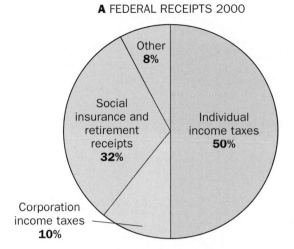

A FEDERAL RECEIPTS 2000

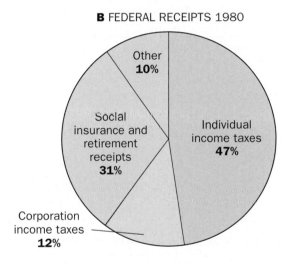

B FEDERAL RECEIPTS 1980

FIGURE 36.2   *The Composition of Government Revenues*

The relative importance of different sources of government revenue has remained fairly constant.

Factors Contributing to the Changing Budget

There are seven main factors that lie behind these broad trends in outlays and receipts.

Federal Taxes   During the 1970s, the federal government collected taxes representing between 17 and 18 percent of GDP. In 1980 and 1981 that percentage rose to over 19 percent. (Remember, 1 percent of a multitrillion-dollar economy will be tens of billions of dollars.) Tax cuts

enacted early in the Reagan presidency pushed the federal take back to its historic range of 17 to 18 percent. Tax increases in 1993 reversed this, and by 2000 federal tax receipts represented 20.6 percent of GDP, the highest level since 1944.

Defense Spending   Federal defense spending fell during the 1970s, as the Vietnam War came to an end, dropping from 8 percent of GDP in 1970 to 4.5 percent in 1979. In 1979, though, the Soviet Union invaded Afghanistan, and President Carter called for a large defense buildup. After Ronald Reagan was elected president in 1980, he followed through on those plans. From 1983 to 1988, defense spending averaged 6 percent of GDP. With the end of the Cold War, there have been reductions in defense spending. By 2000 it had fallen to just slightly less than 4 percent of GDP. Though the threat of small wars in various parts of the world has kept the "peace dividend" smaller than many had hoped, the reduction in defense spending as a percentage of GDP played an important role in the deficit reductions after 1993.

Caps on Discretionary Spending   Beginning with the 1991 Budget Control Act, caps have been placed on discretionary spending—spending other than for interest on the debt or for mandated entitlement programs. The caps in the Balanced Budget and Taxpayer Relief Act of 1997 lowered projected future spending significantly. The projections that the U.S. government will have budget surpluses over the next decade assume these caps will continue to restrict spending. However, with surpluses in the offering, Congress may decide to relax these self-imposed caps.

Higher Social Spending on the Elderly   As the elderly population in the United States has grown, not only absolutely but also as a proportion of the population, federal expenditures on programs like Social Security and Medicare (providing health care to the aged) have expanded dramatically. These programs averaged 4.5 percent of GDP in the 1970s but increased to over 6 percent in the 1980s and nearly 7 percent in the 1990s. These programs are projected to continue to grow, with significant implications for the federal budget. A central question in the current debate over the budget surplus is how much should be set aside to help pay for future Social Security and Medicare expenditures.

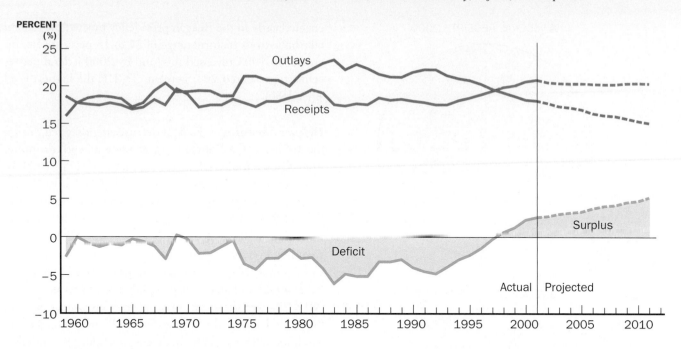

FIGURE 36.3   *The Federal Deficit and Surplus as a Percentage of GDP (1959–2010)*

The federal deficit as a percentage of GDP reached a peacetime high of 6 percent in 1983. The surplus reached 3 percent of GDP in 2000.

SOURCES: *ERP* (2001), Table B-79, and Congressional Budget Office.

Increasing Health Care Expenditures   Through Medicare and Medicaid (the government program providing health care to the poor), the government has assumed an increasing share of total health care expenditures, to the point where the federal government now pays about 37 percent of all health care expenditures. Health care expenditures themselves have soared. Through the 1980s and early 1990s these expenditures were increasing at close to 12 percent per year, doubling in six years. A number of initiatives undertaken during the administrations of George H. W. Bush and Bill Clinton have brought the rate of increase down to below 5 percent.

Interest Payments   Like other borrowers, the federal government pays interest. During the 1970s, federal interest payments represented about 1.5 percent of GDP. But from 1983 to 1990, they exceeded 3 percent of GDP. The main reason was the increasing debt. As the debt rose, so did the interest the government had to pay. Now, with the federal government running a surplus, the amount it owes falls each year, reducing the interest payments that must be made. Current projections suggest interest payments may fall below 2 percent of GDP within five years.

Strong economic growth   One of the biggest factors in turning the federal government's budget from a deficit to a surplus was the exceptionally strong economic growth the U.S. economy experienced in the 1990s. After the recession of 1990–1991, the economy grew for the rest of the decade and into 2001. As incomes in the economy rise, the federal government's tax receipts grow. A recession would threaten the surpluses that are currently being projected, because as total income in the economy declines during a recession, the government's tax revenues would also decline.

Factors Not Contributing to the Changing Budget

In a sense, any expenditure contributed to the deficit—if that expenditure had been reduced, other things being equal, the deficit would have been smaller. But some factors that were commonly blamed for the deficits of the 1980s and 1990s did not deserve the attention they received. For instance, polls suggested that many Americans believed welfare payments and foreign assistance were at fault. Yet general welfare payments, such as Aid to Families with Dependent Children (AFDC) and food stamps, account for less than 4 percent of the federal budget, and their share of the budget has fallen in recent years. Foreign assistance (foreign aid) accounts for only about 1 percent of the federal budget. Welfare payments and foreign assistance played little role in either the rise or the fall of the deficits.

WRAP-UP

Factors Affecting the Federal Budget Outlook

1. Taxes as a share of GDP fell in the early 1980s and have risen since 1993.
2. Increased defense spending contributed to the deficit, but reductions in defense spending as a share of GDP have contributed to the budget swing to surpluses.
3. Caps on discretionary spending have lowered projected future spending.
4. Social spending on the elderly is a growing fraction of GDP.
5. Health care expenditures have soared, and the government's share of those expenditures has increased.
6. Strong economic growth, particularly in the second half of the 1990s, boosted tax revenues.
7. Interest payments soared as the debt rose in the 1980s and 1990s but will fall in the future as surpluses reduce the debt.

Consequences of Government Surpluses and Deficits

In Chapter 26, we used the full-employment model to explore the consequences of the government's budget for the equilibrium real interest rate. Our focus was on the capital market and the impact of the government's budget on national saving. When the government runs a deficit, spending more than it re-

Internet Connection

The U.S. Debt

The U.S. Department of the Treasury maintains a Web site that allows you to keep track of the total debt of the U.S. government. This site is located at http://www.publicdebt.treas.gov/.

ceives in revenue, it must borrow in the capital market, reducing the amount of saving available for private investment. This dissaving by the government reduces national saving. Figure 36.4A depicts the effect of a fiscal deficit on the capital market in a closed economy. The deficit increases the equilibrium real interest rate and reduces the equilibrium level of investment.

When the government runs a surplus, spending less than it receives in revenue, it increases the saving available for private investment. This saving by the government increases national saving. Figure 36.4B depicts the effect of a fiscal surplus on the capital market in a closed economy. The surplus decreases the equilibrium real interest rate and increases the equilibrium level of investment.

Economists traditionally have argued that government borrowing, just like individual borrowing, does or does not make sense depending on the purpose for which the money is used. It makes sense to borrow to buy a house that you will live in for many years or a car that you will drive for several years. Borrowing allows you to spread out payments, paying for the purchase as you use it. It makes sense to borrow for an educational degree that will lead to a higher-paying job in the future. But if you are paying this year for the vacation from two years ago, maybe you should cut up your credit cards!

Countries are in a similar situation. Borrowing to finance a road, school, or industrial project that will be used for many years may be quite appropriate. Borrowing to pay for projects that are never completed (or perhaps are never started) or borrowing to finance this year's government salaries poses real problems. Many governments have taken on more debt than they can comfortably pay off, forcing them to raise taxes sharply and reduce living standards. Others have simply failed to repay, jeopardizing their ability to borrow in the future.

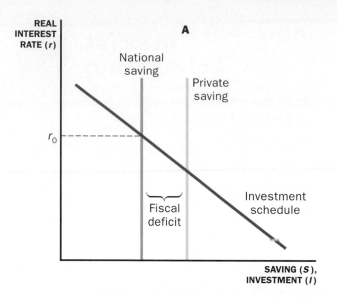

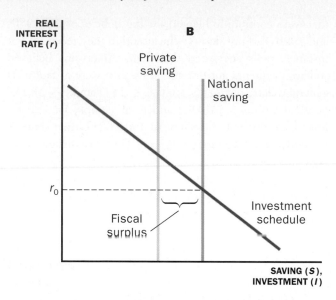

FIGURE 36.4   *The Government Budget and the Capital Market in a Closed Economy*

A budget deficit reduces national saving, leading to a higher equilibrium real interest rate and lower investment, as depicted in panel A. A surplus has the opposite effect, as illustrated in panel B.

Financing government expenditures by borrowing rather than by raising taxes—deficit financing—results in higher levels of consumption in the short run, since disposable income is higher. When the economy is at full employment, higher consumption implies there is less room for investment. To maintain the economy at full employment without inflation, the real interest rate has to rise. Deficit financing leads to lower investment and in the long run, to lower output and consumption.

Reducing the deficit or actually running a surplus has the opposite effect (Figure 36.4B). It allows the real interest rate to fall, stimulating private investment and promoting economic growth and better future living standards.

Deficits and Surpluses in an Open Economy

The effects of deficits and surpluses are different in a small open economy. Such an economy, as we learned in Chapter 26, faces a horizontal supply of saving at the interest rate in the global world capital market, as shown in Figure 36.5. A fiscal deficit results in borrowing from abroad—a capital inflow—without changing the interest rate. Private investment is not crowded out, as would be

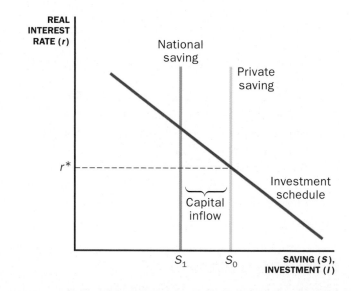

FIGURE 36.5   *A Deficit in a Small Open Economy*

A small open economy faces an elastic supply of saving at the interest rate r^*. The figure is drawn under the assumption that private saving and investment would be balanced at that interest rate. If the government now runs a deficit, national saving is reduced. A capital inflow occurs equal to the deficit.

the case in a closed economy. Instead, the country must pay some of its national income each year to foreign investors as interest on its borrowing. A surplus in a small open economy would have the opposite effect, leading to a capital outflow.

How Future Generations Are Affected by Government Debt

Even though the U.S. government is currently running a surplus, the government owes about $3.4 trillion, or roughly $12,300 per person, as a result of past deficits. By borrowing to finance its expenditures rather than raising taxes, the burden of reduced consumption is shifted to future taxpayers. The U.S. government partly financed World War II expenditures by borrowing rather than by raising taxes by the full amount necessary to finance the war effort. Suppose that the bonds it issued were purchased by forty-year-old workers. Then, thirty years later, when those forty-year-old workers are retired, the government decides to pay off the bonds by raising taxes on those currently in the labor force. In effect, the government is transferring funds from these younger workers to those who were working during the war, who are now seventy and retired. Thus, part of the cost of the war is borne by the generation who entered the labor force *after* the war. The lifetime consumption of those who were forty during the war is little affected. They might otherwise have put their savings into stocks or bonds issued by firms; the war (to the extent it is financed by debt, or government bonds) affects the form of their savings, but not the total amount they have available to spend over their lifetime.

Alternative Views

Though the discussion so far represents the current dominant views, some economists believe that these views overstate the burden of the debt on future generations. Two different reasons are given.

The "Debt Does Not Matter Because We Owe It to Ourselves" Argument

It used to be argued in the United States that the fiscal deficit does not matter because we simply owe the money to ourselves. The budget deficit was compared to the effect on a family's wealth if one member of the family borrows from another. One member of the family may be better off, another worse off, but the indebtedness does not really matter much to the family as a whole. Financing government expenditures by debt, it was argued, could lead to a transfer of resources between generations, but this transfer would still keep all the buying power in the hands of U.S. citizens.

This argument is wrong on three counts. First, even if we owe the money to ourselves, the debt affects investment and thus future wages and productivity, as discussed in Chapter 26. And second, we do not owe all the money to ourselves. The United States financed part of its deficits by borrowing abroad and becoming indebted to foreigners. The consequences of the country spending beyond its means are no different from those of a family spending beyond its means. Eventually it has to pay the price of the consumption binge. In the case of a national consumption binge, future generations have to pay the price.

Third, simply to pay interest on the debt requires high levels of taxes, and taxes introduce distortions into the economy, discouraging work and saving (though there is disagreement among economists about the *quantitative* significance of this effect).

WRAP-UP

Consequences of Government Deficits

1. Some of the burden of current expenditures is shifted to future generations directly.
2. Issuing bonds reduces national saving, raises the real interest rate, and makes future generations worse off.
3. Foreign indebtedness may increase, reducing future standards of living.

Consequences of Government Surpluses

1. Some of the burden of future expenditures is shifted to the current generation.
2. Repaying government debt increases national saving, lowers the real interest rate, and makes future generations better off.
3. Foreign indebtedness may be reduced, increasing future standards of living.

Ricardian Equivalence   As we noted in Chapter 26, there is another argument that the burden of the debt is overstated. If individuals care about their offspring, they may decide to increase their own saving when the government runs a deficit. In this way, they can leave a larger bequest to their children who will face the higher taxes caused by the government borrowing. In terms of our earlier example, the working generation during World War II could have reduced their own consumption and increased their saving to leave more generous bequests to the next generation, who would then be able to pay the higher taxes without cutting back on their consumption. In this view, it does not really matter whether the government raises taxes or borrows. In either case, the current generation will have lower consumption—either because of the higher taxes or because they wish to leave more to their offspring. This view is called *Ricardian equivalence* since it implies there is an equivalence between financing government expenditures through taxes or financing by borrowing.

Most economists do not believe the evidence supports Ricardian equivalence. During the 1980s and early 1990s, when the fiscal deficits were huge, private saving actually declined rather than increased. Proponents of Ricardian equivalence argue that this evidence is not conclusive. A deficit may not lead individuals to save more if they believe the government will cut expenditures in the future rather than raise taxes.

Budgetary Issues

Just as the deficits generated debate over how they should be eliminated, the projected fiscal surpluses have generated a tremendous debate over how they should be spent. At one level, reducing the deficit was a simple matter: either increase taxes or reduce expenditures. Expenditure reductions could occur by cutting or scaling back existing government programs or by making the government more efficient, enabling it to deliver existing programs at lower cost. Using the surplus is an equally simple matter: either pay off the government's debt, cut taxes, or raise expenditures. Basic political debates over what option to emphasize have often made it difficult to reach a consensus on doing anything. For example, all through the years when the deficit was rising, politicians argued that expenditure programs should be cut and the

government made more efficient, and yet remarkably little progress was made until 1993. In contrast, in 2000 and 2001 the government has moved to spend the surpluses projected for future years. In 2000, expenditures rose above the self-imposed caps Congress had passed in 1991 and 1997, and in 2001 the government passed a large tax cut.

Cutting Back on Government Programs

Understanding how government spends money helps explain why reducing expenditures proved so difficult during the 1980s. As we saw from Figure 36.1, discretionary expenditures, the ones Congress and the president can change each year, have become a smaller and smaller proportion of the government's budget. In 2000, these discretionary categories of spending represented only about one third of the total budget. This forces any expenditure reductions to fall disproportionately on a few programs. For example, if nondiscretionary programs are left unchanged, and discretionary spending is one third of the total, a 10 percent cut in total spending would require that discretionary spending be cut by one third.

The deficit reduction debate really became a debate over the size of the government. One side asserted that expenditures and taxes should be reduced, arguing that reducing taxes, especially on capital gains, would stimulate economic growth. The other side argued that these further cuts in expenditures would jeopardize investments in human capital and technology, which had high returns, and therefore such cuts would be counterproductive—growth might actually be retarded.

While there was wide agreement on the desirability of deficit reduction, there remained some who argued that tax reduction was more important than deficit reduction. Even if one could not reduce expenditures, the beneficial effects of lower taxes (increased incentives to work and save) exceeded the detrimental effects of the resulting increased deficits. Most economists remained skeptical of these so-called **supply siders,** believing that there was little statistical evidence in support of large supply responses.

Eliminating the Deficits

Three factors account for the eventual elimination of the deficit. First, policy changes succeeded in reducing

Thinking Like an Economist

Information and Measuring Deficits and Surpluses

The deficits of the 1980s and 1990s were huge. At its peak in 1992, the dollar figure was $290 billion. By 1997, it had been brought down to $22 billion, and in 1998 the government achieved a surplus of $69 billion, its first since 1969. By 2000, the surplus had grown to well over $200 billion. But are these dollar figures the correct way to measure the size and importance of deficits and surpluses? Shouldn't we take into consideration the effects of inflation and the growth of the overall economy?

Robert Eisner of Northwestern University argues for focusing on the overall increase in the *real* debt—that is, the debt adjusted for changes in the price level. This provides a measure of the real value of what the government owes. With total debt outstanding to the public of approximately $3.6 trillion, an inflation rate of 2 percent implies a reduction of the real value of the debt of $72 billion per year due to rising prices. This decrease in the real value of the outstanding debt, in Eisner's view, should be subtracted from any increase in debt due to a deficit. In fiscal 1996, this inflation-adjusted deficit was only $36 billion, compared to the measured deficit of $108 billion. And in 1998, the inflation-adjusted surplus was $141 billion, compared to a measured surplus of $69 billion.

The full-employment or structural deficit takes into account the level of economic activity in the economy, as we saw in Chapter 32. It asks, what would the deficit (or surplus) be had the economy been operating at full employment? For instance, in 1991, as the economy was in a recession, the deficit was officially $269 billion—the largest in history up to that point—but the structural deficit was $191 billion, still

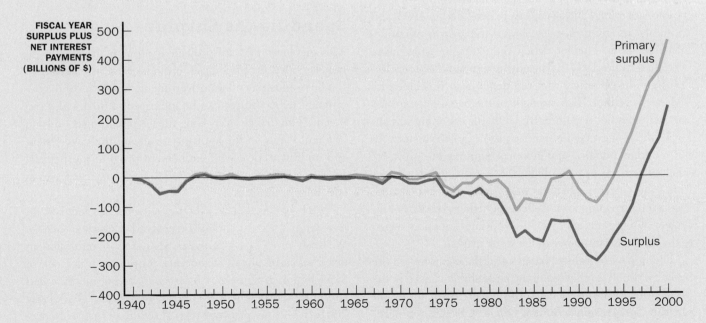

The Primary Surplus: 1940–2000

The primary surplus shows what the federal government surplus would have been if government debt were zero. It is equal to total government revenue minus all government expenditures, excluding interest payments on government debt.

SOURCE: *ERP* (2001), Table B-80.

large by any standards but $78 billion less than the actual deficit. If the economy had been at full employment in 1991 rather than in a recession, tax revenues would have been larger and expenditures smaller; hence, the structural deficit was lower than the actual deficit. In 1998, the economy was in an expansion, so the structural surplus ($31 billion) was less than the actual surplus of $69 billion, reflecting the fact that tax revenues were larger and expenditures smaller as a result of the boom. The Reagan years look particularly bad from this perspective, since, except during wars, the economy had never previously run large structural deficits.

In recent years, as well as the years immediately following World Wars I and II, the U.S. government was saddled with a huge debt. (The debt had peaked at 30 percent of GDP in 1943.) The interest payments alone on the debt totaled almost 3 percent of GDP in 1998. The **primary surplus** is what the surplus would have been had there been no inherited debt; that is, it adds interest payments to the measured surplus. If the government runs a primary surplus, it means that revenues more than cover current expenditures. The government ran a primary surplus in 1989 and has again since 1995 (Figure 36.6).

SOURCE: *ERP* (2001), Table B-80.

expenditures. Second, faster economic growth helped boost tax revenues. Third, even adjusting for economic growth, tax revenues increased more than expected.

Beginning in 1990, spending caps had been put on some types of spending. These caps were extended in 1993, and additional program changes slowed the growth of entitlement spending. Further deficit reduction measures were contained in the 1997 Balanced Budget and Taxpayer Relief Act. The elimination of the deficit also was aided by high tax revenues. The strength of the economy explains part of the higher revenues. By 1999, the economy was enjoying the longest economic expansion in U.S. history. As the economy boomed and incomes continued to grow, tax receipts turned out to be higher than expected. Revenues from some categories of taxes were higher than anticipated, even after correcting for the effects of higher growth. For instance, capital gains tax revenues were large, possibly owing to the strong performance of the stock market.

The impact of policy changes and the economy on the budget outlook is reflected in the large shift it caused in the projections for future deficits. In January 1997, for example, the Congressional Budget Office (CBO), a nonpartisan group of professionals who provide budget analysis for Congress, projected a 1998 deficit of $120 billion. By January 1998, the CBO had revised its estimates and projected only a $5 billion deficit for 1998. In fact, the government ended up having a surplus of $69 billion in that year.

With future surpluses expected if policies remained unchanged, the debate shifted from how to eliminate the deficit to how to use the surplus.

Spending the Surplus

The surpluses that are projected to occur under current policies open up three basic options. First, the surpluses can be used to pay off the government's debt. Second, government expenditures can be increased. Third, taxes can be cut. The debate over using the surplus hinges both on different views on the appropriate size of the government and on how to deal with entitlement programs, especially Social Security, that are projected to have large increases in spending in the future.

Much of the debate over the surplus has focused on how large a tax cut should be enacted. President George W. Bush proposed a ten-year $1.6 trillion reduction in taxes. Congressional Democrats proposed a tax cut of $750 billion, a figure much larger than the one they had supported during the 2000 presidential campaign. In early 2001, Bush's tax plan was passed by the House of Representatives, while the Senate approved a smaller, $1.2 trillion tax cut. The signs of a recession that appeared at the end of 2000 created bipartisan support for a huge tax cut. The Congress also was making plans to increase spending on education, a prescription drug plan for seniors, agriculture, and defense.

It is important to remember that the debates over what to do with the surpluses are debates about spending *projected future* surpluses. If the economy enters a recession, government tax receipts will fall, reducing the projected surpluses. The stock market boom in the second half of the 1990s boosted the government's tax revenues as investors realized huge gains on their stocks. The stock market slide that began in 2000 will sharply curtail this revenue source, further lowering projected surpluses.

The Long-Term Problem: Entitlements and the Aged

Despite the current promising budget outlook, a long-term problem will persist: entitlement expenditures for Medicare and Social Security are likely to soar in the coming decades. The reasons are twofold. First, the number of elderly in the U.S. population will increase dramatically, vastly increasing the number of eligible recipients for Social Security and Medicare. Second, health care costs for the elderly may continue to increase.

The Growing U.S. Elderly Population

The twenty years following World War II saw a huge increase in the birthrate in the United States, producing the generation commonly known as the baby boomers. During the early decades of the twenty-first century, the baby boomers will reach retirement age. At the same time, life expectancy at age sixty-five will also be skyrocketing. In 1935, when the Social Security system was adopted, life expectancy at age sixty-five was only 12.6 years; by 1995, it had increased by almost 50 percent, to 18.2 years; by 2040, it is expected to have increased to 21 years. These population trends will have dramatic consequences, both because health costs tend to be high for the elderly and because of the way the Social Security system is funded.

Social Security Funding   Social Security is funded by payroll taxes. Many people believe that the Social Security taxes withheld from their paychecks are placed in an account with their name and that the benefits

they receive when they retire are paid for from their contributions. This is not how Social Security works. Social Security is actually a "pay-as-you-go" system; the taxes collected from today's workers are used to pay current benefits. The benefits future retirees will receive will depend on the taxes paid by future workers. The financial viability of the system depends on the number of young workers there are for every benefit recipient. This is why the aging of the population creates potential problems for Social Security. The number of elderly will increase by 38 to 44 million by 2040, and there will be more Social Security beneficiaries to be supported by each working-age member of the population, as illustrated in Figure 36.6.

The increase in the number of beneficiaries has been anticipated. Social Security and Medicare tax rates have been set so that revenues currently exceed expenditures, and the difference has been put into a government trust fund, to be used as the baby boomers reach retirement age. In 1998, these so-called off-budget government programs generated a surplus of $99 billion. The on-budget component actually was still in deficit in 1998 by $29 billion. Hence, the total budget surplus of $70 billion was the result of the surpluses generated by Social Security. Despite the large Social Security and Medicare surpluses, the problem is that the amount being set aside is not large enough. As of 2001, Social Security expenditures were projected to exceed revenues in 2016, with the entire trust fund exhausted by 2038.

Budgetary arithmetic provides only two means for addressing the Social Security problem: increasing revenues or decreasing expenditures. Revenues may be increased through higher Social Security tax rates, through increased incomes (resulting from greater productivity), or by tapping general tax revenues. It is estimated Social Security would be financially solid for the next seventy-five years if the payroll tax rate were raised from the current 12.4 percent to 14.5 percent. However, there appears to be little political support for raising the tax rate. Because the federal budget excluding Social Security revenues and expenditures is expected to begin running surpluses in 2001, there is wide support for setting aside some part of these surpluses to fund Social Security. This would help increase the amount in the trust fund that would be available when benefit payments exceed revenues.

There also have been proposals to invest portions of the **Social Security trust fund** in the stock market. Historically, stocks have yielded a far higher return than government

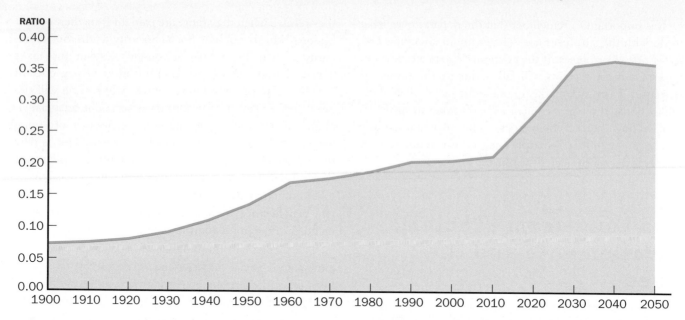

FIGURE 36.6   *Past and Projected Elderly Dependency Ratios*

Elderly dependency is the ratio of the population aged sixty-five and over to those aged eighteen to sixty-four. Elderly dependence is projected to rise dramatically in the twenty-first century.

bonds (in which trust funds are currently invested). If the stock market continues to yield the same high returns, then the solvency of the trust fund can be extended, possibly even permanently, without reducing benefits or increasing taxes. Critics worry about the variability of the returns to the stock market.

Another option is to introduce a system of personal retirement accounts that are individually owned. This type of privatization of Social Security, it is argued, would allow people greater freedom in investing their retirement funds. Linking retirement income more closely to individual contributions—moving away from a pay-as-you-go system—would also increase national saving. This would increase investment and promote faster economic growth.

Finally, Social Security problems could be addressed by reducing future benefits. For example, increased life expectancy, the decline in the relative importance of physical labor in the workplace, and the improved health of the elderly all provide a rationale for restructuring Social Security. Many sixty-five-year-olds could continue to work. Indeed, the Social Security reforms of 1983 increased the normal retirement age to sixty-seven, and there have been proposals to link normal retirement age to longevity—as life spans increase, so would the retirement age.

The Growth of Health Care Costs for the Elderly   Trends in the costs of health care have exacerbated the problem of an aging population. In the 1980s and early 1990s, health care prices increased at a pace far in excess of the increase in the cost of living. Figure 36.7 shows how the index of health care costs has risen relative to the overall consumer price index (CPI) over the last forty years. Total health spending for the elderly has increased even more, with Medicare expenditures increasing at a rate of more than 10 percent per year between 1992 and 1996. Growth has now slowed, but looking ahead, continued spending increases appear unsustainable.

The rate of increase in health care prices and Medicare expenditures seemed to be moderating from 1995 to 1997. At that time, there were large structural reforms in the private health care market—with a rapid expansion of health maintenance organizations (HMOs)—and these might have spillover effects for Medicare. But few expected that these forces alone would contain costs enough to make the problem disappear. And by 1998, health care prices were again rising at twice the rate of the CPI.

A seemingly easy way to address the health cost problem is simply to reduce the reimbursement rate for hospitals and doctors. However, critics of such proposals argue

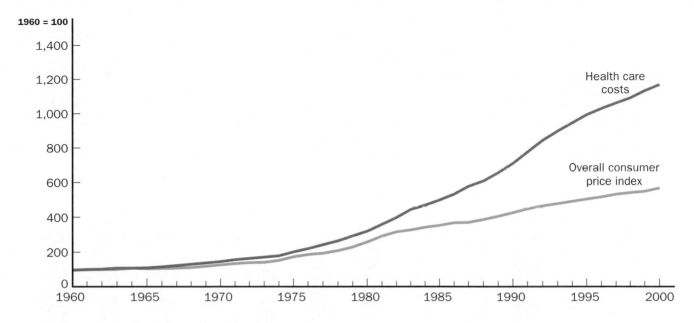

FIGURE 36.7 *Health Costs and the Consumer Price Index (CPI)*

Health care prices have risen more rapidly than the general cost of living. The figure shows how the CPI and an index of health care prices have grown since 1960.

SOURCE: *ERP* (2001), Table B-64.

that there is a limit to this strategy—below some point, either providers will not provide services or there will be a decrease in the quality of the services provided—and we may be near that point. Another way to control public health care costs is to force the aged to pay a larger fraction of their costs, but besides being politically unpopular, putting much of the additional burden on the elderly would push many of them into poverty. Introducing more means testing—making those who can afford it pay more—would not address the more fundamental structural problems, although it would help to reduce the government's costs.

International Perspective

Dependency Ratios

The United States is not the only nation facing the problems associated with an aging population. In many other countries, the number of young workers for every retired worker is also falling. And in some countries, the situation is much more serious than it is in the United States. One measure of the potential seriousness of this problem is to look at the number of individuals over sixty-five years old as a fraction of the population that is between fifteen and sixty-four years old. The chart shows the projected values of this ratio for the year 2010. The Western European countries of France, Germany, Italy, and Spain all face much higher ratios than does the United States. The highest ratio, though, is projected for Japan. In contrast, both Korea and Mexico have much lower ratios.

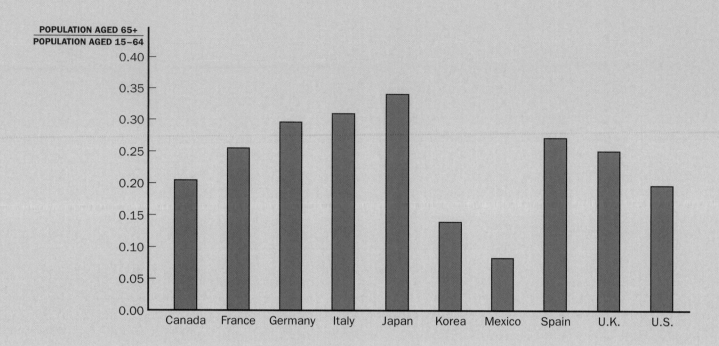

Projected Ratio of Population 65+ to 15–64 Year Olds, 2010

CASE IN POINT

Calculating Your Rate of Return on Social Security

Social Security is a huge program. In 2000, Social Security tax payments amounted to over 4 percent of GDP ($409 billion), more than twice the total individuals contributed to private retirement pension plans. Do these tax contributions represent a good investment from the perspective of the individual worker? This question is at the heart of the debate over whether individuals should have more control over their Social Security contributions and whether some of the Social Security trust fund should be invested in the stock market. Proponents of both types of reforms argue that workers will enjoy higher rates of return than they presently receive.

In calculating the rate of return you can expect to earn on your Social Security contributions, it is important to point out that when you pay taxes into Social Security, these funds are not set aside for your retirement—they are paid out to today's retirees. People who are working when you retire will pay for the Social Security payments you receive during retirement. However, you can still calculate an estimate of the return on your contributions by comparing the lifetime contributions you will make with the expected benefits you will receive.

After this is done, what stands out clearly is that Social Security provides retirement income, but it also redistributes income. Even though Social Security taxes are only paid on the first $72,600 of income (so a college professor pays the same Social Security tax as Bill Gates), the benefit calculations favor low-income workers. Workers in the bottom 20 percent of the income distribution (based on lifetime incomes) can expect a real return of between 4 and 5 percent on their contribu-

In 2000, Social Security tax payments amounted to over 4 percent of the GDP.

to live longer. As a result, rates of return are similar for whites and nonwhites and for college- and non-college-educated workers. ●

SOURCE: Kevin Lansing, "Rates of Return from Social Security," *Federal Reserve Bank of San Francisco, Economic Letter*, No. 99-34, November 12, 1999 (http://www.frbsf.org/econrsrch/wklyltr/wklyltr99/el99-34.html).

tions—those in the top 20 percent of the income distribution can expect a real return of below 1 percent.

Rates of return vary with age—workers born after 1975 who end up in the top 20 percent of the income distribution can expect a negative rate of return on their tax contributions. The poor rate of return for these workers is due to the rising Social Security tax rate—so that they pay higher taxes over their lifetime than workers with similar incomes who were born earlier—and the increase in the retirement age—workers born between 1945 and 1954 can retire and start to receive normal benefits at age sixty-six, while workers born after 1959 can retire with normal benefits at age sixty-seven.

Rates of return on Social Security are higher for women than for men. This is the result of three factors. First, Social Security redistributes income toward low-income workers, and women have historically received lower incomes than men. Second, on average women live longer, so they collect benefits for more years. Third, women are more likely than men to receive spousal and survivor benefits. In fact, Social Security redistributes income toward single-earner families and away from single individuals and two-income-earner families.

There are two factors that do not seem to make much difference for the Social Security rate of return—race and education. College-educated workers have higher lifetime earnings and therefore pay more taxes relative to benefits, but they tend to live longer, thereby collecting benefits for more years. Similarly, whites tend to have higher incomes than nonwhites, but they also tend

Structural reforms have focused on two strategies: improving consumers' incentives, and improving management of care. Most individuals have their most serious medical costs paid for by insurance, and thus have no incentive to economize. Those who focus on incentives argue for more extensive use of deductibles, encouraging the use of major medical and catastrophic insurance policies, which cover individuals for large bills only. Proposals for medical savings accounts would allow individuals to set aside money in a tax-exempt account to meet expenses that they would then have to bear. Critics point out that most of the explosion of health care costs is associated precisely with these major medical expenses, and hence these reforms would not address the central issue. Moreover, medical savings accounts would do little to decrease the government's costs, since individuals would opt for the catastrophic and major medical policies when they are healthy but transfer to the standard programs when they become sick—which is when most of the costs are incurred anyway.

Other structural reforms focus on **managed care.** These reforms recognize that doctors make most of the decisions about health care utilization. The problem is to provide doctors with appropriate incentives. The fee-for-service system, in which doctors are paid for every service they perform, has incentives for doctors to provide more services than needed (especially since typically insurance firms and the government bear the costs, not the patient). Under managed care, the health provider (typically an HMO) receives a fixed fee per year per patient. The health care provider thus has an incentive to ensure that patients receive, for instance, cost-effective preventive care. Medicare reforms in 1983 resulted in hospitals receiving a fixed fee for each incidence of illness they treated; earlier they had been reimbursed on the basis of services performed. The new arrangements provide incentives for them to lower treatment costs. Unfortunately, it also provided an incentive for hospitals to discharge patients out of the hospital as soon as possible. Not surprisingly, posthospital care costs ballooned. One widely discussed structural reform would make hospitals responsible for hospital and

e-Insight

Government Challenges in the New Economy

Information technologies affect the way the government does business just as much as they affect private businesses. In some cases, demand for government-provided services is reduced. For instance, the U.S. Postal Service considered ending Saturday delivery as individuals and businesses increasingly are using electronic mail, or e-mail, instead of "snail mail." In other cases, the demand for government services has increased. An information-based economy demands information, and the government is a major provider of economic data. Shifting from paper-based means of providing access to these data to Internet-based access is a challenge many government agencies face. The U.S. federal government has met this challenge in several ways.

The Environmental Protection Agency (EPA) collects data on drinking water quality, hazardous waste emissions, and brownfield areas containing abandoned or idled facilities that may pose problems of environmental contamination. The EPA has constructed a Web site (http://www.epa.gov/enviro/html/em/) that allows consumers to obtain this information on-line.

Tax publications and forms can be downloaded from the Internal Revenue Service's Web site (http://www.irs.ustreas.gov/). The site recorded almost a billion hits in the first four months of 2000.

The National Weather Service provides on-line access to the official government weather forecasts. This can be found at http://www.nws.noaa.gov/.

College students can now apply for federal grants, loans, and work-study opportunities through the Department of Education's Web site (http://www.ed.gov/finaid.html). The on-line application process cuts down on delays due to errors since the software can identify errors immediately. This gives the on-line process a major advantage over traditional paper forms.

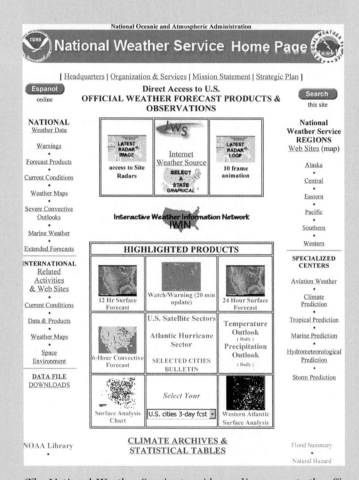

The National Weather Service provides on-line access to the official government weather forecasts (http://www.nws.noaa.gov).

posthospital care, providing them an incentive to manage overall costs, not just the costs within the hospital.

Some critics of these proposals say that the United States will not be able to solve its health care cost problem until it faces up to the underlying cause: rapid changes in technology, which have enhanced the ability to extend life but at a high cost. The changes in technology themselves are a result of misdirected incentives; since life-prolonging innovations will get adopted almost regardless of cost, researchers have little incentive to focus on costs (unlike other areas, in which costs are critical in determining the economic viability of new innovations). Research needs to be more cost conscious, and more of it needs to be redirected to reducing the costs of health care.

Finally, society needs to ask fundamental questions: How much of its resources should be devoted to prolonging life, and how much should be spent on other uses, such as providing better child care and education for the young? Is a $20,000 hip replacement for a ninety-year-old the most valuable use of society's resources? These are difficult and unpleasant questions, but as long as society as a whole bears the brunt of these costs, through its Medicare and Medicaid programs, there is no way of avoiding them.

Review and Practice

Summary

1. The early 1980s were marked by a surge in the size of the federal budget deficits. There were five main causes for the increase: lower taxes, higher defense spending, higher spending on support for the elderly, higher health care expenditures, and higher interest payments.

2. The late 1990s were marked by a turnaround in the federal budget and the first surpluses since 1969. The chief causes were higher taxes, caps on discretionary spending such as on defense, and a booming economy.

3. Government borrowing can be an economic burden for future generations in several ways. First, future generations may have to bear the burden of paying off the debt; there is a transfer from one generation to another. Second, government borrowing can raise real interest rates and crowd out private investment, which will reduce future output and wages. Third, when the money is borrowed from foreign investors, Americans as a whole must pay some of their national income each year to foreigners for interest, resulting in lower standards of living.

4. Government dissaving (deficits) during the 1980s and 1990s were not offset by increased private saving as Ricardian equivalence suggests, and it is not true that

"the debt does not matter because we only owe it to ourselves."

5. Current debates over the use of projected budget surpluses focus on the size of the government and ensuring Social Security solvency. Some argue for tax cuts while others argue for increased spending on high-return public investments such as education, research, and infrastructure.

6. Entitlements—such as Social Security and public health care expenditures—represent a major long-run problem for the federal budget. Factors contributing to the entitlement problem are the aging population, increased life spans, earlier retirement ages, and soaring health care costs.

7. Among the proposals for ensuring continued Social Security solvency are setting aside some of the projected surpluses for Social Security, raising the payroll tax rate, increasing the normal retirement age, and partially privatizing the system.

8. Among the proposals for containing the growth of government health care costs are those that provide increased incentives for consumers to economize in their use of health care services and those that provide improved incentives and responsibilities for doctors and hospitals to manage care more efficiently.

Key Terms

discretionary spending
nondiscretionary spending
entitlements
primary surplus
supply siders
Social Security trust fund
managed care

Review Questions

1. What happened to the size of the budget deficits in the 1980s? Had there ever been such large deficits in peacetime?

2. Name five factors that contributed to the large budget deficits of the 1980s and early 1990s.

3. What is the relationship between deficit spending and the U.S. government's debt?

4. Name three factors that contributed to the elimination of the deficits at the end of the 1990s.

5. What are the consequences of an increased deficit in an open economy? How can borrowing from abroad affect future generations for the better? How can it affect future generations for the worse?

6. Explain the reasoning for the argument that "the debt doesn't matter because we owe it to ourselves"? What is wrong with this argument?

7. What role do entitlements play in the budget outlook for the future? What accounts for the growth of entitlement spending? What can be done about it?

Problems

1. True or false: "Government borrowing can transfer resources from future generations to the present, but it cannot affect the overall wealth of the country." Discuss.

2. Explain how the budget surplus can contribute to long-term growth in a closed economy. Use the saving-investment diagram to contrast the effects in a closed and an open economy.

3. Suppose a country has private saving representing 6 percent of GDP, foreign borrowing representing 1 percent of GDP, and a balanced budget. What is the level of investment? If the budget deficit is 1.5 percent of GDP, how does your answer change? If the budget has a surplus of 2 percent of GDP, how is your answer affected?

4. True or false: "The resources that were spent fighting World War II were spent during the period 1940–1945. Hence, the generations that were alive and paying taxes during that period are the generations that bore the bur-

den of the cost of the war, regardless of how it was financed." Discuss.

5. Does the way the government uses a surplus make a difference for economic growth? Consider the following two cases:

(a) Assume the government reduces income taxes. What is the total impact on national saving, taking into account the reduction in the surplus and the change in private saving? What is the impact on investment? (Hint: how does your answer depend on the interest elasticity of saving?)

(b) Assume the government increases expenditures. What is the total impact on national saving, taking into account the reduction in the surplus and the change in private saving? What is the impact on investment? (Hint: how does your answer depend on the type of expenditures the government increases?)

6. How would the following alternatives for ensuring Social Security solvency affect current national saving?

(a) Increasing current tax rates to build up a larger Social Security trust fund

(b) Pledging to raise taxes in 2038 when the current trust fund runs out of money

7. In most economic activities, people have incentives to choose the most cost-effective ways of doing something. Why might this not be the case in medical care?

8. Japan has a rapidly aging population and the Japanese rely on private savings for retirement. Based on these facts, would you predict that the saving rate in Japan is high or low?

Chapter 37

Development and Transition

Key Questions

1. In what ways, besides their grinding poverty, do the developing countries differ from the United States, Japan, and the countries of Western Europe?

2. How have different developing countries fared over the past half-century? What are the impediments to growth in developing countries? What policies can these countries pursue to improve their standards of living? What policies did the most successful countries pursue? What are some of the alternative strategies for development?

3. What can the more developed countries do to help the developing countries? What is *globalization*, and why are many people skeptical about it?

4. What precipitated the global financial crisis of 1997–1998? What policies deepened the recessions in the countries of East Asia, and why were these policies pursued?

5. How were resources allocated under the old Communist system?

6. What has been the experience of formerly Communist countries in the transition to a market economy? What were the two principle strategies for transition?

*E*very year, thousands of Mexicans risk their lives to cross into the United States. The reason is simple: They seek a way out of their poverty. In the United States, a family of four is said to be in poverty—to have insufficient income for a minimal standard of living—if its income is less than $17,761. This income is about equal to that of the *average* family of four in Mexico! The average income per capita in Mexico is one eighth that in the United States. The minimum wage in the United States is now in excess of $5 an hour. In many developing countries, workers receive a mere $1 a day. Figure 37.1 shows the huge differences in income per capita between developed countries such as the United States and Italy and *less developed countries* such as Ethiopia and Nigeria. These less developed countries sometimes are referred to as the *Third World* and sometimes are called *developing countries*. Unfortunately, many of these low-income countries have not been developing—some have even been declining, with income per capita falling. Today, 4.5 billion people—three fourths of the world's population—live in these developing countries.

Another group of countries also differs markedly from the advanced industrial countries. These are the so-called *economies in transition*—in transition from Communism to a market economy. Figure 37.2 shows how these countries, the most important of which is Russia, have fared since the ending of Communism a decade ago. As a result of the flaws of the Communist economic system, and with the encouragement of the United States and other advanced countries with market economies, people in these countries believed that a transition to market economies would lead to higher standards of living. But in many cases the transitions have yet to bear fruit, and in some cases the results have been disastrous. Russia has seen its income fall by almost half, and the proportion of its population in poverty (defined as an income of $4 a day) has increased from 2 percent to almost 40 percent. To be sure, a few Russians have become wealthy, and a very few have joined the superrich. There are more Mercedes on Russian highways, and one can see more Russians vacationing at the world's most expensive resorts. But the majority of the

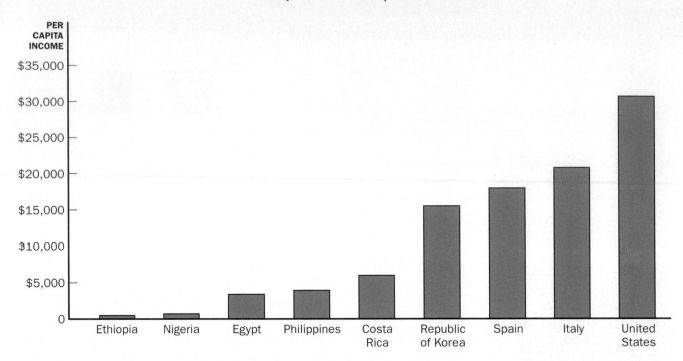

FIGURE 37.1   *Differences in Per Capita Income*

Some middle-income countries such as Costa Rica have per capita incomes up to ten times that of the world's poorest nations, and yet have per capita incomes that are up to ten times smaller than that of the world's wealthiest nations.

SOURCE: *World Development Report 2000/01,* Table 1.

population has experienced a decline in living standards. And in some countries of the former Soviet Union, matters are even worse: in the Republic of Georgia, for instance, incomes are down by 75 percent.

There have been exceptions to this picture, most notably China. China is the most populous country in the world, but a half-century ago was one of the poorest. In the past two decades, it has begun a process of transition to a market economy. Over that period, incomes have soared—growth has averaged 10.4 percent over the decade, and the poverty rate (defined as the percentage of the population with less than $1 per day) has fallen from 80 percent to 12 percent.

This chapter explores the issues of economic development and transition. We will see that many of the challenges faced by developing and transitional economies relate to the process by which the world has become increasingly integrated economically. This process, called *globalization,* has created opportunities for some countries, but it also has been a source of contention and even conflict.

Development

Three fourths of the world's population live in **less developed countries,** or **LDCs.** Statistics cannot convey the full measure of what it means to live in an LDC, but they can provide a start. In the United States, life expectancy at birth is about 77 years. In Peru, it is 65 years; in India, 63 years; and in Nigeria, 52 years. In the United States, 7 infants die for every one thousand live births; in Brazil, 57 die; in Pakistan, 95; and in Ethiopia, 122. The average American completes twelve years of schooling, while the average African gets only five years. India, with a population three and a half times larger than that of the United States, has a GDP roughly one fifth that of the United States. This means that per capita income in India is about 5 percent of that in the United States.

The statistics connect to one another in a vicious cycle. Little or no education, malnutrition, and poor health care

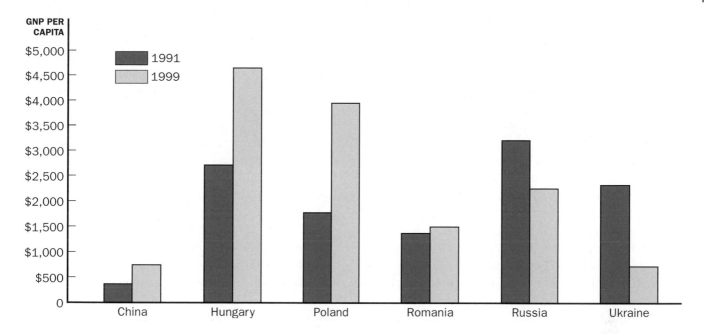

FIGURE 37.2 *Income Per Capita in the Transition Economies*

Some of the economies in transition from Communism to a market economy have fared better than others over the past decade. Countries such as China, Poland, and Hungary have made progress. However, the nations of the former Soviet Union such as Russia and Ukraine have not.

reduce productivity and thus incomes. With low incomes, people in the LDCs cannot afford better education, more food, or better health care. Life is hard in LDCs. In many African countries, whose standards of living were already low, population has been growing faster than national income, so per capita income has been falling. Life is getting worse, not better. The AIDS epidemic has ravaged Africa and threatens much of the rest of the developing world, making a bad situation even worse. Some countries, like Zambia, have seen life expectancy fall by ten years in less than a decade. More than one fourth of the population in southern Africa is infected with HIV.

The United Nations and the World Bank (a bank the major industrialized countries established after World War II that provides loans to LDCs) group countries into three categories: low-income countries, with GDP per capita of $725 or less in 1994; high-income countries, with GDP per capita above $8,955; and middle-income countries, with GDP per capita in between. The low-income countries are the LDCs. The high-income countries are referred to as **developed countries.** Because the basis of their higher level of income is their higher level of industrialization, they also are referred to as the **industrialized countries.** In the Western Hemisphere, hardly two hundred miles lie between one of the richest countries, the United States, with a per capita income of $34,260 in 2000, and one of the poorest, Haiti, with a per capita income of $480.

Internet Connection

The World Bank's Development Goals

The World Bank has established goals for reducing poverty, improving education, reducing child mortality, and achieving other indicators of economic development and improved standards of living. These goals can be found at
http://www.developmentgoals.org/.

The income gap among the high-income countries, including the countries of Western Europe, the United States, Canada, Japan, Australia, and New Zealand, has narrowed considerably over the past hundred years, but the gap between the high-income countries and the low-income countries has not. However, there are signs that change is possible. Some countries have made notable progress in recent years.

First, several countries have moved from the circle of LDCs to the ranks of middle-income countries. These are referred to collectively as **newly industrialized countries,** or **NICs** for short. These success stories include the "gang of four": South Korea, Taiwan, Singapore, and Hong Kong. In the thirty years after the devastating Korean War, for instance, South Korea moved from the category of backward country to that of major producer—not just of simple products such as textiles but of automobiles (the Hyundai) and computers (many of the IBM clones are made in South Korea), the production of which requires a reasonably high level of technological expertise. Even more impressive, Japan has moved from the rank of middle-income country to one of the most prosperous in the world. But the success stories are not limited to East Asia: Botswana, while today suffering greatly from AIDS, has managed to have sustained growth of more than 7.3 percent for thirty years, among the most impressive records anywhere in the world. India, which for decades after independence hardly seemed to grow, has experienced sustained growth of more than 5 percent for a decade.

Second, there have been pockets of remarkable progress *within* the LDCs. In the early 1960s, agricultural research centers around the world (funded largely by the Rockefeller Foundation) developed new kinds of seeds, which under correct conditions enormously increase yield per acre. The introduction and dissemination of these new seeds, accompanied by enormous improvements in agricultural practices, known as the **green revolution,** led to huge increases in output. India, for example, finally managed to produce enough food to feed its burgeoning population and now sometimes exports wheat to other countries.

Third, even the grim statistics for life expectancy—57 years in Bangladesh and 52 years in sub-Saharan Africa (compared to 77 years in the United States)—represent improvements for many countries. But these improvements have a darker side in some countries: a population explosion reminiscent of the Malthusian nightmare. Malthus envisioned a world in which population growth outpaced increases in the food supply. In Kenya during the early 1980s, for instance, improved health conditions enabled the population to grow at a remarkable rate of 4.1 percent a year, implying a doubling of the population every seventeen years, while output increased only at a rate of 1.9 percent a year. Increases in output do nothing to improve per capita income when the population grows even faster.

The 1980s was a particularly hard decade for some of the poorest countries, as Figure 37.3 shows. For example, sub-Saharan Africa basically had stagnated for the previous quarter-century. But during the 1980s, per capita income actually fell by 1.2 percent per year. Per capita income in Latin America had grown at a rate of a little more than 2 percent a year for the previous quarter-century. During the 1980s, per capita income there fell by .3 percent a year. The first part of the 1990s brought renewed hope. Many countries in Latin America democratized, reformed their economies, and experienced a spurt of growth, one that was all too short. A global financial crisis that began in East Asia in July 1997 eventually enveloped the entire developing world, causing deep recessions in many countries, from which they are just emerging.

Life in a Less Developed Country

Just as there are large differences between the LDCs and the industrialized countries, there are large differences among the LDCs. The largest LDC of all, China, has a Communist government. The second largest, India, has an avowedly socialist government, but it also functions as the world's largest democracy. Literacy standards in Costa Rica rank with those of the industrialized countries, whereas more than half of the adult population in sub-Saharan Africa is illiterate. One must be careful in generalizing about LDCs. Still, certain observations are true for *most* of them.

Table 37.1 summarizes some of the most important dimensions of living standards, contrasting the United States, a high-income country; Mexico (its nearest neighbor to the south), a middle-income country; and India, a low-income country.

Incomes and life expectancies in most LDCs are low. A large fraction of the population lives in the rural sector and is engaged in agriculture. Lacking modern equipment like tractors, the farmers work on small plots (an acre or two, compared to more than a hundred acres in the United States). In many cases, they lack the resources to buy productivity-increasing inputs like fertilizer and pesti-

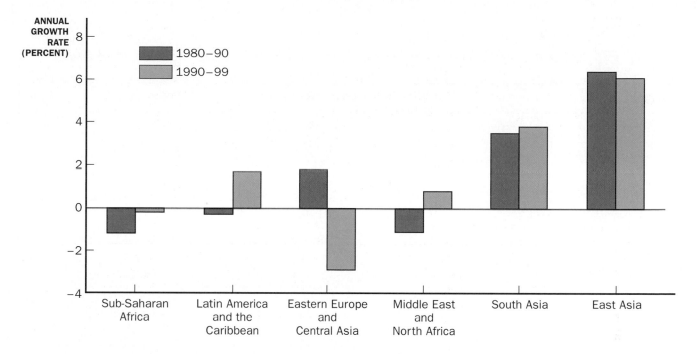

ANNUAL GROWTH RATE (PERCENT)

■ 1980–90
■ 1990–99

Sub-Saharan Africa | Latin America and the Caribbean | Eastern Europe and Central Asia | Middle East and North Africa | South Asia | East Asia

FIGURE 37.3 *Growth Rates in Per Capita Income*

The 1980s were a bad time for many of the poorest nations of the world, as economic growth declined even from the modest rates of the 1960s and 1970s. Except for the Eastern European economies, the 1990s saw a slight improvement in income growth.

cides; on average they use less than half the fertilizer per acre that farmers in more developed countries use. In many countries, most farmers are landless, tilling the landlord's land under **sharecropping** arrangements, in which the landlord gets half the output. In several countries with policies of **land reform,** land has been redistributed to the peasants. Such land reforms were a precursor to the remarkable growth in Taiwan and Japan. In other countries, such as the Philippines and Peru, the land reforms have been only partially successful.

Over the past fifty years, most LDCs have experienced gradual urbanization (Figure 37.4). Those who live in the cities have a much higher standard of living, including access to better education and health facilities. The marked differences between the cities and rural areas have led some to refer to these economies as **dual economies.** While there are large income disparities between rural and urban sectors, there are equally large disparities within the urban sectors, with government workers and those few lucky enough to get jobs in manufacturing earning many times the average wage. These high wages attract migrants

from the rural sector, often resulting in high urban unemployment. Rates in some cities exceed 20 percent.

Part of the poverty in LDCs arises from a lack of resources. These countries have less physical capital per capita and less human capital, with high illiteracy rates and low average number of years of schooling. The lower levels of physical capital per capita are not the result of low saving rates—in fact, the saving rates of most LDCs are considerably higher than the rate in the United States (Figure 37.5). Their high population growth rates mean that they have to save a lot just to stand still.

High population growth rates have another effect. They have increased enormously the proportion of the young, who depend on others for their income. And high rates have made the task of improving educational levels even harder. There is a vicious circle here. Typically, less educated women have larger families. This occurs partly because they are less likely to be informed about family planning, but also because the opportunity cost of having children is lower—they forgo less income. If educational levels can be improved, this vicious cycle can be turned into a virtuous cycle: more educated women have smaller

TABLE 37.1

Standard of Living Measurements in the United States, Mexico, and India

Category	United States	Mexico	India
GNP per capita ($)	30,600	4,400	450
Life expectancy (years)	77	72	63
Agriculture as percentage of GDP	2	5	28
Energy consumption per capita (kilograms of oil equivalent)	8,076	1,501	479
Average annual inflation (GDP deflator, 1990–1999)	1.8	19.3	8.6
Annual average growth of population (%)	1	1.8	1.8
Infant mortality rate (per 1,000 live births)	7	30	70
Maternal mortality rate (per 100,000 live births)	8	48	410
Urban population (% of total)	77	74	28
Television sets (number per 1,000 people)	847	261	69
Personal computers (number per 1,000 people)	458.6	47	2.7

SOURCE: *World Development Report 2000/01.* Data are for the most recent year available, 1999 in most cases.

families, lowering population growth rates. These lower rates reduce the proportion of young and make the task of further improving educational levels easier.

Low educational levels and lack of capital mean that these economies cannot avail themselves of much of the most advanced technologies. With important exceptions, they specialize in low-skill *labor-intensive* industries (those producing products that require much labor relative to the amount of equipment they employ), like textiles.

These problems are compounded by *institutional* failures: The lack of good financial institutions means that what capital is available may not be invested well; the lack of financial markets means that businesses cannot obtain some of the inputs they need; and the lack of good legal systems means that creditors find it difficult to force a recalcitrant borrower to repay, and thus creditors are willing to lend only at high interest rates to compensate them for the risk. All these failures inhibit the entry of new firms and the expansion of old firms.

Many LDCs also are marked by high levels of inequality. The limited incomes are shared even more unequally than are the incomes in the more advanced countries, leading to high levels of poverty. Throughout the developing countries as a whole, the number in poverty, living on less than $2 a day, has increased from 2.7 billion in 1990 to 2.8 billion in 1998, although the number in absolute poverty, living on less than $1 a day, has decreased from 1.3 billion in 1990 to 1.2 billion in 1998.

Some of this inequality is simply due to the law of supply and demand. There is an abundance of unskilled labor and a scarcity of skilled labor and entrepreneurs, so that unskilled wages are low and those who have skills prosper. Indeed, earlier theories suggested that inequality contributed to economic growth. Sir Arthur Lewis, who received the Nobel Prize for his work on development economics, argued that what he called the **surplus of labor** kept wages low and profits high. Workers earning subsis-

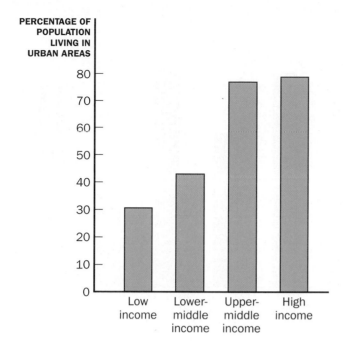

FIGURE 37.4 *Rates of Urbanization*

The percentage of the population living in urban areas tends to be higher in developed countries than in LDCs.

SOURCE: *World Development Report 2000/01*, Table 2.

tence wages could not save, but capitalists could, so that the higher profits contributed to a higher saving rate. In this view, there was a trade-off between growth and equality. Current views are different. Today, many economists believe that growth and equality are in fact complementary, as evidenced by the East Asian miracle.

WRAP-UP

Sources of Problems in Less Developed Countries

A lack of resources, both human and physical, and high population growth, which makes increasing educational levels difficult

The lack of financial markets and inadequate legal systems

A high level of income inequality

The Success of East Asia

The most successful efforts at development, anywhere at any time, have been in East Asia in the decades after World War II. Sustained growth over three to four decades has led to eightfold increases in per capita income or more. There are several ingredients to this success:

- Macroeconomic stability—avoiding for the most part high inflation or high levels of unemployment. Without macroeconomic stability, the private sector cannot thrive. As part of this strategy, governments maintained a high level of fiscal responsibility, eschewing the huge budget deficits that characterize many LDCs.

- High saving rates. With saving rates of 25 percent or more, the countries could invest heavily.

- Smart investment of savings. As important as the high level of saving is the fact that the savings were invested well; other countries with high saving rates (either forced, as in the Communist countries, or the result of a natural resource bonanza, as in Venezuela) failed to do so.

- Heavy investment in education, including the education of women. This investment resulted in a highly skilled labor force that was able to absorb new technologies.

- Heavy investment in technology. What separates developed from less developed countries is not only a shortage of capital but also a "gap" in knowledge. East Asian countries developed technology policies aimed at closing this gap, with remarkable success. Indeed, by the 1990s, students in Singapore and some other East Asian countries consistently outperformed American students on standardized tests in math and science. Some countries, like Singapore, encouraged foreign firms to invest directly, bringing with them access to foreign markets as well as new technology. Other countries, like Korea, focused on licensing new technologies from the more advanced countries.

- Political and social stability, which provides an environment conducive to investment. Government policies were aimed directly at promoting this kind of stability; for instance, governments put pressure on businesses to limit wage differences.

So impressive have the outcomes in East Asia been that many refer to them as the *East Asian miracle*. Some critics argue, however, that there is nothing miraculous—the growth

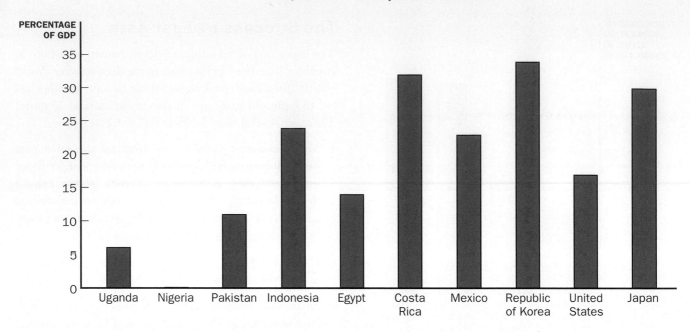

FIGURE 37.5 *Saving Rates*

Saving rates in many LDCs tend to be higher than the rate in the United States, though most are not as high as in some other industrialized countries like Japan.

SOURCE: *World Development Report 2000/01*, Table 13.

can be explained largely by standard economics of the kind that we have studied in this text (see Chapter 27). High saving rates, high investment in both capital and education, and knowledge are part of the standard recipe. Still, there was a miracle: No other set of countries has been able to achieve similar outcomes. In 1997, the region experienced a major crisis, with a depression in Indonesia and recessions in Malaysia, Thailand, and Korea. While some critics questioned whether the East Asian miracle had ever been real, the fact that China weathered the storm so well—its growth only slowed to 7 percent—and the quick recovery of Korea and Malaysia helped to restore confidence in the region and in the kinds of economic policies these countries have pursued.

Underlying these successes were both good policies (such as those that led to macroeconomic stability) and strong institutions (such as the creation of financial institutions that allocated the capital well). Three features of East Asia's development strategy deserve special attention: the roles of government, exports, and egalitarian policies.

The Role of Government.   Perhaps the most distinctive feature of the East Asia model was the balance the coun-

tries achieved between the role of the state and the role of the market. Their governments pursued market-oriented policies that encouraged development of the private sector. They sought to augment and "govern" the market, not to replace it.

They also fostered high saving rates—often in excess of 25 percent (see Figure 37.5). In Japan, more than a third of these savings went into accounts at the postal savings banks established by the government. In Singapore, the government established a provident fund, to which all workers were required to contribute 40 percent of their income.

These governments also influenced the allocation of capital in a myriad of ways. Banks were discouraged from making real estate loans and loans for durable consumer goods. This helped to increase private saving rates and to discourage real estate speculation, which often serves to destabilize the economy. As a result, more funds were available for investment in growth-oriented activities like purchases of new equipment. In addition, governments established development banks to promote long-term investment in activities like shipbuilding, steel mills, and the chemical industry. These interventions have been more controversial, and their success has been mixed. As an example of a success, the steel firms in Taiwan and Korea are among the most efficient in the world. In contrast, the Japanese and Korean governments took a variety of initiatives to promote certain industries, including the computer chip industry. By the early 1980s, Japan looked as if it would completely dominate that market, before Intel and other American producers reasserted American leadership. The dangers of government intervention are often symbolized by the Japanese government's failed attempt to discourage Honda (a manufacturer of motorcycles) from entering the auto market, arguing that there were already too many producers.

Export-led Growth.   A second factor that distinguished the countries of East Asia from less successful LDCs was their emphasis on exports. A growth strategy focusing on exports is called **export-led growth.** Firms were encouraged to export in a variety of ways, including being given increased access to credit, often at subsidized rates.

With export-led growth, firms produce according to their long-term comparative advantage. This is not current comparative advantage, based on current resources and knowledge. It is dynamic comparative advantage, based on acquired skills and technology, and recognition of the importance of learning by doing—of the improvement in skills and productivity that comes from production experience. With exports, demand for the goods produced by an LDC is not limited by the low income of its citizens. The world is its market.

Advocates of export-led growth also believe that the competition provided by the export market is an important stimulus to efficiency and modernization. The only way a firm can succeed in the face of keen international competition is to produce what consumers want, at the quality they want, and at the lowest possible costs. This keen competition forces specialization in areas where low-wage LDCs have a comparative advantage, such as in the production of labor-intensive products. It also forces firms to look for the best ways of producing. International firms often take a role in helping to enhance efficiency. For instance, the clothing store chain Benetton has developed production techniques that combine large production runs with rapid adaptability in style and color. In this way, the firm has been able to take advantage of low-wage LDCs by producing in these countries most of what it sells.

Finally, export-led growth has facilitated the transfer of advanced technology. Producers exporting to developed countries not only come into contact with efficient producers within those countries but also learn to adopt their standards and production techniques. They come to understand better, for instance, why timeliness and quality in production are important.

Fostering Equality.   Another distinctive aspect of East Asia's development strategy is its emphasis on equality. Examples of these egalitarian policies include Singapore's home ownership program; the almost universal provision of elementary and secondary education, which includes women; and the land redistribution programs that were the precursor of growth in several of the countries, including Taiwan and Japan. In many of these countries, the governments also tried to curb excessive wage inequality and to discourage conspicuous consumption by the rich. Their experience has shown that one can have high saving rates without either the oppressiveness of Soviet-style governments or vast inequalities. The equality measures have actually promoted economic growth. The land reforms have resulted in increased agricultural production—the sharecropping system previously in place had had the effect of a 50 percent tax on output. The high educational levels have increased productivity directly and facilitated the transfer and adoption of more advanced technology. More education for women is associated with smaller families, and declining rates of population growth.

WRAP-UP

East Asia's Success

Key ingredients to East Asia's success include macroeconomic stability, high saving rates to finance investment, investment in education and in technology, and political and social stability.

Governments pursued market-oriented policies that encouraged saving and investment.

Growth strategies emphasized *export-led growth.*

Income equality was fostered.

Alternative Development Strategies

The development strategies pursued by East Asia stood in marked contrast to those followed in much of the rest of the world, and many economists attribute, at least in part, the differences in performance to differences in strategies. As the developing countries first experienced independence, many came under the sway of socialism: Government took a central role in planning development. Having been dominated by foreign governments, they worried that opening themselves up to foreign investment would lead to a new form of domination—domination by large multinational firms. Some countries, trying to reduce their reliance on imports, focused on *import substitution* policies, and a few, like Brazil, had a short period of success following that strategy. But by and large, the countries following these strategies stagnated or grew very slowly.

Even before the end of the Cold War seemed to provide convincing proof that the socialist/planning model was badly flawed, the weaknesses for the developing countries seemed apparent. Governments did not do a good job of planning, including managing and allocating resources efficiently. "White elephants" such as huge and inefficient steel mills dotted the landscape. Protectionist barriers were erected, nominally to help support domestic industries, but all too often to allow friends of the government to enjoy high profits insulated from outside competition. In some cases, the inefficiencies were so great that the value of the imported inputs was greater than the value of what was produced, had the output been sold at international prices. Protection had been granted using the *infant industry argument*—the argument that new industries had to be protected until they could get themselves sufficiently established to meet the competition. But in many of the developing countries, the infants never seemed to grow up: protection became permanent.

In the early 1980s a new development strategy emerged. Recognizing the limits of a state-dominated economy, many countries swung to the other extreme, arguing for a minimal role for government. Governments were urged to privatize and liberalize, to sell off state companies and eliminate government intervention. These policies, together with macroeconomic stability, were often referred to as the *Washington consensus*, since they were advocated by the U.S. Treasury and the two international institutions located in Washington, the International Monetary Fund (IMF) and the World Bank. In many cases, these policies proved little better than the older policies in promoting growth over an extended period of time. Reducing tariff barriers led to losses of jobs, and the developing economies were not able to generate new enterprises. The theory was that liberalization would lead resources to move from low-productivity uses to high-

productivity uses, as the theory of comparative advantage suggested; in practice, all too often workers moved from low-productivity jobs into unemployment. All too often the policies that were designed for macroeconomic stability included very high interest rates, so high that new investment to create new jobs was simply not forthcoming.

By the mid-1990s, it became increasingly clear that neither of the extremes—the Washington consensus or state-dominated planning—provided much help. The success of the East Asian countries, even after taking into account the setback of the financial crisis of 1997–1998, stood in marked contrast to the experiences of those who had tried one or the other of the faulty recipes for success. The East Asian countries had been more successful not only in producing growth but also in reducing poverty. Markets were seen to be at the center of development, but government had a vital role as a catalyst for change and in helping to make the markets work better, to transform the economy and society through education and technology, and to regulate the economy so that it could function better. Greater attention was focused not only on how to make markets work better but also on how to make governments work better.

It was recognized that there are a variety of ways by which successful growth strategies can be pursued—not a single recipe existed for all countries—though there were perhaps more roads to failure than to success. The success of Singapore and Malaysia was based partly on attracting direct foreign investment, which brings with it capital, technology, training, and access to foreign markets. (Singapore, with its three million people, was able to attract more investment than India, with its almost one billion people.) In contrast, Korea's growth was based on its own domestic firms, which developed to the point that they could compete internationally. Korea's economy was centered around a limited number of large firms; Taiwan's, around large numbers of small firms. China, as we will see, charted a completely different path, with joint ventures between Chinese firms and foreign firms and with new enterprises created by local authorities at the township and village level—a peculiar blend of public and private enterprise.

The Washington consensus policies, while they corrected the earlier problems of *excessive* state dominance in the economy, underestimated the role of government in providing the basic institutions that make a market economy work, for instance, a legal system that enforces contracts, a financial system that provides credit for new and expanding industries, and an educational system that enhances individual productivity and enables the population to cope with a modern economy.

Development and Foreign Aid

While East Asia managed to generate ample savings to jump-start their economies, the poor economies in the rest of the world have not been able to do so. Within the developing world, there is a widespread view that the developed countries give too little assistance and that the assistance they give has too many strings—undermining the democracies in the developing countries by dictating key elements of policies as a condition for getting aid.

Direct foreign assistance, especially from the United States, has been declining in importance. In 1999, U.S. assistance as a percentage of GDP was lower than that of any other major industrialized country, and in absolute dollars, was surpassed by the amount given by France, Germany, and Japan. Even this does not tell the full story, since a disproportionate part of U.S. aid goes to just two countries, Israel and Egypt.

Today, international capital markets are far better developed than they were fifty years ago. When times are good, countries that provide an investment-friendly atmosphere, like China, have little trouble attracting funds. But when times are bad—as in the global financial crisis of 1997–1998—even the best-managed developing countries find it difficult to raise funds and may be forced to pay back to the developed countries more than they receive. In the best of times, the poorest countries, especially in Africa, cannot access private funds, so there is a huge need for development assistance. And for all of the developing countries, there is a need for technical assistance and help in areas in which the private sector is not particularly interested, such as education and health.

There is an ongoing debate about how effective such assistance has been. There have been huge successes, some supported by private foundations as well as by government. As mentioned earlier, the development of high-yielding crops with the support of the Rockefeller Foundation and the dissemination of the seeds and new technologies throughout the developing world have resulted in a "green revolution," making countries like India self-sufficient in food. But there also have been failures. Food aid sometimes depresses local prices, hurting farmers and discouraging domestic production. Some large projects have been criticized for damaging the environment and resulting in increases in crop yields that were insufficient even to pay the interest on the loans. By and large, statistical studies suggest that the assistance given to countries that have followed reasonably good economic policies (such as stable macroeconomic policies and limited corruption) has been highly productive, but not otherwise.

Globalization and Development

In the half-century since World War II, there have been major efforts at reducing trade barriers. However, from the developing countries' perspectives, the trade liberalization agenda has been driven more by the interests of the advanced industrialized countries, who continue to subsidize agriculture and protect textiles, making it difficult for the less industrialized countries to sell some of the main goods that represent their comparative advantage.

These concerns are but one part of a broader dissatisfaction with globalization and the international economic institutions that help manage it. **Globalization** is the name given to the closer integration of the countries of the world—especially the increased level of trade and movements of capital—brought on by lower costs of transportation and communication. There are three important international economic institutions: the World Trade Organization (WTO), which provides a venue for international trade agreements and resolving trade disputes; the IMF, which was created to help support global financial stability, providing funds to countries in times of crisis, but which has expanded its activities to include assisting developing and transition economies; and the World Bank, which promotes development and the alleviation of poverty in poor and middle income countries.

CASE IN POINT

A Historical Perspective on Globalization

There has been much discussion of globalization, the closer integration of the economies around the world. The most dramatic aspect of globalization is the growth of trade, of exports and imports. But there are other aspects. Workers migrate from one country to another,

International Perspective

Comparing Different Perspectives on Foreign Aid

While support for aid in the United States by and large has been weak, in Western Europe there has been a huge popular movement demanding debt relief for the poorest countries. Many of these poor countries were so swamped under debts that without debt relief, there was little prospect of growth; much of their revenue from exports simply went to paying what they owed. The lenders were at least partly to blame, for many of the projects for which money was loaned did not yield the promised return. In some cases, especially during the Cold War, Western governments and the international financial institutions loaned money, knowing that in all likelihood it would wind up in Swiss bank accounts; they were simply competing for the "loyalty" of corrupt leaders like Mobutu in Zaire (now Democratic Republic of the Congo)—trying to outbid the Soviets—but the people in these poor countries were left footing the bill. Popular pressure succeeded in forcing the governments of the advanced industrialized countries to join the World Bank and the IMF in a huge debt-relief program; in the year 2000 alone, more than twenty countries got several billions of dollars in relief.

multinational firms do business across borders, billions of dollars of capital flow from one country to another, and ideas and knowledge are communicated via the Internet on a continual basis.

It is sometimes forgotten, however, that the world went through a process of globalization once before. In the decades prior to World War I, trade grew enormously, eventually reaching a percentage comparable to that attained more recently. World War I and the Great Depression led to retrenchment. As the economies of the world plunged into a downturn at the end of the 1920s, they erected trade barriers.

Today, there is worry that there might be a backlash against globalization—as evidenced by protest marches in Seattle, Washington, Prague, and Genoa. While many of the marchers saw globalization as threatening their own jobs, others took a more moral stance: They viewed the way globalization had been proceeding as fundamentally unfair, with rich countries dictating to the poor that they open their markets to them, while keeping their own markets protected. After the last round of trade negotiations completed in 1994 (called the Uruguay Round, after the place where it was initiated), the poorest region in the world, sub-Saharan Africa, was actually worse off, while the United States and Europe boasted enormous gains.

Economists argue that free trade allows each country to benefit, as it takes advantage of its comparative advantage. Even unilateral opening up of a market makes the country as a whole better off. But some individuals may be worse off, and typically they are not compensated. Finding ways to ensure that *all* can benefit from lowering trade barriers can convert a situation of conflict into a win-win situation, but few countries have succeeded in doing so.

In poor developing countries, the problems are even more complicated. In these countries, unemployment rates are high, enterpreneurship is limited, and capital is scarce. Bringing down trade barriers can destroy jobs and enterprises quickly, but the country may not be able to make the investments required for it to take advantage of its comparative advantage. Jobs are destroyed faster than they are created. The argument that the country as a whole benefits becomes more questionable: While moving workers from low-productivity employment to higher-productivity employment, based on comparative advantage, would increase national income, moving workers from low-productivity employment to unemployment would lower national income. If opening up trade is to increase incomes, it must be accompanied by other measures to help these poor countries take advantage of their comparative advantage. ●

Trade   American officials, recognizing limited support for aid, often emphasize the importance of trade. For a while, "trade, not aid" even became a slogan. Giving less developed economies access to the U.S. markets is a win-win policy. American consumers win by having a greater variety of goods at lower prices. The LDC benefits by having a huge market for its goods. The United States has a system of preferential treatment for poor countries, called the general system of preferences, or GSP. Of course, as always with trade, some U.S. producers and their workers complain about the loss of jobs to these low-cost competitors. As argued in Chapter 3, the total benefits to trade generally outweigh the losses to certain groups. In many cases, however, these special interests prevail. Many developing countries find that even as they open up their markets to U.S. products, the United States does not fully reciprocate, especially in areas like agriculture and textiles, sectors that are of particular importance to developing countries. While the European Union has not done much better, they have agreed on a striking initiative, offering to eliminate all trade barriers to the lowest-income countries on all commodities except guns.

While the world as a whole, and the LDCs in particular, have much to gain from globalization—after all, we saw how growth in East Asia was spurred by its exports—unless those in developing countries can be persuaded that there is a more level playing field, hostility toward globalization may grow.

The Global Financial Crisis

The dissatisfaction with globalization, which was manifested so strongly in the protests at the 1999 WTO meeting in Seattle, was motivated partially by the global financial crisis that began in Thailand in July 1997 and then spread to Indonesia and Korea, before enveloping Russia and Brazil. Eventually, almost every developing country was touched. Overall, it was the most serious global economic crisis since the Great Depression. The countries most adversely affected faced deep recessions and even depressions: Indonesia's GDP fell by 16 percent, and real wages fell by one fourth or more.

In each country the crisis took a similar form: As investors lost confidence in the country, they took their money out. Each government tried to keep the exchange rate from depreciating, or depreciating too much. Since the foreign debts of many developing countries are denominated in dollars, a depreciation can severely increase the debt burden of the country. To try to prevent its currency from depreciating, the country used up foreign exchange, spending dollars out of reserves to prop up the value of the domestic currency. But there was only a limited amount of funds with which to do this. As soon as this became apparent, bankers who had loaned money to the country demanded that the loans be repaid. Seeing the threat of a precipitous drop in the exchange rate, having no funds to repay the outstanding loans, the country turned to the IMF for assistance. The IMF provided huge bail-out packages (in aggregate, more than $150 billion), but in return demanded cutbacks in government expenditures, increases in interest rates, and a host of other structural reforms, especially in the banking systems. Many banks, already extremely weak, became weaker as the economic downturns led to increasing numbers of nonperforming loans (loans that were overdue). Almost without exception, the IMF programs failed to stabilize the exchange rate, though they did succeed in exacerbating the economic downturns.

Indonesia suffered the most: In an attempt to restructure its banking system, the government closed down sixteen banks and announced that more would be shut down but that depositors would not be insured. Not surprisingly, there was a run on the private banks (that is, all depositors pulled their money out of the banks as quickly as possible), and the already weak banking system was devastated. As Indonesia's crisis mounted, the IMF urged the government to reduce expenditures by cutting food and fuel subsidies for the poor. Given Indonesia's ethnic frictions, these policies ignited social and political turmoil.

The crisis, and the policies used to address it, raised many basic economic issues of the kind that we have discussed in this text. Though many factors contributed to the crisis, some economists have argued that the most important was the removal of the restraints on the movements of short-term financial capital—capital that can come into a country and leave it overnight. This is called *capital market liberalization.* Under pressure from the United States and the IMF, many countries liberalized their capital markets in the late 1980s and early 1990s. Optimism about the region led to huge inflows of capital. But investor sentiments are often highly volatile—as evidenced by the boom in the late 1990s and subsequent bust in 2001 of Internet stock prices or real estate prices. Poor countries have a hard time managing this volatility. Thus, the inflow of capital into Thailand fed a real estate boom. But every real estate boom comes to an end, and as Thailand's came to an end, investors decided to pull their

Indian Engineers in Silicon Valley and Silicon Valley's Capital in India

Globalization and the increasing integration of the world economy can allow both investment capital *and* workers to move across borders, seeking more profitable opportunities. Nowhere is this interchange better illustrated than in the investment by venture capitalists and U.S.-based firms in India's Silicon Valley and the immigration of high-tech workers from India to California's Silicon Valley. U.S. firms are investing in software design and research facilities in India to take advantage of India's well-trained computer workforce and the lower wages in India. At the same time, many engineers from India are moving to the United States to find higher-paying employment.

During the 1990s, the rapid expansion of high-tech jobs in places such as California's Silicon Valley led to an increased demand for engineers and others with the skills the computer industry needed. To increase the supply of skilled workers, Congress expanded the H-1B visa program that allows individuals with certain skills to immigrate to the United States. While potential immigrants can qualify for an H-1B visa in a wide range of occupations, the most common jobs have been in computer-related occupations. According to the U.S. Immigration and Naturalization Service (INS), just under half of the H-1B visas granted between October 1999 and February 2000 were for occupations classified as in systems analysis and programming. The next most common occupation was in electrical and electronics engineering, accounting for 5.4 percent of the visas. (Occupations in economics ranked seventh on the list, accounting for 2.3 percent of the H-1B visas.) Nearly 43 percent of all H-1B visas were granted to individuals from India. Among other countries of origin, China, representing fewer than 10 percent of H-1B visas, was a distant second.

In 2000, Congress increased the number of H-1B visas that could be issued each year from 115,000 to 195,000.

Successful high-tech firms like Infosys, fueled by an influx of American capital investment, are making Bangalore the Silicon Valley of India.

With the bill passing the Senate on a vote of ninety-six in favor and only one opposed, this program to bring skilled workers to the United States enjoyed broad political support. As 2001 opened with the possibility of a recession, and with many high-tech firms laying off workers, it remains to be seen whether the support for this program continues to be strong.

The movement of workers from India to the United States represents just one example of how globalization promotes the flow of resources—in this case human capital—across borders in search of higher returns. The same process is at work in explaining the flow of investment capital from the United States to India. In recent years, such giants as Microsoft, Oracle, Intel, Cisco, and AOL have invested heavily in India. Operating research and development facilities in India has several advantages for these firms. The major advantages are the presence of a well-educated workforce and significantly lower wages. With limits on how many workers can be brought to the United States, it can make sense for a technology firm to move to where the workers are.

Another advantage is the ability to engage in around-the-clock software and product development. Project work does not have to come to a halt when night falls in the Silicon Valley—with a twelve-hour time difference, the workday is just beginning in India, allowing work to switch between a firm's California and India locations. The Internet has helped to make this possible, as a software firm can move new code under development between its California and India locations electronically.

The inflow of capital investment also has helped fuel the development of local high-tech firms in India, and the area around Bangalore is now known as the Silicon Valley of India. Increased capital investment in India provides new jobs for Indian engineers and funds that have allowed local high-tech firms in India to expand.

money out of the country. As they all tried to do that quickly, the country was pushed into crisis.

The standard recipe for a country facing an economic downturn, as Thailand, Korea, and Indonesia clearly did in late 1997, is an expansionary monetary and fiscal policy (see Chapter 32). High interest rates and budget cuts are a sure recipe to exacerbate the downturn. Why then did the IMF prescribe that medicine? The IMF saw the root cause of the problem as a lack of confidence. It believed (1) that if the exchange rate could be stabilized, then confidence would be restored; (2) that high interest rates would lead investors to flock into the country, thus helping to stabilize the exchange rate; and (3) that cutting government expenditures, while it might lead to a temporary reduction in GDP, would also lead to a reduction in imports. A reduction in imports would reduce the demand for foreign exchange and thus also help to stabilize the exchange rate.

To the critics of the IMF, the failure of its prescription came as no surprise. Raising interest rates makes it more attractive to put money into an economy *if in fact the borrowers can repay what they promise*. But investors do not want to put money into a country going into a recession. High interest rates and fiscal contraction would deepen the recession, and a deep recession would make it more likely that borrowers would default. Thus, rather than attracting money into the country, the policies led to capital flight—investors inside the country decided it would be better to take their funds and invest them abroad.

The only two large countries in the world to avoid the global financial crisis were India and China. Both continued to grow rapidly—at between 5 and 7 percent. Both had not liberalized their capital markets, though China had managed to attract huge amounts of foreign direct investment, and India lesser amounts. (When a firm builds a factory in a country, it cannot simply pull up the factory and move elsewhere, when investor sentiment changes. Hence, foreign direct investment is not subject to the same kind of volatility.) China, with its heavy linkages to other countries in the region, was aware that their slowdown would reverberate on it. Worried about a slowdown, it followed classic textbook prescriptions—of the kind discussed in Chapter 32. It increased government expenditures on a host of needed infrastructure projects that at the same time would help its long-term growth.

Today, there is a growing consensus that developing countries should be cautious in liberalizing their capital markets. They should not do so until they have in place strong, well-regulated financial institutions and good macroeconomic management. But even with the best of macroeconomic management, they will still face volatility from sudden changes in investor sentiment. They need to be able to handle that risk, to have safety nets to provide unemployment insurance for those thrown out of work. Most developing countries are far from satisfying these prerequisites.

Concluding Comments

Overall, the divide between the haves and have-nots has not decreased over the past century. There have been successes, where the gap has narrowed, and failures, where it has widened. Policies seem to make a difference: Some countries have adopted policies that promoted increased growth and reduced poverty. Others have pursued policies that led to some growth but had little impact on poverty (or even increased it). Still other countries seem to have stagnated or declined. Unfortunately, the prognosis is for these patterns to continue. China and India are poised to take advantage of the new economy represented by the Internet and information technologies, to further narrow the gap between them and the more advanced industrialized countries. But for Africa, the potential for doing so remains remote. Meanwhile, Africa's already low current standard of living is threatened by the AIDS epidemic and continuing civil strife, conditions that make it difficult to attract foreign capital and that are not even conducive to domestic investment. As a result, the gap with the rest of the world is likely to increase.

The Economies in Transition

As we noted in the beginning of this chapter, there have been two great economic experiments this century. The first was the move from markets to Communism that began in Russia in 1917, which proved an unmitigated disaster. The second was the move from Communism to a market economy, which began in Eastern Europe about 1990 and in China in the late 1990s. This second great experiment also led to disappointing outcomes in most of the countries involved. Before we can understand the reason for these failures, we have to understand the system that prevailed before the transition.

The Communist Economic System

Communism represented an alternative way by which resources were allocated to the market. While there was variation in how the system worked from country to country, the basic system was developed in the Soviet Union, and we describe that system here. Under Communism, the state owned the means of production—the factories, the land, virtually everything except each individual's personal possessions. The government established a vast bureaucracy to determine what was to be produced and how it was to be produced. It decided how many cars would be produced, how many would have two doors, how many would have four doors, and so on. Knowing how much steel would be required to produce cars, tractors, and the myriad of other products using steel, the state calculated the total amount of steel required. It could then calculate how much iron ore would be required. Intricate calculations of this kind allowed it to calculate how much of every good should be produced. It then worked backward, figuring out how much plants in the country should produce. Factory managers were given production quotas—they

WRAP-UP

Development

In LDCs, per capita income is a fraction of that enjoyed in the developed countries.

The newly industrialized countries (NICs) of East Asia have achieved rapid economic growth and have closed the income gap with developed countries. China and India also appear posed to narrow the income gap. Others, particularly countries in Africa, may see the income gap widen even further.

Successful development has been based on macroeconomic stability, high saving and investment (in physical and human capital), and government policies promoting financial markets, strong legal systems, and income equality.

should produce so many tons of steel, or so many nails. Factory managers also were given allocations of inputs with which to produce the output. This system was called **central planning.**

The Failures of Communism

The central planners also decided on wage levels and prices. Consumers did get to choose what to buy, but for many commodities, there was *rationing.* One was only allowed to buy so many pounds of sugar a month. Unfortunately, everything did not go according to plan. Often there were shortages, especially for consumer goods. People had to wait in line for hours to get the food they wanted every day, and there would be month-long waits for consumer durables or a car. Factories also faced shortages: They often could not get the inputs they needed. Deliveries did not occur on time, and often what they got was of inadequate quality. Factories that had been told to produce nails produced nails, but they paid little attention to whether the nails were too brittle or too soft to be used. They had incentives to meet the numerical quotas set by the central planners, but no incentives to produce what others wanted. They figured out ways of getting around the system; if to meet the quotas, they had to obtain more steel, they would find some firm that had been delivered more steel than it needed and make a trade. Managers traded favors with each other a variety of forms of barter occurred. Thus, an underground market developed.

The shortage of consumer goods arose partly because of the emphasis on *development.* In 1917, at the time of the Soviet revolution, Russia was a relatively backward country. In the 1930s, Stalin wanted to push the country forward quickly. He saw the road to success as heavy industrialization, such as building steel mills. The hostility throughout the world toward the Soviet Union's Communist strategy led the country to adopt an inward-looking economic policy; the Communist countries largely traded with each other. They wanted to be self-reliant.

For a while these strategies worked. The Soviet Union grew rapidly, to the point where after World War II it had become one of the two superpowers. It developed missiles and nuclear weapons and even sent the first man into space. By 1956, Nikita Khrushchev, the Soviet Union's leader at the time, could boast that his country, with Communism, would bury the West, with its capitalism. Western textbooks talked about a trade-off between growth and freedom; they granted that the Soviet Union might be able to grow faster, but they asked, was the price, the sacrifice in freedom, worth it.

But the Soviet Union's achievements masked growing problems in its economy: an agricultural sector that was stagnating, and an industrial sector that, outside the military, could not keep up with the rapid pace of innovation in the West. The gap between living standards grew. Mikhail Gorbachev, who became the Soviet Union's leader in 1985, began a process of political and economic reforms, called perestroika, but events got out of control. In 1991, popular protests stopped an attempted military coup, followed soon after by the breakup of the Soviet Union, with each of the so-called republics that had comprised it becoming independent states.

WRAP-UP

The Communist System in the Soviet Union

The government owned the means of production and determined what should be produced and how it should be produced under a system of central planning.

Because the government set wages and prices, they could not function to balance supply and demand. Shortages were common and many goods were rationed.

By the 1980s, the failures of Soviet agriculture and Soviet industry's inability to keep up with rapid innovation in the West led to attempts at economic and political reform and then to the collapse of the Societ Union.

The Move Toward a Market Economy

Russia, and many of the other new republics, quickly moved toward a market economy. They believed that would solve their economic woes. Markets and the price system would replace the inefficient central planners. Private property would provide incentives. Free trade would provide competition, a supply of inputs to Russia's factories, a supply of consumer goods to Russia's consumers, who had been deprived of so much for so long, and a ready market for what Russia produced. The cornerstone of its strategy was thus *privatization* and *liberalization*—eliminating the myriad of constraints that marked the Soviet system. Replacing the inefficient Soviet system thus was bound to raise living standards. The optimists thought it would happen overnight; the pessimists, that it might take six months or perhaps a year.

What happened in the next decade came as a surprise. For most of the countries, growth in the decade since the beginning of the transition has been slower than growth during the decade before the transition. And most have become worse off, as we saw in Figure 37.2. The economy of the former superpower has shrunk to the point where it is comparable with that of the Netherlands or Denmark. Social statistics reflect the deteriorating economic conditions: life spans are shorter, and divorce rates are higher. While 2 percent of the population was in poverty at the beginning of the transition, a decade later the number was estimated to be approaching 40 percent. Today, in many quarters, there is a growing disillusionment. In 2001, in Moldova, one of the small republics most badly hit, more than 70 percent of the voters voted to bring the Communists back to power.

There are some exceptions to this bleak picture: Poland has a GDP today that is 50 percent higher than it was a decade ago, and China, another country making the transition from central planning to a market economy, has seen its income quadruple over the past twenty years.

In this section, we ask what accounts for these transition successes *and* failures? To be sure, each country faced different circumstances at the beginning of the transition, giving some an advantage over others. Poland and several of the other Eastern European countries had a higher standard of living before the move to Communism than did Russia; China had a much lower level of income. The countries of Eastern Europe had easier access to Western markets, and the lure of admission into the European Union helped speed up the reforms required for admission. Some countries, like Uzbekistan, are land-locked, which poses distinct problems. A few countries have been plagued with ethnic conflicts or conflicts with their neighbors (such as the conflict between Armenia and Azerbaijan). Some countries produced commodities, like cotton and gold, that had ready markets in the West; others, for instance, produced parts for Russian tractors or cars, and faced limited markets.

Gradualism Versus Shock Therapy

In the beginning of the transition, many countries faced a problem of extremely high inflation. Under Communism, prices were controlled at levels that were too low, with goods then being rationed. When the restrictions were abolished, prices soared. A first challenge these countries faced was to bring this inflation under control. Many countries adopted a policy that was referred to as *shock therapy*—dramatic reductions in government expenditures and very tight monetary policy. This policy induced deep recessions but did manage to get inflation under control. At this point, two schools of thought developed.

The first argued for a continuation of rapid change. As they said, "You cannot cross a chasm in two jumps." They argued for quick privatization and liberalization. With privatization, the owners of the assets would have an incentive to manage their assets well. Trade liberalization would ensure that there were competing products available from abroad, encouraging efficiency and ensuring that even if there was one, or a limited number, of firms in the domestic market, foreign competition would limit their ability to exercise market power.

The second argued for more gradual change: "crossing a river by feeling the stones." In the battle of metaphors, it was argued that "it takes nine months even to have a baby." The gradualists argued that time was needed to establish the *institutional infrastructure* underlying a market economy, institutions that those in the West simply take for granted, but without which market economies simply cannot function. Earlier, in the context of development, we talked about the importance of legal and financial institutions. There also has to be a tax system in place. Russia is a country rich in natural resources. Selling the resources for a pittance, or giving them away, would leave future governments facing a shortage of revenues unless they could impose taxes on the newly privatized companies. Gradualists also argued that changes were needed not only in the economy but also in the society; change could not be imposed from above, especially in a democracy. For democratic reforms to be durable (sustainable), time would be required to change the mindset of the people, and there would have to be demonstrated successes. The problems confronting Russia and the other countries were particularly severe since the people had been indoctrinated throughout their lives in the evils of capitalism, and since there was little "rule of law"—or at least the kinds of laws required for a market economy—on which to build.

Well-functioning markets require both competition and private property. But if one could not get both simultaneously, on which one should greater stress be placed? Some advocates of rapid change, like Andrei Shleifer of Harvard

University, took the position that the underlying legal structure mattered little; once private property was introduced, owners would create political pressure to create the necessary institutional infrastructure. It was argued that to whom one distributed the state's assets mattered little, since even if the first-round owners were not particularly efficient managers, they would have an incentive to resell the assets to someone who was an efficient manager, or to hire efficient managers.

In the end, the shock therapy approach won in the policy circles, especially in the West. The U.S. Treasury and the IMF pushed for rapid privatization and liberalization. They argued not only for eliminating trade barriers but also for opening up capital markets. Doing so, it was argued, would demonstrate to outside investors that Russia was a business-friendly place in which to invest. To be sure, they said it was important to develop the institutional infrastructure, but they believed that this institutional infrastructure would develop in time.

Not all the countries followed this advice. Poland and Slovenia, having contained hyperinflation, took a more gradualist strategy. China charted its own innovative course of development and transition, but it too was based on gradualism. The decade-long decline of Russia and most of the other countries that followed the shock therapy approach laid bare the weaknesses in this strategy, as compared to that followed by China and Poland.

A Comparison of Transition Strategies

Among the key differences between transition strategies in Russia and China were the following:

- China placed more emphasis on job creation and enterprise than on enterprise restructuring. In China, *local* townships and villages took their savings and created millions of new enterprises. By 2000, while privatization had occurred relatively slowly, these new enterprises produced more than 37 percent of GDP and employed 17 percent of the labor force. They represented a new institutional form: They were not really private, but neither were they like the old government-run, state-owned enterprises.

- China put more emphasis on competition than on privatization. In a sense, the new township and village enterprises were publicly owned, but each had to compete against the other, and this promoted efficiency. Local control and competition helped solve the *governance*

problem. The problem with the old state enterprises was that they suffered from little effective oversight. Government bureaucrats in Moscow or Beijing simply could not keep tabs on what was going on in remote provinces. By contrast, those living in the townships and villages could see what was happening: whether jobs were being created and their incomes were rising, and how they were faring relative to neighbors. This put enormous pressure on managers.

- The gradualist approach built on existing institutions, the communes (townships and village authorities) that previously had been responsible for agriculture. But early on in the reforms, China introduced what was called the *individual responsibility system,* in which land was effectively turned over to the farmers and they reaped the benefit of their own hard work—a standard application of the conventional theory of incentives. The communes then turned their attention from agriculture to industrialization. Putting the new enterprises in the villages and townships meant that there was much less social disruption than would have occurred had the industrialization been centered in urban areas. The contrast with Russia could not have been greater. There, the erosion of *social capital*—a sense of "community" and law and order—had enormous consequences. The entire process of reform was conducted in ways that seemed unfair to the average Russian. While a few oligarchs became billionaires, the government did not pay workers and retirees what was their due. Inflation had wiped out the value of existing savings. Mafia-like activity meant that it was increasingly difficult for ordinary individuals to conduct business. Overall, according to a World Bank study, corruption in the region was second only to that in Africa.

- Privatization of Russia's major revenue sources at bargain basement prices not only lent a sense of unfairness to the whole process, but also, since an effective tax collection system had not been put into place, meant that the government was continually faced with a revenue shortage.

Privatization　It was in privatization that the weaknesses of the transition strategy became most apparent. The problem was that within these countries, given their history, no one had the wealth to buy the firms outright and become efficient entrepreneurs. Thus, there were three approaches.

Thinking Like an Economist

Russia's Failure and the Importance of Incentives

There have been two dramatic economic experiments during the past century. The first began in 1917, with Russia's move to Communism. The second occurred a decade ago, with the move back to a market economy. It was widely thought that after perhaps a short downturn, as resources got redeployed, output would go up. After all, Communism, with its central planning, myriad distortions, and lack of incentives from the absence of a profit motive and well-defined property rights, was operating well below its production possibilities schedule. And with a market system in place, not only should investment increase, but also it should be allocated better.

A decade after the beginning of transition, only three countries out of the nations in Eastern Europe and the former Soviet Union have a GDP as high as at the beginning of the transition, and what went wrong has become a subject of endless debate. Some contend that the reforms went too slowly; some, that they went too fast. Among the factors contributing to the weakening of the economy was the way privatization occurred. *Privatization* is the process of turning over the publicly owned assets to the private sector. Clearly, there is a temptation by those in political power to run the privatization process in ways that give the assets to their friends at low prices. Russia followed this practice, with a few Russians becoming billionaires almost overnight, in return providing financial support for Yeltsin's reelection in 1996. The government received so little revenue from these valuable assets that it could not even pay the aged their pensions. While a few Russians became very, very wealthy, the poverty rate soared, from under 2 percent before the transition to almost 40 percent a decade later. The *hope* was that these new private owners would restart the economy based on market principles. But Western governments (and the IMF and World Bank, the international organizations that provided funds to make the transition easier) insisted that Russia "liberalize" its capital markets, allowing funds to freely flow in and out of the country. This liberalization was viewed to be a hallmark of a market economy. It also would

signal that Russia was committed to becoming a market economy, which would help to attract foreign investors. But it became an almost one-way door. The oligarchs, as the small group of multimillionaires and billionaires who had amassed enormous wealth were called, who were smart enough to figure out how to get so much from the Russian government, had an easy decision given the choice of investing in the United States, where the stock market was booming, or elsewhere in the West, or investing in Russia, whose economy was imploding. In addition, given the widespread view that they had acquired their wealth illegitimately, if they kept their money in the country, a later government might try to recapture their wealth—a fear that was confirmed by the Putin government that succeeded Yeltsin. By general account, several hundred billion dollars left the country. The manufacturing sector was left devastated. The transition had proved that incentives do matter, but unfortunately the wrong incentives had been put in place: Rather than providing incentives for the creation of wealth, incentives had been provided for the stripping away of assets!

Moscow shantytowns reflect the poverty now experienced by many Russians.

First, the assets could be sold to foreigners. Those, like Hungary, that did this have had the most successful privatizations, but many countries have found the idea of selling their assets to foreigners difficult to accept. Second, individuals could be given *vouchers,* which could be used to purchase assets. Originally, there was considerable excitement about this idea, in that it might create a true "people's capitalism" with shares widely held. But then in a firm with many small shareholders, no one would have an incentive to monitor the managers; they would have virtually complete discretion. Then the notion was put forward that the shares could be agglomerated into a holding company, and the holding company would monitor the firm. But then the question was asked, who would monitor the monitor? Unfortunately, these worries proved all too real: In the Czech Republic, originally given credit for the most successful voucher privatization, the managers of the holding companies managed to steal the assets for their own use. Through a series of sham transactions, they "tunneled" out the assets, leaving the other shareholders owning nothing but an empty shell. Third, banks could loan to potential entrepreneurs the money to buy the assets being sold. But again problems were encountered: State banks made loans to friends of the government. In effect, one pocket of the government was giving money to the other pocket—but in the meantime friends of the government became enormously wealthy. In some cases, governments took an only slightly more disguised route: They gave licenses to their friends to open up private banks that were inadequately regulated, and the private banks then provided financing to their friends. When the loans were not repaid, and the banks

went bankrupt, the taxpayers again had to pick up the bill. These abuses were carried to an extreme in Russia, where a few oligarchs wound up owning a vast amount of the national assets. In ten years, Russia managed to create a level of inequality that was almost unrivaled in the world and had taken other countries centuries to build up.

The Future of Transition   The debate about the transition continues to rage. Those who led the reform in Russia and its Asian republics claim that things would have been even worse had there not been shock therapy. They are hopeful that success is "just around the corner." The critics of shock therapy say that China, Slovenia, Poland, and Hungary show that there were alternatives, and that Russia would have fared better if *their* advice had been heeded. They worry about a backlash resulting from the failures—not a return to Communism but to authoritarianism or nationalism, and periodic attacks on parts of the media have been unsettling. They contend that Russia's huge inequality—and the devastation of the middle class—does not bode well for Russia's future. Only time will tell.

In many respects, China has been the most successful transition economy. It has an increasing and thriving private sector, including high levels of innovation in the new economy, but it faces many challenges. It has moved gradually, in part to preserve the authoritarian political control exercised by the Communist Party, and the process of democratization is just beginning. The process of restructuring the large state-owned enterprises lies largely ahead. While all parts of China have seen growth, there is growing disparity between the richest parts, largely along the coast, and the poorer parts, in the western regions.

Meanwhile, most of the countries of Eastern Europe that were part of the Soviet Union are moving toward becoming part of the European Union. They are adapting their legal systems and beginning to integrate their economies with Europe. While the transition may not be an easy one, for them, there is a bright light at the end of the tunnel.

WRAP-UP

Transition Strategies

The two basic strategies the former Communist countries have followed are called *gradualism* and *shock therapy.*

The more gradual reform strategy stresses the creation of competition and the development of the institutional infrastructure necessary for markets to function adequately. Countries following this strategy have fared better over the past decade than those adopting shock therapy.

Review and Practice

Summary

1. In less developed countries, or LDCs, life expectancies are usually shorter, infant mortality is higher, and

people are less educated than in developed countries. Also, a larger fraction of the population lives in rural areas, and population growth rates are higher.

2. In recent years, newly industrialized countries (NICs) such as South Korea, Singapore, Hong Kong, and Taiwan have managed to improve their economic status dramatically. Other LDCs, like India, have expanded food production considerably. But the standard of living in some of the poorest LDCs, such as many African nations, has actually been declining, as population growth has outstripped economic growth.

3. Among the factors contributing to underdevelopment are lack of physical capital, lack of education, lack of technology, and lack of developed capital markets. The factors interact: Low education levels impede the transfer of advanced technology; low incomes make it difficult to invest heavily in education.

4. The success of the countries of East Asia is based partially on activist government policies, which include helping to develop and use markets rather than replacing them; maintaining macroeconomic stability; promoting high levels of investment (including public infrastructure) and saving; providing strong support for education, including the education of women; improving capital markets, which facilitate an efficient allocation of scarce capital; promoting exports; fostering equality; and promoting technology. These policies helped to create a positive investment climate (including for foreign investors) and to reduce population growth.

5. Advanced countries can help LDCs through the provision of aid (capital assistance) and technical assistance, and by opening markets to trade. Recently, debt forgiveness has been a major source of concern.

6. The world faced a global economic crisis in 1997–1998, the worst such crisis since the Great Depression. Capital market liberalization, exposing fragile developing countries to the volatility of investor sentiment, played an important role in bringing on the crisis, and tight monetary and fiscal policies helped to deepen it.

7. Under Communism, the state was responsible for all production: Central planners decided what to produce, how it was to be produced, and for whom it was to be produced. While there were some successes, especially in the early decades, eventually the lack of incentives, the central planners' lack of information, and the distortions that were rife in the system took their toll.

8. The transition to a market economy has not been easy. In most countries, output fell markedly and poverty increased markedly. A few countries fared well.

9. After ten years of transition, it now appears that the countries that rapidly brought inflation down to moderate levels, then took a more gradual approach to broader reforms, with greater emphasis on creating an institutional infrastructure, creating jobs and new enterprises, and creating competition, have done better than those that adopted a more wholesale, shock therapy approach.

10. In many countries, privatization has encountered numerous problems. In some cases, it led to the stripping away of assets, rather than to a restructuring of the enterprise to make it more productive.

Key Terms

less developed countries, or LDCs
developed countries
industrialized countries
newly industrialized countries, or NICs
green revolution
sharecropping
land reform
dual economies
surplus of labor
export-led growth
globalization
central planning

Review Questions

1. List some important ways in which LDCs differ from more developed countries. How have different developing countries fared over recent decades?

2. What are the most important factors inhibiting growth in the LDCs? Why is capital shortage *alone* not the most important factor? How do some of the factors interact with each other?

3. How does rapid population growth make it more difficult to increase a country's standard of living?

4. What are some of the factors that contributed to the East Asian miracle?

5. Why might fostering equality promote economic growth?

6. What are some of the roles that government can play in promoting economic development and growth?

7. What are some of the roles that the advanced countries can play in promoting economic development among the LDCs?

8. What are some of the policies that contributed to the onset of the global financial crisis of 1997–1998 and deepened the resulting recessions?

9. How were resources allocated under the former Soviet (Communist) system?

10. What were some of the problems with the Communist system, and why was the switch to a market economy expected to lead to increased incomes?

11. What were two of the different strategies for moving from Communism to a market economy?

12. How have different countries fared in the transition? How do you explain the different performances?

Problems

1. In the United States, the economy grew by 2.6 percent per year (in real terms) during the 1980s. In India, the economy grew by 5.3 percent during the 1980s. However, population growth in the United States was .8 percent annually, while population growth in India was 2.1 percent annually. Which country increased its standard of living faster for the average citizen? By how much?

2. Nominal GNP in Kenya was 9 billion shillings in 1967 and 135 billion shillings in 1987. The price level in Kenya (using 1980 as a base year) rose from 40 in 1967 to 200 in 1987. And the population of Kenya increased from 10 million to 22 million in those twenty years. What was the total percentage change in real GNP per capita in Kenya from 1967 to 1987?

3. True or false: "LDCs do not have much capital because their rates of saving are low. If they saved more or received more foreign aid, they could rapidly expand their economic growth." Discuss.

4. How might each of the following hinder entrepreneurs in LDCs?

   (a) Lack of functioning capital markets

   (b) Pervasive government control of the economy

   (c) Lack of companies that offer business services

   (d) A tradition of substantial foreign control of large enterprises

5. What is the economist's case for having the government be responsible for providing infrastructure?

6. If many LDCs simultaneously attempted to pursue export-led growth, what would be the effect in world markets on the quantities and prices of products mainly sold by LDCs, like minerals, agricultural goods, and textiles? What effect might these quantities and prices have on the success of such export-led growth policies?

7. Explain how the idea of import substitution conflicts in the short run with the idea of comparative advantage. Need the two ideas conflict in the long run? Why or why not?

8. Why might a family in an LDC face a lower opportunity cost of having more children than a family in a developed country?

9. How might you design a privatization program for an economy attempting the transition from Communism to a market economy?

10. List the pros and cons of globalization.

Productivity and the NAIRU

As new information technologies have spread throughout the American economy, they have boosted productivity growth. Living standards can rise more rapidly when productivity growth increases, as the amount the economy is able to produce from its limited resources of labor and capital increases. Workers enjoy the benefits of this faster productivity growth in the form of bigger wage increases. With higher productivity growth, firms can pay higher wages without seeing their unit costs rise, so faster wage growth does not translate into an increase in the inflation rate.

But the productivity growth that the U.S. economy has enjoyed since the mid-1990s has raised a puzzle for policy-makers. Why has the unemployment rate been able to fall to levels not seen since the late 1960s without igniting inflation? Put another way, why has the nonaccelerating inflation rate of unemployment, the NAIRU, apparently fallen?

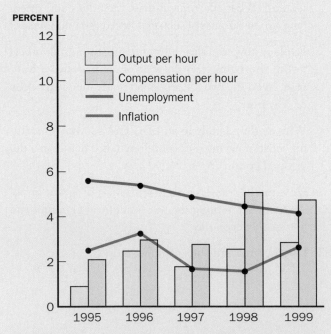

Productivity and Labor Costs: 1995–1999

Faster productivity growth does not have to reduce the NAIRU. If productivity growth rises from, say, 1.5 percent to 2.5 percent per year, workers can demand that their wages increase by 1 percent more each year. Nominal wages will rise at a faster rate, reflecting the faster productivity growth, but this will not raise firms' labor costs and will not be inflationary. If an unemployment rate of 5.5 percent was consistent with steady inflation before, it should still be consistent with steady inflation after the increase in productivity growth. A fall in unemployment below this level would lead to more rapid wage increases, increases that exceed the new, higher rate of productivity growth, and inflation should rise. The controversy facing policy-makers in the 1990s was in understanding why this did not happen as the U.S. unemployment rate fell from 5.6 percent in 1995 to 4.0 percent in 2000.

One argument points to the two factors that contribute to faster wage growth. First, decreases in unemployment cause wages to rise faster. Second, faster productivity growth also causes wages to rise faster. Only the first factor raises labor costs and is inflationary. But what if, for some reason, the second factor is not operating? If workers are slow to recognize the increase in productivity growth, the second factor may not play a role. According to this argument, the decline in unemployment in the late 1990s did increase wage growth, but it did not lead to inflation because the faster productivity growth failed to translate into faster wage growth. As a consequence, the unemployment rate fell and inflation remained steady.

Since this argument is based on the idea that workers only slowly come to recognize that productivity growth has increased, the fall in the NAIRU will only be temporary. Once workers (and firms) fully realize that productivity growth has risen, wage demand will adjust, and the NAIRU will return to its earlier level.

The first chart shows the growth rate of productivity (output per hour) and labor compensation during the late 1990s. The unemployment rate and inflation rate are also shown. Productivity growth rose significantly in 1996 and 1997, but not until 1998 did labor compensation begin to grow significantly faster than productivity. Declining unemployment contributed to faster wage growth, but because workers were perhaps slow to recognize the new, higher rate of productivity growth, wage increases remained moderate.

If this argument is correct, then the impact of new economy technologies on the NAIRU will be short-lived. As workers demand bigger wage increases, both because of higher productivity growth and because of the tight labor market reflected in very low unemployment, wage growth will exceed productivity growth. Unless unemployment rises, as it started to do in 2001, inflation will increase. The rate of unemployment that will be consistent with steady inflation, the NAIRU, will return to its earlier, higher levels.

The 1970s saw a productivity slowdown, so we might expect to see a pattern of unemployment, wages, and inflation that is the reverse of the pattern seen in the 1990s. The second chart shows what actually happened in the United States between 1975 and 1979. Productivity growth fell, but the growth rate of labor compensation per hour remained well in excess of productivity growth. Inflation rose dramatically.

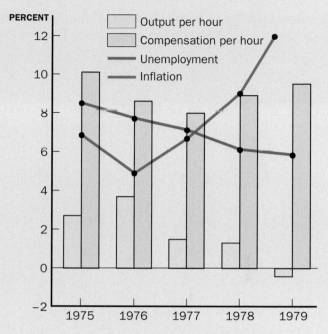

Productivity and Labor Costs: 1975–1979

Glossary

absolute advantage: a country has an absolute advantage over another country in the production of a good if it can produce that good more efficiently (with fewer inputs).

acquired endowments: resources a country builds for itself, like a network of roads or an educated population

adaptive expectations: expectations that respond or adapt to recent experience

adverse selection: the phenomenon that, as an insurance company raises its price, the best risks (those least likely to make a claim) drop out, so the mix of applicants changes adversely; now used more generally to refer to effects on the mix of workers, borrowers, products being sold, and so forth resulting from a change in wages (interest rates, prices) or other variables

affirmative action: actions by employers to seek out actively minorities and women for jobs and to provide them with training and other opportunities for promotion

aggregate consumption function: the relationship between aggregate consumption and aggregate income

aggregate demand-inflation curve: the curve that shows the negative relationship between inflation and spending

aggregate expenditures schedule: the relationship between aggregate expenditures and national income for a given real rate of interest

aggregate saving: the sum of the savings of all individuals in society

antitrust: laws that discourage monopoly and restrictive practices and encourage greater competition

appreciation: a change in the exchange rate that enables a unit of currency to buy more units of foreign currencies

asset price bubbles: asset price increases that are based solely on the expectation that prices will be higher in the future and not based on increases in the actual returns yielded by the asset

asymmetric information: a situation in which the parties to a transaction have different information, as when the seller of a used car has more information about its quality than the buyer

automatic stabilizer: expenditure that automatically increases or tax that automatically decreases when economic conditions worsen, and that, therefore, tends to stabilize the economy automatically

average cost: total costs divided by total output

average tax rate: the ratio of taxes to taxable income

average variable costs: total variable costs divided by total output

backward induction: see *rollback*

basic competitive model: the model of the economy that pulls together the assumptions of self-interested consumers, profit-maximizing firms, and perfectly competitive markets

basic research: fundamental research; it often produces a wide range of applications, but the output of basic research itself usually is not of direct commercial value. The output is knowledge, rather than a product; it typically cannot be patented.

beggar-thy-neighbor policies: restrictions on imports designed to increase a country's national output, so-called because they increase that country's output while simultaneously hurting the output of other countries

benefit taxes: taxes that are levied on a particular product, the revenues of which go for benefits to those who purchase the product

Bertrand competition: an oligopoly in which each firm believes that its rivals are committed to keeping their prices fixed and that customers can be lured away by offering lower prices

bilateral trade: trade between two parties

block grants: grants to states, which are given considerable discretion in how the money is spent

boom: a period of time when resources are being fully used and GDP is growing steadily

borrowed reserves: the reserves that banks have borrowed from the Fed

budget constraints: the limitations on consumption of different goods imposed by the fact that households have only a limited amount of money to spend (their budget). The budget constraint *defines* the opportunity set of individuals, when the only constraint that they face is money.

capital deepening: an increase in capital per worker

capital gain: the increase in the value of an asset between the time it is purchased and the time it is sold

capital goods: the machines and buildings firms invest in, with funds from the *capital market*

capital goods investment: investment in machines and buildings (to be distinguished from investments in inventory, in research and development, or in training [human capital])

capital inflows: money from abroad that is used to buy investments, to be deposited in U.S. banks, to buy U.S. government bonds, or to be lent in the United States for any reason

capital market: the various institutions concerned with raising funds and sharing and insuring risks, including banks, insurance markets, bond markets, and the stock market

capital outflows: money from the United States that is used to buy foreign investments or foreign government bonds, to be deposited in foreign banks or lent in foreign countries for any reason

cartel: a group of producers with an agreement to collude in setting prices and output

causation: the relationship that results when a change in one variable is not only correlated with but actually produces a change in another variable; the change in the second variable is a consequence of the change in the first variable, rather than both changes being a consequence of a change in a third variable

central planning: the system in which central government bureaucrats (as opposed to private entrepreneurs or even local government bureaucrats) determine what will be produced and how it will be produced

certificate of deposit (CD): an account in which money is deposited for a preset length of time and yields a slightly higher return to compensate for the reduced liquidity

chain-weighted real GDP: the method of calculating real GDP in which the percentage increase in output from each year to the next is calculated by comparing the value of output of both years in the earlier year's prices

circular flow: the way in which funds move through the capital, labor, and product markets between households, firms, the government, and the foreign sector

classical dichotomy: the independence of real variables from changes in nominal variables

closed economy: an economy that neither exports nor imports

Coase's theorem: the assertion that, if property rights are properly defined, then people will be forced to pay for any negative externalities they impose on others and market transactions will produce efficient outcomes

collusion: when firms act jointly (more nearly as they would if there were a monopolist) to increase overall profits

command-and-control approach: the approach to controlling environmental externalities in which the government provides detailed regulations about what firms can and cannot do, including what technologies they can employ

commercial policies: policies directed at affecting either imports or exports

comparative advantage: a country has a comparative advantage over another country in one good as opposed to another good if its *relative* efficiency in the production of the first good is higher than the other country's.

compensating wage differentials: differences in wages that can be traced to nonpecuniary attributes of a job, such as the degree of autonomy and risk

complement: two goods are complements if the demand for one (at a given price) decreases as the price of the other increases

constant, diminishing, or increasing returns to scale: when all inputs are increased by a certain proportion, output increases in equal, smaller, or greater proportion, respectively; increasing returns to scale are also called *economies of scale*

constant returns to scale: a production function has constant returns to scale when equiproportionate increases in all inputs increase output proportionately.

consumer price index: a price index in which the basket of goods is defined by what a typical consumer purchases

consumer protection legislation: laws aimed at protecting consumers, for instance by assuring that consumers have more complete information about items they are considering buying

consumer sovereignty: the idea that individuals are the best judges of what is in their own interests and promotes their well-being

consumer surplus: the difference between what a person would be willing to pay and what he actually has to pay to buy a certain amount of a good

contingency clauses: statements within a contract that make the level of payment or the work to be performed conditional upon various factors

corporation income taxes: taxes based on the income, or profit, received by a corporation

correlation: the relationship that results when a change in one variable is consistently associated with a change in another variable

countercyclical policies: policies designed to keep the economy at full employment by smoothing out fluctuations

countervailing duties: duties (tariffs) that are imposed by a country to counteract subsidies provided to a foreign producer

Cournot competition: an oligopoly in which each firm believes that its rivals are committed to a certain level of production and that rivals will reduce their prices as needed to sell that amount

credit channel: effect of monetary policy on output through its effect on credit availability

credit rationing: credit is rationed when no lender is willing to make a loan to a borrower or the amount lenders are willing to lend to borrowers is limited, even if the borrower is willing to pay more than other borrowers of comparable risk who are getting loans

cross subsidization: the practice of charging higher prices to one group of consumers in order to subsidize lower prices for another group

crowding out: a decrease in private investment resulting from an increase in government expenditures

currency board: a system in which the exchange rate between the local currency and foreign currency is fixed by law

cyclical unemployment: the increase in unemployment that occurs as the economy goes into a slowdown or recession

dead weight loss: the difference between what producers gain and (the monetary value of) what consumers lose, when output is restricted under imperfect competition; also, the difference between what the government gains and what consumers lose, when taxes are imposed

deflation: a persistent decrease in the general level of prices

demand: the quantity of a good or service that a household or firm chooses to buy at a given price

demand curve: the relationship between the quantity demanded of a good and the price, whether for an individual or for the market (all individuals) as a whole

demand deposits: deposits that can be drawn upon instantly, like checking accounts

demographic effects: effects that arise from changes in characteristics of the population such as age, birthrates, and location

depreciation: (a) the decrease in the value of an asset; in particular, the amount that capital goods decrease in value as they are used and become old; (b) a change in the exchange rate that enables a unit of one currency to buy fewer units of foreign currencies

depression: a strong downward fluctuation in the economy that is more severe than a recession

devaluation: a reduction in the rate of exchange between one currency and other currencies under a fixed exchange-rate system

developed countries: the wealthiest nations in the world, including Western Europe, the United States, Canada, Japan, Australia, and New Zealand

diminishing marginal utility: the principle that says that as an individual consumes more and more of a good, each successive unit increases her utility, or enjoyment, less and less

diminishing returns to scale: the principle that as one input increases, with other inputs fixed, the resulting increase in output tends to be smaller and smaller

discouraged workers: workers who would be willing to work but have given up looking for jobs and thus are not officially counted as unemployed

discretion: the ability to make explicit policy decisions in response to macroeconomic conditions

discretionary spending: government expenditures that are decided on an annual basis

distribution: the allocation of goods and services produced by the economy

diversification: spreading one's wealth among a large number of different assets

dividends: that portion of corporate profits paid out to shareholders

division of labor: dividing a production process into a series of jobs, with each worker focusing on a limited set of tasks; the advantage of division of labor is that each worker can practice and perfect a particular set of skills.

dollarization: abandonment of the domestic currency in favor of the U.S. dollar

dominant strategy: strategy that works best no matter what the other player does in a game

dual economies: separations in many *less developed countries (LDCs)* between impoverished rural sectors and urban sectors that have higher wages and more advanced technology

dual use: technologies that have both a civilian and a military use

dumping: the practice of selling a good abroad at a lower price than at home, or below costs of production

dynamic efficiency: an economy that appropriately balances short-run concerns (static efficiency) with long-run concerns (focusing on encouraging R & D)

dynamic inconsistency: the problem of whether a government will actually carry out a promised course of action

earned income tax credit: a reduction in taxes provided to low income workers based on the amount of income they earn and the size of their family

economic rent: payments made to a factor of production that are in excess of what is required to elicit the supply of that factor

economies of scope: the situation that exists when it is less expensive to produce two products together than it would be to produce each one separately

efficiency wage: the wage at which total labor costs are minimized

efficiency wage theory: the theory that paying higher wages (up to a point) lowers total production costs, for instance by leading to a more productive labor force

efficient market theory: the theory that all available information is reflected in the current price of an asset

entitlements: programs that provide benefits automatically to individuals meeting certain criteria (such as age)

entry deterrence: the reduction of competition by preventing other firms from entering the market

entry-deterring practices: practices of incumbent firms designed to discourage the entry of rivals into the market

equilibrium: a condition in which there are no forces (reasons) for change

equilibrium price: the price at which demand equals supply

equilibrium quantity: the quantity demanded and supplied at the equilibrium price, where demand equals supply

European Union: an important regional trade bloc that now covers most of Europe

excess demand: the situation in which the quantity demanded at a given price exceeds the quantity supplied

excess reserves: reserves that banks hold beyond what is required

excess supply: the situation in which the quantity supplied at a given price exceeds the quantity demanded

exchange: the act of trading that forms the basis for markets

exchange efficiency: the condition in which whatever the economy produces is distributed among people in such a way that there are no gains to further trade

exchange rate: the rate at which one currency (such as dollars) can be exchanged for another (such as euros, yen, or pounds)

excise taxes: taxes on a particular good or service

expansions: a period in which real GDP is growing

expected return: the average return—a single number that combines the various possible returns per dollar invested with the chances that each of these returns will actually be paid

experimental economics: the branch of economics which analyzes certain aspects of economic behavior in a controlled, laboratory setting

export-led growth: the strategy that government should encourage exports in which the country has a comparative advantage to stimulate growth

exports: goods produced domestically but sold abroad

externality: a phenomenon that arises when an individual or firm takes an action but does not bear all the costs (negative externality) or receive all the benefits (positive externality)

factor demand: the amount of an input demanded by a firm, given the price of the input and the quantity of output being produced; in a competitive market, an input will be demanded up to the point where the value of the marginal product of that input equals the price of the input.

federal funds market: the market through which banks borrow and lend reserves

federal funds rate: the interest rate on overnight interbank loans

Federal Open Market Committee (FOMC): the committee of the Federal Reserve System that sets monetary policy

financial investment: investment in stocks, bonds, or other financial instruments; these investments provide the funds that allow investments in *capital goods.*

fiscal deficit: the gap between the government's expenditures and its revenues from sources other than additional borrowing

fiscal surplus: the amount by which government tax revenues exceed expenditures

fixed costs: the costs resulting from fixed inputs, sometimes called *overhead costs*

fixed exchange-rate system: an exchange rate system in which the value of each currency is fixed in relationship to other currencies

flexible or **floating exchange-rate system:** a system in which exchange rates are determined by market forces, the law of supply and demand, without government interference

flows: variables such as the output of the economy *per year;* stocks are in contrast to flows; flows measure the changes in stocks over a given period of time.

four-firm concentration ratio: the fraction of output produced by the top four firms in an industry

fractional reserve system: the system of banking in which banks hold a fraction of the amount on deposit in reserves

free-rider: someone who enjoys the benefit of a (public) good without paying for it; because it is difficult to preclude anyone from using a pure public good, those who benefit from the goods have an incentive to avoid paying for them (that is, to be a free-rider).

free trade: trade among countries that occurs without barriers such as tariffs or quotas

frictional unemployment: unemployment associated with people moving from one job to another or moving into the labor force

fringe benefits: compensation that is not in the form of direct cash to a worker, such as health insurance, retirement pay, and life insurance

full-employment deficit: what the deficit would be if the economy were at full employment

full-employment level of output: the level of output that the economy can produce under normal circumstances with a given stock of plant and equipment and a given supply of labor

gains from trade: the benefits that each side enjoys from a trade

game table: table showing the payoffs to each player of a game

game theory: theory designed to understand strategic choices, that is, to understand how people or organizations behave when they expect their actions to influence the behavior of others

game tree: diagram used to represent sequential games

GDP deflator: a weighted average of the prices of different goods and services, where the weights represent the importance of each of the goods and services in *GDP*

General Agreement on Tariffs and Trade (GATT): the agreement among the major trading countries of the world that created the framework for lowering barriers to trade and resolving trade disputes; established after World War II, it has been succeeded by the World Trade Organization (WTO).

general equilibrium: the full equilibrium of the economy, when all markets clear simultaneously

general equilibrium analysis: a simultaneous analysis of all capital, product, and labor markets throughout the economy; it shows, for instance, the impact on all prices and quantities of immigration or a change in taxes.

gift and estate taxes: taxes imposed on the transfers of wealth from one generation to another

globalization: the closer integration of the countries of the world—especially the increased level of trade and movements of capital—brought on by lower costs of transportation and communication

green GDP: a measurement of national output that attempts to take into account effects on the environment and natural resources

green revolution: the invention and dissemination of new seeds and agricultural practices that led to vast increases in agricultural output in *less developed countries (LDCs)* during the 1960s and 1970s

gross domestic product (GDP): the total money value of all final goods and services produced within a nation's borders during a given period of time

gross national product (GNP): a measure of the incomes of residents of a country, including income they receive from abroad but subtracting similar payments made to those abroad

horizontal equity: the principle that says that those who are in identical or similar circumstances should pay identical or similar amounts in taxes

horizontal merger: a merger between two firms that produce the same goods

human capital: the stock of accumulated skills and experience that make workers more productive

imperfect competition: any market structure in which there is some competition but firms face downward-sloping demand curves

imperfect information: a situation in which market participants lack information (such as information about prices or characteristics of goods and services) important for their decision making

imperfect substitutes: goods that can substitute for each other, but imperfectly so

implicit labor contract: an unwritten understanding between employer and employees that employees will receive a stable wage throughout fluctuating economic conditions

import function: the relationship between imports and national income

imports: goods produced abroad but bought domestically

incentives: benefits, or reduced costs, that motivate a decision maker in favor of a particular choice

income approach: the approach to calculating GDP that involves measuring the income generated to all of the participants in the economy

income effect: the reduced consumption of a good whose price has increased that is due to the reduction in a person's buying power, or "real" income; when a person's real income is lower, normally she will consume less of all goods, including the higher-priced good.

income elasticity of demand: the percentage change in quantity demanded of a good as the result of a 1 percent change in income (the percentage change in quantity demanded divided by the percentage change in income)

income-expenditure analysis: the analysis that determines equilibrium output by relating aggregate expenditures to income

incomplete markets: situations in which no market may exist for some good or for some risk, or in which some individuals cannot borrow for some purposes

increasing returns to scale: the principle that as one input increases, with other inputs fixed, the resulting increase in output is larger and larger

individual income taxes: taxes based on the income received by an individual or household

industrialized countries: see *developed countries*

industrial policies: government policies designed to promote particular sectors of the economy

infant industry argument for protection: the argument that industries must be protected from foreign competition while they are young, until they have a chance to acquire the skills to enable them to compete on equal terms

inferior good: a good the consumption of which falls as income rises

infinite elasticity: the situation that exists when any amount will be demanded (supplied) at a particular price, but nothing will be demanded (supplied) if the price increases (declines) even a small amount

inflation: the rate of increase of the general level of prices

inflation shocks: events that produce temporary shifts in the SRIA curve

inflation targeting: policies designed to stabilize the economy through countercyclical policies while ensuring that average inflation remains low

information: the basis of decision making that can affect the structure of markets and their ability to use society's scarce resources efficiently

infrastructure: the roads, ports, bridges, and legal system that provide the necessary basis for a working economy

intellectual property: proprietary knowledge, such as that protected by patents and copyright

interest: the return a saver receives in addition to the original amount she deposited (loaned) and the amount a borrower must pay in addition to the original amount he borrowed

interest-rate parity condition: a condition assuming perfect capital mobility where expected returns are equal across countries in equilibrium

inventory investment: firms' investment in raw materials or output on hand

investment: from the national perspective, an increase in the stock of capital goods or any other expenditure designed to increase future output; from the perspective of the individual, any expenditure designed to increase an individual's future wealth, such as the purchase of a share in a company. (Since some other individual is likely selling the share, that person is disinvesting, and the net investment for the economy is zero.)

investment function: the relationship between the level of real investment and the value of the real interest rate; also called the *investment schedule*

job discrimination: discrimination in which disadvantaged groups have less access to better paying jobs

joint products: products that are naturally produced together, such as wool and mutton

labor force participation decision: the decision by an individual to seek work actively, that is, to participate in the labor market

labor force participation rate: the fraction of the working-age population that is employed or seeking employment

labor market: the market in which services of workers are bought and sold

land reform: the redistribution of land by the government to those who actually work the land

law of supply and demand: the law in economics that holds that, in equilibrium, prices are determined so that demand equals supply; changes in prices thus reflect shifts in the demand or supply curves.

learning by doing: the increase in productivity that occurs as a firm gains experience from producing and that results in a decrease in the firm's production costs

learning curve: the curve describing how costs of production decline as cumulative output increases over time

less developed countries (LDCs): the poorest nations of the world, including much of Africa, Latin America, and Asia

life-cycle saving: saving that is motivated by a desire to smooth consumption over an individual's lifetime and to meet special needs that arise in various times of life; saving for retirement is the most important aspect of life-cycle saving.

liquidity: the ease with which an investment can be turned into cash

loanable funds market: the market in which the supply of funds is allocated to those who wish to borrow; equilibrium requires that saving (the supply of funds) equals investment (the demand for funds).

long run: a length of time sufficient to allow wages and prices to fully adjust to equilibrate supply and demand

long-run aggregate supply curve: the aggregate supply curve that applies in the long run, when wages and prices can adjust fully to ensure full employment

long-run inflation adjustment curve: curve depicting the relationship between the inflation rate and output in the long run, with full adjustment of inflationary expectations

luxury taxes: excise taxes imposed on luxuries, goods typically consumed disproportionately by the wealthy

M1, M2, M3: measures of the money supply: M1 includes currency and checking accounts; M2 includes M1 plus savings deposits, CDs, and money market funds; M3 includes M2 plus large-denomination savings deposits and institutional money-market mutual funds.

macroeconomics: the top-down view of the economy, focusing on aggregate characteristics

managed care: a health care system in which the health care provider, in return for a fixed fee per year, manages the care of the individual, including decisions about whether a specialist is required

managerial slack: the lack of managerial efficiency (for instance, in cutting costs) that occurs when firms are insulated from competition

marginal benefits: the extra benefits resulting, for instance, from the increased consumption of a commodity

marginal cost: the additional cost corresponding to an additional unit of output produced

marginal product: the amount output increases with the addition of one unit of an input

marginal propensity to consume: the amount by which consumption increases when income increases by a dollar

marginal propensity to import: the amount by which imports increase when income increases by a dollar

marginal propensity to save: the amount by which savings increase when income increases by a dollar

marginal rate of transformation: the amount of extra production of one good that one obtains from reducing the production of another good by one unit, moving along the production possibilities curve

marginal revenue: the extra revenue received by a firm for selling one additional unit of a good

marginal tax rate: the extra tax that will have to be paid as a result of an additional dollar of income

marginal utility: the extra utility, or enjoyment, a person receives from the consumption of one additional unit of a good

marketable permits: a permit issued by the government, which can be bought and sold, that allows a firm to emit a certain amount of pollution

market clearing price: the price at which supply equals demand, so there is neither excess supply nor excess demand

market demand curve: the total amount of a particular good or service demanded in the economy at each price; it is calculated by "adding horizontally" the individual demand curves (that is, at any given price, it is the sum of the individual demands).

market economy: an economy that allocates resources primarily through the interaction of individuals (households) and private firms

market failures: situations in which a market economy fails to attain economic efficiency

market structure: term used to describe the organization of the market, such as whether there is a high degree of *competition,* a *monopoly,* an *oligopoly,* or *monopolistic competition*

market supply curve: the total amount of a particular good or service that all the firms in the economy together would like to supply at each price; it is calculated by "adding horizontally" the individual firm's supply curves (that is, it is the sum of the amounts each firm is willing to supply at any given price).

matching programs: programs in which federal outlays depend on state expenditures

medium of exchange: an item that can be commonly exchanged for goods and services throughout the economy

merit goods: goods that are determined by government to be good for people, regardless of whether people desire them for themselves or not

microeconomics: the bottom-up view of the economy, focusing on individual households and firms

monetary policy rule: the systematic relationship between the central bank's setting of policy and the variables that it reacts to, such as inflation, cyclical unemployment, or the output gap

money: any item that serves as a medium of exchange, a store of value, and a unit of account

money multiplier: the amount by which a new deposit into the banking system (from the outside) is multiplied as it is loaned out, redeposited, reloaned, etc., by banks

monopolistic competition: the form of imperfect competition in which the market has sufficiently few firms that each one faces a downward-sloping demand curve, but enough that each can ignore the reactions of rivals to what it does

monopoly: a market consisting of only one firm

monopoly rents: see *pure profit*

moral hazard: the principle that says that those who purchase insurance have a reduced incentive to avoid what they are insured against

multilateral trade: trade between more than two parties

multiplier: the amount equilibrium output increases when the aggregate expenditures schedule shifts by a dollar

mutual fund: a fund that gathers money from different investors and purchases a range of assets; each investor then owns a portion of the entire fund.

Nash equilibrium: game equilibrium when both players execute their dominant strategies (that is, neither player would change his strategy if offered the chance to do so at the end of the game).

natural endowments: a country's natural resources, such as good climate, fertile land, or minerals

natural monopoly: a monopoly that exists because average costs of production are declining beyond the level of output demanded in the market, thus making entry unprofitable and making it efficient for there to be a single firm

natural rate of unemployment: the unemployment rate when the economy is at potential GDP and cyclical unemployment is zero

net capital inflows: total capital inflows minus total capital outflows

net domestic product (NDP): GDP minus the value of the depreciation of the country's capital goods

neutrality of the money supply: the idea that changing the money supply has no real effects on the economy, which is a basic implication of the full-employment model

newly industrialized countries (NICs): nations that have recently moved from being quite poor to being middle-income countries, including South Korea, Taiwan, Singapore, and Hong Kong

nominal GDP: the value of gross domestic product in a particular year measured in that year's prices

nominal rate of interest: the percentage return on a deposit, loan, or bond; the nominal rate of interest does not take into account the effects of inflation.

nominal wage: the average wage not adjusted for changes in the prices of consumer goods

nonaccelerating inflation rate of unemployment (NAIRU): the unemployment rate at which expected and actual inflation are equal and inflation remains stable

nonborrowed reserves: the difference between total reserves and borrowed reserves

nondiscretionary spending: expenditures that are determined automatically, such as interest payments and expenditures on entitlements

nonpecuniary attributes: aspects of a job other than the wage it pays

nonrival goods: goods whose consumption or use by one person does not exclude consumption by another person

nontariff barriers: barriers to trade that take forms other than tariffs (such as regulations which disadvantage foreign firms)

normal good: a good the consumption of which rises as income rises

normative economics: economics in which judgments about the desirability of various policies are made; the conclusions rest on value judgments as well as facts and theories.

North American Free Trade Agreement (NAFTA): the agreement between Canada, the United States, and Mexico that lowered trade and other barriers among the countries

oligopoly: the form of imperfect competition in which the market has several firms, sufficiently few that each one must take into account the reactions of rivals to what it does

open economy: an economy that is actively engaged in international trade

open-market operations: central banks' purchase or sale of government bonds in the open market

operating procedures: the manner in which a central bank chooses to implement monetary policy

opportunity cost: the cost of a resource, measured by the value of the next-best, alternative use of that resource

opportunity set: a summary of the choices available to individuals, as defined by budget constraints and time constraints

output gap: the percentage deviation of actual GDP from potential

Pareto efficient: a resource allocation is said to be Pareto efficient if there is no rearrangement that can make anyone better off without making someone else worse off.

partial equilibrium analysis: an analysis that focuses on only one or a few markets at a time

patent: a government decree giving an inventor the exclusive right to produce, use, or sell an invention for a period of time

payroll taxes: taxes based on payroll (wages) that is used to finance the Social Security and Medicare programs

perfect competition: a situation in which each firm is a price taker—it cannot influence the market price; at the market price, the firm can sell as much as it wishes, but if it raises its price, it loses all sales.

perfectly mobile capital: capital that responds quickly to changes in returns in different countries

Phillips curve: the trade-off between unemployment and inflation such that a lower level of unemployment is associated with a higher level of inflation

piece-rate system: a compensation system in which workers are paid specifically for each item produced

plant and equipment investment: purchases by firms of new capital goods

portfolio: an investor's entire collection of assets and liabilities

portfolio channel: effect of monetary policy on output through its effect on prices of various assets, in particular the prices of stocks

positive economics: economics that describes how the economy behaves and predicts how it might change—for instance, in response to some policy change

positive externalities: phenomena that occur when an individual or firm takes an action but does not receive all the benefits

potential GDP: a measure of what the value of GDP would be if the economy's resources were fully employed

present discounted value: how much an amount of money to be received in the future is worth right now

price: the price of a good or service is what must be given in exchange for the good.

price ceiling: a maximum price above which market prices are not legally allowed to rise

price discrimination: the practice of a firm charging different prices to different customers or in different markets

price dispersion: a situation that occurs when the same item is sold for different prices by different firms

price elasticity of demand: the percentage change in quantity demanded of a good as the result of a 1 percent change in price (the percentage change in quantity demanded divided by the percentage change in price)

price elasticity of supply: the percentage change in quantity supplied of a good as the result of a 1 percent change in price (the percentage change in quantity supplied divided by the percentage change in price)

price floor: a minimum price below which market prices are not legally allowed to fall

price-level targeting: a rarely adopted policy designed to achieve a stable price level

price system: the economic system in which prices are used to allocate scarce resources

price taker: firms that take the price for the good or service they sell as given; the price is unaffected by their level of production.

primary surplus: the sum of the measured surplus and interest payments on the debt

principal: the original amount a saver deposits in a bank (lends) or a borrower borrows

prisoner's dilemma: a situation in which the noncooperative pursuit of self-interest by two parties makes them both worse off

private marginal cost: the marginal cost of production borne by the producer of a good; when there is a negative externality, such as air pollution, private marginal cost is less than social marginal cost.

private property: ownership of property (or other assets) by individuals or corporations; under a system of private property, owners have certain property rights, but there may also be legal restrictions on the use of property.

privatization: the process whereby functions that were formerly undertaken by government are delegated instead to the private sector

producer price index: a price index that measures the average level of producers' prices

producer surplus: the difference between the price for which a producer would be willing to provide a good or service and the actual price at which the good or service is sold

product differentiation: the fact that similar products (like breakfast cereals or soft drinks) are perceived to differ from one another and thus are imperfect substitutes

production efficiency: the condition in which firms cannot produce more of some goods without producing less of other goods; the economy is on its production possibilities curve.

production function: the relationship between the inputs used in production and the level of output

production possibilities: the combination of outputs of different goods that an economy can produce with given resources

production possibilities curve: a curve that defines the opportunity set for a firm or an entire economy and gives the possible combination of goods (outputs) that can be produced from a given level of inputs

product market: the market in which goods and services are bought and sold

product-mix efficiency: the condition in which the mix of goods produced by the economy reflects the preferences of consumers

profits: total revenues minus total costs

progressive: describes a tax in which the rich pay a larger fraction of their income than the poor

property rights: the rights of an owner of private property; these typically include the right to use the property as she sees fit (subject to certain restrictions, such as zoning) and the right to sell it when and to whom she sees fit.

property taxes: taxes based on the value of property

protectionism: the policy of protecting domestic industries from the competition of foreign-made goods

public good: a good, such as national defense, that costs little or nothing for an extra individual to enjoy and the costs of preventing any individual from the enjoyment of which are high; public goods have the properties of nonrivalrous consumption and nonexcludability.

pure profit: the profit earned by a monopolist that results from its reducing output and increasing the price from the level at which price equals marginal cost; also called *monopoly rents*

quantity equation of exchange: the equation $MV = PY$, which summarizes the relationship between the amount of money individuals wish to hold and the dollar value of transactions

quota rents: profits that result from the artificially created scarcity of quotas and accrue to firms that are allocated the rights to import

quotas: limits on the amount of foreign goods that can be imported

random walk: a term used to describe the way the prices of stocks move; the next movement cannot be predicted on the basis of previous movements.

rational choice: a process in which individuals weigh the costs and benefits of each possibility and in which the choices made are those within the opportunity set that maximizes net benefits

rational expectations: expectations based on an understanding of the structure of the economy and fully using all available information about the economy

rationing systems: any system of allocating scarce resources, applied particularly to systems other than the price system; rationing systems include rationing by coupons and rationing by queues.

real exchange rates: exchange rate adjusted for changes in the relative price levels in different countries

real GDP: the real value of all final goods and services produced in the economy, measured in dollars adjusted for inflation

real investment: the investment that is part of aggregate expenditures, such as the purchase of new factories and machines

real product wage: the wage divided by the price of the good being produced

real rate of interest: the real return to saving, equal to the nominal rate of interest minus the rate of inflation

real wage: the average wage adjusted for changes in the prices of consumer goods

recession: two consecutive quarters of a year during which GDP falls

regional trade blocs: immediate neighbors that not only agree to eliminate trading barriers, but also to facilitate the flow of capital and labor

regressive: describes a tax in which the poor pay a larger fraction of their income than the rich

regulatory capture: a term used to describe a situation in which regulators serve the interests of the regulated rather than the interests of consumers

relative price: the ratio of any two prices; the relative price of CDs and DVDs is just the ratio of their prices.

relatively elastic: a good is said to be relatively elastic when the price elasticity of its demand is greater than unity.

relatively inelastic: a good is said to be relatively inelastic when the price elasticity of its demand is less than unity.

rent seeking: the name given to behavior that seeks to obtain benefits from favorable government decisions, such as protection from foreign competition

repeated games: games that are played many times over by the same players

reputation: the "good will" of a firm resulting from its past performance; maintaining one's reputation provides an incentive to maintain quality.

reservation wage: the wage below which an individual chooses not to participate in the labor market

residential investment: households' purchases of new homes

restrictive practices: practices of oligopolists designed to restrict competition, including vertical restrictions like exclusive territories

retained earnings: that part of the net earnings of the firm that are not paid out to shareholders, but kept by the firm

revenue curve: the relationship between a firm's total output and its revenues

revenues: the amount a firm receives for selling its products, equal to the price received multiplied by the quantity sold

right-to-work laws: laws that prevent union membership from being a condition of employment

risk aversion: the avoidance of bearing risk

rival goods: goods whose consumption or use by one person excludes consumption by another person

rollback: approach of starting from the end of the game and working backward to determine the best strategy, often used for strategic interactions that occur a repeated but fixed number of times

royalty: a fee charged by a patent holder that allows others to use its patent

rules: automatic adjustments of policy in response to macroeconomic conditions

sales tax: a tax imposed on the purchase of goods and services

scarcity: term used to describe the limited availability of resources, so that if no price were charged for a good or service, the demand for it would exceed its supply

search: the process by which consumers gather information about what is available in the market, including prices, or by which workers gather information about the jobs that are available, including wages

seasonal unemployment: unemployment that varies with the seasons, such as that associated with the decline in construction in winter

sequential game: a game in which players take turns and each can observe what choices were made in earlier moves

sharecropping: an arrangement, prevalent in many *less-developed countries (LDCs)* in which a worker works land, giving the landowner a fixed share of the output

shortage: a situation in which demand exceeds supply at the current price

short run: a length of time during which wages and prices do not fully adjust to equilibrate supply and demand

short-run aggregate production function: the relationship between output and employment in the short run, that is, with a given set of machines and buildings

short-run inflation adjustment curve: positively sloped curve that shows the rate of inflation at each level of output relative to potential GDP, for a given expected rate of inflation

short-run inflation-unemployment trade-off: the trade-off between low unemployment and stable inflation in the short run occurring when low unemployment forces nominal wages to increase faster than productivity

signal: to convey information, for example a prospective worker's earning a college degree to persuade an employer that he has desirable characteristics that will enhance his productivity

sin taxes: excise taxes on alcohol and tobacco

slope: the amount by which the value along the vertical axis increases as the result of a change in one unit along the horizontal axis; the slope is calculated by dividing the change in the vertical axis (the "rise") by the change in horizontal axis (the "run")

social insurance: insurance provided by the government to individuals, for instance, against disabilities, unemployment, or health problems (for the aged)

social marginal cost: the marginal cost of production, including the cost of any negative externality, such as air pollution, borne by individuals in the economy other than the producer

Social Security trust fund: government trust fund that collects the difference between Social Security tax revenue and expenditures, which was created in anticipation of an increase in the number of beneficiaries

static efficiency: the efficiency of the economy with given technology; taxes used to finance basic research and monopoly power resulting from patents cause a loss in static efficiency

statistical discrimination: differential treatment of individuals of different gender or race that is based on the use of observed correlations (statistics) between performance and some observable characteristics; it may even result from the use of variables like education in which there is a causal link to performance.

sticky prices: prices that do not adjust or adjust only slowly toward a new equilibrium

sticky wages: wages that are slow to adjust in response to a change in labor market conditions

stocks: variables like the capital stock or the money supply stock, that describe the state of the economy (such as its wealth) at a point of time; they are contrasted by flows.

store of value: something that can be accepted as payment in the present and exchanged for items of value in the future

strategic behavior: decision making that takes into account the possible reactions of others

strategic trade theory: the theory that protection can give a country a strategic advantage over rivals, for instance by helping reduce domestic costs as a result of economies of scale

structural unemployment: long-term unemployment that results from structural factors in the economy, such as a mismatch between the skills required by newly created jobs and the skills possessed by those who have lost their jobs in declining industries

substitutes: two goods are substitutes if the demand for one increases when the price of the other increases.

substitution effect: the reduced consumption of a good whose price has increased that is due to the changed trade-off, the fact that one has to give up more of other goods to get one more unit of the high-priced good; the substitution effect is associated with a change in the slope of the budget constraint.

sunk costs: costs that have been incurred and cannot be recovered

supply: the quantity of a good or service that a household or firm would like to sell at a particular price

supply curve: the relationship between the quantity supplied of a good and the price, whether for a single firm or the market (all firms) as a whole

supply shocks: unexpected shifts in the aggregate supply curve, such as an increase in the international price of oil or a major earthquake that destroys a substantial fraction of a country's capital stock

supply siders: economists who emphasize the importance of aggregate supply, in particular the responsiveness of supply to lower taxes and regulations; some argue that lowering tax rates leads to such large increases in inputs of capital and labor that total tax revenues may actually increase.

surplus: the magnitude of the gain from trade, the difference between what an individual would have been willing to pay for a good and what she has to pay

surplus of labor: a great deal of unemployed or underemployed labor, readily available to potential employers

sustainable development: development that is based on sustainable principles; sustainable development pays particular concern to environmental degradation and the exploitation of natural resources.

tariffs: taxes imposed on imports

tax expenditure: the revenue lost from a tax subsidy

tax subsidies: subsidies provided through the tax system to particular industries or to particular expenditures, in the form of favorable tax treatment

theory: a set of assumptions and the conclusions derived from those assumptions put forward as an explanation for some phenomena

thin markets: markets with relatively few buyers and sellers

time constraints: the limitations on consumption of different goods imposed by the fact that households have only a limited amount of time to spend (twenty-four hours a day); the time constraint defines the opportunity set of individuals if the only constraint that they face is time.

time inconsistency: a phenomenon that occurs when it is not in the best interest of a player to carry out a threat or promise that was initially designed to influence the other player's actions

time value of money: the fact that a dollar today is worth more than a dollar in the future

total costs: the sum of all fixed costs and variable costs

total factor productivity analysis: the analysis of the relationship between output and the aggregate of all inputs; total factor productivity growth is calculated as the difference between the rate of growth of output and the weighted average rate of growth of inputs, where the weight associated with each input is its share in GDP.

trade creation: new trade that is generated as a result of lowered tariff barriers

trade deficit: the excess of imports over exports

trade diversion: trade that is diverted away from outside countries as a result of lowering tariffs between the members of a trading bloc

trade-offs: the amount of one good (or one desirable objective) that must be given up to get more of another good (or to attain more of another desirable objective)

trade secret: an innovation or knowledge of a production process that a firm does not disclose to others

transactions costs: the extra costs (beyond the price of the purchase) of conducting a transaction, whether those costs are money, time, or inconvenience

transfer programs: programs directly concerned with redistribution, such as AFDC, TANF, and Medicaid, that move money from one group in society to another

Treasury bills (T-bills): short-term government bonds that are available only in large denominations

trusts: organizations that attempted to control certain markets in the late nineteenth century; they were designed to allow an individual or group owning a small fraction of the total industry to exercise control.

unemployment rate: the ratio of the number of people seeking employment to the total labor force

union shops: unionized firms in which all workers are required to join the union as a condition of employment

unitary elasticity: a demand curve has unitary elasticity if the demand for the commodity decreases by 1 percent when the price increases by 1 percent. If demand has unitary elasticity, then expenditures on the good do not depend at all on price. A supply curve has unitary elasticity if the supply of the commodity increases by 1 percent when the price increases by 1 percent.

unit of account: something that provides a way of measuring and comparing the relative values of different goods

utility: the level of enjoyment an individual attains from choosing a certain combination of goods

value added: the value added in each stage of production is the difference between the value of the output and the value of the inputs purchased from other firms

value of the marginal product of labor: the value of the extra output produced by an extra unit of labor; it is calculated by multiplying the marginal product of labor times the price of the good which is being produced.

variable costs: the costs resulting from variable inputs

velocity: the speed with which money circulates in the economy, defined as the ratio of income to the money supply

vertical equity: the principle, that people who are better off should pay more taxes

vertical merger: a merger between two firms, one of which is a supplier or distributor for the other

voluntary export restraints: restraints on exports that are self-imposed by an exporting country, although often in response to a threat that if such constraints are not imposed, the importing country will impose import quotes

voting paradox: the fact that under some circumstances there may be no determinate outcome with majority voting: choice A wins a majority over B, B wins over C, and C wins over A

wage discrimination: paying lower wages to women or minorities

World Trade Organization (WTO): the organization established in 1995 as a result of the Uruguay round of trade negotiations; replacing GATT, it is designed to remove trade barriers and settle trade disputes

zero elasticity: the situation that exists when the quantity demanded (or supplied) will not change, regardless of changes in price

Credits

pp. 4, 5 © Novastock/Picturequest; **p. 13** Martin Fleming/Corbis; **p. 13** These materials have been reproduced by W. W. Norton & Company with the permission of eBay Inc. Copyright © eBAY Inc. All rights reserved; **pp. 24, 25** © Dana White/Picturequest; **p. 35** Joseph Sohm, Chromo-Sohm/Corbis; **p. 39** Mike Dobel/Masterfile; **pp. 46, 47** Buddy Mays/Corbis; **p. 55** courtesy Intel Corporation; **p. 57** AFP/Corbis; **pp. 66, 67** © Bob Daemmrich/Picturequest; **p. 72** Bob Rowan, Progressive Image/Corbis; **p. 75** Martyn Goddard/Corbis; **pp. 86, 87** AP/Wide World Photos; **p. 94** Reuters NewMedia Inc./Corbis; **p. 103** John Hicks/Corbis; **pp. 108, 109** © Novastock/Picturequest; **p. 115** Robert Holmes/Corbis; **p. 124** Marc Muench/Corbis; **pp. 132, 133** © Vecto Verso/Picturequest; **p. 143** © Pictor International/Picturequest; **p. 147** © IFA Bilderteam/eStock Photos; **pp. 156, 157** © IFA/Picturequest; **p. 164** AP/Wide World Photos; **pp. 172, 173** © Richard Pasley/Picturequest; **p. 178** R.W. Jones/Corbis; **p. 188** © Gilles Peress/Magnum Photos; **p. 192** Patrick Bennett/Corbis; **pp. 202, 203** AP/Wide World Photos; **p. 211** © Jan Staller/Corbis Stock Market; **p. 216** Library of Congress; **p. 221** Reuters NewMedia Inc./Corbis; **pp. 226, 227** © Peter Southwick/Picturequest; **p. 233** Kevin Fleming/Corbis; **p. 236** Steve Raymer/Corbis; **pp. 240, 241** AP/Wide World Photos; **p. 248** AFP/Corbis; **p. 254** Reuters NewMedia Inc./Corbis; **p. 260** AFP/Corbis; **pp. 268, 269** AP/Wide World Photos; **p. 274** AP/Wide World Photos; **p. 277** Philip James Corwin/Corbis; **pp. 286, 287** © Mark Richards/Picturequest; **p. 293** Richard T. Nowitz/Corbis; **p. 294** Corel CD-ROM, image #506082; **pp. 302, 303** © Rachel Epstein/Picturequest; **p. 304** AP/Wide World Photos; **p. 312** AP/Wide World Photos; **pp. 316, 317** © Charles Gupton/Picturequest; **p. 320** AP/Wide World Photos; **p. 326** AFP/Corbis; **p. 340** Reuters New Media Inc./Corbis; **pp. 344, 345** Reuters NewMedia Inc./Corbis; **p. 351** AP/Wide World Photos; **pp. 364, 365** Reuters New Media/Corbis; **p. 369** courtesy Golf Carts Fore You, Hudson, FL; **p. 376** Reuters New Media/Corbis; **pp. 382, 383** © David Ryan/Picturequest; **p. 391** Bettman/Corbis; **p. 396** Nik Wheeler/Corbis; **pp. 402, 403** © Pictor International/Picturequest; **p. 405** Peter Kornicker/Corbis; **p. 409** © Ewing Galloway, Inc. All rights reserved; **pp. 420, 421** © Richard Nowitz/Picturequest; **p. 427** Galen Rowell/Corbis; **p. 430** Kevin R. Morris/Corbis; **pp. 440, 441** Morton Beebe, S.F./Corbis; **pp. 452, 453** © Tom Carroll/Picturequest; **p. 462** Reuters Newmedia Inc/Corbis; **p. 465** Gary Braasch/Corbis; **pp. 488, 489** Adam Smith Productions/Corbis; **p. 504** Philip Gould/Corbis; **pp. 514, 515** AP/Wide World Photos; **p. 524** Courtesy PBS Danmark A/S; **pp. 544, 545** Pablo Corral V/Corbis; **p. 562** Kevin R. Morris/Corbis; **pp. 568, 569** © Pictor International/Picturequest; **p. 573** Courtesy Burlington Industries; **p. 573** Sheldon Collins/Corbis; **p. 586** AP/Wide World Photos; **p. 593** © Todd Powell/Picturequest; **pp. 598, 599** © Mark Richards/Picturequest; **p. 604** Laura Dwight/Corbis; **pp. 624, 625** © David Stover/Picturequest; **p. 640** Peter Kornicker/Corbis; **pp. 650, 651** Reuters NewMedia Inc./Corbis; **p. 659** UPI/Corbis; **p. 661** Bob Krist/Corbis; **pp. 672, 673** AP/Wide World Photos; **p. 684** Roger Ressmeyer/Corbis; **p. 685** AP/Wide World Photos; **pp. 694, 695** Reuters NewMedia Inc./Corbis; **p. 698** Reuters NewMedia Inc./Corbis; **p. 703** AP/Wide World Photos; **pp. 716, 717** AP/Wide World Photos; **p. 727** Joel W. Rogers/Corbis; **p. 728** Darrell Gulin/Corbis; **pp. 736, 737** AP/Wide World Photos; **p. 749** AP/Wide World Photos; **p. 752** Reuters NewMedia Inc./Corbis; **pp. 758, 759** AP/Wide World Photos; **p. 777** Walter Hodges/Corbis; **pp. 784, 785** AP/Wide World Photos; **p. 799** Craig Aurness/Corbis; **p. 800** Courtesy National Oceanic and Atmospheric Administration; **pp. 804, 805** The Purcell Team/Corbis; **p. 818** AP Wide/World Photos; **p. 824** Peter Turnley/Corbis.

index